The Gallery of Meissen Animals

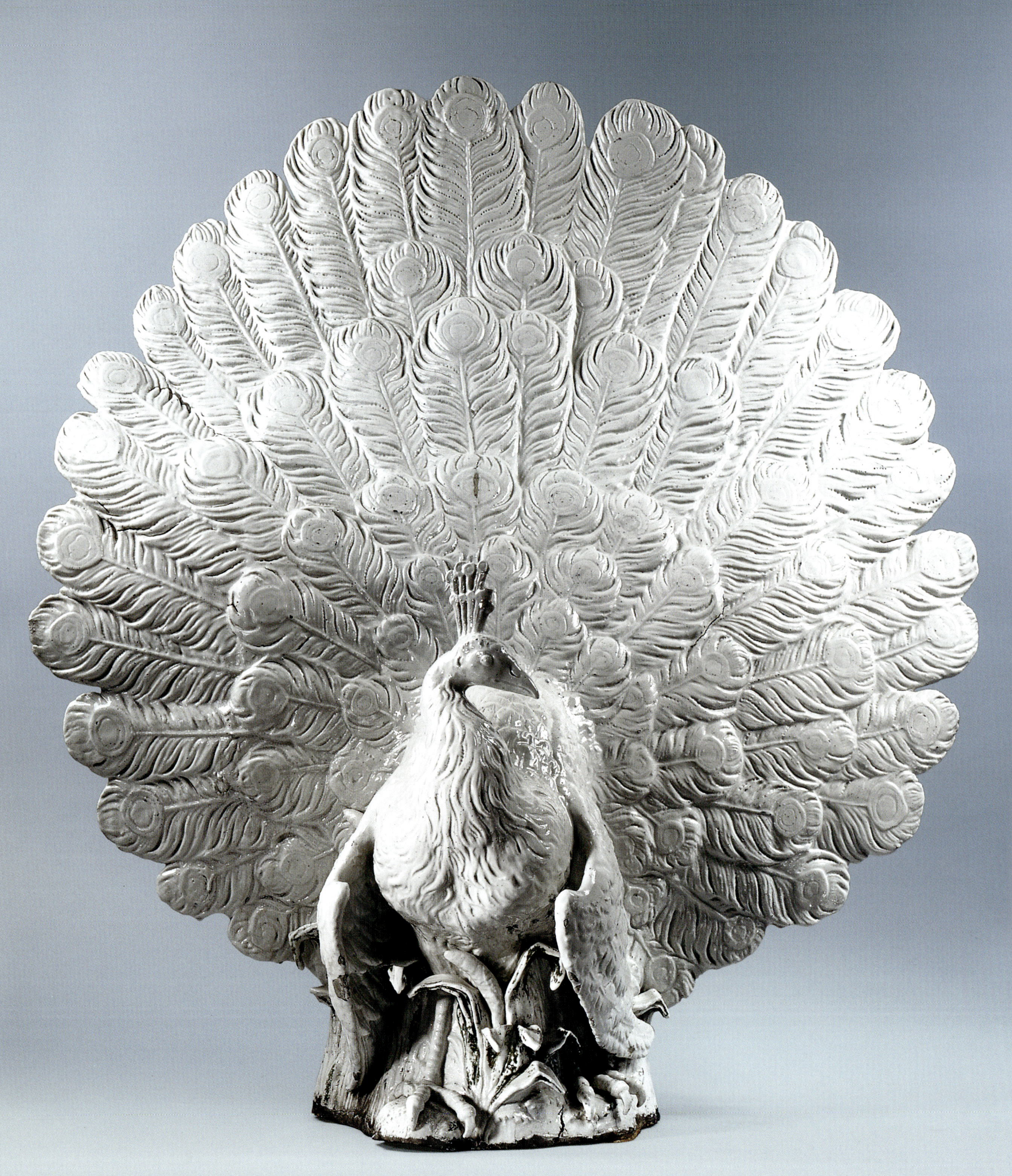

Samuel Wittwer

The Gallery of Meissen Animals

Augustus the Strong's Menagerie for the Japanese Palace in Dresden

Translated by John Nicholson

Photographs by Hans Bach, Jürgen Karpinski, and Peter Mookhoek

HIRMER MUNICH

This book is dedicated to the devoted porcelain-lovers listed below,
to whom the author offers his warmest thanks for their support and practical help,
without which it could not have been published in English translation.

Michele Beiny Harkins

The Arnhold Foundation
Richard Baron Cohen
Lady Kate Davson
Patricia and Samuel Grober
Malcolm Gutter
Patricia and Rhodes Hart
Michael Harkins
Masao Iketani
Doris and Stanford Marks
Rosemarie Pauls
The Pauls-Eisenbeiss Foundation
Pamela and Nicholas Roditi
Linda and David Roth
Melinda and Paul Sullivan

Contents

Preface *9*

Definition of the subject *9*
Sources *9*
The book: a short guided tour *10*
Acknowledgments *11*

Introduction

The historical background to the large animal figures *14*

Saxony in the Augustan period 1694–1763 *14*
A brief history of the Meissen porcelain manufactory 1710–1740 *15*
The porcelain collection of Augustus the Strong *17*

Aspects of the Baroque interior *19*

The fashion for chinoiserie *19*
The porcelain cabinet and the "Porzellanschloss" *21*

Animal sculpture in the late Renaissance and Baroque *25*

Animals in painting and sculpture *25*
Sixteenth-century miniature animal sculptures *26*
The Versailles maze *27*
Animal sculpture in Baroque gardens *29*
Animal sculpture in the Baroque interior *29*

Part One
The Palace and the Animals:
Fundamentals of their genesis and appearance

The Japanese Palace *32*

Building chronology *32*
Architectural decoration *35*
The history of the planning and furnishing *37*
The Japanese Palace in topographical works and travel reports *53*
The Japanese Palace as depository *55*
The end of the project *56*

The porcelain animals for the Japanese Palace: the cultural, technical, and artistic conditions *59*

The general foundations *59*
Animals at the Dresden court *60*
The orders for animal figures for the Japanese Palace *66*
The artists and craftsmen involved *69*
The production of the porcelain animals – the technical aspects *75*
Signatures and markings *108*
Attribution of the models *112*
Models, antecedents, and sources of inspiration *119*
The presentation of the animal figures in the Japanese Palace *130*

Part Two
The Palace and the Animals:
The historical and topographical context

The Japanese Palace and Augustus the Strong's overall plan *134*

The development of the royal collections *134*
Commerce and science in Saxony *134*
The Japanese Palace as a metaphor for economic and cultural wealth *135*
The Japanese Palace in Augustus the Strong's overall plan *137*

The Animal Gallery: its structure and interpretative levels *141*

The animal world as seen by the Baroque court, with particular reference to Dresden *141*
The animals in the gallery *144*

Part Three
The Palace and the Animals: Content and effect

The Japanese Palace: a claim to power in bricks and stone *154*

Court ceremonial and social structuring *154*
The Japanese Palace as a model residence *156*
Excursus. Shine: An attempt to explain the Baroque enthusiasm for porcelain in the Baroque era with reference to aesthetic and socio-historical factors. *159*
Was the Japanese Palace a "porcelain palace"? *163*

The animal figures: form and effect *166*

Art and nature in the Baroque: a short survey *166*
Johann Gottlieb Kirchner and Johann Joachim Kaendler: a comparison of their conceptions of animal sculpture *173*
Kaendler's large animal figures: individual analyses *183*

Part Four
The Animals and the Palace: What is their "meaning" and how are they related?

The animal figures as sculptures *206*

The vital importance of the surface *206*
"Rightness" for execution in porcelain *207*
The "meaning" of Kaendler's animal figures *208*

The animal figures and the model Residence: two mutually formative works of art *212*

The suitability of Kaendler's animal figures for the Japanese Palace *212*
Why did the King need these porcelain animals? *215*

Postlude

The animal figures and their artistic influence in the tide of time: a short summary *218*

The Meissen large animal figures in the late eighteenth, nineteenth, and twentieth centuries *219*

Sales and gifts in the eighteenth century *221*
Sales in the nineteenth and early twentieth centuries *223*
The modern realizations of animal figures in the Meissen manufactory in the nineteenth and twentieth centuries *230*
Imitations and forgeries *233*

Notes *240*

Appendix

Sources *262*
List of the unprinted sources, with their abbreviations *284*
Reference list *288*

Catalog

Introduction *298*
Quadrupeds and creatures of fable *303*
Birds *326*

Glossary *365*

Indexes *371*

Preface

The broad foundations for this book were provided by a doctoral thesis written under the supervision of Prof Dr. Gottfried Boehm and entitled "Tiere für das Schloß des Königs – Die Menagerie aus Meißener Porzellan für das Japanische Palais in Dresden. Ein Beitrag zur Verflechtung von Kunst und Kulturgeschichte in der ersten Hälfte des 18. Jahrhunderts," ("Animals for the King's Palace: The Meissen porcelain menagerie for the Japanese Palace in Dresden. A contribution to the correlation of art and cultural history in the first half of the eighteenth century."), which was approved *summa cum laude* by the *Philosophisch-Historische Fakultät* of Basel University on February 22, 2000, and awarded the university's faculty prize in the same year. The German-language original of the present volume appeared in 2004 as the first number in a new series brought into being by the Gesellschaft der Keramikfreunde e.V., and was likewise published by Hirmer, Munich.

Definition of the subject

The present publication is a study of two aspects of the art of the first half of the eighteenth century which have hitherto been accorded little attention in art history generally: animal sculpture, and porcelain as art.

Published in 1935, Carl Albiker's comprehensive account of the Meissen animal figures of the eighteenth century covered their development through to the decline in artistic quality after the Seven Years' War (1756–1763). This overall perspective on the subject had the advantage of being able to present and draw attention to all its very varied aspects. The catalog-like approach, however, inevitably meant that the same kind and measure of consideration was accorded to works of very different character and artistic quality. Furthermore, Albiker could do nothing more than hint at those aspects of (Saxon) cultural history which had led to animals being represented in porcelain in the first place, and at aspects of the subject beyond the bounds of the manufactory.

Within the corpus of Meissen animal figures, however, there is one well-defined group of works which provides a suitable opportunity for identifying precisely these kind of cross-relations, and the indisputably high quality of these works furthermore allows us on occasion to make light of the strict boundary customarily observed between figurative works of art on the one hand and porcelain objects on the other. This is the group of animal figures, in part life-size, ordered in 1730 by the Prince Elector of Saxony and King in Poland Augustus the Strong for the Japanese Palace in Dresden. The fact that work on this order was only carried on for six years makes it possible to study them in depth without having to resort to the kind of simplifications about developments in the history of art that sometimes have to be made when dealing with longer periods of time.

The intention of the present publication is to investigate and to present a general survey of the attitudes of Dresden court society to the animal world and to art in its various forms, such as can be observed for the 1730s. Against this backdrop, attention is focused on the manufacture of the porcelain animals and the attendant circumstances, on the way in which the creative minds involved understood art and saw the animal world, and on the place of the animal figures in their intended home, namely the Japanese Palace, with a view to establishing the significance of the Meissen large animal figures in and also after the period in which they were created.

It has to be admitted that the expression "large animal figures" is not an entirely happy one, as it implies certain limitations on the potential of the material, and does not reflect the fact that such figures as the Canary were anything but large. In literature on the subject, however, the term has gained currency for figures between 50 and 130 cm in height and is thus appropriate for the majority of the figures ordered for the Japanese Palace. It is used in the present publication in order to avoid misunderstandings when references are made to research done to date, and to distinguish the group of works under study, even though it does include figures less than 50 cm in height, from other Meissen animal figures of a later date.

Sources

Literature on eighteenth-century Meissen porcelain would fill several bookcases. As far as general surveys are concerned, however, four cover all the ground, all published within a period of a little less than a quarter of a century.[1]

The situation is different with regard to articles and smaller books on clearly-defined topics. In this category there are a good number of excellent studies by a small group of authors who are constantly increasing the state of knowledge on a variety of aspects of the subject.[2]

Surprisingly enough, while Meissen animal figures, and particularly the large animal figures for the Japanese Palace, are described and accorded illustrations in almost every one of the more general books on Meissen, no more than a handful of texts have been published that go into these works in any depth. While Jean Louis Sponsel devoted a good deal of space to them in his book on Kaendler's display pieces ("Kabinettstücke"), his publication of 1900 was a pioneer work which understandably contains some facts which have since been found to be wrong, or were wrongly interpreted by Sponsel. This was followed in 1915 by a small study of the large animal figures by Ernst Zimmermann in which he revised certain aspects of Sponsel's work. It was not until 1935 that the first monograph on Meissen animal figures appeared: the book by Carl Albiker mentioned above. In 1959 it was published in a second, much shorter version with the author's own text cut out, leaving only the illustrations, to which were added the modelers' working reports. Since 1959 there has been Josef Horschik's article of 1977 presenting new insights into the painting of the animal figures, which Rainer Rückert adopted in 1992, complementing it with the publication of important source material on the court lacquerer Reinow.

The sources for the art and culture of Dresden's so-called Augustan Age (1694–1763) have been the object of extensive research and documentation; over a period of decades a number of researchers systematically quarried the archives and published both texts and pictorial material. However, there are still gaps, one of which is the history of the Japanese Palace. Furthermore, it is now important that the somewhat narrowly focused perspective hitherto characteristic of publications on art in eighteenth-century Dresden should be broadened, so that these art works can be situated in a wider context; accordingly, the present study is particularly concerned to relate one specific group of works to the wider Saxon cultural context.

As no detailed studies have in recent times been devoted either the Japanese Palace or to the large Meissen animal figures made for the palace, it was vital to make a close study of the original sources and to scour them thoroughly for references to these subjects. The extant documents relating to the building of the Palace are preserved in the *Sächsisches Hauptstaatsarchiv* (State Archive of Saxony) in Dresden. The Meissen manufactory was subordinate both to the king and to a number of intermediate bodies set up by the king, and the related documents are accordingly found in two places: firstly, at the *Sächsisches Hauptstaatsarchiv*, which was the recipient of the archives of all the royal administrative bodies, and secondly at the Meissen Manufactory Archive which itself goes back to the time of the factory's foundation and has correspondingly extensive holdings.

Research for the present publication involved examination of material for the period 1729 to 1740 not only in these archives but also in the *Sächsische Landesbibliothek* (Library of Saxony), and also of plans at the Dresden *Landesamt für Denkmalpflege* (Department of Historical Monuments for Saxony). In all cases, access to the sources was excellent, as all the documentation could be examined in one place and also – especially in the case of Meissen porcelain – in its entirety and without any great complications. Furthermore, of all the collections of Meissen large animal figures, the largest by far is the one in Dresden.

The book: a short guided tour

The intention of the author in composing this monograph has been to investigate, in all their aspects, two art works that are intimately related to one another: a specific and very largely homogeneous group of porcelain animal figures, and a palace. This double subject brought with it an immediate problem as to how the book should be structured; given their respective importance as works of art and the present state of research in each case, a whole book could legitimately be devoted to either subject alone. The book thus had to incorporate consideration of a great variety of art historical and cultural matters. I would ask specialists in the history of court culture and the associated visual arts to bear patiently with what to their minds will certainly seem superfluously long treatments of matters from these fields; my reason for explaining these things at length is that specialist literature on these subjects, coming as it does from the world of arts and crafts, has only recently begun to develop a methodology of the kind long since current in art history.

The Introduction deals first of all with the history of Saxony and of the Meissen porcelain manufactory in the first half of the eighteenth century. Descriptions of the porcelain collection of the Saxon electors are followed by a general account of animal sculpture focusing on the last decades of the seventeenth century and the first of the eighteenth. Finally, attention is paid to the *chinoiserie* fashion in the Baroque, and a section on the porcelain cabinet provides the reader with a bridge into the book's core sections.

In order to give full consideration to the mutual influences observable between the figures and the palace architecture, the accounts of the two main subjects are not interwoven in one continuous text but kept separate. The core of the book is divided into four sections, each of which is divided into distinct parts dealing with the Japanese Palace and with the large animal figures respectively. The relationships between these respective parts reflect the actual relationship between the palace and the animal collection, with the discussion of the palace providing the backdrop for a more focused appreciation of the porcelain figures:

1. The first of the book's four main parts ("The Palace and the Animals: Fundamentals of their genesis and appearance," pp. 32–132) devotes an initial chapter to the genesis and development of the Japanese Palace in Dresden. A survey of the general circumstances surrounding the order submitted by the king for animal figures in Meissen porcelain to be housed at the palace is

followed by a series of chapters on the figures' technical and artistic genesis.

2. Part Two ("The Palace and the Animals: The historical and topographical context," pp.134–153) discusses the place of the palace and the figures in their historical context. A first chapter investigates the way the Japanese Palace relates to the royal collections generally and leads on to a broader survey in which the complex formed by the palace and two further buildings is seen to have a particular significance all of its own. This perspective provides a logical bridge to a discussion of the place of the animal gallery in the context of the building. This is in its turn followed by thoughts on attitudes towards animals at court, which lay the ground for a first tentative general interpretation.

3. Part Three ("The Palace and the Animals: Content and effect," pp.154–205) is principally concerned to investigate how the palace and the animal figures in effect impress the human mind and sensibility; the broader perspective of the previous section is now narrowed to focus on the objects per se. For the palace, this involves investigating the way in which ceremonial was used to structure life at court, and relating this to whole project's underlying concept. Parallel to this discussion, the animal figures are investigated individually and considered in the light of certain basic aspects of (Baroque) art.

4. Part Four ("The Animals and the Palace: What is their 'meaning' and how are they related?", pp. 206–216) offers an interpretation of the palace and the animal collection that draws on the observations made in the previous part. Looking for answers to questions regarding the quality of the animal figures and their underlying artistic concept makes it possible to establish not only their position in the history of art, but also their significance for the Japanese Palace project as a whole. This finally yields insights into the project's two principal "master artists" – Johann Joachim Kaendler and Augustus the Strong – and into the works they created. The interweaving of "object art" (the animals) and "the art of interior decoration" (the palace) is shown to have created an ensemble that, firstly, could not have been brought into being either in any other place than Dresden or at any other time than this, and, secondly, not only made a profound impression on the contemporary world but also – astoundingly enough, given that centuries have passed since the works were banished from their intended home – continues to make a similar impression on receptive sensibilities today.

5. "Postlude" gives an account of the history of the palace and the figures since the middle of the eighteenth century, covering the ways they have been seen in the course of time (their "Rezeptionsgeschichte"), the fate of the building and collection, and other questions such as forgeries.

6. The book is rounded off with an appendix made up of a number of select sources, a bibliography, and a catalog. While constituting a comprehensive inventory of the large animal figures, the Catalog also presents in an orderly form the mass of detailed information that accumulated in the course of research. The general subject of animal sculpture in the Baroque is only discussed in brief in the Introduction, for the reason that, as research has established, the similarities that can be observed between the Meissen figures created for the Japanese Palace and other extant Baroque animal sculptures are merely formal in character and do not provide evidence of common conceptual ground. Given that large-scale animal sculptures were, as we shall see in greater detail later, as a rule bound up with certain commissions for certain locations, and that there was not the kind of large open market for these works that there was, for instance, for paintings, more importance has been accorded to the conceptual background than to formal parallels, which are generally more or less coincidental in character.

Acknowledgments

As the fruit of nine years' work that began tentatively and varied in intensity as time went on, this study could not have been undertaken or completed without the help of a great number of institutions, specialists, colleagues and friends. As these acknowledgments can only include the study's most important benefactors (listed in chronological order), heartfelt thanks are also extended to all those who have given support in any way but are not mentioned by name here.

I owe a particular debt of gratitude to Prof. Dr. Gottfried Boehm, Basel, for his fatherly supervision of this doctoral thesis, for his open ear and stimulating suggestions, and for his readiness to oversee a study that is peripheral to the central fields of art history. My thanks also go to Dr. Bernd Wolfgang Lindemann, who likewise helped me with valuable comments and criticism.

A generous bursary from the *Schweizerische Nationalfonds* from early 1998 to the fall of 1999 enabled me to conduct research in Dresden over a period of seven months, and to visit a number of important collections in the United States of America. In this respect, I owe a particular debt of thanks to the Basel University Research Commission.

My sincere thanks also go to those institutions in Meissen and Dresden which allowed me for the most part unrestricted access to their unique collections, first and foremost to the staff of the Meissen Porcelain Manufactory: Ute Fischer, then working in the Archive, the present archivist Dr. Peter Braun, Dr. Hannes Walter and Uwe Marschner, the mold archivist Herr Rost, and Herr Keil from the depository. I owe a debt of gratitude to Frau Petrasch of the Sächsische Hauptstaatsarchiv for her caring, knowledgeable and untiring efforts on my behalf, and am obliged to the Landesamt für Denkmalpflege for allowing me access to the plan drawings.

My thanks are due to the staff of the Porcelain Collection in the Zwinger who were constantly ready to allow me access to the animal figures and followed the course of my work with encouraging interest and many helpful suggestions. Particular thanks are extended to the collection's director Dr. Ulrich Pietsch, who lightened my burden by clearing away the bureaucratic obstacles along my path to the figures and sources. I am likewise particularly indebted to the head restorer Martin Walcha and his colleague Heike Ulbrich, who were at all times unstinting in their support and advice on technical matters, and worked with full commitment during the photographing of the figures. My thanks are also due to Dr. Elisabeth Schwarm-Tomisch for pointing me in the direction of the *Archiv der Staatlichen Kunstsammlungen* with its archivist Bärbel Arnold, who supported me generously in my research work. Dr. Klaus-Peter Arnold is to be thanked for allowing me access to archive material belonging to the *Sächsische Porzellan-Manufaktur Dresden GmbH* in Freital.

In the most advanced phase of my work, I received assistance of a very special kind from Maureen Cassidy-Geiger, whose numerous insights and critical comments helped me not to lose the thread in the arguments that run through the book, and who at the same time enabled me to incorporate some highly interesting cross-references. I owe her a very special and personal debt of thanks.

I have a double debt of gratitude to Michele Beiny-Harkins, New York. During my studies for my doctoral thesis, her interventions gave me unlimited access to important private collections and museum holdings. Secondly, this book would never have appeared in English translation had it not been for her organizational flair and untiring commitment. Thank-you, Michele.

For valuable suggestions and an unforgettable initiation into the essential character and structure of the Meissen Archive, I am likewise indebted to Claus Boltz, Berlin.

To the photographer Hans Bach I owe not only a debt of thanks but also a hymn of praise for the great skill and feeling with which he reflected my particular view of the animal sculptures in his photographs. My thanks also go to Sebastian Kuhn of Sotheby's and Paul Tippett of Christie's for the active support they gave to my research endeavors.

It would not have been possible for the original German-language version of this book to have appeared in such a comprehensive form had it not been for the generous financial support of the Basel University Dissertation Fund and the commitment to the project shown by the *Gesellschaft der Keramikfreunde e.V.* and its President, Dr. Reinhard Jansen.

Particular thanks are also due to two staff-members of the publishing-house of Hirmer, Munich, for their commitment to the book: Jürgen Kleidt for his constant support and organizational assistance, and to Peter Grassinger for creating a design that is such a convincing reflection of the book's subject matter.

My sincere thanks likewise go to John Nicholson for his sensitive and expert translation, and for taking the trouble of entering into a genuine collaboration with the author on the production of this English-language version.

I would also like to thank Lady Kate Davson for subjecting the whole text to an eagle-eyed critical reading, and for her invaluable suggestions.

I am profoundly grateful to Marcus Köhler for having been a constant source of inspiration to me, and for giving me indispensable support when I was finalizing the text and seeing it through to publication.

My greatest debt of thanks is to my parents for their untiring and unconditional support. Had they not shown such great understanding, this project would never have come to fruition.

Introduction

The historical background to the large animal figures

Saxony in the Augustan period 1694–1763

In 1694 – the year of the accession to power of Friedrich Augustus I as Prince Elector, following the unexpected death of his brother – Saxony was one of the largest and most flourishing principalities of the Holy Roman Empire of the German Nation.[3] It was a land rich in mineral resources (not for nothing does "Erzgebirge" mean "ore mountains") and boasted high standards in the field of manufacturing.[4] The population had a relatively large degree of freedom in comparison with those of other parts of the Empire. There were fine traditions of craftsmanship, and members both of the middle classes and of the nobility had acquired considerable wealth by engaging in trade; the Leipzig trade fairs were well known far beyond the borders of Saxony.

This was the background against which Friedrich August made his bid for the royal crown of Poland and was in 1697 elected as Augustus II, King in Poland (fig. 1), in spite of competition from such great powers as France and such rising powers as Prussia. For the sake of clarity, he will in the present publication always be referred to as Augustus the Strong, the name with which he has gone down into history. Poland was at this time the second largest country in Europe and although Poland and Saxony shared no common border, the young elector-king hoped to be able to join the two states together in a real union. As things turned out, this was prevented by the strong and influential Polish nobility, so that the only union that came into being was a personal one. Nor was he able to turn Poland's electoral monarchy into a hereditary one, which would have given the Saxon electoral dynasty royal status, which was why he and, later, his son were not entitled to call themselves kings "of Poland" but only "in Poland."

Augustus's rise to become ruler of the extensive and highly regarded kingdom of Poland not only gave Saxony access to the sea but also brought about changes at home. One of the most important points was that in order to assume the Polish crown Augustus the Strong had to convert to Roman Catholicism, which was a far from unproblematic step for the supreme head of a land that had been the cradle of the Protestant Reformation. He had to assure the Estates that they would not have to convert along with him. Even his wife resisted the pressure to convert, with the result that while he was king in Poland, she was not queen. As a result, the court at Dresden was partly Catholic, but held sway over a population of Protestant subjects. In the artistic field, the changeover brought with it a new and wide-ranging variety of challenges.

A second important point was that the Elector of Saxony now commanded a degree of status and prestige which put him into the first rank of European princes. And whenever the Elector's status and prestige had to be made evident for all to see and feel, then the symbolic elements in the forms used had to be made to fit the new status quo; accordingly, his family history was scoured for all the outstanding events, important personalities and high honors that could be recruited to serve this end.

A third central point had to do with the places where power was displayed. Together with its lord, the court had to travel to and fro between Dresden and Warsaw, with French as the international lingua franca being complemented by not just one but two local languages, German and Polish. The most influential families of the two countries were encouraged to enter into dynastic alliances. Ruling his kingdom in Poland caused Augustus the Strong more problems than he had reckoned with; from 1704 to 1709 he even had to resort to a temporary laying down of the Polish crown in order to be able to participate in the Great Northern War.

The marriage of his only legitimate offspring, Friedrich August, to the Emperor's daughter Maria Josepha, was not only an expression of his newly-acquired power, but also a tactical move which brought strength to his political arm, with the House of Wettin establishing dynastic links with the House of Habsburg in a way that would not have been possible before Augustus the Strong's change in religious affiliation. The crown prince had been brought up under the strictly Protestant influence of his mother. On his unusually long grand tour, however, he secretly converted to the Catholic faith, thus paving the way not only for the great wedding but also preparing the ground for Augustus the Strong to pursue his intention of establishing an hereditary dynasty in Poland. These factors were what made the wedding celebrations of 1719 into a comprehensive and (to borrow an appropriately musical expression) "through-composed" demonstration of Saxony's claims and aspirations.

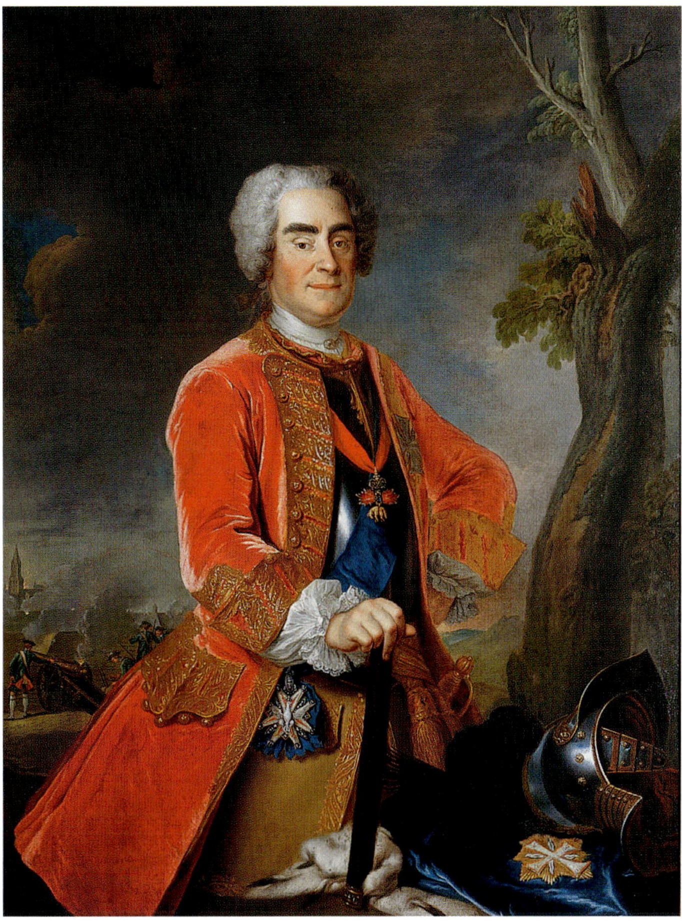

1 Louis de Silvestre (atelier), Augustus the Strong ca. 1730, private collection in Switzerland

On February 1, 1733, Augustus the Strong died in Warsaw. His son, now Prince Elector Friedrich August II, presented himself as a candidate for the Polish throne and one year later, on 14 January, 1734, he was crowned King in Poland as Augustus III (fig. 2). Here he shall be referred to throughout as Augustus III, even though this is strictly speaking incorrect for the period from February 2, 1733 to January 13, 1734.

His reign was a period in which the arts flourished, but also one in which bad political decisions were made and defeats suffered in war, the responsibility for which can be attributed in part to two influential ministers, Count Alexander von Sulkowski and Count Heinrich von Brühl. After the disaster of the Seven Years' War (1756–1763), in the last year of which Augustus III and Count Brühl both died while in exile in Warsaw, Saxony lost its links with Poland and slumped to a position of insignificance in the Empire as a whole, bringing to a close the seventy-year-long "Augustan Period" and that flowering of art and culture in Saxony which even in our own day still constitutes an integral part of Dresden's character and renown.

A brief history of the Meissen porcelain manufactory 1710–1740

In 1708, porcelain was (re-)invented by a team of specialist craftsmen, scientists, and researchers in Dresden. The secrets of porcelain production had been sought for centuries all over Europe, and experiments with ceramics had brought forth a number of optically similar surrogate materials.[5] But until the alchemist-turned-ceramicist Friedrich Böttger, the mathematician and physicist Walther Ehrenfried von Tschirnhaus, the metallurgist Gottfried Papst von Ohain, and a number of foundrymen from Freiberg succeeded in finding the right paste mixture and production techniques for the manufacture of a genuine European hard porcelain,[6] this costly and relatively rare material could only be acquired, at great risk, trouble, and expense, from countries in the Far East.

In 1710, when Europe's first porcelain works was established at the Albrechtsburg in Meissen by decree of Augustus the Strong, these pioneers had not yet got beyond their first experimental phase. It was only in 1713 that production was able to serve a wider

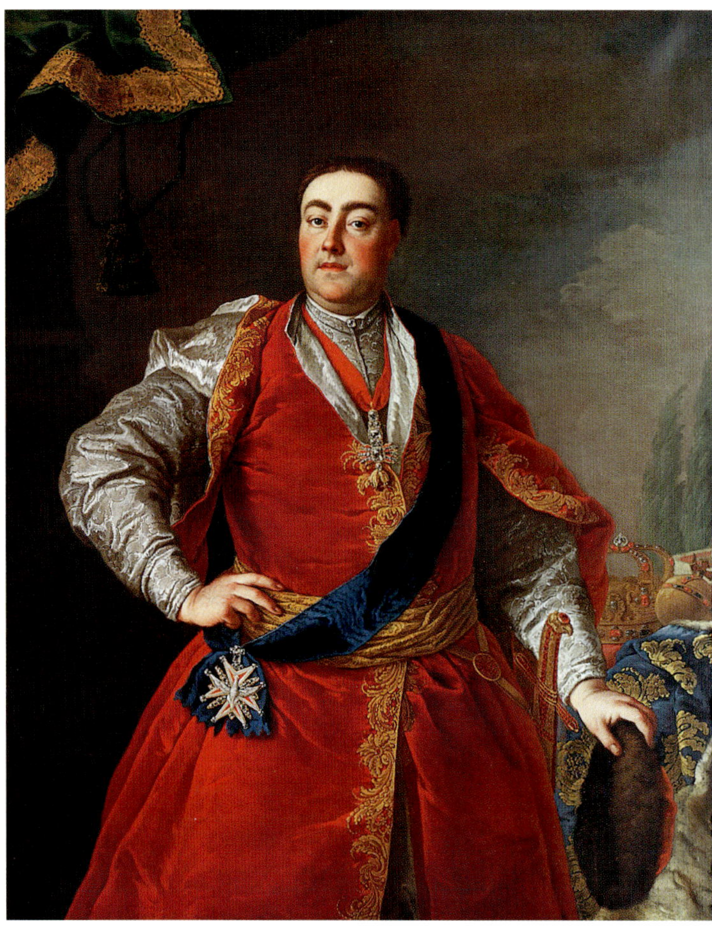

2 Louis de Silvestre (atelier), Augustus III in his Polish robes ca. 1737/40, Historisches Museum Basel, loan from the Pauls-Eisenbeiss-Stiftung

market. In its first decade, the enterprise was mainly preoccupied with the improvement of its paste recipes, glazes, and firing techniques, with the development of a blue that could be used with success in the underglaze painting that was so admired in the Far Eastern goods, and with the invention of fusible colors for porcelain and other ways and means of decorating its wares. On the artistic level, a new palette of forms closely tailored to the special character of the new material was being developed to complement the wares copied directly from Far Eastern models. Another imperative, which economic necessity made into a constant concern, was the preservation of the "arcanum," that corpus of indispensable knowledge on matters ranging from the necessary raw materials and how they were to be prepared and made into paste, to furnace-building, firing techniques, and the production and correct application of fusible colors ("enamels"). Böttger died in 1719. A year later the manufactory engaged a painter fresh from Vienna, Johann Gregorius Höroldt, who developed, in collaboration with the arcanist Samuel Stöltzel and in an astoundingly short time, a wide range of fusible enamel colors. Although the extent to which Höroldt was involved in the actual preparation of the colors cannot be established for certain, he was definitely responsible for developing the correct technique for applying them, and there is no doubt that he is justly known – most of all for the decorations he invented – as the father of European porcelain-painting.[7] Although he was at first not actually a staff-member of the manufactory, he directed an atelier of his own in the Albrechtsburg and charged princely prices for the work done by his sub-enterprise.

Böttger had, by royal appointment, held the title of Administrator at the manufactory, but after his death in 1719 an Inspector was installed who was to pass on monthly reports on the situation at Meissen and the problems currently being faced by the enterprise to a board of directors, the so-called Manufactory Commission.[8] In 1730 a scandalous affair[9] led to the manufactory being reorganized and given the structure that is valid for the period dealt with in this volume. Höroldt's atelier was integrated into the manufactory, but he himself was effectively put in charge of running the whole enterprise; as such he was answerable to the three-man commission, which provided him with his link, via their superior the official director of the manufactory, to the king himself. The manufactory was to report on the state of affairs at Meissen and make its requests on a monthly basis in a "Rapport" to the Commission. The Commission passed on these monthly reports, and any matters which went beyond its own competence, to the director, who presented them to the king and transmitted decisions and queries back to the manufactory via the Commission. In the period that concerns us here, the Commission found itself dealing with two matters of vital importance for the continued existence of the manufactory, namely the provision of sufficient firewood and the preservation of the arcanum. The fact that the king retained main responsibility for the supervision of the enterprise reflects the importance accorded to it by both Augustus the Strong and his successor Augustus III.

All these levels of authority are of importance in connection with the royal orders for the Japanese Palace and thus also for the large animal figures themselves. The documents which record their doings provide a clear picture of the influence they brought to bear on the whole process, with the desire of one agency to "color" the matter in hand being reflected in the little re-formulations it carried out before the text was passed on to the next competent authority. Given the host of problems that the production of life-size animal figures was bound to bring in its wake, it is important that these sources be subjected to particularly thorough critical analysis.

This is particularly the case for a certain corpus of records which provides us with by far the most extensive source of information for the technical difficulties encountered during the production procedures for the large animal figures. Having been appointed as modeler at the manufactory in 1731, the gifted and ambitious sculptor Johann Joachim Kaendler won the respect of all concerned in a very short time, but in his endeavors to retain overall supervision of the white-ware production process he ran up against opposition from Höroldt. And disagreements between the two over competence and responsibility in technical matters led to the conspiracy which has gone down in Meissen history as the "Reinhardt affair" of 1734, which exploded when the Inspector of the manufactory Inspector Johann David Reinhardt and Kaendler put together an extensive compilation of complaints centering on the accusation that the enterprise was suffering as a result of Höroldt's ignorance of production procedures. The "gravamina" will be quoted from extensively later on. The documents brought forth by the special commission set up to investigate the case – including minutes of their interrogations of staff members, Höroldt's counter-arguments in his own defense, and Kaendler's suggestions for improvements – provide a lively, many-faceted, and very human picture of an enterprise of this kind, and their meticulous wealth of detail makes them into a written source of the very highest order. As a result of the affair, Kaendler had his fields of responsibility extended and Inspector Reinhardt was put into prison.

Still discontented some years later and by now *Modellmeister*, Kaendler undertook a second offensive against Höroldt in 1738/1739, rolling out a number of his complaints a second time. The related records are of particular interest because production of the large animal figures had by then been brought to a close, and they contain a retrospective summary of the experience that had been gathered in the course of the project. However, the subsequent internal restructuring of the manufactory is not of interest in the context of the present publication.

The section devoted to the technical genesis of the large animal figures will consider the production process and the organization of its various stages. By way of concluding this section, it should be noted that in the course of the third decade of the eighteenth century the Meissen porcelain manufactory established itself as a flourishing producer of luxury wares that was quite capable of holding its own against increasing competition from other manufactories. From 1730 onwards, the high quality of the painting was complemented by an equally outstanding standard of sculptural work.

The porcelain collection of Augustus the Strong

In boasting a *Kunstkammer* that contained a number of pieces of Far Eastern porcelain, Augustus the Strong's predecessors as electors of Saxony were no different from other rulers of their time. As early as 1595, the *Kunstkammer* inventory contained descriptions of sixteen such pieces, eight of which are preserved to this day in the Dresden Porcelain Collection.[10]

When in the second half of the seventeenth century – the dark days of the Thirty Years' War now a thing of the past – "porcelain fever" broke out among the German princes, the House of Wettin was once again no exception to the general rule and its collection grew accordingly. By contrast with earlier days, mass imports from the Far East now enabled them to acquire larger single lots. Like his brother Elector Johann Georg IV, Augustus the Strong bought Far Eastern porcelain from Dutch dealers at the Leipzig Trade Fair, or, outside the times of the fairs, from representatives of Dutch companies.[11] Although it can no longer be established how extensive these purchases were,[12] it is certain that they were in no proportion to later ones, and it is likewise uncertain whether the pieces purchased were for the elector's own use, or destined to be presented to others as gifts.

A bill issued in Amsterdam in 1700, on the other hand, does show that certain pieces clearly were intended to be used as gifts by Augustus the Strong, by then Elector of Saxony and King in Poland,[13] and a year previously there is evidence of Raymond LePlat acquiring a number of pieces for the Dresden court.[14] And of the other pieces recorded as having been delivered in the first decade of the eighteenth century, it would seem that a portion of them were finally given away as presents.[15] It is not clear exactly when Augustus the Strong began purchasing larger lots of Far Eastern porcelain in order to build up his own collection;[16] remarkably enough, however, it would seem that the really sizeable purchases of whole collections of Far Eastern porcelain only began once Saxon porcelain was already being produced in Meissen. The claim often made that Augustus the Strong was in the second decade of the century already thinking of a large porcelain palace will be given critical consideration at a later point.

We may assume that this relatively late start on the building up of a collection of Far Eastern porcelain was triggered off by the Saxon elector's visit to Berlin in 1709. In the course of the amusements provided at the "meeting of the three kings," the Prussian king Friedrich I took his high-ranking guests on excursions to such destinations as Oranienburg, Caputh, and Charlottenburg, all palaces boasting porcelain rooms in which Augustus the Strong was confronted not only with huge quantities of Far Eastern porcelain – almost certainly the most extensive collection in the hands of any single German prince – but also with the exceptionally refined and highly political iconography of sovereignty that was an integral part of these three famous rooms.[17] Augustus the Strong's desire to collect porcelain was certainly given powerful stimulation both by the experience of these powerfully impressive rooms in 1709 and also by the most important development of the following year, namely the prospect of his soon being able to produce porcelain in his own right. The fact that this coveted material, so long closely associated with wealth, status and prestige, was now becoming available to him in apparently unlimited quantities resulted in his mind becoming even more focused on porcelain than was normal among princes of his time. This "addiction" to one of the finest and most exclusive of all artifacts is reflected in the answer Augustus the Strong gave to Count Flemming on May 22, 1726, when the latter offered to sell him the contents of his orangery in Übigau: "Orange-trees are like porcelain, you know. Once you have got the bug, you can never get enough of them, and you want more and more."[18]

The realization that he was in a position to make a name for himself which no other European prince could hope to emulate, and to put together a collection which would eclipse even those of King Friedrich I ("King in Prussia"), Duke Anton Ulrich of Braunschweig-Wolfenbüttel, or Landgravine Maria Amalia of Hessen-Kassel not only stimulated his commitment to the development of his own manufactory but also had the effect of redoubling his activities as a purchaser of Far Eastern porcelain.

Around 1715 Augustus the Strong's collection grew in leaps and bounds through acquisitions from four sources: purchases and gifts, firstly from the Saxon nobility, and secondly from other potentates; wares bought on the open market; and European porcelain resulting from his commissions to the manufactory at Meissen.

Between 1715 and 1730, Augustus the Strong acquired – or had himself presented with – various quantities of Far Eastern porcelain from: Count Flemming; Kriegsrat (War Councillor) Raschke; Geheimrat (Privy Councillor) Rechenberg; Oberkammerherr (Head Chamberlain) Count Vitzthum; Oberlandbaumeister Count Wackerbarth (cabinet minister, responsible for building); Gerichtsrat (Councillor of the Law Courts) Manteuffel; Voivode Chemetowski; and the elector's former mistress Countess Tetschen.[19]

One of the most celebrated acquisitions he made from another potentate's collection was without doubt the set of one hundred and fifty-one porcelain pieces from the Prussian collections at Oranienburg and Charlottenburg that he acquired early in 1717 in exchange for six hundred soldiers from the Saxon army. Among the porcelains from Schloss Oranienburg were the eighteen large vases that later became famous as the "dragoon vases." In 1723 Augustus the Strong had more vases of the same kind bought for him in Amsterdam.[20]

Augustus sometimes used his ambassadors as buying agents in order to get his hands on certain special pieces being offered in the porcelain trade. In 1715 Raymond LePlat bought Far Eastern porcelain in Paris,[21] and a year later Count Lagnasco is to be found doing the same in Amsterdam.[22] The latter was in fact principally in Amsterdam to buy warships for the Polish fleet, but he returned to Dresden laden with 76 large cases of lacquered furniture and porcelain, acquired from 11 different dealers at a total price of over 20,000 talers.

Similar sums exchanged hands when acquisitions were made from local dealers, especially for wares from the Dresden firm belonging to Elisabeth Bassetouche. These included porcelain bought in 1721 for the Dutch Palace, and in 1730 for the Zeithain camp; finally, in 1757, Augustus III bought the firm's entire holdings for the royal collection.[23] The stock was valued at 17,000 talers, but the king reduced the price to 6,754 talers.

This relatively late example of a large addition to the collection is however an isolated case, and it can be assumed that the greater – and most important – part of the Far Eastern porcelain in Dresden accrued during the time of Augustus the Strong. As we shall see, the Japanese Palace project had from 1725 onwards given these treasures a specific context within which to fulfill a very definite purpose, with large sums being invested in making the palace fit to house them. Given that the project had in spite of all this been given up for good around 1740, having such huge quantities of porcelain did not seem to make very much sense any more. The general attitude of the day and age to Far Eastern porcelain had also changed, and it was no longer appropriate to expand the collection in the way Augustus the Strong had done.

Aspects of the Baroque interior

The fashion for chinoiserie

Of the factors which gave the early modern period its particular character, there were two which exerted a heightened influence on European culture after the close of the Thirty Years' War, that is, in the second half of the seventeenth century. Common to both these factors was a re-orientation with regard to the perception and definition of distance. Just as the boom in Far Eastern trade meant that geographical and cultural distances appeared in a new light, the age of Absolutism saw the emergence of a new and more subtle differentiation of closeness and distance in politics, society, and the economy. The ever-increasing links with far-flung lands heightened the West's view of itself as the center of the world. Likewise, absolutist princes considered that their own personages constituted the center of the systems they ruled over – they considered themselves to be a real presence in society from the smallest detail through to the overall whole, and saw everything in relation to themselves.

After Vasco da Gama had discovered the maritime route to India around the Cape of Good Hope in 1498, Portuguese ships began to bring back from the Far East, in relatively small quantities at first, goods which had hitherto only reached Europe by way of the grueling and dangerous old trade routes. In 1517 Portuguese ships first reached Canton.[24] The other maritime powers which followed Portugal's example included Venice, Spain, England, France, and, with particular success, the Netherlands.[25] The East India companies, whether founded by princes or private individuals, set up trading posts in the target countries, building warehouses in which to gather together the luxury goods which were so avidly longed for back in Europe. Business centered on spices, tea, textiles, and arts and crafts. Wares that had not been the object of a specific order were offered at auction and easily found buyers with pockets to suit.

Founded in the Netherlands in 1702, the United East India Company was conspicuously active in the porcelain trade, and brought – particularly from the mid-seventeenth century on – hundreds of thousands of small handleless teacups, or tea-bowls, together with plates and vases, in their ships to the Netherlands. There, having been acquired by the agents of princes from all over Europe, they finally found their way in relatively small lots into princely reception rooms and curiosity cabinets.[26] Among the wares brought back from the Far East were items for everyday use made to European models, including spittoons, chamber pots, and flowerpots.

So it was that the courts of the absolutist princes came to house collections of all the obtainable objects that had any connection whatsoever with Chinese and Japanese culture. As already mentioned, the second half of the seventeenth century saw the general character of European culture undergoing a fundamental change. Tiring of its delight in the charm of the single curious item, the spirit of the day was now concerned with how to make comprehensive presentations of large and varied masses of material. In other words, the quest of the day was for arranging things in a fresh way. The curiosity cabinets, colorfully thrown together so as to accord each item its own measure of undivided attention, were ill adapted to the challenge thrown down by the recent advances in the classification of the natural world.[27] One possible alternative was the bringing together of – in the broadest sense – like with like. This was the background to the genesis of rooms, usually small ones, containing collections of products of Far Eastern culture, lacquerwork and artifacts in stone, porcelain, paper, and textiles, little worlds with an appeal that was primarily aesthetic.

However, the intention was not to produce an exact copy of a Far Eastern model. An imitation would not have been appropriate to the end in hand; if the objects of which this little world was composed were to appear exotic and out of the ordinary, then a room of this kind had to be adapted to the European eye. Only so could it give visual expression to its three main messages. Firstly, the aura of mystery that surrounded the distant origins of the objects and their mainly unknown production techniques was to suggest that their owner possessed a corresponding degree of understanding and knowledge, all the more to be admired for being quite unquantifiable. Secondly, although the foreignness of the aesthetic could not be made to fit in either with familiar models or with conventional teachings on beauty, it nevertheless gave the impression of being at one with itself, and thus was evidence of perfection of taste. And finally, the sheer quantity, quality, and variety of these rare and costly artifacts was unmistakable proof of the owner's wealth, power, and connections. The very fact that these items were documented in travel reports and legends as playing an important role in the lives of such legendary rulers as the Grand Mogul of India or the Emperor of China also played a part in surrounding their new owner with a fabulous aura of a quasi-spiritual kind, even though this was in its turn no more than a backcloth to the stage-set that presented the prince's power in visible form.[28]

Lacquerwork panels, and artifacts in soapstone, porcelain, silk, and exotic woods went to make up interior decors which were not obliged to obey any European architectural canon, and which sometimes even played merry havoc with the architectural context in which they were set. Positioned at select points on impressive enfilades, these cabinets were evidence of the prince's own modernity and cultural refinement, and helped to maintain a certain distance between his own person and the other, lower orders that peopled his court.[29] It is indicative of the intimate character of these treasure-trove-like cabinets that they were not placed among the *antichambres* but usually at the far end of the state rooms, often after the state bedroom,[30] thus making access to these precious Far Eastern objects into a privilege and sign of particular favor. Even the three most important porcelain cabinets of the Prussian elector-kings, in Caputh, Oranienburg, and Charlottenburg – which were in fact so big that they actually should be called rooms rather than cabinets – were all situated behind the state bedroom.

It was not only luxury goods which were brought back to Europe, but also literature describing what travelers saw and experienced in China and Japan.[31] Books on Asia filled whole libraries in the seventeenth and eighteenth centuries, and constituted a collecting field which a number of princes cultivated avidly. At the beginning of the eighteenth century, Berlin boasted one of the largest China libraries of the day. This resulted in a burgeoning of knowledge about Far Eastern culture which not only influenced the culture of the European courts, but also promoted new perspectives on politics and society.

In the wake of such events as the revocation of the Edict of Nantes in 1685, which was to turn the fact of France's unity as a state into a political unity, leading thinkers began to engage in open criticism of feudal, absolutistic values. They were all familiar with the idealizing discourses on politics and society that had been brought forth by the far-off realm they knew as the "Reich der Mitte." Without any knowledge of the Christian faith, China had clearly attained high levels of culture and ethics; it was a land where life was allegedly governed by reason alone and became a model onto which all kinds of ideals could be projected. China was "of all Earth's parts the noblest."[32] Even the European princes, in their efforts to keep a hold on absolute power, saw the Emperor of China or the Grand Mogul of India as ideal rulers, wielding unlimited power. Although the critics and the criticized held diametrically opposed views on the responsibilities incumbent on European rulers, both parties regarded the Far Eastern model as an ideal. In this respect there was a happy symbiosis between the fashions cultivated in material things and the lines of thought being pursued by the intellectuals. The creators of late-seventeenth- and early-eighteenth-century chinoiserie cabinets took individual artifacts from the Far East and put them together in such a way as to form a self-consciously exotic counter-subject contrasting with but also complementary to the familiar home culture; likewise, early Enlightenment authors used gobbets of Far Eastern philosophy to back up the criticisms they were leveling at the absolutists.[33] The parallels between the two were only apparent, as the two parties were enlisting the wisdom of the Orient to serve two quite different ends. While the princely cabinet – for all its much-praised and uncontested beauty – was no more than a curiosity that corroborated the European canon of harmony and symbolism proclaimed in the surrounding rooms, the writings which the early Enlightenment thinkers peppered with elements from other cultures were quite definitely aimed at the subversion of the status quo.[34]

The school of thought that exerted the greatest influence on the thought of the European critics was Confucianism. With his "utopian alternative to the existing order" which intended "not to dissolve the classical feudal hierarchy governing the relations between the rulers and the ruled, but to resolve its social contradictions and transform them into pure harmony,"[35] Confucius had an obvious appeal for early Enlightenment thinkers with their ideal of a virtuous ruler who was to be wise and responsible in the execution of his duties.

As there were practical limits to the exercise of pure and undiluted Absolutism, the material goods of the far-off kingdoms began to be seen in a somewhat different light. In very simple terms, the purely aesthetic value judgments of yesteryear were superseded by ones more concerned with substance and meaning. As the knowledge available became broader-based and incorporated a greater familiarity with the overall cultural context of the objects in hand, collectors became less and less content with throwing together miscellaneous exotica to form an eye-catching display, however magnificent, and correspondingly more concerned to integrate these treasures into their own system of values.

This manifested itself in a second wave of chinoiserie in which the overall composition was supplemented by freely invented motifs "à la chinoise," reinforcing the style's theatrical dimension in a very European way.[36] This led on the one hand to an increase in fantastic, bizarre, and exaggerated components, but also made it possible for the first time for designers to pursue programs of decoration incorporating thoroughly European iconographies, while at the same time inhabiting – or appearing to inhabit – the same world of Far Eastern forms as before. This shift in approach took place around 1720 and continued to make itself felt until well into the second half of the eighteenth century.[37] This is a phenomenon which we shall have to bear in mind when we consider the iconographical program pursued in the Japanese Palace, as insights into that program will in their turn be important for an in-depth understanding of the porcelain animals themselves.

The changes in the use to which Far Eastern artifacts and culture were put during the period of development from feudal to enlightened absolutism make it clear that the history of seventeenth- and eighteenth-century exotic interior decor cannot be regarded in purely aesthetic terms as a development of the fashion for chinoiserie. On the contrary, the changes in question are themselves a reflection of intellectual developments taking place at the time.[38]

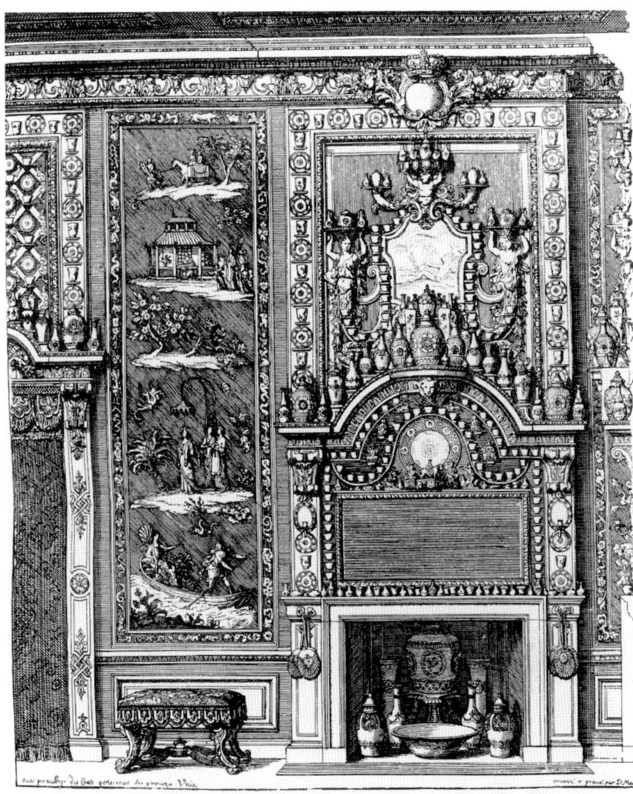

3 Daniel Marot the elder, design for a chimney-piece from *Nouvelle Cheminées Faittes en Plusier en Droit de la Hollande…* (Amsterdam, 1712)

The porcelain cabinet and the "Porzellanschloss"

We have relatively little concrete evidence concerning the actual use to which Far Eastern porcelain was put in the seventeenth and early eighteenth centuries, even in the case of the wares used for the consumption of those relatively new and fashionable beverages, tea, coffee, and chocolate. Whenever porcelain tableware is mentioned in contemporary inventories, it is always in connection with locations which had an element of "show" about them, whether they were, for instance, show-kitchens or chimney-pieces in private apartments. While this fact does not exclude the possibility of the wares being put to functional use, it does restrict this to a very exclusive context. In the second half of the seventeenth century, it was only in regions such as the Netherlands where imports made tea, coffee, and chocolate readily available in large quantities that porcelain was put to widespread use for the consumption of hot drinks. Likewise, we have hardly any evidence at all for the use of porcelain as tableware at German courts around 1700.[39] Precious metals and faience were preferred to Far Eastern porcelain plates and dishes, in spite of the availability of the latter in the requisite quantity and variety of shapes. In some sources it is not possible to know exactly what material is being referred to, as for instance when the chronicler of the inauguration banquet at the Dutch Palace in Dresden in 1717 writes that the guests "all had their fare served to them on Dutch porcelain."[40] It cannot be determined whether the expression "holländisches Porzellan" was here used to mean faience, as it indeed customarily was, or whether the tableware used was genuine Japanese porcelain, as has been suggested recently.[41] It was however certainly the case that on special occasions porcelain was put out for show on sideboards, together with equally costly vessels in precious metals.[42] It was only with the appearance on the market of the porcelain tableware service as such, that is to say around 1730 with the development of the European porcelain manufactories and the concomitant changes in dining habits,[43] that dinner services were commissioned from the East India companies with the intention of their being put to practical use.

For our purposes, however, the fact that in the late seventeenth and early eighteenth centuries porcelain was primarily used as an element in interior decoration is one of some significance. The high value set upon porcelain as a means of demonstrating and reflecting wealth and status derived not only from its origin and

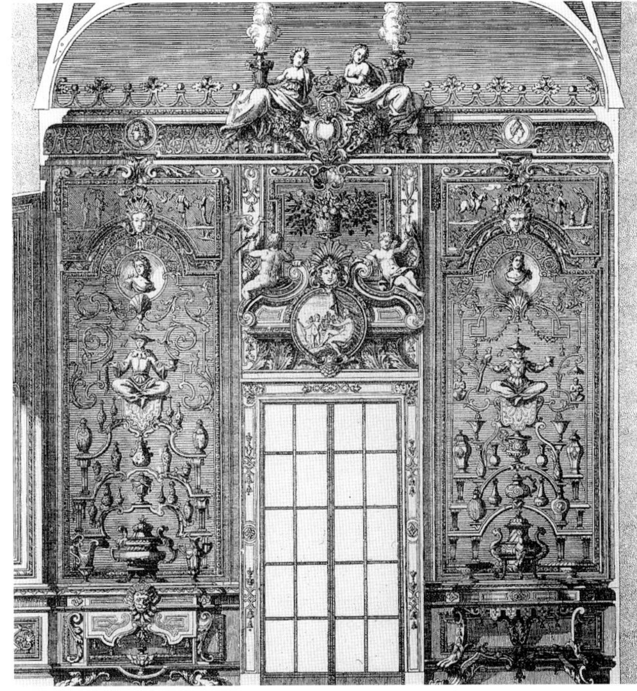

4 Paul Decker the elder, detail of a design for a collection cabinet, from *Fürstlicher Baumeister…* (Augsburg, 1711–16)

rarity but also – as will be shown in greater detail elsewhere – from the visible characteristics of the material itself (see Excursus on "shine," pp. 159–163). Surprisingly enough, the first homogeneous form of porcelain presentation was not invented at princely courts, but developed in the more bourgeois Netherlands, incorporating stylistic elements from France. This was in part the result of the availability of imported porcelain in almost any quantity and quality, but this particular way of arranging the porcelain can also be explained in terms related to the particular character of Calvinist ethics.[44]

The middle of the seventeenth century saw the adoption in the Netherlands of the French fashion for setting mirror surfaces on ceilings and, particularly, above fireplaces.[45] Insofar as they were available, Far Eastern lacquered panels provided another kind of shining, if not reflective, surface, and were used in the same rooms. In the Netherlands consoles were fitted to the fireplace mantels and the Far Eastern porcelain arranged thereon was reflected – and apparently multiplied – in the mirror. The Far Eastern porcelain shone and glowed all the more brightly for being set in dark, paneled rooms. Over and above the aesthetic impression that they made, they were evidence of their owner's interest in the culture of foreign lands and thus to a zest for education – China, after all, was considered the home of eternal wisdom – and also to a passion for collecting.[46]

In the Protestant Netherlands, this last aspect did not simply reflect wealth, but also served as a proof of the owner's capability in financial matters, an attribute considered little short of a high virtue. Especially for the dealers and merchants, making a show of these fragile treasures was tantamount to a material demonstration of their trustworthiness in business matters. And last but not least, as it enabled the eye to see the object from all sides without it having to be moved, thus ushering the beholder into the total presence of the whole, the mirror not only satisfied the rich citizen's desire for magnificence but also – particularly in the Protestant Netherlands – had a second, "transcendental and symbolic" significance as a pointer towards "the light" as understood in a religious sense.[47]

Copperplate engravings of the kind which attained fame in the works of Paulus Decker and Daniel Marot (figs. 3 and 4) ensured widespread familiarity with this way of displaying porcelain and finally led to distinct regional variations in the fashion.[48]

The Prussian porcelain cabinets, both formally and chronologically speaking, stood somewhere between the Dutch mode of presentation and the south German mirror cabinet ("Spiegelkabinett").[49] The first of these, and one of the first in the whole of Europe, was the one constructed by Luise Henriette von Nassau Oranien, the wife of the Great Elector, at Schloss Oranienburg. All we know about the fittings and furnishings from the inventory of 1699 is that the room had gilded blue leather wall-hangings and a large mirror.[50] The fact that from 1695 the Elector of Brandenburg had a mirror-making workshop in Neustadt an der Dosse at his disposition provided ideal conditions for the interiors to be fitted

5 Jean Baptiste Broebes, porcelain room in Schloss Oranienburg (Augsburg, 1733)

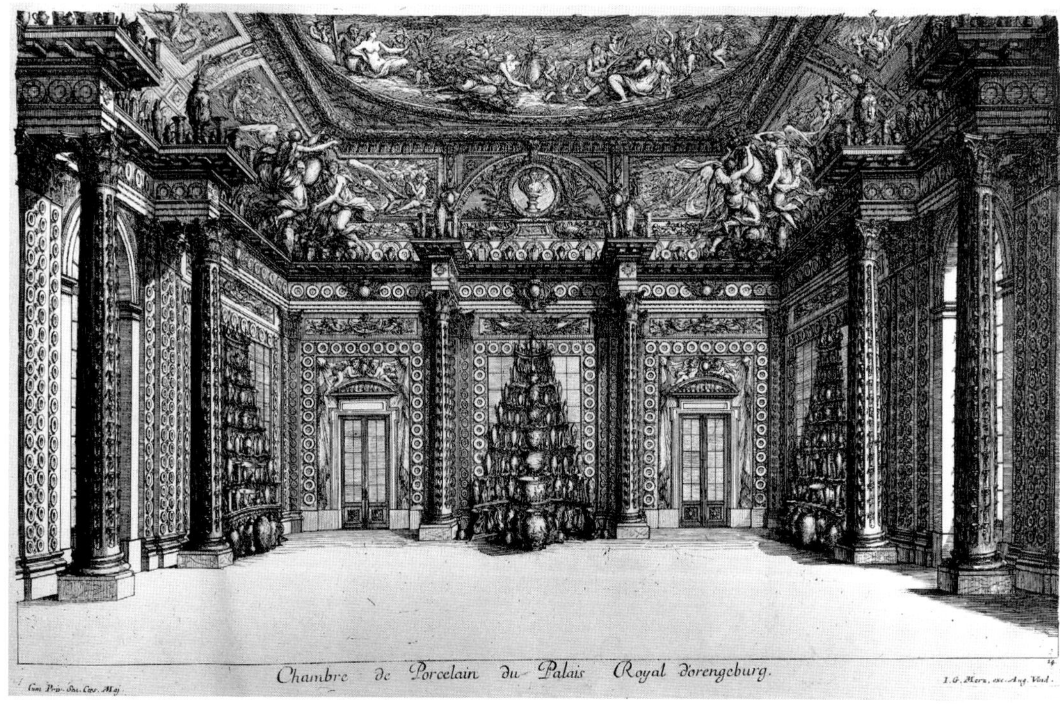

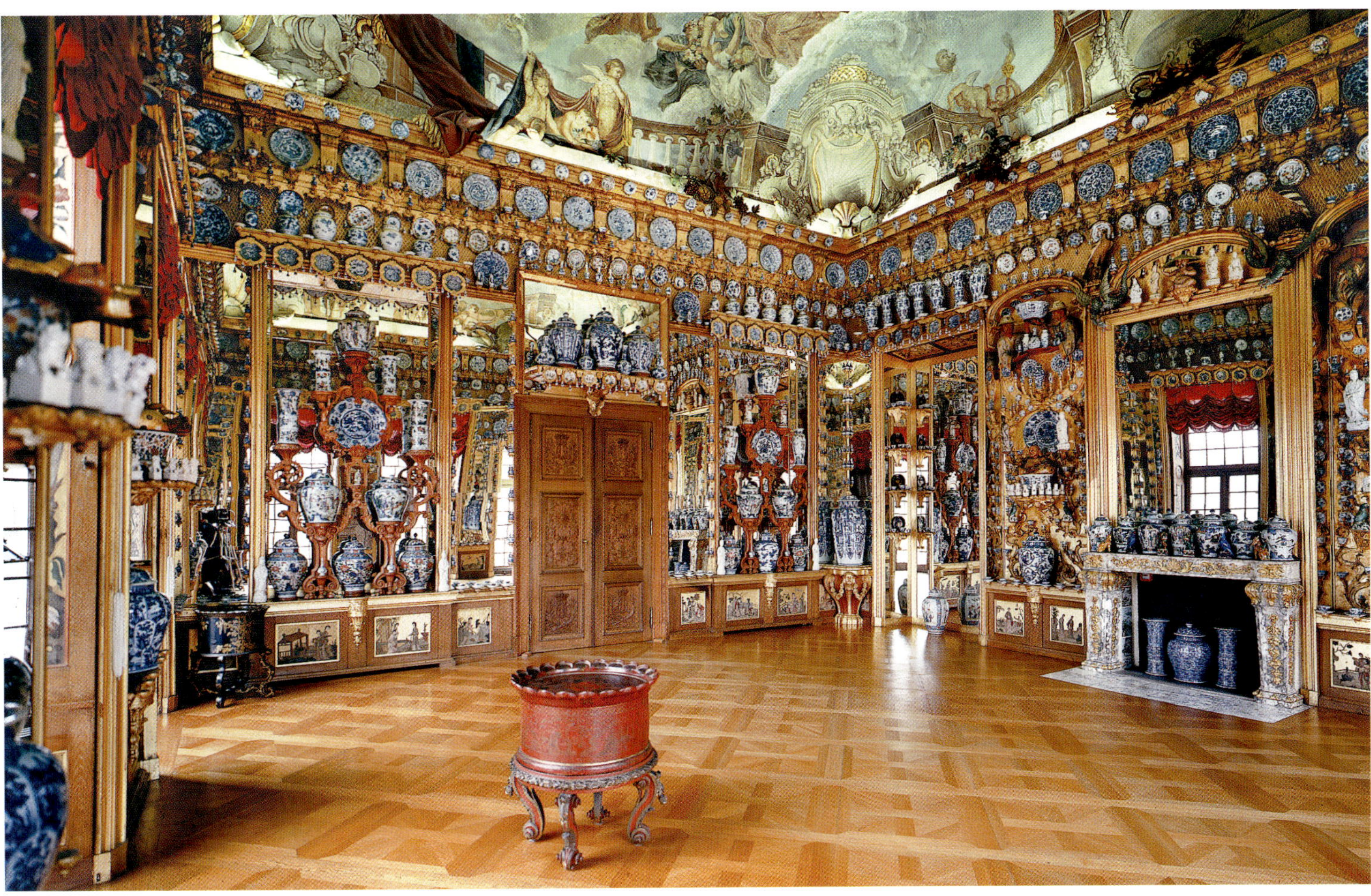

6 Porcelain room in Schloss Charlottenburg, Berlin (1997)

out lavishly with mirrors,[51] and the rebuilding of Schloss Oranienburg bore fruit in a *Porzellankammer* of a sumptuousness which put all its predecessors into the shade (fig. 5).

Against walls generously fitted out with mirrors, Far Eastern porcelain dominated the room, piled up on richly sculpted etageres. The whole impression was given its distinctive finish by a specifically Prussian invention, namely the incorporation of plates and smaller vessels in long rows and geometrical forms into the architectural forms articulating the walls – the beams, cornices, pilasters and even the fluting on the freestanding columns seemed to be made out of porcelain pieces, with the weight-bearing parts of the walls situated behind them. Every detail of the room was quite visibly executed in the costliest of materials.

But the mirrors were intended to do more than to show the objects from all sides at once and effect an illusory "multiplication"; by reproducing and opening up the whole room, they turned it into an allegory of an infinite macrocosm within which the decoration on the Asian porcelains – likewise shining, but opaquely so – engendered a similarly "infinite" microcosm. The beholder was torn hither and thither between the close-sighted perspective born of the wish to examine the intricate painting on the porcelains and the far-sighted perspective necessitated by the desire to grasp – *in uno ictu mentis* – the real length and breadth of a room that was deprived of its lines of demarcation by the mirrors; all the while the elevated and noble character of the prince all the while was strongly impressed upon the eye and mind of the beholder, not only directly and rationally (the iconographical program inherent in the room's decoration, coats of arms and so on) but also indirectly and emotionally (the impression made by the room). The visitor to the Schloss Charlottenburg porcelain room of 1706 (fig. 6), the direct successor of that at Oranienburg, is subjected to an experience of space which affords illuminating insights into what all this magnificence was intended to achieve. Both these rooms were also special examples of their kind in that they were the largest and architecturally most elaborate rooms in their respective suites, and were also situated beyond the state bedroom where in the tradition of the German Baroque one would expect to find nothing more than a small *Kunstkabinett*. Both rooms further-

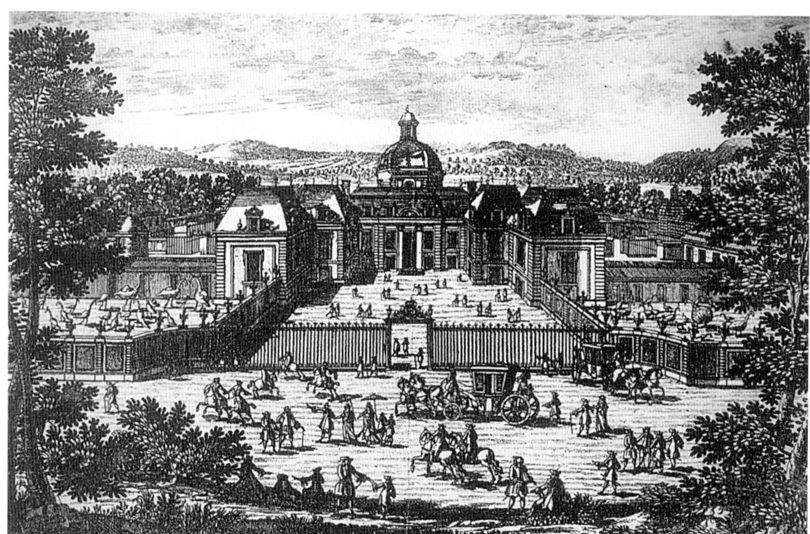

7 André Pérelle, the *Trianon de Porcelaine*

more offered direct access to the chapel and were topped with ceiling paintings incorporating images of sovereignty related to the specific situation of Prussia at the time and coordinated with the lavish decoration of the walls.[52] As we shall see in greater detail later on, this form of porcelain room, calling as it did for a large porcelain collection and home-produced mirrors, was to be subjected to further development of a particular kind at the Japanese Palace in Dresden.

As the porcelain cabinets and rooms were not alone in providing inspiration and models for the Japanese Palace, it will not be out of place to take a brief look at another genre which derived from the enthusiasm for chinoiserie, namely the *Porzellanschloss.*

As has now been well established, the second half of the seventeenth century saw France developing its own manner of using mirrors for symbolic effect and to heighten impressions of power and wealth.[53] While the Hall of Mirrors at Versailles had a certain – albeit limited – influence on similar creations in southern Germany, the porcelain palace built at one end of the transverse arm of the large canal at Versailles became a widely imitated model. The Trianon de Porcelaine opposite the menagerie was commissioned by Louis XIV for Madame de Montespan in 1660 as a tea-house with a front courtyard, wings on either side, and its own garden.

The stimulus for Europe's first *Porzellanschloss* had been given by various reports of the porcelain pagoda in Nanking, regarded at the time as the eighth wonder of the world. When in 1669 Johan Neuhof published his impressions of imperial China, he described this many-storied tower clad in porcelain tiles and backed up his description with an illustration.[54] It was, however, not until the second quarter of the eighteenth century that this illustration and other similar ones had an influence on the outer appearance of the pleasure buildings in European parks and gardens.[55]

The Trianon de Porcelaine had been built with a complete Baroque front elevation, the only Chinese elements being the color, the materials used, and ornamentation. The whole creation, including its fittings and certain parts of the garden, was executed in blue and white, that is to say in the color scheme in evidence on the most sought-after Chinese porcelains of the time.[56]

The special thing about the Trianon, however, was its ceramic decoration. Large vases were placed on consoles on the facade, and the balustrades and garden were likewise adorned with large-size vessels. In addition, faience panels were set into the outside walls, the floors inside were laid with blue-and-white tiles, and the engraving by Pérelle suggests that the roof was also covered with (again, blue and white?) glazed roof-tiles (fig. 7).[57] As Far Eastern porcelain was neither available nor suitable for this kind of architectural decoration, it was decided to use faience produced in the Dutch manner at the newly-founded manufactory in Trianon.[58] But even these tiles proved not to be durable enough and suffered so greatly under the weather conditions that the tea-house was rebuilt in 1687 and extended to form the Trianon de Marbre.

Although Augustus the Strong did see the Trianon de Porcelaine on his grand tour – but before the rebuilding and thus very likely with its original beauty much impaired – it cannot, as will become clear, be regarded as having been a direct source of inspiration for the Japanese Palace in Dresden. It is nevertheless worth noting that this little building was the first European realization of the idea of a *Porzellanschloss,* and that its conception at a time of burgeoning enthusiasm for chinoiserie was directly influenced by the existence of Far Eastern porcelain at the court of an absolutist prince long before the fashion for porcelain cabinets had developed in other parts of Europe.

Animal sculpture in the late Renaissance and Baroque

The depiction of animals has been as constant a phenomenon in the history of art as has the depiction of human beings or plants, and the resulting works of art have been as various as the factors motivating the artists involved. A systematic history of animal depiction, however, has yet to be written. Such publications as make a certain claim to comprehensiveness, such as *Das Tier in der Kunst* ("The Animal in Art") by Reinhard Piper,[59] do no more than list a selection of works of art in which an animal is depicted in some form or other, and venture no judgments as to what might have motivated an artist to depict a certain animal in a given context. This procedure may be justifiable if the animal is treated simply as a motif and no relevance is attached to the nature of the animal in question and of the animal world generally. If this is the case, however, the study will never yield real insights into the intentions lying behind any given work. And yet it is particularly true of animal representation that study of the way in which the artist goes about depicting a subject can tell us fundamental truths about that artist and his or her attitude to the world as created by God. Even cursory study of the art of past ages shows that animal depictions have always provided receptive vehicles for a wide range of projections and concerns. The similarities between mankind and the animals have justified using animals allegorically and symbolically (having them represent virtues, for example); the differences, on the other hand, have justified holding them firmly at a distance, even presenting them as belonging to a world far removed from that of our common experience (beasts of fable, for instance).

The study of the animal as a valid object for art historical reflection is still at the stage where scholarly investigations are limited to certain periods, genres, and motifs.[60] And yet there is one line of thought which recurs leitmotif-like in many of these investigations, a line of thought made up of two components: firstly, a feeling that animals are essentially very like human beings, and secondly, the certain knowledge that they are in fact quite different. The way art relates to the animal world and the forms in which animals are depicted are both dependent on cultural background. What is independent of the cultural context is the perception of each species of animal as being either close to or far away from man, whether in purely superficial terms or at a deeper, more essential level, and the first categorization of the animal world that results from these perceptions. Another category which would likewise be independent of cultural context would be the respective animal's usefulness to man, and another its dangerousness.

These three aspects – similarity, usefulness, dangerousness – are in themselves evidence of the way in which human perception classifies and interprets the animal world. Only that form of natural science which arrives at its structuring of the animal world through the comparison of physiological and anatomical details can claim to be operating with any large degree of objectivity. Although we nowadays have the basic equipment to be objective in these things, we can still see from our own judgments that we are strongly influenced by other categories deriving from the direct relationship between animals and man. Who, on seeing a lion, for instance, does not first of all think of such qualities as "power," "superiority," or even "kingship," before giving a thought to the connection between this beast and the domestic cat?

Accordingly, any artistic genre in which an animal or animals constitute a major or even secondary subject can only be understood with reference to the way in which animals were seen by the contemporary world. The following survey of the general forms of animal representation from the late sixteenth to the eighteenth century, the period which gave birth to the objective zoology referred to above, may formally not be much more than a simple enumeration but it incorporates an attempt to distinguish the various intentions and motivations of the various artists involved.

Animals in painting and sculpture

Animals play a part in various genres of Baroque painting. The visual effect of their forms and surfaces (antlers, plumage, coat etc.) were investigated in the still life, and the animal world was presented in all its variety in such depictions as the Garden of Eden, Noah's ark, Orpheus with the animals, and other such subjects; meticulous accuracy was invested in study-like works which aimed to shed light on the microcosm of, for instance, a bird's wing, and rare species or particularly valuable specimens were accorded animal portraits. France and the Netherlands developed local genres

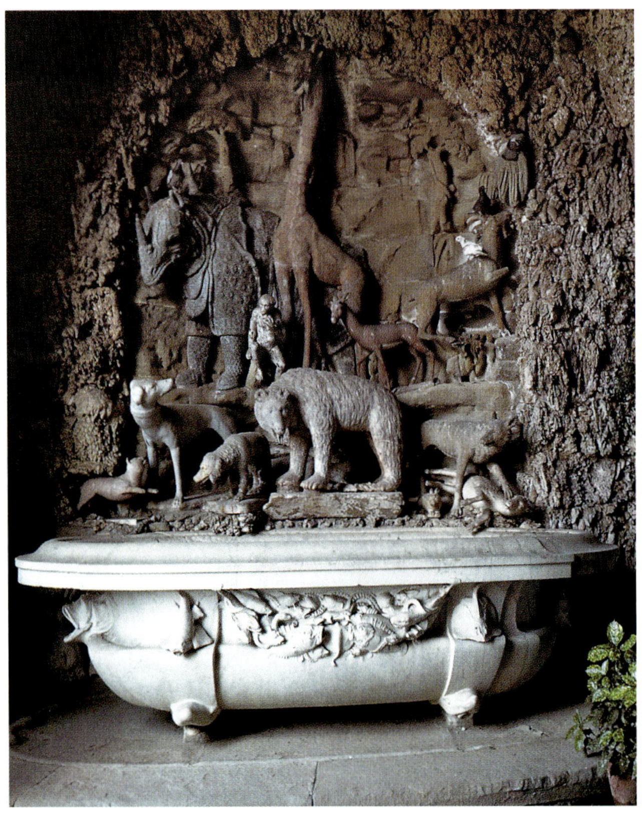

8 Giovanni da Bologna (Giambologna), bear niche from the animal grotto in the villa gardens in Castello, 1565–1569

all of their own such as the animal fight (France) and fowl (Netherlands).[61] Painters such as Melchior de Hondecoeter, Jan van Kessel, Jan Fyt, Jan Weenix, Frans Snyders, Roelant Savery, and Jean Baptiste Oudry – to mention but a few of the more famous names – made a specialty of the one or other aspect of animal depiction, some even achieving their fame first and foremost as animal-painters.

Although one might suppose that animals were as widespread a subject in three-dimensional as in two-dimensional art, sculptors had in fact much greater difficulty with animal representation than painters and graphic artists. One reason for this may be that the sculptor is generally restricted to the representation of one animal, or at the most a few animals, which automatically rules out a number of genres and subjects much favored by painters. The execution of a composite subject such as Orpheus with the animals is a disproportionately more demanding task for a sculptor than it is for the painter, whose very medium always has a certain inherent unity to it. Baroque sculpture thus concentrated rather on saints, rulers, allegories, and architectural elements. Comprehensive surveys such as Piper's on animals in art, and Carl Blümel's on animals in sculpture,[62] show a conspicuous lack of three-dimensional animal representations from the seventeenth and early eighteenth centuries. If, however, one changes one's perspective and looks for examples independent of an "autonomous" tradition, then it is possible to identify animal sculptures that not only have a certain amount in common with the Meissen large animal figures but are also part of the Meissen figures' motivic background.

Sixteenth-century miniature animal sculptures

The fact that the post-medieval world set greater store on earthly values and on their reflection in art led to a new evaluation of the animal world, and to a greater degree of attention being accorded to animals in art. The demonic, or even simply bizarre, element in the bestiaries of the Middle Ages gave way to a vision that saw the animal world as a possible link between the microcosm and the macrocosm, and as a realm in which the divine in creation could be perceived directly, without the need for scholarly or literary mediation.

This was, for instance, the point of view held by artists in northern Italy and France who used molds made directly from small animals to cast animal figures that were faithful and detailed reproductions of their respective live models. Among those who used this method was Andrea Briosco, known as Riccio, who produced little bronze animals in early-seventeenth-century Padua.[63]

9 Giovanni da Bologna (Giambologna), figure of a monkey, bronze, ca. 1570, Musée du Louvre, Paris

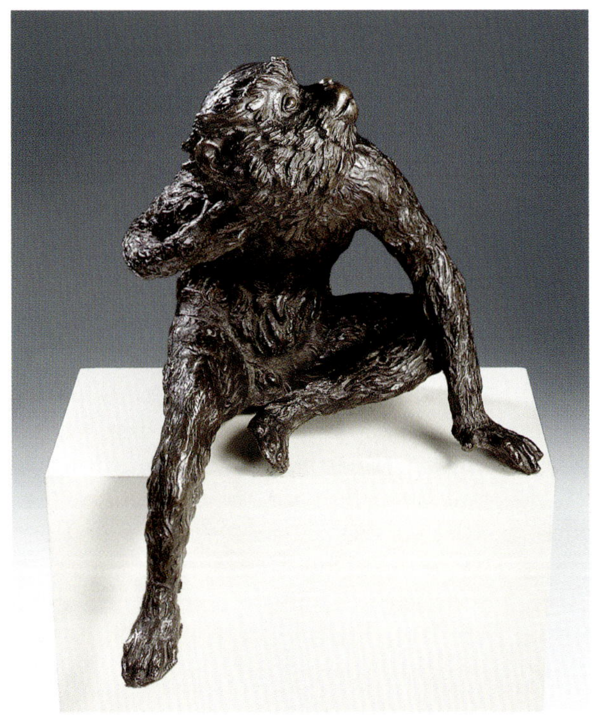

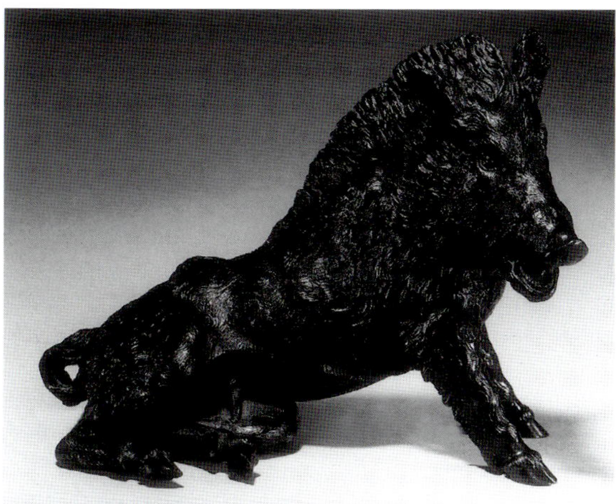

10 Antonio Susini (attrib.), wild boar of Mount Erymanthus, bronze, beginning of seventeenth century

In France, in the middle of the sixteenth century, Bernard Palissy decorated dishes with brilliantly lifelike clay moldings of lizards, snakes, fish and snails, all shimmering with transparent colored glaze. Sadly, only fragments have survived of a principal work from the hand of this "premier poitier du Roi," a whole grotto in Paris populated with a vast multitude of these nature moldings.

It was likewise for a grotto, the *Grotta degli animali* at the Villa Medici in Castello that, around 1567, Giambologna and his workshop created a number of life-size bronze bird sculptures to complement the animal sculptures in stone by Niccolò Tribolo.[64] Giambologna was in fact involved on a number of occasions in the production of animals destined for grottoes or large fountains (fig. 8).[65]

In addition to figures such as these, which were part of a larger concept and only made sense in that context (Giambologna's Monkey [fig. 9], for instance, was part of the Samson the Philistine fountain in the court of the Casino next to San Marco in Florence), late Renaissance Mannerists from northern Italy also made bronze animals which were neither cast from molds taken from nature nor intended to stand in a larger overall context. The selection of animals was restricted to those which were suitable as symbols for power, skill in the fight, beauty, or elegance – for, that is to say, noble virtues. The horse and the bull were much-loved motifs, both presented in "classical" poses. Or copies were made of classical originals, a particularly important example of which was the Roman figure of the sitting boar of Mount Erymanthus (fig. 10).

North of the Alps life-size bronzes were made most notably by the circle of artists around Hubert Gerhard in Munich, likewise at the end of the sixteenth century, conspicuous examples being a pug-bitch and hunting hounds (Bavarian National Museum). These latter belonged to a large fountain, and the pug-bitch might well have been a portrait of a specific dog, especially as the pug was associated with a certain specifically courtly symbolism.[66] Other animal figures done at this time in Germany or the Netherlands, mostly large or small bronzes, tended to be styled in accordance with northern Italian models.

To sum up, the sixteenth century, particularly its second half, saw the animal taking up a position of considerable importance in the repertoire of small sculpture. Although these sculptures were for the most part naturalistic in execution, the figures were not simply done for their own sake, but were decorative elements in larger overall schemes, or were linked to some kind of moral ideal.

While it cannot be claimed that these animal sculptures were direct forebears of the Meissen animals, it is in the present context nevertheless illuminating to consider the development of the animal motif in Baroque sculpture.

The Versailles maze

One of the Baroque's most important and sizeable creations in the field of animal sculpture was to be found in the park of Versailles, where in 1673/74 a total of thirty-nine fountains were constructed

11 "The Monkey as King," fragment of a figure for a fountain in the labyrinth at Versailles, lead with vestiges of painting, ca. 1673, Château de Versailles

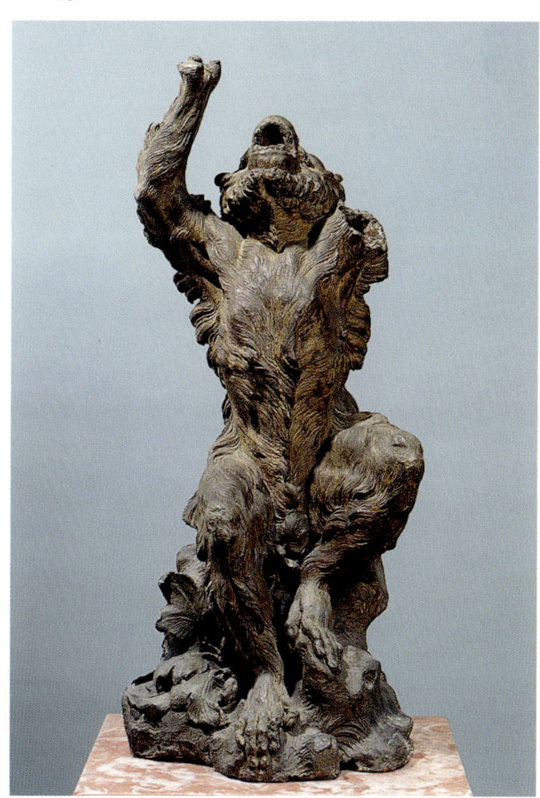

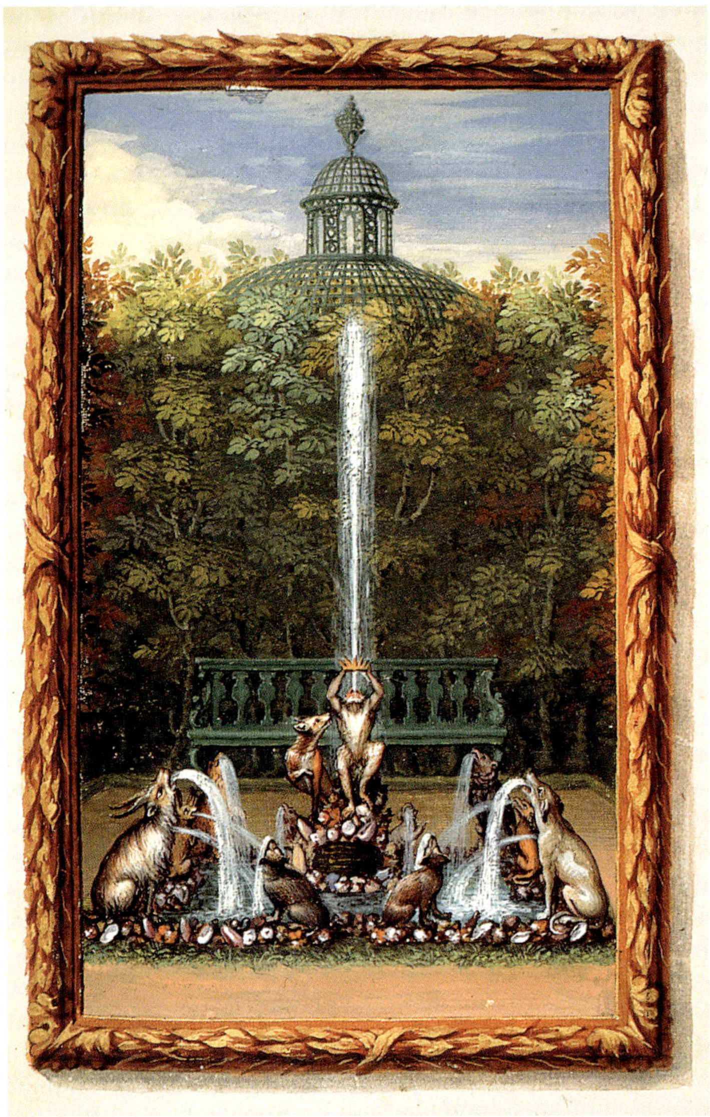

12 Jacques Bailly, "The Monkey as King," gouache after a fountain in the Versailles labyrinth, ca. 1677

at every fork or crossing of the paths in a maze of hedges designed by André LeNôtre und Charles Perrault.[67] Every fountain had as its subject one of Aesop's (or, rather, La Fontaine's) fables, and a total of eighteen sculptors were commissioned to make the necessary animal sculptures in lead (fig. 11).[68] Each figure was painted naturalistically and was put together with trellises, grotto elements, shells and smooth-cut hedges to form a composition in which it also had to function as the water-spout in the fountain: "for the water which they spout at one another not only makes them seem all the more lively and active, but also endows them with what one might call their voice, enabling them to express their excitement and their thoughts" (fig. 12).[69] Appended to the fountains were titles and four-line poems deriving from the respective fables of La Fontaine, and the entrance to the maze was flanked by figures of Aesop and Eros, emphasizing the source of the stories. The ensemble was taken apart when the park was reconstructed to a new design in 1775, but a number of the figures have survived and are kept in the Versailles depository.

Shortly after the maze was constructed, copperplate engravings were made of the animal figures and of the whole complex, which was instrumental in making animal groups from fables into a commonplace of park sculpture throughout Europe (figs. 13–15).[70] Two aspects of the Versailles fountains, which Augustus the Strong certainly saw on his grand tour, are of particular significance in relation to the Meissen animals. Firstly, the individual animals had to be executed in a posture and with spouts which allowed the various fountains of water to make up one large and effective overall water choreography. And secondly, they were not created freely and then made to combine with each other in some way, but had from the very beginning concrete compositional roles to fulfill, both to give visual expression to the content of the fable, and also to ensure that the play of the water at the fountain in question fitted in with the overall plan. These figures cannot be considered examples of free animal sculpture, dependent as they were on the story being told and to the greater whole of which they were but a part. As a quintessential example of a little cosmos sufficient unto itself, the maze naturally appealed to the Baroque predilection for artificial but highly suggestive worlds. The line of thought ran from the perception of the individual animal as part of the natural world, through openness to the fable and its moral, to a binding together of the individual statements into a coherent ideal with limits laid down by the maze. However, no comprehensive art historical study has yet appeared on the maze at Versailles.[71]

13 Johann Baptist Hofmann, "The Monkey as King," detail from an unrealized ideal plan for the palace gardens at Hildburghausen, ca. 1720

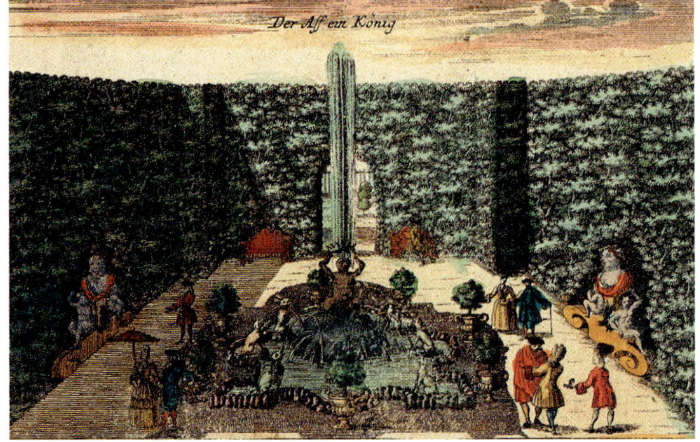

Animal sculpture in Baroque gardens

In the Baroque, animals continued to find favor as motifs for grottoes and fountains, just as they had done in the sixteenth century. A number of seventeenth-century Spanish gardens had large, mountain-like fountain constructions which were decorated with animal figures in accordance with their overall theme. The garden at Abadia had a Parnassus topped by a figure of Pegasus, and Aranjuez had a mount of Diana with the goddess of the hunt and wild animals.[72]

Single animal figures in gardens were used to make heraldic references to their owners, or as general symbols for strength and power, with lions playing a particularly important role in this respect. Alternatively, as in the case of the park of Chiswick House in the first half of the eighteenth century, they were simply copies of classical originals.[73] For Chiswick House, the copy of the Boar of Mount Erymanthus was given a figure of a wolf as a counterpart.

What has already been established in relation to sculptures illustrating animal fables thus also holds true for all animal sculpture done for Baroque gardens: the figures cannot be seen as autonomous or even purely decorative works of art, but had to fit into overall schemes and contexts, or served to refer to higher matters, to which they were subordinated in all respects from their formal execution right down to the expressions on their faces.

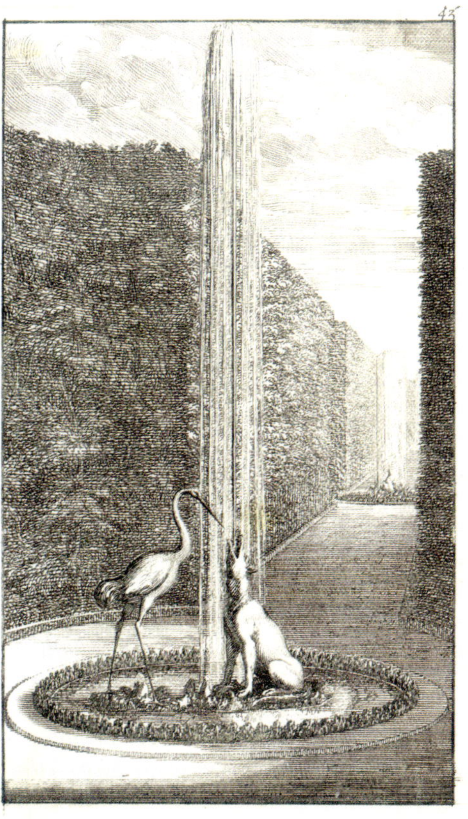

14 Sébastien Le Clerc, "The Wolf and the Crane," engraving after a fountain in the Versailles labyrinth, 1677

Animal sculptures in the Baroque interior

Animal sculptures were not only intended to put out in the open air, but also had a place of their own in the architectural context, or in interiors.

In this sphere too, we find likenesses of animals being used for the projection of ideas and concrete concerns. Heraldic animals such as eagles, lions, and horses were given symbolic and signpost functions, when placed, often in ornamental surroundings, on such locations places as facades and bannister posts on grand staircases, over doors and fireplaces, or next to thrones.[74] In these cases, the image of the animal was decorative but could at the same time symbolize virtues, or, according to its context, refer quite clearly to the bearer of the respective coat of arms. But animal sculptures also had similarly representative roles to play in other more ephemeral contexts, on drinking vessels, for instance, or in the case of small bronzes: "The intention was a particularly charming one, namely to induce associations, multiple meanings, and a consequent multiplicity of possible explanations."[75]

This dual pattern of likeness (the animal itself) and symbol (significance as a reference) played a role in every animal representation, whether in the open air or in interiors. Quite apart from individual figures, myths and themes such as the hunt or Paradise could also be used as vehicles for statements that could be read from the behavior and interaction of all the animals. Particularly

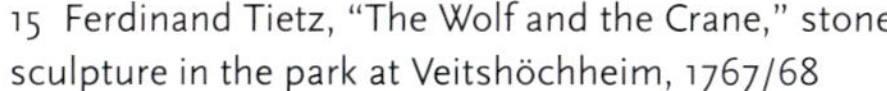

15 Ferdinand Tietz, "The Wolf and the Crane," stone sculpture in the park at Veitshöchheim, 1767/68

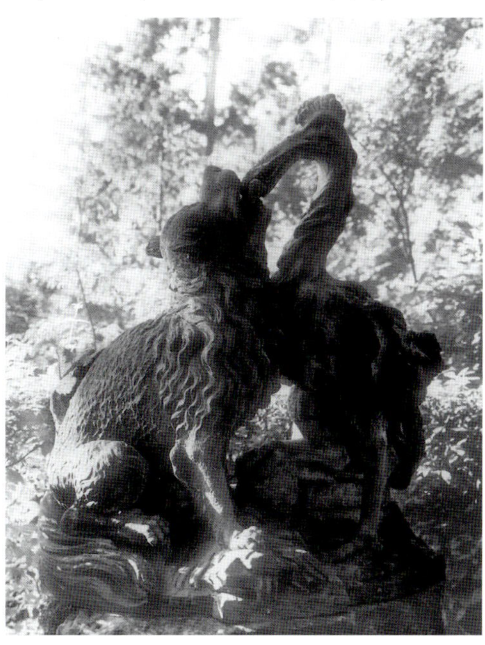

fine examples of this are offered by the two wooden pulpits sculpted by Michiel van der Voort in the Abbey of St. Bernard on the Schelde (1713, now in Antwerp Cathedral) and in the Norbertine convent in Liliëndal (1723), depicting the earthly paradise with a multitude of naturalistically rendered birds and small animals.[76]

What is important is that when used instead of the written word, coats of arms, or ornament animal figures were effective means of creating multiple layers of meaning, and were furthermore more decorative than human representation would have been. It is highly illuminating that when animal sculptures with a primarily representative function were replaced by anthropomorphous or human figures, then the figures chosen to replace them were ones which according to the mind of the time had a status between man and the animal world, such as creatures of fable or certain ethnic groups such as black Africans.

Wherever animal figures appeared, whether they were freestanding, or decorating a table, supporting a console, or done as reliefs running round a cylindrical tankard, the purpose was never that the beholder should learn more about the animal as a living being. As a motif, the animal was always the communicator of an allotted statement, or of a message written clearly upon it for all to understand. It served as an illustration of statements to do with human behavior, which thereby received a quasi-natural status (the fountains at Versailles, for instance), as allegorical symbols for the senses, the continents, the virtues and vices, for the orders of society, as religious symbols (dove, lamb, pelican), as emblems of saints or mythological figures, or as representatives of a world formed by man.

As we come closer to attempting an interpretation of the Meissen large animal figures made for the Japanese Palace, it will be important to bear in mind the place that animals traditionally had in art, and to remember that the animal was represented in a way that was to a large extent independent of its real appearance – but not, it should be noted, its real posture – and that the Baroque invested this tradition with a greater capacity for multiplicity of meaning.

The Palace and the Animals: Fundamentals of their genesis and appearance

The Japanese Palace

Building chronology

It was in the year 1714 that Field Marshall and Privy Cabinet Minister Count Jakob Heinrich von Flemming bought several plots of land on the right bank of the Elbe and had a small palace built, with a garden. On account of the manner of its furnishing it became known as the Dutch Palace. The architect was most likely Matthäus Daniel Pöppelmann.[77] Count Flemming did not take up residence in the palace himself, but let it shortly after it was ready at the end of 1715 to the envoy extraordinary of the Netherlands in Dresden, Johan van Haersolte Heer van Kranenburg, who died in 1716. In May 1717, Augustus the Strong acquired the palace from his minister in exchange for a palais in the Pirnaische Gasse, and had it newly furnished by the *ordonneur des cabinets* Raymond LePlat. The work was finished within a matter of weeks, and there was a grand inauguration celebration on August 15.[78] Whether the palace already had the French-style three-wing layout,[79] or whether it was still at this time simply a nucleus which the king then extended into a three-wing building, is a question which need not be dealt with here, especially as the sources offer nothing in the way of conclusive evidence on the matter.[80]

Augustus the Strong supplemented the furnishings with an abundance of, among other things, lacquered furniture, ceramic works of art, and in 1717 had parts of the *Kunstkammer* installed in the attic story: "His Royal Majesty bought the palace for a large sum of money in 1717 on account of its splendor and excellent situation, and has preserved it for posterity under the name of the Japanese Palace. [...] Having done this, he had the world-famous *Kunstkammer* brought to this palace three years ago from Neu-Dresden for the sake of the good air,[81] accommodating it two staircases up in nine rooms specially adapted for the purpose, where it has been put into the finest order [...]."[82] This source is the first one to refer to the building by its new name. The terms "Dutch Palace" and "Japanese Palace" were used synonymously in written sources throughout the eighteenth century, though the latter expression became the more common of the two after the reconstruction at the end of the 1720s. In a letter of March 27, 1732, Count Wackerbarth even suggested to the king that he might rename it the "Japanisch-Meissnisches Palais," especially since there was nothing comparable to be found anywhere throughout the Netherlands, which is another clear indication that the appellation "Dutch" was not a bow in the direction of the first resident, as is repeatedly claimed in literature on the subject, but simply a reference to the style of the furnishings.[83]

The first highpoint in the history of this palace was the first of the nine fully coordinated planet celebrations mounted in and around Dresden in connection with the marriage of the crown prince Friedrich August II to Maria Josepha, the daughter of the Habsburg emperor.[84] Guests from all over Europe arrived at the Dutch Palace on September 10, 1719, to attend this opening celebration, at which the crown prince was to be invested with the Order of the Golden Fleece. It was fully intended that the guests, many of whom were seeing the palace for the first time, should be bowled over with amazement at the magnificence of the furnishings and decorations, particularly as this and the subsequent celebrations of this quite exceptional dynastic union were also intended by the Elector of Saxony to be seen as demonstrations of his own political legitimacy.[85] We shall at a later stage consider whether Augustus the Strong already had this event in mind when he acquired the Dutch Palace, or whether he was motivated to make the acquisition by other factors.

It was certainly the case that the palace was repeatedly used as a venue for court festivities in the first half of the 1720s; the terraced garden, amply decorated with Italian Baroque sculptures and large ceramic vases, certainly provided an attractive alternative to the other royal gardens in Dresden (fig. 16).[86] As early as 1719 the site itself was being exploited to give an extra dimension to the firework displays which were such an indispensable part of the conclusion of any Baroque court celebration, with the fireworks being set off on the Elbe so that the lights were mirrored in the water. The garden terraces, rather like boxes at the opera, provided an ideal vantage point from which the assembled company could enjoy the display at a safe distance.

In 1722 the acquisition of neighboring plots made it possible to extend the area in front of the palace to reflect its owner's royal status. There were also slight changes made to the interior, such as the construction of a show-kitchen in the basement.[87] This semi-functional room, of a kind for which there was a widespread fash-

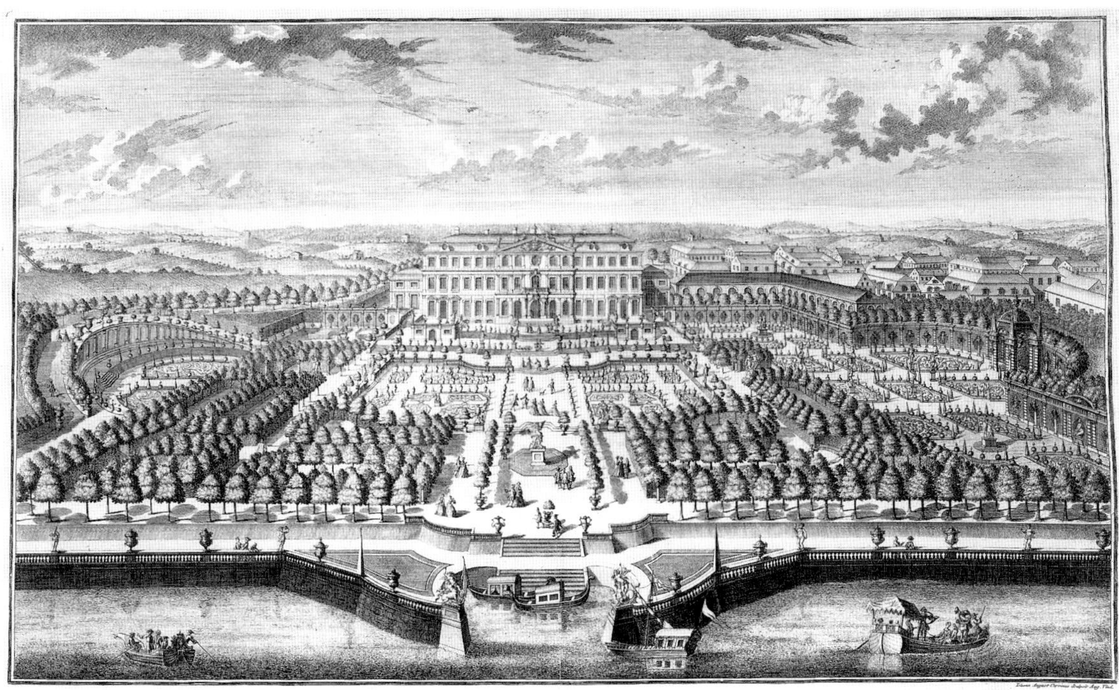

16 Johann August Corvinus, view of the Dutch Palace from the Elbe, with the gardens (1727)

ion, also extended the palace's capacity for accommodating porcelain, glass, silver, and lacquerwork. We know from the inventory of 1721 that the porcelain kept in the kitchen and adjacent rooms was arranged according to color, a fact to which we shall return later.[88] The claim made hitherto in literature on the subject that Augustus the Strong was by about 1720 already intending to make the Dutch Palace into a large-scale porcelain palace cannot be upheld if account is taken of a plan, hitherto overlooked, kept at the *Landesamt für Denkmalpflege* (Department of Historical Monuments of Saxony) in Dresden (fig. 27).[89] This slightly cut-about ground plan for a central-plan building is part of a series of plans for an extension which was to have made Schloss Pillnitz into a kind of "Saxon Versailles,"[90] and is apart from a few details identical to a second draft dated by Walter Hentschel to around 1722.[91]

The remarkable thing about this document is its ink entries, which repeat words already written underneath in pencil in the hand of Augustus the Strong himself. He put his own ideas forward in the case of many other projects, making sketches or "correcting" drawings offered for his perusal, and here he was doing precisely this. The entries, such as "grün Porzellain," relate to the plan to furnish an entire story with his collection of Far Eastern porcelain. Annotations of this kind relating to the distribution of the various porcelain groupings were also made on the series of plans for the Japanese Palace. And this hitherto unpublished plan can furthermore be seen as related to a letter of 1721 in which Count Wackerbarth suggests to the king that Schloss Pillnitz could be converted into a porcelain palace, with a facade – doubtless in imitation of the Trianon de Porcelaine – clad with Meissen tiles.[92]

However, the extensive reconstruction plans for Pillnitz came to nothing, and Augustus the Strong subsequently turned his attention to Großsedlitz and – but only from now on, that is to say, after 1725 – to the extension which was to convert the Dutch Palace into the Japanese Palace. Even though Count Flemming had been commissioned to buy houses on the Meißener Gasse in 1722, this had only been in order to extend the palace garden.[93]

Augustus the Strong's contemporaries do not seem to have found anything unusual about his failure to pursue the Pillnitz project, and this was indeed a fate it shared with most of his building plans. A character sketch penned by Count Flemming in 1722 shows how well he knew the king's passion for building, and what an acute judge he was of his master's abilities in this field: "After the gallant attentions he pays the ladies, the thing that gives him most pleasure in life is putting up buildings, whether military or secular, and all are agreed that he has a considerable understanding of both these skills. He has however not yet brought a single one of his buildings to successful completion. His craving for the approval of all those around him often causes him to change his plans, with the result that he makes many fine starts, but brings nothing to fulfillment."[94]

Some authors have assumed that the palace had been extended by a mezzanine in 1723.[95] Recent research, however, has shown that this was not the case.[96] The first ground for these authors'

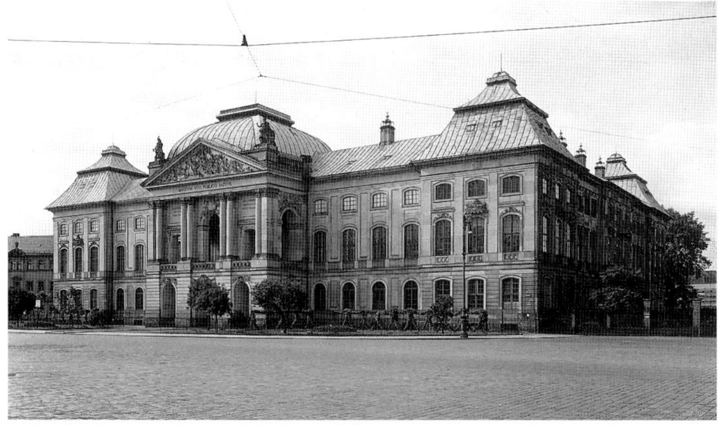

18 Japanese Palace, the portico side (before 1945)

assumption was a letter written to Augustus the Strong in which the writer, Count Wackerbarth in his function as *Generalintendant des Bauwesens* (Director of Building), recommends very highly that this conversion be carried out.[97] The second piece of evidence to which they appealed was the engraving of the palace by Johann August Corvinus (fig. 16). In this instance, however, the inclusion of a mezzanine can be explained by the fact that it was at that time quite normal practice to incorporate elements as yet only planned into architectural prints and drawings; Alexander Thiele, for instance, incorporated Pöppelmann's extension plans into his depictions of the Zwinger. The engraver would have had access to drawings relating to the addition of a story; as we know from Wackerbarth, these had already been made by Longuelune.

This suggests that the planning for the extension of the Dutch Palace did not really get under way until 1725, which is also the first year for which there is circumstantial evidence to make an intensification of planning activity seem plausible, namely the sharp growth in the porcelain collection taking place at the time, and the failure of the Pillnitz project in the same year.

The first designs for the extension show precisely the kind of French-style three-wing construction which was at the time the very epitome of a modern, comfortable palace. Plans made a little later, however, by a group of architects from the *Oberbauamt* (Chief Building Office) show that preference had been given to an enclosed, four-wing layout of the kind that was in fact finally carried out. On March 19, 1727, Augustus the Strong gave his official approval to the execution of a plan with four wings and projecting corner pavilions. The palace was then promptly partially cleared out, and on April 9 the foundation stone was laid,[98] with building materials being brought to the site.[99] Amazingly enough, work apparently stopped immediately afterwards. In any case, when the Prussian king Friedrich Wilhelm I visited the palace in January 1728, it was still possible for him to "feel great admiration for the large stock of precious porcelain."[100] By 1729, however, when a start was finally made on the building work proper, the project had changed once more,[101] possibly under the influence of Jean de Bodt, who had in 1728 succeeded Wackerbarth as director of building in Dresden.[102]

However, the decision in favor of a four-wing construction was adhered to, and Johann Georg Keyssler described the state of affairs when he visited Dresden in October 1730 as follows: "This beautiful palace [i.e., the Dutch Palace] is now to be pulled down and rebuilt as a four-cornered building with four entrances. Overseeing this choice building project are General Bodt and Saxony's three *Oberlandbaumeister* [chief architects], Pöpelmann, Longlue and Knevel"[103] (fig. 17; cf. Source 2). Keyssler, who will be of importance to us as an eye-witness in other contexts, was in fact partly mistaken, as the *corps de logis* of the Dutch Palace was not actually pulled down, but incorporated into the Elbe-side wing of the new building, the only change effected being to the structure of its rooms. The old staircase, for instance, remained as it had been before.

After a substantial sum of money had been made available for building in 1729,[104] the project proceeded apace. By August 1730 the side wings and the Neustadt-side wing had almost been built, and the Elbe-side wing had been roofed.[105] The following two years were to see the completion of all further building, and a bill for the stucco ceiling of one of the three galleries was submitted as early as September 1732.[106] When Augustus the Strong died in Warsaw on February 1, 1733, the exterior of the palace he had always made a point of visiting whenever he left for or arrived from Poland was complete, and plans had been laid for the execution of the interior.

Work still had to be done on the portico, but the financial outlay decreased steadily. When, as we shall see later, Augustus the Strong's plans for the interior were given up around 1740, the only outstanding expenses were those for the building of certain elements essential to keeping the building in good order, namely landings, fireplaces, floors and ceilings.[107] Apart from urgently

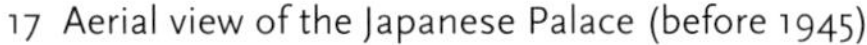

17 Aerial view of the Japanese Palace (before 1945)

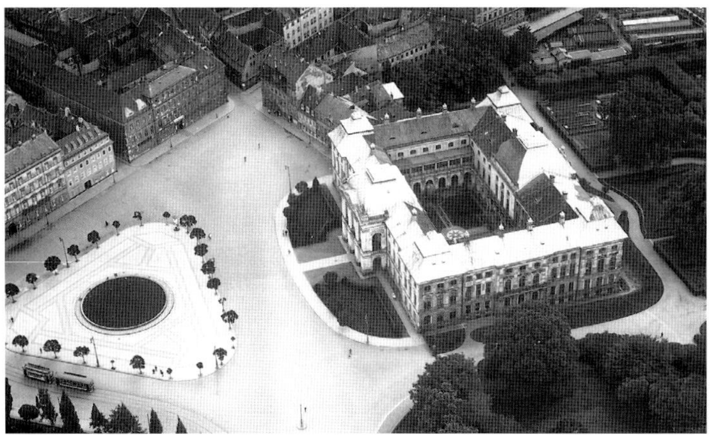

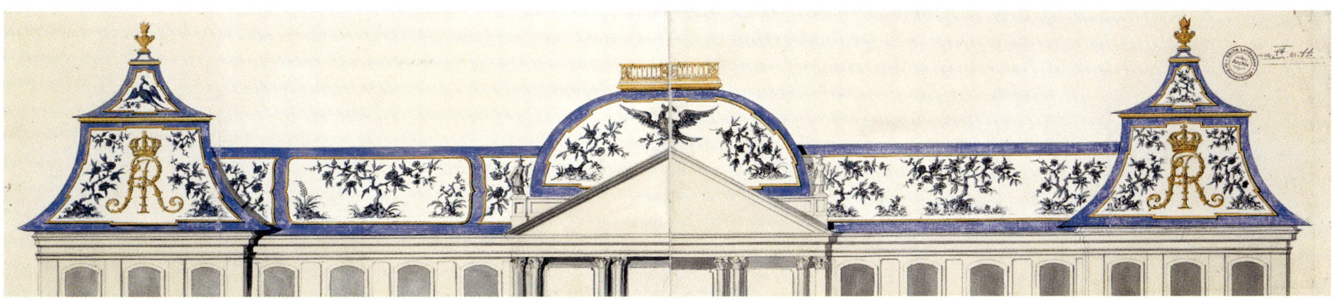

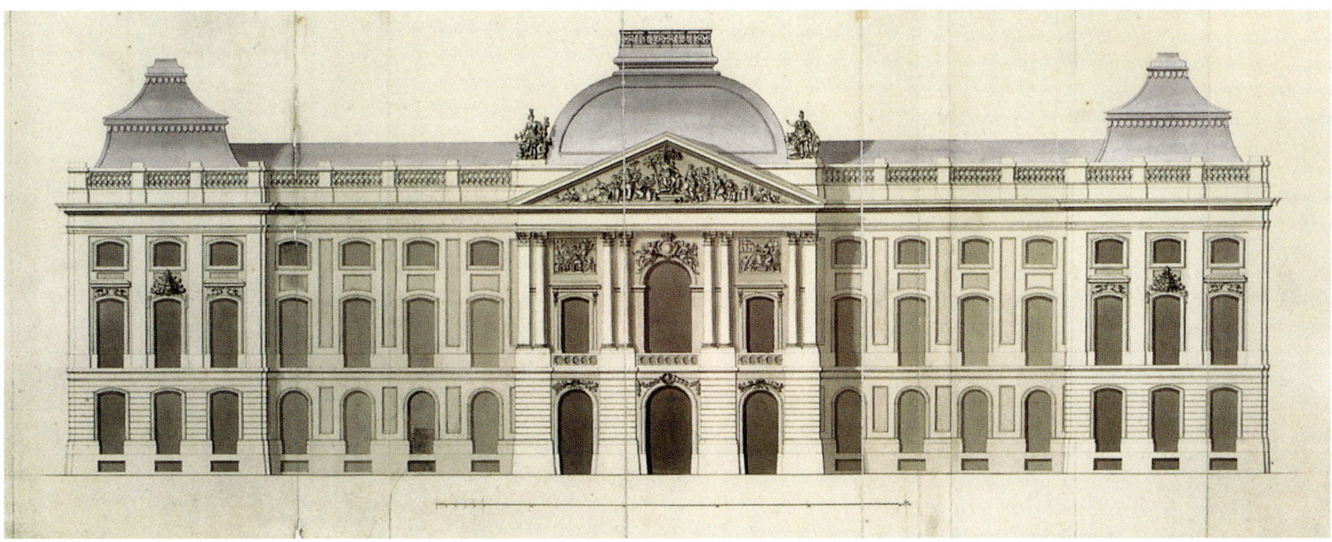

19 Design for a painted roof on the Japanese Palace, ca. 1730

20 Jean de Bodt, design for the main facade of the Japanese Palace, ca. 1730

needed repair work, no further work was done on the palace, and in the Seven Years' War it was even used to store straw.[108] Only in 1782 was it actually put to a definite use, and functioned as a "museum usui publico patens,"[109] accommodating the collection of antiquities and, from 1786, the numismatic collection and the state library, now Saxony's *Landesbibliothek*.

Architectural decoration

The sequences of ground and floor plans show that the Japanese Palace was from the beginning clearly intended to accommodate Augustus the Strong's Far Eastern collections, in which porcelain formed the most important element, both in terms of quality and of its general significance. The fact that the building was to be a repository for highly precious Far Eastern treasures was also to be visible in its external appearance, most conspicuously in the corner pavilions with pagoda-like roofs that would be clearly visible from far off (fig. 18). Some of the facade and roof designs contained even more exotic formulations of the pagoda motif,[110] but were not executed because preference was given to a design better calculated to harmonize the two elements. In one large-scale design, the roofs were to be painted with stylized "indianische Blumen" and birds in white and blue, and furthermore to be adorned with large royal monograms in gold (fig. 19).[111] This proposal is reminiscent of the Zwinger, the roofs of which were first of all painted in blue to fit in with the blue-white-gold color scheme of the rest of the building, a characteristic color triad to which we shall return with interest later on.

The pagoda motif was also taken up in the two-stepped baldacchinos which, sculpted in stone above the corner pavilions' middle windows, stand out in playful contrast to the otherwise rather flat-looking facade. Little baldacchinos of this kind with lobed edges were an indispensable part of the repertoire of motifs of Régence ornamentation, and in Dresden they were ubiquitous not only in architecture but also in arts and crafts, and interior decor. In the case of objects derived from chinoiserie, like the baldacchinos on the Japanese Palace, the basic forms are generally

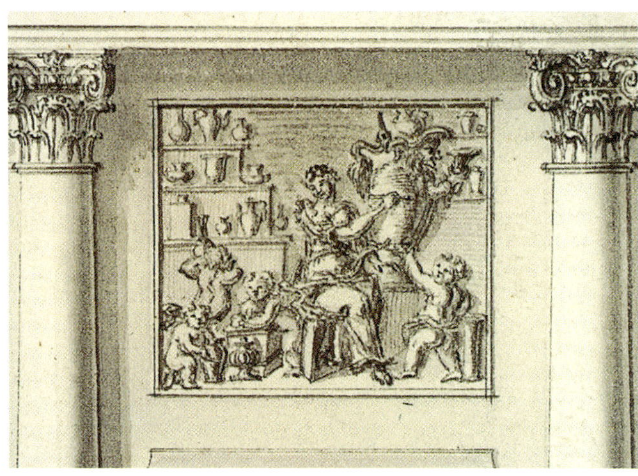

21 Jean de Bodt, design for the left-hand relief on the Japanese Palace portico, with an allegory of porcelain-painting, ca. 1730

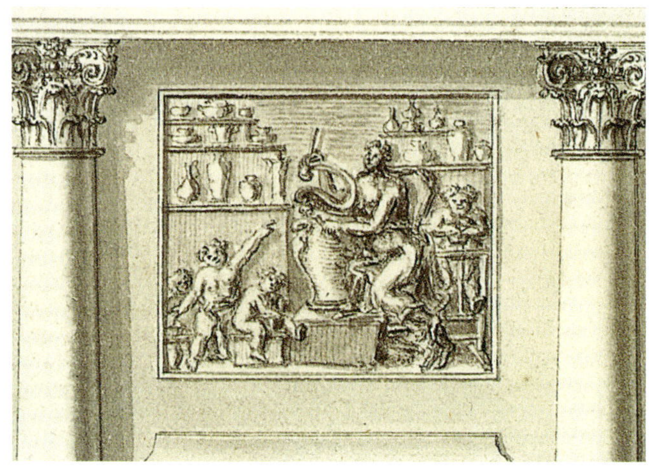

22 Jean de Bodt, design for the right-hand relief on the Japanese Palace portico, with an allegory of vase-making, ca. 1730

more *mouvementé*, and the "lobes" of the valances are rendered in a less tactile fashion and with greater freedom (with leaves, or feathers) than when the motif appears in other contexts.

The most important reference to the identity of the building, however, is given by the relief on the pediment above the Neustadt-side portico, which represents Minerva enthroned as the goddess of trade being offered porcelain treasures by representatives of Far Eastern countries on the one side and Saxony and her followers on the other (fig. 139). A very precise and detailed drawing appended to the designs for the interior of the former office of the Lord Marshall shows two particularly interesting reliefs[112] which were to have filled the gaps between the columns of the portico that were noted by Hasche: "An element of filling which has however not yet been sculpted takes up the remaining space up to the architrave."[113] They were never executed but the drawing is very precise in its details. The two relief designs relate to working stages in the manufacture of porcelain and show classically styled women in workshops with putti as assistants. The right-hand relief (fig. 22) can be interpreted as an allegory of vase-modeling, and the left-hand one (fig. 21) as symbolizing porcelain-painting. It is of particular interest that the two principal figures are both working on examples of exactly the same kind of large and striking "grotesque vases" as were in fact produced in Meissen at the beginning of the 1730s and destined to stand in the great gallery, which ran along

23 Johann Gottlieb Kirchner after Jacques Stella, grotesque vase, model 1730 or 1731, Dresden Porcelain Collection

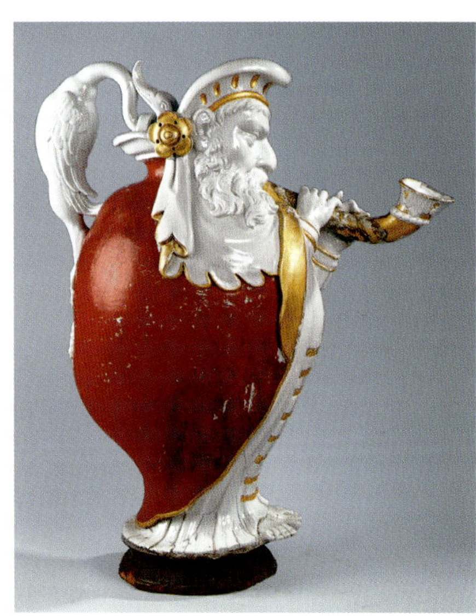

24 Johann Gottlieb Kirchner after Jacques Stella, grotesque vase, model 1730 or 1731, Dresden Porcelain Collection

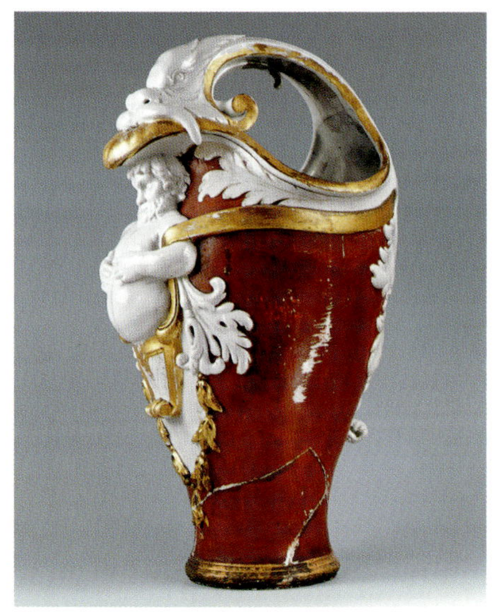

the second story directly behind the place where these two reliefs would have been located (figs. 23 and 24). The draughtsman who did the design for the facade was clearly familiar with these pieces and with the plans for furnishing the palace with porcelain. The fact that these vases were produced in Meissen after copperplate engravings from Jacques Stella's *Livre des Vases* (1667) also suggests that the draughtsman himself would also only have had a print to work from. The fact that not just any vases but these specific ones were chosen for the external decoration for the building indicates that there was a very close connection between the internal and external aspects of the building, a connection which, as we shall see, had an important role to play in the palace's overall iconographical program.

The inner courtyard, finally, made use of a feature well known in Dresden at this time, namely monumental herm pilasters; here they provide support for three sides of a balcony, but since around 1720 they had also been a much-admired feature on the *Wallpavillon* (rampart pavilion) of the Zwinger (figs. 25 and 26). But while the figures supporting Balthasar Permoser's herm pilasters in the Zwinger are bearded fauns hung about with fruit and flowers, those for the Japanese Palace take the form of pot-bellied, grinning "Chinamen" adorned with ornamental hangings made up of various stylized exotic weapons and tools. These outlandish figures were certainly inspired by figures of Chinese divinities from the porcelain collection, and were very likely done after models made by the court sculptor Johann Christian Kirchner.[114]

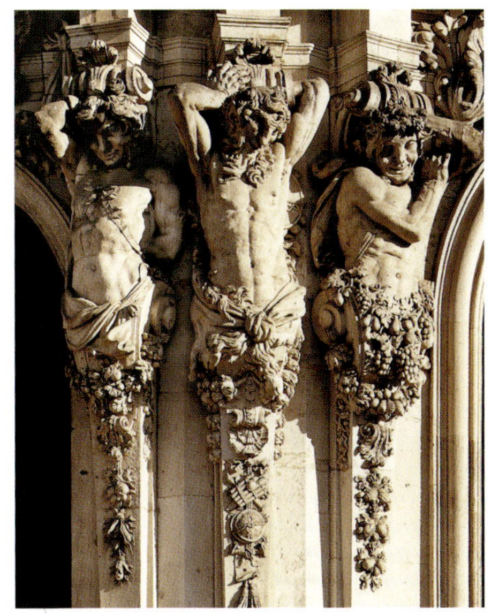

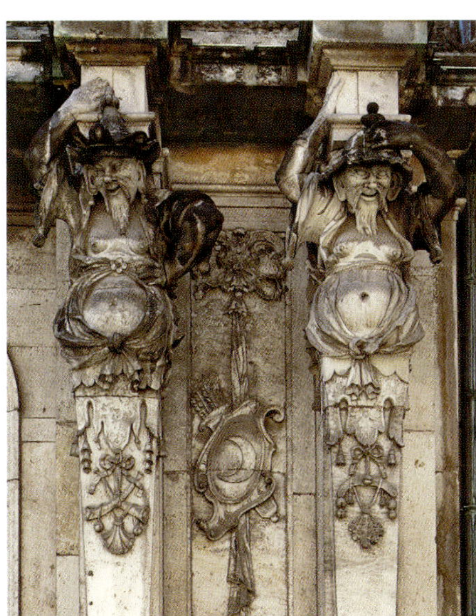

25 Balthasar Permoser, faun herms on the rampart pavilion of the Zwinger, ca. 1720

26 Johann Christian Kirchner (attrib.), Chinaman herms in the inner courtyard of the Japanese Palace, ca. 1730

The history of the planning and furnishing

The sequences of ground and floor plans

When, around 1725, the project of a "Saxon Versailles" in Pillnitz had been given up for good, and the idea of a porcelain palace had transferred its focus to the Dutch Palace, an intensive phase of planning started which is still documented in a whole series of ground and floor plans.[115] However, these plans are of more than simply historical interest as in many instances they also bear handwritten annotations on the function and decoration of individual rooms, thus giving us information not only on the course taken by the architectural planning, but also on the development of a concept for the fittings and furnishings of the interior. Given that these annotations were in many cases made by Augustus the Strong himself, with some sketches coming in their entirety from the king's hand, we can quite confidently say that the scheme for the presentation of the porcelain was conceived ahead of the plans for the building. In other words, what we have here is not a collection which was to be distributed around an already existing scheme of rooms; rather, the architecture was planned so as to create rooms ideally suited to the realization of the presentation concept in an arrangement that would give visible form to a quite specific order of things. This procedure can be observed in many other plans conceived under the aegis of Augustus the Strong, in the distribution of the natural history collections in the Zwinger galleries, for example, or in the path of the tour around the Green Vaults. The only element that was subject to the rules of proportion followed by the architects was the size of the various rooms and galleries, with the result that – as we shall see later in greater detail – the acquisitions for the collection and the orders sent to Meissen were made in accordance with a well-defined need for specific quantities of porcelain.

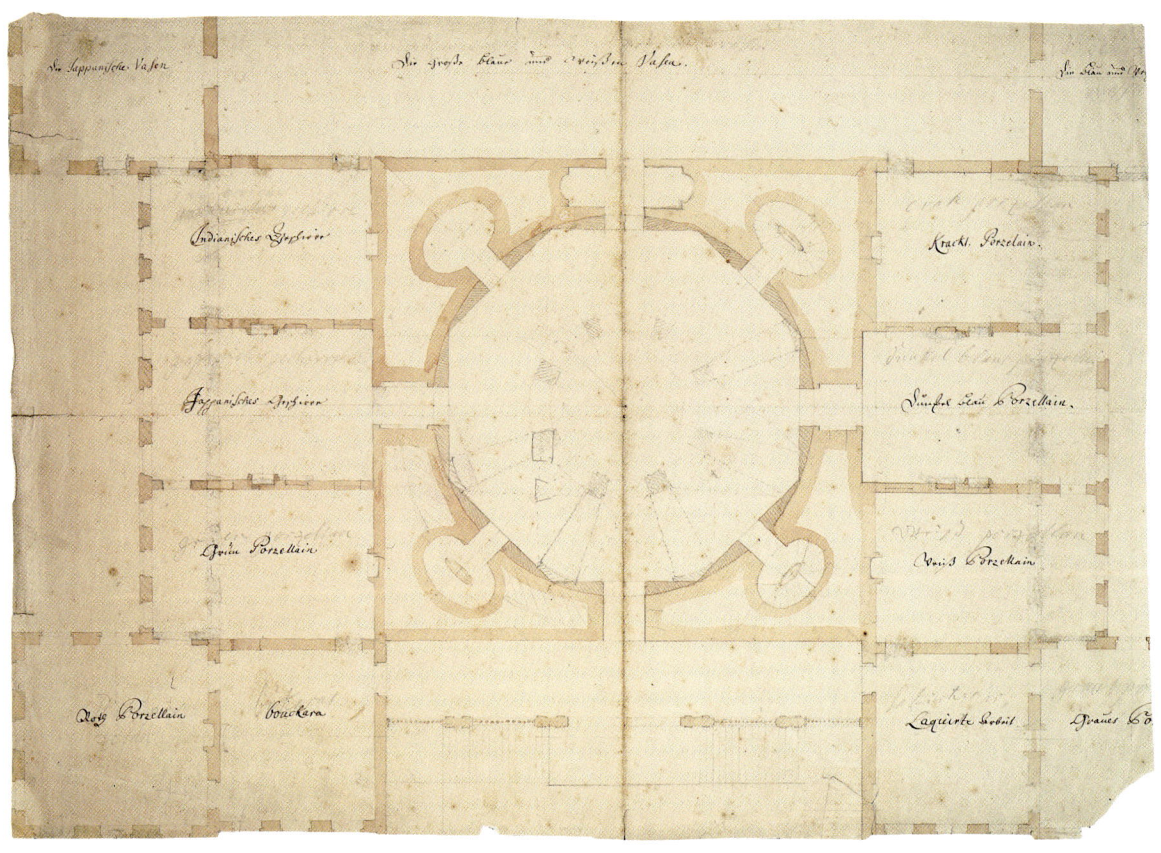

27

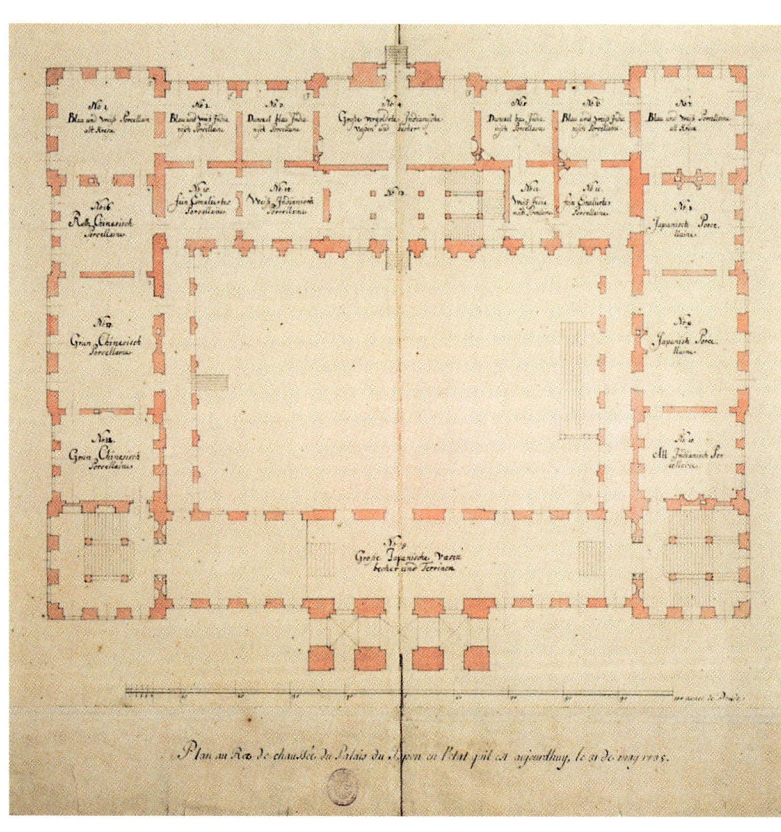

28

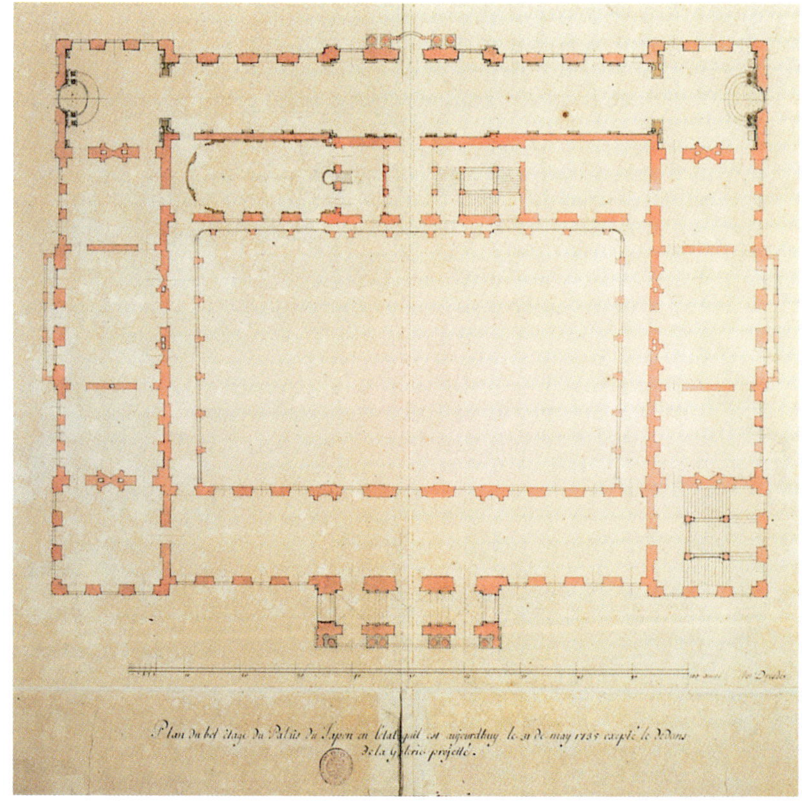

29

27 Ground plan design for a project of Augustus the Strong for Schloss Pillnitz, with indications as to the distribution of the porcelain collection, ca. 1722

28 Zacharias Longuelune, Japanese Palace, ground plan (ground floor) with indications as to the distribution of the porcelain collection, dated 1735

29 Zacharias Longuelune, Japanese Palace, floor plan (upper story), dated 1735

The intention of gathering together the whole collection of Far Eastern porcelain under one roof and allocating it according to aesthetic criteria to the rooms of one building – rather than using the collection to furnish each one of a number of residences with a porcelain cabinet of its own, for instance – can first be seen in the design for Schloss Pillnitz (fig. 27), which envisaged individual cabinets arranged around a large central room and devoted to such categories as "Japponisches Geschirre" ("Japanese wares"), "grün Porzellain" ("green porcelain"), and "Krackt Porzelain" ("*kraak* porcelain")[116], with a long gallery being designated to accommodate "large blue-and-white vases."[117]

The clockwise sequence of porcelain categories which is evident on the Pillnitz plan – red, green, Japanese and "Indian" wares, Japanese vases, large blue-and-white vases, gilded vases, and finally *kraak*, dark blue, white, and gray porcelain – reappears on one of the first designs for the extension of the Dutch Palace.[118] Although this design was not made for a centrally-designed building but for a three-wing construction, it was likewise suggested that the side-wings should contain a sequence of cabinets, while the central tract was accorded a gallery for the "large vases and orange-pots," that is to say, for porcelain fish-basins put to an alternative use as jardinières for lemon-trees.[119] Augustus the Strong had possibly taken this idea for a gallery from Paulus Decker's *Der fürstliche Baumeister*, which contains a design for an interior gallery with orange-trees. The king had had this book sent to him in Warsaw by Pöppelmann in 1713.[120]

In 1727 at the latest, however, the projected three-wing building was replaced by a four-wing version. The king may well have realized that the most suitable layout was one with a clear sequence of cabinets which gave the visitor no other option than that of following a predetermined path. For while in the case of the central plan for Pillnitz (fig. 27) it had been possible to enter all four wings from the round central hall, and in the three-wing plan for the Japanese Palace the row of cabinets had relatively wide corridors running parallel to them which allowed the visitor to sidestep the sequence of rooms, the ground and floor plans for the four-wing palace finally built consist almost exclusively of enfilades (figs. 28 and 29). Only on the ground floor of the Elbe-side wing were the rooms joined to one another in a somewhat freer manner. The courtyard-side corridor on the ground floor, and likewise the balcony in the upper story of the two side-wings only communicated with the middle room by means of a rather narrow opening, probably only meant to be used by servants.

As the development of the planning for the four-wing project was also governed by the projected ordering of the porcelain in the interior, special consideration shall now be given to this aspect of the genesis of the palace.

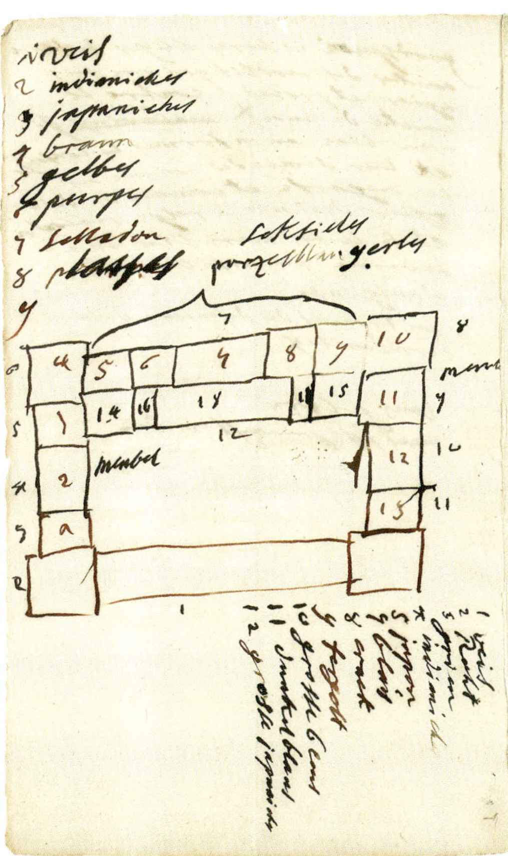

30 Sketch of the distribution of the collections in the Japanese Palace, in Augustus the Strong's hand, ca. 1728

The plans for the ground floor: It was most likely around 1728 that Augustus the Strong made his first scheme for the distribution of the porcelain on the ground floor (fig. 30).[121] The rooms are numbered, and the numbers correspond to a list above the sketch. In the same plan he also numbered the rooms a second time, with a legend written in below the drawing. He bracketed together the whole sequence of rooms on the garden side, and made no entries for the courtyard-side rooms of the Elbe wing. From this it may be concluded the second legend, which only corresponds to the first one in two points, refers to the upper story. It is also the case that number 12, which refers to the courtyard facade of the Elbe wing, or in the case of the upper story to the rooms giving out onto the balcony, has the entry "large Japanese," which agrees with elevations from the same period (fig. 35). The entry for the other side of the wing indicating that "seksiche porzellain gerten" ("Saxon porcelain gardens") were planned is one to which we shall return with interest at a later point.

This sketch was followed by a ground plan (fig. 31), which proposes a different sequence for the groups of porcelain, with some of the entries in ink crossed out in pencil and changed by the hand of Augustus the Strong.

One significant change can be located on a list drawn up at a later date which stated expressly that the ground floor was only to be furnished with Far Eastern porcelain. The list (Source 1)[122] is to

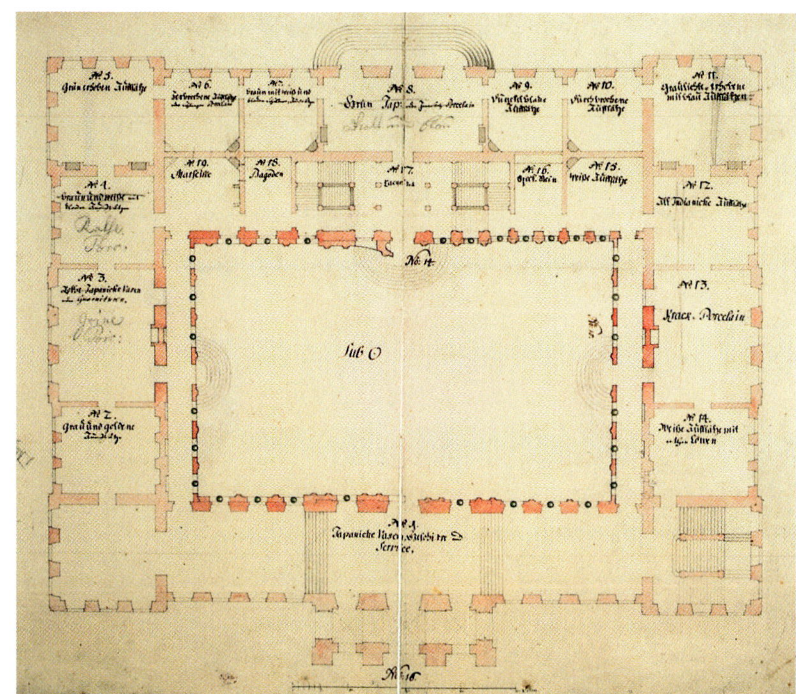

31

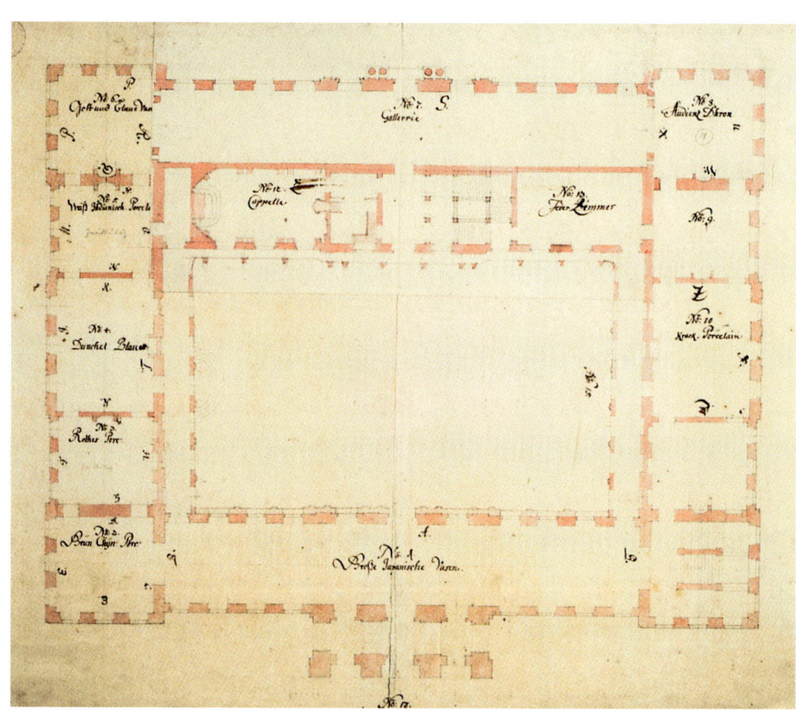

32

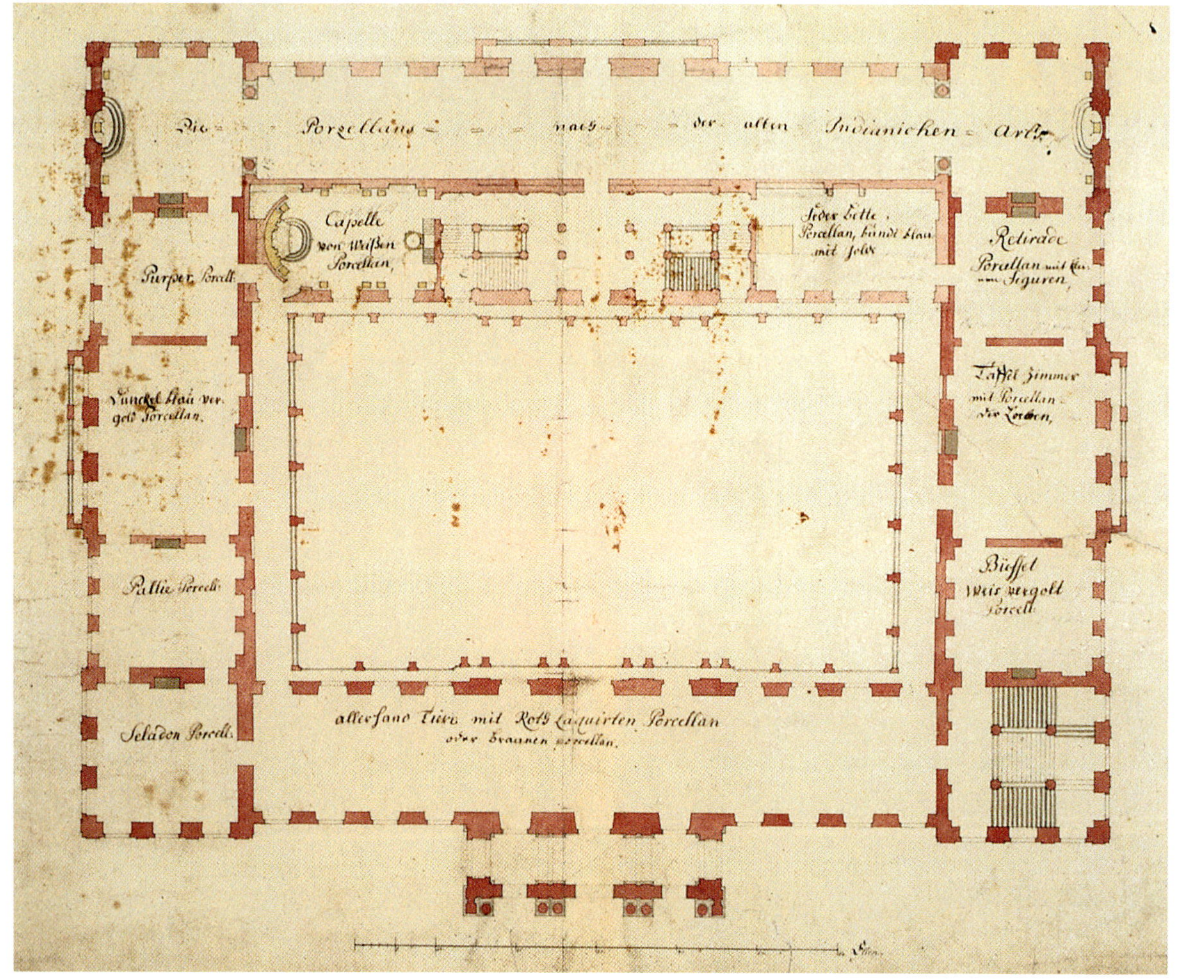

33

31 Japanese Palace, projected ground plan (ground floor), before 1730

32 Japanese Palace, projected floor plan (upper story), before 1730

33 Japanese Palace, projected floor plan (upper story), 1730

be found between the designs for the walls of the former office of the Lord Marshall and is thus clearly closely associated with the ground and floor plans. The title, "Specification of the rooms on the first floor [= ground floor] of the Japanese Palace and how His Royal Majesty of most blessed and glorious memory most graciously intended to furnish them," makes it fairly certain that it dates from 1733, as in that year a number of documents were drawn up for the benefit of the new king Augustus III, describing other projects left behind by his late father, who had died in February, and the various stages which they had reached. This one, however, as can be ascertained from comparison with the course of planning for the upper story, only details the state of affairs that had obtained in 1730. The particular value of the list, which takes account of Augustus the Strong's corrections on the previous ground plan (fig. 31), lies in the information it provides regarding the materials and colors to be used for other elements of the interior decoration.

That Augustus III made hardly any changes to the concept laid down by his father is shown decisively by the last of the extant ground-floor plans with entries related to the porcelain (fig. 28), which is dated by Zacharias Longuelune with the following annotation: "Plan au Rez-de-chaussée du Palais du Japon en l'etat quil est aujourdhuy le 31 de may 1735" ("Plan of the ground floor of the Japanese Palace in the state in which it is today, May 31, 1735").

The floor plans for the upper story: Our point of departure for the planning of the upper story is the sketch from the hand of Augustus the Strong considered above (fig. 30). It distinguishes the porcelain on both stories according to color, but not to provenance (Far East or Meissen). Although some of the entries give some indication of provenance, for the ground floor, for instance, "Japanese [porcelain]," and for the upper floor "*kraak* [porcelain]," other terms are less easy to interpret in terms of Far Eastern porcelain, and contain references to such fashionable ground colors being developed and improved on at Meissen at precisely this time as "yellow-colored" and "celadon-colored" porcelain on the ground floor, and for the upper story the entry "green," which could however also be interpreted as a category of Chinese porcelain. This juxtaposition of rooms with Far Eastern and Meissen porcelain is repeated on a floor plan (fig. 32) that very likely belongs to the plan illustrated as fig. 31. But this mixing up of the two went even further – one order list for porcelain from Meissen (Source 4) dated March 28, 1730, which corresponds quite well in its data with the ordering of this ground plan, suggests that it was in some cases also intended to bring Far Eastern and Meissen porcelain together in the same room. In this instance, dishes and vases in the "Japanischer Facon" after models delivered are ordered for the cavetto and piers of the Neustadt-side gallery, although the floor plan specifies that this gallery was to contain "large Japanese vases."[123] It should however not be forgotten that when porcelain cabinets were being fitted out, it was quite normal to use European ceramic copies, for the sake of symmetry, to complement genuine Far Eastern wares.

The separation of the porcelain according to provenance, that is to say the allocation of the Far Eastern wares to the ground floor and the Meissen wares to the first story, as the inventory of 1721 tells us had largely been the case in the Dutch Palace, only became a feature of the planning for the Japanese Palace in 1730.[124] The first piece of evidence for this is a floor plan for the upper story (fig. 33) which is also the first instance of "all sorts of animals with red-lacquered porcelain or brown porcelain" being planned for the large Neustadt-side gallery. In October 1730, furthermore, Johann Georg Keyssler's travel report recorded the current state of planning, which involved only a few changes in the west wing.

From the year 1733 we also still have detailed written lists of the porcelain requirements for the upper story, which are preserved together with the plans and elevations for the Lord Marshall's office (see Source 13) and – like the ground floor description of the same year already mentioned – show no deviations from the state of planning at the end of 1730. And this is the reason why no trouble is taken to include any entries regarding the distribution of the porcelain in the last floor plan for the upper story, entitled by Zacharias Longuelune "Plan du bel êtage du Palais du Japon en l'etat quil est aujourdhuy le 31 de may 1735 exepté le dedans de la Galerie projetté" (Plan of the bel étage of the Japanese Palace in the state in which it is today May 31, 1735, except for the interior of the projected gallery)[125], which forms the effective conclusion of the planning as reflected in extant sources.

The projected interior designs

The many variants and stages which the ground and floor plans went through in the course of the architectural developments were accompanied by elevation drawings devoted not only to the design

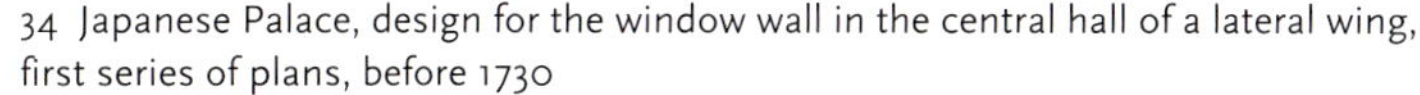

34 Japanese Palace, design for the window wall in the central hall of a lateral wing, first series of plans, before 1730

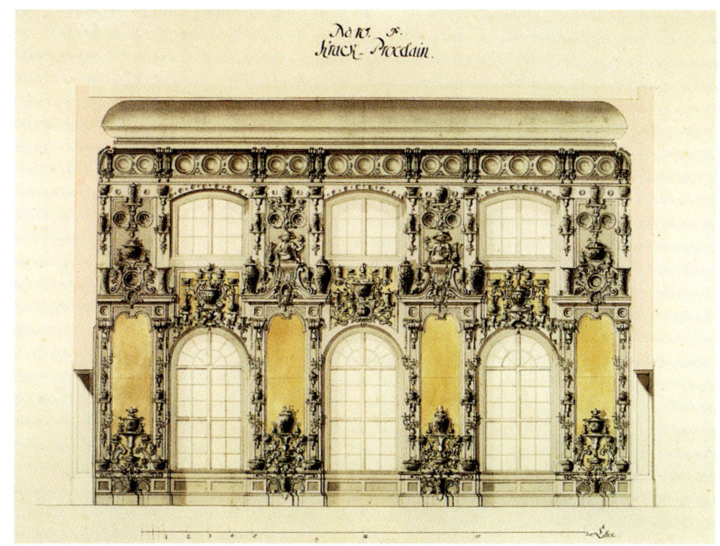

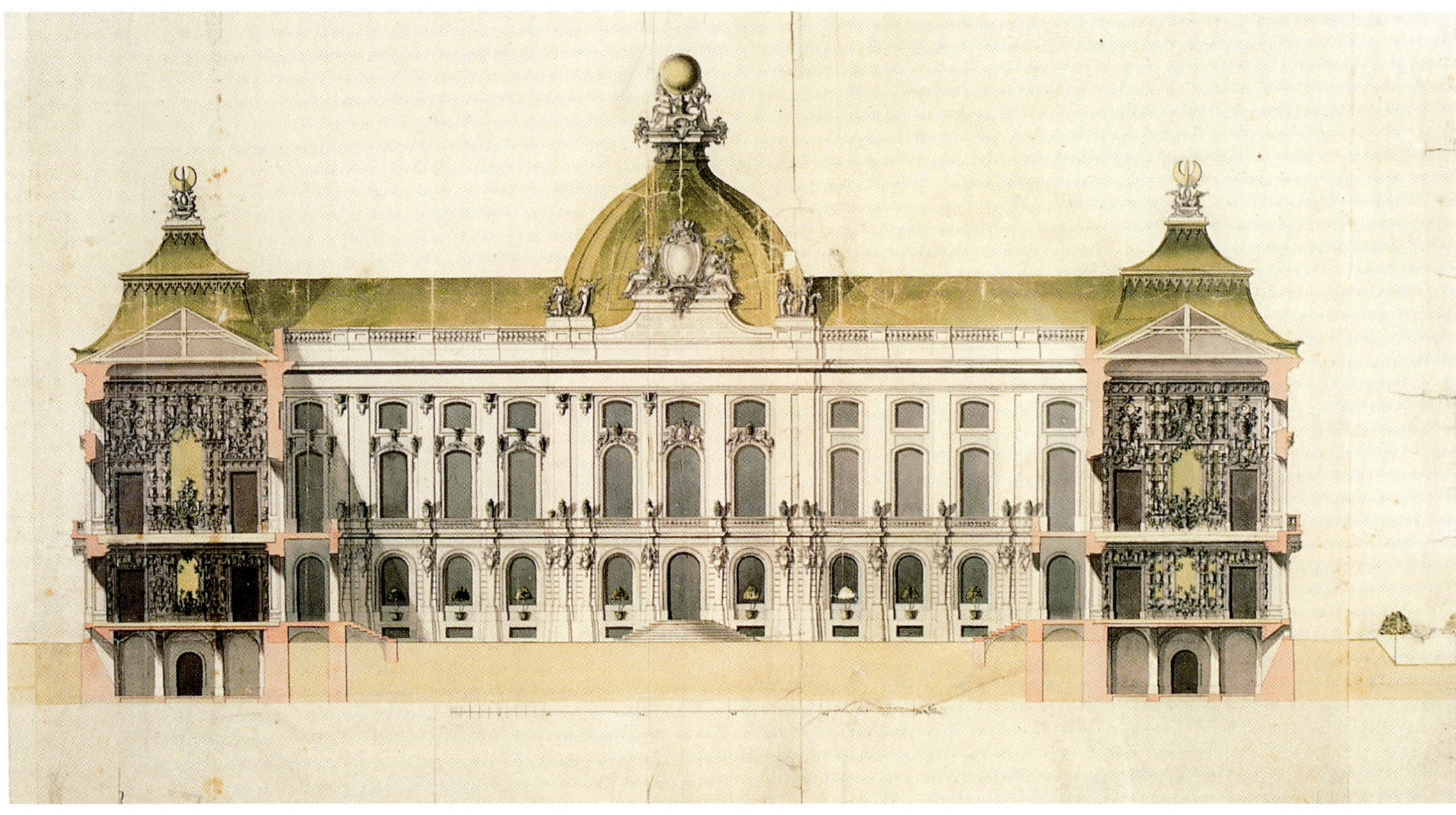

35 Japanese Palace, cross-section through the courtyard and lateral wings, ca. 1728

of the facades and roofs, but also to the decoration of the interiors.[126] Whole sequences of the latter have been preserved in folders in the State Archive of Saxony. Once again, the careful, extensive, and comprehensive planning is evidence of the importance attached to the project by the king.

One is immediately struck by the fact that in the whole of this palace, with its two principal floors, linked by two staircases, containing thirty-two rooms, only a small number of rooms had a clearly defined function: according to the lists and ground and floor plans, three bedrooms, a chapel, a dining room, and a room for the throne at one end of a gallery. The rest – three large galleries and twenty-three rooms – were apparently general in character, which was, even by the standards of the state apartments of the time, an extraordinary number of antechambers and larger rooms *en enfilade*. At the *Landesamt für Denkmalpflege* in Dresden, preserved in a folder together with the designs for the Japanese Palace, is a ground plan of the palace basement with entries concerning the various departments of the kitchen and cellar area. Although it is too faint to be reproduced here, it nevertheless represents clear evidence that these rooms were designed with a view to making it possible to put on large court festivities at the palace.

The elevations with the designs for the walls can be divided into two groups, with the first group consisting of designs for rooms in the upper story.[127] Each one of these twenty-five ink drawings, some of which have bold coloring in pink for the sections through the walls, and in yellow for the mirror surfaces, has next to its title, which indicates the respective porcelain group, a number and a letter (fig. 34). The number corresponds to the room numbering of the floor plan, most likely drawn shortly before 1730, which indicates that the upper story was to contain mainly porcelain of Far Eastern provenance (fig. 32). On this floor plan the letters with which the walls are marked relate to those on the respective elevation designs. The designs for the walls are rendered in great detail, with the drawing even sketching in the decoration on the porcelains, which sometimes even makes it possible for us to recognize individual pieces.

We do not know from whose hand this group of elevations came. In a letter of 1732, Jean de Bodt notes that in 1729 he employed the draughtsman Johann Adam Rothe on account of the many building projects being carried on at the same time.[128] Hentschel is convinced that Rothe was the author of these plans for the arrangement of the porcelains,[129] and thus was also the "unknown German architect" to whom Franz[130] ascribed the first group of elevations. Even though this attribution has a certain plausibility in terms of the timing – the first group of plans and the associated ground plan can both be dated around 1730 – it is not clear from de Bodt's letter whether Rothe was employed to make the designs, or simply to do the final stages of the drawing. May, furthermore, makes the point that the draughtsman must rather have been working for Pöppelmann or Knöffel, as they would have been responsible for the interior designs.[131]

A cross-section through the palace courtyard and two side-wings (fig. 35), principally concerned with showing the design for the courtyard-side facades and roof shapes of the Elbe wing, shows an arrangement of the porcelain in the ground floor and upper story rooms which corresponds in detail to that in the first group. As this design has to be ascribed to one of the three palace architects, and also because of the importance of the project, it can be assumed that while all the principal architects were to busy themselves with the matter of how the porcelain was to be arranged, they may well have had their drawings finished by assistants whose identity remains unknown to us.

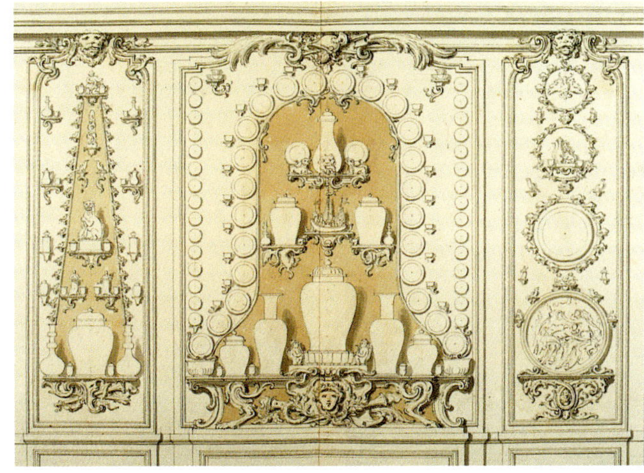

37 Zacharias Longuelune, Japanese Palace, design for a wall in a room on the ground floor, ca. 1735 (detail)

36 Matthäus Daniel Pöppelmann (?), Japanese Palace, pencil design for a wall on the upper story, unfinished, first series of plans, before 1730

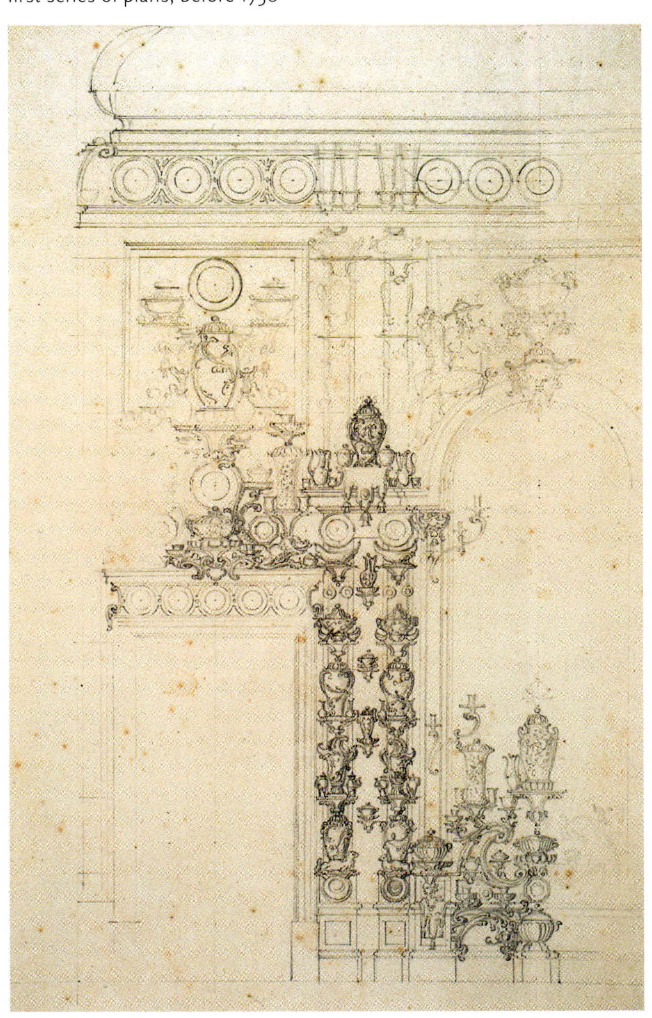

While this group of elevations has a fairly uniform character, it does contain one highly illuminating drawing (fig. 36), which may well have been a design which was never passed on for detailed finishing. Partially still in pencil, the unfinished drawing shows the design for the end wall of the middle hall in the west wing. Remarkably enough, the unfinished pencil drawing includes vases which at this time, around 1730, did not yet exist in ceramic form, and certainly not as "*kraak* porcelain," but were planned to form part of this room, as we know from the fully-drawn elevation (fig. 34). While, for instance, the two vases on the third level of the wall between door and mirror could still be interpreted as being Chinese pieces with lavish European bronze mountings, the two pieces are both also reminiscent of designs in the style of Meissonier. Vases such as the ones first executed in this early Rococo form in precious metals were, however, familiar through prints at the time of the first group of plans, which makes it quite possible that the draughtsman was simply using this task as an opportunity to show off his knowledge of the latest French trends in design. The draughtsman responsible for finishing off the design of the window-side of the same hall (fig. 34), on the other hand, must have been more familiar with the characteristic forms of Far Eastern porcelain and thus restricted himself to doing renderings of such dishes and vases as were actually available to be displayed there. This is of particular interest because the second group of elevations, which are mainly of rooms on the ground floor, were exclusively the work of Zacharias Longuelune.

The procedure by which the architect simply sketched the interior and passed his sketch on to a draughtsman for detailed finishing was quite in accordance with contemporary practice. It should also be remembered that the architects had knowledge of other

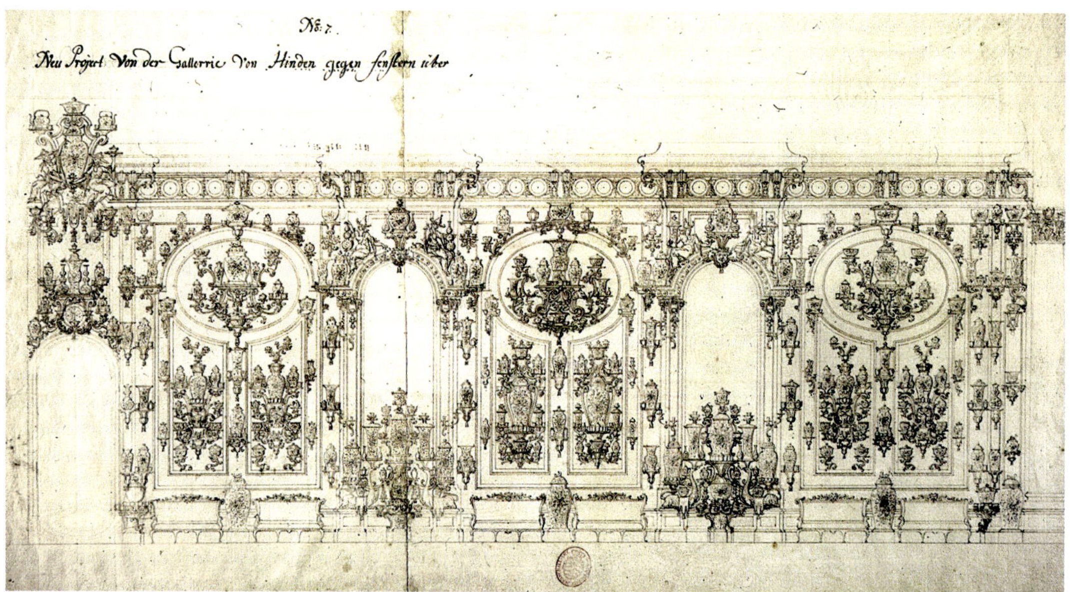

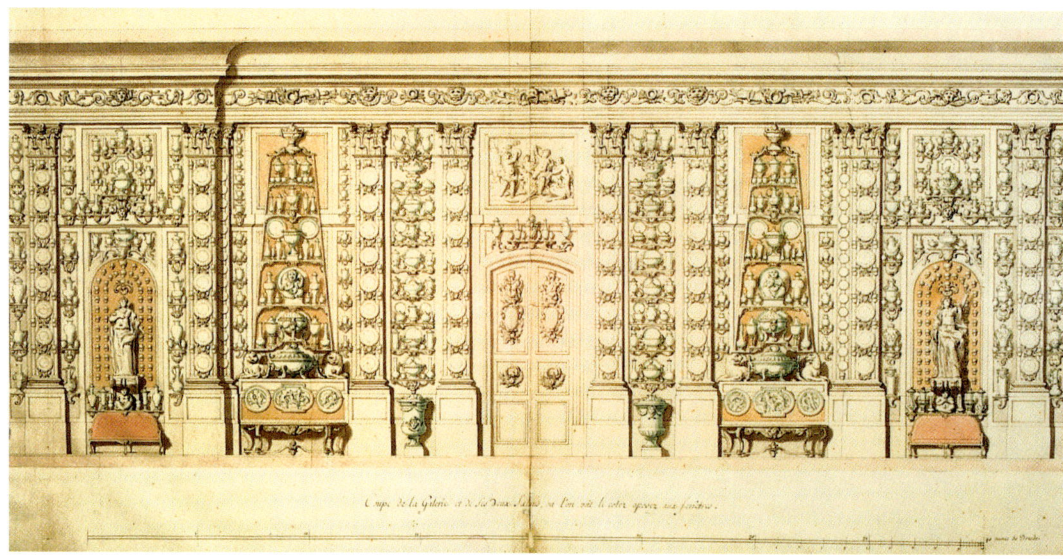

38 Matthias Daniel Pöppelmann (workshop of), Japanese Palace, design for the Elbe-side gallery, first series of plans, before 1730 (detail)

39 Zacharias Longuelune, Japanese Palace, design for the Elbe-side gallery, ca. 1735 (detail from the middle section)

comparable rooms: Pöppelmann had not only seen the porcelain cabinet in Schloss Salzdahlum, near Wolfenbüttel, in 1715 (and had very likely made sketches of it)[132], but had in 1718, before the fitting out of the *Turmzimmer* (Tower Room) of the Dresden residence, been sent by Augustus the Strong to Berlin to study the cabinet in Charlottenburg (fig. 6), which the king had also seen on his visit in 1709.[133] And on January 30, 1730 – that is to say in the most intensive phase of the planning for the Japanese Palace – the privy councillor Starcke was likewise sent to Berlin with two draughtsmen with a commission to make drawings of the porcelain cabinet and chapel.[134]

The elevations of the second group,[135] which were the work of Zacharias Longuelune, are accompanied by a list of contents allocating the designs to nine rooms on the ground floor. Each room has a ground plan and elevations of all four walls, all in duplicate (fig. 37). Also included are plans for the upper story: wall elevations for the large Elbe-side gallery (with the throne),[136] and for the chapel,[137] and for a number of important furnishings.[138] There is a further floor plan which corresponds to this series of designs from a second planning phase, which only overlaps with the first group in the case of the large Elbe-side gallery.[139] The drawings date from around 1735.

The two series of designs for the Japanese Palace are not only separated from one another by two years in time, but also represent two fundamentally different points of view on how to exhibit porcelain. The difference is well demonstrated in the following comparison of two elevation drawings both concerned with the same wall of the Elbe-side gallery, namely the wall opposite the windows, in the upper story.

In the design made around 1730 (fig. 38), the porcelains are allocated to lavishly carved console constructions, each with a number of levels, which tower up in concentrated groups in the lower third of the large mirrors. Each of the wall surfaces between the mirrors is dominated by three such constructions, two of which are at the same height, in front of the vertical panels, and one higher up in front of the horizontal oval panel above. The wall as a whole, furthermore, has porcelain, single pieces or pairs, strewn around it in a somewhat random arrangement. The upper parts of the mirrors act as a restful counterbalance within the whole composition, and give the wall its distinct overall rhythm by offsetting the predominant pattern of little constructions. This having been said, it should of course not be forgotten that in reality the mirrors would reflect the decoration of the opposite wall.

In the case of the first group of elevations, which he ascribed to Pöppelmann, Fichtner quite rightly concluded that the draughtsman was not focusing his attention exclusively on the wall he was drawing, but was aiming to get a feeling for the room as a whole and to take into consideration all the factors which gave the space its own particular character: "The elevation drawings of the interiors allow us interesting insights into the artist's creative process, giving us the impression that the manner of arranging the porcelain was not determined by the characteristics of the individual pieces but by a feeling for the room as a whole. As a result the window side of the room, being darker and indirectly lit, was given the larger, more conspicuous vases, while an abundant array of porcelains both large and small were allowed to run wild on the well-lit wall opposite."[140] By contrast with Longuelune's design for the long south gallery, which gives the same amount of porcelain to each wall, the first design gives the window wall only larger vases, and of these only a small number.

Longuelune's design of 1735 also differs from the earlier design in being fundamentally geometrical and linear (fig. 39). The porcelains are aligned in chains along the architectural divisions or the paneling, or simply stand alone on individually allocated single consoles or console tables. The arrangements are framed by the contours of the pilasters and reserves between them. The overall rhythm is determined by the aligning of the individual pieces. Longuelune was already familiar with the appearance of the vases and dishes, and with the quantities available, as the porcelain collection was by this time already stored at the Japanese Palace, and worked with the natural laws of optics by making the vases get smaller the higher they were placed. The actual weight of each piece is made clear by its having its own individual console tailored to support it, and even the rows of plates aligned along the surface divisions form satisfyingly coherent wholes.[141] The overall effect created by this celebrated ordering is static.

The design in the first group of plans, by contrast, has the largest pieces standing out at particularly exposed points, at the peaks of the console constructions in front of the mirrors, above the mirrors' rounded tops, or right in the middle of the panels between the mirrors. As a result, the upper parts of the walls even have more conspicuous objects than the lower parts. The kind of rows that abound in Longuelune's design are only in evidence in the cavetto at the very top.

It is a remarkable fact that this wall design, all the elements of which are embedded in a swirl of carved mounts and multiple consoles, nevertheless gives an impression of "stability" without having the kind of clear tectonic structure characteristic of its counterpart. The secret is that the carved elements cover whole areas of the wall like a net in which the porcelain pieces seem to be anchored; consequently, the eye does not perceive them as being held up by any supporting structures, but rather as adhering to – or even emerging from – the wall surfaces. The designer's playful lightness of touch makes the porcelains leap out at the beholder from within the decoration covering the wall, and furthermore allows them to determine the overall color of the room; the resulting lively overall dynamic charms the eye in a delightfully carefree and exotic way that is quite at variance with the very European orderliness of Longuelune's composition. In the first group of plans, the porcelain does not simply "furnish a room": it is instrumental in determining the room's own special character.

However, the use of porcelain as an integral part of the interior decor depends on the immediate availability of certain quantities of different sizes and types of porcelain. That Longuelune was quite aware of the obstacles to production at the Meissen manufactory is shown by the reasons he gives in his "Explication" (Source 3) for the design chosen for the throne gallery on the upper story of the Elbe wing: "And it is all designed in such a way as to make it possible to increase or decrease the number of porcelains without changing the overall composition."[142] He clearly recognized the weakness of his additive approach to arranging the porcelain, and incorporated eye-catching decorative elements in non-ceramic media into many of his rooms: "[...] statues and medallions have been put opposite the windows, in order not to be constantly repeating the vases, to avoid a simple arrangement which would look too much like a well-stocked warehouse, and to present the eye and the mind with amusing objects, which – as it were – speak for themselves."[143] It is clear from the last part of the sentence that Longuelune, true to the preference for French classicism he displayed in his work in Dresden, did not think that porcelain appealed greatly to the mind or to our deeper feelings. He was not capable of seeing the porcelains as a constitutive part of the room, but considered them rather as single objects for which he was simply to create a showcase. This attitude was a significant one: he was

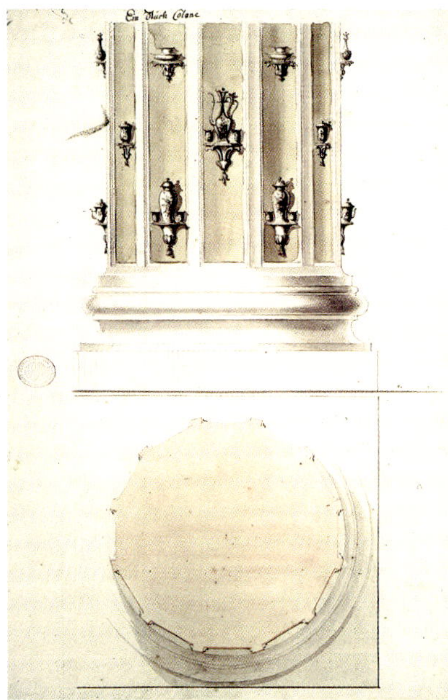

40 Zacharias Longuelune, Japanese Palace, design for the columns in the Elbe-side gallery with small consoles for porcelain, ca. 1735

distancing himself from the Baroque idea of porcelain and mirror cabinets that was a real presence in the first group of plans, and was creating what one might call a "proto-museum-like" home for the Far Eastern porcelain on the ground floor of the Japanese Palace.

At this point one has to ask what the sources of inspiration for the designs were, and to what extent Augustus the Strong introduced his own ideas into the design process. Two events should not be forgotten in this connection: Augustus the Strong's visit to Berlin, and the phenomenon of Prussian artists defecting to Saxony. In 1709 Augustus the Strong betook himself to Berlin with King Frederik IV of Denmark to form an alliance against Sweden. The extensive festivities mounted in the course of the "Dreikönigstreffen" included visits to the palaces of Oranienburg, Caputh and Charlottenburg and to their respective porcelain rooms, which were not only the most important of their kind in Prussia and but also had a very particular political dimension to them as well.[144] As has already been noted, the advent of the most important planning phase for the Japanese Palace reminded Augustus the Strong of the visits he had made in 1709 and prompted him to dispatch draughtsmen to Berlin. The time that had elapsed since then had seen a number of important personalities making the move from the Prussian to the Saxon court. When, after the death of the Prussian king Friedrich I in 1713, his son Friedrich Wilhelm I decided in favor of a more economic and less ostentatious court household, one of the figures to transfer to the service of Augustus the Strong was the experienced Master of Ceremonies Johann von Besser, who had played a central role in matters regarding status and protocol at the Prussian court and was now given corresponding duties at the Saxon court. The architect Johann Friedrich Eosander von Göthe, the creator of the Charlottenburg porcelain cabinet, likewise left Berlin in 1713, finally coming to Dresden in 1722, where he certainly met up with a number of his old friends, even though he was not involved in the Japanese Palace project. Johann von Besser was not the only figure indispensable to the project: Zacharias Longuelune also came to the Saxon court from Prussia in 1713, and Jean de Bodt finally made the move in 1728. Longuelune's designs in particular use motifs which would have been familiar to him from earlier times. Filling the fluting on the columns of his design for the throne-room with porcelain on little consoles was a direct bow in the direction of the porcelain room at Oranienburg (fig. 40), and the most important room at Oranienburg, the large orange room, contained just the same kind of carillon with inverted Far Eastern porcelain bowls as he now designed, together with a playing mechanism and done in Meissen porcelain, as a pendant to the throne in the Japanese Palace.[145] While the architects' designs were not unqualifiedly innovative, there is no doubt about the novelty of the characteristic aspect that Augustus the Strong introduced into the design of the interiors: the grouping of the porcelains according to color. All this shows clearly that the significance of the interior designs for the Japanese Palace lies less in the way they are composed and presented than in the way the collections were organized and the function they were now expected to fulfill. This is a matter to which we shall return at a later point.

The fittings and furnishings

It is no easy matter to establish from the sources what decoration work was actually carried out on the interiors. The primary sources are of little assistance and surprisingly enough, given the size and importance of the project, not a single folder of bills, orders, or

41 Raymond Le Plat, cross-section of the Dutch Palace on the occasion of the *souper* on September 10, 1719, for the electoral prince's wedding, after 1720 (detail)

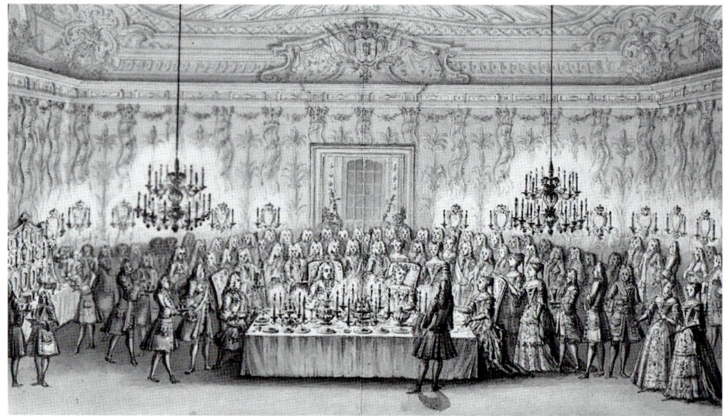

commissions is to be found in all the records of the State Archive of Saxony. One possible explanation for this is that the payments may have been made from the king's privy purse, the records for which are no longer extant. One further possibility is that the records for the Japanese Palace may have been transferred – in an act symbolic of its "deprivatization" – from the royal archive to the city's buildings archive when the palace was converted for use as a public museum and library in 1786, in which case they would have been destroyed along with the entire City Buildings Archive ("Städtisches Bauarchiv") when the police building was stormed in the course of the political unrest of 1830.

In the case of the preceding building, the Dutch Palace, we still have a detailed cross-section of the building (fig. 41),[146] a printed summary by a contemporary chronicler,[147] and finally an extremely comprehensive inventory of all the rooms with their fittings and furnishings.[148] For the Japanese Palace, however, we have comparatively few reliable documents, one of which is the list of 1733 mentioned above (Source 1), which was appended to the elevation drawings and is no more than a concisely formulated account of the state of the project.

The entries give information for all the rooms on the ground floor, specifying which groups of porcelain were intended to be displayed in each one and also, in greater or lesser detail, the materials and colors to be used for the wall coverings. In 1733, when the list was drawn up, Longuelune had not yet made the 1735 elevations for the ground floor, but the wall designs from the first group of plans (upper story, before 1730) were no longer valid, as it had in the meantime been decided to restrict the Far Eastern porcelain to the ground floor. The descriptions in the list thus relate to a planning stage for which there are no extant drawings. As the following example shows, the intention was most likely that the no longer valid, but still existent, designs for the upper story would simply be adapted for the rooms on the ground floor.

Figure 42 shows the pre-1730 design for the room with "dark-blue porcelain," which was at that stage the middle room in the east wing of the upper story. After the Far Eastern porcelains that had been destined for this room were transferred to the ground floor and distributed over two rooms, the list describes the decoration in their new home as follows: "No:7 [=No:9] dark-blue Indian porcelains, with lacquered friezes, the fillings in white satin, upon which large Indian figures in bright colors very cleanly painted."[149] The description corresponds exactly to the elements in the drawing, on which one can distinguish the large painted figures used as wall-filling. The decoration of the two rooms (on the ground plan Nos. 7 and 9) with the same wall-coverings and paneling that were to have been used for the one room in the upper story was possible because the ground-floor rooms were not only smaller but also lower, not having a mezzanine.[150]

Confronted by a muddle of invalid wall elevations and a descriptive list for the projected distribution on another floor of the elements shown on those elevations, Longuelune decided to bring order out of chaos by making an entirely new design for the whole ground floor. Whether it was his intention to reinstitute the earlier designs as valid proposals for a now ill-defined upper story is not clear from the sources. That the design for the upper story around 1735 did not go into any greater detail than to specify the placement of the color groupings of Meissen porcelain is regrettable for our purposes because that was where the animal figures were to have been displayed. But that is a matter to which we shall return later.

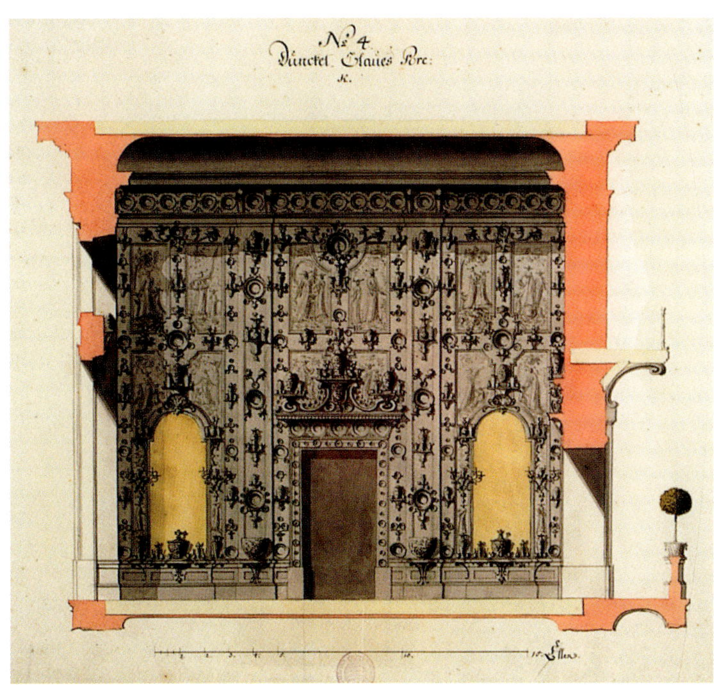

42 Japanese Palace, design for an upper-story room with dark blue porcelain, first series of plans, before 1730

The problem we face as a result of all this is that we have neither extant plans nor descriptive lists from which to make any deductions as to what work was actually undertaken in connection with the extension project. And although a number of eighteenth-century travel reports and descriptions of Dresden provide us with general information, they do not make a clear distinction between plans and the actual state of affairs obtaining at the time.

However, there are indications that some of the fittings for the Dutch Palace were incorporated into, or adapted for, the new building. A letter exists in which the painter Isaak Augustin Wiwild complains that his pension has not been paid, backing up his petition by pointing out services rendered in the past. Sadly he does not give an exact indication of when he did his work for the late king, i.e. Augustus the Strong, not only in the Green Vaults but also at the Japanese Palace, where he "drew and painted in colors wooden wall-paneling, animals, birds and the like."[151] The inventory of the Dutch Palace from 1721 describes the vestibule as having been "decorated with gilded frames, and with Indian figures and animals, painted life-size,"[152] which accords well with Wiwild's account of his own work. The entries on the ground plans and in the lists related to the new planning mention the old vestibule and stairwell only once, referring to them as "lacquered."[153] This, and the fact that no changes were made to this stairwell apart from a certain re-ordering of its windows, suggest that in this instance the decoration of the Dutch Palace survived the rebuilding.

But new furnishings must also have been designed and produced for the new palace. In March 1737, the architect Jean de Bodt made the proposal that part of the 6000 talers made available for the palace in that year could be spent on "the gilding of the étagères and console tables for the porcelain."[154]

One further important source is the above-mentioned extensive list of furniture, works of art, and textiles which were transferred from the Japanese Palace to the Residence in 1759.[155] The intention was most likely that they should be put to good use either in the extension of the Taschenbergpalais, the residence of the crown prince which had had a western side-wing and a further building at the back added to it by Julius Heinrich Schwarze during the Seven Years' War, or for the furnishing of an apartment in the Rococo style for Augustus III in the Residence.[156] If this list, which also contains information about the textile fittings for whole rooms, is compared with the description of the 1733 project for the ground floor of the Japanese Palace and the 1721 inventory for the Dutch Palace, quite astounding correspondences may be noted, such as the following.

According to the 1721 inventory, the room to the west of the central hall of the upper story of the Dutch Palace contained a white satin wall-hanging, "on which all manner of Indian animals, flowers and ornaments, colored and embroidered in gold" were to be seen, and the ground-floor room to the left of the vestibule was designed as a "cabinet hung with linen, lacquered in green and gilded in the Saxon manner." Although a number of rooms had hangings in white taffeta or satin, only this one was accorded an embroidered rather than a painted wall-covering.

On the basis of the 1733 list it is clear that shortly before his death, Augustus the Strong, or his architect, intended to combine the two elements mentioned in the central room of the converted palace's west wing, which was to be decorated "with green linen lacquered bands painted with golden dragons and ornaments, done quite new by the lacquerer Schnellen, the fillings covered in sheets of white satin from India, with golden ornaments, birds and flowers in multi-colored silk, finely embroidered."[157] These sheets, to be used as wall fillings, appear again after many years in the list of 1759 when "a sheet of white Indian satin, richly embroidered with gold and colored flowers," together with six identical pieces and "twenty-five green lacquered bands by Schnellen, with Indian figures in gold, six ells long" were removed from the Japanese Palace.[158]

Although further comparisons would certainly enable us to identify more fittings and furnishings stored in the new building after the Dutch Palace period, in none of these cases would it be possible to deduce whether our period saw the elements in question actually installed in the rooms, or whether they were simply stored in the palace after having been taken down from the walls.

The porcelain in the period of the palace reconstruction

This is true not only of the great number of Far Eastern porcelains which had been housed in the building since the days of the Dutch Palace, but also for those delivered from Meissen from the early 1730s onwards. Although the chronicler writes in 1733 that not only the *Kunstkammer*, which had been accommodated in the attic story, but also "the other precious objects including the incomparable porcelain [...] had been taken to a safe place, so that they might not be damaged,"[159] another source makes it clear that a great many of the porcelains still remained in the palace. In 1731 the palace major-domo Martin Teuffert made a submission asking for reimbursement of expenses on cleaning materials, for he had had to pay 16 talers per year "for the cleaning of the rooms with their porcelains and other objects to be found there."[160] Another piece of evidence for porcelain being present – however it was arranged – in the palace at the time of the reconstruction is a list of 243 Far Eastern porcelains transferred in August 1730 from the premises of the Dresden porcelain-dealer Elisabeth Bassetouche and the audience chamber at the Residence to the Japanese Palace, for which Teuffert issued an acknowledgment of receipt at the same time as he put in his request for reimbursement.[161] As research has shown, a number of the particularly impressive pieces were certainly "evacuated" from 1727 on and put on display in the so-called Tower Room at the Residence.[162] But the fact that a significantly larger portion of the stock of Far Eastern porcelain was left on the premises, as were the textile and wood coverings from the former Dutch Palace now incorporated into the new building, shows that those responsible thought it would not be long before the work on refurbishing the interior would be under way. Building work, however, was to be interrupted by the death of Augustus the Strong.

His successor Augustus III, however, did not give up the project. The 1733 list describing the ground-floor rooms, which has already been mentioned a number of times, gave him information as to the current plans for the distribution of the Far Eastern porcelain, and it was in fact only after his accession to the throne that the plans inherent in this list were given concrete and practicable form in Longuelune's designs. Longuelune's concept likewise incorporated the throne gallery into the overall iconography of the palace, a matter to which we shall return later. Furthermore, the orders for Meissen porcelain for the upper story were to increase greatly under Augustus III, during whose reign they were indeed to reach proportions quite comparable to those of his father's Far Eastern collection.

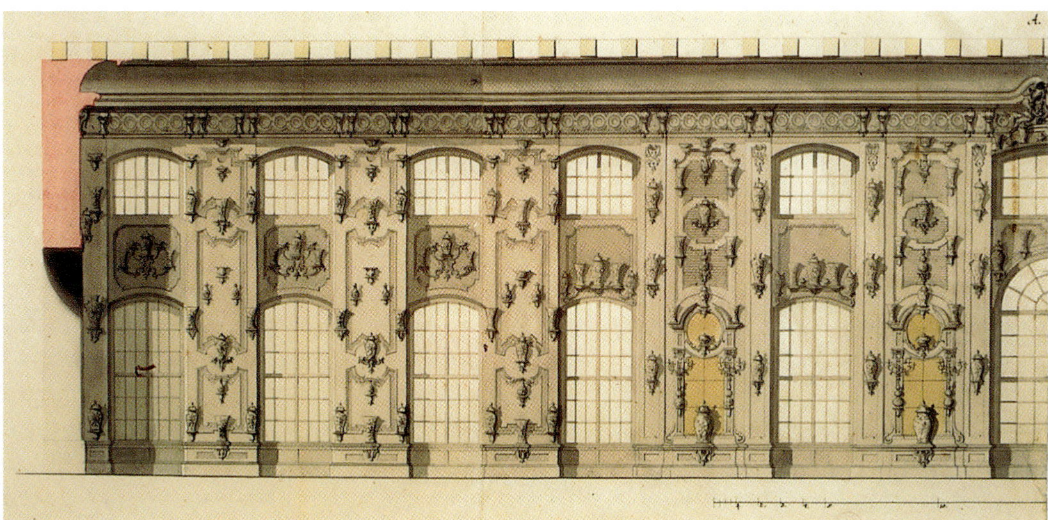

43 Japanese Palace, design for the window wall in the Neustadt-side gallery, before 1730 (left-hand half)

The porcelain orders

As we have seen, the definitive concept for the distribution of the porcelain in various groupings on the two stories had taken shape by the middle of 1730 at the latest. But the interaction between the royal collection and Meissen, which had of course existed right from the foundation of the manufactory, had increased steadily from the mid-1720s onwards, when the project of a "porcelain palace" on the site of the Dutch Palace first took shape, and then all the more so when the beginning of building work came in sight (1727/29), and plans began to include ever larger quantities not only of Far Eastern but also of Meissen porcelain.[163] Although the Dutch Palace still housed Meissen porcelain and Böttger stoneware, and even, after 1723, pieces "executed in the Japanese manner,"[164] Augustus the Strong is at the end of 1728 to be found ordering 300 large dishes which were to be executed in accordance with a model provided, but however "only with simple painting."[165] This order is certainly to be seen in connection with the beginning of the elevation plans, as dishes painted simply – and thus also quickly – would fit well in frieze-like rows into the cavettos at the top of the walls (fig. 43), where, almost thirty-six feet from the ground, the detail on the painting could in any case hardly be distinguished by the human eye.[166]

Towards the end of the decade a backlog of orders would seem to have accumulated at the manufactory, also including orders for porcelain to be executed from works of art provided as models. On the occasion of an order to the manufactory for vases "to furnish the rooms," the palace major-domo Martin Teuffert is to be found making an official statement that he "will in the future come more often, in order to bring over a great variety of good models for the use of the factory."[167] In consequence, the last two months of the year 1729, for instance, were to see five large lots being delivered to Meissen, with pieces chosen from those Far Eastern porcelains which were in spite of the architectural work being housed at the palace. A list of these wares mentions vessels and dishes "of old Indian porcelain," "*kraak* wares," "of Japanese porcelain," and "of green Chinese porcelain."[168] But it was not only porcelain that was being sent to be copied at the Albrechtsburg, as the December report of the manufactory makes clear: "[...] all sorts of galanterie and make-up boxes are being produced, and in addition no fewer mirror-frames and small coffee-tables, with models for some of these being sent here from the Royal Palace in Dresden."[169]

The following example demonstrates the closeness of the links between the royal collection, the manufactory and the planning for the interiors of the Japanese Palace. Around 1727 a Japanese "Vogelbauer vase" (or at least a detailed drawing of one) must have been sent with a batch of Far Eastern porcelains as a model to Meissen, where no efforts were spared in overcoming the technical difficulties involved in copying this – to our minds – somewhat ludicrous combination of vase and bird-cage, as a report of the manufactory inspector records: "Besides, the first large piece in the form of a Vogelbauer has been done to perfection here at the manufactory, of which in all fifty are to be produced for his Royal Majesty."[170] The fifty pieces mentioned could be related to an undated order in which the palace major-domo calls for altogether 530 porcelains and fifty of each of two different kinds of painted Vogelbauer vases, one of which corresponds to the description from the pen of the inspector.[171] A list already mentioned from March 28, 1730, is in a number of points identical with this order, which also contains indications of the rooms for which the vases were to be produced (Source 4).[172] According to the list, the intention was to put them in the Neustadt-side gallery on the upper story, very likely together with the Japanese originals. However, the manufactory was not technically equipped to deliver the fifty pieces at short notice, and it had in the summer of the same year been decided that the gallery was to be used for the animal figures. It can no longer be established where the twenty-one Vogelbauer vases gradually delivered through until the end of 1731 were to be displayed after the separation of Far Eastern and Meissen porcelain,[173] but Longuelune's meticulous elevations allocate twenty-four Japanese examples of the genre to the garden room on the ground floor.

The orders for the upper floor clearly reached a highpoint at the time of a detailed list, a copy of which is appended to the folder with Longuelune's plans and drawings for the former Lord Marshall's office.[174] Strangely enough, it is dated 1736 on the covering sheet, and it has not been established whether or not it is a later copy of the original, which is to be found in the manufactory archive at Meissen, dated November 26, 1733, and bearing the signature of Count Sulkowski (Source 13).[175] The listing is divided up into eleven sections for eleven rooms, with each section detailing the porcelain requirements for each wall, in many cases even giving the measurements of the porcelain in question. This gives one the definite impression that the planning for the upper floor had reached an advanced and detailed stage. Unfortunately, there is no other evidence – as we have seen from study of the planning history – to support this impression. It is true that the color sequence of the porcelain groups corresponds to Keyssler's descriptions of the rooms of October 1730, but no elevations exist, nor indeed even sketches. It may safely be assumed that elevations of this kind, with the exception of the one made in 1735 by Longuelune for the Elbe-side gallery, never even existed. In any case, Count Sulkowski, who was from 1733 responsible for the orders for the Japanese Palace under Augustus III, found it necessary to make the following annotation in the margin of the copy which he had signed and dated: "I give my word that so many pieces are necessary for the furnishing of the Japanese Palace from N 1 to 11,"[176] which is at the very least evidence of his desire to clear up any doubts in advance. Given the quantities ordered, one can quite understand that such doubts might well have arisen. The order lists for the eleven rooms are preceded in the records by an "Extract of the appended specifications about the Saxon porcelain which has been required for the furnishing of the 11 rooms to be found on the upper floor of the Royal Japanese Palace, what is already finished and what still has to be produced," in which a summary is given of the forms of the 25,215 porcelains ordered.[177] It also records exactly how many pieces of these various sorts were already to be found in the Japanese Palace, namely 3,835. The list states that 15,676 pieces were at the manufactory warehouse and ready to be painted, and "only" 5,704 pieces were still to come off the production line.[178]

All these records can only be understood in connection with the death of Augustus the Strong and his son's accession to the throne.[179] Certain parties were concerned to convince Augustus III of the necessity of continuing the project, and clearly used this "whitewashing" of the real state of planning to this end. After all, no concrete design had at that time as yet been projected for the Meissen porcelain. These parties could well have included: Zacharias Longuelune, who as leading architect was concerned to see his work brought to completion, the major-domo Martin Teuffert, whose position was intimately linked to the status of the palace, and Count Alexander von Sulkowski, who as *Oberstkämmerer* (Lord Chamberlain) was responsible, among other things, for this prestigious project and – as we shall see – also derived personal material advantage from this office.

This detailed document of November 26 receives additional significance when considered in connection with a listing dated November 18, 1733 (Source 12) according to which Sulkowski, Teuffert and Pflugk were at the manufactory warehouse a good week before the large order and reserved a total of 35,798 porcelain pieces [!], "for the furnishing of the Royal Japanese Palace."[180] These porcelains, however, were all white and still had to be decorated. As the allocation of porcelains to various rooms in the palace was done according to color, the manufactory still had to know how many pieces in any given form had to be decorated in which ground color or style, and what still had to be produced in the way of molds. This information was provided by the detailed order list of November 26, 1733. The fact that the listing for the painters contained 10,582 fewer porcelains than had been reserved a week before may be the result of it having been put together by the planners of the upper floor, who certainly had detailed knowledge of the design, although sadly no drawing of this design has survived to the present day. The following example is given to show the vague and uncoordinated manner in which the planning was carried out. Out of the 35,789 porcelains carefully reserved by Sulkowski on November 17, 1733, the order of November 26 called for a total of 366 for the window-wall of the carillon room alone (Source 13). However, the relevant elevation by Longuelune and his collaborators, dated 1735, hardly shows half of that number, even on a generous count. This shows the deficient coordination between those designing and those placing the orders, and indeed begs the question of the authorship of the order lists.

It is not quite clear who could have put together the lists to which Sulkowski gave his seal of approval, that is to say, who had the job of turning the king's concept for the porcelain into reality. One possibility is that the author was Martin Teuffert, the palace major-domo, who did claim, in a letter he wrote to Augustus III two months after the latter's accession, that he had been given legitimate authority for the porcelain orders during Augustus the Strong's lifetime.[181] Although he was the link between the palace and the manufactory, it is not clear how far the authority he had been given actually went, or whether he was not trying to use the changeover to create a more important position for himself. The records would rather suggest the latter, as before 1733 Teuffert was in fact only regarded as a messenger, as for instance in the manufactory report ("Rapport") for October 1731: "Various models and drawings which his Royal Majesty wished to be conveyed to Meissen have been brought here by Major-Domo Teuffert,who arrived here at the factory on the 31st of this month from Dresden."[182] In the above-mentioned letter to Augustus III, furthermore, Teuffert made a proposal that the upper story should be speedily furnished with such porcelains as were either available or adaptable for the purpose, which neither accorded with the ideas of Augustus the Strong as they can be deduced from the elevation drawings nor showed any great understanding of the artistic concept behind the plans. And his suggestion that three or four palace pieces should be added to each and every firing in order to hurry progress along towards the desired end only shows the undue influence exerted upon him by manufactory managers who had been driven to the absolute limits of their working capacity. In connection with the orders Teuffert would thus rather have played the role of a secretary, coordinating the orders and checking the deliveries.

As far as the reign of Augustus the Strong is concerned, it was certainly the case that the king, whose involvement with his collections was an intensely personal one, made his own comments on his architects' proposals and on the associated order lists for porcelain – just as he did for the building plans – before giving his approval, sometimes making his own lists of what was required, a number of which have survived to this day. In some lists, the title also specifies that the king originally gave the orders by word of mouth, very likely after consultation with architects familiar with the space available.

His son Augustus III followed a different procedure in that he made Count Sulkowski into a middleman with responsibility for the deliveries, even giving him a relatively free hand in this field. Any corrections made after 1733 to the contents and quantities of the orders will therefore very likely have been the result of consultations between Sulkowski and the architects. As can be seen from the example related to the carillon room, these consultations were by present-day standards somewhat poorly coordinated. If one attempts to correlate the 1733 list and the elevation drawings, which is quite justifiable in that the former would appear to relate to the latter, then it becomes clear that much more porcelain was ordered than it would have possible to accommodate on the basis of the first group of designs, or even of Longuelune's detailed representation of the throne gallery. And although the quantities specified in the orders would thus seem to have been generous estimates, the manufactory was still expected to fulfill them to the letter.

Unlike Teuffert, whose suggestion that the furnishing of the palace should be done as quickly as possible reflects the resistance provoked by the project at Meissen, the ambitious Count Sulkowski refused to reduce the orders. In this he was setting his face against the manufactory, which not only had to meet the king's orders, but also had to keep up production of the so-called "currenten Waaren," the retail wares which actually brought them an income. It was not just the enormous quantities which were a burden on the manufactory, but also the one-off pieces (over-sized items, wall decorations, organ pipes, and so on) which called for elaborate experiments to be carried out before they could go into production. A contemporary overall calculation for the period 1725 to 1733 reveals that while porcelain with a total value of 48,426 talers, 8 groschen and 5 schillings was delivered to the king, the only payment made was one of 500 talers, in 1727.[183] The bill from the end of December 1732 alone, entitled "for the animals and birds hitherto delivered to the Japanese Palace" and appended to this calculation, amounted with its 10,134 talers and 20 groschen to more than a fifth of Augustus the Strong's total porcelain debts. This scenario led to a rupture within the enterprise itself between the artists and the management, with the former benefiting from the opportunity to experiment given them by the challenging commissions, while the latter were extremely worried about the manufactory's dire financial situation.

The pronouncements coming from the manufactory at the beginning of 1732 were still optimistic, although both management and staff were fully aware of the technical problems they faced. With regard to the large-size pieces, "the manufactory's arcanists were hopeful that these [the life-size apostle figures] and the other large vases or *garnitures* that have been ordered by His Royal Majesty, would from then on without exception come out well, as a result of the increasing number of new techniques that have been learnt for handling the figures when they are glazed or fired." And further on, the same report emphasizes that there is hope of success in the form of innovative new objects: "From now on certain bells are to be produced for use in a carillon, and an experiment has been made with organ pipes, in the knowledge that newly invented porcelain pieces will be certain to bring further pleasure to His Royal Majesty."[184]

When the next order list arrived at the manufactory, where the mood was if not exactly carefree still conscientiously focused, the accompanying communication from Augustus the Strong must have come across like the thundering of a mighty drum-roll:

"Augustus, by the grace of God King in Poland, Duke of Saxony, Jülich, Cleves, Berg, Engern and Westphalia, Elector,

Best councillors, dear and faithful ones, given that we have decided that the new front gallery in the upper story of our Dutch Palace at Neustadt, Dresden, is to be furnished with the appended specification, drawn up by us personally, of nine hundred and ten porcelain pieces, it is now our most gracious desire that measures should be taken in accordance with this order so that the porcelain pieces specified therein should in the course of time be produced in our factory at Meissen and delivered, and that the bills should be written off accordingly. This is our will and mind, and you may be sure of our continued grace and favor. On this day in Warsaw, April 2, 1732, Augustus Rex."[185]

The accompanying list (Source 6) lists 910 large vessels and figures, arranged in groups according to their intended locations in the gallery, suggesting that the king had consulted an architect regarding the room's size and capacity.[186] The list is furthermore dated "Neustadt bey Dreßden den 25. Febr: 1732," and is now not kept, as one might expect, appended to the letter in the Meissen Archive, but rather in the records of the *Geheimes Kabinett* (Privy Council) in the State Archive in Dresden. It was thus drawn up *in situ* at the Japanese Palace, possibly in the presence of the king, with the fair copy being sent on later, as Augustus the Strong left Dresden three days later for Warsaw.[187] The still extant copy of the list for the records of the Privy Council remained in Dresden, while the (lost?) original, very likely signed by the king on April 2 together with the order, was sent to Meissen from Warsaw.

This listing of the porcelain required for one single room was a clear indication of what quantities of porcelain might later be ordered for the other rooms. Furthermore, the manufactory was now stretched way beyond its capacity, not only economically but also technically; at this stage, after all, there was still great rejoicing over every large-scale piece that came through the firing safe and sound, and every such occasion was noted in the records.

The manufactory commission, as the prime addressee of the king's instructions, replied immediately on April 19, promising to take advantage of the spring and summer when the long daylight hours would allow extensive overtime.[188]

The manufactory's first reaction was to draw up a list of the members of staff who were to work exclusively on the order and to append it to the next monthly report sent to Dresden (Source 21). It should be noted that they listed all the leading artists and craftsmen, including, for instance, not just one but both of the Meissen modelers. One monthly report contains an indication that the manufactory commission, which played a mediating role between the manufactory and the privy council, had demanded that a list of this kind be drawn up: "[...] a high commission has requested information as to how many persons are to work for his Royal Majesty [...]".[189] But as they were regularly instructed to cancel the bills for the royal orders, which were then left unpaid, other orders had to be taken on to ensure the financial survival of the enterprise, and it was never possible to operate consistently with the projected division of labor.

The pressure on the manufactory to raise production levels increased as a result of intrigues conducted by courtiers seeking to gain Augustus the Strong's favor by working on him at his weakest spot, namely his porcelain palace project. On September 3 and 10, 1732, a total of thirty-one large crates of finished pieces were delivered in two lots to the Japanese Palace.[190] It is fairly sure that the wares delivered included the vases that are the subject of a drawing indicating their intended location over a fireplace in the gallery, made by Privy Councillor Count Heinrich von Brühl and sent at the beginning of September from Warsaw.[191] In order to fulfill his wish as completely as possible, a number of additional undecorated vases were delivered to the Japanese Palace on September 4 and 7.[192] The intention behind all this was that the king should be pleasantly surprised when, on his return from Warsaw, he made his customary visit to the palace to inspect the work that had been done there. That these pieces did indeed find their way to their intended location is confirmed in an eye-witness report written by Jonas Hanway, who visited the palace around the middle of the century: "The long gallery in the second story had already two marble chimney-pieces, each adorned with near 40 very large pieces of porcelain [...]."[193] On October 23, Augustus the Strong returned to Dresden and visited the Japanese Palace one day later.[194] In the case of a number of pieces, however, he expressed dissatisfaction with the quality of the glaze and paste, upon which the manufactory commission asked the arcanists what might have been behind the defects, and what could be done to bring about an improvement.[195] In their reply, the arcanists did not mince their words: "The three arcanists and others engaged at the manufactory have truly devoted every possible effort to the production of the 910 large vases and figures, as is shown by the fact that some of these have come out well from the firing and have been delivered to the Royal Palace in Neustadt, Dresden. Experience, however, has shown that the recipes first thought to be suitable do not bring the expected results, not to mention the fact that many of the large pieces of this kind develop fire-cracks even in the low firing, or are damaged later in the high firing. [...] the arcanists are concerned about continuing to work in this manner on such large pieces, and are more inclined just to put one large figure into the firing at a time, to avoid excessive amounts of paste, work, and wood being wasted, and to ensure the continued production of small pieces, for the good of the manufactory finances."[196]

Up to this point it had been thought that the orders could be met by employing more staff; now that the technical shortcomings had been singled out for criticism from high places, it was clearly necessary to find a new tactic for ensuring that the manufactory could be free to work for its economic survival.

Shortly afterwards, on November 8, the king visited the manufactory while passing through the Meissen area, and inspected the works and warehouse. He was clearly unconvinced that there were limits to the manufactory's production capacity, as December 17 saw the submission of another order, this time solely for large animal figures (Source 10).[197] In order to clarify Dresden's expectations with regard to the deliveries, Count von Brühl wrote the following to the management of the manufactory in a letter of December 28, 1732: "In accord with the most gracious verbal command of His Royal Majesty in Poland and His Serene Highness the Elector of Saxony [...] all porcelain that is produced in the Meissen porcelain factory for His Royal Majesty shall from now on be made from fine white paste and is to have little painting, in the old Far Eastern manner, or if some fine enameling has been ordered, [...] then likewise only very little [painting] should be done."[198] Meissen responded by promising to devote every conceivable effort to the matter, and by requesting somewhat more time in which to meet the order.[199]

On February 1, 1733, Augustus the Strong died in Warsaw. By February 13, Augustus III was already wanting to know from the manufactory what his father had ordered and what was still outstanding.[200] At the end of February he decided to give a positive response to the manufactory's request, and Count Sulkowski granted the enterprise in Meissen more time.[201] The arcanists in turn submitted their request to the commission that they "should not be given too short a time,"[202] following which Augustus III personally told the manufactory that although the work on the 910 pieces ordered by his father was to go ahead, he was giving them five years to fulfill the order in its entirety.[203]

The fact of Augustus III's allowing more time, in the early part of 1733, must be seen in connection with the re-orientation of the whole porcelain palace project. The heir to the throne had had himself informed exactly about the state of planning and the work done to date, and the result was a fairly confusing picture. As a certain amount of time would in any case have been necessary to put the mass of drawings, inventories, and partially valid and partially out-of-date lists into order, a promise of this kind was quite in the king's interest. Another factor was that Count Sulkowski, who had been entrusted with the re-organization of the project, had an interest in endowing his job with as great a degree of prestige as possible. This having been the case, it comes as no surprise to find that the next order list issued half a year later wastes not a word on the 910 porcelains for one gallery, to be completed in five years, calling instead for "only" 750 vases and animal figures for the gallery, but flies in the face of any possible objections by demanding a sum total of 25,215 pieces for the whole of the upper story. Another clear sign of the project's being totally re-planned after the accession of Augustus III is provided by the new designs by Longuelune for the ground floor and throne gallery. Even as late as December 28, 1736, Augustus III is to be found emphasizing his commitment to completing what was by then his own project: "Now that we are having a variety of buildings constructed at our hunting palace, Hubertusburg, and we are no less decided to complete the conversion of the palace here in Neustadt, we have set aside the sum of one hundred thousand talers for the purpose; and we thus herewith graciously command that from the above sum, [...] six thousand talers in the year 1737 [...] and fourteen thousand and twenty talers in the year 1738 shall be paid out in case for the completion of the palace in Neustadt, or [...] shall be taken from the monies placed at our free disposal [...]."[204]

Evidence for a new start having been made, at least on the planning, is also provided by a report of the manufactory commission from the beginning of 1737: "[...] and Court Commissioner Höroldt gives his assurance that from this month onwards, there will be a delivery every week of a number of the still outstanding royal porcelains prescribed for the gallery and rooms to be refurbished in the Japanese Palace."[205]

This new wave of planning also explains why the end of the 1730s saw recurrent apologies on the part of the manufactory for the delays in delivery, combined with the king's insistence that the orders, which by now were no longer being changed, were still valid.[206] This second attempt at the completion of the palace very likely failed on account of the fall from grace of Count Alexander von Sulkowski, who was dismissed from his ministerial position on February 5, 1738.[207] A more detailed account of the wider repercussions of this political event will be given when we consider the orders submitted for animal figures.

This short account of the orders and deliveries begs the question as to the actual appearance of the upper story of the palace once they had taken place. In this connection it should be noted that at the time of Augustus the Strong's death several thousand pieces were already standing in the rooms there, and that many more thousands were delivered in the years that followed. The lists, however, do not indicate how the pieces were exhibited.[208]

Now that consideration has been given to the architectural drawings, the designs for the fittings and furnishing, and the order lists, attention should also be paid to another important source of information about the project and its execution – travel reports and topographical descriptions.

The Japanese Palace in topographical works and travel reports

Great works of art – in both senses of the word – always attract a great measure of attention. Hardly a single travel book or topographical work concerned with Dresden has ever failed to give space to the Japanese Palace, even though only its exterior was actually brought to completion. The interior, which was shown to visitors for a small fee in the period before the building became a museum, contained many works of art but hardly any rooms complete with all their fittings and furnishings, for the palace – unlike the Zwinger, the Residence, or the Green Vaults – had been left in its unfinished state. This is probably the reason why it has always acted as such a powerful stimulant upon the fantasies of its visitors: the "king's dream of a porcelain palace"[209] has tended to make its visitors dream dreams of their own. Extreme caution thus has to be exercised when evaluating these sources.

A first, short description of the Dutch Palace was published in 1720 in the periodical *Der Neu-erscheinende Postillon*.[210] It gave a particularly detailed account of the ceiling painting in the upper story's central room, which showed Hercules as leader of the muses. In fact, it was painted over before (or at the latest in) 1721, to match the sumptuous wall-hangings, as we know from the inventory of that year: "The ceiling is done in well-executed stucco work and painted like the wall-hangings in the middle [...] NB: Under the ceiling which has now been painted in the manner of the wall-paintings is a another painted ceiling which tells a story."[211] This did not prevent Johann Christian Hasche, when writing a description of Dresden over sixty years later, from citing the picture as still adorning the ceiling of the room – which itself by this time no longer even existed in its erstwhile form – and ascribing it to the former court painter Louis de Silvestre.[212] This kind of uncritical reproduction of elements from earlier writings is typical of all the eighteenth-century descriptive literature related to the Japanese Palace. Hasche's description is dependent on earlier writings in a number of other instances, and he quarried large quantities of text from what is one of the most "authentic" and certainly the most important printed source for research into the Japanese Palace project, namely the travel report written by the scholar Johann Georg Keyssler (Source 2).[213]

On his travels all over central Europe in the years 1729 and 1730, Keyssler stayed at courts great and small alike and wrote an account of all that seemed to him worthy of note in the social, political, economic, scientific, scholarly, and artistic fields. His eighty-sixth letter, dated October 23, 1730, is devoted to Dresden; he describes the art collections, some in considerable detail, and gives an exposé of the form the palace was to take according to the plans current at the time. His informant must have been someone with detailed knowledge of the elevations and plans with inscriptions relating to the distribution of the porcelain groups, and very likely a member of the *Bauamt*.

As Keyssler stayed in Dresden in the middle of the conversion phase,214 he quite correctly used the future tense when writing about the arrangement of the Far Eastern porcelain on the ground floor and of the Meissen porcelain in the upper story, but some of his successors were not so scrupulous in this respect. In 1744, three years after the first publication of Keyssler's report, Carl Christian Schramm published his *Neues Europäisches Historisches Reise-Lexicon*.[215] Although his account of the Japanese Palace includes a reference to the large quantity of porcelain, "which is in the future to be given an even more magnificent and choice ordering," the way he alternates between indicative and subjunctive gives the reader the definite impression that six rooms in the upper story were already fitted and furnished. The most blatant example of his distortion of the facts is his description of the gallery on the Neustadt side: "It is already furnished with all kinds of birds and animals from inland and abroad, in porcelain and mostly in their natural size and color."[216] Here he was putting Keyssler's report, which ran as follows, into the present tense: "It [= the first room] is to be furnished with all kinds of birds and animals from inland and abroad in pure porcelain, in their natural size and color; the figures which have already been finished are of such artistry and beauty that one cannot admire them enough." Schramm thus turned Keyssler's small number of finished pieces into a whole fully-furnished gallery. And this in its turn misled Benjamin Gottfried Weinart into making the following claim in his *Topografische Geschichte der Stadt Dresden* of 1777, by which time the porcelain was in fact in the cellars, whither it had been consigned for safety's sake during the Seven Years' War: "The first gallery in the upper story […] was already really furnished with all kinds of birds and animals from inland and abroad in porcelain, mostly in their natural size and color."[217]

Even before the publication of Keyssler's account, a report on the Japanese Palace had appeared in the *Sächßisches Curiositäten Cabinet* of 1733.[218] In many parts the author reproduced, almost verbatim, passages from the article in *Der Neu-erscheinende Postillon*, calling the palace a "Saxon Escorial", and also referring, as so many did after him, to the invisible ceiling painting quite as if it was still there to be admired. He makes no mention whatsoever of the porcelain having been rearranged. Neither did either of two descriptions of Dresden from 1735[219] and 1737[220] have very much to say on the subject, though the latter description clearly owed much to the Baron von Pöllnitz, whose letters had gone into their third printing in the same year.[221]

Pöllnitz praised the sumptuous marble statues which had been acquired in Rome from Cardinal Albani and now decorated the garden, confessing himself highly impressed by the quantity of Far Eastern porcelain in the palace: "The rooms of this palace […] are all cabinets for Japanese and Chinese porcelain. I do not believe that all the dealers in Amsterdam together could offer one so much rare and ancient porcelain as there is here,"[222] thus providing the literature on the palace with another fallacious leitmotif, which was to crop up just as regularly as the "Saxon Escorial." The "Antiquarius des Elbstroms," whose work appeared in the same year as Keyssler's, that is to say 1741, translated Baron von Pöllnitz's French into German with, "all the rooms are furnished with Japanese and Chinese porcelain."[223] All the eighteenth-century descriptions of the Japanese Palace were thus based on two principle sources, published in 1720 and 1741 respectively.[224]

Keyssler was not able to give any more than a rough idea of how the porcelain was to be arranged, but certainly worked from the elevations, according to which not only porcelain but also mirrors and "ornaments," that is to say most likely gilded consoles and decorative elements, were to adorn the walls. He also mentioned elements that were in fact later realized such as the carillon and the decoration of the inner courtyard with vases on consoles. The latter feature is also shown in a cross-section through the courtyard (fig. 35), and is documented by a listing from the hand of Augustus the Strong himself, in which he enumerates "12 large beakers under the galleries, 12 large urns on the balcony walls, 38 middle-size urns on the balustrades," and finally "36 large urns, and 8 large bowls in the courtyard wall-sections"[225] and a further 196 large vessels of various kinds, most likely Far Eastern in origin.[226]

However, Keyssler also wrote also about porcelain furnishings that in fact never got any further than the experimental phase, such as the life-size apostle statues and porcelain organ-pipes for the chapel,[227] and also about projects that were never even started. An altar 6.7 meters high was, for instance, to be made entirely out of porcelain, as were large relief pictures for the chapel and parts of the throne itself, as we also know from Longuelune's explanatory note accompanying the design for the throne room. It is quite understandable that plans such as these caused tongues to wag, and that the resulting rumors provided a powerful stimulus for the fantasy of following generations. In the records of the Meissen company archive, for instance, there is a copy of a newspaper entry from 1740, which runs as follows: "According to news from Dresden, the so-called Japanese House, hitherto roofed with copper, is to be tiled with fine Meissen porcelain."[228] Johann Christian Müller, visiting Dresden in 1744, was told a similar story by the palace guardian, namely that the "outside walls of the building were to have been covered with porcelain decorations,"[229] a claim that was taken by a scholarly publication of 1956 as suggesting that there had actually been a firm project to give the inner courtyard a cladding of porcelain panels.[230] In a newspaper article of 1932 Rauda also contrived to dream up a project for porcelain chairs and tables, possibly interpreting the word "jeridon," which appears in the sources, as a small piece of furniture known in modern usage as a "Gueridon." The Meissen records, however, use "jeridon" to mean "Girandole," a large table candelabra. After Keyssler, the travel reports of greatest interest to us are the ones by Johann Christian Müller and Jonas Hanway, and as they describe the palace as it was around the middle of the century, they will be dealt with in greater detail in the section that follows, which is devoted to the period when the Japanese Palace functioned as a depository.

If Hasche's regurgitation of ill-digested earlier reports led him to construct an idealized palace which was in fact never executed in reality, then the nineteenth and the twentieth centuries – particularly the latter – outdid him by losing touch with the last remnants of the original intention behind the palace, treating it as a pure work of art and a vehicle for the projection of their historicizing understanding of absolutism. Those who followed this line of thought considered that the palace belonged in the category of porcelain pleasure-houses and backed up their interpretation with carefully chosen sources: "Augustus II's prime intention was to decorate the Japanese Palace therewith [with porcelain] as a summer residence […]. The collection of Far Eastern porcelain here is now unique in Europe, and has been so ever since the porcelain from a similar cabinet in Meudon was disposed of after the death of Louis XIV."[231] The real nature of the building was hardly recognized and the seriousness that lay behind it was mistaken for megalomania. The palace remained "a princely dream, dreamt by a *gloire*-hungry and overweening king in a bid to outshine the Sun King of Versailles."[232]

The view of the palace inherent in the written sources also explains why no further buildings have been conceived along the same lines as the Japanese Palace in Dresden. After all, an unfinished project, misrepresented by its appraisers, can hardly be expected to stimulate others to venture down the same path.

The Japanese Palace as depository

Collation and comparison of all the drawings, porcelain orders, and descriptions leads one to the conclusion that certain elements of the work on the interior *were* carried out – the building records, for instance, refer to stuccoed ceilings – but that the fittings and furnishings, whether these were pieces of furniture, mirrors, and wall-hangings from the Dutch Palace, or the Far Eastern and Meissen porcelain, were simply stored in the rooms. In his suggestions of April 16, 1733, as to how the project might be brought to a speedy conclusion, the major-domo Teuffert stated that the pieces that had belonged to Count Hoym were "stored here" and were intended for use in the throne gallery,[233] and "likewise […] a quantity of brown Saxon porcelain […] which would have been perfectly sufficient to decorate one room, and no less a quantity of white Saxon porcelain, which would likewise suffice for one room."[234]

One very valuable source is the description of the Japanese Palace which the Stralsund pastor Johann Christian Müller included in his memoirs (Source 27). Although he visited Dresden in March 1744 and only composed his memoirs towards the end of the 1750s, it seems that he made use of notes that he took at the time, as the account is wonderfully detailed and only contains minor mistakes. On the state of the palace interior he writes as follows: "First of all, we were taken to the large hall which had been designed to be a mirror-room. A start had already been made on fitting it with mirrors, which ran a number of yards along one side, and this mirror-wall had been fitted from top to bottom with carved and gilded pedestals not far from each other on which various four-footed animals and birds of prey in porcelain were standing, done life-size according to nature […]. In one room there was a large number of porcelain animal figures of this kind, which were to be accommodated in the mirror-room. In another room there were large bowls and porcelain vessels with very clear depictions of whole battles, or the most pleasing of landscapes and scenes *en miniature*, all fired in the most beautiful colors. And in a long room there was a long table on which stood two rows of porcelain figurines […]. I was told that the manufactory did not offer such pieces on the open market, but that they were made for the king and used as gifts for other courts. We were shown the rooms, of which one was red and another blue, the third green and the fourth yellow; the walls were to have had porcelain standing on them and were to have been decorated with sets of pieces in precisely those colors. We were shown into a very long room which the late king of blessèd memory had intended to be his audience chamber, and in which the throne, decorated with statues, was to have been done entirely in porcelain. Standing here were also a large number of porcelain bells, all of which rang with a particular note, as they were to have been used to make a carillon for this room. It would have been a most valuable instrument as very many of the bells fired had been no use, because it had been very difficult to get the pitch absolutely right. From the upper rooms we were taken down to the basement rooms, all with large high vaults and large columns as in a church, which were intended as wine cellars. Now they were being used to store the exceptional stock of Chinese porcelain. We were told that there were enough plates and dishes for a table with three hundred guests."[235]

This description makes it clear that the interior was far from complete. Although some mirrors had been delivered and, most likely, fitted one full year before Müller's visit,[236] none of the attempts at completing the furnishing of the palace was ever successful. It is possible that after having given up the plans, Augustus III intended to make the rooms into a kind of "ceramic gallery" for exhibition purposes, for he continued to have important display pieces ("Kabinettstücke") from the Meissen manufactory delivered directly to the palace and entered into the inventory, not to mention also the famous porcelain flower bouquet from Vincennes, which had been given to Augustus III in 1749 by his daughter Maria Josepha, who was married to the Dauphin.[237] One can on the other hand hardly imagine a work of such high artistic quality as the large crucifixion group being delivered as a pure display piece for exhibition in a museum-like context. It may have been the case that this work, modeled by Kaendler for the Catholic court church built in the period 1738–1754 and consecrated in 1751, was for a variety of possible reasons not put up in the church, and was finally reiterated in the palace inventory for want of a more practical solution. Müller's description also shows that the rooms were partially used as interim storage space for the king's orders, noting as he does that there were figure groups standing on tables and waiting to be used as gifts. For these reasons it must be assumed that the only function the palace now had was as a place where the king could show his guests these collected treasures, explaining their provenance, providing other information and presenting gifts. More simply put, the Japanese Palace had become something along the lines of a branch of the Meissen manufactory, maintained for the exclusive benefit of the king. Although this thesis cannot be proven unambiguously from the sources, confirmation that the palace was unfinished and had a depository-like character can be found in the writings of Jonas Hanway, who visited the palace ten years later on a return journey from China that took him through Persia and Russia.[238] His description, which has never been quoted in the literature on the Japanese Palace, is quite free from the influence from earlier writings: "The vaults of this palace consist of fourteen apartments, filled with China and Dresden porcelain; one would imagine there was sufficient quantity to stock a whole country, and yet they say, with an air of importance, that 100,000 pieces more are wanted to compleat the intention of furnishing this single palace, which is not large. [...] The long gallery in the second story had already two marble chimney-pieces, each adorned with near 40 very large pieces of porcelain, of birds, beasts, and vases, ranged to the height of above 20 feet in a most superb taste, the figures being all made so natural, that I could conceive no idea superior in this kind. All sorts of rich hangings, glasses, tables, chairs, &c. are brought into the apartments, but kept packed and covered, the walls remaining bare for four years. The palace in general is unfinished, and it may be presumed that the King himself is tired of the vanity of an unnecessary variety, and of such a profusion of expensive baubles."[239] (For the complete text see Source 22.)

So when Weinart writes, in 1777, that "all these plans for beautification [...] have remained unfulfilled, with the exception of a few remaining rooms which have retained something of their former splendor," then he can only be praising the immovable features, which with the exception of Pöppelmann's stairwell and parts of the entrance hall were destroyed when the building was converted for use as a library.[240]

In the period up to the Seven Years' War, the palace thus remained in an unfinished state, with some parts having a depository-like character; the major-domo, Teuffert, guided visitors around the latter parts,[241] where they were at least able to see "vessels, figures, groups of foreign and local porcelain unsorted on tables and on the floor,"[242] even if they could not experience the rooms as they were intended to be enjoyed. In the winter of 1774/75, by way of preparation for the palace being put to a new use, the two floors were given a final clearing-out and it was proposed that the porcelain should be left in the cellars until the Zwinger pavilion became vacant with the moving of the library, at which point it could be accommodated there. "From amongst the still remaining movable objects, particularly the very many beautiful old lacquered pieces could possibly be brought there [to the Zwinger pavillon], if they were not taken to the Residence or to any other electoral schloss."[243] That the palace also served as a "depository" is also shown by a submission made in 1787 by Count Marcolini in which he called for a new home to be found for the porcelains, not least because the cellars were unsuitable for storing them, and also because they were now "no longer to be regarded as furnishings, but as works of art [!]."[244] One year later, at least two of the principal pieces of the collection, the "carillon in Meissen porcelain" and "a large porcelain bouquet of flowers with its container, standing on a bronze pedestal," were to be found in the marble hall of the Zwinger.[245] The greater part of the porcelain collection, however, was to remain in the cellar rooms for almost a whole century longer, while the use of the upper floors as storage space for luxury items was brought to an immediate end.[246]

The end of the project

It may at first seem surprising that such an extensive and important project as the furnishing of the Japanese Palace with porcelain was apparently jettisoned so suddenly. As we shall see, the orders for and deliveries of animal figures for the large Neustadt-side gallery began in 1730 and ended in 1736. Deliveries of tableware can be shown to have continued into the year 1738.[247] Porcelains delivered to the palace after that year were destined for the king, but were no longer intended to be housed permanently at the palace.

It would be rash to attribute the termination of the *Porzellanschloss* project to a lack of interest in porcelain on the part of Augustus III. After all, Augustus III's reign did see yet another extensive revision of the plans, and greater pressure than ever before being exerted on the Meissen manufactory for the fulfillment of the orders. In my opinion, the real reasons for the interruption of the project are to be sought in two matters which the literature on the subject has hitherto hardly ever associated with the palace. The first is related to an occurrence at the court in the year 1738, and the second to the situation at the manufactory in 1739.

In an order issued on April 9, 1733, that is to say a good month after the death of Augustus the Strong, Augustus III informed the manufactory directorate of his will as follows: "We [...] also most graciously desire, that of the said wares, you would have all that is indicated to you by our master of the stables and treasurer Count Sulkowski provided also for us, to the extent that this is confirmed by him in person [...] and this should all be put onto our bill."[248] This effectively made Count Sulkowski, the great friend of Augustus III's younger days, into the most important person with regard to the Japanese Palace.[249] And it was indeed he, as we saw, who signed the thick bundle of detailed order lists dated November 26, 1733, that clarified the concept for the upper story of the palace.

Sulkowski had in addition ordered porcelain for his own use and had had it delivered to the palace. Among this porcelain was an extensive dinner service that is one of the most important Meissen services of the first half of the eighteenth century. As the king had specified that all the orders he signed were to be met without payment, Sulkowski was able to get his own porcelain free simply by ordering it with the palace as the delivery address. All he had to be sure to do in addition was to instruct Teuffert not to enter the wares in the palace inventory. We should not be too quick to pass judgment on this procedure, however, as it was quite possibly all done with Augustus III's agreement, the king being present when the service in question was first used, at the wedding of Sulkowski's wife's sister, the Baroness von Stain zu Jettingen, to Count Lubomirski on February 28, 1737.[250] This occasion is furthermore of note as the first documented occasion of a Meissen service being used for the main courses and dessert.[251] Maureen Cassidy-Geiger has demonstrated convincingly that the forms used for the service were deliberately derived from silver of the royal silver chamber, and that the service was intended, with the full knowledge of Augustus III, to be used by the first minister as his dinner service for official state functions.[252]

On February 5, 1738, Sulkowski was informed of his dishonorable dismissal. The influential and enormously powerful minister had, for whatever reasons, fallen from favor and from office. Two days later, Wichmannshausen from the Commission sent a very hastily penned letter to Höroldt demanding a compilation of various passages from the manufactory records: firstly, all the passages in which the king had granted "any powers regarding porcelain matters" to Count Sulkowski; secondly, the respective communications from the king to the Commission; and thirdly, an exact list of all porcelains delivered to Sulkowski, whether paid for or not.[253] The answer was issued one day later, the desired passages from the records having been compiled by Johann Friedrich Fleutner, the minutes secretary of the manufactory Commission and a Meissen district official. Logically enough, however, he had not been able to find the orders for Sulkowski's personal use in the records, but noted that when he had asked Höroldt, the latter had told him that the wares produced for the count had been ordered verbally either by Teuffert or by Wolff, the count's master of the kitchen, and that they had been delivered to the Japanese Palace as specified.[254] The Commission had thus clearly been circumvented, with Höroldt's knowledge. Furthermore, as the palace was part of the king's residence, Sulkowski, by making orders that went beyond the measure that he was allowed (the dinner service), was guilty of deceit. The extent of the deliveries to Sulkowski was recorded in a list drawn up by Höroldt, likewise on February 8, 1739.[255]

As a result of the affair, it became clear that as Sulkowski's personal orders had got in the way of the orders for the palace, they had been in part responsible for the slow progress being made on the project in general. And as a result of Count Sulkowski's dismissal, furthermore, someone had to be found who could acquire a quick overall grasp of the situation and take the project in hand.

Augustus III decided to assign this task to the highest-ranking man in Saxony apart from himself, Count Heinrich von Brühl.[256] In so doing, however, he tipped the project out of the frying-pan right into the fire, as would soon become abundantly clear, for Count Brühl was just as much of a porcelain addict as his predecessor had been. Back in 1733 he had already been entrusted with general responsibility for the manufactory, and authority over the commission. And even in 1737, the king had extended Brühl's privilege of not having to pay anything for porcelain from Meissen. What Sulkowski had obtained through deception, Brühl thus acquired officially. And in the same year, he commissioned the manufactory to make the service that subsequently became not only the most celebrated set of tableware ever created, but also a unique artistic creation in its own right: the Swan Service.[257] Production of this service, composed of more than two thousand pieces, was to last a number of years. The models, all devoted in their plastic decoration to the element water, displayed a delight in detail never before seen on tableware, and the technical difficulties involved in their production were quite as unprecedented. For Modellmeister Kaendler and his fellow-modeler Eberlein the commission constituted a new challenge which not only offered them greater artistic satisfaction than any before, but also marked a turning-point in the design of porcelain tableware and the prestige attached to the table service as a porcelain genre in general. A year before Brühl commissioned the service, Kaendler had already started modeling small-scale figures and groups with contemporary themes, that is to say, just the works that established a definitive tradition of porcelain sculpture which has, variations in quality notwithstanding, survived down to the present day. There were various reasons for this first tentative turning away from large-size figures. One of these was certainly that the smaller format was more appropriate to the material and its technical demands. Another reason was related to the emergence of new locations for displaying porcelain (dining tables, mantelpieces, consoles, and chests of drawers) which brought groups into being which would have been much too small for a building like the Japanese Palace but were well suited to forming part of the décor in a private room. A role was also played by the transition that was taking place from the world of the Baroque, with its inherently stately character, to that of the Rococo, with its greater potential for intimacy. And last but not least, when not working on specific commissions, the modelers could now choose their subjects for themselves, which resulted in the depiction in porcelain of a cross-section of contemporary society.

It would seem to me important that with the smaller format the modeler could allow himself many more liberties than had been the case with the monumental porcelain figures, and still be sure that the figure would come through the firing. This partial liberation of form from technical considerations brought forth a genuinely sculptural mode of expression of a refinement that had hardly existed in connection with any other material before, and an unprecedented scope for virtuosity on the part of the modeler. These new expressive possibilities, which came into full blossom in the Swan Service (the creation of which brought about the discovery of porcelain's capacity for pictorial relief, for instance) did however stretch the manufactory's artists to their limit.

Despite the passage of time, the orders for the Japanese Palace had still not yet been met, and once again hefty disputes broke out among the leading heads at the manufactory. When Brühl summoned the Commission in order to clear up the points of contention, he was rather more prudent than Sulkowski had been, noting "en passant" that blame for the delays in delivery could not be put on him, as work on his service was only to be done after the end of the working day.[258] As is shown by a draft letter from Damian Pflugk, a member of the Commission, dated one day after this meeting, that is to say July 6, 1739, those present insisted that they never for a moment thought that there was any connection between the commission for Brühl's service and the difficulties being experienced in meeting the orders for the Japanese Palace. Pflugk, however, was so bold as to remember an episode that was relevant to the matter in hand: "Afterwards, I remembered the following, that about three weeks ago, Court Commissioner Höroldt came to visit me at my lodgings, and I asked him ~~how things were going at the manufactory, and~~ whether the work was still being continued on the pieces ordered for the Royal Dutch Palace, and whether a few such pieces were still being put into each firing, as appropriate, to which the Court Commissioner replied in the negative; when I continued by asking why work was not still being done on the pieces for the palace, he replied that as long as work was still being done on the service for Brühl, the work for the palace had to wait. I cannot refrain from making this known, in order that light may be shed on the present situation."[259]

This statement fits very well into the overall picture in that the manufactory's last delivery of animal figures to the Japanese Palace was made in 1736, and the last proper delivery list dates from 1738. Comparison of the last interim total for porcelain delivered to the palace, drawn up in 1736, and the inventories of 1770 and 1779 shows that the only animal figures to be delivered to the palace after 1736 were four Orioles, which must have been brought to Dresden in the wake of a clearing out of the warehouses carried out in June 1743. The manufactory had complained of having too little storage space, whereupon the Commission made a tour of inspection and decided that the wares that were no longer offered on the open market – in other words, the porcelain that was reserved for the king – should be sent to the palace: yet another demonstration of the depository-like character of the palace after 1738. It was thus suggested that "such vases, animal figures, and other large porcelain pieces which were either trial pieces, pieces which were not allowed to be sold, or pieces which had some defect" should be brought to the palace, "to be placed high up, or be put to some other good use."[260] Given the order for mirrors placed in the same year, 1743 perhaps saw another attempt to bring at least one room to completion.

In spite of these later spurts of activity, it would seem that after the recasting of the plans the project of making a *Porzellanschloss* out of the Japanese Palace gradually wilted from around 1735 onwards and finally gave up the ghost around 1740 in the wake of the fall of Count Sulkowski and competition from the service ordered by Count Brühl. These two intimates of the king needed porcelain in order to confirm their high rank as ministers and leading position in the social order. Both impeded the royal project with their orders and sought to use the leading lights of the manufactory for their own ends. They took advantage of Höroldt's concern for the financial viability of the manufactory, and of the fact of his constant opposition to the production of the animal figures on account of their cost and technical difficulty. And they fully exploited the fact that as time passed Kaendler perceived more and more potentially fruitful challenges, and more hope of positive artistic developments in the field of small porcelain figures, in the large dinner services for Sulkowski and Brühl, and in the project for a larger-than-life porcelain statue of Augustus III on horseback that had germinated in his mind as early as 1734.

The fact that Augustus III was finally not able to carry the day was partly due to the great influence the two ministers exerted upon him. In my opinion, however, a more important reason was the new role that art was called upon to play during his reign.

The porcelain animals for the Japanese Palace: the cultural, technical, and artistic conditions

The general foundations

The Meissen porcelain manufactory's second decade of existence was a phase of artistic consolidation and technical innovation. Fundamental techniques of porcelain manufacture, notably such decorative techniques as gilding and overglaze painting, were developed further and ever more surely mastered. New inventions were made, not only in the sphere of molding and shapes but also in that of the painted motifs, which were increasingly well adapted to the particular qualities of a material that had only been available for a relatively short period. Painting developed particularly rapidly at the hands of the porcelain-painter Johann Gregorius Höroldt, who had only come to Meissen in 1720, and of the "technician" Samuel Stöltzel.[261] By 1730, many of the purely technical problems had been solved and the enterprise was also flourishing artistically.

In the light of these successes, the promises that Johann Friedrich Böttger had made to Augustus the Strong in his formal announcement of the invention of porcelain in 1709, exaggerated though they had been in the light of the technical status quo of the time, finally began to seem feasible. The possibilities that then seemed to be opening up had been so captivating – and so particularly appealing to the mind of a Baroque prince – that they even found their way into the foundational charter of the Meissen manufactory, printed and published in 1710. It was fully intended "that in the future, given the right design and production, white porcelain of this kind [...] shall be able to surpass Asian porcelain by far, not only in beauty and quality, but also in variety of shapes and large pieces, some even solid, such as statues, columns, services and so on."[262]

It was this unbroken faith that not only these but also other large-scale pieces could be successfully produced that resulted in the instruction to Johann Jacob Irminger, the court goldsmith responsible for inventing the shapes of the early period,[263] that "architectural elements [...] for the embellishment of our follies and other edifices [...]" should also be designed and produced in porcelain, after consultation with the *Bauamt* (Building Office).[264]

Behind all this was the fundamentally absolutist insistence that everything, all the materials included, was to be put at the service of the Prince's "creative will"; in the case of porcelain the technical limits were clear, but this was no reason for discouragement. When it came to the planning of the Japanese Palace, which while it could not have been dreamt of without Augustus the Strong's collecting mania would also have been equally unthinkable but for the technical improvements made at the manufactory, architectural features and furniture in porcelain once again came to be accepted as desirable goals. After all, the manufactory's first decade had seen the mastery of overglaze painting being pursued with great intensity, and yet in vain, and then after 1720 this mastery had proved attainable in a surprisingly short period of time. Why should the present zealous endeavors to surpass the Far Eastern model not be crowned with similar success, and likewise the concomitant claiming of the material for the Baroque? This attitude, unclouded by the slightest doubt on the part of the elector's ever demanding court, was one of the preconditions which led to orders for such large-scale pieces as the "life-size" animals.

One further precondition for the project of a gallery of porcelain animals was latent in the very idea of the Japanese Palace as conceived from 1730 on. As we will see, almost every one of Augustus the Strong's royal seats boasted one of the animal enclosures which customarily formed part of the princely estates of the time (large poultry-yard, menagerie, fish-pond gardens, and so on). Animal collections of this kind were an integral part of princely lifestyle, and since the Italian Renaissance they had become an ever more indispensable means of reflecting the wealth and standing of a princely family.[265] Augustus the Strong's palace was not simply some kind of pleasure-dome, built to house porcelain and promote European-Asian cultural exchange: with its throne room, it was quite clearly intended to be a kind of second, porcelain residence. When this is taken into account, it is quite comprehensible that it had to have its own menagerie. And once this had been decided, it was only consistent that the animals in this collection should be in porcelain – the material that was to reign supreme here – and that the wall decorations and tableware should also accommodate animals of both exotic and domestic origin.

A third factor which may have contributed to the idea of a gallery of porcelain animals were those animal figures which Augustus the Strong saw on his grand tour; these included, as mentioned above, the Mount of Diana in the gardens of Aranjuez, and the animals by Giambologna.[266] The many fountains with animal sculptures in the labyrinth at Versailles will also have made a powerful impression upon him.[267]

Further evidence of Augustus the Strong's creativity and innovative powers is provided by the fact that his concept for animal figures in a gallery of his porcelain palace was not derived from iconographical commonplaces associated with depictions of animals (Noah's ark, the Garden of Eden, Diana, Orpheus, and so on); neither did he adhere to traditional decorative schemes (grottos decorated with animal sculptures), nor did he set any store by illustrating literary or moralizing subject-matter (animal fables and emblems). On the contrary, the project for a gallery with animal figures in Meissen porcelain developed directly from the specific conditions obtaining at the court in Dresden, as will be shown by the following account of its attitude and approach to animals in general.

Animals at the Dresden court

The representation of animals at festivities

The culture of the Baroque court was a culture of celebration. The outlay on festivities mounted at the Dresden court under the rule of Augustus the Strong was vast, not only in terms of money, but also in terms of time and logistical work; contemporary sources regard the court of the Elector of Saxony and King in Poland as one of the most splendid in all the Holy Roman Empire, and this testimony has only been confirmed by historians of later generations.[268] Every opportunity was used to to glorify the Prince in pageants, tournaments, and markets, and to impress Saxony's importance and capability upon the local populace, the nobility, and visitors from abroad. When mounted as parts of larger court festivals, these events had two main advantages over the customary festive entertainments such as redoubts, operas, excursions, and hunts. Firstly, they made an impact on a broader section of the population; secondly, as "mobile pictures," they had greater potential for communicating iconographic subject-matter, and thus of making programmatic statements.

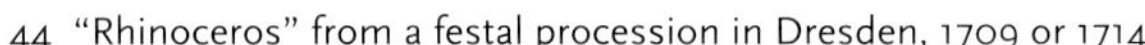
44 "Rhinoceros" from a festal procession in Dresden, 1709 or 1714

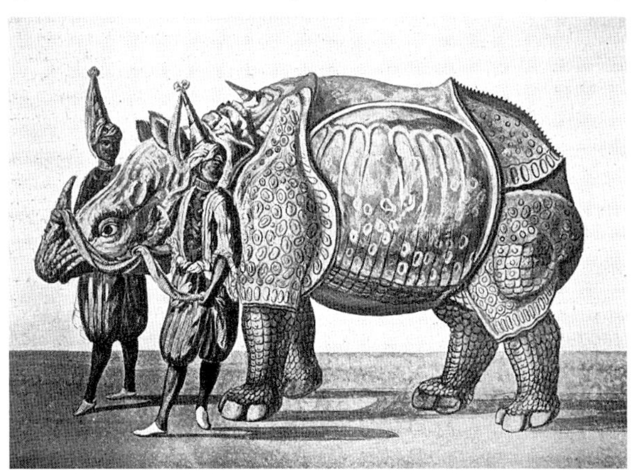

On such occasions, living animals were among the properties exploited to the full for their symbolic value, and to demonstrate wealth. According to Johann Michael von Loen's report of a hunting party at Moritzburg on August 14, 1718, those present at the beginning of the spectacle, which lasted several days, witnessed a solemn procession in which "some two hundred men in costume were divided into four sections representing the four continents of the world [...]. They were accompanied not only by a great number of rare treasures and plants from foreign lands, but also by a variety of foreign animals such as lions, tigers, bears, parrots, all manner of monkeys, and the like."[269] If a certain species was not available, then a solution was improvised through masquerade or mock-up; when a camel was called for in a pageant of the continents to symbolize Asia, a horse was sometimes disguised for the purpose.[270] If a disguise of this kind was not possible, as in the case of the unicorn for instance, machine-like constructions were resorted to, made from a great variety of materials; a print (fig. 44) exists as evidence of this practice being followed at the Dresden court.[271]

Animals owned by the prince were also put on display, particularly the more exotic ones, in cages or on chains. In the coherent programmatic choreography of the event in question, they represented the "savage" world of the animals, subjected to the order dictated by the rule of the absolutist ruler. While the nobility were impressed by the animals' financial value, the exotic aura the animals radiated was a particular source of fascination to the members of the local populace required to attend processions as spectators, who would not usually have had access to the menageries where the animals were kept.

Menageries in the Baroque: the example of Versailles

There are various possible reasons for keeping animals: nourishment, protection, entertainment, and the demonstration of status being only a few of the factors that characterize relationships between humans and animals. Variations in wealth and social status do not bring about essential changes, but only changes of emphasis.

From Roman times through the Middle Ages and into early modern times, indigenous wild animals (game) were kept in enclosures to supply meat, for home consumption, for sale, and for the entertaining of guests in a style appropriate to the standing of their owner, with the balance between these three ends varying from case to case. For Italian Renaissance princes, an important element was the opportunity afforded by enclosures for observing animals in the "parco"; for the grandees of the Baroque, a central reason for the establishment of deer-parks and the like was to breed game for their hunting parties. In both cases, the difference in motivation was reflected in the form taken by the respective enclosure, but did not affect the enclosure's fundamental importance as a status symbol.[272]

Likewise, individual princes and the more important towns and cities had always kept wild or exotic animals in moats, cages, or outhouses. While in Roman times such animals were used for entertainment or for inflicting punishments, the Middle Ages increasingly exploited their symbolic potential, with the municipalities, for instance, putting them to good use in their coats-of-arms.[273] In the Renaissance and Baroque, exotic animals were not only highly-coveted luxury items but also an indispensable element at any princely court worthy of the name. Whether kept in cages or enclosures, they were a visible expression of the prince's far-reaching connections and also an attraction for his visitors, some of whom will have reacted to them with feelings of sheer unthinking amazement, while others will have found them and their behavior worthy of studious observation. Early modern man's particular interest in the workings of nature meant that exotic animals became the object of scientific research. The Renaissance approach of experiencing the world through the observation of individual phenomena finally gave way to Baroque man's preference for taking possession of the world by making visible representations of the order that he perceived in it.

Correspondingly, increasing importance was accorded to the formal aspect of how animals were to be presented. While the game parks were primarily designed to meet the requirements of new methods of hunting, for instance through the creation of avenues laid out in star formations to make progress easier for those riding to hounds, collections of animals were presented in a new way which reflected a certain perceived natural order and thus provided another means of articulating the theories and values of Absolutism. The Versailles menagerie triggered off a redefinition of the word "menagerie," which was from then on most frequently used to refer exclusively to collections of exotic animals as opposed to animals kept for practical purposes.[274] Between 1663 and 1670, a complex was built at the southern end of the canal axis of the park at Versailles with a pavilion-like "menagerie-château" at the hub of a number of animal enclosures (fig. 45).[275] It was an innovation when the extensive animal collections of the kings of France were brought together in these enclosures: until that point it had been the custom at French and German courts for the various groups of animals to be kept at a number of different locations.[276] But now, from the various sectors of the pavilion's upper story, the onlooker was able to see mammals, birds, and fishes all at once, allocated to various sectors of the menagerie. Visitors were not expected to be concerned with thoughts of animal fights, or the hunt, but rather to enjoy feeding their eyes and minds on an encyclopedic presentation of the variety of the animal world.

The French king's guests were not placed right at the middle of this spectacle simply for practical reasons: it was imperative that they should feel it a special privilege to be in this central and raised

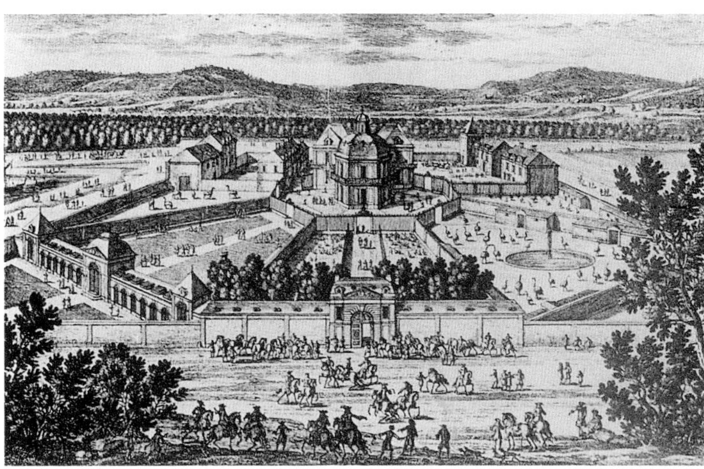

45 André Pérelle, the Versailles menagerie, view from the north-west

position. They felt as if they were surrounded by all the living beings that nature had to offer, and the radial layout of the enclosures gave them the impression that nature in all its variety was oriented towards them. Their view of the animals was thus given a certain panoramic character that defined and gave value to their own position.

In addition, the visitor to Versailles had to be made conscious of the direct connection between the king's claim to power and the view of the animal world offered to them; the large canal built in 1668 was like an umbilical cord providing a direct connection between the menagerie and the palace that was the "core of the Absolutist world-view." Ruling from his palace, King Louis XIV saw his subjects as directly related to his own self, which was why he saw himself as the embodiment of the State, standing opposite and towering over a hierarchically structured population; likewise, visitors to the menagerie were in a similar position vis-à-vis the world of the animals. Putting the matter in somewhat simple terms, one could thus regard the Versailles menagerie as a "model of the absolutist view of the state." The much-loved animal fights and hunts to hounds, by contrast, emphasized the hierarchical element and were for this reason put on in different contexts.

The layout of the Versailles menagerie became the definitive model for eighteenth-century court menageries, including those in the German-speaking lands. Many of its features, in particular the centrally-positioned pavilion surrounded by enclosures, were imitated (in more or less expensive versions), and also found their way into works of architectural theory as elements of large-scale garden design.[277]

Animal-keeping in Dresden

No palace in Dresden could be compared with Versailles, either in respect of size, magnificence, or symbolic value. None of the endeavors aimed at making such royal seats as Moritzburg, Pillnitz, or Großsedlitz into counterparts of that of the French king got any further than the planning stage. This was also the case with the planning of the menageries. Complexes for the accommodation of the animal collections were not only planned in association with the large building projects: designs were also made which cannot be attributed to any particular palace. One of the earliest of these, from around 1704, is derived from a sketch made by Augustus the Strong himself; it is an idiosyncratic complex and does not copy the two most famous concentric menageries of the time, those at Versailles and in Vienna.[278] Pöppelmann also designed a substantial extension of the *Jägerhof* (hunting depository) in Neustadt and submitted plans for a menagerie in the *Schmeltzgarten* that are likewise based on an idea sketched out by Augustus the Strong.[279] Both these designs adopted features from the Versailles model, but neither complex was actually built. In the case of Dresden, it would almost seem that the centralization of the component parts of a Baroque court household was merely planned on paper, with precisely the opposite being put into practice, namely an extremely well-considered distribution of those parts at various locations. This can be demonstrated not only with reference to the animal enclosures, as will be done below, but also to some of the more important aspects of the architectural articulation of power, a phenomenon which will be considered in another chapter.

In the first half of the eighteenth century, the court kitchen was provided with fish from the court fish-ponds; situated in Dresden itself, these were also home to exotic waterbirds.[280] The enclosure for edible fowl and game at the king's kitchen gardens in Ostra likewise also housed exotic animals.[281] The *Großer Garten* (Great Garden) contained a pheasant reserve, where pheasant-shoots were occasionally put on for members of the court. The elector's menagerie was at the *Jägerhof* in Neustadt on the right bank of the Elbe. Known as the *Löwenhaus* (lion-house) the menagerie did not reflect the wealth and status of its owner in the way its Versailles or Vienna counterparts did: when thinking of the *Löwenhaus*, we should rather imagine a conglomeration of sheds, stables, cages, and little courtyards in which particularly savage beasts were kept. The doors of the stables opened onto the *Hetzgarten*, a park used for animal fights and hand-to-hand hunting.[282]

The remainder of the *Jägerhof* was lavishly and magnificently fitted out, in accordance with the high status attributed to the hunt by the rulers of Saxony; for visitors and participants in the hunt, the stables, the storerooms for hunting equipment, and the reception rooms were a tangible demonstration of the high standard of hunting in Saxony. This environment meant that seeing the exotic and indigenous wild animals at the *Löwenhaus* was quite a different experience from that associated with such menageries as the one at Versailles, and this difference was compounded by the different form of presentation. The sight of a fierce animal kept in captivity in the immediate vicinity of all the trappings of the "art of animal-killing" was a singular testimony to the grace and power of a king who commanded the obedience even of wild beasts. This is made all the clearer by the fact that the animals from the *Löwenhaus* were again and again used, even as late as the 1740s, in animal fights. In this case, the onlooker–animal relationship could not have that model character which played a significant role in the menageries of Louis XIV and Prince Eugene of Savoy. The practice of keeping beasts of prey at the Dresden hunting lodge had its roots in a much more ancient tradition – the medieval tradition of the bear-pit-type animal enclosure – which explains why, as in so many instances, Augustus the Strong's plans to change the form and character of the tradition could never actually be realized.

Augustus the Strong had a number of animal enclosures and animal collections of various sizes outside Dresden, a piggery on the *Dresdener Heide* (Dresden Heath), and a bear-pit at Schloss Augustusburg. The most important animal enclosures were at Moritzburg, a much-favored hunting palace with such features as an enclosure for wisents,[283] a large deer-park with star-layout avenues for hunting local game, and most especially a large aviary for exotic birds. This was just one of a number of locations which Augustus the Strong planned to extend to such an degree that it would have surpassed – and indeed further developed – the Versailles menagerie. On his grand tour, Augustus the Strong passed through Paris twice, and on the second occasion, returning from Spain, he paid a visit to the menagerie on September 25, 1688: "At seven in the morning the Count [Augustus travelled incognito] betook himself to Versailles to take his leave of Monsigneur le Dauphine [sic] and Mons. le Duc de Orleans, inspected the menagerie and the Trianons, and took the Princes of Hanover with him to dinner."[284] From then on, Moritzburg was not simply to possess a menagerie to house animals – its entire surroundings were to be turned into one huge, outsize menagerie.

Accordingly, plans were laid for the surrounding woods to be embellished with a system of sightline avenues converging at the terrace in front of the east-facing dining room wing. Most of these sightlines were to train the eye of the beholder on animal enclosures, which Augustus the Strong positioned on a sketch in his own hand, designating them as follows: *Hellberg*, monkeys, squirrels, amphitheater, pheasantry, aviaries, waterbirds, menagerie.[285] Although only parts were actually executed,[286] the project shows that Augustus the Strong was by no means content to follow the example of his predecessors in restricting his animal collections to locations in and around Dresden. While the traditional ordering was not to be given up, it was to be enriched with a new and unique menagerie-world in which – so it would appear from the plan and its partial realization – the individual enclosures were to be constructed along the lines of specialized menageries of the Versailles kind, a concept all the more astounding given that the prime activity at Moritzburg was hunting local game. Although it was modified in later generations, the pheasantry pavilion can still give us some idea of this concept. The individual menageries were to be positioned in the countryside around Moritzburg to make it look as if the castle had been placed in their midst like some outsize Versailles-style observation pavilion. This would have meant that the idea behind the Versailles menagerie as discussed above would have been realized even more dramatically at Moritzburg, as the two principal hierarchical levels (animal–onlooker = enclosure–pavilion; and onlooker–King = pavilion–castle) would have been combined in a coherent and consistently followed concept of spatial centralization.

But as the main role of the castle was to function as one of the most important centers for the court's hunting activities, this plan was conceived as a kind of *summa* of all the various ways in which man encountered and interacted with the animal world at the Dresden court. Both the whole process of rearing, hunting and serving game – "applied animal-keeping," as it might be called – and also its counterpart, "artificial animal-collecting," were to be practiced in interrelated areas in such a way as to bring about a harmonious ordering of the whole animal world with due justice being paid to its usefulness, its delightfulness, and its sheer beauty.

The special attention paid by Augustus the Strong to the development of Moritzburg, and the dimensions he foresaw for the hunting palace are related to the fact that as Margrave of Meissen he also held the elevated office of *Reichsoberjägermeister*, (Imperial Master of the Hunt). As senior huntsman of the Holy Roman Empire he was designing a complex which was to reflect not only the enormous prestige of his office, but also Moritzburg's status as a kind of "supreme Imperial hunting lodge."[287]

An account of the various places where and ways in which animals were kept at the court of Dresden would not be complete without mention of the animals occasionally displayed in the city, or of their keepers and showmen. Such animals as dancing bears, parrots, monkeys, and even camels were to be seen relatively regularly at the public markets and squares, and the appearance of such rarities as a giraffe, an elephant, or a rhinoceros was an event which attracted the attention even of members of the court. The court diary of April 5, 1747, reports on a rhinoceros which traveled through all Europe with its keeper and also paid a visit to Dresden: "A Dutchman has arrived bringing with him a living rhinoceros, which he shows to people for money."[288] As is clear from the famous picture by Pietro Longhi which depicts this very beast during its stay in Venice, presentations of this kind were veritable social events, and thus can in a certain sense be regarded as temporary menageries.[289]

The procurement of wild and exotic animals

As has been suggested above, the idea of commissioning porcelain animals for the Japanese Palace cannot be understood without reference to the king's extensive animal collections, and especially the collections of exotic wild animals. The seventeenth century had seen a particularly rapid increase in general familarity with the fauna of other continents, as the scientific knowledge of the time was committed to print in works of natural history and disseminated in court circles.[290] The Baroque era's appetite for the exotic and bizarre was well catered for by its scientists' increasingly zealous investigations into the natural world; research was being conducted on more and more individual species, and ever greater quantities of new material were being made available to the reading public. As in previous generations, there was still a lively interest in acquiring – whether in pictorial, taxidermic, or living form – the better-known animals such as the lion, elephant, parrot, or monkey; now, however, the mind of the time was also especially fascinated by individual rare and strange species. While this same curiosity and encyclopedic zeal had also been a driving power behind the *Wunderkammer* of the Renaissance, it now led to items leaving the intimate context of the cabinet or small chamber and being classified in accordance with modern science; they were now to be shown in a more decorative and impressive *mise en scène*. There was a veritable symbiosis between those making progress in the research field ("producers of knowledge") and those with an appetite for the unique ("consumers of knowledge"). In this encyclopedic context, science was harnessed to the ends of entertainment, education, and princely self-glorification.

The links between scientific research and systematic ostentation at court are exemplified in the procurement of non-exotic animals; those which symbolized princely virtues, or had exceptional aesthetic appeal, were much used by the elector as gifts.

Animals as gifts: Augustus the Strong's own animal collection was also enriched through gifts, as two specific examples will show. At a dinner in 1725 in Berlin, King Friedrich Wilhelm I of Prussia asked the Saxon ambassador whether the "aurochs" he had presented to Augustus the Strong some time before was in good health. When the ambassador said he did not know whether the beast was still living, Friedrich Wilhelm told him about another large "aurochs" which had gone as a gift to the English king, and could now be viewed by the public on Sundays in a London park. If Augustus the Strong so wished, he would be happy to present him with another.[291]

A pair of lions, two tigers, and an "Indian cat" had clearly had an adventurous journey when, sent from Stockholm as a gift from the King of Sweden, they arrived in November 1731 at the *Löwenhaus* in Dresden, where they "were most fortunately transferred from their boxes into safe keeping". The lion-keeper made a note of the state in which the animals arrived, reporting that "the lion and lioness, and also the two tigers, are good-looking beasts, excepting that the lion has only one eye."[292] He furthermore wished to know what was to be done with "the man who had accompanied the animals and who had taken off their iron neckbands," and how he was to remunerate him for his good offices. In his account of the life of Augustus the Strong, David Fassmann later reported that the man was an "enfranchised serf," and that this "native of Holstein was so accustomed to dealing with these animals that he was perfectly capable of taking them wherever he wanted." Fassmann also tells us that the animals had originally "been sent by the Dey of Algiers as a present for the King of Sweden."[293]

The list of instances of animals being given as presents could be extended *ad infinitum* – Augustus the Strong was even prepared to part with porcelain to acquire rare beasts, as is shown by an exchange in the course of which he received arctic foxes and polar bears from the Russian Tsarina.[294] Precisely because wild animals were shifted here and there and given away as presents, there developed a trade – very like that in Far Eastern porcelain – which thrived upon the princes' passion for collecting.

Trade in animals: As well as dealing in luxury goods from far-off lands, the Dutch East India Company also carried on a sideline in animals and birds, particularly the latter, given the difficulty of transporting the larger animals over the long sea journey. It was thus not only lacquerwork, tea, and porcelain that were on sale in Amsterdam, but also parrots, exotic hens, and the like. One of Augustus the Strong's officials, Count Lagnasco, made a list with descriptions of the birds offered there.[295] Among them were a great variety of parrots, which are described, with great attention to their entertainment value, as "speaking well, whistling, singing, and playing the trumpet." Also offered for sale were a young ostrich, flamingos, and a creature referred to as a "Jahrvogel," from the description possibly a toucan. Although the list is not dated, it is followed by another almost identical list, annotated with prices. It seems that Augustus the Strong was interested in buying and wanted a rough idea of the costs involved, as this second list was attached to a letter to the king dated February 16, 1717.[296] The letter's reference to grossly inflated prices,[297] is borne out by the sums concerned – a crane, referred to as a "Cronvogel," was offered for a thousand gulden, and a very beautiful cockatoo for three hundred. Keyssler was also astounded at the prices put on these birds and animals. In his account of the *Löwenhaus*, he refers, clearly highly impressed, to "two leopards, each of which is worth around two thousand talers."[298] Annotations to the list show that these prices were actually being paid; in the interim period between the two lists, the flamingos, the "Indian" geese, the "Jahrvogel," and the two particularly fine talking and whistling parrots were indeed sold. We can only speculate as to who bought them, as the annotation "have been sold to the Tsar" has been crossed out and replaced with the more discreet formulation, "are no longer present."

Augustus the Strong also purchased animals in person; at the 1729 Leipzig Spring Fair, for instance, he bought a lioness, a tiger, and a baboon.[299] Such much-visited trade fairs must have been ideal places for dealers in luxury goods and animals to do their business.

However, the creatures offered for sale did not all come from far-off lands – some were rarer breeds from European countries. Only a few weeks before his death, shortly before his last journey from Dresden to Warsaw, Augustus the Strong bought two white peacocks, three rock partridges, and a hen capercaillie from a Tirolean traveling dealer.[300]

Not only dealers profited from the Saxon elector's passion for collecting animals. King Friedrich Wilhelm I of Prussia, one of the few commercially-minded rulers of the early eighteenth century, once enquired of Augustus the Strong whether he might be interested in a number of lions and other animals whose keep was proving rather expensive. When an answer was delayed by the elector's absence, Friedrich Wilhelm entrusted these animals to his lieutenant-general Borck, who attempted to mediate by offering them to Count Flemming in a letter of January 16, 1714.[301] It is not known whether the Prussian king's bid to sell the animals met with success.

The Saxon menageries grew in size not only through gifts and purchases from the trade, but also through orders for direct acquisitions. At the same time as taking steps to get his hands on classical sculpture in Rome, Augustus the Strong also submitted an order through Count Wackerbarth to a certain Monsieur Thioly for African deer, which were if necessary to be brought directly from Africa: "For the rest, the King believes that he commissioned you to procure some African deer that have legs more slender than a little finger. His Majesty has therefore ordered me to remind you of this in case you have not been able to have some brought from Africa, failing any other means of acquiring them, and asks how one could be surer of obtaining them."[302]

Meissen porcelain was occasionally offered in lieu of money for the acquisition of live animals, as in the case of the polar bears and arctic foxes which the king wished to be delivered to him through the hands the Saxon ambassador in St Petersburg.[303] In another instance, the much-traveled Zürich silk manufacturer Johannes Escher vom Glas received two Meissen services in 1730 from Augustus the Strong as remuneration for having procured him two eagles from the Swiss Alps.[304] Another enterprise undertaken for the sake of acquiring animals was the first Saxon Africa expedition.

The Saxon Africa Expedition 1731–1733

As early as 1718, having moved to Genoa, where he had made enquiries about the purchase of African animals, the Saxon consul in Venice reported that "[...] not a single one is to be found, neither in this port, nor in those nearby,"[305] and concluded that, as these tiger skins and wild animals were so fervently desired, steps should be taken to obtain them directly from Africa.[306]

Thirteen years later, this suggestion became reality in the form of the costly Saxon Africa Expedition, led by Johann Ernst Hebenstreit and lasting from 1730 to 1733.[307] Its goal was first and foremost the scientific investigation of the flora and fauna, and human culture of northern Africa, which however did not prevent its brief from including the collection of plants and African wild animals, and their transport to Dresden: "Before sending them back, he

[Hebenstreit] shall buy the living creatures *in duplo* or *in triplo*, so that if one perishes on the way, then there will still be one or two living; and he shall take on hands, or slaves and moors, to transport and take care of the animals [...]. He shall be sure to have drawings and paintings made of everything, and to send the depictions back at regular intervals; as to what he cannot bring away alive, he shall endeavor to conserve the skeletons and skins; he shall keep an orderly journal and make note of everything that is of interest [...]."[308]

In order to fulfil these requirements, Hebenstreit traveled with a botanist, an "anatomist," a mechanic, a draughtsman, and a painter.[309] It is no longer known exactly what they finally brought back to Dresden in the way of descriptions, drawings, herbaria, skeletons, and other animal parts, because the *Naturalienkabinett* (natural history collection) in the Zwinger, where a good part of these things were preserved, burned down in 1849. Gurlitt's writings include references to taxidermally preserved animals, corals, herbs and grasses, and "boughs of Tripolitanian wood for turning."[310]

Some reports and lists of the living animals have however survived to the present day. An entry in the court diary notes that one of the members of the expedition returned in October 1732: "Herr Buchner has brought back a young lion, two ostriches, and other animals from Africa."[311] However, the expedition was cut short following the death of Augustus the Strong on February 1, 1733, and the remaining participants set about transporting their acquisitions back to Dresden.

The company left Tunis on April 17 but unfavorable winds meant that their ship did not arrive in Hamburg until three months later, as is documented by a letter of July 13, 1733, from the botanist Christian Gottlieb Ludwig to Count Brühl in which he laments the loss of a number of animals: "If our journey had not been so protracted and grueling, I have no doubt that we would have been able to bring home a good number of the animals which have been lost."[312] Nevertheless, as his listing shows (Source 23), he was still bringing home an impressive number and variety of living birds and animals.[313] Ludwig was afraid that they might still face difficulties on the onward journey from Hamburg: "[...] if I am fortunate enough to be able to bring them [the animals] as quickly as possible to Dresden, I believe I shall lose no more," but he expressed particular concern, "that the many custom-houses to be passed can do much damage, not as a result of the duties to be paid but of the unpacking necessitated by the examination of our curious collection of beasts. I would kindly ask you to help me by providing a pass to overcome this problem, or to deal with the matter as you may see fit."[314] From the list attached to the "Pass issued by the Prince Elector, for various foreign animals to be transported from Hamburg to Dresden, as listed herein, Dresden on July 31, 1733," it is clear that the dead creatures were also to be brought to Dresden, as it includes not only the animals listed by Ludwig as still living, but also those which had perished.

The natural history collection

Exotic and rare creatures kept in menageries were also of interest for scientific study after they died, and also suitable for public and official display.[315] This was the case with respect to the *Naturalienkabinett* in Dresden no less than elsewhere: "The *Thier-Cabinet* is certainly the largest one in existence, and presents as great a variety of animals as one can possibly imagine. Stuffed, they stand there as if they were still living."[316]

There is clear evidence that in the early seventeenth century the attics of the Residence in Dresden already housed an anatomical collection containing human and animal skeletons, presented according to an iconographical concept oriented around the Garden of Eden.[317] When the Zwinger was refurbished as a "Palast der Wissenschaften" ("palace of the sciences") at the beginning of the 1730s, the elector's natural history collections were accorded a new and pre-eminent degree of importance. Their galleries presented not only the latest discoveries of science but also a number of curiosities. On view for visitors were minerals, fossils, plants, and anatomical specimens, and then, housed in the *Kronentorgalerie*, stuffed birds and fish in the first two galleries devoted to the animal world, after which the visitors proceeded along a didactically conceived path to the collections of shells, corals, and amber.[318] The position accorded to the latter collections, displayed in and around a grotto room, testifies to the high value set upon the particular beauty of conchylia at this time.[319]

This was followed by the third and final gallery, devoted to mammals: "Immediately after this [the grotto] comes a gallery in which the rare animals are exhibited, now stuffed, which in their lifetime were kept in Dresden."[320] After having beheld many individual animal parts such as skeletons, preserved organs, eggs, horns and so forth, the visitor was now confronted with whole animals in preserved form. The degree of *mise en scène* involved is reflected in such descriptions as "a crocodile creeping out of its egg (the size of a goose's egg),"[321] or "a wolf tearing apart and eating a deer."[322] A letter also survives which is of particular interest given the few extant documents on the *Animalienkabinett*.

A letter of July 17, 1733, to Augustus III, son and heir of Augustus the Strong, finds the court taxidermist ("Hofwildstaffierer") Gottfried Gebhardt, requesting the confirmation of his continued employment, and back-payment of his salary, which he has not received for full four years: "His Royal Highness your dearest father – God rest his soul – most gracefully saw fit to have me commissioned with carrying out the final work on his stuffed animals."[323] The manner in which the taxidermist continues his epistle gives us an idea of the influence he brought to bear on the appearance of the stuffed animals, and thus on the effect that they had on visitors: "It is thus my most heartfelt desire to do all in my power to use new, strange, and natural ideas and inventions to create a harmonious and impressive whole out of the gallery, and to put these precious rarities into perfect condition." Participating in this *mise en scène* were animals that had died in the menageries, notably lions, tigers, monkeys, a zebra, a pelican, and a cassowary, with the birds being accommodated in the first *Animaliengalerie*, and the quadrupeds in the third. The second, between the *Kronentor* and the Mathematical Pavilion was dedicated to water animals, that is to say fish, crustaceans, seals and so on.

The degree of attention paid to the natural history collections in descriptions of Dresden is evidence that they were accounted almost as important as the art collections: "One would be hard put to find such a complete collection, or one with so many rare animals, not only stuffed, but also with their skeletons standing there to boot. How regrettable that hairy animals are so difficult to keep in good condition! Some have already suffered greatly. The gallery is ninety-five ells long and houses three rows of four-footed animals, almost all of which passed a portion of their lives at the Jägerhof in Dresden."[324] Among these were "a tiger royal, which Hebenstreit brought from Africa." In 1806, Merkel had the following to say about the animals' general state of repair: "The gallery immediately following is remarkable for its rare animal skeletons. The stuffed animals have been somewhat gnawed by the tooth of time."[325]

If it is the case that all the various royal collections were closely bound up with one another, this was particularly true of the natural history and art collections.[326] The porcelain animals created for the Japanese Palace constitute one of the best examples of this correlation of art and nature, and cannot be understood without reference to the phenomenon described above, the animal-collecting pursued so passionately at the Saxon court.

The orders for animal figures for the Japanese Palace

The time-frame of the commission

We do not know for certain who exactly first had the idea of making a gallery fitted out with large animal figures in porcelain as part of the concept for the Japanese Palace. The well-attested creativity of Augustus the Strong in other fields makes it likely that he himself set the project in motion.[327] This thesis is corroborated both by his passion for animals, and by the fact that he made sketches of his own ideas for the Japanese Palace as well as for the menageries. Whether or not other individuals contributed to the advancement and development of the project in the course of the commissions and deliveries of the animal figures, particularly after his death, must remain a matter of speculation.

A second question we cannot answer with certainty is when exactly the idea was born. It can be assumed that the first orders for the Japanese Palace were communicated verbally to the manufactory, and that any notes that had been made about them were either not archived, or were lost, or both.

Apart from the order already referred to for 300 dishes with modest painting, placed in 1728 with no mention of any specific destination,[328] the earliest clear evidence of orders being made for the Japanese Palace is a listing of March 28, 1730, "specifying the pieces of porcelain which His Royal Highness in Poland and his Serene Highness the Elector of Saxony has most graciously ordered to be made in his own factory in Meissen for the Dutch Palace" (Source 4).[329] The first item was an order for 200 dishes in the Japanese manner for the cavetto of the gallery containing the large Japanese vases. This data accords with the state of planning as it appears in the floor plan (fig. 32), as do the list's remaining pieces of information. In this instance there is no mention of animals, whether for this gallery on the Neustadt side of the upper story, or for any other locations.

Similarly, references were made to large vases and other items of tableware in connection with the re-appointment of Johann Gottlieb Kirchner as modeler on June 1, 1730, but there was no mention of animal figures. In his Dresden report dated October 23, 1730, on the other hand, Keyssler not only gives an account of the animal figures project but also claims that has already seen a number of them in the finished state; the decision to go ahead with the gallery of porcelain animals must therefore have been taken in the summer of 1730.

It was one year later, on June 22, 1731, that Johann Joachim Kaendler entered service as modeler at the manufactory. He claimed later (1734) that he had been employed to model "all kinds of 'Indian' birds and animals."[330] In September 1731 it is noted that the two modelers are both working on animal figures; finally, appended to the Commission's report of December 17, 1731, comes the first list of animal figures, some already finished and some still in production (Source 5). From this progress report onwards, animal figures are mentioned in orders and delivery lists in connection with the Japanese Palace right through until 1736.

Although the order for the Neustadt-side gallery drawn up on February 25, 1732, and signed by Augustus the Strong in Warsaw on April 2 (Source 6) only distinguished between "animals" and "birds" when allotting figures their respective locations within the gallery, another undated list exists which is almost identical and refers to certain figures by name (Source 7). The compiler of the latter list, however, did not restrict himself simply to those animals which had existed as models or completed figures since December 1731: as well as eagles, parrots, and monkeys, the order also includes peacocks.

The picture that emerges here shows that manufactory and the palace-planners exerted an influence on each other, as indeed they clearly did in many later instances as well. While the royal patron issued orders for animals to be executed in porcelain, the manufactory's modelers also produced models which had not been ordered,[331] and it is certain that Augustus the Strong consciously allowed this element of freedom, as is shown by his order from Warsaw which speaks of "all manner of large and small animals." This means that both sides were announcing their requirements and delivering their products as they saw fit and were able, which made the orderly and purposeful planning of the gallery a very difficult matter. We cannot be sure whether this first extant order for animal figures deliberately used general formulations in order to permit a certain artistic freedom (technical feasibility would certainly not have been taken into consideration), or whether the planners, still uncertain early in 1732 as to how the project was to develop, were perhaps inclined to wait and see before committing themselves to more specific decisions.

Subsequent lists mention only specific animal names: about half a year after the large order for the gallery, for instance, the manufactory appended to the Commission's report an inventory of the animal figures at that point in Meissen, (Source 8), some of which were fresh from the mold and thus still unfired ("roh"), some low-fired ("verglüht"), some glazed and high-fired ("gutgebrannt"), and some even enameled, with fired overglaze colors ("emailliert"). This encouraging manifestation of the manufactory's progress very likely led to the order on November 18 of the same year for a total of 132 figures of 33 different quadrupeds, and 120 figures of 28 bird varieties, mainly in series of four (Source 9).

This was not only the first decisive increase in the quantity of animal figures ordered: it was also the first time that the order was accompanied by a specific selection of species. Furthermore, this selection was to remain essentially the same, even as regards the sequence in which the species were listed. At first sight, this sequence seems quite fortuitous, as it is neither alphabetical nor related to the chronology of production, nor is it in accordance with size, origin, monetary value, or any perceptible zoological principle. It could possibly have been a hierarchical "pecking order," starting with such animals as the lion and elephant, and such birds as the ostrich and eagle, and proceeding to creatures not held in such high regard.

This time the manufactory responded a month later, on December 17, 1732, by issuing a new listing that specified not the production stage reached for the various animals but rather the progress with respect to actual deliveries (Source 10). Included were those animals which had appeared for the first time in the previous order but which still had not gone into production. The order had also increased in size: most of the 28 quadrupeds and 30 birds listed were now to be produced in series of eight rather than four, bringing the total up to 184 quadrupeds and 214 bird figures, of which 36 and 70 had actually been delivered.[332]

The following February brought with it the death of Augustus the Strong. As we have noted, his successor Augustus III made enquiries about the Japanese Palace project and the orders involved, which he finally confirmed, allowing the manufactory somewhat more time to fulfill them. That summer Teuffert, the palace majordomo ("Bettmeister"), paid a number of lengthy visits to the Meissen manufactory, accompanied by the book-keeper of the manufactory's office in Dresden.[333] Finally, on November 17, 1733, Count Sulkowski,[334] Teuffert, who may be regarded as the "co-ordinator" of the orders, and von Pflugk, a member of the manufactory Commission, betook themselves to the Meissen warehouse to select further pieces for the palace (Source 12).[335] Amongst the total of 35,798 pieces of porcelain in the warehouse were 16 enameled large animals,[336] and 150 white birds and 200 white quadrupeds of all different sorts and sizes.

It was a mere nine days later that the long list was drawn up with eleven chapters allocating the porcelain pieces to eleven rooms on the upper story of the palace (Source 13). At this point, the orders for animal figures reached an all-time high, with 296 figures of 37 different quadrupeds, and 292 of 32 different bird varieties, mainly in series of eight, to be housed in one single gallery. This effectively defined the general framework and established the parameters for the realization of the animal gallery.

In the meantime it had become clear from the deliveries actually made by the manufactory that these technically demanding figures could not be turned out at the rate that had been hoped for; as a result, one and a half years later, early in 1735, the order for animal figures was reduced by almost a half on the occasion of a further interim production report (Source 17). That no further reductions were made is shown by the very last of the extant interim reports, dated March 1736 (Source 19).

Back in Dresden, it was certainly dawning on those responsible for the plans that the order placed in 1733 was also oversized in view of the space available in the gallery. On December 19, 1734, when Kaendler submitted the suggestions for improvements he had drawn up during a crisis at the manufactory[337], he pointed out that he had already enquired of the Commission, "whether the Herr Bettmeister might not profitably give thought to the question of how big each figure should be, so that when it comes to installing the porcelain there will be no difficulties resulting from the manufactory never having received notification of the requisite measurements."[338] He continued by making the aesthetic point, "that the lion, elephant, and aurochs are very much the same size, which means that they will not go together very well."[339]

The sequence of order and delivery lists containing references to animal figures comes to an end with the delivery list for the year 1736 (Source 20). As is clear from a glance at the 1770 and 1779 inventories, 1736 was the last year in which animal figures were delivered to the porcelain collection at the Japanese Palace.[340]

It should at this point be noted that the heavier porcelain figures were not always conveyed to Dresden on the *Marktschiff* (market ship), as was the case with other consignments.[341] A bill for the payment of porters dated December 22, 1734, shows that crates were sometimes carried the whole way: "Ten talers and sixteen groschen [...] carriers' wages for 16 men with 8 crates of various porcelain pieces: birds and animals which for reasons of space could not be kept in Meissen any longer, and which have to be carried to the Royal Japanese Palace on account of their being dangerously fragile, paid to me in full by *Herr Hoff factor* Chladni [...]. Each man 16 groschen, Christian Hermann and fellows."[342]

In spite of the ample source material, it is not easy to deduce from the lists how many animal figures were in fact produced, which has sometimes led to wrong figures being quoted in the literature on the subject. In his important work of 1911, for instance, Karl Berling wrote: "In 1734 it proved possible to deliver 439 animals to the Japanese Palace, 16 each of the 33 quadruped varieties and 27 bird varieties, and furthermore 5 quadrupeds and 23 birds for which there had been no specific commission."[343] As his source, he refers his readers to the appendix of his work of 1900, which gives a correct rendering of the list of February 18, 1735, (Source 17). But his figure of 439 animal figures (according to the list, 469 were delivered up to this point) is just as incomprehensible as his claim that the animals were delivered in series of 16. He had furthermore miscounted the bird species: 28, and not 27, are listed. Berling's figures were adopted uncritically by Rückert in his much-quoted reference work,[344] and thus crop up again and again in the literature on this subject.

Until the steady stream of deliveries finally dries up in 1736, it is possible to work out numbers from the lists, but these also make it clear that there were also disappearances before 1736, especially in the case of the smaller figures (birds).

Deliveries	Source No.	Quadrupeds	Birds
1731 and 1732	11	63	98
1733	14	5	54
1734	16	51	143
5.3.–17.12.1735	18	34	90
1736	20	7	27
Total		160	412
Interim totals: delivered			
up to 17.12.1732	10	36	70
up to 18.2.1735	17	132	337
up to January 1736	19	159	319

At first sight there would seem to be no contradiction between the sum of the individual per annum deliveries on the one hand and the totals taken from the sources. But if one subtracts the 27 birds delivered in 1736 from the sum of the birds delivered in the individual years (412 figures in all), then one ends up with an apparent 385 birds delivered up to December 17, 1735; however, according to the historic interim total for the end of January 1736 (one and a half months later), there were only 319 bird figures to be found at the Japanese Palace. Either the compiler did not count the pieces correctly, or a number of them were taken from the Japanese Palace and used for decorative purposes at other locations, in the Tower Room at the Residence, for instance, or at Moritzburg.

After the Japanese Palace project had been given up, the use of the palace as a kind of "depository" for the royal porcelain collection led to many of the items being moved around. The bird figures, being smaller and more easily transportable, were especially liable to be transferred to new homes. The large and cumbersome animal figures – which, as we shall see, had been given a most unsuitable cold painting to boot – were less suitable for decorative purposes than the little birds with their brilliant overglaze colors. By the time of the inventory of 1770,[345] there were no more than 110 quadrupeds left at the Japanese Palace, and a mere 224 bird figures.

The information value of the order and delivery lists

As is clear from the *compte rendu* given in the last section, the delivery lists constitute a highly interesting source from which to deduce the size of the order and the progress made at the manufactory. Three of the lists even give information about the prices of the figures, in spite of which it should be noted that neither Augustus the Strong nor Augustus III ever really intended to pay for the porcelain in full (Sources 16, 18, 20).

It is clear that the prices were calculated according to the technical difficulty and amount of work involved, and that no account was taken of artistic or other factors. At 129 centimeters, the cassowary was not only the tallest but also the most expensive piece, with its price of 309 talers constituting almost exactly one third of what Kaendler earned in a year as *Modellmeister*.[346] At that time a "finely enameled clock-case, with pedestal" made for the king cost 80 talers, and a service with six tea-bowls, slop-bowl, teapot, coffee-pot, tea-caddy, and sugar-bowl, all painted with "Japanese figures" cost 50 talers.[347] The next most costly after the cassowary, namely the aurochs (265 talers), the bear (209 und ein Drittel talers), and the pelican (204 talers), not only called for large quantities of porcelain paste but were also particularly difficult to fire successfully because of their height and shape. Even today, cracks starting at the bases of such figures are visible proof of the pressure to which the base was subjected when the paste softened during the firing process. This means that the prices for the animals were assessed according to the same main criteria as those applied for tableware, that is to say, quantity of paste used, degree of difficulty, and time. According to an analysis of all the bills submitted to Augustus the Strong for deliveries from 1725 to 1733, the king received porcelain deliveries to the value of around 26,740 talers from 1731 to 1733, and of this sum around 10,134 talers, that is to say almost half, were for "animals and birds delivered to the Dutch Palace".[348]

The order and delivery lists provide an important key to understanding the overall concept underlying the palace. The present author's intention is to use the November 1733 table, which represents the order at its largest (Source 13), to investigate the choice of animals. The table names 37 different quadrupeds and 32 varieties of bird. The former can be divided into 16 exotic and 11 European wild animals, 6 domestic and 3 fabulous animals, and a court-jester. As the bust of the court-jester Joseph Fröhlich – "4 Joseph figures" – only appears in this table, it constitutes a special case which will not be given consideration here.[349] Of the fabulous animals, the unicorn likewise appears only in this table, while the sphinx and the dragon featured permanently in the animal orders and did in fact go into production.

That all the exotic animals except for elephant, rhinoceros, and camel were represented in Dresden, either in living form in the royal menageries or preserved in the taxidermic collection, is proven by records of expenses on animal food in the accounts, by inventory lists, and by references in secondary literature. An "Affricanische Esel" ("African donkey," i.e. a zebra) had arrived in Dresden with the other surviving animals from the Africa expedition only shortly before the November 1733 table was drawn up; the same is true of the chameleon, though no living specimens had survived the journey. Nevertheless, the species of which the lists are composed were not so directly related to events in the royal animal collections as one might suppose. The zebra and the chameleon, for instance, were already well known from zoological books, and already featured on the first detailed order list of November 18, 1732, one year before the arrival of the animals from Africa.

One can observe a similar pattern amongst the 32 species of bird, of which 12 can be regarded as exotic and 20 as native to Europe; in 1733, in fact, all the bird species were represented in the collections, either living, in Dresden or at Moritzburg, or stuffed in the natural history gallery. The composition of the order list of 1733 thus gives a fairly exact reflection of that of the royal animal collections.

By contrast with the quadrupeds, there is amongst the birds one (earlier) case of an observable and direct connection between the development of the animals collections and the orders sent to Meissen. The list of 17 December, 1732, contains a unique instance of the eight peacocks being classified as four colored peacocks and four white ones. At the end of November, Augustus the Strong had acquired two live white peacocks from a "Tirolean" dealer, and the nuance in the order submitted three weeks later was clearly an indication that these two peacocks were regarded as exceptional specimens of their kind (see Source 10).

Finally, there is no observable tendency for the orders to develop from better-known species to less familiar ones: exotic and domestic birds and animals rub shoulders from the very outset. All that varied was the quantity of species, and the quantities in which the individual pieces were ordered. It may thus be concluded that while the concept changed between early 1732 and the fall of 1733 from a gallery of tableware with animals to an animal gallery with some vases, the plan from the very outset – that is to say from summer 1730, when animals were first talked about – was to create a porcelain likeness of a modern princely menagerie.

Nomenclature

When studying the listings, we are in certain individual cases confronted with problems of nomenclature. The names used for the porcelain figures are the ones customarily used at the time for their living counterparts, and it is not always easy to establish which animal or bird was the original behind the porcelain figure.[350]

If a zoological term had not yet been established for an exotic species, then the bird or animal was sometimes named according to its country of origin, as is the case with the "African donkey"[351], or the "Indian deer." Some species owed their names to their conspicuous features: examples include the "Löffelgans" ("spoon goose"),[352] the "Kropfvogel" ("crop bird"),[353] and the "yellow and black bird"[354]. Some were Germanizations of foreign-language names, such as "König von Wawous,"[355] or "Barognittchen"[356]. Eighteenth- and nineteenth-century lexicons are helpful in the case of certain terms now obsolete.[357] The "indianischer Raaben" ("Indian raven"), for instance, is the macaw, "Calcuzschen Hänen" ("Calcutta cockerels") are turkeys, and the "Lerchenstößer" ("lark-basher") is the sparrow hawk. One bird whose identity it has not been possible to establish for certain is the "Krescher" – a contemporary list of expenses on food for exotic birds refers to a "Krisker oder Kletpapagey," which suggests that the bird in question, which while it was among those ordered cannot be shown to have been executed in porcelain, was a species of parrot (Source 28).

The Meissen large animal figures have also been of interest to zoologists endeavoring to identify species. The listings contain references to a quadruped known as the "Waldteuffel" ("wood-devil"), which must be a monkey. Hasche is among the authors who have pointed this out, in his description of the animal gallery: "Opposite the snakes are all kinds of monkeys, 'und Waldteufel'."[358] By studying the numbers of figures delivered and the sizes recorded in the inventories of 1770 and 1779, and by comparing the lists, it has been possible to confirm what the standard works have hitherto supposed to have been the case, namely that the "Waldteuffel" was indeed the mandrill (fig. 207).[359]

The artists and craftsmen involved

Modelers before 1727

As we have seen, the decision to use the large Neustadt-side gallery of the Japanese Palace to house the porcelain animals was made in the summer of 1730. The success of this project, quite unprecedented in the history of porcelain, was clearly going to be dependent on the master modeler ("Modellmeister") having not only the requisite artistic capabilities but also a particular flair for the techniques of porcelain manufacture and for the particular characteristics of the material.

Since its foundation in 1710, the manufactory had mainly produced copies of Far Eastern porcelain and tableware derived from models made by the court silversmith Irminger. When it came to producing figurative pieces in the European style, molds were made from goldsmiths' models or from works by sculptors from

Dresden.[360] No sculptor was employed on a permanent basis in Meissen until 1727, and the manufactory's molders ("Former") were at best potters who were capable as a minimum requirement of shaping ornaments and decorations and applying them to porcelain pieces. Although much discussion continues to be devoted to the small number of pre-1727 figurative porcelain pieces which do not derive from any known Far Eastern or European original in porcelain or any other material, or from a printed original, the question as to who actually designed them still remains unanswered.[361]

Johann Gottlieb Kirchner

The first sculptor to be permanently engaged by the manufactory was Johann Gottlieb Kirchner,[362] the brother of the Dresden court sculptor Johann Christian Kirchner. He applied to be taken on as a modeler at the manufactory in March 1727, and started work on April 29. What was new about Kirchner's brief was that he was not simply to deliver models for the manufactory to execute, as the Dresden sculptors had done, but was to be in charge of and responsible for the realization of the models in porcelain. This means that he was one of the first European sculptors to have to familiarize himself in depth with the technical procedures and difficulties inherent in porcelain production, and to have to take account of the character of the material in his own creations.

The statics of a work to be executed in porcelain are quite different from those encountered in other kinds of sculpture. Though a trained sculptor, Kirchner first had to get to know the limitations imposed by what was technically feasible in porcelain production, and one manufactory report makes it clear that he did indeed take pains to master the difficulties: "[...] the said Kirchner still needs to observe the molders to see the correct way of handling the paste so that, when working with the paste, he will know how to take account of the considerable shrinkage that takes place during firing, for paste cannot be handled in the same way as wood or stone; thus far he has often run up against problems when taking moldings in paste and putting them together to form a whole piece."[363] As a result of the difficulties he had with the material, however, Kirchner's commitment waned and the manufactory became less and less happy with his performance. Lengthy absences from his place of work, and his allegedly unsteady life were among the factors that led to the manufactory's decision to discharge him after just one year's employment,[364] :"[...] and we thus see ourselves forced to dismiss the said sculptor Kirchner, for the reason that during his employment he has not used his working time so industriously as he promised to do, and, furthermore, has recently fallen victim to an illness that he has brought upon himself through his disorderly way of life [...]."[365] Kirchner did not seem to mind this at all, as "he let it be understood, among other things, that it was against his character to continue to work on little pieces in clay, and that he was more accustomed to working in stone and to creating large statues."[366]

Kirchner moved to Weimar, where he became court sculptor, and his place was taken, at the king's request, by Johann Christoph Ludwig Lücke.[367] This choice resulted in greater dissatisfaction;[368] it was claimed that a good molder would have been better, George Fritzsche for instance, who could make better models and could at the same time teach the other molders a thing or two.[369] In January 1729 it was Lücke's turn to be dismissed.

It is not clear who was subsequently responsible for model-making, but the manufactory probably made do with designs made by sculptors who were not permanently employed, as is suggested by a goblet modeled early in 1729 by Christian Kirchner the brother of the first modeler, and then executed in porcelain by Fritzsche.[370]

A year later Johann Gottlieb Kirchner was engaged at the manufactory for a second time, reassuming his duties on June 1, 1730. One important factor behind Kirchner's reinstatement was certainly the fact that the Japanese Palace project was now taking more definite shape, with building now under way in Dresden and the orders were flowing in. If the king's vision was to become reality, then the manufactory had to engage a modeler who had a certain degree of familiarity with the material. Kirchner at first worked primarily on large vases, and then, not long after his new start, on animals.[371] When, one year later, a second modeler of the same age, Johann Joachim Kaendler, was engaged to work alongside Kirchner, it became clear to the latter that his new colleague was more at ease with porcelain than he himself was, with the result that on March 18, 1732, Kirchner asked to be discharged for a second time, because, "[...] now in my second year at the manufactory, I am carrying out the job with which I was most graciously entrusted, in accordance with my instructions, loyally and conscientiously; nevertheless, as a young man and trained sculptor I am eager to see rather more of the world, and to cultivate my knowledge and skills, so that I may become all the more capable of pleasing Your Majesty with my most humble services [...]."[372] One only has to read between the lines a little to see that Kirchner felt uneasy at having to work alongside an artist who obviously had a far greater talent for working with porcelain than he did; resentful at only having been entrusted with "few functions," he felt that he was underestimated and not being challenged to give of his best. His application was at first rejected, as all the skills available were required for the palace project. Kirchner's morale sank even lower in the wake of further complaints and reprimands, and on April 28, 1733, he was discharged for a second time.

Johann Joachim Kaendler

Johann Joachim Kaendler was born in Fischbach on June 15, 1706, the son of a pastor.[373] After his apprenticeship with the Dresden sculptor Johann Christian Feige, he completed his training as a journeyman with the court sculptor Benjamin Thomae,[374] being appointed court sculptor in his own turn in 1730.

The records show that Augustus the Strong in person had noticed him, or at least that someone had drawn the king's attention to the young artist. Kaendler's awareness that being appointed to this position was a privilege is evident in the proud statement he gave in connection with the denunciation affair or "Reinhardt affair" of 1734 in which he and Inspector Reinhardt leveled complaints against Court Commissioner Höroldt: "After I had had the especial privilege of working in the *Grünes Gewölbe* for six years on the production of a great number of ornaments, it was His Majesty the late King's gracious pleasure to engage me as Modellmeister at the royal porcelain manufactory, and to have me instructed to invent all manner of Indian animals and birds along with all kinds of ornaments, and to make clean models of them, and furthermore to instruct all the factory-workers, especially the apprentices, in drawing and modeling, so that they might work more skillfully on all the porcelain pieces in production."[375]

Kaendler was of course giving a somewhat exaggerated account of his duties. Neither was he *Modellmeister* at the beginning, nor did his briefing include giving instruction to the apprentices: he was only entrusted with these functions after Kirchner's departure. The manufactory records of 1731 simply state that more hands were needed on account of the "retail wares, and the many other large pieces of tableware being made according to the drawings and models hitherto accepted by the factory." They continue: "Given that those large pieces which His Royal Majesty wishes to have manufactured according to certain models and drawings could hitherto not be produced by Modellmeister Kirchner alone, Johann Joachim Kentler, sculptor, arrived here at the factory on June 22, His Most Gracious Highness having commanded that he make all kinds of figures, not only in wood but also in clay, and begin on the work of modeling."[376]

Two things are particularly clear from these sources. Firstly, Kaendler's appointment was directly related to the orders for the large Neustadt-side gallery of the Japanese Palace, and secondly, he was not regarded as an assistant for Kirchner but rather as a modeler in his own right. Although Kirchner, who had already been at the manufactory for a relatively long period of time and was thus a known quantity, was promoted to *Modellmeister* when Kaendler arrived, he had his workroom on the third story (the European "second floor") of the Albrechtsburg, whereas Kaendler set himself up in the so-called "molder's room" on the fourth story ("third floor").[377] This is an important point, as the competition between these two artists of the same age was, as we shall see, to have a direct influence on the animal gallery project.

New though it was to him, the medium does not seem to have caused Kaendler any difficulties.[378] It was only in the case of his first piece, an eagle, that he seems to have made several different models. In the course of the denunciation affair, Höroldt claimed that "he [Höroldt] had at the beginning had to instruct Herr Cändler as to how to construct the pieces so that they did not sag in the firing,"[379] to which Kaendler replied, "that Herr Herold had not been on the staff any longer than the questionee [Kaendler],[380] and had therefore not been in a position to instruct him; Kirchner had given him most of his instruction, and when he asked his father-in-law Eckbrechten,[381] he was told that he should pay attention to the position of the center of gravity so that the pieces did not fall over in the firing. This advice he had taken to heart, as it explained why the first pieces, the eagles, had been spoiled in the firing, and at that time Herr HoffCommissarius Herold had had just as little understanding of these things as Kaendler."[382]

It is indeed astounding how quickly Kaendler mastered his new material. Apart from Kirchner and his small number of assistants, there was nobody at the manufactory who could have had experience and knowledge of how porcelain behaves when fired. Within only a few months Kaendler had not only acquired a good understanding of the material but had also surpassed his fellows in his feeling for porcelain's hidden potential. A large proportion of eighteenth-century figurative German porcelain was to be indebted to his particular talent for coaxing the most subtle expressive nuances out of the material while concealing from the beholder the technical snags and pitfalls that had to be overcome during production. In his mastery of the material, Kaendler attained a perfect synthesis of idea and technique.

From the very beginning Kaendler demanded a higher salary than that received by the "veteran" Kirchner, and as it did not take long for Kaendler's talent and worth to be recognized, September 1731 saw the Commission making the following recommendation in a petition to the king: "A short time ago it was Your Royal Majesty's pleasure to recruit one further modeler by the name of Jochim Kendlern at the porcelain manufactory, to the end that he, together with the Modellmeister already in service, Kirchner, should engage in the production of the large vases and many kinds of animals ordered by Your Royal Majesty. Since, as Your Royal Majesty has also been perceptive enough to notice, there has been no reason at all for any complaint whatsoever about Kendler's industry and skill, and given that he has asked for an annual salary of 400 talers and accommodation in the manufactory, it is now expected that this matter shall be regularized. The Commission considers that it would in this case be well worth granting Kendler this salary of 400 talers; of this, the sum that Modellmeister Kirchner receives per annum, namely 300 talers, should be paid out monthly by Manufactory Inspector Reinhardt, and the remaining 100 talers should be handed to him by Hoff-Factor Chladni from manufactory funds in Dresden, in secret, so that Kirchner should not be given reason to claim more for himself."[383] Naturally enough, Kirchner soon became aware of this evasion, and when he found out that Kaendler was receiving 100 talers more from another source, he demanded the same for himself.

Related to this is an oft-quoted source which has generally been used quite uncritically as evidence regarding the regard in which the two artists were held by the manufactory. In a petition to the king dated March 26, 1732, the Commission enquired as to whether they should grant Kirchner the supplement or not. In the petition it is claimed that Kirchner, "is accorded praise from all

46 Johann Joachim Kaendler, handle of a tureen from the service made for Count Sulkowski, model ca. 1737; Historisches Museum Basel, loan from the Pauls-Eisenbeiss-Stiftung

sides when his name is raised at the manufactory, and it is agreed that he understands his work well, he is a useful member of staff, and he surpasses the other modeler Kändler, not only in his creations but in other respects as well."[384] This claim that Kirchner was a superior artist to Kaendler only tells us that cliques had formed within the manufactory, which is also evident from all the records of the time. Given the important positions the two modelers held in the enterprise, and their differences in character and approach, side-taking and partisanship was practically inevitable. It is quite conceivable that the Commission was given this picture of Kirchner by Höroldt. Samuel Stöltzel, on the other hand, who as arcanist was certainly in a good position to make an assessment of Kaendler's feeling for technical matters, made it clear which side he was taking during the denunciation affair of 1734, stating in evidence that he could not understand Höroldt's hatred of Kaendler, "given that [Kaendler] was from the beginning so good and was given priority over the modeler Kirchner, whom I also considered to be a skilful worker."[385] In July 1735, Höroldt, who had come out on top after the denunciation affair, could not resist having Kaendler sent a written reprimand on account of his alleged laziness.[386] The impression given by the work reports and the number of models he completed, however, is one of an artist almost possessed, giving of himself unreservedly and making models at an astounding rate, and his huge number of works furthermore included a good number of original creations which are not only of the very highest quality but were also to have a formative influence upon the development of European porcelain figures generally.[387]

His own assessment of his achievements is preserved in comments he committed to paper in 1739 when asserting his right to certain permissions and privileges in the course of a further power struggle with Höroldt. On the occasion of this second offensive he knew he would be supported by his powerful protector Count Brühl. With his typical self-assurance and proneness to exaggerate, he wrote that if only he were to be allowed more freedom, "Your Royal Majesty would have the pleasure of being able to order far more exquisite and splendid pieces. I do not write this unthinkingly, and have such knowledge of the matter that I am quite aware of what I could achieve; I am not boasting when I say that I can cope with all the physical work that would be demanded of me, as indeed all those working at the manufactory [...] could not but attest; further, they would surely agree that when I started work eight years ago, I could not find in the works a single handle that was properly made, let alone a whole piece, and that it was only through my hard work, creating, thinking, working and studying, for no-one could help me at all in this respect, that I found out how to make figures and pieces of tableware in such a way that they stay upright in the fire."[388]

Kaendler's self-assessment is interesting for two reasons. First, it shows the pride of an artist who right at the very beginning of his career in porcelain was recognized by his contemporaries as having carried off a brilliant achievement in the form of the animal figures, thus putting porcelain into the same league as any other material used for making large figures. This awareness of his own worth is also apparent in a request submitted some thirty years later, reminding his addressee that he was owed "the modest sum of 1000 talers [...] for the porcelain figures and animals modeled for the so-called Dutch Palace in Dresden in the years 1731, 1732, and 1733."[389] Secondly, this quotation makes it clear that Kaendler regarded the creativity he invested in the kind of tableware we nowadays consider of secondary value as no less important than his more spectacular technical achievements. While we would never accord the same importance to a tureen handle (fig. 46) as to the virtuosic, life-size figure of the carrion-devouring vulture (fig. 153), the creator nevertheless applied himself to the two pieces with equal seriousness. This is not to suggest that Kaendler would have considered them of equal artistic value; however, the comparison which his own words provokes us to make underlines the fact that his particular treatment of detail is a powerful element in the effect made by the whole.

It would take a whole book to do justice to Johann Joachim Kaendler's achievements over and above the field of the animal figures. The present book will therefore content itself with considering the "thunderous drum-roll" that brought the genre of monumental porcelain figures into being, a development which paved the way for the flowering of European figurative porcelain in the period through until his death in 1775.

Johann Friedrich Eberlein

After Johann Gottlieb Kirchner had left the manufactory at the end of April 1733, the responsibility for the creation of new figures and tableware was put in the sole hands of the new *Modellmeister* Johann Joachim Kaendler. Augustus III, after his accession in 1733, gave the manufactory somewhat more time to fulfill the orders for the Japanese Palace, but still held fast to the plans that had been made, "in accordance with the verbal order, because of the production of the large pieces," also apparently demanding the "engagement of a modeler necessary to the fulfillment of the same,"[390] subsequent to which the Commission asked the manufactory for its opinion on the matter.

The answer they received shows that the manufactory had confidence in Kaendler's capacity for hard work and high productivity: "The factory does not consider it necessary to engage a new modeler in the place of the recently departed Kirchner, for the reason that all the outstanding pieces still remaining to be modeled can well be done by Kaendler, especially since the manufactory has two young men, Schmieder and Krumbholz, who are skilful repairers and can well be used as such, having even been given instruction in the art by Kaendler."[391] And that was the end of that, until pressure for the delivery of the outstanding pieces of tableware and of the figures for the Japanese Palace increased in the course of the new concept brought in by Longuelune shortly before 1735.

It was around this time, on February 9, 1735, that the Dresden sculptor Johann Friedrich Eberlein –whether by luck or good judgment – submitted his application to be taken on at the manufactory. Eberlein, who was born in Dresden in 1695, had until this point mainly been active as a member of the team working on the "Golden Rider," the equestrian statue of Augustus the Strong, and was now in need of a new job.[392] He was immediately taken on for a trial period.[393]

The sources make it clear that Eberlein's trial period was directly linked with the order for the Japanese Palace and with the manufactory's drive to meet the order's requirements: "The arcanists conducted an investigation together with Herr Kaendler as to whether the latter was capable of doing the work commissioned by the King and the other work all on his own. The said Modellmeister […] made his statement and has promised to execute the outstanding pieces for the Royal Japanese Palace, and to carry out the ordinary work within three months, for a fee, as he will have to work from early in the morning until well into the evening. The arcanists, however, considered it a matter of the greatest necessity, both for the sake of the royal orders and of the other work, of which more and more is being ordered each day, that the sculptor who applied to us, Eberlein, should be taken on for a trial period, as a result of which Eberlein did indeed present himself on the 18th inst., and began work."[394]

When Eberlein was engaged on a permanent basis as "Kaendler's Adjuvante"[395] on April 18, 1735, he was granted an annual salary of 144 talers, which was a little more than a third of what Kaendler received. This established for the first time a hierarchy among the modelers, with the terms "Modellmeister" and "Modelleur" now reflecting an assessment of their status, and not simply – as had been the case with Kirchner and Kaendler – length of experience.

This new configuration, which made Kaendler the teacher and Eberlein his pupil, had a far-reaching effect on the creative work of the manufactory's new sculptor, and it is no disrespect to his undisputed artistic talent to note that the influence of Kaendler is constantly evident in all his pieces. This artistic closeness to his teacher has sometimes given rise to the suggestion that Eberlein, particularly in his animal figures, may simply have finished off works which had already been given their basic shape and form by Kaendler.[396] This cannot be proved from the sources, and Eberlein can arguably be credited with more independence than this suggestion would infer; in any case, his works are positive evidence of the emergence of a new, unified style at the Meissen manufactory.

If in the years before 1727 the models had been made by a variety of artists, and between 1727 and 1731 mainly by Kirchner, then the keynote of the years 1731 to 1733 derives from two antithetical understandings of the matter in hand, Kirchner's and Kaendler's. In the years that followed, modelers were without question more influenced by Kaendler's captivating style, which was also the predominant one; at the same time, however, the manufactory was also coming to recognize that the enterprise was best served by a corps of artists who, while being capable of a great range of subtle nuances, still adhered to a relatively unified overall stylistic concept, especially as the manufactory's increasingly frequent large commissions were calling for more and more new forms. The large services for Count Sulkowski and Count Brühl are two good examples of sets in which a great variety of different pieces all had to be quite clearly parts of one whole. One single artist would have taken too long to complete a large set of this kind, but through the collaboration of a number of artists sharing a common stylistic vision, it was possible for these and similar orders to be executed more quickly. This approach was also applied to the other artistic department, that is to say to the painters, who were likewise successfully trained to decorate the pieces in as uniform a manner as possible.

Similar conclusions had evidently been arrived at in connection with the large animal figures for the Japanese Palace. Although, as we shall see, Kirchner had at first taken responsibility for the quadrupeds, and Kaendler for the birds, a similar division of labor turned out not to be possible at the advanced stage reached in 1735. When Eberlein modeled a turkey-hen in August 1735, for instance, it was not just in a formal sense that it was be a pair to the turkey-cock Kaendler had made two years earlier – it also had to match it stylistically (figs. 179–180).

The other sculptors engaged by the manufactory prior to 1750 played no part in the production of the animal figures for the Japanese Palace. While there is evidence that Johann Gottlieb

Ehder (at the manufactory from 1739) and Peter Reinicke (from 1743) produced or carried out changes on animal models, these models were not directly related to the king's order.[397]

On July 26, 1732, the manufactory paid Christian Gottfried Böhme, a sculptor from Weimar, the sum of 18 talers for his "large pieces executed during his trial period,"[398] including a large lion which he was said to have "bossiert," which in the usage of the time could have meant either that he made a model for a lion, or that he acted as a "repairer," putting the moldings together and doing the finishing on the assembled piece.[399] It was very likely the latter that was the case, as at this time the manufactory already had two sculptors making models. This source is nevertheless of interest as it shows that "repairing" was not considered beneath the dignity of a sculptor. Böhme was supposed to take up a post in the department for large tableware after an interim period of two months, but he did not appear, very likely remaining as court sculptor in Weimar.[400]

The individuals involved in the production process

It should not be forgotten that the production process for the porcelain animals was made up of several stages carried out by different individuals. The sculptors Kirchner, Kaendler, and Eberlein made the models, from which other craftsmen then made plaster molds; other individuals ("molders") used these molds to take moldings in porcelain paste, and then others ("repairers") were responsible for putting the whole figure together. As will be shown when we consider the joins on the figures and the working over of detail on the surface, this last stage had a not insignificant bearing upon the final appearance of the figure. For this reason, brief consideration will now be given to the individuals involved in the realization of the animal models as porcelain figures.

After the order for 910 porcelain pieces for the Neustadt-side gallery of the Japanese Palace, the Commission requested a "specification of those employees who are to work exclusively on the porcelain pieces ordered for the new front gallery of the Royal Dutch Palace."[401] According to this specification, drawn up by the manufactory in April 1732, "to this end, the following persons are nominated by Court Commissioner Höroldt as follows:

1.	Kirchner	
2.	Kentler	as modelers ["Modellirer"]
3.	Geithner sen.	
4.	Lohse sen.	
5.	Grund	as throwers ["Dreher"]
6.	Lücke	as repairer ["Poussirer und verputzer"]
7.	Fritzsche	
8.	Albrecht	
9.	Krumbholz	
10.	Schmahl	
11.	Schmieder	
12.	Müller	as molders ["Former"]"[402]

The first thing that strikes one is that it was the most capable and experienced members of staff who were chosen for listing in the specification. This was certainly done in order to keep up appearances, and to show the Commission that the order was being taken seriously and being given priority treatment. It is equally certain that these individuals cannot have worked exclusively for the royal order, as they also had to make sure that production of the other stock wares was maintained.

Carl Friedrich Lücke was employed at the manufactory as a molder and repairer and worked particularly closely with Kirchner; however, as he was discharged along with Kirchner in April 1733, the division of labor specified in this list cannot have been kept up for very long.[403] The records show that those mentioned as being "molders" were not only responsible for taking the porcelain paste moldings correctly, but for the most part also functioned as repairers, assembling the moldings to form whole pieces.

In 1733, when considering whether Kirchner should be replaced, the manufactory came to the conclusion that they would be sufficiently served by Kaendler as a modeler, and Johann Friedrich Schmieder and Carl Friedrich Krumbholz as skilled repairers. Schmieder was clearly involved in the production of the large animal figures; when questioned in connection with the denunciation affair of 1734, he stated that the coarseness of the paste used made it difficult to put the figure together and work over the individual parts.[404] We know that in 1732 Krumbholz worked together with Christoph Müller for two weeks assembling "two large vases, a large monkey, and a large bird."[405] In 1734, however, the same Müller gave in evidence that when working on the large figures, he had only dressed joins and had not had anything to do with the "embellishments."[406]

Johann Christian Wittich is also mentioned in connection with the "grobe Masse," the paste used for the large figures, but all that is stated is that he was at the time working on a "bust."[407] That Andreas Schiefer was also involved in taking moldings and assembling animal figures is shown by the fact – to which further consideration will be given later – that his initials appear on a bustard, and his molder's mark, a little cross with four dots, on a cat.

Although the name of Johann Gottlieb Schmahl (senior) is included in the list of employees who worked on the 910 pieces of porcelain, he changed position to work at the kilns a year later, and was therefore not among the molders mentioned in the records as being questioned in 1734.

In spite of so many individuals evidently having been involved in the production of the animal figures, it is as a rule unclear how many figures each individual actually worked on, with George Fritzsche and Friedrich August Albrecht being two notable exceptions, appearing as they do to have been the two main individuals responsible for taking moldings for the animal figures.

George Fritzsche, who had worked at the manufactory since 1719, was on a number of occasions accorded special praise as one of the best and most experienced molders. Before 1727 he had also made the models for figures and (small) animals.[408] One piece of evidence of his having worked on the large animal figures is contained in Johann Georg Schlicke's statement of 1734 that he, Schlicke, had worked for two years on the large pieces, together with Fritzsche and using the coarse paste.[409] Höroldt's response to Kaendler's suggestions for improvements provides further evidence. Kaendler had praised the talents of the molders and had taken Höroldt to task for having managed them poorly, in response to which Höroldt made a statement on March 26, 1735, giving his assessment of each thrower and molder in turn and reserving particular criticism for Fritzsche, who had been repeatedly praised by Kaendler: "[...] when the large pieces were ordered about four years ago, Fritzsche was among those who did not want to have anything to do with them, doubting that they could be executed successfully. I, however, spoke to the molder Albrecht, telling him that he should take the moldings for the first big piece (a dragon), and the credit for the success of this piece cannot be claimed by Fritzsche, as he, along with a number of others, had to learn the art of making larger pieces, as he had in his whole life not even seen a large figure, let alone made one. Most of the pieces for the Royal Palace which turned out well were of Albrecht's molding and making, and Albrecht did just as many pieces as Fritzsche, while at the same time having to give instruction to Schiefer, Müller, and Schlicke, in spite of only receiving ten talers per month, while Fritzsche received twelve talers on account of his age."[410]

We have even more extensive information about the work of the Höroldt protégé Friedrich August Albrecht. In 1739 he applied for a rise in salary, claiming that he was particularly well qualified, and that back in the days of Augustus the Strong, "when these large and troublesome pieces for the Porcelain Palace were first invented, when all the other workers, even the best of them, had been having their doubts and had constantly been saying, 'Nothing will come of it,' I was the one who, because I showed enthusiasm and attention, was entrusted with this work by [...] Höroldt, who also promised me that I would be well paid for my trouble, and that was how it happened that from that point on I took the moldings for most of the pieces, and in any case for the most important pieces delivered to the Royal Palace."[411] Albrecht furthermore claimed that he had been in advance of his fellow-workers in discovering the right way of going about this work, and that the latter had learnt a lot from him in this respect. And if he was now requesting a pay rise, this was because "I had been encouraged by my superior to do this work with promises that I would be well paid for it, even to the extent that Hofkommissar Höroldt gave me a ducat from his own pocket for me on the occasion of the first so-called dragons and other pieces." His application was turned down, and he repeated it the following September in even clearer terms: "[...] in respect of my work, I would refer you to my superiors, who will be dutiful enough to confirm in all conscience that I was the one who invested such artistry and pains in all the most considerable porcelain pieces invented by Kaendler, Modellmeister to his Royal Majesty, which are now to be found in his Japanese Palace, animals, vases, birds and the like, [...] taking the moldings for the same and assembling them."[412] Given that in 1736 Albrecht was being almost as well paid as the sculptor Eberlein, and was furthermore frequently praised by Kaendler as one of the best molders, we may justifiably regard his claims as credible.[413]

The records show that at least eight different molders and repairers were involved, to various degrees, in the realization of the models delivered to them by the three modelers. The molders and repairers had a formative influence on the final appearance of the animal figures, and they felt the pressure of the orders for the Japanese Palace just as much as the arcanists and modelers did. They too were obliged to work overtime, which they did not resent as it provided a welcome source of additional income. And they too found themselves caught between the parties composed of individuals vying with one another for positions of influence and power at the manufactory. The only reason why it is not possible to pay adequate tribute to the role of the molders and repairers in the production of the figures for the Japanese Palace is that although they indeed had important and formative tasks to perform, their section of the production process – which we shall consider in greater detail in the following sections – was an anonymous one.

The production of the porcelain animals – the technical aspects

Given the size and production capacity of the Meissen manufactory, technical problems inevitably constituted a major obstacle to successful porcelain production. It was only possible to start thinking along artistic lines once the production processes had been established and the material had been mastered. In the context of the large animal figures, it was not just a matter of developing suitable pastes and glazes, but also, for instance, of achieving greater efficiency at the mills where the raw materials were ground. Not least because of the animal figures, the consumption of paste at Meissen rose in the course of the 1730s, but the raw materials still had to be ground to a certain degree of fineness, and still had to be stored for a certain length of time once they had been processed into a paste. The manufactory's milling works thus had either to operate more quickly or have the capacity to take on larger quantities at once.[414] This problem is highlighted by the report to the Commission of October 1731, in which the manufactory calls for an extra horse for the glaze mill because glaze is not being produced in sufficient quantity, and the mill will have to be kept going day and night.[415] At the end of November, a blind horse arrived at the manufactory from the royal riding stables, requisitioned by Teuffert, the major-domo.[416] The same problem was faced with respect to the kilns, which were of great interest to the management, not only with regard to their capacities but also because of the possibility of saving wood through the implementation of new designs.

The history of the Meissen manufactory in the 1730s shows that the orders for the Japanese Palace, the first commissions for large table services, and the demand for astounding quantities of porcelain for the French and Ottoman markets brought about a decisive change in the relationship between technical knowledge and the use made of that knowledge for efficient production. Artistic ideas were no longer a function of the current technical possibilities; now, it was the artistic ideas which called the tune, and the technical developments followed in their wake.

As the development of the manufactory between 1731 and 1736 was driven by the endeavors related to the animal figures for the Japanese Palace, and as these figures cannot be properly appreciated without reference to the techniques of porcelain manufacture, the following sections will be devoted to the fundamentals of these techniques and to the demands they made.

The making of the model and the molds

The manufacture of porcelain figures in the eighteenth century was an art "ex negativo"; in serial production, the individual parts of the figure were always taken from plaster molds. To reach this decisive stage of production, it is first necessary to have a model.

In porcelain production, the first condition a model has to fulfill is that it must be possible to take a plaster mold from it. Astounding quantities of plaster were required to take molds from the large models; in July 1732, for instance, 35 metric hundredweight of plaster were bought for 49 talers and 14 groschen for the large pieces alone.[417] For molds to be taken, the model can either be cut up into single pieces without overhanging parts, or plaster negatives can be taken from separate sections of one whole model, which is a highly troublesome procedure.

When the term "model" ("Modell") appears in the sources, it has to be regarded critically. When, for instance, we read in the Meissen records that, "[…] all sorts of *galanterie* and make-up boxes are produced, and in addition no fewer mirror-frames and small coffee-tables, with models for some of these being sent here from the Royal Palace in Dresden,"[418] then one can be certain that what was being referred to were prototypes for the modeler to copy, rather than items from which molds were to be taken. And when we read that a number of Far Eastern porcelain pieces from the royal collection were put at the disposal of the manufactory for modeling purposes, and know that the pieces which resulted from this modeling can today still be compared directly with their originals in the Dresden Porcelain Collection, then it is clear that the modelers did not take molds from the Far Eastern pieces but rather made copies in clay before proceeding to production in porcelain.

When the manufactory received drawings from which figures were to be made, then the prototype first had to be executed in three-dimensional form. This was also the case with sculptures. Although the records contain numerous references to models carved in wood, the material most frequently used was clay, which was also the most suitable one: "If the nature of the piece, whether a figure or a piece of tableware, is such that it is ordered frequently, then a model should be made in clay to make production easier."[419]

In the case of the very large animal figures, however, this led to a stability problem. The large quantity of wet clay which was necessary for the model of the bear (fig. 202), for instance, could not have been handled if it had not been hollow underneath: otherwise it would have distorted under the pressure of its own weight. More exact insights are afforded by another instance, this time a smaller figure. In 1735 Kaendler is to be found complaining that the manufactory still owes him money for materials he used when modeling a heron four years before: "At the all-gracious behest of his majesty the most blessèd King of most glorious memory, I the undersigned had, in the year 1731, to model, life-size, the white heron that was at that time to be seen live in the courtyard of the Royal Palace in Dresden, for the porcelain manufactory, standing amongst rushes with frogs and fishes. To that end I had to purchase for 36 groschen the iron and screws which had to be incorporated into its body so that it did not sag, and furthermore the clay used and the pedestal on which it stood."[420]

All this makes it clear that in the context of porcelain production the word "model" developed quite a different meaning from the meanings it had in the other fields of the plastic arts.

A further factor to be taken into account by the modeler at a porcelain works is that the model has to be made bigger than the size intended for the end product, as the porcelain will shrink by up to a sixth of its size during drying and firing. That is to say, the model is an outsize version of the final figure.

Furthermore, the form of the model must be fully thought-out and realized in detail, as once its surface has given birth to a plaster mold, it is only possible to make the smallest corrections. The modeler also has to bear in mind, particularly in the case of figurative pieces, that when the piece is glazed its lines will lose a good measure of their sharpness. This means that a model made to be used in porcelain production has to be exaggerated in all its aspects, as it will only give birth to the figure envisaged by the modeler after it has been taken out of its creator's hands and sacrificed in the production process. The model itself will not be preserved and its artistic value will be measured from the resulting porcelain figure. However, the process itself has a certain creative and artistic life of its own, as we shall see; consequently, what is most personal about the artist's style is only perceptible "in copy" in the end product. As a good modeler will be aware of this factor and will allow for it in his modeling, we may regard it as an essential characteristic of a model made for porcelain that it must, as a result of the path that lies before it, incorporate a certain formal augmentation, or exaggeration, of the original artistic idea.

This imperative is made less problematic by a second characteristic of a model in clay, namely that the medium of the model and that of the final artefact are extremely similar. The fact that the model is made in a ceramic material means that the conditions that governed its own creation and the characteristics that it acquired as a result of those conditions will also be present in the figure subsequently executed in porcelain. If serial production was not intended, the modeler could indeed perfectly well create his work of art directly in porcelain paste. This is a very different scenario from the one in which a clay model is finally executed in bronze. The rightness of clay as a material for a model to be executed in porcelain leads to an organic unity of expression and effect; in other words, it means that the modeler's feel for the material is still apparent in a very direct way in the final porcelain piece. In spite of all the intermediary stages involved in the execution, there is still an intimate connection between the point of departure (model) and the destination (porcelain figure), and it is indeed only because this is the case that we, on the basis of the end product, can make any meaningful statements whatsoever about the artist's original idea.

A clay model made by a stone, wood, or metal sculptor is something quite different, its primary intention simply being to establish the basic composition of the sculpture-to-be; as such, it is more a kind of plastic sketch than a model in the present sense of the word. Knocking up this kind of impromptu three-dimensional *aide-mémoire* was something which the modelers of the Meissen animal figures also sometimes did. In his working report of November 1732, Johann Gottlieb Kirchner noted that while in Dresden, he had "made, *en plein air*, the roughest of models" of three wild cats and a porcupine.[421] This was doubtless nothing very different from the kind of bozzetto that as a sculptor Kirchner was certainly used to making. That Kaendler also made figures of this kind is shown by his working report for June 1734, in which he states that while in Moritzburg he made "small models of the 'Indianischer Geyer' [griffon vulture], the 'Gackedu' [cockatoo], the crane, and the 'König von die Wawon' [king vulture]."[422] These three-dimensional designs were actually "models for models," rather than models in the strict sense. When the model has been used for the purpose of making molds, it only any longer exists "in negativo"; once this stage has been reached, however, the work with the porcelain paste can begin.

The porcelain paste

The records related to the manufacture of the large animal figures show particularly clearly that a porcelain paste is not a clearly defined material, but a mixture composed according to a recipe that varies according to the nature of the piece being produced. The component substances – the clay body, a flux, and an opening additive (a non-melting or hardly melting substance that makes the paste less plastic, or "shorter"), and – are given separate preliminary treatment, cleaned, ground, and then mixed with water to form a paste.[423]

In the Meissen of the 1730s, the most-used paste – the "ordinaire" – was composed of roughly 60% kaolin, 20% opening material (finely ground low-fired porcelain shards), and 20% feldspar as a flux.[424] As, however, large vases and figures could not be fired successfully when the paste was made according to this recipe, other more suitable mixtures had to be found. When the solution was found, it was – as in earlier related problem cases such as the paste for tableware with blue underglaze painting – thanks to a combination of data culled from experience, results of empirical experiment, and pure good luck.

If the main problem during the first years after the large animal figures went into production had been how to get a figure through the firing process in a more or less stable and undamaged state,[425] the problem topping the agenda towards 1734 was that of the color of the figure after the high firing. These two matters were directly related. While the success rate was raised by changes in the paste recipe made to reduce the formation of cracks and avoid breakages during firing, the extra opening additives introduced had a detrimental effect on surface quality, and the figures had neither the whiteness nor the smoothness of true porcelain.

Statements by Kaendler quoted in a report of Höroldt's dated October 28, 1734, extant only in fragments, indicate that Count Sulkowski was far from pleased with the appearance of the finished animals in the Japanese Palace.[426] Speaking as the official in

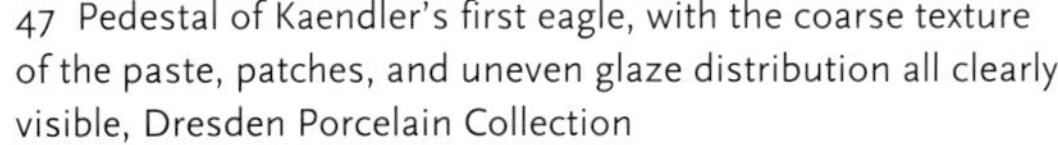
47 Pedestal of Kaendler's first eagle, with the coarse texture of the paste, patches, and uneven glaze distribution all clearly visible, Dresden Porcelain Collection

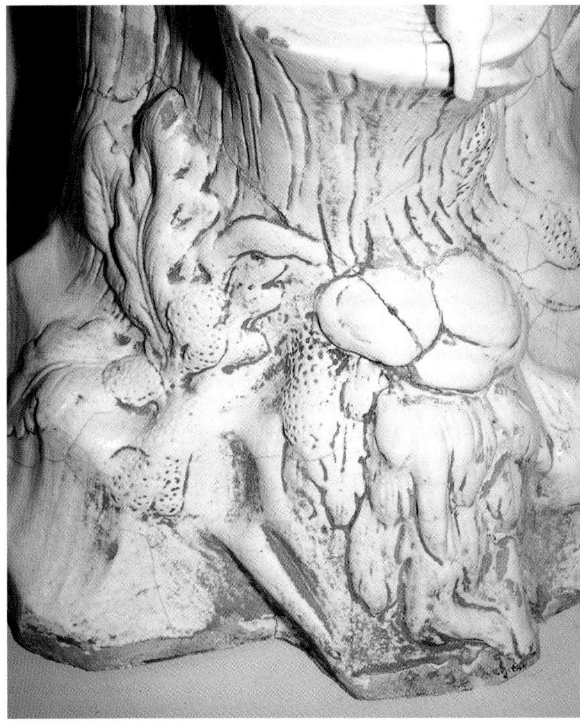

charge of the fitting out of the palace and the associated deliveries, the Count had complained, "that the paste was bad and only good for pottery," to which Höroldt responded as follows: "I wanted to take responsibility for finding out what it is in the paste which makes it black. One should do tests and experiments to see how to succeed in making the animals stand up properly." It was not in fact the case that the paste was black, but the appearance of a good number of the surviving figures make it quite understandable why Sulkowski was reluctant to call them porcelain (fig. 47); with their dirty grey, or brown, spotted surfaces they are a far cry from the pure white of porcelain.

The unsightliness of the figures became one of the principal causes of dissatisfaction in the context of the denunciation affair raging around Höroldt at the time. Kaendler described the problem in his written allegations:

"§1: The paste which Hofkommissar Höroldt had prepared was of such low quality that the workers at the manufactory called it clay rather than porcelain paste; in spite of all the complaints, he had most of the pieces for the King made from this paste, much to the disadvantage both of his Majesty and of the manufactory,

"§2: This paste has a thoroughly grey and unsightly appearance, as if sand had been strewn over the fired pieces; it has none of the beauty and smoothness typical of real porcelain. It is impossible to produce anything decent out of this paste, because it is so coarse and sandy; it does not hold together properly, and cracks when worked upon for any length of time."[427]

Upon which "Hofkommissar Höroldt expressly informed the Commission that the porcelain paste for the large pieces was made from the same ingredients as the so-called good paste from which the small pieces of tableware were made, and that it was made coarse in texture so that it would hold together better."[428]

In fact both were right. On the one hand, when the allegations against Höroldt were investigated, it was found that the paste was indeed turning out dark and grey.[429] On the other hand, Höroldt's records show that in 1734 foreign substances were no longer being added to the paste. As early as February 5, 1734, the two arcanists had written to Höroldt and Dr. Petzsch as follows in an account of their new inventions: "[...] we are working on the invention of a paste, as there have been indications that the pieces made with this paste hold together better in the low firing [...]"[430]

The progress made in this decisive year is demonstrated by a number of recipes for paste mixtures for large porcelain pieces, the recipes having survived in the arcanists' records in the archive of the porcelain manufactory. While one can deduce from them that sand or clay was indeed added as an opening agent to the paste used for the earlier animal figures, they also confirm what Höroldt stated in his own defence, namely that in 1734 foreign substances were no longer being added to the paste. This led to a slight improvement in the color, which for the painter and arcanist Höroldt was certainly the most important factor after that of successful firing. Kaendler on the other hand was more concerned about the paste being of a consistency conducive to his fine and detailed surface work. When he complained about the grey color he also laid particular emphasis on the coarseness of the paste being made for the animals, hinting that this was what had frequently led to drying cracks. The extant records show the reasons for this granular consistency.

Höroldt's recipe book contains several mixtures for pastes to be used for large porcelain pieces, and these are of particular interest because he also wrote comments on their quality after completion of the firing process. On January 9, 1734, for instance, he did a test on a paste, "which could be used for large pieces or animals, and which should on account of its coarseness hold together well and not break in two in the firing."[431] In addition to Colditz clay and "Siebenlehnscher Stein" (i.e. feldspar), it also contained "Corbitzer Scheyer Sand" (scouring sand from a place called Corbitz) as an opening agent. His comments confirm that with its admixture of scouring sand, this paste did not make for a very porcelain-like end product; the test piece turned out yellow, and the Corbitz sand produced a great number of iron specks. Six recipes follow on fols. 44a–45a in which the sand is replaced by ground porcelain shards. These "low-fired shards, crushed until they were like grains of sand and then passed through a fine sieve,"[432] turned out to be an ideal opening agent; although the paste remained relatively granular, its color was markedly whiter.[433]

Sadly, the notes made on these two pages, to which we shall return in the section on markings on the animal figures, bear no date, but as we shall see, links to certain animal figures show that they originated in the year 1734. The experiments continued, and one year later it was possible for a table of the improvements and inventions of 1735 to contain the following statement: "A new paste has been found and since this invention a number of large pieces have been made successfully; indeed, without this paste it would not be easy to make a success of any pieces."[434]

It is not easy to say which direction developments had taken, and how this later paste was composed. In addition to those of Höroldt's notes which are relevant for the large animal figures, we also have the notes made by the arcanists Samuel Stöltzel and Dr. Petzsch.[435] Although Stöltzel dated one paste 1736, he apparently only had it used to make tableware.[436] In Dr. Petzsch's notes on the arcanum, by contrast, there is a recipe for a "coarse paste": "This paste was given its particular name because the coarsely crushed porcelain shards [...] are mixed into the so-called spoon paste [...]."[437] Although the book has been dated "after 1736" by Helmuth Gröger, and "after August 1737" by Rainer Rückert,[438] it is still possible that the recipe in question was at that time already tried and tested, and was only transcribed from notes no longer known to us when the knowledge of the arcanum was committed to writing. And as one can see from the large animal figures produced in 1735 and 1736 – after which, of course, they were no longer produced at all – these years did see great progress with regard to the purity and whiteness of the paste (fig. 136).

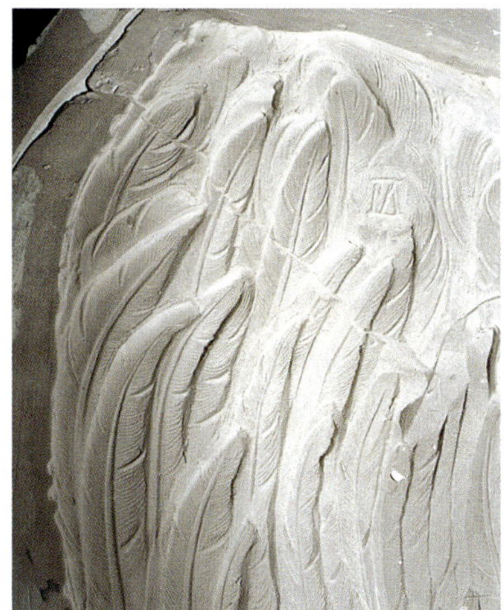

48 Mold-half for the body of the cassowary, twentieth-century plaster mold, produced during the revival of the model, Meissen, mold store (detail)

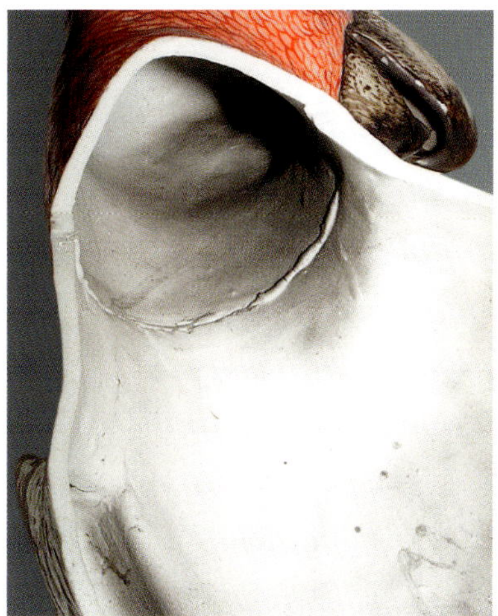

49 View into the head of a broken macaw, with a repairer's join clearly visible, Dresden Porcelain Collection

Again and again, however, the development of the paste did suffer setbacks; each and every stage of the production process – preparation of the paste, glazing, firing – was fraught with risks and could have a decisive influence upon the final appearance of the porcelain pieces in question.

It was not only the proportions of the mixture that could have a decisive bearing on the appearance of the fired porcelain pieces; this was also true, for instance, of the quality of the preliminary treatment given to the component substances. According to Dr. Petzsch's description of the preparation process for the "coarse paste" that was his particular variant for the animal figures, the *Siebenlehner Stein* (feldspar) was first separated out, then washed, "calcined" (burnt down), separated out once again, crushed, ground, wetted, dried, and then finally sieved. The manufactory report for June 1733 reveals that the quantities of paste used for the large animal figures had led to stocks running low; this was how it came about "that the paste-workers made too hasty a job of wetting and cleaning the material and did not take care to carry out the procedure as they should have, which had the negative consequence that some of the porcelain pieces produced since then have come somewhat dark out of the high firing, and lack the pleasing white color."[439] It was very likely these impurities which led to the animal figures of 1733 and 1734 repeatedly emerging from the kiln with dark spots (fig. 58). As nobody could come up with a satisfactory explanation, Höroldt, during the denunciation affair of 1734, put the blame for the "pinckertge Masse" ("spotty paste") onto the arcanist Samuel Stoeltzel,[440] who defended himself against the accusation by pointing out that in July 1734 when there had been a particularly large quantity of spotty pieces he had not even been present at the weighing of the components of the paste and he had no explanation for the phenomenon either.[441]

All the problems surrounding the color, graininess, and plasticity of the paste used for the animal figures were only associated with the large pieces. The Pied Wagtail modeled by Kaendler in February 1733, 25 centimeters in height, was naturally made from a different paste from that he had used half a year before for the Cassowary, 129 centimeters in height (fig. 172). This explains why, for instance, the herons delivered at the end of 1732 are very white and make a genuinely porcelain-like impression; looking at these figures, one would not think that the manufactory was having any problems with the paste (fig. 187). But a glance at the pelican on which work was begun at the same time is enough to see what was giving the manufactory cause for concern (fig. 185). The two figures are nevertheless almost the same height, which shows that in choosing the paste, it was not only the height of the piece which was taken into account; consideration was also given to certain factors related to the shrinkage which took place in the kiln, as we shall see when we come to our section on firing.

The molding

Once the paste had been mixed correctly and let lie for a while, it then became the material finally used by the respective craftsmen – throwers, molders, and repairers – to make pieces of tableware and figures. The molder would press a slice of paste into each of the two separate mold-halves of which each individual part was made up (fig. 48), removed the superfluous paste, coated the edges with slip and pressed the two halves exactly together. After a short time the plaster had absorbed a measure of water from the paste,

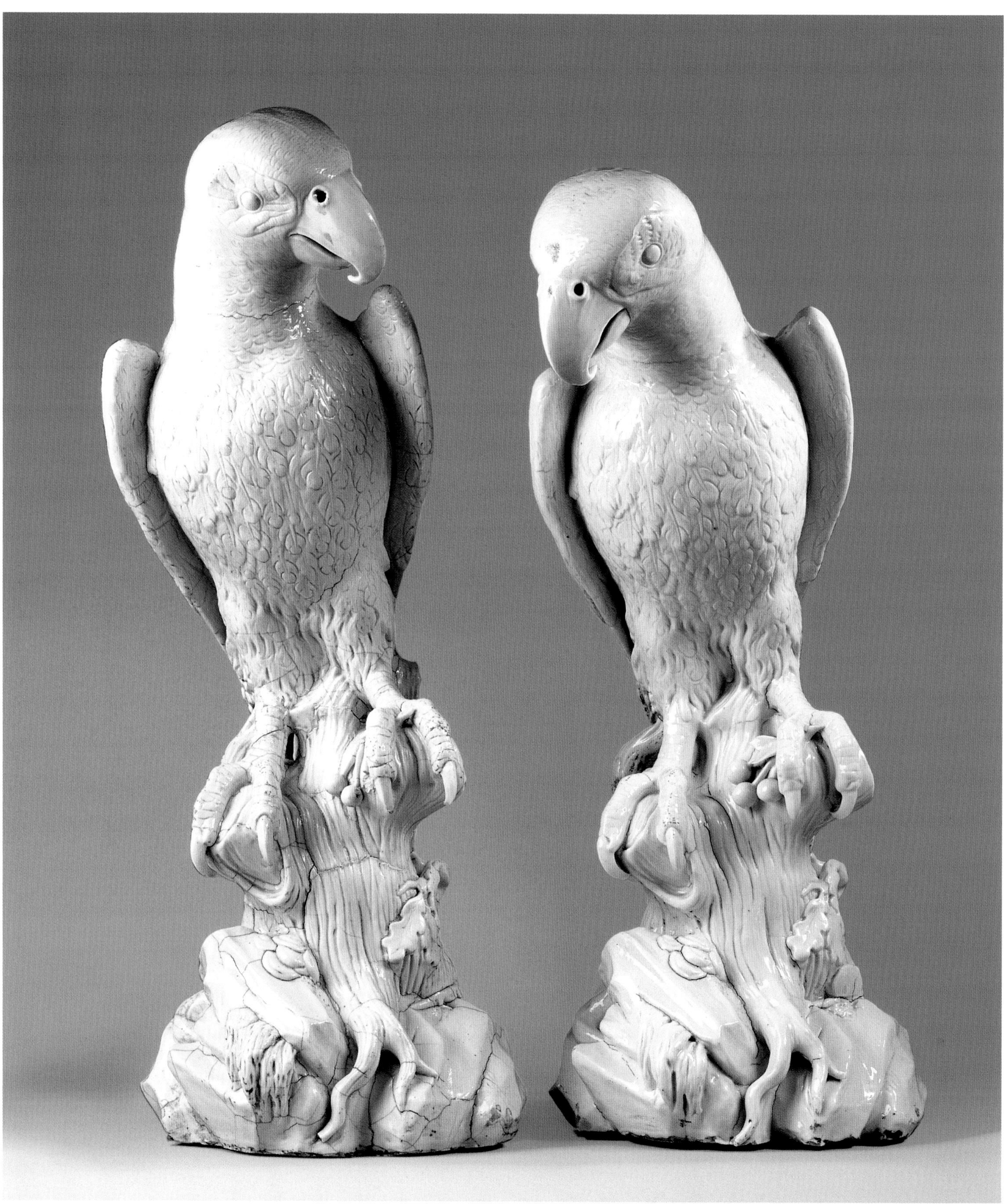

50 Johann Joachim Kaendler, two sitting macaws, the heads attached differently, model 1731, Dresden Porcelain Collection

and the part could be extracted from the mold without difficulty. Likewise using slip, the repairer then assembled the still wet parts to form the figure. On the outside the joins were smoothed over, but were left as they were on the inside (fig. 49). The repairer then touched up all the detail, sharpened the edges, and if necessary put in surface details not present in the mold such as hatching. Freely modeled trimmings are hardly ever to be found on the animal figures. Even the leaves decorating the branch pedestals were taken from molds. The repairer finally made a number of holes in the figure so that the air inside it would be free to expand during the firing and would not cause a rupture. Although some of these air-holes would be positioned so that they could not be seen, or made at "logical" points, for instance in noses or ears, there are many animal figures where they are distributed, sometimes in conspicuously large numbers, in a quite arbitrary fashion.

This procedure opened up possibilities for ringing the changes on one given model, while at the same time also setting limitations on how far these variations could be taken. If two parts did not interlock but had a level interface, it was possible to rotate one of the parts slightly. When this technique was applied to the sitting macaw, no problems were encountered; the head was put on as a single piece, and the result was one macaw looking to the right and one to the left (fig. 50). However, the repairer who wanted to achieve the same effect with Kaendler's 1731 eagle (fig. 163) had to do fundamental retouching on the moldings which were to look to the right; after the quarter-turn, the flaming feather structure, which was already incorporated into the mold, no longer matched the neck, and the repairer had to do some modeling in order to achieve a seamless join. Nevertheless, the very fact that this was

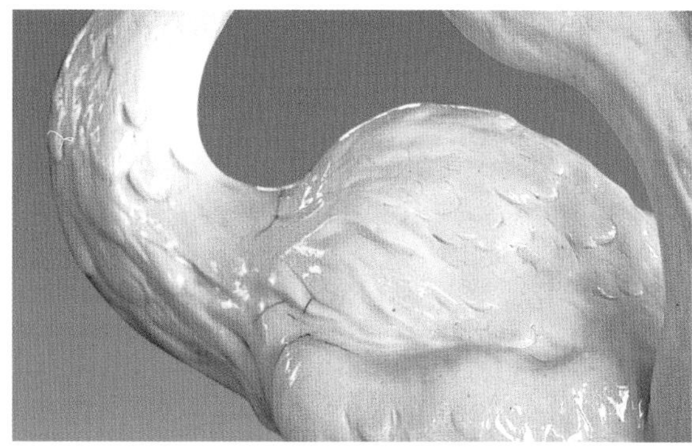

51 Detail of the lower neck on a preening heron, with the feather-structure smudged over, Dresden Porcelain Collection

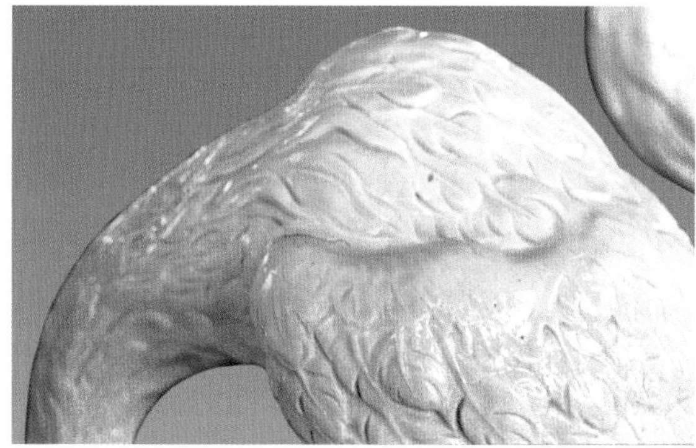

52 Detail of the lower neck on a heron with fish, Dresden Porcelain Collection

53 Johann Gottlieb Kirchner, Mother-Monkey with young, three different repairings, model most likely 1731, Dresden Porcelain Collection

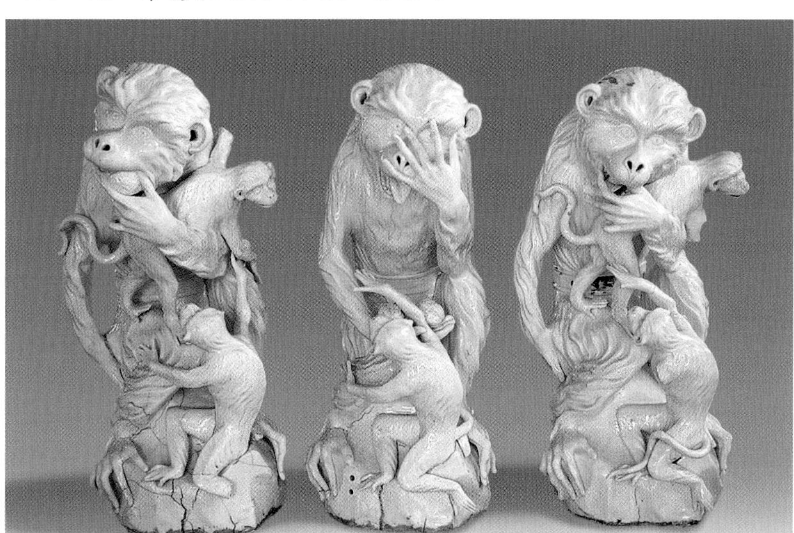

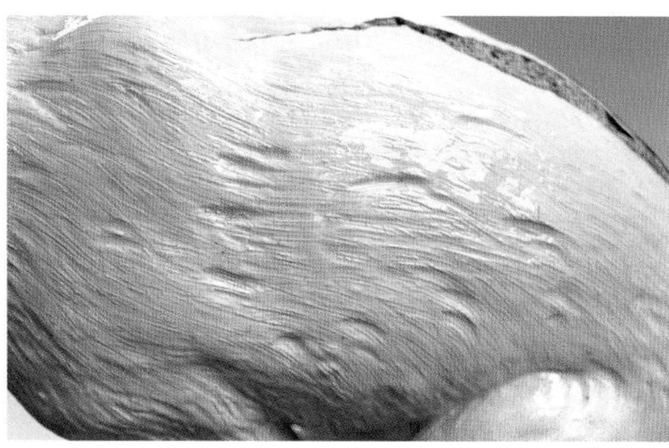

54 Detail of a cat's coat, done with a riffling iron, Dresden Porcelain Collection

possible meant that a matching pair could be made without the modeler having to model two different heads. In this case, when the variant was being made, it was accepted that the *contrapposto*, or balanced asymmetry of posture, was only guaranteed in the eagles looking to the left, and that the optical balance was disturbed in the case of those looking to the right.

Those figures with more extensive variants display even clearer indications of having been retouched; this is the case with the Heron, for which Kaendler modeled two different necks and heads to be attached to the same body. While one heron is busy preening its feathers (fig. 187), the other one holds a fish in its beak (fig. 188). Close examination of the retouching marks visible on the neck joins of the surviving herons shows that the heron with the carp was the original version, and that the heron preening its feathers was the variant. The feathering of the latter is smeared at the join (fig. 51), while in the case of the former the surface detail on the moldings matches perfectly (fig. 52). For several of his birds (the Swan, for instance, figs. 70 and 71) Johann Friedrich Eberlein made two different necks for the same body.

As repairing is an additive procedure, it was also occasionally possible – insofar as it made sense to do so – to leave moldings out or to include extra ones, a fine example of this being the Mother-Monkey (fig. 53). The one with only one young monkey holds a nut in her right hand in front of her stomach and is holding her head with her left hand. In the two other examples of the piece in the Dresden Porcelain Collection, the mother is not only holding a second young monkey on her left arm, but she is also scratching her backside with her right hand and raising her left hand to her mouth – in one case with a nut, and in the other without. The young monkey at the feet of the mother-monkey with a nut is furthermore reaching up to its mother's arm. These things apart, the young monkeys, the pedestals, and the bodies and the heads of the mother-monkey are all identical; that is to say, they came from the same mold. Given the refinement and lively variation inherent in these figures it must be assumed that the artist himself put his hand to the paste, or at least worked out the various interpretations for his model in collaboration with the repairer. The changes are so far-reaching that a craftsman responsible only for realizing the model could not have been allowed to have undertaken them on his own initiative.

In the case of most of the animal figures, however, no variants were made, and it is possible to compare examples of the same piece down to the finest detail, the way the strands of hair go to make up an animal's coat, for instance, without finding any differences beyond the fact of the glaze being somewhat thicker in parts on the one piece than on the other, or a corrugation here and there, added by the repairer to refine the overall structure (fig. 54), a matter to which we shall return with interest in the section on forgeries.

Thus far we have considered some of the aesthetic consequences of the repairer's work; now we shall turn our attention to a number of concrete historical facts related to the order for animal figures which make it clear how very important the molding process was.

Taking moldings and assembling them to form a figure in porcelain paste was – and still is – a highly demanding task, with far-reaching consequences for the end product. In the case of the large animals, the wall of the hollow figure had to be of even thickness, and what is more, gradually get thinner towards the top. The problem was familiar not only to the experienced molders, but also to the modelers. In 1734, Kaendler had the following to say on the subject: "It is remarkable that as a result of Hofkommissar Höroldt doing his job so badly, it was not ensured that the porcelain pieces had sides of uniform thickness; instead, porcelain pieces were two inches thick at some points, at others half an inch, or even a quarter of an inch, and if anyone needs to have this proven to them I am ready to show them a number of large broken pieces which were ruined because of this failing. This kind of unevenness results in the different surfaces not being compatible with each other; as the thin points cannot resist the pressure from the thicker points then the whole thing tears in two in the fire. This is what caused the large cracks on the pieces for the Royal Palace, as was dutifully and officially noted, but nothing changed as the present Commission did nothing to remedy the situation."[442]

For the molders this problem was a technical obstacle which could be overcome with sufficient experience, but for the repairers it was an aesthetic challenge. Kaendler accused Höroldt, who allotted the tasks, of always having six to eight copies of the same animal molded straightaway, with the result that there was no opportunity to learn from observing the behavior of the figure in the kiln. Höroldt's answer was that a procedure of this kind would last too long, especially since a number of weeks had to be allowed to let the piece dry, and time was short. But he continued by arguing that there were also artistic reasons for his way of going about things, "because the molder has to learn from the first one [molded figure] in the series how he is to manage to get the thickness and thinness right, because he cannot think about the problem properly while the pieces are still in the mold, and must actually see the pieces before he can work out a solution."[443] According to this argument it was also important for the repairer to have a number of further identical figures to assemble, so that he – given that by that time he could no longer refer to the artist's model, which of course no longer existed – could establish how best to assemble the individual pieces. To help him there were markings made on the joins, but it was possible for a given part, a head for example, to be attached at a slightly different angle, which was sometimes done, as described above, in order to achieve variants.

Another area in which the repairer had to acquire experience was related to the moistness of the moldings; if drying cracks were to be avoided, it was of the greatest importance to ensure that the pieces to be assembled to form any one figure should all be, approximately, equally moist. In his criticisms of Höroldt, Kaendler claimed that this task had sometimes been carried out unsatisfactorily, having been entrusted to a less gifted craftsman working against the clock, and one can well understand his indignation, born of a true artist's concern to see his model executed as faithfully as possible.[444] These craftsmen were furthermore specialists, with a special understanding either of taking moldings (especially regarding the thickness of the walls), or of repairing (assembling and finishing). It was incomprehensible to Kaendler that Fritzsche, who was the best molder, should be used as a repairer, as repairing and taking moldings called for quite different technical and aesthetic capabilities.[445]

It was for practical reasons such as these that the craftsmen involved with the large animal figures worked as a team. As we have already seen, the molder Christoph Mueller and the repairer Carl Friedrich Krumbholz formed a team, if not permanently, then for a certain length of time at least. In 1732, when George Fritzsche was first used as a repairer by Höroldt,[446] Johann Georg Schlicke worked with him as molder. In order not to waste time, animal figures were usually manufactured by a team of this kind: "These large pieces are never signed, as it is easy to find out who the repairer was, as normally any one certain model is always realized by the same man [or team]."[447]

We can verify this statement by examining the three cats in the Dresden Porcelain Collection, one of which has a marking indicating that it was the work of the repairer Andreas Schiefer. It is indeed the case that on all three figures the texture of the fur is suggested by a distinctive detailed hatching. In the case of this figure this surface detail was to be executed by the repairer, while in many other figures it was already incorporated in the mold (fig. 54). Because of the coarse and granular consistency of the paste, the execution of such fine strokes as these caused the repairers the greatest problems, as did the retouching of the smaller details. But the degree of gravity they attributed to these problems varied according to which party they supported in the denunciation affair.

The statement made by the Höroldt protégé Albrecht was reported as follows: "It was not possible to execute the small strokes so exactly in the coarse paste, but on the other hand many of the animals were smooth, as far as this was possible with the coarse paste. Even with the fine paste,[448] the fine strokes could not be done as well as they could in clay."[449] In saying this he was clearly making a stand against Kaendler's demand that the porcelain moldings should accord with his clay model right down to the finest details.

Johann Friedrich Schmieder is reported as having given a different account of the problem: "[...] the coarse paste resulted in bad figures because it was impossible to do any decorative strokework on them at the repairing or retouching stage; it was only possible to use a sponge or a cratching brush, and the paste was so coarse, containing little pieces like grains of scouring sand, that when he was working, pieces were torn out and he had to use a little curved knife. The pieces made from such a coarse paste would neither have stood up to the firing, and if they had then they would not have had a good appearance."[450] Johann George Schlicke, who worked with Kaendler's favorite Fritzsche, backed him up with the effectively exaggerated claim that when he was doing the finishing, pieces not only broke out of the paste, but also sometimes tore open his skin causing blood to run down over his fingers.[451]

All these statements make it clear that Kaendler was not the only one to be dissatisfied with the way his models were being executed. After all, the repairers could see for themselves what degrees of finesse and effectiveness was being achieved in the small figures.

Once the figures had been assembled and given their finishing touches, they still had to be left in the air to dry out completely before being fired. Dr. Petzsch had the following to say about this stage: "Once they have been molded, these pieces [the large ones], are left for six or eight weeks in the molders' room or the storeroom, with some being left even longer according to how the thick or thin the body has been made."[452] After this drying period, the pieces were subjected to the *Glühbrand*, or low firing, at 800–900 °C, which gave the piece a certain firmness, so that, still being porous, it could absorb the glaze without dissolving in it.

The glaze

The distinction between body and glaze is a familiar feature of almost all types of ceramic production. As well as sealing the porous ceramic body, the glaze also preserves any decoration already applied, or it may be applied for purely aesthetic reasons. In the case of European hard porcelain of the kind manufactured in Meissen, the glaze is not applied to seal the body, but rather to make pieces destined for everyday use easier to clean and more hygienic, and, especially in the case of figurative pieces, to allow for permanent, eye-catching decoration with fired enamel colors. The enveloping flow of the glaze around the ceramic body not only puts a smooth

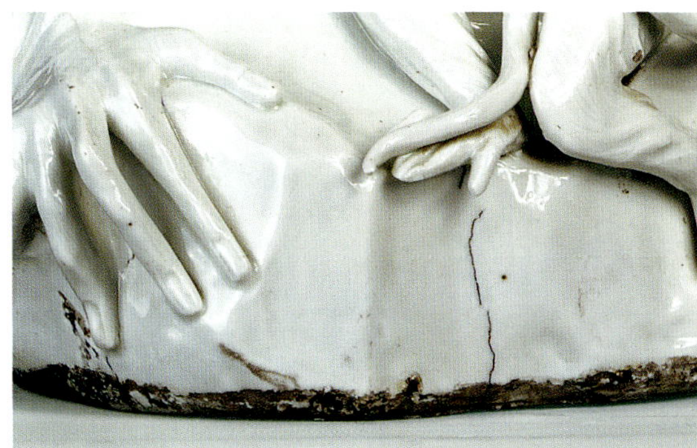

55 Unglazed ring around the bottom of a monkey figure, Dresden Porcelain Collection

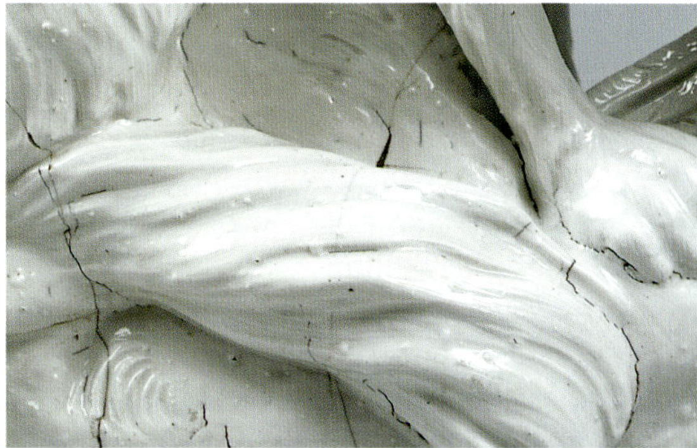

56 Glaze with small bubbles in the glaze on the tail of a fox, Dresden Porcelain Collection

surface on any sharp points or edges, but also gives the piece the glorious shine typical of true porcelain.

Essentially, porcelain glaze is made of the same substances as the paste, but in different proportions, and the raw materials have to be given the same kind of preliminary treatment as those used for the paste. At Meissen there was a special glaze-mill precisely for this purpose. The finely ground ingredients are mixed in the right proportions and then thinned down with water to form a more or less liquid glaze.

In the case of small pieces, the glaze was normally applied by immersion. Having been fired once, the body was relatively stable, but it was still absorbent enough to take in a certain amount of the liquid, leaving behind a powdery layer of glaze on the surface. In the case of the large animal figures, there were a number of reasons why immersion was not possible. Firstly, it would have necessitated huge tubs and equally huge quantities of glaze slip; furthermore, after their first firing, the heavy figures were riddled with cracks and were to be carried around as little as possible.

Dr. Petzsch's highly detailed description of the glazing procedure for the large animal figures covers twenty-three pages of his arcanum notebook and was probably written in the mid-1730s.[453] It relates how the smaller figures were dipped in the slip by two men working together, and how glaze was subsequently applied with a brush to the places where the figures had been held. It was all much more complicated with the larger figures: "Those figures, particularly animals and birds, which are too big to be dunked in the glaze by two workers, or indeed too delicate to be picked up, have to be as it were basted." The piece was placed on a wooden stretcher above an empty tub, together with the "low-fired lid," that is to say a tray-like platter, on which it had stood for the firings. The lid-shaped underpiece had to be covered with a layer of "gravel" ("Kiesel"), possibly crushed chamotte, so that the base of the figure would not be fired into one with the platter when superfluous glaze ran off the piece in the high firing. Petzsch gives a detailed account of the importance of the platter being made of the same paste as the figure, so that they would shrink to the same extent during firing. Had the piece been placed directly on the floor of the kiln, then the relatively large pressure of its own weight would have been in opposition to the shrinkage, which would have led to cracks at the base.

One worker then gave the glaze slip a protracted and energetic stir while another fetched ordinary clay to make small slabs, and lengths in the shape of thin sausages. The small slabs were used to close up the orifices of "animals with open jaws" and any small holes were stopped with paper plugs, so that the glaze would be prevented from running into the inside of the hollow figure, "from which it would be impossible to pour out the glaze quickly, and cracks would result." Two fellow-workers then took the lengths of clay and laid them along the edge of the base of the figure, "pressing them firmly onto the underpiece and figure and giving them an extra coat of slip to make sure that none of the glaze would end up under the figure." The workers were then to wash their hands to prevent any clay from contaminating the glaze.

Two workers, or perhaps three, depending on the size of the figure, now filled jugs with glaze and stood on either side of the figure; if it was a long animal, then an additional worker stood at its head. Each worker had a wet sponge to hand, "in case the flow of the glaze should congest at any point, so that he could mop it up." If the figure had overhangs, then the workers also had basins with glaze. When all is ready, they put two stools by the tub, especially if it is a tall figure and they consider that without stools they will not be able to cover the figure with glaze properly. They then stir the glaze with spatulas, climb with their glaze-jugs onto the stools, and pour glaze onto the figure, each from his respective side, until they see that the glaze is starting to run down [that is to say, when the biscuit stops absorbing glaze]. When those with the basins full of glaze notice that parts, mainly below overhanging sections, are not covered with glaze, they pour or sponge it on from their basins." When the figure was saturated, that is to say, when the glaze started running off the figure, then the glazers got up on their stools again and mopped up any pools of glaze which

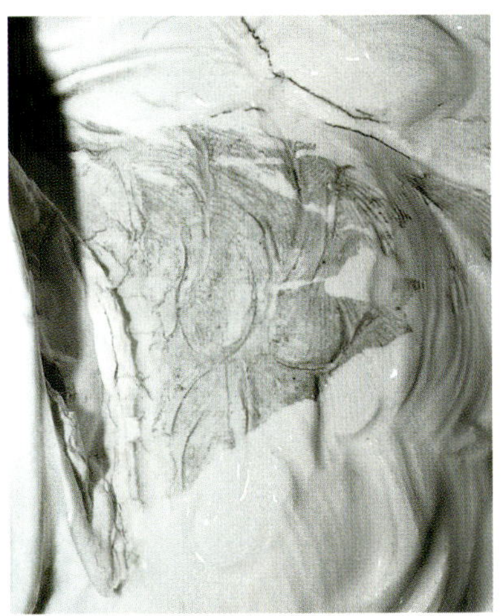

57 A patch that remained unglazed on the wing of a cockerel, Dresden Porcelain Collection

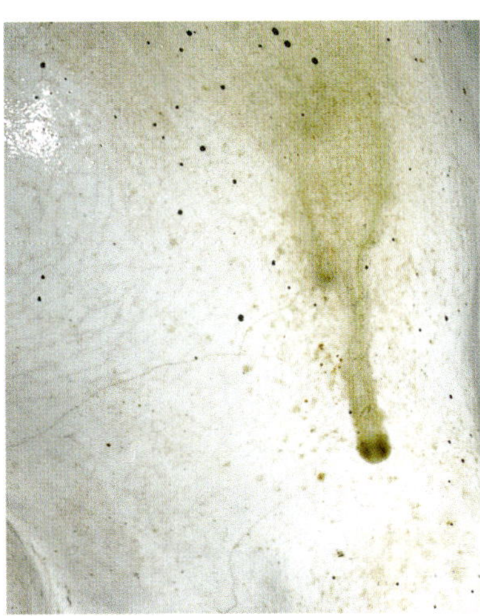

58 Discoloring in the glaze, a drip, and black spots on a leopard, Dresden Porcelain Collection

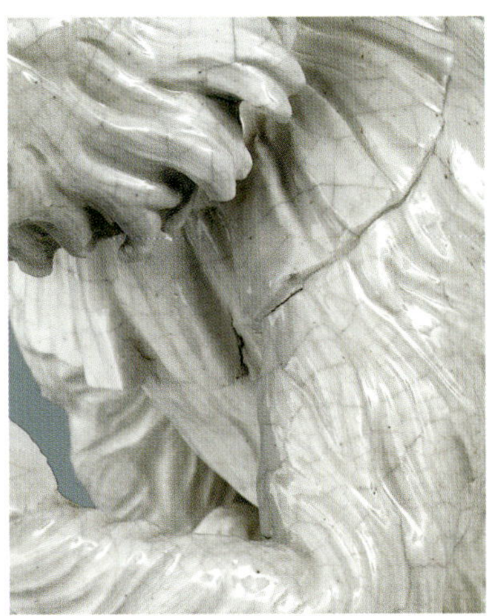

59 Head of a monkey wearing a ruff, with crazing in the glaze, Dresden Porcelain Collection

had formed in the depressions. Superfluous glaze was likewise mopped off the stretcher and the underpiece.

"Finally, they take out the little slabs and remove the pieces of clay from the figure, cutting them away with knives where the sausages were pressed so hard that they stuck to the foot of the figure." Glaze was then applied with a brush at points the flow had not reached, and to those edges onto which the disks had been pressed. Once the glaze had dried, the figure could be handed over for the high firing.

The animal figures still show the marks of these steps having been carried out. Almost all the large pieces have an unglazed strip along the base where the clay sausage was applied to prevent the figure from sticking during the firing (fig. 55). Although the glazers were supposed to take great care over any overhangs not reached by the glaze, it is still common to find unglazed patches on the animal figures (fig. 57), allowing us to see clearly the sharpness of the surface work done by the repairers. In the case of some figures which are open on the underside, the glaze reached a short way up into the inside cavity, but the animals remained as a rule unglazed on the inside, as required by Petzsch.

An account has already been given of the difficulties encountered in the quest for a porcelain paste suitable for large figures, and the difficulties encountered in the quest for a suitable glaze were very similar. The historical sources, however, do not always differentiate between paste and glaze, and it is often reported that the porcelain pieces are simply poor in their overall appearance, not beautiful to look at, discolored, and so on.

In the case of the some of the large animal figures from the first years, it is a fact that body and glaze cannot easily be distinguished (fig. 47); the glaze on some of the early animals is cloudy and porous, with a leathery, matt surface.

On one occasion in October 1732, having returned from Poland the day before, Augustus the Strong betook himself to the Japanese Palace, where he expressed criticism both of the paste and of the glaze of the animal figures he saw there.[454] The glaze was neither whitening the gray body nor countering its coarse texture.

As had been the case with the paste, the manufactory started a wave of experiments, evidence for which is visible on the pieces today in the form of discolorations, dripping (fig. 58), crazing on the surfaces (fig. 59), and little bubbles (fig. 56). The baneful fact that mistakes made during assembly usually only became apparent after firing is reflected in the monthly report of the Commission for August 1734, according to which of the twenty-five firings made by Dr. Petzsch in the course of the month, five brought forth spotty porcelain, "with a sandy glaze," all of which had to be rejected as "brac."[455] It did sometimes happen that the causes were recognized; in a report of an investigation dated July 20, 1739, for instance, it was pointed out that "some time before" a certain amount of iron had been ground off the glaze-mill, contaminating the raw materials and giving the glaze a yellow color that only became visible after the firing.[456]

Two particularly conspicuous glaze-related phenomena can still be observed on figures today, the first on the Lion in the Metropolitan Museum of Art, New York (fig. 61). The somewhat matt and strongly crazed glaze of this figure has a distinctly blue coloring, the greenish shade of blue being particularly clearly recognizable in all the depressions where the glaze layer is somewhat thicker than elsewhere. The paste is furthermore very granular, and large parts are covered with a fine brown net-like veil (not crackle). The reason for the blue coloring has not been established with certainty. The mishap perhaps came about because someone had the idea that the addition of small amount of blue would make a dirty

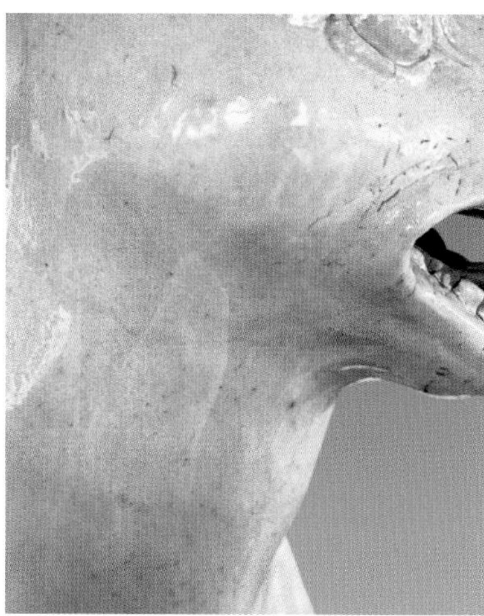

60 White shading with paintbrush traces, a consequence of Höroldt's instruction that unglazed pieces should be given a coat of white slip made from tableware paste, seen here on a lynx's neck, Dresden Porcelain Collection

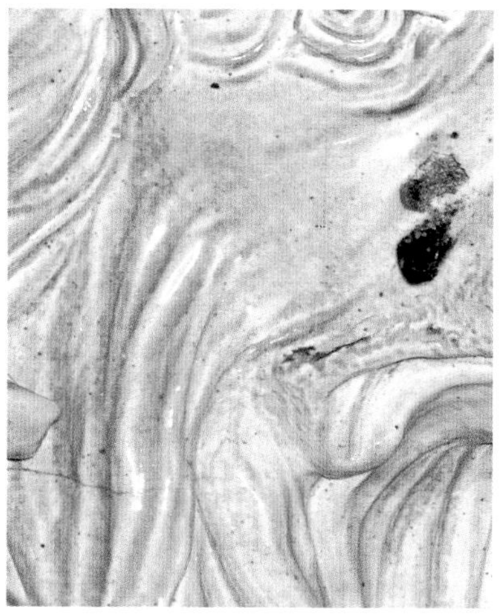

61 Bluish discoloring in the glaze and a large iron stain on the head of a lion, Metropolitan Museum of Art, New York

paste look whiter. Or it could have been a genuine accident. Traces of cobalt could have remained as impurities in the mills where the glaze was prepared, giving it a blue tint; or unintentional friction on the iron bars of the mill could have resulted in a fine iron dust, or indeed rust, ending up in the glaze mixture, which would have had the same effect. Similarly, reduction-roasted iron oxide, that is to say iron oxide burnt in the absence of oxygen, is used in Far Eastern ceramics to color glazes blue and green.[457] As this lion was otherwise successfully fired and was in any case to be painted with cold colors, it was retained while the other pieces spoiled by this faulty glaze were rejected. According to the arcanists' complaints in the reports for the months September to November of 1732, (when, as we know from a list, two lions were being prepared for firing),[458] it had been noted, "that after certain recent firings, the glazes of some porcelain pieces delivered were greyish and looked as if they had been sprayed with blue."[459] We cannot be certain whether this statement refers to the lion or just to another similar occurrence, especially as the – admittedly rather simple – records only refer to tableware, and furthermore to the "blaue Masse" ("blue paste") used for wares to be painted in underglaze blue: "if the black coloring and blue spraying effect persist, and given that pieces affected in this way have been found in almost all recent firings, which causes great damage to the manufactory, then it must be asked, given that these things have never been noted in the so-called blue paste, what can be the reason for these things. OberMeister H. Stölzel assures us most certainly that the spottiness on the wares can be remedied [...] if the raw materials are cleaned more thoroughly, and that it should not last longer than four weeks more."[460]

We are better informed about a second phenomenon apparent on the figures. It is illuminating that efforts were made to use the glaze to whiten the greyish appearance of the paste. The extent to which glazes were used to which tin had been added to make them a cloudy white color has yet to be established.[461] It is true that according to Stöltzel's notes on "how the porcelain pastes and glazes were prepared by the undersigned," made in a report dated April 9, 1731, "a beautiful shiny white color was acquired in firing by a fluid glaze" consisting of one part Colditz clay, one part quartz, one part English tin ash, and other ingredients.[462] We do not know whether this glaze was later used for the large animal figures; there is indeed even reason to doubt this, as a glaze made according to this recipe would have destroyed not only all the fine linework, but also the impression of depth, and thus the last vestiges of any typically porcelain-like effect. It was rather the case, as we know from the report of Kaendler's accusations, that Höroldt used another method to try to make the animals look whiter: "Finally he [Kaendler] recalls that the Herr Hofkommissar had the palace pieces painted five or six times over with good paste, which ruined all the artistry expended upon them even before the glaze was applied."[463] Although this evidence that Höroldt was simply using the old ceramic technique of applying a layer of *engobe*, or slip, one can well imagine how the coat of slip must have filled up the fine linework on the body. On some figures remnant traces of the brushwork are still clearly visible below the glaze (fig. 60).

The firing process and the problem of shrinkage

"Artistic sculpture is an especially good and praiseworthy thing when applied to the making of pieces in porcelain. While there are great differences between wood, stone, and clay, there is a world of difference between these and porcelain. In wood, stone and clay, the figure remains exactly as it leaves the sculptor's hands, but in the case of porcelain, it is only in the all-transforming heat of the fire that it is finished and brought to perfection."[464] In this blithe and seemingly self-evident statement, Höroldt put his finger on what was in fact one of the manufactory's central problems in connection with the large animal figures. With its temperatures of around 1400°C, the high, or smooth, firing was indeed the stage which determined whether the laborious work of the modeler, formers, and repairers was to bear fruit or come to nothing. The preparation of the paste apart, the stages which preceded the full firing were not in essence different from those used in other fields of art ceramics. In the case of porcelain, however, the "magical effect of the fire" ideally transformed the unattractive, light brown to light grey biscuit with its powdery layer of glaze into a brilliantly white, shining material with chemical and physical properties quite different from those it had before the firing.

The kilns used in Meissen in the first half of the eighteenth century were horizontal tunnel-kilns. The gases heated by the fire burning under the opening at the front of the kiln wafted through the tunnel and escaped at the back up the chimney.[465] As this resulted in a variety of different temperatures in the firing area, a good measure of experience was needed to know what positions were best for the various kinds of pieces with their different thicknesses and paste compositions. Findings from archaeological excavations in the Albrechtsburg castle courtyard have, in combination with the relevant records, made it possible to establish the chronology of the various kiln-housings.[466] The construction of a new kiln was not only necessitated by money or space; as there was a constant need for greater capacity,[467] the technical requirements also became more and more demanding. The large porcelain pieces ordered for the Japanese Palace also required a new measure of kiln space: "Although the various large vases and all kinds of large birds [...] which have been ordered by Your Royal Majesty have been brought through to a certain production stage, they cannot be high-fired and brought to complete perfection until the new kilns have been constructed. In the meantime a test has been carried out with a vase in the one already existing large kiln, and it has turned out quite well [...]."[468] However, the practice hinted at here of firing large pieces at the same time as normal tableware was not an ideal one. It involved the use of a number of different pastes, and the size of the large pieces would furthermore seem to have disturbed the firing process: "[...] or the fire in the kilns which had been changed to accommodate the large pieces was not steady enough."[469] According to the Commission's report of December 1731, two new and larger full-firing kilns were in the process of being constructed, and they went into operation in 1732, at first as low-firing kilns.[470] They must have been of a size to correspond with the demands of the Japanese Palace project, as in his 1734 catalog of criticisms of Höroldt, Kaendler lamented the fact that, "the large full-firing kilns, built to Höroldt's specifications, brought about more damage, as a great number of empty saggers had to be used, and the porcelain did not fire as well as it had done before, cracking and turning out dark, and grey, and too thick [...]."[471]

The saggers referred to here by Kaendler were cylindrical lidded containers into which the objects were put for the full firing; they protected the wares from flying ash and flames, and their insulating properties also ensured that the wares cooled slowly after the firing. The fact that they were thrown on the wheel meant that there were limits to how big they could be; even two sagger-throwers together could not have achieved the size that would have been necessary for the large animal figures,[472] which were protected in the kiln using a method of which the arcanist Dr. Petzsch wrote a detailed account, as he had done for the glazing procedure.[473]

The firers fetched the glazed animal figures from the *Glasurstube* (glazing room) and lifted the piece "into the kiln on its stretcher, and then took the greatest care over removing it from the same; lifting it onto the lid [= underpiece], they then placed it on the prepared ground." This prepared ground inside the kiln consisted, according to the height of the animal, of one or more layers of old tableware saggers, placed tightly against each other with their joins being covered over with clay. It was intended that the figure should reach almost up to the ceiling of the kiln. Sausage-like lengths of clay were pushed beneath the underpiece to ensure that the figure did not wobble and stood exactly upright. The figure was then surrounded with "little saucer, bowls, or plate saggers, all of which had to be old [that is to say, fired and not subject to further shrinkage]," all the gaps once again being sealed with clay. The structure was then topped with an arch-shaped piece, and the space between the arch and the wall of saggers was filled in with further small saggers, shards, and bricks, all sealed up with clay. It was only at the back, towards the flue, that the filling was not sealed up, allowing the air inside to expand and to cool more efficiently once the firing was over.

In this way, an oversize sagger was built around the figure and right up to the ceiling of the kiln. This was a very laborious procedure which also involved at least those saggers on the side also being filled with wares to be fired. "Wares to be fired are to be put into as many of the saggers as possible, and these surround the large pieces."[474]

Kaendler had an interest in all the production stages which his models were to pass through and would naturally have been interested in seeing this procedure. In 1734, however, he still did not have access to the firing house, a restriction which was to become an important bone of contention in the denunciation affair. His criticism of Höroldt was that woodcutters and bricklayers were working in the firing house and thereby causing a great deal of damage, "in that finished pieces had to pass through such inexperienced and clumsy hands, which was why most of the pieces for the King had lost legs, ears, or snouts."[475] The situation was particularly frustrating for the artist in that when he was designing a model, he had to take account of the vagaries of the firing process and to accept the limitations that these brought with them.

All ceramic materials shrink during the production process. While the paste shrinks relatively little when drying, its shrinkage during firing can be considerable. When porcelain is subjected to full firing, it undergoes a change in its microstructure (fusion), which causes it to shrink by up to one sixth of it volume, and to lose its porosity and become waterproof. Those responsible for the manufacturing process were of course fully aware of this transformation, and the modelers had to learn to make models which took account of the way in which the paste shrank, or to find other solutions to this problem.

In the case of the large figures, the fact that the contraction of the paste was in opposition to the figure's own weight often led to cracks at the base. This explains how it happened that Kaendler, during the denunciation affair, presented the Commission with a new invention which involved "the placing of rollers under the large pieces to prevent them being torn apart at floor level where the weight from above made them incapable of tolerating shrinkage to the degree the upper parts could, and demonstrated it with rollers brought along for that very purpose."[476] As he himself said, he had been given the idea by his father-in-law, the Dresden faience-manufacturer Eggebrecht, who had used this technique when producing large wares in Berlin. He added that it would also be possible to use ball bearings, but there is no evidence that this invention was ever tried out.

That the manufactory was aware of one further aspect of shrinkage suffered in the kiln is shown by Höroldt's note to the effect that "the paste shrinks more in the vertical than in the horizontal plane, as we have found out from bitter experience."[477] He accused Kaendler of making models which did not take sufficient account of this phenomenon, the explanation for which is the simple fact of the force of gravity. And as can be seen from the modeler's suggestion of using rollers, Kaendler did indeed work on the assumption that in most cases it was the techniques that had to be made to fit his artistry, and not vice versa.

The pernicious effects of shrinkage are still visible on most of the large animal figures. Kaendler's models for the Heron (fig. 187) and the Pelican (fig. 185), for example, were made within months of each other. Although the two figures are roughly the same height, the former is more vertically structured and the latter, especially at the base, more horizontally orientated. While most of the herons fired successfully, and it was therefore possible to use a paste which gave the figure a finer appearance, the sheer volume of the pelicans, and the large surface area of the base, resulted in extensive cracks.

Along with the color and granularity of the paste, these cracks constituted one of the main problems encountered in the manufacture of the large animal figures. And in addition to the problems already described related to unsuitable paste compositions, both the low and the high firings were fraught with hidden dangers which could lead to the figure partially breaking at the side.

One cause of cracking in the light firing was moisture on inside surfaces which had not been exposed to the air enough to dry out properly. Those responsible for the manufacturing process were aware both of the problem and of its causes; in February 1732 they stated that although a number of elephants and rhinoceroses had been done in paste, they had not yet dried out for long enough to be fired.[478] The drying phase, particularly in the case of the animal figures, could sometimes be several weeks long, but as the pressure of orders increased, those responsible often did not wait this long before firing them. In March 1735, Kaendler modeled a large bittern,[479] and the first three figures were full-fired in May.[480] Given that there were a good number of procedures to be carried out between the model stage and the light firing, it is likely that the time allowed for drying was far from generous. This is borne out by Kaendler's criticism: "Many accidents can be avoided at the manufactory if the wares are given enough time to dry, which has often not been the case, the wares being put into the kiln still damp and as a result very liable to split."[481]

The cracking problem was a different one when it came to the full firing, the point of which was to bring the figure to fusion point, that is to say to that relatively circumscribed temperature zone at which the structure of the paste changes, becomes more dense, "vitrifies," or in other words, turns into porcelain. If higher temperatures than this are reached, the figure enters the dangerous zone in which the material softens and becomes deformed. The bigger a piece is, the heavier is the pressure of its own weight on the lower parts, where there is a correspondingly greater danger of deformations, or at points under very great pressure, of actual ruptures. In the case of the animal figures it was particularly the bases which ended up with multiple gaping fissures (fig. 67), as the modelers were quite aware: "As for the bases on which the figures stood, it was his [Kaendler's] wish that they should always be made rather thick and fat, so that they would hold better in the firing."[482]

The limitations dictated by the material were however not just ones of overall size, but also of thickness, the large animals having to be hollow, as solid figures would never have survived the firing. In order to make the figures stable, particularly in the perilous base area, experiments were carried out using various designs and support constructions.

62 Lion with completely open base, Dresden Porcelain Collection

63 Lion with partially open base, Metropolitan Museum of Art, New York

64 Lion with closed base, Dresden Porcelain Collection

65 Interior of a sitting macaw with a cylindrical support structure to stabilize the figure during firing, Dresden Porcelain Collection

66 Interior of a monkey with grape, with buttresses to stabilize the figure during firing, Dresden Porcelain Collection

67 Base of a fox, with large holes for better air circulation in the kiln, Dresden Porcelain Collection

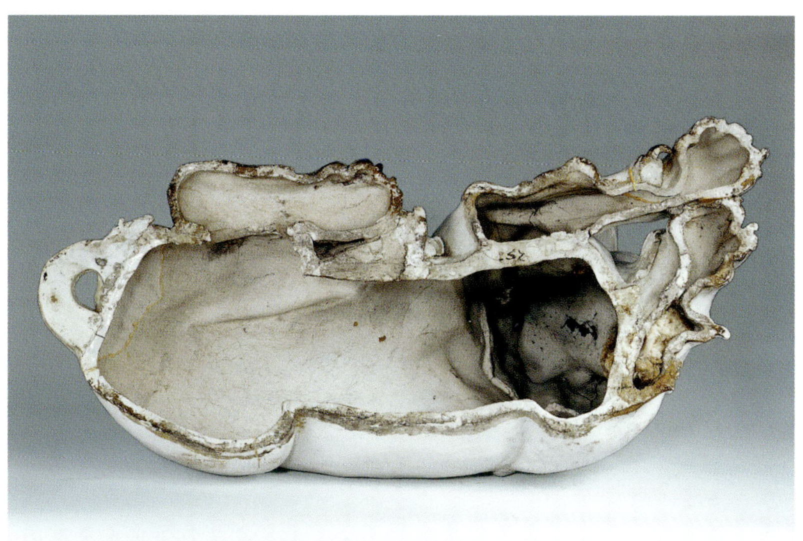

62

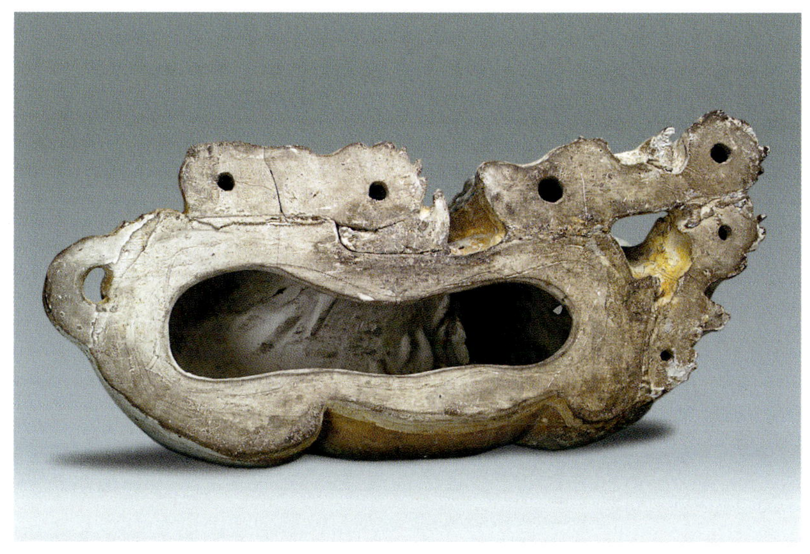

63

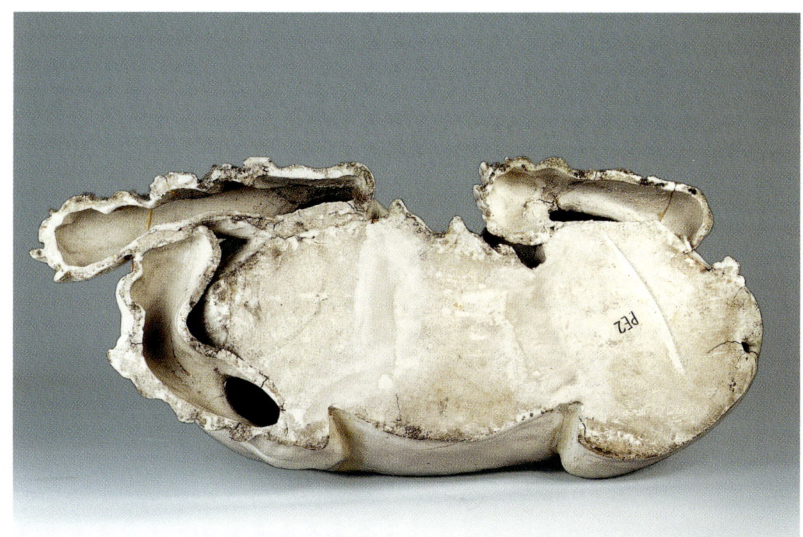

64

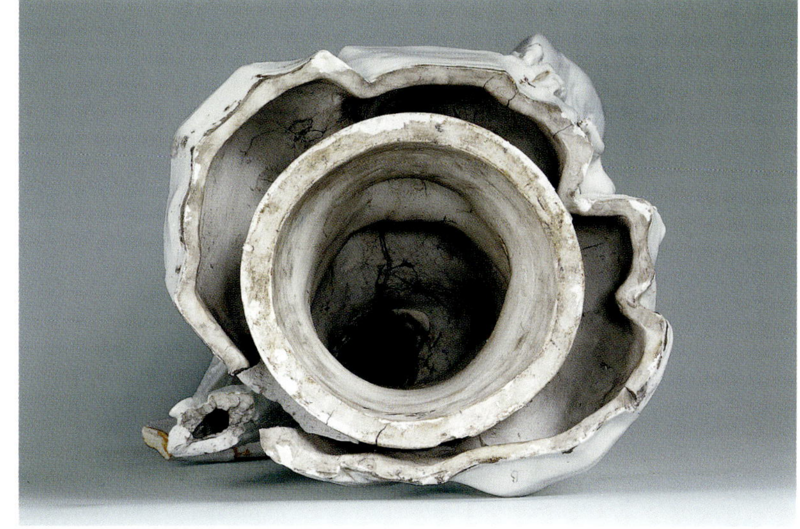

65

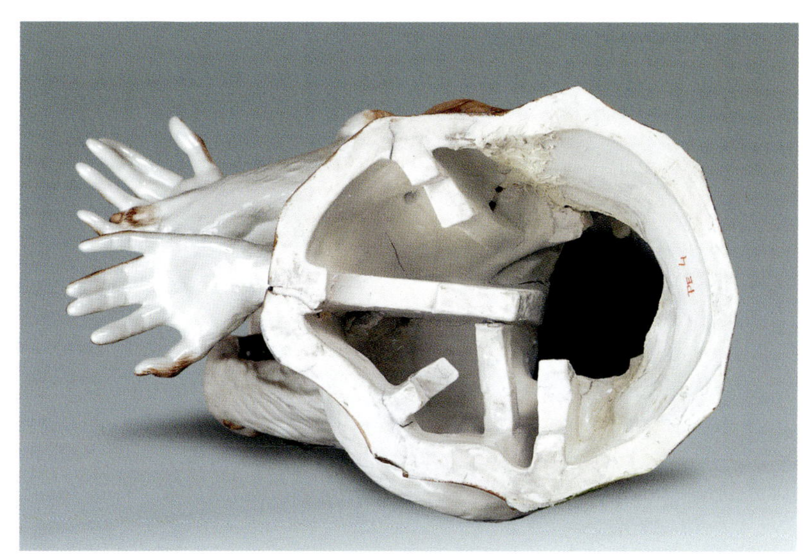

66

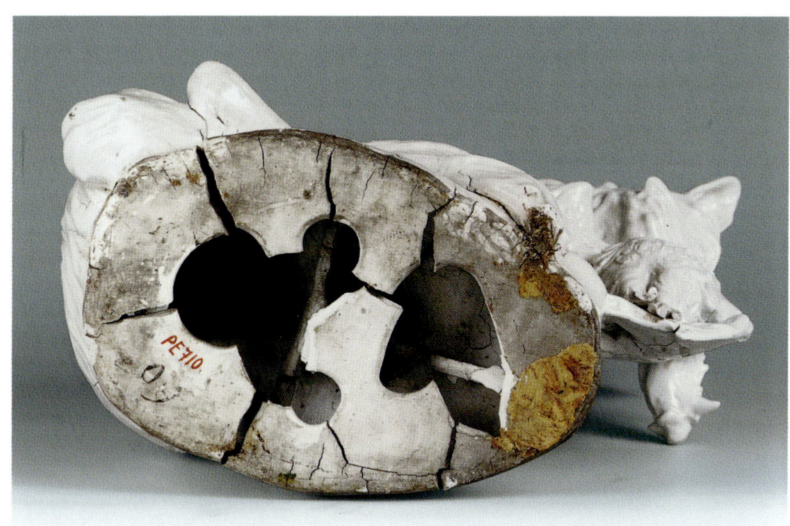

67

Some of the figures have completely open bases (fig. 62), and some have a plate extending over part of the bottom (fig. 64); alternatively, these two solutions are combined in a broad edging positioned along the side of the base with the intention of preventing vertical cracks (figs. 63 and 67). It was not the case that one kind of base was used uniformly for all the pieces made from one particular model; on the contrary, various bases were tried out on successive executions of the same model.

A further means of stabilizing the figures was the bracing up of the inside of the base with plates and cylinders, a technique used particularly for the middle-size figures. It was especially the case with birds and monkeys sitting on rocks or tree-trunks that their weight was situated directly above the cavity of the base, and it was this weight that the buttress-like plate of paste (fig. 66) – or, in the case of bigger figures such as the Macaw, larger cylindrical structures (fig. 65) – was intended to support. Interior scaffolding of this kind provided a partial solution to the problem of figures having a tendency to fire-cracks at critical points, which in the case of any one model could however only be fully recognized once a number of pieces had failed in the firing.

All these stabilization measures had to be taken in the course of the molding and assembly of a figure. But even before that, the particular behavior of porcelain in the kiln had to be taken into consideration in the modeling, unless the modeler wanted to see all his works come to grief in the firing. This applied not only to the base area but also to the figure's whole composition and structure. Every horizontal part which was not anchored or supported in some way had a tendency to sag and tear in the firing. In the case of very tall models, furthermore, the volume of paste had to decrease constantly towards the top.

Höroldt complained emphatically that Kaendler did not take account of these limitations in his models, which was why his figures were destined to fail from the outset: "Kaendler was shown the pieces that had gone wrong so that he might learn from them how not to make the same mistakes in the future."[483] The whole unhappy story of the large animal figures was the result of "Kaendler's bad composition, and nothing else."[484] And although Kirchner's carefully conceived models may have resulted in rather static-seeming figures, it was indeed the case that they did not bring with them the kind of problems which Kaendler's did. On the other hand, one only has to take a closer look at some of Kaendler's first animal figures to see quite clearly that Höroldt simply wanted to put the blame onto someone else for the failure of certain pieces. Kaendler had indeed come up against real difficulties in his first two genuinely large models, the first eagle (1731), and the one of a wisent fighting with a wild boar. In the former case, it was the slightly raised wings which threatened to be an obstacle to success (fig. 163), and in the latter it was the wisent's free-standing legs, which were relatively thin in comparison with the overall mass of the figure (fig. 116). Quite apart from the smaller animal figures from his first creative year, the heron he modeled in March 1732 shows that even at this early stage he already had a complete grasp of the way in which the material behaved (fig. 187). The bird's thin legs, which could on their own never have borne the weight of the body in the kiln, are supported by rushes. This way of holding bird figures up by putting supports between their legs was practiced in earlier (and smaller) Far Eastern porcelain pieces; Kaendler translated the technique into his own formal language, and by deciding in favor of rushes with their richly varied and articulated surface he furthermore avoided the unsubtle uniformity of a conventional cylindrical support.

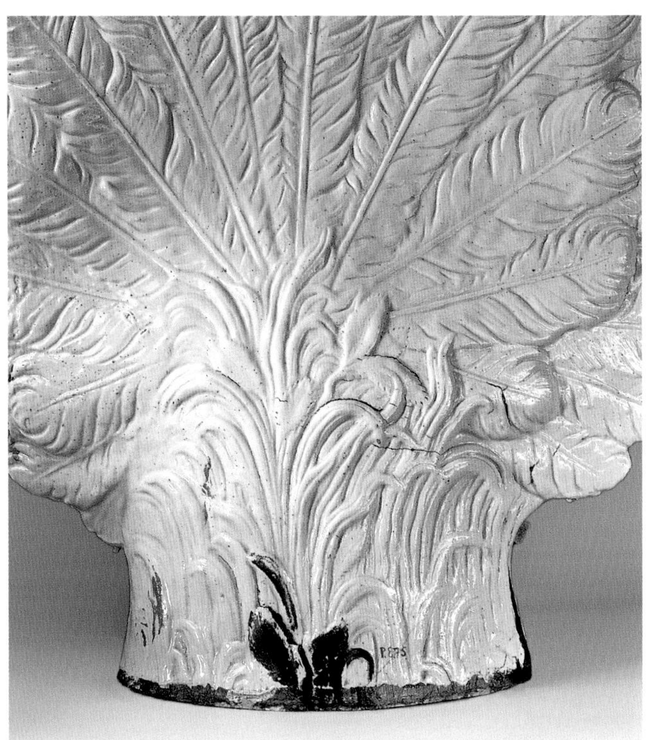

68 Peacock displaying, seen from behind, Dresden Porcelain Collection

In neither of the versions does the heron have to bear its characteristic long neck unsupported, as the neck is either attached to its plumage, or directly connected to the base through the fish. The nanny-goat's head (fig. 78) is linked by her tongue to the back of the kid, and once again this gives the impression of being artistically rather than technically motivated. Kaendler's reports on his work as a modeler are also proof that his years of experience had taught him the demands of sound modeling: "Modeled a life-size peacock [...] the base of which is almost entirely made like pure grass, which provides a good anchorage for the large unruly tail"[485] (fig. 68); furthermore (fig. 69), "a she-wolf sitting on her back legs [...] sitting under her are two young wolves, the one rather larger than the other, which are primarily there to make the whole thing more stable in the firing."[486]

The other modelers of animal figures also had to take account of these porcelain-related technical demands; evidence of their efforts can be seen in Kirchner's Fox, whose head is supported by the chicken it is holding in its mouth (fig. 166), or in the Swan, for which Eberlein modeled a second neck bent forward to make it "safer" than the one held up straight (figs. 70 and 71).

As we have seen from Höroldt's recriminations, however, Kaendler was not always prepared to let technical considerations call the tune, and of his models, three in particular show that he was on occasion quite prepared to tempt providence. In spite of being double-walled and getting thicker towards the bottom, the large fan of the Peacock (fig. 150) still exerted a heavy weight on the base and ran the risk of not retaining its equilibrium in the kiln. But as this pose is the one which is most characteristic of the peacock, Kaendler was not prepared to forego it. Similarly, when he modeled his second eagle figure (1732), he stretched one wing disconcertingly high into the air, so that a slight irregularity in the work of the molders or a small mistake in the regulation of the heat was sufficient to throw the piece off balance in the firing and destroy it for good (fig. 165). Höroldt made it clear that he had no sympathy for Kaendler's love of treading perilously narrow paths between glorious success and miserable failure, criticizing him for having "ignored the dictates of simple common sense in modeling the wing, with the result that there was no possibility of firing the piece successfully."[487] It is indeed the case that no historical example of this work has survived. The third piece to involve a high degree of risk was his figure of a macaw climbing down a tree-trunk and stretching its long tail-feathers full 123 cms into the air (fig. 182). And as he once pointed out in connection with another figure, Kaendler made sure to position the figure's "centrum gravitatis" correctly.[488] In these three models Kaendler was pushing his material to its absolute limits, but in spite of their being so fraught with risks and troublesome to produce, they were not actually beyond the bounds of technical possibility.

Although the pieces spoiled in the firing made these limits quite clear to him, he did not give up the search for new solutions. The order for the Japanese Palace had specified that the animals should be life-size, which, for reasons already given, was not possible in all cases. Kaendler's eye was however offended by dimensions which were not true to life, and in 1734 he is to be found requesting "that an experiment should be carried out to see whether it really was impossible to make life-size renderings of the large animals such as the deer, aurochs [wisent], African donkey [zebra] and the like."[489] As it was clear to him that such figures could not be executed in one piece, he made the following suggestion: "It would seem quite possible for the animals, however big, to be cut down the middle and fired in two halves, which would then be joined together with iron and filling, with the joins being painted over so that nobody will notice. In this way, it will be thought that the piece has been made in one."[490] Although permission was given and the Commission repeatedly asked for the experiment to be carried out, the idea never came to anything. The animal gallery project was terminated after 1736, and Kaendler furthermore wanted to apply his concept of a monumental porcelain figure made in a number of parts to the projected larger-than-life equestrian statue of Augustus III.

When one bears in mind the many difficulties that beset the production of the large animal figures, the works existing today must in spite of all their visible shortcomings be regarded as minor miracles of ceramic technology. Every single one had to survive the dangerous firing process, and in many cases, the works only got as far as the Japanese Palace thanks to special measures which will be given closer attention below. Even today, their cracks mean that the animal figures are in serious danger every time that they are moved from place to place.

It was this factor which caused Kaendler, disappointed at the defects which had appeared in his works during firings, to issue an unequivocal warning to the effect that "the major-domo of the Royal Palace must pay the greatest attention; he will not be sure, when moving the one or the other piece around, that it will not fall apart in his very hands. It has already happened to us at Meissen with a figure which had just been fired and was due to have its cracks filled by one of our workers that when it was simply moved

69 Johann Joachim Kaendler, She-Wolf, model 1735, Dresden Porcelain Collection

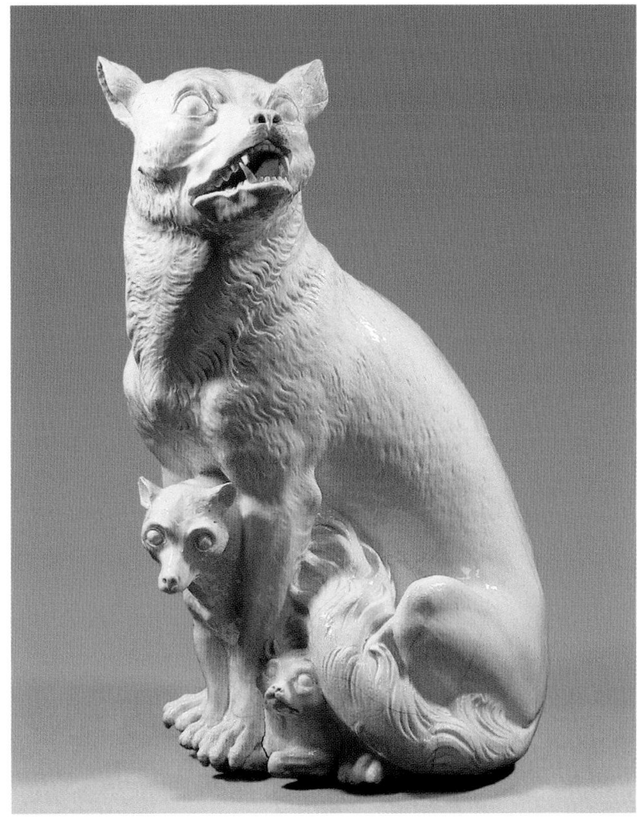

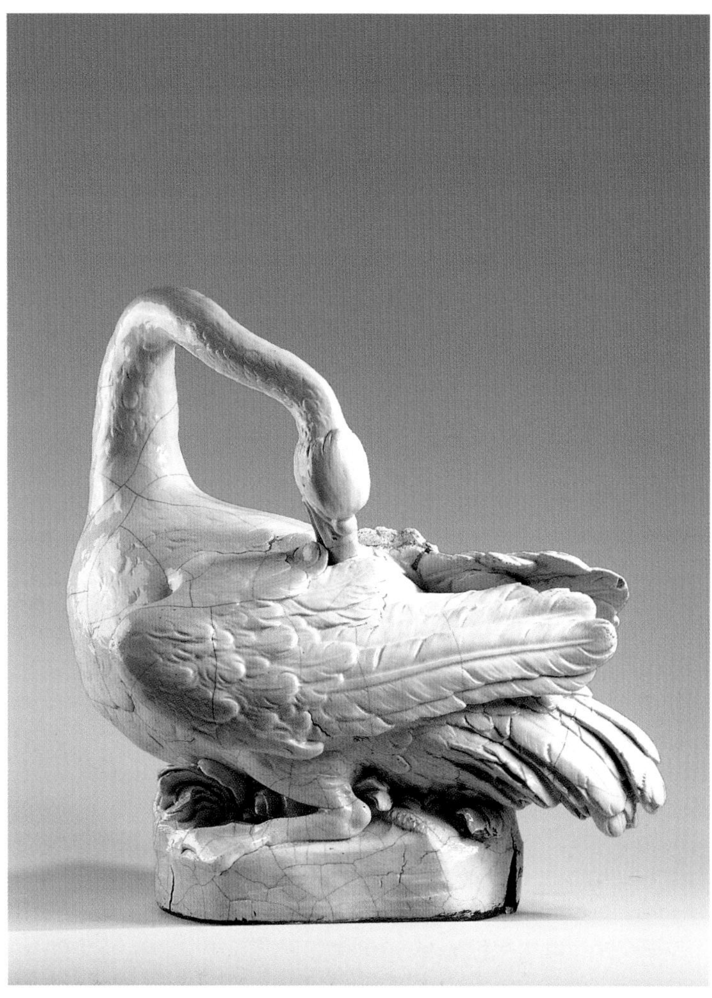

70 Johann Friedrich Eberlein, Swan with head turned back, model 1735, Dresden Porcelain Collection

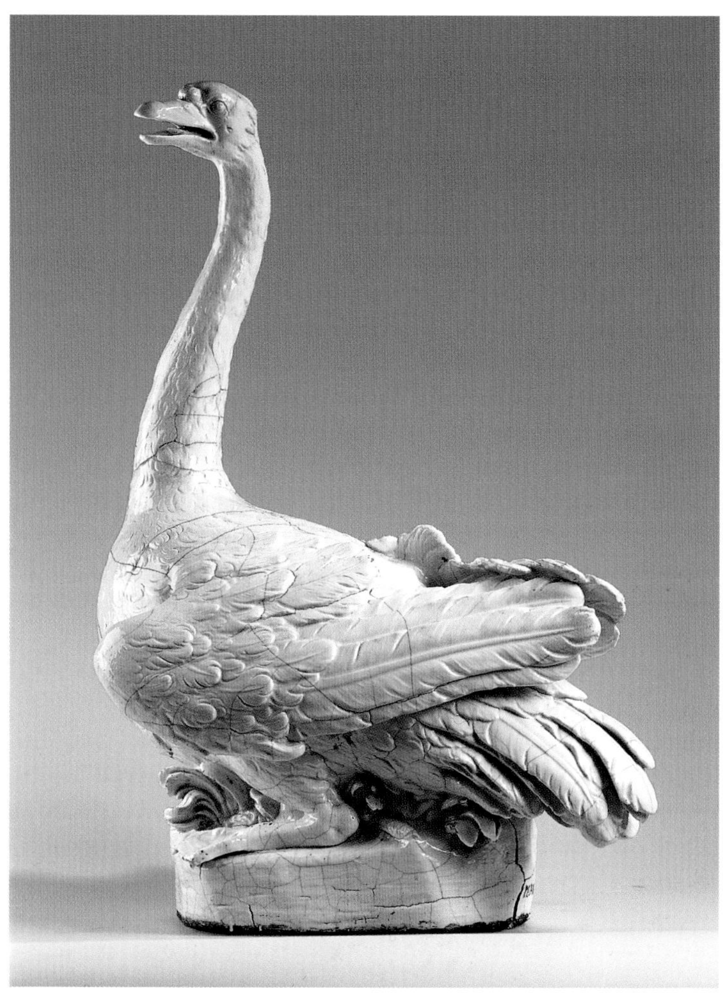

71 Johann Friedrich Eberlein, Swan with raised head, model 1735, Dresden Porcelain Collection

a little, a big piece fell out of the base, and it is to be feared that this may happen to some of the pieces in the Palace, which would be a great loss."[491]

A certain proportion of the large animal figures were irreparably destroyed in the full firing. It is not possible to establish the exact losses because there are only occasional references to lost animal figures in the records. However, even the fragments seem to have been so highly valued by the factory managers that they were only partially ground down to be used as opening material in the paste, the other pieces being preserved in a room in the Albrechtsburg. During the hearings in the course of the denunciation affair in the fall of 1734, Kaendler emphasized that the Commission would certainly understand his complaints if he were allowed to show them the spoiled figures; then he would be able to demonstrate the incompetence with which Höroldt had allotted the various jobs and overseen their execution. And after their session of October 26, the members of the Commission finally betook themselves, accompanied by the arcanists Höroldt, Stöltzel, and Petzsch, and Modellmeister Kaendler, to the "glory-hole where the large quantity of ruined porcelain was to be found."[492] Höroldt was the one who "opened the door to a room three staircases up, in which stood about twelve large Palace pieces that had been ruined in the kiln, lions, eagles, and other similar beasts, including various vases that were defective after the light firing." Finally, the molders were also summoned. All those present disclaimed responsibility for the damage done, insisting that their work was of the highest quality, and putting the blame onto the others. There was some logic in this: weaknesses could be found in all the stages of production – in the models, the paste, the repairing, or the firing – and it was in fact the sum of all these working stages which determined the success, or in these cases the lack of success, of the end product.

Repairing the cracks with filling

After successful firing, figures with severe cracks had to be stabilized and protected from further damage. The simplest way of doing this was to use a strong, sticky filling capable of holding the parts of the body together as well as just bridging the gap. The cracks, which according to a statement of Kaendler's dating from 1734 were so large "that one could put one's hand through them,"[493] were, likewise in Kaendler's words, "repaired by an apprentice, at the order of Hofkommissar Höroldt, with a resinous filling... and partially even made good with wood and plaster."[494] Höroldt claimed in his own defense that "given that the large pieces did not hold and could not yet be produced without cracks, it was better to repair them than to break them and throw them away,"[495] and added that "Kaendler made the filling himself, and even gave the orders as to how the filling should be done, having even done it himself at the beginning."[496]

This does indeed seem to have been the case: as the molder Johann Christian Wittich mentioned in a begging letter of December 1, 1734, among other things, he had, as Kaendler would confirm, been much engaged with the "filling of larger holes and cracks on large pieces."[497] That another molder, Paul Wildenstein, had to carry out these "restoration measures" is clear from his own statement: "Regarding the large pieces, I can say that I had to do so much filling that I often did not know how to repair the cracks, which were so large that I had to fill them with wood and then spread the filling on top of the wood."[498] In the case of some animal figures the old filling may well have been replaced in the course of restoration; in other cases, however, such as the vultures in the collection of the Marquess of Bath at Longleat, the brown-black, resinous-looking fillings are still in evidence (fig. 72).

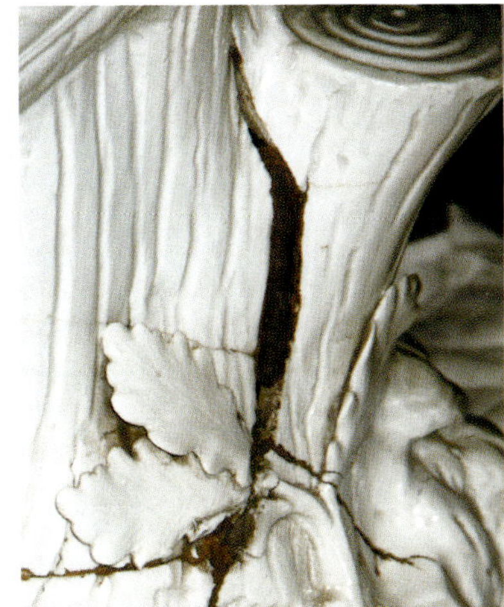

72 Crack with original filling on the pedestal of a king vulture, Rockefeller Collection, Kykuit

If, however, a large animal figure emerged safe and sound from the firing with few enough cracks to allow it to be made ready for transport to the Japanese Palace, thought then had to be given to the next problem, which was that Augustus the Strong had ordered the figures "in their natural size and color."[499] In the case of most of the severely fissured large animal figures it was quite unthinkable that they should be decorated with fusible overglaze colors because that would have entailed a third firing. And the risk that the figures would come to grief if exposed to high temperatures a third time was just too great.

The painting of the figures with cold colors

Two publications have been devoted to the painting on the Meissen large animal figures, the first being Josef Horschik's 1977 summary of research on the subject until that date.[500] The special thing about his account is that he pleaded that the cold painting on the animal figures should not be seen with modern eyes, arguing that this was one particular respect in which Baroque aesthetics differed from those of our own time. Although this is basically a valid point, he was only able to arrive at his conclusions because he was, apparently, not familiar with what, as we shall see, the manufactory records have to say on the subject. The second publication, by Rainer Rückert, was devoted to the court lacquerer Christian Reinow and his work on some of the animal figures.[501]

As mentioned above, it was considered too risky to paint the large animal figures with fusible overglaze colors (enamel colors) and subject them to a third firing. In 1734, Höroldt defended the decision to paint the figures with cold colors with the argument that, "as is well known, the pieces were painted with oil varnish because it was at that time not yet possible to fire them with enamel colors."[502]

The cold colors used on the animal figures at the manufactory were oil paints. Horschik pointed out that in eighteenth-century usage "both cold colors and fusible colors were known as enamel colors."[503] This is confirmed by the fact that a number of the lists accompanying the animal orders make no distinction between the two terms. While in March 1735 only "painted" ("bemahlte") large animal figures were delivered to the Japanese Palace, come July it was "enameled or painted" figures ("emailirte oder bemahlte"), and come September only "enameled" figures ("emailirte"), including a number of cranes and a she-wolf figure which we know for certain to have been painted with cold colors.[504] When Horschik assumes on the basis of this evidence that the same pigments, produced by the manufactory itself and available in ample quantities, were used for the cold painting as for the enamel colors, he would at first sight seem to be making an illuminating point.[505] Technically, this would have been quite possible, if only the less durable oils used as binding agents for the enamel colors were replaced by ones with stronger binding power. They would however have had to purchase a number of extra pigments, because the metal oxides used in porcelain-painting are not in the unfired state capable of producing all shades of every color.

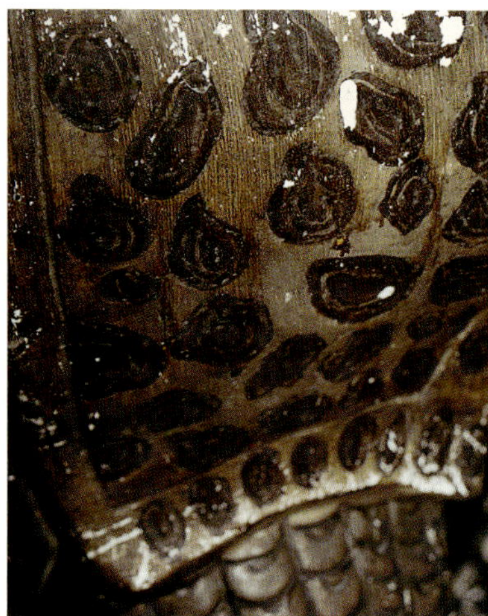

73 Detail of the oil-painting on a rhinoceros, with various color-shades

Especially, these pigments could not have produced such a powerful fiery red as can be seen glowing behind the jaws of the She-Wolf (fig. 77). It is also very possible that those few colors which were laborious and expensive to produce would in principle not have been used for the expansive cold-painted surfaces. However, there is on the whole very little to be said against his thesis. Nevertheless, the reason why some of the cold-painted animal figures are described as "enameled" could also quite simply be that the compilers of lists and writers of records were unfamiliar with the production process and that their relative ignorance of technical terms led them to use "colored," "painted," and "enameled" ("bunt," "gemalt," "emailliert") indiscriminately.

While Horschik was principally concerned with the pigments, Rainer Rückert devoted his attention to the question of the binding agent. His studies of the court painter Reinow led him to the conclusion that the cold painting on the animal figures was not done with oil colors but with lacquer paints, which he backed up by quoting a source from the Meissen manufactory records containing an exact definition of what was understood by lacquer. The document in question, however, dates from 1791,[506] and the fact that this definition was committed to writing then does not necessarily mean that the same binding agent was being used back in the 1730s almost sixty years before. His second argument was that when Reinow wrote in his notes about "lacquer varnish" ("Lackfirnis") in connection with the animal figures, he would as court painter certainly have known the difference between oil and lacquer paints.[507] Rückert was certainly right in saying this of Reinow, whom we shall meet again later, although he did not take account of the fact that the lacquer varnish referred to by Reinow was being used to give a shining finish to figures which had already been painted in Meissen, a fact to which we shall likewise return later.

One cannot conclude from the Reinow records that the animals were "lacquered" in the present-day sense of the word, for the only paints referred to in connection with the animal figures in the Meissen records are oil paints, and the painters of the Meissen manufactory would certainly have known just as well as Reinow did what kind of paint they were using, and what kind of binding agent.

We can assume that all but a very small number of the large animal figures were color-painted, as the order submitted by the king made it clear that he wanted to have all the animal figures painted in the same colors as their natural counterparts. Closer examination of the 113 large animal figures (over 40 cms high) in the Dresden Porcelain Collection reveals that on 55 of them one can still clearly see larger or smaller remains of earlier cold painting. Six figures are still almost completely painted. In the case of comparable figures in other collections, even more than half have traces of cold painting. Furthermore, the descriptions in the inventories provide evidence that most of the pieces which are now entirely white were originally cold-painted, and that the paint has since been removed.

We should be wary of equating the impression given by the colors today with the figures' original appearance. The surfaces are now dirty and the colors have changed in the course of the past two hundred and sixty years; for one hundred of these the figures were exposed to damp in the basement of the Japanese Palace. The final coat of varnish documented by Reinow has tended to darken the colors; in the case of the Rhinoceros, which shows finely nuanced painting under bright light, the slightly metallic shine may have been produced by an admixture of bismuth, which would also provide another explanation for the oxidization of the colors (fig. 75).

Quite apart from the ravages of time, even in the eighteenth century opinions varied on the quality of the cold painting. Inspec-

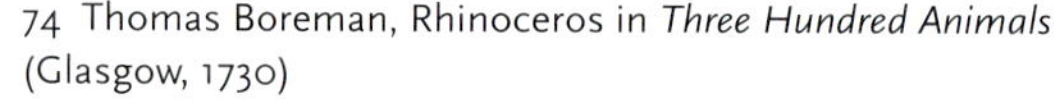

74 Thomas Boreman, Rhinoceros in *Three Hundred Animals* (Glasgow, 1730)

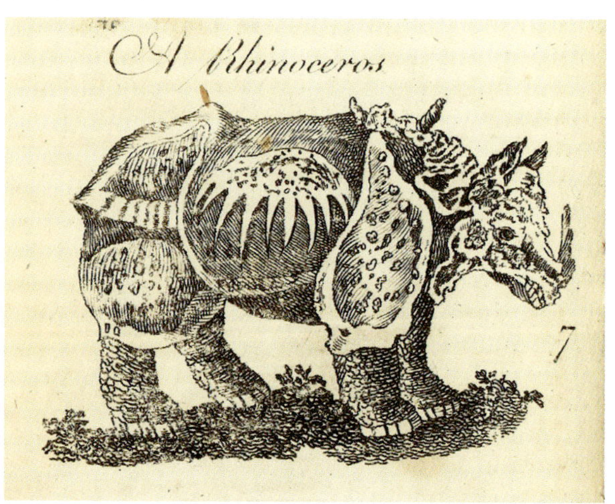

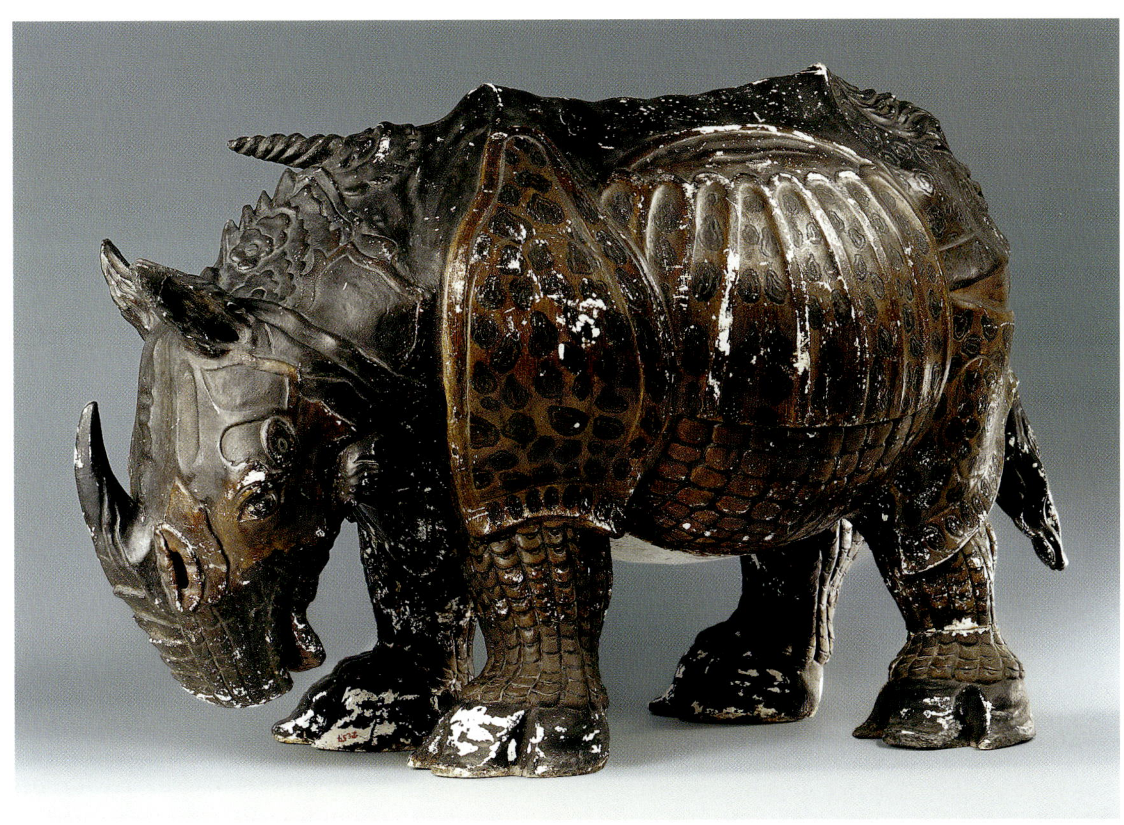

75 Johann Gottlieb Kirchner, Rhinoceros, painted with oils, model 1731, Dresden Porcelain Collection

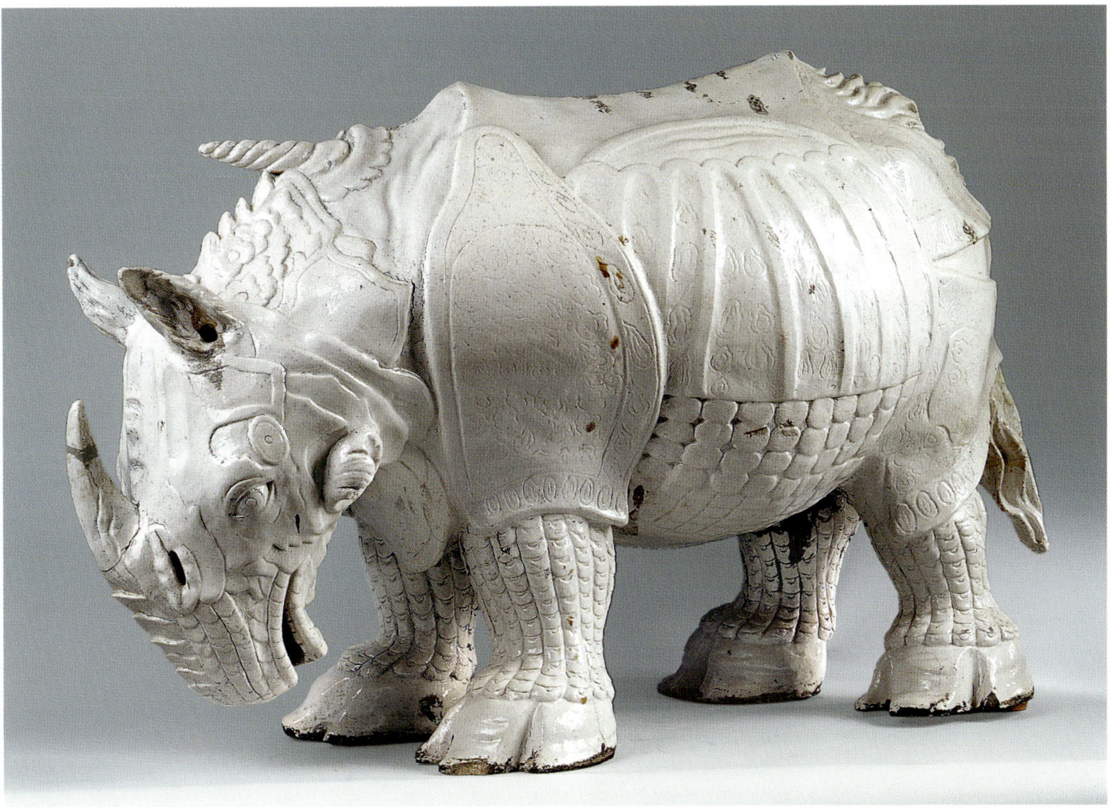

76 Johann Gottlieb Kirchner, Rhinoceros, model 1731, Dresden Porcelain Collection

tor Reinhardt, the compiler of the manufactory's monthly reports to the Commission, wrote in his report for November 1733 that eight crates with large animal figures had been sent to the Japanese Palace, but that "the pieces, on account of their size and partially because of small cracks [...] had not been enameled but painted with oil colors, and were therefore by no means good to look at."[508] Höroldt was angry at this disparaging statement and insisted a number of times that Reinhardt was not entitled to make judgments of this kind.[509] Reinhardt, however, repeated his statement half a year later in the hearings connected with the denunciation affair, in which he and Kaendler were Höroldt's two principal opponents. It was, he said, very much to the discredit of the manufactory that the large animal figures, "given that their cracks and fissures had been repaired with filling, were subsequently only painted with oil colors, and not enameled with colors as other porcelain wares were."[510] Once again, Höroldt reacted by claiming that Reinhardt was acting above his station in expressing his opinions in this way.[511] In his own defense he argued that cold painting was the only technique with which the king's order could be fulfilled, but the poor quality of the products meant that this argument fell on deaf ears in Dresden. Count Sulkowski had taken Kaendler to task, claiming that "the colors were not true to life,"[512] and Kaendler also reports Bettmeister Teuffert's statement of July 1734, according to which "the porcelain pieces were so badly made that when His Royal Majesty saw them, he expressed himself most ungraciously on the subject of the bad oil-painting, with which he was clearly very displeased."[513]

77 Johann Joachim Kaendler, She-Wolf, painted with oils, model 1735, Dresden Porcelain Collection

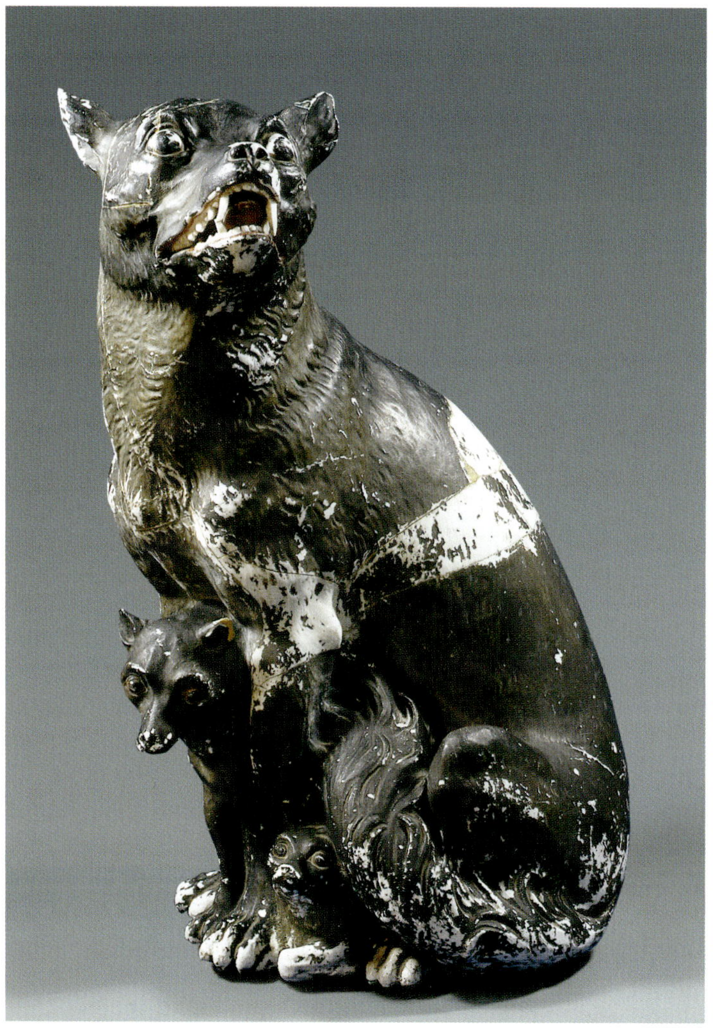

These statements, whether from the one or the other party, make it quite clear that nobody was really happy with the cold painting, which did indeed completely conceal the real charm of the material. Horschik's argument that Baroque man did not find the cold-painted colors so disturbing to the eye as modern purists do is thus over-simplified. In Horschik's defense, it is not clear from the relevant sources whether the criticism delivered by Count Sulkowski and Augustus III was directed at the quality of the cold painting, or at the practice itself, although a document dated January 5, 1733, may shed some light on this question: "At the most gracious command of the King of Poland and Elector of Saxony, all the animals and birds which are to produced for the Japanese Palace in Neustadt at the King's porcelain manufactory in Meissen, are, according to their kind, to be painted and enameled in the fire, but in such a way that there is still much white porcelain to be seen"[514] (fig. 78). This instruction is directly connected with another one issued to the manufactory only eight days before, on December 28, 1732, to the effect that only porcelain wares "in a fine white paste and with little painting" ("von schöner weißen Massa und wenig Mahlerey") were to be considered as suitable for the royal deliveries.[515]

The change in taste apparent here, which Horschik also noted in connection with this document, shows that it was not only on enameled porcelain that the king was keen to have a greater measure of the treasured shining white, but generally. When, as in the case of the large animal figures, this the principal attraction or porcelain is hidden with a layer of paint which for all its lacquer varnish can never approach the brilliant shine of porcelain and furthermore deprives the surface of any depth, then eighteenth- and twentieth-century aesthetic sensibilities react alike. And that the manufactory did indeed comply with this requirement is shown by the Goat from the Dresden Porcelain Collection (fig. 78, and illustrated in Horschik's book), which is painted only in large patches, and also by a Golden Pheasant with a base with leaves and grass painted on quite independently of the relief work (fig. 79).

It would on the other hand be going too far to claim that the eighteenth-century eye would have been happiest – as some modern eyes might be – if the animal figures had been pure white and entirely undecorated. The fundamental intention behind the naturalistic painting was that it should bring out the particular char-

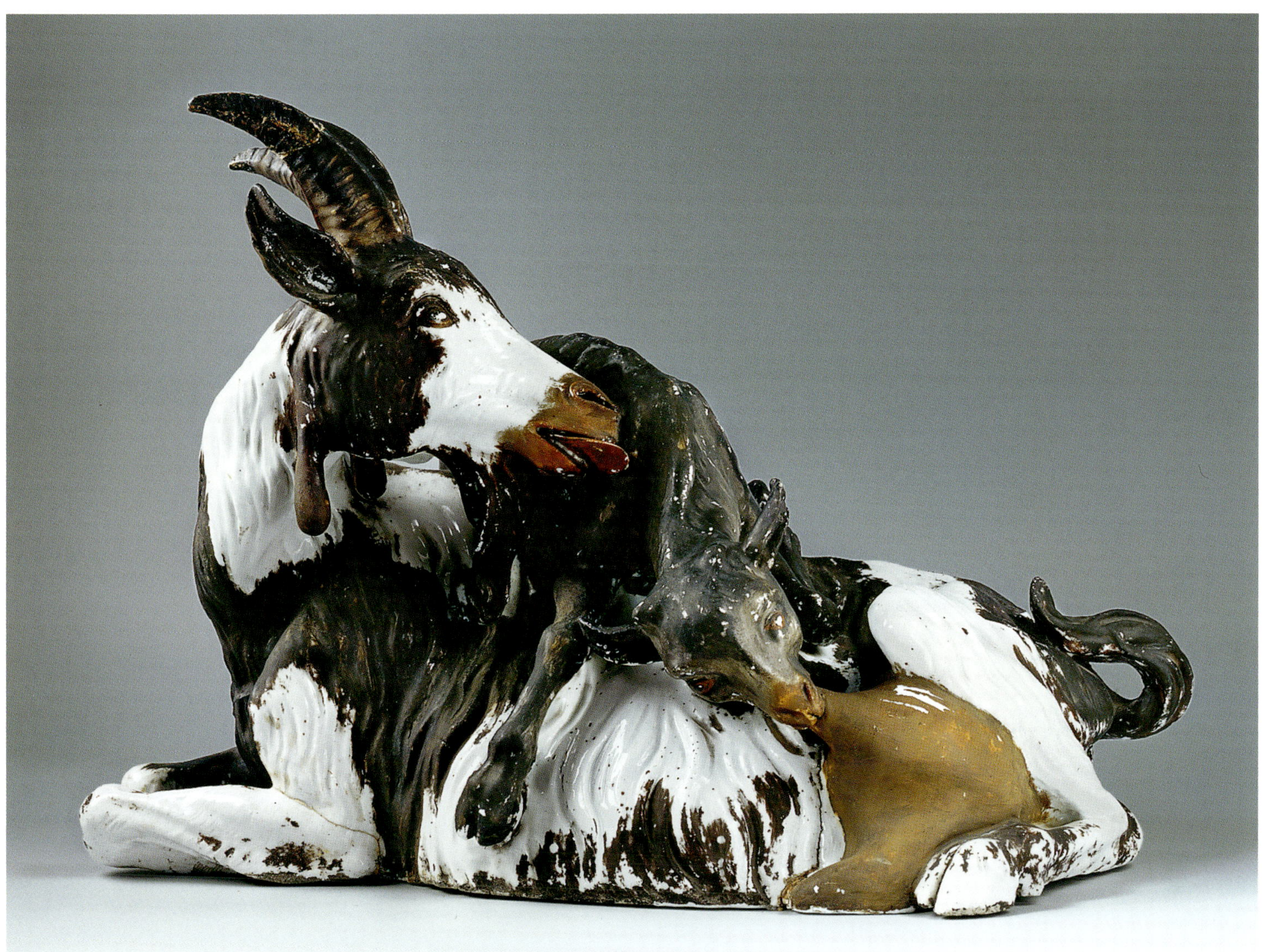

78 Johann Joachim Kaendler, Nanny-Goat, partially painted with oils, Dresden Porcelain Collection

acter of the material; equally, it was to have been executed in shining fused enamel colors, just as it was on tableware.

If Kaendler was critical of the quality of the cold painting, then this was particularly because it detracted from the merit of his own work on the original models. Although Gröger was exaggerating when he reported that Kaendler was constantly fighting against Höroldt's color decorations,[516] he was right that what Kaendler had in mind when modeling his figures was that lively interplay between shine and shadow that is typical of a skillfully modeled glazed porcelain surface. After all, Kaendler was a sculptor and was quite used to thinking in terms of sculptural effects. Although, as Horschik notes, Kaendler saw the deadening effect of the cold painting when he was still in his first year at the manufactory, he continued his finely articulated surface work, not only for the sake of being true to nature, as Horschik suggests, but also because he considered this the best way to ensure that the material was used to best effect. Kaendler's figures, as we shall see on other occasions, are not naturalistic animals that could just as well have been done in wood or stone but happen to have been executed in porcelain; on the contrary, they show very clearly Kaendler's talent for expressing his ideas in forms that were, to use a modern term, "materialgerecht": in short, "right" for the material in hand. Kaendler's particular approach to decoration with enamel colors will be discussed at a later stage.

The state in which the cold painting has come down to us means that we can no longer venture a judgment as to its original quality. A few small vestiges at hidden points (fig. 80) suggest that it was relatively finely applied, with the intention of achieving

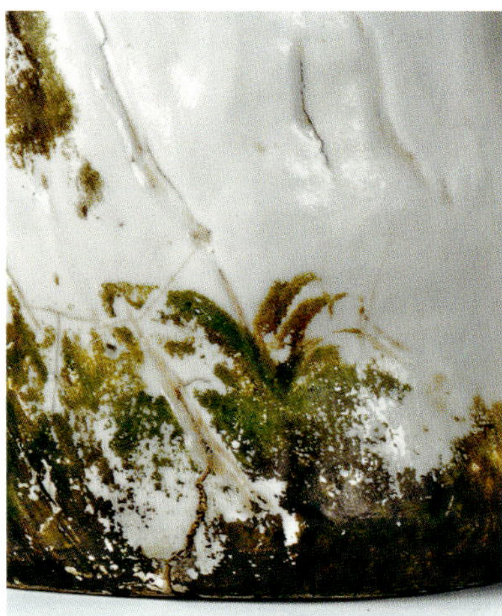

79 Grasses painted on with oils on the pedestal of a golden pheasant, Dresden Porcelain Collection

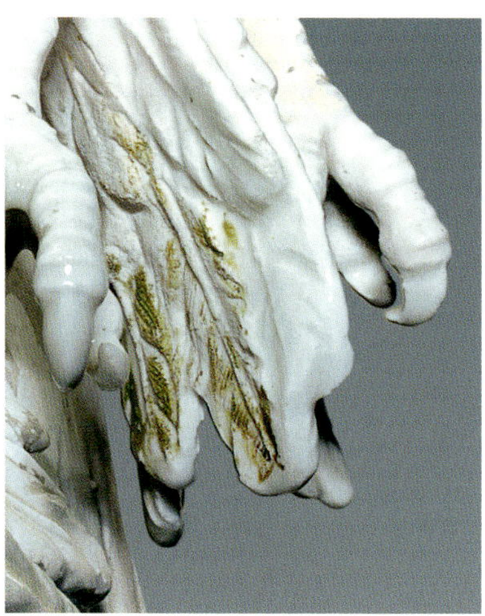

80 Oil-painting on the feathers of a cockatoo being devoured by a vulture, Dresden Porcelain Collection

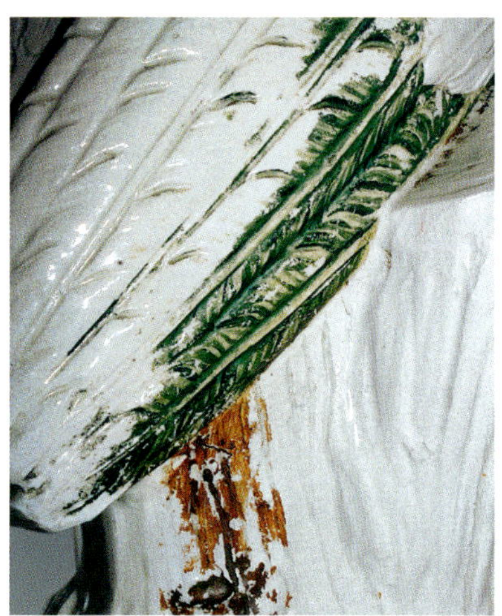

81 Vestiges of oil-painting on a king vulture, Victoria & Albert Museum, London

shading and nuance. This is particularly well shown by a Vulture from the collection of the Marquess of Bath, auctioned in the summer of 2002 at Christie's. Various tones of blue, red, and green are seen to have been applied in a variety of shadings, sometimes with fine and sometimes with more generous brush-strokes. This begs the question as to who at the manufactory could have been responsible for doing the painting (fig. 81).

Astoundingly enough, the records contain no clear indication, possibly for the reason that during the two controversial affairs of 1734 and 1738/39 the arcanists, modelers, molders, and repairers were required to make official statements about their work, but the painters were not. Nevertheless, one would still expect to find a record of some kind: perhaps a manufactory painter boasting about having the job of painting such important animal figures, in some such context as a demand for overtime payment. After all, the painters were mentioned by name in the accounting books even when all they were being paid for was painting doors, staircases, or sentry boxes at the Albrechtsburg.[517]

One possibility – a purely speculative one – is that it might have been the painter and lacquerer Johann Gottlieb Mehlhorn, whose father and brother had been painters at the manufactory for some time before him and frequently worked on the arcanum.[518] In April 1734 he was commissioned by the manufactory to fill the cracks in a Pietà and paint it, clearly in cold colors.[519] Finally, after having done a period of probation, Mehlhorn was finally engaged at the manufactory as a painter, solemnly affirming "that he was prepared to comply with all requests to do not only normal painting but also lacquering, with which he was familiar by virtue of his chosen trade."[520] In the early part of 1735, however, he was sent to prison in the wake of an affair in which his family had become embroiled. It is however not possible to say whether animal figures were also given to him for painting before 1735, or whether he painted any animal figures at all during his period at the manufactory.

Although no name from within the manufactory can be indubitably linked with the cold painting of large animal figures, this can be done in the case of one painter from Dresden. On March 4, 1734, the court painter Reinow submitted a bill for 124 talers and 16 groschen for having cold-painted and lacquered 31 animal figures and 17 other porcelain pieces which he had received from the Japanese Palace. This piece of source material has been dealt with in depth in an article by Rainer Rückert.[521] Reinow may have been given the commission much earlier, as according to the records of the Meissen castle guard he had visited Höroldt for an hour on the afternoon of September 11, 1732.[522]

One interesting aspect of the bill of 1734 is its indication that Reinow was asking for 3 talers for 12 pieces of porcelain that from the context can only have been animal figures, "which had come [to Dresden] already painted," and which he had "treated with lacquer varnish."[523] In other words, Reinow was responsible for applying a final coat onto a number of animal figures which had already been painted in the manufactory in Meissen with oil colors. While this gave the piece a high shine, the effect could certainly not compare with the softness and depth of enamel colors. However, the very fact of the task entrusted to Reinow does show what trouble was taken to make the large animal figures colorful and porcelain-like in appearance, and how much was spent on trying to achieve this effect.[524] It is not known whether Reinow received further figures from the palace for painting, but this one order does also reveal that even before 1734 a small number of purely white animals had been delivered to the Japanese Palace which he was called upon to paint.

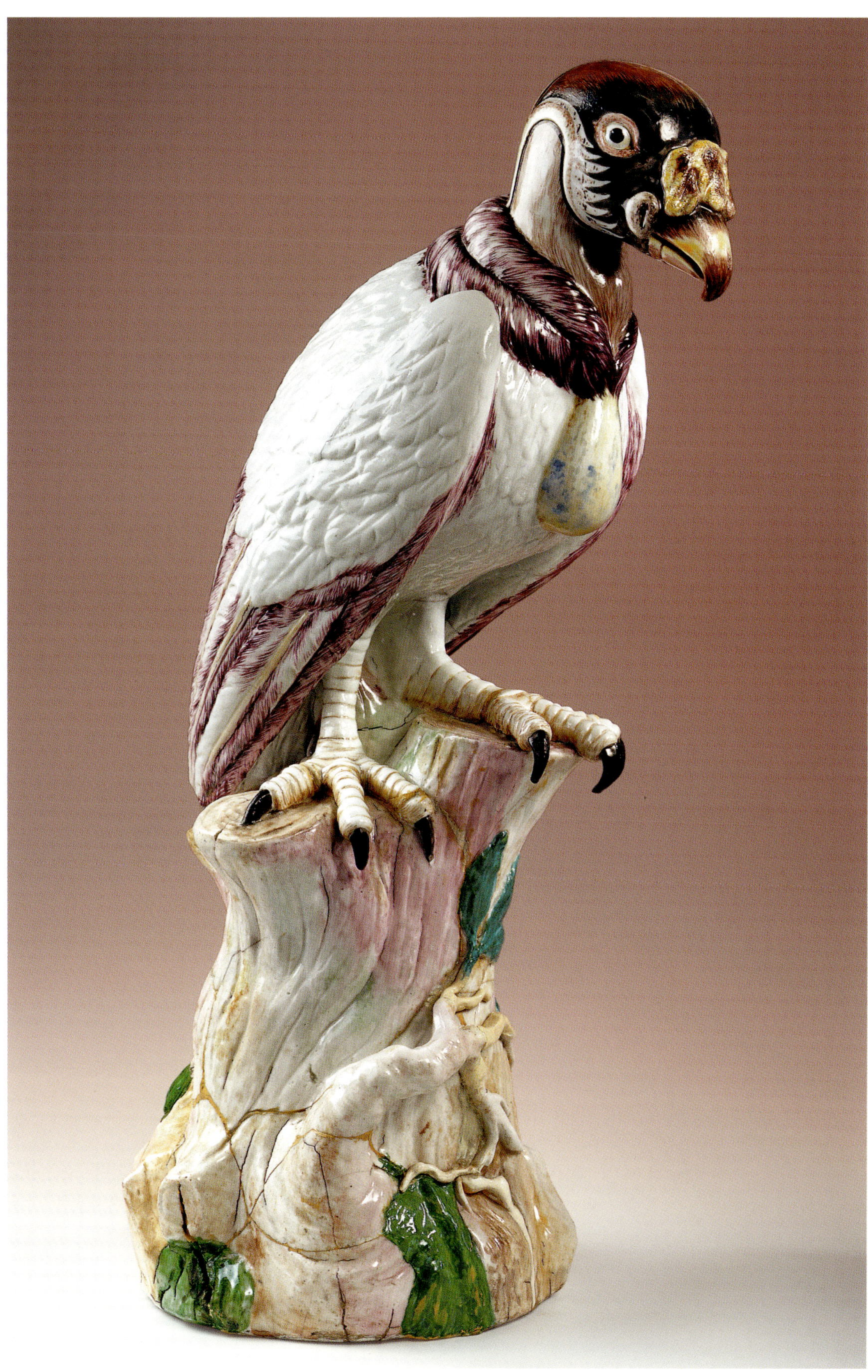

82 Johann Joachim Kaendler, King Vulture (1731) decorated with enamel colors, Dresden Porcelain Collection

Decoration with enamel colors

By no means all of the animal figures made for the Japanese Palace were cold-painted: many were decorated with fired enamel colors.

There are several synonymous expressions for this form of decoration, all derived from technical aspects of the procedure. Painting with enamel colors is sometimes known as "overglaze painting" ("Aufglasurmalerei"), because the color is applied to the glazed, full-fired piece, as opposed to "underglaze painting" ("Unterglasurmalerei"), which is done before the piece is glazed. The colors are known as "muffle colors" ("Muffelfarben") because the pieces are put into the firing in "muffles" (here referred to as "saggers"), which protect the colors from the direct heat of the fire. The third German expression, "Schmelzfarben" ("melting colors"), finds its English equivalent in "fusible colors," which with its reference to the firing process and its clear opposition to "cold painting" is the most apt expression for the colors themselves and will thus be used for preference here. The fourth expression, "enamel colors" ("Emailfarben"), is a slightly unfortunate one as it can be confused with the closely related practice of enameling on metal; in the following, however, the verb "to enamel" will be used for the decoration of porcelain with enamel colors, reflecting the general use of "emaillieren" in the historical documents.

It was primarily the smaller animal figures that were decorated with enamel colors, as there was no great risk involved in subjecting them to one further firing. Enamel colors were also used for the middle-size figures (between 30 and 50 cm in height).[525] Of the larger figures (over 50 cm), however, this risk was only taken in a very few cases, when the figures had emerged relatively crack-free from the full firing.[526] These were the following: a Mandrill (fig. 207); one example of the King Vulture of 1731, the model re-

83 Johann Joachim Kaendler, King Vulture (1734), Dresden Porcelain Collection

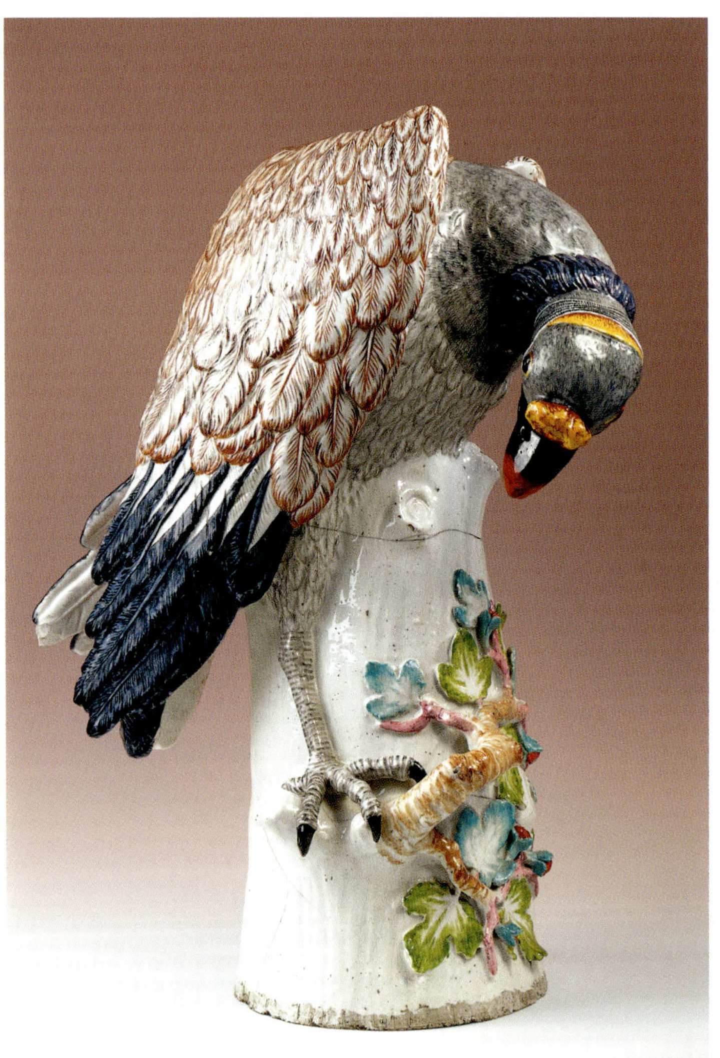

84 Johann Friedrich Eberlein, Eagle Owl with dead pigeon, decorated with enamel colors, model 1735, Metropolitan Museum of Art, New York

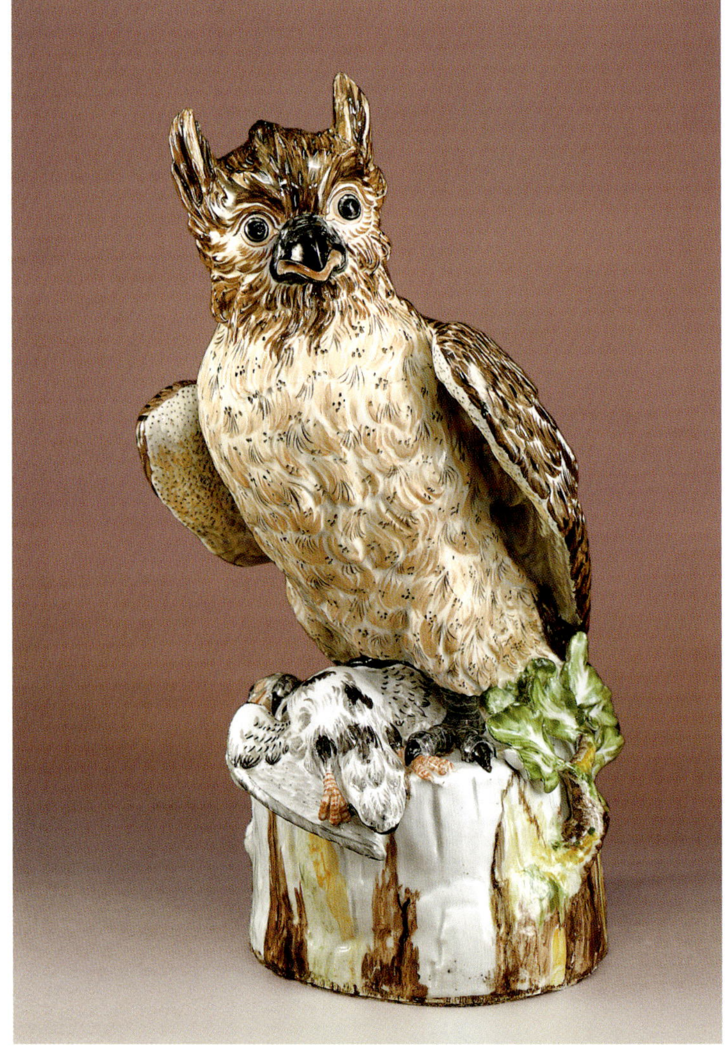

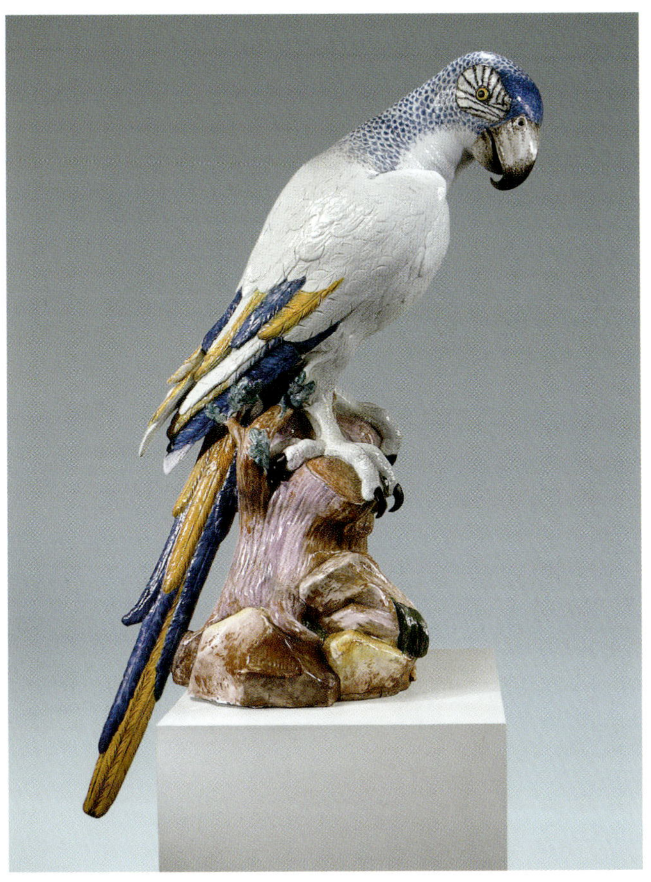

85 Johann Joachim Kaendler, Macaw (1731) decorated with enamel colors, Rijksmuseum Amsterdam

The instruction was quoted in the section on cold painting as evidence for the general desire that the typical characteristics of porcelain (white and shining) should be more in evidence on the animal figures. While figures decorated with enamel colors had the desired level of shine, this form of decoration met with a problem that occurs in any kind of painted sculpture, namely that the two-dimensional character of the painting detracts from the figure's plasticity, that is to say, from its inherently three-dimensional character.

This can be demonstrated very well for the Meissen animals by looking at three particular monkey figures. These figures have been chosen in spite of the doubts that have been cast on their originality, and the suggestions that the painting on two of these figures is not original but was carried out at a later stage will be dealt with in the section on forgeries. One could find parallels in other undisputedly original figures, particularly from among the birds, but the fact that the three monkeys have very similar coat structures makes them particularly suitable vehicles for the demonstration of the effects that result from the various kinds of painting.

In the case of the Monkey wearing a ruff (fig. 89), the body is colored with an even layer of very shiny black-brown enamel. In the case of the Marmoset (fig. 88), a monochrome ground was given structure by being painted with fine brushstrokes in a darker shade. In the Monkey taking snuff (fig. 87), on the other hand, the painting of the monkey's body is restricted to the head, fingers, and toes, and otherwise to its belt. The coats of all three monkeys were done sculpturally by the modeler. Both in the case of the ruff-

ferred to as a "Kropfvogel" ("crop bird," fig. 82); several examples of the King Vulture of 1734 (fig. 83), and of the Bittern (fig. 174); and a few examples of the Macaw sitting on a tree-trunk (fig. 85), the Golden Pheasant (fig. 98), and the large Eagle Owl (fig. 84).

As is shown by the manufactory report dated August 18, 1732, it was particularly the first period that saw experiments with enamel colors being conducted on large figures: "On August 7, the first elephant figure was delivered to the warehouse from the firing house, and although it already had a few cracks, Hofkommissar Höroldt was of the opinion that it could pass for a good piece and could now be enameled."[527] According to the inventory of 1770, of the four elephant figures that had been delivered to the Japanese Palace, one was white with lacquer painting, and three were brown. None of the four examples known to us today is enameled, which suggests that the attempt referred to in the report was not crowned with success. That it was nevertheless hoped that all the animal figures could be decorated with enamel colors is shown by the instruction issued at the beginning of 1733 and quoted above, to the effect that all the animal figures were to be enameled, but in such a way as to leave a large part of the surface white.

86 Johann Gottlieb Kirchner, Temple of Venus with its strongly colored marbling, model 1727, Metropolitan Museum of Art, New York

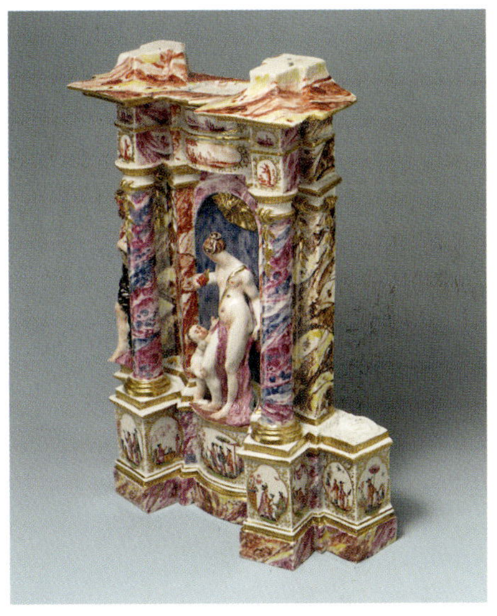

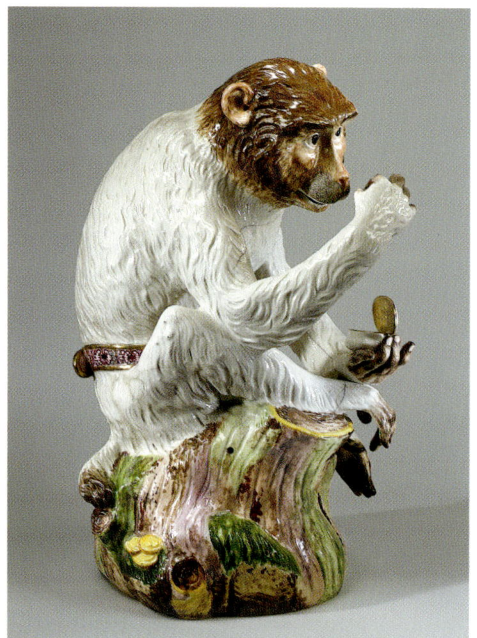

87 Johann Joachim Kaendler, Monkey taking snuff, decorated with enamel colors, model possibly 1732, Rijksmuseum Amsterdam

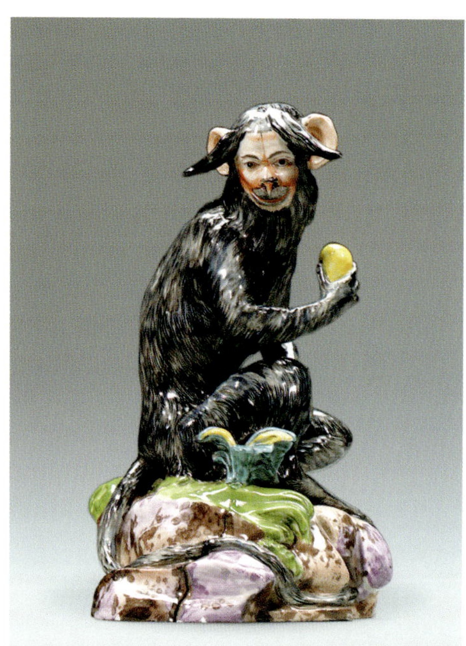

88 Johann Joachim Kaendler, Marmoset, decorated with enamel colors, with AR-mark, model 1731, trade

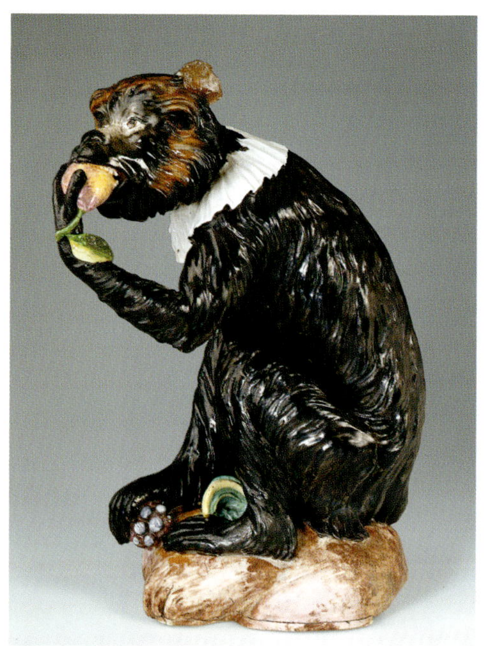

89 Johann Gottlieb Kirchner, Monkey wearing a ruff, decorated with enamel colors, model 1731, Musée Ariana, Geneva

wearing monkey, which is black, and in that of the snuff-taking monkey, which remained largely white, the plasticity of the strands of hair was brought out purely and simply by the light-and-shade effects of the relief. In the first case the hair is more or less black and thus bears a greater similarity to the natural original, while in the second the information as to the actual natural color of the monkey is restricted to the painted areas mentioned above. But there are also differences in the effect produced by these two procedures. The dark painting on the ruff-wearing monkey counteracts the sculptural effect of the relief by reducing the contrast between the shadowy furrows and the prominent, brightly lit ridges. When the figure is white, however, the relief is more effective, and the eye picks up the smallest and slightest shadow. In other words, relief work in white has the greatest capacity for contrast, which explains why the surface of the Monkey taking snuff has a liveliness about it which is lacking in the rather static Monkey wearing a ruff.

Between these two lies the brushwork done on the Marmoset, which covers the monkey's whole body and is linear in conception. It uses painterly means to try to bring about something that is already been brought about sculpturally, and positively competes with the modeler's carefully worked relief. The decorator was not content simply to bring out the relief by, for instance, emphasizing the shadows in the furrows with strokes placed closer together; on the contrary, he had in his mind's eye an evenly-growing coat of animal hair and did his painting accordingly. This approach was quite the opposite of artistic, for in an artistic rendering, the main point is not to recreate an animal's coat but to give the beholder the optical impression of one. The kind of painting used here actually counteracts the work of the modeler, and the final effect is consequently not natural but, rather, artificial.

What Augustus the Strong had demanded in his order was – put somewhat more freely – that the animals should be rendered as naturalistically as possible, but in a material that in the mind of the time was one of the most artificial of all. The porcelain palace was to surprise its visitors with a menagerie of shining animals that on closer inspection would turn out to be *objets d'art* in porcelain. When his successor Augustus III came to the throne, there was a slight change in this way of seeing things. Augustus III was certainly just as great a connoisseur of art as his father had been, and had somewhat more refinement and a greater feeling for intimacy. While Augustus the Strong went to great lengths in order to realize his all-embracing collecting plans and to create *mises en scène* for showing off his works of art (well exemplified in the overall project for a porcelain menagerie), these priorities had to be moderated under Augustus III to allow more attention to be paid to the particular significance and effect of each individual work. In the realm of art in Dresden, preference was given to the microcosm of detail over the Absolutist macrocosm of broadly-based programmatic works. In rather simple terms, the taste-determining, instrumentalizing, conceptual way of thinking of the father had developed into the taste-forming, more personal connoisseurship of the son. It should however not be forgotten that

Count Brühl also played an important role and exerted considerable influence. The demand made of the manufactory that there should be more white showing on the animals came from the pen of Count Brühl and was indeed even made shortly before Augustus the Strong's death.

If one moves on from this thesis to the idea that Augustus III (with Brühl busy in the background) paid more attention to the individual animal and its relationship to the whole animal gallery, rather than – as we shall see his father had done – subjecting the collection of porcelain animals in the Japanese Palace to an overall artistic concept that also affected a number of other palaces and castles, then one can also begin to see more clearly the real reason behind the call for more visible white that was to be of such importance for the character of the animal figures created during Augustus III's reign. Their beholders' eyes and minds were now to be impressed not only by the likeness of the figures to their natural models, but also by the supremely artificial character of the material in which they were made. While in the cases of the Monkey wearing a ruff and the Marmoset with its painted-on coat structure

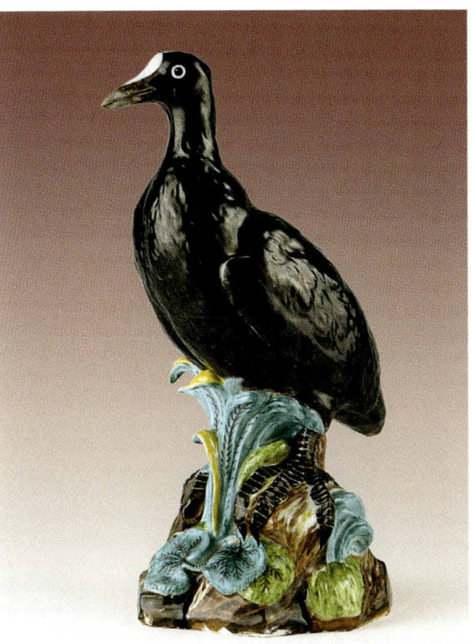

91 Johann Joachim Kaendler, Coot, model 1731, formerly Dresden Porcelain Collection

90 Johann Joachim Kaendler, Great Crested Grebe, model 1734, Dresden Porcelain Collection

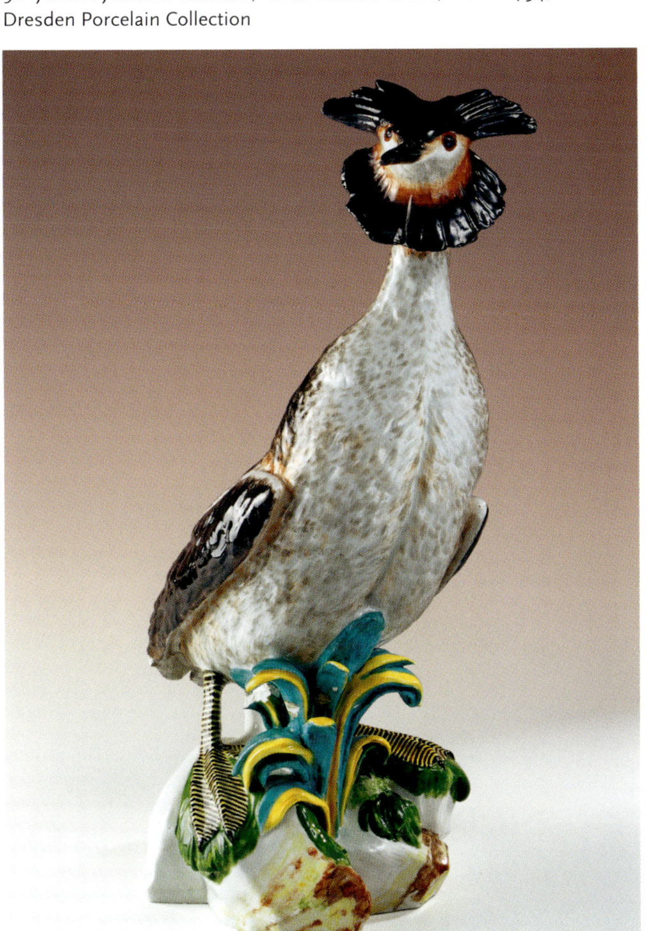

the efforts to imitate nature actually work against the sculptural characteristics of the medium, the Monkey taking snuff, executed in the wake of the demand for more white porcelain to be visible, combines these two tendencies. This gives the figure a pleasing balance: the very sculptural coat and the fact of its color zones only being suggested are a sign that we are being trusted to call nature to mind and to fill in the missing colors for ourselves. There are two "real presences" in the figure: the natural monkey and the material in which the monkey's likeness has been done.[528]

This is also a vindication of Sulkowski's and Augustus III's condemnation of cold painting; for all its efforts to imitate nature, it put too much trust in eye-catching externals and not enough in the beholder's knowing eye.

As in the case of the cold painting, the very existence of animal figures decorated in enamel colors begs the question as to their originator. The practice of suggestive, partial coloring was not practiced in any other field of the sculptural arts at the time and must have been "invented" by someone, even if the invention was motivated by the instruction quoted, and thus perhaps by the king himself. As with the cold painting, however, the records give us no definite answer. Rainer Rückert, who made a close study of the painting on the faces of eighteenth-century Meissen figures, suggested that at least some of the first enameled animal figures could have been painted by Höroldt.[529] He claims that this was the case with, for example, the Coot (fig. 91), the Great Crested Grebe (fig. 90), the Rose-Ringed Parakeet (fig. 127) and the Osprey

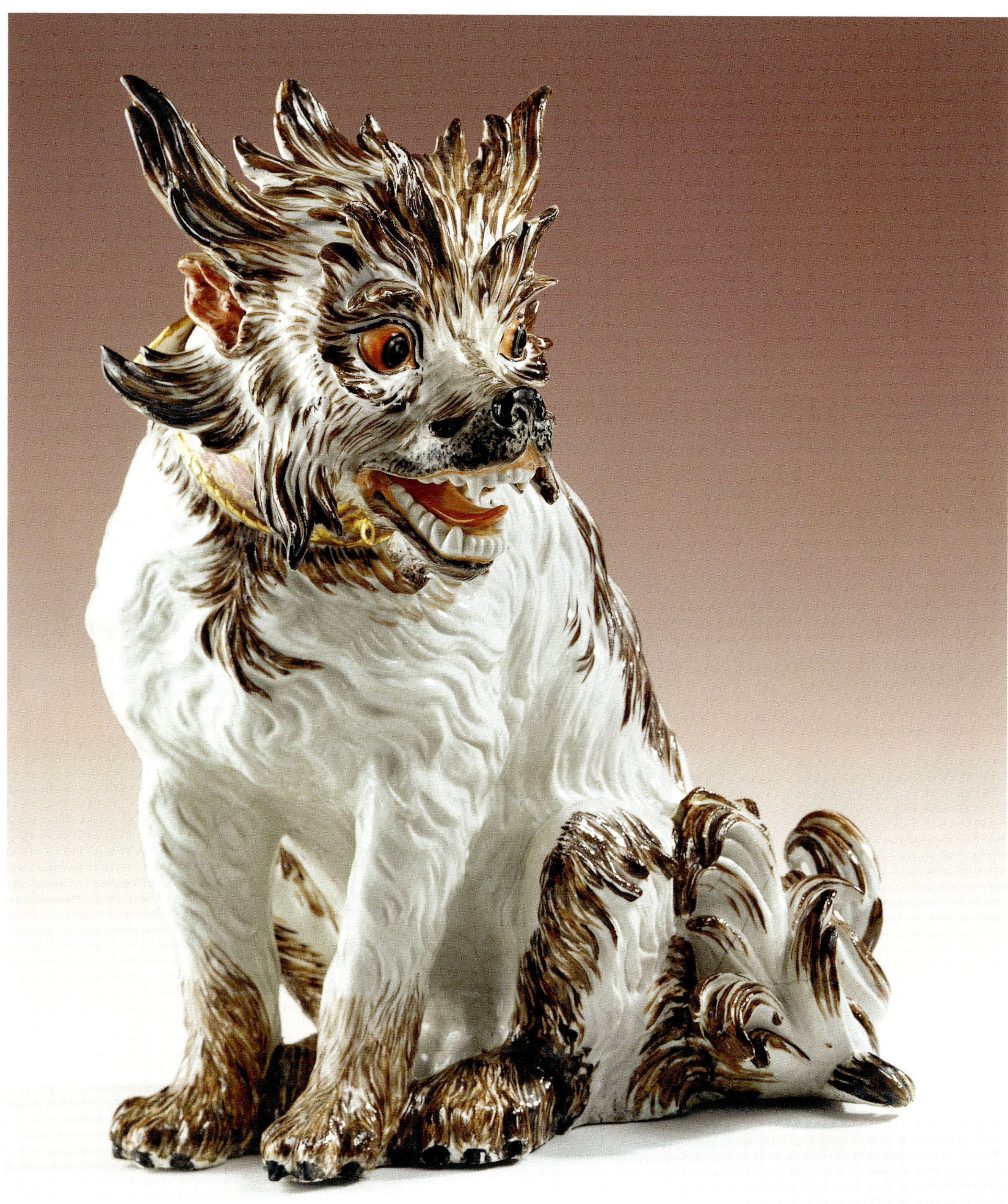

92 Johann Joachim Kaendler, Bolognese Dog, model most likely 1734, Dresden Porcelain Collection

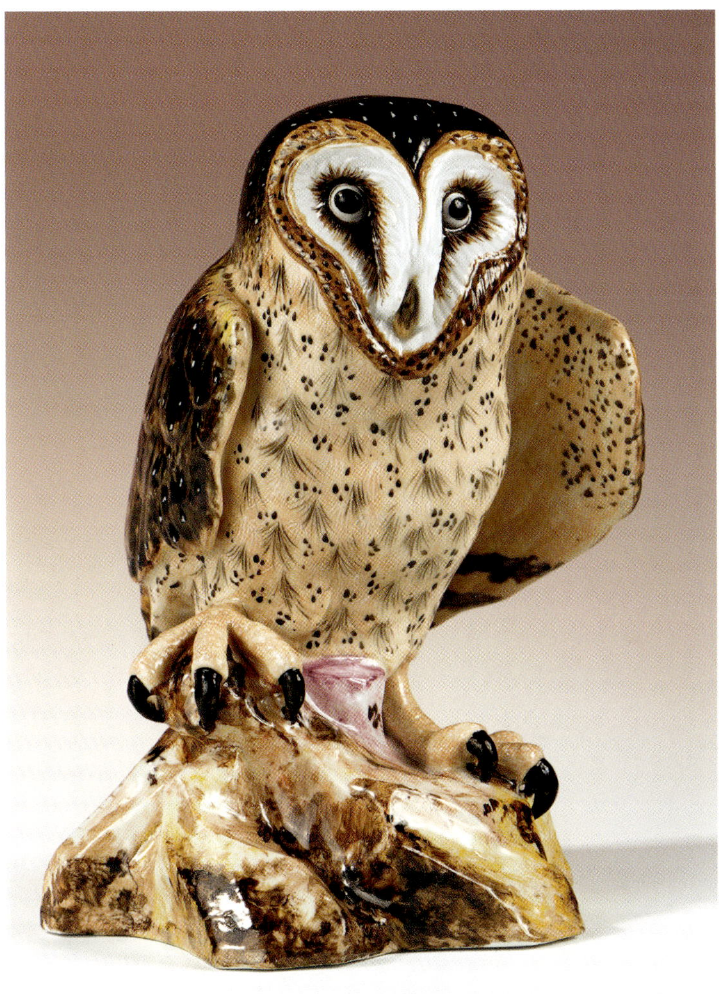

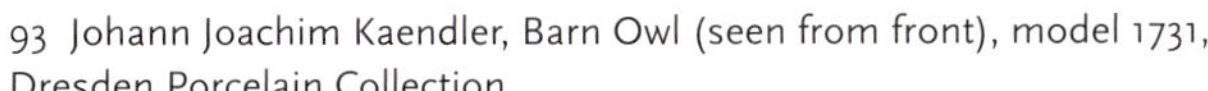

93 Johann Joachim Kaendler, Barn Owl (seen from front), model 1731, Dresden Porcelain Collection

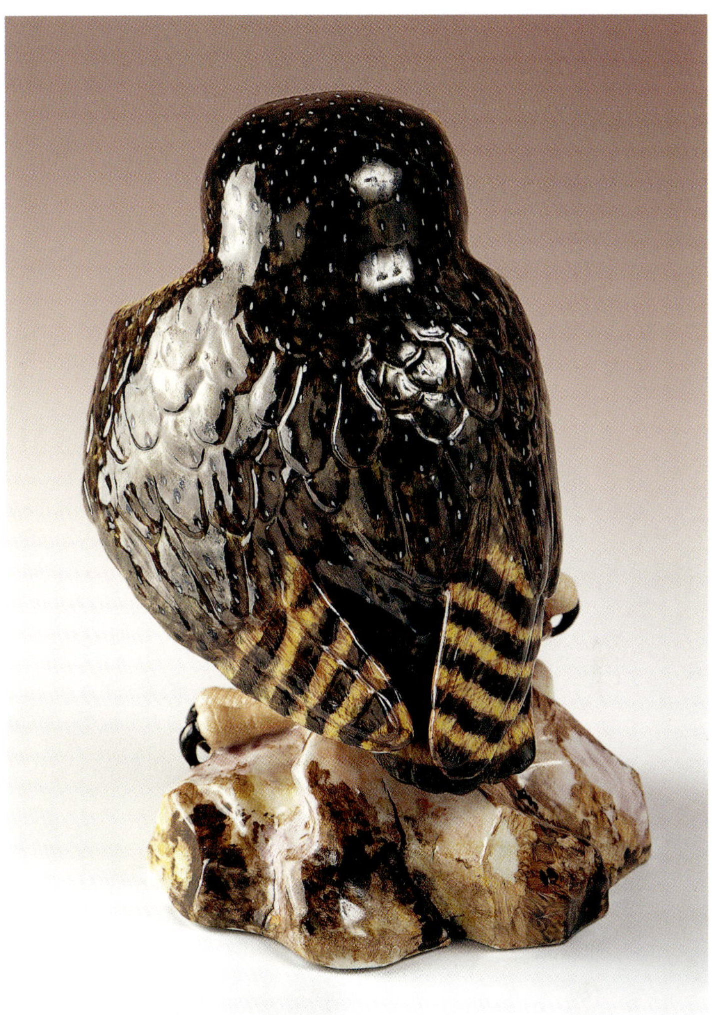

94 Johann Joachim Kaendler, Barn Owl (seen from behind), model 1731, Dresden Porcelain Collection

(fig. 97), and also with such larger figures as the Eagle Owl (fig. 84) and the Bolognese Dog (fig. 92). I know of no records to support this theory. Although, for example, Höroldt is recorded as "boasting to the same person [the king] that he is not only producing and enameling the large Apostles and other large figures, but also producing four times as much tableware in the new large kilns,"[530] he was talking of his role as manager of the manufactory, and not as repairer, painter, and firer. And there is also the much-quoted statement of Höroldt's recorded in the same context in October 1734 to the effect that he was himself no longer laying hands on brush or paint, which of course may have been an exaggeration.[531]

Although the present author cannot answer the question as to the identity of the decorators, there is no mistaking the great differences in the quality of the enameling done on the animal figures. Examples range from the highly effective and faithfully rendered plumage on the Barn Owl (figs. 94 and 95), through the less

95 Barn owl, stuffed specimen, Museum of Natural History, New York

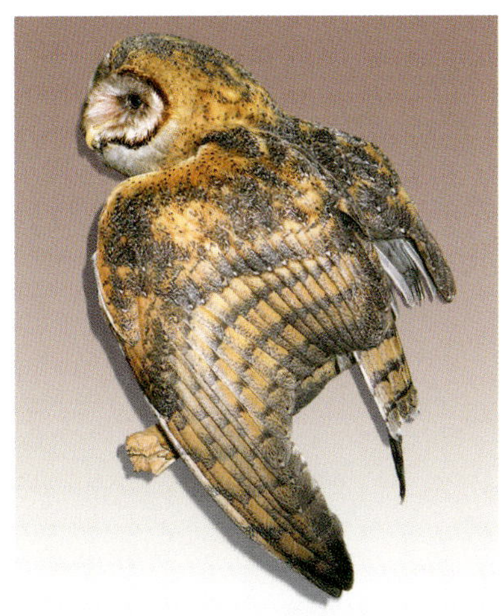

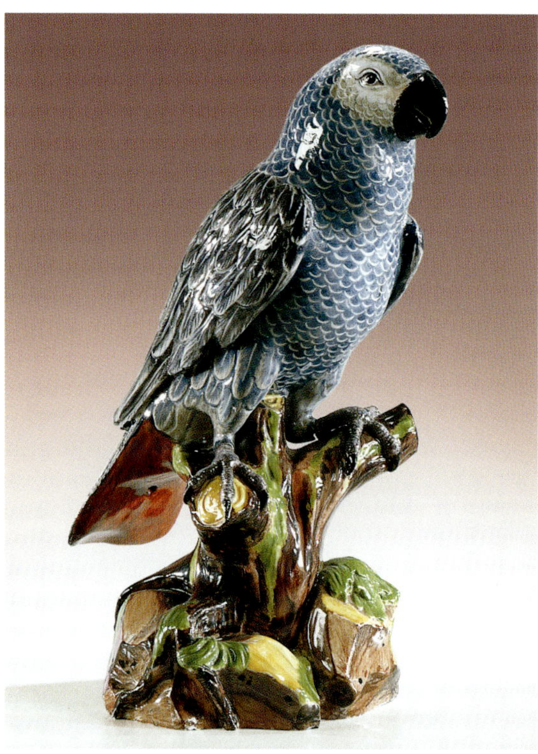

96 Johann Joachim Kaendler, Gray Parrot, model 1731, Rijksmuseum Amsterdam

original model. This fundamentally painterly approach to decoration is a far cry from what we generally associate with the best of Meissen figure-painting.

Our idea of Meissen figure-painting, however, is derived from the famous and exceptionally finely painted small-size figures (shepherds, Commedia dell'Arte figures, crinoline groups) modeled by Kaendler after 1736, by which time the large animal figures had gone out of production. While the former, as small figures, were only to be looked at from near to, this was never the case with the animal figures, which, as the manufactory was fully aware, had to be painted in such a way that they would be best seen from a distance, and as we know from Keyssler's report, the gallery was only a little less than eleven meters high. This may well explain the general tendency towards large expanses of single colors and the lack of very fine shadowing and internal linework. The strongly contrasting color-tones, powerfully applied, functioned in rather the same way as those used on colorful painted figures designed to stand on baroque high altars.

These factors make it clear that the difficulty of making judgments about the colored decoration of the animal figures is not primarily to do with the period in which they were created but rather with the way we see things now, and our modern-day expectations.

refined and somewhat more schematic color application on the Gray Parrot (fig. 96) and the monochromatic coloring of the Coot (fig. 91), to clumsily executed plumage in the cases of the Rose-Ringed Parakeet (fig. 127), the Falcon (fig. 122), the sitting Macaw (fig. 85) and the Golden Pheasant (fig. 98). As enameled examples of all these bird figures were delivered to the Japanese Palace before December 1732, they clearly all originated at roughly the same time. The pedestals, most often tree-stumps, are painted with the same kind of strongly contrasting, non-naturalistic patches of color as are also to be found on Far Eastern animal figures.

In the early 1730s the manufactory had had very little experience in the decoration of sculptural figures; in fact, hardly any work had been done in this field at all. Comparison, for instance, of the quality of the decoration (marbling) on the Temple of Venus (fig. 86), which was executed before 1730, with that on the large sitting Macaw (fig. 85), does reveal parallels in respect of choice of color and brushwork. The color application, technically speaking comparable to that used in watercolors, is either very patchy with stark contrasts, or quite the opposite. Darker strokes usurp the role of the surface relief, which consequently suffers a decisive loss of depth. The fact that powerfully contrasting color combinations make the piece lively and eye-catching is only further evidence of the use of more or less bright or dark color-tones to oust the typically sculptural play of light and shade that was a feature of the

97 Johann Joachim Kaendler, Osprey with fish, model 1731, Dresden Porcelain Collection

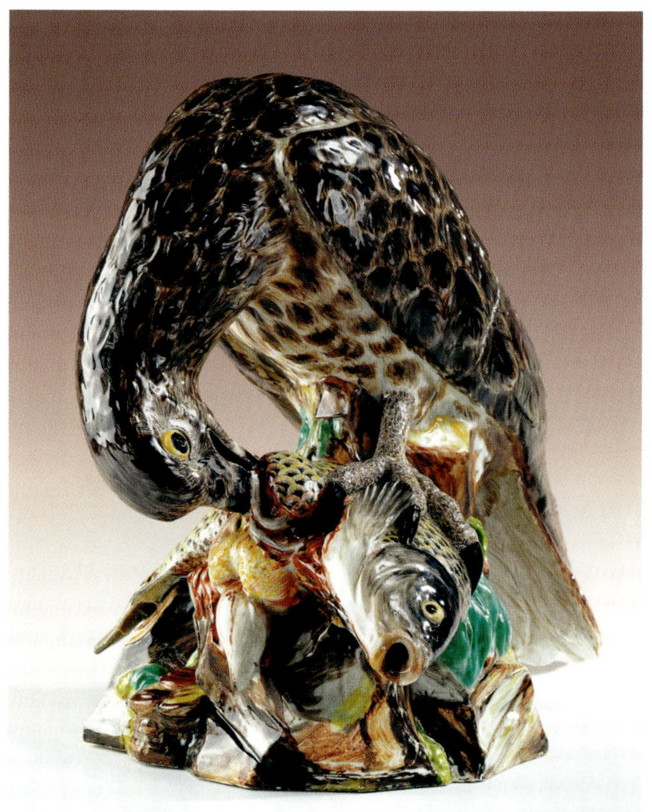

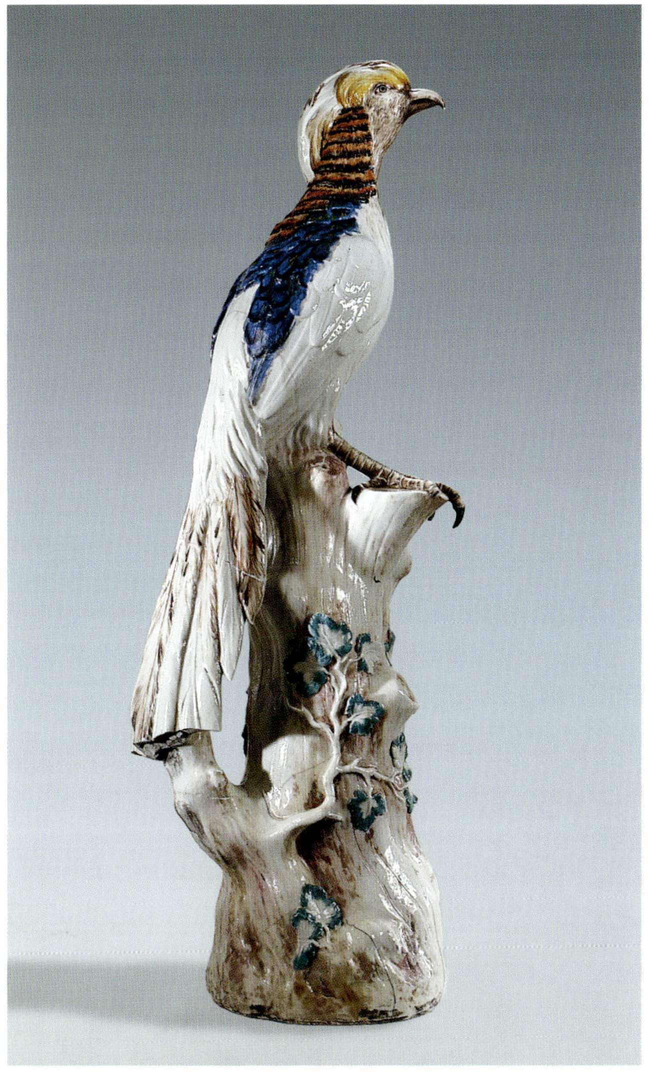

98 Johann Joachim Kaendler, Golden Pheasant, model 1731, Rijksmuseum Amsterdam

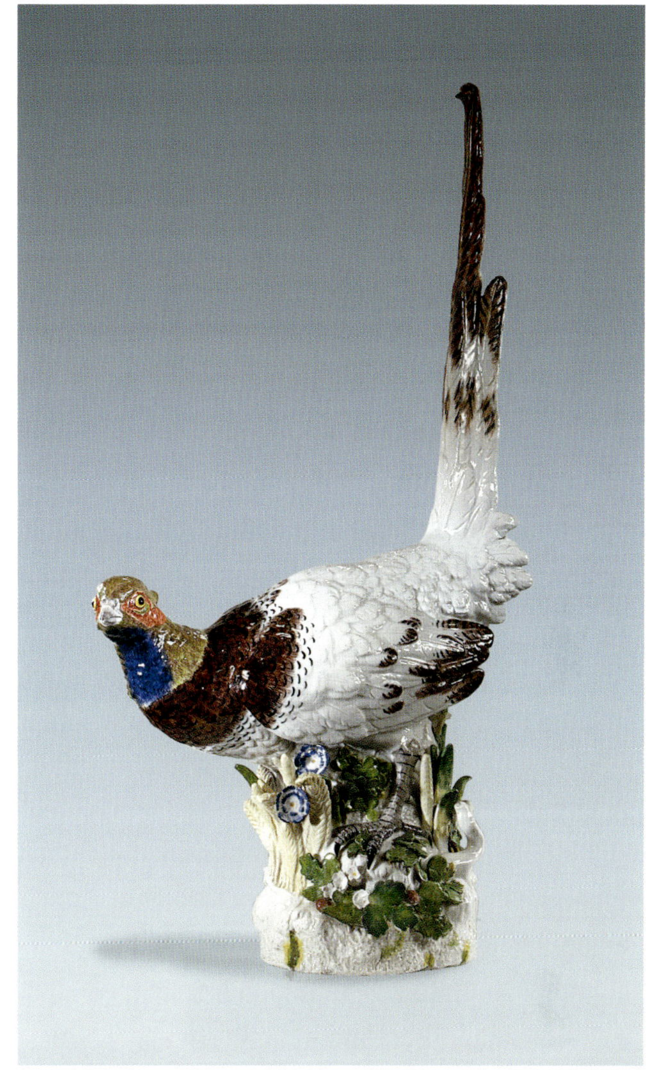

99 Johann Joachim Kaendler, Pheasant, model 1735, Rijksmuseum Amsterdam

In the case of the Golden Pheasant (fig. 98), for example, it is relatively difficult for us to free ourselves not only from the visual habits of the past (which have in any case only been passed down to us in fragmentary form) but also from the conditioned taste of our own time, and to follow as objective a path as possible in trying to see sense in the figure's patchy painting and pedestal decoration. And yet the rather strange flesh color that dominates the figure's tree-trunk is also to be found in small remnants on other Japanese Palace animals that were nevertheless painted with oils.

True, Count Sulkowski is in 1734 recorded as complaining about the postures of the palace animals and the "unnatural" way in which they were painted; and speaking as the official in charge of the realization of the Japanese Palace project, it was with Kaendler in particular, as has already been noted, that he was expressing dissatisfaction. However, it should be noted that he was referring to the figures painted with oils, and furthermore that the manufactory was still engaged in the quest for the best means of decorating the animal figures. When one compares such figures as the blue-painted and black-shaded parts of the sitting Macaw (fig. 85) and the Golden Pheasant (fig. 98), both decorated in 1731/32, with the corresponding parts of the Pheasant (fig. 99) done in June/July 1735, there is no mistaking the extent of the technical development that had taken place in the few intervening years.

The chapter on the forgeries of the large animal figures will give further consideration to the question of the decoration with enamel colors – original or not, authentic or false.

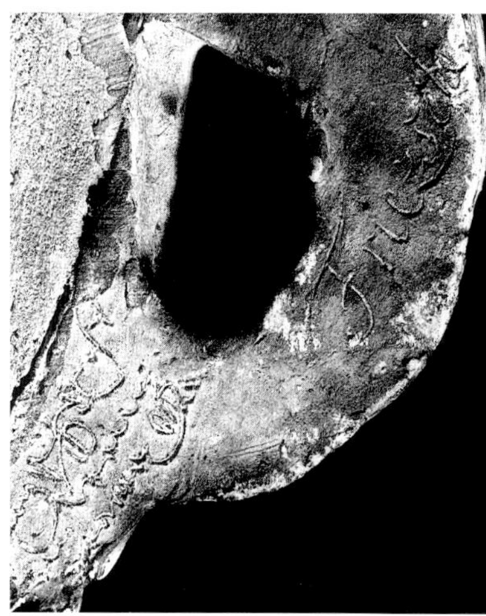

100 George Fritzsche, signature incised on the underside of the tail on a porcelain lion, Longleat Castle

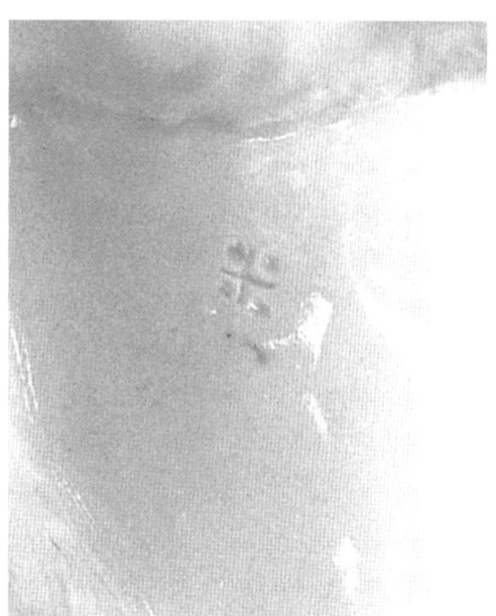

101 Andreas Schiefer, molder's mark on a cat, Dresden Porcelain Collection

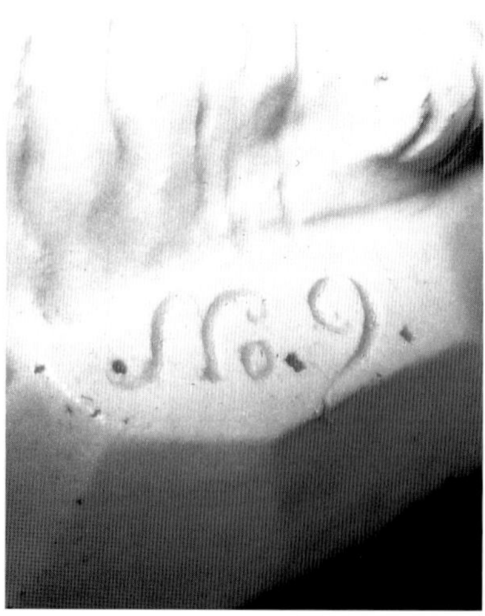

102 Paste-recipe number – No:9 – incised on a king vulture, Longleat Castle

Signatures and markings

The study of marks, signs, and signatures on eighteenth-century Meissen porcelain has now developed into a research field in its own right. The intention in the following section is simply to record the kinds of markings found on the animal figures made for the Japanese Palace in Dresden in the period between 1731 and 1737.

Signatures

Name signatures, or even simply initials, of painters, modelers, and repairers are very rarely found on Meissen porcelain. Mass production called for uniformity of execution, and it was only in exceptional cases that there was any scope for personal stylization. This was particularly true of the painting, as even when a service was painted by a number of different painters it still had to give the impression of being "all of a piece." This uniformity was attained through in-house schooling and working procedures that essentially consisted of copying and reproducing. The painter did not function as an artist but rather as a member of a team, which explains why pieces signed by painters are such a rarity, and why those that do exist are all single specimens.[532]

In the case of the sculptors engaged as artists, on the other hand, the reason why they were not required to sign their work was very likely because no more than two sculptors were creating new models at any one time, which was indeed the case for the period of the orders for the Japanese Palace.[533] It should furthermore not be forgotten that in the relatively circumscribed context of a court such as that of Dresden the artist's signature was accorded far less attention than on paintings, prints, or drawings destined for the international market.

As far as we know, the only two signatures to appear on Meissen large animal figures are signatures of repairers. The one, "Friezsch," refers to George Fritzsche and is scratched into the bottom of the tail of the Lion in the collection of the Marquess of Bath at Longleat (fig. 100). The second signature consists simply of the letters "A S" and is likewise scratched into the still unfired paste. It appears on the lower half of the beak of a Bustard and refers, as Maureen Cassidy-Geiger rightly noted, to the repairer Andreas Schiefer. There is supposedly also a privately-owned Bustard in Italy with "A S" cut into the paste, which is further evidence that any one model was usually only worked on by one repairer.[534] The signatures on the Lion and on the Bustard show that the respective craftsmen felt a certain pride in having been involved in their production.

Molders' marks

Impressed marks, which were given comprehensive treatment in a study of 1996, served a different purpose.[535] On the one hand, they made it easier to check the work of the respective molder; on the other hand, they were an indication of the paste used, which also helped the firer to position the work in the kiln in such a way that the temperature would be right for the paste in question. Although the arcanist Dr Petzsch recorded in his notes that the large animal figures were not marked for the simple reason that one could always find out who had been responsible for the figure and thus establish which paste had been used, the Dresden Porcelain Collection does have a cat with a molder's mark, once again one used by Andreas Schiefer (fig. 101).[536] The Porcelain Collection also contains a shard of feather-structure with an incised cross, but these are as yet the only instances of a molder's mark on a (larger) animal figure made for the Japanese Palace.

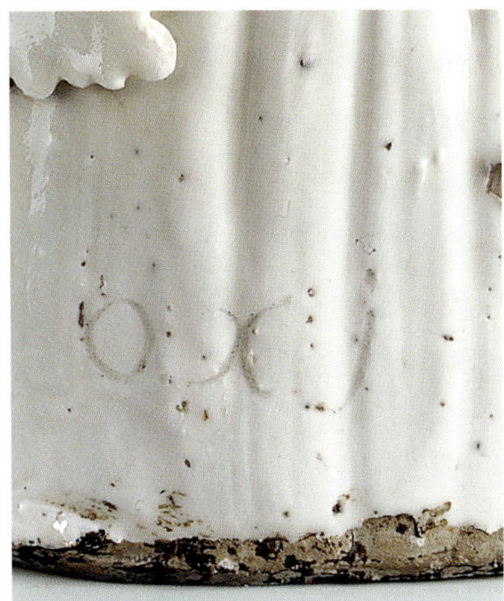

103 Marking – OXi – on the tree-stump pedestal of a sitting peacock, Dresden Porcelain Collection

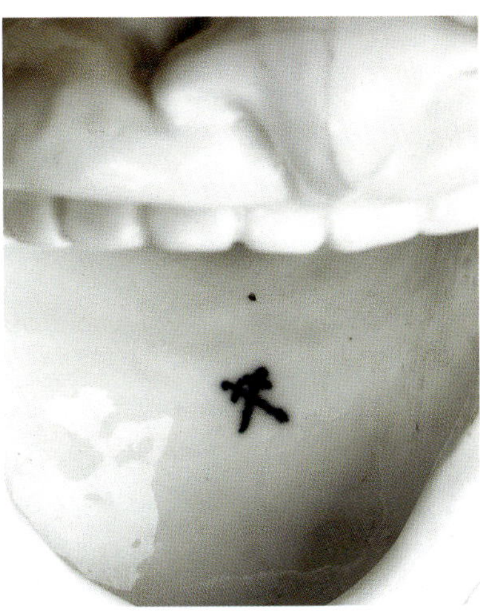

104 Swords mark in the lower jaw of a dragon, Dresden Porcelain Collection

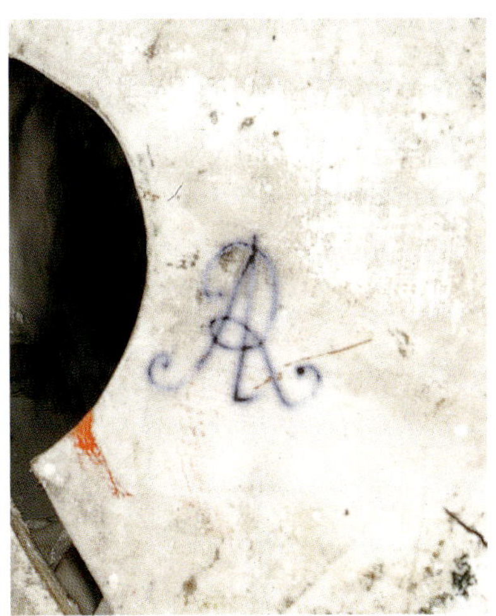

105 AR-mark on an owl, Dresden Porcelain Collection

Terms for the various pastes

A similar scenario is suggested by incised letters and numbers to be found on the pedestals of certain large animal figures. As they are relatively conspicuous and not hidden, it has been supposed in the literature on the subject that they were molder's numbers which served to facilitate monitoring of the craftsmen's work.[537] However, Rainer Rückert has come closer to the truth with his suggestion that these marks were in fact connected with glaze tests.[538]

Clues to the solution of this mystery are to be found in the extant notes on paste recipes. Once a piece had been given its final shape and form it was not subjected to its first firing until it had dried for a number of weeks, in the course of which further changes were made to the paste recipe. When the time came for the high firing, it was important to know what results the respective recipes had yielded, and to this end the abbreviations for the various pastes used in the arcanists' recipe books were scratched into the body of a number of test pieces. These signs, which were only of importance for the production process, were then covered over when it came to the painting.

An example of the King Vulture of 1731 (standing) in the Pflueger Collection in New York has the incision "N: 08" on it. Other examples of this figure, in the Rockefeller Collection in Kykuit, New York, and in the possession of the Marquess of Bath at Longleat, are marked "No: 9" (fig. 102); one further vulture at Longleat has "No. 6." and the mark "4.0" is found on an eagle in Copenhagen. These markings correspond to those associated with certain paste recipes in Höroldt's notes: "No:O.8./4 parts Schnorr's earth/one part stone/2 parts of the above low-fired porcelain shards, crushed."[539] The following note was added later in red ink: "is a beautiful paste and shall from now on be used for large animals and vases, holds better than the other pastes on account of the crushed body, or 'Graubeln'."[540] The recipe is not dated. Although the King Vulture ("Kropfvogel") was created in the fourth quarter of 1731, seven further examples of the figure were produced in 1734, and delivered; this paste recipe could thus well have been developed in the summer of 1734, as is also suggested by the evidence to be found in the notes.[541]

The above entry in Höroldt's recipe book is followed by a further recipe for the production of large figures: "No:O.9./5 parts Schnorr's earth/1 part Siebenlehner stone/2 parts of the above low-fired porcelain body, crushed."[542] Further down on the same page, Höroldt finally made a note of the results achieved at the firing: "NB: the above paste No.O.8 is the best so far and shall be used, for the reason that the large animals and vases will not hold upright with the ordinary paste, which is why this paste has been made with crushed low-fired shards. It holds the large pieces together so that they no longer rupture in the shrinking, as we know the pieces produced hitherto have done." This is corroborated by the fact that the crouching bird from the Rockefeller Collection contains a quarter more kaolin than the standing vulture from the Pflueger Collection.

The conclusion that paste No. 8 was the most suitable for the animal figures is later confirmed by Höroldt in connection with a good recipe for the production of normal tableware: "Furthermore, from now on, the same paste shall be used as for the large animals, recorded above as No:O.8. 4 parts Schnorr's earth/one part Siebenlehner stone/2 parts low-fired body crushed to the size of coarse sand and sieved accordingly."[543]

While one further mark, "O X i", has only been found on one model so far, namely on the Peacock sitting on a high tree-trunk, it does appear on all known examples of this figure (fig. 103).[544] Although the mark does not appear in any arcanum-book in exactly the same form, Höroldt did make notes of a whole series of paste recipes numbered from 4 to 9, each preceded by the "O" which appears in the above examples. On the page before these recipes, under "No:X.i." (the Roman numeral XI) he made a note of a paste test dated 1734.[545] And the fact that the model of the Peacock was created in April 1734 makes it highly probable that there is a direct link between the mark on the figures and the recipe.[546]

The Billy-Goat in the Victoria and Albert Museum, London, has a "Z" – or possibly an "N" – incised on the underside of the hoof of its outward-turned right front leg. If this mark is interpreted as a "2", it could be related to the marking on the Nanny-Goat in the Dresden Porcelain Collection that has a "3" incised on the underside of the hoof.[547] The significance of these markings, however, has yet to be explained. The same is true of the letters "B I F" incised on the back of the pedestal of a Griffon Vulture, also in the Dresden Porcelain Collection.

Manufactory marks

From 1723 on, the Meissen manufactory had with a greater or lesser degree of regularity marked its wares with signs in underglaze blue. The various markings, which included the blue crossed swords still used today, were intended to distinguish the pieces decorated at the manufactory from those done by the independent decorators ("Hausmaler"), and later to distinguish all pieces from those of other manufactories.

The animal figures detailed in the order lists of the 1730s were however produced exclusively for the Japanese Palace. According to Keyssler, writing in 1730, thought was even given to the idea of breaking the plaster molds after the completion of the commission, so that "these animal figures may for ever remain rare and costly."[548] However, this was not carried through, as is shown by the fact that a number of mold-sections survived into the twentieth century. But as there was no intention of putting the figures up for public sale, it was not thought necessary to mark the animals with the manufactory sign. This, however, only applied to the large figures, as small birds such as the parrots, canaries, magpies and so on were already being sold to third parties around 1740, and were normally marked with the crossed swords. Markings are sometimes to be found on middle-size figures, even though they were also intended exclusively for the Japanese Palace; in some cases we find the crossed swords, and in the case of models from 1731/32 also the mark "AR" ("Augustus Rex") in underglaze blue.

The crossed swords have as yet only been found on a Turkey-hen and three Coots, on the Marmoset in the Dresden Porcelain Collection, and on a large number of small-size figures (birds) from the period, either in other collections or being offered for sale. The smaller examples of the Dragon have the crossed swords on their lower jaws (fig. 104). The AR mark is to be found on: one Osprey eating a carp, one Owl (with a mouse), two Barn Owls, two Rose-Ringed Parakeets, one Gray Parrot, one Coot, two Great Crested Grebes, one Marmoset, three Monkeys (wearing ruffs), two Monkeys (with chains), and one Dragon. Of these, all are enameled, with the exception of two Owls, one Grebe, and the Dragon (fig. 105).[549]

If one considers the whole range of the figures, including all sizes, types of decorations, and markings, and takes account of the fact that – as we shall see in greater detail later on – the small animal figures were also sold on the free market from the middle of the 1730s onwards, then a relatively clear picture emerges which for lack of source material can nevertheless only be presented as follows. It must have been common knowledge amongst all the employees of the manufactory and all its branches that the large animal figures were being made solely for the Japanese Palace and thus for the king, and the fact that such extraordinary porcelain was in production will certainly have been a subject of general conversation. There was thus no need for these pieces to be marked with a "trademark" for protective purposes. However, the AR-mark was applied (as a reminder, as it were) to the smaller figures also made for the project. From the point in time when some were allowed to be produced for third parties, which only happened with a few models, the figures produced required the manufactory marking, the crossed swords. This can be particularly clearly seen in the case of the Marmoset or the examples of the Rose-Ringed Parakeet.

Inventory numbers

An inventory of the collection in what was then known as the "Holländisches Palais" was kept from 1721 onwards.[550] There are no extant inventories from the period immediately after the conversion of the building into the "Japanisches Palais." The Dresden Porcelain Collection and the State Archive of Saxony each have a five-volume catalog, from 1770 and 1779 respectively, listing the items in the porcelain collection and other works of art, ordered by numbers in various categories.[551] These inventories show clearly the degree of importance accorded to these collections. Far from being regarded simply as an accumulation of decorative pieces, the porcelain in the Japanese Palace almost had the same standing as specialist collections do in our own time: the numbering in the record-books was not simply done with "serial numbers," as was customary for porcelain inventories, but inventory markings were also attached to the pieces themselves.

In the case of the Far Eastern and Meissen tableware and small figures, the numbers were from 1732 on at the latest incised into the undersides with glass-cutting tools, with the incisions sometimes also being colored black. In 1996, Rainer Rückert published a record found by Joachim Menzhausen according to which the glassmaker Johann Daniel Springer received, at the end of May 1732, a relatively large sum (135 talers) for incising inventory numbers in porcelain pieces. Nowadays, these numbers are generally known as "Johanneum numbers," after the second home of the porcelain collection, the Johanneum in the Dresden stables building.[552] However, no extant animal figure provided with a number

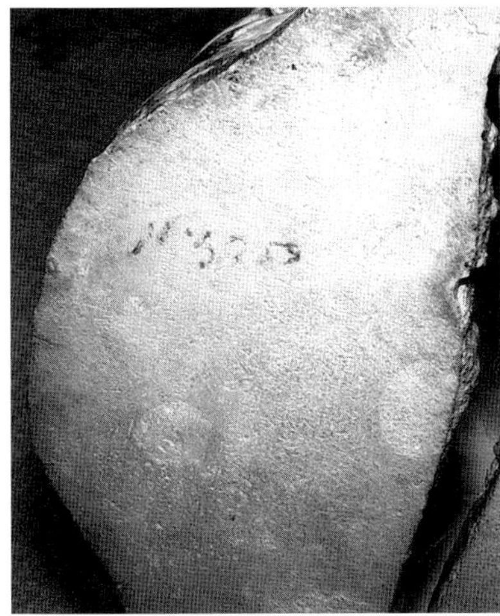

106 Royal collection inventory number ("Johanneum number") N-320 on the underside of a king vulture, Longleat Castle

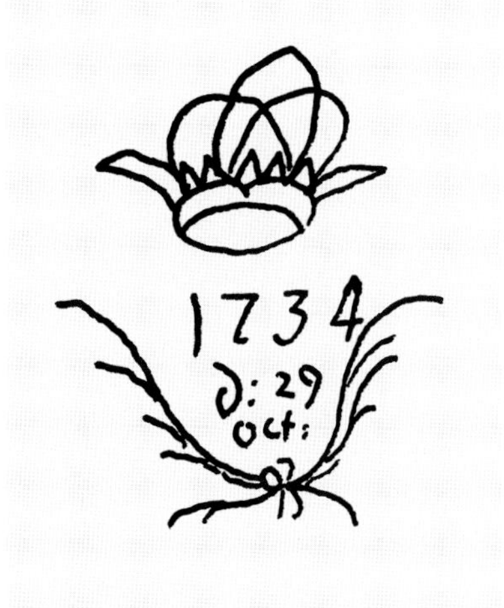

107 Elaborate date mark inside the tree-stump pedestal of a king vulture, Rockefeller Collection, Kykuit

in the inventory books has an incised inventory sign, although there are several pieces that have an inventory number, or part of an inventory number, painted on them in black (fig. 106).

Datings

The Rockefeller Collection in Kykuit, New York, contains an example of the 1734 King Vulture that is a unique case in that on the inside of the base it has an exact date, which was incised into the paste before the first firing: "1734 d:29 oct:" (fig. 107). This highly unusual dating mark has even led to the work being considered a forgery.

The figure was definitely produced in the manufactory, as comparison of the detail with a proven original shows. No forger would have copied such things as the angle and details of every single feather, all a sixth bigger to allow for the shrinkage. As for the idea that it might have been a later execution, perhaps carried out at the beginning of the twentieth century when the large animal figures went back into production at the manufactory, one would have to explain how a repairer of that time could have had such exact knowledge of the way in which dates and numbers were written in the first half of the eighteenth century, and how he could have known that this date was a possible one for the King Vulture. Given that the model was made in June 1734, the first examples would indeed have been ready for firing the around the end of October. All these points make a later execution at the manufactory at the very least highly unlikely.

The inventories of 1770 and 1779 both list one King Vulture under the number N=321-W and five under the number N=273-W, all described however as being "reddish and blackish-grey," or "blackish-grey birds [...] also painted in a reddish color."[553] All the other known copies apart from the figure in the Rockefeller Collection are decorated with enamel colors as in the description (fig. 83). It may therefore be supposed that this white figure was the one referred to as N=321-W, and that it was decorated in the same colors as the others, but had perhaps been cold-painted. It is not unusual to find that cold painting has disappeared without trace; as it was often harmful to the figure, it was in many cases deliberately washed off at some later date.

There are thus no compelling arguments in favor of regarding this work, with its characteristic dating mark, as a forgery. Just as repairers occasionally left indications as to their names on their pieces, there are also other pieces of Meissen porcelain with hidden date marks, such as a large candlestick from the Swan Service which, when it was broken, was found to have "1740 29May" incised on the inside of the base-plate.[554]

When one takes into account that the Commission had been in session at the Albrechtsburg from October 26 to 28, 1734, and that the repairers had had to make their official statements regarding the accusations brought against Höroldt, it is not so far-fetched to think that the repairer was so acutely aware of the importance of these events as to want to cut the date into the paste for posterity.

Mention should finally be made of one case noted by Carl Albiker, though all other trace of it has disappeared: "The figure known as the Marmoset [...] is a little monkey, marked in one old example with the year 1726."[555] Albiker however leaves us quite in the dark as to where the figure was to be found, and what form the date mark took. The date itself cannot be correct, given that the model was not created until 1731, and may simply have been misread, or may have been a forgery; whatever the truth may be, the case is all in all a very dubious one.

Attribution of the models

General problems of attribution and dating

As has been made clear, the animal figures were serial products, manufactured in a number of distinct stages with various specialists making their own contribution to the respective figure's final appearance and character. One problem inherent in this is that a given artist's characteristic style or personal "handwriting" can no longer be recognized in the details, which means that stylistic attributions can only be made on the basis of compositional characteristics noted in other animal figures where the authorship is proven through written evidence.

There are similar problems when it comes to dating figures. The date of the creation of the model always has to be distinguished from that of the completion of the production process; in the case of the large animal figures, the two dates were separated by at least three and sometimes as many as six months. For the animal figures made for the Japanese Palace, written sources often help us to determine the date of the creation of the model, or at least the period in which it was created. Information about the production of individual pieces is given by firing reports and delivery lists, insofar as they are still extant.

Modeler attributions made certain by work reports

From 1731 onwards, the manufactory demanded of the modelers that they make short summaries of their work, the so-called work reports.[556] From 1732 these were submitted monthly, though for the first half of the 1730s we do not have all those compiled by the artists engaged on the large animal figures, namely Kirchner and Kaendler. The only artist whose animal figures are documented in their entirety in work reports is Eberlein.

The oft-quoted modelers' work reports are not only useful for establishing authorship and datings, but also often contain detailed descriptions with plentiful evidence regarding the artists' intentions, way of working, and knowledge of technique.

This may be demonstrated by one example. In the summer of 1734, Kaendler spent some time in the natural history gallery ("Animaliengalerie") at the Zwinger studying certain exotic animals, in preserved form, that could not be observed live in the royal menageries. When he returned to Meissen, the items he brought with him included a bozzetto of a "goat of atonement, or scapegoat, such as the Jews had."[557] In January 1735, he translated his sculptural sketch into a fully-fledged model: "A large figure for the Palace, to be known as the Goat of Atonement, or Scapegoat, modeled in clay, wondrous in appearance, and in its natural size."[558] (fig. 108) Kaendler must have been inspired by the little drama created by the taxidermist Gottfried Gebhardt involving an exotic ram which was supposed to have some connection with the scapegoat of the Old Testament.[559] The taxidermal collection also contained a further exhibit, described by Keyssler when he was visiting the *Animaliengalerie* in October 1730 as "a large Babylonian sheep with very broad and fat back."[560] Kaendler made a model from this exhibit in December 1734: "A large Indian sheep with two horns which grow out of the sheep's eyes in a wondrous way."[561] (fig. 109) The resultant figure was later referred to in delivery lists as an "Indian sheep." These two taxidermal specimens, the form and history of which must have exerted a certain fascination upon Kaendler, are an eloquent testimony to the direct connection that existed between the various animal collections at the Dresden court.

For models which written sources enable us to date and attribute to a specific modeler (9 models by Kirchner, 59 by Kaendler, and 8 by Eberlein) the relevant records are quoted in the Catalog. In spite of this corpus of reliable evidence, the literature on the work reports has on occasion thrown up fallacious interpretations leading to wrong conclusions, particularly in connection with Kaendler.

There still exists an undated list from Kaendler's hand, with the following heading: "What I have produced since June 22 for the order made by His Majesty to the Royal Porcelain Manufactory is the following: [...]" (fig. 110, Source 24).[562] The list enumerates seven bird models which other sources show to have been his first works at the manufactory. As the modelers' regular monthly work reports do not start until 1732, and Kaendler was first engaged at the manufactory on June 21, 1731, it has hitherto been assumed that the list was a retrospective summary of his work during his first half-year at the manufactory. This assumption was corroborated by the fact of the list being bound into the volume of records for the year 1732. It is however remarkable that Kaendler concludes his listing with the following note: "At the present I am working on the following: [...] an aurochs killing a wild boar," (fig. 116). Furthermore, the manufactory report for October 1731 also runs: "[...] not only an elephant but also an aurochs of considerable size has been modeled, from which molds are to be made in the coming days."[563] Kaendler must therefore have written his list

108 Johann Joachim Kaendler, Scapegoat, model 1735, copy from the Meissen revival ca. 1922

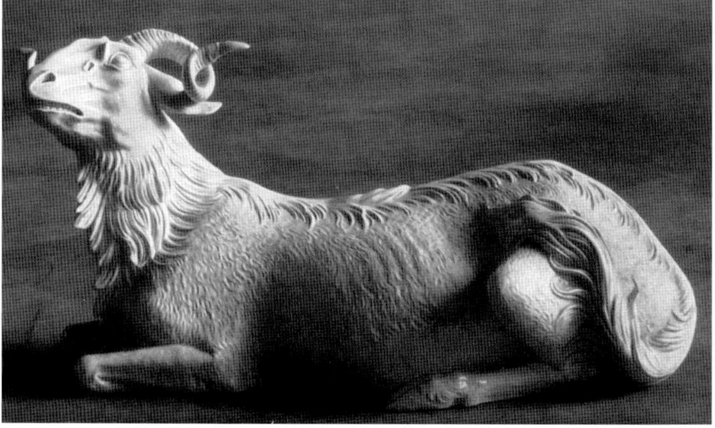

at this point in time, October 1731, at the latest; accordingly, it only describes the models which he made in his first quarter-year at the manufactory.[564] However, the gap in direct written documentation of Kaendler's models for the period October 1731 to the early months of 1732 can be shown to correspond clearly to a group of animal figures that have significant stylistic features in common with models which we know for certain to have been from his hand.[565]

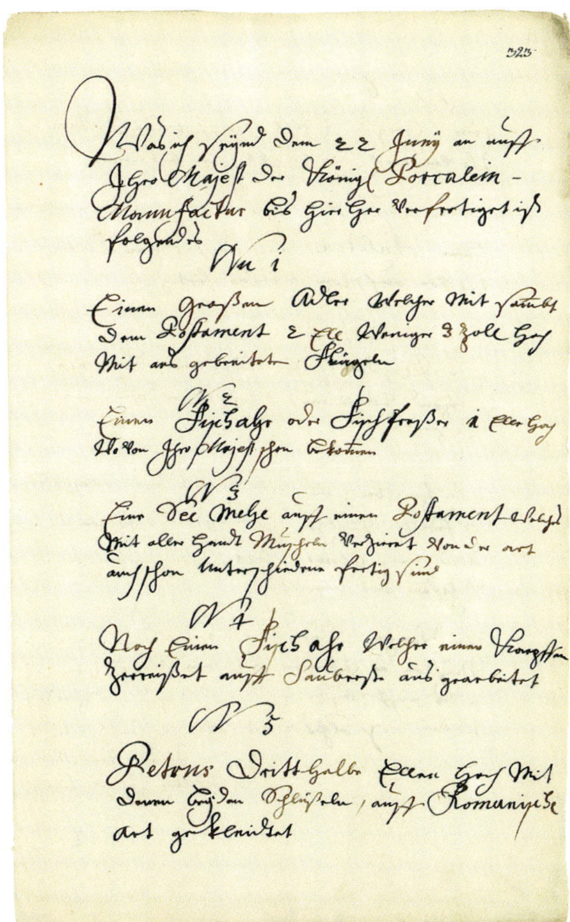

110 Johann Joachim Kaendler, work report with a list of the animals he modeled for the manufactory between June and October 1731 (detail)

The models that can be attributed with certainty through written records are the following, with their dates:

Johann Gottlieb Kirchner: Dragon[566] (1730), Bear (Oct. 1732), Fox (Oct. 1732), Bustard (Nov. 1732), Leopard (Jan. 1733), Lynx (Jan. 1733), "Tiger" (which came to be known as a sitting Lioness; Jan. 1733), Pied Wagtail (Feb. 1733).

Johann Joachim Kaendler: Eagle, first model (June 1731), Wisent Fighting with a Boar (Oct. 1731), Owl (before Oct. 1731), Barn Owl (before Oct. 1731), Kestrel (before Oct. 1731), Osprey (before Oct. 1731), Osprey with a fish (before Oct. 1731), Gull (before Oct. 1731), Coot (before Oct. 1731), Monkey (Feb. 1732), Heron (March 1732), Macaw climbing downwards (May 1732), Squirrel (Aug. 1732), Cockerel (Aug. 1732), Hen (Aug. 1732), Nanny-Goat (Aug. 1732), Dog, scratching itself (Sept. 1732), Canary (Sept. 1732), Cassowary (Sept. 1732), Tit (Sept. 1732), Swallow (Sept. 1732), Turtledove (Sept. 1732), Eagle, second model (Oct. 1732), Pelican (Oct. 1732), Pigeon, on nest (Oct. 1732), Bird's Nest (Jan. 1733), Bird of Paradise (Jan. 1733), Woodpecker (Jan. 1733), Pair of Pigeons (Jan. 1733), Turkeycock (Jan. 1733), Magpie (Feb. 1733), Bullfinch (Feb. 1733), Green Woodpecker I (Feb. 1733), Tit (Feb. 1733), Golden Oriole I (July 1733), Green Woodpecker II (March 1734), Peacock, displaying its train (March 1734), Golden Oriole II (March 1734), Peacock, on a tree-stump (April 1734), Sparrowhawk, with a lark (April 1734), King Vulture (June 1734), Vulture Devouring a Cockatoo (Sept. 1734), Great Crested Grebe (Oct. 1734), Cockatoo (Oct. 1734), Exotic Sheep (Dec. 1734), Scapegoat, or "goat of atonement" (Jan. 1735), Cock Pheasant (Feb. 1735), Hen Pheasant (March 1735), Bittern (March 1735), Jerboa (April 1735), Sable (April 1735), Crane (April 1735), Guinea Hen (April 1735), She-Wolf (April 1735), small Parrot (July 1735), Kingfisher (Sept. 1735), Roller (Sept. 1735), Jay (Nov. 1735), Hoopoe (July 1736).

109 Johann Joachim Kaendler, Exotic ("Indian") Sheep, model 1734, Dresden Porcelain Collection

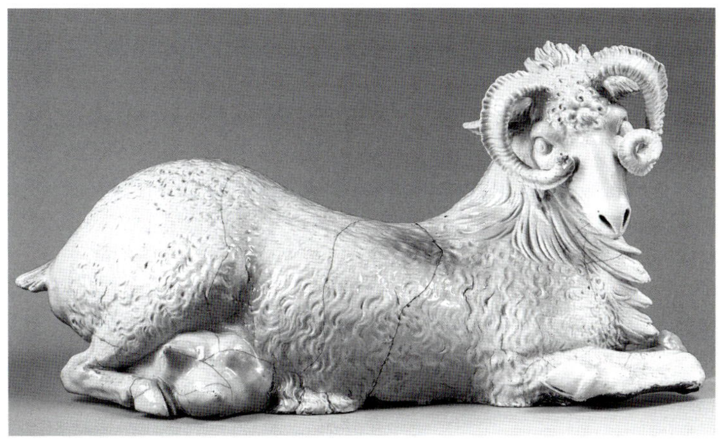

Johann Friedrich Eberlein: Chamois (April/May 1735), Swan (April/May 1735), Eagle Owl, with pigeon (April/May 1735), Sheep (June/July 1735), "Stork" (June/July 1735), Sheep II (Aug. 1735), Sparrow (Aug. 1735), Turkeyhen (Aug. 1735).

Attributions on stylistic grounds

It has hitherto been assumed in literature on Meissen that of the models that cannot be attributed for lack of written sources, the ones that are less naturalistic, less concerned with effect, and less "expressive" must have come from Kirchner's hand. What this highly subjective approach does not take into consideration is that Kirchner was also a trained sculptor, as is clear from the fact that even before his first departure from Meissen he was engaged

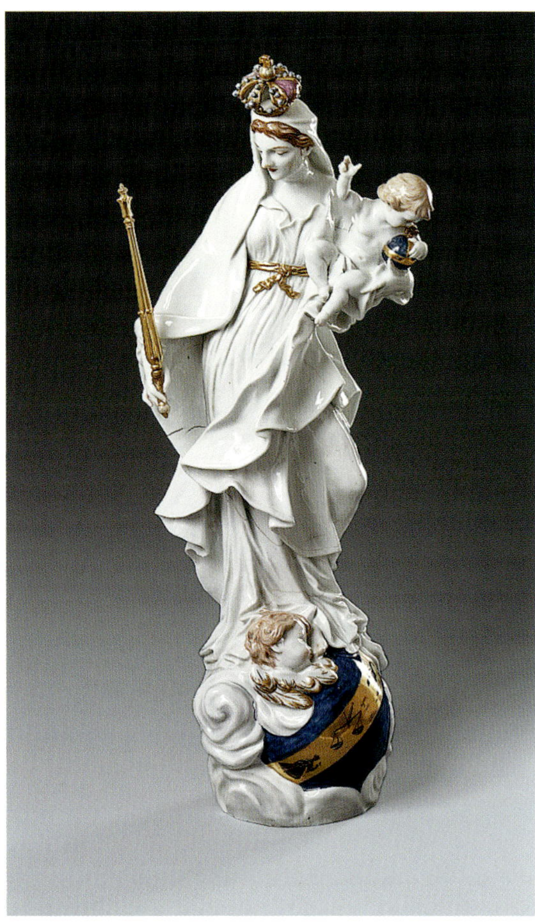

111 Johann Gottlieb Kirchner, Madonna on Orb, model 1732, Dresden Porcelain Collection

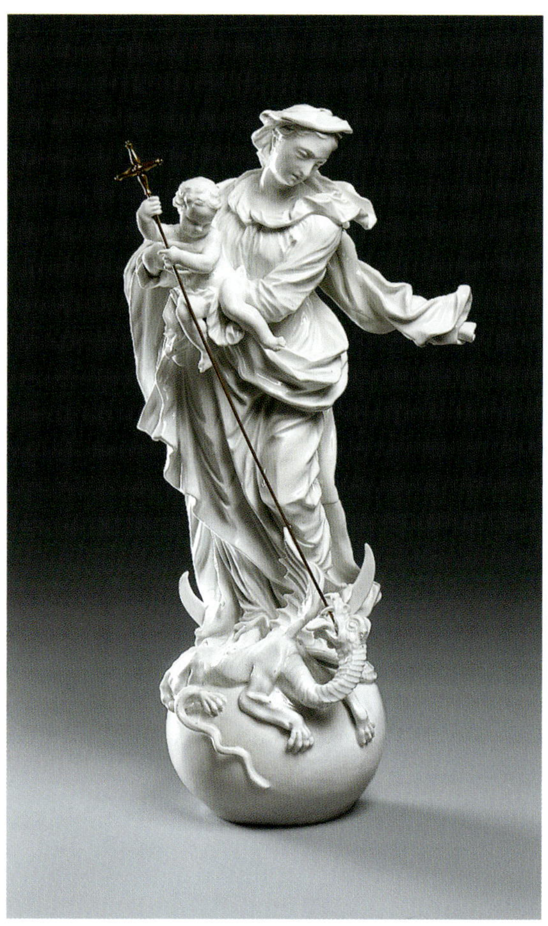

112 Johann Joachim Kaendler, Madonna on Orb, model 1738, Dresden Porcelain Collection

to become Court Sculptor in Weimar. A comparison between Kirchner's Madonna of 1732 (fig. 111)[567] and Kaendler's of 1738 (fig. 112)[568] shows that, while one could not claim that the former was as convincing or as "expressive" as the latter, Kirchner was quite capable of doing very decent and thoroughly contemporary creative work.

The sculptor Carl Albiker, whose book on the Meissen animal figures was intended to open porcelain-lovers' eyes to the quality of Kirchner's work, restricted himself in his arguments largely to the models which can be attributed to Kirchner without any doubt. The intention in what follows is to use the most striking differences between Kirchner's and Kaendler's work to make attributions for those figures for which we have no evidence in the written sources.

In instances where a bird or animal was done as a pair but there is only written evidence for one of the two figures, it can be assumed that the other figure was also modeled by the same artist. One example is the Billy-Goat, which forms a pair with Kaendler's Nanny-Goat of August 1732.

Another way of coming closer to a reliable attribution is to examine the execution of certain aspects and details such as the pedestals, body surfaces, or eyes. In his first three months at the manufactory, Kaendler made a number of bird models that all had one feature in common: detailed pedestal designs incorporating elements from the respective bird's natural habitat. As a rule, these consisted of stones and branches embellished with little tufts of grass and mushrooms, and in the case of water birds, reeds, rushes, and shells. The fact that these motifs also appear on the impressive gravestone sculpted by the artist for Gottfried Keil in 1732 shows how typically Kaendleresque these little "landscapes" are.[569] Exactly the same feeling for variety of detail is observable on, for instance, the Monkey taking snuff, the Marmoset, or the Gray Parrot, which all have pedestals decorated with the same stock motifs. The animals that we know for certain to have been done by Kirchner were mostly modeled without a pedestal, or stand on relatively uninspiring platforms, as do his fox, mother-monkey, and cat (fig. 113). The rock-like structure on which the mandrill is sitting and the bustard's clumsily executed tree-stump are equally tentative and ill-defined. Only in the case of the Monkey wearing a ruff (fig. 89) did Kirchner follow Kaendler's example, but his attempt to make something more interesting out of his very ponderous base by putting in a tuft of grass does not really integrate it into the figure as a whole.

While these obervations are in themselves reason enough to attribute these last three models to Kirchner, a number of other features provide us with further evidence. The coats on Kirchner's animal figures are mostly modeled in flowing strands: there is no great difference between the coats on the Fox (fig. 166) and the Bear (fig. 203), or indeed between these and the mane on the Lion (fig. 159). The same structure covers the whole surface evenly, and all these animals furthermore show a remarkable preference for parting their hair down the middle. This treatment can also be observed on the Mandrill (fig. 207), the Monkey wearing a ruff (fig. 89), and the Mother-Monkey (fig. 147). Kaendler, by contrast, differentiates between the coats of his various long-haired animals. The body-hair of the Billy-Goat (fig. 196), for instance, is shaggier than that of the Nanny-Goat (fig. 195), and the hair on the Wisent (fig. 116) is longer on some parts of the body than on others.

These observations are valid not only for the animals and their coats of hair, but also for bird figures. Comparison of Kirchner's Bustard (fig. 173) and Kaendler's Eagle of 1731 (fig. 163), for instance, shows in the former an uninspired repetition of scales that at best bear a certain resemblance to feathers, as against a lively and differentiated treatment of the surface in the latter. And in Kaendler's Cassowary (fig. 172), which was modeled a month before Kirchner's Bustard and certainly influenced it, one can also observe subtle differentiations between the various parts of the bird's skin and between the various kinds of feathers.

Of Kaendler's first models, two are devoted to one and the same bird, the osprey; the one is in a somewhat stiff, upright posture, and the other is devouring a fish (figs. 114 and 115). Both figures show that Kaendler was not content with superficially exact representation, but considered the bird better depicted when engaged in an activity typical of its species. In the second version he not only filled out the base with elements from the bird's natural habitat, but also emphasized the fact that the osprey is a bird of prey. This line of thought, applied to a different model, would suggest that the remarkable figure of two dogs fighting was also inspired by the artist's interest in animal behavior, and thus originated shortly after he depicted a wisent locked in combat with a wild boar in the last quarter of the year 1731.

Amongst the large animal figures there is a recognizable group with distinctive s-shaped eyebrows that give their eyes an almost human look. Notable examples are the Lion and Lioness, and the Mandrill, none of which is attributable on the strength of a written source. But as the distinctive s-shaped eyebrows are a feature of Kirchner's elephant and (by means of strands of hair) of his bear, fox, and ruff-wearing monkey, we can be reasonably certain that the first-mentioned figures were his work too too.

This leads us to the most difficult criterion for distinguishing Kirchner's and Kaendler's work: the general artistic approach to and understanding of the species in hand. When it comes to making a model, different ways of looking at any given animal will lead to different interpretations. The animal in question can either be seen as reflecting the human perspective, or as representing the natural world. In the former case, the lion will be seen as a majestic creature, king of the animals, but in the latter it will appear as a powerful feline predator. While for some the mother-monkey will be the foolish and self-obsessed creature depicted by Aesop and his successors,[570] for others the monkey will not be a literary figure but a real one, expressing its curiosity and delight in imitation in the way it plays with a snuff-box. Kirchner and Kaendler also had two very different ways of looking at the animal world, and more detailed consideration will be given to this fact at a later stage.

In the cases of the figures which are not attributable from the written sources, the findings made during the study of the technical, stylistic, aesthetic and interpretational differences between the two modelers and their work have been used for the attributions made in the Catalog.

113 Johann Gottlieb Kirchner, Cat, model most likely 1732, Dresden Porcelain Collection

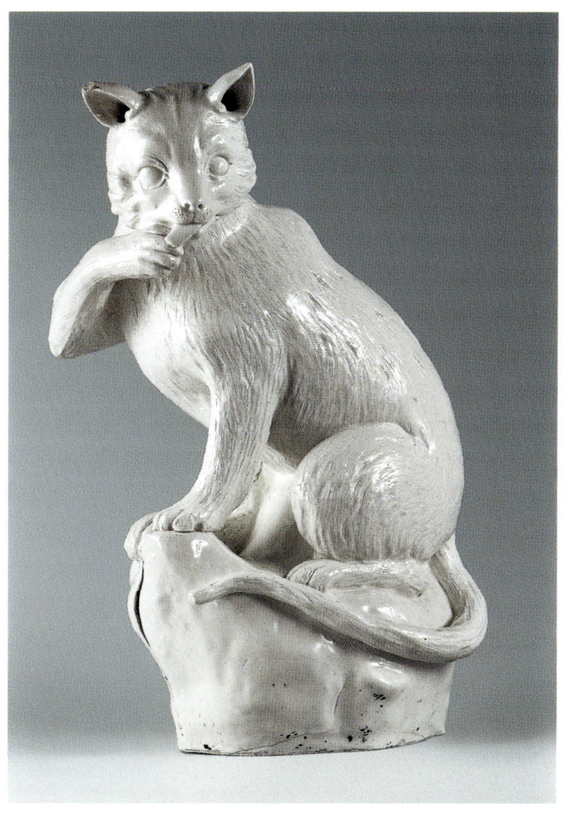

Kaendler as modifier of models made by Kirchner?

Given that these two artists worked on the same project, in the same manufactory and physically near to one another, in a medium which was for both of them alike a relatively new one, it is astounding to find that they contrived to produce such different work and did not exert more influence upon each another. When Kirchner was making his only large bird figure, the Bustard, he certainly took a look at the Cassowary which Kaendler had modeled only a short time before, and the latter's influence is easily recognizable. In all the other figures, however, there a very few parallels of this kind.

There is nevertheless a widely-held theory that after Kirchner's departure, Kaendler reworked models made by his erstwhile colleague that at that point only existed in the form of plaster molds and had not yet been used for taking moldings in paste. There is no source material whatsoever to back up this theory, and it can even be refuted satisfactorily on purely technical grounds. Clay models have to be cut up for molds to be made from them, and can no longer be used once this has been done. Nor can a clay model be put to any good use once it has stood for a while and dried, as is confirmed by a note made by Kaendler in a written submission of December 15, 1738, during his second offensive against Höroldt: "I would soon have finished Mr. Schmiedel's portrait, but was prevented from continuing on it until the end, so that my work was in vain and has to be done all over again from the beginning."[571]

This being the case, Kaendler could only have recreated the model by using the technique known as "aufreparieren" (or "erneuern" from its use as a means of renewing worn-out or incomplete mold sets). In this procedure, moldings are taken in ordinary modeler's clay and then "repaired" (assembled and dressed) to recreate the model. Given the pressure on the artists to create genuinely new models, and the fact that Kaendler's understanding of his art was fundamentally different from Kirchner's, it is highly improbable that he would have done this.

It has also been suggested that the two artists worked together, which is likewise unlikely, as Kaendler's work was at first devoted to birds while Kirchner concentrated on quadrupeds. We can certainly assume that Kaendler's first quadruped, namely the Wisent

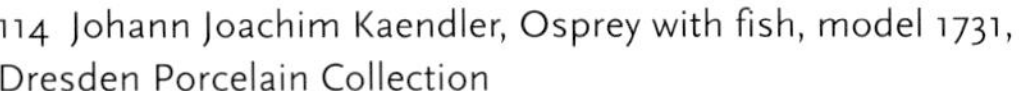

114 Johann Joachim Kaendler, Osprey with fish, model 1731, Dresden Porcelain Collection

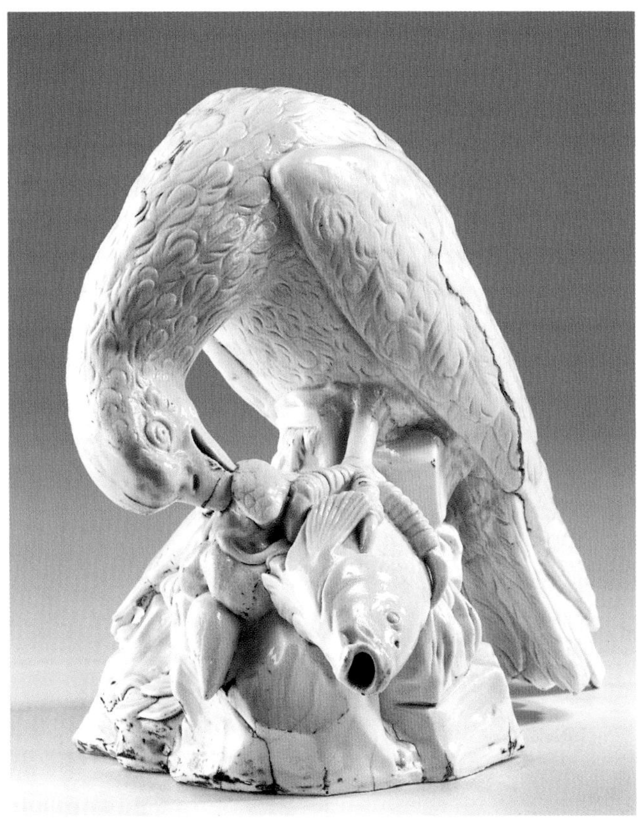

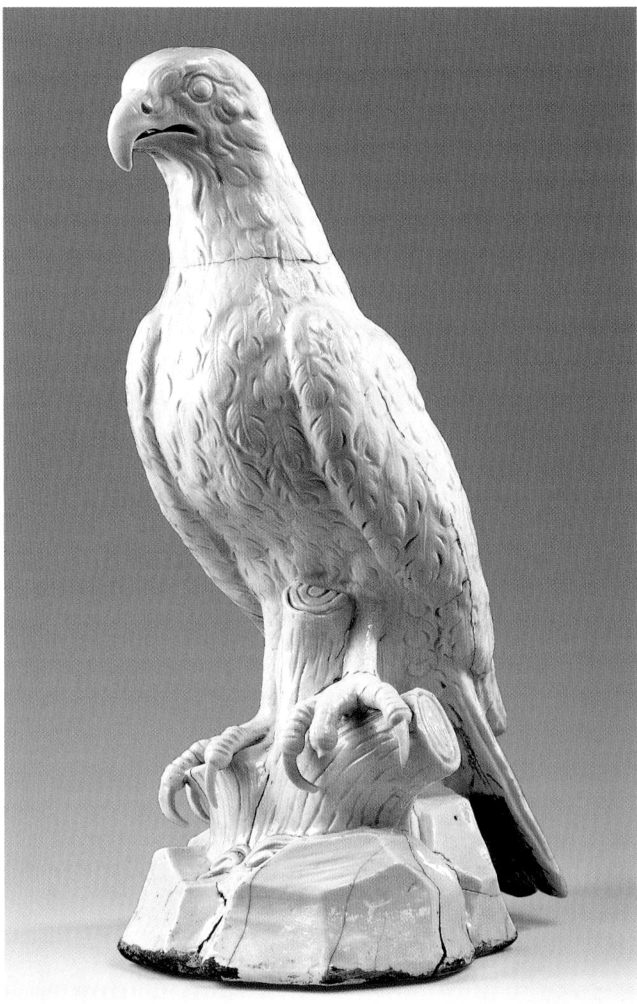

115 Johann Joachim Kaendler, Osprey, model 1731, Dresden Porcelain Collection

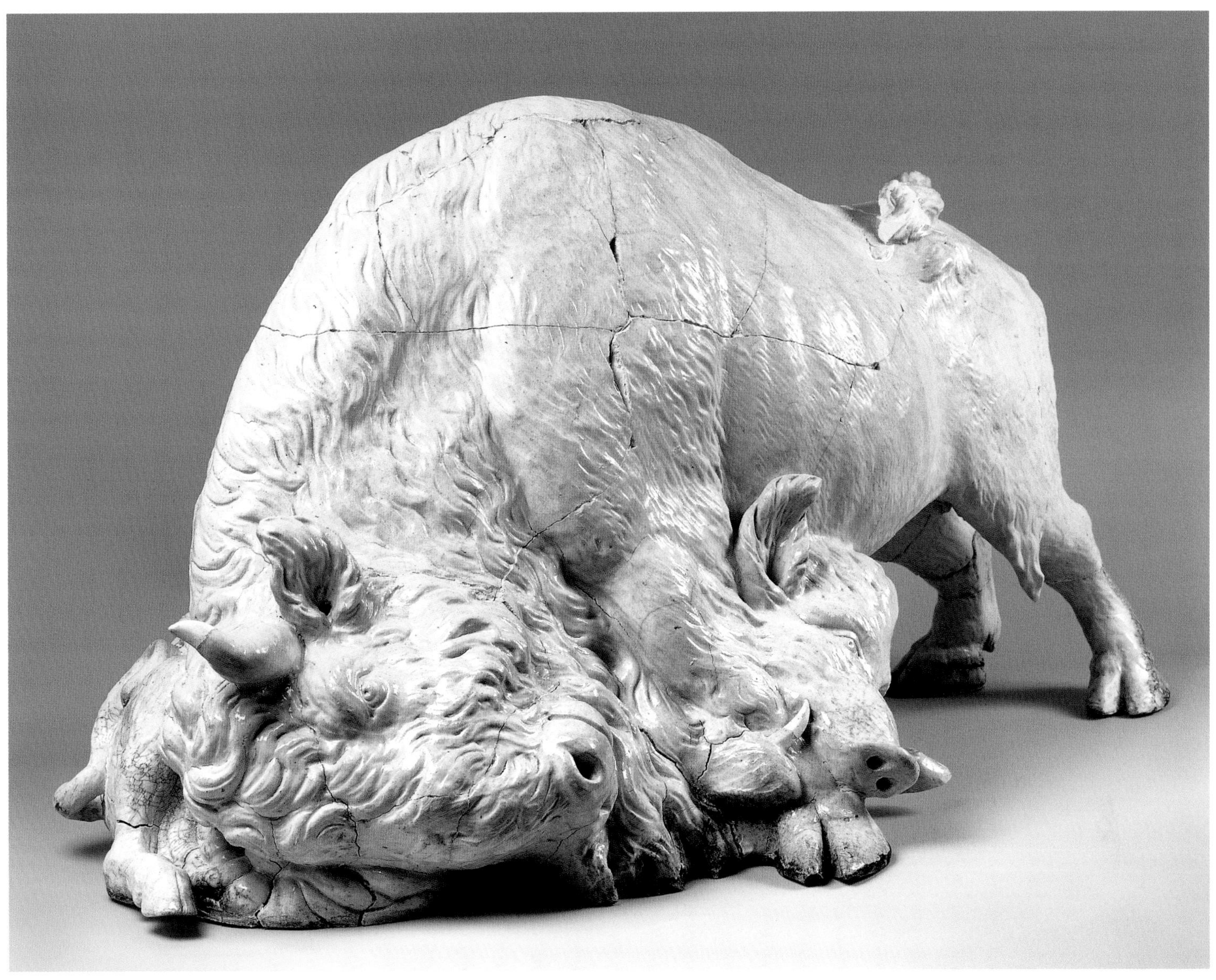

116 Johann Joachim Kaendler, Wisent Fighting with a Boar, model 1731, Dresden Porcelain Collection

Fighting with a Boar (fig. 166), was his work and his alone, as we know from the records that Kirchner was busy at that time on the Elephant.[572] There is not a single figure that offers evidence of a co-operation between the two artists, who were if anything competitors rather than collaborators.

Questions of dating

Having considered which of these two main artists were responsible for which of the models of unproven authorship, we must now turn to the question of dating. When models are not mentioned in the monthly work reports, it is only rarely the case that the sources offer evidence of their date. One case is the Elephant, which is mentioned in the General Report of the Commission for October 1731: "not only an elephant but also an aurochs has been modeled, both considerably large."[573] In most cases the best we can do is to infer a *terminus ante quem* from the delivery lists for the Japanese Palace, and datings made in this way are indicated as such in the Catalog.

Those of Kaendler's works that display clear stylistic parallels to his first models must have originated in that fourth quarter of 1731 for which there are no extant work reports or other written sources. These include not only the figure of two dogs fighting that continues the theme of animals engaged in internecine combat first exploited by Kaendler in his Wisent Fighting a Boar, but also

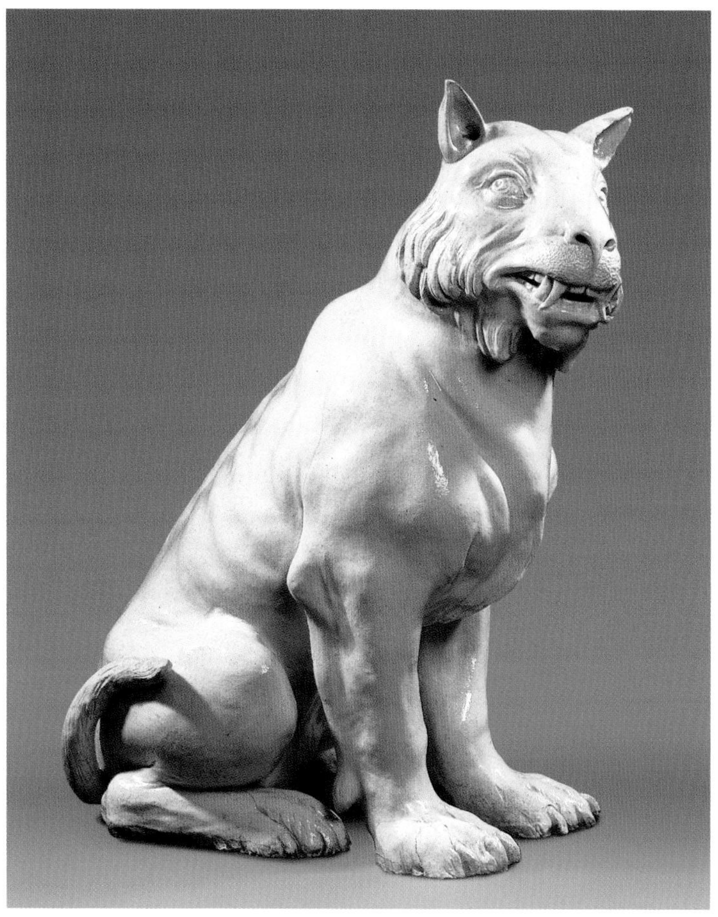

117 Johann Gottlieb Kirchner, Lioness sitting ("Tiger"), model 1733, Dresden Porcelain Collection

some of the smaller birds and monkeys. The models in question are dated "October to December 1731" in the Catalog.

The following particularly confusing example is intended to demonstrate the problems that arise when an attribution is made on stylistic grounds and then used as evidence for a dating.

According to the respective working report, Kirchner created three models in January 1733, a leopard, a tiger, and a lynx, all life-size;[574] according to his own report, he had made bozzetti for all three at the *Löwenhaus* in Dresden the previous November. The three models he referred to have hitherto unanimously been associated with three figures of sitting feline predators; in comparison with the other animals, these three figures seem unnatural and crudely executed, an impression only emphasized by the cold painting having been washed off, revealing the figures' unsightly paste. While the Lynx (fig. 119) is without doubt the animal it claims to be, some of Kirchner's contemporaries clearly had their doubts when it came to the "Tiger" (fig. 117), as although Kirchner refers to a "tiger" in his work reports and "tigers" appear in the order lists, there is no record of a Tiger, as such, ever having been delivered. The solution to this puzzle is that the compiler of the lists recorded this figure as a sitting Lioness, in spite of it bearing no resemblance to the lying Lioness (fig. 160). That this was the case is shown by the fact that the two inventories of 1770 and 1779 enumerate eight lionesses under the number N=253-W, five lying and three sitting. Comparisons of size, and the fact that there are more than three indisputably original executions of all other models of sitting feline predators, confirm that the figure identified as a Lioness was in fact Kirchner's "Tiger." Both in what follows and also in the Catalog, the model will therefore be referred to as a sitting Lioness, in accordance with the eighteenth-century view, even though the artist may well have had another animal in mind when making his model.

As we know from the delivery lists, the three realizations of Kirchner's model must have been delivered together with the five lying Lionesses between January 1 and October 22, 1734, that is to say at the same time as the Lynx and the Leopard. This takes us on to the real problem of this group of three wild cats. It is true that leopards, lynxes and tigers were repeatedly called for in the order lists from November 18, 1732, onwards, and that the respective models were made by Kirchner shortly before his departure in January 1733. The delivery list for the period March 7, 1733, to October 22, 1734,[575] records 5 leopards, 5 lynxes, and 8 lionesses, of

118 Johann Gottlieb Kirchner, Leopard, model 1733, Dresden Porcelain Collection

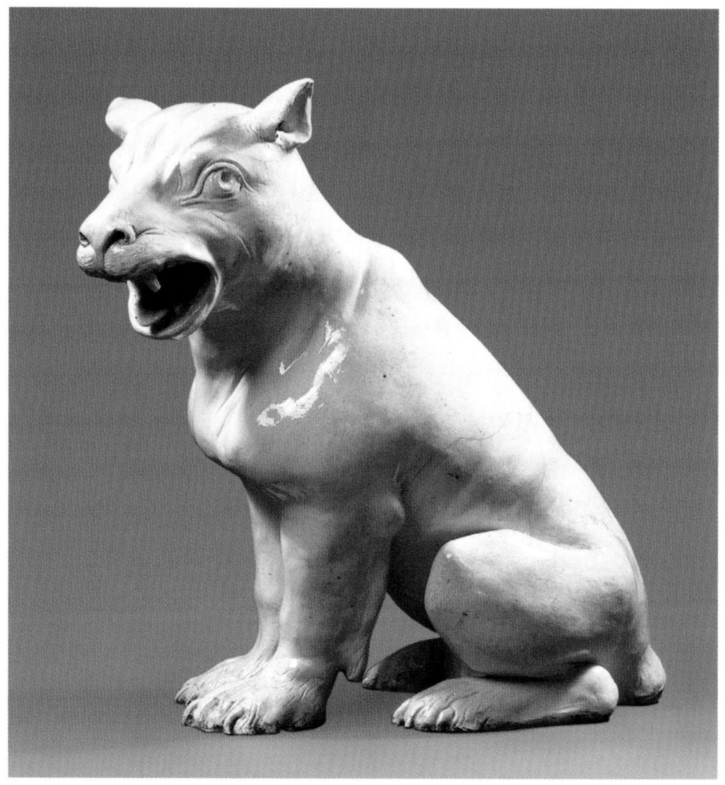

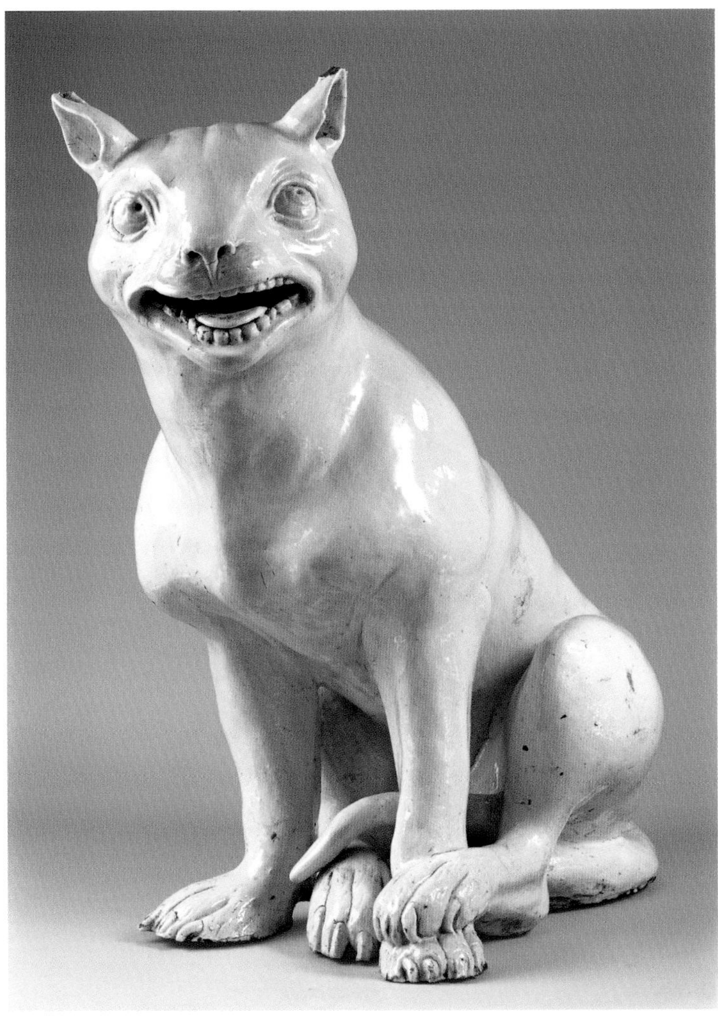

119 Johann Gottlieb Kirchner, Lynx, model 1733, Dresden Porcelain Collection

which 2 leopards, 2 lynxes, and 5 lionesses were taken to the palace in August 1734. This could lead one to conclude that the remaining 3 leopards and 3 lynxes had already been produced in March 1733, which would tally with the usual period of two months between the creation of the model and the assembly and finishing of the figure in paste. However, the summary list of the porcelain pieces actually delivered to the palace in 1733 mentions neither leopards nor lynxes nor lionesses.[576] It must therefore be assumed that the management of the manufactory at first did not want to go through with the execution of Kirchner's somewhat clumsy models, Kirchner himself not of course being any longer in a position to push production ahead. In July 1734 Kaendler himself made studies of a tiger in the *Löwenhaus* in Dresden. When it was finally decided that Kirchner's models should go into production, one important reason may have been that the project had been extended under Augustus III and Count Sulkowski in the winter of 1733, and the manufactory was under great pressure to deliver in accordance with the order. The fact that the summer of 1734 saw work being done on these models although they were no longer stylistically consonant with the works already produced is shown not only by the delivery lists but also a statement made by Höroldt. Replying on March 26, 1735, to the accusations leveled at him by Modellmeister Kaendler, he charged his opponent with not even knowing enough of statics to be able to make stable animal figures, as was shown by "the Tiger only recently 'poussiert', which [...] could not even stand up to the low firing, and fell in two,"[577] which shows that in 1734 – Höroldt was defending himself against charges made the year before – work was indeed done on a "Tiger" at the manufactory. It should be noted that Höroldt was using the word "poussieren," in accordance with common parlance at the time, to mean the taking of moldings.

Models, antecedents, and sources of inspiration

Porcelain-making is a reproductive art, not merely because works of porcelain are very seldom one-off creations and the molds can be used again and again to produce smaller or greater numbers of the same wares, but also because original creations are not the norm: the forms, shapes, and decorative elements are usually derived from pre-existing types. This is one thing among others that porcelain-making has in common with other arts and crafts.

Types – or, in a second sense of the word, "models" – were collected at the Meissen manufactory from the very beginning, whether on paper or in sculptural form.[578] The whole business of stock types played a central role in porcelain-painting, as the porcelain-painters were not trained "high-art" painters but craftsmen who had learned to copy stock motifs and patterns in the manufactory's own drawing school. It was a different matter with the modelers, however, for whom the models and types were intended to provide inspiration rather than to be copied. Nevertheless, porcelain works were on occasion executed as exact copies from prints or drawings, whether out of interest on the part of the modeler, or in response to the wish of a customer.

Our study would thus not be complete if it did not look into the works that inspired the modelers to create the large animal figures for the Japanese Palace.

Far Eastern porcelain animal figures

As has already been pointed out, the manufactory was from its foundation onwards repeatedly sent Far Eastern porcelain pieces from the royal collections, to be used as models. The existence of copies of these made at Meissen shows that these models also included animal figures.[579] Nonetheless, in the context of the porcelain menagerie in the Neustadt-side gallery of the Japanese Palace, copying the Far Eastern model was – by contrast with what was the case for certain pieces of tableware or vases – precisely not the point of the exercise. The animal figures were to be given forms all of their own, and their monumental size was to make them unlike anything that had been known in China or Japan.

It is however quite probable that the modelers did take note of the example of the Far Eastern porcelain birds when they faced the particular problem of how to do birds' legs, which are, being thin, not suitable for carrying the weight of a porcelain bird's body, particularly at the critical moments during the firing. The bird's body needs to be supported. Chinese porcelain birds as a rule had a substructure to rest upon: a tree-trunk, or a pile of leaves, or a rock, on which the legs were only rendered in relief (fig. 120). Most of the Meissen bird figures employ a similar system, with the difference that the legs are done in the round, and the pedestals have more detail to them. One might be tempted to see this as an element shared by two traditions using the same material, but it should not be forgotten that Kirchner and Kaendler were trained sculptors, and that stone birds require supports in just the same way and for just the same reason as porcelain birds do. Furthermore, a support in the form of a substructure between the birds' legs is, and always has been, a fairly obvious solution.

It may thus be concluded that while the Far Eastern tradition of porcelain figure-making – in particular as regards the birds – may have provided useful ideas for the solution of technical problems, the solution applied in Meissen had just as strong roots in the traditions of European sculpture.

Of the Far Eastern pieces to hand at the Meissen manufactory, there is only one that is of interest as far as Kaendler's figures are concerned. This is a Japanese eagle figure now only existent in the form of a number of copies made at Meissen (fig. 121); a detailed account of the relationship between the Meissen eagle and the original Japanese eagle figure was published in 1979.[580] Two sources indicate that the figure had already been produced at the manufactory before Kaendler's time. Firstly, a list dated April 7, 1731, found in the house of the disgraced minister of state Count Hoym includes "two large eagles, enameled."[581] This is backed up by a passage in Höroldt's written defense of March 26, 1735, which confirms "that a number of years ago, his Royal Majesty gave the factory two 'Indian Eagle' figures, not big ones but rather about three quarters of an ell in height, to be copied."[582] This statement is directly related to Kaendler's complaint that Höroldt had simply had animal figures painted cold once their cracks had been repaired with filling. Höroldt's reaction was to draw attention to precisely these Japanese eagle figures as examples of Far Eastern work which were likewise "full of cracks, which had simply been filled, and the whole figures had been painted with water-colors, which one could still wipe off with a wet finger."[583]

The Meissen copies, which are in two sizes and two versions, one looking to the left and one to the right, must therefore have been part of the product range by 1730 at the latest, and were almost certainly, as Winfried Baer was justified in surmising, among those animal figures which Keyssler admired at the Japanese

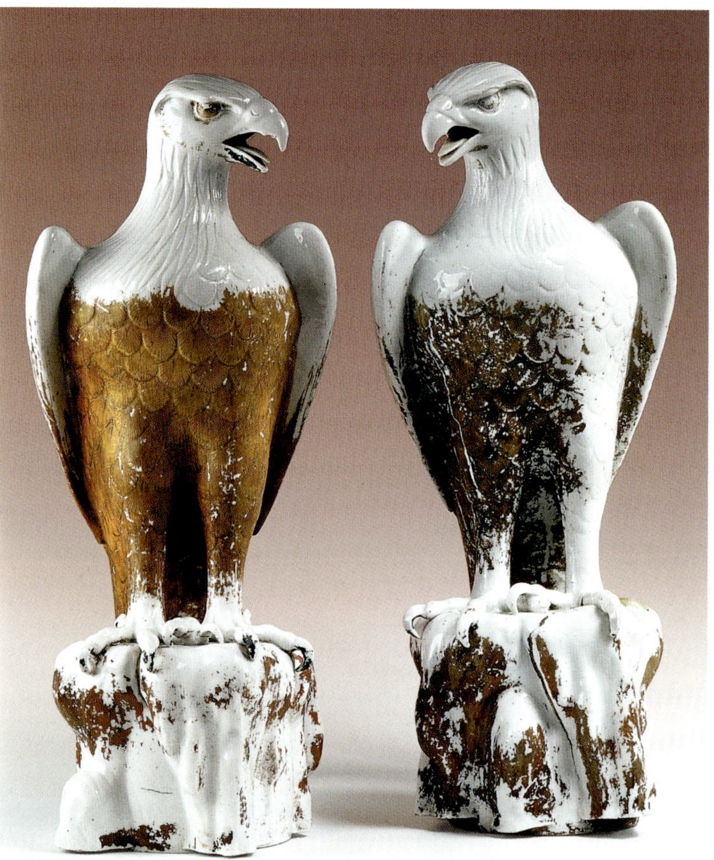

121 Eagle, Meissen copy of a Japanese original, ca. 1728, Dresden Porcelain Collection

120 Bird in *émail sur biscuit* from the chimney-piece in the Charlottenburg porcelain room, China ca. 1700

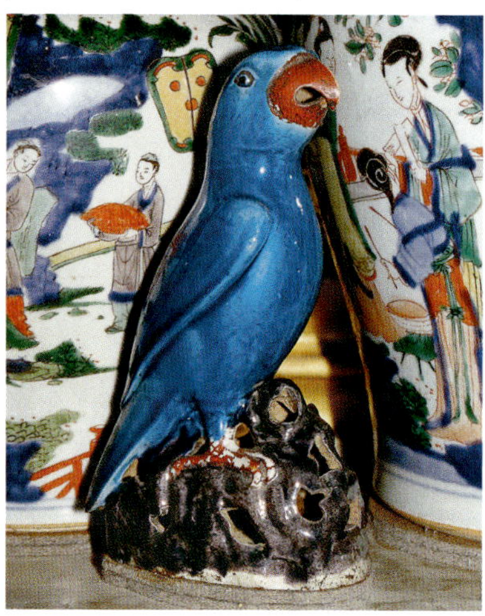

Palace in October 1730.[584] It is however far from easy to locate these copies in the delivery lists, as they would have fallen into some such ill-defined category as "birds of prey," and there was little distinction made between various kinds of eagles and falcons. These copies of Japanese eagle figures were in all probability delivered as "falcons."

During his first year at the manufactory, Kaendler only modeled two birds of prey which bear any comparison with the eagle copied from the Japanese original, namely the Kestrel ("Falke" in German, but clearly a kestrel; fig. 122), and the Osprey, which he modeled in two versions (figs. 114 and 115). However, Kaendler's models and the Japanese counterparts differed greatly, not least in the way they solved the above-mentioned technical problem of how the weight of the bird's body was to be supported. Kaendler's birds have their bellies resting on tree-stumps, with their fanned-out tail-feathers being stabilized, like those of the Far Eastern birds, by being joined with struts to the base. Their legs, unlike those on the Japanese figures, are modeled in the round and relatively thin, but as they straddle the tree-stump they are relieved by the body of having to carry any weight themselves. However, these differences are minor ones in comparison with those related to the modeling of the surfaces. In the Japanese Arita-ware figure, the eagle's plumage is suggested with the same very simply patterned relief that can also be seen on the Meissen copy, but when Kaendler came to model his birds of prey, he did them with a wealth of lively surface detail. Far from consisting simply of repeated scale-like units, the osprey's breast is made up of a multitude of distinct feathers, each rendered in relief with its outline, shaft, and individually modeled vane. This commitment to achieving a naturalistic effect is thoroughly European, and is reflected not only in the plumage but also in the bird's whole posture. The parallels between the Japanese eagle figure, or rather its Meissen copies, and the first bird figures made for the Japanese Palace are thus too slight, and in any case too restricted to one technical matter, to substantiate the idea that the former functioned as a model for the latter. Models in this sense – sources of inspiration – are more likely to be found in another field: that of zoological illustration.

122 Johann Joachim Kaendler, Kestrel, model 1731, Rijksmuseum Amsterdam

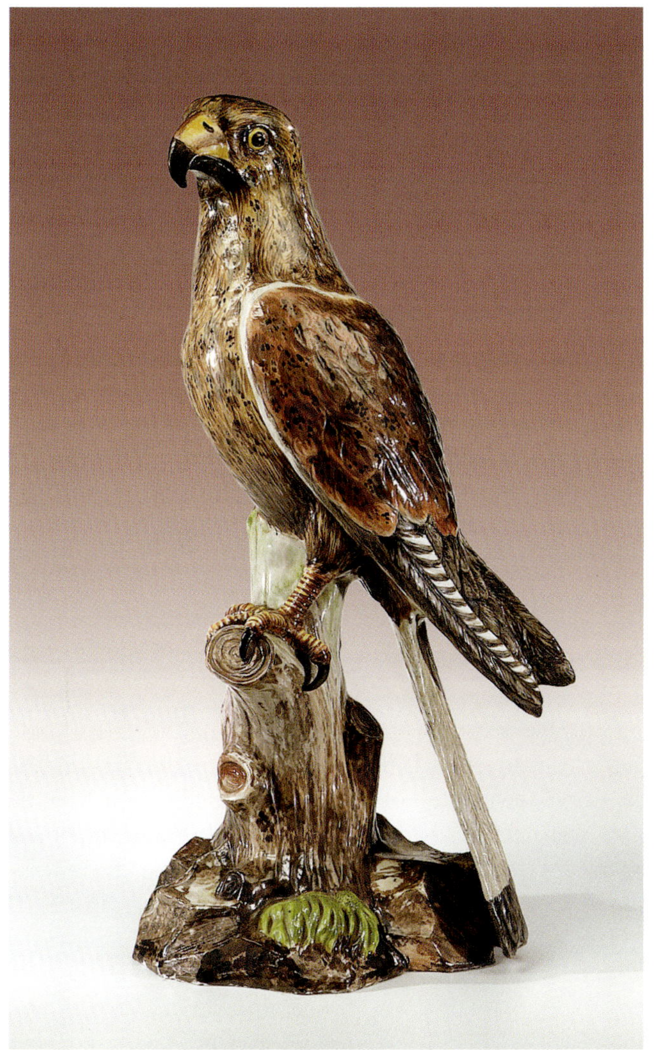

Zoological illustration

The mid-sixteenth century saw a change in the approach to depicting animals in scientific books, with illustrations now also being designed to aid in the identification of European species.[585] This approach distanced itself from the purely descriptive (and sometimes fantasy-ridden) bestiaries of the Middle Ages and laid the foundations for the kind of genuinely scientific, more objective, research-oriented depiction that had already developed in the field of botany. As classification began to be conducted with an ever finer degree of differentiation, it became clear that significant limitations were imposed by the lack of finesse of the woodcut as a medium. Another drawback was the lack of awareness of the concept of species; draftsmen were not aware which were the most important characteristic features, and made too much of certain particularly conspicuous elements such as the hoopoe's crest or the ears and trunk of the elephant.[586]

The new understanding of natural science that established itself around 1700 brought about a further change in the zoological depiction of animals. Purposeful research into the animal world, including the collecting, dissecting, and classifying of animals, was no longer left up to individual researchers and their patrons, but became a systematic scientific field in its own right.[587] This brought in its wake an increase in the number of illustrated natural histories and monographs being published.[588] Furthermore, the copper-plate engravings which had since the mid-seventeenth century been the normal medium for illustrations in books made it possible to achieve the requisite degree of precision in the rendering of detail.

123 Eye surround on Macaw (sitting), Dresden Porcelain Collection

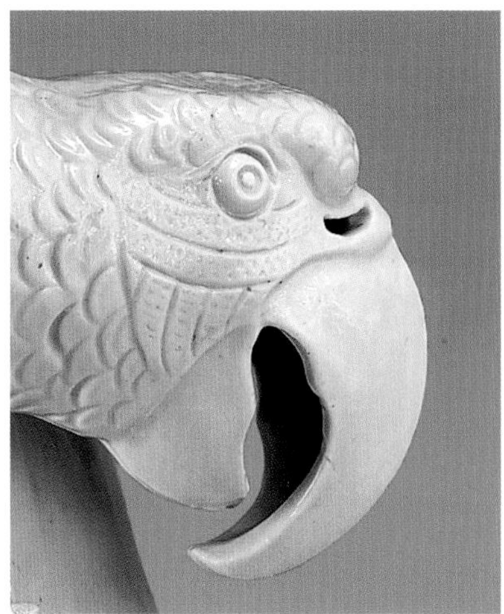

124 Eye surround on Macaw (downward-climbing), Dresden Porcelain Collection

The passion that absolutist princes had for collecting animals has already been described, and they were equally passionate in their enthusiasm for acquiring works of zoological literature for their libraries. These copper-plate menageries complemented the live and taxidermal menageries – and in Dresden's case, the sculpted menageries as well. The oldest catalog of what was formerly the Royal Library in Dresden contains numerous examples of such books, many of which are lavishly illustrated.

A number of pieces of evidence clearly show that the artists engaged on the large animal figures were inspired by animal illustrations, both in and out of books. In connection with Kaendler's engagement as modeler, the manufactory report for the month of June 1731 mentions that "those large pieces which his Royal Majesty wishes to be produced from certain models and drawings,"[589] could not be done by Kirchner alone, and that Kaendler had already made three models, one of which was a large eagle figure. The report for February 1732 also mentions that the King had sent models and drawings for "all kinds of birds and exotic animals hitherto produced in the factory."[590] And that the modelers themselves were also at pains to acquire prints and drawings of animals is shown by the fact that a small sum was paid in 1733 out to Kaendler to reimburse him for purchases he had made at the end of January of that year, namely "56 copper-plate engravings with all kinds of birds, to be used when necessary at the factory."[591]

That Kaendler was influenced by prints and drawings is clear from a number of his early bird models, but it has not been possible to identify any actual drawing or print that definitely inspired any given work. To take one example, in the winter of 1731 Kaendler made the model for a "large raven of the Indian kind," that is to say for the sitting Macaw (fig. 85). In doing so, he very probably made use of a print, even though he had that very year made drawings of exotic birds in the Moritzburg menagerie. That he took his cues from a print is suggested not only by the bird's somewhat stiff posture, but also and especially from a detail in the modeling of the head: both eyes are rendered with a surround so modeled as to stand out from the surface, a feature which is not evident on any live macaw (fig. 123). The solution to this riddle is that whatever print Kaendler took his cues from must have used a fan-like pattern to render the light-colored area surrounding the eye of the macaw. As a sculptor, Kaendler interpreted this little area in sculptural rather than chromatic terms. Later, however, he clearly had the opportunity to study a live macaw on a visit to the *Jägerhof* in Dresden or the menagerie at Moritzburg, as a result of which he was able to create the model of a macaw making its way head-first down a tree-trunk, a model bursting with life and very close to nature (fig. 182). And what is more, he also got the eye right (fig. 124).

Although it is thus very probable that printed works were among the models, archetypes, and other visual aids sent to the manufactory, the thorough screening of around 45 zoological books and print series from the period 1650 to 1730 has not trougth forth any notable finds. However, when one considers that the sources to be examined include not only the 140 animal books and print series listed by Bridson and White for this period but also all manner of other graphic representations of animals such as depictions of Paradise, illustrations for travel books and collections of fables, ornaments, and emblems, it becomes clear that this search for graphic antecedents is no minor undertaking. Even the graphic collection of the manufactory archive at Meissen, which was until very recently not accessible to researchers, does not contain – or no longer contains – any relevant prints or drawings.[592]

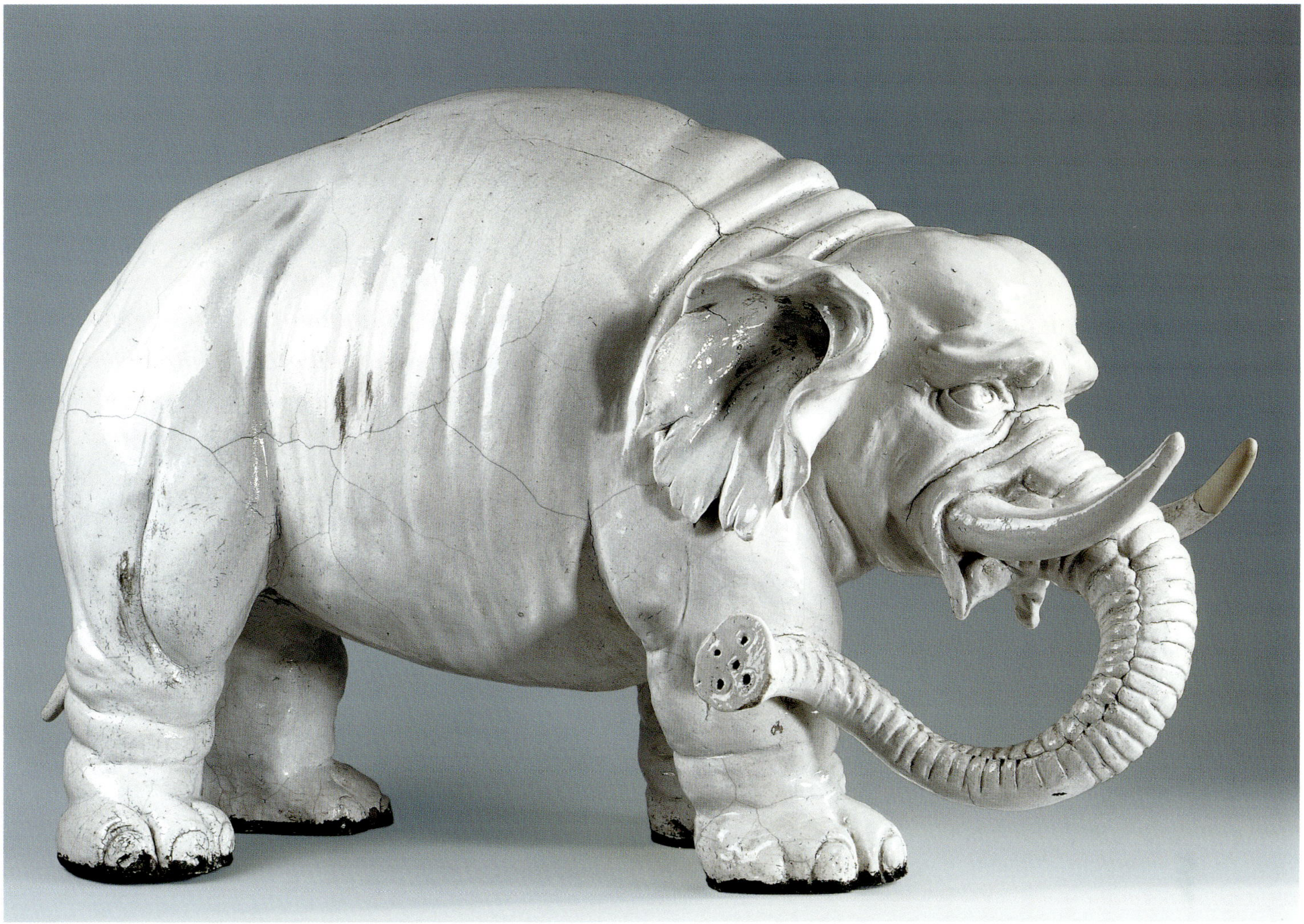

125 Johann Gottlieb Kirchner, Elephant, model 1731, Dresden Porcelain Collection

Research has however established a number of very close possible associations between Meissen animals and graphic antecedents. Thomas Boreman's animal book, published in Glasgow in 1730, could well have provided Kirchner with a source of inspiration for his Elephant (figs. 125 and 126); especially the proportions and the idiosyncratic rendering of the ears evident in the print seem to have been adopted by Kirchner for his model. The elephants in other depictions of the time have quite differently proportioned body volumes, head sizes, leg lengths and so on. When doing his Rhinoceros (fig. 76), Kirchner may well have returned to Boreman (fig. 74), whose rendering is of course quite clearly in the tradition of Albrecht Dürer's famous woodcut of 1515.[593] As most of the animals to be modeled could be studied live in or around Dresden, one cannot in these cases expect there to be such a close correspondence between models and graphic antecedents as is observable in the cases of the Rhinoceros and the Elephant.

126 Thomas Boreman, Elephant, from *Three Hundred Animals* (Glasgow, 1730)

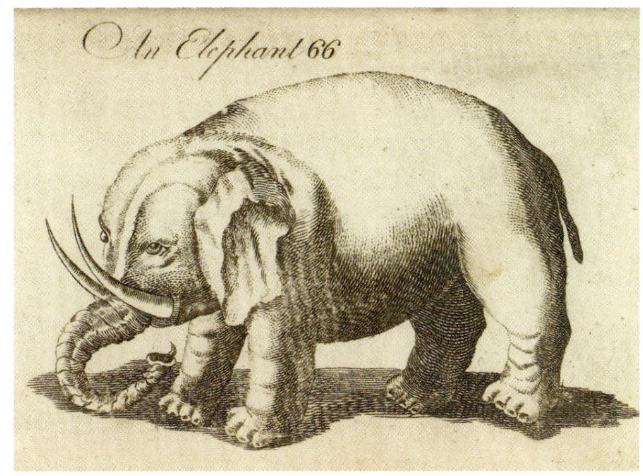

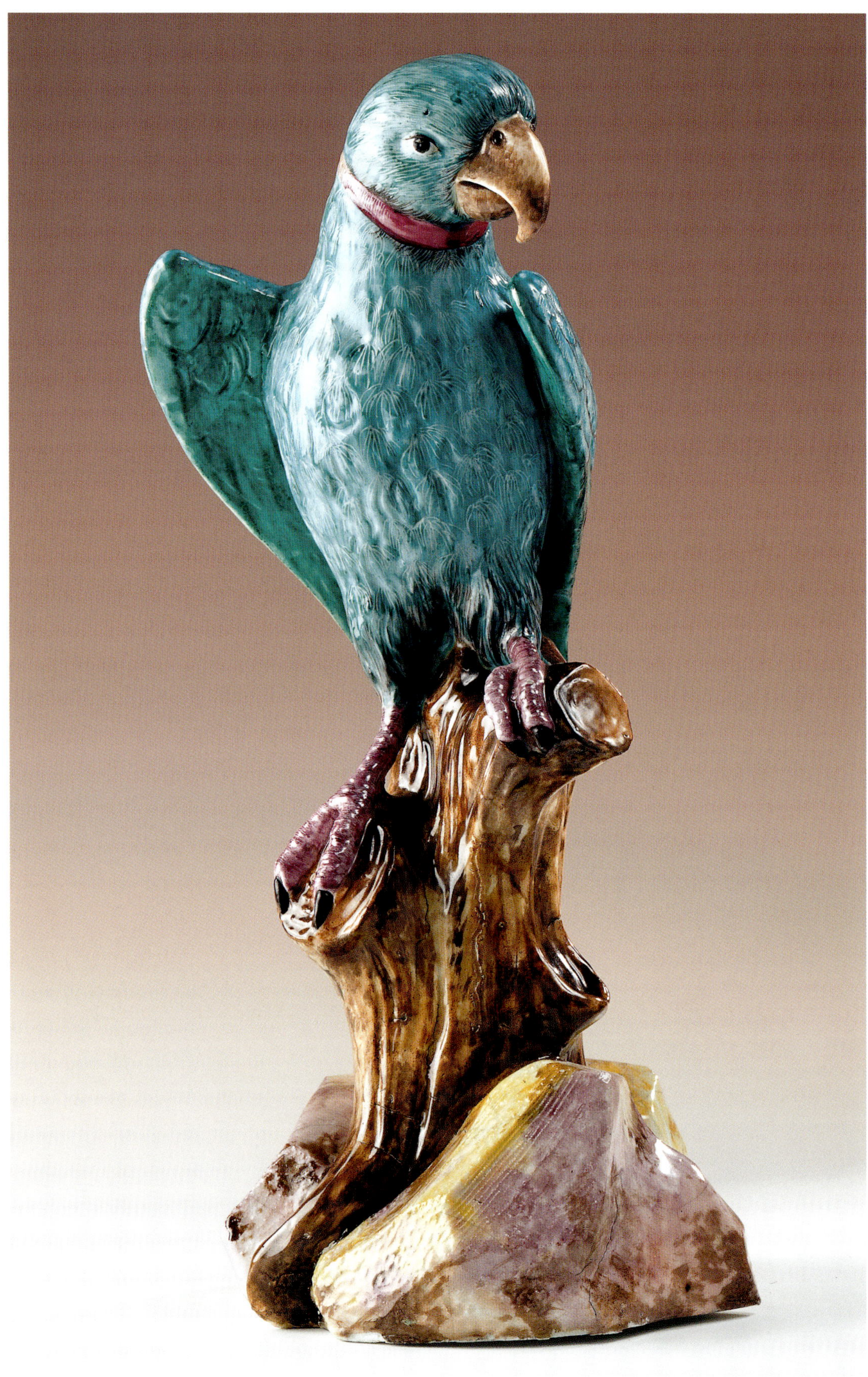

127 Johann Gottlieb Kirchner, Rose-Ringed Parakeet, model most likely 1731, Dresden Porcelain Collection

Kirchner's Lion, for instance, has certain characteristic features, but not the overall posture, of a lion in a print by Stefano della Bella from the "diversi animali" collection; the crossed front paws, the tail tucked under the hind leg, and the intently serious raised eyebrows are more essential to Kirchner's lion than, for instance, its head, which is, unlike that on the print, turned to one side (figs. 159 and 160). This is particularly worthy of note because it is precisely in respect of these features that della Bella's print differs somewhat from lions by other artists. Many other subjects, on the other hand, such as the bear licking its paws, the owl with a mouse, or the eagle owl with a pigeon, are stock types which appear again and again in a great variety of works.

Associations of this kind are even more clearly evident for the earlier bird figures than they are for the quadrupeds, and the stiffness of Kaendler's first models (figs. 115, 122, and 128) can, as we have seen in the case of the Macaw, be put down to the artist having drawn his creative inspiration from a print. A particularly illuminating example of this, written up in detail in the Catalog (p. 358), is provided by the two King Vulture figures of 1731 and 1734. But even the idea of making the base of many of the figures into a representative slice of the bird's natural habitat could have been inspired by practices followed in animal books. Animals are often represented in landscapes in such genres as print series, which were not strictly zoological but were rather supposed to give a panoramic survey of the animal world in all its wonderful variety.[594]

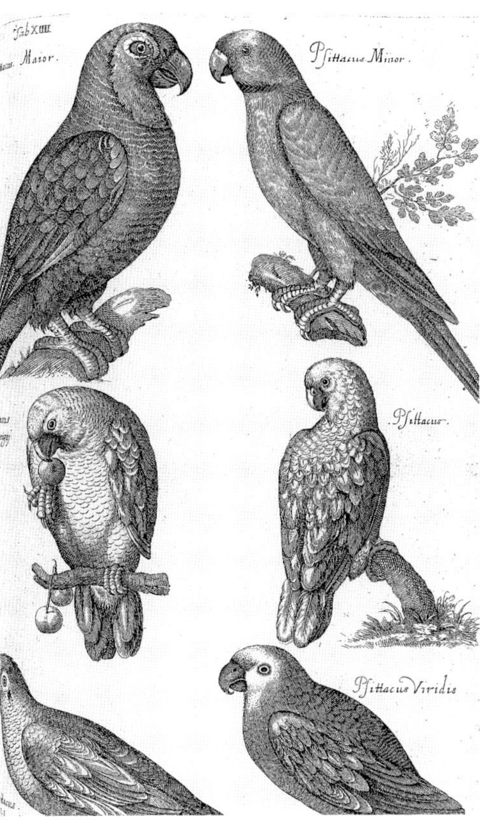

129 Matthäus Merian the younger, Parakeet, from John Jonston, *Historia naturalis de avibus* (Frankfurt, 1650)

128 Johann Joachim Kaendler, Gull, model 1731, formerly Dresden Porcelain Collection

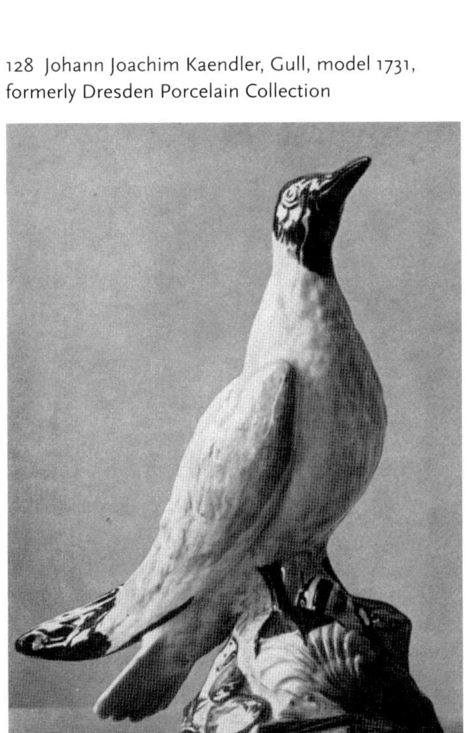

Attention should finally be drawn to a special case among the Japanese Palace animals with graphic antecedents, namely a sitting, horned grotesque figure that is detailed in the delivery lists and inventories as a "Drache" ("Dragon"). Two variants exist, a larger one (ca. 68 cm) with boldly modeled front paws (fig. 133), and a smaller one without front paws (ca. 56 cm; figs. 130 and 132).

The smaller of the two appears to have been a fairly faithful copy of the copperplate engraving of a grotesque jug-like vessel that appears among the illustrations in Bernard de Montfaucon's *L'Antiquité expliquée et représentée* (fig. 131).[595] Montfaucon assumed that it dated from antiquity and put it in one plate together with a number of Roman vases, entitling the page "Grands vases pour tenir du vin ou d'autres liqueurs." Although he goes on to relate that he saw the originals in the garden of the French ambassador in Rome,[596] it is not quite clear whether he is referring to the creature of fable or just the large classical vases. It is worth noting the existence of several small bronze sixteenth-century *aquamanilia* exactly like the one in the engraving, which could just as well have served as Montfaucon's model.[597]

While the porcelain version from Meissen is related to the large grotesque vases also ordered for the large animal gallery and modeled at the beginning of the 1730s after engravings in Jacques

Stella's *Livres des Vases* of 1667 (figs. 23 & 24),[598] it is nonetheless clear from the delivery lists and inventories that it was neither referred to as an "Untierkrug" ("monster jug"), as it often is now, nor regarded as a vessel: on the contrary, it was considered as a representation of a dragon and reckoned among the animal figures.

A number of pieces of evidence in the records indicate that this was the first of our animal figures to be modeled: for instance, it is explicitly referred to as such by the molder Albrecht in the context of a pay claim.[599] All eleven copies were delivered to the Japanese Palace in the course of the years 1731 and 1732. The garlands adorning the figure's lower neck, which in Montfaucon's engraving are a reference to its use as a wine-jug and consequently consist solely of grapes and vine-leaves, are transformed into a lavish floral border. As this did not form part of Kirchner's model, it

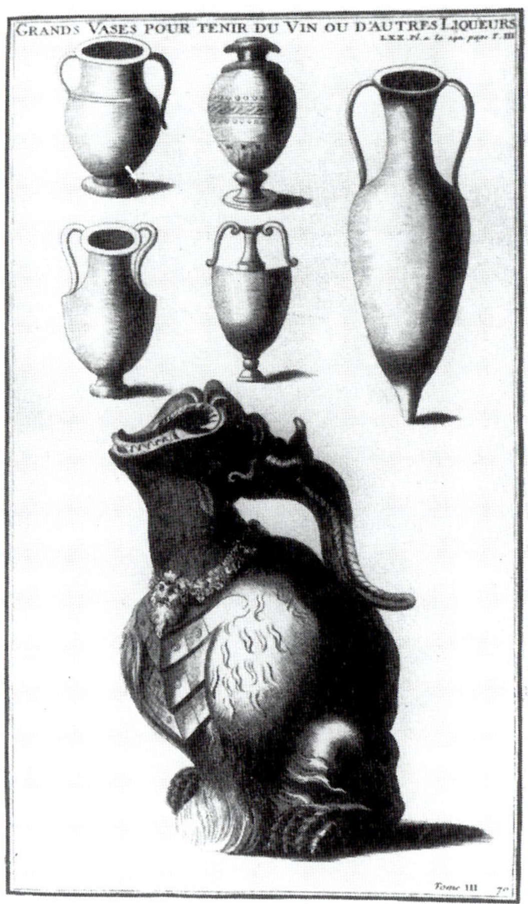

131 Berard de Montfaucon, engraving with jug in the form of an animal, from *L'Antiquité expliquée et représentée* (1719–1724)

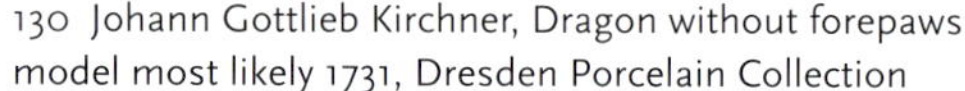

130 Johann Gottlieb Kirchner, Dragon without forepaws, model most likely 1731, Dresden Porcelain Collection

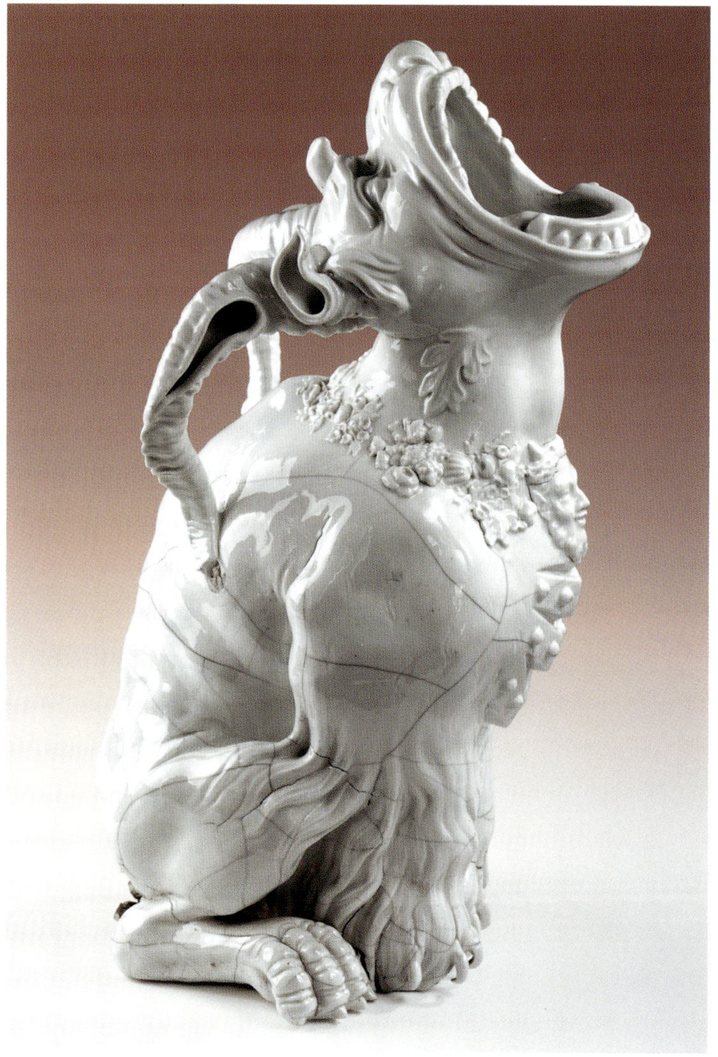

is each time different in composition, with the garland sometimes made mainly of fruit and sometimes mainly of flowers. The individual moldings, joined together like the links of a chain around the dragon's neck, were taken from stock molds that had already been used for decorating vessels in the Böttger period fifteen years earlier; common to several of the dragon figures is, for instance, a little bouquet of roses and other flowers which we know were modeled between 1715 and 1720 (figs. 134 & 135).

The question remains, however, as to why two versions of the model were produced. While the larger of the two dragons differs from its graphic antecedent in respect of the front paws and the shape given to the horns, the differences in the case of the smaller one are restricted to the coat around the upper thigh, which in the case of one enameled copy (fig. 132) the decorator endeavored to improve by painting on shaggy strands of hair. One remarkable fact cannot be overlooked, namely that the difference in size between the two figures is the same as that in porcelain shrinkage (one sixth), which suggests one possible genesis story for the smaller version, namely that plaster molds were made from a

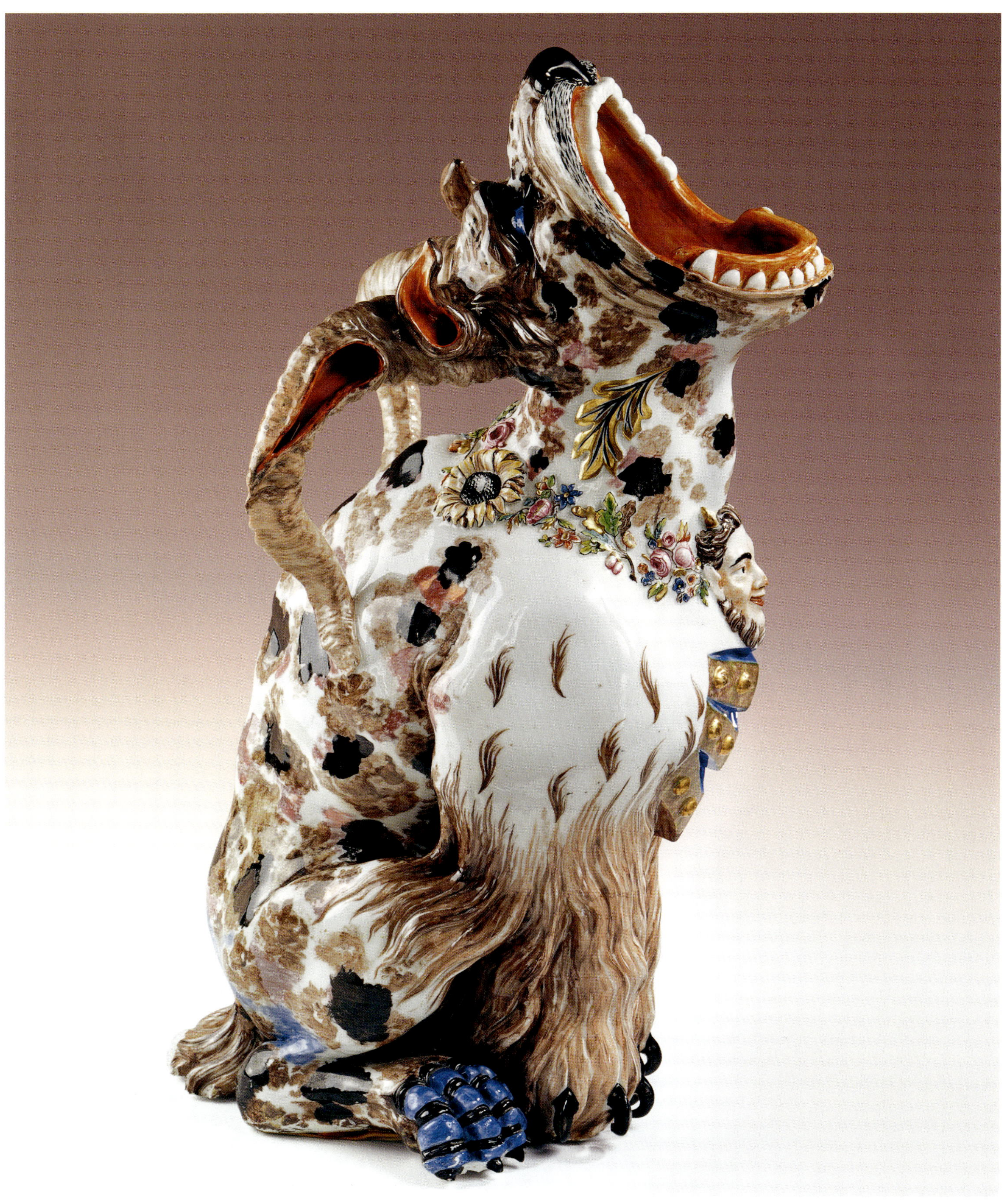

132 Johann Gottlieb Kirchner, Dragon, decorated with enamel colors, model most likely 1731, Dresden Porcelain Collection

133 Johann Gottlieb Kirchner, Dragon with forepaws, model most likely 1731, Pflueger Collection, New York

high-fired figure and used to mold a clay model, which was then reworked before providing the molds for the production of another porcelain figure. This was before the introduction of the systematic separating of original and working molds that later became customary. If one of the most important molds for a certain figure was broken, all that could be done was either to have a completely new model made, or to take the short cut of taking casts from a high-fired figure, in which case all the new figures would be a sixth smaller than in the first instance. If this procedure was followed in the case of the Dragon, then it is quite possible that the molded shaggy strands of hair were lost and the other changes made. Account should also be taken of two pieces of circumstantial evidence which support the thesis that the larger variant was modeled and went into production first, and the smaller one afterwards: the smaller ones are all glazed on the inside and have the crossed swords on the inner lower jaw, while the larger ones are all unglazed inside and some have the AR mark on the bottom.[600] As there was a general preference for having the animal figures in pairs at the palace, we can also assume that the production of a second Dragon would have been on the agenda, which would still of course not rule out the possibility of the smaller figure having been a "re-model" of the larger prototype.[601]

Models from nature, living and taxidermal

The modelers did not draw their inspiration exclusively from depictions and figures of animals and birds, either provided by the King or purchased directly: they also went out of their way to study natural specimens, both live and stuffed, with Augustus the Strong's animal collections offering them ample opportunity to make drawings and bozzetti.

In the fall of 1734, Kaender re-submitted a request for reimbursement of expenses incurred on a journey that he had made in 1731 to Moritzburg and Dresden, where he made drawings of exotic birds and a wisent (erroneously referred to in the sources as an aurochs).[602] The accounting books indicate that he was in Moritzburg on August 6, 1731, and in Dresden from September 25 to 27.[603] That Kirchner followed his example is shown by his (Kirchner's) working report for November 1732, according to which he "made [four] very rough models *en plein air*,"[604] in Dres-

134 Detail from the neck of the Dragon (fig. 132) with a garland of flowers in relief, Dresden Porcelain Collection

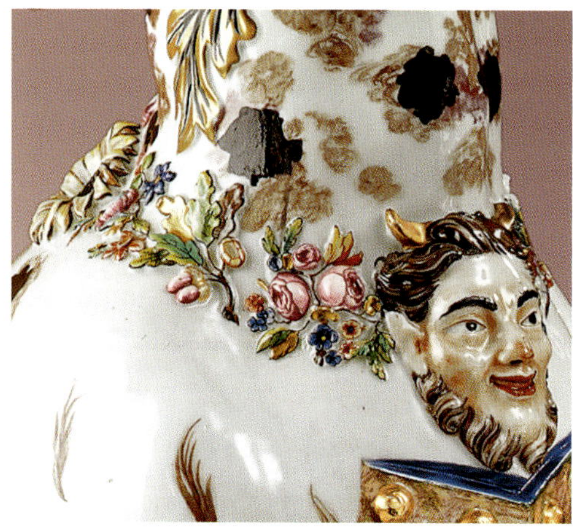

135 Teapot with a bouquet of flowers in relief, ca. 1715–1720, Dresden Porcelain Collection

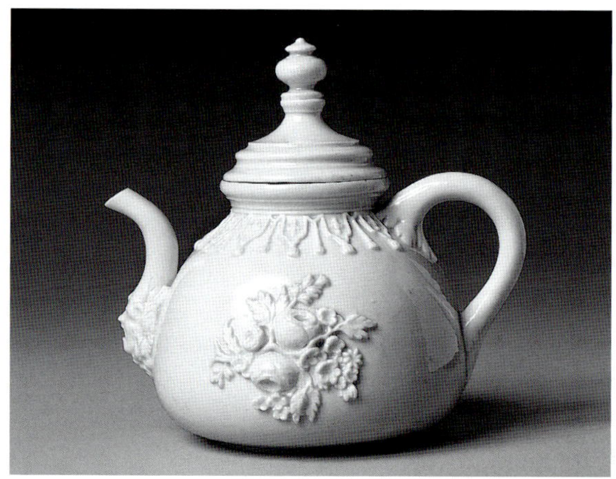

den (i.e., at the *Jägerhof*). These were of a leopard, a tiger, a lynx, and a porcupine.

In June 1734 Kaender returned for two days to Moritzburg, making a bozzetto of a king vulture, from which he proceeded to make a life-size model before the month was out.[605] While at the menagerie he was clearly even more fascinated by the sight of another vulture (a griffon vulture) holding fast to a dead cockatoo. Although in his record of having made the bozzetto he simply described it as being of the "Indian vulture with the cockatoo"[606], the extent of his fascination is clear from the detailed description contained in the report he made after having completed the large model: "I have made a model of the large Indian vulture that can be seen living in Moritzburg. Together with the pedestal, which I have done as a tree-stump overgrown with leaves and grass, it is one ell and twelve inches high, truly wondrous to behold on account both of its strange appearance and also of it having just caught a cockatoo, another exotic bird about as big as a large pigeon; it is holding the mortal remains of this bird torn apart at its feet, and in its beak the bird's innards as if it was on the point of eating them."[607] This figure, one of the most impressive of all his models, was created while he was still under the impression of what he had seen at Moritzburg.

Between this stay at Moritzburg and the modeling of the griffon vulture ("Vulture Devouring a Cockatoo"), he made a list of the studies that he had made in the king's various animal collections; this list constitutes the most detailed source for this aspect of his activities. It was appended to the monthly manufactory report for July 1734 and is entitled: "Specification of the foreign animals and exotic birds, to be found in part in the *Löwenhaus* and *Bärenhaus*, and in part in the *Kunstkammer*, of which I made both accurate and correct drawings and rough models between July 4 and 26, so that when the same are executed as large figures at the Royal Porcelain Manufactory they may turn out to be all the more natural and beautiful for having been made after these bozzetti and drawings" (Source 25).[608]

The list enumerates twenty-nine birds and animals, including eight quadrupeds and a bird from the *Jägerhof*,[609] and eleven quadrupeds and eight birds from the *Animaliengalerie* (the natural history collection at the *Kunstkammer*). It is unclear what No. 29 – "a creature of fable" – may have looked like. It is illuminating that Kaendler also made bozzetti of the animals of which Kirchner had already made large models.[610] With the exception of the Bear, these models by Kirchner are precisely those rather unsubtle models which were, surprisingly, not executed in porcelain until more than a year after Kirchner's departure in 1734 (see above for the explanation). It is quite possible that at this point in 1734, Kaendler was intending to do further models of these animals himself.

Some of the birds and animals mentioned in the list can be directly linked to a figure finally executed in porcelain. The "Indianische Rattze" is the Jerboa (modeled April 1735, fig. 167); the "Indianische Schaf" is the Exotic Sheep (modeled December 1734, fig. 109),[611]; the "Versühn oder Sünden Bock welchen die Juden gehabt" ("Goat of atonement or scapegoat which the Jews had") is the Scapegoat (modeled January 1735, fig. 108); the "Zobel" is the Sable (modeled April 1735, fig. 136); and the "Indianische Ente mit einem Hals Kragen" is the Great Crested Grebe (modeled October 1734, fig. 90).

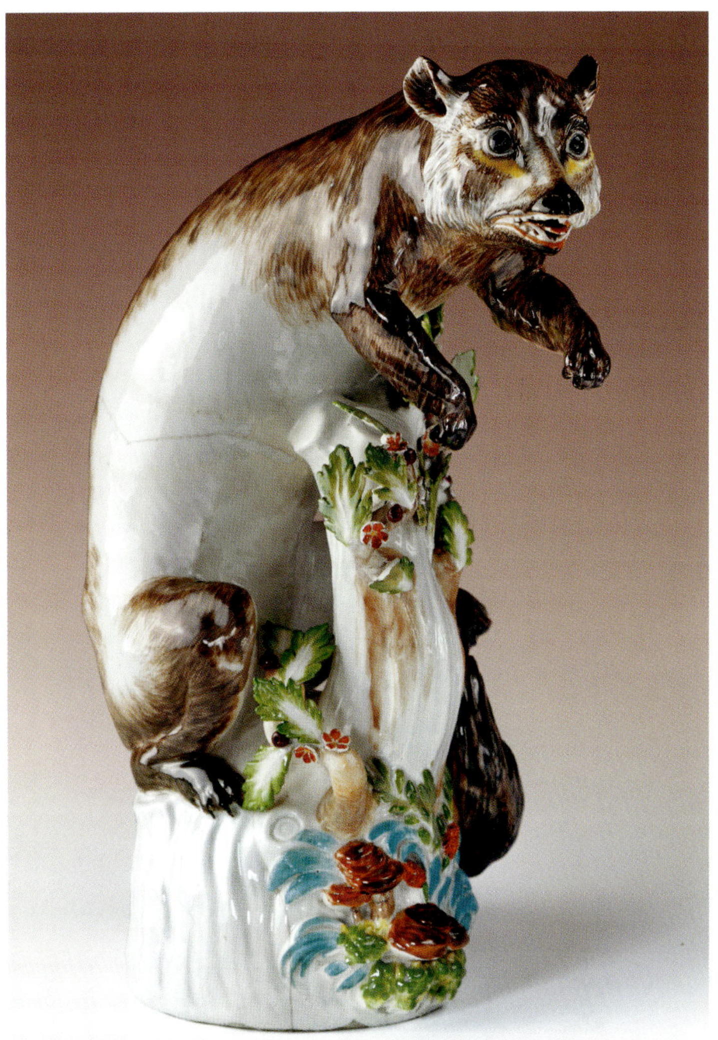

136 Johann Joachim Kaendler, Sable, model 1735, Dresden Porcelain Collection

In 1736, Augustus III, as we know from his own writings, commissioned the court painter Christian Reinow to make further drawings in the natural history collection, "to be used for executing life-size porcelain figures for the Royal Japanese Palace".[612] Why he should have done this is puzzling, as of the thirteen animals which Reinow, "drew according to life and painted with watercolors," eleven had already been drawn by Kaendler in studies made two years before, and seven had in the meantime already been executed in porcelain and delivered to the Japanese Palace.[613]

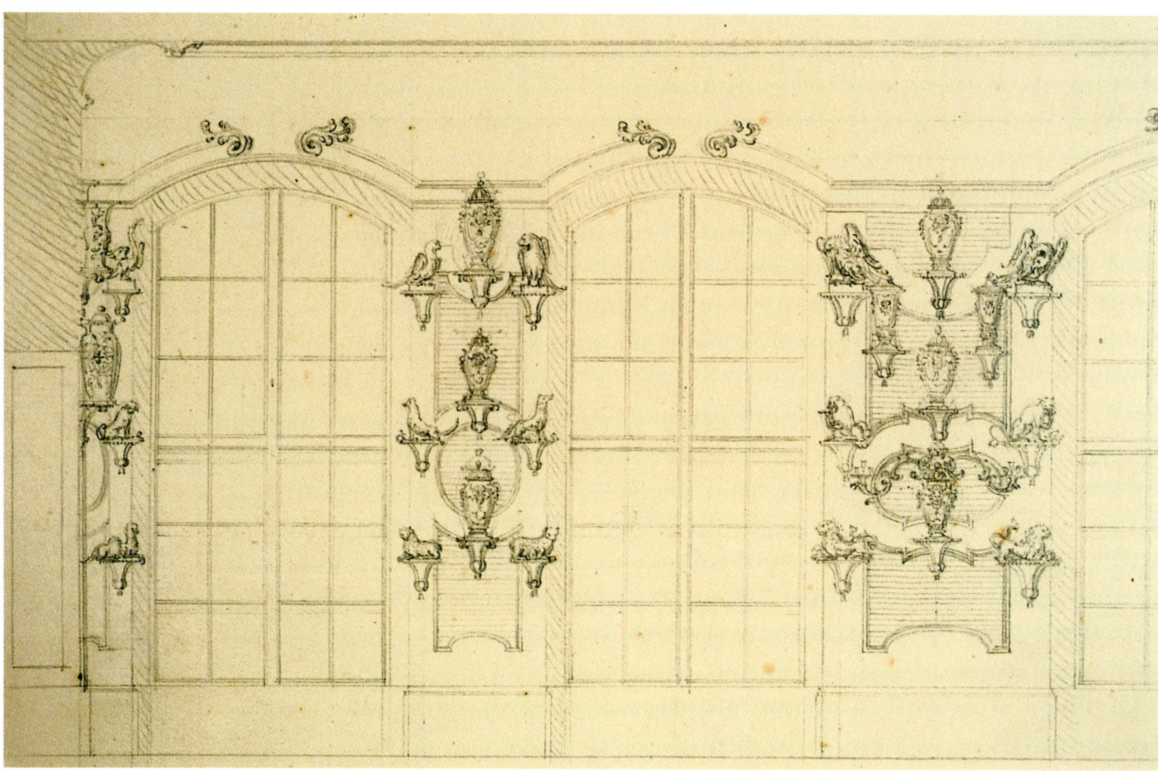

137 Matthäus Daniel Pöppelmann, design for a room with animal figures, first series of plans, ca. 1727 (detail)

In any case, the drawings were by this time no longer of any use to the manufactory, and Höroldt "moderated" Reinow's claim of 47 talers and 16 groschen down to 43 talers.

Having considered the circumstances attendant on the orders for animal figures and their production in Meissen, we shall now return – as it were in the company of the finished porcelain figures – to the Japanese Palace.

The presentation of the animal figures in the Japanese Palace

After the decision had been taken in 1730 to house the Far Eastern porcelain on the ground floor of the Japanese Palace and the Meissen porcelain separately on the upper story, the new plan of the Neustadt-side gallery (upper story) specified that the large Japanese vases formerly planned were to be replaced by "all sorts of animals [...]" ("allerhand Thiere [...]," see fig. 33). This decision on the exact use of the gallery was not to change again, as can be seen from the order and delivery lists which were sent to and fro between the palace and the manufactory calling for both larger and smaller animal figures for "the upper story of the front gallery."[614]

As the first series of elevation drawings of the walls was made shortly before 1730, the sections devoted to the long gallery still have the large vases (fig. 43); the project to furnish the palace with almost life-size animal figures in porcelain thus only came into being after concrete plans had been drawn. The reason why the draftsmen did not revise their drawings and make new designs for the gallery with animal figures may have been that they did not know what the animals were going to look like. Or perhaps they made a conscious decision to wait until they could be certain what size the animals were to be.

The planning became more specific when, a year later, a good number of models could be admired in Meissen and some finished figures had even already been delivered to the palace. In the order list of February 25, 1732, (Source 6), which called for 910 pieces for the gallery, there is even an approximate specification as to where the animal figures (not as yet individually named) were to stand: "On the four broad walls above the chimney-pieces [...] 40 animals of various sizes [etc.], between the arches of the windows [...] 22 birds of various sizes [...]" Although no corresponding draft plan has survived, it is clear from this source that it was planned to distribute the figures over the walls, most likely on console brackets. This is also suggested by an entry in the log of the Meissen castle guard, which noted every visit made by outsiders. It records that on May 28, 1732, Major-domo Teuffert came to the manufactory together with a bricklayer and a master carpenter.[615] It is possible that they came to inspect the largest models, none of which had as yet been delivered to the palace, in order to be able to design correspondingly stable and spacious console constructions for them to stand on.

When, half a year later on November 18, 1732, quite specific species of animals were ordered, mostly in sets of four (see Source 9), the only pieces which were allotted to the "6 broad and 12 narrow walls between windows" and the two side-walls were the 156 vases destined to stand in the gallery. There does not seem to have been any concept for the distribution of the animals, unless a *placement* was drawn up separately and subsequently lost. When the new concept for the presentation of the porcelain was drawn up in 1735, the only draft plan made by Longuelune for the upper floor was one of the throne gallery, so that we can now only speculate on how the animals were to be distributed in the space available.

Nonetheless, our speculations are assisted by three written sources. The first is related to the suggestion made by Kaendler on December 19, 1734, but never pursued, that life-size large animals might be produced in two or if necessary more separate parts. Regarding the presentation of such monumentally large figures as a life-size "aurochs," he noted "that such animal figures as these [...] could well be placed around the walls between the windows, which would also mean that the walls in the Royal Palace would not have to be fitted out with such large brackets and console constructions."[616]

The other reference is related to two chimney-pieces in the large gallery, which we know were decked out with vases and animal figures. Jonas Hanway described them as follows in his report (Source 22): "The long gallery in the second story had already two marble chimney-pieces, each adorned with near 40 very large pieces of porcelain, of birds, beasts, and vases, ranged to the height of above 20 feet."[617]

The best description we have of the work in progress is the one by Johann Christian Müller, whose report of 1744 (see Source 27) refers to a mirrored wall that "had been fitted from top to bottom with carved and gilded pedestals not far from each other on which various four-footed animals and birds of prey in porcelain were standing, done life-size according to nature. I can remember a bird of prey with a mauled hen lying before it, its blood-bespattered frame and innards clearly visible, all as natural as if it was living, right down to the colors. [...] The figures I admired included a large she-goat, lying down with a couple of kids hanging on its udder; a wild boar on the point of getting its tusks into a hunting-hound that had sunk its teeth into one of its legs; a beautiful, large swan, and a peacock with its fan fully spread etc."[618]

The only pictorial source we have is an uncompleted design drawing which Gerhard Glaser thought came from the hand of Pöppelmann himself (fig. 139).[619] It is, however, not clear which room the drawing depicts. The cavetto on the drawing is evidence against there having been a mezzanin area immediately above, and in favor of this being a room on the ground floor, which is also suggested by the porcelain pieces which feature in the drawing: animal figures and vases stand on consoles on three of the fully drawn wall sections between the large arched windows. The shape of the vases and the fact of their being adorned with masks and decoration in relief identifies them without doubt as large vases from the Böttger period made from designs by Raymond le Plat and executed in white porcelain and red-brown stoneware (fig. 138). As one would expect in such a detailed design drawing, the draftsman was clearly concerned to reproduce the exact proportions, correcting the size of a number of the vases sketched in, as is clearly visible in the case of the lowest vase on the middle one of the three sections on which porcelain is drawn in. If the height of the room is calculated from what we know to have been the size of the said porcelain vases, then the result corresponds fairly exactly to that of the ground-floor rooms of the Japanese Palace.

On the drawing, however, the room has five windows, which was not a feature of any room in the Japanese Palace. The solution to this discrepancy lies in the fact that the original plan for a three-wing extension of the Dutch Palace was replaced by a four-wing design signed by Augustus the Strong and dated March 19, 1727, on which the middle room of the Elbe-side wing does have five windows.[620] And the fact that the King made an additional note on the plan that this constituted the end of the planning stage, and that the building should be constructed exactly so, provides a plausible explanation for Pöppelmann's having subsequently given thought to the way in which the porcelain was to be displayed in the elevation under consideration. But as it turned out, further

138 After Raymond Le Plat, vase with mascaroons, ca. 1725, Dresden Porcelain Collection

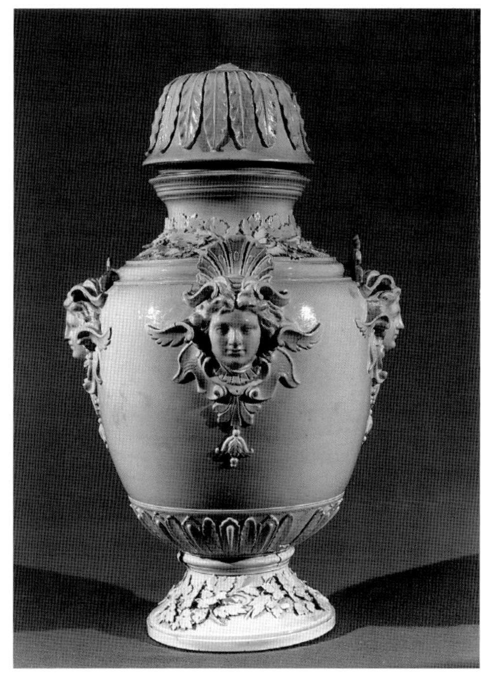

changes were in fact made to the plans before building work actually began in 1729 and Pöppelmann's drawing, made at some point between March 1727 and 1729, was laid aside uncompleted, together with a selection of other designs and detail drawings.

Even though the porcelain figures that the drawing was concerned with were most likely Far Eastern ones, it is still of considerable interest for what it tells us about the way the animals were to be presented. The draftsman intended not only birds but also four-footed animals to be placed like vases on wall consoles, for preference in complementary pairs. As we have already seen, consideration was later given to displaying the figures in the large gallery on sills and consoles. Given the quantity of figures ordered, there would in fact have been no alternative to putting the animals together with the vases up on the walls, although it would be illuminating to work out whether the area of wall available would actually have been able to acommodate the vases plus all the 588 figures.

This disproportion between the number of figures ordered and the rooms intended to house them may have been what in the nineteenth century gave rise to the opinion that the animal figures ordered were in part intended to be used for garden decoration. As Graesse wrote in his 1873 guide to the Porcelain Collection, "The reason why these figures were produced was that they were put in the gardens in place of marble statues; this is also the reason why they are now so extremely rare and command such truly fabulous prices."[621] It may be that Graesse derived this notion from the general use of animal figures in stone or metal for decorating gardens, as there is nothing to support his theory in the Japanese Palace sources. Or he might have been taking his cue from Keyssler's account (see Source 2), which described the status quo of the planning in 1730 as follows: "The garden is likewise to be enlarged and to be extended two hundred feet further into the Elbe. Its *bassins* are to be done in marble, and its many statues to be in marble and porcelain."[622] Keyssler does not reveal how it was thought that this could be done, or with what particular statues and figures. If Graesse knew Augustus the Strong's sketch for a ground plan with its reference to "Saxon porcelain gardens" (fig. 30), then this may have led him to dream up a garden teeming with porcelain animals. And it is a tribute to the particular charm of this fanciful notion that it crops up again and again throughout the literature on Meissen.[623] Augustus the Strong's reference to a porcelain garden was in fact to an extent a reflection of the state of affairs at the time: as is shown by the view of the Dutch Palace by Corvinus as seen from the Elbe (fig. 16), there were an impressive number of large vases along the balustrades and edged beds in the inner sections. A list in the archive of the Dresden Porcelain Collection calls for a large number of "blue and Japanese porcelains," altogether 207 vases and pots, which are allotted in the king's own fair hand to various terraces, staircases, and *bassins*.[624] And inventory marginalia provide definite proof that in the first half of the 1720s the garden did house, temporarily at least, a quantity of large Far Eastern porcelain vases and tubs, a number of which, including some very old ones, were on various occasions blown over by the wind and broken.[625] But once the Dutch Palace has been converted into the Japanese Palace, none of the relevant travel reports make any mention of porcelain standing in the garden.

Even at that time it was well known that ceramic figures are far from durable and thus unsuitable for decorating gardens. In 1720, Leonhard Christian Sturm gave a detailed account of this problem, also noting how it was possible to make terracotta figures more resistant to wind and weather: "Wooden and clay statues are all too destructible [...]. And terracotta figures are no use whatsoever, because they lose any fine linework and clean edges in the firing, so that private persons who wish to have inexpensive statues standing in the open air in their gardens are advised to have statues made in clay covered with a roof so that while they may be exposed to gentle sunlight and the soft caress of dry air, it may yet be possible to protect them from biting wind or scorching sun. When they are completely dried out, they can be given another mild firing without losing any significant detail, and painted with oil colors as soon as they come out of the kiln."[626] For all that porcelain is harder, denser, and more resistant than terracotta, porcelain figures would still also suffer greatly from being left in the open air, as is indeed recognized by the Meissen manufactory at its present-day home, where it is only in summer that recently made examples of the animal figures are put out to adorn the courtyard of the Triebischtal factory. And it was for just the same reason that Fürst Adam Friedrich von Seinsheim, back in 1768, had no other option with his garden sculpture but "to give them a coat of paint like Saxon porcelain has, now and then finishing the decoration with a little gilding; after which they are varnished to make them look as if they were made of porcelain."[627]

The Palace and the Animals: The historical and topographical context

The Japanese Palace and Augustus the Strong's overall plan

The development of the royal collections

The *Kunstkammer* of the electors of Saxony was set up in the year 1560,[628] and differed in no way from other historic art and curiosity cabinets. It contained a broad range of objects: all kinds of *naturalia*, works of art, coins and medals, books, mechanical devices, curiosities, and the like. We know from the inventory of 1595 that it also contained sixteen pieces of Chinese porcelain, which had come into the collection five years earlier as a gift from the Grand Duke Ferdinand I of Tuscany to Elector Christian I of Saxony.[629]

At first, the *Kunstkammer* was housed in the Residence, but it was enlarged on a number of occasions and finally transferred to a provisional home in 1710.[630] Like other princes of the time, Augustus the Strong was interested not only in art but also in science, and he planned to subject the collection to thorough reorganization and rearrangement. When he inherited the collection, it was displayed according to a scheme that was basically decorative in character, and this was no longer in tune with the spirit of the times. Modern scholarship called for a new approach, as did the Baroque thirst for order and predilection for schemes that reflected the way things related to each other and to an overall whole. The natural history collections were now to be arranged systematically, and the art collections likewise had to be displayed in accordance with a variety of new criteria such as aesthetics, wealth, and iconography. Even before 1718, Augustus the Strong himself made a design for what would effectively have been a museum, housing the holdings of the former *Kunstkammer* on two floors.[631] Various factors prevented his design from being realized. Having been divided up a number of times, the natural history collection finally found a home shortly after 1730 in the rooms and galleries of the Zwinger.[632] Other parts of the *Kunstkammer* had been taken to the attics of the Dutch Palace as early as 1717. The *Kunstkammer* only ever contained a relatively small number of porcelain pieces, and the thirty-four pieces remaining when the *Kunstkammer* was dissolved in 1832 were transferred to the porcelain collection,[633] which had evolved as a separate entity. At first housed in the Dutch Palace, which was then rebuilt to become the Japanese Palace, it expanded enormously under Augustus the Strong. In 1721, it became the first specialized collection in Dresden to be given its own inventory, even in advance of the collection of paintings.[634] But in spite of this relative independence, the porcelain collection was directly affected by the development of the other royal collections and the overall concept governing the way they were housed. If the function of the porcelain collection within this overall concept is to be understood correctly, it is first necessary to look at the roles played in Saxony by commerce and science.

Commerce and science in Saxony

In the first half of the eighteenth century, Saxony had one of the most advanced economies in the whole of the Holy Roman Empire. Leipzig's geographical situation at the crossroads of important north-south and east-west trade routes was a vital factor in the city's significance as a venue for trade fairs. Mineral resources and a high level of technical development made Saxony capable of an at least partial realization of the mercantilist ideal. From 1694 on, the country's development was driven forward by its forceful ruler Augustus the Strong, who was indeed one of Europe's mightiest figures in the political, social, and cultural fields. Manufacturing flourished during his reign, with international artists working on the extension of the Residence and critical discoveries being made by scientists and scholars in their various spheres.

The development of manufacturing in Saxony is particularly relevant to this study.[635] As the manufactories had their origins in middle-class or princely initiatives, they were not subject to the restrictive regulations of the guilds and differed greatly from the traditional small craft workshops. Division of labor, at that time a new way of organizing the work process, raised levels of production, and the concomitant specialization had a beneficial effect on quality. As the manufactories were not administered by master craftsmen tied to the guilds, they now had greater freedom to be active on the open market. Another important result was that they had access to a wider range of artists, and were in closer contact with the newest fashions and available models, particularly through the trade fairs.[636]

The manufactory was particularly well suited to porcelain production, which calls for artists and craftsmen with a great variety of skills and techniques. When European porcelain was in its first years, other models of production such as that used for pottery workshops would have been impracticable. The big ceramics producers such as the Dutch, French, and Mediterranean faience firms were organized along manufactory lines, as were the Far Eastern producers. When the Meissen manufactory was founded under royal protection, it was consciously set up along these same lines, and was from the very beginning designed for a relatively large turnover and range of products. The foundational charter has a pertinent passage in this respect: "This is one of the principal means which We have found, namely that if this country is to be given back a sound diet and flourishing trade, then this is first and foremost to be achieved through manufactories and commerce."[637] Augustus the Strong furthermore made it clear that he was referring to the misfortunes brought about by the Northern War, and that he was intending to remedy them by promoting trade. The intention was that Saxony should compete with the Far Eastern porcelain manufacturers and that the land should be enriched by the monies that would flow in in ample quantities from abroad. The motivation behind the founding of the Meissen manufactory was to just as great a degree commercial as it was artistic. This is just one instance of the link between art and commerce that was so typical of the Baroque era.[638]

As has been pointed out, science and scholarship flourished in Saxony no less than commerce did, with the universities of Leipzig and Wittenberg both situated on the Elector's territory. The exchange of the most recent scientific findings was promoted by the development of Leipzig into an important center for the book trade and publication of periodicals. The *Acta Eruditorum*, Germany's first scholarly scientific journal, was founded in Leipzig in 1682, and in the 1730s Leipzig likewise fathered the first universal lexicon.[639] The philosopher and mathematician Walther Ehrenfried von Tschirnhaus, "by his entry into the service of the Elector [...] was instrumental in promoting a close association between science and the court of Dresden. He was at the very vanguard of the early Enlightenment and among those involved in the initial debate on the ideals of Germany's academic institutions [...]."[640]

Tschirnhaus furthermore owned a glassworks that produced, among other things, large-size burning glasses, which were intended to be of service to scientists and to promote the development of new enterprises. And when, shortly after Tschirnhaus's death, Johann Friedrich Böttger and his fellows finally discovered the secret of porcelain production, they only did so by continuing Tschirnhaus's experiments, which had been conducted with the help of precisely these burning glasses.

This episode is ample demonstration of the ubiquitous close association between science and art already noted in the sphere of commerce. Between them, science and art set the scene for the invention of European porcelain, the former as necessary condition and the latter as goal. And while the artistic aspect of porcelain was in the foreground in the Japanese Palace project, we are certainly correct in assuming that contemporary minds saw this aspect as very closely interwoven with such matters as scientific prowess and economic development.

The Japanese Palace as a metaphor for economic and cultural wealth

In this general context it is worth taking a further look at the layout of the palace interior and at the structures and ordering as they are reflected in the plans. As has already been seen, the ground floor was from the summer of 1730 onwards to be reserved for porcelain of Far Eastern origin and the upper story for products of the Meissen manufactory. The latter ranged from more or less strict copies of Far Eastern models, through what one might call paraphrases, such as the "indianische Blumen" and "Korean lion" *décors*, to pieces with decoration that was thoroughly European in origin and inspiration. This division can be applied equally well to the forms.

The visitor to the palace was thus enabled to make direct comparisons between very similar pieces from Europe and the Far East, and to become acquainted with creations that were pure Meissen. In this respect a clean break had been made with the kind of compilers of porcelain cabinets who, when short of the Far Eastern porcelains necessary to make up a symmetrical whole, happily made do with faience copies, or even with pieces made of lacquered wood. Had the plan for the upper story of the Japanese Palace been brought to fulfillment, the vast variety of forms and decorations would have made it into something akin to an outsize parade of all the lines produced by the Meissen manufactory. The king knew very well that once his foreign guests had had their appetites aroused by such a magnificent display, they would be sure to make enquiries at the manufactory's branch in Dresden about acquiring similar pieces for themselves. This was in his own interest as well: after all, he was the manufactory's proprietor. The only snag for the guests was that the pieces displayed in the two most magnificent rooms of the upper story, namely the animal figures in the gallery on the Neustadt side, and the vases and other pieces "so nach Alt Indianisch-differenter Arth gemahlet" ("painted in various ancient Indian styles") in the Elbe-side gallery, were reserved exclusively for the king himself. A decree issued by Augustus III on November 26, 1733, and signed by Sulkowski, expressly stated that such items and *a fortiori* also whole services, "were no longer to be produced for anyone, or sold to anyone, whoever they may be."[641] This meant that to receive, for instance, a vase of this kind as a gift was an extraordinary sign of the king's favor.[642]

The connection between the Japanese Palace and commerce suggested by this scenario is not only confirmed by the iconographical program for the palace, but is also shown to have been

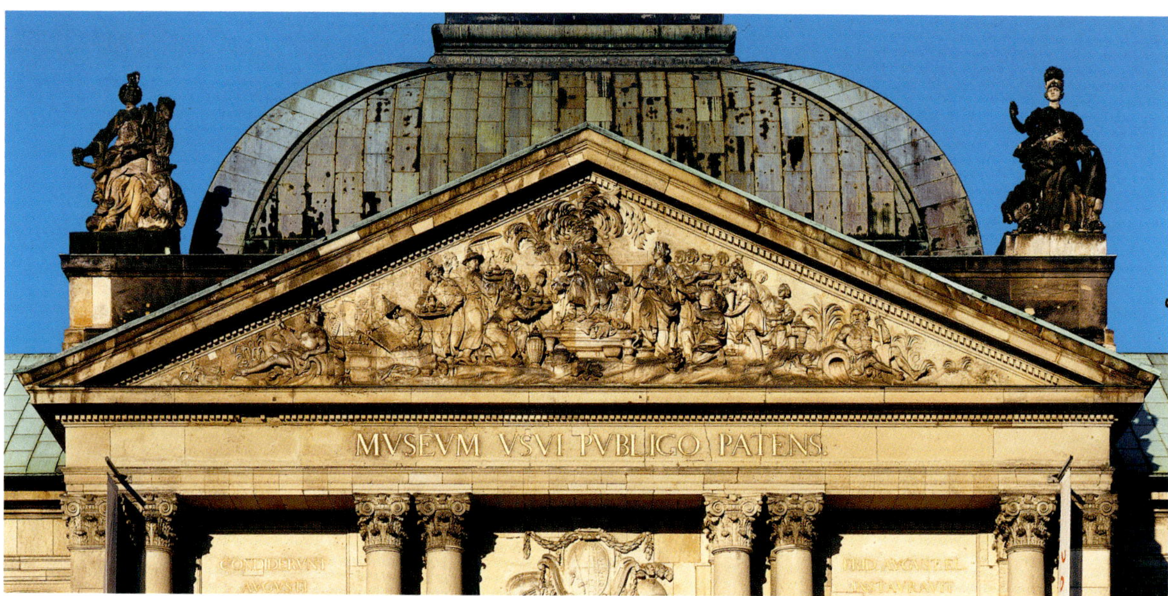

139 Japanese Palace, relief on the pediment over the portico (2001)

fully intentional. Even before entering the building, the visitor could not fail to notice above the entrance portico the pediment relief in which representatives of the two porcelain-producing continents of the world – Asia and Europe – come to the feet of Saxony enthroned to present her with their treasures (fig. 139). Standing on the molding above and behind the pediment were Minerva on the European side, and a corresponding figure representing Far Eastern trade on the Asian side.

While these thoughts were fairly unambiguously conveyed by Jean de Bodt's sculptural decoration in the entrance area, they were even more unmistakable in Zacharias Longuelune's plan for fitting out the large Elbe-side upper-story gallery with a carillon and throne pavilion. It was drawn up in 1735 and is further proof of the importance of the changes in planning brought about under Augustus III. Longuelune wrote a long and very detailed description of his concept for this wing, giving the reasoning behind all the constituent elements (Source 3). He suggested that the ceiling of the carillon pavilion should be painted with a representation of foreign nations,[643] and that above the throne Minerva and Neptune should be depicted arguing the toss about the name to be given to the city of Athens, as this theme would allow for the inclusion of all the gods of antiquity.[644] For the ceiling of the gallery in between he proposed the following: "The ceiling of the long gallery between the two rooms is to be divided into three parts, with the middle part representing Saxony and Japan engaged, in the presence of Minerva, in a dispute on the merits and perfection of the works made in their porcelain manufactories. They are to be accompanied by Emulation, Taste, Imitation, Painting, and Sculpture, and by all the elements which contribute to the beauty of these kinds of works. The goddess shall put the crown, the prize for the winner of the dispute, into the hands of Saxony, while Jealousy and Spite make signs to advise Japan to have her porcelain vases loaded back onto the vessels which brought them."[645]

Longuelune suggested that the theme of Saxony winning the contest for the most favored porcelain would offer many opportunities for allegorical representation and offer the beholder the kind of food for thought that would be quite appropriate at this point. He then continues: "The two other parts of the ceiling are to represent on the one hand the arts and the manufactories established in Saxony, and on the other such beneficial natural products as grow and are produced in the land; this is all to be done allegorically, with little elaboration, and to be executed nobly and in the grand manner."[646]

This program not only gave Meissen porcelain a position of honor between Art and Nature, but also demonstrated its importance as a commodity by showing the Far Eastern porcelain manufacturers, as the losers of the contest, being forced to take their wares home with them. Having been depicted in the entrance pediment as being allowed to join Europe in laying their wares at Saxony's feet, they have now forfeited their position as market-leaders. Conversely, while the entrance area presented Saxony, representing Europe, on the same level as the revered continent of Asia, the throne gallery emphasized Saxony's primacy. Having started the tour of the palace by admiring, with still relatively unbiased minds, the Far Eastern collection on the ground floor, the visitors would continue through the animal gallery and the adjacent rooms and cabinets of Meissen porcelain. Standing as it were together with the foreign nations (ceiling of the carillon pavilion), opposite the prince on his throne under the gods (ceiling of the throne pavilion), they would hear the gentle tinkling of the carillon and would have no choice but to be of one mind with the message of the ceiling painting. After all, there can be no better demonstration of a country's economic might than the fact of its having broken a long-standing foreign monopoly.

Even as early as Meissen manufactory's foundational charter of January 23, 1710, Augustus the Strong is to be found expressing the wish, or rather, intention, "that in the future [...] white porcelain of this kind [...] shall be able to surpass Asian porcelain by far, not only in beauty and quality, but also in variety of shapes [...]"[647] This was the result of a debate about the quality of the new invention that had lasted almost a whole year: Böttger, in his memorandum to the king of March 28, 1709, announcing among other things the invention of European porcelain, had proudly referred to the "fine white porcelain, together with the very finest glaze and painting, which is if not better than the Asian wares, then at least as good."[648] In the subsequent investigation conducted by a commission specially constituted for this purpose, great importance was attached to the question of how good Böttger's porcelain was in comparison with its Far Eastern counterpart.[649]

The extent to which the superiority of Saxon porcelain became a commonplace is shown by a text in which this topos is used to amusing effect, Rudolph Friedrich von Wichmannshausen's description in five parts (published in Schoettgen 1736) of the festive illumination of Dresden put on from August 7 to 9, 1736, to celebrate the return of Augustus III from Poland. In the fifth part of the unpaginated text, which gives a detailed description of the illuminated symbols and honorific pictures that the citizens of Dresden put into their windows, he makes a special mention of the pictures displayed in the windows of his apartment by Teuffert, the major-domo of the Japanese Palace. The pictures included: "Ein Indianer in Lebens-Größe mit bunt gezirtem Habite, welcher eine Porcellaine Aufsatz-Urne vor sich auf einem Postament stehend hatte, mit Ueberschrifft: 'Was ich durch meinen Witz zu allererst gemacht – Hat Sachsen nach der Zeit vollkommen ausgedacht'; [...] Ein Europäer in Lebens-Größe, mit einem roth mit Gold bordirten Kleide, welcher einen grossen Trinck-Becher, oder Willkommen mit des Königs von Pohlen Portrait, in der rechten Hand hatte, mit der Ueberschrifft: 'Japanisch Porcellain, und was Chineser reichen – Muss unserm Sächßischen an Kunst und Güte weichen'." ["A life-size Oriental clad in colorfully decorated garments, with a porcelain urn standing on a pedestal in front of him and the superscription: 'What I first made with wit and great invention/Saxon brains have raised to sheer perfection.' ... And a life-size European in a red robe edged with gold, holding a large drinking beaker in his right hand to welcome the King of Poland depicted thereon, with 'Porc'lains from Japan and far-off China/ Must now admit that Saxon wares are finer' written above."]

This constant insistence on the merits of the home-produced porcelain should not mislead us into thinking that no great value was any longer set on Far Eastern porcelain, which Augustus the Strong acquired in large quantities to form a collection that was subsequently expanded even further under Augustus III. It was precisely because the imported products were still so coveted in Europe that the local Meissen porcelain, by virtue of its being considered superior, acquired a status much higher than would have been accorded to wares that were simply a worthy ersatz for what had been available until then. The palace iconography incorporated this eclipse of the Far East in that it presented Asia and Meissen on an even footing at the entrance to the palace, but then in the throne room showed Meissen porcelain bathed in the glorious splendor of the ruler and rising victorious over the still highly-valued wares of the Far East. Parallel to this, the Elector of Saxony who occupied the throne was at the same time ruler of the huge kingdom of Poland and had to defend his status against those who resisted his claims. By symbolically putting foreign powers firmly in their place, European porcelain, proof of Saxony's inventive genius, redoubled the splendor of the Saxon sovereign and at the same time underlined the land's economic and cultural prosperity. This was the basic statement made by the Japanese Palace, and it will become even clearer and more comprehensible in the following section, in which we shall consider the significance of the palace in the overall context of Augustus the Strong's program of palace-building in Saxony.

The Japanese Palace in Augustus the Strong's overall plan

In the State Archive of Saxony are preserved notes made in the year 1716 by Augustus the Strong in which he sketched out an overall plan for his palaces in Saxony.[650] This plan is very illuminating for the present discussion, even though it was drawn up more than ten years before the initiation of the Japanese Palace project. It was conceived in connection with the planned publication of an "Atlas Royal" which was to make a record of the state of the Saxon-Polish union at the time.

This draft concept for the overall plan contained two parts. The first included the more remote palaces, and the second more detailed one covered only those in and around the *Residenzstadt* Dresden. To quote Monika Schlechte: "Close examination of the order in which those [palaces] in the immediate vicinity of the Residence are put reveals that an attempt was being made to establish an intellectual scheme similar to the one familiar from the history of architecture for the architectural styling of a whole country, systematically relating the already existing palaces and *maisons de plaisance* to each other, and making a number of disparate elements into a coherent whole."[651] The structure of this thematic organization of the palaces was not firmly defined. Nor was it based on a purely theoretical concept: on the contrary, it incorporated the buildings that were already in existence. This justifies the assumption, even in the absence of a direct documentary source, that even such buildings as had a direct relationship to the Residence and were later bought and converted by the king – such as the Dutch Palace – were already in his mind, or at least at the back of his mind, when he drew up the plan in 1716.

There is evidence of a second phase of activity from the mid-1720s on aimed at the creation of a symbolic net of interrelations between the royal palaces. In 1726 Großsedlitz was officially declared the property of Augustus the Strong (who had in fact acquired it through a middleman back in 1723), and from 1727 it provided the venue for the celebration of the king's name-day on the feast of the Order of the White Eagle, the highest Polish order. Moritzburg was from 1727 onwards likewise given new fittings and furnishings, and its pheasantry was built in 1728 as the first of a number of projected menageries. In the same year the Zwinger was converted for use as a "Palais des Sciences," and 1728/29 saw the beginning of the building work on the Japanese Palace.

The buildings mentioned in Augustus the Strong's draft overall plan were each allotted their specific functions. Pillnitz was to be a *chevalerie*, Cossebaude a hermitage, and Sternburg a "Belvedere"; the palace in the *Großer Garten* was to be dedicated to the god Mercury, the hunting palace Moritzburg was to be a temple to the goddess Diana, and so on.[652] For certain buildings he furthermore specified what textiles were to be used and what style was to be followed in the fittings and furnishings, laying down, for instance, whether the furniture was to be in the French, English, Turkish, or Chinese taste, in accordance with the function of the palace in question.

Comprehensive planning, which always gives the planner and designer a particular opportunity to see how component parts relate and fit together, was of formative importance for the overall plan that finally emerged. It was certainly intended that the plan should be carried out, but even the planning itself was taken enormously seriously, for what was going on in the prince's mind was a sign of his talent for perceiving higher structures. His ideas for plans were generally regarded as the prime tangible manifestation in the world of mortal senses of the fact that the prince was a "higher" being.[653] At first these ideas were only visible on paper or in the form of a model, but even at that stage they were compelling evidence of the penetrating insights and power of their originator even if the plans were not actually, or only partially, carried out. Although Augustus the Strong's overall plan was not carried out in full, a number of events are evidence of its partial realization, such as the festivities in honor of the Order of the White Eagle in Großsedlitz, the peasant weddings in Pillnitz, and the hunting parties in Moritzburg.[654]

The idea, however, had been born, and as a glance at Augustus the Strong's creations clearly shows, it lived on in other forms and was constantly adapted and expanded. This is not only shown by the use of the palaces for court festivities, but also the symbolism and articulation of the fittings and furnishings.

Monika Schlechte has demonstrated this with reference to the layout of the hunting palace of Moritzburg. Moritzburg's designation as a temple of Diana formed the first plane of the symbolic association of the palace with its function. The four ponds around the palace were named after figures of classical mythology from

140 The marble-paved upper courtyard at Versailles (2002)

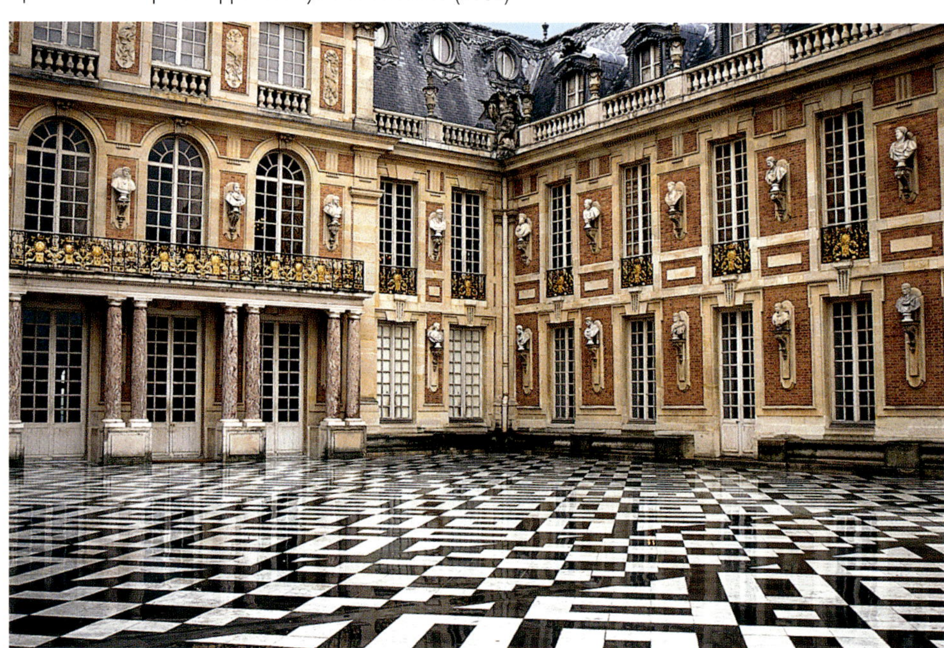

stories relating to the goddess Diana (Endymion, Actaeon, and so on), and precisely these figures and their relationship to the patroness of the palace reappear in the paintings on the wall-coverings in the "Monströsensaal" inside the building. There is thus a link stretching from the macrocosm of the overall plan to the microcosm of the interior decoration.[655] The patronal presence of the goddess Diana permeated the buildings right down to the descriptive explanations of the historical pictures hanging in the palace; various configurations of symbolism and iconography were thus woven together into one coherent whole.

Although there are clear links between this iconographical level and the overall plan, there are greater complexities to be discovered in the palace's interior. Among the items that formed an integral part of the interior at the hunting palace of Moritzburg were the most prestigious items of the extensive and impressive antler collection of the electors of Saxony; these were brought to Moritzburg in 1725 when the electoral collections at Augustusburg were being ordered anew and exhibited in a manner appropriate to their perceived importance. Most of the larger rooms at the Moritzburg still have their leather wall-hangings to this day. However, the antlers were not only treasured for their preciousness, nor was the leather only used for the wall-hangings because it was technically suitable. In the overall scheme of things at the palace, the antlers and the luxurious, expensively processed animal skins share a certain basic common identity in that they are both animal trophies. The one material comes from cattle raised and slaughtered for man's benefit, and the other from an animal hunted for its meat, and both materials are among the last parts of these animals to be put to good use by man. That they have the character of trophies is emphasized by the imposing way they are displayed, and also by the significance of their home as a center of hunting.

One further small part of the antler collection, on the other hand, was housed in the *Animaliengalerie* (natural history collection) in the Zwinger.[656] These, however, were not the antlers of royal stags but rather malformed freaks of nature. Similar misshapen antlers were also preserved as special rarities in the Moritzburg "Monströsensaal," where they were attractive not so much for their scientific interest, as was the case in the *Animaliengalerie*, but for their oddness. While the trophies at Moritzburg were, by virtue of being juxtaposed with living creatures in the runs and menageries, pointers in a very general sense to the life-preserving, or life-destroying, power of the prince, the trophies in the Zwinger – Mother Nature's building blocks, as it were – were by virtue of their juxtaposition with stuffed animals indicators of the prince's knowledge of and insights into the natural world.

When the Japanese Palace came into being, it did so on the opposite bank of the Elbe from the Zwinger, and at the same time as the Zwinger was being turned into a "palace of science." The animal world also had a place of honor in the Japanese Palace, in the first gallery of the upper story. It is surprising to find that the very obvious connection between the two buildings in the light of the significance of the animal world in the Baroque has hardly ever been pointed out in the literature to date.

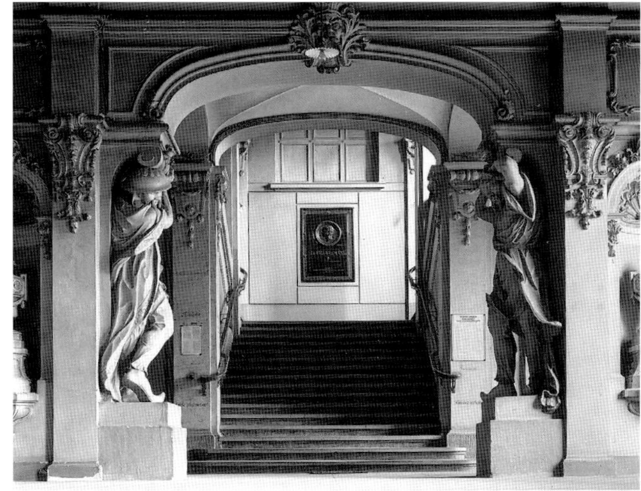

141 The Chinaman atlantes in the entrance hall of the Japanese Palace (before 1945)

There is abundant evidence that the Zwinger as a building had metaphorical significance of the kind associated with gardens, and this matter has been the object of scholarly discussion.[657] Its original purpose as an orangery, combined with the powerful allusion to Augustus the Strong in the form of the Hercules Saxonicus on guard on the *Wallpavillon* ("rampart pavilion") make the interpretation of the Zwinger as a Saxon garden of the Hesperides most plausible. The presence of the element Water in the cascades of the *Nymphenbad* and in the ornamentation on the *Wallpavillon* is complemented by symbols of the element Earth in the form of ample hangings of fruit and faun-like herm pilasters, once again on the *Wallpavillon* (fig. 25). Even the way the building is articulated has a certain "vegetative" quality: the design plays havoc with the architectural canon of geometrical forms, deforming the moldings and turning the open gables into so many interchangeable building blocks. The apparently rampant decoration on the building winds itself around the framework of the windows and pilasters, transforming the structure into an image of organic growth in stone. It is in stark contrast to the cool and strictly geometrical structure of the Japanese Palace with its conscious turning away from all that is natural: only the fat-tummied Chinaman herms in the inner courtyard offer a touch of cheerfulness, their laughter seeming to appeal for a little humanity in the face of the intellectuality that is so much in evidence in the building's caculated structure (fig. 26).

Although both buildings are constructed around an inner court, the impressions they make are quite different. The fact that the Zwinger court is surrounded by relatively low buildings – on special occasions the open space on the Elbe side was built up into a kind of fourth wing with temporary constructions – makes it a stark contrast to the Japanese Palace courtyard, which almost has the character of an interior. If the basically curvilinear form of the Zwinger speaks to us of Dionysiac organic growth, then the appeal of the Japanese Palace lies in the Apollonian spirit that permeates its rationally ordered rectangular forms. The plan to give the palace courtyard a marble floor – like the courtyard at Versailles that Augustus the Strong may well have seen on his grand tour (fig. 140) – would have reinforced its *Festsaal*-like character still further.

The decoration of the Zwinger with statues of classical divinities draw attention to the first (quite un-Christian, it goes without saying) incarnations of the divine being in nature and have their counterparts in the Chinese figures in the courtyard and entrance hall of the Japanese Palace (fig. 141), exotic Far Eastern gods representing the world as formed by man.

The collections simultaneously allocated to the two buildings can be related quite directly to the basic structure and character of the two buildings as expounded above. The natural history collections in the Zwinger corresponded to the garden symbolism apparent in the architecture. The scientific element present here, the presentation of nature and the affirmation of its aptness as an object of research, raised the flag of intellectual discourse. The encyclopedic range of animal specimens of the *Animaliengalerie* represented the natural world in all its infinite variety. The Japanese Palace, by contrast, decorated as it was with clearly man-made artifacts in an iconographical program relating to trade and Saxony's cultural achievements, reflected in its every detail the taste and connoisseurship of its owner. The sub-text to the costliness and rarity of the collection had nothing to do with research into the natural world: it was related to the universality of the claims asserted by the ruler of the Saxon lands, the most important aspect here being his capacity for sheer pleasure and self-gratification. While the Zwinger and its collections were a suitable setting for thought and intellectual encounters, the milieu created in the Residence-like Japanese Palace was one that favored the kind of encounters beloved of connoisseurs and lovers of pleasure. The range of animals in the Japanese Palace may not have been encyclopedic, but it was a choice and representative selection that not only spanned a broad technical and artistic gamut but was also, as we shall see, replete with allusions to the contemporary social order. If – to use modern-day terms of reference – the Zwinger's chosen focus was on the natural world, then that of the Japanese Palace was on the world of culture. This antithesis was quite in the tradition of the *Kunstkammer* and *Wunderkammer*, the contents of which were also divided up into *naturalia* and *artificialia*, drawing a line between the things created by God and the things created by Man. At the Zwinger and the Japanese Palace, however, this Renaissance division of things was given monumental proportions and rather more concrete terms of reference through the comparison-inviting contraposition of the organic creativity of nature and the artistic creativity of the Saxon prince.

While the Zwinger was used to display Saxony's predominant source of wealth, namely its natural resources, the Japanese Palace was to house items related to its other major asset, namely the combination of its highly-developed manufacturing technology with its prowess in commerce.

If this account has focused primarily on the antitheses between the two buildings, there were also parallels, such as the herm pilasters already mentioned, that invited the world to compare as well as to contrast. Another parallel was the fact that the roofs of both buildings were painted – or were to have been painted – in the same colors,[658] so that the visitor standing on the bridge and looking to the two banks of the Elbe would have recognized in the two eye-catching blue-roofed buildings the two cornerstones of Saxony's prosperity and culture.

Using the Zwinger to house parts of the royal collections was a solution to which Augustus the Strong had only resorted *faute de mieux*, once it became clear that the project for an all-embracing museum was not going to be realized. However, the fact that the alternative solution led in its turn to a quite specific kind of furnishing and conversion of the Japanese Palace reinforces the thesis that the idea of an overall plan for the royal palaces and *maisons de plaisance* was still alive around 1730, and that it exerted an influence on the ordering of the collections. The three different animal presences in the prince's three outstanding building complexes provide us with a particularly clear demonstration of the subtle differentiation that went into giving each building its own particular character, and into setting each building in its own relation to the others and to the whole.

The presentation of Augustus the Strong's might at Moritzburg (mastery over animals) was complemented by a demonstration of his education (knowledge about the animal world) at the Zwinger, and of his taste at the Japanese Palace (presentation of animals). While these three places, seen together, provided a representative picture of Saxony's natural and economic resources, each one also had its own particular political, scientific, and artistic slant – insofar as politics, science, and art can ever be considered in isolation from each other, which is a particularly moot question for the Baroque period.[659]

The intention in the following section is to investigate the extent to which the animal gallery at the Japanese Palace was – or was planned to be – structured so as to reflect these concerns and priorities. But in order to establish this, it is first necessary to make certain points regarding the particular relationship between man and the animal world in the context of the Saxon court.

The Animal Gallery: its structure and interpretative levels

The animal world as seen by the Baroque court, with particular reference to Dresden

Certain elements in man's dealings with the animal world are universal: they have been in evidence – and continue to be in evidence – in all countries of the world and at all times. And the Saxon court in the first half of the eighteenth century was no exception to this general rule.

In many instances, animals are suppliers of food and are themselves edible; such animals are either bred and raised to supply man with food at a later stage, or are shot or captured in the wild, their edible parts then being collected and prepared for the table. The Dresden court had, to mention only a few examples, its own fishponds, a pheasant reserve in the Great Garden, and a number of enclosures for keeping farm animals at the kitchen gardens in Ostra. The fact that animals are a source of food gives them a particular value in man's eyes, so that they can represent a kind of "capital." This applies not only to food-supplying animals, but also to those that bring their owners other less direct benefits, providing protection, or reflecting something important about their masters and mistresses. Although such wild animals such as lions and bears were by the beginning of the eighteenth century no longer kept as signs of power in cages or pits in the city fortifications, they were still to be seen in the city, at first on the *Altmarkt* and then in the *Jägerhof* in Neustadt. In these instances the focus was on what one might call their ideal value, which was compounded by the fact that animals are so suitable as vehicles for symbolism: similar to man in many respects, they are nevertheless different enough to be able to act as a kind of hinge, linking our quasi-objective experience of the world with the intellectual ideas we come up with when endeavoring to explain that world. And the metaphysical relations between mankind and the animals, made manifest in allegory, emblem, and symbol, are in their turn complemented by the relations operating in the strictly physical sphere where man and the animals are distinguished from each other – or brought closer to each other – through scientific research.

Animals can also be called upon to fulfill roles in which they stand side-by-side with their owners, offering them protection or amusement, or engaging with them in teamwork, as in the hunt. Two examples can be drawn from the Dresden context. The Meissen porcelain figure of the huntsman Johann Georg Wenzel, modeled in 1744 by Kaendler, shows Wenzel as part of Princess Maria Anna's retinue, accompanied by her own personal guard-dog. This unusually large figure is now held in the Porcelain Collection in Dresden.[660] The source for the second example is an undated handwritten document, certainly from the first half of the eighteenth century, in which an animal, most probably a monkey, is either being offered for a certain price, or being delivered to its purchaser; the note contains eleven words to be used as commands to make the monkey, for instance, perform somersaults, blow kisses, or play the soldier.[661]

Common to all these examples is the fact that man is the master of the animal, whether the animal in question is being honored and respected, being used to make a statement, being put on display, being trained to be useful in a certain way, or is being put to death. If man stands in fear of the animal's unpredictability or superior strength, then taming the animal and keeping it in captivity is always tied up with an attempt on man's part to give visible form to his anthropocentric world-view. Ever since Aesop, the lion had been regarded as the king of the animals and was a symbol for the highest princely virtues; in Baroque allegories it was also often used to represent the continent of Africa (the "wild" continent). At the royal menageries, however, it was not presented as a hierarchical counterpart to the prince – by, for example, being housed in a centrally situated enclosure – but as a wild and dangerous animal was, rather, put under lock and key together with other such beasts. While the prince granted the lion its status as ruler of the animal world, he paid himself back in the same coin by claiming a share in that position himself, and demonstrated his ultimate superiority over the lion by subjecting it to a humiliating captivity. The way we treat (wild) animals in our possession can reveal a great deal about our culture and about our understanding of the society in which we live.

Animal collections

The animal collections of Augustus the Strong and Augustus III have already been described in a fair measure of detail. Live animals could be seen in their respective sheds, enclosures, and menageries, and the various kinds of game in their reserves. The hunting palaces of Moritzburg and Hubertusburg housed vast collections of trophies taken from local game killed in the hunt. The natural history collection in the *Animaliengalerie* complemented these trophies with taxidermal exhibits that ranged from single limbs and organs to whole specimens, stuffed or otherwise preserved, with pride of place being accorded to those that were particularly bizarre or exotic.

In all these cases the relationship between man and the animals was, as suggested in the introductory comments above, far from being a purely objective one: on the contrary, it was strongly subjective. With its strong belief in God-given hierarchies, Baroque society naturally had a particular interest in the hierarchies that governed the animal world. Although the prince had no reason to doubt the God-given nature of his own standing, he was nevertheless concerned to use every opportunity to confirm and emphasize it through his cultural and intellectual achievements, and through feats of physical skill and strength. While there did not seem to be such a thing as a cultural or intellectual hierarchy in the animal world, a hierarchy of sorts could be established by observing how the various animals fared when pitted against each other in the fight.

Animal fights

One possible way of effecting a confirmation of this world-view was to put on animal fights, which were also a much-loved source of entertainment. In securely enclosed areas, or in specially built arenas, animals were let loose upon each other, notably those endowed with particular strength (bears, lions, wisents), with particularly aggressive temperaments (wild boar, dogs), with particular skills (monkeys), or with exceptional defense mechanisms (porcupines), not forgetting the "victims" (cattle, horses, donkeys). Sitting in rows or boxes, the guests observed the course of events. For the great festivities in Dresden, an arena was specially built for this purpose at the *Jägerhof*, as we know from contemporary prints.[662] Some architectural features were well suited to being used as arenas, such as the courtyards at the palace, stables, and *Jägerhof*. Augustus the Strong's plans for a large and permanent arena for animal fights were not realized. At that time, Vienna boasted one such permanent arena known as the *Hetztheater*,[663] and in 1693 the architect Johann Arnold Nering built a "Hetzgarten" in Berlin.[664]

When necessary, the animals were aroused to greater aggression with firecrackers, or by dogs, or by the infliction of wounds. The contemporary commentator Julius Bernhard von Rohr had the following to say on the subject: "The animals are all let out at once to the pleasant sound of horns. At that point they will have just been made more aggressive by being beaten with red-hot irons, being pinched on the ear, by having little arrows fired at them which stick into their ears, and by having firecrackers thrown amongst them, etc. When they have only been captured recently and are still a little wild, this provides a very amusing way of passing the time. [...]."[665] When the dogs had chased themselves into a state of exhaustion, they were exchanged for others; after the fight, the wounded or "worthless" animals were killed, and the exotic ones taken back into captivity. The greater the importance of a festivity, the more precious were the animals brought in for the fight from the menageries and cages.

Animal fights were much loved at the Saxon court. The reports of these spectacles in the court journals and chronicles sometimes went into considerable detail. On February 8, 1740, for instance, in honor of the birthday of the Russian Tsarina Anna Ivanovna, a "Kampff-Jagen" was mounted at the Jägerhof from nine-o'-clock to one-o'-clock in the afternoon, in the presence of "fremden Ministers und viele Hohe Fremde" ("foreign ministers and many high-ranking dignitaries from abroad"), not to mention the royal family and court. Iccander described the event as follows: "In the arena were a lion and lioness, a panther and a leopard, a tiger, a lynx, three bears, a wolf, a wisent ["Auerochs"], two buffaloes, a cow with its calf, a female mule, a stallion, two wild horses, and twelve large wild boar. The lion and one of the two bears immediately laid into two pigs, and having done for them devoured half of their meat straight off the bone. The leopard went for the calf. With a thrust of its horns the wisent tore open the belly of the mule. One of the bears attacked the wolf, tossing it into the air a number of times, upon which the latter ran away and took refuge among the pigs. The king then shot the lynx, and the whole event came to a most pleasurable conclusion."[666]

However, the fight did not always run so smoothly. If expectations were not fulfilled, the reports made no bones about the ensuing disappointment; on occasion, the lion would fail to get the upper hand over all the other animals, or animals supposed to be enemies turned out to be quite happy to leave one another in peace: "After lunch, His Royal Highness the Prince Elector had two badgers baited in the palace gardens on the Taschenberg. As it had been claimed that there was a natural antipathy between tame pigs and badgers, and that they would immediately attack one another, six tame pigs were driven towards the two badgers, but there was no sign of hostility."[667]

When the fight ran according to expectations, two things will have impressed the spectators in particular. Firstly, while the behavior of the animals was driven by pure feeling, it still seemed to confirm a certain hierarchical ordering. Secondly, the spectators were reassured of how different they were from the animals: for they were able to control their feelings through the exercise of reason. Animal fights thus made it possible to see the animal world, or at least that little slice of it that was put on show on these occasions, as a kind of model of the human world, while at the same time showing the superiority of the latter over the former. And after all, whenever the king chose to do so, he could of course intervene with a well-aimed shot from his gun.

Hunting

The court related to animals in a different way when it came to the hunt. A perfectly mounted court hunt in the Baroque era was a big event that required long preparation and well-thought-out choreography. As a rule, the most important festivities ended with a hunt of this kind.

The electors of Saxony loved the hunt, both for its own sake and also as a means of self-glorification. Various kinds of hunting were practiced in the woods around Dresden in the first half of the eighteenth century.[668]

The most important hunting technique was the so-called "Deutsche Jagd" (or "eingestellte Jagd"), which was a drive, or battue. The game was driven by beaters into an enclosed area marked off with cloths or fences, and then let through an opening into a second enclosed area where they were exposed to the guns. The participants could then shoot the animals down from a pavilion. It is recorded that a total of 394 head of game were shot at an event of this kind during an electoral wedding in 1719.[669] This form of the hunt also allowed for women to participate. The game that had been shot was prepared for the table in the court kitchens. There were also water-hunts in which the animals had even less opportunity to defend themselves, as they were driven into the water where they were shot at from gondolas. Drives of these two kinds took place principally in Moritzburg and Hubertusburg.

The "Parforce-Jagd" was a form of coursing. A single animal, normally a royal stag, was chased by the hunters, in coaches or on horseback and accompanied by dogs, until it was exhausted and easy prey. These hunts also called for detailed preparatory organization, so that the participants could change their horses and dogs and take refreshments at appropriate moments. Special systems of lanes were cut through the woods (creating "hunting stars") to make it easier for the participants to follow the animal in the chase. This form of hunting called for a large number of trained personnel, and was correspondingly costly.

Hawking was also practiced in Saxony for hunting small game and wild birds. Ducks were also captured as well as being shot, and birds were also shot from hides.[670] In the pheasant reserves in the Great Garden there were pheasant-shoots, and the Saxon court even went in for a form of hunting barely worthy of the name known as "Prellen" ("tossing"). This involved small game (foxes, martens, beavers) being driven from their cages over an area on which long narrow nets were stretched out, with ladies and gentlemen holding these at either end. When an animal ran out it was tossed into the air by a powerful tug from the ends of the net: off went the guns, and the animal fell dead on the floor.

Augustus the Strong and Augustus III thus not only had a variety of animal collections, but also practiced a variety of forms of hunting. As has been pointed out, hunting was at once a form of amusement and also a way of procuring food. It also provided a welcome opportunity to show guests the abundant riches of the Saxon woods.

The hunt was also a means of creating and confirming distance between social groups. Hunting in Saxony was divided into high, middle, and low ("die Hohe Jagd, die Mittlere, die Niedere"), and there were regulations specifying who was entitled to shoot what. While the High Hunt, which by decree of Augustus the Strong included capercaillie, swan, bustard, crane, pheasant, and bittern, was exclusive to the ruler, the Middle Hunt could be bestowed on certain persons.[671] Granting or taking away the right to shoot certain animals was the prerogative of the prince and was thus a demonstration of his superiority. The same was true of the privilege of being allowed to hunt a certain animal from the royal herds with hounds, an honor which the prince bestowed on important guests as evidence of the favor in which he held them.

But hunting also gave the prince the opportunity to confirm his status through his personal prowess. When he demonstrated his accuracy in shooting at drives, his skill in riding to hounds, or quite simply his physical strength, he was not just showing that he was superior to the animals but also to his own noblemen. And he was always able to count on being able to do this, given that no courtier would have dared to outdo him as they were more inclined to when playing games. Johann Michael von Loen, who in his "Kleinen Schriften" not only gave his readers portraits of high-ranking personalities active at the court of Dresden around 1718, but also gave detailed descriptions of a variety of festivities, testifies to the elector's demonstration of his twofold superiority – over men and over animals – in a report on a two-day hunting party that took place in August of that year at Moritzburg. He describes the end of the drive as follows: "Three hundred stags and deer having been shot, those which remained were set free at the king's command, the net (enclosing the shooting area) being let down at the end of the shoot."[672] The animals were thus granted a reprieve, by grace of the king. The evening saw another form of hunting being practiced: "We then came to the greatest entertainment of the hunting day, with over a hundred wild boar being killed, in the course of which the King gave a quite admirable display of his world-famous skills, both with the iron grab and with the deer-catcher. Nobody except Graf Moritz von Sachsen was able to emulate him.[673] But as others were rash enough to follow suit, the spectators were given cause for hearty laughter when the boars turned these clumsy heroes head over heels in piles, or drove them around holding in vain to their iron grabs."[674]

The hunting practiced by the court has justifiably been described as a sublimated form of warfare, as has the jousting that was still practiced in the Baroque era. As the prince no longer had to demonstrate his right to his social position by leading his armies into battle or by engaging in feuds and warmongering, he needed other ways and means of proving the authenticity of his status. In the conspicuous outlay of personnel, time, and expense, and in the clear evidence of the prince's abilities, any potential opponents were given ample proof of the caliber of the man they were thinking of opposing. In the hunt, the prince could make a twofold impression upon those present, on the one hand presenting them with a spectacle that was extravagant and theatrical in the extreme, and on the other hand showing his own personal prowess, just as Augustus the Strong clearly did by fighting at close quarters with the wild boar.

The Saxon court in the first half of the eighteenth century thus went about its dealings with living animals in a number of different ways: some animals were kept and looked after in menageries, some were bred and raised, or driven together from the hunting ground, to be killed, and others were let loose upon each other. However, the common feature in all these kinds of animal-keeping was that the animals were drawn into an overall scenario that made it clear where power lay, and were allotted roles to play in a newly-ordered world-picture. The royal stag, for instance, was looked after with the greatest care up until it was chosen to be the huntsmen's "opponent," for whose benefit it was to symbolize the urge for freedom in full but hopeless flight. The same applied to the animals that were not shot in a drive: graciously let loose into the woods at the end of the day, their reprieve only lasted until the next shoot, when they would be called upon to play the victim once again. And it was particularly true in animal fights, where the animals were selected for their entertainment value and to play their allotted roles as victor or as vanquished.

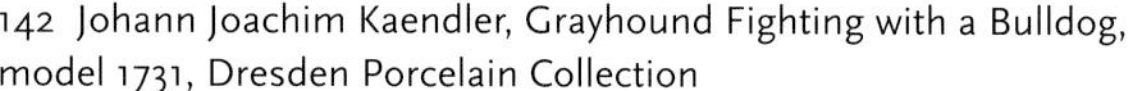

142 Johann Joachim Kaendler, Grayhound Fighting with a Bulldog, model 1731, Dresden Porcelain Collection

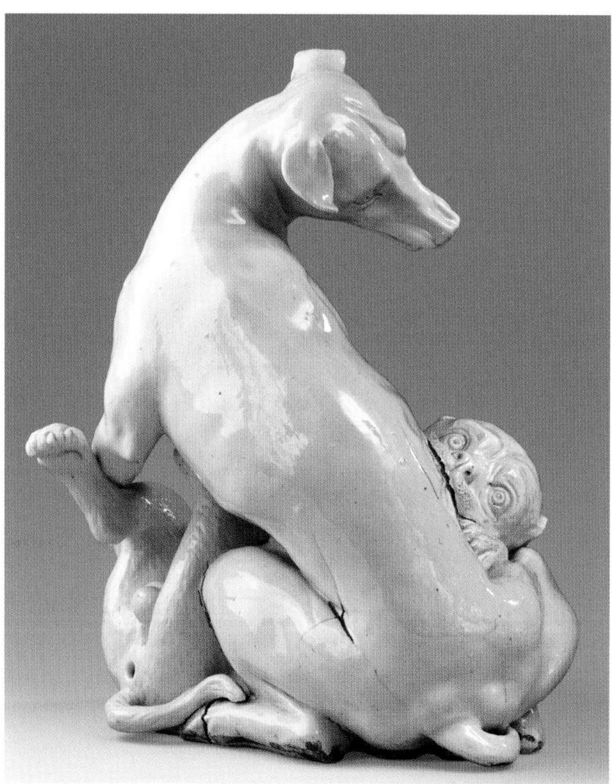

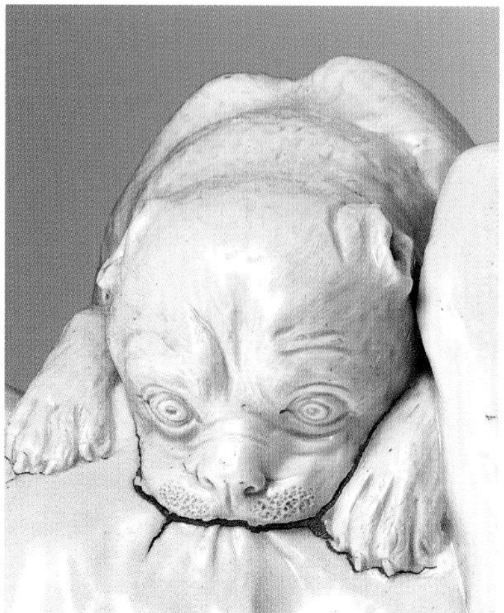

143 The bulldog, a detail from the fighting dogs, Dresden Porcelain Collection

We shall now proceed to investigate the extent to which these tendencies are reflected in the animal figures made in porcelain for the Japanese Palace.

The animals in the gallery

The composition of the porcelain menagerie

Given the genesis of the Meissen large animal figures, it is hardly surprising that the commission as a whole was structured in the same way as a contemporary menagerie. As we have seen, many of the exotic animal figures were modeled from live animals or taxidermal specimens, in or from the Moritzburg menagerie or the Löwenhaus in Dresden. The composer of the lists certainly took his cues from these animal collections. As is shown by the example of Versailles, for which we still have detailed inventory lists, Baroque menageries were not exclusively composed of exotic creatures, but also had local animals, albeit in smaller numbers, both farmed and wild.[675]

In the order lists we find all the most important quadrupeds and birds from the High, Middle, and Low Hunt, and also domestic animals, exotic animals, and creatures of fable. The stock thus gives a more or less representative picture of the whole known animal world, with the one limitation that it only covers mammals and birds. If one examines how they are represented, it is possible to establish certain types based on activities and behavior.

This begs the question as to the extent to which the modelers proceeded along intentional lines, that is to say, whether they had some kind of overall concept in mind when creating the individual models, and if not, then how it was that the type groups grew up. With one exception the animal figures were ordered simply by

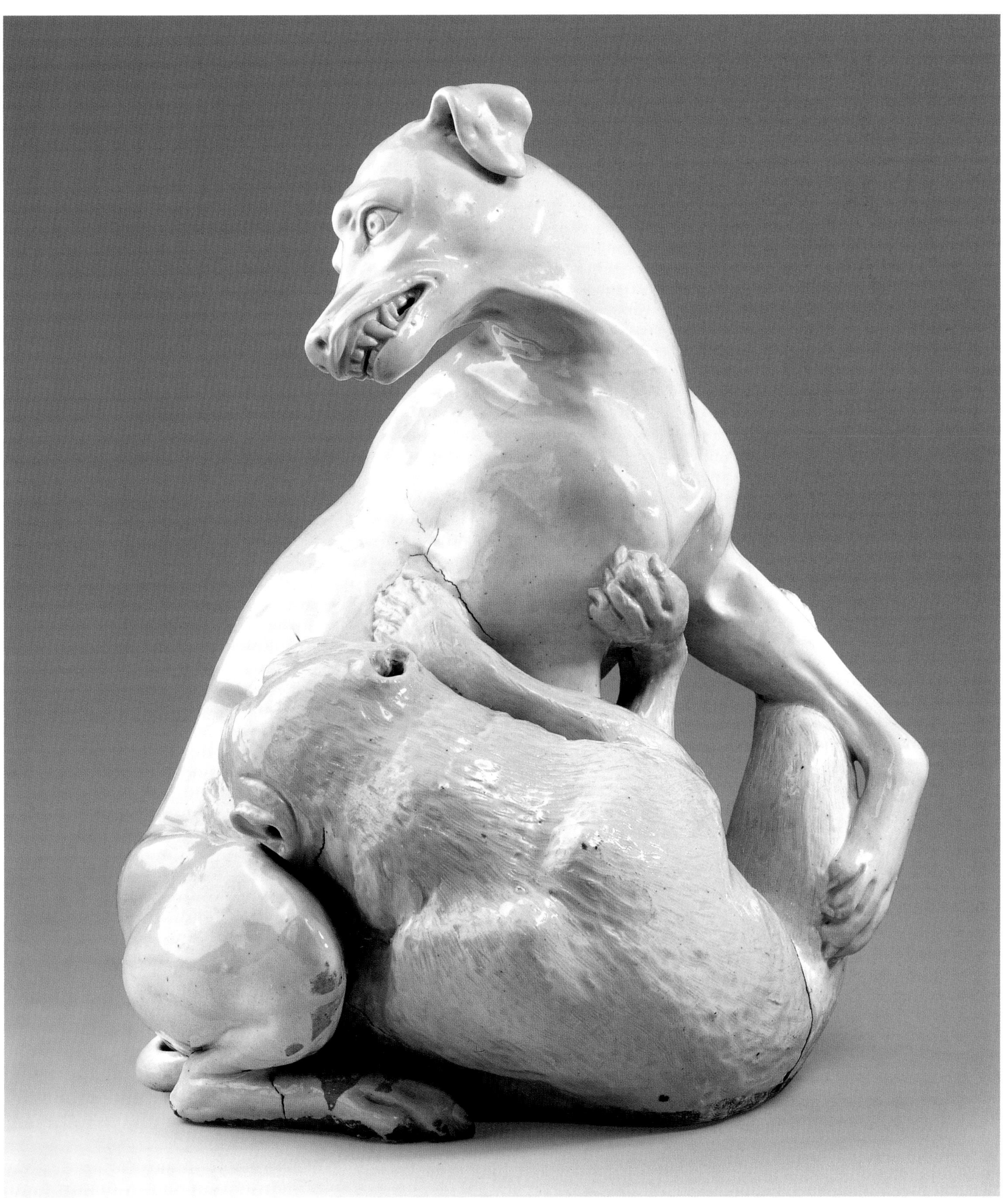

144 Johann Joachim Kaendler, Grayhound Fighting with a Bulldog, model 1731, Dresden Porcelain Collection

name, without any specification being made as to their posture or attributes.

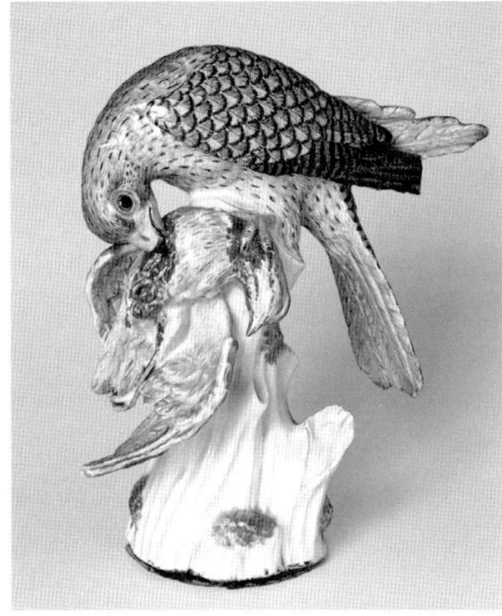

146 Johann Joachim Kaendler, Sparrowhawk devouring a lark, model 1734, Neues Palais, Potsdam

Creation according to types

When the figures were commissioned, it was specified that the animals should be done in their natural size, posture and color. This specification could best be fulfilled through the execution of a kind of "type portrait." That meant that in addition to being a good external likeness, the model had to express something of the "character" generally associated with the animal in question. The modeler thus had to find the posture most typical of the animal, with its most important nuances, and possibly also come up with characteristic attributes. This was made easier by the fact that adding an object is not the only way of incorporating an attribute: characteristic actions or activities can also be considered as attributes. In an animal gallery it was not necessary that the visitor should be able to distinguish fox A from fox B, but rather that the Fox should be markedly different from the Bear, not only in its external appearance, but also in its character traits. At a later stage we shall pay more detailed attention to the different ways in which the Meissen modelers responded to this challenge.

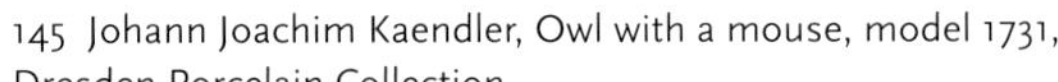

145 Johann Joachim Kaendler, Owl with a mouse, model 1731, Dresden Porcelain Collection

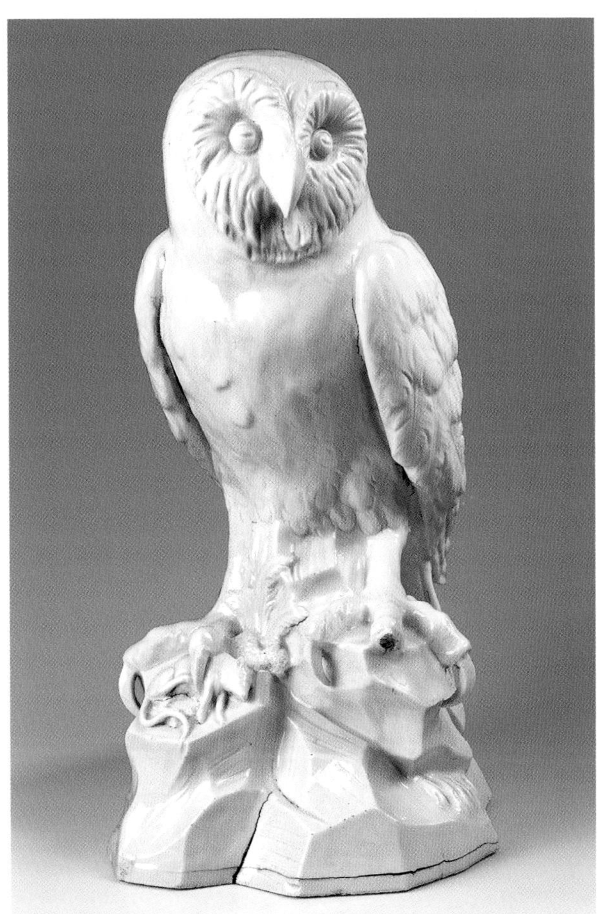

A number of the animal figures created for the Japanese Palace illustrate this process of characterization by creation according to types – or "typification" – particularly well. The following examples are intended to demonstrate that certain principal relationships that man has with the animals – "fighting," "hunting," "protecting," and "caring" – also find expression in this corpus of porcelain figures. These actions and activities derive from instincts or drives common both to mankind and to the animals.

Kaendler's earliest models include two of animals fighting. The one shows a wisent and a boar locked in combat (fig. 116), and the other a greyhound and a bulldog likewise fighting tooth and nail (fig. 144). It was quite possible that a boar and a wisent may have been pitted against each other in an animal fight mounted at the court. And as we have seen, Kaendler studied the wisents at Moritzburg in his very first summer as a modeler at the Meissen manufactory. We do not know whether he was ever actually witness to an animal fight, but this clearly seemed to him to be such an appropriate way of depicting the wisent that he was even prepared to take measures to overcome the disproportionate difference in their sizes. Kaendler could just as well have fulfilled the order for a wisent by modeling it on its own. However, it was not simply for reasons of statics (the interlocking animals stabilize the figure as a whole) that he chose to portray it fighting. By making the wisent proportionately smaller, he makes the boar seem more threatening, and a more credible challenge to its larger opponent. The fight is thus made more dramatic, as it is not possible to distinguish a clear winner or an obvious loser. Both animals are presented as totally immersed in the struggle for survival. Exactly the same is true of the two dogs, in which aggression and determina-

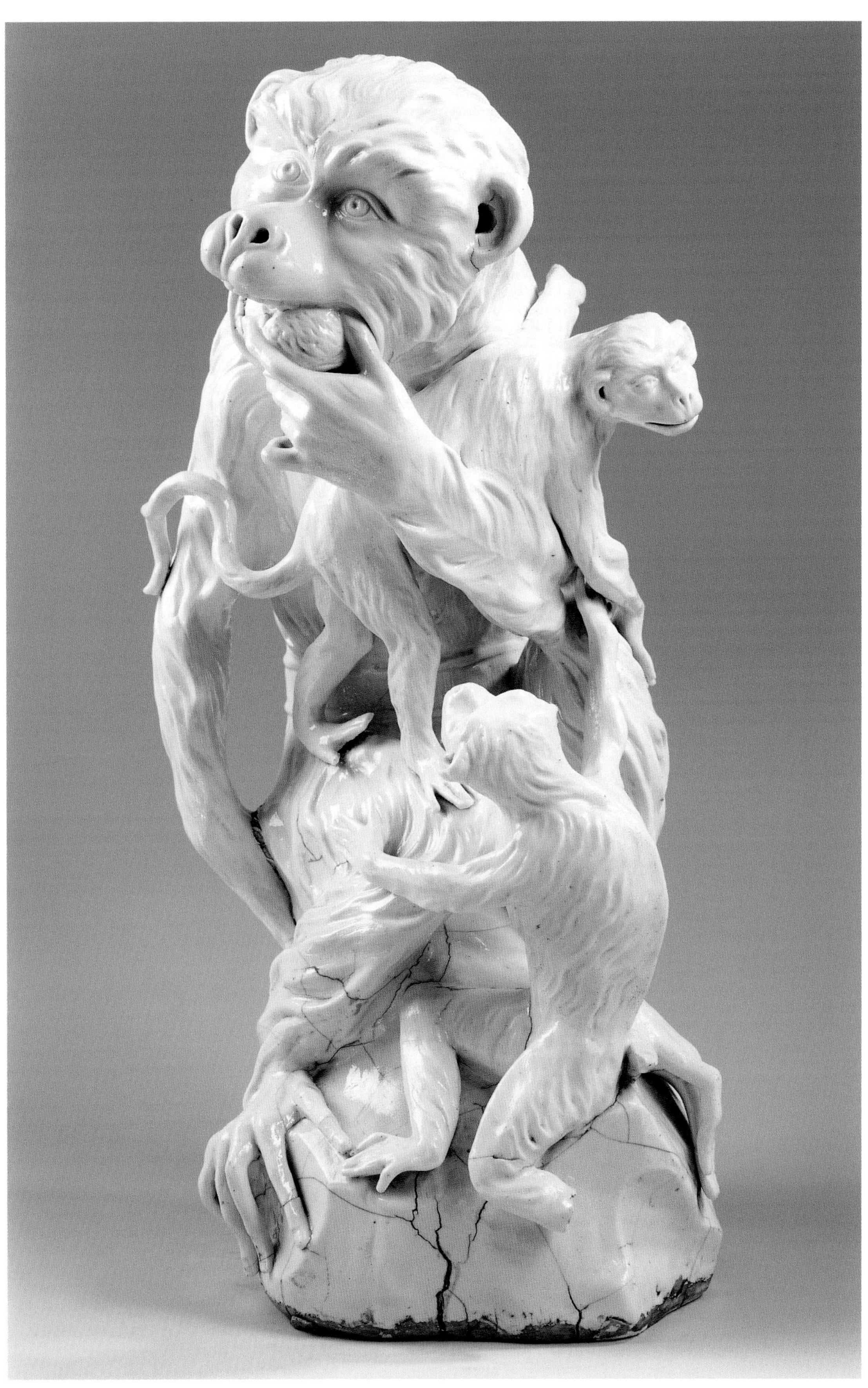

147 Johann Gottlieb Kirchner, Mother-Monkey, model most likely 1731, Dresden Porcelain Collection

tion to win the fight to the death are powerfully expressed by such features as painful physical dislocations and bared teeth (fig. 144).

Both in nature and in the animal gallery, the case of two equally matched animals fighting is quite a different matter from the unequal struggle that takes place when one animal hunts another. Many of the figures show animals with prey they have hunted down, and in these cases the roles of victor and victim were predetermined. The exact points at which the prey is shown being snapped up are chosen in such a way as to bring out particular characteristics in the predator: the long, elegantly curved neck of the heron is shown off to best effect when it is catching the little carp at its feet (fig. 188), and the large bill of the pelican is at its most impressive when it is pointing directly upwards on the point of swallowing a plump little fish (fig. 185). The look in the fox's eye is so lifelike because when we look at the figure it is as if we have just caught him red-handed with his stolen chicken (fig. 166). The statuesque and magisterial posture of the owl standing over the mouse he has caught (fig. 145) is in stark contrast to the osprey shown pecking voraciously at a fish with the sharp beak typical of birds of prey (fig. 97).

Certain animals were modeled twice, one of the two versions showing the animal involved in an activity typical of its species. The figure of a crouching osprey devouring a fish (fig. 114) is a better depiction of an osprey than the one in which the bird is simply seen standing on a tree-stump (fig. 115). However, Kaendler modeled both figures in the same year. In a first work report recording his earliest pieces of work he writes: "N[o.] 2, a 'Fischahr' or 'Fischfreßer' one ell high which His Majesty has already received," and "N[o.] 4, another osprey tearing a carp apart, an impeccable piece of work,"[676] (Source 24). This makes it clear that Kaendler's first figure, with the bird sitting on its perch, was executed in the manner of a zoological depiction: we recognize it as an osprey because of its size and proportions, the shape of its head, and so on. In the second figure, however, he broadens his perspective on the osprey and tells us more about the bird, presenting it with its prey, and not on a tree but on a rock. This additional information about the bird's habits and natural environment makes us all the better equipped to distinguish it other birds of prey, such as the sparrowhawk shown plunging its beak into a dead lark (fig. 146).

148 Johann Joachim Kaendler, Hen, model 1732, Dresden Porcelain Collection

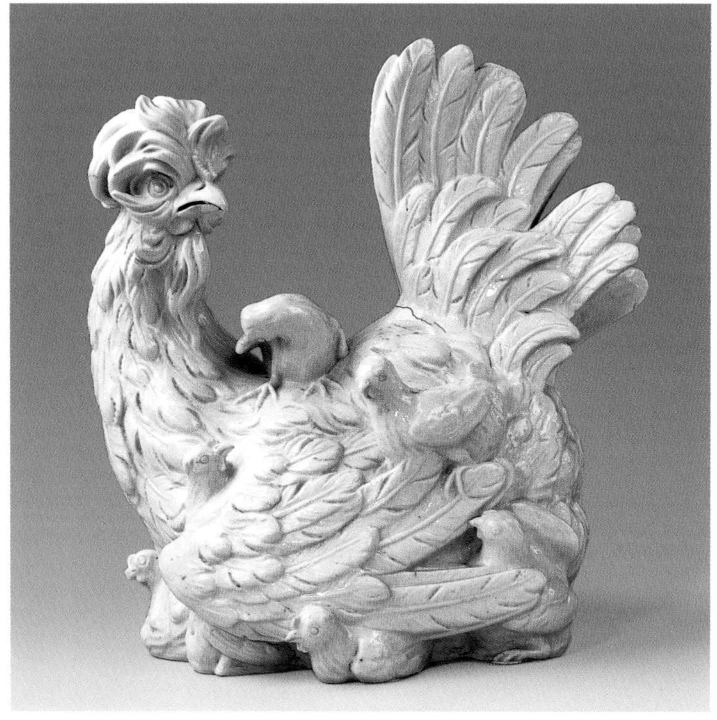

Another type into which a number of figures fall is provided by the theme of protecting and caring. As in the case of animals fighting and animals clutching their prey, the relationship depicted is one between two individual animals, focusing exclusively on mothers tending their young. When two different species are presented together they are often fighting, whereas two members of the same species are most often shown united by bonds of affection.

Eloquent examples of this are the nanny goat, represented licking and giving suck to her kid (fig. 195), and the hen (fig. 148) and the hen-pheasant, both rendered giving motherly protection and warmth to their chicks. Another form of the "mother-child" relationship is shown by the she-wolf (fig. 69). While it is no surprise to see a farmed animal such as the she-goat giving milk, one expects a wolf to show a certain measure of aggression; accordingly, the she-wolf protects her young as wolves do, growling and baring her teeth.

In the fourth "mother-type" among the animal figures, we see a telling portrayal of the most fundamental character trait of the animal in question. The mother-monkey (fig. 147) with her young – according to the version, one or two in number – does not seem to be the slightest concerned about her babes, but simply lets them scramble around over her. The one at her feet is looking up and stretching out a hand towards her, but she is too self-absorbed to respond to him: in short, she is typical of her species. This point was also made by one of the fables chosen as the subject of a fountain in the Versailles labyrinth, the fable of the mother-monkey that suffocates her young one "out of love." In his German-language edition of the prints Krauss appended the following four-liner to this fountain: "Durch all die grosse Lieb, der Aff scheint weggerücket/Das junge an der Brust, wird gar von ihm versticket/Wer preiset allzuviel sein eigen Werck und That/Hat sattsam unterdrückt sein guten Nahm und Staat."[677] ["Distraction has o'ercome the loving monkey-mother/The darling on her paps she's now contrived to smother;/She who was so foolish her good works to over-rate,/Has now wrought needless damage on her good name and state."]

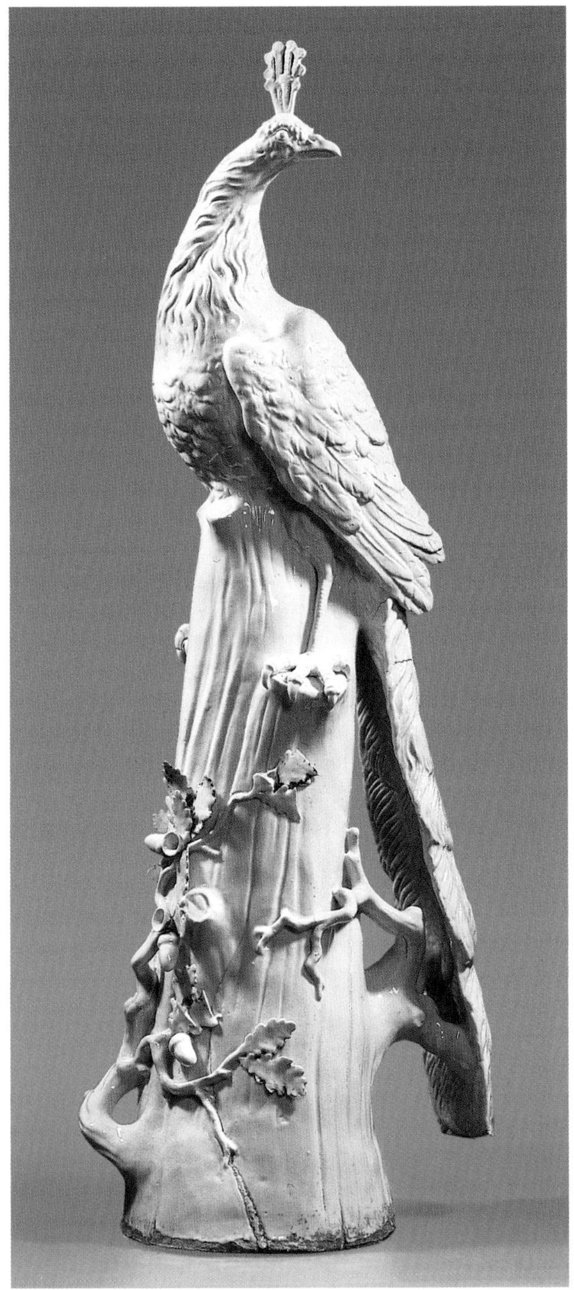

149 Johann Joachim Kaendler, Peacock sitting on a tree-stump, model 1734, Dresden Porcelain Collection

In addition to animals that are fighting, devouring their prey, or protecting their young, we also find animals engaged in an activity directed solely at themselves. But even within this category there are distinctions to be noted, such as the difference between the cat and the bear: while the cat raises its paw to lick it with its tongue (fig. 113), the bear holds its paw on the ground and bends over to lick it (fig. 202). Similar distinctions are to be found, without going into any greater detail at this point, among the birds depicted preening themselves (heron, bustard, swan) and in the dog scratching itself (fig. 170).

In all these cases the modelers chose characteristic activities to bring out the particular character of the respective animals, but there are also figures in which the animal is "characterized" by other means. In March 1734 Kaendler created the model of a peacock displaying its fan, and only a month later did another peacock, this time sitting on a tree-stump (figs. 149 and 150). In combination, the two figures give a vivid impression, comprehensible even to the beholder who has never seen a peacock before, of the unique ability of the peacock to spread out its train in a fan, and thus also give the peacock a special place of its own in the animal world presented by the porcelain menagerie.

Finally, even Kaendler's crane has pointers to character traits, which can be understood with just a little background knowledge. This long-legged bird differs from those in the heron or bustard figures not only in its external appearance but also in that it holds a stone in its right claw. "8 cranes with a stone" was what was called for in the order-list of December 17, 1732,[678] (Source 10), and when Kaendler finally modeled the figure in April 1735, he fulfilled the requirement exactly (fig. 151). As the son of a pastor, Kaendler was familiar with the (Christian) idea that the crane sym-

150 Johann Joachim Kaendler, Peacock Displaying, model 1734, Dresden Porcelain Collection

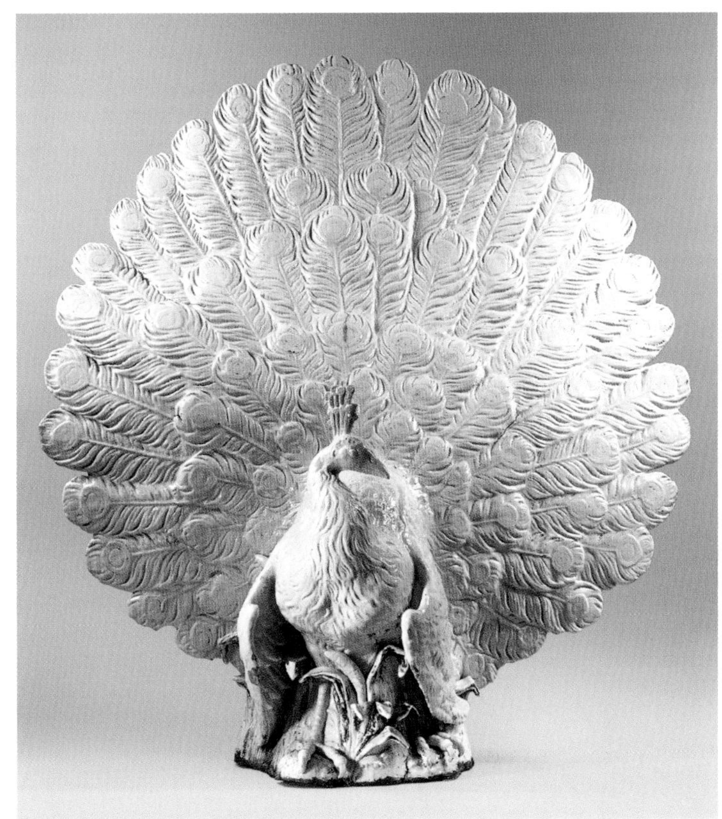

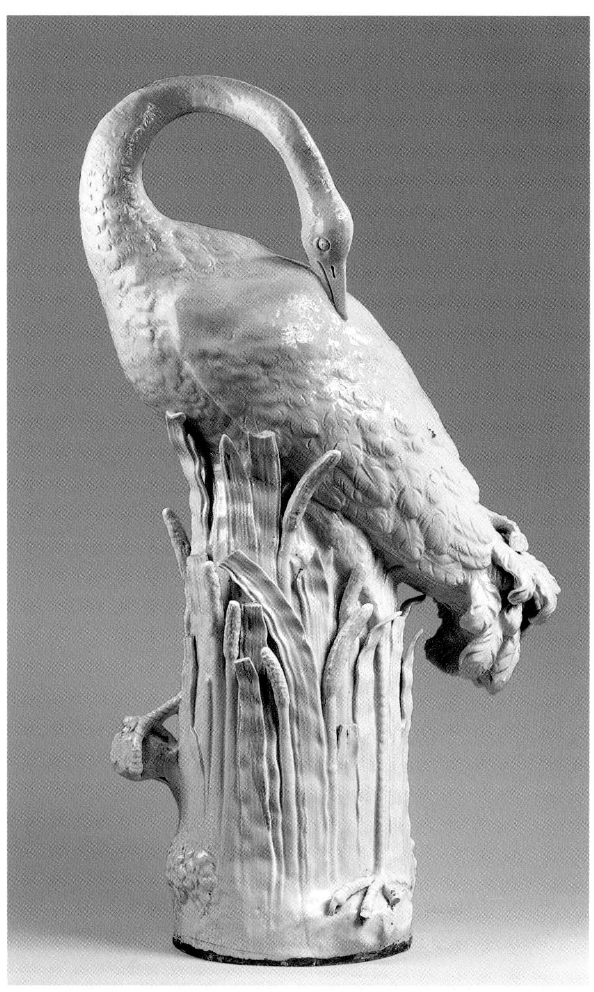

151 Johann Joachim Kaendler, Crane, model 1735, Dresden Porcelain Collection

bolized vigilance: it held a stone so that when it went to sleep it would drop it and immediately wake up again. The association between the crane and the stone goes back to Pliny the Elder's *Natural History*, which not only mentions the motif of vigilance but also provides another explanation for the stone, namely that before taking off to fly over the Black Sea, cranes would pick up a stone as ballast, then dropping the stone over the sea when they got tired, either to lose weight, or to use their allegedly sensitive ear to test whether they were still over the sea or had already reached land. Aristotle contested this interpretation, but stated that the crane's stone could be used as a testing stone in the production of gold. In his *Universallexikon*, Johann Heinrich Zedler attributed another significance to the stone: he stated that the crane was "above all a symbol of vigilance," in that it stood on one leg in order not to fall asleep, but also continued: "They lay no more than two eggs, between which they are wont to place, in the nest, a stone."[679] The extent to which the crane was regarded as a symbol of vigilance is also documented by an amusing picture which was to be seen in the window of the apartment of Friedrich Gottfried Gerber on the Alter Markt on the occasion of the illumination of Dresden on August 9, 1733: "Ein Kranich, mit der Beyschrifft: Vigilat, oder: Des Königs Gnad und Recht, der Schutz gerechter Waffen, Wacht stets vors gantze Land, daß es kann sicher schlaffen."[680] ["A crane, with the inscription: Vigilat, or: By royal grace and right, protector of weapons blest/Keeps watch o'er all our land, that we may sleep at rest."] Kaendler made implicit reference to this attribute of the crane's by depicting it with its beak already in its plumage, on the point of going to sleep.

The various kinds of characterizations combine to constitute an interpretation of the sector of the animal world represented in the corpus of figures. It is divided up into (1) the hunters and the hunted, (2) the protectors and the ones they protect, (3) animals shown eating, and finally (4) animals with particular abilities. Some figures cannot be accommodated in this type-scheme, and are distinguished simply by their external features rather than by any "intrinsic" character derived from the behavior characteristic of their species. In other words, the animals are in part presented in their traditional roles (the thieving fox, the vigilant crane, the cleanly cat), and in part as representatives of a type (predatory animals, protecting and caring animals, fighting animals, and so on). Others are not portrayed in such depth but are simply presented as they meet the eye, although there are cases where even inactivity can also be a kind of characterization: "The lion is known – on account of his nobly joyful temperament, his courage and strength,

152 Johann Friedrich Eberlein, Chamois, model 1735, Dresden Porcelain Collection

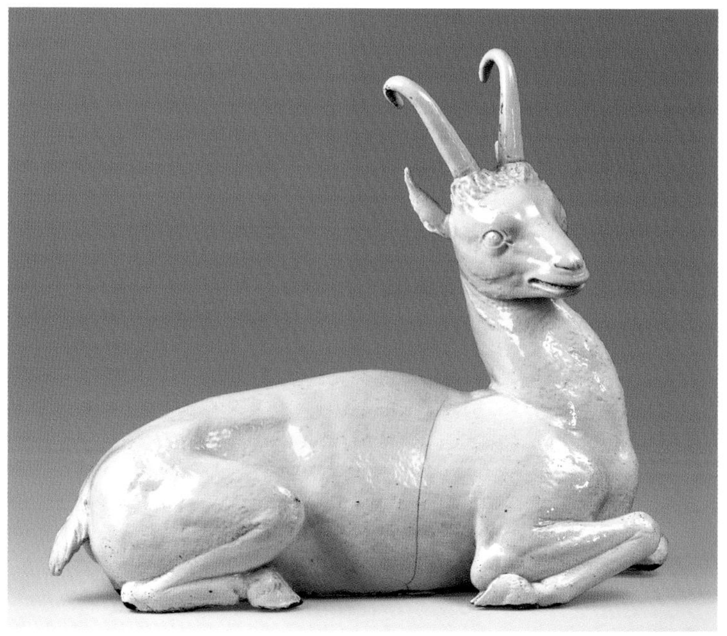

his magnanimity and fearlessness – as the king of the all the wild animals."[681] As king of the animals, the lion was thus not primarily intended to have the expression of a terrifying beast of prey, but precisely that of the strong, courageous and unapproachable prince. More detailed consideration will be given to Kirchner's Lion at a later stage, and likewise to the lion as a topos.

Of all the animals modeled for the Japanese Palace, only a few – the sheep, the chamois, and the king vulture, to mention three – are represented in a state of inactivity. In these instances, the visitor to the gallery is invited to be a beholder (of a static figure) rather than – as in the majority of cases – an observer (of something going on).

All three modelers produced figures that contain neither a behavioral element nor any indication as to the animal's status in the natural world, as one can see by looking at Kirchner's Lioness (fig. 160), Kaendler's King Vulture (fig. 82), and Eberlein's Chamois (fig. 52). This in itself gives the lie to the idea that there was from the very beginning a unified concept for the presentation of the animals in the gallery, drawn up with the express intention of creating such a rich variety of characterizations. On the contrary, the artists had to find their own solution for each and every one of the models, which were created in a random sequence over a period of six years. In some cases the solutions were determined by behavioral clichés attributed over time to the animals by man through experience or deriving from a literary tradition (for example, the fox as the stealer of chickens), and in some cases by the observation of living specimens (for example, the vulture with the cockatoo).

An analysis of the figures conducted in accordance with their physical similarity to living specimens would yield scientific results and would not take account of the artistic dimension. A survey of the "emotions" suggested by their postures and expressions would on the other hand certainly lead to a fallacious anthropomorphism, although a few figures are actually anthropomorphic in character, a fact we shall look into in greater depth at a later stage. However, the modelers' great achievement was to tread the narrow path between purely objective ("zoological") depiction and subjective ("artistic") interpretation of the animals as living beings with particular behavioral tendencies (hunters, protectors, food-providers, fighters, and so forth): as a result, our attention is drawn to parallels with the human world where the same patterns of behavior are also present.

The animal world and the world of men

Our account of the relation between the individual figures and the animal gallery as a whole has hitherto been made from the perspective of the creative artists. Behind the artists, however, stood the king, who was the prime mover in the drawing up of the order lists, deciding – or having someone decide – which species were to be modeled. As has already been pointed out, the composition of the other royal animal collections had a great influence on these decisions. Nevertheless, we are still left with the question as to the deeper purpose of the project. Was the animal gallery to become a kind of porcelain art-menagerie that, while it could not hope to be quite so correct as the taxidermal exhibits in the *Animaliengalerie*, would nevertheless in the final analysis be more impressive? Or was it supposed to have an encyclopedic character, which would symbolically raise its owner to the position of lord over the whole animal kingdom?

The very fact that the animal figures were commissioned specifically for the Japanese Palace suggests that the porcelain menagerie's raison d'être bore some relation to the concept behind the building that was to be their home. When the idea for an animal gallery was born in the summer of 1730, the planning for the palace was already very far advanced. So it was not a matter of ordering a number of animal figures that were to be displayed at some as yet unspecified location: on the contrary, the animal figures were destined for this particular location and nowhere else, and because they were for the Japanese Palace, they could not possibly be in any other material than porcelain.

As was shown in the last chapter, the Japanese Palace had a very specific role to play in Augustus the Strong's overall concept for his buildings and collections: it was to present the Saxon economy and Saxon culture, brought together in the form of art. Everything that was going to be on show on its two floors was intended to epitomize man's highest achievements in the technical, economic, and aesthetic fields.

The animal gallery incorporated a particular emphasis on the artistic dimension, as is shown by the fact that the very first order lists for the animal figures also include large vases. The sources show that the vases ordered were the monumental grotesque vases modeled by Kirchner, shortly after his return to the manufactory, from copperplate engravings in Claudine Bouzonnet's "livres de vases" published with illustrations by her uncle Jacques Stella in 1667; the vases were subsequently lacquered in red and gold by Reinow (figs. 23 and 24). As has been shown, the plan had been to integrate these vases into the allegorical reliefs on the outer facade of the gallery. Given the combination of vases and animals, one might be forgiven for thinking that they had something to do with a garden, were it not for the fact that the vases were quite bizarre and had forms entirely untypical of elements used in garden decoration at the time. They are different from other contemporary vase designs in that they are neither vehicles for reliefs, whether informative or decorative in character, nor purely graphic fantasies: the body of the vase is done like a human body, which makes the vase anthropomorphic in character and turns it into a kind of figure. This aspect of these very old-fashioned-looking vases must have been the reason why Stella's illustrations were used as models. In this connection, it should be noted that in the Baroque the vase was regarded as the symbol *par excellence* of the art of antiquity, and also that as the most artificial and unnatural object of all, the vase clearly symbolized human creativity. Stella's transformation of the vase into an intermediate thing between a vessel and a figure emphasizes the association with human creativity. The counterpart to human creativity, however, is divine creativity, which was understood as having culminated in mankind and in mankind's nearest relatives, the animals. The combination – in porcelain, one of the most precious materials of all – of animal figures as metaphors for the divine creation (of nature) and vases as metaphors of man's creativity (in art) formed a "cosmos of creativity." This constituted the perfect introduction to a tour around the rooms displaying Meissen porcelain, which far from being simply so much decoration and extravagance was, in the specific context of the Japanese Palace, a powerful indicator of Saxony's (creative) power.

It was at the same time impressed upon the visitor to the gallery that the ruling prince was not only lord over the arts but also over the (higher) animals, subjecting them to the demands of his overall plan. Another factor that should be taken into consideration in this connection is that the Baroque mind was just as familiar with animals being used to symbolize human matters as it was with the idea of the animals representing the natural world. Animals were used to represent a whole range of phenomena from the (princely) virtues to the continents of the world.

Quite apart from this kind of ambiguity, which is only pointed out to show how accustomed the Baroque mind was to perceiving things in two ways at once, the porcelain animals of the Japanese Palace also naturally enough included species weak and strong, savage and tame, local and exotic, with all being associated with the instinct-driven activities enumerated above. Some of these animals were shown fighting each other ("dueling," one might even say), some preying on others, some feeding or protecting their progeny, and others taking special care over their appearance, showing themselves off for all they were worth and even controlling their feelings. In short, they were all engaged in activities that were not only characteristic of the animal world, but were – as they still are – of fundamental importance in the human world, at court as elsewhere.

The animals were furthermore all shown as types rather than as individuals, and represented particular standings in the hierarchy of the animal world. The members of the court invited to spend time in this gallery were not only accustomed to suppressing their animal natures and controlling their feelings, but were also conditioned by a way of thinking that accorded greater value to social origins than to personality: while due recognition was accorded to particular achievements, real respect was reserved for hierarchical status. This paradoxical combination of a code of behavior that was in its preoccupation with self-control quite unlike that of the animals and a social structure that was in some respects so de-individualized as to be somewhat similar to the animal world made for a multitude of interesting associations. Parallels between man and the animals in literary or emblematic form were a veritable *idée fixe* ("Be as clever as the fox and not foolish or vain like the raven"), but the more cultivated one was, the more one was to distance oneself from the animals, being educated in good manners and being taught to control one's feelings, and so on. A multitude of instances show men and women of court society using study of the animal world and all that it stood for as a means to understand themselves better; comparing themselves with the animals and marking parallels between humans and animals was a ubiquitous and constant practice, even in the visual arts.[682]

Why the precious world of court society was to be confronted with a precious cross-section of the animal world can perhaps be better understood if one considers the problems that Augustus the Strong met when trying to enforce absolutist rule. He never succeeded in establishing the kind of absolutist system of rule that prevailed in France.[683] The Saxon and Polish nobilities were not to be reconciled, unwilling to let themselves be forged into one entity. Even in Saxony, the estates succeeded again and again in asserting their claims. In the electorate, Augustus the Strong had no Church to underpin his power, as he had converted to the Catholic faith for the sake of the Polish crown. It was thus vitally important for him to permeate the area in Dresden in which the court moved with symbols of his claims to absolute power, and use this omnipresent sign-system, just as other Baroque princes did, to make his authority appear self-evident and unchallengeable.

In this light it becomes easier to grasp the deeper significance of the animal collection in the Japanese Palace, which was not intended to be seen in the context of natural history, but rather in that of human culture. As well as being seen as a work of art, as a technical achievement, as one further animal collection among many, and so on, the porcelain menagerie was also to be seen as an image of the natural subjection of the court hierarchy to the power of the king. The Orpheus motif was used in connection with Augustus the Strong to evoke similar connotations and it is quoted here as evidence for the animal gallery's inherent ambiguity. It is another demonstration of the king's claim to absolute power, which is made explicitly with regard to the animals as representatives of the natural order, but is also to be understood as applying to human society ordered in its various estates by God himself. In his report of a hunt at Moritzburg in 1718, Johann Michael von Loen describes the following interlude: "A French singer who was leading the procession then welcomed the whole royal court with a song in his own language, adding in praise of the king that it was no wonder that, under such a goodly monarch, even the wildest of beasts changed their natures and lay at his feet as tame as pets."[684]

In order to shed further light on this first step towards an interpretation of the animal gallery, a step that was based on the general relationship of man (at court) to the animal world, we must now consider the organization of human life at the court, and then see how that organization relates to the Japanese Palace and its porcelain animals.

The Palace and the Animals: Content and effect

The Japanese Palace: a claim to power in bricks and stone

Court ceremonial and social structuring

In the second half of the seventeenth and early eighteenth centuries, the German-speaking lands of Europe saw printed, in quick succession, a number of tracts and books that investigated the ways in which members of court society related to one another and to the outside world beyond the confines of the court; these writings identified certain rules and put them down in print.[685] A whole branch of historical research is now devoted to these scholarly works on ceremonial, and they have become the object of particular interest in our own day.[686] This new research is founded on the pioneering investigations conducted by Weber and Elias, whose general studies of the structures of court life in the Baroque have opened up a research field that has till now been accorded little attention but is now attracting the interest not only of historians but also of sociologists.[687]

The period between 1680 and 1730 saw renewed discussion of the concept of learning – "Gelehrsamkeit" – in the lands of the Holy Roman Empire.[688] The reason offered for a general turning away from the "antiquarian ideal of the Humanists," with its focus on bookish learning,[689] was that the new theories should be founded on the observation of and reflection upon the real world, and not just be reinterpretations of historical currents in science and philosophy. This resulted in the development of the scholarly and scientific discipline known as etiquette, or ceremonial. This discipline analyzed certain areas of court life and laid down how things were to be done in those areas; it recorded existing traditions, and its own observations and theorizing exerted an influence on how the ceremonial structures developed in the course of time. This theorizing regulated the life of the various estates in such an all-permeating way that it was reflected in almost all every statement made by any member of the ruling class. As the intention of the following account of the function of ceremonial is to provide background information for consideration of the animal figures, it necessarily presents a highly complex body of knowledge in a somewhat simplified form.

While the Baroque court was on the one hand the place where political power was exercised, it was also the place *par excellence* where power was represented in symbols.[690] However, these two aspects cannot be separated from one another, as there was a kind of symbiosis between power experienced "physically" and power experienced "psychologically." The symbolic dimension of the former was merely shorter-lived than that of the latter, with its images of power carved in stone and wrought in iron. It was precisely at the points where these two spheres overlapped that ceremonial came into play, giving short-lived or repeated instances of the practical exercise of power forms that would endow them with visible permanence and validity. In other words, while ceremonial imposed regulations and demarcations upon dealings at court, it at the same time laid down the way in which these dealings were to be made visible, audible, tangible and so on. As a consequence, the central theme of literature on Baroque ceremonial was the making visible of the realm of divine grace.[691]

This led to the development of a whole system of signs and pointers, a repertoire of sensory experiences that communicated very direct and concrete facts and messages to the minds of the initiated. This coding took a variety of forms ranging from pure bodily posture, through behavior (gestures, "manners," and the like), to completely regulated procedures and complexes of procedures (celebrations, rites of passage, and so on). Each and every one of these elements had a meaning or a purpose behind it. Ceremonial made visual impressions and living beings into a coherent unity: intentions and consequences were first and foremost communicated symbolically (by such things as the color of a certain dress in a certain context, or a certain manner of greeting) rather than being realized in concrete form.

The ruler-subject relationship

As a result, ceremonial had a significant influence on the way members of the court saw themselves and the world around them. Its signs could have a negative or positive influence on one's social standing; they were clear indications of one's place in the established order. Courtiers could, by virtue of privileges granted them, effect a positive change to their symbols, improving, for example, their coat of arms when they were raised to a higher level of the nobility; the loss or withdrawal, on the other hand, of possible modes of self-affirmation led to a humiliating and visible personal devaluation.

The system assumed the existence of a strong hierarchy, which it also contributed to perpetuating. Rank and status were distributed and re-allocated through the dispensing or withholding of favors by those on the higher rungs of the social ladder. One of the most important functions of ceremonial was the regulation of the way members of the court conducted their dealings with one another. The existence of standard signs indicating status meant that – whatever else he or she might be besides – every individual that frequented the court was a "standardized" member of court society.

At the same time, the laying down of modes of behavior (etiquette) gave courtiers more scope for distancing and reserve. Control over one's feelings was proof of one's ability to hold the world at arm's length. An inconspicuous but integral part of this ability was a certain talent for symbolism: "natural" behavior (that is to say, unpredictable behavior: feelings, instincts, reflexes) was replaced by a network of codes and patterns which could communicate real meaning to those who were capable of deciphering and interpreting the signals being emitted.

If the individual was invested with a certain rank in the overall order of things, then it was ceremonial that maintained order among the ranks. As Julius Bernhard von Rohr put it: "If subjects are to recognize the King's Majesty, then they must first understand that he holds the highest power and authority, and order their actions in such a way as to reflect that power and authority. The common man, who cleaves to his outward senses, and makes little use of reason, cannot on his own conceive what the King's Majesty is, but through the things that he sees with his eyes, and which impinge upon his other senses, he comes to a clear understanding of His Majesty, and of his power and authority."[692]

In his important treatise on ceremonial, Rohr explained the importance of figurative symbolization in terms of the human capacity for appreciating an abstract concept. Accordingly, the means used by ceremonial for regulating relations *at* the court were different from those it used for regulating relations *to* the court. The world of the initiated courtier was a far more delicate one than the external world; the subtle nuances inherent in the way the court functioned were lost on those outside, who simply saw the court as an undifferentiated whole. For the courtier, the power of the prince was evident in such things as where he was placed at table; from the *placement* he could deduce where he stood in the king's favor. For the peasant, it was the outward magnificence of the court which spoke most eloquently of the power of the prince, which he then of course felt in real terms when it came to the forced labor of the corvée (doing duty at drives, for example). For the particular concerns of the present study, it is important to note that there were, as Rohr suggested, two fundamentally different kinds of sensibility towards the symbolic.

The nobleman moving in court circles had no option but to accept symbolic acts and a symbol-oriented way of thinking as a part of his environment, and indeed to assimilate it so that it was part of his very self. For the man beyond the bounds of the court, on the other hand, the representation of power was simply something with which he was confronted, and not something he felt part of. The world outside the court also made use of signs and symbols, in the detail of its traditional clothing ("Tracht"), for instance, or in non-verbal communication. But the central difference was that the signs were traditional and regional, while at court they were contrived and "international." The collective understanding of what was behind the signs, while being so essential for the survival of those signs, was something quite different from the knowing objectivity and distanced reserve that were typical of the court. The lower orders preserved their symbols in order to maintain a time-hallowed identity, while the court created symbols in order to forge new identity.

This means that if we are to investigate the animal gallery of the Japanese Palace with an eye to its being a symbolic presentation of human society, as was suggested we might in the previous chapter, we should not forget that whenever the nobility were confronted with new things, they were conditioned to scour them immediately for deeper levels of symbolic significance, to interpret them, and to work out where they themselves stood in relation to the new phenomenon. After all, essential aspects of the nobleman's social existence depended solely on his ability to recognize symbols and to put them to good use for his own ends.

At the apex of a society that was organized, maintained and directed by ceremonial stood the prince as the prime mover of significant acts and signs. One of his most important tasks was to maintain and refine ceremonial and all the visual symbols of his power and supremacy. His influence had to be omnipresent at court, no less in the menageries than in its parks, no less in architecture than in the political sphere. It was ceremonial that made it possible for him to achieve this. The means he used derived from the universal principle of "geometricization," the principle of *creating* order by *putting* things in order.[693] This geometrical principle was as much in evidence in park design and fortress construction as it was in music and ballet, or in art and architecture.[694]

Ceremonial as reflected in the architecture of the palace

The correlation of ceremonial and geometry is most clearly perceptible and best researched for architecture, particularly that of royal and princely residences.[695] Versailles is the prime example of a palace in which ceremonial is reflected in architecture, and it offers us much food for thought. The importance of its central room, Louis XIV's bedchamber, and the transparent significance of the equally central procedures that formed part of the bedchamber ceremonial, the "lever du Roi" and the "coucher du Roi," are now familiar enough not to need anything more than a passing mention here.

As Volker Bauer has rightly pointed out, however, the architecture and ceremonial of the French model were by no means so exactly copied by the princes of the Holy Roman Empire as one might assume from, for instance, a reading of the book by Norbert Elias.[696] The example of Dresden alone shows that even Augustus the Strong, who was one of the richest and most splendor-loving of all German princes, never intended to create a "Saxon Versailles" in the sense of a copy. However, as has already been noted in the chapter on Augustus the Strong's overall plan, his absolutist aspirations were reflected in his architecture, but within the limitations of local circumstances; more detailed attention will be paid to this matter below.

Court society – divided as it was into a range of variously privileged groups, all of which had the right to give outward and visible expression to their respective positions – had to be accommodated in the residence in such a way as to reflect clearly the relations of its members to their superiors and to the prince himself. The forms taken by these palaces, or at least by their staterooms, were to an extent determined by the demands court society made on them, but they can – conversely – also be seen as mirroring the prevailing social order.[697]

The further forward a member of the court was allowed to advance in the sequence of antechambers, the higher was his or her social status. "The furniture and tapestries differ from room to room. Those in the first antechamber are not so fine or costly as in the last one."[698] This gradation from antechamber to antechamber was also evident in the way the rooms were furnished and the comfort of their furnishings, in the degree of warmth (heating), in the choiceness of the materials used, and in the character of the iconographical programs, all of which became more magnificent the closer they were to the prince. The organization and ordering imposed on society by palace architecture led Peter Baumgart to conclude that the Baroque palace "was not simply a reflection of court culture, aesthetics, and art, but rather an architectural realization of the prince's intent to rule, and a demonstration of his political will."[699]

In Dresden, however, building a whole newly-conceived residence was not a possibility. Although the staterooms of the old one had been redesigned after the fire of 1701 and rebuilt in accord with current needs, the mere fact that the palace was not part of a coherent complex of architectural gardens and buildings standing in front of the city gates meant that it could not stand comparison with the many new residences that had arisen in the German principalities at the end of the seventeenth and beginning of the eighteenth centuries. The palace in the Great Garden was relatively small, and for all its extraordinarily innovative character the Zwinger was likewise no more than a very compressed Baroque complex in the immediate vicinity of the Residence.

The fact that the Elector of Saxony and King in Poland had to find his own solutions to his own problems in Dresden, the capital and the seat of his court, is in my opinion a particularly cogent reason for looking at the costly reconstruction of the Japanese Palace in precisely this light.

The Japanese Palace as a model residence

The tour

"Rulers such as Louis XIV were always to be approached in person. One would present one's concerns and requests, and once his busy and attentive entourage had given him the arguments for and against, he would make his decision. The energies he needed were in a certain sense piped in to him; he was somewhat passive and used them as he saw fit. He did not need to have – nor did he in fact have – any great ideas of his own; he was well supplied with the ideas of others, and he knew how to put them to good use."[700] What Norbert Elias writes about the Sun King was also to an extent true of the many German princes of the Baroque who simply put their trust in the expertise and taste of their architects, court artists, and decorators. In the case of Augustus the Strong, however, numerous notes and sketches testify not only to the personal influence that he exerted on new projects but also to instances where the original idea was actually his own. Given his bold attempt, soon after his unexpected accession to the electorate of Saxony, to effect a union with the kingdom of Poland, it was a more urgent matter for him to undertake innovative projects than it was for many of his peers. Above all in his building projects he was often the one who had the original core idea, which was then developed further by a staff of architects, artists, and others. And that he reserved the right to make final decisions himself is shown by the simple fact that for a number of projects he put on competitions in which the leading architects of the *Hofbauamt* (Court Buildings Office) were to take part.

We may justifiably assume that the concept for the Japanese Palace was pre-eminently the idea of Augustus the Strong: the porcelain collections it was to house were very close to his heart and he visited the palace regularly to keep himself *au courant* with building progress. It was furthermore to be the cornerstone for the new showcase Dresden that he planned to build on the far side of the River Elbe in Neustadt.[701]

The palace has all the essential features of a residence. On both stories, the rooms in the side wings were constructed *en enfilade*, thus giving the impression of being antechambers and of forming part of a set of princely apartments (fig. 29). The ground floor of the main, Elbe-side wing contained the *Gartensaal*, which could be used as a dining room, and the upper story contained the long gallery, which was not only large enough to be used as an assembly room for the whole court, but with its adjacent throne room was also clearly designed as an audience chamber. There were also plans for a chapel and state bedchamber looking onto the inner courtyard. Adjoining the throne room and bedchamber was furthermore a room which on one floor plan is designated as a "Retirade" (fig. 33),[702] which Rohr comments upon as follows: "Nobody is permitted to enter the 'retraites' and 'retirades' except persons of princely rank present at court, including relatives, ambassadors and ministers."[703]

Let us now imagine the path that would have been trodden by a visitor to the palace, just as we did when considering the iconographical program. For the upper story, it would have begun with the staircase in the western corner pavilion on the Neustadt side. As will be shown below, the old staircase by Pöppelmann in the Elbe-side wing can for reasons connected with ceremonial only have been intended for use by the prince and certain of the most elevated personages from his entourage.

Once visitors had reached the upper story, they would then have had to pass along the Neustadt-side gallery with its animal figures before entering, at the pavilion at the north-eastern corner, the first of four rooms *en enfilade*. If one assumes that these rooms were to function as antechambers, one cannot but be struck by two things in particular. Firstly, there was a relatively large number of them; and secondly, as they were all designed to be richly decorated porcelain cabinets, there was no indication of a hierarchical gradation in their fittings and furnishings.

This series of rooms had a different kind of gradation. When Augustus the Strong annotated floor plans with indications regarding his porcelain, he was always concerned to arrange the pieces in groups that each had one predominant color. Nevertheless, it is noticeable that he repeatedly changed the order of the colors, which is at least proof that the color sequence was not fortuitous. Although one might suppose that his re-groupings were motivated by aesthetic considerations, the very fact that symbolism was so ubiquitous at the court, even in small details, suggests that the sequence of colors, especially in a building so permeated with ceremonial as a king's palace, might well have had a special significance.

However, the sequence of colors finally laid down for this project – red, green, yellow, blue, puce ["Purpur"] – cannot be related coherently to any such conventional allegorical scheme from the Baroque as the one involving the elements (brown for earth, white for water, blue for air, and red for fire)[704] or the architectural orders (black for Tuscan, green for Doric, yellow for Ionic, red for Roman, white for Corinthian).[705] A treatise on painting printed in the Netherlands in 1707 does however give us an illuminating clue to the solution. In the fourth book of his famous work of instruction for artists, Gérard de Lairesse records the associations that are to be made with certain colors: "These primary colors also have their significances and particular characteristics."[706] White generally stood for light, and black for darkness, and furthermore, "yellow for splendor and glory, red for power or love, blue for divinity, puce ["das Purpur-rothe"] for authority and the highest powers, violet ["das Blaulicht-rothe," literally "bluish-red"] for subjection, and green for subservience."[707]

The hierarchical structure is obvious and is to be interpreted as follows for the sequence of rooms in the east wing of the Japanese Palace. First of all, the visitor entered the animal gallery with its red porcelain, where he prepared himself for the procedure known as "Antichambrieren" and hoped that the prince would be gracious, showing love rather than exerting authority. According to the seniority of his rank, he would be able to penetrate beyond the stages of subservience (green), perhaps through to glory (yellow), or even to the blue room symbolizing the divinity of the prince. This was followed by the chamber that with its puce porcelain would have impressed upon him the complete authority of the ruler, whom he would then finally see in person upon entering the glockenspiel pavilion, seated in state on the throne at the other end of the long gallery.

This is by no means to suggest that the visitor would have recognized or deciphered the symbolic significance of the sequence of colors. What is more, the question is irrelevant, given that the structure of the Japanese Palace was, as we shall later see more clearly, to be an ideal model of a princely residence and was in any case finally not brought to completion. The important point is that the series of antechambers was conceived and planned as a hierarchically graded enfilade.

The visitor was now coming nearer to the throne, and if he was a member of the circle closest to the prince, he could, as we know from Rohr's account, also enter the west wing's first room, which was often used also served as a "Retirade" for more private consultations; he could then either proceed to the dining-room in the middle room of the wing, or go through a door into the state bedchamber, before leaving the apartments in the direction of the old staircase. The layout of the rooms forced the visitor to follow the path described, a path that is fully in accord with the conventional sequence of rooms that made up state apartments in German princely residences of the Baroque, as can be confirmed by examination of the studies made by Hugh Baillie, who established a typology on the basis of numerous residences in Spain, Germany, France, and England.[708]

As we have seen, when Augustus the Strong was making plans for a museum, he opted for a central-plan building in which the visitor could at any moment leave one cabinet and find his way to another cabinet of his choice through the central hall. The Japanese Palace, by contrast, was never intended to be a central-plan building, as this would have deprived it of its model character.

The Animal Gallery: the correlation between its situation and its general significance

In Part Two, consideration was given to attitudes to animals at court and whether the gallery of porcelain animals could possibly be understood as an allegory for (court) society. Having presented the thesis that the Japanese Palace was a model princely residence – the "ideal of a residence" – we are now in a better position to give a satisfactory answer to this question.

The "role-playing" the courtier was involved in had nothing "playful" about it, apart from certain somewhat theatrical elements (pose, gesture, cutting a fine figure, and so on); on the contrary, it was a deeply serious matter.[709] His life was determined by rules. His station determined what clothes he was allowed to wear and when, how he was to behave in his dealings with his fellow-courtiers, what he was allowed or had to own,[710] and where and when he was expected to act on his own initiative. Such procedures as hat-doffing, hand-kissing, and greeting were nothing but clearly prescribed, ballet-like procedures. Life in the context of this highly self-controlled world had however certain similarities to the art of rhetoric in that the point of the exercise was to highlight the standard messages conveyed by the signals in an eye-catching and convincing way. The non-verbal forms of communication in particular made up a kind of de-individualized backcloth against which the more perfect smile, the more elegantly executed bow or curtsey, and the more finely formulated compliment combined to convey ever subtler facets of the courtier's personality. If one regards the codification of life at the court as a form of aestheticization, then the factor most calculated to raise the individual's prospects of social advancement – over and above what was prescribed on the ceremonial level – was style.

The spheres of human activity that were subjected to categorical regulation were thus precisely those that the mind of the time regarded as the ones man had in common with the animals, that is to say, all spheres except that of the mind.[711] The intellect was the only faculty by virtue of which one could break through the external stereotypes and acquire real individuality. This apart, the nobleman at court was thus first and foremost a representative of his social class and family, just as the animals in a menagerie were seen as representatives of their species. It was not the courtier's or the animal's individuality that determined his standing, but rather the fact of his belonging to a particular group.[712]

The point of the "animal world collection" assembled in the Japanese Palace was not to give a religious or scientific account of the creation of the world Creation based on the notion that the grandeur of the natural or created world can also be perceived in its smallest and least spectacular elements.[713] The selection was neither encyclopedic – neither fishes, nor arthropods, nor amphibians were represented – nor philosophical or religious. The collection of porcelain animals had the power to fascinate because it was exotic, because it performed what seemed technically impossible, and because it had a capacity to surprise. However, this does not provide a full explanation of why the project was driven on with such determination and resolve in spite of the extreme demands it made on all concerned. It is striking that the animals chosen came to a very large extent from those species which contemporary science regarded as "perfect animals": "Perfect [animals] are not only those which have more organs or parts of the body than others but also broadly speaking those in which one can distinguish the male from the female, such as dogs, cats, sheep, cattle, deer, bears, elephants, lions and the like, with the differences being rather less clear in the case of feathered birds."[714] Accordingly, the menagerie in the palace gallery was thus composed of the "perfect animals" presented by Zedler's account as superior to the others and worthy of a higher place in the hierarchy. Speaking in somewhat black-and-white terms, they were not the *hoi polloi* but rather the upper echelons of the animal world.

Baroque sculpture of the "public" kind only involved human representation in the context of certain well-defined fields, all related to élite groups: saints, mythological and allegorical figures, and rulers. If society was to be represented, or alluded to, in the context of the kind of model palace we are regarding the Japanese Palace as having been, then it was clearly necessary to find a very special means of doing so – society, after all, was the very heart of the Baroque residence. As there were other locations in Dresden where animals evidently were representatives of the natural world, it is quite possible that putting them into a princely residence was precisely that very special means of making them represent human society.

One further thought should be brought into consideration at this point. As Norbert Elias found in the case of Versailles, "that society, which [...] was boxed up together in one place and made all the more complex by all the king's functions as ruler and representative of the state, at the same time determines the shape and form of the royal palace intended to accommodate it."[715] In this respect, however, Versailles and Dresden differed in that Dresden had no princely residence large enough to attract the whole of the nobility to the capital en masse and to accommodate them once they were there.[716] As in other capitals in the Holy Roman Empire, the leading noble families had their own palais's in the vicinity of the Residence. If the Japanese Palace did have the model character we are proposing for it, then thought must have been given as to how it was to accommodate the nobility. It is significant that at the very point when Augustus the Strong's final concept for the project took firm shape and form, that is to say in the summer of 1730, the king not only already had clear ideas as to the sequence of colors for his "antichambres" but was also putting in his order for animal figures which represented the élite of the animal world; in doing so, he was clearly opting for an overall staging which with its (at least) two planes of significance was calculated to contribute to the palace's capacity to fulfill this function. The collection of animal figures was entirely of a piece with the king's other animal collections and could well have been read as a kind of variation on the familiar animal scenario: as art animals for the artistic residence, as it were. Alternatively, it could quite plausibly have been read as yet another instance of animals being used to symbolize man, and consequently as representing a "society," in which case other motives, such as the desire to create an entirely new genre of sculpture, would have been quite secondary in comparison, quite apart from the fact that the desire to make art history could just as well have been brought to fulfillment by other projects such as the planned furnishing of the chapel with life-size apostle figures.

This thesis is also supported by the very positioning of the animal gallery. The figures were not to be distributed disparately throughout the whole series of rooms as interchangeable decorative pieces; the visitor was to be greeted by a coherent array of animal figures vibrant with internal relations. Located at the beginning of the tour through the "European department," the animal gallery was furthermore located where under other circumstances the Guard Chamber would have been. Presented in this thematically loaded way, the animal gallery compelled – or rather would have compelled – the visitor to look for a meaning behind it very much as we do today, and to expect much more from it than simply fine craftsmanship and high artistry. Given that animals in Baroque art usually stood for human qualities and values, or even human types, and given that this animal collection was designed and arranged with such a high degree of artifice, a mind of the time would have been much more likely to see it as referring to human society than as a natural history collection.

It has been shown that the type-categories of the Meissen large animal figures (hunting, fighting, caring and protecting, and so on) can be seen as corresponding to activities pursued in and around a princely residence. Now that we have established connections between the figures as type-portraits and members of a court so formatively influenced by ceremonial, and have seen the significance of the gallery as part of a model residence, we shall now proceed to investigate how it was possible for a parallel of this kind to be established – a legitimate question indeed, as this could never have been the case with a collection of stuffed animals of the kind displayed in the *Animaliengalerie*.

Among the ideas presented by Milos Vec in his article on the discipline of ceremonial is the notion that the legitimacy of the Absolutist prince was based on two apparently antithetical conditions: naturalness "in being" and unnaturalness "in doing."[717] The prince could on the one hand lay claim to the "natural rights" due to him as the highest-born member of the nobility, and as one who was by his very nature the impersonation of "majestas." On the other hand, he redoubled his unassailability by uniting in his own person a whole range of the noblest and most abstract qualities and virtues. The fact of his living on another level, not only physically but also in a certain sense also spiritually, the evidence for which was the control that he exerted over nature, confirmed the view that he was an unnatural or even supernatural figure. Members of various sectors of the nobility also laid claim to these two qualities, in correspondingly diluted form, as a means of distancing themselves from lower social orders.

If we consider the animals against the background of these two planes – relating on the one hand to natural status in society, and on the other to an ability to maintain or improve social status by self-control and knowledge of present claims and possible future aspirations – then an interesting parallel emerges: a comparison can be made between the material porcelain, which as the *nec plus ultra* of artistry and artifice raises every porcelain object far above the common and banal, and the self-stylization of court society and its members. Another element that is in accord with this view of things is the naturalistic character of most of the porcelain animals, which we shall consider in due course.

If the fact of porcelain being an élite material is one that supports the notion of the animal gallery as a visual representation of court society, then this is a very suitable moment for an excursus devoted to the visual character of porcelain and to the consideration of certain related socio-historical matters.

Excursus

Shine: An attempt to explain the Baroque enthusiasm for porcelain with reference to aesthetic and socio-historical factors.

Explanations offered hitherto for the porcelain fashion of the seventeenth and eighteenth centuries

The enthusiasm for porcelain that increased so dramatically in the second half of the seventeenth century has hitherto been explained with reference to a variety of cultural-historical factors. One of the most common explanations is based on the material's exotic origin – until towards the end of the first decade of the eighteenth century porcelain was only available from the Far East – and thus its relative rarity, which made it a costly luxury ware. Owning porcelain was not only a demonstration of good taste, but also of being well connected, well educated, and very well heeled.

However, this was not only true of the Baroque period, as porcelain had been finding its way to Europe in small quantities ever since Marco Polo had returned from China at the end of the thirteenth century, and had been valued especially highly for a number of centuries for precisely the reasons enumerated above. Furthermore, the demand for porcelain did not abate with the mass imports that became more and more common in the course of the seventeenth century: on the contrary, it became even greater. And from 1710 on, when European porcelain came onto the market, all the greater availability did was to fuel the enthusiasm still further.

As a result, by the middle of the eighteenth century at the latest porcelain was no longer an exotic rarity. It thus cannot be argued that the constant increase in the interest in porcelain from the end of the Thirty Years' War through to the beginning of Neoclassicism was principally and constantly driven by porcelain's exotic origin and consequent rarity and costliness.

A further explanation that repeatedly appears in the literature has to do with the ideal qualities of the material for use at table (easy to wash and keep clean, neutral in taste, poor thermal conductor or good thermal insulator, colorful decoration), particularly for the consumption of tea, coffee, and chocolate, the luxury hot drinks of the time. These qualities did indeed play a very important role in the general development of table culture and made a significant contribution to porcelain's triumphant success, but it was only in the second quarter of the eighteenth century that porcelain was in widespread functional and decorative use on the dining-tables of the nobility.

It is thus possible to see two counter-currents at work in the value accorded to porcelain. Porcelain was at first prized for its rarity and exoticism, but as it became more common it was the functional qualities of the material which drove up demand. But even these two arguments can only be upheld with certain qualifications, as the one only applies to porcelain's decorative value and the other first and foremost to tableware. These lines of thought thus fail to offer fully satisfactory explanations for the steady increase in porcelain's popularity and the great efforts invested in Europe in its imitation or second invention.

When Johann Friedrich Böttger wrote his "Unvorgreiffliche Gedancken" ("Original Thoughts") in April 1709 with the aim of convincing a royal commission of the qualities of his inventions, he enumerated three qualities calculated to arouse desire for possession: "Firstly beauty, secondly rarity, and thirdly these two combined with usefulness. Three such qualities make a thing pleasing, costly, and necessary."[718]

The aspects of rarity and usefulness have been covered comprehensively in the literature hitherto, but no publications have ever considered the beauty of porcelain in any depth. It will thus be particularly worth our while to devote attention to the first of Böttger's three factors, and to see if there is any connection between the specifically aesthetic qualities of porcelain and the enthusiasm that the material provoked. It would seem to me to be a particularly fruitful approach if we wish to see how the phenomenon of shine relates to the importance accorded to porcelain in our particular period.

The phenomenon "shine"

"Shine" is a highly complex phenomenon that exerts a formative influence on human perception. It has been and continues to be the subject of scientific, theological, and philosophical studies.

Shine is visually perceptible as reflected light on material surfaces. It is a highly intensive and concentrated colorless brilliance. The variety of kinds of reflection results in various distinct kinds of shine: an object may shine, or it may shimmer, or it may sparkle, and so on. In our perception these various forms of shine become an integral part of the material, and in our minds and memories we identify the shine with the respective material itself: the luster of velvet is velvety, the shimmer on silk is silky, and when something is described as pearly, what we think of is the delicate off-white sheen typical of the pearl.

Regardless of the source of light, it is generally true that the more compact, even and colorless the light reflection is, the more even and smooth is the surface of the object, the result being a more intensive shine. When the eye sees a surface with a high shine, then the mind automatically assumes that the material concerned is hard, because the reflections themselves would seem to be coming off a densely and impermeably structured surface, as is shown by the reflection of light on a dark-blue glass, which is not light blue, as one might expect, but pure white. But these reactions are only feelings stemming from visual impressions. When we see a highly polished apple or a piece of sandstone, our tactile memory assures us that for all its shine the former is a soft object, and that the latter is relatively hard in spite of not having a shiny surface. When confronted with a given object, the human mind is fully capable of tempering the impression made by appearances with knowledge derived from experience, and of distinguishing the one from the other. This is particularly evident in connection with the phenomenon of "shine."

At this stage another point should be made, namely that things which are, or appear to be, comparatively hard are, or appear to be, more durable. This statement, too, would appear to be backed up our visual experience: such inorganic natural materials as precious stones, marble, and metals are as a rule not only shinier but also more durable than their organic counterparts, such as bird feathers, leather, or fruits. The exceptions, such as ice, need not concern us here. The fact that we have hitherto only considered natural materials leads us on to the third element in our quite subjectively oriented line of thought, an element likewise based on what we feel to be the case, namely that things we are given by nature are different from those we produce by artifice. We tend to regard shiny materials as not entirely "natural," because they are comparatively good at resisting nature's "ashes to ashes" cycle of growth and decomposition, of integration and disintegration. The dominant role which shine plays in the distinction we make between "natural" and "artificial" is made clear by the following example.

Wood shines relatively little, is felt to be soft rather than hard, is only moderately imperishable, and is suggestive of nature and naturalness. If the pores that are responsible for its characteristic shimmer are closed with a polish, wood can be given a very intensive shine with a great density of reflected light; this has the dual effect of making the human eye perceive it as hard rather than soft, and of preserving the material and making it less perishable, because its increased density fends off elements seeking to penetrate its fibers. Ultimately, the polish, which in fact infringes wood's natural structure, gives it an artificial appearance. The difference between the look of unpolished wood and the look of polished wood, which changes our perception of the wood from natural to artificial, is derived solely from the change in the wood's shine.

Shine and its importance in the Baroque interior

When we call to mind an interior from the late seventeenth or early eighteenth century, and consider which of the materials used in it shine, then we will come up with a list that includes the following: glass, mirror, enamel, (precious) metals, tortoiseshell, ivory, pearls, coral, glazed ceramics, polished or cut stone and stone imitations, polished leather, lacquer, polished wood, varnished sculpture and paintings, silk, and velvet. These materials, which shine to differing degrees, can be divided into two groups: those which are naturally shiny, and those which shine as a result of having been treated. When reading the list, one immediately notices that the materials are either relatively rare, and thus costly, or they have been subjected to a technically demanding and laborious (and thus also costly) treatment.

But it is precisely because there is a difference in the degree of shine and costliness between waxed and polished wood, between linen and silk, and between tin and silver that one can – with certain reservations and a few exceptions – see that shine was a commodity available to differing degrees in different social classes. Our line of thought thus arrives at a further station, this time economic and social in character: things with a high shine are not only harder, less perishable and more artificial in the sense of being produced by artifice, but also more costly and – in a sense – élitist.

A further point is that the shinier a given material has become, the more costly was the treatment that made it so. A cut and polished glass set the prosperous merchant more than a cut above the ordinary mortal who had to be content with a blown glass. But the prosperous merchant was in his turn put in the shade by those who drank from ground rock crystal glasses that sparkled with all the colors of the rainbow. To a visitor entering a relatively dark room, the measure of shine to be perceived therein was a reliable indicator as to the social standing of the master of the house. When high-ranking personages were figuratively described as "radiant," or "splendid," these figures of speech were quite literally true of their material possessions.

The ability of the shiny surface to reflect and brighten the smallest light source – the fact that it is a light-multiplier – was grist to the nobility's mill in that it helped them to emphasize their social pre-eminence by turning the night into day. They may have had hefty bills to pay for the candles that illuminated their reception rooms at night, but the costly candlelight was used to best advantage by being reflected in (likewise costly) glass or metal chandeliers and in the various ubiquitous shining sufaces.[719] But the shining surfaces made the day last longer even without candles. If, whiling away the sunset hour in some Baroque palais or stately home, one resists the temptation to turn on the electric light, one can still be fascinated by the dying away not just of the daylight but of the room itself. The first elements to be lost in the gloaming are contours and color values, but porcelains, mirrors, and precious metals can still be made out for a time, at first as objects but then only as spots of reflected light, and then even those fade away to leave the final "a niente" to the cut-glass pendants of the chandeliers.

It was certainly no coincidence that at precisely this time Netherlandish still-life painters devoted themselves intensively to this intermediate stage between light and darkness, between appearance and disappearance, painting pictures that can justifiably be called studies in shine. Shine was also consciously used in Baroque churches as an alternative to direct lighting.[720]

The special character of porcelain shine: its two layers, mirror effects, and luminosity

If one is to account for the eighteenth-century enthusiasm for porcelain in terms of material and aesthetic qualities, then we must first establish what its optical qualities actually are, first and foremost with reference to glazed white porcelain.

The two layers: Porcelain consists of two layers, an opaque white core (the body), and a transparent glaze ranging in color from milky to entirely colorless. The eye can penetrate the outer layer, but not the body. The layer of glaze is most clearly visible in small depressions and grooves where, having accumulated during the firing, it is thus somewhat thicker than in other places. These two optically distinct layers are what makes porcelain different from other white ceramics common in the Baroque period.[721] Back in 1936, Fritz Fichtner described the effect of the two layers as follows: "The lively shimmering light on a fine glaze – whether spreading itself generously over a large smooth surface, or creating deep shadows, or bursting into an almost audibly sparkling bouquet on a finial, ridge or other small plastic elevation – demands the highest artistic sensitivity. Porcelain only comes to life in light, it drinks in the light which, once under the glaze and on the white body, acquires a magical life of its own and is refracted many times over before finally shining out once again through the surface."[722]

Mirror effect: That the surface is not porous but entirely sealed brings about the kind of intensive, concentrated emissions of reflected light that one otherwise only sees on glass. The very word "glaze" is a reference to this similarity. However, porcelain differs from glass not only in the non-transparency of the body beneath the glaze but also in that it has a different mirror effect. With the exception of polished metals such as gold and silver, it is a general rule that the darker a smooth, shiny surface is, the more it will behave like a mirror. Transparent, colorless glass has a noticeably greater mirror effect than porcelain (unless of course it is held in front of a white surface, which is broadly speaking a simulation of the structure of porcelain).

If one compares porcelain with other materials that have a similarly high degree of shine, such as silver, glass, lacquer, and so on, one finds that while porcelain shines in the same way as they do, it does not have the same mirror effect. Because of the white body, porcelain gives a very meager pictorial reflection of its surroundings, but nevertheless shines light back in full measure.

It may furthermore be observed that the more perfect a mirror effect a material has, the more it disappears in the consciousness of the beholder – the "selflessness" of the mirror is an age-old topos. The charming experience of seeing one's surroundings in a distorted reflection in the bulging side of a silver coffee-pot, which distracts one's attention from the pot itself, is not one that one can enjoy with a coffee-pot in white porcelain. In spite of being just as shiny, the porcelain coffee-pot remains its own material self.

These two aspects – the effect of depth brought about by the two layers, and shine without mirroring – are the two principal characteristics of porcelain.

Luminosity: When we look at a clay model made for a porcelain figure, it is the play of light and shade on its surface that tells us what it is made of and enables us to see its exact shape. This is in fact true of any sculpture, and indeed of any object whatsoever. If the clay model in question is executed in glazed porcelain then the contrast between light and shade is heightened, with shining, light-reflecting sections alternating with sections which appear to be matt because they are in the shade. A similar effect can be observed on, for instance, a polished stone sculpture.

Regarded from the point of view of the human eye, the porcelain object, being two-layered, seems only to start after its actual surface, that is to say, when the line of vision has gone through the transparent glaze and meets the white body. At the same time, the rays that are reflected from the real surface towards the human eye seem in their concentrated form (as "shine") to lie in front of the material substance of the object. Between the point where the reflection actually takes place and the opaque surface of the body is a layer – albeit a very thin one – that has a blurred no-man's-land quality to it, deriving from the unclarity as to where the surface actually lies.

Conversely, it is as if the porcelain object begins to form itself for the eye of the beholder only to dissolve in the intermediary zone described above, before then becoming pure light in the points of reflection (in the shine). The line of demarcation between "matter-filled" form and air-filled space cannot be drawn exactly. This is the case without the kind of mirror-reflection that we observe on the silver coffee-pot, for the apparent dissolution of the coffee-pot's contour is the result of its surroundings being reflected on its surface, that is to say, of external forces working on the pot, and not of an effect emanating from the pot itself. In the course of his deliberations on the phenomenon of transparency, Ludwig Wittgenstein found that it is impossible to imagine something which is at the same time both white and transparent. However, this is precisely the combination that characterizes the porcelain surface: the body is an even opaque white, while on the surface there are pools of pure light. Opaquely transparent, the porcelain object is luminous, as if it were itself a source of light.[723]

The aesthetic qualities enumerated here are not sufficient to explain the degree of enthusiasm that was felt for porcelain in the Baroque and Rococo periods. Another factor that could be investigated in greater detail is the significance of the color white. The subject that I would like to turn to at this point, however, is the great enthusiasm that the Baroque had for the life-giving element of water. The motion characteristic of waves is integral to Baroque ornament and has an important place in the Baroque repertoire of forms. The mirror qualities of water surfaces were deliberately used in architecture to create eye-catching symbolic symmetries. Scientists devoted themselves to Neptunism (according to which all life came out of water), and shells, corals, amber, and other things taken from water were no longer kept as single pieces in cabinet cupboards, but collected in large quantities and put together to form wildly imaginative grottoes. Gardens were given new dimensions of life and movement by the shine and sparkle of fountains and other aquatic creations.

It would be difficult to overlook the similarities between the shine on porcelain and the shine on water. The surface of glazed porcelain has a permanently wet look to it, as if water was constantly lapping at its glaze. By being associated with water, the characteristic appearance of porcelain described above receives an additional dimension, an immaterial and elemental character proper to hardly any other material – as a result, it is almost as if the special appearance peculiar to porcelain was born out of the life-founding element of water.

It should be noted that the only material that had a similar degree of metaphysical import for the European mind was gold, an important point if one is to understand the sense in which porcelain was described – somewhat too often, admittedly, for the expression not to tarnish a little as time went by – as the "white gold of the eighteenth century."

The characteristic qualities of porcelain and their relation to court society in the Baroque period

In order to put the observations made about the aesthetic qualities of porcelain into the cultural-historical context and thus move towards a more solid explanation of the Baroque enthusiasm for porcelain, we must now give brief consideration to two further characteristics of the material.

In spite of being even denser than steel, porcelain has a structure that makes it sensitive to pressure and very fragile. There are on the other hand almost no limits to the forms into which the paste can be molded. The plasticity of the clay-like paste, which hardens when fired and provides the ground for a never-fading shine, is deceptive: the final product is in fact extremely brittle and fragile.

This combination of characteristics would seem to me to be a positive invitation to compare porcelain and the (court) society of the eighteenth century for possible structural parallels.

"In the châteaux of France, mirrors served to provide self-images for a society which not only found that the mirror embodied its ideals as perfectly as porcelain did – beautiful, costly, and fragile – but also developed it into a subtle means of exercising power."[724] What Loibl hints at here has in fact much deeper roots.

Much has been written on the subject of shine. For example, Baroque princes and courtier alike were greatly concerned, as we are now all aware, to make as resplendently "shining" an impression as possible and to earn optimum ratings on the "shine" scale (priorities which have turned out not to be exclusive either to the Baroque period or to the nobility).

The aspect of fragility is more complex. The system regulating Baroque court society was based on the granting or withdrawal of grace. The possession of wealth, beauty, or intelligence was of no advantage unless a person higher in the hierarchy recognized these assets and attributes, was gracious enough to promote them, and also made the party being promoted aware of the favor-bestowal network he was dependent on for his advancement. To put it rather more dramatically than is strictly necessary, one only had to give offense to the wrong person for one brief moment for the fragility of one's social existence to become disconcertingly apparent. It was not necessarily so that the offender would fall from favor entirely, but even a change in one's allotted placement at court events was sufficient to take a few degrees of shine off one's general aura and standing. This parallel with fragile objects, which for all their splendor can go to glory in the space of one careless moment, is made even more salient in the case of porcelain by one further factor.

The immaculate white of the porcelain paste had a counterpart in the make-up used by persons of standing. Make-up emphasized delicacy of appearance and gave facial traits a certain pictorial quasi-imperishable, character that suggests a parallel with painting in pastels. In the eighteenth century, pastels were almost exclusively used for portraits, which could aptly be described as powdered, made-up paper. The gestures and movements that courtiers trained themselves to carry out with a maximum of supple elegance had, in the make-up on the courtier's face, a counterpart which in its capacity for controlling the expression of feelings was no different from the immutable poses of porcelain figurines, whose swirling virtuosity, apparently so *mouvementé*, is in fact nothing but rigidly frozen modeling.

This accords with the courtier's practice of interrupting gestures by striking a meaningful pose, freezing briefly before proceeding to the next movement. This practice was a means of bringing about the "fruitful moment" that was the goal of all those who had to put themselves on show, and lent to the appearance of the person in question a figurine-like quality in the sense remarked on with regard to porcelain. It was by through *savoir faire* in the labyrinthine codes of court behavior that courtiers set themselves apart from the uninitiated that made up society outside the court; their lives were so shot through with the art of illusion that the illusion itself became a mirror of real life.

This leads us to the last of the parallels between court society and porcelain to be drawn in this excursus. The raw materials necessary for the production of porcelain can be found naturally and are not in themselves "precious" substances; only knowledge of the right processing technique can turn these unprepossessing materials into a top-quality artistic product. And even the owner of a product of of this kind had to use it in a way that demonstrated connoisseurship, another quality which the Baroque nobleman exploited to distinguish himself from lesser mortals.

A composite of pulverized stone and clay-like substances, porcelain is furthermore a material which appeals to three of man's five senses: sight, touch, and – because it gives a ringing sound when struck, making it suitable for carillons – hearing. The social structures of the time made it an asset, and indeed at some moments a vital necessity, to be able to charm, to beguile, and generally to hold one's fellow human beings under one's sway. If a gentleman had gracious movements, polished manners, a resonant voice, witty conversation, and a sense of rhythm in declamation, and could back them up with a well-groomed appearance, perfect clothing, and fragrant perfumes, then he had all the basic elements for cutting a fine figure in society; as barometers of his refinement these things paved the way for success and advancement. The notion of "refinement" is particularly germane to the present context: with its connotation of ennobling what would otherwise be ordinary, it not only applies to man, but also to the stone and clay of which porcelain is made.

A porcelain object, whether colored or white, will automatically catch our eye when we enter the room in which it is placed; in just the same way, the courtier strove to focus attention upon himself and to make a positive impression by the correctness and elegance of his appearance, with a view to augmenting the social capital that was so crucial to his existence. The ability of porcelain to drink in light and give it out again in a concentrated luminous glow, and in so doing to reflect upon its surroundings an equal measure of its own glory, was something that would certainly – for obvious reasons – have struck a familiar chord in the minds of all those whose lot it was to live out their lives at a princely court in the Baroque era.

End of Excursus

Was the Japanese Palace a "porcelain palace"?

We must now consider the question why, of all the buildings built or rebuilt by Augustus the Strong, it was the Japanese Palace that was given the character of a residence by its sequence of upper-story rooms. One would expect a palace filled with exotic treasures and set in spacious gardens to be something more in the nature of a *Lustschloss*, devoted purely to life's pleasures: "When fitting out their princely residences and pleasure-domes, they [certain princes] are not content with what the most outstanding masters of France, Italy, Holland, and England offer them, but feel compelled to bring new inventions from Turkey, China and other lands outside Europe, for the embellishment both of the architecture and of the furnishings."[725]

Julius Bernhard von Rohr's somewhat negative evaluation of the aesthetically motivated incorporation into court culture of decorative Far Eastern works of art was not shared by all his contemporaries; other writings from the period, such as John Stalker's *Treatise of Japaning and Varnishing* of 1688, contained expressions of euphoric admiration, here quoted in a rendering from a German translation: "The Europeans should no longer pride themselves on their mistaken assumption that they have left the rest of the world behind them with their stately palaces, costly temples, and other elaborate buildings. Ancient and modern Rome are to admit the superiority of one land, namely Japan, which alone has surpassed the proud Vatican in beauty and magnificence."[726]

Sources such as these show that when contemporaries were confronted with chinoiserie elements interpolated into buildings or interiors, they looked for a meaning behind the way the elements had been executed and the exact location chosen for the foreign body. Magnificent interiors decked out with Far Eastern works of art – whether genuine, imitation, or simply chinoiserie – were sometimes used to make a calculated impression upon visitors. But chinoiserie frequently also sprang simply from an uninhibited and capricious creativity, or from sheer delight in the decorative superficiality, follies, and amusements proper to the *Lusthaus* or *Lustschloss*; indeed, the Trianon de Porcelaine at Versailles, the Favorite at Rastatt, and the Pagodenburg garden pavilion in the Nymphenburg palace park were to all intents and purposes likewise no more than generously-sized *maisons de plaisance*.[727]

It would be just as misguided to conclude from the Japanese Palace's having been designed to house the royal porcelain collection that it was just another "Porzellanschloss" than it would be to think of it as nothing more than a museum. For reasons related not only to its size and expense but also to its containing elements typical of a residence, the Japanese Palace – unlike its predecessor the Dutch Palace – would never have been suitable for the less formal socializing that went on beyond the bounds of official court life.[728] The mere fact of it having a throne room, antechambers, and a state bedchamber disqualified it as a *Lustschloss*, in which there was generally speaking no place for such features as enfilades of ceremonial rooms. Von Rohr wrote of the hunting lodges and *Lustschlösser* that "there are commonly certain strict ceremonies which are taboo in the residences at court; and in general one feels that there is greater freedom, and less formality."[729]

But the transferral of residence-like structures into a building that had been a place for the enjoyment of aesthetic pleasures ("Lustschloss") had a certain bearing on the style in which the prince was to present himself and go about his state duties. Inevitably, the complex as a whole began to assume the model character already noted more than once in these pages. Indeed, this was the only possible way of coping with the discrepancy between the older external form (the Chinese-style *Lustschloss*) and the new interior (the princely residence designed to be an evident center of rule and government).

In this form the Japanese Palace was suitable neither as a substitute "modern" residence, nor as a location for the occasional ceremonial, as and when required. But given that its decoration and furnishings gave it a close link with Far Eastern culture, which was then put firmly in its place by its European rival, it not only imparted to its owner the dazzlingly unapproachable aura of an Oriental prince, but also imported this same aura directly into the field of European court culture. This view is also supported by the fact that the exterior of the palace was designed to bring about a balance between Far Eastern (decoration, roofs) and European elements (articulation of the overall structure). The Japanese Palace was primarily conceived neither a setting for masquerades and junketings nor as an ersatz residence, but in its fusion of a Far Eastern ideal and model formulations of the external signs of European rulership was a direct – and precisely programmed – expression of the claims and aspirations of Augustus the Strong and his son and heir.

This being the case, it was clearly intended that the palace should actually be used on particularly important state occasions, which, as we have seen, would have been perfectly possible, given the ceremonially correct sequence of rooms. It was certainly no coincidence that the decision to structure the interior as a ceremonial enfilade in the manner typical of residences was made precisely at the moment when, around 1730, the architects failed in their last attempt to push through a large-scale extension of the old castle (the "Residence") in accordance with a plan drawn up by Longuelune.[730] The intention to extend the residence was now to be implemented in the palace currently being rebuilt over the river in Neustadt.

To make a connection between this insight and Augustus the Strong's overall plan, it should be recalled that the Zwinger was a symbol for the prosperity of Saxony, which did indeed owe a good deal of its wealth to its natural resources. And although the iconography of the Japanese Palace was first and foremost associated with trade, as a whole it went further than this, pointing with its model structure to a projected future in which Saxony would take its place among the major powers of the world.

The seriousness of intent with which Augustus the Strong went about giving symbolic expression to his claims and aspirations vis-à-vis such highly respected absolutist rulers as the Sun King, the Grand Mogul of India, and the Emperor of China can also be observed in other works that he co-conceived or inspired.[731] They were directly dependent on the claims to power and personal predilections of the prince, which brings us to a further reason for the final renunciation of the project of the "Japanese Palace as a *Porzellanschloss*."

A number of aspects of an explanation have already been given consideration. Technical difficulties led to the manufactory being seriously behind with its deliveries and the modelers had to discontinue their work on the animals when they started working on the Swan Service. It was just at this juncture that Count Sulkowski, the coordinator of the whole project, fell from grace, and his successor Count Brühl put the manufactory to work for his own ends. Although Longuelune's new design for the interior of around 1735 was an attempt to tread a more "fashionable" and more intellectual path, the artistically sensitive Augustus III was fully aware that it had inevitably led to the collection being presented in a somewhat depository-like manner. Longuelune himself would seem to have had only a limited enthusiasm for porcelain, and no great sympathy for a project based on a series of porcelain rooms. From his description of the design for the throne-gallery it is clear that he not only found the quantity of porcelain vases boring but also considered it to be of no artistic value whatsoever. He thought that the mind needed things (iconographical elements) that had something to say: "On this same side statues and medallions have been put opposite the windows, in order not to be constantly repeating the vases, to avoid a simple arrangement which would look too much like a well-stocked warehouse, and to present the eye and the mind with amusing objects, which – as it were – speak for themselves." (Source 3)

The period in question also saw changes in Saxony's political and cultural circumstances. New generations came to power in three major countries bordering on Saxony and Poland, and there were new ideas about how the power of the state should be given formal expression.[732] A number of German princes had weakened their standing by keeping courts with levels of officialdom and ceremony in excess of their financial means and political status.[733] In other cases, the new trends in the courts of the day led to a certain skepticism about ceremony and all that it stood for.[734] The fact that most princes now expected a greater measure of privacy in their lives meant that the old signs, symbols, ceremonies, and rules of behavior were now formalities and void of any real meaning. It was not that the political claims and aspirations had changed, but rather that there were new ways of means of giving them visible expression.[735]

Seen in this light, the Japanese Palace was a building without a future. It was less and less suited as a vehicle for the expression of political aspirations which were in any case hardly realistic any more, and changes in the general understanding of symbolism meant that it was no longer understood as anything more than an ostentatious and extravagant folly. Jonas Hanway's travel report from the middle of the century makes it quite clear that it was quite impossible, for outsiders at least, to see the real character and significance of the still unfinished Japanese Palace project: "The palace in general is unfinished, and it may be presumed that the King himself is tired of the vanity of an unnecessary variety, and of such a profusion of expensive baubles."[736]

Commentators led by superficial similarities to place the Japanese Palace in the tradition of the porcelain pleasure-domes and to put the magnitude of the project down to a misguided prince's exaggerated self-esteem rather than to the specific circumstances of the time are victims of the loss of relevance suffered by the palace around the middle of the eighteenth century. In a sense, this explains the fact that while the animal figures are widely admired as technical and aesthetic masterpieces, it is very difficult for scholars and art-lovers to divine their real and deeper significance. For this very reason we shall now proceed to investigate the animal figures as works of art.

The animal figures: form and effect

Art and nature in the Baroque: a short survey

Nature "has its own inherent beauties and orderings, and her rules must be followed. For this reason, Nature is the pattern and example of all arts [...]. Nature contains within itself the foundations of all works with regular proportions and also the designs that lie behind all the ornaments that we find pleasing; the rules of art are not created by the arts themselves, but are rather already drawn up in the works of Nature. The arts are thus never more perfect than when they are representing Nature itself."[737] What Johann Christoph Gottsched had to say in 1760 on the relation between art and nature highlights one of the central insights of the fundamental change in the understanding of art that had come about more than two hundred years earlier. The question as to the relation between art and nature followed on from the question as to the relation between art and God (without replacing it); for the mind of the thinking beholder, it was indeed in a certain sense the "Urfrage" – the primary question – posed by the art works of the Renaissance and Baroque. "Art and nature" was one of the most important conceptual pairings to occupy the human mind in the sixteenth, seventeenth, and eighteenth centuries.[738]

In the wake of the re-discovery of the art works of antiquity, the art of the Renaissance combined a new outlook on what art was all about with the development of a new basis and new means for going about artistic creativity. One prime example of this was perspective. As a result, nature became in a certain sense reconstructible; in other words, it became possible to create a second form of reality with a suggestive power that made the beholder see it as natural, but still at one remove from nature itself. By bringing together and elaborating upon a great variety of ways of encountering and perceiving nature, art became one of the principal vehicles for the realization of the goals of "naturalistic encyclopedism."[739] In this sense, nature provided art with a treasure-trove that was at once an infinite source of inspiration for the inventive power of the human mind and spirit and at the same time a kind of "laboratory" in which man could experiment with his own capacity for experiencing the world. Artistic skill derived from the individual artist's ability to make the imitation of nature bear fruit in meaningful works of art.

Towards the dawn of the Baroque era, this process accelerated as artists employed their virtuosity not only to simulate reality but to create their own reality. Works of art no longer derived their life-blood from mediating between nature and the beholder: their *raison d'être* was now something more than simply to refer to objective reality. The crux of this change lay in a new appeal to the beholder's emotions.

Artistic virtuosity and the conscious representation of feelings – "affects" – combined to give works an emotional appeal on two fronts. The formal dynamic and general mood of the work had to reflect the chosen theme and also arouse the emotions of the beholder through their somewhat amplified dramatic character. Nature was no longer just an invisible element in the background: it was now present in the work of art and could be experienced with a high degree of immediacy. The proportions and character of the execution were laid down by the work of art itself, which meant that work and beholder could meet on the emotional level. The encounter with a work of art thus increasingly became a way for the beholder to experience and become more aware of his or her own self; in the ideal case there was a one-to-one correspondence between what was exceptional and elevated about the work and the emotions evoked in the beholder. To transcend the level on which art simply mediates nature, however, there had to be a certain exaggeration in the execution of the work – not as an end an itself, but as a catalyst – so that the border could be crossed from the work being seen rationally to the work being experienced in ways beyond the bounds of reason. "Art is Nature's complement, a second mode of being that makes Nature incomparably more beautiful, aiming as it always does to outdo Nature in all its works. It is Art's pride and joy that it adds another world – an art world – to that of Nature."[740] The potential that Baltasar Gracián, writing in the second half of the seventeenth century, saw in art went far beyond the capacity for reconstructing and interpreting reality that had previously been attributed to it. He hinted that art works have multiple layers of reference and symbolism that can be appreciated in full by the beholder, either through intellectual perception or through emotional experience, or through a combination of the two.

Concettismo and rhetorical structure

Gracián was one of the originators of *concettismo*,[741] that is to say the theoretical explanation of art that saw works of art as encoded signs, each work of art bearing within it references to further interpretative levels.

According to *concettismo*, while the work of art is formally speaking an imitation of nature, it provides the artist with a foundation for further references and allusions which go well beyond the objective reality of the subject-matter. The work becomes a relay station that gives visible form to intellectual substance, inspiring the mind and stimulating the emotions. The work of art brings together three planes of reference, in themselves linked by a complex multitude of interrelations: the plane of the creation of the work (the artist), that of the concept behind the work (the person who ordered it, the place it was ordered for), and that of the way in which it is experienced (the beholder).

The Baroque theory that art has multiple layers of symbolism leads to the dissolution of the border between intellectual perception and the experience of works of art in real life.[742] Both – philosophy and art – evoke pictorial perceptions in the broadest sense: in other words, they work through images. The concept specifies how the "two natures" should be linked together in one work; in so doing, it raises the power of the work to refer, and controls the perception of what the work has to say. But if the higher meaning inherent in the work is to be made comprehensible, then the work's message has to be unequivocal and regular – as we have already noted, emotions can also be controlled. The "technique" used to this end in Baroque art was a kind of rhetoric.

Rhetoric, the art of fine speaking, lays down the structural framework and procedures to be followed if a speech is to be made as convincing as possible. The procedures of rhetoric also played a role in the pictorial art of the Baroque.[743] Typically, the procedure involved presenting the structure and theme of the subject-matter, assessing a variety of theses, and then proceeding to convince the audience with arguments linked up with and/or distinct from the conclusions previously drawn. In Baroque art, the stimulation of emotions in the beholder was particularly favored as a means to this end, as for the Baroque mind emotional involvement was the key to understanding the work in question: the feelings it aroused were regarded as part of its "argument."

We have already encountered one example of a rhetorical structure in an architectural context, namely the path trodden by the visitor to the upper story of the Japanese Palace. In that instance it is possible to discern three different levels, all of which function according to one rhetorical system:

1. The visitors are first confronted with the Palace's underlying theme in the relief on the portico pediment (or rather with one important aspect of its theme, namely porcelain). They then make their way through rooms that constantly subject them to new experiences and perspectives on the subject. When they finally find themselves face-to-face with the palace's owner on his throne, the prince's very presence and the powerful messages being delivered by the ceiling paintings cannot fail to convince them of his economic might. This also explains why, after the portico relief had presented Saxony and Asia on equal terms with each other ("exordium," presenting the theme), it was only after the visitor had made his tour and seen Far Eastern and European porcelain presented to him in close proximity (argumentation) that the ceiling painting in the throne room took the side of European porcelain (peroration, designed to convince). Clearly, the Japanese Palace was to be read as a proof of the superiority of Meissen porcelain.

2. In parallel with the above, having first been confronted with the initials and coat-of-arms of the owner, visitors were then treated to the animal collection (reference to nature), works of art (culture), and music (carillon), all demonstrations of the wealth and good taste of Saxony and irrefutable proofs of the all-embracing might of its ruler.

3. On a third level, visitors could not fail to be surprised that a "Porzellanschloss" (by definition a "maison de plaisance") should be so vast. The explanation for this anomaly was then given them in the ceremonial sequence of the staircase, first gallery, enfilade of antechambers, throne-room and state bedchamber, all clear indications of the power wielded by the prince.

The three rhetorical strands, at once parallel and interwoven, thus lead to three likewise interwoven and mutually supporting messages: on the material level the iconographically substantiated superiority of Saxon porcelain, on a second level the might of the prince as attested by a multitude of sensory images, and then on a final third level the fact that was to be impressed on each and every visitor to the palace, namely the greatness of the prince holding court within its walls.

This example provides us with a good demonstration of the interpenetration of the will to make a statement (concept) and the way of making the statement understood (rhetoric). A synoptic look at the three levels as exemplified by the figures in the animal gallery shows the visitor being put through a process that is rhetorical in character, first of all examining the works in their material aspect (the work of art simply as an object), then admiring their appeal to the senses (the object as a work of art), and then coming to

	1st level material	**2nd level** sensory	**3rd level** intellectual
Palace	superiority of Meissen porcelain	cultural wealth of Saxony, power of the prince	the prince's political and social pretensions
Animal figures	porcelain/ object	work of art/ animal	part of the palace/ representative

Schematic presentation of the concept and rhetorical structure of the Japanese Palace

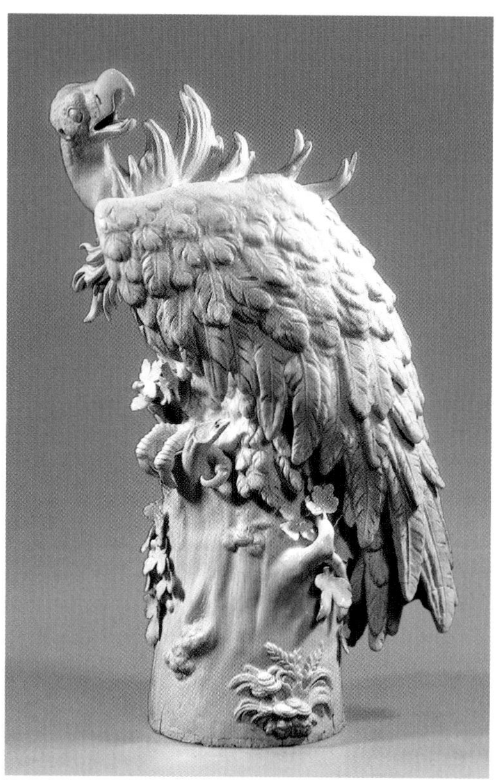

153 Johann Joachim Kaendler, Griffon Vulture (without cockatoo), model 1734, Dresden Porcelain Collection

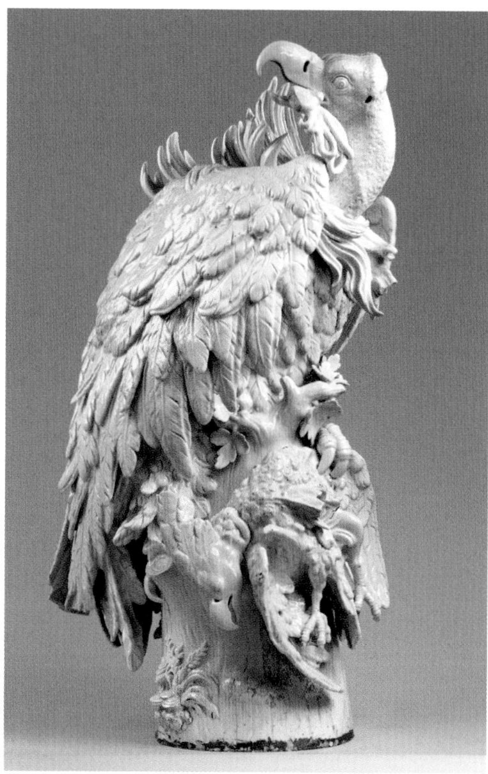

154 Johann Joachim Kaendler, Vulture Devouring a Cockatoo, in profile, model 1734, Dresden Porcelain Collection

a more intellectual awareness of their higher "nature" (the work of art as a concept, or part of a concept). The visitor was thus first invited to consider the works in the light of the technical difficulties and artistic challenges entailed in their having been executed in porcelain, and was then led on to consider what their deeper meaning might be. In short, the visitor realized the following three things in succession: a) it is a porcelain figure (art), b) it is an animal (nature), and c) it is part of a greater and more complex whole.

In order to ensure that the concept was read correctly and that the visitor did not interpret the symbols according to his or her own whim, the whole had to be given a calculatedly rhetorical structure. The artistry that gave the animals their own particular shape and form also had to function as a part of the argument. This was the critical point at which the visitors' thoughts transcended the perception of purely material things (the porcelain in itself), and at which they were made to realize, as they made their way through the palace, that the animals could be seen as a symbolic representation of society, a realization which was necessary to their being able to interpret the palace in accordance with our third level.

We shall therefore now proceed to a first single-work study, with the intention of looking more deeply into the microcosm of the palace, and of showing up the role played by the rhetorical structure that is evident within the animal figures as a group. In so doing, we intend to use this one isolated example to demonstrate the rhetorical power of the animal figures, before proceeding to further studies that will show how these particular animal figures were able to sustain the Japanese Palace's underlying concept.

An example: Vulture Devouring a Cockatoo

Johann Joachim Kaendler created the model for this figure in September 1734 after having observed a vulture devouring a dead cockatoo in the menagerie at Moritzburg (figs. 154 and 155). Johann Christian Müller saw the figure in the palace in 1744 and described it in his memoirs as "a bird of prey with a mauled hen lying before it, its blood-bespattered frame and innards clearly visible, all as natural as if it was living, right down to the colors."[744] The second version ("without cockatoo") is simply a variation of the same model but without the cockatoo (fig. 153).

The life-size vulture is crouching on a tree-stump. Its talons are holding fast to the branch-stumps and at the same time clasping a dead cockatoo, with a number of the individual claws piercing the cockatoo's spread wing and others holding the dead bird by the neck. Sundry elements of foliage and cockatoo plumage cover the transition from the tree-stump to the bird. This vertically oriented sculpture culminates in the vulture's backward-straining neck and head.

To the eye of the beholder looking at the figure from the front, this verticality is interrupted by the dead bird at the vulture's feet. While the cockatoo's left wing is spread out horizontally under the vulture, its right wing hangs down in such a way as to form a

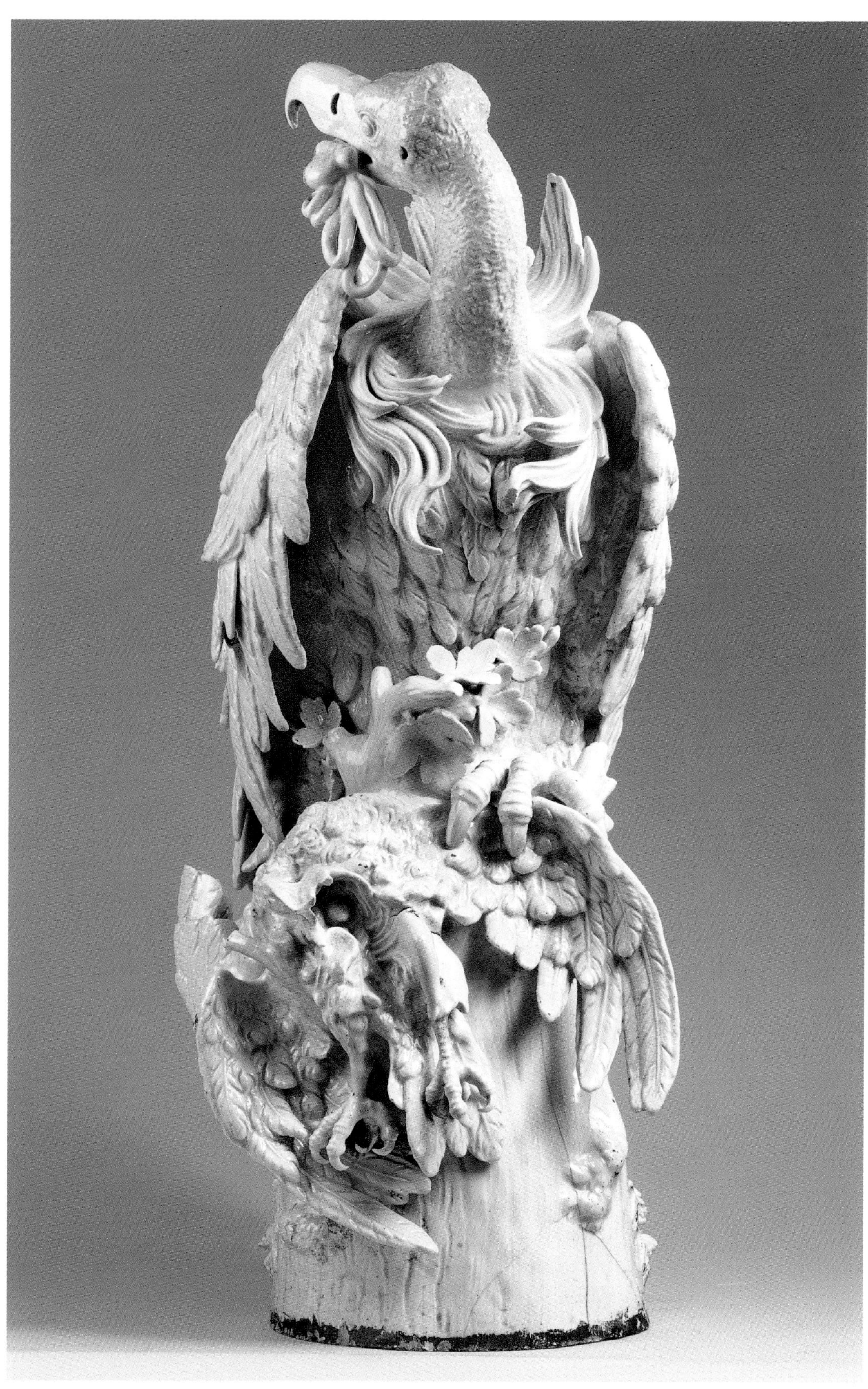

155 Johann Joachim Kaendler, Vulture Devouring a Cockatoo, seen from the front, model 1734, Dresden Porcelain Collection

three-quarter circle from wing-tip to wing-tip, the two legs hanging limply down within. Even a momentary glance at the flat, two-dimensional cockatoo is enough to tell us that "something is not quite right with it." As the eye moves upwards from the disk formed by the bird, it meets the body of the vulture enclosed in two folded wings as if in a shell. Even when seen from the front, this expansively three-dimensional arrangement is in stark contrast to the flatness of the cockatoo's wings.

The vulture's breast feathers are conventionally done, overlapping like scales, but immediately above the breast they explode into a proudly virtuosic ruff of flame-like plumage, tongues of fire licking around the vulture's bare, wrinkled, boldly thrusting neck. Following the upward movement, the beholder cannot quite see the whole of the turned head, and has to move a little to the left to get a full view.

Our sightline slightly adjusted, we now see the whole head from the side and immediately realize that held in the vulture's huge beak is the cockatoo's heart, its innards trailing down behind (fig. 154). Having been forced by the composition to follow this upward path, our eye reverts to its point of departure: from the vulture's backward-turned, static head, we backtrack via the heart and innards, upstanding neck feathers, and vulture's chest, following a natural path down along the lines of the plumage. More lively down at the wing-tips, the vulture's plumage guides us back to the cockatoo. However, as we have moved slightly to the left, we are now in a position to take in the cockatoo's head, which was previously hidden behind the lower wing. From this point of view, the flat disk formed by the wings is as it were pierced by its ribs, prominently visible through its gaping breast: what we now have before us is a cockatoo carcass, replete in all its three dimensions.

If one disregards the cockatoo's characteristic crest, there is a certain similarity in the heads of the two birds, particularly in the shape of their beaks, added to which they are modeled in roughly parallel postures. All this invites the beholder to draw comparisons between them. While the cockatoo's head is hanging down, grasped at the neck by a powerful talon, the vulture's head is the culmination of its muscular, curving neck. The figure successfully incorporates a vivid contrast between what is living and what is lifeless. And it is precisely because it is a depiction of life and death that it appeals to us in a particularly emotional way. The attention of the beholder is not only caught by the birds' various energy centers, their plumage, for instance, and especially their wings, but also by the two birds as living beings, that is to say, by the subject matter. The dramatic concept behind the figure has two particularly important features. Firstly, the depiction is generally somewhat exaggerated, especially in such features as the flaming feathers on the vulture's neck; and secondly, it anticipates that the beholder, guided through the composition along the lines described above, will ultimately see the critical connection between the heart in the vulture's beak and the cockatoo's gaping breast. Once the eye of the beholder has taken all this in, it is no longer just a likeness of two birds involved in what is after all a common enough incident, but an event captured in a well-timed snapshot that compels us to take sides. The sharp, blade-like edge of the vulture's beak, holding the soft contours of the cockatoo's inner organs in a pincer-like grip, the passion and vehemence with which it is turning its head from out of the wildly unkempt snake-like shags around its neck – all this is in such stark contrast to the limp and lifeless head, wings, and talons of the hapless cockatoo.

The vulture, in spite of its unquestionable superior strength, seems to be wrenching its head to one side out of fear that the beholder might snatch its booty from its beak. The figure's dynamic energy, which derives from the torque in the vulture's head, makes a constant appeal to the attention of the beholder, demanding that he or she react in a strongly emotional way, either with disgust, nausea, or admiration. The body of the cockatoo, calmly circular as it hangs in repose, evokes contrastingly peaceful emotions – pity, or awe. Both areas of the figure, the dynamic head above and the inanimate shell below, are capable of striking a chord in the soul of the beholder.

This way of building up emotional tension accords with a rhetorical procedure. Once we have recognized the basics of what we have before us, the formal and narrative aspects of the figure begin to constitute an "argument," which in its turn compels us to resolve the tension by deciding on our own position with regard to the event depicted. The theses and arguments presented by the figure cannot but evoke a certain response in the beholder. The beholder knows that the little bird was once living and is now dead; furthermore, the heart is not only a vital organ but also one with a very special emotional connotation. The vulture has, it is clear, torn the cockatoo's heart out. For all that the vulture lords it over its victim, we do not see it as enthroned in majesty, but rather as a savage cutthroat. And this also means that whatever the formal echoes, the figure has nothing in common with a Pietà.

The beholder who sees the birds as a depiction of two exotic species can maintain a certain objectivity and can even go so far as to admire the noble savage in the vulture. However, because there is nothing closer to human kind than the animals, we cannot but feel pity for the cockatoo. Torn hither and thither by the scene depicted, we are receptive to the rhetorical structure of the figure; we may even forget that the figure is an inanimate object, and invest it through our emotional involvement – for a moment, if not longer – with real life. In this sense a second reality is revealed to us, a reality that by virtue of being such a magnificently deceptive imitation not only has the character of an end in itself but also draws us – in spirit – into the work and demands that we (as witnesses at the scene of the crime) respond. The beholder is moved to participate in the work of art.

This first work analysis is a telling example of the astounding quality that is to be found in a good number of the Meissen large animal figures. Although animals were ubiquitous elements in the emblematic and symbolic art of the Baroque, they only served as pointers in an overall "argument" intended to guide the mind of the beholder to a meaning behind the image that was to a very large extent independent of the animal depicted.[745] While the figures on the animal fountains in the labyrinth at Versailles are, formally speaking, the ones most closely related to the Meissen animals, the Versailles animal figures only served to illustrate a moral and the beholder indeed had to be familiar with the moral in advance (or had to acquire this familiarity by reading the appended text) if he or she was to understand the sculpture at all. All the viewer had to do was to decipher a predetermined concept.

This was by no means the case with the Vulture Devouring a Cockatoo, which did not have a literary or emblematic background and does not necessarily have a moral, or demand a moral interpretation. The point of the work is to tell a general story about life and death and not to illustrate the fable "The Cockatoo and the Vulture." It is the birds themselves that we are confronted with; they constitute the focus of the work and are not there simply to illustrate a pre-formulated and pre-interpreted motif.

While it was true of the vast majority of the animal figures that they were to be appreciated for their own sake rather than as pointing to a deeper meaning, the concept for the gallery as a whole was indeed one which had symbolic character and was consciously designed to guide the mind of the visitor to a variety of levels of meaning. The animal gallery was thus a collection of "value-free" works in an overall context that was quite the opposite.

The freedom that the modelers enjoyed at Meissen rubbed off on their creations: the figures were made in such a way as to present the respective animal to the beholder in as direct and as natural a way as possible. No animal had any obligation to symbolize anything; all they had to do was to take their beholders beyond mere admiration and to stimulate them to an emotional response. Once this had taken place, the astounded and fascinated beholder was ready to fall under the spell of the collection as a whole, at which point it was the collection as a whole that offered the beholder levels on which deeper meanings might be perceived. So when Count Sulkowski and the king objected that certain figures had poor colors and posture, this was in part because substandard figures could never be more than simply objects: a substandard figure that was not a good likeness of a real animal could never play a part in the interior décor in the way that the vases and plates did.

We shall find ourselves returning to these basic structures again and again when we look at other figures, but before proceeding to further individual analyses, we now propose to consider the understanding of art that was beginning to develop in Europe in the period around 1730, an understanding which had its own way of relating nature and art.

The change in the relationship between art and nature after 1730

Our consideration of the essential character of Baroque art has hitherto been derived exclusively from the visual arts: painting, sculpture, and architecture.[746] The change in the approach to the creation of ornament that came about in the 1730s did not take place in these fields but rather in that of "decorative" or applied art; it had to do with the new understanding of the "nature of forms" that we nowadays attempt to categorize with the designation "Rococo."[747]

Because the "Rococo" has hitherto mostly been investigated from the point of the history of style, the change in question has

156 Johann Joachim Kaendler and Johann Friedrich Eberlein, parts of the Swan Service (1737–1741), Dresden Porcelain Collection

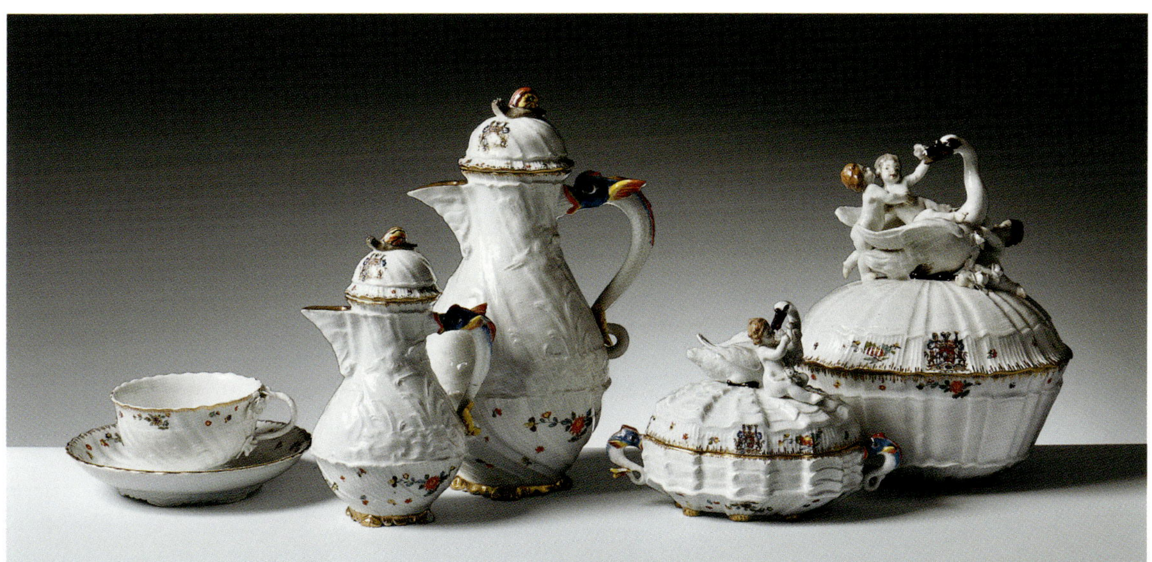

generally been explained in very limited terms as deriving simply from aesthetic whim or the practice of playing around with traditional forms; what has not been understood is that the new development has to be seen in the larger context of a general and more far-reaching new assessment of nature and "naturalness" in the first half of the eighteenth century.[748]

The following quotation from Paul Hofer is offered as one characteristic example of the ill-considered and negative view of the Rococo which has sadly become so widespread: "The Rococo is fundamentally different from the Baroque. The great 'Welttheater' has disappeared like a puff of smoke; on the new shallow stage all we see are the insubstantial neo-mannerist *divertimenti* of a sublime musical and spiritual – but now no longer sculptural – culture. In respect of form, the porcelain figures of the eighteenth century and the miniature bronzes of the sixteenth belong to the same family. And everywhere we see an identity between the two stages of style in evidence before and after the Baroque."[749]

Although there is no doubt that the animal figures for the Japanese Palace are sculpture and thus "visual art," it is also the case that they were created in an arts and crafts environment and, what is more, by the same hands that modeled items of applied art (from coffee-pots to tobacco jars) incorporating the very stylistic changes that led to the Rococo. The production may have been broken off in good measure because of the huge load of work demanded of the Meissen manufactory by the Swan Service, but it should not be forgotten that its creation and production (1737–1741) was a pioneering achievement, and that it was to become a stylistic prototype for a whole new genre of porcelain (fig. 156). It would certainly be wrong to think that Kaendler only discovered the Rococo attitude to nature when applying his mind to the Swan Service, and that when he did so he simply – like many a later historicizer – took a quick crash course in the graphic antecedents and regurgitated their detail as frills and trimmings. On the contrary, this new feeling for the relation between nature and form had certainly been maturing in his mind for some time before.

Around 1730 a playfully creative school of ornamentation spread from France that had certain structural elements in common with the grotesques of the Mannerists. While its basic building blocks, the shell form and the C-scroll, were elements that had been used in Baroque ornamentation, they were now to be combined in a quite different manner. The new dogma of asymmetry led to vexing distortions. The Rococo forms fought for freedom from the principles and standards of architecture; underlying the movement was an inherent tendency towards the "playful dissolution of all tectonic forms."[750] The deformalization, the emphasis on flow, and the general avoidance of repeated rhythms combined to suggest that the new forms belonged to a world of organic growth, a world of natural proliferation (figs, 157 and 158).[751]

But it would be misleading to claim that the naturalness of the Rococo consisted simply in its use of natural elements (shells, wings etc.). To combine the non-representational with the representational is a basic principle of any grotesque. But unlike the motifs of "Knorpelwerk" (auricular style), which come across as deformed surface, unlike "Bandelwerk" (strapwork), in which the net-like structure is more important than the detail, and unlike acanthus, which in spite of being rendered very naturalistically in the Baroque was still always subordinate to the overall formal context, rocaille had an inherent compositional freedom that could not be made to correspond to any Baroque teachings on art and harmony. The only law that could be established was the law of complete irregularity and of the surprise value of the unpredictable.[752]

With respect to the understanding of nature evident in the Rococo, this meant that the formal procedures were no longer rooted in rules derived from the observation of nature; on the contrary, composition was practiced in accord with the very principle of natural creation, in a constant bringing forth of recognizable elements (shells, wings etc.) and their immediate deformation and dissection into smaller parts.

For the student of how Rococo decoration is perceived, the interesting implication of all this is that although rocaille is made up of natural elements such as shells and rocks that are the very epit-

157 Franz Xaver Habermann, *Autumn*, rocaille fantasy (Augsburg: Johann Georg Hertel)

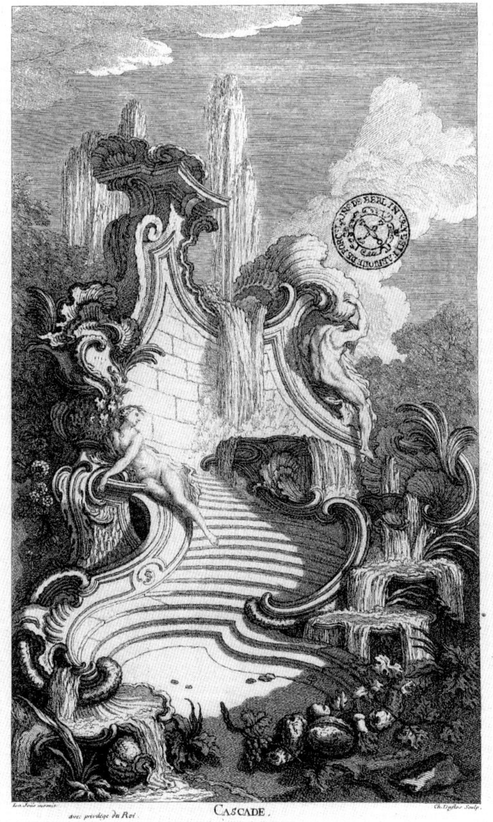

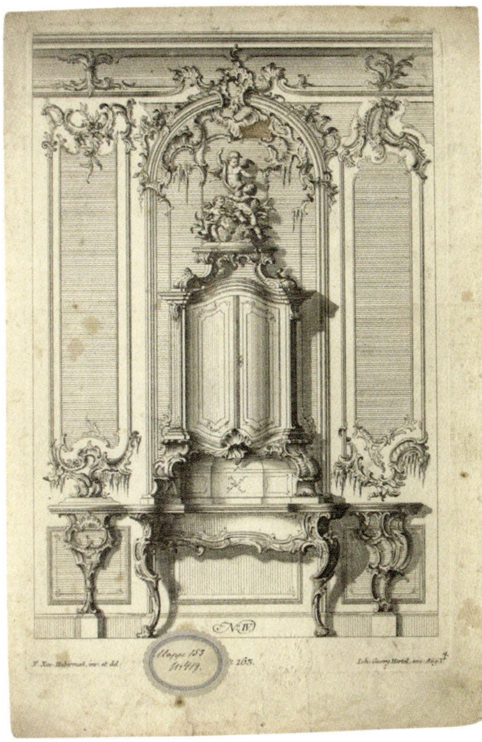

158 Franz Xaver Habermann, design for a writing desk (Augsburg: Johann Georg Hertel)

ome of formal stability, it creates an impression of fluidity in the mind of the beholder, who breathes life into the work and makes it positively unstable by following the energies of the curves. What gives the impression of movement and "natural" growth is in fact a deconditioning of material and form that takes effect when the work is perceived by the human eye. This fascination and stimulation both spring from the strong impression of instability given by a juxtaposition and intertwining of hard but deformed elements that are not designed to bring about emotional involvement (for which there is in any case too little concrete narrative), but rather to give the beholder a sense of great underlying creative energies.

The very referencelessness of Rococo ornamentation does of course lay it open to the charge of being nothing but self-indulgent eye-teasing – effect for effect's sake – and shallow display. What this charge fails to see, however, is that rocaille was born in a time in which science (the science of the early Enlightenment) was devoting itself increasingly to the investigation of fundamentals (energies rather than mechanisms) and was the child of a society that was embarking on a new interpretation of the notion of individuality. One might even go so far as to suggest that rocaille brought about the break with the idea (born of a hierarchical, religious mindset) of art as a "speculum mundi," and that it was rocaille that paved the way for a completely new attitude to meaning and perception in art. After all, rocaille did full justice to the fundamental truth that our perception of the world consists of a mass of fragmentary impressions and that the dimension which we know as nature is nothing other than a joining together of many single phenomena as observed in the human mind. This view was, for example, expressed in Leibniz's theory of monads, which took God as its point of departure and recognized God as highest being, responsible for the creation and organization – for the principle – of the world, but at the same time regarded man as capable of participating in the divine activity by exercising a vicarious creativity of his own.[753] It was thus not so much nature as a phenomenon but rather how nature came into being – its genesis – that was now of greatest interest, and this it was that led to rocaille imitating a principle rather than reproducing a structure.

The extent to which the change in man's understanding of nature that was becoming manifest in art around 1730/35 is reflected in the Meissen large animal figures can be seen particularly clearly if one makes a comparison between the two principal *Modellmeister*, Johann Gottlieb Kirchner and Johann Joachim Kaendler. Although they were the same age, they held different views about the way nature and the animal world related to art, the one adopting a position that we may designate as traditional, and the other cultivating a more progressive and innovative approach.[754] This difference is now to be demonstrated with two comparisons, the first comparison involving an animal and a bird that were both among the highest-ranking traditional symbols of rule and government, and the second being intimately related to the incorporation in the figures of anthropomorphic, and thus hierarchical, traits.

There was a third modeler active at the manufactory at the time when work was being done on the commission for the Japanese Palace, Johann Friedrich Eberlein; he was responsible for modeling a small number of the animal figures, and was very much influenced by Kaendler. His understanding of the animal figures was not very different from that of Kaendler, and we may assume that he also received correction from Kaendler, to whom he was a kind of assistant. Although this is frequently claimed to have been the case for Kirchner, there is no proof that this was ever so with regard to the animal figures. Their fundamental artistic concepts were, as we shall see, very different.

Johann Gottlieb Kirchner and Johann Joachim Kaendler: a comparison of their conceptions of animal sculpture

Symbolically loaded motifs: the lion and the eagle

At the time the animal figures were ordered for the Japanese Palace, the lion and the eagle – king of the beasts and king of the skies – had long been used as symbols closely associated with the public demonstration of power and authority. They were omnipresent in heraldic devices and at central points on princely buildings, usually firmly attached to all manner of finials, and to coats

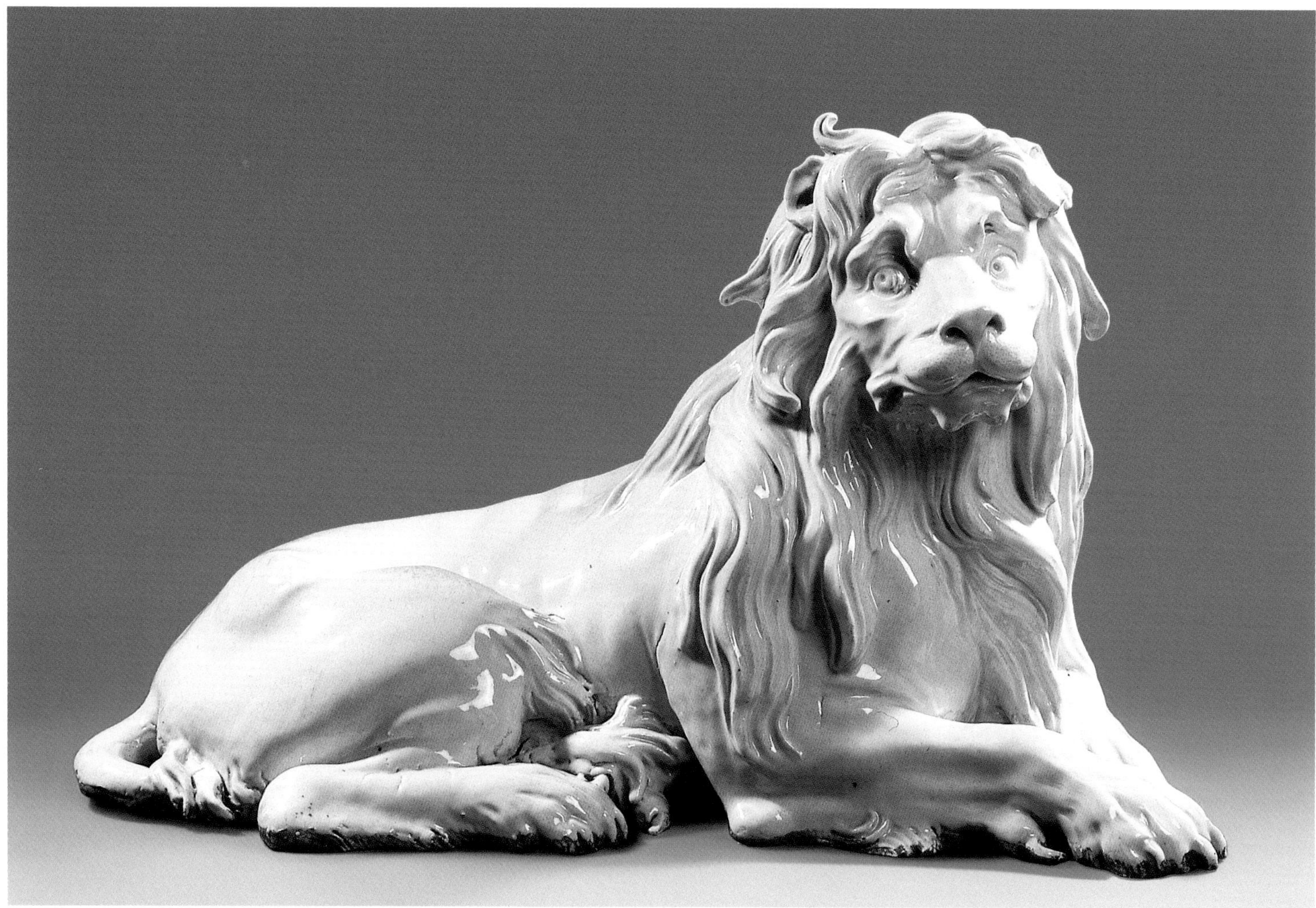

159 Johann Gottlieb Kirchner, Lion, model 1732, Dresden Porcelain Collection

of arms, roof-beams, banister-posts and the like. At the time the lion and eagle models were made, there were live specimens of both at the *Jägerhof*, so that both Kirchner and Kaendler could well have seen them live before putting their hands to the clay.

Kirchner's Lion

Johann Gottlieb Kirchner almost certainly did his model of a lying lion in the first half of the year 1732 (fig. 159). The fact that its raised head is turned to the right means gives it a "best side": the beholder sees more of the lion when looking directly at the right flank than from any other standpoint. The lion's body is smooth, without any sculptural suggestion of a coat, but ribs, muscles, and skin-folds can be discerned on its back and loins. By contrast with the smooth surfaces representing the parts where the lion's coat is short, the legs, the end of the tail, and above all the mane are rendered sculpturally with long, powerfully modeled strands of hair. Of the tail, which is partially hidden under the right hind leg, all we can see is its beginning and its tassel-like tuft. So far, then, Kirchner's Lion looks quite the part.

The jaws are closed and there are no teeth to tell us that the lion is a dangerous beast of prey. The eyes are wide open and the lion is glancing to the right. The eyebrows are rendered as a decorative and prominent pair of symmetrical bolsters, as if the lion were raising them and at the same time knitting them in a pronounced frown. This considered and quite unspontaneous expression makes the physiognomy thoroughly human, an impression made even more marked by the execution of the mane, which with its center-parting, and long, shaggy waves of flowing hair has an unmistakable likeness to an unkempt full-bottomed Baroque wig.

The animal's whole posture is static, but not limp. The tail is securely fixed in place by virtue of being tucked under a hind leg, the paws are accurately placed, and the raised head is attentive and observant. A turning movement runs throughout the body to the eyes, creating a highly effective build-up of tension and vigor start-

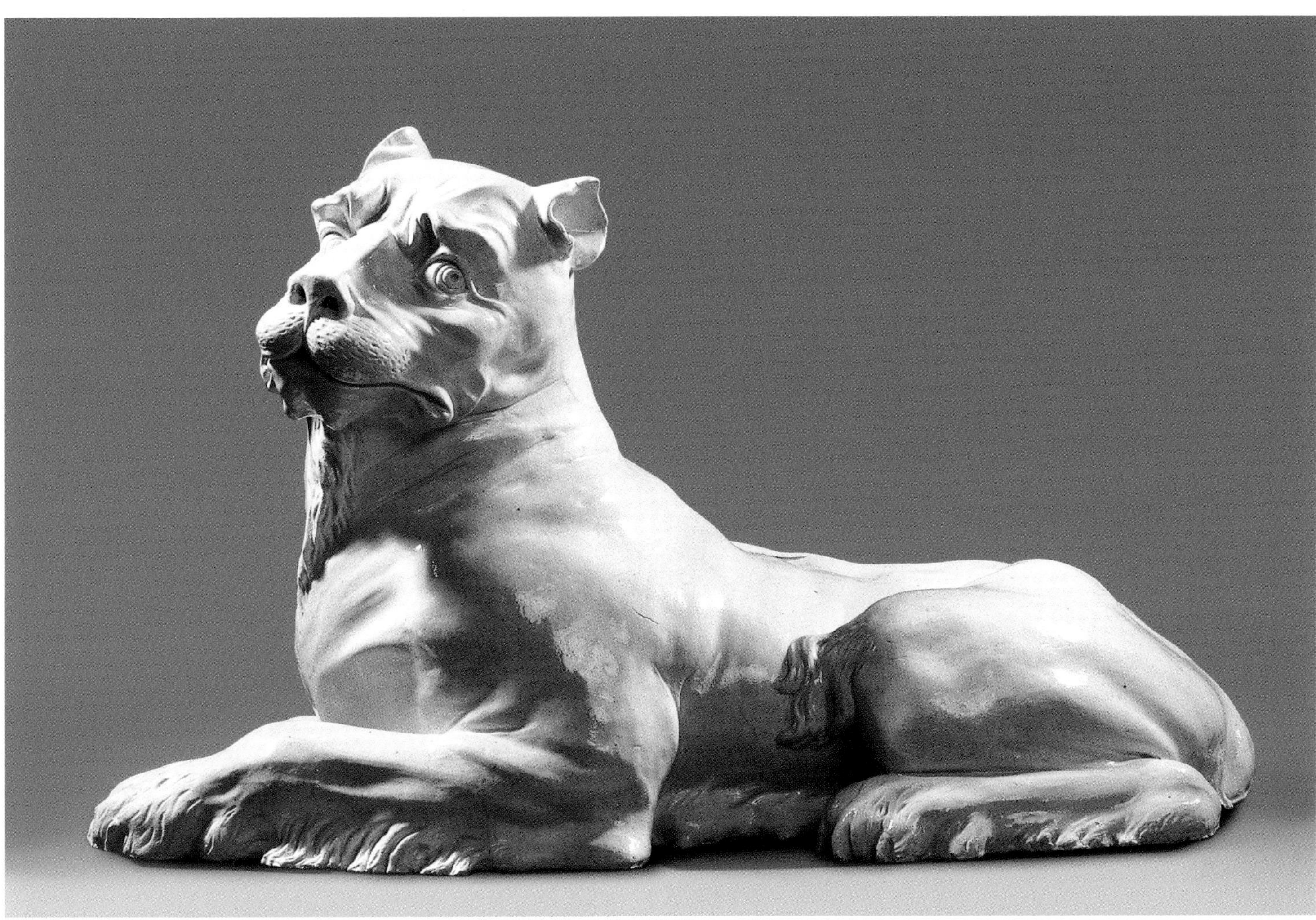

160 Johann Gottlieb Kirchner, Lioness, model 1732, Dresden Porcelain Collection

ing from the perfectly inert tail, continuing through the backmuscles along the waves of the mane, and culminating in the lion's sideways glance. This the composition's sole dynamic axis is enhanced by the figure's uninterrupted outline. This lion stands before us in a pose which is well-considered but not in any way stiff or tense.

The animal only seems to be active in its eyes: even the tip of its tail – always atwitch on a live lion – is held still, a clear sign that it has its feelings and reflexes fully under control. The calm but watchful pose gives the beast a certain natural superiority and majesty, underlined by the meaningful look in the tightly-focused eyes. Even in humans, a combination of patronizingly raised eyebrows with such a frown as this bespeaks a moment of the greatest concentration, and it is a combination which in its refined artificiality makes Kirchner's lion a figure with real stage presence.

The typical characteristics of the lion as a wild animal are thus quite absent from this depiction; no huge paws or sharp-toothed jaws for the dangers posed by this predatory carnivore, no tense muscles or nervously twitching tail to indicate its vigilance and readiness to pounce. Here the lion embodies a different ideal, and one proper to a human king: control of the emotions and reflexes, a well-considered and dignified pose, and a proud look in the eyes to give an impression of personal strength and superiority.

With respect to the imitation of a natural lion, Kirchner does not go any further than is necessary for the animal to be immediately recognizable; neither, however, does he follow the heraldic tradition of the stiffly sitting or standing heraldic lion, which for technical reasons alone would have been problematic in a figure this size. His concept was quite literally to embody a human king in the king of the animals. The figure's appeal and power to charm lie in the courtly but considered pose and in the highly expressive eyes. Kirchner's recipe for this sculpture, one might say, was to combine a minimal measure of the lion's physique with the psyche of the ideal king. Kirchner's Lion is a symbolic lion, executed

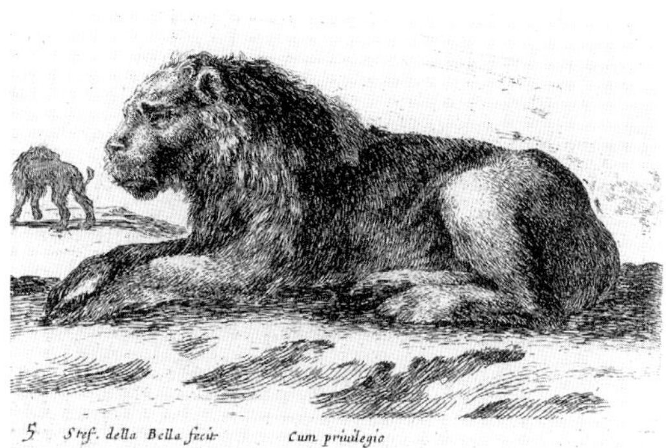

161 Stefano della Bella, lion from the *diversi animali*

pictorially, an attempt to build a bridge between nature as seen by the human eye and nature as interpreted by the human mind. His rendering comes from treading a narrow path between two spheres: it is in the truest sense of the word an "inter-pretation," for while the rationally-minded beholder sees the figure as a lion, the emotionally sensitive beholder will surely see it as a king.[755]

In this sense, Kirchner's way of handling the lion motif is fully in accord with the Baroque approach to depicting animals. In his representation, the animal is not an autonomous being presented in a scientific illustration, but rather the embodiment of a notion or a statement which the beholder can decipher through a combination of careful thought and sensitive feeling.

Kaendler's eagles of 1731 and 1732

Johann Joachim Kaendler modeled a large eagle figure in the first weeks after he started work at the Meissen manufactory in June 1731. One porcelain eagle made from his model was very probably delivered to the Japanese Palace before the end of the same year (figs. 162 and 163). In order to make up complementary pairs, some of the seven figures were produced with the head turned to its left, and the others with the head turned to its right. The bird is sitting upright, its wings slightly spread, on a tree-stump growing out of a rock.

Eagle figures are to be found at cornice level at various points on the Zwinger in Dresden, where they may be read as direct symbols for the Polish crown, in the arms of which the white eagle appears in two fields. The Zwinger was one of the buildings that Kaendler's teacher, Benjamin Thomae, had worked on. Eagle figures were also a feature of the interior decoration of the Green Vaults,[756] to which Kaendler also had access for his work, a fact which caused Otto Walcha to suggest in his account of Kaendler's appointment in Meissen that the artist had come to the notice of Augustus the Strong while working on precisely these eagles: "Kaendler's interpretation of heraldic beasts showed so much elegance and vitality that the king could not desire a better artist for the design of his monumental porcelain."[757] This, however, cannot be proved.

There is no doubt that in his choice of a posture for his first model for a porcelain animal figure, Kaendler was influenced by the heraldically styled eagles to be found on the princely buildings – frontal pose with head to the side, wings spread, and legs turned slightly outwards. But the artist cannot be charged – as he sometimes has been – with having simply executed an heraldic eagle in porcelain: "The eagle figure presented Kaendler with something of a problem, as he could not model it in the naturalistic manner that he applied to his other birds. Eagles were not part of natural history, but were still shrouded in an ancient metaphysical notion that saw them as a supernatural being symbolizing the power of the state. [...] A naturalistically executed eagle figure would not have been monumental in character, and yet this was precisely what it had to be if its real significance was to be expressed."[758]

These suppositions are purely speculative. As this was Kaendler's first model, it can hardly be claimed that the artist was in this instance unable to follow a naturalistic line on the grounds that a naturalistically executed eagle would not have done justice to the special position occupied by the eagle in the hierarchy of the animal world as seen by the human mind. At this stage, as is clear from his earliest work at Meissen, Kaendler still had to become familiar with a new material and a new subject: he would still take a while to develop his undisputed genius as a modeler of porcelain animals. However, Albiker was quite right to assert that such a symbolically loaded motif as the eagle had a certain "bias."

The bird is standing on two tree-stumps emerging from one trunk, its left leg on the somewhat higher of the two, and its right

162 Johann Joachim Kaendler, Eagle looking to its left, model 1731, Dresden Porcelain Collection

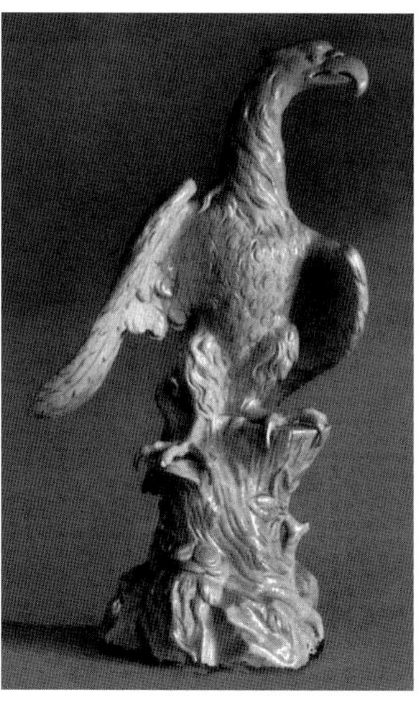

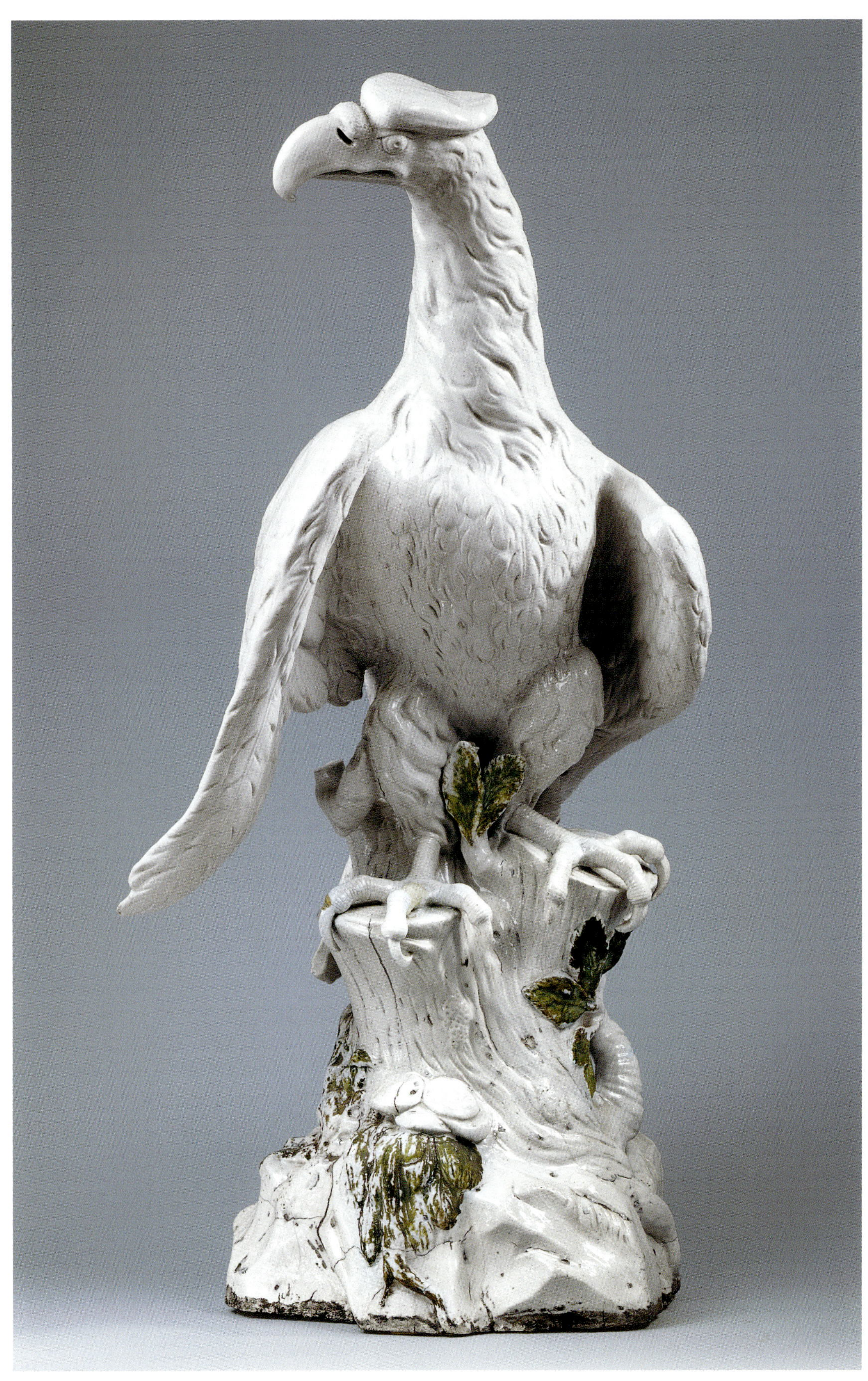

163 Johann Joachim Kaendler, Eagle looking to its right, model 1731, Dresden Porcelain Collection

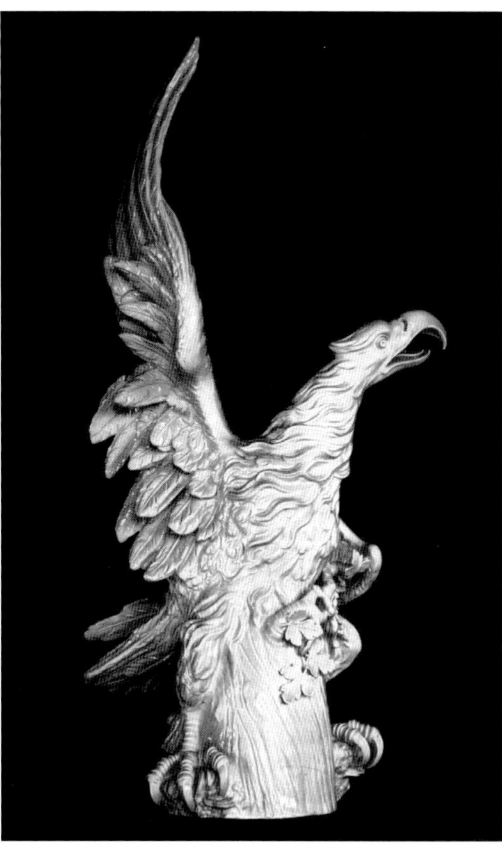

164 Johann Joachim Kaendler, Eagle beating one wing, model 1732, modern realization from the early twentieth century, Meissen, present whereabouts unknown

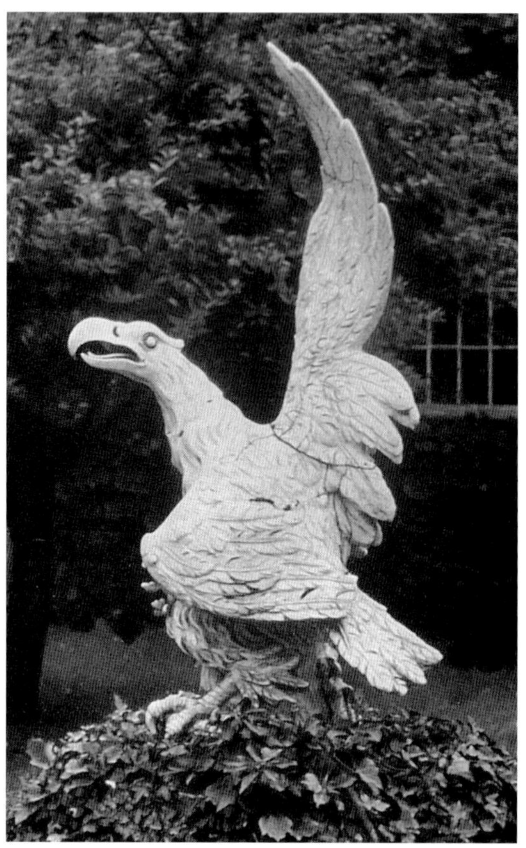

165 Johann Joachim Kaendler, Eagle beating one wing, model 1732, modern realization from the early twentieth century, Meissen, present whereabouts unknown

leg on the lower one, resulting in a slight contrapposto.[759] Its right wing is somewhat more spread than the left wing. In Kaendler's original model [i.e. fig. 162], the fact that the bird is looking to its left is calculated to underline the overall dynamic of the composition, which from the beholder's point of view goes from bottom left to top right. When the head is turned in the direction Kaendler intended (i.e., to its left), then the left leg (placed higher and braced for lift-off) and the right wing (raised somewhat more than the left wing) make it clear that the eagle is on the point of spreading its wings and taking to the air. The eagle is not done frontally to emphasize the open breast, as is the case in the heraldic depictions, but is rather the consequence of the eagle's preparing for lift-off. Comparison with the heraldic eagle modeled in roughly the same size by Kaendler in 1747 (illustrated in Albiker) clearly shows the difference between the traditional symbolic version and this figure; the 1731 eagle betrays no concern to display any attributes, which would in any case have been a difficult proposition given the posture in which the bird is depicted.

Kaendler's particular way of handling this so richly symbolic bird is even more evident in his second eagle model, executed one year later in October 1732. 135 cm high in the fired state, it was the tallest of all the animal figures (figs. 164 and 165), with the eagle's fully spread right wing thrusting high into the air. This explains why the model was never successfully fired in the eighteenth century, and why Kaendler's second eagle never figured among the deliveries to the Japanese Palace. In 1921, however, Karl Hubert Stein modeled and molded the figure anew, and one example came safe and sound through the firing. After being exhibited in the manufactory's display hall, the porcelain figure then stood in the inner courtyard, where it was photographed in the post-war period by Helmut Gröger.[760] The figure's whereabouts is now unknown, but the photographs published by Albiker and Gröger make it possible to compare this figure with Kaendler's first eagle.

At first sight it would seem as the second eagle was simply a variant of the first, depicted as it would have been a moment or two later: the right wing is now raised on high, the feathers spread out, the legs, neck and head stretched out and ready for flight. The oblique dynamic axis of Kaendler's first composition (eagle looking to its left) is now expanded into a similarly asymmetrical figure with an even greater measure of dynamism and energy. Because of their different dynamics, the bird and the tree-stump come across as being quite independent of each other. That they are combined at all seems to be a mere technicality.

The posture is spectacular in many respects. The figure has been invested with such a degree of suspense – in both senses of the word – that it seems to depict the very last moment at which the bird can still keep its balance. In a technical sense this was also literally true: only if such a daringly modeled wing as this is relatively free from irregularity and unevenness does it have any chance of surviving the critical initial stage of the firing when the paste softens.

The eagle's momentum is given powerful expression by the execution of the plumage. The flame-like strands of feathers along the neck seem to be fluttering in the wind. The powerful air currents caused by the vehement upward motion of the wings has put the lower wing into a disorderly ruffle. Because almost every feather is rendered individually, and some individually sculpted, and even the internal structure is executed in sharp relief, the consequent strong contrast of light and shade promote the impression of vigorous upward movement. This eagle's posture (wildly dissonant and crying out for resolution, one might say) and lively temperament (extravagantly expressed in the mass of restless detail) put it worlds away from the eagles of traditional heraldic devices. This, however, did not prevent Kaendler from describing it as follows in his work report: "...a large eagle spreading its right wing high into the air, at the same representing the graciousness of a great and noble lord."[761]

It is in general wrong to put too fine an interpretation on the texts in Kaendler's work reports, but in this case the work report makes his intentions quite clear. The figure was to be two things at once: on the one hand the depiction of a particular bird species, and on the other hand a symbol of sovereignty. It lay however in the nature of the beast that he could not proceed as Kirchner had done with the lion and compensate for changing the traditional heraldic pose with an anthropomorphizing physiognomy. As Kaendler had to achieve his goal through the use of appropriate posture, he took the opposite path. Taking as his point of departure his first eagle, which in spite of certain innovative elements was in purely formal terms still quite close to the general scheme of the symbolic eagle, he proceeded to give absolute priority to emphasizing the animal itself, at the expense of the symbol.

The qualities that man believed he saw in the eagle, and which were what made the eagle a suitable symbol of sovereignty, are here expressed in forms. The powerful virtuosity of the outstretched beating wing combines with the apparently endless variety of small feathers to give a highly impressive and unified overall picture; equally enthralling is the extreme physical exertion of an animal at the very limit of its ability to power to keep balance. Finally, the figure displays a fascinating range of contrasting surfaces from the linear structures of the tree-stump through the ruffled wing plumage to the fluttering strands of plumage on the neck, a dramatic gradation of external forms which is intended to captivate the eye and, ideally, to transport the beholder into an exalted state of admiration and excitement. When confronted with such a superabundance of information and impressions, even the beholder who is not aware of the symbolic significance of the eagle will take the unbridled vigor of the sculpture as indicative of the character that is to be attributed to the bird. Nor will even an unknowing eye fail to remark that the right-hand side of the bird's body is stretched to the full, creating the largest possible span between right claw to right wing-tip, and that when this extreme level of tension, which in a certain sense defines the eagle's spatial territory, is resolved, the bird will quite inevitably take to the air. The effect of the bird's forward-straining eyes and prophetically beating wing is to extend the "is-space" defined by the eagle's wings, tail, talons and neck into a "will-be-space" (a "virtual" space) that it has not yet reached but to which it is reaching out to claim. For – to make what seems to me to be a very important point – if one were only interested in the narrative aspect of the sculpture, then the eagle could be on the point of folding its wings and settling onto the tree-stump. This does not negate the interpretation proposed thus far: if the eagle's extremely extraverted gesture can be seen as leading one way or the other, then the beholder is figuratively speaking compelled to wait for the next moment, or – as the next moment will never come – to accept the eagle's Janus-like position, with all its possibilities, as a definitive part of its character. The eagle's pose is thus a statement about the scope of its power, and not a narrative indication of what it is going to do next.

Whether the beholder takes all this as referring to the eagle as a species of bird, or follows Kaendler's cue and sees the eagle's omnipotence as a representation of the graciousness, that is to say the power, of a great and noble lord, is left entirely up to the beholder in question. The two "natures" – that of formal imitation and that of the work's symbolic significance – can only become one for the beholder through a process of emotional involvement. In this respect it is more important that the beholder should feel the eagle's absolute hold in its own strength, on the space it is laying claim to, and on its present momentum – its poise – than that he or she should be familiar with *idées reçues* about the position attributed by man to the eagle in the animal world.

Although the ranges of pictorial possibilities inherent in these two traditional symbols of power are quite different, and only allow of a limited degree of comparison (it is for instance not possible to invest the eagle with a human facial expression), these examples do constitute a clear demonstration of the contrast between the conceptions followed by Kirchner and Kaendler respectively.

If we understand the term "image" ["Bild"] as the vehicle that bears the weight of symbolism inherent in these two animals, then Kirchner is seen to be a "sculptor of images" ["Bild-Hauender"] and Kaendler a "builder of images" ["Bild-Bauender"]. Figuratively speaking, Kirchner takes a lion and minimizes its appearance and details until all that is left are the elements which are necessary for his image of what the lion is to stand for. Every point of Kirchner's sculpture is an intellectual reference to the qualities of a human king; his lion is the result of a mental picture of kingship and all its inherent qualities. Kaendler's procedure, on the other hand, is an additive one: the way he composes brings out such individual elements as the large beak, the spreading wings, and the powerful talons, and such primary traits as strength and the proverbial "eagle eye," combining them with a superabundance of detail into an overall picture that is so impressive that one might be tempted to accuse him of exaggeration. The beholder who approaches the sculpture intellectually will always end up thinking about the species of the eagle, but the eye that sees the figure with an openness to its emotional impact will penetrate to the eagle's underlying symbolism. The "image" that Kaendler conjures up is one that is built up in and through the porcelain figure, which works both as a catalyst and as a source of inspiration. Kaendler's eagle evokes an image of the very essence of what it means to be a king.

The terms "sculpt" for Kirchner's from-without-to-within approach and "build" for Kaendler's from-within-to-without procedure are not merely metaphorical: they also reflect an important truth about their respective approaches to handling their medium, as Handt and Rackebrand suggest: "While Kaendler's bird and animal figures are unimaginable in any other medium than porcelain, most of Kirchner's animals could be executed just as successfully in clay or stone."[762] Although, as we shall see in a number of instances, it is indeed the case that Kaendler makes more than Kirchner does out of the fact that modeling is a "building" process, it would be unfair to Kirchner to suggest that the stylistic difference between the two artists resulted only from this factor. As the comparison of the lion and eagle figures shows, Kirchner's specific style does not result from lack of skill with porcelain or a deficient understanding of the medium, but from a different attitude to the motivic tradition. The extraordinary degree to which Kirchner gives his lion human traits makes his figure a positive *pièce de résistance* of the Baroque, an almost exaggerated demonstration of how one single work can be invested with a multiplicity and variety of levels of meaning. Kirchner takes a number of essential features from the motivic and symbolic planes and brings them together in visual form. Kaendler, by contrast, puts greater trust in our sensibility: he bombards us with densely compacted motivic components until the excess of visual impressions causes the inner eye to seek relief on the metaphysical plane of ideas and meaning. Taking a step or two beyond the bounds of naturalistic expression by the exaggerated depiction of individual components (talons, beak, and so forth) is a technique which we have already met in our considerations of the fundamental elements of the Rococo.

The highly naturalistic impression given by Kaendler's wing-beating eagle derives from a multiplicity of detail and its abundance of pulsating dynamic energy. From a purely motivic point of view, however, his figure is far from being an unqualifiedly strict imitation of a natural eagle, but what he does convey with incomparable vitality are the forces of nature that flow out of the finely graded mass of individually distinct feathers, through the flaming neck-plumage and up to the high thrust of the beating wing, a transforming flood ensuring that the principle – and not the detail – is foremost in the beholder's consciousness. This is not of course to suggest that Kaendler's Eagle is, stylistically, a work of the Rococo. However, what this particular work does show is that at this threshold stage Kaendler was an active contributor to the slow process by which eighteenth-century man arrived at a new understanding of the place of nature in art.

Anthropomorphic tendencies: the Fox and the Jerboa

Comparison of the very loaded lion and eagle figures – loaded because these motifs were traditionally used as symbols of power – led to consideration of the extent to which they are anthropomorphic. Most authors have regarded Kirchner's tendency towards non-naturalistic depiction as a shortcoming, quoting as evidence animal figures that most obviously incorporate human features, such as the Lion and the Lioness (figs. 159 and 160) and the Elephant (fig. 125). As a consequence, authors have commonly divided up Kirchner's work into various categories, reckoning the group of figures considered to be most naturalistic, such as the Bear (fig. 203), to have been executed under the influence of Kaendler.[763]

Although Albiker is one of the few writers to have seen positive qualities in Kirchner's figures, the only explanation he could come up with for the various human features in the Lioness and the Fox was that Kaendler must have remodeled the heads of these animals after Kirchner had left the manufactory.[764] As has already been pointed out, this can be ruled out, both for technical and for artistic reasons.

Light can however be shed on the question of "various workgroups" in Kirchner's oeuvre by going more deeply into the general matter of anthropomorphism, as we shall now see in an examination of Kirchner's figure of a fox carrying a chicken in its jaws. This figure is to be compared with Kaendler's figure of a jerboa on a corn-sack. Both figures are life-size, and – most importantly for our investigation – both are presented as thieves, stealing something from man.

Kirchner's Fox

In October 1732, Johann Gottlieb Kirchner modeled "a fox, devouring a chicken, life-size" (fig. 166)[765], crouching on an oval pedestal only just big enough to accommodate it. In its mouth it is holding a dead chicken; Kirchner cleverly modeled the bird's wings hanging down onto the pedestal so as to give the fox's head the support it would need for the firing. The animal is given further support by a tree stump hardly visible under its belly. The surface of the figure is boldly sculpted, with the fox's coat and the chicken's plumage

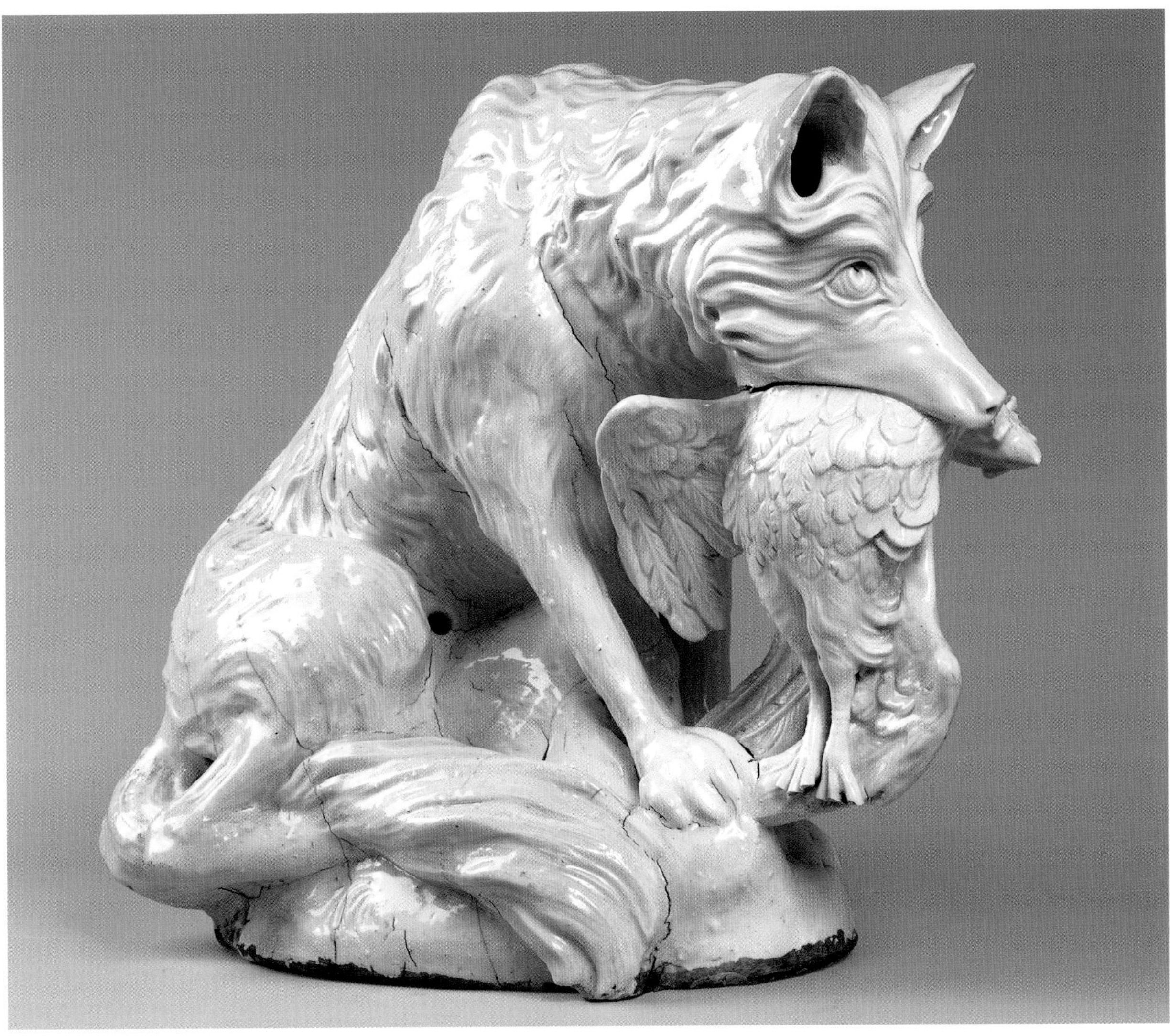

166 Johann Gottlieb Kirchner, Fox with chicken, model 1732, Dresden Porcelain Collection

rendered in flowing waves and finely-drawn scale-like feathers respectively.

As with Kirchner's Lion, the most important compositional line in the Fox is its outline. When seen from the front, it runs from the tip of the fox's tail via a number of initial short curves over one hind leg and the back to the base of the neck, towards which the stiffly-stretched front legs are also aligned. The fox's head and the hanging chicken take the line full circle and back to its point of departure, giving the figure a markedly static character. The fox is at rest – it has apparently been sitting in this position for a while already and does not seem to be on the point of changing its posture.

The head is lowered, but the eyes are raised – the fox is clearly looking at someone, and that someone is looking at the fox. Neither on the look-out nor lost in thought, its attentively focused look is highlighted by sharply pricked ears. When we consider its look in the light of what it has just done, namely killed and stolen a chicken, it also begins to look distinctly shamefaced.

This is the crux of the story the figure is telling. With its still posture and alert but obedient look, the fox is behaving like a trained dog that knows that it has done something forbidden. That it has pulled in its tail suggests its abashment as it waits for a reaction from its unseen counterpart. Kirchner has endowed his fox with a degree of awareness that – as a wild animal – it cannot have. Its crouch is not the tensed posture of a real fox thrown onto the *qui vive* by an impending danger (threats from the chicken's owner, for instance): Kirchner's fox comes across as a sulky creature that would drop the chicken at once if it were challenged to do so.

Kirchner has not carried out his anthropomorphization by giving the fox a tendentially human physiognomy, but rather by depicting it as man traditionally likes to see it: as a shamefaced but shameless thief. The character inherent in the figure corresponds to the human character-type generally attributed to the fox by man and reaffirmed time and time again in phrase and fable.

Kaendler's Jerboa

In April 1735, Johann Joachim Kaendler modeled, from a bozzetto he had made from a live specimen in the fall of 1734, "an Indian rat, as can be seen alive in the Royal Lion-House, modeled with the pedestal done as a corn-sack open at the top, with the rat eating from it," (fig. 167).[766] Like Kirchner's fox, Kaendler's jerboa is in the act of thieving and is looking someone in the eye.

However, the figures have as many significant differences as similarities. There is a distinct sense of instability as the jerboa leans so far over its booty that the sack leans alarmingly far forward of its center of gravity. The whole volume of its body is held up by two spindly legs and is almost as big as the sack itself. It is using its tail as if it was a balancing-pole; coiled between its hind legs and over its back, the long thin wavy tail is an indicator of the precariousness of the mouse's balance and conveys to the beholder a strong sense of the scene's momentariness.

167 Johann Joachim Kaendler, Jerboa on a corn-sack, model 1735, Dresden Porcelain Collection

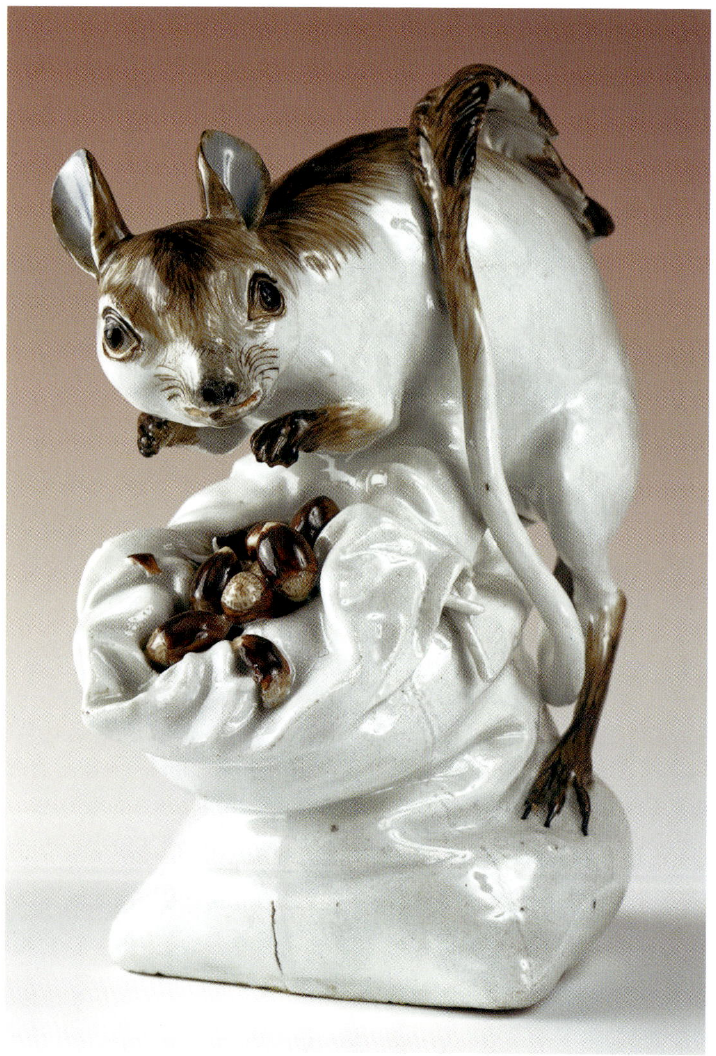

The mouse has looked up from the sack, but it is not looking up. It does not seem to be thinking about what it is doing; it has rather simply been disturbed. Its outline, running from the hind legs over its back to the head, suggests rather that it is simply keeping its head down than experiencing any sense of shame. In combination with the impression given by the tail, the overall effect is one of a tension which will probably be resolved by the mouse disappearing in the twinkling of an eye.

These two heraldically neutral figures show the two modelers' different approaches clearly, just as the lion and eagle figures did. Kirchner's animal sculptures are projections of interpretations; he refuses to be satisfied with giving a characteristic, or even scientifically faithful, depiction of the animal in hand. The animal's possible symbolic significance and the question as to what it might be thinking or feeling lead to the animal having human traits imposed on it, which it its turn results in Kirchner's figures being strangely stiff and inert. Posture and activity are not really determined by the nature of the animal itself, which leads to a gaping discrepancy between the figures' external form and the mood they convey. This approach can be well understood in the context of the Baroque tradition of animal sculpture, according to which an animal could only be depicted or only had to be depicted if there was some kind of higher meaning to be conveyed. An animal had to have something to point to, or a message to convey. If it simply pointed to itself – a Lion that was nothing other than the likeness of a lion – then it did not qualify as art. Animals had at least to embody virtues – the horse standing for elegance, or the bear for strength, for instance – or had to relate to the kind of literary or cultural traditions we have already considered. As Kaendler's work report on his first eagle figure attests, he too sometimes intended to bring out symbolic associations. However, his approach to depicting animals differed from Kirchner's in that he did not project meanings onto his animals, but strove for a depiction that was positively saturated with a range of the respective animal's actual characteristics. For any one model he would aim to forge a whole from characteristic external details, postures, patterns of behavior, and elements from the animal's natural habitat, using discreet hyperbole to underline the most important elements. He conveyed an animal's characteristic movements by making some parts of his composition more highly charged than others. He made sure to depict his animals in situations that corresponded to their behavior. And he would understate or bring out details in accordance with their importance of the motif in question.

We have seen that for his first pieces of work, which followed each other in rapid succession from the point of his engagement at the manufactory onwards, Kaendler worked from zoological depictions submitted for the modelers by the king. Accordingly, the

Gull, the Great Crested Grebe, the Osprey, and the Kestrel were all modeled according to a similarly stiff and static concept, immobile on pedestals decorated (see the Gull) with references to their natural habitats. The figure of an owl with a mouse in its talons (fig. 145) was a common topos in the zoological illustrations of the time, the mouse being an indication that the owl was a bird of prey.[767]

Yet as early as the Wisent, and quite definitely in the case of the Heron that constitutes the first high point of his artistry as a modeler for porcelain, Kaendler was modeling from life. Having begun by working from zoological illustrations – depictions made to help in the identification of animals which thus embodied a more objective perspective on animals than that inherent in the symbolically oriented artistic tradition of animal depiction – he then adopted a phenomenological approach, which he automatically applied to all his models thereafter.

In his research into the Meissen porcelain animal figures, Carl Albiker proceeded on the assumption that all artistically autonomous animal depiction – the natural bronze casts made by the Mannerists, for instance, and then symbolism-free zoological illustration, which he unqualifiedly categorized as art – was a central catalyst for scientific progress: "It was the visual arts, and above all painting, that paved the way for science. The proof of this is to be seen in the progress made in science in the eighteenth and nineteenth centuries. The work of all the animal-depicting artists, however important they were for the times in which they lived, and however important we can now see them to have been for the development of art, was essentially nothing other than preliminary work done in a spirit of self-sacrifice for a higher goal, namely the paving of the way for scientific progress."[768] While natural science clearly was, as has been noted, an integral ingredient in the creation of the Meissen large animal figures, the above analyses seem to me to show that for this group of works the case was quite the reverse of the process proposed by Albiker. The more objective perspective on natural phenomena and the increased interest in investigating and explaining them brought about a change in the way eighteenth-century man saw the world, and this made itself felt in the field of artistic creativity just as markedly as in other fields, and indeed even more markedly and more tangibly because the creation of an art work is ultimately a processing, a re-casting, of reality.

The symbiosis between art and natural science in the time of the large animal figures is demonstrated particularly strikingly by Kaendler's work, which shows the artist evolving a more "modern" perspective on the animal world than the one adopted by Kirchner (which should not, as Albiker rightly stressed, mislead us into writing Kirchner off as a bad sculptor).[769] But the objective viewpoint which Kaendler used as a foundation for building up his particular tensions and creating his specific visual effects make his animal figures more universal than Kirchner's, and more adept at transcending the time and place of their creation.[770]

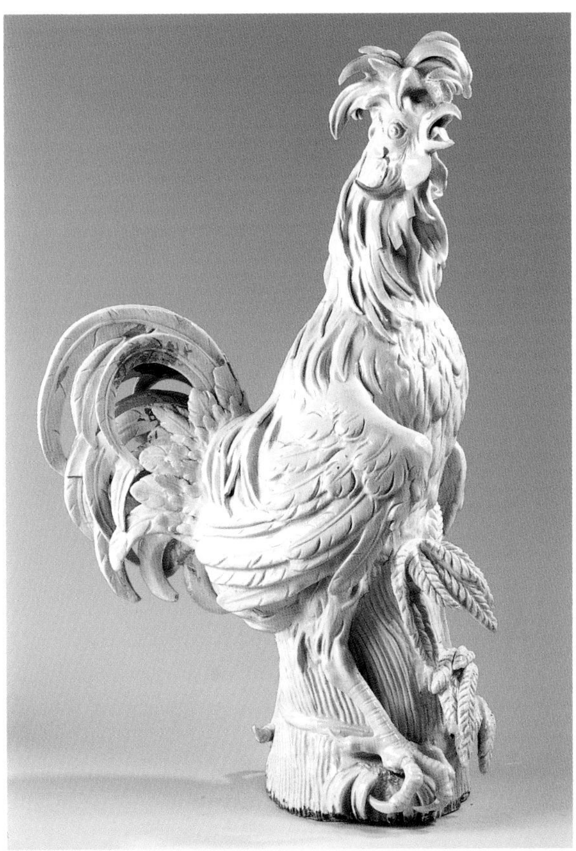

168 Johann Joachim Kaendler, Cockerel, model 1732, Dresden Porcelain Collection

Before continuing our investigation of Kaendler's art, we shall now turn our attention to a number of further works with a view to highlighting further aspects of the animal figures themselves. Each section will focus on two or three figures in order to shed light on one aspect of plastic artistry.

Kaendler's large animal figures: individual analyses

The figure in relation to the space it stands in, with reference to single-viewpoint and multi-viewpoint figures: the "Paduan" Cockerel and the Dog scratching itself

Cockerel

In August 1732, Johann Joachim Kaendler modeled "a cockerel, life-size" (fig. 168).[771] The bird is standing with its legs apart over a bound sheaf of corn; stretching its head far into the air with its beak wide open, it is clearly crowing.

The lower section that provides the cockerel with the support it needs is marked all around with close vertical serrations and is girded with a narrow band. Underneath the cockerel's breast, the evenness of the serrations is broken by a number of ears of corn: the pedestal is clearly a sheaf.

When the bird is looked at from the side, its plumage is divided up into differently structured areas. A disorderly bunch of feathers, "planted" on the cockerel's head, fans out in all directions. Similar narrow feathers surround the neck, but now all parallel and covering the bird's back in three lots. On the bird's sides, below these cascades of plumage, broader feathers with multiple splits in the vanes combine to form its wings. These lead in a broad curve to the contrary motion of the long, sickle-shaped tail feathers, which spurt out of an opening formed by a ring of smaller feathers. The figure is thus made all the more emphatically three-dimensional by a suggestive use of lines and outlines in a number of different areas.

Only a few points of the figure thrust out into space: the cockscomb on the bird's head, the ears of corn, and the flat, sickle-shaped tail feathers. These areas contrast with the compact round form of the bird's body, and at the same time accentuate three of the bird's most significant aspects: the exuberantly arched wad of tail feathers show that the bird is a cockerel, the ears of corn bursting out of the sheaf show that it is a domestic cockerel, and the crown of feathers standing in for the comb tell us what it is doing, namely crowing for all its might as only a cockerel can. As these three points are the only ones at which we can see through the figure, they also accentuate the plastic character of the figure, not consisting merely of modeled surface but of an abundance of eye-catching overlaps, overhangs and other fully three-dimensional sculptural elements. Furthermore, as the ears of corn, the head feathers and tail feathers are all bunches, they stand out effectively from the orderly flow or serrated linearity of the rest of the figure. The clear contour running around the pedestal is thereby exploded by powerfully directional "vectors" that make the figure as a whole all the more spatially expansive.

All the signals sent out to the beholder by the figure can be picked up from a viewing-point slightly to the side of head-on. This is also the point of view from which the three explosive areas are seen at their most sculpturally effective, and from which the relatively massive body of the cockerel, animated only by the bas-relief plumage, is at its least bulky. Although the figure is done in the round, with an equal degree of detail on all sides, this is its best viewing angle: seen from this point of view, it has the most to say for itself, both artistically (greatest possible expansiveness in all directions in space, balance of masses, and the like) and also from the point of view of "content" (execution of detail, posture, what the cockerel is doing, and so forth). The figure is thus ideally suited to stand on a wall-console and was almost certainly intended for display on some such fitting in the Japanese Palace. In its interaction with the space in which it stands, it has a great deal in common with such features of the Baroque sculptural tradition as niche figures or figures intended to stand against specific backgrounds: statues of saints in churches, for instance, or sculptures designed to adorn topiary walls. We do not know what works Kaendler executed when he was apprenticed to Thomae, but they certainly will have included a goodly number of sculptures for buildings and interiors in Dresden. When figures are firmly anchored to a certain place within a well-defined larger context, it is for obvious reasons almost always the case that they are best seen from one particular side.[772]

In the Baroque, there was an opposite number to the figure with a best viewing side, namely the figure that could in principle be seen from all sides and incorporated a turning movement directed out into the space around it. This compositional form for free-standing sculptures depicting movement required for its perfection "a good turning of the limbs, and movement in the head, the arms, hands and feet."[773] Figures designed according to this principle demand that the viewer walk around them, physically traversing their greater – or "coextensive" – space. Every point of view affords the beholder new insights into the subject matter, with the result that only the circumambient eye appreciates the work fully, at the same time making the free-standing figure into a truly – in both senses of the word – "moving" work of art.

Certain factors inherent in the great gallery of the Japanese Palace meant that it was not possible to display figures of this kind in the proper way. This was certainly something that the Meissen modelers were fully aware of, with the result that most of the figures are executed in such a way as to have one, more or less wide, best viewing angle. There is on the other hand also a relatively small group of animal figures which gain from being displayed in the round. While the circumambient eye does not see very much more in the basic subject matter of the Wisent Fighting with a Boar (fig. 116) or the Two Dogs Fighting (fig. 144), the stories the figures tell are bound to become more dramatic if the beholder is on the move and thus constantly gaining new insights into the work. It is a requirement of a figure depicting a fight that the beholder should be able to see how the two protagonists are pitted against one another at the given moment, and this is only possible if the viewing eye sees them on the move. This explains why the particularly emotive fighting motif is among those subjects that are particularly often executed in accord with the principle that the beholder should view the work when following a path right round the figure. The following section is thus devoted to the investigation of just such a figure in precisely this light.

Dog scratching itself

In September 1732, Kaendler modeled "a dog, lying"[774] (figs. 169 and 170). The subject of a dog scratching its throat with one hind paw had already been treated more than two hundred years before by Peter Vischer the Elder, in a bronze figure about 6 cm high (fig. 171).[775] Kaendler did not however take his cue from Vischer's dog, which is sitting, but chose rather to have his dog lying down, the effect of which, first and foremost, is to emphasize the horizontal plane. The dog is lying on its right flank, in such a curved posture as to be able to scratch its throat with its left hind-paw. Folds in the skin indicate the point where the paw is scratching.

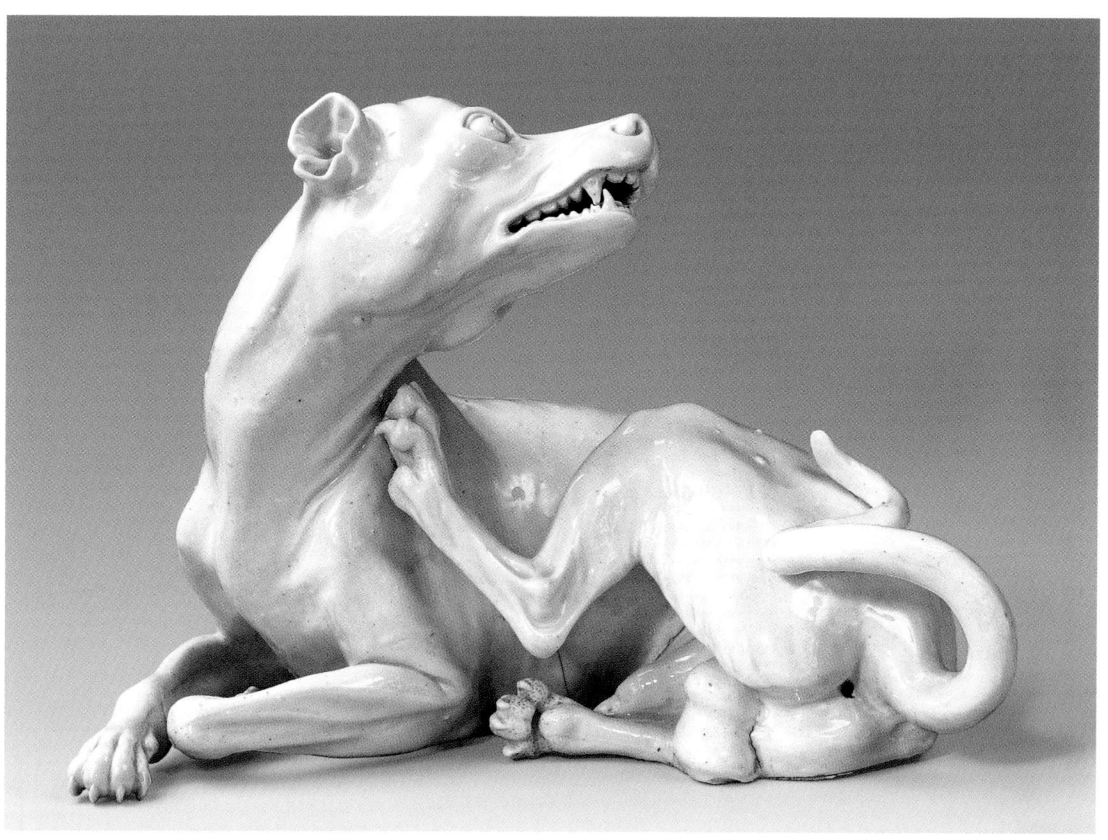

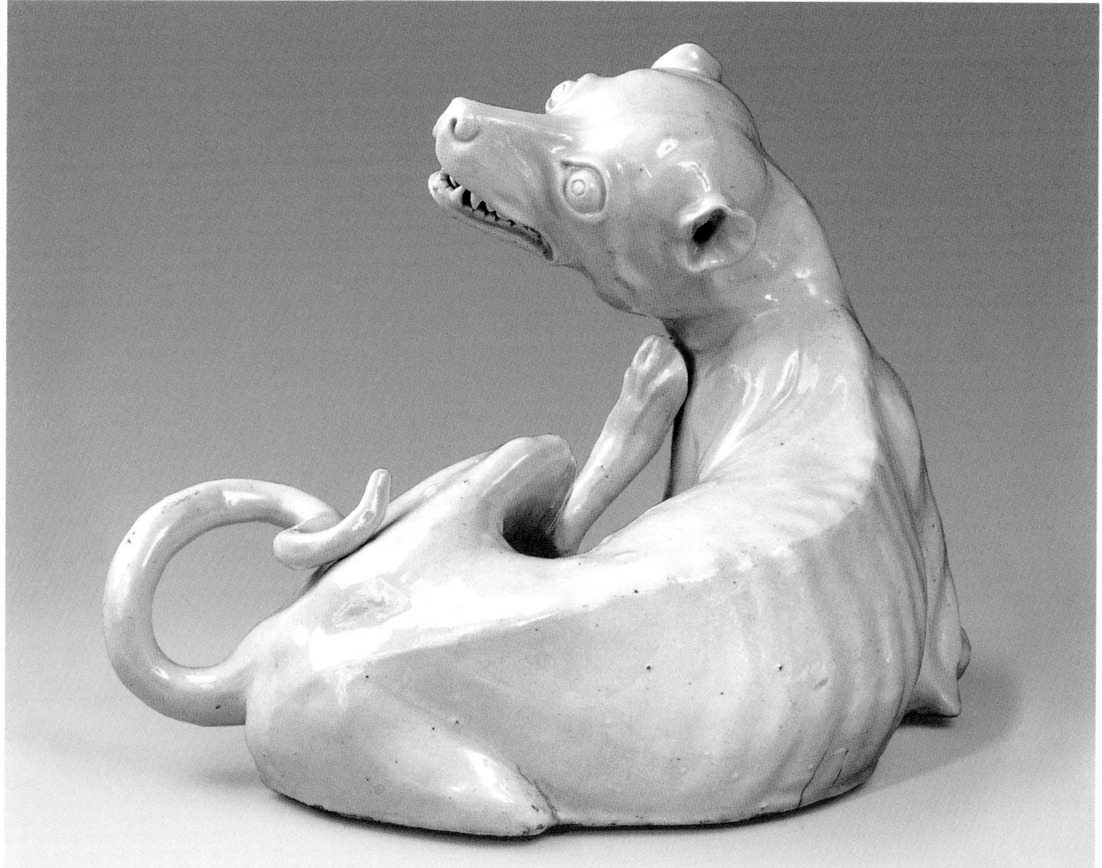

169 Johann Joachim Kaendler, Dog scratching itself, front view, model 1732, Dresden Porcelain Collection

170 Johann Joachim Kaendler, Dog scratching itself, view from behind, model 1732, Dresden Porcelain Collection

The dog's head is turned backwards and the muzzle slightly opened.

If the figure is looked at from at the angle from which it would seem to afford the most information, that is to say at a right angle to the leg that is doing the scratching, the viewer cannot but notice one particularly dominant compositional line. Beginning at the front legs, it follows a large fold in the skin to the scratching paw and then makes a sharp zig-zag along the hind leg before arriving at the base of the tail. This line is based on the right foreleg and the left hind leg. Once the eye has taken in the sense of space engendered by a variety of vectors, its attention is next drawn to the vigorously spiraling tail, which according to the angle is seen as a curl or number of curls allowing one to see through to beyond the animal's hindquarters. If one really wants to see the way the tail is held, then one has to move 90° to the right to look at the dog at an angle from which what had been a sharply zig-zag compositional axis is now a straight line; from the new standpoint it is the tail's turn to form a zig-zag, with round curves moving from left to right. Its tip leads the eye to the sharp ridge formed by the dog's spine and invites the viewer to take a further step to the right, in order to be able to see the whole of the dog's back and to have a full view of the dog from behind (fig. 171).

The vectors in the legs and the spiraling of the tail are now cancelled out but open up two gaps one can see through, which amplify the figure's overall volume. The spine forms a line leading in a purposeful spiral sweep from the base of the tail (bottom left) to the tip of the muzzle. Caught in the wake of this swirl, the viewer moves once again to the right to stand front on to the dog's right shoulder blade, from which point the animal, limbs and torso, is seen as one more or less closed and bulky mass. Finally, the turning movement of the head prompts a few further steps around the figure to give the eye a full view of its highest point, the muzzle, and to return the beholder to the original point of departure.

171 Most likely Peter Vischer the elder, Dog scratching itself, bronze, ca. 1500

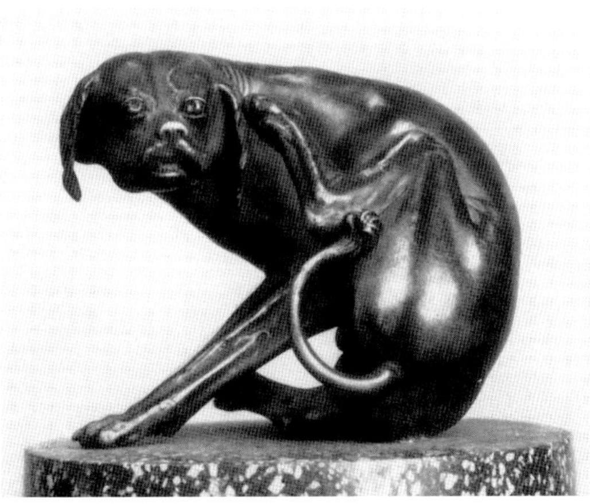

The path around the figure thus leads from the flat plane of the scratching leg via the serpentine movement of the tail to the upwardly spiraling sweep of the body. By imitating the turning movement of the whole figure, the coiling tail acts as a kind of route-plan for the eye that is seeking to comprehend the figure in its fullness. It gathers up the multiplicity of different vectors in the legs and channels them into the more composed and concentrated bulk of the dog's upward-turning body.

The more closed the figure appears to its circumambient beholder, the more the beholder can see of the muscular tension that underlies the dog's turning movement. On the legs side the eye is torn hither and thither by the restless variety and multiplicity of vectors, overlaps, and gaps, but when the eye comes round to the back and the composition settles down and becomes more restful it is also given a more detailed view of the surface relief. The prominent vertebrae and ribs lead on to neck muscles that are so tensed that they cause a slight opening of the dog's muzzle. While it is at first an effort to see order in the variety of visual impressions and combinations, we are gradually relieved of the task by the increasingly visible physical exertion demanded of the dog. And this process is carried through best if we follow the energy lines of the figure by walking around it as described. If we look at the figure from what we might imagine to be its best viewing side, then we only see the beginning and end of a development are thus miss out on an essential part of the figure's inner logic.

Detail and surface between instrumentalization and ornamentalization: the Cassowary, the Bittern, the Turkeycock, and the Billy-Goat

No description of the large-size animal figures would be complete without reference to their fascinating wealth of surface detail. The sources do not give any indication as to whether, or to what extent, Kaendler took account of the shine that his models would have when executed in porcelain, that is to say whether he consciously pursued a different concept from the one he would have applied to carved figures. This question is to be considered in the light of the following analyses, which examine certain aspects of Kaendler's particular way of executing his surfaces.

Cassowary

In September 1732, Kaendler modeled "the bird known as the cassowary, life-size" (fig. 172).[776] At 129 cm high, it is the largest of the animal figures preserved from the eighteenth century. The bird is standing with a powerful pair of legs astride a tree-stump overgrown with leaves and small branches. Its body is covered with long, narrow feathers, rendered in a wavy flowing relief. This lively vertical structure is interrupted on each side by a small horizontal wing. The surface of the long extended neck is covered in small boil-like lumps, true-to-life as the cassowary's neck is in reality knotty and unfeathered; down the front of the neck hangs a long loose drop-shaped wattle of skin. The small bald head with its

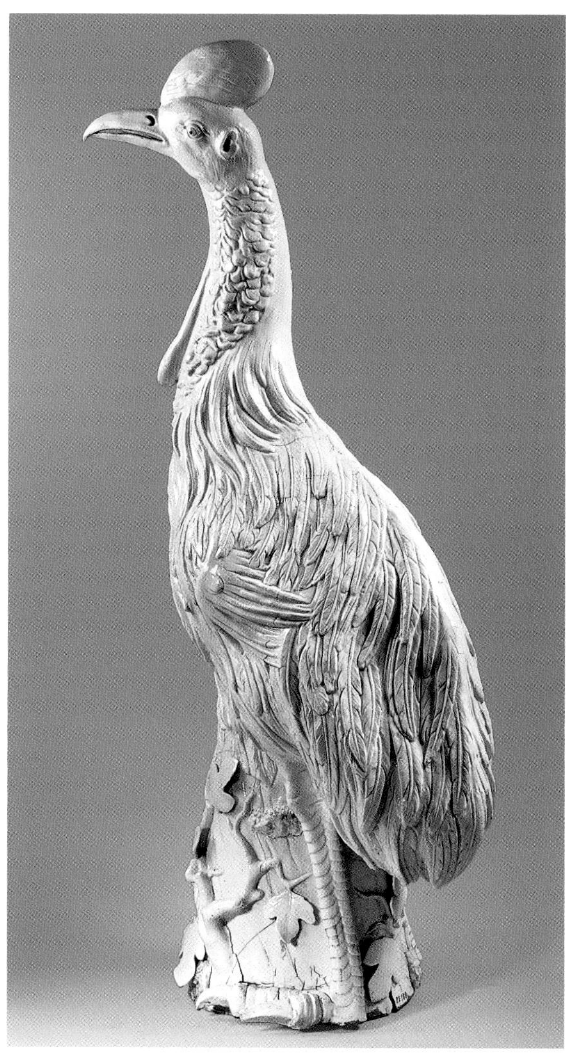

172 Johann Joachim Kaendler, Cassowary, model 1732, Dresden Porcelain Collection

diminutive eyes and sharp beak is crowned with the flat helmet-like disk from which the bird receives its German name "Helmkasuar" ("helmet cassowary").

Kaendler uses a variety of sculptural techniques to bring out the differences between all these physical features, which in reality are distinguished by their various colors.[777] He took the structures from nature, but not their degree of elaboration.

Casting one's eye over this compact closed-form figure from top to bottom, one notices a general increase in the plasticity of the surface. Starting with the smooth, crested head, the surface becomes somewhat less even at the neck before acquiring a lively structure in the plumage, which is furthermore given greater texture and depth by the suggestion of overlapping feathers. And applied to the tree-stump, finally, are numerous decorative elements, some of which are fully sculpted. As it moves down the figure, the eye consequently notes a constant increase in the play between light and shade, the play being at its most lively at the base, that is to say at the point which carries the greatest weight, both optically and in physical fact. Likewise, the movement from closed to more open form also relieves the figure of a certain degree of weightiness, although these surface effects are in themselves not enough to hide the voluminous monumentality of this particular figure. This example does however show how Kaendler used the contrast between highly-worked and less highly-worked structures to guide the eye of the beholder and to create a certain overall effect. Although Kirchner modeled his Bustard at the same time as Kaendler was working on his Cassowary and was certainly influenced by Kaendler's figure, there is a striking difference between the skillfully differentiated surfaces of the Cassowary and the repetitive structures of the Bustard (fig. 173).

Bittern

Kaendler made the following entry in his work report for March 1735: "For the Palace, the bird known as the bittern which is the same size as a heron and on account of its thickly feathered breast and other features is wondrous to behold, done sitting in such

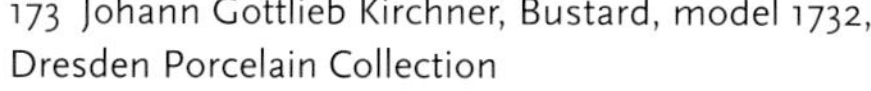

173 Johann Gottlieb Kirchner, Bustard, model 1732, Dresden Porcelain Collection

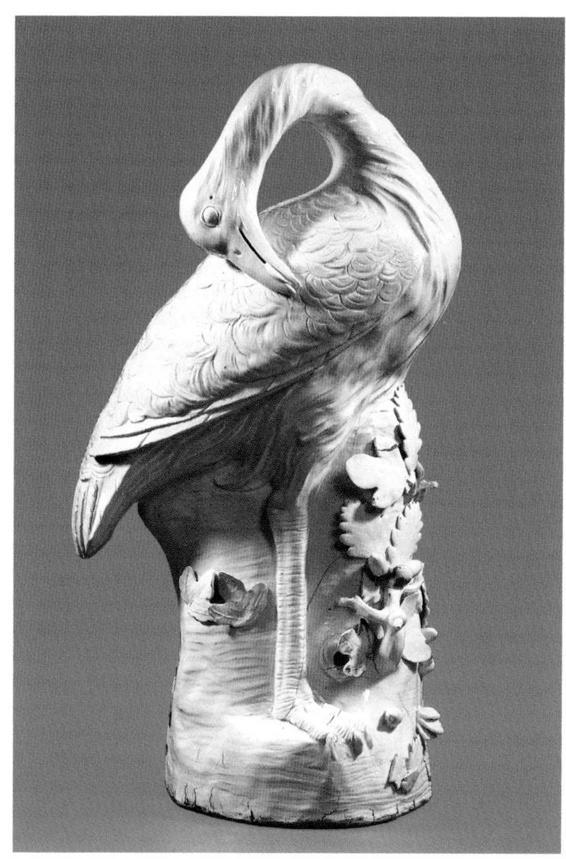

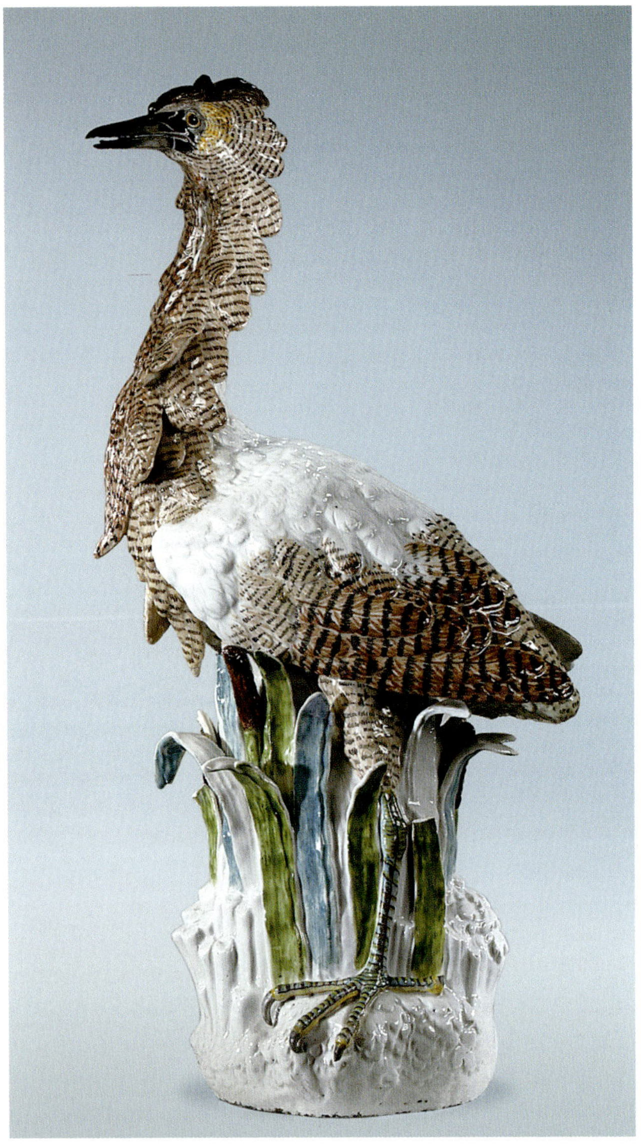

174 Johann Joachim Kaendler, Bittern, model 1735, Rijksmuseum Amsterdam

reeds, rushes and grass as are wont to grow in ponds" (fig. 174).[778] The importance that Kaendler attached to the bittern's features is clear from this description, and he used a correspondingly wide variety of techniques for the model's various surfaces.

The simple oval base is covered with a low relief consisting of overlapping scale-like trefoils. Kaendler would certainly have come across this motif for depicting waterweed in the context of his earlier work, on the edge of the bassin of the Nymphenbad fountain in the Zwinger, for instance. A thick bunch of broad flat rushes rises from the waterweed; at the back and front of the base there are two clumps of reeds cut back low down. The bulk of the bird's body sits horizontally over the vertical rushes, its wings closed with the feathers in bas-relief. The bird's long neck is modeled with distinct feathers, ruffled up and fanned out wide, leading up to a small head with a long sharp beak. All these surface structures accord in their form with the features of a real bittern, but the degree of plasticity and sharpness of line with which they are executed were determined by the artist himself.

Kaendler also makes use of an element from the bittern's natural habitat to conceal a technical necessity: he encircles the structure supporting the bird with lifelike rushes, which at the same time creates a parallel between the surface structuring of the pedestal and the bird itself. Looked at in isolation, the pedestal consists of a somewhat massive bas-relief foundation supporting a little stage-set of rushes; the latter are staggered at the bottom like flats so as to give an impression of depth and volume, but gain in plasticity as they leave the foundation behind them, growing tips that are finally quite distinct and free-standing. This progression from a dense bulk representing a mass of waterweed to an exact number of "liberated" free-standing rush-tips is repeated in the organization of the bird's plumage in the transition from body to neck. It is a sculptural realization of the development from from drawing to modeling, from sign to genuine likeness.

This sculptural parallelism means that there is a particularly close relationship between the pedestal and the bird itself. Before we see how this relates to a narrative element latent in the figure, we shall at this point investigate the artistic means the modeler used to forge a satisfying link between a foundation conditioned by technical factors and the actual figure resting upon it.

Most of the porcelain quadrupeds are lying down, some are sitting, and only three – the unicorn, elephant, and wisent – are

175 Johann Joachim Kaendler, Pair of small bitterns, model 1750, Rijksmuseum Amsterdam

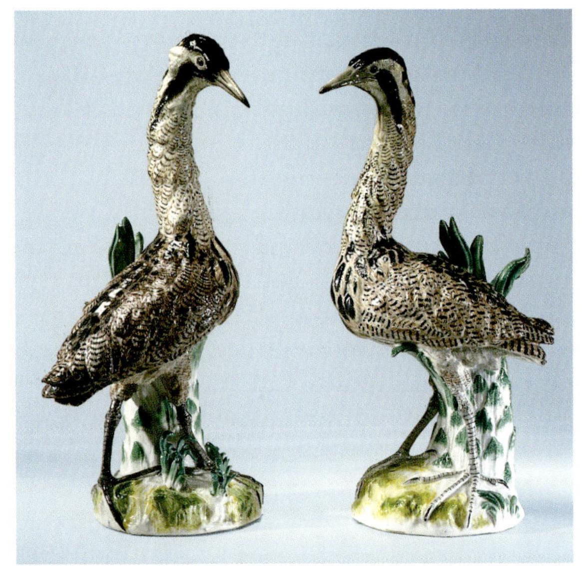

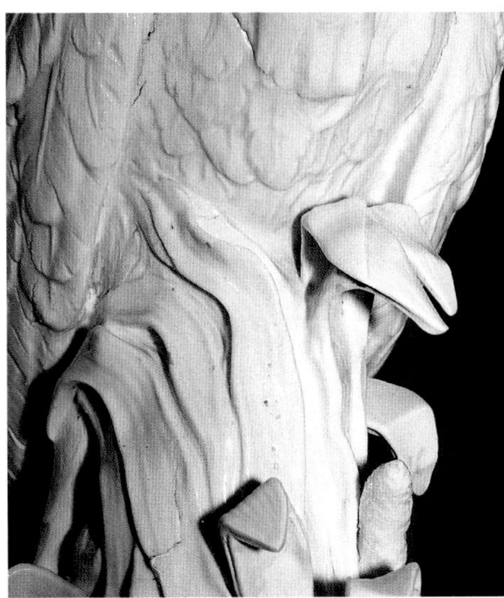

176 Transition area from pedestal to body on a heron, Dresden Porcelain Collection

standing. By virtue of its large undersurface area and horizontal orientation, a figure of an animal lying down has no need of a base. In the case of figures of sitting animals the decisive factor is most often the thickness of the front legs and the question as to whether they can go through the shrinking process in the firing without deforming under pressure from the weight of the body. Apart from the monkey figures, which are a special case, there are only two figures of sitting animals that have pedestals, namely the Fox and the Cat. In these two cases, however, the pedestals were not attempts on the part of the modeler to place the animals in their natural habitat: in fact they are little more than roughly kneaded lumps of paste. One could on the other hand hardly imagine a large-size bird figure that did not have some kind of support between or behind its legs. One way of making supports less conspicuous was of course to use a different or stronger color to bring out the legs at the expense of the support; our concern here, however, is with the structural means used by the modelers to conceal the technical necessity of their pedestals and to ensure that they formed a real part of the artistic whole.

In the case of some of Kaendler's earliest bird figures, the beasts look as though they have been positively skewered by their supports (Kestrel, fig. 122). Others, however, such as the Coot (fig. 91), betray his first tentative efforts to hide the join between the bird and the support with a few leaves, a technique which he uses again and again (in the Great Crested Grebe, for instance, fig. 90). It was particularly suitable for water-birds, as a cylindrical support column lent itself well to being clothed in a sleeve of reeds or rushes, with the curved or hanging tips of these growths contrasting with and thus distracting from the geometrical and suspiciously support-like shape of the lower section. Johann Joachim Kaendler used this method for the first time on the Heron (see fig. 176, and figs. 187 and 188) and re-used it for a number of further figures such as the Bittern.

In the case of non-aquatic birds, the most obvious solution was to use rocks or branches, just as Far Eastern modelers had done (in more abstract fashion) with their bird figures. In a number of cases, such as the Cassowary and the downward-climbing Macaw, Kaendler did not support the body with a clump of reeds, ears of corn, or the like, but stuck the bird on the stump with a few feathers covering the join (fig. 177); in these cases we are forced to accept that the tree-stump comes to a convenient end where the bird's body begins. There are a number of figures – among them the Peacock (on a tree-stump), the Pheasant, and the Macaw just referred to – where this solution has been used more convincingly than in the case of, for instance, the Cassowary. Even in this last case, however, comparison with Kirchner's Bustard modeled two months later (fig. 173) highlights Kaendler's skillful application of leaf-decoration to transform the closed form of the pedestal into a feature boasting strong contrasts of light and shade; in so doing he makes the pedestal seem less heavy and distracts the eye from the potentially embarrassing zone at and around the join. But Kaendler was fully aware that an over-detailed decoration of the pedestal might in turn lead to the eye being distracted from the main subject; as a result, as he himself put it, he "wanted to be sure that more finishing touches and details should be applied to the top of the figures, so that the eye would be attracted to them and not so much attention would be paid to the pedestal."[779] As a bird, the bustard did not lend itself to Kirchner's favored practice of psychologizing by physiognomizing, and it is surprising that it is one of his weakest works; indeed, it can only really be understood as an attempt on his part to emulate Kaendler's birds.

To summarize, while in the case of the Bittern Kaendler contrives to guide the eye towards the point of transition from the pedestal to the bird (out-turned tops to the rushes), in the case of the Cassowary he distracts the eye from that point by applying con-

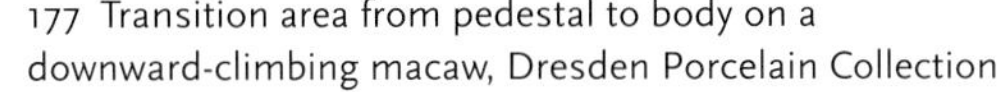

177 Transition area from pedestal to body on a downward-climbing macaw, Dresden Porcelain Collection

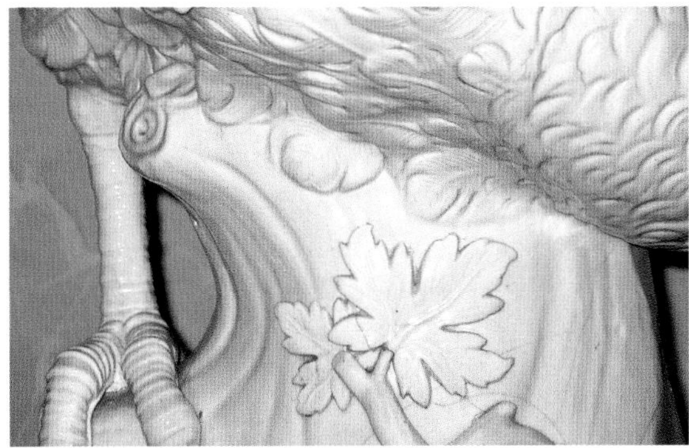

spicuously eye-catching decoration to the adjacent areas. One important element in the solution he used for the Bittern (the rush-tips) mirrors an important anatomical feature of the bird (neck-feathers), so that the eye jumps to and fro between these two zones and skips the problematic join area. In the Cassowary, on the other hand, the pedestal and the figure are both part of one progression (degree of plasticity) that sweeps from the base upwards and fuses the two into one optically convincing unified whole.

These examples show how the modelers used a variety of degrees of surface-working to help solve artistic problems. We now have to consider how far these techniques become ends in themselves, or – to put the matter more positively – to what degree they are used to impart character to the bird or animal in question.

Turkeycock

In January 1733, Johann Joachim Kaendler modeled one further roughly life-size bird model: "a turkeycock, life-size"[780] (fig.789). It was somewhat unusual that Kaendler used the term "Truthahn" in his work reports, as the more common terms were "Welscher Hahn" or "Calcuzscher Hahn," which are also the ones used in the order and delivery lists. Grimm's dictionary derived the latter term from the Indian port of Calcutta, claiming that the French words for turkeycock and turkeyhen – "dindon" and "dinde" – indicated the bird's Indian origin ("de l'Inde").

Kaendler chose to model his turkey at a characteristic moment of grandiose self-display, fanning its tail and spreading its body feathers to make itself as expansively voluminous as possible. This display of densely puffed-up plumage is the turkey's way of showing his strength and in real life it does lead to the feathers standing up from a surface that is otherwise smooth. This is of course good news for the sculptor modeling for porcelain, because he cannot do the individual feathers with thin disks, but has in any case to resort to a scale-like, overlapping structure. In order to avoid a too regular, fir-cone-like effect, the feathers in Kaendler's model, while being quite correctly flattened over at the end, almost all have at least one split on the vane. The powerful lateral spread visible in the fan, the wings and even in the smaller feathers is thus mirrored and continued – exaggerating reality – down into the figure's smallest constituent part.

178 Detail of plumage on a turkeycock, Dresden Porcelain Collection

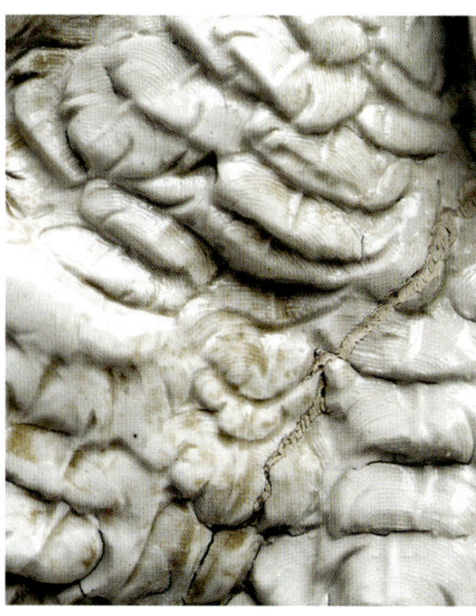

After the molds had been taken, the repairer gave every single feather its fine structure with a riffler. As glaze fills such tiny indentations as these, they are visible on the figures in their present condition, but they would not have been visible on the oil-painted figures that were delivered to the Japanese Palace. Even the application of fusible enamel colors would have covered the fine riffling, so that the figure-painter would have had the job, as with other bird figures, of painting onto the feathers an imitation of the fine line-drawing.

The great importance that Kaendler attached to the preservation of the sculptural detail of his models is shown clearly from one of the complaints leveled at Höroldt in the fall of 1734, namely that the manufactory director had instructed the repairers to restrict their work on detail to smoothing over the joins. As Kaendler put it, Höroldt "was not concerned with art."[781] Kaendler on the other hand was insistent that the repairers should not be deterred by any difficulties from doing this intricate line-drawing, so that the figures would be "sufficiently artistic." Whether a figure was being looked at from a distance or examined close-to, it was to overflow with just as ample a measure of detail as the corresponding natural specimen would.

One of the main problems in the realization of these micro-structural details lay in the consistency of the paste, which in the case of the animal figures was not of the finest. When questioned in the fall of 1734, Johann Friedrich Schmieder's explanation for the unsatisfying quality of the animal figures was that because the paste was too granular, "it was impossible to do any decorative work on them at the repairing or retouching stage; it was only possible to use a sponge or a cratching brush, and the paste was so coarse, containing little pieces like grains of scouring sand, that when he was working, pieces were torn out and he had to use a little curved knife."[782]

As has been noted, the Meissen large animal figures were created in an environment devoted primarily to the production of – in the very best sense of the word – decorative works of art. Porcelain objects – tableware apart – were first and foremost intended to fit into and enhance pre-existing interior designs. A concept closely related to "decorative" is "ornament." Considered in isolation, many a natural microcosm is distinctly ornamental in character, one example that springs to mind in the present context being a bird's plumage.

Although we do not know what pieces Kaendler sculpted at the Green Vaults before he started working at Meissen, they would cer-

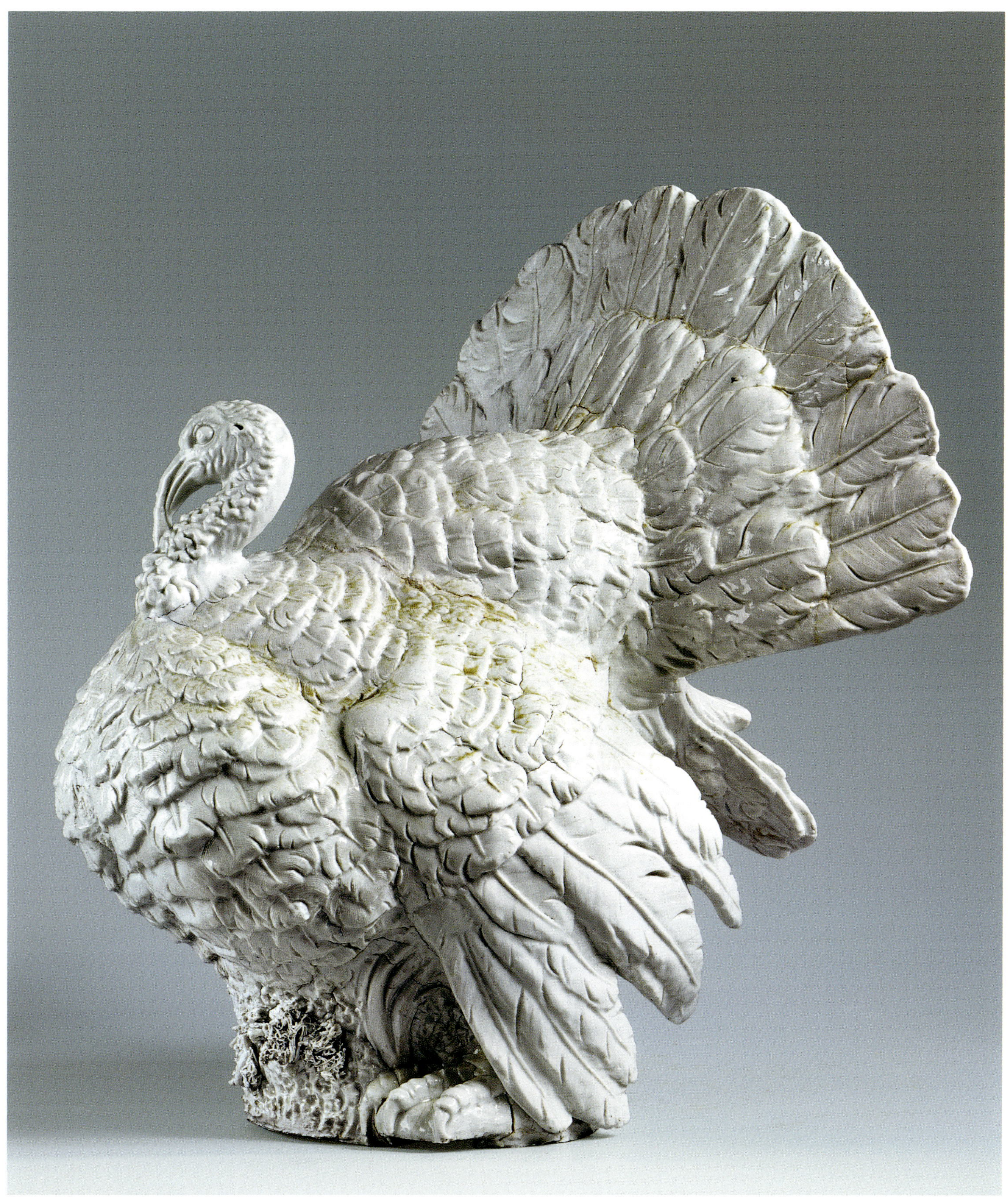

179 Johann Joachim Kaendler, Turkeycock, model 1733, Dresden Porcelain Collection

tainly have been mainly ornamental in character. Even at Meissen he did some purely ornamental work, such as the crowned initials of Augustus the Strong in November 1732 to adorn the porcelain warehouse,[783] and he later worked on the housing of the carillon.[784] It is certainly justifiable to see a connection between Kaendler's purely ornamental work and the attention he devoted to the smallest details of his animal figures. The "cosmos" of an ornament – strictly ordered so that its constituent elements are nicely balanced but nevertheless do not combine to "tell a story" – is a field of the visual arts with rules of its own, devoted to the depiction of energy *tout pur*. As we have seen, Kaendler brought his figures to life not only by modeling the animals in postures with telling compositional lines but also by the priority he gave to the treatment of their surfaces. Every detail was of importance to him, not because he was concerned to achieve a one-to-one imitation of nature, but as a means of holding the beholder's attention and guiding the eye around the figure. On one bird figure we saw him making the feathers stand up more in one area than in another, and on another figure certain flowing waves of an animal's coat were brought into sharper relief than others.

This is just as much the case with the Turkeycock. We have already noted that a strikingly large proportion of its feathers have split vanes (fig. 178). These vertical notches inject an extra measure of life into the surface by offsetting the relatively regular scale-like surface structure of the horizontally-oriented feathers. This effect is compounded by the feathers' likewise somewhat exaggeratedly prominent shafts, as can be seen particularly well in the breast area. By making the shafts so prominent, he achieved an optical balance between the individual feathers and the plumage as a whole; at the same time he contrived to make the most of the purely ornamental aspect of the plumage while still giving a detailed rendering that was true to nature. The turkey's plumage is not only gloriously decorative, but is the bird's entire decoration, which for Kaendler meant that every single feather had to be finely and delicately worked so as to reflect the filigree structure evident in nature. One feature of a great number of Kaendler's large animal figures is a small surface area which is so intensely and decoratively worked that if one looks at it for long enough, it develops a kind of ambiguity, at one moment appearing to be no more than a faithfully rendered feature of a certain natural species and at the next coming across as pure decoration. Examples are the throats of the Cockerel (fig. 168) and the Vulture Devouring a Cockatoo (fig. 153),

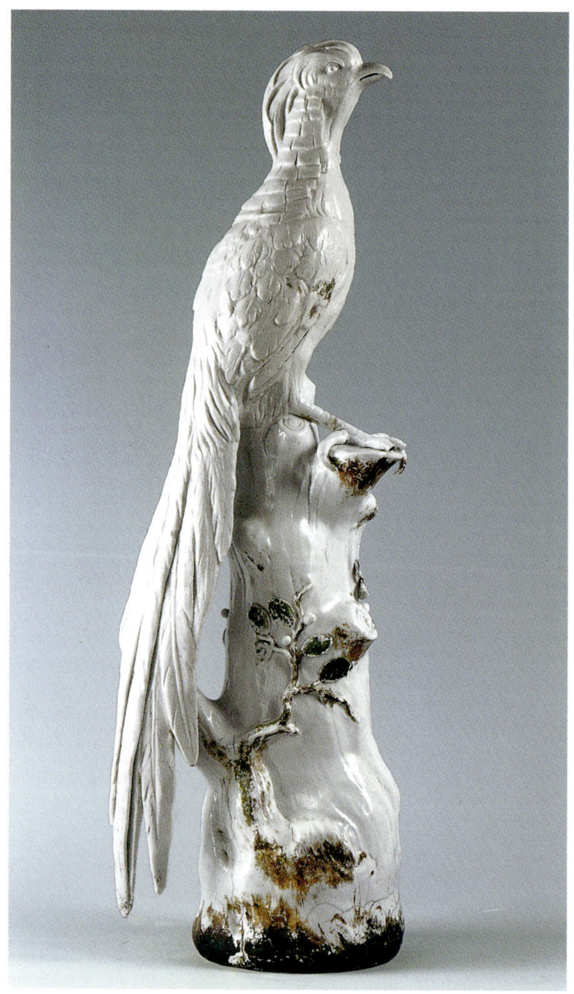

181 Johann Joachim Kaendler, Golden Pheasant, model 1731, Dresden Porcelain Collection

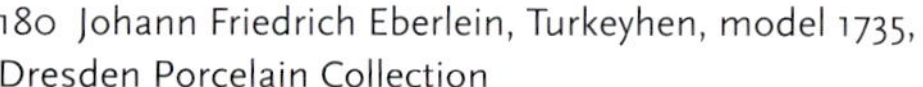

180 Johann Friedrich Eberlein, Turkeyhen, model 1735, Dresden Porcelain Collection

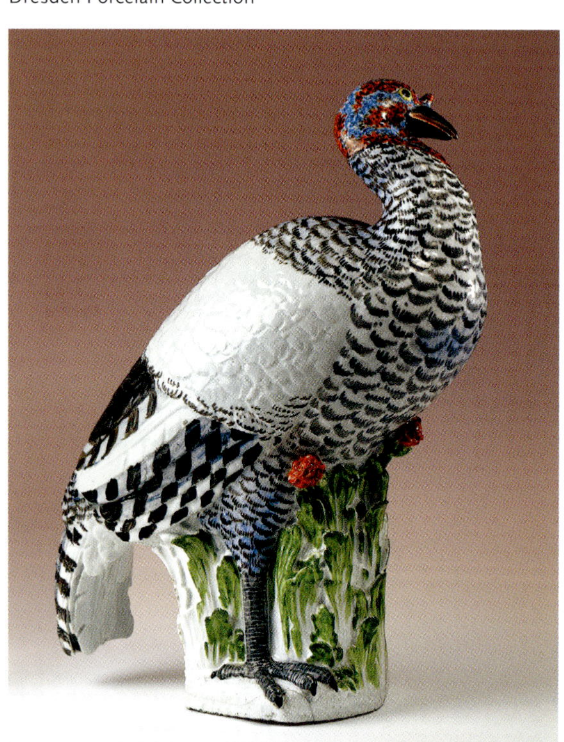

the feathers in the nape of the Golden Pheasant (fig. 181), and the locks on the forehead of the Indian Sheep (fig. 109).

Given that Kirchner only ever bothered to bring out, or indeed even to model, details that were absolutely necessary to make it clear what animal the figure was intended to represent, this is a point on which Kaendler's and Kirchner's approaches were diametrically opposed. Kaendler's partially ornamentalized surfaces have such a life of their own that they constantly entice the eye to focus on the detail, so that we can quite easily be convinced of the "reality" of the work on the merits of one small part regarded for a moment quite independently of the figure as a whole. Once the eye has discovered the riffling on the turkey's feathers, half-hidden under the glaze, it cannot resist returning close to the surface to enjoy the effect again and again. The Turkeycock also confirms the principle that it is such ornamentally organized structures as these that constitute the basic elements of our visual perception.

Billy-Goat

Our studies of the Bittern and the Cassowary have shown how Kaendler treated his surfaces in such a way as to give visual preeminence to certain areas and to distract the eye from other problematic areas such as the join between the animal and its pedestal. The example of the Turkeycock has shown the capacity of his elaborately rendered detail to take on a life of its own and come across as ornament. In the following study of the Billy-Goat, the intention is to look at Kaendler's treatment of surface in the context of the figure as a whole.

The Billy-Goat (fig. 196) is to be regarded as a pendant to the Nanny-Goat, and both are figures that only really need to be looked at from one side. It is not mentioned in any of Kaendler's work reports, but the fact that it is a direct companion piece to the Nanny-Goat indicates that it must also have been modeled in the summer of 1732. The fact that the two figures are related in a narrative sense, and not just on the natural and formal levels, is a matter which will be given consideration when we come to study the Nanny-Goat.

The animal is lying on his left side with his forelegs bent back, and is looking backwards over his left shoulder. His head is crowned with two mighty, spiral horns and his shaggy, long-haired coat hangs down in wavy strands on both sides of his spine. These strands are not all executed with the same degree of elaboration but combine to create a flowing river of hair running down the goat's flank; however, as they bear no relation to the figure's main compositional lines and meet both spine and floor at right angles, they only serve to confirm the static effect of the stretched-out body. As far as these respects go, the goat is a picture of repose.

A typical "goatee" beard is growing from under the animal's chin, flowing in a striking serpentine diagonal down in front of the his upper breast. This clump of hair is not only exaggeratedly long but also has a greater degree of plasticity that makes it stand out from the rest of the coat. The beard furthermore constitutes the first section of an arc which continues over the bridge of the nose and is taken up by the spiraling horns. The beard is pivotal to the figure as a whole, belonging formally to the coat and body, but compositionally to the head. The beard also imparts a strong energy and sense of direction to the turn: the fact that the hair of the beard is still clinging to the breast tells us that the goat's head has only just been turned. The suddenness of the turn draws our attention to the goat's eyes and gives them an especially intense focus. The spiral horns echo the turn of the goat's head, anchoring it in its new position. And the horns are echoed too, distantly, by the tail tucked in at the far end of the goat's restful, idle body.

Kaendler thus modeled the surfaces on his goat in such a way as to exert an important influence on the way we see the figure. The contrast between the homogeneous ("all-over") fleece and the dynamic flow of the beard overflows onto another plane in the strenuous posture and the energetic turning of the head. The antithesis is mirrored on a third, lower plane in the contrast between the relaxed, restful body and the alert, focused look in the goat's eyes.

The fact that Kaendler lavished such attention on his detail suggests that his general approach was considerably more far-reaching than that of a naturalistic imitator. For Kaendler, modeling the surface was an essential means of endowing a sculpture with character; his surfaces emphasize what the work has to say to us, and guide the beholder's eye around the figure. While the *grandes lignes* serve to give a composition its overall shape and anchor it in space, these and other effects are subtly underlined – or initiated – by finely modeled surfaces.

This brings our train of thought to a further aspect central to the effectiveness of any given work of art and one directly linked to our visual appreciation of a work in space: the dimension of time.

The relationship between the suggestion of movement and the time dimension: the downward-climbing Macaw and the Pelican

In our study of Kaendler's figure of a dog scratching itself, we not only discovered that walking around a figure gives us a better feeling for its circumambient space, but also saw that we came to an ever greater appreciation of the work's complexity as we proceeded with our circumambulation. However, this kind of time dimension – the time that it takes for us to appreciate a work – is a quite different thing from the time dimension that is inherent in the work itself, as we shall now see.

Between October and December 1731, Johann Joachim Kaendler made a model of a macaw sitting on a tree-stump (fig. 50). This dating is derived from two pieces of evidence: firstly, the reference in a list of December 17, 1731, to four "Indian ravens" already standing as finished porcelain figures at the manufactory, and secondly, the absence of any Indian ravens in any of Kaendler's own lists of the models he made from the day he started work at Meis-

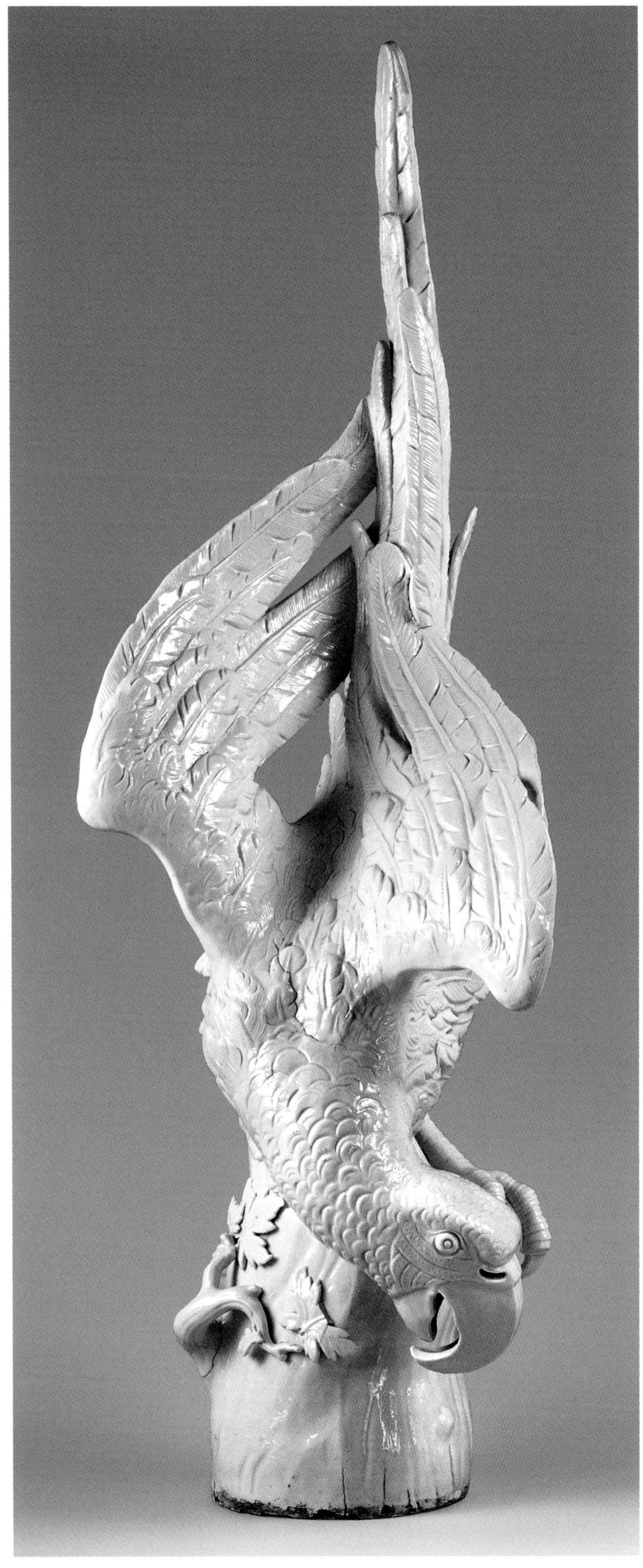

182 Johann Joachim Kaendler, Macaw climbing downwards, front view, model 1732, Dresden Porcelain Collection

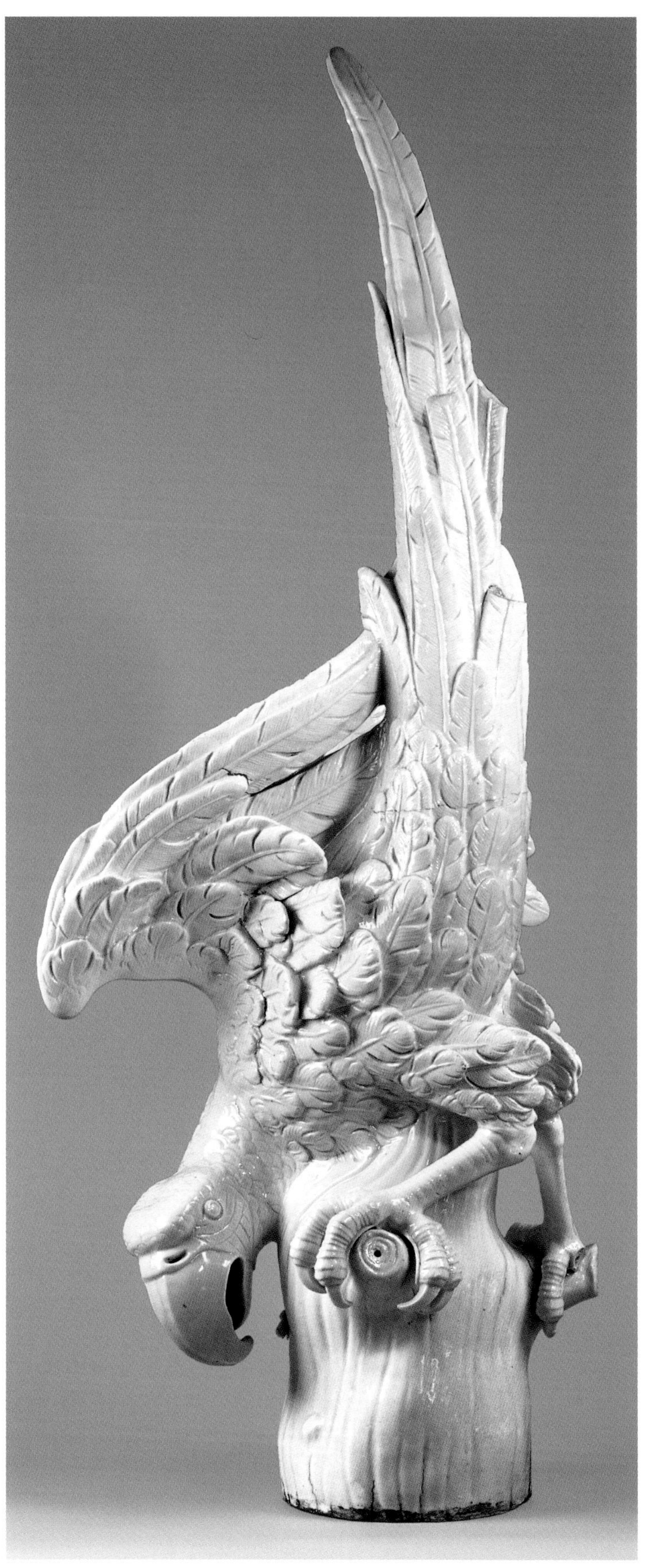

183 Johann Joachim Kaendler, Macaw climbing downwards, side view, model 1732, Dresden Porcelain Collection

sen (June 22, 1731) until his completion of the Wisent Fighting with a Boar in October of the same year, or from January 1732 onwards.

Stylistically speaking, the figure has one of the pedestals made out of a combination of rock and tree that are typical of Kaendler's early works. He modeled the figure from an as yet unidentified engraving. The "ruff" around its eye a three-dimensional rendering of the (two-dimensional) engraving, which evidently did the area around the eye with colors and/or cross-hatching. Further evidence that Kaendler did not model the figure from either a live or stuffed specimen is provided by the wrongly-shaped beak and the beak's perforation with two round holes with raised edges.

The whole concept underlying the figure is in crass contradiction to the character of the movement-loving macaw, as Kaendler must have noted when he first saw live specimens, either at the Moritzburg menagerie or at the *Löwenhaus* in Dresden. This was what stimulated him to do the second macaw model referred to in the manufactory report for May 1732: "The modeler Kaendler has made a large raven of the Indian kind."[785] The difference between his two macaw models could hardly be greater: in the second version he not only got all the anatomical details right, but also modeled the bird in a posture which captures its character perfectly.[786]

Macaw climbing downwards

This downward-climbing macaw has its talons around two cut-off branches on a tree-stump which serves both as a pedestal and as a technical support (figs. 182 and 183). Its breast is resting on and covering the upper surface of the tree-stump, its slightly turned head is thrust downwards, and the tail-feathers are pointing vertically upwards. Seen from the front, that is to say from the side with the bird's head, the macaw seems to be about to climb down the tree-trunk. The wings are roughly half open, and their tips touch the tail-feathers leaving gaps one can see through between the wings and the tail. As the talons are not quite on the same level and the neck and head are bent to one side, the bird has a kind of *contrapposto* which is carried through to the wings, one of which is held higher than the other. The dynamic character of the composition tells us quite unmistakably that the bird is on the move.

The figure's after-firing height of 125 cm puts it among the tallest of all the animal figures. Only if certain technical conditions are fulfilled can a porcelain object of this size be fired successfully in one piece,[787] the following being three of the most important: the figure must decrease in volume towards the top, the thickness of the walling must increase towards the bottom, and the unsupported horizontal elements should be kept to a minimum. When the temperature reaches vitrifying point and the paste softens slightly, then the figure must be able to hold all the unsupported highest points in equilibrium. In the light of these criteria, the downward-climbing Macaw wins all the prizes for perfect technical construction.

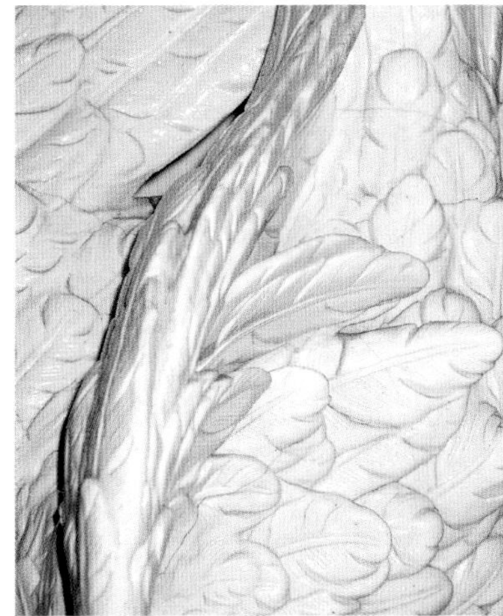

184 Feathers on a downward-climbing macaw, deliberately ruffled to support the freestanding wing, Pflueger Collection, New York

This requirement was mentioned when we were considering Kaendler's spectacular second eagle figure; it was modeled only half a year after his second macaw and the two figures have a number of similarities. As in the case of the eagle, there is a parallel between a technical matter and the figure's subject matter: like the paste at vitrifying point, the macaw is in a delicate state of equilibrium. The bird's wing-tips seem not just to be touching the tail but also to be pressing on it, actively holding it aloft like "flying" buttresses; and at the same time they are "balancing poles" for the macaw. The ruffling of the feathers under the wings likewise has two functions. In technical terms, they support the wing; in visual terms, their erect posture contributes to the excitement of the moment (fig. 184). This bird has nothing of the repose of Kaendler's first macaw: it is clearly on the move and if it has stopped, then it has only done so in order not to lose its balance. The fact of its having stopped makes it all the clearer that it is in motion; the "fermata" it is holding fuses the "before" and the "after" into one. Quite devoid of pose, this figure captures a highly charged moment of pure concentrated time – "bird time."

For the beholder, the time dimension is important for another reason. The bird's body is in the shape of a long drop, the round end made visually more interesting by the slightly turned head. Because the alert-eyed bird has its head – and thus the greater part of its weight – down, we assume that the macaw is going downwards. The arch formed by the two wings, their surfaces touching at the tip, creates a kind of suction current that sweeps the eye upwards towards the spine and up to the tail-feathers. Our eye is helped along this channel by the way the feathers are rendered: on the head and neck they are in low relief, around the wings they are in *mezzo rilievo*, and the tail-feathers are free-standing. This, the suction-channel wings, and the tapering off of the figure towards the top all combine to accelerate the upward movement of the eye. The real substance of the figure seems to be concentrated into the very tips of the tail-feathers. If the eye is to slip back down again, rather than being ejected into outer space at the top, then it has to swim against the current and do battle with the figure's surface vectors and powerful upward taper.

So while the drop-shaped macaw has a low center of gravity, its compositional lines flow upwards and together. The parrot's downward search for balance – "bird-time" – is thus set against the "beholder-time" measured by the upward acceleration of our eye. We, however, can make a distinction between the two modes of perception and skip from the one to the other at will; this bringing together of two apparently opposed time dimensions puts us into a state of mind similar to that of the macaw as it seeks to keep its balance in that precarious position. Again and again caught up in the upward movement, the eye – more or less promptly – switches back to the head where it is once again caught up in the flux of the compositional lines. Escaping from this circle is only possible with a conscious effort and for a short period of time. Beholder and figure become one in a shared experience of time.

Pelican

Kaendler's practice of choosing a specific moment in time as part of his portrayal of an animal's character is now to be illustrated by a second example. According to the monthly report for October 1732, he had modeled "a large 'spoon goose' devouring a carp"[788] (fig. 185). As the pelican is an extremely voluminous bird, the modeler was confronted by a number of technical difficulties, and all five extant copies have multiple fire-cracks on the bottom edge of the walling, caused by the weight of the figure during the firing. Such difficulties as these and the large quantity of paste required explain why this bird figure was at 204 talers the fourth most expensive of all the animal figures. At the time of production, this sum was the equivalent of half of Kaendler's annual salary.

The bird is modeled sitting, the head tipped so far as to be leaning on its back. In its scissor-shaped bill it holds a fish, only half of which – the tail end – can be seen. Once again, the posture can be explained in terms of technical requirements, as the body somehow had to hold up the weight of the pelican's large head and bill.

The beholder has no trouble in taking in the figure's relatively simple construction. The eye is led along a simple curve that be-

185 Johann Joachim Kaendler, Pelican, model 1732, Dresden Porcelain Collection

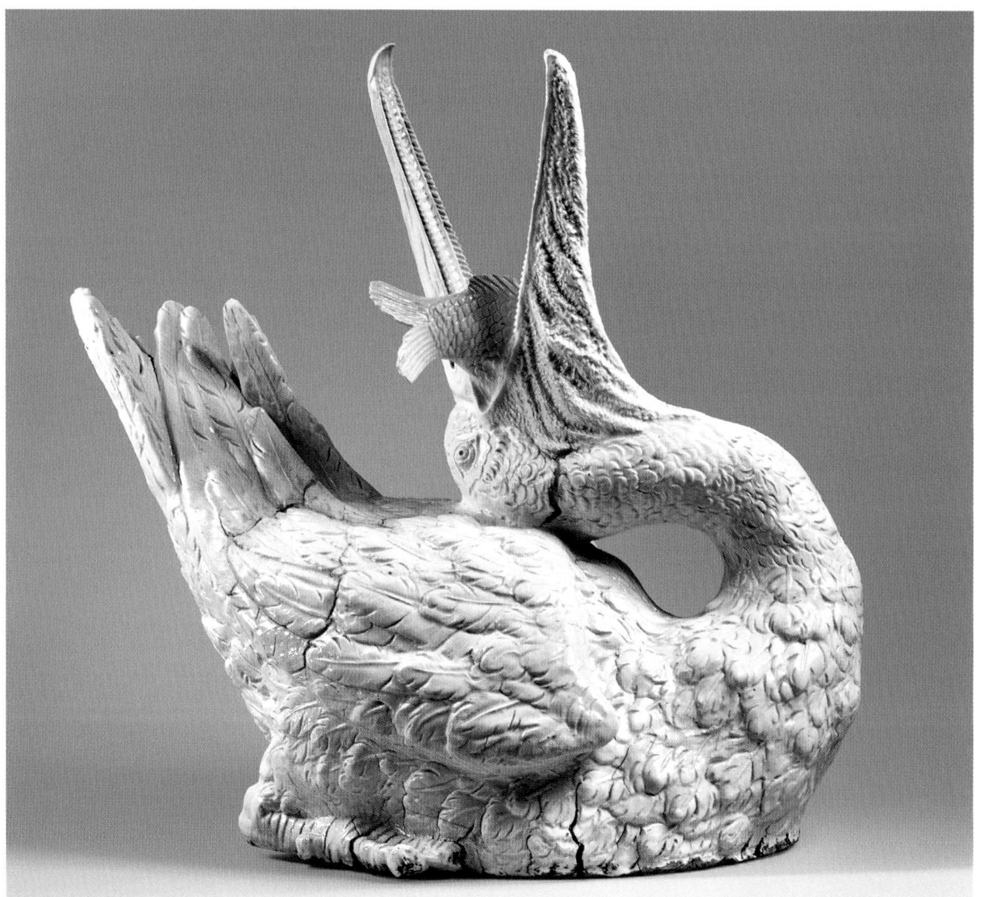

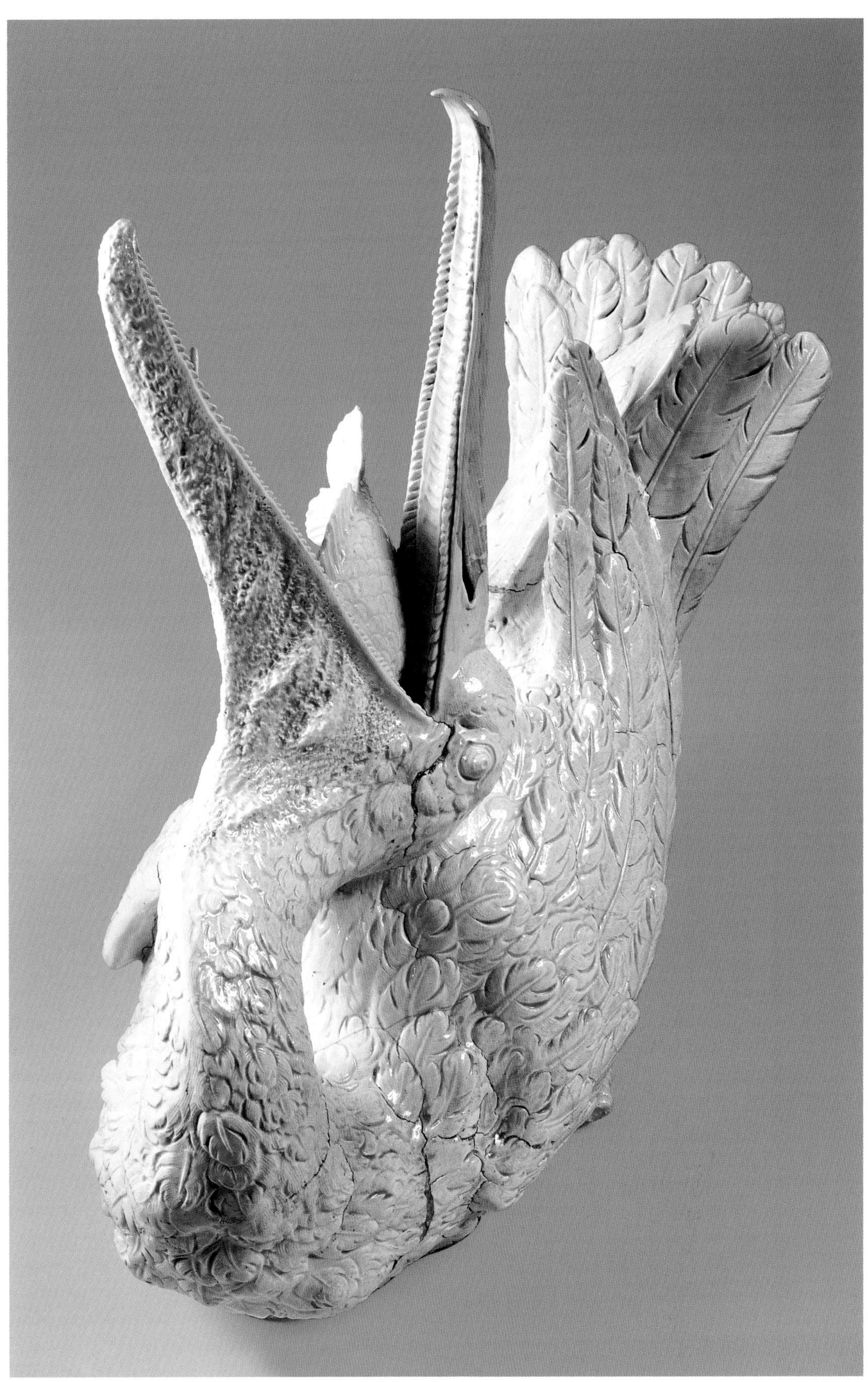

186 Johann Joachim Kaendler,
Pelican, model 1732,
Dresden Porcelain Collection

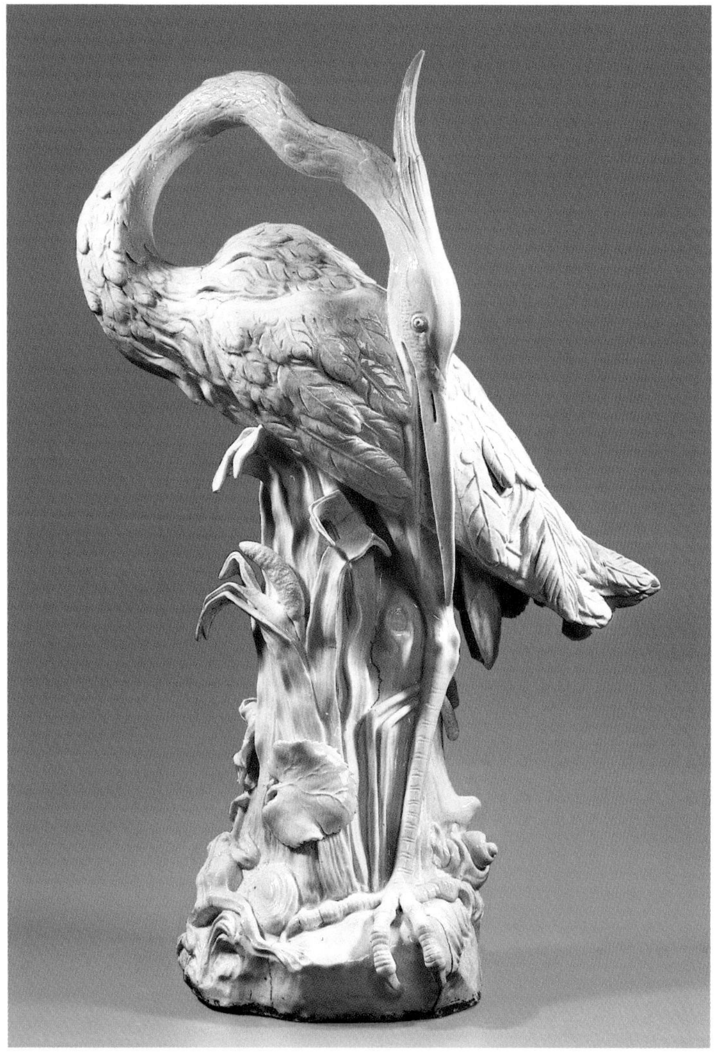

187 Johann Joachim Kaendler, Heron preening, model 1732, Dresden Porcelain Collection

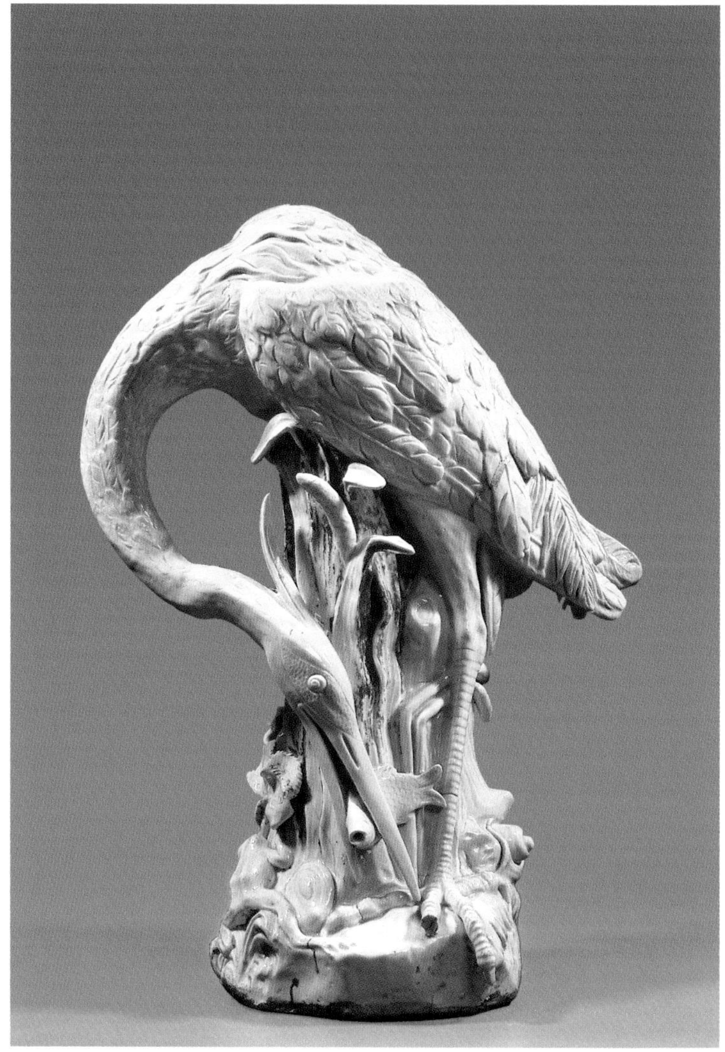

188 Johann Joachim Kaendler, Heron with fish, model 1732, Dresden Porcelain Collection

gins at the tail and dips down and around the neck and back up to the head, where the flowing curve is brought to an abrupt end by the strongly vertical bill. At this point the moving eye – "beholder-time" – meets another time factor, namely the activity the bird is engaged in. One would at first imagine that the wide-open lower part of the pelican's bill was large enough for the rest of the carp to be swallowed up a moment later. But while the bill is open, it is countered by the hermetic closed-form mass of the pelican's body. This massiveness is underlined by the close-lying feathers, rendered only in relief, and by the crossed wing-tips (fig. 186) that echo the scissor shape of the bill. If the fish is to pass on into this closed body, then it will have to pass through the gullet, which – for all that its sinuous curve makes it an ideal conductor for the eye of the beholder – does not in this position seem to be a really logical channel between bill and stomach. The compensation for this is that the stomach is on the same axis as the fish, but directly underneath it; the fish is however prevented by the nature of things from continuing downwards on this axis, which puts it very definitely in its place and ensures that it is there to stay.

In that the eye of the beholder is hurried along to the pelican's head where it is stopped in its track by an active vertical with a very definite "no entry" sign on it, the whole process of the pelican's devouring of the fish is frozen into a pose. This is not a pose that embodies any abstract quality – dignity, elegance, or the like – but one that simply depicts the particular way that a pelican eats. If we put ourselves into the place of the pelican for a moment, then we can quite imagine that a simple movement of the head would be enough for the fish to be swallowed whole, but there is nothing in the composition that is crying out for this kind of resolution. The powerful curves and clear lines, the charming peep-hole formed by the tilting of the head, and the parallelism between the tail-feathers and the bill combine to make the pelican a picture of unruffled repose and, compositionally speaking, a coherent and self-sufficient whole.

In the Macaw, form and content are mutually enhancing: together they contrive to give us a clear idea of the bird's nervous agility. Here, they are at odds, but most effectively so, as this very opposition eloquently reflects both the sheer weight of the pelican and also its ponderous, phlegmatic character.

In the above studies, we have often noted that the animals give the impression that they are engaged in doing something. Quite apart from the consequences this has for the time-dimension inherent in the animal figures, this begs the question as to which artistic category these works belong to. Are they portraits or genre pieces?

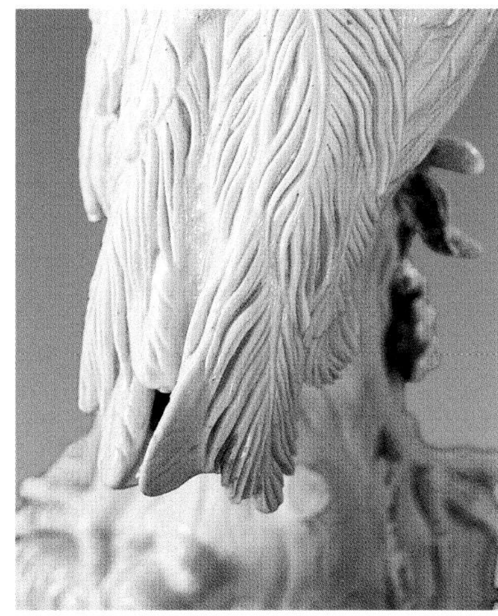

189 Tail feathers on a heron, Dresden Porcelain Collection

The relationship between character portrayal and general narrative elements: the Heron and the Nanny-Goat

Heron

It is clear from the relevant manufactory report that Kaendler modeled the Heron in March 1732: "Modeler Kentler has modeled a large heron."[789] Two different necks were made for the figure, so that in one version the heron is preening its plumage (fig. 187), and in the other it is holding a carp, or in some cases a frog, in its beak (fig. 188).

In May 1735, however, we find Kaendler claiming reimbursement for expenses he had incurred on working materials – clay and metal to make a support structure – for a large heron that he had modeled for the porcelain manufactory in response to the verbal order of Augustus the Strong: "[...]in the year 1731, I the undersigned had to model, life-size, the white heron that was at that time to be seen live in the courtyard of the Royal Palace in Dresden, for the porcelain manufactory, standing amongst reeds with frogs and fishes."[790]

If one disregards the curious fact of Kaendler having to bear the expenses for working materials himself, one might imagine that he had made his heron model in the first half-year of his employment and then simply revised it the following March, the month for which it appears in the manufactory report, which is indeed the sequence of events that has generally been presented in the literature to date. However, this is to overlook the document appended to Kaendler's demand in which the manufactory refuses to reimburse him, for the following reason: "According to the arcanists, at the time Herr Kaendler did the work in 1731, he was not yet employed in the service of the king at the factory, but was at that point only seeking to commend himself to us. Consequently, the manufactory is not obliged to fulfill his request for reimbursement."[791]

We cannot say for certain what this first heron looked like that Kaendler made before June 1731, most likely as a test piece for Augustus the Strong, or what the manufactory did with it. However, what we can say for sure is that the heron figure realized in porcelain with two variant necks was the figure referred to in March 1732, and that it was not a revision of an earlier heron figure but a completely new creation. This can be substantiated on stylistic grounds, as this figure has nothing in common with the comparatively stiff figures that Kaendler modeled in the first months of his employment at the manufactory. Furthermore, the technical problems involved in modeling a heron for realization in porcelain are solved with such a degree of skill that this particular model could not have been the work of a sculptor who had little or no experience of the difficulties presented by this demanding material. See-

190 Dominikus Aulicek, Heron, Nymphenburg manufactory ca. 1765–1770, Metropolitan Museum of Art, New York, Untermyer Collection

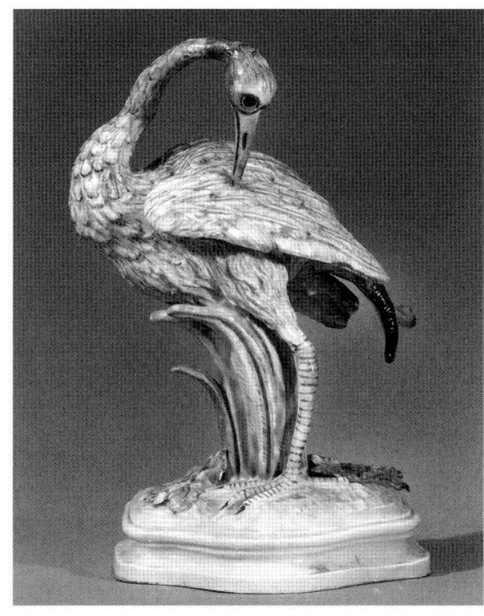

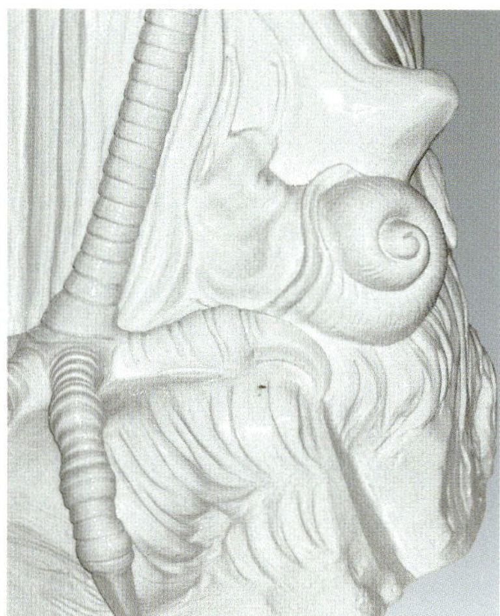

191 Snail on the pedestal of a heron, Dresden Porcelain Collection

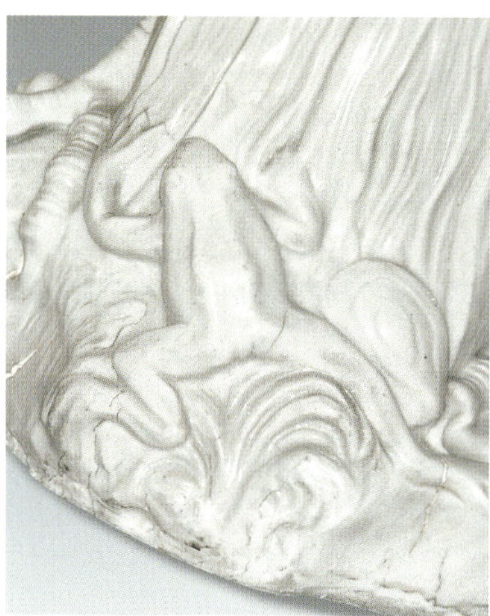

192 Frog on the pedestal of a heron, Dresden Porcelain Collection

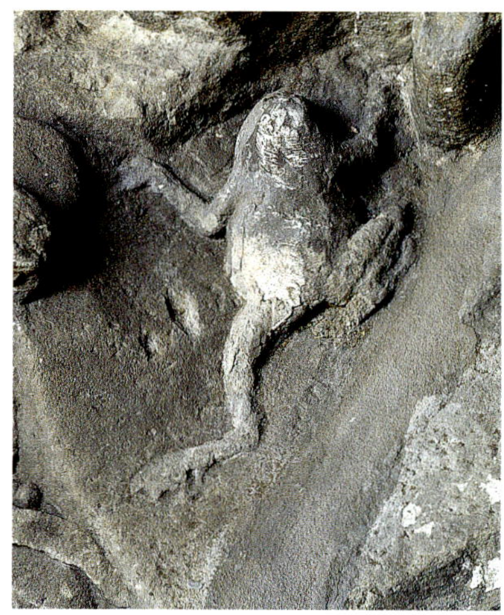

193 Johann Joachim Kaendler, frog on the tombstone for Gottfried Keil, 1732, Meissen City Museum

ing that Kaendler's description of his 1731 heron model does accord exactly with the model he made the following year, one can at the most argue that the first model may have still been existence at the manufactory a year later, and that it provided a certain inspiration for the second model. It had after all been a depiction of a real live specimen.

In this connection, it is in any case noteworthy that when the young sculptor came to Augustus the Strong's notice (whether the king noticed him personally, or whether a recommendation came from a third party), the king asked him to do an animal model as his test piece. This is clear evidence that of all the wares being produced by his manufactory in 1731, the king accorded the highest priority to the animal figures.

The figure in which the heron is holding a carp (or a frog) in its beak is the original version (fig. 188) and shows the bird standing on an angular rock pedestal. Its body is supported by a tree-stump, to the front of which there are rushes reaching up to the bird's breast, where its body is modeled as a diagonal mass, covered all over with feathers in relief. The long neck leads in a sinuous line down to where a small carp is caught in the heron's beak.

The eye is initially accelerated along this principal line up the vertically-structured rushes and the leg that is standing in front of the tree-stump, only to reach a stopping point on the lower surface of the heron's trunk where the energies so effectively channeled by the rushes are dispersed in all directions by their downward-turned tips (see detail in fig. 176). The leg, however, provides an effective link to the heron's trunk, where the eye is at once slowed down and given room to wander over the plumage. The surface, which is otherwise compact in spite of the relief of feathers, opens up towards the tail in a few intricately worked "heron feathers" (see detail in fig. 189). At the opposite end the eye gathers speed again, guided along the elegant curve of the neck until it meets the axis running between the head's long crest feather and the tip of the beak. There it comes upon the carp which with its bent body and wide-open mouth is a kind of signpost leading back to the eye of the beholder.

This sequence thus contains two cycles each made up of the same pattern of acceleration and dispersal, once in the space of the pedestal and once on the bird itself. The tree-stump is thus paired to the legs that would in reality bear the bird's weight, and the somewhat unruly rushes find their parallel in the vibrant elasticity of the neck. Correspondingly, the pedestal has a dual function: technically it stabilizes the figure, and optically it rehearses and echoes the composition of the heron. Initially, its evident weight-bearing role makes it an inseparable part of the whole, but it proceeds to take a back seat when we focus on the heron's head and the captive fish.

There are two further elements that belong to the pedestal. On one side a frog is hurrying away into the rushes (fig. 192), and on the other a large snail is embarking on a slow path up the side of the tree-stump (fig. 191). This frog, used here as an element typical of the heron's natural habitat, was also used in 1732 by Kaendler "in retrograde" on the tombstone of Gottfried Keil, where it joins worms and sundry other creatures reminding us of the transience of our mortal bodies (fig. 193).[792]

These two little creatures bear no compositional relation to the heron, nor do they allude to any literary source (a fable, or the like). They are simply extensions of the rushes and the tree; standing between the heron's legs, they symbolize the two elements in which the heron is at home, water and earth. Inconspicuously executed, they are entirely without eye-catching features: the snail's shell, for instance, is done simply and without desire for effect. They are clearly not intended to distract the eye of the beholder. They are "extras," used to help set the scene for the little drama of the heron catching the fish.

The sculptor does not have the same means of depicting an animal's habitat that are available to an artist doing a painting or drawing. If the sculptor wishes to include elements to give greater definition to the natural environment, then this has to be done directly in or on the figure itself. And elements added in this way can only be pointers or aides-memoire for the beholder. Such a limited, two-dimensional representation of nature cannot be anything more than a blueprint of reality indicating that stage left is water, and stage right is land. Or, to use other terms of reference, they are intended to signify a landscape or an environment. If the elements are understood in this way, then it is quite possible to see what relevance they have to the protagonist figure, as we have done. However, it also means that elements introduced to support and clarify the picture of nature have to be very understated, as is the case with the frog and snail.

The principal compositional lines lead the eye towards the part of the model where there is both the most drama and also the greatest sense of the figure catching the heron at a specific moment in time. The point where the fish is caught gasping for breath between the two halves of the heron's hard beak, that is to say where the drama is coming to a climax, is also a point of rest even for the eye of the most restless beholder. Kaendler focuses on the action and arranges the whole composition in such a way as to ensure that the eye treads and re-treads the two-stage path described, always ending up at the scene of the drama and only taking in the rest of the sculptural information, such as the snail and the frog, *en passant*. The main goal of the composition is not to waste our time on environmental details, but rather to give us a performance of the lightning stab of the heron's beak, and then to allow us as many encores as we care to enjoy. What we are given is not a glimpse of nature at a particular place when some event happens to be going on, but rather an insight into nature at one very particular moment.

If we now return to the question of how we are to categorize the animal figures, we cannot but conclude, given the observations that we have made, that they are not genre pieces in the broadest sense of the expression. Although the bare bones of a "narrative" can be grasped with ease, the emphasis is not on the fact that a heron is catching a fish; the allusions to the place where this is happening are used to give further information about the heron (they are "attributes"), but not as a traditional means of underlining what is going on.

This being the case, it would be most appropriate to put the figure into a category that was, as we have noted, of considerable importance for the animal figures: the zoological illustration. The

194 Johann Joachim Kaendler, Nanny-Goat and yeanling, with remains of cold-painting, model 1732, Dresden Porcelain Collection

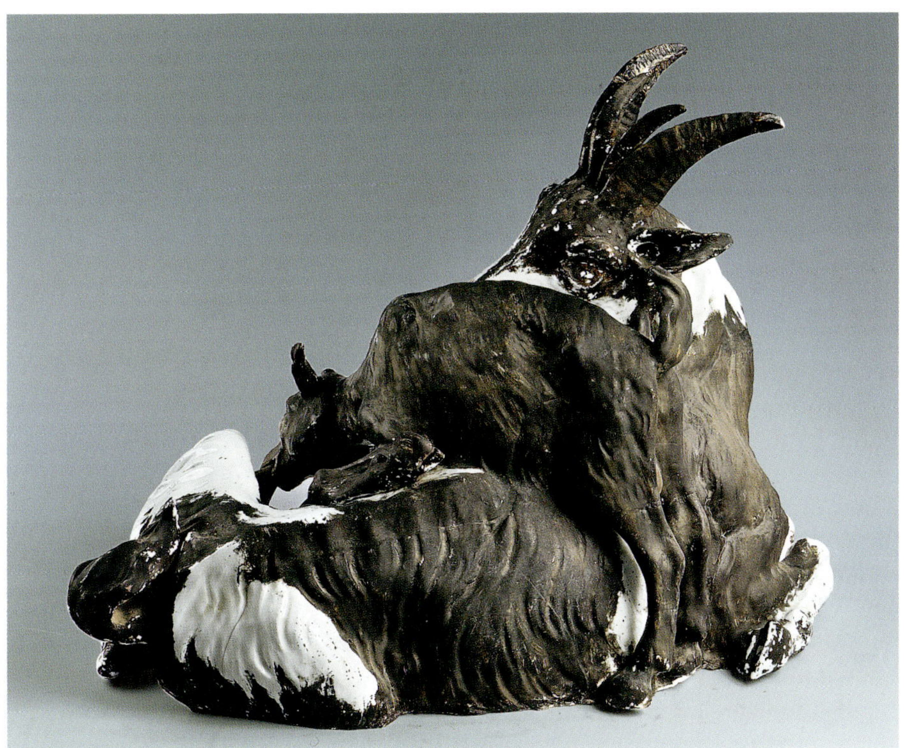

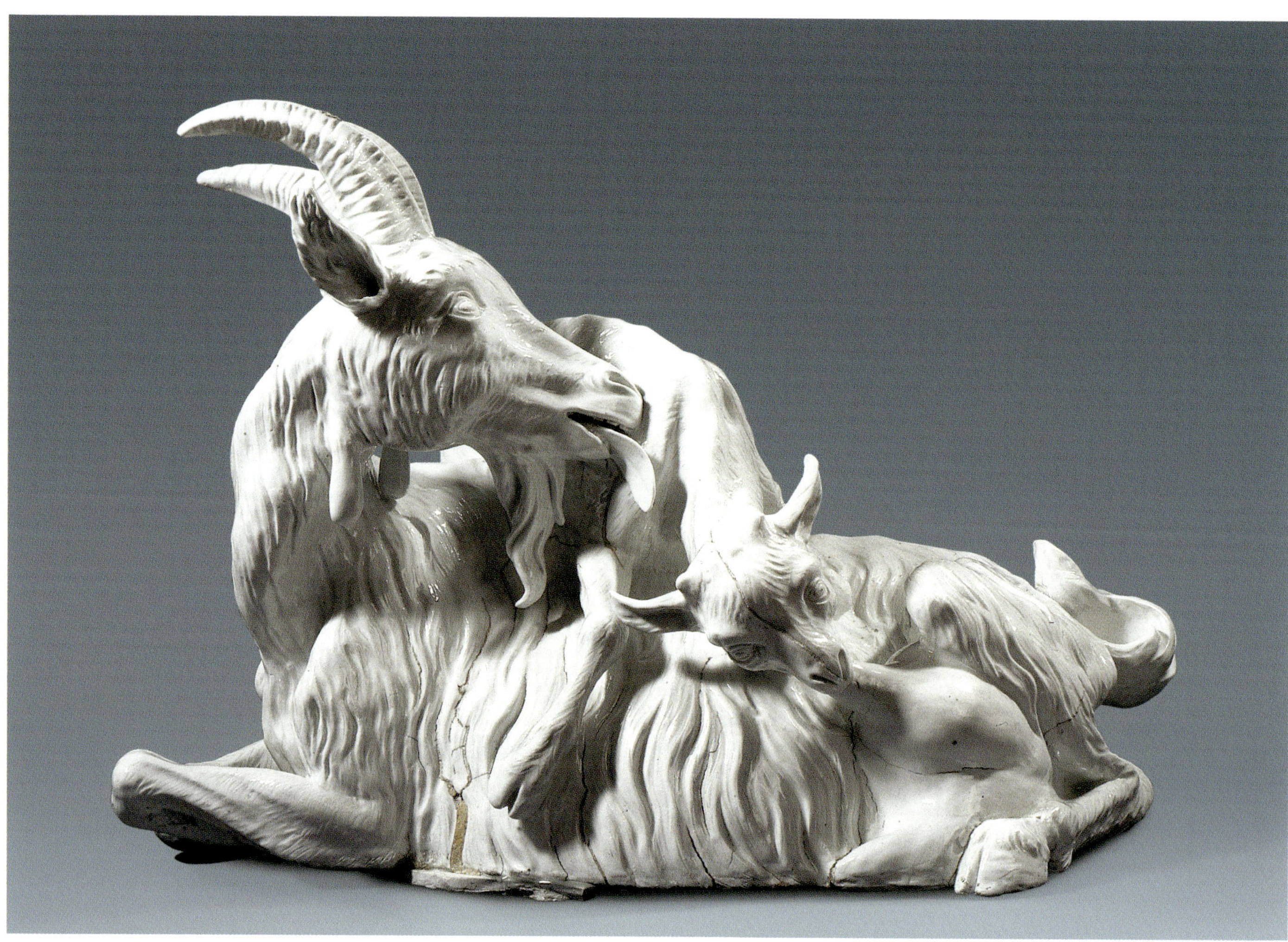

195 Johann Joachim Kaendler, Nanny-Goat and yeanling, model 1732, Dresden Porcelain Collection

animal's habitat is only rendered in a small, limited excerpt, and our attention is guided entirely to the animal itself. But in this instance Kaendler is doing more than a pure zoological illustrator would; as a sculptor and artist, he was concerned to go beyond the kind of externally and anatomically exact depiction of the animal that would help the ornithologist to recognize this species on sight. The emphasis of Kaendler's characterization of the heron is on the bird's skill at catching fish, and if he is to impress this quality on the viewer as convincingly as possible, he has to arrange the animal's energies in such as a way that the viewer will be aware of the way they are going at the critical moment when the fish is caught. And sculpture, with its specific potential for bringing alive the play of light and shade and so on, is a particularly suitable medium for doing just that.

While the bird figures require technical supports, which Kaendler was able to exploit by using them to put the bird into its natural setting, it was a different matter with most of the quadrupeds, which have the advantage of being able to do without a support of this kind: their setting is real space, that is to say the beholder's space. This is to be borne in mind as we turn our attention to one last example in order to look for confirmation of the observations we have made, and to explore them in greater depth.

Nanny-Goat with kid

As the manufactory report for August 1732 puts it: "Modeler Kentler, for his part, has modeled and made ready … a nanny-goat with a kid," (fig. 195).[793]

The nanny-goat is lying full-length with her forelegs bent back at the knee; with her head turned back over her left shoulder, her posture is a mirror-image of the billy-goat's (fig. 196). A kid is lying across her back and feeding from its mother's distended udder; for her part, the mother is stretching her tongue far out of her mouth and licking her kid's body.

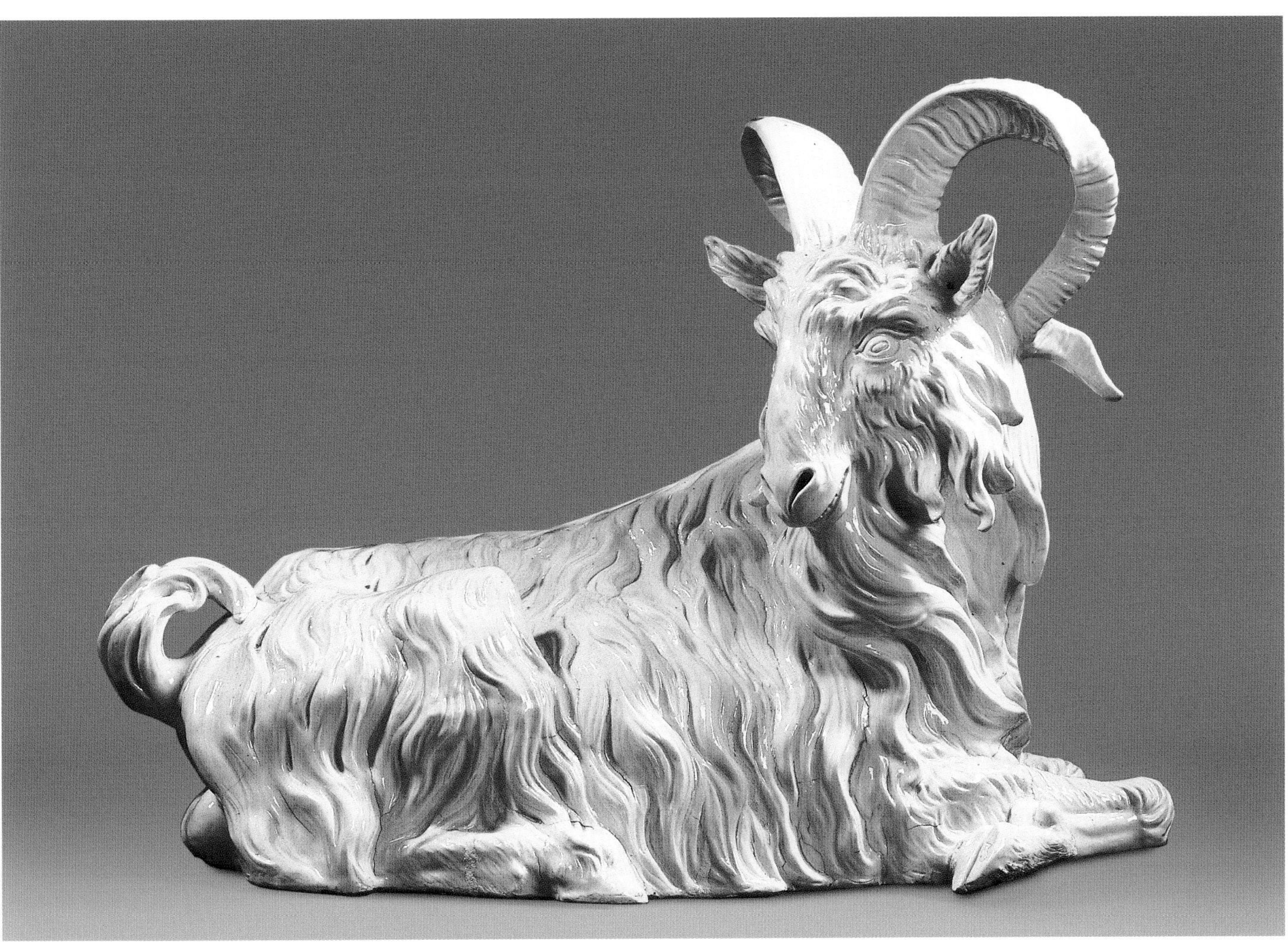

196 Johann Joachim Kaendler, Billy-Goat, model 1732, Dresden Porcelain Collection

Her coat is made up of waves of hair that run vertically all over her body, even – unlike the billy-goat – on her head, where her goatee beard hangs straight down. The two drop-shaped lobes of skin below her cheeks contribute to the feeling of repose that emanates from this static, vertically structured composition. The figure has a strong diagonal axis running from the nanny's horns[794] via her muzzle and tongue, along the kid's head to the udder. This axis forms a straight or S-shaped line according to the viewer's position, and incorporates all the points of the figure where something is going on.

If we are to understand this little scenario fully, we have to be familiar with certain of the goat's habits, as Kaendler himself certainly was, seeing that such animals as goats were a common feature of domestic life in the eighteenth century, even in the towns. The key point is that as a rule, a she-goat only licks its young immediately after they are born, in order to clean the newborn's coat of blood and mucus. By massaging the chest she also encourages the yeanling's respiration and her licking generally stimulates the circulation of the blood. This is not simply an outpouring of maternal affection, but rather an action of life-preserving importance. A mother-goat will not clean a stillborn kid. For its part, the yeanling follows its natural instincts and reaches for the udder and the milk that will provide it with its first nourishment, a potent image of strength and growth to maturity.[795]

The nanny-goat's tongue is thus to be understood as a sign to which Kaendler clearly wishes us to pay special attention: to this end he makes it somewhat longer than would strictly speaking be realistic, using the technique of selective exaggeration that we have often noted in his figures. It has a pivotal function, mediating in terms both of form and of content between mother and kid. The nanny-goat has given birth to her kid, which as a yeanling is still physically bonded to her; this physical closeness and dependence is expressed in the way it lies across its mother's back (see also fig. 194). If our eye proceeds from the udder to the kid's head close by and thence to the tongue, then we cannot but note that the tongue is the only channel for the tender loving care being lavished by the *alma mater* on its little yeanling. Her eyes are gazing beyond the kid's back, her absent-minded look suggesting that her licking is a reflex, prompted by instinct.

Nevertheless, the Nanny-Goat was conceived as one of a pair, and when the nanny and billy are set up as a pair, their eyes do indeed meet. We do not have to try to read feelings into this meeting of the eyes: the important thing is that the two animals have their minds on each other. Then it becomes clear that the nanny-goat's tongue has a second pivotal function, that of forming a bridge between a physical and a mental relationship. Given that the physical contact between the nanny and her yeanling is the most intensive form of the one relationship and direct eye contact is the most intensive form of the other, there is a strong temptation to read human ideas of love and morality into this pair of figures; however, whether this was the intention of the artist is at the very least questionable.

The prime message conveyed by the group's particular rhetorical structure and by its arguments (the lines of the composition) is that what we are looking at is a depiction of two quite different, but equally important, forms of communication in the broadest sense of the word. In itself, the look in the nanny-goat's eyes can equally well be taken as expressing affection and desire, or the desire to impress, or vigilance. What all these have in common, however, is that they are instances of one living being energetically making or seeking contact with another. A look can create relationships that are neither physical nor physically apprehensible. If one sees this in a very general sense and applies it to the essence of nature, then the look can be regarded as corresponding to all those invisible forces of nature which have an effect on us and which we can experience: in this particular porcelain group, it represents the fundamental principle of the effect of things and phenomena.

The intimate physical involvement of the yeanling with its mother could not be depicted in a more definitive and static way. The only compositional line towards or along which the eye is guided is the one depicting this intimate bonding between the two beings. Considered once again in a very general sense, this bond also stands for a fundamental aspect of nature: it points us to the cycle in which all natural substances are constantly being transformed but are always present and apprehensible in some form or other. Accordingly, the unshakable bond between the mother and its young one here stands for the basic principle of the existence of things and phenomena.

The recognition that we came to through our examination of the Heron, namely that Kaendler's animal figures resulted from an "insight into" and not a "looking at" nature, is confirmed by close attention to this goat family. If we set aside all interpretations and symbolic meanings (the family, the goat as a symbol of Bacchantic lust, and so on) and concentrate solely on that which is formally present, it becomes clear what an all-embracing and at the same time precise eye for nature Kaendler had. In his animal figures he expresses with great sensitivity the feelings he had when confronted with the living animals in their natural state.

To point out that Kaendler's animal figures express basic principles of nature is not of course to make the absurd suggestion that he consciously injected scientific or philosophical perceptions into his pair of porcelain goats. The apprehensible presence of the two principles of "existence" and "effect" in his animal figures is a result of his fundamental purpose, which was not to tell a story, but to capture the essential character of the animals he modeled. The way in which he did this, enabling those who enjoy his figures to replace looking at nature with looking at art, may however without exaggeration be counted as one of the most outstanding artistic achievements of the eighteenth century.

The Animals and the Palace: What is their "meaning" and how are they related?

The animal figures as sculptures

In Part One, we considered a number of factual matters related to the large animal figures created for the Japanese Palace: the manufacturing process and techniques, "models" (in the sense of sources of inspiration), the artists and craftsmen themselves, and so on. In Part Two, we broadened the perspective, giving consideration to the cultural-historical context (with particular reference to the various royal animal collections) and to attitudes to animals at the court of Dresden. The lion's share of Part Three was then devoted to studies of individual animal figures, which were examined with a particular view to establishing the characteristics of Johann Joachim Kaendler's works in this field.

At this point, we shall broaden our perspective once again to consider what all these insights tell us about Kaendler's art, and what it is about this group of works that gives them their perennial charm and fascination. To do this, we now have to switch back from things to ideas, from the factual to the theoretical plane.

The vital importance of the surface

We have hitherto considered the meaning ("Bedeutung") of the animal figures for the Japanese Palace on two levels: firstly, on the level of their (narrative) form and, secondly, on the level of the immediate impression the figures make on us. The narrative element in the animal figures does not usually extend beyond the representation of a particular moment in time made manifest in a little scenario involving two animals (vulture and cockatoo) or in the specific posture of a single animal (dog scratching itself). However, as these cases show, the moment the artist has captured is a "fruitful moment," which not only enables us to follow the story-line backward to see what has just happened and forward to see what is going to happen, but also gives us insights into the essential character of the animal in question.

The narrative dimension is made all the more suggestive by compositional means, notably the varying degrees of elaboration accorded to the detail, the selection of certain areas for especially elaborate treatment, and the alignment of the main compositional axes. These combine to enliven the overall structure and to guide the eye and mind towards the recognition of essential truths about the animal concerned. The impression thus made on us has consequences for our perception of the primary level of meaning, the figure's subject matter ("Inhalt"), as for instance in the figure of a macaw climbing downwards which we cannot look at without having a vivid feeling of the precarious balancing act the bird is performing. However, the two levels of meaning (subject matter and effect) are not brought into association with one another by virtue of a symbolic interpretation of certain features, as we noted was the case with, for instance, the posture and physiognomy of Johann Gottlieb Kirchner's lion. The means used by Kaendler for the mutual energizing of subject matter and effect are ones that are and always have been sculptural means *par excellence*: spatial expansion ("Raumergreifung") and surface treatment. Together, these give the figure in question that lifelike "charge" that enables us to see it in itself, undistracted by "material considerations" related to the medium porcelain.

The surfaces of the figures play a central role in this process. The surface is where Kaendler lays down his optical guidelines, and it is on the surface that such lines are picked up by the compositional axes and then carried on over the whole object. These processes result in the sculpture being enveloped in a kind of "magnetic field" that catches our eye and gives us in return not only insights into the structure of the work but also stimulating hints for a better understanding of the subject matter. When writing about modern sculpture, Gottfried Boehm coined the expression "plastischer Raum": "What we perceive as plastic space is nothing other than the extended effect of the vectors we perceive on the surface."[796] In Boehm's view, the surface of a sculpture is like a skin or membrane,[797] which "not only shows us externals, but also speaks to the beholder's eye and mind of what is internal, telling us about the weight, mass, density and structure of the body that lies beneath the surface, that is to say, how the body is made up with respect to the expressive values that lie hidden in the darkness of its materiality."[798] This way of looking at a figure does however assume that there is no intention to deceive the beholder as to the material of which the sculpture is made, and that the material used is not subjected to any processing by the artist. In the above paragraph we noted that Kaendler's figures enable us to free ourselves from an exclusive preoccupation with the material in which the figure is executed, so that when we see Kaendler's Macaw, we are more likely to exclaim "look, a macaw," than "look, a porcelain macaw." However, it is not so much the sequence of our observations that determines whether form has the upper hand over matter, but rather the relationship between the two observations that comes into being once they have been made. For if the notion of plastic space is to have any relevance, it is fundamentally important that "form should not subordinate matter, but liberate it."[799]

The prime implication of this is that the artist should create his work in a way that is completely "right" for the material concerned. This leads us on to the fascinating question as to whether it is possible for sculptures that are as "naturalistic" as the animal figures to be "right" for the material, or in other words, whether our perception of the form a figure takes and our perception of the material can be held in equilibrium.

"Rightness" for execution in porcelain

As we have seen, while Kaendler definitely did his surfaces in accord with what he saw of the respective bird or animal *in natura*, he only imitated nature insofar as this practice resulted in the best possible sculpture, and insofar as it contributed to guiding the eye and mind of the beholder as he wished. The Kaendleresque surface is thus not given its particular treatment with a view to realizing a pre-interpreted mime, as is the case with Kirchner's Lion or Fox, as it is only effective in a formal sense, and not on the level of subject matter. As it is on a sculpture's surface that we encounter the material it is made of – after all, it is only thanks to their surfaces that we can perceive objects in the first place – then the answer to the question whether it has been made in a way that is right for the raw material will not only depend on the way the figure is shaped as a whole, but also (or even solely) on the way the artist has done the surfaces. In order to preclude the objection that in figurative sculpture matter is in any case totally subordinated to form, it will now be wise to differentiate and to consider the question on the two levels mentioned above: firstly with respect to "subject matter" and then with respect to "effect."

With respect to subject matter, whether a figure is "right for the material" depends on whether the artist has proved capable of imitating other surfaces solely by structuring the material in hand, as the painter does with color. If, in the case of the animal figures, the artist were able to imitate such things as reeds and rushes, horn, feathers and fur by making the surfaces softer and rounder, more or less dynamic, and so on, or by shaping the features especially thickly or thinly, then we could clearly say that his figures were "right for the material" in this sense. However, this would be to exclude the other way of looking at the problem, which is to be described below. Although the modelers who made the animal figures disposed over a number of means of varying and differentiating their surfaces, those means were clearly inadequate to the task of imitating other materials convincingly. The glaze cannot be given a patina or a polishing as marble or bronze can, which limits the scope for nuance, and homogenizes the overall effect. As we are now considering the specifically sculptural dimension, the painting done on the figures in order to compensate for this "shortcoming" is not of interest, especially since painting is a technique with limited potential when applied to porcelain.

The second kind of "rightness for the material" is to be observed in the way a given figure comes across as a whole. The principal means used in this respect are not so much form and contour, but rather relief and line-drawing. Relief results not only in an intensification of the effects of light and shade, but also in those light reflexes that are of such decisive and specific importance for porcelain. Differentiation in the relief is a magnificent way of bringing porcelain alive, as is admirably shown by the surfaces on the animal figures. The great variety of structures in the relief brings about an equal variety of light reflexes, lengthy ones alternating with sparkling points, sharply demarcated beams alternating with diffuse pools. Each structure yields its own kind of light-show, stimulated by form but ultimately deriving from the material. From this point of view, a typical Kaendler animal – its abundant variety of surface structures injecting a kaleidoscopic (and thus non-figurative) dimension to its appearance – is ideally "right" for the material of which it is made. The same is true of the line-drawing. The reason why line-drawing is a fruitful means of exploiting porcelain's "two-layeredness" is that filling incised lines with transparent glaze gives an effective impression of depth, the most illuminating example of this being the feather structures scratched into so many of the bird figures (see fig. 57). Kaendler was clearly aware of the softening effect of the glaze, which while it imparts depth also takes away something from the sharpness of the drawing, and it was at his express instruction that this line-drawing was put in by the repairers. In his catalog of complaints of 1734, Kaendler lamented that Höroldt only instructed the repairers to work over the joins and did not allow them time to apply more delicate finishing touches to the figures; and he furthermore complained that fine line-drawing was in any case practically impossible because the paste was too coarse and granular.

Finally – and particularly in a study of the animal figures – consideration should be given to a third aspect of "rightness for porcelain," namely the extent to which porcelain is an intrinsically suitable medium for this particular kind of subject matter. An animal is first and foremost an organic being, and thus one that can move of its own accord. Constant changes of posture – and thus constant changes in the appearance of contours and surfaces – are an integral part of the way animals look. This being the case, a plastic medium such as the clay used for making porcelain models clearly provides the ideal material for the depiction of a living being. Modelers build their models: formless clay shapes up at the touch of their gifted hands. Clay can be shaped in almost any conceivable way and enables the artist to seek out the form he or she is looking for. Unlike carver-sculptors, for whom one slip of the chisel can render a piece of marble or wood useless for the work they have in mind, modelers in clay are always free to go back and correct.[800] It is thus not entirely correct to speak of clay-modelers subjugating or exercising mastery over their material, just as it is not strictly correct to say that marble-sculptors are at the mercy of the stone. The hand of the modeler engages in a direct dialog with a compliant material that – so to speak – positively rejoices at the touch that gives it shape and form.

This is precisely the characteristic that makes a material ideal for the depiction of animals, because seeking after eloquence of form – all inevitable limitations notwithstanding – is an entirely different process from the one in which a pre-determined formal idea is to be imposed as exactly as possible on a material that cannot be re-shaped and re-formed. To model is to shape organically, to build up, to bring about a marriage between a creative idea and a piece of pliant, submissive clay.

Putting it in somewhat black-and-white terms, one might say that while the sculptor in marble liberates the work from the stone, the modeler subdues the work in the clay.

This makes it clear why clay – the modeling medium *par excellence*, plastic in the real sense of the word – is the ideal medium for the depiction of the naked living being, and thus also the ideal medium for animal figures.

Our consideration of these three aspects of material-attuned craftsmanship may be summarized as follows. Precisely because porcelain does not allow for a successful imitation of materials and textures (feather, horn, and so on), our attention is drawn primarily to the particular character of the working material. Although our attention constantly jumps between recognition of the subject and recognition of the material in which the subject is rendered, the fact that the material has a rich life of its own (light reflexes, its "fluidity") and an organic, plastic quality that is still in evidence even when it is in the fired state, the material does not compete with the motif, but positively joins forces with the movement inherent in the figure's composition.

To say that Kaendler worked in a way that was right for the material is thus not to say, inverting what has been said above, that the material is mastered by form, nor to suggest that this rejection of the mastery of material by form implies the dominance of material over form, as has been the general tendency in the modern era. In Kaendler's animal figures, the material with all its particular characteristics form make a significant and positive contribution to the overall effect. Just as the clay being used to make the model enters into dialog with the artist's hand, the porcelain surface, alive with all its characteristic depth and light-reflective qualities, enters into a dialog with the subject matter, which is for preference not a coffee-pot, but rather a living being. In this sense, Kaendler's animal figures can be regarded as "models" of the kind of artistry that is absolutely right for porcelain.

The "meaning" of Kaendler's animal figures

"With his finely differentiated and detailed surfaces, and those subtle contours, eye-catching overhangs, and spirited gestures that never lose touch with the appearance of the figure as a whole, Kaendler was fully in tune with the artistic spirit of the late Baroque and with the period's zest for spatial dynamism and natural expressiveness. In spite of the immediacy of his depictions of movement in porcelain, Kaendler did not really create images of nature, but rather subjected his figures to an artistic concept that was entirely his own, characterized by a calculated building up of the component parts and self-contained composition."[801] In a formal sense, Pietzsch (writing here about a madonna figure) was certainly right in proposing this as a basic feature of Kaendler's art. And we have already pointed out a number of times that "naturalism" (a problematic enough term at the best of times) is not the right term for the classifying the animal figures, giving formal reasons why this is the case just as Pietzsch does in the above passage. The ornamentalization of the surface and the exaggeration of select elements in order to guide the eye are just two features which belie the notion that Kaendler's figures are faithful representations of natural exemplars. However, the animal figures also have a dimension that lies above and beyond the imitation of outer appearance: they also contrive to reflect the inner nature (the sensibility, the "character") of the animal they depict. While Kaendler's animal compositions are, as has been noted, fully in tune with the canons of late Baroque art, we should not forget that they also have "expressional subject matter." For when we look at them, do we not also see, communicated through externals, something akin to an "image of the animal's inner nature"?

In the individual analyses, we constantly found ourselves making reference to the animal's present state and activity: the fish-swallowing pelican, the dog straining to scratch itself, the cockerel stretching upwards and crowing, and so on. None of these, however, has anything to do with inner states in the sense of rendering the "character" or "nature" of an animal. When, coming face-to-face with the precariously balanced macaw, we catch ourselves saying "yes, that's just what a cheeky macaw looks like," then we must remember that we are putting our own interpretation on the bird. And the fact that the macaw holds it head up high when climbing downwards is no real reason for assuming that it has inner feelings that have anything to do with the human notion of "cheekiness." When we see a member of a certain bird or animal species, we commonly transfer it into the broad context of our own experience, and take certain of its norms of behavior as indicating that it has a certain character or feels certain feelings; in fact, we have no reason for supposing that this is true of the particular animal we are looking at – in this instance, this particular macaw. The practice of building up character-portraits from successive interpretations is ubiquitous in our culture. It turns animals into inexhaustible vehicles for our moral and ethical projections.

The opportunities provided by this tendency were exploited to the full by the art of the Baroque. With its disposition towards putting things into order and making every element refer to a further order, it naturally leapt at the chance of seeing animals as symbols for a whole range of other phenomena: the natural world as a whole, certain affective states, (human) character traits, aesthetic principles, the power of God, and many other abstract ideals according to the respective context. Representations of animals had to incorporate pointers to the realities they were intended to symbolize. Kirchner's animal figures are fine examples of the capacity of the Baroque work of art to reflect – or even to create – *Weltanschauung*. We have already examined his techniques for doing this in our studies of the majesty-radiating lion and of the guilt-feeling fox. These figures are made up of symbolic references that constantly point us away from the depiction of nature to other ideals and values. As far as external appearance was concerned, all that was necessary was that the species should be recognizable, for the real meaning of the Baroque animal figure lay on a different plane entirely.

And in Kaendler's case? His more mature animal figures are absolutely lacking in pegs on which to hang human interpretations. Nor, however, are they such perfect copies of nature that they could be taken for casts. Looking at a figure by Kaendler, we are somewhat taken aback to find that what we have before us is at once a work of art (the figure's external appearance) and at the same time an animal (from the effect it has on us). However, it is not the external appearance that deceives us into thinking that the figure really is an animal (as would be the case with a *trompe l'oeil* figure, or one that achieved a perfect imitation of detail): the illusion results from the energies that the external appearance sets in motion. If the sculpture interprets the externals of the animal, or indeed changes the natural appearance of the animal, it only does so up to the point where the artist's emphases have succeeded in bringing the inner nature of the animal to the surface, where it can then impinge on our perception. The reason why this mechanism works so well is that while we may have certain intellectual ideas about the animal concerned and are thus capable of using the animal at our pleasure for symbolic purposes, on the emotional level we still have a strong sense of the animal's essential integrity and inviolability. When we use an animal as a vehicle for our projections (attributing character, symbolic value, or whatever), we also have the intelligence to know that our point of reference is no longer the animal itself, for we have made the animal, or our depiction of the animal, into a sign for something else.

And this is precisely what Kaendler does *not* do. He observes the animal as a living sculpture in its own right, and captures it at what seems to him to be its most telling moment, when it is most "itself."

He is entirely uninfluenced by the conventional images of the animal: his hand is guided by his feeling for what is special and what is charming about the animal at the particular moment that he has chosen. He is interested in the animal as a living being, which he observes and finally illustrates in his model. If we judge the figures as works of naturalism, then we are bound to end up complaining about the elements of exaggeration, or at best admiring the artist's virtuosity. But if we open our feelings to the animals, then we are sensitive to their inner charge and immediately grasp the essential point, namely that a Kaendler animal figure is not intended to be an image but a "Du" (a "thou"): a living being that can look one in the eyes. This is very well demonstrated by the downward-climbing macaw, which is so precariously balanced as to make us feel we are losing our balance too, but is also the case with other models as well.[802]

Kaendler's animals allow us to come close and to get to know them, without letting the whole exercise become overshadowed by symbolism, or by the emotions that they arouse in us. When we put our questions to the animals, they do not give us irrational answers, as religious art does: on the contrary, our question-asking only leads us back to ourselves. Our dialog with the animal figure leads us to conclusions about the animal figure itself and not to conclusions relating to higher value systems of which they are merely symbols. Our eyes are guided around the figure by the surface treatment and compositional lines, and emotions are aroused in us (a sensual process, and thus thoroughly Baroque), but we cannot take refuge in any higher values or meanings. We cannot intellectualize our emotions any more than we can when we are confronted with a real live animal: we have to find other ways of coming to terms with the being before us. Never are we given the chance to see through to some kind of narrative plane, to dwell on secondary meanings, or to be edified, as we do with heraldic images of animals, or in the literary field with the fable, or with such religious symbols as a dove in a church. If we are looking for meaning in this sense of the word, a Kaendler animal will give us no joy: however long we look at it, it will always remain an animal. At the same time, however, we are also prevented from going to the other extreme of leisurely and pleasant appreciation of the sheer beauty of the figure (cf. ornaments, objets d'art), because in the object in question we recognize an animal, a living being. Once we have come so far, we are certainly aware that Kaendler's animal figures are not stand-ins but the real thing, not representation but presentation.

The fact that to arrive at this insight we need to go through this process of logical thought is in itself a demonstration of how natural and unpretentious these works are. With the possible exception of the wing-beating eagle, their appeal lies not in the grand passions that they depict or evoke, nor in the emotionally charged theatrical gesture, but rather in their delicate sensitivity towards the nature of the animals they depict.

This is a very un-Baroque characteristic, particularly in the court context: the intention is not to impress, enthrall, or deceive (porcelain in any case hardly lends itself to trompe-l'oeil), but rather to suggest things that require sensibility to be appreciated. It would of course be highly audacious to claim that Kaendler's animal figures were Baroque art in their composition and general formulation, but un-Baroque in the realization of the fundamental idea behind them: the art we know as Baroque encompasses a multitude of currents ranging from "emotional propaganda" to coolly calculated classicism. Nevertheless, all these currents do have one thing in common: they all aim to answer questions about meaning and purpose.

Again, this is quite emphatically something that Kaendler's figures do *not* do. As tangible "reality," Baroque sculpture was reserved for representative use (it had to stand for something), which ruled "out of court" works of art that stood for nothing but what they depicted. Why, then, was such a notable exception made in the case of Kaendler's Japanese Palace animals? I believe that the answer is first and foremost to be found in his biography. As has already been noted a number of times, we do not know what pieces Kaendler worked on during his period of training.[803] He definitely worked on stone: his tombstones from the 1730s were clearly done by a hand experienced in sculpting sandstone. We also know for certain that he carved wood, not only during his training but also after he came to Meissen. As a practitioner of the plastic arts, he was just as familiar with these techniques as with modeling, but we do not know what motifs he sculpted. The Dresden sculptors had a great deal to do with architectural decoration in the broadest sense of the expression, and with interiors. We can thus assume that Kaendler gained experience in sculpting stone, most likely at the Zwinger, and in carving wood, among other things, at the Green Vaults.

What all these fields had in common was that the work was fundamentally decorative or even purely ornamental in character: the pieces were intended to play a supporting part in a greater whole, and it was very rarely the case that they even achieved a kind of semi-autonomy as works of art in their own right, as did, for instance, the Hercules Saxonicus on the rampart pavilion at the Zwinger. With their decorative character, these pieces of work – and particularly their purely ornamental elements – called for great aesthetic sensitivity, and a fine feeling for subtleties of line and for the distribution of focal points. The sculptor not only had to bear the overall context in mind but also had to pay close attention to such designs as were already in existence, such as architects' plans. In this sense, the role of the artist was to "illustrate" elements that were part of a greater whole. This is not to suggest that the court sculptors were not capable of original creative work, but in order to do work that was subordinate to a higher overall concept they had to develop a feeling for striking a balance between the immediate effect of the piece in hand, its "representative" function, and its relation to the whole. If we consider Kaendler's mature work with this in mind, it is clear that the young artist became thoroughly competent in these procedures and that they still had a formative influence on his approach in later years.

In the summer of 1731, when Kaendler arrived at the manufactory in Meissen to take up a position primarily oriented towards the creation of large animal figures, he first turned his hand to birds, taking his inspiration, as has already been noted in detail, from zoological depictions. By this time, these depictions were already "illustration" in the strict sense of the word, worlds away from the highly symbolic, cosmologically loaded bestiaries of medieval times. The contemporary interest in the infinite variety of the natural world and the concomitant concern to discover its underlying order called for maximum precision in the rendering of detail, and an objectivity that was to be disembarrassed of all possible value judgments. Classification was conducted more or less in accordance with the hierarchy attributed to the animal kingdom, but the main point was not only to examine individual animals and species, but also to examine each species as representative of its genus or family. The parallels with the general scheme of things governing ornamental sculpture are unmistakable.

As the "spirit" of the zoological illustration is likewise unmistakably present in Kaendler's first bird and animal figures, it comes as no surprise to find that he retained his objective, analytical approach in the later works done from natural specimens, whether stuffed or, as in many cases, in the menageries. In the menageries, the objective approach was now supplemented by the highly important fact that he had observed the animals live. The challenge he now faced was to bring the same high degree of observation and perceptiveness to capturing the character of the animal as manifest in its movements that he had shown when rendering motionless externals. As an artist whose natural aesthetic sensibility had been heightened by his training as a sculptor at the court, Kaendler was certainly aware that by elaborating upon externals in the right way he could contrive to give clearer expression to inner character. This is to be borne in mind when we consider certain typical features of Kaendler's work, notably his compositional lines, and his habit of singling out certain areas for special accentuation and certain features for calculated exaggeration. These elements are thrown out of shape and optically weighted in such a way that they take charge of the beholder's eye and guide the mind towards recognition of the nature of the animal in question.

While Kaendler was fully aware that the animals he was modeling were to be displayed in a gallery, there are no signs that he took any account of the demands of their future home, apart from a few pairs that are well suited to being exhibited symmetrically. It was perhaps a great stroke of good fortune that no rigid concept was drawn up for the animal gallery, and that the artist was not compelled to suit any of the figures to particular locations.

This is also one of the reasons why Kaendler's figures – which we have described as abounding in very special aesthetic qualities but lacking in any reference to extraneous levels of meaning – cannot be dismissed as superficial and decorative. Every one of his animal models was the result of a personal encounter with a source of inspiration. In some cases the source of inspiration was a print, but in most cases it was a living specimen. The very fact that he focused so intensely on what was special about each bird or animal belies the notion that the moving spirit behind the figures was essentially decorative; this having been said, we may gladly admit that the unprogrammatic nature of the individual animals did leave Kaendler free to make them gloriously decorative to boot.

And yet the figures strike us as being very much more than simply excellent likenesses: they also speak to us on the emotional level, giving us a powerful impression of the inner character of the animal in question. The distinction between these two facets becomes all the clearer when one examines the successes and failures of Kaendler's forgers and imitators. Kaendler achieved an ideal synthesis that can be observed in many another sphere of art: his figures are aesthetically pleasing (decoration) and impinge on the eye in such a way as to stimulate the heart and mind in equal measure.

With this group of works, Kaendler was plumbing new depths: he saw the animals in a new way and developed means to express his vision in his figures. As has been noted, he had been given an ideal schooling for this task by his early career. Nothing was definitively laid down apart from the selection of species to be modeled (and even this he did not adhere to unfailingly), and the new material that he was to use was ideally suited to his artistic goal. Furthermore, with a small number of exceptions, he was not in the least influenced by the conventional traditions of animal depiction, and could follow his own vision more or less as the spirit moved him.

These ideal external conditions meant that there were no hindrances to the development of his artistic talent. The new way of seeing the animal world that had been stimulated by the development of natural science, the challenge presented by a young material that still had a wealth of inherent potential, a theme that was not weighed down by tradition (in this material), and the artist's own highly refined sensitivity: all these things combined to give birth to strikingly new creations far beyond the bounds of convention.

How is it that these works have so effectively retained their power to impress and, unlike the much less immediately comprehensible small figurines, have constantly been accorded such high regard? The answer is to be found in their unbiased honesty with regard to the motifs, their way of illustrating the animal in such a way as to engage our attention and give us new insights into its essential character, and – last but not least – the exceptional decorative quality of certain outstanding figures. And unlike Kirchner's large animals, it is only in a formal sense that Kaendler's are typical of their era (*mouvementé*, bursting with energy): quite unconventionally, Kaendler was on the non-formal level so resolved to convey the real character of his natural subjects that his creations never began to "lie." Irrespective of cultural developments and changes in the way people have seen art, our view of animals always has two components: one that is based on unmediated, "true" experience, and one that is culturally conditioned, not concerned to see the animal objectively but rather to construct some kind of relationship between the animal and mankind. While the first component was one of the most important foundations of natural science, it could not lay claim to such a foundational position in the sphere of art. The animal casts of Mannerism, the studies of the German masters, and – in the field of ceramics – even the works of Palissy owed their birth more to the spirit of science than to an urgent need to be artistically creative.

It may be considered as one of Kaendler's major achievements that he bridged these two fields for sculpture. In so doing, he broke with convention and freed animal sculpture from its two traditional functions: symbolism and science. When making his models he succeeded in distancing himself from his creation to such an extent that his eye would only monitor the composition while his hand shaped the living being that the composition was to frame. Kaendler put his finger on this aspect of his art in a statement that is just as valid for nature as it is for art, made in the course of one of his suggestions for improvements: "Es [ist] nicht zu beschreiben, Weil [= wie] die Natur durch die Formen gantz gewaltig arbeitet." ("It is beyond the power of words to express how mightily nature works through forms.")[804]

Our point of departure at the beginning of this book was the Japanese Palace, which constituted the reason why the animal figures were created in the first place, and it is to the Japanese Palace that we shall now return in order to draw our final conclusions. What was the general reaction to Kaendler's art as manifest in the animals? As works of art, how do the individual animal figures relate to the Japanese Palace?

The animal figures and the model Residence: two mutually formative works of art

As was noted at the beginning of this study, consideration of the artistic concept underlying the animal figures entails taking account of two points of view: that of the modelers, who brought forth single animals or pairs in a fairly fortuitous sequence over a period of about six years, and that of Augustus the Strong, who commissioned the figures. The fact that he and his collaborators planned to incorporate the figures as one ensemble into a certain specific context, the Japanese Palace, was considered reason enough for according the animals and the palace an equal measure of attention. Now that we have given a comprehensive factual and circumstantial account of the two entities, the moment has finally come to investigate how the animals and the palace relate to each other in terms of their "meaning" ("Bedeutung").

At first it would seem difficult to find any kind of common denominator. As noted above, the modelers did not take very much account of where and how the figures were to be displayed. Although they did do matching pairs and most of the figures were done with a front and a back, it is by no means the case, for example, that roughly half of the figures were done looking downwards because they were to be displayed on consoles high up on the walls. In each and every case, the modelers went about their business without regard for external factors, considering the figure in question as a fully autonomous work of art.

The king – to mention just the most important person involved on the court side, for simplicity's sake – took these works of art as his basic building blocks and put them together to form a comprehensive and coherent whole. Although this procedure had a certain amount in common with the way in which a princely gallery of paintings was built up, there was a difference in that the building that was to house the animals was founded on a very specific and all-pervasive concept. Visitors were not primarily intended to focus their attention on individual works, or even dwell on the relationships between the figures in the gallery: the main intention was that the individual work should be seen as subordinate to the palace as a whole and – to put it in more concrete terms – as an aspect of the palace as a model residence.

The mind of our own time naturally considers the animal figures best investigated with the tools and insights of art history, and the palace with those of cultural history.

An account has already been given of the role envisaged for the animal figures: like the plates and vases in other rooms, they were to be displayed on walls, on consoles, tables, and very likely also on pedestals. This having been said, it should be noted that there was an important difference between the non-figurative wares and the animals: whereas the plates and vases were a showcase for porcelain as a material, a demonstration of the potency of the Saxon economy, and also a color-coding device for the conscious structuring of the model Residence, the animal figures were important for one additional reason, namely that they were likenesses of living beings. As the animals were somewhat more than just objects, they were interpreted as proofs of Saxony's high standard in things artistic, as representatives of the natural world, and also – within the model residence – as a metaphor for parts of human society. Meaning was accorded them that went beyond their literal and primary significance: a typically Baroque procedure.

As we have seen, Kirchner clearly designed his animals so that they could be interpreted as referring to things above and beyond their immediate subject matter. Their very style and expressive qualities positively encouraged the beholder to see them as images of moral and ethical values, or even of hierarchical positions. We have also noted that this powerfully referential dimension is conspicuously absent from Kaendler's later animal figures.

It now remains for us to establish the extent to which Kaendler's figures were suited to their intended home in the Japanese Palace, and whether credit can still be given to the thesis that the animal gallery had a deeper general significance and further roles to play on other levels.

The suitability of Kaendler's animal figures for the Japanese Palace

In a certain sense, the Japanese Palace animals are quite the reverse of the display piece created by the goldsmith Dinglinger depicting the birthday of the Grand Mogul, in itself a vehicle for a multitude of coded references to political and cultural events.[805] The piece itself was exhibited in the Green Vaults, where the objects on display had nothing in common with each other except for the exceptional artistry that had gone into their making and the costliness of the materials in which they were made. In spite of many of them being shot through with symbolism, they were not subordinate to an all-embracing overall iconographic program.

In the Japanese Palace, on the contrary, a multitude of – in the best sense of the word – decorative, iconographically insignificant objects were put together to form an ensemble that was anything but purely decorative or lacking in higher meaning. With its multiple levels of meaning, the palace was something quite different from the traditional porcelain room. In the case of the porcelain room, the microcosm–macrocosm dimension was summoned up by the abundance of intricate detail within a large overall context: the collection's appeal to the senses combined with its strictly structured but lively ordering to speak to the visitor of a certain cosmic and universal order. In the case of the Japanese Palace, the two elements were consciously combined so as to underpin a specific claim, with splendid and costly decoration effectively designed to reflect not just any prince's standing, but that of one in particular: Augustus the Strong (and later Augustus III), Elector of Saxony and King in Poland.

In his characterization of the Baroque, Harald Olbrich has identified fields of tension of just this kind – highly charged areas deriving their character from contrasting extremes – as a fundamental feature of the period. For Olbrich, the Baroque is positioned "between a highly developed sensitivity for the individual element, right down to the smallest detail, and a capacity for rational or emotional apprehension of the world as a whole... between a new quality of perception and skepsis about the capacity of the senses... between the demands of the individual and those of the social order."[806] In the field of tension, however, the one extreme does not exclude the other. On the contrary, the two poles usually appear simultaneously, promoting what one might call an awareness of the relativity of things. To return to our specific context, the visitors to the Japanese Palace could, according to the measure of their knowledge and sensitivity, flit to and fro between focusing on such detailed elements as the plumage on a porcelain bird and dwelling on the model character of the palace as conceived by Augustus the Strong, either intuitively feeling that they had seen the same essential scenario at the Zwinger, or rationally reflecting on the relation between the individual figures and the palace as a whole. The visitors were also free to tap into a number of other levels of meaning. Three that were valid for the palace have already been investigated: "porcelain palace," metaphor for art and commerce, archetypal residence. Discerning visitors found themselves confronted by a whole complex of references that were articulated by the building and its contents but at the same time went far beyond them. If the visitor, or rather the visitor's capacity for interpreting things, was thus the tower from which this whole cosmos could be viewed, then what the visitor saw – the "image" – was the key to the tower.

The fact that Kaendler's figures were relatively precise in their detail and at the same time devoid of any specific program or "meaning" was propitious to this approach. The visitors could, if the spirit moved them, still see Kaendler's animals as representatives of human moral values, though this would have been a very intellectual and interpretative train of thought incompatible with committed admiration of the works as sculpture. If so inclined, they could well see the pair of goats with their young one as representative of the "family," as was indeed suggested in our study of the figures. However, if the group set them reflecting on the relation of the animal to the natural world, then they would dwell on those rational and irrational relationships which we identified as two of nature's basic principles in our study of the goats above.

Kirchner's figures, however, generally made no allowances for changes of perspective of this kind. In his rendering of the lion, for example, he took it so much for granted that it would be regarded as a symbol for a ruler that the beholder is hard put to see a real live lion in the figure at all. While a gallery of Kirchner animals would have fulfilled and underpinned the last intention of the project (palace as archetypal residence, animals as representatives of human society), it would not have promoted the other levels of meaning at all, if only for the reason that when the Baroque eye sought to evaluate sculpture as art, it set great store by external similarity to the natural original, as is shown by Sulkowski's criticism of the unsubtle postures of some of Kirchner's early animal figures.

To shed further light on the quality of Kaendler's figures in this particular respect and to show how suitable they in fact were for the Japanese Palace, one further thought has to be taken into account.

As been pointed out, the period of production of the Japanese Palace animals also saw the development of the form of ornament we know as rocaille. Rocaille is nothing other than the logical result and continued development of a certain way of apprehending the world: without any apparent mediation, it plunders nature's treasury of forms for elements such as shells and wings, transcribes them into a matrix of higher aesthetic and formal relationships (line, curve, and so on) and finally puts a variety of these units together into a coherent composition. While it is perfectly normal to find this basic tendency towards abstraction in an ornamental style, the remarkable thing about rocaille is that the basic natural components remain clearly recognizable. This leads us to something that one could, for want of a better expression, call rocaille's "third dimension": in part, it leaves off being purely imitative and transmutes into an irrational and non-figurative energy flow that always finally turns back into an element rooted in the real world.

As a system of forms, rocaille involves elements identical with natural originals being interspersed with and joined by variable, fluid sections not formally identical with any natural originals but nevertheless essentially natural in character. This explains how

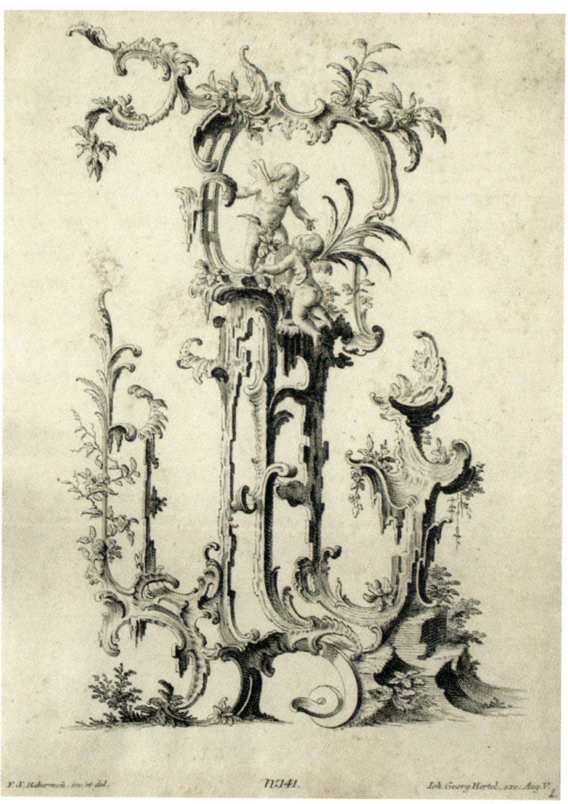

197 Franz Xaver Habermann, rocaille fantasy (Augsburg: Johann Georg Hertel)

rocaille can promote fantasy and free association with other levels of meaning without totally losing touch with reality. If we lose track of our thoughts or our feelings in the "sur-realism" of the overall construction, then we can always get our bearings on the *terra firma* of one of the purely imitative features before venturing out afresh into the swirls that lie between them. In other words, it is a constant variation on a theme, the theme being a metamorphosis in which we are thrown hither and thither between our reason ("I recognize the shell") and our feeling (our eye is drawn on in the general flow), and which enables us to experience the ornamental design as a composition with a higher meaning and to see it as a coherent and comprehensive whole.

If the elements were to be presented in an interpreted form – as was indeed the case with the well-proportioned and pre-processed ornamental forms of the Baroque and Régence (acanthus, scroll, and so on) – then our intellectual and emotional reaction would be that the object of the exercise was to satisfy the human desire for harmony, or that it had all been done to accord with a specific artistic concept. Both the detail and the overall composition would in this case be presenting nature in an interpreted, abstract, cultivated form. Rocaille, by contrast, is genuinely illustrative in character, but at the same time goes much further than this: it not only presents individual forms but is also constructed in such a way as to give a visual scheme of nature's underlying forces. It is even capable, in spite of the apparent rigidity of its basic building blocks, of breathing further life into elements that in themselves already speak to us of what is most lively about nature itself. It is the paradox of an artificial phenomenon that comes across as being very natural that gives rocaille its particular charm and fascination.

Parallels can be drawn between rocaille and three aspects of the present study: porcelain as a material, Kaendler's animal figures, and the way these figures relate to the Japanese Palace.

In the excursus on "shine" in Part Three, it was noted that the special character of porcelain is related to the paradox that porcelain paste has an almost unlimited capacity for being shaped and molded while the fired porcelain object is very hard and brittle. Furthermore, even in the hard and brittle state, the object still conveys something of its former plasticity: one can still imagine how tractable and how easy to shape it must once have been. Although a porcelain piece is actually a rigid structure, it speaks to us of movement; although the medium "dies" (in the kiln) it rises immortal from the ashes with an eternal capacity for effects that abound in life, light, and liveliness. Another polarity inherent in porcelain is the relative simplicity of its basic materials and the highly artificial character of the end products.

Precisely this is true of Kaendler's later animal figures: the natural original is imitated in the overall shaping and the treatment of the surfaces, but with varying degrees of faithfulness, as a result of which the mind is alerted and the eye is guided along lines that are powerfully suggestive of the presence of a real living being.

And finally, when *in situ* at the palace, Kaendler's mature animal figures always allow the beholder either to see them as standing in for the living beings of the natural world or to see them as opening up interpretative paths to the palace's other levels of meaning. The figures come from the very core of the natural world, but the artificiality of their material and their ornamental function in a specific interior means that while they can be read in various ways, they still remain self-evidently and transparently natural whatever interpretations they may give rise to. The interpretative freedom that the figures allow is what makes it possible for us to perceive the overall concept on various levels, and to intuit the fullness of what they stand for.

A more traditional animal figure of the kind Kirchner produced would be too one-dimensional to achieve this, because it is so preoccupied with pointing to higher values. Kaendler's models are quite different because they allow us to focus on higher values if we will, but at the same time leave us free to pursue a number of other perspectives as well. Far from being programmatic or didactic set pieces, they are components of the natural world and thus can be appreciated both emotionally and rationally. Integrated into a highly complex system, they testify to the mastery of nature inherent in human creativity and to man's ability to take elements from nature and put them together into thought-provoking and meaningful compositions.

Here it is helpful to pursue the comparison touched upon above between the animal gallery and a gallery of paintings, in which each painting likewise has its own fund of meaning, capable of being developed along its own particular lines. As a representation, the painting has, among other things, a referential function, a core content that is intellectual in character. While the putting together of a collection of paintings in a gallery will first and foremost be done in accordance with formal criteria, they can be so arranged to make their content, or even simply their motifs, amount to an overall statement: an iconographical program, for instance, or an ancestral gallery, or a showing of the work of a particular artist. If the decision is made to give the gallery a certain overall theme, then each picture will lose something of its own particular immediate impact, while the aspect that is of especial importance for the gallery as a whole will be brought to the fore. The acknowledgment of the one (overall program) will always be to the detriment of the other (the particular cosmos of the individual picture), the latter losing something of its autonomy and being relegated to a subordinate role.[807]

As individual works, Kaendler's animal figures in the gallery of the Japanese Palace make their impact on a quite different level. It is not just that they are complete in themselves as formal entities: their details – the microcosm – are also purely formal in character, devoid of the kind of referential content that a painting has, and lacking in the kind of references to human values inherent in a classical sculpture. On the emotional level, however, they do allow us insights into the character of the motif. In the overall context of the gallery, the emotional experience of the individual work triggers off an intellectual appreciation of the meaning of the whole. If we wish to appreciate the animal figures *in toto*, then we have to look into the context in which they were intended to be set, which immediately leads to our making interpretations, to which our emotional feelings about any single animal can no longer make any useful contribution.

In this sense, a gallery of Kirchner animals – in which the quest for meaning would begin with the individual work and soon enough find the answers it is looking for – would seem to have more in common with a gallery of paintings. But this is only partially true, as the mind of the beholder quickly comes to the limits of what a Kirchner figure has to say about the character of the animal concerned. Kaendler's animals, on the other hand, strike a fine balance between the effect of the individual piece and the overall context, because the two levels of appreciation are approached along quite different channels and offer quite different insights and experiences. When we consider Kaendler's animals in the context of the gallery, our appreciation is enriched by a whole new dimension. In this sense, it is precisely because they were created as autonomous works that they are such ideal foils for the levels of meaning inherent in the Japanese Palace. These animals are not just an aspect of one of the palace's levels of meaning: they are "arguments" which effectively underpin every one of the palace's rhetorical structures and have a contribution to make however we read the palace's underlying concept.

Why did the King need these porcelain animals?

Whether Augustus the Strong saw from Kaendler's first heron, done in the spring of 1731, how suitable the modeler's artistry was to his own concept for an animal gallery must remain a matter for speculation: the figure has not survived, nor do we know whether Kaendler's particular approach to modeling animals had begun to take shape at this stage. However, it is very likely that this test piece was very much in accord with the kind of animal figure that the king had had in mind a year earlier when decided that his "porcelain palace" should contain an animal gallery. For one thing, the king never troubled to define exactly how he wanted his animals to be done. And to make a somewhat pointed distinction, what he asked for were not animal figures, but simply animals. Linguists may object that this *bon mot* fails to allow for the freedom with which the German language was used at the time, but it does provide an apposite illustration of what the king's fundamental intention certainly was.

His requirement that the animals should be lifelike – "in their natural size and color" – was intended to highlight the links between the gallery, and thus the whole Japanese Palace, and other key locations where his power and authority were given visible expression: it has already been pointed out how closely the gallery is related to the natural history collection in the Zwinger, which was effectively an integral part of the Dresden *Residenzschloss*, and to Schloss Moritzburg. Furthermore, only animal figures are capable of the kind of openness and ambiguity that the king wanted: another reason why Kaendler's approach was the right one for the king's purposes. And this ambiguity, logically enough, was what so effectively made the message associated with the animal gallery all the more far-reaching and comprehensive.

Augustus the Strong was particularly dependent on mechanisms of this kind, with their potential for presenting him as an elevated and superior being. They were of course part and parcel of the propaganda machinery of any absolutist prince, but the particular position to which Augustus the Strong as Elector of Saxony had risen by acquiring the Polish crown and forging dynastic links with the Imperial house meant that the means he used to give public expression to his claims to power had to be doubly convincing. Their goal was not simply to underpin the rights he had inherited by birth: they also had to be credible enough to lend legitimacy to his new pretensions.

Writing about the celebrations for the wedding of the future Augustus III with the Emperor's daughter Maria Josepha in 1719, Monika Schlechte put it as follows: "The pretensions expressed [by the wedding] constituted not only a quantitative but also a qualitative questioning of the old order of things. No expense or trouble was spared to shed doubt on the practicability of everything that belonged to the status quo, and new possible orientations were sought high and low: in the dynastic tradition of the elector's own family, at the outstanding historical and present-day European courts, and in the most important events in European history. These constituted the concrete and ideal foundations for the reputation won for Saxony by Augustus the Strong of being home to one of the continent's leading courts."[808] Study of this wedding alone is enough to demonstrate that Augustus the Strong was under exceptional pressure to innovate. Tradition had to be given a certain retouching, and increased emphasis had to be put on the importance of the present. He could not simply copy an already existing system, such as that of France, as his goal was to underpin new pretensions and to present the new claims that he himself had made for Saxony. A new standard had to be set, and where there was no historical claim to assert in support of the new standard, then a new "truth" had to be forged to take the place of reality.

This is precisely how we are to see the raison d'être of the Japanese Palace: built as an artificial model of a princely residence, it stood for an equally artificial claim, imparting validity and permanence to that claim by the very fact of its real existence.

Porcelain – universally admired, historically rare, a recent invention that was the Saxon elector's personal property – was the ideal material for expressing and propagating the claims being made. Enlisting politically value-free but nevertheless living beings – animals – to the cause effectively raised Saxony's new potential onto a "natural" and highly generalized plane and made it possible to propound the new lines of thought more clearly.

Setting foot in the animal gallery, the visitor was greeted with a many-faceted statement that may be paraphrased as follows: "Nature, Art, and Society are at the service of this Prince: represented in His very own material in this porcelain menagerie, they hereby comply to His claims and aspirations."

The innovativeness that was so characteristic of Kaendler's animal figures and led to the formulation of a genuinely original artistic style well outside the bounds of convention was in full accord with the innovativeness that was characteristic of Augustus the Strong's public artistic ventures. When figures that plumbed the nature of the animals they depicted came together with a palace that gave visible expression to its owner's highest claims and aspirations, the place that was chosen for their rendezvous was a gallery: the Gallery of Meissen Animals.

Postlude

The animal figures and their artistic influence in the tide of time: a short summary

For the purpose of a history of the artistic "reception" of the Meissen animal figures in the eighteenth century, the pieces ordered for the Japanese Palace are best divided into two groups: the ones that from the mid-1730s onwards were allowed to be sold to third parties, and those that were reserved for the royal collection.

Given that the large Meissen figures were not produced for sale and there were no illustrations of them in circulation, it was in the eighteenth century only possible to admire them in situ at the Japanese Palace. It was thus not really possible for the large figures to exert any influence on the creations of other manufactories, and the great technical difficulties involved in their production was in any case sufficient discouragement to anyone thinking of imitating them. As a result, eighteenth-century porcelain firms restricted themselves to imitating or drawing inspiration from the technically less problematic smaller figures (mainly birds) that Meissen had offered on the open market since the 1730s. These were better known to customers generally and more saleable than the large ones would have been.

It is hardly possible to draw up a catalog of all the "derivatives" of the Meissen originals, "derivatives" being understood not only as strict copies – of which there were enormous numbers, done by almost all eighteenth-century porcelain firms (fig. 190) – but also works that were in some way or other inspired by the Meissen figures. Almost every modeler who applied himself to making a small bird figure took his cues from a figure by Kaendler and his fellows, or from a figure that derived from Kaendler. The Meissen creations exerted a formative influence on the whole approach to making small animal models, and with certain notable exceptions continued to do so until the end of the nineteenth and beginning of the twentieth centuries. Kaendler's way of turning his birds' support structures into little natural habitats and his habit of decorating branches with nests, fruit, or little animals became standard features even of porcelain animal figures that were not strictly speaking copies. The little artificial gardens that began to appear in the elaborate wooden paneling, stucco, and painting of Rococo interiors provided an apt setting for the smaller birds and animals that Kaendler had made so popular.[809] As far as the larger figures are concerned, the literature on the subject does contain a reference to the Cockerel being copied by the Vienna manufactory around 1750.[810] A number of other figures earlier considered to be eighteenth-century copies, such as a mandrill with the Frankenthal mark,[811] have turned out on closer inspection to be forgeries in the modern sense of the word, and will be considered below in the relevant section.

The nineteenth century brought a change in the way the animal figures were seen, and there was a corresponding shift in their "reception." At the same time as the appearance of Neo-Rococo in England around 1820, historicists were already calling for the re-creation of the major works of past ages.[812] The fact that porcelain-making is a reproductive process made this all the more feasible. The re-creations executed at Meissen are a specific aspect of the history of the animal figures' "reception" and will thus be treated in a section of their own, like the forgeries. It is nevertheless quite true that along with the rise of historicism in the nineteenth century there was a corresponding rise in demand for large animal figures "à la Meissen." Many smaller manufactories, particularly in Thuringia and Bohemia but also in France and England, brought forth veritable menageries of birds, monkeys, dogs, and the like, and it would take a whole book to give an adequate account of all these. What they all have in common is that they were inspired by the example of the large animal figures made for the Japanese Palace. The large animal figures could now be studied properly: the Porcelain Collection was from 1833 onwards open to the public, housed in a Japanese Palace that now functioned as a museum, and the sale of duplicates had made it possible for Meissen animal figures to be admired elsewhere in Europe, and not only in Dresden. But the actual production of animal figures of this size was still as problematic as ever, with the paste and the firing presenting just the same technical problems as they had at Meissen back in the 1730s.

The Meissen large animal figures in the late eighteenth, nineteenth, and twentieth centuries

When the animal figures were first brought to the Japanese Palace from Meissen, they were simply stored there, as the fitting out of the interior was not advanced enough for them to be put on display as had been planned (Sources 22 and 27). A comparison between the 1736 list (interim total of figures delivered to date; Source 19)[813] and the first inventory thereafter (1770)[814] shows that animal figures were repeatedly removed from the Palace, whether temporarily or permanently, some to be used as gifts, and some to be put on display elsewhere, for instance in the Tower Room of the Residence (fig. 189). With a few exceptions (Elephant, Fox, Cockerel, Cassowary) these were middle-size or small figures. The inventories of 1770 and 1779, for instance, only mention one cat, although there were four in 1736, and three have survived to form part of the present-day Porcelain Collection. It should also be noted that there must have been occasional breakages in the period 1736–1770.

The following is a list of those animal figures that were at the palace after the last delivery in 1736 but no longer appear in the inventory of 1770, with account being taken of the figures listed in the 1769 inventory drawn up specially for the Tower Room: 11 monkeys, 1 macaw, 5 coots, 2 Bolognese dogs, 2 squirrels, 1 elephant, 10 magpies, 8 owls/barn owls, 8 pheasants, 2 foxes, 6 bullfinches, 1 dog (scratching itself), 4 cockatoos, 1 cassowary, 3 cats, 3 rollers, 1 mandrill, 12 tits, 2 cockerels, 11 parrots, 1 bird of paradise, 6 guinea fowls, 10 “Raubvögel” (“birds of prey”), 4 bitterns, 1 sheep, 1 swallow, 1 parakeet, 1 woodpecker, 3 sparrowhawks, 5 jerboas, 5 doves, 1 turkeyhen, 3 eagle owls, 3 sables.

198 Tower Room of the *Residenzschloss* in Dresden (1896)

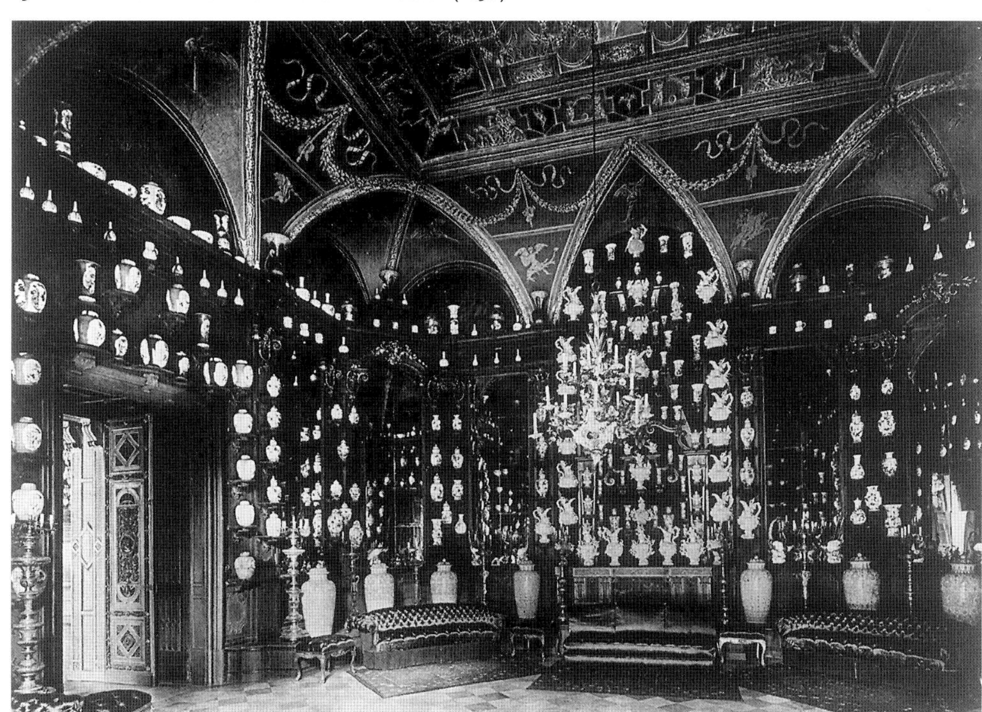

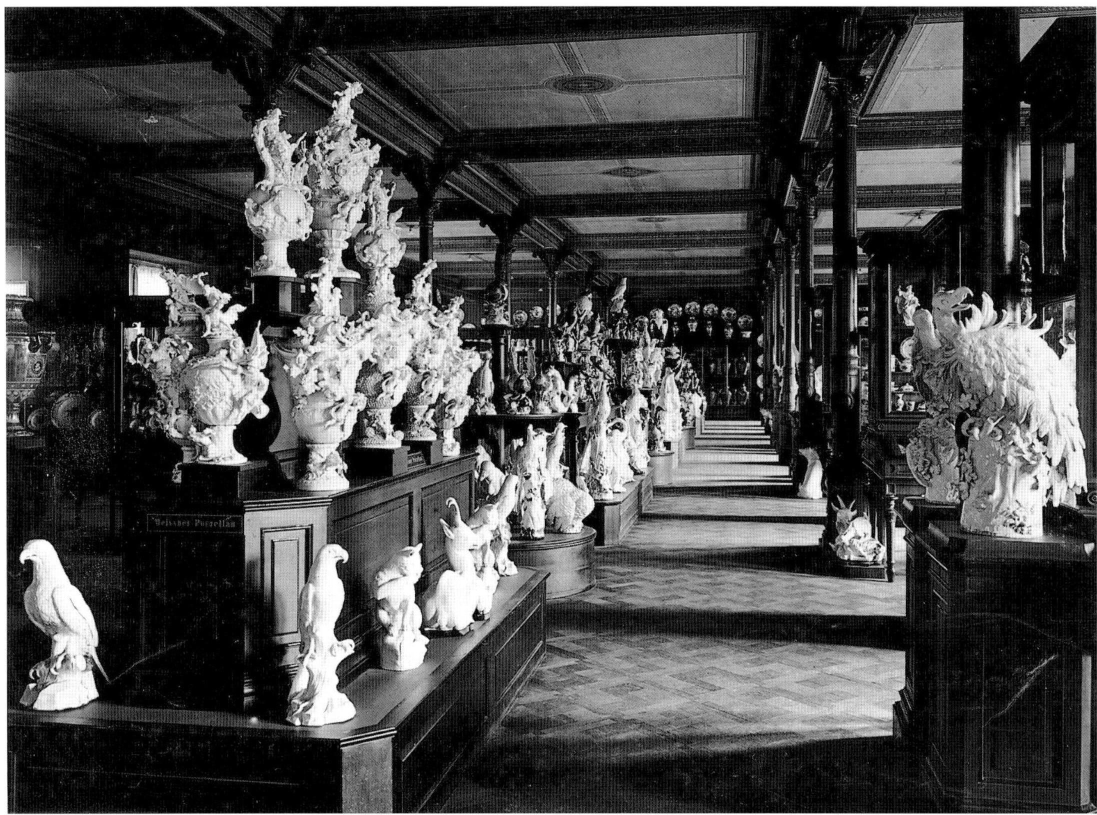

199 The Porcelain Collection in the main hall of the Johanneum, Dresden (ca. 1900)

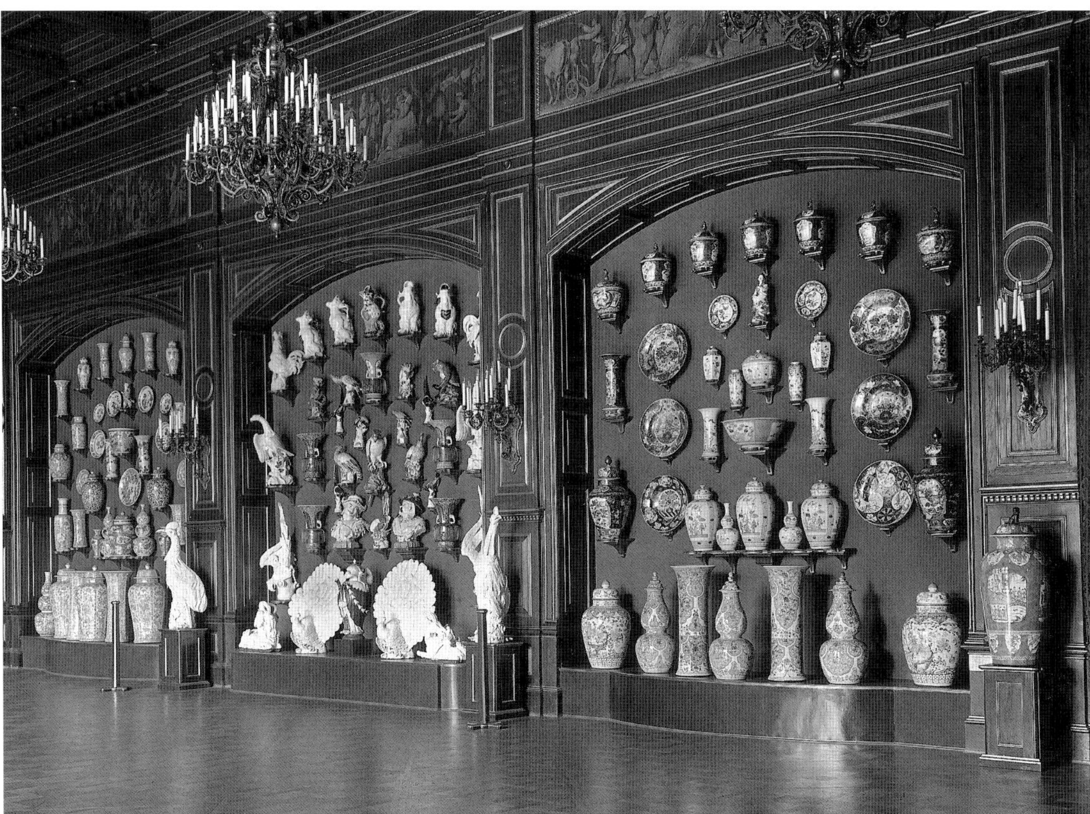

200 Banqueting hall of the *Residenzschloss* in Dresden (ca. 1920)

The losses and removals in the period 1770–1779 can be deduced from the inventory entries for the respective years. These reveal that one squirrel, two kingfishers, one pelican, and one woodpecker were broken, and two canaries were simply removed. A note entered into the inventory of 1779 at a later date furthermore tells us that a cassowary "fell in two during cleaning."

It is still unclear why so few of the large animals were removed in the second half of the eighteenth century. Taken out of the obsolete "Porzellanschloss" context, a single large animal figure would have been an eminently suitable decorative element in any number of interiors at the royal palaces. But it was only after the end of the monarchy, when the Residence became a museum,[815] that – in addition to the installation of the Porcelain Collection in the Johanneum (fig. 199) – a porcelain gallery was set up in the castle banqueting hall and animal figures were displayed in one of the wall-niches (fig. 200).[816]

However, the large animal figures remained together in one place until the beginning of the Seven Years' War in 1756, and while we do not know how the palace collections were arranged and displayed, the large animals were certainly among the most outstanding treasures that visitors were able to admire there. After the changes and chances of the war, they were left in the palace cellar as part of the royal collection, which was from that time on regarded as fit for display in a museum. As Count Marcolini proposed in 1787, the porcelain deserved more worthy accommodation, "as they are no longer to be regarded as furnishings ["als Meuble bestimmt"], but as works of art."[817]

Marcolini had a project to transfer the porcelain collection to the rooms in the Zwinger that had formerly housed the library, but it came to nothing. Instead, the porcelain remained in the cellar of the Japanese Palace, with some of the animal figures being used as decoration for other parts of the building. When the director of the Sèvres manufactory, Alexandre Brongniart, was visiting Dresden in 1812, he was even misled into thinking that the animal figures had from the very beginning been intended to be used to decorate the grand staircase: "Among the manufactory's monumental creations were a series of animal figures produced around 1730 [...] destined to decorate the grand staircase that led to the electoral library in Dresden, underneath which are a great number of large rooms containing a collection of innumerable porcelain pieces from Meissen, China, and Japan."[818] In 1876 the animal figures was transferred with the remainder of the collection to the former stable building known as the Johanneum, which also housed the collection of paintings. In the Johanneum's high, bright rooms, the animal figures were for the first time exhibited in a worthy setting, and they were seen to fine effect. However, even before the First World War, Ernst Zimmermann planned to transfer the collection to the Zwinger, where a part of the collection was finally put on display in 1939. After the war, it was only in 1962 that what remained of the collection was made accessible to the public as the "Porzellansammlung im Zwinger."[819]

Sales and gifts in the eighteenth century

During the period when animal figures were being delivered to the Japanese Palace, the accounting books of the manufactory's branches in Dresden, Leipzig, and Warsaw had headings for animal figures, just as the books of the Meissen warehouse itself did. But even when the branch accounts mention large and small animals or birds, the prices quoted give conclusive evidence that the figures were small or even very small ones as compared with the animals made for the palace. The manufactory report for May 1736 also states that the large quantity of orders submitted made it necessary for overtime to be done, so that "there should be no shortage of retail wares, and of the small animal, bird, and other figures that are offered for sale."[820]

However, it was always intended that the order for a menagerie originally submitted by Augustus the Strong and then continued by his son should remain unique. As we have seen, these large animal figures were not to be produced for or sold to third parties. But as the demand for animal figures continued, some of the royal large animal figures were offered for sale to a wider range of customers after 1740, but in a smaller format (figs. 175 and 202). As from the second half of the 1730s, furthermore, there was a veritable deluge of new, decorative small animal figures, including a particularly large number of birds.[821] Like the figurines, they were done either at the free will of the modelers, or formed part of orders. For example, Kaendler made several smaller parrot models for the French market: "made a model of a parrot in clay, of the

201 Johann Joachim Kaendler, two birds of paradise with inventory numbers from the royal collection, model 1733, Arnhold Collection, New York

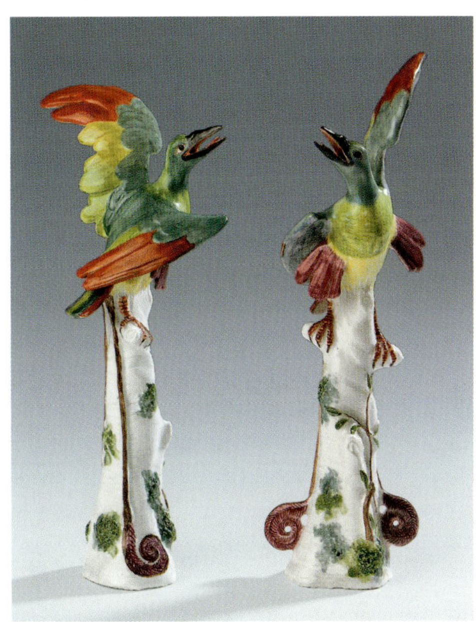

large kind, for Mr. Huêt […].”[822] After 1735, permission was given for a number of the smaller bird figures originally modeled for the Japanese Palace to be offered on the open market (figs. 146 and 201). This helps us to explain why the Jay, for instance, which Kaendler referred to in his work report for October 1735 as "belonging to the Royal Palace,"[823] was in May 1740 given additional elements: "also modeled in clay, various oak-leaves and other features to decorate the Jay,"[824] or why in February 1737 it was necessary for a new "neck and head [to be] made for the Guinea Fowl, to vary it,"[825] when the last examples had been delivered to the Japanese Palace in July 1735, and no further guinea fowls appear in the inventories of the collection thereafter.[826]

Nevertheless, the sources do provide evidence of one case, unique in the eighteenth century, of an exception being made and of middle-size palace figures being sold directly to a customer by the manufactory, after permission had been obtained from the king. In 1735, the manufactory asked the Commission whether it might be allowed to fulfill an order submitted by the imperial master of the stables. When the Commission passed the enquiry on to Count Brühl for him to present it for Augustus III's consideration, they appended the following letter to their missive:

"Most humble submission:
The Colonel High Steward has ordered, for the Imperial Master of the Stables, Graf von Altheim, a set of six porcelain animal figures, namely:
2 monkeys
2 parrots, and
2 magpies
from the warehouse in Dresden, and in such dimensions that the monkeys are one ell tall.

Given that His Royal Majesty has most graciously given permission that on request birds may be given to private parties in such measure as the French merchant Huet has received them to date;[827] and although to this day nobody has received even a single one of the monkeys, which have all been delivered to His Royal Majesty's Indian Palace from the porcelain manufactory here; it remains for His most gracious Majesty to decide: whether the above-mentioned figures, among which Hoff-Factor Chladni reckons that a monkey of this kind should be priced at between 130 and 150 talers, should be produced for and delivered to Graf von Altheim. Meissen, August 23, 1735."[828]

The answer came back from Warsaw on September 3, to the effect that the two monkeys were to be produced to Count Altheim's order.[829] Sadly, which monkey model it was that he had ordered cannot be deduced either from the source or from the price proposed by Chladni: although we know of a monkey that was priced at 86 talers and 12 groschen when it was delivered to the Japanese Palace in the same year, we have no information either as to its size or as to which monkey it was.[830] However, it is clear that Count Altheim's monkey must have been one of the royal models. This

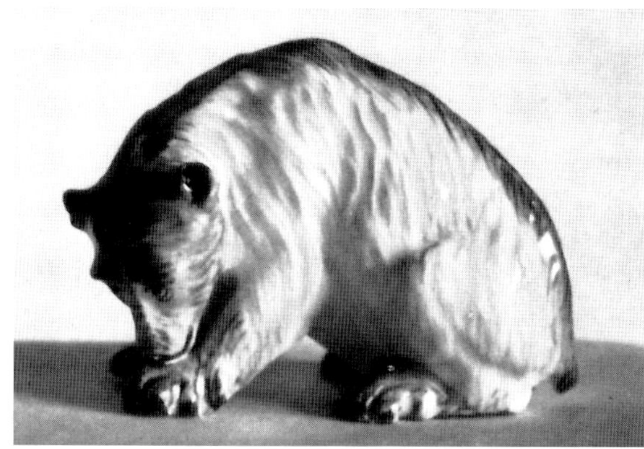

202 Johann Joachim Kaendler, Bear (8 cm high), model 1741

source not only constitutes important proof of the free sale of the smaller models, but is also the only piece of evidence we have for a larger animal figure being sold to a third party.

We likewise still only have one piece of documentary evidence for large animal figures being used by the king as gifts. A long list of gifts, all pieces taken from the Dresden warehouse for use as gifts to important personages, includes four larger porcelain figures that were delivered to the king's half-brother Moritz von Sachsen on September 3, 1737. All these pieces were otherwise strictly reserved for the king:

"At the verbal order of His Royal Majesty in Poland and Highness, Elector of Saxony, the following pieces were delivered to Count Moritz in Saxony:
2 large Vogelbauer pieces, defective
1 large owl, and
1 large monkey, both defective,
for 100 talers in all,
Maurice de Saxe HvBrühl."[831]

It is surprising enough that large (albeit defective) copies of figures reserved for the king should apparently have been standing around in the manufactory's warehouse in Dresden. There is also an indication for 1734 that some deliveries were not brought directly to the Japanese Palace but first passed through the Dresden warehouse. The branch accounts book mentions the following costs: "Ten talers and sixteen groschen ('10 T 16 Gr') carriers' wages for 16 men with 8 crates of various porcelain pieces: birds and animals which for reasons of space could not be kept in Meissen any longer, and which have to be carried to the royal Japanese Palace on account of their being dangerously fragile, paid to me in full by *Herr Hoff factor* Chladni […]. Each man 16 groschen, [signed] Christian Hermann and fellows."[832] Receipt was confirmed by the major-domo: "The above- listed porcelain was on His Royal Majesty's most gracious order rightly delivered to the

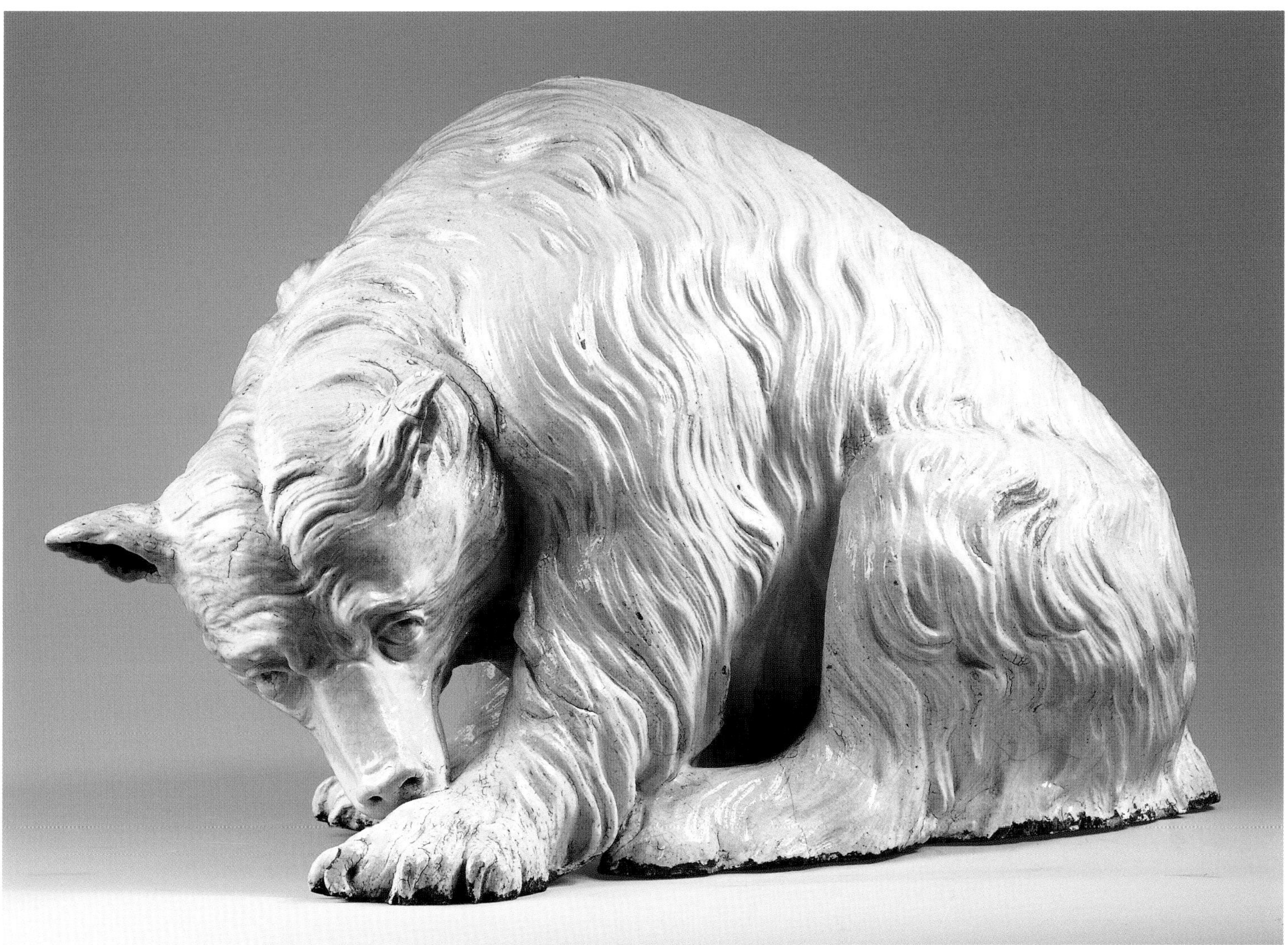

203 Johann Gottlieb Kirchner, Bear, model 1732, Dresden Porcelain Collection

Royal Japanese Palace, for which delivery 10 talers and 16 groschen was paid out, as I hereby confirm, Martin Teuffert, Major-Domo."

This source is the only one of its kind in all the account books. However, we may assume that even though they were not offered for sale, the large animal figures will nevertheless have been displayed at the sales rooms, as decoration and as proof of the manufactory's technical and artistic prowess. That this was the case for the Meissen warehouse is shown by a description of the banquet in the Albrechtsburg put on by two commissaries representing the king in the course of the homage paid by the town of Meissen to Augustus III on his succession to the throne. During the whole banquet, "the entire newly-built porcelain warehouse was open, decorated in blue and gold [...] where it was possible to see not only an astonishing quantity of all kinds of large and small wares, most precious vases and garnitures, and a variety of beautiful groups,[833] but also lions, panthers, bears, monkeys, parrots, and other local and foreign animals and birds, all life-size."[834]

Sales in the nineteenth and early twentieth centuries

The sales, gifts, and breakages of the eighteenth century were relatively minor in comparison with the casualties suffered by the collection of animal figures in the nineteenth and early twentieth centuries.

In 1833, Gustav Klemm, Secretary of the Royal Library, was appointed "Inspektor" of the Porcelain Collection, which was thus finally turned into a museum collection in the full sense of the expression. Klemm's intention was to extend the collection into a kind of universal museum for the ceramics of all the countries and peoples of the world. In order to raise the necessary funds for this project, and "in order to create space," he drew up a list of 4,875 duplicates.[835] He furthermore raised objections to the long rows of similar pieces that had been a necessary part of the fittings and furnishings in the Japanese Palace's earlier days. The "limitless mass" gave the rooms "the deadly appearance of so many storehouses."[836] Duplicates were subsequently not only stored in separate cellars but also sold to interested parties.

Lists were repeatedly drawn up of the pieces being offered for sale. One such catalog – "of the duplicate pieces from the 'Royal Porcelain and Vessels Collection' that could be disposed of,"[837] – is undated and was very likely used over a long period of time. It shows clearly how the prices asked for the animal figures rose in accordance with demand: the initial price of 120 talers quoted for a "Peacock, striding forward, displaying [...] its train, 44 1/2 inches high" was first raised to 200 and then to 300 talers. The pieces were in part priced in collaboration with the director of the Meissen branch in Dresden, which caused the relevant ministry to issue a regulation dated June 21, 1854, specifying that the duplicates were only to be offered to other collections, i.e. other museums, and were not to be sold on the open market.[838] This statement was not uncontroversial at this particular time, as will become clear from the following concrete examples. The same document also demands that a number of unspecified pieces be removed from the stock of duplicates and restored to the permanent collection. This slight change in policy may well have come about as a result of a change in the directorate in 1853. In 1852 Gustav Klemm was appointed *Oberbibliothekar*, and was succeeded in 1853 as director of the Porcelain Collection by Theodor Graesse, hitherto "Inspektor" of the numismatic collection.[839] 1854 furthermore saw the accession to the Saxon throne of a new king, Johann, who as a monarch of exceptional artistic sensitivity was possibly of one mind with Graesse in wishing for a new approach to the curation of the royal collections. The sales of large animal figures ceased, and from now on the catalogs of duplicates concentrated on such pieces of tableware as, for instance, Böttger porcelain and stoneware.[840] Graesse's 1873 guide to the collection does however make a reference to the sales of animal figures, stating that particularly the animals "are infinitely rare and exchange hands for truly fabulous prices."[841] When the collection came to be moved to the Johanneum in 1876, Graesse was finally called upon to make a decision as to what he thought should be done with the "stock of duplicates still stored in the basement of the Japanese Palace," and to consider "whether these pieces could not be used for decorative purposes, to surround doors and windows in the collection's new premises."[842] This makes it clear that the reserve of duplicates was by this time regarded not so much as a stock of pieces to be sold, but rather as the collection's depository. Not until 1912 were catalogs of duplicates once again drawn up with prices, these also including large animal figures, as we shall see below.[843]

Before we turn our attention to a few examples of sales, it is worth considering the background to the increasing interest in and demand for the large animal figures. In France, the restoration of the monarchy by the Bourbons brought about a turning away from the Empire style and a reawakening of interest in the forms that had been current in France's glorious Rococo. In the 1820s, George IV's English court was generally very Francophile and followed France's example. "Second Rococo" interiors happily mixed "genuine" historical pieces and historical copies, eloquently testifying to their owners' monarchist credentials. Dealers went to great lengths to satisfy the demand for works from the middle of the eighteenth century, adding a new component to the notion of what was "antique." When it was not possible to acquire a sufficiency of either old or suitable pieces, then new fittings and ornaments were manufactured in the neo-antique style to produce the desired effect in the new interiors.

The manufactory at Meissen was also influenced by the widespread thirst for items that unmistakably had the patina of history upon them. Shortly after 1820, the interest of English dealers in Rococo pieces was so great that many traveled to Dresden and Meissen and personally explored the mold-stores and modeling rooms of the Albrechtsburg for eighteenth-century models.[844] The sale to England of figures re-created from seventy- to eighty-year-old models soon developed into a considerable source of income for the manufactory, which from then on offered an assortment of historical figurines and tableware parallel to its contemporary range, as it indeed still does. In the second quarter of the nineteenth century, Rococo pieces sold to English dealers constituted almost half of the manufactory's foreign business, or eight per cent of its total sales.[845] The catalogs offered "porcelain pieces in the English taste" (fig. 210), and wares "in the old French style."

Around 1840, the advent of a second Rococo in Germany aroused increased demand amongst German dealers for Meissen porcelain of this kind. Incited by the interest shown by their customers, antique-dealers often bought eighteenth-century white porcelain pieces and had them painted in the historical style. The Dresden dealer Löw Mayer played a particular role in this connection, buying Meissen rejects ("Brack" or "Ausschuss Porzellan") and very probably having them painted before offering them to his customers; his practice was to obtain information, partly through hotel employees, about the arrival of foreigners in Dresden and then to busy himself with providing them, especially the English, with the kind of porcelain they were looking for.[846] He was able to get better prices for "genuine, old" works: the Meissen administrators reported in 1857 that "many buyers, and most notably all English buyers have set particular store by the wares not having been manufactured recently, but being remnants of earlier times."[847] It is amusing to note that in its zeal to accommodate this preference, the manufactory sometimes conveniently "forgot" to have new pieces marked with the Meissen crossed swords. This is the case, for instance, with a number of examples of the Bolognese Dog that the manufactory reintroduced into its range and offered in various sizes in the above-mentioned catalogs in the mid-1820s. The reduced-size figures that they produced are remarkably good copies of the larger figures from the 1730s (fig. 92), not only in respect of detail, but also in the color and style of the decoration. Only around the collars was the original luster ground replaced by a simple puce with a strapwork ornament in relief.[848]

But Rococo models were not only in demand among dealers but also among private individuals. Travelers often made enquiries about specific eighteenth-century models, particularly large ones, after they had viewed the porcelain collection in the Japanese Palace vaults. The enthusiasm for porcelain that could overcome the visitor to the collection is well conveyed by the diary entry for March 25, 1847, made by Mary Wilson when visiting Dresden with her sister Anne: "We went after dinner to see the collection of Porcelaine at the Japan palace [...]. I should think there is a specimen of every pattern ever made in China, large animals and birds and teapots enough to satisfy the most enthusiastic lover of old china."[849]

However, only very few of the much-admired large animal figures (they are found worthy of especial mention in all the documentary sources) were still being produced by the manufactory, with the result that the only way of satisfying the interested foreign visitors was to sell them such historic animal figures as were possessed by the collection in multiple copies (which was the case with most models), either directly from the stock of duplicates of the Royal Collection, or through the manufactory's Dresden branch.

In the earliest proven case of a sale of animal figures from the collection after its transformation into a museum in 1833, two elephants were sold to the Dresden banker Michael Kaskel on May 11, 1835.[850] The receipt sadly includes no indication of the size of the figures or the price paid, but later lists make it clear that they must have been smaller figures that had not been produced in connection with the orders for the Japanese Palace.

The first instance of large animal figures being disposed of was an exchange of porcelain with the Sèvres manufactory in 1836/37.[851] The "Catalog of the pieces from the 'Königl. Sächs. Porzellan- und Gcfässe-Sammlung' in Dresden given away to the Royal French Porcelain Manufactory at Sèvres"[852] is divided up into fifty-one sections that together form a representative showcase of eighteenth-century Meissen porcelain. In addition to Böttger stoneware and porcelain, Far Eastern imitations, and tableware and figures from the middle of the century, the list also contains a rhinoceros, a peacock, a vulture (devouring a cockatoo), a pelican, a bear, a dragon referred to as a "lion vase," and one of the large grotesque vases by Kirchner. Although all these pieces can still be admired in the Musée National de la Céramique, they must have had a rough ride from Dresden to Sèvres, as the relevant correspondence shows. On April 7, 1837, the then director of the collection in Sèvres wrote to Klemm to confirm receipt of the consignment, but also had to add that "we regret to inform you of the following: 1. the complete breakage of the pelican in numerous pieces, 2. some damage on the peacock and rather more on the vulture, and 3. the fracture of the right hind leg of the rhinoceros," concluding that most of the damage could be repaired, "but the pelican is entirely lost."[853] Contrary to his assertion, it did prove possible to put the pelican back into one piece.

This exchange was followed by a number of direct sales. As has been mentioned, the collection and the manufactory's sales branch in Dresden worked together on setting the prices. The manufactory's agent, Johann Carl Friedrich Teichert, furthermore acquired from the stock of duplicates a considerable number of animal figures to offer for sale. On April 17, 1849, for instance, he received one example each of the Pelican, Dragon, Hen, Turkeycock, Cockerel, and Monkey taking snuff, and furthermore one eagle, one vulture, and two herons.[854] A number of the animal figures have their inventory numbers appended on the receipt. That a special account was set up for the money received from these sales is shown by the letter on the subject written to Klemm by Weitersheim, who was the minister of state responsible for the matter and the president of the Royal Collection for Art and Science: "Given that His Royal Majesty, in response to your application of 21 January of this year, deigned to give his permission for the sale of nine animal figures in Meissen porcelain from amongst the duplicates of the 'Königl. Porzellan- und Gefäßesammlung' for the sum of 555 rt [rt, rthl = *Reichsthaler*], you are hereby instructed to dispose of the figures in question in return for payment of the sum concerned, and to pay the sum in to the separate fund of the Royal Collections and to enter the sale of the figures in the inventory of duplicates."[855] The sources make it clear that Klemm himself had proposed selling these animal figures, and that he had done so in order to raise funds to acquire, among other things, "20 hindustani bronze vessels," which he had been offered by a certain Herr Petersen in June 1848.[856]

Evidently spurred on by this acquisition, the agent Teichert took the initiative of applying to the president of the royal collections, on December 5, 1850, for his permission for the purchase of a further 18 animal figures for a certain sum. Immediately after having submitted his request, however, he must have made certain amendments, as von Wietersheim's reply of December 7 makes it clear that Teichert was now wanting 20 figures and two vases for the sum he had originally offered: "With respect to your application, dated December 5, for the purchase of 18 animal figures from the stock of duplicates of the Royal Porcelain Collection by Teichert, agent at the Dresden offices of the Royal Porcelain Manufactory, originally for the price of 800 rthl, the application then being changed to 20 animal figures and 2 red vases for the same sum, I hereby give you to understand that the application cannot be granted. The items listed by Teichert are priced at 1,370 rthl exclusive of the two vases, and that these prices are not disproportionately high is sufficiently clear from the fact that on February 3,

1849, the same Teichert of his own free will paid the sum of no less than 555 rt for 9 such animal figures."[857] The existence of an unsigned receipt for the transaction, listing a pelican, two turkeycocks (one defective), a lion, a lynx, a rhinoceros, a nanny-goat, a bear, a cockerel, a kestrel, a hen, a large vulture, an elephant, three herons (one defective), and three macaws, is a first indication that the sale never took place.[858] Comparisons of the numbers of figures in stock (with reference, for instance, to the lynx or the bear) also show that this second sale never took place. The records, however, offer no further reasons as to why this was the case.

All in all, however, an exceptional amount of business seems to have been done in 1850. On June 6, Klemm received permission to sell two herons and two macaws to the Dresden antique-dealer Moritz Meyer.[859] Klemm intended to use the proceeds of this deal to buy a pair of Chinese vases from the Dresden court antiquary Wolf. And on June 10 he is to be found making the following communication to the director of the Royal Collections: "Mr. Marks from London is at present in Dresden and offers the following prices for the following items, payment in cash exclusive of taxes: 1 broken heron 35 rt, 1 tiger entirely defective 60 rt, 1 billy-goat defective 80 rt, 1 monkey very defective 70 rt; he [Mr Marks] would like to be informed of your decision tomorrow."[860] Permission was given, at a price of 110 talers in all, because "the collection has several well-preserved examples of all the figures, and the sale can be regarded as advantageous."[861] Interestingly enough, the confirmation of receipt of the four figures was not signed by the buyer, who had by this point (June 21) already left Dresden, but by Helena Wolfssohn.

From 1843 Helena Wolfssohn successfully ran a workshop in which white porcelain was painted in the Meissen style, offering the resulting pieces for sale. She obtained the undecorated pieces from a number of different manufactories and her name has risen to notoriety in the literature on account of the legal battle she had with the Meissen manufactory over her use of the AR mark.[862] It is not so well known that she was also a dealer in antique porcelain. The year 1850 not only saw her handling Mr. Marks's acquisition, but also submitting a "catalog of the animals that the undersigned wishes to purchase from the 'Königliche Samlung' [sic!]," in which 22 animal figures are listed at a total price of 1,290 talers.[863] When she finally took possession of the figures, they were only 21 in number, as is shown by the receipt she signed on January 8, 1851, the missing figure being a billy-goat that she finally declined to take because of its poor condition:

"2	Hens with young	à 50.–	Rt 100.–
1	She-wolf		60.–
2	Lions	à 100.–	200.–
1	Pelican		80.–
1	large Monkey, defective		70.–
1	Vulture with hen [cockatoo], defective		90.–
1	Macaw ["Arras"] with wings spread, defective		90.–
1	Heron in the reeds		35.–
2	Billy-goats in the form of jugs	à 40.–	80.–
3	Herons	à 35.–	105.–
2	Turkeycocks	à 30.–	60.–
1	Nanny-goat with kid		80.–
1	Fox		50.–
1	Macaw ["Arras"]		60.–
1	Macaw [ditto] decorated with enamel colors		50.–
			1210 Thlr
	Discount		30 Thlr
			1180 Thalers."[864]

At the same time as acquiring, on January 7, 1851, this impressive number of animal figures (for a no less impressive sum of money), she wasted no time at all in submitting a further list in which she applied to purchase further animals, this time in exchange for porcelain pieces in her own possession:

"Catalog of the animals that the undersigned wishes to obtain from the 'Königliche Samlung' in exchange for other items in porcelain:

1	Pelican	80.–
1	Billy-goat in the form of a jug	40.–
1	Lion	100.–
1	Lioness	90.–
1	Turkeycock	30.–
1	Elephant	150.–
1	Bear	120.–
1	Fox	50.–
1	'Arras'[865]	30.–
5	'Arras' all defective à 30.–	150.–
		840.–."[866]

The value of the oriental, Far Eastern, and European ceramics that Klemm intended to acquire in exchange from Helena Wolfssohn was estimated at only 400 talers, resulting in a very complicated calculation which also took account of 30 talers discount, of the 70 talers she had apparently paid for the billy-goat that she decided to leave at the collection, and of a cockerel offered at 60 talers as compensation.[867] Even if we do not go into any further detail here, this example shows that the gentlemen of the Royal Collection engaged in quite serious porcelain-dealing, which is also reflected a few years later in 1854 when the custodian Tauschert is to be found receiving a gratuity of 25 talers for the extra work and inconvenience caused him by "the recent increase in the sale of duplicates."[868]

The series of sales transactions carried out in the second quarter of the nineteenth century comes to a provisional end with an enquiry made by the collector Prince Anatol Demidoff, who expressed an interest in purchasing several "animal figures and other items of Meissen porcelain now to be found in the stock of duplicates of the 'Königl. Porzellan- und Gefäße Sammlung'." The king proved agreeable, and on March 5, 1853, Klemm was presented by the director of the Royal Collections with a price-list to use as the basis of his negotiations with the prince, which were to constitute one of the last undertakings of his long period in office.[869] While most of the figures in the list were roughly as highly priced as those sold in previous years, two figures in particular stand out as being offered at exceptionally handsome prices, possibly in part because of the prominence of the buyer: a peacock at 500 talers and a rhinoceros at 400. The prince declined to pay these prices, paying instead a total of 490 talers on July 7, through the agents Bassenge & Co., for a cockerel, a hen, two herons, two kestrels, a bustard, a vulture, and the two busts of the Dresden court-jesters Fröhlich and Schmiedel.[870]

As suggested above, the records provide us with no evidence for any further sales of large animal figures in the whole of the second half of the nineteenth century. However, the figures that had been sold prior to 1853 made their way in the trade and caused a stir wherever they were offered for sale, as for instance at a Christie's sale in 1858. A total of 19 days between April 19 and May 12 saw "The Magnificent Collection of Works of Art and Vertu formed by Mr. David Falke on New Bond Street" being put up for auction,[871] with a collection entitled "fine old white Dresden figures from the Japanese Palace at Dresden" going under the hammer on April 28:

"1443 A goat reclining, small life size
1445 A jug, formed as a monster, 27in high (15£ 10 S; Saxby)
1446 A Pelican with a fish, 32in high (11£; Saxby)
1448 A Bird, 28in high (7£; Saxby)
1449 A pair of hens with chickens, 13in (7£ 10 S; Falck)
1450 A ~~Swan seated~~ Stork on a pedestal of reeds, 34 in (12£ 10 S; Doc. Falck)
1451 the companion (11£; D. Davis)
1456 A Figurc of a Lion reclining, small life size
1457 A figure of an eagle on stem, 29in (3£ 10 S; Bowdon)
1265 Two monkeys, 22in
1267 A pair of foxes (15 S; Falck)."[872]

The prices and buyers (mainly dealers) were noted in the copy of the catalog now kept in the Christie's archive: one is struck by the astoundingly low sum that the large eagle went for, while the price paid for the two foxes is perhaps an indication that they were small ones. David Falke was possibly the gentleman referred to in a record of the Porcelain Manufactory of January 24, 1852, in which it is noted that an application from a London dealer named Falk had had to be turned down by the Dresden branch, on the grounds that the "English wares" were not allowed to be sold undecorated, and the painting department was unable to decorate them on account of their services already being in very high demand.[873]

So it was that even in the nineteenth century Meissen large animal figures passed through the trade into private collections, where they have in part remained to this day.[874]

Ernst Zimmermann, who was at first a directorial assistant and then became Director of the Porcelain Collection from 1912 to 1933, was the next director to sell and exchange large animal figures from the Dresden collection. In the petition he submitted on October 3, 1912, he gave as his justification the fact he would use the proceeds – in this first instance from the sale of duplicates from the Böttger period – to buy small figures and tableware by Kaendler, which he noted were poorly represented in the collection.[875] By this time, the early-nineteenth-century project of extending the collection into a comprehensive museum of ceramics was clearly no longer on the agenda: the main concern was to build up a fully representative collection of Meissen china. That the collection should have been short of any items by Kaendler may well seem surprising but can be explained by the fact that the Dresden Porcelain Collection evolved from the wares held at the Japanese Palace: figures used for table-decoration and certain elements of the great services, on the other hand, were kept at the court confectioneries and in the silver-pantries respectively, and examples were not automatically received into the collection. In December 1912, Zimmermann reiterated that his list only contained wares whose absence or loss would not have a noticeable effect on the collection, and pointed out that visitors to the collection as he planned to have it exhibited in the Zwinger would only be tired out by a superfluity of identical pieces. His concluding remark indicates that even at this point he must have been thinking of selling large animal figures: "With regard to the valuations set on the individual pieces, it should be noted that those made for the monumental pieces can at present only be regarded as estimates, as these works have hitherto hardly ever been offered for sale."[876] The continuing correspondence makes it clear that Zimmermann was thinking of mounting a large auction. When Privy Councillor von Seidlitz expressed reservations, fearing that the collections could forfeit their unique character, Zimmermann countered by drawing his attention to the sale of works from the *Kunstkammer* and *Mathematisch-Physikalische Sammlung* in 1834, to the 568 paintings successfully auctioned off in three sales between 1859 and 1861, and to the 420 prints and drawings from the *Kupferstichkabinett* that had been sold in 1904. He very wisely refrained from referring to any of the earlier sales from the Porcelain Collection; "[...] with regard to the concern that if monumental works were to be sold, the Collection would no longer be the only place where such figures could be seen, it should be noted that this is by no means the case now. Two of the large Meissen animals are held by the ceramics museum in Sèvres; two others are in the possession of Freiherr von Miltitz of Schloss Siebeneichen near Meissen and are currently being offered for sale by Lepke in Berlin […]."[877] The loss of certain large figures would hardly be noticed, as "of the 200 large Meissen animals, it is only intended to put up 14 […] for sale." At the beginning of 1914, it was decided to entrust the auction-house Lepke with the sale, and to ask Julius Brinkmann to make the estimates. The outbreak of war interrupted proceedings, but work was resumed immediately the war was over. Ernst Zimmermann drew up a list that included not only Japanese Palace animal figures of all sizes, but also examples of Kirchner's grotesque vases and one of the vases with the portrait of King Louis XV of France. On October 7 and 8, 1919, the first sale with porcelain and arms from the Dresden collections was held at Rudolph Lepke's in Berlin. In his enthusiasm, Seidlitz wrote in the foreword to the sale catalog that the animal figures had been intended for the garden of the Japanese Palace. A report by Adolph Donath also relayed some misleading information about the animal figures: "The mere fact that large white-glazed figures from the Kaendler period had never previously been offered for sale on the open market made this auction into a major event."[878] Donath nevertheless gave an evocative and atmospheric account of the sale, describing all those attending, listing who bought what and for how much, and noting that the most expensive item at the sale had been a 1734 King Vulture, which he referred to as a "Kronengeier" ("crown vulture"), bought by Rasmußen from Copenhagen for the sum of 178,000 marks. All fifteen animals in the catalog were sold, and most of these can still be identified in collections today. Encouraged by the success of the sale, Zimmermann paved the way for a second auction, which was held by Lepke on October 12 and 14, 1920, this time in Dresden (at the *Kunstverein*), with paintings, arms, ivories and porcelain from the erstwhile royal collection now known as the "Staatliche Sammlungen." The proceeds were to be used to make further acquisitions. Once again, Adolph Donath gave a detailed report.[879] Of the twelve porcelain animal figures all were sold with the exception of the Rhinoceros and the Cat; this time the highest-selling piece was a monkey, for which bidding opened at 20,000 marks and did not cease until the hammer fell at 360,000. This figure now belongs to the Rijksmuseum, Amsterdam.

In the settlement made at the end of the monarchy, the items granted to the House of Wettin included six animal figures. In 1920 the Ligner Foundation made an offer of 45,000 marks for a king vulture, but the records of the art collections do not make it clear whether the sale ever took place.[880] In the remaining instances in which Ernst Zimmermann disposed of Japanese Palace animal figures during his period in office, the pieces in question were exchanged for figurines and tableware from the 1730s and 1740s that he was keen to acquire to fill gaps in the collection. In December 1730, for instance, the art firm Hermann Ball received two "damaged" birds of paradise and a tit in exchange for a clock housing by Kirchner.[881] In January 1931, a peacock (on a tree-stump) was sold to the Berlin art-dealer Arthur Wittekind, with the justification that the collection had four more examples of this figure. In exchange, the collection inventory was made the richer by a clock painted with chinoiseries, a "small, painted old Meissen porcelain statuette of King Augustus the Strong around 1725," and a huntsman figure.[882] In October of the same year, Wittekind made a further offer, this time of a crinoline group made from a model by Kirchner, the so-called "Herzdosenkauf" ("the purchase of a heart box"). The piece had come from the collection of Baron Goldschmidt-Rothschild of Frankfurt, from whose family the porcelain collection had already acquired a copy of the Sofa-Group. Wittekind offered an additional 2,000 marks in cash and received in return a large bittern and a parrot, which must have been a rose-ringed parakeet on account of its AR mark and blue-green coloring.[883] In July 1932, Wittekind received a large eagle in exchange for the lady with a fan from the "Kusshand-Gruppe" plus 1,000 marks in cash.[884] In a letter to the relevant ministry dated September 30, 1932, Zimmermann is to be found reporting enthusiastically that he might be able acquire an example of Kaendler's figure of the huntsman Wentzel; he knew of only two other specimens of this model, both in the collection of Hermine Feist in Berlin. As Wittekind was prepared to put down a further 3,000 marks on top of the Wentzel figure without expecting to receive anything more than one additional rose-ringed parakeet in exchange, Zimmermann thought it necessary to mention that the Berlin dealer had bought his Wentzel figure in London for a very good price at an auction of the Ernest Cassel collection, and that this was why he was able to make such a reasonable offer to the collection. But the value of the figure, he added, was many times higher than that of the parakeet.[885]

This was the last exchange made for the purpose of adding to the collection's holdings: shortly after the Nazis came to power, Ernst Zimmermann found himself the object of a long list of accusations. The archive of the Dresden Art Collections contains a copy of his letter of self-defense, from which one can reconstruct the accusations brought against him. Zimmermann had to justify his alleged special relations with Jewish dealers and explain why these dealers had been allowed to purchase antique (German) porcelain. He was furthermore made responsible for the fact that now, i.e. since the two sales of 1919 and 1920, foreigners no longer needed to come to Dresden in order to see certain figures (the animal figures). Zimmermann's response was that even previously the Porcelain Collection had not had a monopoly in this field, and that of the four large animal figures that Freiherr von Miltitz had had in Siebeneichen, two had been on display before the auctions at the *Schloßmuseum* in Berlin. But all his reasonings were in vain. On December 2, 1933, Ernst Zimmermann received a curt communication that the curator Dr. Fichtner would take over the direction of the Porcelain Collection, and that he was to be thanked for his thirty years of service.

As far as the present author is aware, only one large animal figure has been sold since World War Two, namely the colorfully painted Golden Pheasant acquired in 1963 by the Rijksmuseum, Amsterdam.[886] Today, of the 53 middle-size and large animal models (that is to say, over 40 cm tall), the Dresden Porcelain Collection possesses 107 figures in all, which is a little less than half of the number attested to in the 1779 inventory of the royal collection.

The Meissen large animal figures that have taken their leave of Dresden in the past two hundred years are now dispersed in public and private collections all over the world. Few and far between, however, are the collections that boast a sizeable group of animal figures, surely not least as a result of the high prices that these "incunabula" of European porcelain sculpture have always fetched. It is a striking fact that many of the animal figures no longer in Dresden are notable for the high quality of their paste, and for their state of preservation. In the sales of duplicates described above, it would seem that those in authority were willing to offer well-preserved pieces for sale, in order to maximize the proceeds. This is also confirmed in the foreword to the 1919 sale catalog, which states that "the fire-cracks which are to be seen on all the large Meissen animals offered for sale [...] are to be seen in just the same way on the majority of the specimens preserved in the collection," and that this was so "because there were such insurmountable difficulties involved in the production of such large pieces."[887]

A comparatively high number of the figures sold have ended up in England, which can be explained by the particular interest in Rococo porcelain shown by English travelers to Dresden in the first half of the nineteenth century. As historical "curiosities" the animal figures will furthermore have been particularly attractive to the taste of these travelers, who were particularly interested in acquiring originals and not contemporary executions of old models. In the case of the collection of the Marquess of Bath at Longleat, the history of the pieces can be followed right back to the time of their acquisition.[888] Until 2002, there were ten large animal figures at Longleat, from amongst which a Fox and a Turkeycock were then sold at auction and acquired by the Getty Museum, one Vulture came into the possession of the Victoria and Albert Museum, and one further Vulture went into the trade. Raby Castle also has an old collection of five figures.[889] The collection of Lord Hastings, however, was dispersed by auction in 1950.[890] While the Lion and Lioness in the Metropolitan Museum, New York, came from the Earl of Longford's Irish castle of Tullynally, other figures have ended up in a variety of English museums.

But a good number of other museums and collections accessible to the public (some only periodically) in and outside Europe now have large animal figures on display that originally belonged to the Dresden collection:

Amsterdam, Rijksmuseum: Monkey wearing a ruff, Monkey with a chain, Monkey taking snuff, Macaw (sitting), Golden Pheasant, Gray Parrot, Kestrel (2 specimens), Cockatoo
Berlin, Kunstgewerbemuseum: Eagle, Heron (both on loan from the Dresden Porcelain Collection)
Detroit, Institute of Arts: Crane
Edinburgh, Royal Museum of Scotland: Lion
Geneva, Musée Ariana: Monkey wearing a ruff
Hamburg, Museum für Kunst und Gewerbe: Mandrill
Cologne, Museum für Angewandte Kunst: Macaw sitting, Lynx
Kopenhagen, Danske Kunstindustrimuseum: 2 Eagles, King Vulture (1734), Cockerel
Kykuit, Rockefeller Collection: King Vulture (1731, 2 specimens); King Vulture (1734)
London, Victoria and Albert Museum: King Vulture (1731), Billy-Goat
Longleat, collection of the Marquess of Bath: Elephant, Fox, King Vulture (1731)
Los Angeles, Getty Museum: Fox, Turkeycock
Moscow, Kuskovo Palace: Elephant
Munich, Bayerisches Nationalmuseum, Schneider Collection in Schloss Lustheim: Macaw (sitting), Lioness (sitting), Crane
New York, Metropolitan Museum: Bolognese Dog, Lion, Lioness (lying), Eagle Owl, Nanny-Goat
New York, Pflueger Collection (in future: Boston, Museum of Fine Arts): Dragon, Macaw (sitting), Macaw (downward-climbing), Kestrel, King Vulture (1731, 2 specimens), Peacock (on tree-stump), Heron
Nuremberg, Germanisches Nationalmuseum: Fox (on loan)
Paris, Musée du Louvre: Bolognese Dog
Philadelphia, Museum of Art: Nanny-Goat, Billy-Goat
Pittsburgh, Carnegie Museum of Art: Monkey wearing a ruff
Raby Castle: Eagle, Griffon Vulture (without cockatoo), Pelican, Turkeycock
Rouen, Musée de la Céramique: Chamois
Sèvres, Musée National de la Céramique: Bear, Dragon, Vulture Devouring a Cockatoo, Rhinoceros, Pelican, Peacock Displaying
St. Petersburg, Hermitage: Cockerel
Turin, Museo Civico: Leopard, Bustard, She-Wolf
Waddesdon Manor: Turkeycock, Nanny-Goat
Warsaw, National Museum: Cockerel
Vienna, Museum of Applied Art: Bear

The modern realizations of animal figures in the Meissen manufactory in the nineteenth and twentieth centuries

In his report on the Japanese Palace of October 1730, Keyssler wrote as follows: "[...] and in order that these animal figures may for ever remain rare and costly, their molds are to be broken."[891] This intention was quite clearly not put into practice in all cases: when at the beginning of the twentieth century, under the direction of Max Adolf Pfeiffer, the manufactory made moves to take figures from Augustus the Strong's menagerie back into production, it did actually prove possible to produce four different models of which there were no original examples still in existence (figs. 108, 165, 204, and 205).[892] As some of these appear in the work reports as having been modeled but are not mentioned in the delivery lists or inventories, we may assume that they were never originally realized as porcelain figures.

The re-working and bringing back into production of large animal figures began in Meissen in 1915, some being produced with surviving sets of molds (or parts thereof), and some being copied from original specimens held in museums. The first "re-creations" were of a number of bird figures, and work continued until 1936, when one of the monkey figures was "copied from an original porcelain figure in Paris."[893] Fortunately, the manufactory model-books contain exact information for most of the animal figures as to which models were taken back into production and when, and as to whether the old molds were still in existence at the time: if not, they had to be re-made, or if only in part, then the missing ones had to be re-made to make up the set. This information is included in the entries for the individual figures in the Catalog. The information provided in the model books tells us that whole sets of molds for a total of 31 large figures were re-made during Max Adolf Pfeiffer's period in office, using original figures in the Dresden and other porcelain collections. The figures in question were: Monkey wearing a ruff, Monkey with chain, Monkey taking snuff, Mother-Monkey, Macaw (sitting), Wisent Fighting with a Boar, Bear, Coot, Heron (with carp), Heron (preening itself), Fox, Great Crested Grebe, Two Dogs Fighting, Dog Scratching Itself, Cassowary, Cat, King Vulture (1731), Gull, Rhinoceros, Peacock (on a tree-stump), Marmoset, Exotic Sheep, Sheep, Barn Owl, Swan, Osprey, Sphinx, Doves, Eagle Owl, She-Wolf (not completed), Sable.

204 Johann Gottlieb Kirchner (?), Leopard (lying), reworked revival piece from the early twentieth century

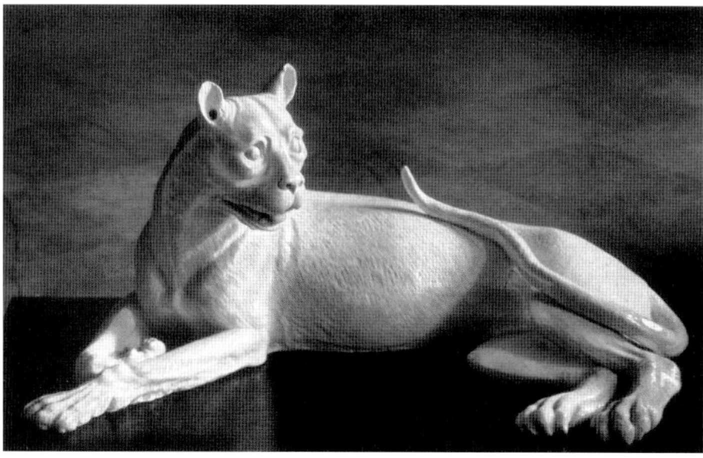

In twelve cases, the modelers had to make new molds of some sections of the figure in question, as only some of the molds had survived, but not the whole set. When there was a historical figure available, this was used for the re-making of the molds; in the absence of a historical figure, the modelers were free to recreate the mold as they thought fit. The twelve cases were: Eagle (sitting), Eagle (beating one wing), Macaw climbing downwards, Bolognese Dog, Vulture Devouring a Cockatoo, Leopard (head and legs re-modeled), Cockerel, Pelican, Peacock Displaying (*Urform* partially extant), Bittern (*Originalform* partially extant), Scapegoat (original set of working molds had to be completed), Bustard. For German terminology, see Glossary.

Of particular interest are the eight large animal figures that, as the model book tells us, had to be "renewed" ("aufrepariert," "erneuert") in the 1920s. This procedure is used to recreate a model and produce fresh working molds when the old set has become worn down or incomplete. In the case of these figures, we may assume that the sets of molds were complete, and that the manufactory could at that time have used them to produce further figures. They were the following: Elephant, Chamois, Lioness (lying), Lion, Lynx, Mandrill, Billy-Goat.

For eight further large animal figures, the model book sadly contains no indications as to whether molds survived, and if so, then to what extent: Owl, Pheasant, Golden Pheasant, Crane, King Vulture (1734), Guinea Fowl, Turkeycock, Nanny-Goat.

The high mold number of the large Turkeycock, B 145, would suggest (if one is to place uncritical trust in the chronological order of the numbers) that it is to be dated around 1776. The fact that the period after the ending of the project also saw another middle-size bird figure, the Guinea Fowl, being produced for the open market suggests that the very attractive Turkeycock may well have been brought back into production with the same end in mind. And we do know of a number of turkeycock figures that are decorated in the style of the second half of the eighteenth century; these were without doubt produced in Meissen and are marked with the Meissen swords.[894] Their pedestals are however somewhat differently executed from those on the five examples delivered before 1736 to the Japanese Palace. In place of the remarkable support structure of the original model, which incorporates two projecting "consoles" for the bird's claws, the later version has a stump made of rock or earth, which widens out at the bottom into a base on which the turkey is "standing." On all these later figures, however, the

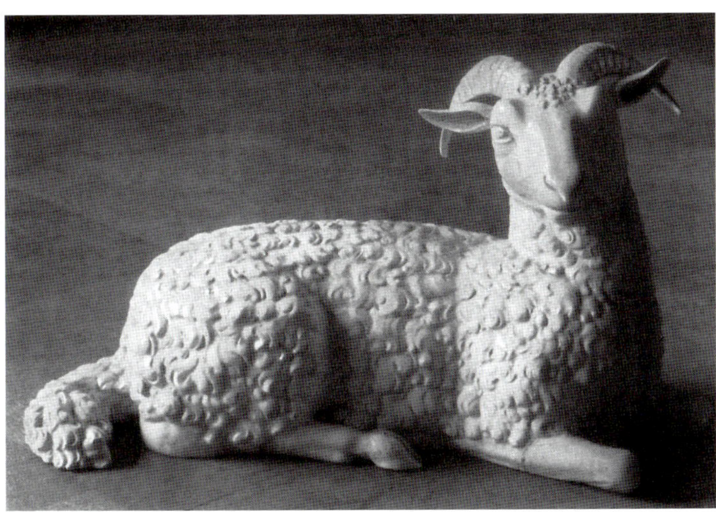

205 Johann Friedrich Eberlein (?), Ram, revival piece from the early twentieth century

surface of the bird is, down to the smallest details, identical with the figures from the 1730s. It is thus quite possible that the later turkeycock model was produced in the last quarter of the eighteenth century with the original molds (or in the case of wear and tear with copies), and that at this time a new pedestal was designed, with the whole model being given a new mold number.[895] When at the end of the nineteenth century the Potschappel manufactory in Freital copied the Meissen Turkeycock (a matter to which we shall return later), they used the structure of the second pedestal but transformed it into a little rockscape.

The question does naturally enough arise as to whether copies of some of the large-size figures (over 50 cm high) were not perhaps also produced in the nineteenth century. This is particularly possible in the case of the figures for which the molds were simply "renewed" in the 1920s. However, this is only corroborated by written evidence in two instances, the Bolognese Dog (fig. 92) and the large Mandrill (fig. 208). As we have seen, these two models were offered in the manufactory price-lists from 1826, if not earlier. One heavily painted version of the Mandrill, most likely produced about the middle of the nineteenth century, was sold at auction in 1998 (fig. 209).[896] Another Mandrill, acquired by John Bowes in Dresden in 1865, is now in the Bowes Museum.[897] In both cases, the base is not the original rock but rather a tree-stump, perhaps because the original mold had not been preserved. When Karl Hubert Stein re-worked the model for production in 1928,[898] he adopted the tree motif.

This style of decoration in powerful, opaque colors that cover the whole of the figure's surface is also in evidence on a Monkey

206 Johann Friedrich Eberlein, Sheep, model 1735, Dresden Porcelain Collection

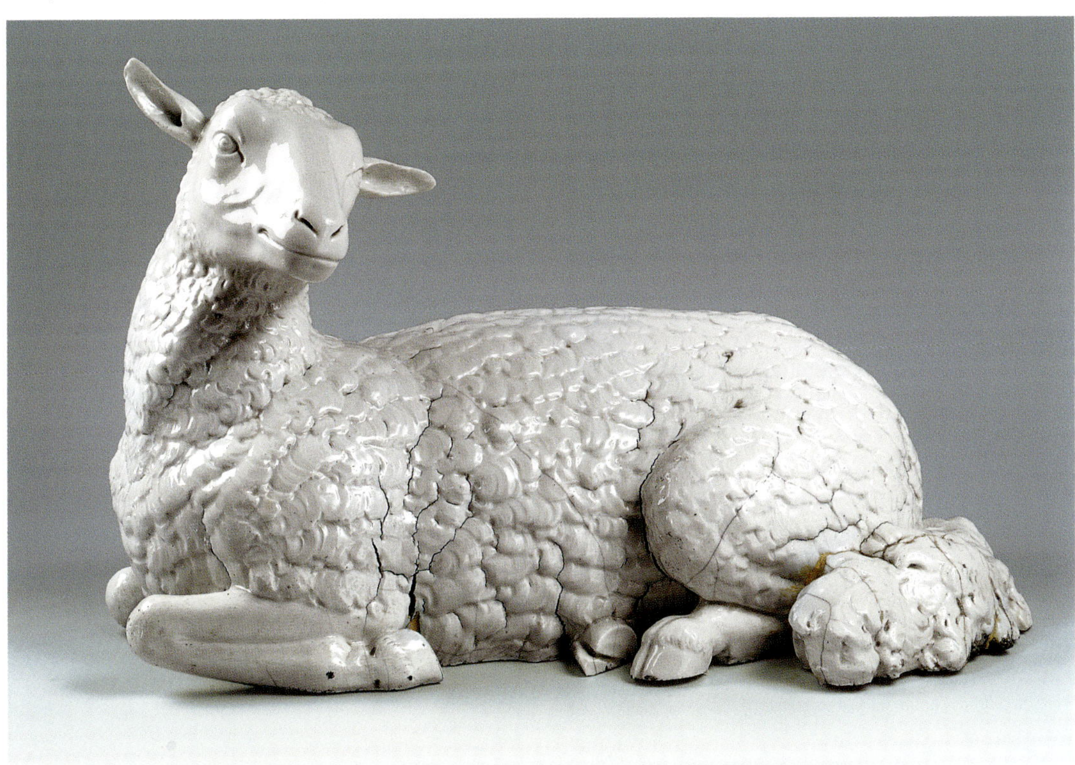

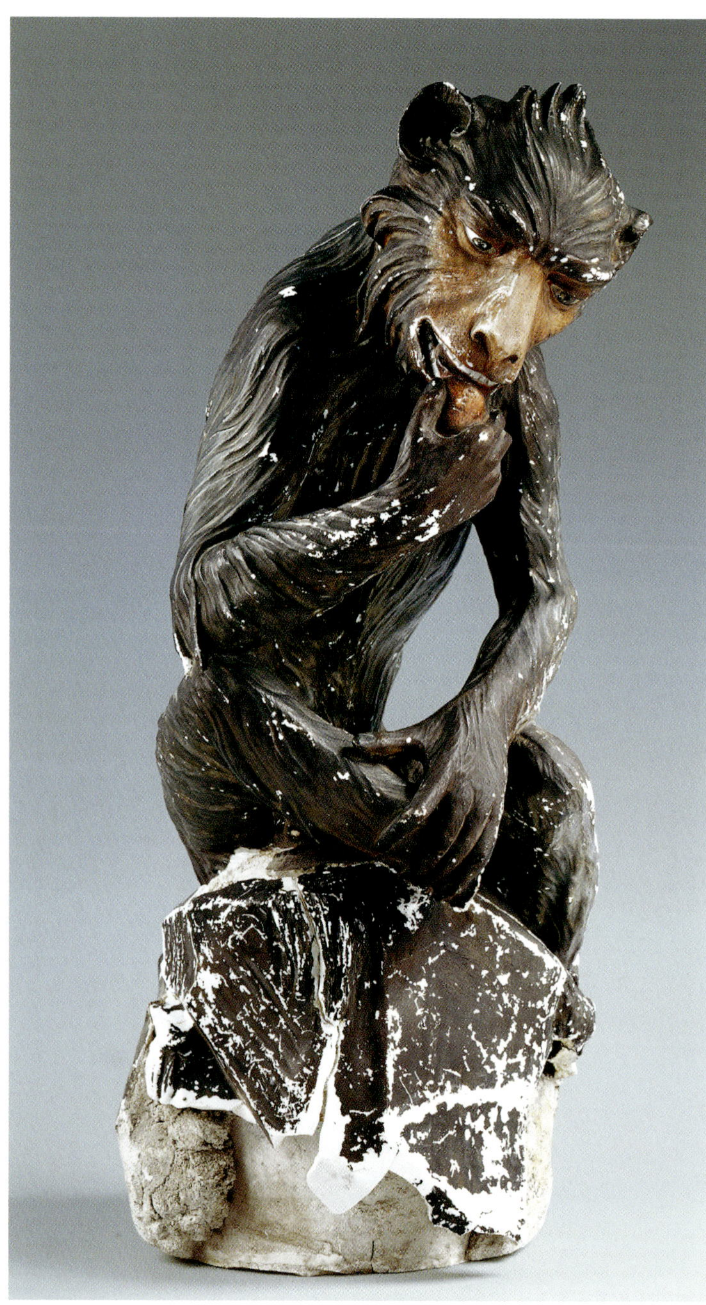

207 Johann Gottlieb Kirchner, Mandrill, painted with oils, model 1731, Dresden Porcelain Collection

taking snuff that was already recorded in a catalog of the collection of Sir William Holburn and is now the museum of the same name in Bath.[899] When this figure was manufactured, the Meissen mark was also conveniently "forgotten," as we saw had been the case with a number of the Bolognese dogs produced for sale in the mid-nineteenth century. Two more monkeys are similarly decorated: one is now in the possession of the Mendelssohn family,[900] and another is notable for having been unadventurously described in an auction catalog as "deutsch," in view of its missing mark and conspicuous decoration.[901] A fourth figure has been mistaken in print for a work of the Samson manufactory, also on account of its unusual decoration and lack of marks.[902] If one looks more closely at this series of examples of the Monkey taking snuff, it is noticeable that they differ from the proven originals held in the Dresden Porcelain Collection and Rijksmuseum. In the later figures it is not immediately obvious whether the monkey is actually taking the snuff, as the right hand is not quite in front of the nose. And the thumb and forefinger of the left hand are much closer together, not leaving so much room in between for the snuff-box. The long, finely articulated fingers on the eighteenth century figures are altogether more expressive, pointing as they do in various directions rather than lying in a uniform row as in the later figures. Further differences can be noticed in the transitions from the coats to the tree-stumps, which are likewise somewhat differently rendered. Even these small differences are enough to deprive the nineteenth-century monkeys of the sparkling wit of their forebears from the eighteen century: while the latter's lively inquisitiveness is clear from the way they hold the snuff between thumb and forefinger, stretching out the remaining fingers in an affected gesture reminiscent of polite ladies drinking tea (this posture is more noticeable on the Dresden monkey in fig. 215 than in its Rijksmuseum counterpart in fig. 87), the later figure looks somewhat bored, weary, and unfocused. Rather than imitating man, as the original Meissen monkey does, it only copies the hundred-year-old porcelain figure.

If one bears these factors in mind, then there is no doubt that the example of this model in the Schneider Collection in Schloss Lustheim near Munich (Bayerisches Nationalmuseum) is from the nineteenth century. However, one is surprised by the manner of its decoration, which is quite different from that of the other completely painted specimens. The painting of its pedestal, clearly demarcated areas in strongly contrasting colors, derives without doubt from the Monkey taking snuff in the Dresden collection, now preserved in the Rijksmuseum (fig. 87). The Munich figure was accordingly most likely produced at Meissen in the first half of the nineteenth century, when the Amsterdam monkey was still in the Japanese Palace, where as the only painted example was then the model for a copy requested by a private customer. One further Monkey taking snuff from the (late) nineteenth century was originally left undecorated, but was then painted in the twentieth century by a hand not belonging to the Meissen manufactory; as this decorator chose to do a slavish imitation of the painting on the Munich monkey, this case will be treated in the section on forged decoration. However, it should be noted that during Pfeiffer's revival of the Japanese Palace animals at Meissen, it was decided to eliminate the slight changes that the passage of time had wrought upon Kaendler's original, and to make the new series conform as strictly as possible to the 1730s originals preserved in museums.

The Billy-Goat was also occasionally executed in the nineteenth century, as is shown by the existence of a fully painted example in the collections of the National Museum in Stockholm, which also explains why the molds only had to be "re-modeled" when it came to the figure being taken back into production in 1922. The same is true of the Cockerel, the plaster molds for which were completed and changed one year before. The Cockerel also exists in likewise heavily painted examples from the late nineteenth century, with a pedestal that differs slightly from the original, and marked with the Meissen swords.[903]

The last example in this section is also one of the most puzzling. It is a King Vulture (1734 model), which has already appeared twice in the trade and differs, in the way it is holding its head and in the execution of the pedestal, so strikingly from the eighteenth-century examples that one might easily take it for a forgery. On its unglazed base, furthermore, is a mark that is no more than a shadow of the Meissen crossed swords.[904] However, the figure is painted in the same way as the originals from the 1730s. One further example of this version has the same head and pedestal but decoration that was clearly forged; however, it has a much clearer crossed swords mark and the incised model number 1768.[905] Albiker would seem to have been familiar with this variant back in 1935, as he describes it in his book of that year.[906] However, all the realizations of the early twentieth century are exact copies of the original models of the 1730s, so that one can only assume that in the second half of the nineteenth century the Meissen manufactory offered a King Vulture that differed quite considerably from Kaendler's original model and was then readapted to conform with the original during the revival in the early twentieth century under Pfeiffer.

These are the only nineteenth-century re-productions of original Japanese Palace animal models that the present author has actually seen with his own eyes, which of course does not exclude the possibility that others were done in that period.

In conclusion, reference should be made to the problem of "the absence of marks," which also arises in connection with the Meissen re-productions of the twentieth century. Although most of these have both the crossed swords mark in underglaze blue and also the impressed marking "weiß" ("white," indicating that it was originally sold undecorated), there is also evidence of pieces that are quite indisputably twentieth-century Meissen products, but on which there is no sign of a manufactory mark or any indication as to where they were produced. On a vulture in a private collection in north Germany, for instance, there are no marks at all, and the same collection contains another vulture on which the mark was clearly later sanded away, as can easily be seen from the damaged glaze.

At this point distinguishing between a re-production and a genuine forgery becomes not so much a scholarly as an ethical undertaking. This perilous matter is to be the subject of our next, and final, chapter.

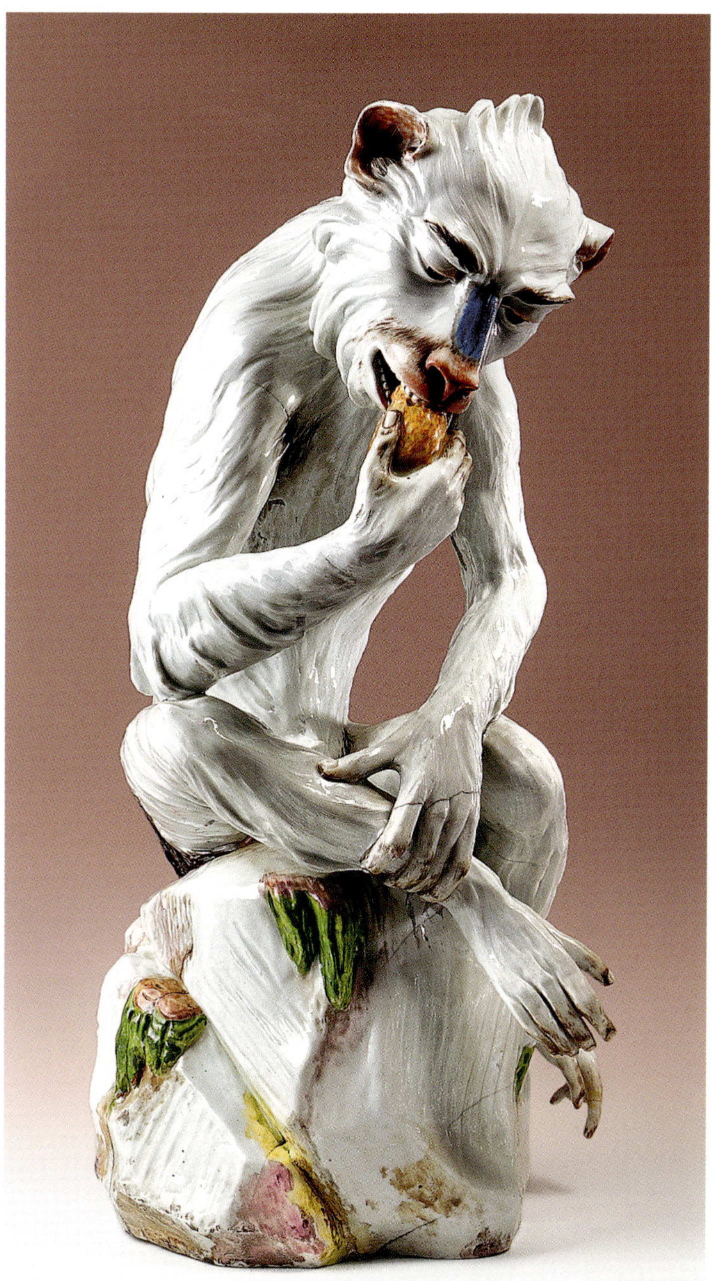

208 Johann Gottlieb Kirchner, Mandrill, decorated with enamel colors, model 1731, Dresden Porcelain Collection

Imitations and forgeries

The question as to whether a certain porcelain piece is an original or a forgery is exceptionally complex, and one that cannot be discussed exhaustively in words. It is not just that in most cases we have no absolutely reliable indicators, and that even the expert's judgment or the connoisseur's eye can err as they examine the

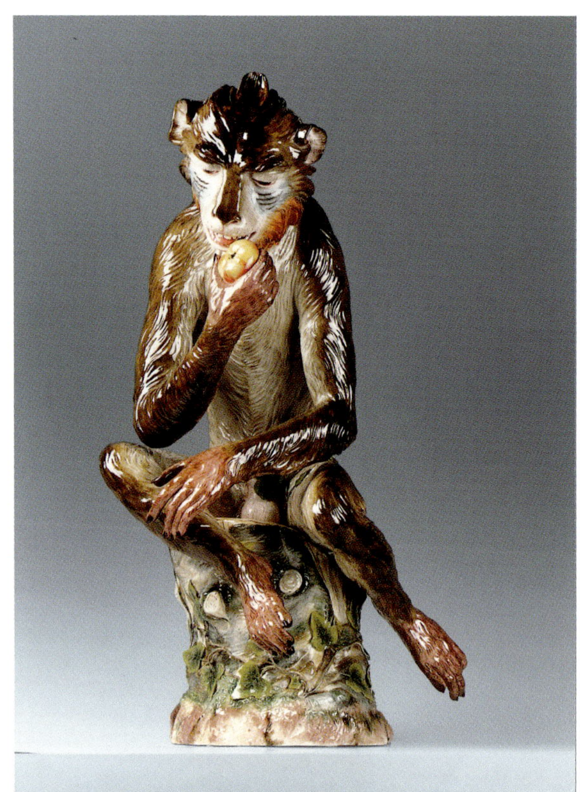

209 Mandrill, a Meissen product from the mid-nineteenth century

paste, the glaze, the plastic quality, and the technical details of any given piece. We even have to apply a certain differentiation to defining what a "forgery" exactly is. However, there is an exceptionally lively interest in recognizing forgeries of the Meissen large animal figures, especially since the question is far from being merely academic: often astoundingly high sums of money are also at stake.

The following account is not to be understood as applying to the smaller figures. As has been mentioned, certain figures, particularly the smaller birds and the monkeys, were not only produced almost uninterruptedly at the Meissen manufactory, but were also roughly imitated, with varying degrees of inspiration, in similar compositions by many other porcelain works in the eighteenth and nineteenth centuries. Clarifying whether all these innumerable works are to be classified as forgeries, or paraphrases, or copies would require an apparatus going beyond the boundaries of study by far. It should furthermore not be forgotten that the word "forgery" has itself undergone changes in meaning since the eighteenth century.

The large animal figures (over 40–50 cm high) are likewise not so immediately affected by this problem: the technical difficulties involved in their production meant that in the late eighteenth and early nineteenth centuries the smaller manufactories never even considered attempting the naïve imitations that they undertook with respect to the smaller figures. The second half of the nineteenth century, however, was to see rapid developments in ceramics technology generally and a rise in demand for the art of the Rococo: these two factors naturally made the animal figures increasingly interesting to forgers. As we have seen, there is also no evidence for any large animal figures having been sold from the royal collection in Dresden in the second half of the nineteenth century, and only a few models were in production at the Meissen manufactory. What are we to regard as a "forgery" in this context? Is the word only to be applied to those copies of Meissen animals that were made by other manufacturers and then marketed as originals? How are we to describe those figures which were produced at a later period by other manufactories, but in spite of slight variations from the original can still easily be mistaken by uncritical porcelain-lovers for Meissen originals from the 1730s? What are we to say of figures that were produced in Meissen for the Japan-

210 Price-list with wares for the English market, ca. 1826

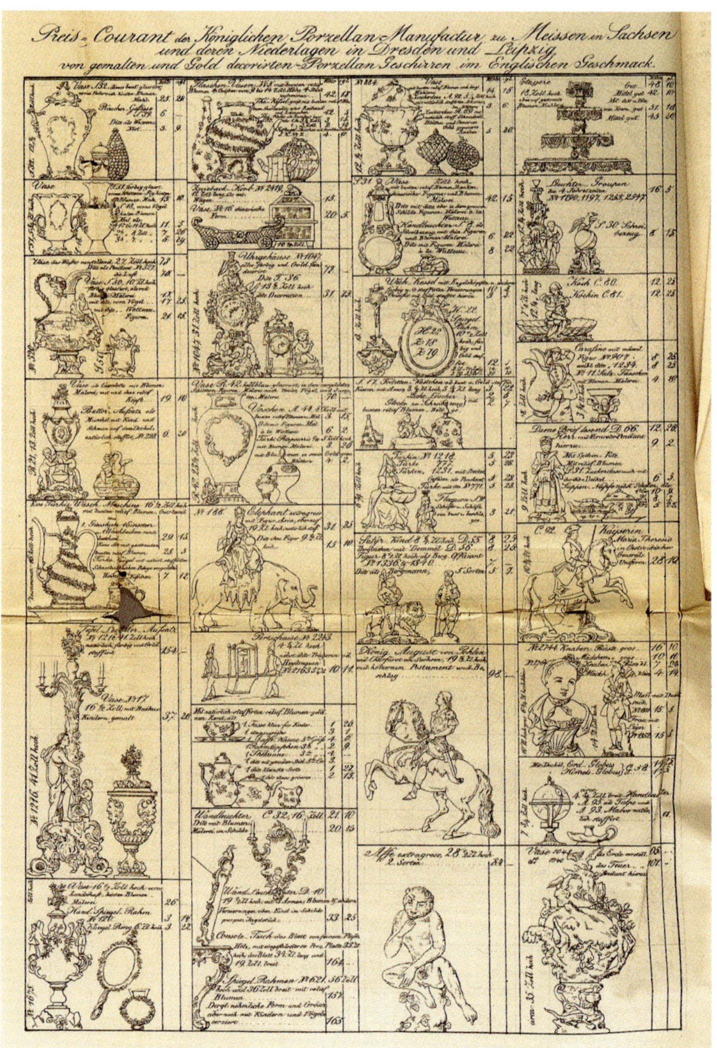

Preis-Courant der Königlichen Porzellan-Manufactur zu Meissen in Sachsen
und deren Niederlagen in Dresden und Leipzig
von gemalten und Gold decorirten Porzellan Geschirren im Englischen Geschmack.

ese Palace in the time of Augustus the Strong and Augustus III but were decorated later, and elsewhere, with enamel colors? Drawing the line between quotation and copy is at the best of times a very tricky business, and the scholar intending to investigate Meissen large animal forgeries – or, for that matter, any category of porcelain forgeries[907] – is well advised to divide the matter into two parts: forgeries of the models, and forged decoration.

Forgeries of models

The first question to be considered is whether long experience and expertise is really necessary for detecting forgeries, or whether it cannot perhaps also be done through the simple means of subjecting the figure in question to direct detailed comparison with a proven original. At this point, the author wishes to qualify the opinion that he has expressed in a number of lectures and in one publication to the effect that forgeries can be identified or excluded by the meticulous one-to-one comparative examination of all such details present in the plaster mold as strands of animal hair or individual feathers.[908] It is of course true that the repairer never has such a great degree of freedom as to be able to re-shape whole sections of hair-strands or feathers, which means that a detailed comparison of the feathers or the coat structure, or of their proportions, can enable us to make judgments with a considerable degree of certainty. However, a copyist who has an original eighteenth-century figure at his disposal, and not only has a high degree of familiarity with porcelain production techniques but is also a good modeler, can use methods practiced in sculpture to produce a clay model that is about a sixth larger than the original and will thus yield a final porcelain figure that will be an exact copy, capable of deceiving even the expert eye through its rendering even of the smallest details. This, however, is a highly labor-intensive process and calls for a high degree of skill and sensitivity. The results of applying this bafflingly demanding technique can best be seen in certain figures copied by the Meissen modelers of the 1920s from originals in the Dresden collection.[909] The profound respect and admiration that the master-modelers of today's manufactory have for the achievements of their forebears is an indication of the degree of skill and artistry that one needs to make an exact copy using this process.

Even when a forger has negotiated this first hurdle, he still has to succeed in getting the figure safely through the firing, the perils of which can hardly be underestimated, as is shown by the fact that even in the twentieth century the Meissen manufactory was not always entirely successful in eliminating fire-cracks: there is a guinea fowl from the early part of the century kept in the Dresden collection for instance, with a back that is seriously disfigured by a gaping fissure.

Finally, the forger has to make sure his paste corresponds to that used in the original. As we saw in Part One, the final appearance of the paste was a problem that faced arcanists and repairers alike. Only around 1735 was a recipe found for middle-size figures that resulted in an approximately pure white color and a consistency that was not too granular. A forger must be able to imitate this very particular paste in order for the forgery to give the impression of having been produced in the 1730s.

Finally, constructional features and marks left by the production process can also assist us in our detective work. In order to be able to copy the inner support construction typical of any given figure, the forger would have had to have a historical original to hand, or must have had the opportunity to examine an original thoroughly. The advisability of exercising caution before committing oneself to a judgment is shown by the example of a group of real experts who doubted the authenticity of one of the two painted kestrels in the Rijksmuseum on the grounds that it is, firstly, heavier than its fellow, and, secondly, clearly bears the impression of a piece of coarse linen on its unglazed undersurface. This impression is apparently often to be found on figures from the French firm Samson. However, it should not be forgotten that the craftsmen of the Meissen manufactory responsible for executing the models in porcelain were constantly on the lookout for new ways of responding to the difficult technical conditions and the unpredictable behavior of the paste. Nor is the weight of the figure a reliable criterion, as a kestrel figure was not "mass-produced" to the extent coffee-cups, for instance, were. The textile impression, which most likely resulted from the figure having been put on a piece of linen to dry, is not an indicator of a forgery, as it can also be observed on the King Vulture in Copenhagen, on the Mandrill in the Museum für Kunst und Gewerbe in Hamburg (acquired directly from the Dresden collection at the 1919 auction conducted by Lepke), and on one specimen of the Sheep in the Dresden Porcelain Collection (inv. no. PE 976). This instance shows that while deviations from the technical norm commend us to subject figures to closer examination, they should not spur us on to overhasty conclusions.

These considerations show that only the larger and longer-standing porcelain manufactories can ever have been capable of overcoming the artistic and technical difficulties inherent in the copying, or "forging," of original porcelain figures. As far as the present author can see and judge, really good forgeries of the large Japanese Palace animal models are thus a relatively rare phenomenon. The findings on this front can conveniently be divided into four categories:

1. Figures that originated outside the Meissen manufactory but which quote Meissen models, and, through the absence of any mark or through the presence of a mark used at Meissen, intentionally give the impression of having been made at Meissen:

Even before 1900, the Potschappel porcelain manufactory in Freital near Dresden had in its production range (as well as a number of smaller examples) at least four models that were copied from Meissen large animal figures, some specimens of which either have no marks or are misleadingly marked and are thus have to be regarded as forgeries.[910] They are illustrated in some turn-of-the-century sales catalogs preserved at the manufactory (fig. 211). Inspection of these catalogs reveals that while the Cockerel is roughly the same height as its Meissen prototype, its feathers are done in lower relief and also differ from the original in respect of certain structural details. Close comparison also shows that the bunch of feathers on the cockerel's head is differently conceived. The pedestal is high in proportion to the overall figure and the partially free-standing ears of corn are likewise differently set. The overall appearance nevertheless accords closely with the Meissen originals. The Potschappel copies of the Turkeycock and Turkeyhen are somewhat smaller than their Meissen counterparts and can be recognized for what they are by the slightly different rock design used for the pedestal. The precision with which all the details of feather structure have been imitated is nevertheless astounding, and it comes as no surprise to find that their absence of marks and their imitative decoration has led to their being considered Meissen originals from the second half of the eighteenth century.[911] However, the most common Potschappel forgery is the Mandrill (figs. 211 and 212). It was variously offered as a small figure, as a middle-size figure about 47 cm high, and in the size of the Meissen original. As this figure was also sold by Meissen in the nineteenth century, the Freital modelers will have had no problem obtaining a Meissen mandrill to copy. Instead of Kirchner's original rock pedestal, the Freital version has the tree-stump used in the nineteenth-century Meissen figures. An unmarked specimen from the trade, with the addition of an abundance of flowers applied to the pedestal, shows that the Potschappel model differs from the original particularly in its facial expression. In the records of the Dresden Porcelain Collection, there is a photograph of just such a figure with a note from the restorer Richard Seyffarth on the back to the effect that he did not consider the piece, which he had just restored for the dealer Max Siegwald, to be Meissen. Whether the Potschappel manufactory did any further imitations of large Meissen animals, omitting to give them marks and thus making them into forgeries, is not possible to say with certainty.

There is a figure of an osprey in existence, the provenance of which it has as yet proved impossible to ascertain.[912] It is very similar to Kaendler's model, but somewhat larger, and spoiled by an unsuccessful attempt to imitate the style of decoration of the earlier Meissen birds. Its flat, unglazed bottom has a small hole in the middle, with the crossed swords to one side. In this respect it imitates a technical feature that appears on such Meissen figures from the early twentieth century as a Guinea Fowl from around 1920 now in the Dresden Porcelain Collection.

As a counternote to these potentially misleading forgeries, it should be noted that some forgeries are so clumsily done as to be (unintentionally) comical. This is the case with a Marmoset unmarked which in spite of the earnest attempts of the forger is so distorted that it requires something of an expert eye to identify the figure of which it is supposed to be a forgery.[913]

2. Figures produced outside the Meissen manufactory in imitation of Meissen models but with small deviations or with signs that they are copies:

When describing the copies of large Meissen animal figures done in Potschappel – which are forgeries by virtue of their absence of marks – we saw that close comparison revealed small deviations from the respective originals. The porcelain firm Samson, founded by Edme Samson in Paris in 1845, achieved notoriety among experts and porcelain-lovers alike for its perfect copies, and specialized in museum copies that had particular signs to mark them out as such.[914] However, many Samson copies later had these signs removed, which made them into forgeries.

The firm marketed copies of at least five of the large animal figures, including one version of the Mandrill (fig. 214). The figure is only a little more than 52 cm high and thus significantly smaller than the Meissen original. The posture and facial expression of the animal are better done than in the Potschappel copy, but the coat is very unsubtly structured and poorly modeled. This is also true of the plumage of the Samson Bittern, which was produced in the correct size, but is with regard to the pedestal design, the rushes, and the feathers, a much simplified version of the original.[915] Even the decoration is such a free rendering of the Meissen original that nobody would mistake it for an original even if a special "G" mark had not been added to identify it as a copy. The Samson Cockerel gets somewhat higher marks, although it likewise has a simplified coat of plumage and a new contour to the pedestal.[916] The Samson Guinea Fowl, by contrast, is very close to Kaendler's original, not only in its proportions and measurements, but also in its modeling.[917] Achille Bloch's version of Kaendler's Monkey taking snuff

211 Potschappel manufactory sales catalog with a mandrill in three sizes, and turkeyhen and turkeycock, ca. 1900, Potschappel Archive

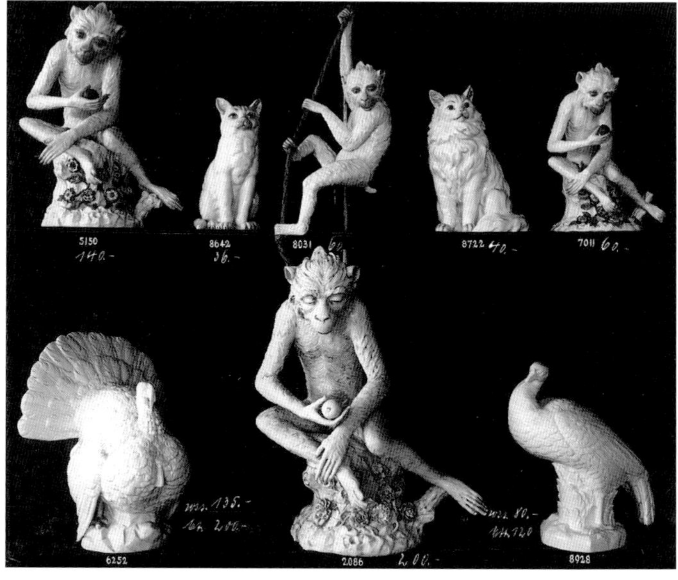

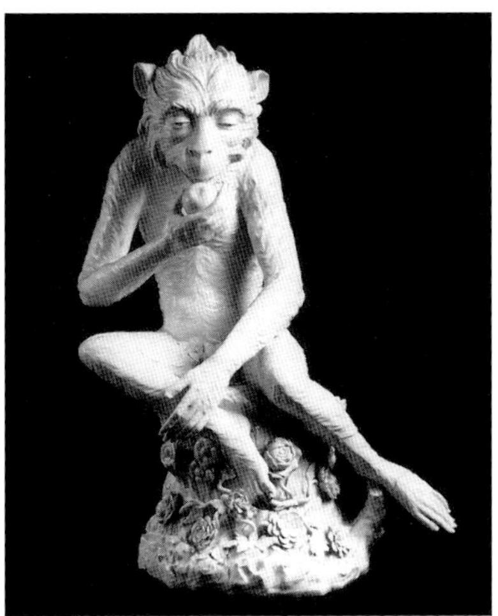
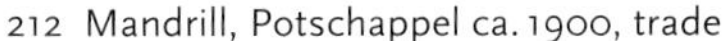

212 Mandrill, Potschappel ca. 1900, trade

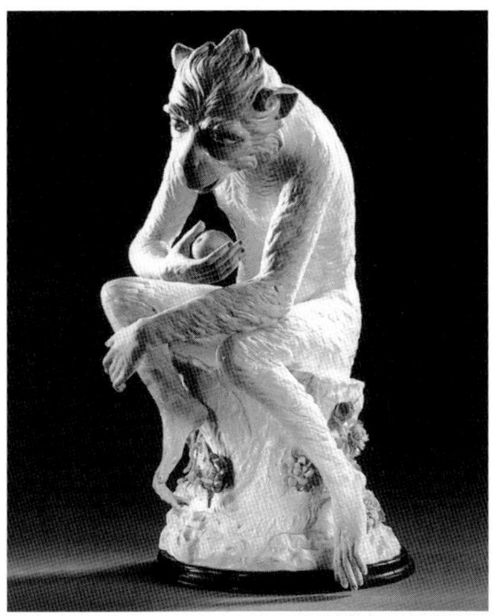

213 Mandrill with Frankenthal mark, Samson ca. 1900, trade

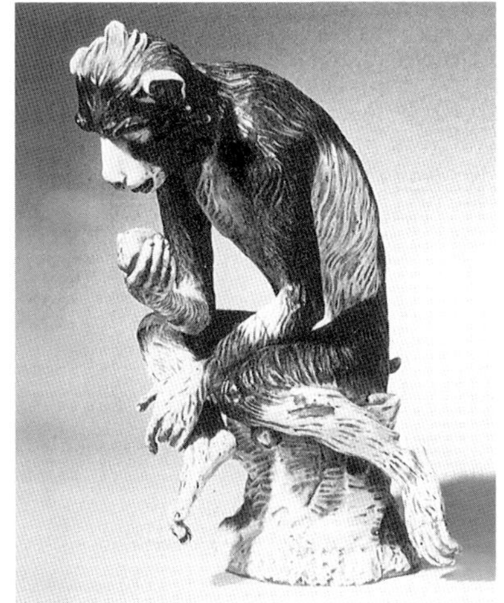

214 Mandrill, catalog for the sale of wares from the Samson manufactory warehouse

from the end of the nineteenth century differs so clearly from the original that it is not so much a copy as an "interpretation" (figs. 215 and 216).[918] The monkey is not holding a snuff-box but a pomegranate, and the snuff-taking gesture has been changed accordingly. The coat and facial expression also differ from those on the Meissen original. The privately-owned example illustrated here bears on the back of the base Bloch's own allusion to the Meissen swords, namely a pair of crossed arrows with their tips pointing downwards. One further Bloch Monkey sold at auction in New York, with a pedestal decorated in imitation of historical figures, was furthermore signed AB.[919] Remarkably, in spite of being solely inspired by the Meissen Monkey taking snuff, this charming figure is still a highly original creation in its own right.

3. Figures not produced at the Meissen manufactory, quoting Meissen models exactly, and claiming through their marks to have been made at other eighteenth-century manufactories:

Very confusing are the small number of porcelain animals that are to be reckoned as unqualified forgeries because they have marks indicating a provenance other than their real one. The curious thing about them is that although they clearly aim to imitate Meissen originals exactly, they claim to have been made in other eighteenth-century manufactories. Mention shall be made of just four of these somewhat scurrilous forgeries: a middle-size Mandrill produced by Samson bearing the upright lion that was the customary Frankenthal mark between 1755 and 1762 (fig. 213);[920] a Potschappel Mandrill of the same size, marked with an impressed arrow, thus purporting to be a work from about 1745/50 from the Bow manufactory;[921] an unpainted Potschappel Cockerel bearing on the inside of the pedestal a mark (not clearly legible on account of the blue having run) in the form of a stylized crown with three letters underneath;[922] and finally a figure recently offered at auction, a small version of the Bolognese Dog that has the Nymphenburg's Bavarian shield of arms, but is of uncertain provenance.[923]

In the first chapter of the Postlude it was suggested that our account of forgeries might also extend to considering those nineteenth- and twentieth-century animal figures produced at Meissen on which the manufactory conveniently omitted to apply the Meissen mark. While this practice was not questionable in a juridical sense, it would go beyond the bounds of the present study to discuss the complicated matter of its ethics.

Figures with forged decoration

Much more problematic than the matter of forged animal models is that concerning figures that originated in Meissen in the 1730s but were only decorated later and not at Meissen. In the section on the original decoration of the figures with enamel colors it was seen that the often brightly colored and "patchy" decoration was determined by the optical habits and technical conditions prevailing at the time. The unexpected and new challenge of having to decorate monumental porcelain sculptures for a huge gallery led to solutions which had nothing in common with the meticulous painting practiced on precious pieces of tableware. On account of the thick brushwork and sometimes apparently clumsy decoration in strongly contrasting colors on some enameled Japanese Palace animal figures, it has sometimes been thought that they were only decorated later and not at the time they were originally produced. The uncertainty deriving from this impression has sometimes led to large museums consigning such figures to their depositories as "forgeries." When one considers that there was great demand for animal figures in the nineteenth century, and that in Dresden of all places there were decorating studios where no compunction was

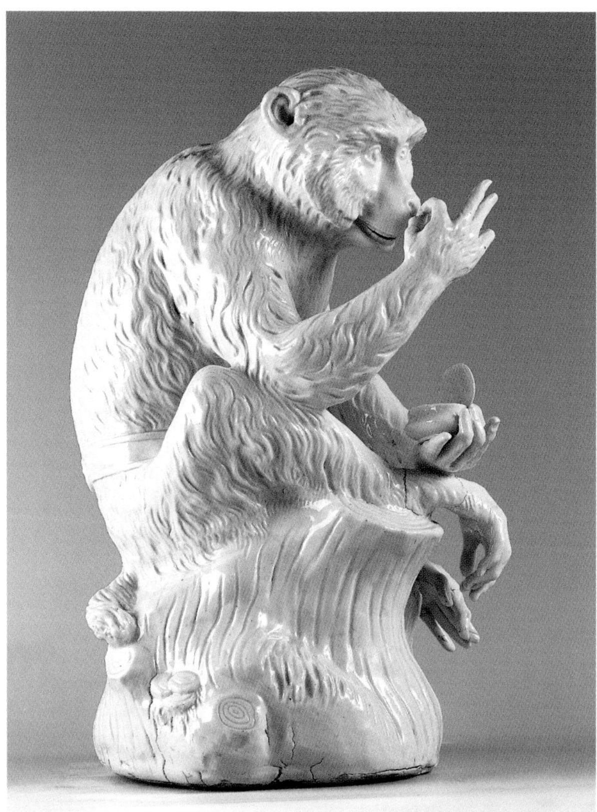

215 Johann Joachim Kaendler, Monkey taking snuff, model most likely 1732, Dresden Porcelain Collection

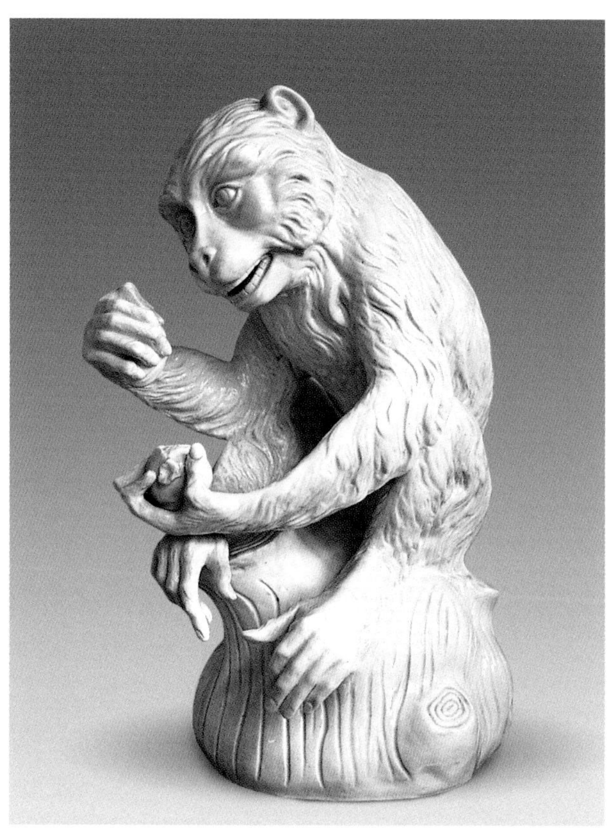

216 Monkey with pomegranate, Achille Bloch manufactory, end of nineteenth century, private collection

felt about painting old white tableware in historical styles, one can quite understand curators' fears that the figures entrusted to their charge might well have unauthentic decoration.

If one makes a survey of all the enameled animal figures that were produced for the Japanese Palace between 1731 and 1736, one immediately notices great differences in the technical and artistic quality of the painting. Everything is there, from dull, matt areas to radiant shine. To the eye examining the Rijksmuseum's Golden Pheasant, thickly applied and almost opaque yellow patches inserted into back-feathers bathed in fluid blue and underlaid with dark purple suggest a clumsy and unconvincing attempt to liven up the dark area with bright highlights. If one compares this painting with the refined decoration done four years later on the Pheasant, with its delicate balance between the painterly and the sculptural in the rendering of the plumage, one is immediately able to see the development that had taken place (figs. 98 and 99). And one cannot fail to observe that the smaller figures, even in the early period, are better and more coherently decorated than the large figures, on which the depressions are still painted with dark colors in an attempt to accentuate the shadows.

The supposition that the large animal figures that have strongly contrasting, broadly applied, unnatural colors were painted later and thus could be considered forgeries with respect to their decoration oversees the fact that these figures were decorated at a time when the great technical steps forward were only just being made. The limited format of the small pieces of tableware was becoming a thing of the past, and a new approach had to be developed that would be suitable for the decoration of large figures with colors that are in themselves not really suitable for covering large areas. The fact that such large-size figures as the Mandrill, the Golden Pheasant, and the vultures were decorated in enamels show that there was sufficient kiln capacity for this kind of decoration, and that the figures not too excessively affected by fire-cracks could well have been decorated in this way. That this did not happen was connected with the aesthetic results, which the eyes of the time did not find any more convincing than we do, as porcelain-painting is closer to painting with watercolors than to painting with oils: areas are given their shading primarily by differentiated thicknesses of application (layers) and not through colors being worked into each other. Another factor is that the pigments for porcelain-painting are relatively costly.

A further point to be noted is that the few genuinely large animal figures decorated in enamels still in existence today are, even when one exercises caution over the language used, definitely so described in the delivery lists, in the eighteenth-century inventories, or in the records of nineteenth-century sales.

In the general context of forgeries of the original animal figures of the 1730s, the later forging of the painting looms considerably less large than that of the models.[924] However, one case of the former aspect may be mentioned by way of conclusion. A specimen of the Monkey taking snuff offered some time ago in the trade attracted attention because while it was decorated in a way comparable to the Rijksmuseum figure, and was even almost identical with the figure in the Schneider Collection in Schloss Lustheim near Munich[925], the body, certain technical features, and the detail of the modeling suggested that it originated in the nineteenth century. However, the whole of the figure's glaze showed regular crackle, and of a kind that was quite different from that to be seen on the relevant, crackle-affected example of this figure in the Dresden Porcelain Collection, but quite the same as the crackle on old figures that have been "restored" with an enamel treated so as to melt at low temperature, and have thus been subjected to one additional firing. The conditions created by a modern gas or electric kiln are not the same as those created in the original kilns, particularly in respect of heating-up and cooling-down times, and can thus bring about tensions that sometimes result in the cracking of the glaze. Logically enough, this can also happen when a porcelain piece is given an inexpert extra firing that has nothing to do with restoration, but is carried out in order to fix enamel colors. The hesitant character of the brushwork applied to this monkey, the slavish copying of pedestal detail from the Munich example, the slight deviations in color tones, and certain illogical peculiarities (the tip of the tail is painted over in purple rather than being highlighted in brown) also combine to suggest that it is not an original nineteenth-century decoration carried out at the Meissen manufactory, but rather a later addition. Ironically, when the forger took the Munich figure as his exemplar, he unwittingly chose a figure long held to be an original from the 1730s that was in fact only a copy. At the time of the revival of the animal models under Pfeiffer, the Meissen manufactory made a happier choice, copying the decoration on the Amsterdam figure, as is shown by the examples of their twentieth-century copy in the depository of the Meissen *Schauhalle* and by another example from the trade.[926]

The labors undertaken at the Meissen manufactory in order to revive Augustus the Strong's porcelain menagerie and the effort invested by those who have endeavored to copy or forge the animals both go to show how timeless the interest provoked by these figures is. While collectors of Kaendler's *Kleinplastik* from the 1730s and 1740s have long since lost any kind of personal relationship with the world of the eighteenth-century courts that these figures directly illustrated, the animal figures have retained a great deal of their essential and immediate appeal. For the enthusiast as for the scholar, for collectors and dealers as for museum curators, for the occasional museum-visitor as for the connoisseur, they remain precisely what they would have been if the Japanese Palace project had been brought to full and final fruition: a challenge as much to the gut as to the head. Given the increasing lack of respect for culture in our own day, one can only hope that we will not wake up one day to find that the Meissen animals have abandoned our museums and returned to the wild.

NOTES

1 All four are based on research into source material in Meissen and Dresden, and are the following: Berling 1900, Zimmermann 1926, Rückert 1966, and Walcha 1973.
2 See the publications by Boltz, Cassidy-Geiger, Pietsch, and Rückert.
3 On Dresden's "Augustan period," see Schmidt/Syndram 1997.
4 Forberger 1958.
5 Plaßmeyer 2001.
6 On the development of the Meissen paste from lime porcelain to feldspathic porcelain, see Goder 1978.
7 Pietsch 1996.b.
8 Rückert 1990, 41–42.
9 Boltz 1980.
10 Fichtner 1939 and Ströber 2004. On one of the extant pieces, see the article by Friedrich Reichel on the Dresden phoenix jug in Pietsch 1998, 24.
11 Reichel 1972.a, 47.
12 Ibid. The relevant document was, according to Reichel, a war loss suffered by the SächsHStA.
13 Ibid., 45.
14 Schwarm-Tomisch 2002.a, 63.
15 Ibid.
16 Reichel 1972.a, 45.
17 Wittwer 2000.a, 2001.a, and 2004.
18 "Ne scavez vous pas qu'il est des orangers comme des porcelaines, que ceux qui ont une fois la maladie des uns ou des autres ne trouvent jamais qu'ils en ayent assez et que plus ils ent veulent avoir." Quoted from Sponsel 1900, 10.
19 On the dates and extant lists, see Sponsel 1900, 10ff.; Fichtner 1939 and Reichel 1972.a, 48ff.; on Chometowski in particular, see Reichel 2002.
20 Reichel 1972.a, 49 (with delivery lists for the objects) and Reichel in Pietsch 1998, 45; see also Wittwer 2001.a.
21 Sponsel 1900, 10.
22 Heres 1991, 84.
23 Reichel 1972.a, 48.
24 Schmidberger 1990, 14.
25 On the porcelain trade, see Treue 1953, 1954, and 1958; Howard/Ayers 1978; and Jörg 1990.
26 Even before the foundation of the United East India Company, the Kunstkammer of Archduke Ferdinand II at Schloss Ambras contained, in 1595, 233 Chinese porcelains (Schmidberger 1990, 14), and one hundred years later the Oranienburg porcelain room contained several thousand pieces of blue-and-white porcelain; see Wittwer 2001.a.
27 Daxelmüller 1995, Scheicher 1995.
28 Wittwer 1999, 2000.a and 2001.a.
29 On the importance of the spatial and social distancing mechanisms at and around the courts in the absolutist Baroque period, see Elias 1997.
30 Württemberg 1998.
31 Buttlar 1996, 1. On the influence of the literature on China, see Köllmann 1954, cols. 450–452, and Walravens 1987.
32 Beutler 1680, 241. On the early Enlightenment's understanding of China, see Reichel 1972.a, 2 and 17; Hsia 1985 provides material in particularly ample measure.
33 For the example of Dresden, see Warncke 1989.
34 The work of Beutler (see note 32), for instance, the Elector's secretary, mathematician, and director of the *Kunstkammer*, was dedicated – certainly with a view to their education – to the sons of the Elector George III that is to say, Johann Georg (IV) and Friedrich August (I), later known as Augustus the Strong; see Schlechte 1988.
35 "...in einem utopischen Gegenentwurf zur bestehenden Ordnung ...die klassische Feudalhierarchie zwischen Herrscher und Beherrschtem zwar nicht auflöste, doch deren soziale Widersprüche beseitigen und in Harmonie verwandeln wollte"; Vogel 1996, 188.
36 On the three "phases" of the fashion for chinoiserie, see Köllmann 1954. He proposes for the period ca. 1670–1730 a form of chinoiserie that primarily copied and imitated, and suggests that the chinoiserie prevalent during the Rococo period from ca. 1730–1760 received its free and creative character at the onset of the Enlightenment. In the third period from ca. 1760–1820, chinoiserie followed the tendencies of Romanticism.
37 Köllmann 1954.
38 First steps towards this kind of comprehensive new interpretation of the fashion for chinoiserie, going beyond Köllmann's purely aesthetic categorizations, are to be found, for instance, in Buttlar 1996 and Vogel 1996.
39 Cassidy-Geiger 2005.
40 "bey denen Tafeln... alle mit holländisch Porcelain serviret"; court journal 1717, quoted from Schwarm-Tomisch 2002.a, 46.
41 Ibid.
42 Seelig 1995, 15–21 and 31–38; Wittwer 2001.b. The "use" of porcelain in seventeenth-century still-life painting would in itself be a subject worthy of discussion, and shows parallels to the function of sideboards, even though the still-lifes in question did not reflect a scene that existed in reality.
43 Reinheckel 1990.
44 Loibl 1989, 81.
45 Loibl 1989, 80, and Lohneis 1985.
46 Loibl (p. 81) described the rooms: "begehbare Sammlungsschränke," or "walk-in collection cabinets."
47 Loibl 1989, 80.
48 This ambiguity was present, playing a slightly different role, in such contexts as the mirror-cabinets, mainly small in size and South German, which developed in the first half of the eighteenth century; see Glaser 1983, Lohneis 1985, and Loibl 1989. Some of the most important are, or were: Merseburg (1712–1714), Weikersheim (1717), Weißenstein, nr. Pommersfelden (1719), Wiesentheid (1724), Fulda (1724–27), the Munich Residence (1731–33), Würzburg (1736–44), Ansbach (1739).
49 Reidemeister 1934, Wittwer 2001.a.
50 Wittwer 2001.a, 232.
51 Loibl 1989, 82.
52 Wittwer 2000.a and 2001.a.
53 See also Loibl 1989, 82.
54 Neuhof 1669, 276–277.
55 Temple 1990 and Vogel 1996.
56 On the Trianon de Porcelaine, see Gothein 1988, 2:162ff.
57 See Vogel 1996, 192; Vogel assumes that the roof was covered in "ceramic roof-shingles of such an exalted quality as to suggest, aesthetically and associatively, an intended emulation of the famous porcelain pagoda of Nanking."
58 Gothein 1988, 162.
59 Piper 1921; for a more recent work with a similarly survey-like structure, see List 1993.
60 Clarke 1986, Oettermann 1982; a list of all the titles would be too long for inclusion here, but it would certainly include studies devoted to medieval bestiaries, animal representations in architectural sculpture, Baroque animal pictures of the Netherlands, English horse paintings, and Mannerist and nineteenth-century animal bronzes; for a detailed bibliography, see List 1993.
61 On the animal in Dutch painting, see Müllenmeister 1978.
62 Blümel 1939.
63 Andrea Riccio, whose real name was Briosco, lived from 1470 to 1532 in Padua; see also Liebieghaus Frankfurt 1985.
64 On a little owl figure in the manner of Giambologna, see Krahn

1995, 124; on the animal grotto of the Medici villa, see Rietzsch 1987, 47.

65 Krahn 1995, 380–382; on the decoration of grottoes with animals generally, see Rietzsch 1987, and Maué 1995; on Giambologna generally, see Gibbons 1995.

66 Krahn 1995, 464–466.

67 Gothein 1988, 151–154.

68 G. Weber 1985, 306; see also Cassidy-Geiger 2003.b with a listing of the sculptors involved.

69 "…denn das Wasser, das sie einander zuspeien, scheint ihnen nicht nur Leben und Aktion zu verleihen, sondern es dient ihnen auch gleichsam als Stimme, um ihre Erregung und Gedanken auszudrücken." From a description by Charles Perrault, quoted from Hansmann 1983, 109; see also Perrault 1990.

70 Two versions of a guidebook appeared in 1677 and 1679 respectively, with texts by Charles Perrault and prints by Sébastien LeClerc, engraved after paintings and gouaches by Jean Cotelle II. The gouaches are reproduced in Pincas 1996, and Salmon 2001, 34–35. A Dutch edition by Pierre Mortier from around 1680 complements LeClerc's engravings with further material on each side to achieve a landscape format; one example is illustrated in Cohen 2000, 108. The German edition by Johann Ulrich Krauss used LeClerc's engravings unchanged and simply added a translation of the four-line verses, see Krauss 1975, while Jacques Bailly made magnificent gouaches of the engravings, see Cassidy-Geiger 2003.b, ills. 8 and 11. LeClerc's engravings were used once again, slightly changed, in a projected view made around 1720 by Johann Baptist Homann for a garden at Schloss Hildburghausen, which was however never executed in this form; both leaves of the projection are kept at the Potsdam collection of plans of the Stiftung Preußische Schlösser und Gärten Berlin-Brandenburg, and the plans are discussed in Paust 1996, 108–112 and ill. 32. On the animal figure groups inspired by the example of Versailles, see for example the four groups in the park at Veitshöchheim; Lindemann 1989, 295–301.

71 According to G. Weber 1985, 306–307, preparations are being made for a catalog of the extant works.

72 Gothein 1988, 1.388–390.

73 Davis 1991, 72–76 and 89–92.

74 For just one example, the reader is referred to the famous "Solomonic" silver lions next to the throne in Rosenborg.

75 "Assoziation, Mehrdeutigkeit und daraus folgende Vielfalt möglicher Erklärungen waren beabsichtigt und sind von besonderem Reiz." Karl-August Wirth on animal-form drinking vessels, quoted from Lehne 1985, 48.

76 These pulpits are described in detail in Tralbaut 1946. I am grateful to Wolfram Koeppe, New York, for drawing my attention to these works, which would certainly deserve in-depth studies.

77 May 1987, 90; Johann Rudolf Fäsch has also been suggested, see Joachim Menzhausen in Kopplin 1998, 8; on the question of the architect and for a detailed building history, see Schumann 1885, Gurlitt 1903, Fichtner 1939–41, Franz 1953, Heckmann 1972 und 1986, and Schwarm-Tomisch 2002.a; I am particularly indebted to Walter May's publication of 1987.

78 As Flemming himself never actually moved into the finely situated palace, it has been suggested that when he acquired the plot and built the palace he was all the time a middleman acting on behalf of Augustus the Strong. This was a practice which we know the king followed in other instances. See Heckmann 1972, 164; and Schwarm-Tomisch 2002.a.

79 May 1987, 90.

80 See, for instance, Heckmann 1972, 165.

81 After the great fire of 1685, the part of the city on the right bank of the Elbe till then known as "Alt-Dresden" was rebuilt and renamed "Neustadt" by Augustus the Strong in 1732.

82 "Das propre Palais… haben 1717. Ihro Königl. Maj. wegen seines vortrefflichen Splendeurs und Situation umb ein großes Geld an sich erkauffet und unter dem Nahmen eines Japanischen Palais der Nachwelt aeternisiret … Nachdem auch vor 3. Jahren die in aller Welt berühmte *Kunstkammer* aus Neu-Dreßden81 in dieses Palatium 2 Treppen hoch in 9 absonderlich darzu adaptirte Zimmer wegen der allda befindlichen guten Lufft gebracht und in schönster Ordnung rangiret worden." Anonymous 1720, 35 and 38; on the history of the *Kunstkammer*, see also Heres 1991.

83 Schumann 1885, 116, note 9.

84 H. Bauer 1992, 126–135.

85 This was the sense in which Fritz Fichtner referred to the palace as "größte Schaubühne damaliger Diplomatie" ("the greatest theater of diplomacy of its day"); Fichtner 1940, 492.

86 On Dresden's gardens, see Jöchner 2001.

87 Hofmann/Tradler 2003, 79.

88 Schwarm-Tomisch 2002.a, 64.

89 Landesamt für Denkmalpflege Dresden, M6. XIII Bl. 2.

90 Hentschel 1969, 30–34.

91 Ibid.; the plan published by Hentschel as fig. 34 bears the classification number: SächsHStA, OHMA Cap. VI, Nr. 17, fol. 21a, b.

92 Reichel, 1972.a, S. 98.

93 Gurlitt 1903.

94 "Nächst der Galanterie bereitet ihm die Baukunst, und zwar die militärische wie profane, am meisten Vergnügen, und alle Welt ist sich darüber einig, dass er von alle beiden ein Menge versteht. Indessen hat er noch kein Bauwerk zu Ende geführt. Die Sucht, den Beifall aller für sich zu haben, lässt ihn häufig den Plan ändern, sodass er vielerlei anfängt, aber nicht vollendet." Quoted from Schurig 1907, 1.

95 Franz 1953, and in his wake particularly Heckmann 1972 and 1986.

96 May 1987, 90.

97 See Heckmann 1972, 171–172.

98 Franz 1953, 38; Heckmann 1972, 175ff.

99 Schwarm-Tomisch 2002.b, and Hofmann/Tradler 2003, 80.

100 "über den grossen Vorrath des daselbst befindlichen pretieusen Porcellains eine grosse Admiration spühren lassen"; Iccander 1726–1735, in this instance no. 110, 1729, 267.

101 The question as to his influence and that of the architects Matthäus Daniel Pöppelmann, Zacharias Longuelune, and Johann Christoph Knöffel has been discussed in detail in the literature; see Gurlitt 1903, Franz 1953, Heckmann 1972 and 1986, and May 1987.

102 Kuke 2002, esp. 224–227.

103 "Dieser schöne Pallast [= the Dutch Palace] wird anitzt niedergerissen und ins Viereck mit vier Eingängen wieder aufgeführet. Die Aufsicht über solchen kostbaren Bau haben der General Bodt und die drey Oberlandbaumeister Pöpelmann, Longlue und Knevel." Keyssler 1751, 1320.

104 Schumann 1885, 117 n. 10.

105 Ermisch 1935, 17.

106 Schumann 1885, 117

107 Ibid.

108 Hasche 1783, 2:180; anonymous 1799, 54, and Rauda 1932.

109 This inscription "museum usui publico patens" ("museum open for the benefit of the public") was put on the portal when the building was put to its new use.

110 Franz 1953, ills. 77–79.

111 Landesamt für Denkmalpflege, M16.VII Bl. 11.

112 SächsHStA, OHMA Cap. II, 16.9.

113 "Eine Füllung, deren Verzierung aber noch nicht ausgehauen, nimmt den übrigen Raum bis unter den Architrav ein." Hasche 1783, 2:185.

114 Löffler 1962 and Gurlitt 1903 consider the herm pilasters to have been entirely Kirchner's work, an ascription which Asche 1966 is right to doubt. Asche suggests that although Johann Christian Kirchner made the models for the pilasters, these (or at least a number of them) were completed after his death in 1732 by Matthäus Oberschall and Johann Gottlieb Kirchner; see Asche 1966, 237–239, 334, 337. The latter was the brother of Johann Christian and was at this time still Modellmeister at Meissen; Schumann refers to the herm pilasters as an invention of Pöppelmann, which does not exclude the possibility of his idea being put into practice by others; Schumann 1885, 44. This theory is corroborated by an as yet unpublished cross-section through the two gallery wings (north-south) that has two such Chinese herms sketched in pencil over two undecorated pilasters of the courtyard-side facade of the east wing. On the grounds of the roof-forms (not executed) and the roughly drawn arrangement of porcelain in the interior, this design can be attributed to Pöppelmann and dated around 1727. The courtyard facades, and thus the Chinese herms as well, had to wait until the mid-1730s to be completed; see Heckmann, 178.

115 On the evolution of the planning, see Gurlitt 1903, Fichtner 1939–1941, Franz 1953, Heckmann 1972, and May 1987, summarized in Träger 1991. The plans are now mostly kept in the SächsHStA, with some at the Landesamt für Denkmalpflege and the Sächsische Landesbibliothek, Dresden.

116 The expression "Krackt Porzelain" most likely refers to the typical

Chinese blue-and-white porcelain of the seventeenth century that we know as "*kraak* porcelain."
117 "große blaue und weißen Vasen"; the expression can be taken as referring to such large palace vases as, for instance, the "dragoon vases" which had been in the royal collection since 1717.
118 Landesamt für Denkmalpflege, M6.I. Bl. 5. A slightly different version of this plan is illustrated in Heckmann 1972, 172 fig. 174.
119 "Großen Vasen und Orangen Töpffe"; a number of these, which are still preserved in the Porcelain Collection in the Zwinger, had holes drilled in them to allow water to flow away.
120 Glaser 1983, 35.
121 SächsHStA, loc. 2097 Nr. 49, fol. 12.
122 "Specificatio dererjenigen Zimmer, welche Ihro Majth. der höchstseeligste König glorwürdigsten Andenckens, im Japanischen Palais, und zwar in der Ersten Etage [= ground floor], auf nachbeschriebene Arth aus meubliren zu laßen, allergnädigst intentioniret gewesen"; SächsHStA, OHMA Cap. II, Nr. 15, Anlage C.
123 SächsHStA, loc. 1341, Vol. IV, fols. 383a–384a.
124 On the distribution of the porcelain in the Dutch Palace, see the descriptions of the rooms in the 1721 inventory, recently published in Cassidy-Geiger 2004, 60–65.
125 SächsHStA, OHMA Cap. II, 15.2, the last part of which is concerned with the large gallery in the upper story of the Elbe-side wing, the throne gallery, to which Longuelune devoted an explanation several pages long in his design.
126 See Franz 1953, Träger 1991.
127 SächsHAStA, OHMA Cap. II, 15.26.
128 Letter of 7. 11. 1732; SächsHStA, loc. 2214, Vol. II, fol. 44b.
129 Hentschel 1969, 68.
130 Franz 1953.
131 May 1989, 203.
132 Reichel, 1972.a, S. 73; the gallery created in 1709 with the collection of around 8000 Far Eastern porcelains belonging to Duke Anton-Ulrich von Braunschweig-Wolfenbüttel was one of the most famous porcelain cabinets of its day, see also especially Ströber 2002, 9–24.
133 Glaser 1983, 32.
134 Ibid.
135 SächsHStA, OHMA Cap. II, Nr. 15.5–15.25.
136 SächsHStA, OHMA Cap. II, Nr. 15.22.
137 SächsHStA, OHMA Cap. II, Nr. 15.24 and 15.25.
138 These are series of designs for the throne and the carillon; SächsHStA, OHMA Cap. II, Nr. 15.23.
139 SächsHStA, OHMA Cap. II, 15.4.; this ground plan corresponds more exactly with the elevations than fig. 28 in respect of the positioning of the fireplaces and the distribution of the doors. Longuelune maybe delivered this plan later, after he already had the ground plan illustrated in fig. 28 and the elevations.
140 "Interessante Einblicke in das künstlerische Schaffen gewähren die Aufrisszeichnungen von Innenräumen, sie lassen nachfühlen, dass man sich bei der Aufstellung nicht von Werten der Einzelstücke bestimmen, sondern vom Raumgefühl leiten liess: die dunkleren Fensterseiten mit Gegenlicht erhielten grössere, sinnfälligere Vasen. An den gut beleuchteten Rückwänden entwickelte sich der ganze Reichtum grosser und kleiner Porzellane." Fichtner 1936.b.
141 That plates were not only placed on consoles but also hung freely on the walls is shown by a list drawn up in 1759 that contains various items taken from the palace. These included "eight 'Assietten' [= large round platters] in Saxon porcelain, painted with yellow lions, and bordered with gilded silver bands; forty-nine matching plates," ("Acht Assietten, von Sächß. Porcell. mit gelben Löwen gemahlt, und Silbernen und vergoldeten Bändern eingefaßt; Neun und Viertzig Stk. dergl. Teller") SächsHStA, loc. 895, fols. 8b–9a. The vermeil (gilded silver) edgings around the pieces from the court service decorated with yellow lions suggest that these could have been fixtures for hanging them up, especially as one ground plan (fig. 28) has the entry: "dining room with lion porcelain" ("Taffel Zimmer mit Porcellan der Löwen"). Plates hung on the wall in this way had been a feature of the Oranienburg *Porzellankammer* (1695) and of the Charlottenburg *Porzellankabinett* (1706).
142 "Et le tout est composé de la maniere que l'on pourra augmenter ou diminuer le nombre des Porcelaines sans changer la Composition générale." SächsHStA, loc. 895, fol. 1b/a; more detailed consideration will be given to this description of the concept for the throne gallery at another point.
143 "On a mis… vis à vis des fenêtres des statuës, et des Medaillons, pour ne pas tôujours repéter des Vases, et éviter un simple arangement, qui auroit trop l'air d'un riche Magazin, et pour presenter aux yeux, et à l'esprit des objets amusants, et qui/: pour ainsi dire:/parle." Ibid., fol. 1b/a.
144 On their political aspects, and on the similar problems Friedrich I and Augustus the Strong faced as they sought to give their claims legitimacy, see Wittwer 2004.
145 Wittwer 2001.a, 34 and 127.
146 The drawing by Raymond Le Plat shows in a longitudinal section of the Dutch Palace the *placements* in the individual rooms at the wedding celebrations of 1719, but was very likely done later from memory, as suggested in May 1989 where it is cautiously dated between 1720 and 1732. The section has been published a number of times; see, for instance, Cassidy-Geiger 1995, 15. The drawing itself is kept in the *Kupferstichkabinett* in Dresden, inv. no. Ca 202.
147 Anonymous 1720.
148 "Inventarium über das Palais zu Alt-Dreßden Anno 1721"; Staatliche Kunstsammlungen zu Dresden, inventory no. 324, Porcelain Collection, Zwinger, published in Cassidy-Geiger 2004, 60–65.
149 "No:7 [= No:9] Dunckel blau Indianisch Porcellaine, mit laquirten Friesen, die Füllungen von weisen Atlas, worauf Indianische Große Figuren von bunten Farben sehr sauber gemahlt." SächsHStA, OHMA Cap. II, Nr. 15, Beilage C.
150 At this point it is of interest to note that in the first group of plans for the upper story it was intended to put in intermediate ceilings in some of the cabinets in the lateral wings (but not in the central rooms) and to separate off the mezzanine, in order to preserve the proportions of the rooms.
151 "Japanischen Palais zu Neustadt bey Dreßden, Schäffte [= wooden wall-paneling], Thiere, Vögel und dergleichen gezeichnet und illuminiert" SächsHStA, loc. 379 Verzeichnisse, fols. 78a–79a.
152 "mit Indianischen gemahlten Figuren und Thieren in Lebensgröße und vergoldeten Leisten bekleidet"; Inventarium über das Palais zu Alt-Dreßden Anno 1721, Staatliche Kunstsammlungen zu Dresden, inventory no. 324, Porcelain Collection, Zwinger (Cassidy-Geiger 2004, 60–65).
153 "Lacquirt"; ground plan, SächsHStA, OHMA Cap. II, no. 3p, see fig. 31.
154 "die Vergoldung der Etageren und Schränke für das Porzellan"; Kuke 2002, 226 (from: SächsHStA, loc. 557, fols. 173f.).
155 SächsHStA, loc. 895, fols. 5a–20a: "Specification Dererjenigen Meublen, so auf Ihro Königl. Hoheit des Chur-Printzens allergnädigsten hohen Mündlichen Befehl, aus dem Königl. Japan. Palais auf das Königl. Schloß von 9ten bis den 14. Aug. 1759 sind gebracht worden" ("Specification of the items which were brought on the verbal order of His Royal Highness the Prince Elector from the Royal Japanese Palace to the Royal Residence from August 9 to 14, 1759"), published in Cassidy-Geiger 2004, 69–74.
156 Stimmel 1998, 419, and Syndram 2001, 71.
157 "mit grün leinewandnen laquirten Banden, worauff goldene Drachen und Zierathen gemahlt, von dem Laquier Schnellen verferttiget, so ganz neu, die Füllungen von Indianischen weisen Atlas Decken, worein goldene Zierathen Vögel und Blumen von bunter Seide, sauber gestickt." SächsHStA, OHMA Cap. II, no. 15 Beilage C, Raum 13 (see Quelle 1). The Dresden court lacquerer Martin Schnell had since 1710 carried out numerous pieces of work for the court, central to which was his extensive collaboration on the Dutch Palace. In my opinion, the additional comment "all new" ("so ganz neu") does not preclude the possibility that they were first used in the Dutch Palace, as the expression has to be considered in juxtaposition with the many Asian paper and textile hangings which as well as being "exotic" were also surrounded by an aura of antiquity by virtue of their association with the time-hallowed ancient civilizations of the East. On Martin Schnell, see Kopplin/Haase 1998.
158 "25 grün lackirte Banden von Schnellen, mit goldenen Indian. Figuren, 6 El. lang"; SächsHStA, loc. 895, fols. 5a–20a: "Specification Dererjenigen Meublen… " (see n. 155 above).
159 "die andern Pretiositäten nebst den incomparablen Porcellain…, damit kein Schade geschehen möge, in Sicherheit geschaffet"; Iccander 1734, 231.

160 “zu renovierung derer Zimmer ingleichen zu Aussauberung des dasigen Porcelains und was sonst allda befindlich”; SächsHStA, loc. 1341, Vol.V, fols. 1a/a–1b/a.
161 SächsHStA, loc. 1341, Vol. IV, fols. 417a–418a.
162 See Zimmermann 1905, and Reichel 1972.b.
163 For the first sketch, see fig. 30.
164 “auff Japanische Art ausgeführet”; Pietsch 1996.a, 28.
165 “mit ganz schlechter [= schlichter] Mahlerey”; BA, IAa.12, fol. 249b.
166 Keyssler states that the ground-floor rooms were to be 20 feet high, and those on the upper story 38 feet high (Keyssler 1751, 1320), with one Saxon foot being equal to 28.3 cm.
167 “zum ausmöbliren der Zimmer” … “künfftighin öffters anhero kommen und allerhand gute Modelle zum Nutzen der Fabrique überbringen werde”; BA, IAa.12, fol. 314a/b.
168 “von alten Ind.Porcelain,” “CrackGuth,” “von Japanischen Porcelain,” [and] “von grünem Chynesischen Porcelain”; SächsHStA, loc. 1341, Vol. IV, fols. 324a–328b.
169 “So werden auch allerhand Galanterie- und Schminck-Kästgen, nicht weniger Spiegel-Rähmen und kleine Kaffee-Tischgen gefertiget, und sind theils Modelle hierzu aus dem Königl: Palais von Dreßden anhero übersendet worden.” BA, IAa.16, fol. 198b.
170 “Sonst ist nunmehro bey der Fabrique das erste große Auffsatzstück in Form eines Vogelbauers … zur perfection gebracht worden, davon in allem 50 Stücke vor Ihro Königl. Maj. gefertiget werden sollen.” Pietsch 1996.a, 29–30.
171 SächsHStA, loc. 1341, fol. 11a.
172 SächsHStA, loc. 1341, Vol. IV, fols. 383a–384a.
173 Pietsch 1996.a, 30.
174 SächsHStA, OHMA Cap. II, Beilage D.
175 BA, IAa.19, fols. 347a–369a; The lists have been published with commentaries (Cassidy-Geiger 1996.a), but Maureen Cassidy-Geiger only had access to the copy dated 1736 kept at the Sächsisches Hauptstaatsarchiv.
176 “J’ateste qu’on a besoin de tent de pieces pour l’ameublement du Palais du Japon depuis le N 1 jusqu-à 11.” Ibid., fol. 348a; the indication “numbers 1 to 11” refers to the 11 room-related chapters of the list.
177 “Extract Derer nach beygelegten Specificationes über dasjenige Sächß. Porcelain, so zu Ausmeublirung des Königl. Japanischen Palais der Obern Etage in die daselbst befindlichen 11. Zimmer erfordert wird, auch schon bereits vorhanden und noch zu verferttigen ist.” Ibid., fols. 345a–346a.
178 According to this source, the warehouse even contained more of certain types of wares than had been ordered (it is stated that there was a surplus of 22,253 porcelains), but these also had to be used to meet orders from normal customers.
179 The presentation of the status quo also included an account of the monetary worth of all the porcelain (not just the porcelain delivered to the Japanese Palace) that had been delivered to Augustus the Strong, which for the period from November 12, 1725 until his death in 1733 was calculated to amount to the sum of 47,926 talers, 8 groschen, and 5 pfennigs, BA, IAa.19, fols. 127a–128a.
180 “zum ausmöbliren des Königl. Japanischen Palais”; BA, IAa.19, fols. 342a–343a.
181 BA, IAa.19, fols. 160a–161b.
182 “So sind auch durch den Herrn Bettmeister Teufferten, welcher am 31. huj. aus Dreßden bey der Fabrique alhier sich eingefunden, abermahlen verschiedene Modelle und Zeichnungen, so Ihro Königl. Majth. gefördert wissen wollen, überbracht worden.” BA, IAa.16, fol. 109b.
183 SächsHStA, loc. 1342, fols. 107b–108b (appendix to the Commission’s report for January 1733).
184 “von denen Hrn. Manufactur-Arcanisten die Hoffnung gemachet, daß diese [the life-size apostle figures] und andere große Vasen oder Auffsätze, welche von Ihro Königl. Majth. verlanget worden, bey immer mehr und mehr erlernten Handgriffen, wie solche sowohl in Brennen als Glasuren tractiret seyn wollten, hinführo ohnfehlbar gutbleiben würden.” “So werden auch voriezo gewiße Glocken gefertiget die zu einem Glockenspiele dienen sollen, dergl. ist auch eine Probe mit den Orgel-Pfeiffen vorgenommen worden, umb Ihr:Königl.Majth. durch solche neu inventirte Porcellain-Stücken, eine ziemliche Freude zu machen.” BA, IAa.16, fols. 229b–234a. A whole book could be written simply on the endeavors undertaken at Meissen for the sake of the porcelain carillon and the porcelain organ for the chapel. While the carillon was actually produced, in spite of the greatest difficulties, and delivered in 1737 to the Japanese Palace, all that still remains of the porcelain organ are a few test pipes, which are now kept at the Porcelain Collection in Dresden.
185 “Von Gottes Gnaden Friedrich August König in Pohlen, Herzog zu Sachßen, Jülich, Cleve, Berg, Engern und Westphalen, Churfürst, Beste Räthe, liebe getreue, Demnach Wir die neue fordere Gallerie in der Obern Etage Unsers Holländischen Palais zur Neustadt bey Dreßden mit dem in beykommenden von Uns eigenhändig Verzeichniß Specificirten porcelainen Geväß zusammen Neunhundert und Zehn Stücken besezen zu laßen entschloßen; Alß ist Unser gnädigstes Begehren, Ihr wollet Krafft dieses die Verfügung thun, daß in Unserer Fabrique zu Meißen sothanes Porcelain-Geväß nach und nach gefertiget und dahin geliefert, auch in Rechnung also passirlich verschrieben werde. Hieran geschiehet Unser Wille und Meynung und Wir verbleiben euch mit Gnaden gewogen. Datum Warschau den 2. April 1732, Augustus Rex.” BA, IAa.17, fol. 59a. The expression “in Rechnung also passirlich verschrieben werde” means that the pieces were to be written off in the annual account, and indicates that the king had no intention of paying for them.
186 SächsHStA, loc. 1341, Vol.VI, fols. 198a–200a; an undated variant of the list, similarly constructed but only calling for 726 pieces, is furthermore kept at SächsHStA, loc. 1341, the relevant pages being paginated in pencil, fols. 29a–30a, published here as Source 7.
187 A detailed diary of Augustus the Strong’s travels and stays away from Dresden can be found in Schmidt/Syndram 1997, 49–53.
188 SächsHStA, loc. 1341, Vol.VI, fol. 262a; further on, there is indeed an entry by the manufactory reporting to the commission on extra expenses incurred for overtime work; ibid., fols. 342a–343b.
189 “so haben ja selbst eine hohe Commission einbefohlen, wie viel personen vor Ihro Königl. Majestät arbeiten sollen”; IAa.17, fol. 238a.
190 BA, IAa.18, fols. 244b–245b.
191 BA, IAa.17, fol. 238a.
192 Ibid.
193 Hanway 1753, 2:227. That he saw figures as well as vases is an interesting fact to which we shall return at a later stage.
194 BA, IAa.17, fol. 259a/b.
195 BA, IAa.17, fols. 260b–261a.
196 “Haben sich zwar die drey arcanisten nebst denen andern fabricanten zeithero alle Mühe gegeben, nach der von Ihro K. M. unterm 2. Aprili a.c. erfolgten declaration, die 910. Stück große Vasen und anderen Stücken porcelaine in Arbeit zu nehmen, inmasen sie denn auch einige davon würckl. gutgebrennet und sie in das Königl. Palais nach Neustadt bey Dreßden geliefert, alleine es hat die Erfahrung gewiesen, daß man mit deren Zubereitung überall so, als man wohl anfänglich vermeynet, nicht reussiret, denn zu geschweigen, daß gar viele von solchen großen Stücken gleich in Verglüh-Feuer Riße bekommen, oder sonst in Guthbrennen zu Schaden gegangen, … machen sich die arcanisten selbst nunmehro ein Bedencken, in so großen Stücken weiter so starck zu arbeiten, sondern nur nach und nach eine dergleichen große mit einzusetzen, damit nicht zuviele Massa, Arbeit, Holtz vergeblich aufgewendet, sondern dafür der Cassa zum Besten in kleinern Stücken gearbeitet werden könne.” BA, IAa.17, fol. 296a/b; A copy of these “puncta” was appended to a submission of December 30, a copy of which is to be found in the same volume, fols. 346a–363b.
197 BA, IAa.17, fols. 335a–336a.
198 “Auff Sr. Königl:Majth: in Pohlen und Churfürstl:Durchl: zu Sachßen allergnädigsten hohen mündl: Befehl … künfftig ein alles Porcelain, so in der Meißnischen Porcelain-Fabrique vor Ihro Königl: Majth: verfertiget wird, von schöner weißen Massa und wenig Mahlerey, nach der alten Indianischen Porcelain-Arth, oder so von der feinen emailirung etwas bestellet wird, … ebenfalls wenig [Malerei] darauf verfertiget werden [soll]”; BA, IAa.17, fol. 334a.
199 BA, IAa.17, fol. 340a; this answer is dated 29 December, 1732.
200 BA, IAa.19, fol. 51a/b.
201 BA, IAa.21, fol. 49a.
202 “eine nicht allzu kurze Zeit eingeräumet werde”; SächsHStA loc., 1342, Vol.VIII, fol. 21a/b.
203 SächsHStA loc., 1342, Vol.VII, fols. 4a–5a.
204 “Nachdem Wir bey Unserm JagdSchloße, Hubertusburg, verschiedene Gebäude ausführen, Wir nicht weniger das in Neustadt allhier befindliche Palais ausbauen zu laßen in Gnaden entschloßen sind, und hierzu eine Summe von Einmalhundert Tausend Thalern destiniret

haben; So begehen Wir hiermit gnädigst, ihr wollet die Verfügung thun, daß von ermeldter Summe... Sechstausend Thaler im ao: 1737 und... Vierzehen Tausend und zwanzig Thaler 16 gr. in dem 1738ten Jahre, zu Ausbauung des Palais in Neustadt... baar bezahlet, oder ...von denen zu Unserer freyen Disposition ausgesezten Geldern bestritten und verrechnet werden"; SächsHStA, Spezialreskripte 1736, 469.

205 "und es wird von Seiten des Hoff-Commissarii Höroldts, daß mit ietzogem Monath an, gewiß bey einer ieden wöchentlichen Lieferung von denen noch übrigen rückständigen Königlichen Geschirren, wie solche in die neu anzulegende Gallerie und Zimmer besagten Jappanischen Palais destiniret sind, einige Stücke von hier abgehen sollen, versichert." SächsHStA, loc. 1342, Vol. IX, fol. 238b.

206 For one typical instance, see BA, IAa.25a, fol. 1b.

207 See Rückert 1990, 268–269.

208 With the exception of the carillon already mentioned, which was installed in December 1736 in the place planned for it in the eastern Elbe-side pavilion of the upper story; on this, see BA, IAa24a, fol. 402a/b.

209 "Königstraum von einem Porzellanschloß"; Rauda 1932.

210 Anonymous 1720.

211 "Die Decke ist von sauberer GipßArbeit und in der mitten, wie die Tapeten gemahlet... NB! Unter der Decke so vorjezo nach Facon der Tapeten gemahlet worden, ist ein anderer gemahlter Blafon so eine Historie vorstellet." Inventarium über das Palais zu Alt-Dreßden Anno 1721, Staatliche Kunstsammlungen, Porcelain Collection, Zwinger, fols. 35 & 36; see also Cassidy-Geiger 2004, 63.

212 Hasche 1783, 2:180.

213 Keyssler 1751.

214 This however did not prevent him from seeing the so-called dragoon vases in the upper story (of the old Dutch Palace); Keyssler 1751, 1319.

215 Schramm 1984.

216 "welches doch nach der bereits gemachten Disposition künftig in eine noch prächtigere und wohl auserlesene Ordnung gebracht werden soll" ..."Diese ist bereits mit allerhand sowohl einheimischen als ausländischen bunten Thieren und Vögeln von Porcellain, meistentheils in natürlicher Größe und Farbe meubliret." Ibid., cols. 434–438. [cf. Keyssler: "Es wird solches [= the first room] mit allerhand sowohl einheimischen, als ausländischen Vögeln und Thieren von purem Porzellan, in ihrer natürlichen Größe und Farbe meublirt, und kann man an denenjenigen Stücken, welche schon fertig sind, die Kunst und Schönheit nicht genug bewundern."]

217 "Die erste Galerie des obersten Stockwerks... war schon würklich mit allerhand sowohl einheimischen als ausländischen bunten Thieren und Vögeln von Porcellain meistentheils in natürlicher Größe und Farbe meubliret." Weinart 1974, 340–343.

218 Iccander 1734.

219 "Among other things, the large Japanese Palace with its beautiful adjacent gardens is well worth going to see, as it not only contains many curiosities, but is furthermore so skillfully built that one cannot admire it enough." ("Unter andern ist der grosse Japanische Pallast nebst seinen daran stossenden schönen Garten Betrachtens werth, der nicht nur viele Curiosa in sich fasset, sondern auch dermassen artig gebauet ist, daß man ihm nicht genug ansehen kann.") Anonymous 1735, 477.

220 Anonymous 1737.

221 Pöllnitz 1737.

222 "Toutes les chambres de ce Palais... sont autant de Cabinets de Porcelaines du Japon & de la Chine. Je ne crois pas que tous les Magasins ensemble d'Amsterdam puissent fournir autant de Porcelaines rares & anciennes, qu'il y en ici." Pöllnitz 1737, 121.

223 Unlike other authors, he does at least quote his source. The quotation is taken from Klemm, 1834, 70–71.

224 That is to say, the article in *Der Neu-erscheinende Postillon*, and Keyssler's report (Keyssler 1751), and to a slight extent also the letters of Baron Pöllnitz. Further examples of sources derived from the above include: von Loen 1749.b, 46–47; Daßdorf 1782, 152–153; Anonymous 1799, 53–54.

225 "12 grosse beger [= Becher] unter die gallerien, 12 grosse urnen an der mauer auf die altanen, 38 mitel urnen auf die gellender« »36 grosse urnen, 8 Kieble [= Kübel] an die chesten in hove." The combination of Augustus the Strong's personal handwriting and orthography – once aptly described by Friedrich Reichel as "adventuresome" – means that on occasion one can only guess the meaning of certain words. I read this phrase, "8 Kieble [= Kübel] an die chesten in hove" as meaning "an die Kästen im Hofe" ("in the courtyard wall-sections"), and as referring to the eight sections of wall on the courtyard side of the Elbe wing, which are in fact shown in the cross-section (fig. 35) as having eight little trees in tubs.

226 SächsHStA, loc. 2097, no. 49.

227 An account of the experiments on the production of the life-size apostles with which Kirchner and Kändler were involved for so long would fill a whole book. The Porcelain Collection in Dresden has some surviving examples of test organ-pipes.

228 "Den Nachrichten aus Dreßden zufolge würde man das bisher mit Kupfer gedeckte so genannte Japanische Hauß mit feinem Meißnischen porcellain auf Ziegel-Arth decken laßen." This announcement appeared in the *Hallische Zeitung*, No. 88 of July 28, 1740, and the transcription is held under BA, IAa.26, fol. 301b; this information probably resulted from an indiscretion, as Kaendler did in fact do some work in 1740 on porcelain tiles, without however making any mention of any particular building in his notes, BA, IAb.14, fol. 102a and fol. 130a. In the design for the roof of the Japanese Palace already mentioned (fig. 19), however, the intention was clearly that the surface should be painted, and not tiled with porcelain.

229 "wie die Mauern des Gebäudes mit porzellanenen Zieraten von außen hätten sollen belegt werden"; Müller 1907, 2:97.

230 Handt/Rackebrand 1956, 5.

231 "August II wollte vorzüglich damit [viz. with porcelain] den Japanischen Palast zum Sommeraufenthalt dekoriren... Die hiesige Sammlung des Asiatischen Porzellans ist iezt einzig in Europa, seit dem ein ähnliches Kabinet zu Meudon, nach Ludwigs XIV Tode, vereinzelt ward." Merkel 1806, 27–28.

232 "ein fürstlicher Traum, den maßloser Ehrgeiz und Ruhmsucht, der Drang, den Versailler Sonnenkönig zu überbieten, dem König vorgaukelte"; Rauda 1932.

233 "allhir in Vorrath"; the reference is certainly to porcelain from the so-called Hoym-Lemaire affair; see Boltz 1980.

234 "ingleichen... eine Quantitat von braun Sächß. Porcelain..., welches zu Meublirung eines Zimmer vollkommen genug, nicht weniger eine große Quantitat von weiß Sächß. Porcelain so ebenfalls zu einen Zimmer employret." BA IAa.19, fols. 160b–161a.

235 Müller 1907, 2:97 (see Source 27).

236 In June 1743a contract was concluded with Johann Friedrich Thielmann, the tenant of the Dresdener Spiegelschleife mirror manufacturing firm, for the production of 320 mirrors, of which only 316 were delivered, leading to a court case lasting several years; SächsHStA, Spezialreskripte 1748, no. 623 and Spezialreskripte 1750, no. 134. See also Schwarm-Tomisch 2001.b, 182.

237 My attention was drawn to these important late deliveries by Elisabeth Schwarm-Tomisch in her article Schwarm-Tomisch 2001.b, 183–184.

238 I am obliged to Maureen Cassidy-Geiger for drawing my attention to this source.

239 Hanway 1753, vol. II, 226–227; Hanway's work was translated into German in 1754 and published in Hamburg/Leipzig with the title *Herrn Jonas Hanway zuverläßige Beschreibung seiner Reisen*... However, his reports about cities such as Danzig, Berlin, and Dresden were omitted on the grounds that they were too superficial and that more detailed literature had already been published on these subjects. Only the reports on China, Russia and the United Provinces were considered as having sufficient substance; see ibid. 415–416.

240 "alle diese entworfenen Verschönerungen... bis auf wenige Zimmer, so noch etwas von ihrer alten Pracht haben, unerfüllt geblieben [sind]"; Weinart 1974, 343.

241 Anonym 1737, 21.

242 "Gefäße, Figuren, Gruppen aus fremdem und heimischen Porzellan ungeordnet auf Tischen und auf dem Fußboden"; these were the words used by Rauda in his 1932 interpretation of Müller's report.

243 "Eben dahin könnte von den noch vorhandenen Mobilien absonderlich den zahlreichen und schönen Stücken von alten Lack dasjenige gebracht werden, was nicht auf dem Residenz oder andern ChurFürstl. Schlößern gebracht wurde." SächsHStA, loc. 2407 Doubletten, fol. 27b; the request was granted; see ibid., fols. 44a–45b.

244 "iezt nicht mehr wie sonst als Meuble bestimmt, sondern als Wercke der Kunst anzusehen [seien]." Ibid., unpaginated leaves in the

Appendix: "Extrakt eines Alleruntertänigsten Vortrags vom 30. Mai 1787."

245 "Glocken-Spiel von Meißnischen Porcellain" [and] "ein großes Porcellainenes Blumen Bouquet nebst darzu gehörigen Topf, so auf einen pronceau [= bronzenen] Postament stehet"; ibid., unpaginated leaves in the appendix; the bouquet of flowers, however, did come back and receives attentive consideration in the nineteenth-century descriptions of the Porcelain Collection, as early as Merkel's in 1806.

246 One of the earliest descriptions of the porcelains at this location, written thirty years before the appearance of the first printed guide to the collection, is to be found in Merkel 1806, 27–30. Merkel also noted in his account that two rooms on the ground floor were not made available for the newly installed collections and library, but continued to be used for objects which were sensitive to damp, such as the bed made with the feathers of exotic birds – the "feather-bed of Augustus the Strong," Merkel 1806, 30. On the subject of the feather-bed itself, see Cassidy-Geiger 1999.

247 Boltz 1996, 6–7.

248 "Wir ... begehren auch gnädigst, ihr wollet an dergleichen Geväßsen dasjenige, was von Unserm OberStallmeister und Cämmerer Grafen Sulkowski auch in Zukunfft angezeiget wird, vor Uns ferner verabfolgen laßen inmaßen das, was dergestalt von ihm attestiret werden wird ... in Rechnung Krafft dieser passiret." SächsHStA, loc. 1342, Vol.VII, fol. 4a/b.

249 On Sulkowski's exciting life and meteoric career, see Rückert 1900, 268–269.

250 Cassidy-Geiger 2005.

251 Information kindly supplied by Maureen Cassidy-Geiger.

252 At a symposium in Berlin in March 2002, Maureen Cassidy-Geiger proposed the theory that the first porcelain services for Sulkowski, Brühl and others were possibly thought of as "substitutes" for silver services in a material appropriate to their standing as ministers; see Cassidy-Geiger 2005.

253 BA, IAa.24d, fol. 86a/b.

254 BA, IAa.24d, fols. 89a–90b.

255 BA, IAa.24d, fols. 87a–88a.

256 On Brühl's life, see Rückert 1990, 267–268.

257 See Pietsch 2000.

258 Records for 5 July, 1739; BA, IAa.25a, fol. 2a/b.

259 "Nachdem mir aber beyfället, daß, als der HoffCommissarius Herr Hörold von Meißen ohnlangst und ohngefehr vor drey Wochen bey mir in meinem quartir sich befunden, ich ihme ohngefehr gefraget, ~~wie die Arbeit auff der Fabrique ver~~ ob denn auch noch continuiret werde mit der Arbeit, welche in das Königl. Holländische Palais bestellet worden, und ob man noch immer in allen Bränden einige stücke, so darzu gehörig mit ein gesezet würden, mir ermeldeter Herr HoffCommissarius darauff mit nein geantworttet und als ich fort gefahren, warumb denn nicht an denen Pallais stücken auch gearbeitet würde, er wiederum repliciret, daß diese Arbeit, so lange an dem Bruhl~~schen~~ Serviçe gemachet würde, anstehen und wartten müste; so habe dieses zu einiger erläuterung nicht verhalten und dahin stellen sollen." BA, IAe.5, fol. 314a/b.

260 "Vasen, Thiere und andere große Porcelaine-Stücken, so zum Theil in abgewichenen Jahren daher zu Probe gefertiget worden, theils nicht verkauffet werden dürffen, auch sonst einigen Mangel an sich haben, zum Aufsetzen in der Höhe, und zu andern Gebrauche"; quoted from Boltz 1996, 6–7; the relevant sources are printed in the same work, on p. 99. See also Schwarm-Tomisch 2001.b, 182–183.

261 See Pietsch 1996.b.

262 "dass in Zukunft bei rechter Einrichtung und Veranstaltung dergleichen weißes Porzellan ... dem Indianischen an Schönheit und Tugend, noch mehr aber an allerhand Façons und großen auch massiven Stücken, als Statuen, Columnen, Servicen u.s.w. weit übergehen möchten." Quoted from Zimmermann 1908, 322.

263 On Irminger, see Rückert 1990, 82–83.

264 The whole of the Instruction of June 25, 1712, is published in: I. Menzhausen 1982.a, 85–87.

265 It is of particular interest in the context of the Japanese Palace that on occasion a figure of a court jester is mentioned together with the exotic animals. There is a Perugian chronicle which states that a noble lord's entourage should include not only horses and dogs, but also court jesters and exotic animals; see Burckhardt 1860, 290. The Dresden court was one of the few which had, in addition to the usual dwarfs, a court jester. Two specimens of a Meissen porcelain bust of the court jester Joseph Fröhlich, a figure whose influence should not be underrated, were delivered to the Palace together with a number of animal figures and appear in the relevant delivery lists among the animals, as does a figure of the apostle St. Peter (see Source 11). However, that this was the case was probably to do with the format, and cannot be taken to suggest that there was any intention of displaying the figure together with the animals. The two busts were in 1734 finally cold-painted by by the court painter Christian Reinow, see Rückert 1992/1993, 47. On Fröhlich's life and the art works depicting him, see Rückert 1998.

266 See Bräss 1901, 5.

267 Maureen Cassidy-Geiger has even claimed that the labyrinth at Versailles was the decisive source of inspiration behind Augustus the Strong's commission for a porcelain menagerie, see Cassidy-Geiger 2003.b. Although they have some formal features in common (the composition of the peacock displaying its fan, for instance) which can also of course have been taken from nature, and although Augustus the Strong was certainly not oblivious of this famous section of the garden at Versailles, his menagerie contained no echoes, as we shall more clearly later, of the literary sources that were such an important element in the Versailles labyrinth.

268 On court festivities generally, see: I. Weber 1985; Schnitzer/Hölscher 2000.

269 "ungefehr zwey hundert verkleidete Männer aufzogen, welche in vier Hauffen zertheilet waren und die verschiedene Völkerschaften der vier Theile der Welt vorstelleten ... Sie führten auch allerhand Seltenheiten von fremden Schätzen und Erdgewächsen mit sich; wie auch verschiedene ausländische Thiere, als Löwen, Tieger, Bären, Affen, Meerkatzen, Papagayen und dergleichen." Loen 1749.b, 56–57.

270 Warncke 1989, 171, and Rieke-Müller 1995 and 2000.

271 Illustrated in Sponsel 1900, 68. Sponsel furthermore refers to pictures of the Dresden "Karrusselfeste" of 1709 and 1714 illustrating not only "fremden Volksstämme" (foreign tribes) but also artificial elephants and unicorns; see Sponsel 1900, 64.

272 Paust 1996, 24–38.

273 Paust 1996, 38–41.

274 Paust 1996, 17.

275 On the Versailles menagerie, see especially Paust 1996, 54–80; and Loisel 1912, vol. 2.

276 Loisel 1912, 2:103.

277 On German menageries in the Baroque and on theoretical menagerie concepts, see Paust 1996, 81–161 and 162–172 respectively.

278 See illustration and commentary in Hentschel 1969, 19–21.

279 Heckmann 1954, ills. 3 and 5.

280 In connection with his commentary on the Meissen Pelican, for example, Sponsel mentions a print (19a) from a volume of engravings, "In- und ausländische nach dem Leben gemahlte Vögel, verfertiget zu Frankfurth am Main von Matthia Merian ao. 1659" ("German and foreign birds painted from life, engraved in Frankfurt am Main by Matthäus Merian in 1659"). He states that an engraving with the following title had been inserted into the copy held at the Kupferstichkabinett in Dresden: "eine große Löffel Gans in den Dresdener Königl. Fischgarthen zu sehen 1728" ("a large pelican, as seen at the royal fishponds in Dresden in 1728"); Sponsel 1900, 65. In the summer of 1998, however, the volume of Merian engravings Sponsel saw in 1900 was sadly not to be found at either the Kupferstichkabinett or the Sächsische Landesbibliothek.

281 Nickel 1996, 13; Nickel only gives a short account of the transformation of the seventeenth-century menagerie into the eighteenth-century game reserve. But the existence of local game for court consumption and also of "Indian" game is attested by bills for animal feed in the court household account books, see SächsHStA, Rentkammer-Akten, Ausgaben, under the heading "Ausgabe auf Fütterung derer Auer, Bähre und andern Wildprets, sowohl in denen Thier- und Bähren-Gärten, als auch sonst"; this heading appears in all the volumes examined by the author (1727–1738) and contains details of game in Ostra; see, for example, vol. 244, January–June 1731, fols. 57b–60a.

282 Keyssler 1751, 1322.

283 These animals appear to have been bred specifically to be introduced to Saxony. There is a list of decrees issued by Augustus III in the first year and a half after the death of his father which includes the following item: "July 21, 1733, a decree that nobody should presume to lay hands on or do harm to the wisents ["aurochses"] and other animals which have been let out into the open," ("Den 21. Julii 1733. ein Mandat, daß derer ins freye gelassenen Auer- und anderer Thiere sich niemand anmassen oder solche beschädigen solle"); Iccander 1735, Part Two, section LXXVIII, § 7, 275.

284 "Frühe nach 7. Uhr fuhr der Herr Graff nach Versailles von Monsigneur le Dauphine und Mons. le Duc de Orleans Abschied zu nehmen, besahe daselbst die Menagerie und Trianoren und brachte die Prinzen von Hannover Abends mit zur Tafel." SächsHStA, loc. 754, fol. 85a. The diary of his travels does not reveal whether he had visited the menagerie on his first visit, although this is highly likely.

285 Schlechte 1995, 28–29; see also Hensel 1998, 62–63. For Moritzburg generally, see Schlechte 1984 and 1985. I use the term "menagerie" in a broader sense than as a place where animals were kept for purposes other than hunting; when Augustus the Strong marks one *point de vue* on the plan for a system of avenues "Menagerie" then he presumably meant exotic four-footed beasts as opposed to birds.

286 On the pheasantry, see Eissenhauer 1992 and Hensel 1995.

287 Krünitz 1778–1858, here vol. 28, the article on "Jagd", 138 and 185–187. My thanks go to Marcus Köhler, Berlin, for drawing my attention to this point.

288 "Ist ein Holländer allhier angekommen, welcher einen lebendigen Rhinoceros anhero gebracht um solchen allhier von Geld sehen zu lassen." SächsHStA, OHMA, O. IV, record 129 (kindly pointed out by Maureen Cassidy-Geiger).

289 Particularly on the traveling unicorns, see Clarke 1986.

290 Nissen 1966/1978.

291 The ambassador reported this offer in a letter to Count Flemming: SächsHStA, loc. 681, Vol. CCLXI, fols. 225a–228a.

292 "auch ganz glücklich aus denen Kästen in die Fänge eingefangen" ... "daß der Löwe und Löwin, wie auch zwey Tieger recht gut aussehen, außer daß der Löwe nur ein Auge hat." SächsHStA, loc. 589, fol. 6a/b.

293 "mitgekommenen Menschen" ... "die eisernen Halß-Bänder abgenommen" ... "frey gegebenen Sclav" ... "so ein gebohrner Holsteiner, und um diese Thiere dergestalt gewohnt gewesen, daß er sie, wohin er gewolt, frey fortragen" ... "Dey zu Algier Ihro Majestät dem König von Schweden zum Praesent überschicket"; Fassmann, 986; quoted from Pietsch 1997.b, 92. Fassmann, however, is wrong in giving the date of this event as 1726.

294 See Boltz 1995.

295 "Deux Louris tres beaux qui parlent bien, sifflent, chantent et jouant dela trompette fort privez"; SächsHStA, loc. 380, fol. 312a/b.

296 Ibid., fol. 240a; the list is published in Rückert 1992/93, 51.

297 Ibid., fol. 236a.

298 "zween Leoparden, deren jeder bey zwey tausend Thaler kostet"; Keyssler 1751, 1322.

299 Hensel 1992, 37. On further purchases at the Leipzig Fair, see Hertel 1980, 87.

300 Fichtner 1940, 495; from the form of the note, Fichtner very likely quoted from an entry in the court journal dated January 12, 1733. In the court accounts the Tirolean dealer appears half a year previously: "2 talers 16 groschen to the Tirolean on account of the rock partridges, by receipt of November 22," ("2 Thlr 16gr Warttegeld, dem Tyroler wegen der Steinhühner, vermöge Quittung vom 22. Novembr: 1732"), SächsHStA, Rentkammer-Akten, Ausgaben, no. 246 Jan–July 1733, fol. 383b. In the next order for animal figures, the list of December 17, 1732, there is, correctly, a distinction made between white and colored peacocks.

301 SächsHStA, loc. 681, Vol. XXI, fols. 2a–4b.

302 "Au reste le Roi croit vous avoir donné commission touchant des cerfs d'Afriques, qui ont les jambes plus mines qu'un petit doigt, C'est pour cela que S. M. m'a ordonné de vous en faire ressouvenir si vous ne pouviez pas trouver d'en faire venir de l'Afrique au cas qu'il n'y en eut pas a avoir autrement, et comment en pourroit les faire transporter ici avec plus de sureté." SächsHStA, loc. 3422, fol. 38b, a draft letter of Wackerbart's from October 6, 1721 (kindly pointed out by Maureen Cassidy-Geiger).

303 On the exact circumstances of the exchange, see Boltz 1995.

304 Schnyder von Wartensee 1994/1955.

305 "on n'en trouve aucune ny dans ce port-icy, ni dans ceux des environs"; excerpt from a letter of November 13, 1718; SächsHStA, loc. 589, fol. 1a/b.

306 He furthermore indicates that he will soon be sending 12 mules ("mulets") with drivers to Dresden.

307 See Loisel 1912, 60; Gurlitt 1924, 296–298; Hensel 1998, 64–65; according to Sponsel 1900, 65, an expedition of this kind had already been made at the order of Louis XIV.

308 "Die lebendigen Thiere soll er in duplo oder triplo kauffen und abschicken, damit wenn eines unterwegs crepierete, man doch die andern lebendig hätte; auch soll er zu Fortschaffung und Warttung der Thiere Personen annehmen oder Sclaven und Mohren kauffen ... Er soll fleissig alle Sachen abmahlen lassen und die Schildereyen iederzeit überschicken, desgleichen was er nicht lebendig fortbringen kann, die Sceleta Häute gut zu conserviren suchen, auch sein Journal in guter Ordnung halten und alles notable bemerken." From the *Instruktion* given to Hebenstreit, quoted from Hensel 1998, 64, where it appears without clear indication of the author's source.

309 Hensel 1998, 64.

310 "Ästen tripolitanischen Holzes für Drechslerarbeiten"; Gurlitt 1924, 298.

311 "Hat Hr. Buchner einen jungen Löwen, 2. Strauß-Vögel und andere Thiere aus Africa anhero überbracht." SächsHStA, OHMA O. I, 3, Dresdener Hofjournal 1732– Oct 1734, entry for October 27, 1732, fol. 18a.

312 "Wenn unsere Reise nicht so langwierig und verdrüßlich gewesen wäre, so zweifle ich nicht wir hätten noch eine gute Anzahl Thiere erhalten können, welche wir biß itzo verloren haben." SächsHStA, loc. 589, fols. 8a–9a.

313 For further information on animals collected in Africa, see Loisel 1912, 60.

314 "wenn ich Gelegenheit habe sie [the animals] aufs schleunigste nach Dreßden zu bringen, so glaube ich keines mehr zu verlieren." ... "daß die vielen Zölle nicht etwan in Ansehung des Aufwands sondern in Ansehung des Aufpackens bey Untersuchung der gesammelten Curiosorum vielen Schaden thun können. Ich bitte Sie wollen mir durch einen zu diesem Ende gemachten Pass zu hülffe kommen, oder die Sache so einrichten wie es Ihnen am besten deucht." ... "Churfürst. Paß, auf verschiedene, nach beyliegender Specification, von Hamburg nach Dreßden ... zu schaffender fremder Thiere, Dreßden den 31. Julii 1733." SächsHStA, loc. 589, the pass is on fol. 2a, and the list on fol. 5a.

315 The latter was especially the case if a portrait had been painted of them during their lifetime, as is attested by a number of paintings still preserved in Dresden; the list of the paintings restored to the House of Wettin by the state of Saxony on September 9, 1999, includes such animal pictures as "Der vogel Cis" ("the bird 'Cis' "), the "Großtrappe" ("great bustard"), the "Fettschwanzwidder" ("fat-tailed ram"), the "Vielfraß" ("glutton," apparently a kind of marten), and the "Kronenkranich" ("crowned crane"); see Patrimonia, 18/2000, *Für Sachsen erworben. Schätze des Hauses Wettin* (KulturStiftung der Länder); information kindly supplied by Maureen Cassidy-Geiger.

316 "Das Thier-Cabinet ist wohl das gröste und praesentiret allerhand Thiere, die man nur erdencken kann. Dieselben sind alle ausgestopfet und stehen da, als ob sie lebeten." Anonymous 1735, 471–472.

317 Heres 1991, 35; the 1727 inventory of the Anatomiekammer lists 113 skeletons and parts of skeletons; the holdings were transferred in 1733 to Wittenberg University; ibid., 73.

318 A ground plan of the Zwinger with entries regarding the collections in the year 1755 is published in Heres 1991, 106.

319 On artificial grottoes, on turning spaces into grottoes, and on the importance of the shell shape, see also Rietzsch, 1987.

320 "An dieselbe [the grotto] stößt eine Galerie, worinnen die raren Thiere, so in Dresden lebendig gewesen, ausgestopft aufgestellet sind." Keyssler 1751, 1312; on Keyssler's description of all the Zwinger galleries, see ibid., 1306–1314.

321 "Crocodil, wie es aus seinem Ey (das die Größe eines Ganseyes hat) auskriecht"; Keyssler 1751, 1309.

322 "Wolff welcher einen Hirsch zerreiset und frist"; from a list with animals from the *Animaliengalerie*, which Kaendler studied in the summer of 1734, BA, IAa.22, fol. 227b: There he also found "ein Fabl Thier," which is perhaps rather to be categorized as a "Wolpertinger."

323 "Ew. Königl. Hoheit in Gott ruhender Hochtheuersten Herrn Vaters Königl. Mayth. hat allergnädigst gefallen mir die Verfertigung derer ausstaffirten Thiere ... auftra-

gen … zu laßen." … "Also trage annoch äuserstes Verlangen, alle meine Kräffte dahin anzuwenden, daß ich durch neue selzame und natürliche Vorstell- und Erfindungen eine sehenswürdige Harmonie von der ganzen Gallerie herstellen und diese kostbaren Raritäten in vollkommenen Stand sezen möchte." SächsHStA, loc. 379, fols. 30a–31a.
324 "Vollständiger und mit raren Thieren, die nicht nur ausgestopft, sondern auch in Skelettern zugleich dastehn, wird man schwerlich was finden. Schade, daß harichte Thiere so schwer zu erhalten sind! Manche haben schon viel gelitten. Die Gallerie ist 95 Ellen lang und enthält in dreyfacher Reihe harichte vierfüßige Thiere, die meist alle, bis auf einige wenige, zu Dresden im Jägerhof gelebt haben." Hasche 1783, Bd. II, 317.
325 "Die darauf folgende Thiergallerie zeichnet sich durch die seltensten Thier-Skelete aus. Die übrigen ausgestopften Stücke hat der Zahn der Zeit etwas zernagt." Merkel 1806, 48.
326 Pictures, for example, were incorporated into the galleries in the Zwinger, or particularly extraordinary natural history exhibits were integrated into display pieces. It would certainly be worth investigating the links in greater detail.
327 This was also Sponsel's opinion, Sponsel 1900, 42.
328 BA, IAa.12, fol. 249b.
329 SächsHStA, loc. 1341 Vol. IV, fols. 383a–384a.
330 "umb daselbst allerhand Arthen von Indianischen Thieren und Vögeln"; BA, IAe.2, fol. 3a. In the report on his engagement in the summer of 1731, however, there is only a general statement that he was "to make all sorts of models, not only in wood, but also in clay" ("allerhand Modelle, sowohl aus Holz, als auch aus Thon verfertigen soll"). BA, IAa.16, fol. 5a.
331 This was the reason why from 1735 on special listings were made of the animal figures that were delivered but had not been ordered.
332 However, a kind of interim total, incorporating all the deliveries of animal figures for the years 1731 and 1732, does not tally with this result; in the cases of some animals there are such great discrepancies that we either have to assume that there were large deliveries between December 17 and the end of the year, or that the list was not made until the spring; BA, IAa.20, fol. 64a/b.
333 This can be deduced from the logs of the Meissen castle guard, according to which the two came to the manufactory for seven days from March 22, 1733, and for four days from April 11. On February 1, the day of Augustus the Strong's death in Warsaw, Teuffert's wife also arrived for a four-day stay in Meissen. Teuffert and Rost also stayed in the Albrechtsburg in 1734, for instance from April 18 to 19; SächsHStA, loc. 14636 Vol. III, fol. 5b, 33a, 6a, and Vol. IV, fol. 22a; I am indebted to Maureen Cassidy-Geiger for this information and for her transcription from the records of the castle guard.
334 On his life, see Rückert 1990, 267–269.
335 SächsHStA, loc. 1342, VII, fol. 8a/b; which is identical with BA, IAa.19, fols. 342a–343a.
336 The source refers to them as "emalirt" ("enameled"), which in the context of the animal figures would normally mean decorated with fired overglaze colors. But most of the animals were, as we shall see, only decorated with cold colors. The list was drawn up by the manufactory bookkeeper, Johann Georg Heymann, who most likely used the expression in order to distinguish these colored figures from the white ones that follow immediately after.
337 This crisis in 1734 came about as a result of a denunciation in which various members of the staff blamed Höroldt for everything that they thought was going wrong at the manufactory; the records related to this crisis give us profound insights into many matters which while they would otherwise have been considered of little importance were in the context of the crisis regarded worthy of record. See esp. BA, IAe.2, sowie BA, IAe.3.
338 "ob nicht gut were daß von H. BettMeister im Königl. Ballais eine überlegung gemacht würde wie groß ein jedes Stück sein sollte, damit sich bey der Möblirung nicht Hinderungen finden möchten, indem man Niemahlen ein rechtes Maß zu Balläis Stücken auf die Fabrique bekommen." BA, IAe.5, fol. 190b.
339 "daß der Löwe, Elephante und AuerThier fast einerley Größe haben, wie solche im Porcelläin gemacht worden, welches den nicht alzu wohl zusammen Accordiren möchte." Ibid., fol. 191a.
340 Meissen porcelain was delivered to the Japanese Palace right up until the Seven Years' War, but we may assume that it was used for quite different ends from those of the animal gallery project, which was finally given up around 1740, see for example I. Menzhausen 1988, 7; a list dated January 14, 1737, signed by Sulkowski on behalf of Augustus III, details a large number vases and pieces of tableware which were to be delivered to the palace together with 30 unspecified large and small figures and birds, BA, IAa.24c, fol. 32a/b; however, it is clear from the context that they were for some other room than the gallery. In January 1738, the Commission went on to make the assurance that "the greatest and most dutiful care is being taken regarding the pieces ordered by Your Royal Majesty for the Japanese Palace, and whatever is required for the Royal Court," ("und es wird vor die von Ihro Königlichem Majestät zu Dero Jappanischen Palais bestellte Geschirre, auch was sonst vor Dero Königliche Hofstadt verlanget wird, pflichtschuldigstermaßen gesorget"); BA, IAa.24d, fol. 1b. The subsequent list no longer mentions any animal figures.
341 The records refer a number of times to crates which fell off the market ship and were later found by third parties in Dresden and recorded as "gefunden," see BA IAb.11, Rapport November 1738, fols. 235b–236a, or SächsHStA, loc. 1342, Vol. X, fols. 61a–68a.
342 "Zehen Thaler Sechzehn Groschen … Träger Lohn vor 16 Mann mit 8 Kästen allerh. Porcel: Vögel und Thiere, welche wegen vieles Raumes in Meißen nicht länger aufbehalten werden können und der Gefahr und Zerbrechlichkeit halber haben herauf ins König. Japanische Palais getragen werden müßen, seynd mir von dem Herrn Hoff factor Chladni richtig bezahlt worden … Auf iedene Mann 16 Gr gerechnet, Christian Hermann und Consorten." SächsHStA, loc. 520, Vol. 1734, unpaginated, bill no. 165.
343 "1734 konnten 439 Tiere in das Japanische Palais geliefert werden, und zwar von den bestellten 33 Vierfüßler- und 27 Vogelarten je 16, außerdem aber 5 Vierfüßler- und 23 Vogelarten, die nicht verlangt worden waren." Berling 1911, 24.
344 Rückert 1966, 18.
345 Boltz 1996.
346 To provide further guidelines, Otto Walcha calculated that in 1710 a bushel ("ein Scheffel") of wheat (= ca. 105 liters) cost 2 talers 20 groschen, and that one kilo of butter cost 7–8 groschen (1 taler = 24 groschen); Walcha 1973, 25.
347 "fein Emaill. Uhr Gehäuse nebst einem Postamente" … "Japonischen Figuren"; SächsHStA, loc. 1342, Vol. VII, fol. 107b.
348 SächsHStA, loc. 1342, Vol. VII, Anlage H, fols. 107b–108b.
349 "4 Josephs Figuren"; for more detailed information about Fröhlich, see Rückert 1998.
350 Albiker also went into the problem of historical nomenclature, Albiker 1935, 31.
351 Zebra; Hasche listed just such a one in his description of the natural history collection in the Zwinger: "The beautifully striped zebra, or American wood-donkey" ("Der schön gestreifte Zebra oder amerikanische Waldesel"), Hasche 1783, 2:318.
352 Pelican.
353 King vulture.
354 Golden oriole.
355 King vulture; the designations "roi des vautours" and "king of the vultures" customarily used for this bird in eighteenth-century French and English ornithological works turned into "König von Waiwou," "Wau Wau" and other similar expressions in German; see Hensel 1998, 69–70, and information given in the relevant catalog entry in the present volume.
356 Likewise a Germanization, from the English "parakeet."
357 Particularly Zedler's *Universallexikon* and Grimm's *Wörterbuch*.
358 Hasche 1783, 2:304–311.
359 See, for example, Schnorr von Carolsfeld 1974, 1:106; Sponsel, however, did not translate the term with "Mandrill," but rather with the mysterious expression "großer Kronenaffe," and Zimmermann (1926, 105 and 1929, 28) referred to the animal as a "Pavian" (baboon).
360 Asche 1970 and 1971.
361 See Zimmermann 1914, Rückert 1996.
362 Born 1706 in Merseburg. On his life, see Rückert 1990, 114, and Zimmermann 1929.
363 "hat erwehnter Kirchner voritzo noch nöthig, daß er zuerst die rechten Vortheile von denen Formern absehe, wie er mit der Massa wegen der starcken Schwindung im Feuer arbeiten und poussiren soll, denn diese läßet sich nicht als ein Holtz oder Stein tractiren, dahero es ihme

auch bisher offte contrair ergangen, wenn er eine Figur aus Massa poussiren und verputzen wollen." Rapport of July 12, 1727, BA, IAa.10, fol. 324a/b.

364 On Kirchner's general habits and behavior in the manufactory, see esp. Walcha 1961.

365 "so sehen wir uns doch veranlaßet, gedachten Bildhauer Kirchnern um deßwillen nunmehro zu dimittiren, weil er nicht alleine währenden diesen seinen engagement die Arbeits-Stunden so fleißig, als er vorher versprochen nicht abgewarthet und nun vor einer kurzen Zeit in eine Krankheit, die er sich durch seine unordentliche Lebens-Arth über den Halß gezogen, verfallen." Report of the Commission to the king, March 15, 1728; SächsHStA, loc. 1341, Vol. IV, fol. 131

366 "gab derselbe unter andern auch so viel zu vernehmen, wie daß es wieder sein naturell sey, ferner solche kleine Stücke in Thon auszuarbeiten, sondern er sey vielmehr gewohnet, in Stein zu arbeiten, und große Statuen zu verfertigen." Rapport of April 24, 1728; BA, IAa.12. fols. 104b–105a.

367 The report of March 15 already quoted (see n. 365, above) stated a further reason for Kirchner's dismissal, namely that "it is the gracious intention of Your Royal Majesty to have another modeler, the journeyman sculptor Lücke, engaged, who has by the generous support of Your Majesty spent some time gaining experience in foreign countries and has thus made himself all the better qualified for the work for which he has already proved himself to be qualified," SächsHStA, loc. 1341, Vol. IV, fol. 131b; on Lücke's life, see Rückert 1990, 119.

368 The Rapport of September 25, 1728, claims that Lücke had until that point only done small jobs, and that he was not even capable of making a model in wood; BA, IAb.1e, fols. 293b–294a.

369 Rapport of December 4, 1728, BA, IAa.12, fol. 234a/b. Eulogies for the long-standing craftsman Fritzsche, whom we know to have been responsible for models before 1727, have to be seen in the human context obtaining at the manufactory: on the personal level, Lücke was "not on the best of terms with the manufactory people here," ("in keiner guten harmonie mit denen hiesigen Manufactur-Leuten"), quoted from Rückert 1990, 119. Other instances show that judgments about the abilities of fellow-staff at the manufactory naturally varied greatly according to who was talking about whom and in what context.

370 Manufactory report of April 25, 1729; BA, IAa.12, fols. 352b–353a.

371 Keyssler had of course seen some finished animal figures in October 1730.

372 "bereits 2. Jahr mich darbey [at the manufactory] befinde, und die mir allergnädigst aufgetragene wenige Function meiner instruction gemäß, ohnrühmlich treulich und gewißenhafft verwaltet, Gleichwohl als ein junger Mann und würcklicher Bildhauer begierig bin, nach etwas mehrers in der Welt zu sehen, und meine Wißenschafften zu excoliren, damit capabler werde, Ew:Königl: in zuKunfft mit meinen fernern allerunterthänigsten Diensten aufzuwarthen"; SächsHStA, loc. 1341, Vol.VI, fol. 205a.

373 On Kaendler's life, see Anonymous 1775 (= Source 26); Gröger 1956; Ducret 1956 (dates-and-facts biography); Rückert 1990, 112–113, J. Menzhausen 2002.

374 J. Menzhausen 2002, 3.

375 "Es haben Ihro Mayt. der höchstseel. König Allergnädigst beliebet, nachdem ich vorhero die besondere Gnade gehabt in die 6. Jahre lang in dem sogenannten Grünen Gewölbe viele ornamenta zu verfertigen, mich als Modell-Meister bey hiesiger Königl. Porcelain-Fabrique verpflichten und constituiren zu laßen, umb daselbst allerhand Arthen von Indianischen Thieren und Vögeln, sammt anderen nur vorkommenden ornamente zu inventiren und in saubere Modelle zu bringen, wie auch die Fabricanten, sonderlich aber die Lehrlinge in Zeichnen und poussiren aufs beste zu unterrichten, Daß selbige bey allen vorkommenden Porcelain-Stücken desto geschickter zu arbeiten seyn möchten, an mich anweisen laßen." BA, IAe.2, fol. 3a/b.

376 [on account of the] "currenten Waaren und vielen anderen großen Geschirren nach denen bishero bey der Fabrique eingegangenen Modellen und Zeichnungen" … "Nachdem diejenigen großen Stücke, welche Ihro Königl. Mayth. nach einigen gewißen Modellen und Zeichnungen gefertiget wißen wollen, bishero nicht von dem Modell-Meister Kirchnern alleine bestritten werden können, und aber Johann Joachim Kentler, ein Bildhauer, auf Königl: allergnädigsten mündlichen Befehl, am 22. Juny bey der Fabrique allhier sich eingefunden, daß er allerhand Modelle, sowohl aus Holz, als auch aus Thon verfertigen soll, der auch sogleich die Arbeit im poussiren angefangen." BA, IAa.16, fols. 4b–5a.

377 Walcha 1973, 89.

378 Ulrich Pietsch has made the point that as a sculptor Kaendler would have been used to making clay models (bozzetti) for sculptures in stone; Pietsch 1997.a, 77. In this regard, two further things should be borne in mind: firstly, if this was true of Kaendler, then it will also have been true of Kirchner; and secondly, the astounding thing about Kaendler's first months at Meissen was not so much the skill with which he used the modeling stick, but how quickly he grasped the particular demands made by models to be realized in porcelain.

379 "daß er [Höroldt] H. Cändler in Anfange abrichten müßen, wie er die Stücke stellen sollte, damit sie sich im Feuer nicht senckten"; BA, IAe.3, fol. 208a.

380 Höroldt's painting business, which was a sub-enterprise of the Albrechtsburg, had only been integrated into the Meissen enterprise and into the department responsible for producing the whiteware; the "Referent" (see German text in n. 382) was Kaendler, that is to say, the party making a statement at the hearing.

381 Peter Eggebrecht was a manufacturer of faïence in Dresden; on his life, see Rückert 1990, 79–80.

382 "H. Herold sey nicht länger bey denen Fabricanten als Referente, u. habe ihn also nichts weisen können sondern Kirchner habe es ihn das meiste gewiesen, ingleichen habe er von seinen SchwiegerVatter Eckbrechten sich sagen laßen, daß er bey denen Stücken das centrum gravitatis in acht nehmen müße sonst fiehlen sie in Feuer umb u. dieses habe er mit hergebracht, es wäre andem, daß die ersten Stücken so Adler gewesen, in Feuer eingangen, allein H. HoffCommissarius habe solches damahls so wenig als Referent verstanden." BA, IAe.3, fol. 274a/b.

383 "Hierüber ist Ihro Königl. Maj. höchstgefällig gewesen, noch einen Modellier Nahmendlich Jochim Kendlern, vor kurzer Zeit in die Porcellain Fabrique darum einweisen zu laßen, daß derselbe insonderheit die von Ihro Königl.Maj. bestelte großen Vasen und allerhand Arthen Thiere mit dem bereits in Diensten stehenden ModellMeister Kirchnern verfertigen solle. Da nun an seinem Fleiße und Geschickligkeit, wie Ihro Königl.Maj. Selbst es höchsterleuchtet bemercken werden, nichts auszusetzen und er in angefügten allerunterthänigsten memoriali zu seinem Jährl. Tractament 400.Thl.-. samt einer freyen Wohnung in der Manufactur begehret, wird darüber solche Anordnung erwarttet, und hält man von Seiten der Commission dafür wie es ohnmaßgeblich wohl gethan seyn dürffe, wenn Kendlern im Fall ihm dieses tractament à 400.Thl. accordiert werden sollte, nur 300.Thl.-. als soviel der Modell-Meister Kirchner jährl. genießet durch den Manufactur Inspector Reinhardten gegen seine Quittung, nach und nach monathlich ausgezahlet, die übrigen 100.Thl.-. hingegen denselben durch den Hoff-Factor Chladni aus der Dreßdnischen Cassa, um Kirchnern zu einer mehreren praetension nicht Anleitung zu geben in der Stille gereichet würde." SächsHStA, loc. 1341, Vol.V, § VI, fol. 457a/b.

384 "bey angeregter fabrique durchgehends das Lob erlanget, daß er seine Arbeit wohl verstehe, und nutzbar zu gebrauchen ist, auch den andern modellirer Kändlern, nach seinen inventionen und sonst übertrifft." SächsHStA, loc. 1341, Vol.VI, fol. 203a/b; which is identical with BA, IAa.17, fol. 47c/a.

385 "da er [Kaendler] doch anfänglich so gut und den Modellier Kürchnern weit vorgezogen wurde, welchen ich doch auch vor einen geschickten Menschen hielt." Stöltzel's statement of March 21, 1735; BA, IAe.5, fol. 247a.

386 *Registratur* for July 30, 1735, BA, IAa.23, fol. 168b.

387 On the work reports, see Pietsch 2002.

388 "Ihro Königl. Majt. zu Dero besonder hohen Vergnügen weit kostbarere und herrlichere Stücken verlangen können, welches ich bedächtig schreibe, masen ich solches Werck dergestalt kundig bin daß ich sehr wohl weiß wie hoch es zu bringen, und jederzeit ohne allen Eiteln Ruhm alles bey der Cörperlichen Arbeit auf mich ankommen, welches alle bey der Manufactur befindl. Personen … bezeugen müßen, wie ich bey meinem Antritt vor 8 Jahren im

Werck nicht einen rechten Henkel noch anders Stücken gefunden sondern durch fleisiges Inventiren, Nachdenken, Arbeiten, und Studiren ausfündig gemacht, wie die Modelle und Geschirre Einzurichten, daß solche im Feuer halten und stehen müßen, wozu mir Niemand nichts helffen können." SächsHStA, loc. 1342, Vol. X, fols. 486b–487a; on these suggestions for the improvement of the manufactory, and on Kaendler's overestimation of the technical possibilities of the material, brought about in part by his hard work and great achievements thus far, see also Sponsel 1900, 125–127.

389 "einer Ergötzlichkeit von 1000 Thlr ... vor die ins sogenannte Holländische Paleis nach Dreßden schon Annis 1731, 1732, 1733 modelirte Porcellaine Figuren und Thiere"; SächsHStA, loc. 1344, Vol. XVIII, fol. 349b.

390 "beschehenen mündlichen Anordnung wegen Beförderung derer großen Geschirre" ... "Annehmung eines darzu nöthigen Modellirers"; report of June 19, 1733, SächsHStA, loc. 1342, Vol. VII, fol. 129a/b.

391 "Einen neuen Modellirer aber an des lezthin abgegangenen Kirchners Stelle wieder anzu nehmen, findet man von Seiten der Fabrique nicht nöthig, indem alle diejenigen Geschirre, so annoch ermangeln und zu poussiren vorkommen möchten, von dem Modellirer Kändler gar wohl gefertiget werden können, da doch überdieses auch noch 2. junge Leute, als Schmieder und Krumbholz bey der Manufactur sich befinden, welche in poussiren ebenfalls gar geschickt und zu solcher Arbeit durch Anführung vorhernbesagten Modellirer Kändlers zugebrauchen sind." Extract from the manufactory report of June 12, 1733, appended to the report of June 19, see n. 390, fol. 133a/b.

392 Eberlein's letter of application is given in full in Goder 1989, 105.

393 For greater detail on Eberlein's work in Meissen and on his life, see Goder 1989, and Rückert 1990, 105.

394 "Ist von denen Hrn. Arcanisten, mit dem Modellmeister Kändler, wegen alleiniger Bestreitung der bestellten Königs- und andrer Arbeit, Vernehmung gepflogen worden. Es hat auch gedachter Modellmeister ... sein Erklährung gethan und versprochen, binnen 3. Monathen, die rückständigen Stücken ins Königl: Jappanische Palais, neben der ordinairen Arbeit, sauber zu verferttigen, wenn ihm, da er über die tägl: Zeit früh und Abends sitzen müste, dafür eine Ergötzlichkeit gereichet würde; jedoch erachten insoweit die Hrn: Arcanisten vor höchst nöthig, zu Beförderung sowohl der Königl: als andrer Arbeit, welche tägl: immer mehr und mehr bestellet würde, den sich angegebenen Bildhauer, Eberleinen, auf eine Probe anzunehmen, gestalt er denn am 18. hujus, angetretten und zu arbeiten angefangen hat." Rapport for April 1–15, 1735, BA, IAa.24, fols. 121b–122a.

395 "Adjuvante Kaendlers"; Rückert 1990, 105.

396 Berling 1911, 43; Berling is of the opinion that Eberlein had a certain independence in the treatment of detail. Jedding 1979, 82, is more cautious and interprets the closeness of Eberlein's style to Kaendler's as a sign of his adaptability and capacity for subordination.

397 On this, see Albiker 1935, or (for the work reports) Albiker 1959.

398 "zu einer Probe gefertigten großen Stücken." BA, V2.12, fol. 30b.

399 Rückert 1990, 103.

400 Ibid.

401 "Specification Dererjenigen Fabricanten, welche allein an den Porcellain Geschirren arbeiten sollen, so in das Königl: Holländische Pallais und zwar zu der neuen fördern Gallerie erfordert werden"; Rapport for April 1732, BA, IAa.18, fol. 85a.

402 "sind von dem Hr. Hoff-Commissario Hörolden, zu dem Ende, nachstehende Persohnen hierzu denominiret worden, als ..."; for their dates and further activities at the manufactory, see Rückert 1990.

403 Not to be confused with the sculptor Johann Christoph Ludwig Lücke.

404 Hearing of October 27, 1734, BA, IAe.3, fols. 347b–348a.

405 "zwey große Vasen, einen großen Affen und einen großen Vogel," SächsHStA, loc. 1342, Vol. VII, fol. 30a; the reference to the animals assembled is connected with the affair surrounding "den alten Mehlhorn" ("old Mehlhorn"), who claimed, *inter alia*, that he had invented a non-shrinking paste that would guarantee the successful firing of the large figures (on this point, see the Commission's report to the king dated December 30, 1732, ibid., fols. 15a–19a, and the adjoining detailed commentary given by the arcanists dated. December 28, 1730, ibid., fols. 29a–32a). The monkey and the large bird mentioned in the quotation were made ready in Mehlhorn's paste as test pieces, but the kiln, likewise Mehlhorn's work, collapsed during the firing, so that "of all the pieces the only ones to come out undamaged were a large baboon and an Indian bird; these were, it has to be admitted, not perfectly fired, but it will be possible to fire the two pieces again in another kiln." Record for December 17, 1732, ibid., fol. 50b.

406 Hearing on October 27, 1734, BA, IAe.3, fol. 387a.

407 "BrustStücke"; hearing of October 28, 1734, BA, IAe.3, fol. 392a/b.

408 Rückert 1990, 107.

409 Hearing of October 28, 1734; BA, IAe.3, fol. 389a/b. This explains why, two and a half years before, Schlicke himself was not yet mentioned in the list of those working on the order for the Neustadt-side gallery.

410 "und sind die großen Stücken nur ohngefehr vor 4. Jahren gegeben worden, und hat Frizsche so wohl als andere nicht daran gewolt, sondern gezweifelt, daß es möchte praestiret werden, ich dennoch aber habe den Former Albrechten zu geredet, daß er das erste große Stücke/:welches damals ein sogenannter Trache war:/ ausgeformet, welches auch gerathen, und hat sich Frizsche nichts zuzuschreiben, denn er selber wie andere an denen großen Stücken hat erst lernen müßen, weil er Zeit seines Lebens dergleichen nicht gesehen, geschweige gemacht gehabt. Im Königl. Ballais sind die meisten Stücken, so gerathen, von Albrechten gemacht und geformet, und hat derselbe dergl. soviel verfertiget, als Frizsche, auch anbey Schiefern Müllern und Schlicken unterweisen auch unter richten müßen, ungeacht er 10. Thlr. jener aber Frizsche, als ein Alter, 12. Thlr. monathl. Tractament genießet." The account that Höroldt gave in response is to found in full under BA, IAe.5, fols. 194a–245a; the quotation on Fritzsche and Albrecht under ibid., fol. 227a/b.

411 "gleich bey inventierung dieser großen und mühsamen porcellain-Ballais-Stücken, mir, da alle Fabricanten, auch die sonst besten Arbeiter daran gezweiffelt und immer gesagt: daraus wird nimmermehr nichts, dergleichen Arbeit bey verspürter Lust und Auffmercksamkeit von ... Hörolden unter Versprechung guter Belohnung anvertrauet worden und von mir auch nachhero die meisten und wichtigsten Stücken so zeithero ins Königl. Ballais ... geliefert, geformet." Letter of July 9, 1739, BA, IAb.12, fol. 147b.

412 "hiernechst von meinen Vorgesezten unter Versprechung guter Beförderung, wie gedacht, zu dergleichen Arbeit encuragiret worden [sei], dergestalt, daß auch der Hoff-Commissarius Hörold mir ein Ducaten aus seinem eigenen Beutel bey denen erstern Stücken, als sogenannten Trachen und dergl., genießen laßen," ... "beziehe mich meiner Arbeit wegen ferner auf meine Vorgesezten, die Pflicht und Gewißenhafft zu attestiren sich nicht entbehren werden, daß ich die allerconsiderablesten Porcellain-Stk. so künstlich und mühsam sie auch nur von Ew. Königl. Majth. Modell-Meister Kändlern bis anhero eingeführet worden, und davon die in Dero Jappanischen Balleis befindlichen Thiere, Vasen, Vögel und dergleichen . . ., geformet und gefertiget habe." BA, IAb.12, fol. 207a/b.

413 Eberlein received 144 talers, Albrecht 120; see Rückert 1990, 101.

414 The Mehlhorn affair of 1732 sheds light on the urgency of the situation generally, in that credit was even given to "old Mehlhorn" when he claimed that he had invented a better paste and a better kiln (see n. 405 above), and also a better mill. The hand-operated mill that he designed was built by the manufactory mechanic, but also proved useless; SächsHStA, loc. 1342, Vol. VII, fol. 29b.

415 BA, IAa.16, fol. 98b.

416 Ibid., fol. 152b.

417 BA, IAa.18, fol. 152a.

418 "auch allerhand Galanterie- und Schminck-Kästgen, nicht weniger Spiegel-Rähmen und kleine Kaffee-Tischgen gefertiget [werden], und sind theils Modelle hierzu aus dem Königl: Palais von Dreßden anhero übersendet worden." Rapport for December 1731, BA, IAa.16, fol. 198b.

419 "Erfordert der Sache Beschaffenheit, daß zum öfftern ... von solchen Geschirren und Stücken, die ... bestellet worden, um selbige desto leichter zu gewinnen, mit Dohn ein Modell gemacht werde." BA, IAa.15, fol. 183a.

420 "Auf Allergnädigsten hohen mündlichen Befehl Ihro Majt: des höchst Seeligsten Königes Glorwürdigsten Andenkens habe ich endes bemelter im Jahre 1731 dem weißen Fisch Reihger wie er im Königl Schloß Hoffe zu Dresten zurselbigen

Zeit am leben befindlich war, in seiner Natürlichen Größe auf die Porceläin Fabrique zum gebrauch wie er in Schilffe stehet und Frösche und Fische bey sich hat müßen poussiren, Darzu ich daß Eißen und Schrauben welches in deßen Corpore zu seiner Haltung sein muste wie auch den darzu gebrauchten Thon und Postament worauf er ruhet mit 36.gr. bezahlen müßen." Letter of May 31, 1735; BA, IAa.24, fol. 177a.
421 "Modelge auffen gröbste Possiret"; BA, IAa.18, fol. 363a.
422 "den Indianischen Geyer sammbt dem Gackedu, Kranich und dem König von die Wawon ins kleine nach dem leben Poussiret"; BA, IAa.22, fol. 202a.
423 For greater detail on the techniques and technology of porcelain manufacture, see Goder 1978.
424 Goder 1978, 197–198.
425 This shows, for example, that in the Mehlhorn affair of 1732, there was more discussion of the problems of shrinkage and the cracks it tended to bring about, and less discussion of the problem of color; I shall consider the problem of shrinkage in greater detail in the section on firing.
426 "die Masse wäre schlecht und Töpfferzeug" ... "Was die schwartze Maße wäre wollte ich schon verantworthen, man müste ja Probiren Proben machen und sehen wie man es Prastieren könnte damit die Thiere stehen blieben." The fragment, consisting of pages 7–9 of a nine-page letter, is bound into a volume of records in the State Archive, SächsHStA, loc. 1342, Vol. VIII, (archival pagination: VII a–IX a); Berling 1900, 69, quotes the fragment and refers to it as a letter from Höroldt to the Commission. I was not able to establish whether the letter-head and the first six pages were also archived in Berling's day. More serious is the fact that a report drawn up by Sulkowski in person – quoted by Berling with a reference to fol. 51 of the same volume – has now disappeared entirely.
427 "§1: es hat der Hoff-Commissarius Höroldt so eine sehr geringe Masse zubereiten laßen, die von denen Fabricanten vielmehr vor einen Tohn als Porcelain gehalten wird und hat dannoch aller remonstration ungeachtet die meisten Königl. Stücken zu Ihro Mayth. höchsten Schaden und der Fabrique zum größten Nachtheil davon fertigen laßen. §2: Siehet diese Massa gantz grau und unansehnlich aus, als wenn gleichsam lauter Sand auf denen gebrannten Stücken herumbgestreuet wäre, hat also keine Schönheit und Glätte, wie etwan rechtes Porcelain zu haben pfleget, und ist impossible daß aus dergl. massa etwas sauberes kann gefertiget werden, weil selbige so sehr grob, sandkörnicht und nicht beysammenhält, bekommt Riße unter währender Arbeit." BA, IAe.2, fol. 4a/b.
428 "eröffnet H. HofCommissariy Hörold der Commission ins besondere daß die Porcellain Masse zu denen großen Stücken von eben denen Ingredientien als die so genannte gute, daraus das kleine Geschirr gemachet sey, nur daß sie wegen beßerer Haltung grobkörnicht [sei]." BA, IAe.3, fols. 334b–335a.
429 Commission's report to the king of November 1, 1734, SächsHStA, loc. 1342, Vol. VIII, fol. 60a.
430 SächsHStA, loc. 1342, Vol. VIII, fol. 28b.
431 "welche zu Große Thüre [Tiere] oder Stücken gebraucht werden könnte, und von wegen der Gröbe halten und in Feyer nicht in zwey gehen sollte." BA, Pret. 10, fol. 42a.
432 "vergliehteten Massen Schierbel so gröblich wie Sand Körner gestoßen und durch ein dergleichen Sib gesiebet"; BA, Pret. 10, fol. 46a.
433 The Rapport for January 1733 had already referred to similar, successful experiments with ground low-fired porcelain shards, but only for use in the paste for tableware, stating "that pieces that have broken in the low firing can be used for a paste from which good pieces can be made" ("daß die verglüheten und zerrissenen Porcelain Geschirre wieder zu einer Masse gebraucht und gute Geschirre daraus gefertiget werden können"); SächsHStA, loc. 1342, Vol. VII, fol. 106b.
434 "Ist eine Massa erfunden worden, von welcher die zeithero gerathenen, großen Stücken gemacht worden sind, ohne diese Massa aber, würden keine können leichtlich praestiret werden." SächsHStA, loc. 1342, Vol. IX, fol. 45b.
435 On his life generally, and work at Meissen, see Rückert 1990, 52.
436 BA, Pret. 16, fol. 25a.
437 "Diese Massa hat den Nahmen daher, weil die gröblich gestoßenen Porcellaine Schirbel ... unter die folgende so genante Loffel Massa genommen werden"; BA, Pret. 4, fols. 131b–133a. For more detail on Petzsch's arcanum notebook, see Rückert 1996, esp. 62ff.
438 Rückert 1996, 68; this dating can be considered as correct at least for the 44 press marks in the notes.
439 "daß die Massen-Arbeitere beym Schlemmen und reinigen derer Materialien sich übereilet, und nicht das behörige, so darbey zuthun gewesen, beobachtet, als wodurch nachhero der Schade erfolget, daß einige derer Porcellain-Geschirre bißhero in gut-brennen etwas dunckel geblieben, und nicht die angenehme Weiße gehabt." SächsHStA, loc. 1342, Vol. VII, fol. 133b.
440 BA, IAe.3, fol. 199b.
441 Ibid., fol. 234a.
442 "Sonderlich ist auch zu mercken, daß auch durch die schlechte Anstalt des Hoff-Commissarii Höroldt nicht gehörig dahin gesehen worden, daß die Porcelain-Stücken allezeit von einerley Stärcke wären von denen Fabricanten gearbeitet worden, weil an einigen Orten die Stärcke des Porcelains 2. Zoll, an andren wieder 1/2 Zoll, oder gar nur 1/4 Zoll Dicke ist, wovon ich noch zu jedermanns Beglaubigung große zerbrochene Stücke, welche durch diesen Fehler sind zu Grunde gegangen, aufweisen will, Solche Ungleichheit nun, sich nicht mit einander verträget, sondern kan das schwache Ort dem starcken nicht nachgeben reißet also alles im Feuer entzwey, Dieses hat nun Gelegenheit mitgegeben zu denen großen Rißen an den Königl. Palais-Stücken, solches ist zwar von mit pflichtmäßig erinnert worden, aber immer einerley geblieben und bey zeitheriger Commission keine remedur darauff geschehen." BA, IAe.2, fol. 19a.
443 "weil an dem ersten [molded piece] der Former selbst erst lernen und studiren muß, wie er ihm etwa mit der Stärcke und Schwäche zu statten kommet, weil er in der Forme ehe er solches heraus und vor die Augen bekommet, nicht alles so genau überlegen kann." BA, IAe.5, fols. 243b–244a.
444 BA, IAe.2, fols. 6b–7a.
445 BA, IAe.3, fol. 274b.
446 As Kaendler attested in 1734: "The molder Fritzsche has been been putting the finishing touches to figures before firing for two years now," ("der Former Fritzsche sey zum Verputzen seith 2 Jahren gebraucht worden"); BA, IAe.3, fol. 274b.
447 "Diese große Stücken werden niemahls gezeichnet und kan gar leicht der Verfertiger oder Former ... erfraget werden weilen gemeiniglich einerley große Stücken von einem [man or team] verfertiget werden." From Dr. Petzsch's arcanum notes, BA, Pret. 32, 4th bundle; see also Rückert 1996, 66.
448 The "klare Masse" referred to was the "normal" porcelain paste for the production of small objects.
449 "Die kleinen Striche exprimirten sich in der groben Masse wohl nicht so genau, dahingegen wären auch viele Thiere glatt, dabey es wohl angienge von der groben Masse. Es ereignete sich auch in der klaren Masse, daß die klahren Striche nicht so wie in Thone exprimiret werden könnten." Hearing of October 27, 1734, BA, IAe.3, fols. 346b–347a.
450 "es wäre andem daß schlechte Stücke aus der groben Masse gemacht worden weil sich daran kein zier Strich beym Possiren oder Verpuzen anbringen laßen, sondern er sich nur des Schwamms und Kraz Pinsels bedienen müßen, denn weil die Masse so grob gewesen, daß sich Stückgen wie Scheuer Sand darinne gefunden, so wären bey der Arbeit mit dem Beine gleich stücken heraus gerißen worden u. habe er krumme Meßergen brauchen müßen, Die Stücken hätten von solcher Masse auch nicht gehalten noch gut ausgesehen." Ibid., fols. 347b–348a.
451 Hearing of October 28, 1734, BA, IAe.3, fol. 389a/b.
452 "Diese Stücken, wenn sie geformet, bleiben sechs auch wohl acht Wochen in denen Former oder Vorraths Zimmer zu trocknen, stehen auch wohl noch länger, worbey sich apart nach dem Schierbel ob er dücke oder dinne gerichtet wird." BA, Pret. 4, fol. 132a.
453 "Diejenigen Figuren, aber so ingleichen Thiere, Vögel, so entweder nicht von zweyen Personen wegen ihrer Größe mehr können in Glasuren diregiret werden, oder wegen ihres zärtlichen Beleges wohl angegriffen werden, müßen begoßen werden, dieses geschiehet folgendes"/"bey denen Thieren mit Offenen Rachen"/"welche darauß in der Behändigkeit nicht wieder könnte ausgegoßen werden, sondern darinne Rüße verursachete."/"und trücken solche wohl theils auff dem Teckel als auch das Geschirre an und verstreichen es also, damit nichts unter das Geschirre von der Glasur kommen könne."/"wenn sich allenfals [irgend]wo was Glasur an einen Orte stehen bliebe, da sie nicht recht ablieffe damit er solche gleich austuncken könne."/"Wenn nun alles so weit fertig setzen sie zweine Schem-

mel an die Wanne an das Stücke sonderlich wenn es hoch, daß sie judiciren [voraussehen] sie möchten das Stücke nicht recht übergießen können, rühren mit denen Spadeln die Glasur auff, legen die Spadel bey Seite, steigen mit ihren Glasur Kannen auff die Schemmel, und Gießen jeder auff seiner Seite die Glasur über das Stücke herunter, wenn auffgehöret in dem die Glasur herunter läuffet und diejenigen sehen so die Spühlnäppe haben mit angefölleter Glasur daß an einen oder den andern Ort sonderlich unten von der Glasur nichts hinkomme gießen oder schwippen sie dahin von unten aus ihren Spuhlnäppen die Glasur."/"Nunmehro nähmen sie oben die Blatten hinweg und schaben überall den Thon so allenfals an das Geschirre wo sie angelegen angeglebet mit denen Meßern rein ab, wie nicht weniger auch unten die Würstel so angedrücket, da sie den anhangenden Thon von den Fuße wohl abschaben." BA, Pret. 67, vol. 3; there is no pagination, but the passages are taken from the last 23 pages of the volume.

454 BA, IAa.17, fol. 259a/b.

455 "mit einer Sandigten Glassur" BA, IAa.21, fol. 144a.

456 BA, IAa.25, fol. 11a.

457 As kindly pointed out to the author by Malcolm Gutter.

458 See Source 8.

459 "bey einigen bisher gelieferten Porcellain-Bränden und zwar nur an etl. Geschirren wahrgenommen [habe], daß solche an der Glashur grau und wie blau gesprenget ausgesehen [hätten]." BA, IAa.18, fol. 249b. My thanks go to Dr. Braun of the Meissen Manufactory Archive for transcribing this source.

460 "Will das Schwarze und theils wie blau gesprengte an den Porcellain-Geschirren noch nicht gänzlich nachbleiben und sind solche Geschirre bishero fast in allen Bränden zusehen gewesen, welches der Fabrique großen Schaden verursachet, man muß sich wundern, da sonsten dergleichen niemahlen in der so genannten blauen Massa gefunden worden, was es voriezo damit vor eine Beschaffenheit habe, der Ober-Meister H. Stölzel giebet zwar die gewisse Versicherung, daß diesen puncktgen Geschirr durch beßere Reinigung der Materialien ... abgeholffen werden könne, und sollte über 4 Wochen nicht mehr dauern." Ibid., fol. 335a/b.

461 Although Albiker writes that the animals were glazed in white, he gives no source, Albiker 1935, 16.

462 "Pflichtmäßigen Bericht Wie die von Endesbenanntem die Porcellain-Massen und Glassuren zubereitet [werden]"/"eine schöne flüßige Glassur So bis zum Ende des Ofens Schön gläntzend und weiß worden"; BA, Pret. 16. Information by courtesy of Claus Boltz.

463 "Endlich erinnert er [Kaendler], daß H. HoffCommissary die Palais Stücken 5 bis 6 mahl mit guter Masse überstreichen lassen, wodurch die Kunst daran verderbet worden, indem sodann erst die Glasur darauf kommen." BA, IAe.3, fol. 276b.

464 "Was künstliche Bildhauerey anbelanget, so ist solche an- und für sich selbst allerdings zu rühmen wenn man sie von denen Porcellain-Stücken haben kann. Alleine, weil zwischen Holz, Stein und Thon ein großer Unterschied zu machen, so ist Porcellain gegen diese alle gar kein Gleichnüs, jenes bleibt, wie es einmal gearbeitet worden, dieses muß das penetrante Feuer erst vollends zur Perfection bringen." BA, IAe.5, fols. 231b–232a.

465 Schnorr von Carolsfeld 1974, 1:5.

466 Küas 1977.

467 There were 254 firings at the manufactory in 1736 (20 more than in the previous year); SächsHStA, loc. 1342, Vol. IX, fol. 238b.

468 "Sind bishero verschiedene große Vasen und allerhand Arthen große Vögel ... wie solche von Ihro Königl.Majth. verlanget worden, in so weit gefertiget, die aber nicht zum Gutbrennen und zur völligen perfection gebracht werden können, ehe und bevor nicht die neuen Brenn-Öfen hierzu auffgebauet, inzwischen ist mit einer Vase in dem vorhandenen großen Ofen eine Probe gemacht worden, welche auch ziemlich gut geblieben." Report for September 1731, BA, IAa.16, fol. 79b–80a.

469 Walcha 1973, 103; here Walcha is quoting a remark made by Samuel Stöltzel at the beginning of the 1730s: "oder das Feuer in den für die Aufnahme von Grossplastik veränderten Öfen war allzu flattricht."

470 The report for January 1732 only mentions low-firing kilns, in which there were three firings of normal and large wares in the month. According to the report, the fire burned for 34 to 36 hours for a firing of this kind, thus calling for a large quantity of wood (a cost item not to be underestimated, and one which posed major problems at the manufactory). Either further kilns were built for the high firing, or the low-firing kilns proved capable of high firing once they had been tested at high temperatures.

471 "auf seine [Höroldt's] angaben die großen Brenn-Ofen erbaut und dadurch großer Schaden zugezogen worden, indem viel leere Capseln eingesezet werden müsten, das Porcellain auch die Gütte nicht mehr wie sonst habe und zerspringe, sowohl dunckel und grau auch allzu starck ausfalle." SächsHStA, loc. 1342, Vol.VIII, fol. 60a.

472 BA, IAa.16, fols. 107a–109a.

473 One version is to be found more or less in the middle of the bound notes, BA, Pret. 67, Bd.7. There is a description of the same procedure, somewhat differently expressed, in BA, Pret. 32, 4th bundle.

474 "das Stücke in den Ofen auff der Trage hinein, inwendig mit gleicher Behuthsamkeit wiederumb von der Trage ab, daß sie selbiges mit dem Teckel heben, setzen solchiges auff den verfertigten Boden."/"Schälchen, Spühlnap oder TellerKapseln so aber alte seyn müßen zugesezet"/"es werden die Capseln, damit die großen Stücken zu gesezet werden in alle so weit es sich leiden will Geschirre gesezet." BA, Pret. 32.

475 "indem solche gefertigte Stücke durch dergleichen unerfahrene Hände, welche kein Geschicke haben, durch müßten, und von denen meisten Königl. Stücken die Beine, Ohren und Schnäutze und dergleichen abgebrochen worden." BA, IAe.2, fol. 15a/b.

476 "wie vermittelst untergelegter Rollen das Zerreißen derer großen Stücke am Boden wo solche sehr starck waren u. dahero nicht der Schwindung wie oben fortkämen, zu verhindern und demonstriret solches mit herzugebrachten döhnern Röllgen"; BA, IAe.3, fol. 272b.

477 "die Massa von oben herunter ehender in einander schwindet, als von beyden seiten herzu, denn davon hat man ja leider die Erfahrung." BA, IAe.5, fol. 242b.

478 Rapport of February 1732, BA, IAa.16, fol. 283b.

479 BA, IAa.24, working report appended to Rapport for March, fol. 108a.

480 BA, IAa.24, firing report May 1735, fols. 200a–201a.

481 "Kann sehr vieles Unglück bey der Fabrique verhütet werden, wen die Geschirre fein ihre gehörige Trocknung erlangen, und nicht wie bis hero offt geschehen noch feuchte in die öfen getragen werden, da selbige dan leichtl. zerspringen." Probably a criticism from 1738, SächsHStA, loc. 1342, Vol. X, fol. 492b.

482 "An denen Postamenten worauf die Stücke stünden habe er [Kaendler] desideriret daß selbige allezeit etwas starck u. plump gemacht werden müsten, damit sie in Feuer stünden." BA, IAe.3, fol. 274b.

483 "Es wären auch die verdorbenen Stücken Cändler gezeigt worde, sich darnach zu richten und den Fehlern abzuhelffen." BA, IAe.3, fol. 208a.

484 "pure die von Kändlern gegebene üble Stellung." BA, IAe.5, fol. 244a.

485 "Einen Pfau in Lebens Größe modelliret ... deßen Postament Ist fast wie lauter Graß gemacht und giebet solches Graß Dem Großen umschweiffenden Schwantze gute Haltung" Kaendler's work report for March 1734, BA, IAa.22, fol. 99a.

486 "Eine Wölffin in Lebens Größe, sitzet auf den hintern Läufften ... Unter sich aber hat sie 2 Junge Wölffe einen etwas größer als den andern sitzen, welche die Haltung im Feuer hauptsächlich geben müßen." Kaendler's work report for April 1735, BA, IAa.24, fol. 173a.

487 "den Fliegel wider die gesunde Vernunfft so poussiret, daß es ... keine Möglichkeit [gäbe], dergl. Stücke im Feuer zu praestiren." BA, IAe.5, fol. 201a.

488 BA, IAe.3, fol. 274a.

489 "daß Eine Probe gemacht würde, Ob nicht die großen Thiere als Hirsche, Auerthier, Africanische Esel [Zebra] und dergleichen in Lebensgröße könten praestiret werden." BA, IAe.5, fol. 191a.

490 Ibid., fol. 191a/b.

491 "daß der Bettmeister im Königl. Palais mit diesen Stücken sich wird wohl müßen in acht nehmen, indem er nicht sicher, daß wenn er eines oder das andre fort-transportiren soll, daß es ihm nicht in Händen zerfalle; maßen schon dergleichen bey uns in Meißen an einem Stück geschehen, daß als es schon gebrannt gewesen und von einem Fabricanten hat sollen wegen seiner Riße halber verküttet werden, selbiger es nur ein wenig fortgerücket, gleich ein groß Stück aus dem Postament gefallen, welches nun ebenfalls an einigen Stücken im Palais zu besorgen seyn [= zu befürchten ist], und großer Schaden geschehen dürffte." BA, IAe.2, fol. 5a/b.

492 "Unglücks Winckel worinne sich das viele verdorbene Porcellain befindlich"/"ein Zimmer drey Treppen hoch öffnete, worinnen ungefehr 12. große Palais Stücken an Löwen Adlern u. dergl. Thieren stunden die in Feuer verdorben waren, ingl. verschiedene vergliehete mangelhaffte Vasen." BA, IAe.3, fols. 334a–335a.
493 "daß man mit der Hand darzwischen hinein greiffen können"; BA, IAe.2, fol. 6a.
494 "auf Anordnung des Hoff-Commissarii JHöroldt von einem Lehrling mit einer gewißen Hartz-Kütte [Kitt] vermacht, ... Theils sind [sie] auch sogar mit Holz und Gipß zusammen gemacht." Ibid., fol. 5b–6a.
495 "es wäre doch beßer, weil die großen Stücken noch nicht hielten u. ohne Riße noch nicht gemacht werden könnten, daß selbige ehe sie entzwey geschlagen würden noch zu gutte gemacht worden"; BA, IAe.3, fol. 200a.
496 "daß Cändler ja selbst die Kütte darzu gemacht und selbst angeordtnet wie es verküttet werden müßen, auch im Anfange solches selbst gethan hätte"; ibid., fol. 207a.
497 "zeithero mit dem Kitten großer Löcher und Riße an großen Stücken"; BA, IAa.22, fol. 356b.
498 "Wegen der großen Stücken, so kann ich sagen, daß ich so viel habe müßen verkütten, daß ich vielmahl nicht habe gewußt, wie ich die Riße vermachen soll, so groß sind sie geweßen, dann hab ich sie mit Holz müßen auffüttern und die Kütte darüber [gestrichen]." BA, IAe.2, fol. 181b.
499 "in ihrer natürlichen Größe und Farbe"; Keyssler 1751, 1320.
500 Horschik 1977.
501 Rückert 1993.
502 "daß es bekannt genug wäre, wie die Stücken mit Ohlfirnis überstrichen würden, weil es mit den großen Stücken sich noch zur Zeit nicht praestiren laße, selbige im Feuer zu emaliren." BA, IAe.3, fol. 207a.
503 "sowohl kalt aufgetragene wie auch eingebrannte Farben als Emailfarben bezeichnet"; Horschik 1977, 14.
504 BA, IAa.24, fols. 105a–106a; fols. 271a–272b; fol. 314a–315a.
505 Horschik 1977, 15.
506 Rückert 1993, 49.
507 Especially as Dresden was at this time one of the most distinguished centers for painting in lacquer in all Germany; see Kopplin/Haase 1998.
508 "solche Stücken wegen ihrer Größe, und theils der kleinen Rißgen halben ... nicht emailliret, sondern mit bunten Öl-Farben bemahlet worden, daß sie also gar kein gutes Aussehen haben"; Rapport for November 1733, BA, IAa.20, fols. 379a–380a.
509 Höroldt is first found expressing this opinion in the Registratur, February 3, 1734, BA, IAa.20, fol. 430a.
510 "da die Riße an selbigen mit einer Kitte vermacht, so dann aber nur mit Öhl Farben bemahlt und nicht wie andere Porcellain-Geschirre mit bunten Farben emailliert" BA, IAd.3, fol. 147b.
511 BA, IAe.3, fols. 326b–328b.
512 "die Farben getadelt, die Thiere wären nicht nach ihren Farben gemacht." This is clear from the fragment of a letter of Höroldt from October 28, 1734, quoted above, in which he notes Sulkowski's complaints as expressed by Kaendler; see n. 426.
513 "solche Porcelain-Stücke dergestalt schlecht beschaffen wären, daß Ihro Königl. Maj. bey Dero hohen Ansicht über selbige und deren schlechte Öhlfarben-Mahlerey gantz ungnädig gewesen und daran großes Mißfallen bezeiget"; BA, IAe.2, fol. 24a.
514 "Auf Sr: Königl:Majth: in Pohlen und Churfürstl. Durchl. zu Sachßen allergnädigsten hohen mündl. Befehl, sollen alle Thiere und Vögel, so in der Meißnischen Porcelain-Fabrique vor Ihro Majth. in dero Japanisches Palais in Neustadt zu verfertigen, iedes nach seiner Arth gemahlt und in Feuer emailiret werden, iedoch dergestalt, daß an jedem Stück auch viel weißes von Porcelain zu sehen ist." BA, IAa.19, fol. 1a.
515 BA, IAa.17, fol. 334a.
516 Gröger 1956, 30.
517 See, for example, BA, V2.12, fol. 146a: "2 talers for 2 sentry-boxes to be painted red with oils, to the painter Johann Gottfried Mehlhorn, as per receipt of Jan 14, 1732" ("2 Thlr. vor 2 Schilder Häußern mit Öhl:Farben roth anzustreichen Johann Gottfried Mehlhornen dem Mahler laut Quittung vom 14. Jan: 1732").
518 On Mehlhorn's life and for mentions of Mehlhorn in the records, see Rückert 1990, 177 and 178.
519 Ibid.
520 "nicht nur in der ordentlichen Mahlerey sich engagiren, sondern auch zum lacciren, welches er ex professo verstünde, auf jedes mahliges Verlangen gebrauchen laßen [wollen]"; Registratur June 23, 1734, BA, IAa.21, fol. 116a/b.
521 Rückert 1992/1993.
522 SächsHStA loc. 14636, Vol. II, fol. 32a (= records of the Meissen castle guard); information kindly supplied by Maureen Cassidy-Geiger.
523 "so Von meißen Gemahlet Herauf gekommen" ... "mit Lackfirnis über Zogen"; Rückert 1992/1993, 47.
524 The final sum of 127 talers and 16 groschen demanded by Reinow was lowered to 117 talers by Höroldt.
525 For instance, the following figures: Coot, Great Crested Grebe, Rose-Ringed Parakeet, Monkey taking snuff and Monkey with grape/chain, Marmoset, Monkey wearing a ruff, Bolognese Dog.
526 Claus Boltz has pointed out that the reason why the animal figures were not painted with fusible enamel colors was that the only muffle-kilns available for enamel-firing were small ones, but this is contradicted by the fact of there having been a small number of large figures that were delivered to the palace decorated with enamels: as early as the end of 1731 or beginning of 1732, the following figures were standing at the manufactory ready for delivery, resplendent in their enamel colors: a mandrill, a king vulture, a golden pheasant, and a macaw (sitting).
527 "Mann hat auch am 7. Aug. den ersten Elephanten aus dem Brennhauße zum Waaren-Lager geliefert erhalten, welcher, ob er schon einige kleine Riße in sich hat, nach des Hr. Hoff-Commissarii Meynung dennoch vor ein gut Stück passiren und zum emailliren genommen werden könne." BA, IAa.18, fol. 169b.
528 On the practice of partial painting and its effect, see also Albiker 1935, 38–39. He argues that the contrast between naturalistically painted areas and white areas corresponds to the contrast between painting and sculpture, giving as an example a colored bird's leg against a white treestump. Nevertheless, however "naturalistic" this painting may be, the high shine and brightness of the enamel colors will always result in it being perceived as porcelain painting and thus as intrinsically artificial.
529 Rückert 1995–1997, Part 1, 46, n. 63.
530 "allezeit gegen Selbte [die königliche Majestät] sich den Ruhm gegeben, nicht allein die großen Apostel und andere große Stücken zu verfertigen und zu emailliren, sondern auch in denen iezigen großen Oefen 4.mahl mehr Geschirre zu bereiten"; BA, IAe.2, fol. 95b.
531 BA, IAe.2, fol. 170a.
532 See Pietsch 1996.b.
533 Sponsel 1900, 204.
534 Information kindly supplied by Maureen Cassidy-Geiger.
535 Rückert 1996.
536 On Petzsch, see BA, Pret. 32, 4. Bündellage.
537 Morley-Fletcher 1993, 1:32.
538 Rückert 1996, 67.
539 "No:O.8./4 theil Schnorr: Erde/1 theil Stein/2 theil obiger gestoßen, vergliehete Massen Schierbel"; BA, Pret. 10, fol. 45a. The first two ingredients mentioned are "Schnorr's white earth" ("Schnorrsche weiße Erde,"), i.e., kaolin, and "Siebenlehner Stein," i.e., feldspar. The third ingredient was pulverized shards from low-fired pieces made with the same paste recipe.
540 "ist eine Schöne Masse und wird jetzo zu großen Thiere und Vassen gebrauchet, hält beßer als andre Massen wegen der gestoßenen Schierbel oder Graubeln"; an earlier experiment with ground shards in the so-called blue paste is in the same book, page 51a, dated May 1732, but it was not suitable for throwing or molding.
541 This is also suggested by another recipe written down three pages earlier and dated January 9, 1734; the notes made in the book are however not in strict chronological order, as is shown by entries towards the back with earlier dates.
542 "No:O.9./5. theile Schnorrisch-Erde/1. theil Stein Sieb:/2. theil obiger Masse Schierbel" ...
"NB: obige Masse No.O.8. ist vor itzo die beste und wird gebraucht und zwar um deß willen, weilln die großen thiere und Vasse nicht von der ordentlichen Masse stehen wollen, so kombt diese gestoßen vergliehete Masse zu Statten und hält die große Stücken zusammen, daß sie nicht so sehr Schwinden und reißen wie es sichs an den zeithero verferdigten Stücken uns weißet." Ibid. According to this source, the "obige Masse Schierbel" are ground, low-fired shards from failed pieces composed of Paste No. 8.
543 "Ferner wird izo gebrauchet zu den großen Thieren wie vor hero schon stehet als No:O.8. 4. theile Schnorische Erde/1 theil Siebelschen Stein/2. theile von den Groben Grabeln oder ver glieheten Massen

Schierbel so gröblich wie Sand Körner gestoßen und durch ein dergleichen Sib gesiebet." Ibid., fol. 46a.
544 Also on the figure from the Pflueger Collection. When making his inventory of the collection, Morley-Fletcher must have overlooked the marking, which is indeed not particularly clear; Morley-Fletcher 1993, 26.
545 BA, Pret. 10, fol. 43a; it was composed of 14 units of "Schnorr's white earth," to 5 of "Siebenlehner Stein" and 10 of a particular sand.
546 Rückert thought that the prefix "O" was the sign for glaze; Rückert 1996, 66–67. But the "O" could also simply mean "number," in which case the incision "N:O8" would stand for No. 8.
547 Ziege, Inv. no. PE 713.
548 "die Abdrucke der Thiere jederzeit rar und kostbar bleiben mögen"; Keyssler 1751, 1320.
549 The marks are noted in the Catalog below, appended to the individual specimens in the various collections. On the AR-mark and the associated problems, see Boltz 1980, 34–35, and Boltz 1996, 7–8.
550 "Inventarium über das Palais zu Alt-Dreßden Anno 1721"; Staatliche Kunstsammlungen Dresden, Porcelain Collection.
551 On the inventories, see Boltz 1996.
552 Rückert 1996, 90.
553 See Boltz 1996.
554 Information kindly given by Mr. Martin Walcha, head restorer at the Dresden Porcelain Collection.
555 "Ein kleines Äffchen … ist die unter dem Namen Pinseläffchen bekannte Plastik, welche in einer alten Ausformung mit der Jahreszahl 1726 versehen ist." Albiker 1935, 25.
556 Kaendler's work reports are published in Pietsch 2002.
557 "Einen Versühn oder Sünden Bock wie ihn die Juden gehabt"; BA, IAa.22, fol. 227b.
558 "Ein Groß Balläis Stück dem Versühn oder Sünden Bock genannt, Nach seiner wunderlich anzusehenden Gestalt und Arth in seiner Natürlich Größe aus Thon possiret"; work report, January 1735, BA, IAa.24, fol. 32a.
559 Leviticus 16.
560 "großes babylonisches Schaf mit sehr breitem und fettem Rücken"; Keyssler 1751, 1312.
561 "Ein Indianisches großes Schaf mit 2 Hörnern welche wunderlich über des Schafes Augen gewachsen"; BA, IAa.22, fol. 373a/b.
562 see Source 24.
563 "ist voritzo aufs neue nicht nur ein Elephante sondern auch ein Auer-Ochße von ziemlicher Größe poussiret worden, so nechster Tage zum Abformen in Gipß befördert werden soll"; BA, IAa.16, fol. 109a.
564 This had already been noticed by Ernst Zimmermann in 1915, but those who came after him did not take this into account, see Zimmermann 1915, 103.
565 This applies to such figures as the Macaw (sitting), the fighting Dogs, the King Vulture, and a number of smaller figures such as the Gray Parrot and the Rose-Ringed Parakeet.
566 According to the records, this was the first of the animals for the palace, which means that it must have been done in the summer/fall of 1730; we shall return to this point at a later stage.
567 Pietsch 1998, fig. 221.
568 Pietsch 1998, fig. 223.
569 Sponsel 1900, 79–80; Gröger 1956, 105.
570 The moralizing four-liner, appended by Krauss to the engraving of the fountain in the Versailles labyrinth that incorporates a mother-monkey squashing its young one, emphasizes the animal's foolish behavior: "Durch all zu grosse Lieb, der Aff scheint weggerücket, das junge an der Brust, wird gahr von ihm ersticket. Wer preiset allzuviel, sein eigen Werck und That, hat sattsam unterdrückt, sein guten Nahm und Staat." Quoted from Krauss 1975, Plate XI; for an English rendering, see p. 148.
571 "Ms: Schmiedeln sein Portrait, welches von mir schon bald gefertiget gewesen, aber [an dem ich] nicht bis zum Ende habe dürffen daran continuiren, ist also die Arbeit auch vergeblich gewesen und muß von neuem angefangen werden." SächsHStA, loc. 1342, Vol. X, fol. 106a.
572 BA, IAa.16; this has not prevented some authors assuming this figure to have been the work of Kirchner, on the grounds of "stylistic characteristics." See Schnorr von Carolsfeld 1974, 1:106.
573 "voritzo aufs neue nicht nur ein Elephante sondern auch ein Auer-Ochße von ziemlicher Größe poussiret worden"; BA, IAa.16, fol. 109a.
574 BA, IAa.20, fol. 49a.
575 BA, IAe.3, fol. 236a/b.
576 BA, IAa.21, fols. 16a–17a.
577 "zeiget der nur lezther poussirte Tieger, welcher … so gar das Verglüh-Feuer nicht ausgehalten sondern entzwey gegangen"; BA, IAe.5, fol. 231a.
578 On the general subject of the links between "models" (in the sense of original sources of inspiration, or items copied) and works in Meissen porcelain, see Reinheckel 1962, Ducret 1973, Cassidy-Geiger 1996.b.
579 Rückert 1996.
580 Baer 1979.
581 "zwey Stück große Adler email-lirt"; SächsHStA, loc. 32562, no. 120a, fol. 193a.
582 "daß vor etl. Jahren Ihro des höchstseel. Königs Majt. 2 Stk. Indianische Adler zur Fabrique gegeben, umb solche nachzumachen, welche zwar nicht groß, sondern nur ohngefehr 3/4 Ellen hoch gewesen"; BA, IAe.5, fol. 199a.
583 Ibid., fol. 199a/b.
584 Baer 1979, 260; Keyssler 1751, 1320.
585 Nissen 1966/1978, 113.
586 Nissen 1966/1978, 130.
587 French travelers returning from the Antilles in the time of Louis XIV, for example, brought back not only drawings but also whole exotic animals for dissection at the Académie, and published the results, Nissen 1966/1978, 130ff.
588 The best surveys on this point are given by Nissen 1966/1978, and Bridson/White 1990.
589 "diejenigen großen Stücken, welche Ihro Königl. Mayth. nach einigen gewißen Modellen und Zeichnungen gefertiget wißen wollen"; BA, IAa.16, fol. 4b.
590 "bishero in der Fabrique gefertigten großen Stücken an allerhand Arthen Vögeln und indianischen Thieren"; BA, IAa.16, fols. 278b–279a.
591 "vor 56 Stück Kupffer-Stiche mit allerhand Arten Vögeln zum nöthigen Gebrauch bey der Fabrique"; BA, V2.13, fol. 154b.
592 I am grateful to the archivist, Dr. Peter Braun, for this information.
593 On these two animals in art generally, see Oettermann 1982, and Clarke 1986.
594 Nicolas de Bruyn's *Volatilium varii generis* (Amsterdam, ca. 1590) is just one example among many.
595 The work was published from 1719 to 1724; the illustration of the vessel is to be found in Vol. III, in Plate 70.
596 I am grateful to Maureen Cassidy-Geiger for this information.
597 On this point, see Hackenbroch 1955; Hackenbroch 1962, 18–19, and Catalog 21, Sotheby's New York, 10. Januar 1995, Lot 20.
598 Zimmermann 1929, 10–11; on the graphic antecedents, see also Brüning 1914, 76.
599 BA, IAb.12, fol. 148a.
600 See the Christie's London catalog of July 2, 1984, Dragon with AR-mark, from the possession of Lady Carmont.
601 Maureen Cassidy-Geiger suggested that this might have been the case, and her suggestion is supported by the fact that the only two dragons to have been decorated in enamel colors in 1732 (delivery list) do in fact form a matching pair consisting of one larger figure and one smaller one (the smaller one is now in the Dresden Porcelain Collection, and the larger one in the Musée National de Céramique in Sèvres). 6 larger dragons and 5 smaller dragons were produced for the Japanese Palace.
602 BA, IAa.22, fol. 264b.
603 BA, V2.14, fol. 103b.
604 "Modelge auffen gröbste Possiret"; BA, IAa.18, fol. 363a.
605 BA, IAa.22, fol. 202a.
606 "den Indianischen Geyer sammbt dem Gackedu"; ibid.
607 "Einen großen Indianischen Geyer wie er in Moritzburg im Leben Befindlich ist poussiret hat in seiner Höhe mit sammbt den Postament welches in Gestalt eines mit Laub und Graß Bewachsenen Stockes 1. Elle und 12. Zoll, und ist wegen seiner Seltamen Gestalt wunderlich anzusehen zu mahlen er auch einen noch andern Ausländischen Vogel in Größe einer Starcken Tauben Gackedu genannt, geraubet und solchen als Todt neben sich zu seinen Füßen liegen Hat welchen er gantz zerrißen, und davon Das eingeweyde in seinen Schnabel Hat als wolte er es freßen." Work report for August 1734, BA, IAa.22, fol. 315a.
608 BA, IAa.22, fol. 227a. (see Source 25).
609 At the Jägerhof, the exotic animals were accommodated in the "Löwenhaus," while the enclosure for the European wild animals was known as the "Bärenhaus."
610 These are the Lynx, the Tiger, a figure of an "African cat," and the Bear.
611 This stuffed animal was most likely the "large Babylonian sheep

with a very broad and fat back," ("ein großes babylonisches Schaf mit sehr breitem und fetten Rücken,") that Keyssler described from his visit to the natural history collections ("Animaliengalerie") in October 1730; Keyssler 1751, 1312.

612 "zur Nachferttigung von porcelain in das Königl: Japanische Palais in Lebensgrößse, abzuzeichnen" ... "nach dem Leben gezeichnet[en] und mit Waßer farben gemahlet[en]"; the quotation from the manufactory report for August 1736 can be found under BA, IAa.24b, fol. 188b, to which is appended the list dated by Reinow 19 April 1736, BA, IAa.24b, fol. 209a.

613 Namely the She-Wolf, Scapegoat, Bolognese Dog, Exotic Sheep, Sable, Great Crested Grebe, and Guinea Fowl.

614 "die Obere Etage der fördern Gallerie"; see, for instance, the order of 26 November 1733; BA, IAa.19. fol. 347a.

615 SächsHStA loc. 14636, Vol. II, fol. 22b (= records of the Meissen castle guard); I am obliged to Maureen Cassidy-Geiger for bringing this source to my attention.

616 "daß solche Thiere ... gantz ohn Maßgeblich unten in der Gallerie an die Schäffte herum könten gesetzet, mithin nicht so große Consolen oder KrackSteine an die Wände im Königlichen Balläis dürfften angemacht werden"; BA, IAe.5, fol. 191a/b.

617 Hanway 1753, 227.

618 Müller 1907, 2:97 (see Source 27).

619 SächsHStA, OHMA Cap. II, no. 15.27.b.

620 Landesamt für Denkmalpflege, III.1.; illustrated in Franz 1953, fig. 74, text 38.

621 "Der Zweck der Anfertigung dieser Figuren war ursprünglich der, dass man sie statt Marmorfiguren in die Gärten stellte; darin liegt auch der Grund, dass sie jetzt unendlich selten sind und mit wahrhaft fabelhaften Preisen bezahlt werden." Graesse 1873, 6.

622 "Der Garten soll gleichfalls vergrößert und zwey hundert Fuß weiter in die Elbe hineingeleget werden. Seine bassins werden mit Marmor eingefasset, und die darinnen befindlichen vielen Statuen aus Marmor und Porzellan seyn." Keyssler 1751, 1321 (and here Source 2).

623 In Sponsel 1900, 96, for example, and more recently in Pietsch 1997.a.

624 "blauen und japanischen Porcelains"; Staatliche Kunstsammlungen Dresden, Porcelain Collection, Zwinger, in the folder "Verschiedene Specificationen und Belege über Zu- und Abgänge 1700–1876," see also Reichel 1972.a, 77.

625 On these occurrences and further mentions of damage in the inventory, see Reichel 1964.

626 "Die höltzerne und thonerne Bilder sind allzu verderblich ... Hingegen die von Thon gebrannte taugen gar nichts, weil sie in dem Brennen ihre Zeichnung und Sauberkeit verliehren; doch so Privat-Persohnen wohlfeile Statuen in Gärten unter freyem Himmel haben wollen, müssen sie wohl aus Thon bossirte Statuen also unter Dach stehen lassen, daß sie die Sonne beschauen und trockene Lufft frey bestreichen kann, doch daß man die allzu raue Lufft davon abhalten und die allzu starck scheinende Sonne nach Belieben moderiren kann. Wenn sie nun also völlig ausgedrocknet sind, kann man sie noch gelinde brennen, so verliehren sie nichts merckliches an ihrer Zeichnung, und zuletzt mit Oel-Farbe, wann sie eben aus dem Ofen kommen, warm überstreichen." Sturm 1720, 9.

627 "nach dem sächsischen Porcellain kleyden und anstreichen, auch hin und wieder mit Gold auszieren [zu] lassen; nun werden sie mit einem Firnis überzogen, daß sie aussehen, als wenn sie von Porcellain wären." Roda 1980, 235, Source 150; I am grateful to Dr. Burkard von Roda for this piece of information.

628 Heres 1991, 29.

629 Friedrich Reichel, in Pietsch 1998, 24; Ströber 2004.

630 Heres 1989, 102.

631 Heres 1989.

632 Heres 1989, 110, and Heres 1991, 30, 31. Parts of the Kunstkammer were, for instance, on display in the attic story of the Dutch Palace between 1718 and the beginning of work on the conversion. On the development of the Kunstkammer and the ordering system in the Zwinger, see also Schmidt/Schnitzer 2002.

633 Fichtner 1939, I:302.

634 Arnold/Schmidt 1986, 195.

635 See Forberger 1958.

636 See W. Weber 1981.

637 "So haben Wir unter andern ausgefundenen Mitteln, daß die Wiederbringung einer geseegneten Nahrung und Gewerbes im Lande hauptsächlich durch Manufakturen und Commercia befördert werden könne, vornehmlich in Consideration gezogen." From the printed foundational charter of the Meissen porcelain manufactory, of January 23, 1710; the quotation is taken from Zimmermann 1908, 322.

638 On the significance of the promotion of the arts for commerce, and vice versa, in the first half of the eighteenth century, see J. Menzhausen 1989.

639 Schillinger 1997, 141; the reference is to Zedler's Universallexikon, see Zedler 1995.

640 [Tschirnhaus] "förderte durch seinen Eintritt in kursächsische Dienste ... in entscheidendem Maße eine enge Verbindung zwischen Wissenschaft und Dresdner Hof. Er war der Bahnbrecher der Frühaufklärung und einer der Wegbereiter des Akademiegedankens in Deutschland." Schillinger 1997, 141; on Tschirnhaus, see Dresdener Hefte 2 (1983), and Plaßmeyer 2001.

641 "nicht mehr, es sey auch an wen es wolle verferttiget oder verkaufft werden sollen"; BA, IAa.19, fol. 344a.

642 The decree was however corrected by Sulkowski on April 8, 1734, when he specified that of the porcelains with "ancient Indian" painting, only those models were exclusively for the king which had the incised monogram AR, while nineteen models incised with the marking "NB" might be copied for general sale; see Boltz 1996, 7, and Appendix, 13.

643 SächsHStA, loc. 895, fol. 1b.a.

644 Ibid., fol. 1a.b.

645 Ibid., fol. 1b.b. (see Source 3).

646 Ibid., fol. 1b.b. (see Source 3).

647 "daß in Zukunft ... dergleiches weißes Porzellan ... dem Indianischen an Schönheit und Tugend, noch mehr aber an allerhand Façons ... weit übergehen möchten"; quoted from Zimmermann 1908, 322.

648 "guthen weissen Porcellain, sambt der allerfeinsten Glasur und allem zubehörigen Mahlwerck, welches dem Ostindischen wo nicht vor, doch wenigstens gleich kommen solle"; quoted from I. Menzhausen 1982.b, 143.

649 I. Menzhausen 1982, 189–190.

650 Schlechte 1983; the notes are to be found under SächsHStA, loc. 2097 no. 50.

651 "Betrachtet man jedoch die Reihung derer [der Schlösser] in unmittelbarer Nähe der Residenz, fällt folgendes auf: Hier wird der Versuch unternommen, ähnlich wie der aus der Architekturgeschichte bekannte Plan der architektonischen Gestaltung eines ganzen Landes, ein Gedankengebäude zu errichten, das systematisch die bereits vorhandenen Schlösser und Lusthäuser um die Residenz zueinander in Beziehung setzt bzw. aus einer Anzahl von Elementen ein Ensemble schafft." Schlechte 1983, 273.

652 Ibid.

653 On ideal plans laid down in drawings, see Völkel 2001.

654 Schlechte 1983, 273.

655 Ibid., 274.

656 Keyssler was highly impressed and even went so far as to include a whole-page illustration of a particularly bizarre pair of deer antlers in his description; Keyssler 1751, 1308–1309.

657 J. Menzhausen 1980.

658 The blue roofs of the Zwinger can be seen not only in paintings of 1722 by Johann Alexander Thiele (Gemäldesammlung, Dresden), but also in a not so well-known colored drawing by Franz Anton Danreither of 1720 in the Museum Carolinum Augusteum in Salzburg, see Schnitzler-Sekyra 1994, 41–42 (information kindly supplied by Maureen Cassidy-Geiger). During a renovation in the year 1789 the roofs were once again painted blue, as is documented in the travel diary of Daniel Chodowiecki: "The roofs are all blue, and the rest including all the decorations (of which there are very many) are white," quoted from Schnitzler-Sekyra 1994, 42.

659 This system can also be extended to include other palaces, but this would take us too far from the subject of the present publication. One example is Großsedlitz, which provided the venue for the annual feast of the Order of the White Eagle, Poland's highest order. When Augustus the Strong founded the order, he was demonstrating his position in the international political field through his association with Poland, and – by virtue of it being a high-ranking order, comparable with that of the Golden Fleece (Habsburg), of the White Elephant (Denmark), of Saint Andrew (Russia), of the Garter (England), or of the Black Eagle (Prussia) – his claim to equal status with the rulers of the other leading powers.

660 Pietsch 1998, 216.

661 SächsHStA, loc. 589, fol. 4a/b.

662 Illustration in Gurlitt 1924.

663 Roth 1993, 9–13.

664 Lorenz 1998, 34–35; Kuke 2002, 124.

665 "Die Thiere werden auf einmahl, und zugleich, und zugleich unter angenehme Thone von Jagt- und Wald-Hörnern ausgelassen. Vorhero werden sie auf allerhand Art hefftiger gemacht, man schlägt sie mit glüenden Eisen, man zwickt sie in die Ohren, man schießt ihnen kleine Pfeile, so vorn spitzig sind und stecken bleiben, in die Ohren, man wirfft Schwärmer unter sie u.s.w. Wenn sie noch wild und nur neuerlich eingefangen, giebt es einen lustigen Zeitvertreib." Rohr 1990, 870.
666 "Es waren allda ein Löwe und Löwin, ein Panther-Thier und Leopard, ein Thieger, ein Luchs, drey Bähren, ein Wolf, ein Auer-Ochs, zwey Büffel-Ochsen, eine Kuh mit ihrem Kalbe, eine Maul-Eselin, ein Hengst, zwey wilde Pferde, und zwölf grosse wilde Schweine. Der Löwe und der eine von den Bähren ergriffen alsobald zwey Schweine, und nachdem sie mit ihnen fertig, frasen sie selbige halb auf. Der Leopard machte sich über das Kalb her. Der Auer-Ochs gab der Maul-Eselin mit seinen Hörnern einen Stoß, womit er ihr den Bauch aufschlitzete. Einer von den Bähren attaqvirte den Wolf, und warf ihn einige mahl in die Lufft, worauf dieser davon lief und zu den Schweinen seine Zuflucht nahm. Der König erlegte darauf den Luchs, und endigte sich diese Lust in höchsten Vergnügen." Iccander 1740, 66–67.
667 "Nach der Mittags Taffel ließen Ir. Königl. Hoheit der ChurPrinz 2 Dachße in dem Gärtgen des Palais auf dem Taschenberge hezen. Weil auch vorgegeben worden, daß die zahme Schweine und Dachße eine sonderbare Antipathie haben, und einander selbst anfallen solten, so wurden vorhero 6 Zahme Schweine auf diese 2 Dachße getrieben, es hat sich aber dergl. vermuthete Antipathie nicht zeigen wollen." Dresden court journal for November 25, 1734; SächsHStA, OHMA O. I, Nr. 3, Vol. 4, fol. 4b.
668 This listing is based on the account given in Hensel 1992.
669 Schlechte 1985, 24.
670 On shooting from hides with owls as decoys, see Benker 1993.
671 Hensel 1992, 40.
672 "Dreyhundert Hirsch und Rehe wurden auf diese Art geschossen, denen übrigen aber auf Befehl des Königs die Freyheit über das Garn angewiesen, welches man zu dem Ende niederfallen ließ." Loen 1749.b, 59–60.
673 Moritz von Sachsen was an illegitimate son of Augustus the Strong.
674 "Die größte Jagdkurzweil begunte darauf mit den wilden Schweinen, deren über hundert geschlagen wurden. Der König ließ hierbey seine Weltbekante Fertigkeit sowohl mit dem Fangeisen als dem Hirschfänger recht bewunderswürdig sehen. Niemand, ausgenommen der Graf Moritz von Sachsen, konnte ihm solches nachmachen. Da aber gleichwohl auch andre sich dessen unterfiengen, so bekamen die Zuschauer etwas zu lachen, wann diese ungeschickte Helden von den anlauffenden Schweinen übern Hauffen geburzelt, oder sonst mit ihrem Fangeisen herumgetrieben wurden." Loen 1749.b, 60.
675 Loisel 1912, 2:170–183.
676 "N[r] 2 Einen Fischahr oder Fischfreßer 1 Elle hoch wovon Ihro Majest schon bekommen" and "N[r] 4 Noch einen Fischahr welcher einen Karpffen zerreißet auff Sauberste aus gearbeitet" SächsHStA, loc. 1341, Vol. VI, fol. 323a/b.
677 Krauss 1975, Tafel XI.
678 "8. Kraniche mit 1 Stein" BA, IAa.17, fol. 336a; this annotation "with the stone" only reappears once, in an undated list: SächsHStA, loc. 1341, fol. 6b.
679 "Der Kranich ist vornehmlich ein Sinn-Bild der Wachsamkeit,"... "Sie bringen nicht mehr als zwey Eyer zwischen welchen sie in ihren Neste jedesmahl einen Stein zu legen pflegen." Zedler, 15 (1737), cols. 1752 and 1757.
680 Schoettgen 1736, n.p.
681 "Es wird der Löwe wegen seiner edelmüthigen Freudigkeit, tapffern Stärker und Hertzhafftigkeit, auch unerschrockenem Gemüthe, der König aller wilden Thiere genannt." Zedler 1995, 18 (1738), col. 216.
682 This was often done in illustrations to fables. See, for example, Francis Barlow, *Les fables d'Esope et de plusieurs autres excellens mythologistes* (Amsterdam 1714): Fable 24 (p. 51) shows the lion, going hunting with the other animals, as a ruler amidst a variety of character types, and the illustration to Fable 37 (p. 76) likewise shows the rat and the frog engaged in a jousting contest at court.
683 Czok 1991.
684 "Ein französischer Sänger, der den Zug aufführte, bewillkommte darauf die ganze königliche Gesellschaft, mit einem in seiner Landessprache verfertigten Liede und fügte zu des Königs Lob hinzu, wie es kein Wunder sey, daß unter einem so gütigen Monarchen auch selbst die wildesten Thiere ihre Natur veränderten und sich als zahme Geschöpfe ihm zu Füssen legten." Loen 1749.b, 57.
685 The best survey on this subject is given by Vec 1998.
686 This is attested by numerous publications; see Ehalt 1979; Schlechte 1990.a; Holenstein 1992; H. Bauer 1992, 147–181; Berns/Rahn 1995; Vec 1998.
687 See M. Weber 1922 and Elias 1997.
688 Vec 1998, 201.
689 Ibid.
690 V. Bauer 1993, 9.
691 Schlechte 1990.a, 4.
692 "Sollen die Unterthanen die Majestät des Königs erkennen, so müssen sie begreiffen, daß bei ihm die höchste Gewalt und Macht sey, und dem nach müssen sie ihre Handlungen dergestalt einrichten, damit sie Anlaß nehmen, seine Macht und Gewalt daraus zu erkennen. Der gemeine Mann, welcher bloß an den äusserlichen Sinnen hanget, und die Vernunfft wenig gebrauchet, kann sich nicht allein recht vorstellen, was die Majestät des Königs ist, aber durch die Dinge, so in seine Augen fallen, und seine übrigen Sinnen rühren, bekommt er einen klaren Begriff von seiner Majestät, Macht und Gewalt." Rohr 1990, 2.
693 Eichberg 1977 and Brainard 1979.
694 See, for example, Eichberg 1977.
695 Baillie 1967.
696 V. Bauer 1993, 39.
697 Baillie 1967.
698 "Die Meublen und Tapisserien sind nach dem Unterschied der Gemächer unterschieden. In der ersten Antichambre sind sie nicht so kostbar, als in der letztern." Rohr 1990, 73; on ceremonial and decorum see especially Langer 2002.
699 "um mehr als Hofkultur, Aesthetik und Kunst, nämlich um die architektonische Realisierung eines Herrschaftsanspruchs, um die Demonstration eines politischen Machtwillens." Baumgart 1981, 27.
700 "An einen Herrscher wie Ludwig XIV. trat man immer heran; man trug ihm etwas vor, man bat ihn um etwas, und wenn er das Für und Wider aus dem Munde verschiedener, sich um ihn bemühender Menschen gehört hatte, entschied er. Die Energien wurden ihm gewissermaßen zugetrieben; er hielt sich zurück und wußte sich ihrer zu bedienen. Er brauchte keine großen eigenen Ideen zu haben, und er hatte sie nicht; die Ideen der anderen strömten ihm zu, und er wußte sie zu nutzen." Elias 1997, 199.
701 On the palace as the "Residence in the Neustadt," see also Kuke 2002, 225.
702 SächsHStA, OHMA Cap. II, Nr. 3q.
703 "In die Retraiten und Retiraden ist an vielen Orten niemand erlaubt zu gehen, als Fürstlichen Personen, die sich an dem Hofe aufhalten, sie mögen nun den Anverwandten beyzuzehlen seyn, oder nicht, ingleichen den Abgesandten und grösten Ministris." Rohr 1990, 78.
704 Lairesse 1728 (Part One), 4:52.
705 Lairesse 1730 (Part Two), 8:58.
706 "Diese erstbenannten Couleuren haben auch ihre Sinn-Bedeutungen und besondere Eigenschaften." Lairesse 1728 (Part One), 4:42.
707 "Das Gelbe vor [= für] den Glanz und die Glorie, das Rothe vor die Gewalt oder die Liebe, das Blaue vor die Göttlichkeit, das Purpurrothe vor die Authorität oder obere Gewalt, das Blaulicht-rothe vor die Unterthänigkeit, das Grüne vor die Dienstbarkeit." Ibid., 42–43.
708 Baillie 1967, 199; see also Wagner-Rieger 1979.
709 See Brainard 1979.
710 On "conspicuous consumption" see Pallach 1987.
711 There is a very detailed account of the contemporary state of research into the nature of animals in Zedler 1995, vol. 43 (1745) under "Thier," cols. 1334ff.
712 As has already been noted, the emotions and instincts that the courtier was supposed to have a perfect capacity for controlling were used in the animal figures to give each animal its own particular character.
713 On the contemporary interpretation of this idea, see Zedler 1995, vol. 43 (1745), under "Thier," col. 1347.
714 "Vollkommene [Tiere] sind solche, welche nicht nur mehr organa oder Leibestheile haben, als die andern, sondern an welchen man auch meistens den Unterscheid des Geschlechts, ob sie Mann oder Weib sind, gar genau erkennen kann; dergleichen sind Hunde, Katzen, Schaafe, Rindvieh, Hirsche, Bären,

Elephanten, Löwen u.d.g. nur bey dem Federvieh ist es etwas undeutlicher." Zedler 1995, vol. 43 (1745), Artikel "Thier," col. 1360. Among the animals he designated "imperfect" were amphibians and arthropods.

715 "jene Gesellschaft, welche ... ineinandergeschachtelt und durch die besonderen Herrschafts- und Repräsentationsfunktionen des Königs kompliziert, zugleich die Gestalt des Königspalastes bestimmt, der die Gesellschaft als Ganzes beherbergen soll." Elias 1997, 71.

716 I do not intend to go into the question as to whether this was ever the wish of Augustus the Strong. But we do have a beautiful description of a magnificent hunting party held at Moritzburg in 1718, when the participants had to spend the night in carriages, barns, and even in the open air, and on waking the following morning found that all their personal belongings had been stolen; Loen 1749.b, 58–59.

717 "im Sein" and "im Tun"; Vec 1998, 147ff.

718 "Als erstlich die Schönheit, zum andern die Rarität und drittens die mit beyden verknüpfte Nutzbarkeit. Solche drey Qualitaeten machen eine Sache angenehm, kostbar und nöthig." Quoted from I. Menzhausen 1982.a, 84.

719 For the eighteenth century artificial light is synonymous with luxury, as is clearly shown not only by the great expenses incurred for the nocturnal illumination of rooms and, at festivities, even of public places (see the floodlights designed in 1710 by Andreas Gärtner for the *Mathematisch-Physikalischer Salon* in Dresden; Schillinger 1992, cat. no. 3, p. 10), but also for the illumination of whole towns on great occasions. The latter was also a special way to paying tribute, as for instance when the citizens of Dresden lit up streets to mark the return of the elector from Warsaw, illuminating pictures – in some cases, one might even say, images – in his honor. The unaccustomed abundance of light in familiar surroundings made the scene into an image in own right. On the costliness of light and light-sources, see Klappenbach 2001, esp. 11–17.

720 A convincing account is given by Schmid 1997, esp. 16.

721 Except for Delft faïence with its lead-over-tin glaze in imitation of porcelain.

722 "Das lebendige Spiel der schimmernden Glanzlichter einer herrlichen Glasur, das sich einmal über grosse, glatte Flächen behäbig ausbreitet, dann wieder auf engem Raume auf Spitzen, Graten und anderen plastischen Erhebungen zu einer Garbe knisternder Funken entfaltet oder auch als Reflexlichter tiefe Schatten auflöst, erfordert höchstes künstlerisches Feingefühl. Porzellan wird erst im Licht lebendig, es saugt Licht in sich ein, das unter der Glasur, auf dem weissen Grunde ein magisches Leben erhält und schliesslich, vielfach gebrochen, aus dem Werk herausstrahlt." Fichtner 1936.a, 15, 16.

723 On the role of luminosity in wall-fittings in the Rococo, see Köhler 2000

724 "In den Schlössern Frankreichs dienten Spiegel der Selbstbespiegelung einer Gesellschaft, die in ihnen nicht nur gleich dem Porzellan ihre Ideale verkörpert fand – schön, kostbar und zerbrechlich–, sondern sie auch zum subtilen Machtmittel entwickelte." Loibl 1989, 82.

725 "Sie sind bey der Architectur und Ausmeublirung ihrer Fürstlichen Residentz- und Lust-Häuser nicht mit dem zufrieden, was ihnen die sinnreichsten Meister in Franckreich und Italien, Holland und England an die Hand geben, sondern sie müssen auch noch dazu, so wol bey der Bau-Art, als bey den Meublen, aus der Türckey, China, und andern Ländereyen ausserhalb Europa, neue Erfindungen herholen." Rohr 1990, 80–81.

726 See John Stalker: Treatise of Japaning and Varnishing, Oxford 1688. The English rendering is translated from H. Bauer 1991, 1: "Die Europäer sollten sich nicht länger in der unbegründeten Annahme sonnen, sie hätten alle Welt hinter sich gelassen mit ihren stattlichen Palästen, kostbaren Tempeln, aufwendigen Bauten. Das alte und das moderne Rom sollen dem Ruhme eines einzigen Landes weichen: Japan allein hat den stolzen Vatikan übertroffen, was Schönheit und Großartigkeit betrifft."

727 On the pavilion-like pagoda as a type, see H. Bauer 1991.

728 For other instances of the temporary relaxation of ceremonial strictures through the use of well-ordered forms (masquerades, peasant weddings, etc.), see Schnitzer 1995.

729 "sind gemeiniglich manche strenge Ceremonien, die man in den Residentien bey Hofe verspührt, verbannet, und man spühret allenthalben mehr Freyheit und ungezwungenes Wesen." Rohr 1990, quoted from H. Bauer 1992, 82.

730 Syndram 2001, 65.

731 Carsten-Peter Warncke came to a similar conclusion in his very illuminating essay on the display-piece "Der Hofstaat des Großmoguls" ("The Court of the Grand Mogul") in the Green Vaults in Dresden; see Warncke 1989.

732 1740 saw Frederick the Great come to power in Prussia (reg. 1740–1786), and Maria Theresa in Vienna (reg. 1740–1780); 1741 saw the accession to power of Elizabeth Petrowna (reg. 1741–1762) in Russia.

733 Bauer has shown this with reference to the electorate of Cologne, Hannover, and Württemberg; V. Bauer 1993, 96ff. This author also observes a general trend away from officialdom and ceremonial in the eighteenth century, using five categories of court; V. Bauer 1993, 103ff. His five types are: 1. the ceremonial court (absolutist princes, electoral princes etc.); 2. the imperial court as a type in its own right; 3. the patriarchal court (with the prince setting a moral example); 4. the social court (only a limited measure of social distinctions, and not so much politically as militarily organized); 5. the artistic court ("Musenhof"; smaller courts with strong commitment to patronage of the arts, branch families of great dynasties, etc.), see ibid., 55ff. Bauer sees the trend in Germany as proceeding from the patriarchal court at the end of the seventeenth century via the ceremonial court at the beginning of the eighteenth to the social court from around 1740, with numerous exceptions deriving from political or financial factors; see ibid., 78.

734 V. Bauer 1993, 103ff.; this trend can be seen very clearly at the French court under Louis XV.

735 As a result, ceremonial, which had been raised to the status of a science by Rohr, became simply "court law" ("Hofrecht"), that is to say no more than a part of law in general; V. Bauer 1993, 103ff.

736 Hanway 1753, 227.

737 "liegen Schönheiten und Ordnungen, und ihren Regeln muß man folgen. Daher ist sie das Muster oder das Vorbild der Künste ... Die Natur hält die Grundrisse aller regelmäßigen Werke, und die Entwürfe aller Zierrathen, die uns gefallen können, in sich; und die Regeln werden nicht von den Künsten geschaffen, sondern sie sind in dem Beyspiele der Natur vorgezeichnet. Die Künste sind daher nie vollkommner, als wenn sie die Natur selbst vorstellen." Gottsched, Johann Christoph: *Handlexicon oder kurzgefaßtes Wörterbuch der schönen Wissenschaften und freyen Künst* (Leipzig 1760), the article on "Nature" as quoted in Bursche 1977, 146.

738 Jong 1997, 248.

739 Schlechte 1990.a, 26.

740 A rendering from the German translation ("Die Kunst ist die Ergänzung der Natur und ein anderes, zweites Sein, das diese aufs äusserste verschönt, ja sie in ihren Werken zu übertreffen trachtet. Sie ist stolz darauf, eine andere künstliche Welt der ersteren hinzugefügt zu haben.") in Gracián 1957, 61.

741 H. Bauer 1992, 193.

742 Ibid., 189.

743 Ibid., 189–195.

744 "Raubvogel, der ein angefressenes Huhn vor sich liegen hatte, es war das blutige Gerippe und das Eingeweide zu sehen und alles so natürlich, auch von Farbe, als ob es lebte." Müller 1907, 2:97.

745 See Heckscher 1967.

746 Here is not the place to go more deeply into the whole problem of the term "Baroque," which is not only used to designate an epoch but also a style and an artistic concept; on this subject see, for example, H. Bauer 1992 und Tintelnot 1956.

747 On the phenomenon of the Rococo, and for some suggestions as to its interpretation, see H. Bauer 1962, Bursche 1977, and especially Vergoossen 1996.

748 It would take us too far from our present subject to discuss these changes, which had their roots in various branches of the natural sciences. In the field of botany, one may mention Carl von Linné's work of systematization; for an account of the developments in zoology and the changes in zoological illustration, see Nissen 1966, I.

749 "Das Rokoko ist im Grunde nicht mehr barock. Das große Welttheater ist wie Rauch vergangen; auf der untief gewordenen Bühne spielen die gewichtlosen divertimenti eines Neumanierismus von sublimer musikalischer und spiritueller, längst nicht mehr plastischer Kultur. Porzellanfiguren des 18. Jahrhunderts und Kleinbronzen des 16. Jahrhunderts gehören zum gleichen Formgeschlecht. Überall begegnen

sich nun die zwei Stilstufen hüben und drüben des Barock." Hofer 1956, 162.
750 Wölfflin 1965, 3.
751 In his publication of 1977, Bursche quite rightly distanced himself from the opinion, widespread in the literature of the first half of the twentieth century, that Rocaille was the result of an abstraction from forms in art and had no direct connection with the observation of nature; Bursche 1977, 143.
752 Peter Fuhring points out that the period from 1674 on there were a number of printings of Longinus's treatise *On the Sublime* (in Boileau's translation), in which the element of surprise plays a central role; see Fuhring 1998, 28.
753 Leibniz 1720; according to Bursche 1977, 146, the first writer on art theory to be influenced by Leibniz's theory of monads was Johann Christoph Gottsched, but around 1730 the phenomenon of the Rococo was already in evidence – at first in prints – and spreading quickly.
754 I cannot endorse the opinion expressed by Rainer Rückert and others (Rückert 1990, 114, col. 2 – with the suggestion that Kaendler was following in Kirchner's footsteps) that the two artists exerted a far-reaching influence on one another; apart from minor compositional borrowings effected by Kirchner for his Bustard, the figures show that the two artists had quite different attitudes and approaches, as will be shown in the following section.
755 It should be noted that the lion is also regarded as the king of the animals in other cultures, such as China, where lion figures often bear the sign of the Emperor on their foreheads.
756 In 1733 there was a hovering white eagle, made in wood with a crown, in the bronze room, see Heres 1991, 54.
757 "Seine [Kaendler's] Auffassung der in der Heraldik häufig verwendeten Tiere verriet so viel Einfühlung in alles Organische, zeigte so viel Eleganz und Schwung, daß der König sich zur Erschaffung seiner Monumentalporzellane keinen besseren Künstler als diesen aufgeweckten jungen Mann wünschen konnte." Walcha 1973, 89.
758 "Der Adler hat Kändler zu schaffen gemacht, denn er durfte ihn nicht mit derselben Naturalistik behandeln, wie seine anderen Vögel. Die Adler sind nicht in die Naturgeschichte einbezogen, sie sind noch umstrickt von einer alten metaphysischen Vorstellung, welche in ihnen ein Überwesen sieht, ein Gleichnis für die Staatsgewalt... Ein naturalistisch gebildeter Adler könnte nicht monumental wirken, doch gerade das muß er, wenn seine Bedeutung zum Ausdruck kommen soll." Albiker 1935, 51.
759 Ibid., 52.
760 Gröger 1956, fig. 4.
761 "Einen großen Adler, Welcher den rechten Flügel in Die Höhe Von Sich strecket, Deutet zugleich eines großen Herren Gnade an." BA, IAa.18, fol. 323a.
762 "Sind Kändlers Tiere und Vögel nur in Porzellan vorzustellen, so kann man sich die meisten von Kirchners Tieren ebensogut in Ton oder Stein gebildet denken." Handt/Rackebrand 1956, 32.
763 See, for example, Albiker 1935, 27. Albiker, however, takes Kirchner's side, suggesting that he fell foul of a certain interference on Kaendler's part, which led to his later animals being less powerful and less psychological; Albiker sees these figures as attempts at naturalism, but his only evidence for this is Kirchner's treatment of the animals' coats etc.
764 Albiker 1935, 25.
765 "Ein Fuchß, so Eine Hünne frißt, Lebens größe"; BA, IAa.18, fol. 322a.
766 "Eine Indianische Ratze, wie solche in Königl. Löwen Hauße am Leben sind, gefertiget. Deren postament worauf sie ruhet Stellet einen Korn Sack vor, wie er oben offen ist und die Ratze daraus frißet"; BA, IAa.24, fol. 173a.
767 See, for example, the engraving by Barlow, illustrated in Benker 1993.
768 "Durch die bildende Kunst werden der Wissenschaft die Wege geebnet, vor allen Dingen durch die Malerei. Der Erfolg dieser Entwicklung liegt bei der Entfaltung der Wissenschaft im 18. und 19. Jahrhundert. Sämtliche Tiere-bildenden Künstler, auch wenn sie für ihre Zeit eine große Bedeutung gehabt haben, auch wenn sie für die Entwicklung der Kunst heute, rückläufig betrachtet, eine wichtige Stellung einnehmen, haben doch nichts weiter getan, als mit aufopfernder Vorarbeit das Hauptziel, die Wissenschaft, vorbereitet." Albiker 1935, 2.
769 Ibid., 15.
770 Carl Albiker had the following to say on this subject: "Kirchner sees much more to an animal than simply a piece of nature in motion" ("Kirchner sieht im Tier viel mehr als nur ein Stück sich bewegende Natur."); Albiker 1935, 19.
771 BA, IAa.18, fol. 208a.
772 Kaendler's stone sculptures from the 1730s–tombs and memorial stones – also follow this principle; see the account of the tomb for Gottfried Keil, for instance, in Gröger 1956, 102–117; on Kaendler's stone sculptures generally, see also Walcha 1938, Parts 2 and 3.
773 "einer guten Drehung der Gliedmassen und Bewegung des Hauptes, der Aerme, Hände und Füsse"; Lairesse 1730 (Part Two), 265.
774 "einen Hund, liegend"; BA, IAa.18, fol. 263b.
775 One example is to be found in the Kunstkammer in the Badisches Landesmuseum, Schloss Karlsruhe, and is illustrated in Piper 1921, 160, 161; see also Albiker 1935, 54. Two further examples are preserved in the Green Vaults in Dresden, but with a different attribution. See furthermore the copperplate engraving by the "Hausbuchmeister" (end of 15th cent.) with the same motif, illustrated in List 1993, 258.
776 "den Vogel Casuarium in Lebensgröße"; BA, IAa.18, fol. 263b.
777 The cassowary's plumage is blackish brown, and the neck is bright blue with red "wattles" hanging down in front. The legs and helmet are light brown.
778 "Ein Ballais Stück Den Vogel Rohrtummel genannt ist ... wegen seines starck befederten Halßes und andern an sich habenden Eigenschafften wunderlich anzusehen, ist vorgestellet wie er in Schilff-Rohr, Binsen und Graß wie es in Teigen [Teichen] zu wachsen Pfleget sitzet"; BA, IAa.24, fol. 108a.
779 "die Stücke oben desto beßer verputzt wißen wollen damit sie das Auge an sich zögen, u. nicht das Postament so consideriret würde"; BA, IAe.3, fols. 274b–275a.
780 "Einen Truthahn in Lebens Größe"; BA, IAa.20, fol. 51a.
781 BA, IAe.3, fol. 271b.
782 BA, IAe.3, fols. 347b–348a.
783 BA, IAa.18, fol. 364a.
784 See illustration in Pietsch 1998, 208.
785 "hat der Modellirer Kantlern einen großen Raben nach Indianischer Art ... poussiret"; BA, IAa.18, fol. 100a/b.
786 Still to be seen on display at the "Schauhalle" museum at the Meissen porcelain manufactory is a third, as yet unpublished, figure of a large macaw (inv. 3753). According to the mold book, the model for this figure (mold no. 24) was a re-creation with additions, in June 1921 by Karl Hubert Stein, who was responsible for so many of the re-creations done at this time. It is recorded that Stein did his work using parts of old molds, but we no longer have knowledge of any such piece. The close-lying wings, the execution of the tail-feathers, the head (quite different from that of the downward-climbing Macaw), and the kind of detail on the base suggest that Stein took a large degree of license with his model, or even that many parts were done afresh. The sources do not tell us whether this model is related either to an old figure or to eighteenth-century molds; consequently, we do not know whether there is another work by Kaendler lying behind this parrot figure, as the annotation in the mold book "after an old porcelain figure" ("nach altem Porzellanmodell") could be a reference to a nineteenth-century figure done in the style of the eighteenth century.
787 One of the findings of a restoration project illustrates this point tellingly. In the case of some realizations of the Macaw, the long tail-feathers were found to have been produced separately from the rest of the figure and then cemented on once both parts were fully fired. In some instances, however, the manufactory did take the riskier path and succeeded in firing a number of figures in one piece; information kindly supplied by Heike Ulbrich, Dresden Porcelain Collection.
788 "Eine Große Löffel Ganß Welche einen Karpffen Verschlinget"; BA, IAa.18, fol. 323a.
789 BA, IAa.18, fol. 18a.
790 "habe ich endes bemelter im Jahre 1731 dem weißen Fisch Reihger wie er im Königl Schloß Hoffe zu Dresten zurselbigen Zeit am leben befindlich war, in seiner Natürlichen Größe auf die Porceläin Fabrique zum gebrauch wie er in Schilffe stehet und Frösche und Fische bey sich hat müßen poussiren"; BA, IAa.24, fol. 177a.
791 "Die Hrn. Arcanisten sagen, H. Kändler wäre zur selben Zeit, als er ao: 1731. dergl. Arbeith gethan noch nicht bey der Fabrique und in

Königl: Diensten gewesen, sondern hätte sich nur zu recommendiren gesucht, folglich würde ihm die Manufactur Cassa des wegen keine Satisfaction zu thun haben." BA, IAa.24, fol. 137b.
792 It is possible Kaendler's inspiration for the frog he included on the gravestone came from one of the tombstones of the Wettins (Ernestine line), on which frogs feature conspicuously. In this context, Eva Schmidt made an attempt to interpret the frog as a resurrection symbol; Schmidt 1970. However, when one considers that the frog is very similar in appearance to the toad, and that the toad is definitely one of the verminous agents of decomposition that are part of the iconography of death, then one can spare oneself the bother of investigating the frog's pre-Christian associations and of constructing a tradition to suit.
793 "Hingegen hat der Modellirer Kentler ... poussiret und gefertiget 1.) eine alte nebst einer jungen Ziege"; BA, IAa.18, fols. 207b–208a.
794 The nanny-goat has four horns. The process of breeding has deprived the present-day domestic goat of the two smaller horns in the middle, which are now no more than little humps. In one instance (the Meissen Nanny-Goat at the Metropolitan Museum of Art, New York), the repairer omitted to add these smaller horns; in the case of the Nanny-Goat in Philadelphia they broke off at some point, and were transformed into "stumps" by a restorer.
795 For this information my thanks go to Dr. med. vet. Fritz Wittwer of Kleindietwil.
796 "Was als plastischer Raum wahrgenommen werden kann, ist nichts anderes als die Kraft jener Vektoren, die wir an der Oberfläche bemerken." Boehm 1977, unpaginated.
797 Ibid.
798 "außen der Anschauung [anzeigt], was außen, aber auch was innen ist, z. B. wie der von der Oberfläche jeweils umschlossene Körper hinsichtlich seiner Schwere, seiner Masse, Dichte oder Struktur, d. h. hinsichtlich der im Dunkel seiner Materialität liegenden Ausdruckswerte beschaffen ist." Ibid.
799 [dass] "die Form die Materie nicht subordiniert, sondern freisetzt." Ibid.
800 These comments are of course equally applicable to models that are not finally realized in a ceramic medium such as porcelain: to models, for instance, that are to be cast in metal.
801 "Mit einer äußerst differenzierten und detaillierten Oberflächengestaltung, aufgelockerten Konturen, spannungsreichen Überschneidungen und temperamentvollen Gesten, die jedoch das Gesamtbild der plastischen Erscheinung nicht aus dem Auge verlieren, entsprach Kaendler vollkommen dem Gestaltungswillen des Spätbarock und den damit verbundenen Forderungen nach raumgreifender Dynamik und naturgetreuem Ausdruck. Trotz der Unmittelbarkeit der in Porzellan festgehaltenen Bewegungsmotive schuf Kaendler nicht wirkliche Abbilder der Natur, sondern unterwarf seine Plastiken einem eigenen, künstlerischen Gestaltungsprinzip, das durch einen kalkulierten Aufbau und eine in sich geschlossene Komposition gekennzeichnet ist." Pietsch 1997.a, 77.
802 It is of course the case that Kaendler did not always achieve this in the same measure in all of his models. The principle is most particularly evident in his later and more mature palace animals.
803 J. Menzhausen 2002.
804 SächsHStA, loc. 1342, Vol. X, fol. 488a/b. The sentence quoted originated in connection with Kaendler's second offensive against Höroldt of 1738/39, in which he was concerned to demonstrate that it would be financially beneficial for the manufactory if he, Kaendler, were to be put in charge of the molders. He justifies this by saying that a molder was in a position to do as much "Bildhauerei" ("sculpting") as he did in one whole year.
805 On this point, see Warncke 1989.
806 "zwischen entfalteter Sensibilität für das Einzelne bis zum geringfügigsten Detail und rationalem oder emotionalem Besitzergreifen der Welt als Ganzem [...], zwischen neuer Qualität der Wahrnehmung und Skepsis gegenüber der Fähigkeit der Sinne [...], zwischen Individualität und ständischer Ordnung"; Olbrich 1985, 13.
807 See Welzel 1997.
808 "Der damit gesetzte Anspruch stellte Vorhandenes sowohl quantitativ als auch qualitativ in Frage. Mit einem ungeheuren Aufwand wurde alles Vorhandene auf seine Tauglichkeit hin in Zweifel gezogen und nach Orientierungen in der eigenen dynastischen Tradition oder bei herausragenden Höfen und Ereignissen der europäischen Geschichte und Gegenwart gesucht. Damit wurde die substantielle wie ideengeschichtliche Basis geschaffen, die Sachsen in der Regierungszeit Augusts des Starken den Ruf eines kulturellen Leithofes auf dem Kontinent einbrachte." Schlechte 1990.b, 58.
809 As for instance in the "Schmuck-Cabinet" of the electoral princess and later princess elector of Saxony, Maria Antonia, in the Palais Taschenberg; see Kunze-Köllensperger 1997, 35–43.
810 Ducret 1962, no. 53, 152.
811 Sotheby's Paris, 27. 6. 2001, no. 144.
812 Kunze 1982.
813 The figures delivered in 1736 (Source 20) are to be included in the calculation.
814 Boltz 1996.
815 Syndram 2001, 81–82.
816 This is documented by historical postcards.
817 "da sie iezt nicht mehr wie sonst als Meuble bestimmt, sondern als Wercke der Kunst anzusehen [seien]"; SachsHStA, loc. 2407, Acta die Veräußerung derer bey der Churfürstl. Bibliothec befindlichen Doubletten ... auch Anwend. und anderweite Placirung derer jetzt darinnen befindlichen Porcelaines und Mobilien betr. Anno 1774. The letter of May 30, 1787, is to be found in the unpaginated section after fol. 100.
818 "Parmi les objects de grande dimension, la manufacture a fait, vers 1730, une série de grands animaux ... destinés à orner le grand escalier qui conduissait à la bibliothèque électorale située à Dresde, et au-dessous de laquelle sont de nombreuses et grandes salles renfermant une réunion innombrable de pièces de porcelaine de la manufacture de Meissen, de la Chine et du Japon." Brongniart 1844, 379–380.
819 An informative summary of the history of the collection is to be found in Pietsch 1998, 3–15.
820 "an currenten Geschirren, ingl: an allerhand kleinen Thieren, Vogeln und Figuren zum Verkauff kein Mangel vorfalle"; BA, IAa.24b, fol. 148a.
821 Many of these animal figures are illustrated in Albiker 1935 and 1959. Particular mention may be made of the numerous middle-size bird figures possessed by Kurfürst (Elector) Clemens August; see Köllmann 1961.
822 "einen Pappagoy in Thon bossiret große Sorte, vor Mr. Huêt"; Kaendler's work report for May 1740, SächsHStA, loc. 1342, Vol. XI, fol. 193a. For this dealer from Paris Kaendler produced a number of parrots, which in spite of being referred to as "groß" were hardly taller than 35 cm (incl. pedestal).
823 "ins Königl. Balläis gehörig ist"; BA, IAa.24, fol. 343a.
824 "Annoch unterschiedliche Eigel Blätter nebst andern zu behör, Die Eigel Gabichte damit zu verziren in Thon poussiret"; BA, IAb.14, fol. 102a.
825 "Halß und Kopff zu der Perel Henne gefertiget [wurde] um selbige zu verändern"; BA, IAb.9, fol. 35a.
826 A fine survey covering many of these small models is given by the sale catalog Ball/Graupe 1933.
827 To quote Pflugk's letter to Fleuter: "We now finally have permission to sell birds of this kind" ("Nun ist zwahr dergleichen Vögel verkauffen zu dorffen erlaubniß vorhanden"); BA, IAa.23, fol. 199a/b.
828 "Allerunterthänigster Vortrag: Es hat der Obriste Meyer vor den Kayserl: Obrist-Stallmeister Herr-Grafen von Altheim Sechs porcelaine-Aufsatz-Stücke von Thieren, als: 2. Affen/2. Pappegoyen und 2. Elster auf dem Waaren-Lager zu Dreßden und zwar in solcher Maaße, daß die Affen einer Elle hoch werden sollen, bestellet. Nun haben zwar Ihro Königl: Majestät die allergnädigste Erlaubnüß ertheilet, dergleichen Vögel als hier verlanget werden an privatos zuverlassen827, inmaßen der Frantzösische Kauffmann Huet solche zeithero bekommen; Alleine, da von denen Affen noch zur Zeit niemand ein Stück erhalten, sondern selbige insgesamt aus hiesiger porcelaine-Fabrique zu Ihro Königl: Majestät Indianischen Palais geliefert worden; So beruhet zu Ihro Königl: Majestät höchstgefälligen Entschlüßung: ob vor besagten Herrn Grafen von Altheim vorher erwehnte Thiere unter welchen der Hoff-Factor Chladni einen dergleichen Affen auf 130. biß 150. Thlr. dem Preyße nach schätzet, gefertiget und an ihn geliefert werden sollen? Meißen den 23. Aug: anno 1735." BA, IAa.23, fol. 201a.
829 Ibid., fol. 211a.
830 SächsHStA, loc. 520, Vol. 1735, fol. 98b.
831 "Vor Ihro Königl. Majestät in Pohlen und ChurFürstl. Durchl. zu Sachßen, wurden auf allergnädigsten

hohen mündlichen Befehl an den Herrn Grafen Moritz In Sachßen geliefert, als: 2 Stk. große Vogelbauer Aufsatz-Stücken, so defect/ 1 Stk. große Eule und 1 Stk. großen Affen, so alle beyde auch defect, insgesamt vor Thlr. 100.–/Maurice de Saxe/HvBrühl." SächsHStA, loc. 521, Vol. 1737, Appendix P.

832 "Zehen Thaler Sechzehn Groschen, sage 10 T 16 Gr, Träger Lohn vor 16 Mann mit 8 Kästen allerh. Porcel: Vögel und Thiere, welche wegen vieles Raumes in Meißen nicht länger aufbehalten werden können und der Gefahr und Zerbrechlichkeit halber haben herauf ins König. Japanische Palais getragen werden müßen, seynd mir von dem Herrn Hoff factor Chladni richtig bezahlt worden . . ., Dreßden den 22 Decembr 1734 ... auf iedene Mann 16 Gr gerechnet, [gez.] Christian Hermann und Consorten." ... "Obiges Specifirtes Porcelain ist auf Sr: Königl: May: aller gnädigst. hohen Befehl richtig in daß Königl: Jap: Palais gelifert worden und mit 10 Thlr 16 Gr veraccordirt, wirt hirmit Attestiret, Martin Teuffert, BettMeister." SächsHStA, loc. 520, Vol. 1734, bill no. 165; as kindly pointed out by Maureen Cassidy-Geiger.

833 What was meant by the "unterschiedenen schönen Groppen" of 1733 is not clear, especially as the famous small Meissen figure-groups were only produced after the middle of the 1730s.

834 "war das gantz neuerbauete, blau und Gold staffirte kostbare Porcellain-Waaren-Lager offen ... in welchen nebst einer erstaunenden Menge von allerhand groß und kleinen Geschirren, kostbarsten Vasen und Aufsätzen, auch Löwen, Panther, Bäre, Affen, Papageyen, und andere inn- und ausländische Thiere und Vögel in Lebens-Größe nebst unterschiedenen schönen Groppen zu sehen waren." Anonymous 1733, 43. The journal of the Meissen castle guard has the following entry: "On December 17, there was the homage-paying ceremony in the castle, and the warehouse was lit up on the orders of Councillor of the Commission Fleuter and opened, with the nobility being allowed in but, however, a sentry being placed by the entrance." ["den 17. Dec. War die Huldigung auf dem Schloße, da denn auf Befehl des Hn. Commission-Rath Fleuters das Waaren-Lager illuminiret und eröffnet, auch die Noblesse in selbiges eingelaßen worden, vor welches jedoch eine Schildwacht gesezet gewesen."]; SächsHStA, loc. 14636 Vol. III, 1733, fol. 58a.

835 Pietsch 1998, 8.

836 "das fatale Aussehen einer Vorrathskammer"; Quoted from Pietsch 1998, 8.

837 "derjenigen Stücke, welche gegenwärtig als Doubletten von der Königl. Porzellan- und Gefäßesammlung entbehrt werden könnten" ... "Pfau, in schreitender Stellung, den Schweif ... entfaltend, Höhe 44 1/2 Zoll" Staatl. Kunstsammlungen Dresden, Archiv, Akte 10: Akte der königlichen Porzellan und Gefäßesammlung Dresden 1848–1874, fol. 39.

838 Ibid., fols. 86a–88b.

839 Pietsch 1998, 8.

840 Staatl. Kunstsammlungen Dresden, Archiv, record 10, Akte der königlichen Porzellan und Gefäßesammlung Dresden 1848–1874, fols. 220ff.

841 "unendlich selten sind und mit wahrhaft fabelhaften Preisen bezahlt werden"; Graesse 1873, 6.

842 Staatl. Kunstsammlungen Dresden, Archiv, Akte 11: Akte der königlichen Porzellan und Gefäßesammlung Dresden 1875–1876, fol. 18.

843 Staatl. Kunstsammlungen Dresden, Porzellansammlung, "Abgebbare Doubletten 1912–1920" (= Kunstsammlungen Inventare Nr. 351.a).

844 Kunze 1982, 37.

845 Ibid., 42.

846 Ibid., 44; however, if Rococo-style pieces were without defects, the manufactory at first never sold them unpainted.

847 Quoted from Kunze 1982, 43.

848 The specimen in the Metropolitan Museum of Art, New York, is about a quarter smaller than the eighteenth-century originals, but is painted in a deceptively similar manner. One further example, a small one in the possession of the Pauls-Eisenbeiss Foundation in the *Haus zum Kirschgarten* in Basel (historic room in the "Kleiner Kirschgarten"), which would seem to have been made around the middle of the nineteenth century, is more clearly different but likewise has no mark, and has purple rather than luster and a pattern in relief on the collar.

849 Simpson 1987, 50.

850 Staatl. Kunstsammlungen Dresden, Porzellansammlung, "Verkauf und Tausch bei der Königl. Sächs. Porzellan- und Gefäße-Sammlung 1832–1842," fol. 4.

851 On this exchange generally, see Cassidy-Geiger 2003.a.

852 "Verzeichniss der an die Gefässe-Sammlung der Königl. Französischen Porzellan-Manufactur zu Sèvres aus der Königl. Sächs. Porzellan- und Gefässe-Sammlung zu Dresden abgegebenen Stücke"; Staatl. Kunstsammlungen Dresden, Porzellansammlung, "Verkauf und Tausch bei der Königl. Sächs. Porzellan- und Gefäße-Sammlung 1832–1842," fols. 9a–10a.

853 "nous avon à regretter 1. le rupture entier en nombreux morceaux du pelican, 2. quelques avaries au Paon et surtout au Vautour, 3. la fracture dela jambe droite posterieure du Rhinoceros" ... "mais le Pelican est entièrement perdu"; Ibid.

854 Staatl. Kunstsammlungen Dresden, Porzellansammlung, "Verzeichnis der Doubletten der Königl. Porzellan- und Gefäße-Sammlung (um 1850–1854) geführt von Karl August Friedrich Böttcher," unbound sheet in the appendix, fol. 256 (= Kunstsammlungen Inventare no. 347).

855 "Nachdem Se.Königl. Majestät den von Ihnen unter dem 21ten Januar d. J. beantragten Verkauf von neun Stück bisher unter den Doubletten der Königl. Porzellan- und Gefäßesammlung aufbewahrten Thierfiguren, von Meißner Porzellan, an den Factor der hiesigen Königl. Porzellanniederlage Teichert für die Summe von 555 rt – die Allerhöchste Genehmigung zu ertheilen geruht haben, werden Sie hierdurch veranlaßt, die gedachten Figuren gegen den Empfang der Zahlung zu verabfolgen, die Summe an den Separatfond der Königl. Sammlungen einzuzahlen und den Abgang der Figuren im Inventarium der Doubletten zu bemerken." Staatl. Kunstsammlungen Dresden, Archiv, Akte 10 "Akte der königlichen Porzellan und Gefäßesammlung Dresden 1848–1874," fol. 2, letter of February 3, 1849.

856 "20 hindostanische Bronzegefäße"; ibid., fols. 1 and 3. Permission to purchase is granted, but Klemm is only to give Petersen 80 talers instead of the 100 that he asked for. Another letter on this subject makes it clear that the vessels were from the Reding Collection, which had been sold at auction in Hamburg the year before; Klemm's intention was to exhibit the bronzes together with the "Indian clay vessels" ("indischen Tongefäßen"), SächsHStA, Ministerium des Innern Nr. 17261, fol. 45a/b.

857 "Auf Ihre unterm 5ten dieses Monaths wegen des von dem Factor in der Königl. Porzellan Niederlage Teichert gewünschten Erkaufes von 18 Stück Thierfiguren aus den Doubletten Vorräthen der Königl. Porzellansammlung für den Preis von 800 rthl anher erstattete, nachträglich jedoch dahin abgeänderte Anzeige, daß solcher für jene Summe 20 Stück Thierfiguren und 2 Stück rothe Vasen zu erwerben wünsche, gebe ich Ihnen andurch zu erkennen, daß auf dies Gesuch nicht eingegangen werden kann. Die von Teichert bezeichneten Gegenstände sind zusammen auf 1 370 rthl excl. der beiden Vasen taxirt, und daß die Taxpreise gedachter Gegenstände nicht unverhältnismäßig hoch sind, geht zur Genüge daraus hervor, daß solcher dieselben ohne einigen Abzug für die von ihm, laut Verordnung vom 3ten Febr. 1849 erkauften 9 Stück Thierfiguren mit 555 rt freiwillig bezahlt hat." Ibid., fol. 7.

858 Ibid., fol. 8.

859 Ibid., fol. 9.

860 "Ferner befindet sich Hr. Marks aus London hier, der folgende Gegenstände gegen baar Zahlung excl. Taxe zu nehmen wünscht: 1 zerbrochenen Reiher 35 rt, 1 Tieger ganz defect 60 rt, 1 Ziegenbock defect 80 rt, 1 Affe sehr defect 70 rt; worüber er [Mr. Marks] gerne morgen Bescheid haben möchte." Ibid., fol. 10.

861 "die gedachten Gegenstände mehrfach in wohlerhaltenen Exemplaren in der Sammlung vorhanden sind und der Verkauf als ein vortheilhafter bezeichnet werden kann"; ibid., fol. 12.

862 On the Wolfssohn atelier, see Harran 2002, 139–140.

863 "Verzeichnis der Thiere, welche Unterzeichnete aus der Königlichen Samlung [sic!] zu kaufen wünscht"; Staatl. Kunstsammlungen Dresden, Archiv, record 10 "Akte der königlichen Porzellan und Gefäßesammlung Dresden 1848–1874," fol. 38.

864 "2 Hühner mit Jungen à 50.– Rt 100.–/1 Wölfin 60.–/2 Löwen à 100.– 200.–/1 Pelickan 80.–/ 1 großer Affe, defekt 70.–/1 Geyer mit Huhn, defekt 90.–/1 Arras mit ausgebreiteten Flügeln, defekt 90.–/1 Reiher im Schilf 35.–/2 Böcke als Kannen à 40.– 80.–/3 Reiher à

35.–105.–/2 Truthähne à 30.– 60.–/1 Ziege mit Jungen 80.–/1 Fuchs 50.–/1 Arras 60.–/1 Arras bunt mit eingeb. Farben 50.–//1210 Thlr/Rabatt 30 Thlr/1180 Thlr." Ibid., fol. 42.

865 This and the five subsequent "Aras" (macaws) must have been smaller parrots, as there is too great a difference between their price and the price paid in the previous bill (60 talers). This is also confirmed by inventory statistics.

866 "Verzeichnis der Thiere welche Unterzeichnete aus der K. Porcelain Samlung [sic!] gegen andere Porcelain Gegenstände einzutauschen wünscht: 1 Pelickan 80.–/1 Bock als Kanne 40.–/1 Löwe 100.–/1 Löwin 90.–/1 Truthahn 30.–/1 Elephant 150.–/1 Bär 120.–/1 Fuchs 50.–/1 Arras 30.–/5 Arras alle defect à 30.– 150.–//840.–." Ibid., fol. 41; the confirmation followed on January 9.

867 Ibid., fols. 40 and 43.

868 "des in der neuesten Zeit gesteigerten Verkaufs von Doubletten"; ibid., fol. 139.

869 "im Doubletten-Vorath der Königl. Porzellan- und Gefäße Sammlung befindliche Thierfiguren und andere Gegenstände von Meißener Porzellan"; ibid., fol. 62a.

870 Ibid., fol. 66; the two busts are now in Detroit.

871 See Christie's London, Furniture Silver and Porcelain from Longleat, 13. 6. 2002, introductory catalog text to lots 350–353, 98–100; David Falk was also one of the important English dealers who went in search of Rococo models in Meissen after 1823; see Kunze 1982.

872 Ibid. and original catalog in the Christie's archive, 88.

873 SächsHStA, loc. 41843, fol. 179a.

874 At Longleat, for example, and at Raby Castle.

875 Staatl. Kunstsammlungen Dresden, Archiv, record 24/1912, fol. 35b.

876 "Hinsichtlich der Wertangabe der einzelnen Stücke ist dann zu bemerken, daß die für die Monumentalstücke angegebenen Werte, da derartige Stücke bisher kaum je im Handel vorgekommen sind, zur Zeit nur ungefähre Schätzungen sein können." Ibid., fols. 192–193.

877 "was weiter das Bedenken betrifft, daß bei Abgabe einiger Monumentalstücke der Sammlung diese dann nicht mehr allein in der Porzellansammlung zu sehen sein würden, so ist hierzu zu bemerken, daß dies schon jetzt keineswegs der Fall ist. So befinden sich z. Zt. zwei der großen Tiere aus Meißner Porzellan im Keramischen Museum in Sèvres, zwei andere im Besitz des Freiherrn von Miltitz auf Schloß Siebeneichen bei Meißen, die augenblicklich bei Lepke in Berlin zum Verkauf stehen" ... "es ist beabsichtigt, von den 200 großen Meißner Tieren nur etwa 14 ... zur Versteigerung fortzugeben." Staatl. Kunstsammlungen Dresden, Archiv, record 25/1913, fols. 56–60. The number of animal figures in Sèvres was not in fact correct; the two figures of Freiherr von Miltitz finally ended up in the Schlossmuseum in Berlin (only to become war losses).

878 "Diese Versteigerung nun war schon deshalb ein Ereignis, weil hier zum ersten Male jene großen weißglasierten Plastiken der Kaendlerzeit ausgeboten wurden, die bisher noch niemals auf den Markt gekommen sind." Donath 1919, 69; I am grateful to Sebastian Kuhn for pointing out this source.

879 Donath 1920.

880 Staatl. Kunstsammlungen Dresden, Archiv, record 32/1920, fol. 74–75.

881 Staatl. Kunstsammlungen Dresden, Archiv, record 35/1929–1930, fol. 311.

882 "kleine bemalte Altmeissner Porzellanstatuette König August des Starken um 1725"; Staatl. Kunstsammlungen Dresden, Archiv, record 36/1931–1933, I: fol. 10.

883 Ibid., I: fol. 188.

884 Ibid., II: fol. 336.

885 Ibid., II: fol. 361.

886 Blaauwen 2000, catalog 289, 397.

887 "die Brandrisse, die den großen Meißener Tieren eigentümlich sind, ... sich in derselben Weise auf der Mehrzahl der in der Sammlung verbliebenen Exemplare« ... »da der Herstellung so großer Stücke unüberwindliche Schwierigkeiten entgegenstanden"; Rudolph Lepke Berlin, sale October 7–8, 1919, foreword by W. v. Seidlitz, third last section.

888 See Christie's London, Furniture Silver and Porcelain from Longleat, June 13, 2002, introductory text to lots 350–353, 98–100.

889 Published in Morley-Fletcher 1971; the exact point when the acquisition was made is not known (information kindly supplied by Mrs. Simpson, Raby Castle), although there are certain parallels with the 1858 auction at Christie's and the Cockerel was clearly the one offered at the Lepke auction in 1919.

890 Sotheby's, June 6, 1950.

891 "und damit die Abdrucke der Thiere jederzeit rar und kostbar bleiben mögen, sollen die Formen derselben zerschlagen werden"; Keyssler 1751, 1320.

892 This applies to: Eagle (beating one wing), Panther (lying), Scapegoat, Ram.

893 Entry in the manufactory moldbook.

894 See, for example, Museum für angewandte Kunst Frankfurt a. M.; Sotheby's London, November 25, 1997, lot 155 (with Turkeyhen); Sotheby's London, November 21, 2000, lot 33.

895 The Mandrill was also given a newly-designed pedestal when it went back into production.

896 Vienna, Dorotheum, October 6, 1998, lot 295.

897 Information by courtesy of Howard Coutts.

898 BA, IIIH.121; see also catalog in the appendix.

899 Information by courtesy of Lady Lisa White.

900 Porstmann 1998, fig. 7.

901 Sotheby's New York, November 1, 2000, lot 21.

902 Sotheby's Monaco, November 30 to December 2, 1986, lot 1524.

903 Sotheby's London, July 17, 1990, lots 174 and 175.

904 Sotheby's London, July 17, 1990, lot 236 and again December 1, 2003, lot 316.

905 Auction-house Michael Zeller, June 27–28, 2003, lot 1301.

906 Albiker 1935, 41.

907 See Meister/Reber 1980, the chapter entitled "Fälschungen."

908 Wittwer 2000.b, 43.

909 Or, for example, if one compares the large Bolognese Dog from the 1730s and the reduced-size copy from the early nineteenth century in the Metropolitan Museum of Art in New York.

910 See also Hannover/Rackham 1925, III: European porcelain, 109–111.

911 For a Turkeyhen, see auction-house Bergmann, Erlangen, sale 44, March 15, 1997, lot 2332.

912 Auction-house Bergmann, Erlangen, sale 57, March 18, 2000, lot 308.

913 Auction-house Bergmann, Erlangen, sale 65, February 23, 2002, lot 260.

914 On Samson generally, see Slitine 2002, and the three catalogs of the manufactory's collection of models, sold at Christie's London, December 17, 1979, March 3, 1980, and June 16, 1980.

915 See illustration in Slitine 2002, 149.

916 Another example, likewise marked "G" is illustrated in Slitine 2002, 148.

917 Christie's London, June 16, 1980, lot 171.

918 See also Sotheby's Monaco, November 30 to December 2, 1986 (Estate of Mona Bismarck), lot 1522.

919 Christie's New York, April 1–2, 2003, lot 310.

920 Sotheby's Paris, June 27, 2001, lot 144.

921 Weltkunst 37/1968, brochure 22 of November 15, 1968, 1181.

922 Cologne, Rautenstrauch-Joest Museum, from the estate of Max von Oppenheim.

923 The author has not actually seen the figure, and is thus reluctant to express an opinion as its place and date of origin; Neumeister Munich, varia auction April 25–26, 2001, lot 121.

924 Or of the decoration in the case of the Meissen small figures; on this subject, Rainer Rückert is the only author to have published a broadly-based investigation, which concentrates on the problem of the decoration of faces, see Rückert 1995–1997.

925 Auction-house Fischer, Luzern, May 19–22, 1999, lot 1481.

926 Exhibition catalog Haus der Kunst, Remshalden-Grunbach, summer 2001; there a Meissen monkey with snuff-box, a figure made about 1935/45.

Appendix

Sources

1 List with description of the ground floor of the Japanese Palace, 1733
2 Description of the Japanese Palace by Johann Georg Keyssler, October 23, 1730
3 Zacharias Longuelune's description of his concept for the throne gallery, ca. 1735
4 Order list of March 28, 1730
5 Manufactory balance statement of December 13, 1731
6 Order list of February 25, 1732
7 Order list, undated
8 Manufactory balance statement of September 2, 1732
9 Order list of November 18, 1732
10 Interim totals of December 17, 1732
11 Deliveries 1731/1732
12 Animals reserved in Meissen for the Japanese Palace by Sulkowski on November 17, 1733
13 Order list of November 26, 1733
14 Deliveries 1733
15 Deliveries from March 7, 1733, to October 22, 1734
16 Deliveries 1734
17 Interim totals of February 18, 1735
18 Deliveries from March 5 to December 17, 1735
19 Interim totals up to and including January 1736
20 Deliveries 1736
21 List of the modelers, throwers, repairers, and molders, 1732
22 Description of the Japanese Palace by Jonas Hanway, published in 1753
23 Lists with the animals brought in 1733 to Dresden from the Africa Expedition
24 Kaendler's list of his first works, 1731
25 Kaendler's list of the animals of which he made studies in Dresden and Moritzburg, July 1734
26 Obituary for Kaendler from the *Neue Bibliothek der schönen Wissenschaften und der freyen Künste*, 1775 (see Bibliography)
27 The description of the Japanese Palace in 1744 from the memoirs of the preacher Johann Christian Müller from Stralsund
28 From the deeds of the court accounting office relating to the animal collections, first half-year of 1727 to first half-year of 1738

Note

Most of the sources are excerpts from longer texts or lists. This should be taken into account, even when there is no indication to this effect here or no information as to how the source continues.

Source 1
List with description of the ground floor of the Japanese Palace, 1733

[SächsHStA, OHMA, Pläne und Zeichnungen, Cap. II, Anlage C]

Specificatio dererjenigen Zimmer, welche Ihro Majth. der höchseeligste König glorwürdigsten Andenckens im Japanischen Palais, und zwar in der Ersten Etage, auf nachbeschriebene Arth aus meubliren zu laßen allergnädigst intentioniret gewesen, Nehmlich
[Specification of the rooms on the first floor (= ground floor) of the Japanese Palace and how His Royal Majesty of most blessed and glorious memory most graciously intended to furnish them, namely:]

No 1 In der untersten Gallerie. Große Japanische Vasen, Becher und Terrinen, die Schäffte, mit Indianisch vergoldeten Pappier, worauf bunte Blumen und Vögel gemahlt sind. Das Pappier muß durchgehends auf Leinewand gezogen werden.

No 2 Grün Chinesisch Porcellaine und schwarz Indianisch laquirte Banden von Holz, die Füllungen mit Indianisch vergoldeten Pappier, worauf große Figuren von bunten Farben fein gemahlt sind.

No 3 Ebenfalls grün chinesisch Porcellaine aus Auffsäzn und dergleichen bestehend, auch schwarz Indianisch laquirte Banden von Holz, die Füllungen mit Indianisch vergoldeten Pappier, worauff differente Pagoden sauber gemahlt.

No 4 Roth Chinesisch Porcellaine mit schwarz und Gold Indianisch laquirten Banden von Holz, die Füllungen von weisen Indianischen Atlas, worein große Indianische Figuren mit bunten Farben sehr sauber gemahlt. Müssen mit Leinewand gefüttert werden.

No 5 Blau und weiß Porcellain alt Krack-Guth mit laquirten Friesen, die Füllungen von großen und kleinen Spiegeln.

No 6 Blau und weiß Indianisch Porcellaine mit laquirten Friesen, die Füllungen mit dunckel violettnen Atlas-Banden, worein große goldene Drachen und Zierathen gestickt.

No 7 Dunckel blau Indianisch Porcellaine, mit laquirten Friesen, die Füllungen von weißen Atlas, worauf Indianische Große Figuren von bunten Farben sehr sauber gemahlt.

No 8 Das Taffel-Zimmer. Große vergoldete Indianische Vasen und Becher, das Zimmer mit Boiserie und großen Spiegel-Gläßern.

No 9 Dunckelblau Indianisch Porcellaine, mit laquirten Friesen, die Füllungen von weisen Atlas, worauf große Indianische Figuren von bunten Farben sehr sauber gemahlt.

No 10 Blau und weiß Indianisch Porcellaine mit laquirten Friesen, die Füllungen mit duckel violettnen Atlas-Banden, worein große goldene Drachen und Zierathen gestickt.

No 11 Blau und weiß Porcellaine alt KrackGuth mit laquirten Friesen, die Füllungen von großen und kleinen Spiegeln.

No 12 Japanische Porcellaine mit gewürckten Banden, worein von bunter Seide, Gold und Silber Indian. Figuren sehr sauber gewürckt, die Füllungen von weisen Indianischen Atlas, worauf große Figuren mit bunten Farben segr sauber gemahlt.

No 13 Jappanische Porcellaine mit grün leinewandnen laquirten Banden, worauff goldene Drachen und Zierrathen gemahlt, von dem Laquir Schnellen verferttiget, so ganz neu, die Füllungen von Indianischen weisen AtlasDecken, worein goldene Zierathen Vögel und Blumen von bunter Seide, sauber gestickt.

No 14 Alt Indianisch Porcellaine mit dunckel violettnen Sammt-Banden, worein goldene Drachen, und Zierathen fein gewürcket sind, die Füllungen von Spiegel-Gläßern und laquirten Friesen.

No 15 Schlaff-Zimmer. Weiß.Indianisch Porcellaine, das Zimmer ist von Boiserie und roth laquirt, mit erhobenen verguldeten Figuren, Ist zu repariren. Darein, Ein Bette, der Himmel, Crantz und Decke von Indianischen Zeuge mit guldenen reich gestickten Grund, worauf von bunter Seide Blumen, und allerhand Zierathen gleichfalls gestickt, Zwey Vorhänge darzu von weisen Atlas mit darauff gestickten goldenen Nahmen in einem Schilde, worüber eine Crone, und darneben allerhand bundt genehete Zierathen.

No 16 Vor-Gemach. Indianischer Speckstein, die Tapeten von roth und goldenen Blumen gewürckten Stroh-Banden.

No 17 Schlaff-Gemach. Weiß Indianisch Porcellaine die Tapeten von ponceau Indianischen Atlas, worauff goldene Drachen und allerhand Zierathen gestickt sind. Das Bett von eben dergleichen Indianischen Zeuge.

No 18 Vor-Gemach. Schwarz mit Gold von Holz sehr fein laquirte Indianische Vasen, das Meuble von weisen Indianischen Tafft, worauff Blumen und Vögel gemahlt.

Source 2
Description of the Japanese Palace by Johann Georg Keyssler, October 23, 1730

[Johann Georg Keyssler, *Neueste Reisen durch Deutschland, Böhmen, Ungarn, die Schweiz, Italien und Lothringen*, second printing, Hanover 1751; from letter no. 86 of October 23, 1730, "Nachrichten von der Stadt Dresden," the passage on the Japanese Palace, pp. 1319–1321.]

Der Japanische Pallast in Alt-Dresden nahe am weißen Thore, gehörte sonst dem Grafen von Flemming, welcher ihn an den König für hundert tausend Thaler verkauft und etwan zwanzigtausend Thaler daran gewonnen hat. Die Menge des allhier befindlichen einheimischen und ausländischen Porzellans ist nicht zu beschreiben, und wird dasjenige allein, so zum Küchengeräthe gehört, auf eine Million Thaler geschätzet. In einem der obern Zimmer sieht man die acht und vierzig großen Gefäße aus weißem und blauem Porzellan, für welche der König in Pohlen dem itzigen Könige in Preußen ein Regiment Dragoner gegeben hat.

Eine Kammer ist voll von solchem Geschirre, welches Raphael d'Urbino gemalt haben soll. Das röthliche Porzellan, so hier zu Lande gemacht wird und Feuer schlägt, wird nun antiquiret, das ist, man verfertiget keines mehr, damit eine desto größere Rarität mit der Zeit daraus werden möge. Indessen ist die Beschreibung, wie es gemacht werde, an sichern Orten verwahret. Die Fabrike des gemeinen Porzellans [=Fayence] ist nahe vor Dresden, das recht feine und kostbare wird mit vielem Geheimnisse auf dem Schlosse zu Meißen bereitet. Seit anderthalb Jahren ist verbothen, kein ganz weißes mehr zu verkaufen, sondern denjenigen Profit, welchen auswärtige Künstler mit Verguldung und Anmalung derselben machen, im Lande selbst zu ziehen, und werden zu solchem Ende vierzig Maler unterhalten, welche gute Arbeit auch en mignature liefern. Die Gelegenheit zu Erfindung des dresdenischen Porzellans gab die Goldmacherey. Bötticher, der Erfinder desselben starb im Jahre 1719, zu seiner Zeit aber wußte man nur weißes Gut zu machen. Das braune und blaue ist erst im Jahre 1722 erfunden worden. Es steht alles Feuer in dem Gebrauche der Küche aus, und kann man darinnen kochen und backen, was man will; der Rauch läßt sich auch leicht wieder abwischen. Bey der Verguldung hat es ein außerordentliches Feuer auszustehen, und da springen öfters viele kostbare Stücke. Man arbeitet anitzt an einem Service, das aus vier Dutzend Tellern, sechs und dreyßig Schüsseln, sechs Kumpen [=Kummen, grosse Schalen], vier Leuchtern, ein Dutzend Messern, ein Dutzend Gabeln, ein Dutzend Löffeln, vier Gefäßen zu Essig, Oehl, Pfeffer und Senf, nebst der Pyramide, worauf diese vier Stücke gesetzet werden, besteht und vier tausend Thaler gelten soll.

In dem japanischen oder holländischen Hause zeiget man ferner noch ein Paradebette mit etlichen Stühlen aus lauter Federn, wofür dreyßig tausend Thaler gezahlet worden.

Dieser schöne Pallast wird anitzt niedergerissen und ins Viereck mit vier Eingängen wieder aufgeführet. Die Aufsicht über solchen kostbaren Bau haben der General Bodt und die drey Oberlandbaumeister Pöpelmann, Longlue und Knevel. Das prächtige Hauptportal wird insbesondere ein Zeugniß von der Baukunst des erstgedachten Generals ablegen. Die Zimmer des untersten Stockwerkes werden eine Höhe haben von zwanzig Fuß, und mit lauter chinesischem und japanischem Porzellan gezieret seyn. In die Zimmer des obersten Stockwerkes, das acht und dreyßig Fuß hoch werden soll, kömmt kein anderes als meißnisches Porzellan, und bestehet das erste Zimmer in einer Galerie, welche acht und dreyßig Fuß in der Höhe und hundert und siebenzig Fuß in der Länge hält. Es wird solches mit allerhand sowohl einheimischen, als ausländischen Vögeln und Thieren von purem Porzellan, in ihrer natürlichen Größe und Farbe meublirt, und kann man an denenjenigen Stücken, welche schon fertig sind, die Kunst und Schönheit nicht genug bewundern. Das Brustbild des itzigen königlichen kurzweiligen Raths Joseph ist gleichfalls so wohl gerathen, als man von dem geschicktesten Bildhauer verlangen könnte. Zwischen den obgedachten Thieren kommen rothe Gefäße von unterschiedener Erfindung zu stehen, und damit die Abdrucke der Thiere jederzeit rar und kostbar bleiben mögen, sollen die Formen derselben zerschlagen werden.

Das zweyte Zimmer soll mit vielerley Arten Porzellan von Seladonfarbe und Gold besetzet, die Wände aber mit Spiegeln und andern Zierrathen versehen werden. Das dritte Zimmer wird Porzellan von hochgelber Farbe und Gold meubliret haben.

Das vierte ist ein Saal, worinnen dunkelblaues mit Gold geziertes Porzellan Parade machen wird. Das fünfte Zimmer soll Porzellan von Purpurfarbe mit Gold haben. Hierauf folget die große Galerie von obiger Höhe und von zwey hundert und sechszig Fuß in der Länge. Gleich beim Eintritte derselben wird sich ein großer Baldachin zeigen, worunter ein Glockenspiel von Porzellan hängt. Wo sonst der Stuhl seyn sollte, wird eine Uhr, die sechs Fuß in ihrer Höhe hat, stehen, und hinter derselben wird ein verborgener Platz für einen Organisten, der das Glockenspiel regieren kann, angeleget seyn. Diesem Werke gegenüber und am andern Ende der Galerie wird sich der Audienzthron zeigen, der in allem eine Höhe von acht und zwanzig Fuß und drey Stuffen hat. Beyde Seiten werden mit vier Seulen von Spiegelglase prangen, deren Höhe von zwey und dreyßig und der Diameter von anderthalb Fuß ist. Diese Galerie wird mit meißnischem Porzellane nach der alten indianischen Art, die Wände aber mit Spiegeln und andern verguldeten Zierrathen meubliret seyn.

Gleiche Bewandniß soll es mit den Wänden des siebenten Zimmers, welches graues Porzellan mit Golde in sich halten wird, haben.

Das achte Zimmer soll zum Tafelgemache dienen und mit Porzellane von bleu-mourant-Farbe und Golde besetzet seyn. Die Zierrathen der Wände werden mit den zweyen vorhergehenden Gemächern überein kommen, und solche auch in dem folgenden neunten beybehalten werden, welches für das Buvet oder die Schenke von grünem Porzellane mit Golde ausersehen ist.

In dem zehnten oder dem Federzimmer, wird das Bett nebst Tapeten von indianischen Vogelfedern und das Porzellan von Pfirsichblüthe-Farbe und Golde seyn. Die Zierrathen der Wände gleichen den vorhergehenden.

Das eilfte Gemach soll zu einer römischkatholischen Kapelle dienen, und das darinnen befindliche Porzellan, woraus die Kanzel, die Orgelpfeifen, der massive Altar, (so vier und zwanzig Fuß hoch wird) und verschiedene andere Dinge bestehen, von weißer Farbe mit Golde seyn. In diese Kapelle kommen die porzellanenen Statuen der zwölf Apostel beynahe in Lebensgröße und gleichfalls von weißer Farbe, und müssen dergleichen große Stücke über Jahr und Tag stehen, um recht trocken zu werden, ehe sie ins Feuer gebracht werden, widrigenfalls springen sie. Die Wände sollen mit bas-reliefs aus Porzellan gezieret werden.

Die Assicht aus dem japanischen Pallast über die Elbe nach Dresden und den umliegenden Höhen ist vortrefflich, und dieses vermuthlich die Ursache, warum man lieber das schon aufgeführte schöne Gebäude abbricht, als mit Beybehaltung desselben einen andern Platz zu des Königs Absichten wählet.

Der Garten soll gleichfalls vergrößert und zwey hundert Fuß weiter in die Elbe hineingeleget werden. Seine bassins werden mit Marmor eingefasset, und die darinnen befindlichen vielen Statuen aus Marmor und Porzellan seyn. Der Hof des Pallastes selbst wird mit Marmor gepflastert, und die Wände mit großen Gefäßen von Porzellan besetzet.

[The Japanese Palace in Old Dresden, near the White Gate, formerly belonged to Count Flemming, who sold it to the king for a hundred thousand talers, making a profit of about twenty thousand. It contains an indescribable quantity of local and foreign porcelain, and alone the wares for kitchen use are estimated to be worth a million talers. The forty-eight large blue-and-white porcelain vessels for which the King in Poland gave the present King in Prussia a regiment of dragoons are to be seen in one of the upper-story rooms.

One room is full of tableware of this kind, which are supposed to have been painted by Raphael d'Urbino. The reddish porcelain [= Böttger stoneware] made in this country – so hard that one can strike sparks from it, as from a stone – is now considered antiquated and is no longer produced, so that it may in the course of time become an even greater rarity, to which end the description of how it is made is kept safe in a number of places. The factory for common porcelain [= faience] is near Dresden, but the fine and costly porcelain is manufactured in great secrecy in the castle at Meissen. For one and an half years now, it has been forbidden to sell any entirely white porcelain, in order that the profit otherwise to be made by outside artists with gilding and painting may accrue to the land of Saxony. To this end forty painters are employed, who also do good miniature work. The foundations for the invention of Dresden porcelain were laid by alchemy. The inventor, Böttger, died in 1719, at which time it was only known how to make white porcelain. Brown and blue porcelain were only invented in 1722. This porcelain can withstand all the heat of fires used in the kitchen, and one can boil and bake whatever one likes in it. What is more, smoke-marks can be easily wiped off. When it is gilded it is subjected to exceptionally hot firing, which frequently causes costly pieces to crack and break. Work is now in progress on a service to be composed of four dozen plates, thirty-six bowls, six "Kumpen" [meaning "Kummen": large shallow bowls] four candelabra, a dozen knives, a dozen forks, a dozen spoons, four containers for vinegar, oil, pepper, and salt, together with the pyramid on which these four containers are to stand. The whole service is to cost four thousand talers.

In the Japanese or Dutch house one is furthermore shown a state bed with a number of chairs made purely of feathers, for which thirty thousand talers were paid.

This beautiful palace is in the process of being taken down and re-built in a square shape with four entrances. Supervising this expensive building project are General de Bodt, and the three senior state architects Pöppelmann, Longuelune, and Knöffel. The magnificent main entrance will be a particular testimony to the architectural talents of General de Bodt. The rooms on the ground floor will be twenty feet high, and will be decorated solely with Chinese and Japanese porcelain. The rooms of the upper story, which is to be thirty-eight feet high, are to contain nothing other than Meissen porcelain, and the first room is a gallery which is thirty-eight feet high and one hundred and seventy feet long. It is to be furnished with all kinds of local and foreign birds and animals in pure porcelain, in their natural size and color; the figures which have already been finished are of such artistry and beauty that one cannot admire them enough. The bust of the present court jester Joseph has likewise been done as successfully as one could imagine it done by the most skilful sculptor. Between the animals mentioned above are to stand red vessels of various kinds, and in order that these animal figures may for ever remain rare and costly, their molds are to be broken.

The second room is to contain many kinds of celadon-colored porcelain with gilding, and the walls are to be fitted out with mirrors and other ornaments. The third room will be furnished with bright yellow porcelain with gilding.

The fourth is a hall in which there is to be a great show of dark blue porcelain with gilding. The fifth is to house puce porcelain with gilding. This is followed by the great gallery, as high as the gallery mentioned above and two hundred and sixty feet in length. Right at the entrance there will be a large canopy, with a porcelain carillon hanging underneath. Where the chair would normally be there is to be a clock, six feet high, and behind the clock, a hidden place for an organist to play the carillon. Opposite all this and at the far end of the gallery will be seen the audience throne, which is to be twenty-eight feet high in all with three steps. The two sides will be resplendent with four columns in mirror glass, thirty-two feet high, and one and a half feet in diameter. This gallery will be furnished with Meissen porcelain in the ancient Indian style, but the walls with mirrors and other gilded ornaments.

The same will be true of the walls of the seventh room, which will contain gray porcelain with gilding.

The eighth room is to serve as a dining room and is to be fitted out with porcelain in *bleu-mourant* with gilding. The decorations on the walls will be the same as in the two previous rooms, and will also continue in the ninth room which is reserved for the *buffet* and is to be furnished with green porcelain with gilding.

In the tenth room, the bedchamber, the bed and wall-hangings will be of the feathers of exotic birds, and the porcelain will be the color of peach blossom, with gilding. The walls will be decorated like those in the previous rooms.

The eleventh room is to serve as a Roman Catholic chapel, and all the pieces to be done in porcelain are to be white with gilding, that is to say the pulpit, the organ pipes, the large altar (which is to be twenty-four feet high), and various other things. The chapel is also to house porcelain statues of the twelve apostles, almost life-size and likewise white in color. Such large pieces have to dry out for more than a year before they are subjected to firing, lest they should crack. The walls are to be decorated with bas-reliefs in porcelain.

The view from the Japanese Palace over the Elbe towards to Dresden and the surrounding hills is excellent, and this is, I suppose, the reason why preference has been given to knocking down the fine earlier building, as opposed to keeping it and having to choose another site for the carrying out of the King's present intentions.

The garden is likewise to be enlarged and to be extended two hundred feet further into the Elbe. Its *bassins* are to be done in marble, and its many statues are to be in marble and porcelain. The palace courtyard is to be paved with marble, and the walls are to be fitted out with large porcelain vessels.]

Source 3
Zacharias Longuelune's description of his concept for the throne gallery, ca. 1735

[SächsHStA, loc. 895, Acta Chinesische und japanische Porcellaine, auch andere im japanischen Palais aufbewahrte Kunst-Sachen betr., fol. 1 a/a–1 b/b]

Explication de la Galerie du Palais du Japon à la Ville Neuve
Le Trône marqué A sur le plan est décoré d'un ordre Jonique; On a choisi cet Ordre preferablement à un autre, parce qu'il tient le milieu, entre le Dorique et le Corinthien, qu'il participe de la Force et de la Majesté du premier, de la delicatesse de l'autre; et que ces proportions ont une noblesse et une élegance qui semble convenir au Sujet: D'ailleurs il sembloit qu'on ne devoit pas repéter le même ordre Corinthien dont la galerie est décorée, ni du Klocken-Spiel

qui est vis à vis, et c'auroit été une faute contre la varieté que demande ces sortes de compositions, dont les changements d'objets sont les principales beautez.

Dans le fond du Trône, on y a representé en bas relief un grand Palmier, duquel la Victoire vient de cueillir une branche, pour marquer les avantages qui se remporte dans les Batailles, par les Victoires: Cette Figure est acompagnée de plusieurs Genies qui tiennent des Couronnes; ce qui donne à entendre le prix des heureuses reüssites, et des Negotiations qui regardent les interrets de l'Etat.

Les sens de cette Embléme signifie, que les avantages de Guerres, des Victoires, et des Negociations heureuses, qui regardent les interrets des Etats, et des Roïaumes, sont duës, et viennent ordinairement des justes resolutions, et des ordres qui émanent du Trône et du Conseil des Rois.

On a mis dans la Cartouche au dessus du Dais les Armes de Pologne et de Saxe, ornez des Palmes et d'Oliviers; les Têtes, qui l'enrichit, representent les diferentes passions des hommes, pour montrer qu'elles sont assujetties au Trône, qu'elles n'y servent que d'ornements, et les Souverains en y montant, savent les faire taire, en n'écoutant plus que la Sagesse et la prudence; qui sont representées par les deux Statuës qui sont aux deux côtez du Trône. On a mis au dessus de ces Statues des Cartouches entourez de Trophées, où sont les chifres et la devise de Sa Majesté.

J'ai representé dans la frise de l'Entablement un faisseau, avec une lire, melez de Trophées, qui signifient l'Armonie, et la concorde qui régnent dans les Conseils des Rois, et parmi leurs Aliez. Tous les autres ornements de la même Frise ont raport au Sujet.

Si on le juge à propos, ce Trône sera executé de glaces, de la maniere qu'il est exprimé sur le dessein, et s'il se peut la plus grande partie des ornements seront de Porcelaines.

Le Bas-relief qui sera au dessus de la cheminée representera l'Histoire.

On pourra peindre dans le Plafond la dispute entre Minerve et Neptune, touchant la nomination de la Ville d'Athéne: C'est un grand Sujet puisqu'on y peut representer tous les Dieux du Paganisme, et un Peintre savant, y pourra joindre des Ornements et des alégories ingenieuses.

Comme le Salon du Klocken-Spiel, ou doit être l'Orloge est /:pour ainsi dire:/ consacré au Soleil, qui régle les jours et les heures, tous les ornements doivent avoir du raport à Apollon.

Le Dôme, où doit être le Klocken-Spiel, au dessous duquel doit être l'Orloge, sera soutenu et orné par quatre Termes, qui representeront les quatre Saisons de l'année, qui se distingueront par leurs Atributs, soit Fleurs ou Fruits qui naissent dans chaque Saison &ca [=etc.]. Ces Termes seront de meme hauteur que les Colonmes Jonique du Trône, qui se trouvent vis à vis, et feront Simetrie sans repéter les mêmes objets. Le Dôme sera orné en déhors d'une tête d'Apollon, qui reprendra ses raïons, sur deux Cornes d'abondance remplies des Fruits et des Fleurs de tout les Saisons, pour designer ses bien faits: La Frise de l'Entablement sera enrichie de Festons de même sorte. Les deux Bas-reliefs qui seront aux deux côtez du Dôme, seront tirez de l'histoire d'Apollon, et les plus convenables qu'il sera possible de choisir, comme, par exemple, sa dispute avec Martias, et le châtiment qui la suivit, ou autres sujets qui ont leurs significations phisique, par raport aux éfets du Soleil; Ces mêmes Bas-reliefs seront ornez de Trophées qui leur conviennent.

Dans le Bas-relief du Piedestal qui porte l'Orloge. sera representé les instruments qui servoient aux Prêtres des Temples, où Apollon rendoit ses oracles.

Tous les autres ornements, comme ceux de la Frise de l'Entablement du Salon, seront significatifs, par raport au même sujet, comme on peut voir sur les desseins.

Cet ouvrage, /:si on le trouve à propos:/ sera executé de glaces, comme on voit sur les desseins, et s'il se peut une partie des ornements seront faits de porcelaines.

Dans le Plafond du même salon, on pourra y representer les Nations; les diferents Carractéres des têtes de chaque Nation, et leurs habillements diferents, contriburont beaucoup à donner de la Varieté au sujet, joint aux alégories qu'un habile Peintre y saura ájoûter.

La Galerie entre les deux Salons sera ornée de Porcelaines, de la Couleur marquée, sur la repartition qu'on en a fait, et elle sera autant variée par son arangement qu'il sera possible: Et le tout est composé de la maniere que l'on pourra augmenter ou diminuer le nombre des Porcelaines sans changer la Composition générale. On s'est conformé pour la grandeur des Porcelaines, autant qu'on a pû à l'état qui en a été donné.

Ladite Galerie est decorée avec un ordre Corinthien regulier, porté sur deux Zocles, afin de l'éléver, et lui donner plus d'élégance, on a été oblige de se servir de cet expedient, pour eviter de faire l'Ordre du dedans de cette Galerie plus grand que celui du dehors du Palais, ce qui auroit été un defaut inexcusable; cet ordre est canelé comme on le voit sur le dessein. Chaque Pilastre sera orné de plats, dont les Diametres sont conformes à la Specification ils y seront enfoncez et entaillez dans les Pilastres, de sorte que leurs saillies ne choqueront pas les yeux, et il sera necessaire pour qu'ils fassent un bon éfet qu'ils soient rehaussez d'or, a fin que les Pilastres se distinguent et se détachent entiérement par leurs couleurs, de celles des Porcelaines de toute la Galerie.

Les ornements de la Frise ne sont qu'une continuité d'arabesques varriez et mélez de Trophées, de Mascarons, et autres ornements de diferentes sortes comme on peut le voir sur le dessein.

Au milieu de la Galerie, aux côtez oposez aux fenêtres on a ordonné deux Piramides, formées de Porcelaines, sur un fond de glace, afin de repéter les objets: Ces Piramides formeront de grandes parties, et donneront de la varieté à la composition.

On a mis à ce même côté, vis à vis des fenêtres, des statuës, et des Medaillons, pour ne pas tôujours repéter des Vases, et éviter un simple arangement, qui auroit trop l'air d'un riche Magazin, et pour presenter aux yeux, et à l'esprit des objets amusants, et qui /:pour ainsi dire:/ parle.

Les quatres Statuës representeront les Arts qui sont necessaires à la perfection de la Manufacture comme la Peinture, la Sculpture, la Geométrie, la Chimie, ou autres que l'on trouvera le mieux convenir.

Les Medaillons seront ornez de Trophées de diferentes especes, et qui conviennent à la Déesse, qui preside aux Arts, et les Sujets representeront les choses les plus memorables de son histoire, en ce qui regarde les Arts: Comme son Triomphe sur Arachné, et la punition de son Audace, qui fût d'être changée en araignée; le reste se voit sur le dessein.

Le Plafond de la Galerie entre les deux Salons, sera partagé en trois parties, celle du milieu representera la Saxe et le Japon, qui disputent ensemble, en presence de Minerve, sur la preference, et la perfection des ouvrages de leurs manifactures de Porcelaines; Elle seront accompagnées de l'Emulation, du Goût, de l'Imitation, de la Peinture, de la Sculpture, et de tout ce qui contribuë à la beauté de ses sortes d'ouvrages: La Déesse remettra entre les mains de la Saxe, la Couronne, ou le prix de la dispute; et la jalousie, et le depit feront signe, et sugéreront au Japon de faire rembarquer ses Vases de Porcelaines, sur les Vaisseaux qui les ont aportez.

Ce sujet semble convenable et peut être traité d'une maniere noble et grande, et il est susceptible d'ingeniuses Alégories qui est ce que demande ces sortes d'ouvrages, pour donner quelque chose à l'Esprit à deviner.

Les deux autres parties du Plafond, representeront d'un côté les Arts, et les Manifactures établies en Saxe, et de l'autre les productions avantageuses de la Nature, qui naissent, et qui sont produits dans le Païs: Le tout doit être traité alegoriquement, avec peu d'ouvrage, d'une grande maniere, et qui s'aplique noblement.

Ceci n'est que pour donner une légere idée de cette Galerie; L'habilité des Peintres, des Sculpteurs et d'autres Artistes, qui y seront emploïez, y pourra donner des perfections, et des beautez, qui ne peuvent pas bien s'exprimer dans une si courte explication.

[Explanation of the Gallery of the Japanese Palace in Neustadt
The throne marked A on the plan is decorated with Ionic columns, this order having been preferred because it holds the middle place between the Doric and the Corinthian, having something of the strength and majesty of the former, and something of the delicacy of the latter, and because these proportions possess an elegance fitting for the subject in hand. Furthermore, it seemed wrong to repeat the Corinthian order of the gallery decoration, or that of the carillon opposite, and it would have been an offense against the variety called for by this kind of composition, the principal beauty of which lies in diversity.

Behind the throne there is a representation in bas-relief of a large palm tree, from which Victory has just taken a branch to signify the advantages that are to be gained in battles, through victories; this figure is accompanied by several *putti* holding crowns, to be understood as the prize of fortunate success, and of negotiations undertaken in the interests of the State.

The sense and significance of this emblem is that the advantages of wars, of victories, and of happy negotiations affecting interests of States and Kingdoms are due to, and are normally the outcome of, right decisions and of orders proceeding from the thrones and councils of Kings.

Into the cartouche above the dais have been put the coats of arms of Poland and of Saxony, decorated with palms and olive branches; the heads with which they are adorned represent man's various passions, to show that the latter are subject to the throne, on which their only use is ornamental, and furthermore to show that when sovereigns ascend their thrones, they know how to still their passions and listen only to wisdom and prudence, which are represented by the two statues on the two sides of the throne. Above these statues have been put cartouches surrounded with trophies, on which are His Majesty's monogram and device.

In the frieze of the entablature I have put a representation of a fasces, with a lyre and adorned with trophies, which together signify the harmony and concord which rule in the councils of Kings and among their allies. All the other ornaments of the same frieze relate to the same subject.

If it is judged fitting, this throne will be executed in mirrors in the way shown on the drawing, and if possible most of the ornaments are to be in porcelain.

The bas-relief which will be above the fireplace is to represent History.

In the ceiling is to be painted a depiction of the dispute between Minerva and Neptune regarding the naming of the city of Athens. This is a grand subject in which all the pagan gods can be depicted, and a knowledgeable and skillful painter will find scope for ornaments and ingenious allegories.

As the carillon room, where the clock must be, is – so to speak – dedicated to the Sun, which rules the days and the hours, all the ornaments are to relate to Apollo.

The dome where the carillon is to be, with the clock below, will be supported and decorated by four herms representing the four seasons of the year to be distinguished by attributes in the form of flowers and fruits proper to each season, and so forth. These herms will be the same height as the Ionic columns of the throne opposite, thus creating symmetry without repeating the same objects. The dome will be decorated on the outside with a head of Apollo surrounded by rays on two cornucopias filled with fruits and flowers of all the seasons to indicate the benefits he bestows, and the frieze of the entablature will be decorated with festoons of the same kind. The subjects of the two bas-reliefs at the two sides of the dome shall be taken from the story of Apollo, chosen in as fitting a way as possible, such as, for example, his dispute with Marsyas and the ensuing punishment, or other subjects related to the effects of the sun, and these bas-reliefs are to be decorated with suitable trophies.

In the bas-relief of the pedestal carrying the clock shall be represented the instruments used by the priests of the temples where Apollo delivered his oracles.

All the other ornaments, like those of the frieze of the room's entablature, are to be related to the same subject, as can be seen on the drawings.

This work, if it is judged fitting, shall be done in mirrors, as is to be seen on the drawings, and if possible a number of the ornaments shall be in porcelain.

On the ceiling of the same room are to be represented the nations of the world; the different appearances of the heads of each nation, and their various clothes will contribute greatly to giving variety to the subject, combined with the allegories that a skillful painter will not fail to add.

The gallery between the two rooms shall be decorated with porcelains in the color marked and distributed as has been laid down, with as much variety as possible. And it is all designed in such a way as to make it possible to increase or decrease the number of porcelains without changing the overall composition. As far as the size of the porcelain pieces is concerned, we have kept as far as possible to the measurements that we have been given.

The said gallery is decorated with regular Corinthian columns, supported on two pedestals in order to raise it and make it more elegant; we have been obliged to resort to this device to avoid making the order inside the gallery larger than that on the outside of the palace, which would be an unforgivable fault indeed. This order has fluting, as can be seen on the drawing. Set into incisions in each pilaster shall be little shelves of a diameter conforming to the specification, not projecting so abruptly as to offend the eye, and if they are to make a good effect, they will have to be gilded so that they are distinguishable from the pilasters and of a color distinct from those of the porcelains all around the gallery.

The ornaments of the frieze are nothing but a continuity of various arabesques mixed up with trophies, mascarons, and various other ornaments such as can be seen on the drawing.

In the middle of the gallery, on the side opposite the windows, two pyramids have been prescribed made up of pieces of porcelain with a mirror behind in order to multiply the objects. These pyramids will be major elements in the whole and will impart variety to the overall composition.

On this same side statues and medallions have been put opposite the windows, in order not to be constantly repeating the vases, to avoid a simple arrangement which would look too much like a well-stocked warehouse, and to present the eye and the mind with amusing objects, which – as it were – speak for themselves.

The four statues are to represent the arts that are necessary for perfect manufacturing, that is Painting, Sculpture, Geometry, and Chemistry, or such others as may be thought most fitting.

The medallions shall be decorated with various trophies fitting for the goddess who presides over the arts, and the subject matter shall represent the most memorable elements in her history as concerns the arts, such as her triumph over and punishment of Arachne, who for her boldness was changed into a spider; the rest can be seen on the drawing.

The ceiling of the gallery between the two rooms is to be divided into three parts, with the middle part representing Saxony and Japan engaged, in the presence of Minerva, in a dispute on the merits and perfection of the works made in their porcelain manufactories. They are to be accompanied by Emulation, Taste, Imitation, Painting, and Sculpture, and by all the elements which contribute to the beauty of these kinds of works. The goddess shall put the crown, the prize for the winner of the dispute, into the hands of Saxony, while Jealousy and Spite make signs to advise Japan to have her porcelain vases loaded back onto the vessels which brought them.

This subject matter would seem to be appropriate and can be executed in a noble and grand manner, furthermore offering scope for ingenious allegories, which is exactly what is called for by works of this kind, in order to exercise the mind.

The two other parts of the ceiling are to represent on the one hand the arts and the manufactories established in Saxony, and on the other such beneficial natural products as grow and are produced in the land; this is all to be done allegorically, with little elaboration, and to be executed nobly and in the grand manner.

The intention of this account has been to give a slight idea of this gallery. The skillfulness of the painters, sculptors and other such artists as are engaged upon it will bring it to perfection and bestow upon it beauties which cannot be well described in such a short explanation as this.]

Source 4
Order list of March 28, 1730

[SächsStAD, loc. 1341, IV, fols. 383a–384a]

Specification Derjenigen Porcelains, so Ihro Königl. Majt. in Pohlen und ChurFürstl.Durchl. zu Sachsen in Deroselben Fabrique zu Meißen zu dem Holländischen Palais verfertigen zu laßen allergnädigst anbefohlen haben

I. 200 Stück Schüßeln auf Japanische Facon nach dem Model No. I. iede 17. Zoll in Diametro und 2. Zoll tieff mit dem Randen in die

Gallerie wo die Japanischen Vasen zu stehen kommen und zwar zur Corniche.

II. 50. Stück Vogelbauer nach Japanischer Zeichnung und Mahlerey wie auch sonst nach dem Model No. 2. in gedachte Gallerie an die Trumons.

III. 100. Stück dunkel blaue Schüßeln mit weißen Feldern und darin gemahlten blauen Blumen und Landschafften nach dem Model No. 3. iede 17. Zoll in Diametro und 2. Zoll tieff zur Corniche in den Seiten Flügel wo das dunkel blaue Porcelain stehen soll.

IV. 50. Dutzend dergleichen Tassen und Schaalen Iden dergleichen ThéePots, mittel Auffsätze und Bouteillen so incirca zum garniren in gedachtes Zimmer gebrauchet werden dürfften.

V. 20. Stück Vogelbauer von blau und goldenen Porcelain sonst aber nach dem Model w in No. 2. in die beyden Eck-Pavillons wo blau und goldenes Porcelain auffgesezet werden soll.

VI. 200. Stück Schüßeln von weiß und blau ordinairen Porcelain, iede 17. Zoll in Diametro und 2. Zoll tieff, in die hinterste Gallerie nach dem Garthen zur Corniche und wo die großen blau und weißen Vasen stehen sollen.

VII. 60. Stück Assietten von alten Indianischen Porcelain zur Corniche in das Zimmer, wo dergleichen Porcelain rangiret werden soll, iede 10. Zoll in Diametro und 1 1/2 Zoll Tieff.

VIII. 16. Garnituren an Auffsätzen und Bouteillen von dergleichen Porcelain so ohngefähr zum garniren obgedachten Zimmers nöthig sein möchten in circa 1/2 Elen hoch.

IX. 20. Dutzend ThéeTassen und Schaalen von dergleichen Porcelain, gleichergestalt zum garniren gedachten Zimmers.

Dresßden, den 28. Marty. 1730

Source 5
Manufactory balance statement of December 13, 1731 (Catalog: "13 Dec 1731")

[SächsHStA, loc. 1341, VI, Acta die Porcellän Manufactur betr. 1732, fol. 26 a/b] = [BA, IAa.15, fol. 522 a/b]

[Appendix B to the report of the Commission of December 17, 1731]

Verzeichniß Derer nach Ihro Königl. Majth. hierzu absonderl. gegebenen Modellen und Rißen gefertigten großen Geschirren und dergl. so zum Verglühen mehrentheils parat stehen
[Catalog of the large porcelain pieces made in accordance with sketches and models provided by His Royal Majesty, the greater part of which now stand ready for low-firing:]

1.

Was in Thon poussiret und noch ausgeformet werden muss, als:
1. Stück WildSchwein
1. " Elèphant
1. " Rhenocerus
1. " Apostel Paulis 3 1/2 Elle hoch.
und
Ihro Königl.: Majth. zu Pferde

2.

Was in der rohen Massa ausgeformet und verfertiget stehet, als:
3. Stücke heil. Nepomuceni
4. " Indianische Raben, groß
2. " WaldTeuffel
90. " Aufsazstücken, diverser Sorten
3. " große Drachen

[26b]
4. Stück große Schüßeln
22. " große Vasen
21. " Aufsaz Stk. in Form eines Vogelbauers
5. " Spinxhe
3. " Apostol Petri von 2 1/2 Elle hoch
6. " Affen
2. " Indianische Fasahnen
4. " Falcken
2. " SeeMerhen
3. " Fischahr
2. " Kropff Vogel
3. " Adler
2. " FischAnher mit dem Karpffen
3. " Bläßgen
2. " große Eulen

3.

Gut gebranndte Stücken weiß
9. Stück Papagoyen
4. " Spinxhe
1. " KropffVogel

4.

Gut gebrannte und emaill. Stücke
9. Stück große Affen diverser Sorten
3. detto kleine
1. Stück Falcken oder StoßVogel
5. Papagoyen
3. kleine Eulen
1. Taucher

Wiewohl zeithero verschiedene von einigen solchen Stücken auch gut gewonnen, und zum Theil nach Dreßden geschicket worden, theils aber zur Lieferung alhier parat stehen.

Meißen den 13. Dec: 1731.

Source 6
Order list of February 25, 1732

[SächsHStA, loc. 1341, VI, Acta die Porcellän Manufactur betr. 1732, fols. 198 a/b u. 200a]

[198a]
Specification Was in dem Königl. Holländischen Pallais zu der fordern Gallerie in der Obern Etage an Porcelain erfordert wird, als:
[Specification of the porcelain ordered for the front gallery of the upper story of the Royal Dutch Palace:]

Zu denen Vier Stück breiten Camin-Schäfften
4. Roth laquirte Aufsäze jeder von 5. Stücken
24. Stück einzelne große Vasen, differ. Façon
40. Stück allerhand Thiere differenter Größe
40. Stück allerhand Vogel differenter Größe
8. Stück große Terrinen

Zu denen Vier Trumons
40. Stück allerhand groß und kleine Thiere
24. Stück große Vasen, differenter Façon
8. Stück grosse Terrinen mit Deckeln
40. Stück allerhand groß und kleine Vogel

Zu Vierzehn Stück schmalen Schäfften
84. Stück allerhand groß und kleine Vögel
56. Stück allerhand Thiere, differenter Größe
[198b]
28. Stück große Terrinen mit Deckel
98. Stück große Vasen, differenter Façon

16. Stück allerhand Thiere über die Fenster
32. Stück große Vasen desgleichen

Zwischen die Bogen Fenster
22. Stück einzelne Vasen, different
22. Stück allerhand Thiere differenter Größe
22. Stück allerhand Vögel differ. Größe

Auf die zwey schmalen Seiten-Wände
40. Stück allerhand Thiere
12. Stück große differente Vogel
20. Stück detto kleinere
2. Aufsäze über die Thüren jeder von 5 Stücken
36. Stück große Vasen, differenter Façon
30. Stück kleine detto detto
4. Stück große Terrinen mit Deckel

An Schüsseln
120. Stück Schüßeln 2. Zoll tief, 18. Zoll in diam: oben zur Corniche
[200a]
Summa derer von jeder Sorte betragenden Stücken:
30. Aufsaz Stücken an 6. Guarniduren
266. einzelne Vasen differenter Façon
198. Stück allerhand groß und kleine Thiere
198. Stück allerhand groß und kleine Vögel
48. Stück Terrinen mit Deckel
120. Stück Schüßeln
——
910. Stück

Neustadt bey Dreßden den 25. Febr: 1732

Source 7
Order list, undated (Catalog: "Early 1732")

[SächsHStA, loc. 1341, Varia, die Porcelain-Manufactur betreffend, undated, loose leaves, paginated in pencil, fols. 29a–30a]
[Annotation on the lower edge of the page: "1731 Japan.Palais"]

[29a]
Specification was in dem Königl: Holländ: Pallais zu der neuen fordern Gallerie in der Obern Etage an Porcellain erfordert wird, als:
[Specification of the porcelain ordered for the new front gallery of the upper story of the Royal Dutch Palace:]

Zu denen Vier Stück breiten Camin-Schäfften
4 Roth laquirte Auffsäze, jeder von 5 Stücken
12 Stück einzelne große Vasen auf die 4 Camin-Schäffte
8 Stück detto Bechern
8 Stück kleine Schaalen
8 Stück große Terrinen
24 Stück allerhand Thieren
8 Stück große Indianische Raben
8 Stück Papagoys

Zu denen Vier Trumons
24 Stück allerhand Thieren
12 Stück große Vasen
16 Stück detto Bechern
16 Stück kleine Schaalen
12 Stück große Terrinen mit Deckeln
8 Stück große Adler
[29b]
4 Stück große Pagoden
8 Stück große Pfauen
8 Stück kleine Vogel
6 Stück große Thiere über die Bogen-Fenstern
12 Stück große Vasen daneben zusezen
12 Stück Milch Känngen

Zu Vierzehn Stück schmalen Schäfften
56 Stück allerhand Thiere
40 Stück große differente Vogel
36 Stück detto kleinere neben bey zusezen
16 Stück große Terrinen mit Deckel
42 Stück große Vasen
52 Stück große Schaalen
32 Stück detto neben beyzusezen
16 Stück allerhand Thiere über die Fenstern
32 Stück große Vasen desgleichen

Auff die zwey schmalen Seitenwände
36 Stück allerhand Thiere
12 Stück große differente Vogel
20 Stück detto kleinere
2 Auffsäze über die Thüren, jeder von 5. Stücken
24 Stück große Vasen
12 Stück detto Bechern
[30a]
8 Stück großer Schaalen
20 Stück detto kleinere
4 Stück große Terrinen mit Deckel
4 Stück kleine Affen

An Schüßeln Oben zur Corniche
170 Stück Schüßeln, 18. Zoll in diametro, 2. Z. tief

Summa, derer von jeder Sorte betragenden Stücken, als:
164 Stück große Vasen
36 Bechern
60 Stück große Schaalen
76 Stück kleinere detto
40 Stück Terrinen
156 Stück allerhand Thieren
6 Stück große Thieren
8 Stück große Indian: Raben
8 Stück Papagoys
8 Stück große Adler
4 Stück große Pagoden
8 Stück Pfauen
52 Stück große differente Vasen
64 Stück kleinere detto
12 Stück Milch Känngen
4 Stück kleine Affen
20 Stück Schüßeln

Source 8
Manufactory balance statement of September 2, 1732 (Catalog: "18 Aug 1732")

[SächsHStA, loc. 1341, VI, Acta die Porcellän Manufactur betr. 1732, fols. 353b–354a] = [BA, IAa.17, fol. 234ab] = [BA, IAa.18, fol. 188a/b, where it is dated: "18. August 1732"]
[Appendix K to the report of the Commission of September 2, 1732]

[353b]
Specificatio Derjenigen Porcellain-Geschirren, welche theils emaillirt, theils gut gebrannt, theils aber noch roh und unverglühet bey der fabrique zu Meißen vorräthig, und zum Königl:Hollänischen Palais zuliefern dato fertig sind, als:
[Specification of the porcelain pieces which, partly enameled, partly high-fired, but also partly not yet fired at all, are in stock at Meissen and are now ready to be delivered to the Royal Dutch Palace:]

Porcellaine

emaillirte Stücke	Gutgebrannte Stücke	Verglühete Stücke	Rohe Stücke	
5	6	–	–	Affen
2	2	–	–	Eulen
–	10	–	4	Indian: Raben
–	2	–	–	Indian: Fasahnen
–	12	–	–	große Fischreyher
–	3	–	–	Waßer Hühner
–	1	–	–	Seemehe
–	8	–	–	Raubvögel
[354a]				
–	6	2	2	Wald-Teuffel
–	1	–	1	Elephanten
–	1	1	3	große Trachen
7	–	–	–	Papagoyen
–	8	31	51	große Vasen oder Aufsätze
–	–	–	2	Löwen
–	–	2	3	Katzen
–	–	2	1	Hunde
–	–	–	4	Bake
–	–		2	Renoceri
–	–	1	3	Adler
–	–	74	51	große Schüßeln
–	–	2	7	Aposteln worunter 1. Stück von 3. Ellen und 1. Stück von $3^{1}/_{2}$ Ellen lang
–	–	1	–	AuerOchßen

Meißen, den 18. Aug: 1732, Johann Gregorius Heroldt

Source 9
Order list of November 18, 1732 (Catalog: "18 Nov 1732")

[BA, IAa.17, fols. 332a–333a]

Specificatio Dererjenigen Vasen, Terrinen, Thiere und Vogel, so in das Königl: Japanische Palais in die Obere Etage der fordern Gallerie, nach Ihro Königl:Majth. allergnädigsten Resolution und Befehl verfertiget werden sollen, Als:
[Specification of the vases, vessels, animals and birds that are to be produced for the front gallery of the upper story of the Royal Dutch Palace in accordance with His Royal Majesty's most gracious resolution and order:]

1.)
An Vasen
auf 6. breite und 12. schmahle Schäffte, ingl. auf die 2. Seiten Wände
– 156. Stück Vasen von differenter Façon

2.)
An Terrinen
– 44. Stück Terrinen mit Deckel

3.)
An Thieren
4. Löwen
4. Stück Löwinnen
4. Elephanten
12. Affen
4. Spinxe
4. Bären
4. AuerOchßen
4. Reinocerus
8. Pavions
4. Camele
4. Leoparten
4. Tieger Thiere
4. Panther Thiere
4. Luxe
2. Eichhörne
2. Zobel
4. Indianische Hirsche
4. Stachel Schweine
4. Pferde
4. Hirsche
4. Wölffe
4. Affricanische Esel
4. Gemßen
2. Füchße
2. Dachße
2. Hunde
2. Kazen
4. Ziegenböcke
4. Ziegen
4. Schaafe
4. Haasen
4. Gardeleons
4. Indian: Ratten
Thut/132 Stück

4.)
An Vögeln
4. Strauße
4. große Rayher
4. Adler
4. Könige von Wawou
4. Csuarius
4. Löffel Gänße
4. Trappen
4. Krescher
4. Pfauen
4. Schwanen
4. Störche
4. Caloutsch-Hüner
4. dergl. Hähne
4. Vasanen
12. große Raub Vogel
4. Ind: Raben
4. große Eulen
4. Stk. Graniche
4. Falcken
4. Ind. Berl-Hüner
4. Hähne
4. Hüner
4. Papagoyen
4. Auer-Hähne
4. Mandel Krahen
4. Parognitten
4. Türckische Endten
4. Buhu

Summa Summarum
156. Stück Vasen
44. Stück Terrinen
132. Stück Thiere und
120. Stück Vogel

Neustadt bey Dreßden den 18. Novbr: 1732
Martin Teuffert

Source 10
Interim totals of December 17, 1732 (Catalog: "17 Dec 1732")

[BA, IAa.17, fols. 335a–336a]

[335a]
Extract
Was von denjenigen Porcellain-Geschirren so ins Königl. Holländ. Pallais zuverfertigen anbefohlen worden, bereits geliefert, bis dato in Arbeit, und theils noch zu verfertigen sind.
[List of which of the porcelain figures ordered for the Royal Dutch Palace have already been delivered, which are still in production, and which are still to be produced.]

Sollen allergn: anbefohlener-maßen gefertiget werden	Sind geliefert	Sind in Arb:	Müßen noch gefertiget werd.
Stück	Stück	Stück	Stück
4. Löwen	–	2	2
4. Löwinnen	–	3	1
12. Affen	12	–	–
8. Elephanten	1	1	6
8. Spinxe	–	4	4
8. Bäre	–	3	5
8. AuerOchßen	–	2	6
8. Reinocerus	–	1	7
8. Pavions	8	–	–
8. Camehle	–	–	8
8. Leoparten	–	–	8
8. Tieger Thiere	–	–	8
4. Zobel	–	–	4
4. Haasen	–	–	4
4. Taxe	–	–	4
[335b]			
4. Luxe	–	–	4
8. Stachel Schweine	–	–	8
8. Pferdte	–	–	8
8. Hirsche	–	–	8
8. Africanische Esel	–	–	8
4. Wölffe	–	–	4
4. Füchße	–	3	1
4. Hunde	4	–	–
4. Kazen	4	3	–
8. Ziegenböcke	3	1	4
4. Ziegen	2	–	2
8. Wider oder Schaafe	–	–	8
8. Eichhörnchen	2	–	6
An Vögeln			
8. Strauße	–	–	8
8. große Reyher	11	–	–
8. do. Raubvögel	8	–	–
8. Ind: grose Raaben	6	2	–
8. große Eulen	5	–	3
8. Adler	–	1	7
8. sogenannte König Wowous	–	–	8
8. Casuarios	1	4	3
8. Löffel Gänße	–	1	7
[336a]			
8. Trappen	–	1	7
4. Auer Hähne	–	–	4
8. Mandel Kraen	–	–	8
4. Krescher	–	–	4
4. Ind: Raub Vögel	4	–	–
4. Falcken	3	–	1
4. Schwane	–	–	4
8. Pfaue, als 4. bunde			
als 4. weiße	–	–	8
4. schwarze Störche	–	–	4
8. Ind: Berghüner	–	–	8
8. Hähne	2	–	6
8. Hüner mit Coppen	4	–	4
8. Kraniche mit 1. Stein	–	–	8
12. Fasanen	6	–	6
4. Calutsch Hähne	–	–	4
4. do Hüner	–	–	4
12. Papagey	12	–	–
8. Barognitchen	–	–	8
4. Türckische Enden	–	–	4
12. Manninchen	–	–	12
6. Buhu	–	2	4
100. allerhand kleine Vögel	8	6	86

Meißen am 17. Decembr: 1732

Source 11
Deliveries 1731/1732 (Catalog: "1731/1732" or "1732 only")

[BA, IAa.20, fols. 64a–65a]

[64a]
Specification
Dererjenigen PorcellainGeschirre, welche in dem Jahre 1731 und 1732 aus der Königl. Porcellain Fabrique zu Meißen zum WaarenLager nacher Dreßden und ferner in das Holländische Palais nach und nach geliefert worden, als: [Specification of the porcelain pieces that were delivered in the course of the years 1731 and 1732 from the Royal Porcelain Factory in Meissen to the warehouse and then to Dresden and to the Dutch Palace:]

An Weißen
10. Vasen [most likely the large grotesque vases]
9. Drachen
7. WaldTeufel
3. große Affen
6. kleine dto
11. Fischreyher
4. Fasahnen
4. Gluckhüner mit Jungen
12. RaubVögel
4. Hunde
1. Casuarius
10. Raben, Ind:
1. großer Hahn
[64b]
3. weiße Ziegenböcke, it. 2. Ziegen
1. großer Elephant
6. Eulen
3. Waßerhüner
2. SeeMeuben
4. Kazen
2. Papogey
8. Schüßeln
2. Schwalben
1. Adler
5. kleine Spinxe
1. Waßer Taucher
2. Josephs Brust-Stücken
1. Petrus Figur

An emaillirten
2. Drachen
17. Affen
6. Raub Vögel
3. Indianische Raben
3. Manincken
[65a]
3. Fischreyher
2. Grobvogel
5. Eulen
3. Waßerhüner
1. See Meube
8. Papogeyen
4. Tauben
2. Eichhörnigen

Source 12
Animals reserved in Meissen for the Japanese Palace by Sulkowski on November 17, 1733 (Catalog: "17 Nov 1733")

[SächsHStA, loc. 1342, VII, Acta die Porcelaine Manufactur betr. 1733, fol. 8r–8v] = [BA, IAa.19, fols. 342a–343a]
[dated in the title: "17. Nov. 1733"]

Specificatio dererjenigen Porcelain Geschirre so auff Ihro Königl. May. allergnädigsten hohen mündlichen Befehl, und ferner hohen Anordnung des Herrn Geheimbden Raths und Ober-Stallmeisters Reichs-Graffen von Solcowsky Excellenz den 17. November 1733 bey Anwesenheit des Herrn Cammer-Rath von Pflugs, und Bettmeister Teufferts, in dem Königl. Meißnischen Porcelain Waaren-Lager zum ausmöbliren des Königl. Japanischen Palais befunden und ausgesezet worden, als:
[Specification of the porcelain pieces that were found at the Meissen porcelain warehouse on 17 November 1733 in the presence of Councillor von Pflugk and Major-domo Teuffert and were reserved to be used for the furnishing of the Royal Japanese Palace in accordance with the verbal order of His most gracious Royal Majesty and delivered by Privy Councillor and Master of the Stables Reichsgraf von Sulkowski:]

An Emalirten Porcelain Geschirren
4 Casuarii
2 Trappen
3 Welsche Hähne
1 Löffel-Gannß
1 Indianischer Rabe
1 großer Hahn
4 Füchße

An ganz weißen und nicht Emailirten Porcelain Geschirren:
[...]
150 Vögel groß und kleine diverser Sorten
200 Thiere allerhand Arthen groß und kleine
300 Figuren groß und kleine diverser Sorten
[...]
6 Orgel Pfeiffen

[signed] Meißen, den 18. November 1733, Johann George Heymann [book-keeper]

Source 13
Order list of November 26, 1733 (Catalog: "26 Nov 1733")

[BA, IAa.19, fols. 347a–369a] = [SächsHStA, OHMA, Pläne, Cap.II, Nr.15; Beilage zu Grund- und Aufrissen] = [publ. in Cassidy-Geiger, Maureen, "Meissen Porcelain ordered for the Japanese Palace: A transcription of the Specification von Porcilan of 1736," *Keramos* 153 (1996): 119–130]

Meißen den 26. Novembr: 1733
[347a]
No. 1.
Specificatio Dererjenigen Vasen, Thiere und Vögel, so in das Königl. JapanischePalais
in die Obere Etage der fördern Gallerie auf Ihro Königl. Mayt. in Pohlen, und ChurFürstl. Durchl. zu Sachßen allergnädigsten hohen mündlichen Befehl, und fernehohen Anordnung Sr. Excellenz des Herrn Geheimbden Rath und Ober-StallMeisters, Reichs-Grafen von Sulkowsky in der Meißnischen Porcelain Fabrique verferttiget werden soll, als:
[Specification of those vases, animals and birds to be produced in the Meissen Porcelain Manufactory for the upper story of the front gallery of the Royal Japanese Palace, according to the most gracious verbal order of His Royal Majesty in Poland and Highness the Elector of Saxony, delivered by his Excellency Privy Councillor and Master of the Stables Reichsgraf von Sulkowsky:]

An Vasen
Auff 8. breite und 12. schmahle Schäffte, ingleichen auf die 2. Seiten-Wände
2. Garnituren, jede von 7. Stück über die 2. Thüren, roth und Gold gemahlt
148. Stück einzelne Vasen, von differenter Façon, nach obiger Mahlerey

[347b]
An Thieren

8. Löwen	8. Affricanische Esel
8. Löwin	8. Gemßen
8. Elephanten	8. Füchße
8. Spinxe	8. Füchße
8. Bähren	8. Taxe
8. Auer Ochßen	8. Hunde
8. Rheinoceros	4. Kazen
8. Leoparden	8. Ziegen Böcke
8. Camehle	8. Ziegen
8. Pavians	8. Schaafe
8. Tieger Thie	8. Haasenr
4. Luxe	4. Eichhörngen
8. Stachel-Schweine	8. Zobeln
4. Pferde	8. Jardeleons
11. Drachen	8. Indianische Ratten
8. Panter Thier	26. Affen
8. Hirsche	4. Josephs Figuren Brust Stücke
8. Wölffe	11. Wald-Teuffel
8. Affricanische Schafe	4. Einhörner

[348a]
An Vögeln

8. Strauße	8. Granige
8. Adler	8. Falcken
12. Könige von Wawoa	8. Indianische Perl Hühner
14. Indianische Raben	8. Große Hähne
12. Fisch-Reyher	8. Teutsche Hühner
18. Raub Vogel	13. Papegoy
8. Casuarii	8. Auer Hähne
12. Eylen	8. Mandel Grahen
8. Löffel-Gänße	8. Elstern
8. Trappen	8. Türckische Enden
12. Krescher	8. Puhu
8. Pfauen	4. Fisch-Taucher
8. Schwane	2. Krob Vogel
8. Störche	6. Waßer Hühner
8. Calcuzsch Hähne	3. See-Meuben
8. Fasane	24. Taube

[...]
No. 6.
Specificatio
Der Porcelains, Weiß, so nach Alt.Indian.Arth mit wenig Mahlerey versehen, und in das Königl. Japan. Palais in die Obere Etage in den Pavillon nach den Garthen zu, verferttiget werden soll, als
[...]

An die Fenster Seite

4. Stück einzelne Vasen, jede 1 Elle 8 Zoll hoch	10. Stück Assietten, 15 Zoll in diam.
2. Garnituren jede von 5. Stück 1 elle 6 Zoll hoch	6. Stück Assietten, 12 Zoll in diam
2. do. etwas kleinere, 1 Elle hoch	2. Stück Bajoden
2. do. noch kleinere, 18 Zoll hoch	6. Stück Thée-Känngen
6. Stück hohe runde	6. Stück Milch-Krügel
6. Stück achteckigte	6. Stück Coffée-Känngen, Div. Sorten
6. Stück sechseckigte, Bouteillen, div.Sorten	18. Stück Confect-Schälgen
6. Stück viereckigte	196. Stück Coffee-Tassen mit Henkeln u. Unterschalen
	6. Stück Thée-Büchßen

6. Stück SpühlCompen, 10 Zoll hoch
6. Stück Terrinen mit deckeln, rund und passigt
24. Stück Thée-Copgen und Schälgen
12. Stück Butter Büchßen

J'ateste qu'on a besoin de tent de pieces pour l'ameublement du Palais du Japon depuis le N 1 jusqu-à 11.

AJSulkowski

Source 14
Deliveries 1733 (Catalog: "1733")

[SächsHStA, loc. 1342, VIII, fols. 20a–25b] = [BA, IAa.21, fols. 16a–17a]
[= Beilage zum Kommissionsbericht vom 2. April 1734]

[29a]
Specificatio Was vor Ihro Königl.Majestaet in Pohlen und Churfürstl.Durchl. zu Sachßen, an emaillierten Porcelain-Geschiren in Dero Japanisches Palais zu Neustadt aus hiesiger manufactur Anno 1733 geliefert worden, als:
[Specification of the enameled porcelain pieces that were delivered for His Royal Majesty in Poland and Highness the Elector of Saxony to the Japanese Palace in Neustadt from the manufactory here in the year 1733:]

[29b]
1.
An Thieren und Vögeln
den 31. Octobr. 1733
2. Stück nach dem Leben bemahlte Aelstern
den 11. Nov.
2. Stück dergl. Tauben
den 18ten Nov.
4. Stk. große Casuarius mit bunten Farben bemahlt
1. Stk. dergl. Löffel-Ganß
2. Stk. dergl. Trappen
3. Stk. dergl. Welsche Hähne
1. Stk. dergl. Brabander. Hahn
1. Stk. dergl. Indian. Raben
5. Stk. " " Füchßen
2. Stk. kleine Grümpel
2. Stk. " " Schwalben
2. Stk. " " Kohl-Maisen
2. Stk. " " blaue Maisen
den 25. Nov.
4. Stk. Aeltestern, nach den Leben bemahlet
4. Stk. Bachsteltzen, desgleichen
4. Stk. Grümpel, dergl.
6. Stk. Kohl-Maisen
[30a]
6. Stk. Ind. Vögel mit hohen Postamenten
den 23. Dec.
6. Stk. Canari-Vögel mit Nestern

[A second section follows, including green- and yellow-glazed tableware, 55 pieces altogether.]

Source 15
Deliveries from March 7, 1733, to October 22, 1734
(Catalog: "7 Mar 1733 – 22 Oct 1734")

[BA, IAe.3, fol. 236a/b]

[236a]
Specification
Was vor Ihro Königl.Maj. in Pohlen undt Churfürstl. Durchl. zu Sachßen an allerhandt Porcelain-Wahren, sowohl ins Holl. Palais als auch sonsten geliefert worden als vom 7 Marty 1733 bis dato den 22 Oct. 1734.
[Specification of what sundry porcelain pieces were delivered for His Royal Majesty in Poland and Highness the Elector of Saxony to the Dutch Palace and elsewhere from March 7, 1733 to October 22, 1734.]

An Vögeln
4 Casuarii
6 Trappen
2 Löffel Gänse
1 Indianischen Rabe
3 Welsche Hähne
5 Hauß Hähne
14 Elstern
4 Tauben
4 Grob Vögel
7 Spechte
6 gelb und schartze Vögel
7 Vgel auf hohen Postamenten
1 Pfau
6 große und
3 kleine Pappegoy
6 Indianische Vögel
[236b]
4 Gimpel
4 Bachsteltzen
12 Meisen

An Thieren
5 Löwen
8 Löwinn
5 Leoparden
4 Rinoceros
4 Elephanten
5 Bähre
5 Luchße
2 Ziegen
1 Ziegen Bock
6 Füchße

[Here follow several pages of table services, including the Coronation service, and the yellow hunt service.]

Source 16
Deliveries 1734 (Catalog: "1734" or "1734 in toto")

[SächsHStA, loc. 1342, VIII, Acta die Porcelaine Manufactur betr. 1734/35, fol. 78/1a–78/7a] = [SächsHStA, loc. 520, Porcelain Waaren Lagers zu Dreßden Rechnung vom 1. Jan. bis 31. Decembr 1734, fols. 113b–114b]

[78/1a]
Anno 1734 in Dreßden
Vor Ihro Königl. Majestät in Pohlen und Chur-Fürstl. Durchl. zu Sachßen, seynd dieses Jahr aus Dero Porcelaine Lager zum Japan. Palais in Unterthänigkeit geliefert worden, als
[What has been duly delivered, for His Royal Majesty in Poland and Highness the Elector of Saxony, during this year 1734 from the porcelain warehouse to the Japanese Palace in Dresden:]

An Thieren

5	Löwen	106r	530.–
8	Löwin	106r	848.–
5	Leoparden	66 1/3r	331.16
4	Elephanten	197r	788.–
4	Rinoceros	172r	688.–
5	Bäre	209 1/3r	1046.16

5	Luchße	60r	300.–
2	Auer Ochßen	265r	530.–
6	Füchße	66 1/3 r	398.–
3	Ziegen mit Jungen	132 2/3 r	398.–
2	Ziegen Böcke	134r	268.–
2	Eichhorne, als Thee Potte	4r	8.–
	Transport		6134.8

[78/1b]
An Vögeln

6	Adler	136r	816.–
4	Pfaue mit breiten Schweiffen	179r	716.–
5	dergl. mit hangenden Schweiffen	120r	600.–
5	Casuarii	309r	1545.–
6	Trappen	99 1/2 r	597.–
3	Löffel-Gänse	204r	612.–
1	Indian. Rabe		112.–
5	Welsche Hähne	67r	335.–
5	Hauß Hähne	48 1/3 r	241.16.
5	Könige von Wawa	67 2/3 r	338.8
1	Indian. Geyer		95.–
6	Pappegoye	14r	84.–
5	Jakacou	24r	120.–
3	Paroetgen	8 1/4 r	24.18.
4	Tauben	12 1/4 r	49.–
7	Krob Vögel	66 1/3 r	464.8.
13	Paradies Vögel	4 1/3 r	56.8
14	Elstern	11 1/4 r	157.12.
7	Spechte	8 1/2 r	59.12
6	gelbe Vögel	6r	36.–
4	Bachsteltzen	5 2/3 r	22.16.
	Transport		13216.10

[78/2a]

6	Gümpel	3 1/4 r	19.12
14	Meisen	2r	28.–
6	Vogel Nester	4r	24.–
2	Schwalben	2 1/3 r	4.16

[Here follow tableware, *galanteries*, table services, and other wares of indeterminate character.]

Source 17
Interim totals of February 18, 1735 (Catalog: "18 Feb 1735" or "before Feb 1735")

[SächsHStA, loc. 1342, VIII, Acta die Porcelaine Manufactur betr. 1734/35, fols. 125a–127a] = [BA, IAa.23, fols. 90a–92a]
[Appendix E to the report of the Commission of February 18, 1735]

Specificatio was von denenjenigen Porcellain Geschirren so ins Königl. Japanische Palais zu verferttigen allergnädigst anbefohlen worden, bereits geliefert und noch zu verferttigen sind, als:
[Specification of which of the porcelain figures most graciously ordered for the Royal Japanese Palace have already been delivered, and which are still to be produced:]

Benennung derer Sorten, als	soll geliefert werden	ist geliefert worden	Restiren	sind über die Bestallung gel.
An Thieren				
Löwen	4	5	–	1
Löwinnen	4	8	–	4
Elephanten	4	5	–	1
Affen	12	26	–	14
Spinxe	4	8	–	4
Bären	4	5	–	1
Auer-Ochßen	4	2	2	–
Reinocerus	4	4	–	–
Pavians	8	–	8	–
Camehle	4	–	4	–
Leoparten	4	5	–	1
Tieger-Thiere	4	–	4	–
Panther-Thiere	4	–	4	–
Luxe	4	5	–	1
Stachel-Schweinen	4	–	4	–
Pferden	4	–	4	–
Hirsche	4	–	4	–
Wölffen	4	–	4	–
Africanische Esel	4	–	4	–
Gemßen	4	–	4	–
Füchße	2	6	–	4
[125b]				
Dachße	2	–	2	–
Hunde	2	5	–	3
Kazen	2	4	–	2
Ziegen-Böcke	4	5	–	1
Ziegen	4	5	–	1
Schaafe	4	–	4	–
Haasen	4	–	4	–
Eichhörner	2	4	–	2
Zobel	2	–	2	–
Indianische Hirsche	4	–	4	–
Gardeleons	4	–	4	–
Indianische Ratten	4	–	4	–
An Vögeln				
Strauße	4	–	4	–
große Rayher	4	11	–	7
Adler	4	7	–	3
Könige von Wawou	4	6	–	2
große Raub-Vögel	12	18	–	6
Ind:Raben	4	14	–	10
große Eulen	4	11	–	7
Graniche	4	–	4	–
Casuarius	4	6	–	2
Löffel-Gänßen	4	6	–	2
Trappen	4	6	–	2
Krescher [Krischer][1]	4	–	4	–
Pfaue	4	9	–	5
Schwane	4	–	4	–
Störche	4	–	4	–
[126a]				
Caloutsch-Hüner	4	–	4	–
dergl. Hähne	4	5	–	1
Vasanen	4	4	–	–
Falcken	4	18	–	14
Ind:Berl-Hüner	4	–	4	–
Hähne	4	8	–	4
Hüner	4	4	–	–
Papagoyen	4	16	–	12
Auer-Hähne	4	–	4	–
Mandel-Krahen	4	–	4	–
Parognittgen	4	–	4	–
Türckische Endten	4	–	4	–
Buhue	4	–	4	–

Über vorhergehende Bestallung sind annoch an Thieren u. Vögeln so nicht bestellet geliefert worden, als:

An Thieren

Trachen	–	–	–	11
Wald-Teuffel	–	–	–	7
Poloneser-Hunde	–	–	–	5
Crocodille	–	–	–	4
kleine Bähre	–	–	–	3

[126b]
An Vögeln

Krob Vogel	–	–	–	10
Fisch-Taucher	–	–	–	4
Waßer-Hüner	–	–	–	6
See-Meuben	–	–	–	1
Indian:Gayren	–	–	–	5
Elstern	–	–	–	18
Tauben	–	–	–	13
Jackacou	–	–	–	6
Bier-Eulen	–	–	–	12
Ind:Gugucke	–	–	–	6
Lerchen-Stößer	–	–	–	2
Ind:Endten	–	–	–	5
Spechte	–	–	–	7
Paradies-Vogel	–	–	–	17
Paretgen	–	–	–	3
Bachstelzen	–	–	–	6
Gümpel	–	–	–	6
Meisen	–	–	–	23
Vogel-Nester	–	–	–	6
Schwalben	–	–	–	8
Manninchen	–	–	–	3
Canarien Vogel	–	–	–	5
kleine Schwanen	–	–	–	16

[The specification continues with green-glazed tableware.]

Source 18
Deliveries from March 5 to December 17, 1735 (Catalog: "1735" or "1735 in toto")

[SächsHStA, loc. 520, Porcelain Waaren Lagers zu Dreßden Rechnung vom 1. Jan. bis 31. Decembr 1735, fols. 98b–99b]

Anno 1735 In Dreßden
Vor Ihro Königl. Majestaet in Pohlen und ChurFürstl. Durchl. zu Sachßen, wurden zu Dero Japan. Palais vom 5. Marty bis 17 Decembr a.c. in Unterthänigkeit geliefert, als:
[What has been duly delivered, for His Royal Majesty in Poland and Highness the Elector of Saxony, from the porcelain warehouse to the Japanese Palace in Dresden between March 5 and December 17 in the year 1735:]

An Thieren

5	Bologneser Hunde	33 Thlr	165.–
1	Affe	86.12	
6	Indian. Zobel	a 48 $^{5}/_{6}$r	293.–
1	Indian. Schaaf		131.–
9	Indian Ratten	a 7 T	63.–
3	kleine Bäre	1 T 16 gr	5.–
8	Sfinxe	16 $^{1}/_{3}$ r	130.16
1	Wolff		92.8

An Vögeln

3	Lerchen Stößer	10 $^{5}/_{6}$ r	32.12
5	Elstern	a 11 $^{1}/_{4}$ r	56.6
6	Falcken	a 10 $^{5}/_{6}$ r	65.–
10	Bier Eulen	a 6 r	60.–
2	Bachsteltzen	a 5 $^{1}/_{2}$ r	11.–
6	Meysen	a 1 $^{1}/_{3}$ r	8.–

[99a]

Transport			1199.6
4	Paradies Vögel	a 4 $^{1}/_{2}$ r	18.–
3	Löffel Gänse	a 204 r	612.–
1	Krob Vogel		66.8
1	König von Wawa		67.12
4	Indian. Reyer	a 93 r	372.–
6	Indian. Endten	a 48 $^{1}/_{2}$ r	291.–
6	Rohr Dommeln	a 33 $^{1}/_{4}$ r	199.12
5	Fasan Hähne	a 93 r	465.–
6	Fasan Hüner	a 96 r	576.–
7	Berl Hüner	a 21 $^{1}/_{4}$ r	148.18
5	Tauben incl. 1 doppelte	a 12 $^{1}/_{4}$ r	61.6
1	Indian. Jakedow		33.8
3	See Meuben	a 15 $^{2}/_{3}$ r	47.–
6	Kraniche	a 74 $^{1}/_{4}$ r	445.12

[The listing continues with tableware.]

Source 19
Interim totals up to and including January 1736 (Catalog: "9 Mar 1736")

[SächsHStA, loc. 1342, IX, Acta die Porcelaine Manufactur betr. 1736/37, fols. 41a–44a] = [BA, IAa.25, fols. 48a–51a, abweichende Orthographie]
[= Appendix 3 to the report of the Commission of March 9, 1736]

Specificatio Was von denenjenigen Porcellain-Geschirren, so in das Königl. Japanische Palais zu verferttigen allergnädigst anbefohlen worden, bereits bis mit ult:Jan:1736. geliefert und noch zu liefern sind, als:
[Specification of which of the porcelain figures most graciously ordered for the Royal Japanese Palace were delivered up to and including the last day of January 1736, and which are still to be delivered:]

Benennung derer Sorten, als	soll geliefert werden	ist geliefert worden	Restiret noch	Ist über die Bestallung gel.
An Thieren				
Löwen	4	5	–	1
Löwinnen	4	8	–	4
Elephanten	4	5	–	1
Affen	12	27	–	15
Spinxe[2]	4	10	–	6
Bäre	4	5	–	1
Auer-Ochßen	4	2	2	–
Reinocerus	4	4	–	–
Pavians	8	–	8	–
Camehlen	4	–	4	–
Leoparten	4	5	–	1
Tiger-Thieren	4	–	4	–
Panther-Thieren	4	–	4	–
Luxe	4	5	–	1
Stachel-Schweinen	4	–	4	–
Pferden	4	–	4	–
Hirsche	4	–	4	–
Wölffe	4	5	–	1
Affricanische Esel	4	–	4	–
[41b]				
Gemßen	4	2	2	–
Füchße	2	6	–	4

Dachßen	2	–	2	–
Hunde	2	5	–	3
Kazen	2	4	–	2
Ziegen-Böcke	4	5	–	1
Ziegen	4	5	–	1
Schaafe	4	2	2	–
Haasen	4	–	4	–
Eichhörnern	2	4	–	2
Zobel	2	6	–	4
Ind:Hirschen	4	–	4	–
Gardeleons	4	–	4	–
Ind:Ratten	4	9	–	5

An Vögeln

Strauße	4	–	4	–
große Rayhern	4	11	–	7
Adlern	4	7	–	3
Könige von Wawou	4	6	–	2
große Raub-Vögel	12	18	–	6
Ind:Raben	4	14	–	10
große Eulen	4	11	–	7
Graniche	4	6	–	2
Casuarius	4	6	–	2
Löffel-Gänßen	4	6	–	2
Trappen	4	6	–	2
Kreschern	4	–	4	–
Pfaue	4	9	–	5
[42a]				
Schwane	4	3	1	–
Störche	4	–	4	–
Caloutsch-Hähne[3]	4	5	–	1
dergl. Hünern	4	4	–	–
Vasanen	4	11	–	7
Falcken	4	18	–	14
Ind:Berl-Hünern	4	7	–	3
Hähnen	4	8	–	4
Hünern	4	4	–	–
Papagoye	4	16	–	12
Auer-Hähnen	4	–	4	–
Mandel-Krahen	4	–	4	–
Parognittgen	4	–	4	–
Türckische Endten	4	–	4	–
Buhue	4	5	–	1

Über vorhergehende Bestallung sind anoch an Thieren und Vögeln so nicht bestellet geliefert worden, als:

An Thieren

Trachen	–	–	–	11
Wald-Teuffel	–	–	–	7
Poloneser-Hunde	–	–	–	5
Crocodillo	–	–	–	4
kleine Bähren	–	–	–	3

[42b]
An Vögeln

Rohr-Tummeln	–	–	–	6
Ind:Endten	–	–	–	6
Fisch-Taucher	–	–	–	7
Krob Vogel	–	–	–	10
Waßer-Hünern	–	–	–	6
See-Meuben	–	–	–	1
Ind:Gayren	–	–	–	5
Elstern	–	–	–	19
Tauben	–	–	–	13
Ind:Jackedou	–	–	–	6
Bier-Eulen	–	–	–	12
Ind:Guckucken	–	–	–	6
Lerchen-Stößern	–	–	–	3
Ind:Endten	–	–	–	5
Spechte	–	–	–	7
Paradies-Vogel	–	–	–	17
Paretgen	–	–	–	3
Bachstelzen	–	–	–	6
Gümpeln	–	–	–	6
Meisen	–	–	–	23
Vogel-Nester mit jungen	–	–	–	6
Schwalben	–	–	–	8
Manninchen[4]	–	–	–	3
Canarien Vögeln	–	–	–	5
kleine Schwanen	–	–	–	16

[42b–44a]
[Here follow items of green-glazed tableware, some enameled and some for the silver pantries, confectioneries, etc.]
[In Expl. BA the last birds are summarized as follows:]

Gimpel und Meisen	–	–	29
Canarien Vögel und Schwalben	–	–	19
Manninchen und kleine Schwaane	–	–	19

Source 20
Deliveries 1736 (Catalog: "1736")

[SächsHStA, loc. 1342, IX, Acta die Porcelaine Manufactur betr. 1736/37, fols. 243b–245a] = [BA, IAa.24c, fols. 8a–10a] = [SächsHStA, loc. 521, Porcelain Waaren Lagers zu Dreßden Rechnung vom 1. Jan. bis ult. Dec. 1736, unpaginated, but with prices]
[= Appendix 4 to the report of the Commission of January 4, 1737]

[243b]
Specificatio
Derjenigen Geschirre, welche anno 1736 in das Königliche Jappanische Palais allergnädigst anbefohlenermaßen gefertiget und abgeliefert worden, als:
[Specification of those pieces which were produced and delivered according to order to the Royal Japanese Palace in the year 1736:]

[245a]
Zum Jappanischen Palais ist geliefert:
4. Wölffe
2. Gemßen
1. Schaaf
3. Schwahne
4. Buhu
4. Welsche Hüner
6. Mandel Krähen
4. Eiß-Vögel
2. Spechte
2. Paroetgen
2. Eichel Gabichte

38. kleine grün glasurte Suppen Schalen
9. grün glasurte Aufsatz Bouteillen
12. Saladieren
5. Confect-Schaalen
1. großer Punch Napff mit Königl: Wappen, so etwas schadhafft
20. allerhand Spühl-Compen, ohne denen was in Warschau geliefert worden

Samuel Chladni

Source 21
List of the modelers, throwers, repairers, and molders detailed to work on the Japanese Palace orders, 1732

[BA, IAa.18, Acta worinne die wegen Umtrieb der Königl: Porcelain- Manufactur auf dem Schloße zu Meißen abgefaßte Monathsrapports und darauf ertheilte Commissarische Resolutiones befindlich, anno 1732]

Rapport [...] vom 1. biß mit den 30. April: 1732
[66b]
Wird die Specification sub KK mit mehrern besagen, welche Personen von dem Herrn Hoff-Commissario Hörolden darzu denominiret worden, die eintzig und allein an denen jenigen Porcellain-Geschirren, so Ihro Königl:Majth: vermöge allergnädigsten Special-Rescriptes sub dato Warschau den 2. April 1732 und beygefügten Specification an die neue fördere Gallerie des Königl: Holländischen Palais verlangen, arbeiten und nach und nach verfertigen
[67a]
sollen. Wie dann hierzu von gedachten Herrn Hoff-Commissario auf die erforderte Anstalt bereits getroffen worden, daß solche Geschirre, anhalts vorher angefügter Specification, wovon derselbe Abschrifft erhalten, nach aller Möglichkeit gefördert werden sollen.

[85a]
KK
Specification
Dererjenigen Fabricanten, welche allein an den Porcellain Geschirren arbeiten sollen, so in das Königl: Holländische Pallais und zwar zu der neuen fördern Gallerie erfordert werden, und sind von dem Hr. Hoff-Commissario Hörolden, zu dem Ende, nachstehende Persohnen hierzu denominiret worden, als:

1.) Kirchner	
2.) Kentler	Modellirer
3.) Geithner sen.	
4.) Lohse sen.	
5.) Grund	als Dreher
6.) Lücke	als Poussirer und verputzer
7.) Fritzsche	
8.) Albrecht	
9.) Krumbholz	
10.) Schmahl	
11.) Schmieder	
12.) Müller	als Former

Source 22[5]
Description of the Japanese Palace by Jonas Hanway, published in 1753

[Jonas Hanway, An Historical Account of the British Trade over the Caspian Sea [...], London 1753, II:226–227]

[...] The next curiosity is the Chinese palace, so called from the taste of the building, and the intention of furnishing it with porcelain. The ornaments of the architecture, and the relievo in the frontispice, are after the Chinese and Japan manner. The palace stands on the Elbe, and commands a view of the bridge and of the Romish chapel, but it is far from being an elegant building, and is siuated too near the river. The vaults of this palace consist of fourteen apartments, filled with China and Dresden porcelain; one would imagine there was sufficient quantity to stock a whole country, and yet they say, with an air of importance, that 100'000 pieces more are wanted to compleat the intention of furnishing this single palace, which is not large.

Perhaps it may be some indulgence, to a female curiosity at least, to be informed concerning this brittle commodity, which has been so passionately sought by the fair sex. But can this passion be deemed a folly when we see even mighty princes pride themselves in it? Here are a great number of porcelain figures of dogs, sqirrels, monkeys, wolves, bears, leopards, &c. some of them as big as the life; also elephants and rhinoceros's of the size of a large dog; a prodigious variety of birds, as cocks, hens, turkeys, peacocks, pheasants, hawks, eagles, besides parrots and other foreign birds, and a curious collection of different flowers. The apostles near three feet high, are in white porcelain. There is a representation of the crucifixion four or five feet high, with numerous other curious pieces: these last are intended for the Romish chapel, which I have already observed is to be furnished with these rare materials. A clock is preparing for the gallery in this palace, whose bells are to be also of porcelain: I heard one of them proved, and they are sufficient to form any music; but the hammers must be of wood.

A superstitious reverence for this extraordinary production has induced of his majesty to preserve some of the first efforts of the porcelain fabric, and other performances in their several gradations, to the perfection the art is now arrived: nor is this pious concern confined to his own manufactures; here is a great number of plates and dishes of the old porcelain of China, invaluable in the esteem of those whose ideas are refined above common capacities. But what is most amazingly wonderful, are the 48 China vases, which do not appear to be of any use, nor to be any ways extraordinary except their great size; and yet his late Polish majesty discovered such captivating charms in these inanimate beauties, that he purchased them of the late king of Prussia, at the price of a whole regiment of dragoons.

The long gallery in the second story hat already two marble chimney-pieces, each adorned with near 40 very large pieces of porcelain, of bird, beasts, and vasa, ranged to the height of above 20 feet in a most superb taste, the figures being all made so natural, that I could conceive no idea superior in this kind. All sorts of rich hangings, glasses, tables, chairs, &c. are brought into the apartments, but kept packed and covered, the walls remaining bare for four years. The palace in general is unfinished, and it may be presumed that the King himself is tired of the vanity of an unnecessary variety, and of such a profusion of expensive baubles. [...]

Source 23
Lists with the animals brought in 1733 to Dresden from the Africa Expedition

[SächsHStA, loc. 589, Verschiedene in Hamburg auch sonst erkaufte wilde Thiere 1718, fols. 8a–10a]
[The letter is addressed to Count Brühl.]

[8a]
Monsieur
Ich habe schon von Gibraltar aus vom 27. May meiner Pflicht gemäß Ew. Excellenz einige Nachricht von dem Anfange meiner Reise gegeben; nehmlich daß ich den 17. April Tunis verlassen habe, und den 12. May nach Gibraltar gekommen bin. Der Wind hielt mich nach diesem Schreiben noch biß zu dem dritten Juni auf, da wir unsere Reise fortsezten und den 24. Jun. in Deala [?] ankommen. Hier wurden wir wiederum durch widrigen Wind und einige andre Verdrüßlichkeiten biß zum 6. Julii aufgehalten. Endlich sind wir heute den 15. Julii glücklich hier
[8b]
in Hamburg angekommen. Wenn unsere Reise nicht so langwierig und verdrüßlich gewesen wäre, so zweifle ich nicht wir hätten noch eine gute Anzahl Thiere erhalten können, welche wir biß itzo verloren haben. Wovon Sie beyliegende Nachricht unterrichten kann. Die noch übrigen Thiere befinden sich alle wohl, und wenn ich Gelegenheit habe sie aufs schleunigste nach Dreßden zu bringen, so glaube ich keines mehr zu verliehren. Vor die Schiffe wird aber wird wohl Hr. Piher [?] auf dero befehl sorgen, und ich werde hier durch beyhülfe des Hr. Legations Raths und der Hrr. Stemglin meiner Caufleuthe das meinige thun. Bey meiner Reiße nach Dreßden fält noch dieser Rudolph vor, daß die vielen Zölle nicht etwan in Ansehung des Aufwands sondern in Ansehung des Aufpackens bey Untersuchung der gesammelten Curiosorum vielen Schaden thun können. Ich bitte Sie wollen mir durch einen zu diesem Ende gemachten Paß zu hülffe kommen, oder die Sache so

[9a]
einrichten wie es Ihnen am besten deucht. Schlüßlich empfehle ich mich dero Schutze, wo durch ich die Ehre genüße allzeit zu seyn

Ew. Excellenz
Hamburg den 13. Juli 1733 unterthänigst gehorsamster Diener
Christian Gottlieb Ludwig

[10a]
[The list mentions:]
Die 9. Antalops oder Gazellen sind alle gestorben und auch das Adat [?] oder Chevre-Cerf.

ferner sind gestorben:
2. Straußen
1. Löwe
1. Guineisch[6] Schaaf
2. Guineische hühner
alle Chamaeleons

Lebend habe ich also noch.
7. Strauße 2. Männchen 5 Weibchen
2. bunte Esel aus der Saarah
Schaafe mit großen Schwänzen und Hörnern
2. Guineische Schaafe
1. Tyger
1. Löwin
1. Dabba oder Africanischer Wolff
1. Dieb oder Africanischer Fuchs
2. Stachel-Schweine
1. Damoiselle
4. Africanische Mäuße
5. Guinische Hühner
2. Voitour
1. Adler
3. Meerkatzen
2. Affen
allerhand Tauben

[Same record, fol. 2a is the pass mentioned.]
Churfürst. Paß
auf verschiedene, nach beyliegender Specification, von Hamburg nach Dreßden, durch einen Schiffer, welcher von dort aus darzu bedungen werden wird, zu schaffender fremder Thiere. Dreßden, den 31. Julii 1733
FrA
C.Sulk. dde Br.

[In the same record, fol. 5a, there is a list that has no further details but with the one exception of an antelope corresponds to the list in the letter and is thus very likely the specification mentioned in the pass.]

9 Strauß Vögel
2 Junge Löwen
1 Tieger
5 Verschiedene Arthen Affen
1 Chevre Cerf, Audeet genannt
8 Antelopen
3 Aetiopisch Schaff, so an statt Woll Haar tragen
1 Africanischer Wolff
Eine Arth Seeländische Füchse
6 Mauritanische Schaff
Eine Arth seltene Africanische Mäuß
3 arthen Spanische RaubVögel
Africanische Hüner
Einige Arthen Africanische Tauben
Eine Arth Cranich Demoiselle genannt
Einige Chamaleons
3 Stachel-Schwein
2 bunde Esel aus der Sand Wüste

Source 24
Kaendler's list of his first works, 1731

[SächsHStA, loc. 1341, VI, Acta die Porcellän Manufactur betr. 1732, fol. 323a/b]

[323a]
Was ich seynd dem 22 Juny an auff Ihro Majest der Königl Porcalein-Manufactur nis hierher verfertiget ist folgendes:
[What I have made ready since June 22 until now at His Majesty's Royal Porcelain Manufactory is the following:]

Nr 1
Einen großen Adler welcher mit sammbt dem Postament 2 Ell weniger 3 Zoll hoch mit aus gebreiteten Flügeln

N 2
Einen Fischahr oder Fischfreßer 1 Elle hoch wovon Ohro Majest schon bekommen

N 3
Eine See Mehe auff einem Postament welches mit aller handt Muscheln verzieret von der art auch schon unterschiedene fertig sind

N 4
Noch einen Fischahr welcher einen Karpffen zerreißet auff Sauberste aus gearbeitet

N 5
Petrus dritthalbe Ellen hoch mit denen beyden Schlüßeln, auff Romanische art gekleidet

[323b]
N 6
Eine große Eule auff einen Postament wo von auch Ihro Majest schon bekommen

N 7
Einen Falcken auch auff einen Postament wo von auch schon etwas fertig

N 8
Ein Waßer Huhn auff einen Postament sitzend welches mit Schilff und anderen Dingen verzieret

Anitze aber sind in Arbeit Ihro Majest zu Pferdte welches gnädigst anbefohlen worden und ein Auer Thier welcher ein wildes Schwein um bringet
An vorigen Dingen aber habe viele Mühe müßen an wenden bey dem verputzen das alles auff beste in der Maße ausgearbeitet worden

Solches hat mit gröster Unterthänigkeit melden wollen

Johann Joachim Kändler
Bildhauer

Source 25
Kaendler's list of the animals of which he made studies in Dresden and Moritzburg, July 1734

[BA, IAa.22, fol. 227a–227b]

[227a]
Specificatio
Dererjenigen fremden Thiern und Indianischen Vögeln Welche theils in den Löwen und Bären Hauß, theils auch in der Kunst Kammer zu Befinden, und von mir Endes Benannten so wohl in richtige Modelle als auch accurate und richtige Zeichnung vom 4ten bis 26. Jul. gebracht worden, damit selbige wenn solche Stücke bey hießiger Königl. Porcellain Fabrique ins große angefangen werden Desto Natürlicher und Schöner nach solchen gemachten modellen und Zeichnungen poussiret werden können

[Specification of the foreign animals and exotic birds, to be found in part in the *Löwenhaus* and *Bärenhaus*, and in part in the *Kunstkammer*, of which I made both accurate and correct drawings and rough models between July 4 and 26, so that when the same are executed as large figures at the Royal Porcelain Manufactory they may turn out to be all the more natural and beautiful for having been made after these bozzetti and drawings:]

Im Löwen Hauße poussiret

1. Ein Stachel Schwein
2. Einen Lux
3. Ein Tieger Thier
4. Eine Affricanische Katze
5. Einen Indianischen Wolff oder Menschen Freßer
6. Ichnemon oder das Thier was dem Crocodill in Hals grichet [kriecht und dann tötet]
7. Eine Indianische Rattze

Im Bären Hauße

8. Einen Bär
9. Einen Stein Adler

[227b]

In der Kunst Kammer nach dem ausgestopfften Thieren poussiret

10. Einen Affricanischen Esel
11. Ein Indianisches Schaaf
12. Einen Indianischen Wilden Hund
13. Einen Indianischen Zahmen Hund
14. Einen Zobel
15. Einen Viel Fraß
16. Einen Versühn oder Sünden Bock welchen die Juden gehabt
17. Ein Kameel
18. Einen Wolff welcher einen Hirsch zerreiset und frist
19. Ein Murmel Thier
20. Einen Indianischen Ziegenbock

Vögel welche in der Kunst Kammer aus gestopfft seynd, und von mir gezeichnet worden

21. Ein Nimmer Satt so groß als eine Löffel Ganß
22. Eine Indianische Ente mit einem Hals Kragen
23. Einen Paradies Vogel
24. Einen Indianischen Fischreiher
25. Eine Affricanische Ente mit sonderbahren Füßen
26. Einen Indianischen Taucher
27. Ein Indianischer Kibitz
28. Einen Indianischen Teuffel
29. Ein Fabl Thier

Summa 29 Stück

Meißen den 31. Jul. 1734 JJ Kändler

Source 26
Obituary for Johann Joachim Kaendler

[in *Neue Bibliothek der schönen Wissenschaften und der freyen Künste*, XVIII:296–303 (Leipzig 1775)]

Nachricht von Herrn Johann Joachim Kändlers Leben und Arbeiten

Am 17ten May dieses Jahres verlor Deutschland einen seiner größten Künstler, den Churfürstlichen sächsischen Hofkammerkommissär und Modellmeister bey der Porcellainmanufaktur zu Meißen, Herrn Johann Joachim Kändler, im 69sten Jahre seines Alters. Er war zu Seeligstadt bey Bischofswerde in Sachsen, im J. 1706 geboren. Da sein würdiger Vater, der Pfarrer dieses Ortes, die Funken eines lebhaften Genies, und einen Hang zu den schönen Künsten frühzeitig in ihm entdeckte; so hielt er es für Pflicht, diesen Trieb nicht zu ersticken, sondern nur richtig zu leiten. Er machte daher seinen Sohn mit den besten Schriftstellern, mit der Mythologie und den Kunstwerkern des Alterthums bekannt, und mit diesen Vorbereitungskenntnissen übergab er ihn 1723, als der junge Kändler die Bildhauerkunst vorzüglich wählte, der Unterweisung des geschickten Hofbildhauers Thomä zu Dresden. Hier fand der eifrige Lehrling ein weites Feld, seinen Geschmack zu bilden, und seine Talente zu üben. Er legte sich darneben vornämlich auf die Zeichenkunst, studirte die Antiken mit anhaltendem Fleiß, und machte sich dadurch den hohen Grad des Korrekten, des Affektvollen, kurz den wahren Ausdruck der Natur eigen, der alle seine Werke bezeichnet. Seine Fähigkeiten konnten dem großen Kenner und Beförderer der Künste, König August dem II. nicht verborgen bleiben. Als dieser Herr das grüne Gewölbe, diese unschätzbare Sammlung von Kunstwerken einrichtete, ließ er verschiedene seltene Stücke durch unsern Kändler pußiren, und fand seine Arbeit so kräftig und elegant, daß er ihn 1730 zum Hofbildhauer ernannte, und kurz darauf als Modellmeister und Direktor des sogenannten[7] weissen Corps zur Meißner Porcellainmanufaktur setzte. Sein Nachfolger auf dem Throne und im Geschmack, König August der III. würdigte den Künstler gleicher Gnade, und beehrte ihn 1749 mit dem Charakter eines Hofkommissairs.

Es wetteiferten damals die königlichen französischen Porcellainfabriken mit der Meißner um den Vorzug. Kändler aber wußte solches zu behaupten. Er verfertigee (sic!) im Jahr 1750 das bekannte Meisterstück, einen mit Blumenketten, Laubwerk, Figuren und Geschichten ins Erhabene gearbeiteten Rahm, von Porcellain, 7 Ellen hoch, zu einem auf der Dresdner Spiegelfabrik gegossenen Trümeauspiegel, und dazu einen Konsoltisch, ebenfalls ganz von Porcellain. Beide Stücke hatte August zum Geschenk für den König von Frankreich bestimmt. Kändler selbst überbrachte sie nach Paris, und die eifersüchtigen Franzosen ließen dem Geschmack und der Arbeit des deutschen Künstlers alle mögliche Gerechtigkeit wiederfahren.

Im folgenden Jahre that ihm der Premierminister Graf von Brühl, auf Befehl des Königs, den Antrag, das Standbild des Monarchen zu Pferde, en Courbette, von der Größe der an der Allee der Dresdner Neustadt stehenden Statue August des II., mit einem vehältnißmäßigen Piedestal, beides von weissem Porcellain zu verfertigen, damit solches ebenfalls aufgestellet werden könnte. Der Gedanke eines solchen Kunstwerks, welches das einzige seiner Art in der Welt würde gewesen seyn, und bey dessen Ausführung der Ruhm des Künstlers so stark interessiret war, überwand bey unserm Kändler die zahlreichen Schwierigkeiten, die ihm dabey entgegentraten. Er verfertigte dazu ein treffliches Modell von Porcellain, das mit dem Fußgestelle fast 3 Ellen hoch, und gegenwärtig im holländischen Palast besagter Neustadt Dresden zu sehen ist. Der König, zufrieden mit diesem herrlichen Probestück, saß hierauf dem Künstler, und ließ sich von ihm pußiren, bezeugte auch ein ungemein Vergnügen, als er schon 1755. das große Modell in Gips in Augenschein nehmen konnte. Nun arbeitete Kändler mit brennendem Eifer, sein Werk bald in Porcellain darzustellen. Allein der kurz darauf einbrechende lange Krieg hemmte das Unternehmen mit einmal, und ob schon der unsterbliche Churfürst Friedrich Christian, nach wiederhergestelltem Frieden, mit Ernst bedacht war, dieses prächtige[8] Denkmahl seines Vaters vollenden zu laßen; so vereitelte doch sein frühes Ableben diese Absicht abermals, und nunmehr ist der Künstler für dieses Werk auch dahin! Herr Kändler war nie, ohne nur bey vorbesagter kurzem [sic!] Reise nach Frankreich, aus Sachsen gekommen. Er hatte die berühmten Gallerien von Bildsäulen nicht gesehen, worauf Italien so stolz ist, sein Lehrmeister war ein Deutscher, und gleichwohl erreichte Kändler, ohne ausländische Führer, den Gipfel der Kunst glücklich. Seine Arbeiten sind sehr zahlreich, und alle tragen das Gepräge der Meisterhand.[9] In seinen letzteren Arbeiten aber[10] scheint sein Geist seine ganzen Kräfte vereiniget, und sich gleichsam übertroffen zu haben, und Rom und Petersburg werden den Meißner Künstler noch lange bewundern. Sein glückliches Genie verließ ihn niemals. Nie war ihm eine Aufgabe zu schwer, und selbst die Größe der Schwierigkeiten gab seinem Geiste nur einen desto stärkeren Schwung. Seine Einbildungskraft war feurig, seine Ausführung edel, und er besaß die seltene Leichtigkeit, das Eigne und Charakteristische eines jeden Gegenstandes auf den ersten Blick zu ergreifen, und in den angemessensten Zügen wieder auszudrücken. Er bildete seine schönsten Stücke aus freyer Faust, ohne erst Skizen und Zeichnungen davon zu entwerfen. So sicher und so übereinstimmend waren bey ihm Aug und Hand. Seine vorhandenen Zeichnungen sind meisterhaft. In seinen jüngeren Jahren malte er zum Vergnügen in Oel, und seine Familie besitzt verschiedene Stücke,[11] die ihm einen Rang unter den berühmten Malern seines Zeitalters anzuweisen hinreichend wären. Auf sein Herz hatte sein Geschmack den besten Einfluß. Das moralische Fehlerhafte und Häßliche war ihm äußerst zuwider, und keine Rücksicht konnte ihn abhalten, den Abscheu, den er daran empfand, laut zu bezeugen. Er war ein redlicher Vater seiner Familie, ein herzlicher warmer Freund, ein eifriger, nicht zu ermüdender Patriot. Er hatte die alten Schriftsteller in seiner Jugend mit solchem Erfolg studiret, daß sie auch in seinen hohen Jahren noch seine Ergötzung ausmachten, und es ist anmerkungswerth, daß er, als er bereits seinem wichtigen Posten zu Meißen vorstund, noch viele Jahre bey dem um die Meißnische Fürstenschule so verdienten damaligen dritten Kollegen, Hr. M. Weißen, täglich Unterricht zu Erklärung der schwerern mythologischen Dichter nahm. Seine bekannte Uneigennützigkeit und seine treue Zuneigung gegen die Porcellainmanufaktur, deren Flor er durch Fleiß und Anwendung seiner Talente merklich emporgebracht hatte, verstatteten ihm nicht die Vortheile unterschiedener auswärtiger Berufungen anzunehmen; selbst den Ruf des preußischen Monarchen, welcher ihm in dem letzten Kriegsjahre einen ansehnlichen Gehalt anbieten ließ, suchte er abzulehnen. Dieser muntere Künstler behielt die Heiterkeit und Gegenwart seines Geistes bis auf die letzten Augenblicke, und gieng durch einen Schlagfluß plötzlich aus dem Leben, ohne selbst in seinen hohen Jahren die geringste Unbequemlichkeit oder Schwachheit des Alters empfunden zu haben.

[An account of the life and work of Johann Joachim Kändler

On May 17 of this year, Germany lost one of its greatest artists, court commissioner of the electorate of Saxony and master modeler at the Meissen porcelain manufactory, Johann Joachim Kändler, who died in his sixty-ninth year. He was born in 1706 in Seeligstadt near Bischofswerde [present-day Bischofswerda], Saxony. His reverend father, the local pastor, early on discovered in him the sparks of a lively intelligence and an inclination towards the fine arts. Considering it his duty not to stifle his talents but to guide them in the right direction, he therefore introduced his son to the mythology, art, and best authors of antiquity. Equipped with this preparatory knowledge, the young Kändler, out of preference choosing to pursue sculpture, was sent in 1723 to receive instruction from the accomplished court sculptor Thomä in Dresden. Here the keen young apprentice found ample opportunity to form his taste and to put his talents into practice. In addition he concentrated particularly on the art of drawing, applied himself with persistence and industry to the study of classical art, and thereby developed that highly correct and affective artistry – in short, that true and natural expression – that was to be characteristic of all his work. It was impossible that his abilities should remain unknown to that great connoisseur and patron of the arts, King Augustus II. When this ruler set up his inestimable collection of art works in the Green Vaults, he had our young Kändler make models of various rare pieces, and found his work so powerful and elegant that in 1730 he appointed him court sculptor, and shortly afterwards master modeler and director of the "white corps"[7] at the Meissen Porcelain Manufactory. His successor on the throne, Augustus III, who followed his father in matters of taste, accorded the artist the same measure of favor and in 1749 honored him with the rank of court commissioner.

At that time the royal French porcelain factories were vying for superiority over the Meissen manufactory. But Kändler ensured that Meissen kept the upper hand. In the year 1750 he brought to completion his well-known masterpiece, a porcelain frame nobly decorated with garlands of flowers, leafwork, figures, and stories, 7 ells high, done for a large wall-mirror cast at the Dresden mirror factory, with the addition of a console table, likewise entirely in porcelain. Both pieces were intended by Augustus as presents for the king of France. Kändler took them to Paris in person, and the jealous French accorded the German artist just praise for his taste and fine work.

In the following year, the Saxon prime minister Count von Brühl was ordered by the king to commission Kändler to make an equestrian statue of the monarch doing a curvet, in the size of the statue that stands on the avenue of the Neustadt in Dresden, with a pedestal of the appropriate size, both in white porcelain so that they might be put up in similar manner. The very thought of a work of art of this kind, which would have been unique of its kind in the whole world and would have been greatly beneficial to the artist's fame, was sufficient to spur Kändler on to overcome the numerous difficulties with which the task presented him. To this end he made an excellent first model in porcelain, which can at present be admired in the Dutch Palace in Neustadt, Dresden, almost 3 ells high with the pedestal. The king was satisfied with this glorious test-piece and sat to be modeled by the artist; no later than 1755, he was able to see the model in its full size in plaster and expressed the greatest pleasure. Kändler then worked with burning zeal to present him his work in porcelain, but the long war that broke out soon after brought his work to a halt. After peace was made, the immortal Elector Friedrich Christian seriously intended to have this magnificent monument to his father completed,[8] but his own early passing frustrated this intention, and now the artist is no longer with us to be able to do anything about the work himself! Herr Kändler never left Saxony, except for the above-mentioned short journey to France. Although he had never seen the famous galleries of sculptures of which Italy is so proud, and his teacher was a German, Kändler successfully attained to the summit of art without the help of any foreign mentor. His works are very numerous and all clearly show the hand of a master.[9] In his last works,[10] however, his spirit clearly rallied all his powers and he so surpassed himself that Rome and Petersburg will surely long have the highest admiration for the artist from Meissen. His happy genius never abandoned him. Never was there a task that was too difficult for him, and even the greatness of the difficulties tended to stimulate his spirit to even greater achievements. He had a passionate imagination, his work was noble in execution, and he had a rare facility for grasping what was proper to and typical about any given object at the very first glance, and then for expressing these characteristics with the most rightly chosen of features. He did his most beautiful models *extempore*, without having done any sketches or drawings beforehand, his eye and hand were so sure, and the accord between them so great. Such drawings of his as have survived are masterly. In his younger years he took great pleasure in painting in oils, and his family possesses various pieces that would suffice to assure him a place amongst the famous painters of his day.[11] His taste had the best possible influence on his heart. Moral failings and moral ugliness were repellent to him in the extreme, and when he was confronted with them, no consideration would make him refrain from giving loud expression to his repulsion.

He was a sincere father to his family, a warm-hearted friend, and a zealous and indefatigable patriot. As a young man he had studied the authors of antiquity to such effect that he still took the greatest delight in them at an advanced age, and it is remarkable that even when he was occupying his important post at Meissen he still continued for many years to take daily instruction in the explanation of the most difficult mythological poets, from Herr M. Weißen, who rendered such outstanding service as third master at the *Fürstenschule* in Meissen. His well-known altruism and affectionate loyalty to the porcelain manufactory, which only attained to its full flowering through his industry and talent, prevented him from being able to respond to and take advantage of various external calls upon his services: he even deliberately refused the call of the monarch of Prussia when the latter him offered an attractive salary during the last years of the war. This lively artist remained of good cheer and sound in mind to the last and died suddenly of a stroke, without having experienced the discomforts and weakness of old age in the slightest, even in his most advanced years.]

Source 27
Description of the Japanese Palace in 1744 by Johann Christian Müller

["Ein Besuch Dresdens im Jahre 1744, Teil II" ("A visit to Dresden in the year 1744, Part Two") in *Dresdner Anzeiger*, Sunday supplement no. 24, June 16, 1907, Part Two, p. 97.]

Die Beschreibung des Japanischen Palais 1744 ... aus Stralsund
Nach der Handschrift zum ersten Male veröffentlicht und durch Anmerkungen erläutert von O. Scheel, Stralsund

Am Nachmittag besahen wir uns in der Neustadt das kostbare Japanische Palais. Das Portal desselben hatte fast das Ansehen wie das des Rostocker Rathauses. Der geheime Bettmeister, der es uns zeigte, meldete uns, daß es ganz unvollkommen geblieben, weil der hochselige König, ein prachtliebender Herr, darüber weggestorben, dieser aber ein schläfriger Herr wäre, der sich um nichts bekümmere und auf dergleichen Sachen nichts gäbe. Ich habe gemerkt, daß alle Leute hier frei von ihrem Könige reden und fast alle etwas an ihm auszusetzen fanden.

Das Gebäude hatte in seiner Mitte einen viereckigen Hofplatz. Wir wurden zuerst auf den großen Saal geführt, der zu einem Spiegelzimmer bestimmt gewesen. An der einen Seite war auf einige Schritte auch schon der Anfang gemacht, und man hatte an dieser Spiegelwand nicht weit voneinander von unten bis oben kleine vergoldete Postamente von Bildhauerarbeit angebracht, auf welchen verschiedene vierfüßige Tiere und Raubvögel, in Lebensgröße und nach der Natur von Porzellan gebildet, standen. Ich besinne mich eines Raubvogels, der ein angefressenes Huhn vor sich liegen hatte, es war das blutige Gerippe und das Eingeweide zu sehen und alles so natürlich, auch von Farbe, als ob es lebte. In einem Zimmer standen eine Menge solcher Tiere aus Porzellan, die in dem Spiegelsaale hätten angebracht werden sollen. Ich bewunderte darunter eine große liegende Ziege, die an ihrem Euter ein paar junge Zicklein säugend hatte; ein wildes Schwein, das von einem Jagdhunde an dem einen Bein gepackt wurde und demselben mit den Hauern drohte; einen schönen, großen Schwan, einen Pfau mit seinem ausgebreiteten Schweife usw.[12] In einem anderen Zimmer standen große Kummen und Gefäße von Porzellan, auf denen ganze Schlachten oder die angenehmsten Landschaften und Vorstellungen en miniature mit den schönsten Farben, im Feuer gebrannt, aufs sauberste geschildert waren. Noch in einem langen Zimmer war ein langer Tisch, worauf zwei Reihen Puppenwerke aus Porzellan standen, anderthalb oder zwei Quartier höchstens hoch; darunter bemerkte ich Frauenzimmer in langen Kleidern oder großen Reifröcken und junge Herren, ebenfalls in Modekleidern, in allerlei angenehmen, lebhaften Stellungen; besonders war eine auf dem Rasen sitzende Schäferin, bei welcher der Schäfer mit der verliebtesten Miene stand, sehenswert. Man sagte, dergleichen Stücke würden gar nicht aus der Fabrik verhandelt, sie gehörten für den König und würden zu Geschenken an andere Höfe verwendet. Man zeigte uns die Zimmer, deren eines rot, das andere blau, das dritte grün, das vierte gelb war; es hatten die Wände mit Porzellan sollen bezogen und auch mit solchen farbigen Aufsätzen sollen ausgeziert werden. Man führte uns in einen sehr langen Saal, den der hochselige König zur Audienz bestimmt hatte, worin der mit Statuen gezierte Thron ganz aus Porzellan hätte sein sollen. Es standen hier eine Menge Porzellanglocken, deren jede ihren besonderen Ton angab, daraus in eben diesem großen Zimmer ein Glockenspiel hatte werden sollen. Es wäre ein gar kostbares Werk gewesen, da sehr viele Glocken vergeblich gebrannt waren, weil es schwer gewesen, den rechten Ton zu treffen.

Aus den oberen Zimmern führte man uns in die Souterrains oder unterirdischen, die aus lauter großen und hohen Gewölben bestanden, mit großen gemauerten Pfeilern wie in einer Kirche, die zu einem Weinlager bestimmt gewesen. Hier wurde der außerordentliche Vorrat an chinesischem Porzellan aufbewahrt. Man sagte uns, daß es so viele Schüsseln und Teller seien, daß man eine Tafel von 300 Personen damit besetzen könnte. Es waren große Kummen dabei, von denen jedes Stück, es nur aus Italien herzubringen, über 300 Taler gekostet hatte.[13] Da waren eine außerordentliche Menge Teetassen da, von denen viele mit allerhand, und zwar den geilsten Posituren bemalt waren. Wir fliegen endlich heraus aus dem Keller; der Aufseher zeigte uns den Hof und wie die Mauern des Gebäudes mit porzellanenen Zieraten von außen hätten sollen belegt werden. Wir gaben ihm hierauf seinen Dukaten und nahmen von ihm Abschied.

[The description of the Japanese Palace in 1744 from the memoirs of the preacher Johann Christian Müller from Stralsund, published from the manuscript for the first time with a commentary by O. Scheel, Stralsund.

In the afternoon we went to look at the admirable Japanese Palace in Neustadt. The portal looked almost like that of Rostock Town Hall. The privy major-domo who showed us round told us that the reason why it was unfinished was that the late king of blessèd memory, who had been a great lover of magnificence, had died while it was still being completed, and the present king was a sleepy character who took no trouble about anything and was not in the habit of spending money on such things. I have noticed that everyone here speaks quite freely about their king, and when they do so almost everyone finds something to complain about.

The building had a four-cornered inner courtyard. First of all, we were taken to the large hall which had been designed to be a mirror-room. A start had already been made on fitting it with mirrors, which ran a number of yards along one side, and this mirror-wall had been fitted from top to bottom with carved and gilded pedestals not far from each other on which various four-footed animals and birds of prey in porcelain were standing, done life-size according to nature. I can remember a bird of prey with a mauled hen [Kaendler's Vulture Devouring a Cockatoo] lying before it, its blood-bespattered frame and innards clearly visible, all as natural as if it was living, right down to the colors. In one room there was a large number of porcelain animal figures of this kind, which were to be accommodated in the mirror-room. The figures I admired included a large she-goat, lying down with a couple of kids hanging on its udder; a wild boar on the point of getting its tusks into a hunting-hound that had sunk its teeth into one of its legs; a beautiful, large swan, and a peacock with its fan fully spread etc.[12] In another room there were large bowls and large porcelain vessels with very clear depictions of whole battles, or the most pleasing of landscapes and scenes *en miniature*, all fired in the most beautiful colors. And in a long room there was a long table on which stood two rows of porcelain figurines, at the most one and a half or two quarters in height, among which my eye was particularly caught by women in long dresses or large crinolines, and young gentlemen, likewise fashionably dressed, in all sorts of pleasing and lively postures. Particularly worthy of note was a shepherdess sitting on the grass, with a shepherd with the most love-lorn look beside her. I was told that the manufactory did not offer such pieces on the open market, but that they were made for the king and used as gifts for other courts. We were shown the rooms, of which one was red and another blue, the third green and the fourth yellow; the walls were to have had porcelain standing on them and were to have been decorated with sets of pieces in precisely those colors. We were shown into a very long room which the late king of blessèd memory had intended to be his audience chamber, and in which the throne, decorated with statues, was to have been done entirely in porcelain. Standing here were also a large number of porcelain bells, all of which rang with a particular note, as they were to have been used to make a carillon for this very room. It would have been a most valuable instrument as very many of the bells fired had been no use, because it had been very difficult to get the pitch absolutely right.

From the upper rooms we were taken down to the basement rooms, all with large high vaults and large columns as in a church, which were intended as wine cellars. Now they were being used to store the exceptional stock of Chinese porcelain. We were told that there were enough plates and dishes for a table with three hundred guests. There were large bowls, and each one had cost over 300 talers, just for it to be brought from Italy.[13] There was also an exceptionally large quantity of teacups, many of which were painted, with a great variety of highly captivating exotic motifs. We finally emerged from the cellar, and the guardian showed us the courtyard and explained that the walls of the building were to have been adorned with porcelain decorations. We then gave him his ducats and bade him farewell.]

For bibliographical information on Müller's description of Dresden, see Bibliography.

Source 28
Selected entries from the deeds of the court accounting office relating to the animal collections, first half-year of 1727 to first half-year of 1738

[SächsHStA, Rentkammer-Akten (court accounting office), Ausgaben (expenditure); volumes examined: nos. 237 = first half-year of 1727 to no. 254 = first half-year of 1738]

The deeds of the court accounting office ("Rentkammer") contain a wealth of references to expenditure for the feeding of and caring for animals in the electoral menageries. The entries are only worthy of note here if they represent a notable deviation from the normal costs, or if they indicate a major expense that cries out for particular explanation (on a particularly valuable animal, for instance).

The volumes for 1727 to 1732 are entitled:
Rechnung über Ausgabe Geld Bey der Königl: und Churfürstl: Sächs: Renth: Cammer wie auch Was von des Stiffts Naumburg und Zeitz auch andern Sachssen Weydaischen Einkünfften bezahlt [Accounts of monetary expenditure of the Royal and Electoral Accounting Office, and likewise of Stift Naumburg and Stift Zeitz, and what has been paid from other revenues in Saxon Weida]
The volumes for 1733 to 1738 are entitled:
Rechnung über Ausgabe Geld Bey der Königl: und Churfürstl: Sächß: Renth: Cammer in Dreßden, wie auch Was von denen Sachsen-Weydaischen Einkünfften bezahlt [Accounts of monetary expenditure of the Royal and Electoral Accounting Office in Dresden, and what has been paid from other revenues in Saxon Weida].

Each volume records information about the animal collections under four headings:
A = *Ausgabe*
Auf das Löwen- und Thier-Haus in Alt Dreßden
[Expenditure: on the lion- and animal-house in Old Dresden]
B = *Ausgabe*
Auf Fütterung derer Auer, Bähre und andern Wildprets, sowohl in denen Thier- und Bähren-Gärthen, als auch sonst
[Expenditure: on fodder for its aurochses (= wisents), bears, and other wild game, not only in the animal and bear gardens, but also elsewhere]
C = *Ausgabe*
Auf die Königl: Phasan Geheege
[Expenditure: on the royal pheasant reserve (in Ostra)]
D = *Ausgabe*
Auf Fütterung derer im hiesigen Vestungs-Graben befindlichen Schwäne und wilden Enten, sowohl vor das in Morizburg und anderer Orthen vorhandene wilde und fremde Feder-Vieh
[Expenditure: on feed for the swans and wild duck in the castle moat in Dresden, and for the wild and exotic birds in Moritzburg and elsewhere (for instance, in the court fish garden)]

RT = January to June; CL = July to December

Volume call no.	Place	Excerpts and quotations
No. 237/1, CL, 1727	B	There are references to “aurochses” in Moritzburg, and to expenditure on their new sheds.
No. 241, CL, 1729	A	[fol. 419] References to, inter alia: – a tiger, arrived from Weißenfels on 8 Feb 1723, died on 29 May 1729 – a tiger-cat, arrived from England on 30 Sept 1727, died on 30 Mar 1729 – a tiger, arrived from England on 24 July 1724, still alive – a monkey, died on 16 Nov 1729 – further references to: a lioness, a tiger, a lynx, a “Pappian” (= *Pavian*, baboon), an Arabian “Moll”
	C	References to, inter alia: an “indianischer Hirsch” (“Indian deer,” unidentified)
No. 242, RT, 1730	A	references to, inter alia: – a lioness, arrived on 5 Nov 1729, died 15 Jan 1730 – the “Arabisch Thiergen Molé genannt” (the small Arabian animal known as a “Molé”), died on 12 Apr 1730
	B	In Moritzburg, references to, inter alia: “türkische Schwäne” (“Turkish swans”)
No. 243, CL, 1731	A	references to: lions, panthers, tigers, lynxes, baboons, monkeys, porcupines
	B	In and around Moritzburg, references to, inter alia: black storks and two white peacocks, pelicans, herons, Augsburg billy-goats, two African “Schaf-Stehre”(= ?), a cassowary, a parrot, two “Ind. Raben” (= macaws), a “Monien” (= parakeet), two “Wauwaus” (= king vultures), a golden eagle, an “Ind.Geier” (= griffon vulture), a green “Parquitgen” (= parakeet), a “Krirken oder Kletpapagei” (referred to previously on fol. 397b as a “Krisker oder Kletpapagey”), a “Wasser-Falke” (“water-falcon,” unidentified; died).
	C	“Indian” and local wild game
No. 244, RT, 1731	A	[fols. 56a – 57a] Expenditure on feed and fodder: 581 talers for meat, *welches vir die im Löwenhause zu Alt-Dreßden aufbehaltenen wilden Thiere, davon bey der andern Post Ein Tieger, so am 4. Januar: 1729. aus Bayreuth anhero gekommen, und am 27.th Jan: 1731 gefallen, daß demnach von dato an deßen tägl. Fütterung à 6 lb: Rindfleisch cessiret, laut des Herrn Ober-Hof-Jägermeisters von Leubnitz dabey befindlichen Bescheinigung von besagten dato, der Hofe-Mezger, Johann Georg Heyer geliefert, und ich ihm gegen seine beanordnete und von Löwenwärther. Christian Neumannen bescheinigte beyde Specificationes und Quittungen bezahlet.* [“for the wild animals kept in the lion-house in Old Dresden, including a tiger that had come with the other post from Bayreuth on January 4, 1729, and died on January 27, 1731, at which point its daily feed of six pounds of beef ceased, in accordance with the confirmation of that day from Ober-Hof-Jägermeister von Leubnitz, delivered to the court butcher Johann Georg Heyer, both of whom demanded specifications and bills, which I the lion-keeper Christian Neumann confirmed and paid.”] 27 talers 16 groschen for feed, *und ist die Fütterung tägl. umb 2.gr. [...] dahero gestiegen, weil am 23. Martii a.c. ein StachelSchwein ins Löwenhauß gekommen, und von dato an mit deßen Fütterung nach beygehefften Befehl vom 7. April. praes:a. angefangen worden.* [“and the food has increased by two groschen ... because on March 23 a porcupine came to the lion-house and from that date was fed in accordance with the appended order dated April 7.”] 29 talers 9 groschen for feed, *zu Unterhalt und Fütterung derer im Löwenhause zu Alt-Dreßden bishero und aniezo vorhandenen Affen und andere Thiere [...] bezahlet.* [“for the upkeep and feeding of the monkeys and other animals kept to date and at present in the lion-house in Old Dresden.”]

2 talers 8 groschen for feed *statt der angesezten 3.Thlr.6.gr. dem HofeViehmer [...] vor 2. mit Haaren ausgefütterte Halsbänder vor 2. Pavians, und vor 6. Affen desgleichen Bänder, so er in das Königl: Löwenhauß gefertiget.* ["instead of the 3 talers 6 groschen prescribed for the court saddler ... for two neck bands stuffed with hair for two baboons and like bands for six monkeys made for the Royal Lion-House."]

B [fol. 57b]
References are made to feed, material to be scattered ("Streumaterial"), and hedge-cutters' wages in connection with the winter feeding of the "Auerochsen" in Moritzburg; also references to feed for the exotic and other foreign wild game ("Indianische und andere fremde Wildpreth"), both longer-standing ones and recent arrivals, and likewise to the wild veal ("Wild-Kalb") brought to Ostra, meat of the exotic wild game ("Indianischen Wildpreth").
[fol. 59a]
Expenditure on feed:
in March 1731 for feed, 82 talers 16 groschen: *Vor 1. weißen Hirsch, 1. weißes Thier, 6. Zug-Hirsche, auf iedes Stück täglich 6.gr., ingl. vor 1. Indianischen Hirsch, und 3. Indianische Thiere, welche am 26. April 1730 anhero gebracht worden, auf iedes Stück täglich 4.gr.* ["for one white deer, one white animal, six 'Zughirsche' ('draft deer'), each one daily six groschen, and three exotic animals that were brought here on April 26, 1730, each one 4 groschen daily."]

D [fol. 398b]
Expenditure on feed for Moritzburg:
68 talers 23 groschen 7 1/4 pfennigs for: *Fütterungs:Kosten vor zwey schwarze Störche, 2. weiße Pfauen, 1. Löffel-Ganß, 1. Waßer-Falcken, ingl: 3. Augspurgische Ziegen-Böcke, von und mit den 30. Sept: 1730 bis und mit den 27. Jan: 1731* ["feeding costs for two black storks, two white peacocks, one 'spoon-goose" (= pelican), one 'Wasser-Falcken,' and also three Augsburg billy-goats, from 30 Sept 1730 to 27 Jan 1731 inclusive."]
48 talers 8 pfennigs, *an dergleichen auf den Monath Novembr: 1730 zu Unterhaltung der Strauß- und andern Indianischen Vögel* ["for the upkeep of the ostriches and other exotic birds in November 1730"]
3 talers 18 groschen and 9 pfennigs, *auf 121. Tage von und mit den 29ten Setembr: 1730 bis und mit den 27.th January 1731 Fütterung auf 1. Türkischen Schwahn, täglich 9.dn.* ["for feeding one 'Turkish swan' for the 121 days from 29 Sept 1730 to 27 Jan 1731 inclusive, 9 pfennigs daily"]
43 talers 5 pfennigs, *auf 28. Tage, nehmlich vom 1. bis ult: Febr: 1731 vor den Vogel Strauß, Casuarium, 1. Papagoy und andere Indianische Vögel* ["for 28 days, from the first to the last day of Feb 1731 for the ostrich, cassowary, one parrot and other exotic birds"]
69 talers 9 pfennigs, *nehmlich vom 27. Jan: bis 18. May 1731 vor 2. schwarze Störche, 2. weiße Pfauen, 1. waßer-Falcken, 1. Löffel-Ganß, 3. Augspurgische Ziegen-Böcke, 1. andern Ziegen Bock, und 2. Africanische Schaaff-Stehre* ["from 27 Jan to 18 May 1731 for two black storks, two white peacocks, one 'wasser-Falcke,' one 'spoon-goose' (= pelican), three Augsburg billy-goats, two African 'Schaaff-Stehre,' and one other billy-goat"]

No. 246, RT, 1733

A [fols. 51a – 52a]
– Mentioned for the first time: a leopard
In addition 4 talers were spent on six large and eight small neck-bands for baboons and monkeys.

D [fols. 383a – 385a]
Moritzburg pheasantry, mentioned for the first time:
– a "Gagatout" (= *Kakadu*, cockatoo) and "arabische Perlhüner" (guinea fowl)
Also mentioned:
– *50. allerhand Sorten Gänße, als: 38. Stk. Persianische, 11. Stück Pommerische, und 1. Stk. Türkische uts* ["50 geese of sundry kinds: 38 Persian, 11 Pomeranian, and 1 Turkish"]
– 4 bustards, of which one "crepiret" (died) on 17 Mar 1733
– ostriches, cassowaries, king vultures, eagles, "ravens" (probably "Indian," i.e. macaws), various parakeets, parrots, storks, peacocks, herons, billy-goats
– 86 English and 10 Turkish hens
– 176 Turkish, 74 Dutch, 53 "Pommersche" (Pomeranian), and 12 Hungarian ducks

D Further entries relevant to the pheasantry at Moritzburg:
– [fol. 57a] the pheasant-keeper of the "Wörbliz" (sic) region receives money for pheasants delivered
– [fol. 57b] a ropemaker in Pirna receives money for twine and linen for hawk baskets
– [fol. 383b] *2 Thlr 16gr Warttegeld, dem Tyroler wegen der Steinhühner, vermöge Quittung vom 22. Novembr: 1732* ["2 talers 16 groschen to the Tirolean for looking after the rock partridges, as per receipt of 22 Nov 1732"], *und darauf noch 10 Thlr zur Zehrung weil er entlassen wurde* ["and 10 talers in addition for food because he was sent back"]

Nr 247, CL, 1733

B Mentioned for Moritzburg, inter alia:
6 "aurochses," guinea fowl, cranes, exotic birds, ostriches, black storks, pelicans, herons, peacocks, "afrik. Schaafe," billy-goats, vultures, "ravens," "Wauwaus" (= king vultures), parrots.

NOTES

1 It is not clear whether this letter is an i or an e, as it has no dot.
2 In Expl. BA = Sfinxe.
3 In Expl. BA = Calientsche.
4 Sponsel, who published a list of this kind, translates this with "rabbit" ("Kanninchen"), which is certainly wrong.
5 I am grateful to Maureen Cassidy-Geiger for drawing my attention to this source, which only contains the passage on Dresden in the original English-language edition, and not in the German-language translation.
6 "Guinea" = the coastal area of west Africa between the Sahara and the west African coastal desert.
7 "Dieses Corps begreift die Former, Dreher, Pußirer, Verputzer, Bildhauer und alle übrige Arbeiter unter sich, die mit der rohen Masse zu thun haben." ["The 'weiße Corps' includes the molders, turners, repairers, finishers, sculptors, and all others who work on the unfired paste."]
8 "Diese Statue sollte mit dem Fußstücke 17 Ellen hoch werden. Das Modell dazu von Gips ist, wie oben angeführt, schon seit 1755 fertig. Es steht auf dem Vorhofe des Meißner Schlosses, in einem hölzernen Schuppen, und es wäre zu wünschen, daß es an einem schicklichern Orte, zum Besten der Kenner und Liebhaber öffentlich aufbewahret, und wenigstens das Andenken eines so kühnen Vorsatzes, den ein sächsischer Künstler gefaßt hatte, und den er, ohne die eintretenden Hindernisse gewiß ausgeführet haben würde, möchte erhalten werden." ["This statue was to have been 17 ells high with the pedestal. The model in plaster has been ready, as has been mentioned above, since 1755. It stands in the front courtyard of Meissen Castle, in a wooden hut, and it could well be wished that it might be kept in a more appropriate place where it would be accessible to connoisseurs and porcelain-lovers, so that at least the memory of such a bold enterprise might be preserved, an enterprise undertaken by a Saxon artist and one which he would certainly have brought to completion had it not been for the obstacles that arose."]
9 "Eine Beschreibung nur der vorzüglichsten Werke Herrn Kändlers, ungeachtet sie unterhaltend und lehrreich genug seyn würde, wäre zu weitläufig für diese Blätter.
Ich will einige wenige davon anführen:
Der Apostel Paulus in Lebensgröße.
Der sterbende Xaver.
Die Geisselung des Heylandes.
Die Kreuzigung, von verschiedener Größe.
Die 12 Apostel, 24 Zoll hoch.
Ein Glockenspiel ganz von Porcellain.
Viel ausländische Vögel und vierfüßige Thiere in Lebensgröße.
Die Reihe der Kaiser, habsburgischen Stamms, in großen Büsten für den Wienerischen, und fast alle ovidische Geschichte, für den Petersburger Hof."
["A description of the most outstanding works of Herr Kändler, although it would be both entertaining and instructive, would take up too much space for inclusion in these pages. I nevertheless wish to list a small number of them: The apostle Paul, life-size. The dying Xavier. The scourging of the Savior. The crucifixion, in various sizes. The 12 apostles, 24 inches high. A carillon entirely in porcelain. Many foreign birds and four-footed animals, life-size. All the emperors from the Habsburg dynasty, in large busts for the Viennese court, and almost al the stories from Ovid, for the court at Petersburg."]
10 "Diese sind vernämlich: Gellerts Bildniß in Medaillon und Büste. Ferner das Geschenk für den letzt verstorbenen Papst Clemens, nämlich: ein großes Stück, Christus am Kreuze, die Figur 20 Zoll hoch; 6 Heilige 22 Zoll hoch, von einem redenden Affekt. Vier Altarleuchter von herrlicher Erfindung und Auszierung. Noch hat Herr Kändler 40 allegorische Gruppen für die rußische Kaiserin entworfen, und davon 15 mit eigener Hand im wahren Antikenstil, und mit bewundernswürdiger Schönheit und Harmonie ausgeführet." ["These are, namely: the portrait of Gellert as a medallion and as a bust; the gift for the late Pope Clement, a large piece, Christ on the cross, the figure itself 20 inches high; 6 saints 22 inches high, done with eloquent feeling; four altar candlesticks, most marvelously conceived and decorated. Herr Kändler furthermore designed 40 allegorical groups for the Russian Tsarina, modeling 15 of them with his own hand in the true classical style, with admirable beauty and harmony."]
11 "Nur einige davon will ich anführen;
Das Portrait des Michel Angelo, in Rembrantischen Geschmack, vortreflich gemalt.
Zwey Stück 36 Zoll hoch, 30 breit, Paulus, ein Gesicht voller Hoheit; das Gegenbild, der betende Petrus ist in einem rührenden Ausdruck. Simeon mit dem Christkinde auf den Armen; Maria sitzend, Joseph hinter ihr, der Priester vorwärts, und neben ihm ein paar Tauben in einem Kefich. Im Vordergrunde ein Knabe mit einer Fackel, ein geistreiches Gemälde, jede Figur mit dem angemessenen Affekt belebt, und die Erleuchtung sehr schön, ist zwey Ellen hoch, und ein und dreyviertel breit, noch nicht ganz ausgemalt.
Ein Stück mit todtem Federvieh, so natürlich, als es nur ausgedrückt werden kann."
["I would only mention a small number of these: The portrait of Michelangelo, in the style of Rembrandt, exceedingly well painted. Two pieces 36 inches high and 30 broad: Paul, a most noble face, and as a counterpart, Peter in prayer, most movingly expressive. Simeon with the Christ-child in his arms: Mary sitting, Joseph behind her, the priest to the fore and next to him a pair of turtle-doves in a cage. Also in the foreground a boy with a torch, a spirited painting, each figure enlivened with the right feeling, and the lighting most beautifully done, two ells high and one and three quarters broad, not fully painted. A piece with a dead bird, as natural as is humanly possible."]
12 Note by O. Scheel: "Es heißt, daß nach Vollendung der Figuren die Formen zerschlagen wurden, damit die Stücke nicht doppelt hergestellt würden, und damit sie doppelt kostbar und selten sein sollten." ["That is to say that after the figures had finally been produced, the molds were broken so that the figures could not be produced again and so that they might be doubly costly and rare."]
13 It is not clear why Müller gives the size in "quarters" ("Quartier"), a unit normally used for volume rather than length. It is possible that he meant a quarter of an ell (= 14.2 cm), which would correspond to the small-size display pieces produced at the Meissen manufactory.
14 It is possible that majolica is meant.

List of the unprinted sources, with their abbreviations

Abbreviations for the institutions concerned:

SächsHStA	Sächsisches Hauptstaatsarchiv Dresden (State Archive of Saxony, Dresden)
BA	Betriebsarchiv der Staatlichen Porzellan-Manufaktur Meissen GmbH (Archive of the Meissen State Porcelain Manufactory)
PS	Staatliche Kunstsammlungen zu Dresden, Porzellansammlung im Zwinger (Dresden State Art Collections, Porcelain Collection in the Zwinger)
AKS	Archiv der Staatlichen Kunstsammlungen zu Dresden (Archive of the Dresden State Art Collections)

SächsHStA = Sächsisches Hauptstaatsarchiv Dresden

OHMA Oberhofmarschallamt (Lord Marshall's Office)

Abbreviation	Full title
OHMA Cap.II	OHMA, Pläne und Zeichnungen, Cap.II
OHMA Cap.VI	OHMA, Pläne und Zeichnungen, Cap.VI
OHMA Cap.VIII	OHMA, Pläne und Zeichnungen, Cap.VIII
OHMA Cap.IX	OHMA, Pläne und Zeichnungen, Cap.IX
OHMA O.I	OHMA, O.I, Nr.3, Dresdener Hofjournal Vol.3 (1732/33), Vol.4 (1734/35), Vol.5 (1736/37), Vol.6 (1738), Vol.7 (1739)
OHMA O.IV, Akte 129	OHMA O.IV, Akte 129, Schreibkalender, Eintrag 5. April 1747
OHMA TI	OHMA T I., Nr.511A, Verordnungen und Befehle 1705–29
loc.354	loc.354, Hofkassen- und Schatullensachen 1686–1732
loc.379 Direction	loc.379, die dem CabinethsMinister Grafen von Manteuffel aufgetragene Directio über die Bibliotheken[...] Kunstkabinette etc 1720, ferner die Direktionen von Friesen 1727, Sulkowski 1733, Brühl 1738
loc.379 Verzeichnisse	loc.379, Diverse Verzeichniße von Gem[älden] und Schildereinen, ingl. Königl. S[ammlungen], Kunstakademien, Kunstsachen und [Her]steller betr. 1700–1772
loc.380	loc.380, Papiers concernant les emplettes de porcelaines en Hollande [...] 1716–1718
loc.452	loc.452, Correspondenz / Papiere von Beichlingen 1660ff
loc.520 Vol.1734	loc.520, Porcelain Waaren Lager zu Dreßden Rechnung, 1734
loc.520 Vol.1735	loc.520, Porcelain Waaren Lagers zu Dreßden Rechnung, 1735
loc.521 Vol.1736	loc.521, Porcelain Waaren Lagers zu Dreßden Rechnung, 1736
loc.521 Vol.1737	loc.521, Porcelain Waaren Lagers zu Dreßden Rechnung, 1737
loc.557	loc.557, ObermbauAmts Sachen 1735–1743
loc.589	loc.589, Verschiedene in Hamburg auch sonst erkaufte wilde Thiere 1718
loc.676	loc.676, Lettres et relations au Roi, à la Reine, à Sulkowski de Brühl 1734
loc.681 Vol.XXI	loc.681, Correspondenz Graf Flemming, Vol.XXI, 1713
loc.681 Vol.CCLXI	loc.681, Korrespondenz Graf von Flemming, Vol.CCLXI
loc.709 Vol.CCLXI	loc.709, Correspondenz Graf Flemming, Vol.CCLXI
loc.754	loc.754, Diarium Hr:Durchl: des Prinzen Friedrich Augusts Herzog zu Sachßen gethane Reysen in fremde Länder betr. Anno 1687 bis 1689
loc.773	loc.773, Die Reparirung des Schlosses zu Dresden 1717/18
loc.885	loc.885, Varia das Oberhofmarschallamt betr 1728–1761
loc.895	loc.895, Acta Chinesische und japanische Porcellaine, auch andere im japanischen Palais aufbewahrte Kunst-Sachen betr.
loc.949	loc.949, Sachen den CabinetsMinister und General Grafen von Sulkowski betr. 1733–1744
loc.950	loc.950, Die nach Ableben des Cab.Min. Grafen Brühl [...] Taxation des Nachlasses 1763–1765
loc.1295	loc.1295, Acta den Obl.Baumeister Longuelune betr. 1736–49
loc.1341	loc.1341, Varia die Porcelain-Manufactur betreffend, ohne Tag und Jahr

loc. 1341 Vol. IV	loc. 1341, Vol. IV, Acta die Porcellän Manufaktur betr. 1725ff
loc. 1341 Vol. V	loc. 1341, Vol. V, Acta die Porcellän Manufactur betr. 1731
loc. 1341 Vol. VI	loc. 1341, Vol. VI, Acta die Porcellän Manufactur betr. 1732
loc. 1342 Vol. VII	loc. 1342, Vol. VII, Acta die Porcelaine Manufactur betr. 1733
loc. 1342 Vol. VIII	loc. 1342, Vol. VIII, Acta die Porcelaine Manufactur betr. 1734/1735
loc. 1342 Vol. IX	loc. 1342, Vol. IX, Acta die Porcelaine Manufactur betr. 1736/1737
loc. 1342 Vol. X	loc. 1342, Vol. X, Die Porcelaine Manufactur betr. 1738–1739
loc. 1342 Vol. XI	loc. 1342, Vol. XI, Acta die Porcelaine Manufactur betr. 1740
loc. 1344 Vol. XVIII	loc. 1344, Vol. XVIII, Die Porcelaine Manufactur betr. 1760–1762
loc. 2097 Nr. 549	loc. 2097, Nr. 49, Eigenhändige Notizen König Augusts II. von Polen, Meissner Porzellan betr.
loc. 2097 Nr. 50	loc. 2097, Nr. 50, Eigenhändige Notizen König Augusts II. von Polen, Meissner Porzellan betr.
loc. 2214 Vol. II	loc. 2214, Oberbauamtssachen, Vol. II, 1724ff
loc. 2407 Doubletten	loc. 2407, Acta die Veräußerung derer bey der Churfürstl. Bibliothec befindlichen Doubletten [...] und anderweite Placirung derer jetzt darinnen befindlichen Porcelaines und Mobilien betr. Anno 1774
loc. 2407	loc. 2407, Die Unterbringung der Porcelaines und Unterbringung Majoliken 1774
loc. 3315/3316	loc. 3315/3316, Bd. V, Korresp. zwischen Grafen Manteuffel und LeFort 1721-28
loc. 3354	loc. 3354, Correspondenz des Legationssecretairs Rothe zu Berlin mit dem Grafen Brühl 1736–1739, nebst dem Tagebuch über eine Reise nach Dreßden 1738
loc. 3422	loc. 3422, Correspondence du Cte de Wackerbarth avec Msr. Thioly à Rome sur L'achat des statues 1721
loc. 3447	loc. 3447, Schreiben Graf Hoym an August II über einen in Baden gekauften Elefanten 1720 (fehlt)
loc. 8576	loc. 8576, Acta die Abnahme Dr. Joh. Ernst Hebestreits Prof. Phil. in Leipzig geführte Africanische Reise [...] vom 25. August 1731–6. Oct. 1733 betr.
loc. 14636 Vol. II	loc. 14636, Fasciculus die Porcellain Fabrique in Meißen betr., Vol. II, 1732
loc. 14636 Vol. III	loc. 14636, Fasciculus die Porcellain Fabrik betr., Vol. III, 1733
loc. 14636 Vol. IV	loc. 14636, Fasciculus die Porcellain Fabrik betr., Vol. IV, 1734
loc. 32561	loc. 32.561, Rep. XII, 117/118 Acta der Kammerräte der Kommission, Wichmannshausen und Pflug, 1729 (117) und 1730 (118)
loc. 32562 Nr. 5119/120	loc. 32.562, 119/120a.b Acta der Kammerräte der Kommission, Wichmannshausen und Pflug, 1730 (119), 1731 (120a) und 1729-1735 (120b)
loc. 32562 Nr. 5120	loc. 32562, Nr. 5120a, Acta dem Cammer-Collegio aufgetragene Administration und beßere Einrichtung der Porcelain-Fabrique zu Meißen [...] betr. 1731
loc. 33610	loc. 33610, Rechnungen über den Kurfürstl Hofhaushalt
loc. 34944	loc. 34944, Hofbausachen betreffend 1645–1750 (Coll. Schmid. Amt Dresden, Vol. XIb/294)
loc. 35762	loc. 35762, Miscellanea, Hofbau- und andere Bausachen enthaltend Vol. I, ab 1731
loc. 35862	loc. 35862, Allg. Anschläge über Bauten in kgl. Schlössern etc. betr. 1737 (vier Bände)
loc. 35865	loc. 35865, Nachrichten von der Residenzstadt Dresden 1755
loc. 36147	loc. 36.147, Convolut, Meissen 1729–1768
loc. 37284 Vol. I	loc. 37284, die allhier in Dresden befindlichen Kgl. [...] Häuser, Vol. I, 1734–1737
loc. 37284 Vol. II	loc. 37284, die allhier in Dresden befindlichen Kgl. [...] Häuser, Vol. II, 1737–1741
loc. 38186	loc. 38186, Die bey der Kgl. Naturalien-Gallerie zum Ausstopfen annoch benöthigten Vögel u. Thiere 1783
loc. 41843	loc. 41843, Die Verwaltungsprotokolle der Porzellan Manufactur Meissen betr., Vol. V, 1850–1853
loc. 41910	loc. 41.910, div. Schriften Meissen ab 1709
Rentkammer-Akten	Rentkammer-Akten, Ausgaben, eingesehen Band 237 (1. Halbjahr 1727) bis 254 (1. Halbjahr 1738)
Spezialreskripte 1736	Spezialreskripte 1736, Nr. 5469
Spezialreskripte 1748	Spezialreskripte 1748, Nr. 5623
Spezialreskripte 1750	Spezialreskripte 1750, Nr. 5134
Ministerium d. I. Nr. 517261	Ministerium des Innern Nr. 517261, Die Kunstsammlungen und Kunstakademieen betr. 1848–1852
Inventar 1769	Hausmarschallamt R, XVI, Nr. 56, Inventar des Turmzimmers im Dresdener Residenzschloss 1769
Inventar 1770	Hausmarschallamt R, XVI, Nr. 555, Vol. II, Inventarium vom ChurFürstl. Sächßischen Japans. Palais zu Neustadt bey Dreßden und zwar über das Sächß. Porcellain, 1770

BA = Betriebs-Archiv der Staatlichen Porzellan-Manufaktur Meissen GmbH

IAa	Kommissionsakten (Deeds of the Commission)
IAb	Rapporte (Monthly reports of the Commission)
IAd	Kassensachen (Accounts)
IAe	Gerichtssachen (Judiciary matters)
IIIH	Betrieb und Gestaltung (Running of the enterprise and porcelain design)
Pret	Pretiosa

Abbreviation	Full title
IAa.10	IAa 10, Acta Commissionis Die Königl: Porcellain Manufactur auf den Schloße zu Meißen betr. de Anno 1726 item 1727
IAa.12	IAa.12, Acta Commissionis Die direction der Königl: Porcelain Manufactur auf dem Schloße zu Meißen betr: Ao 1728 et 1729
IAa.14	IAa.14, Acta Die dem Cammer-Collegium aufgetragene Administration und beßere Einrichtung der Porcellain-Fabrique zu Meißen [...] betr. Anno 1731
IAa.15	IAa.15, Acta Commissionis Die allergnädigst anbefohlene beßere Einrichtung der Königl: Porcelain-Manufactur auf dem Schloße zu Meißen und deren stärckern Umtrieb betr: Anno 1731
IAa.16	IAa.16, Acta worinne die wegen Umtrieb der Königl: Porcelain- Manufactur auf dem Schloße zu Meißen abgefaßte Monathsrapports und darauf ertheilte Commissarische Resolutiones befindlich, anno 1731
IAa.17	IAa.17, Acta Commissionis Die allergnädigst anbefohlene bessere Umtreibung der Königl: Porcelain:Manufactur auf dem Schloße zu Meißen betr: Anno 1732
IAa.18	IAa.18, Acta worinne die wegen Umtrieb der Königl: Porcelain- Manufactur auf dem Schloße zu Meißen abgefaßte Monathsrapports und darauf ertheilte Commissarische Resolutiones befindlich, anno 1732
IAa.19	IAa.19, Acta Commissionis Die allergnädigst anbefohlene Beobachtung der Königl: Porcelain: Manufactur auf dem Schloße zu Meißen [...] betr: Anno 1733
IAa.20	IAa.20, Rapports Welche von dem Zustande der Porcelain-Manufactur zu Meißen anno 1733 zur Commission erstattet und die resolutiones, so darauf von commissaischer Seite ertheilet worden
IAa.21	IAa.21, Acta Commissionis Die allergnädigst anbefohlene Beobachtung der Königl: Porcelain:Manufactur auf dem Schloße zu Meißen [...] betr: 1734
IAa.22	IAa.22, Rapports Welche von dem Zustande der Porcelain- Manufactur zu Meißen Anno 1734 [...] ertheilet worden
IAa.23	IAa.23, Acta Commissionis Die administration der Königl: Porcelaine-Manufactur auf dem Schloße Albrechtsburg zu Meißen betr: de Ao:1735
IAa.24	IAa.24, Rapports Welche von dem Zustande der Porcelain- Manufactur zu Meißen Anno 1735 [...] ertheilet worden
IAa.24a	IAa.24a, Acta Commissionis Die administration der Königl: Porcelaine-Manufactur auf dem Schloße Albrechtsburg zu Meißen betr: de Ao:1736
IAa.24b	IAa.24b, Rapports Welche von dem Zustande der Porcelain- Manufactur zu Meißen Anno 1736 [...] ertheilet worden
IAa.24c	IAa.24c, Acta Commissionis Die administration der Königl: Porcelaine-Manufactur auf dem Schloße Albrechtsburg zu Meißen betr: de Ao:1737
IAa.24d	IAa.24d, Acta Commissionis Die administration der Königl: Porcelaine-Manufactur auf dem Schloße Albrechtsburg zu Meißen betr: Anno 1738
IAa.25	IAa.25, Acta Commissionis Die administration der Königl: Porcelaine-Manufactur auf dem Schloße Albrechtsburg zu Meißen betr: Anno 1739
IAa.25a	IAa.25a, Acta Commissionis Die Untersuch- und Erörterung einiger, bey der Königl: Porcelaine-Manufactur zu Meißen ao: 1739 geeuserten Mängel und Gebrechen, auch daher beschehene noch beßere Einrichtung sothaner Fabrique betr:
IAa.26	IAa.26, Acta Commissionis Die administration der Königl: Porcelaine-Manufactur auf dem Schloße Albrechtsburg zu Meißen betr: Anno 1740
IAa.29	IAa.29, Acata Commissionis Die administraton der Königl. PorcelaineManufactur auf dem Schloße Albrechtsburg zu Meißen betr. Anno 1743
IAb.1e	IAb.1e, An die zur Königl: Porcellain-Manufactur in Meißen allergnädigst verordnete Commission von Zeit zu Zeit erstattete Rapports, Angefangen mit dem Jahre 1728
IAb.2	IAb.2, An die zur Königl: Porcellain-Manufactur in Meißen als zu beßerung Einrichtung Derselben allergnädigst verordnete Commission von Zeit zu Zeit erstattete Rapports, Angefangen mit dem Jahre 1729
IAb.9	IAb.9, Rapports, Welche von dem Zustande der Porcelain-Manufactur zu Meißen Anno 1737 zur Commission erstattet und von selbiger die Resolutiones darauf ertheilet worden
IAb.11	IAb.11, Rapports, Welche von dem Zustande der Porcelain-Manufactur zu Meißen, Anno 1738 zur Commission erstattet und von selbiger die resolutiones darauf ertheilet worden
IAb.12	IAb.12, Rapports, Welche von dem Zustande der Porcelain-Manufactur zu Meißen, Anno 1739 zur Commission erstattet und von selbiger die resolutiones darauf ertheilet worden
IAb.14	IAb.14, Rapports, Welche von dem Zustande der Porcelain-Manufactur zu Meißen, Anno 1740 zur Commission erstattet und von selbiger die resolutiones darauf ertheilet worden
IAd.3	IAd.3, Acta Commissionis Die defectirung wie auch justification derer von dem gewesenen Inspectore bey der Königl: Porcelain-Manufactur zu Meißen, Herrn Johann David Reinhardten, jetztgedachter Fabrique halber verführten Rechnungen von Ao: 1731. biß Ao: 1734 sich erstreckend
IAe.2	IAe.2, Reinhardische Denunciation-Collectanea 1734
IAe.3	IAe.3, Acta Commissionis Die allergnädigst anbefohlene Untersuchung derer wieder verschiedene Personen bey der Königl. Porcellain-Fabrique zu Meißen denuncirten Puncte betr. Ao:1734
IAe.5	IAe.5, Acta Einige Porcellain-Manufactur-Bedienstete betr. de ao. 1727 bis 1738
IIIH.114/3	IIIH. 114/3, Verzeichnis der Modell in Gestaltung (20. Jh.)

IIIH 121	IIIH 121 Liste der Modellnummern der Vögel von Hösel
V2.12	V2.12, Der Königl:Pohln: und Churf:Sächs: Porcellain-Manufactur zu Meißen Jahr-Rechnung [...] Vom Januar: bis Ultimo Decembris Anno 1732
V2.13	V2.13, Der Königl:Pohln: und Churf:Sächs: Porcellain-Manufactur zu Meißen Jahr-Rechnung [...] Vom Januar: bis Ultimo Decembris Anno 1733
V2.14	V2.14, Der Königl:Pohln: und Churf:Sächs: Porcellain-Manufactur in Meißen Stück-Rechnung [...] Vom 1.sten Januar: bis Ultimo Novbr: Anno 1734
V2.16	V2.16, Der Königl:Pohln: und Churf:Sächs: Porcellain-Manufactur zu Meißen Jahr-Rechnung [...] Von 1. Januarii bis ultmo Decembris 1736
Pret. 4	Pret. 4, Arkanabuch zur Porzellanherstellung (wohl) von Dr. Petzsch; Manuskript, nach 1736
Pret. 10	Pret. 10, Johann Gregorius Höroldt: Versätze für Glasuren und Massen sowie Rezepte für kobaltblaue Unterglasurfarbe
Pret. 16	Pret. 16, Samuel Stöltzel: Versätze für Massen und Glasuren
Pret. 32	Pret. 32, ungebundene, nicht paginierte Arkanaschrift in mehreren Papier-Bündellagen; könnte von Petzsch sein (?)
Pret. 67	Pret. 67, Arcanabuch, Dr. Petzsch (1959 in 3 Bände gebunden)

PS = Staatliche Kunstsammlungen zu Dresden, Porzellansammlung im Zwinger

Abbreviation	Full title
Inventar 1721	Inventarium über das Palais zu Alt-Dreßden Anno 1721 (= Staatliche Kunstsammlungen zu Dresden, Inventare Nr. 5324)
Inventar 1779	Inventarium vom ChurFürstl. Sächßischen Holländischen Palais zu Neustadt bey Dreßden und zwar über Das Sächßis. Porcellain, Vol. II, 1779 (= Staatliche Kunstsammlungen Dresden, Inventare Nr. 5328)
Verkaufs- und Tauschverzeichnis	Verkauf und Tausch bei der Königl. Sächs. Porzellan- und Gefäße-Sammlung 1832–1842
Doublettenverzeichnis 1850/54	Verzeichnis der Doubletten der Königl. Porzellan- und Gefässe-Sammlung (um 1850–54), geführt von Karl August Friedrich Böttcher (= Inventare der Staatlichen Kunstsammlungen Dresden, Nr. 5347)
Doublettenverzeichnis 1912–1920	Abgebbare Doubletten 1912–1920, (= Kunstslg Dresden, Inventare 351 a)

AKS = Archiv der Staatlichen Kunstsammlungen zu Dresden

Abbreviation	Full title
Akte 10	Akten der königlichen Porzellan und Gefäße-sammlung Dresden, Akte 10, 1848–1874
Akte 11	Akten der Königlichen Porzellan und Gefäße-sammlung Dresden, Akte 11, 1875–1876
Akte 13	Akten der Königl. Porzellan und Gefäßesammlung, Akte 13, 1884–1893
Akte 24	Akte die Porzellansammlung betr., Akte 24/1912
Akte 25	Akte die Porzellansammlung betr., Akte 25/1913, p. 56 a–60 b
Akte 28	Akte die Porzellansammlung betr., Akte 28/1916
Akte 30	Akte die Porzellansammlung betr., Akte 30/1918
Akte 31	Akte die Porzellansammlung betr., Akte 31/1919
Akte 32	Akte die Porzellansammlung betr., Akte 32/1920
Akte 35	Akte die Porzellansammlung betr., Akte 35/1929–1930
Akte 36 Vol. II	Akte die Porzellansammlung betr., Akte 36/1931–33, Vol. II
Akte 37 Vol. I	Akte die Porzellansammlung betr., Akte 37/1933–1934, Vol. I

Reference list

Printed historical sources, reprints

anonym 1720
Der Neu-erscheinende Postillon, 1720, no. 3. Dresden, 1720.

anonym 1733
Aufrichtige und umständliche Nachrichten Was bey der Den 17. December 1733. in der Stadt Meissen von denen Aemtern und Städten Meissen, Hayn, Oschatz, Ortrant und Lommatzsch eingenommenen Erb-Huldigungen Den 16. 17. und 18. December d. a. merckwürdiges und solennes vorgegangen. Leipzig: Langenheim, 1733.

anonym 1735
Curieuse Reise-Beschreibung des Herrn Androphili. Leipzig, 1735.

anonym 1737
Dreßdnische Adresse. Oder kurtze Anzeige, was ein curieuser nach Dreßden reisender Passagier [...] zu observiren hat. Dresden, 1737.

anonym 1775
Nachricht von Herrn Johann Joachim Kändlers Leben und Arbeiten. *Neue Bibliothek der schönen Wissenschaften und der freyen Künste* 18:296–303. Leipzig, 1775.

anonym 1779
Inventarium vom ChurFürstl. Sächßischen Holländischen Palais zu Neustadt bey Dreßden und zwar über Das Sächßis. Porcellain, Vol. II. (= Staatliche Kunstsammlungen Dresden, inventory no. 328, Porzellansammlung im Zwinger). Dresden, 1779.

anonym 1799
Neue Ansicht von Dresden. Für Reisende von einem Reisenden. Leipzig, 1799.

Beutler 1680
T. Beutler. *Geographisches Kleinod.* Dresden, 1680.

Boreman 1730
Thomas Boreman. *Threehundred animals.* Glasgow, 1730.

Brongniard 1844
Alexandre Brongniard. *Traité des arts cèramiques ou des poteries.* 2 vols. Paris, 1844.

Cassidy-Geiger 2004
Maureen Cassidy-Geiger. Supplement to the exhibition catalog of the Museum für Lackkunst, Münster, and Schloss Favorite, Rastatt, *Schwartz Porcelain. Die Leidenschaft für Lack und ihre Wirkung auf das europäische Porzellan.* Munich, 2004.

Dassdorf 1782
Carl Wilhelm Dassdorf. *Beschreibung der vorzüglichsten Merkwürdigkeiten der Churfürstlichen Residenzstadt Dresden.* Dresden, 1782.

Decker 1711
Paul Decker. *Fürstlicher Baumeister oder: Architectura civilis (wie grosser Fürsten und Herren Paläste, mit ihren Höfen, Lust-Häusern, Gärten, Grotten, Orangerien und anderen darzu gehörigen Gebäuden füglich anzulegen und nach heutiger Art auszuziren, zusamt den Grund-Rissen und Durchschnitten).* Augsburg, 1711.

Decker 1716
Paul Decker. *Deß Fürstlichen Baumeisters, Oder Architectura civilis anderer Theil, welcher eines Königlichen Pallastes General-Prospect, Grund und Aufzug sammt den vornehmen Gemächern Lust-Brunnen Garten und Lust-Gebäuden ec. vorstellet.* Augsburg, 1716.

Fassmann 1733
David Fassmann. *Das Glorwürdigste Leben und Thaten Friedrich Augusti.* Hamburg, 1733.

Franciscus 1668
E. Franciscus. *Ost- und West-Indischer wie auch Sinesischer Lust- und Stats-Garthen [...].* Nuremberg, 1668.

Gracián 1957
Baltasar Gracián. *Criticón oder über die allgemeinen Laster des Menschen, Teil 1–3* (originally Barcelona, 1664). A new German-language edition, trans. Hanns Studnieczka, with an afterword by Hugo Friedrich. Hamburg, 1957.

Hanway 1753
Jonas Hanway. *An Historical Account of the British Trade over the Caspian Sea, with a Journal of Travels from London through Russia into Persia, and back through Russia, Germany and Holland.* 2 vols. London, 1753.

Hasche 1781/83
Johann Christian Hasche. *Umständliche Beschreibung Dresdens mit allen seinen äußern und innern Merkwürdigkeiten.* 2 vols. Leipzig, 1781/83.

Iccander 1726–1735
Iccander (= Johann Christian Crell). *Kurtzgefasstes Sächsisches Kern-Chronicon.* Dresden, 1726–1735.

Iccander 1734
Iccander (= Johann Christian Crell): Von dem zu Neustadt bey Dreßden in diesem seculo neu-angelegten Königl. Japanischen Palais. *Curiosa Saxonica* I, November 1733, to be found in *Sächßisches Curiositäten Cabinet auf das Jahr 1733*: 227–231. Dresden, 1734.

Iccander 1735
Iccander (= Johann Christian Crell): *Curiosa Saxonica* November 1734, to be found in *Sächßisches Curiositäten Cabinet auf das Jahr 1734.* Dresden, 1735.

Iccander 1740
Iccander (= Johann Christian Crell). *Alte und neue curiosa saxonica,* March 1740, first half, to be found in *Sächsisches Curiositäten-Cabinett auf das Jahr 1740.* Dresden, 1740.

Keyssler 1751
Johann Georg Keyssler. *Neueste Reisen durch Deutschland, Böhmen, Ungarn, die Schweiz, Italien und Lothringen.* Second edition (first edition: 1741). Hannover, 1751.

Klemm 1834
Gustav Klemm. *Die Königlich Sächsische Porzellansammlung. Eine Übersicht ihrer vorzüglichsten Schätze, nebst Nachweisungen über die Geschichte der Gefäßbildnerei in Thon und Porzellan.* Dresden, 1834.

Krauss 1975
Johann Ulrich Krauss. *Der Irrgarten zu Versailles.* Reprint, ed. Helmut Eisendle. Berlin, 1975.

Krünitz 1773–1858
Johann Georg Krünitz. *Oekonomische Encyclopaedie, der allgemeines System der Land-, Haus- und Staats-Wirthschaft.* 242 vols. Berlin, 1773–1858.

Lairesse 1730
Gérard de Lairesse. *Großes Mahler Buch.* German translation of *Het groot schilderboek* (2 vols. Amsterdam 1707). Part One: Nuremberg, 1728; Part Two: Nuremberg, 1730. Trans. J. F. Fritsch as *The Art of painting,* 2 vols. (London, 1738).

Leibniz 1720
Gottfried Wilhelm Leibniz. *Monadologie.* Jena, 1720.

Leibniz 1979
Gottfried Wilhelm Leibniz. *Das Neueste aus China 1697 (Novissima Sinica).* Trans. and ed. Heinz-Günther Nesselrath and Hermann Reinbothe. Cologne, 1979.

Leibniz 1995
Gottfried Wilhelm Leibniz: *Unvorgreiffliche Gedancken.* Reprint in *18th and 19th century German linguistics* 1/1995.

Loen 1749.a
Johann Michael von Loen. *Abbildung des Königs in Pohlen.* In *Des Herrn von Loen gesammelte Kleine Schrifften,* ed. J.C. Schneider, vol. 1, section 2: 187–195. Frankfurt/Main, 1749.

Loen 1749.b
Johann Michael von Loen. *Der Hof zu Dresden im Jahr 1718.* In ibid., vol. 1, section 3: 39–67. Frankfurt/Main, 1749.

Merkel 1806
D.J. Merkel. *Beschreibung von Dresden.* Vol. 5 of *Erdbeschreibung von Kursachsen und den iezt dazu gehörenden Ländern. 3. durchaus verbesserte und vermehrte Auflage. Nach dem Tode des Verfassers größtentheils aus handschriftlichen Nachrichten bearbeitet von Karl August Engelhardt.* Dresden, 1806.

Müller 1907
Johann Christian Müller. *Tagebuch seiner Reise durch Dresden 1744, niedergeschrieben gegen Ende der 1750er Jahre.* Transcribed by O. Scheel and published in the *Dresdner Anzeiger* in two parts as *Ein Besuch Dresdens im Jahre 1744:* 9 June 1907, Sunday supplement 23:93–95, and 16 June 1907, Sunday supplement 24:97–99.

Neuhof 1669
Johan Neuhof. *Gesandtschaft der Ost-Indischen Gesellschaft in den vereinigten Nederländern, an den Tartarischen Cham und nunmehr sinischen Keyser.* Amsterdam, 1669.

Perrault 1990
Charles Perrault. *La labyrinthe de Versailles.* Reprint, edited with a commentary by Jean-Pierre Collinet. Paris, 1990.

Pöllnitz 1737
Baron von Pöllnitz. *Lettres et memoires du Baron de Pöllnitz contenant les Observation qu'il a faites dans ses voyages.* Third edition. Amsterdam, 1737.

Rohr 1990
Julius Bernhard von Rohr. *Einleitung zur Ceremoniel-Wissenschafft der großen Herren.* Second edition (Berlin, 1733). New edition, with commentary, by Monika Schlechte. Weinheim, 1990

Schoettgen 1736
Christian Schoettgen. *Historische Nachricht Von denen Illuminationen, Wie solche zu alten und neuen Zeiten bey allerhand Völckern im Gebrauch gewesen, Bey Gelegenheit der bey Ihr. Königl. Majestäten in Pohlen und Churfl. Durchl. zu Sachsen höchst erfreulichen Ankunfft in Dero Residentz Stadt Dreßden aufgestellten Dreytägigen Illumination.* No pagination. Dresden and Leipzig, 1736.

Schramm 1984
Carl Christian Schramm. Dreßden/Neustadt bey Dreßden. In Schramm, *Neues Europäisches Historisches Reise-Lexicon* (Leipzig, 1744), cols. 349–448. New edition: Leipzig, 1984.

Sturm 1718
Leonhard Christoph Sturm. *Vollständige Anweisung grosser Herren Palläste starck, bequem, nach den Regeln der antiquen Architectur untadelich und nach dem heutigen Gusto schön und prächtig anzugehen [...].* Augsburg, 1718.

Sturm 1720
Leonhard Christoph Sturm, ed. *Nicolai Goldmanns Abhandlung von den Bey-Zierden der architectur, welche durch Mahlerey und Bildhauerey zuwege gebracht werden [...].* Augsburg, 1720.

Weinart 1974
Benjamin Gottfried Weinart. *Topographische Geschichte der Stadt Dresden* (Dresden, 1777). Facsimile: Leipzig, 1974.

Wolff 1995
Christian Wolff. *Vernünftige Gedancken von den Kräften des menschlichen Verstandes.* Reprint in *18th and 19th century German linguistics* 1/1995.

Zedler 1995
Johann Heinrich Zedler. *Großes vollständiges Universal-Lexicon* (Leipzig/Halle, 1733–1750). Second reprint: Graz, 1995.

Literature

Albiker 1935
Carl Albiker. *Die Meissner Porzellantiere im 18. Jahrhundert.* Berlin, 1935.

Albiker 1959
Carl Albiker. *Die Meissner Porzellantiere im 18. Jahrhundert.* 2nd edition: Berlin, 1959.

Arnold/Schmidt 1986
Ulli Arnold and Werner Schmidt. *Barock in Dresden.* Exhibition catalog of the Villa Hügel, Essen. Leipzig, 1986.

Asche 1966
Siegfried Asche. *Balthasar Permoser und die Barockskulptur des Dresdner Zwingers.* Frankfurt/Main, 1966.

Asche 1970
Siegfried Asche. Die Dresdner Bildhauer des frühen 18. Jahrhunderts als Meister des Böttgersteinzeugs und des Böttgerporzellans. *Keramos* 49 (1970): 67–92.

Asche 1971
Siegfried Asche. Supplement to the above essay. *Keramos* 51 (1971): 18–21.

Baer 1979
Winfried Baer. Frühe japanische Porzellanadler und ihre verschiedenen Nachbildungen. In *Staatliche Schlösser und Gärten Berlin. Festschrift für Martin Sperlich zum 60. Geburtstag 1979,* 259–278. Tübingen, 1979.

Baillie 1967
Hugh Murray Baillie. Etiquette and the planning of the state apartments in baroque palaces. In *Archaeologia or Miscellaneous tracts relating to antiquity* 101:169–199. London, 1967.

Ball/Graupe 1933
Hermann Ball and Paul Graupe. *77 Meissener Porzellanvögel und französisches Kunstgewerbe aus einer bekannten Privatsammlung.* Sale catalog 22, 15 March 1933, Berlin.

H. Bauer 1962
Hermann Bauer. *Rocaille. Zur Herkunft und zum Wesen eines Ornament-Motivs.* Neue Münchner Beiträge zur Kunstgeschichte 4. Berlin, 1962.

H. Bauer 1991
Hermann Bauer. *Fernöstlicher Glanz. Pagoden in Nymphenburg, Pillnitz und Sanssouci.* Munich, 1991.

H. Bauer 1992
Hermann Bauer. *Barock. Kunst einer Epoche.* Berlin, 1992.

V. Bauer 1993
Volker Bauer. *Die höfische Gesellschaft in Deutschland von der Mitte des 17. bis zum Ausgang des 18. Jahrhunderts: Versuch einer Typologie.* Frühe Neuzeit 12. Tübingen, 1993.

V. Bauer 1997
Volker Bauer. *Hofökonomie: Der Diskurs über den Fürstenhof in Zeremonial-Wissenschaft, Hausväterliteratur und Kameralismus.* Frühneuzeitstudien NF 1. Vienna, 1997.

Baumgart 1981
Peter Baumgart. Der deutsche Hof der Barockzeit als politische Institution. In *Wolfenbütteler Arbeiten zur Barockforschung* 8, ed. Martin Bircher, 25–43. Hamburg, 1981.

Benker 1993
Gertrud Benker. Die Hüttenjagd mit der Eule. *Kunst und Antiquitäten* 10 (1993): 28 and 30. Munich, 1993.

Berling 1900
Karl Berling. *Das Meissner Porzellan und seine Geschichte.* Leipzig, 1900.

Berling 1911
Karl Berling. *Festschrift zur 200jährigen Jubelfeier der ältesten europäischen Porzellanmanufaktur Meissen 1710/1910.* Dresden, 1911. (Translation: Carl Berling. *Festive publication to commemorate the 200th Jubilee of the first European China Factory, Meissen.* Leipzig, 1910.)

Berns/Rahn 1995
Jörg Jochen Berns and Thomas Rahn, eds. *Zeremoniell als höfische Ästhetik in Spätmittelalter und Früher Neuzeit.* Tübingen, 1995.

Blaauwen 2000
Abraham L Blaauwen. *Meissen porcelain in the Rijksmuseum.* Museum catalog. Amsterdam, 2000.

Bluche 1986
François Bluche. *Im Schatten des Sonnenkönigs. Alltagsleben im Zeitalter Ludwigs XIV. von Frankreich.* Freiburg im Breisgau, 1986.

Blümel 1939
Carl Blümel. *Tierplastik: Bildwerke aus fünf Jahrtausenden.* Leipzig, 1939.

Boehm 1977
Gottfried Boehm. Plastik und plastischer Raum. In *Skulptur*, vol. 1, unpaginated exhibition catalog of the Westfälisches Landesmuseum. Münster, 1977.

Böhmert 1880
Victor Böhmert. Urkundliche Geschichte und Statistik der Meissener Porzellanmanufaktur um 1710–1880. *Zeitschrift der königlich-sächsischen statistischen Bureaus* 26 (1880): 44–93. Dresden, 1880.

Boltz 1980
Claus Boltz. Hoym, Lemaire und Meissen. Ein Beitrag zur Geschichte der Dresdner Porzellansammlung. *Keramos* 88 (1980): 3–101.

Boltz 1995
Claus Boltz. Eisbären und Polarfüchse: 6 Kästen sächsisches Porzellan. *Keramos* 148 (1995): 3–36.

Boltz 1996
Claus Boltz. Japanisches Palais-Inventar 1770 und Turmzimmer-Inventar 1769. *Keramos* 153 (1996): 3–118.

Börsch-Supan 1967
Eva Börsch-Supan. *Garten-, Landschafts- und Paradiesmotive im Innenraum. Eine ikonographische Untersuchung.* Berlin, 1967.

Börsch-Supan 1973
Helmut Börsch-Supan. Die Chinamode in den brandenburgisch-preußischen Residenzen. In the Schloss Charlottenburg exhibition catalog: *China und Europa. Chinamode und Chinaverständnis im 17. und 18. Jahrhundert.* Berlin, 1973.

Brainard 1979
Ingrid Brainard. Der Höfische Tanz. Darstellende Kunst und Höfische Repräsentation. In *Wolfenbütteler Arbeiten zur Barockforschung* 9, ed. Martin Bircher, 379–394. Hamburg, 1979.

Bräss 1901
Martin Bräss. Die Thierfiguren Johann Joachim Kändlers in der königlichen Porzellan-Sammlung zu Dresden. *Dresdner Anzeiger*, Monday supplement, 1901 no. 17, 29 April: 4–6.

Bridson/White 1990
Gavin Douglas Bridson and James Joseph White. *Plant, animal and anatomical illustration in art and science: a bibliographical guide from the 16th century to the present day.* Winchester, 1990.

Brüning 1914
Adolf Brüning. *Porzellan.* New edition. Berlin, 1914.

Burckhardt 1860
Jacob Burckhardt. *Die Cultur der Renaissance in Italien.* Basel, 1860.

Bursche 1974
Stefan Bursche. *Tafelzier des Barock.* Munich, 1974.

Bursche 1977
Stefan Bursche. Die Rocaille als Sinnbild der Natur. In *Anzeiger des Germanischen Nationalmuseums Nürnberg 1976*, 143–150. Nuremberg, 1977.

Buttlar 1996
Adrian von Buttlar. Sanssouci und der "Ewige Osten": Zur Deutung des Chinesischen Teehauses. *Gartenkunst* 8 (1996), no. 1: 1–10.

Cassidy-Geiger 1995
Maureen Cassidy-Geiger. *The Japanese Palace collections and their impact at Meissen.* In the catalog of the 1995 International Fine Art and Antique Dealers Show, New York, 15–24.

Cassidy-Geiger 1996.a
Maureen Cassidy-Geiger. Meissen porcelain ordered for the Japanese Palace: A transcription of the Specification von Porcilan of 1736. *Keramos* 153 (1996): 119–130.

Cassidy-Geiger 1996.b
Maureen Cassidy-Geiger. Graphic sources for Meissen porcelain: origins of the print collection in the Meissen archives. *The Metropolitan Museum of Art, Journal* 31 (1996): 99–126.

Cassidy-Geiger 1999
Maureen Cassidy-Geiger. The "Federzimmer" from the "Japanisches Palais" in Dresden. *Furniture History* 35 (1999): 87–111.

Cassidy-Geiger 2003.a
Maureen Cassidy-Geiger. Meissener Porzellan für das Musée National de Céramique in Sèvres. *Keramos* 179/180 (2003): 3–20.

Cassidy-Geiger 2003.b
Maureen Cassidy-Geiger. Fabled beasts: Augustus the Strong's Meissen menagerie. *Antiques* 164, no. 4 (October 2003): 152–161.

Cassidy-Geiger 2005
Maureen Cassidy-Geiger. *Zeichen und Raum. Ausstattungen und höfisches Zeremoniell in den deutschen Schlössern der Frühen Neuzeit.* Rudolstädter Forschungen zur Residenzkultur 3, ed. Peter-Michael Hahn and Ulrich Schütte. Munich and Berlin, 2006.

Clarke 1986
Tim Clarke. *The Rhinoceros from Dürer to Stubbs 1515–1799.* London, 1986.

Cohen 2000
Sarah R. Cohen: *Art, Dance, and the Body in French Culture of the Ancien Régime.* Dissertation, University at Albany, NY. Cambridge, 2000.

Czok 1989
Karl Czok. *Am Hofe August des Starken.* Leipzig, 1989.

Czok 1991
Karl Czok. *August der Starke: Sein Verhältnis zum Absolutismus und zum sächsischen Adel.* Sitzungsberichte der sächsischen Akademie der Wissenschaften 131, no. 3. Berlin, 1991.

Dauterman 1963
Carl Christian Dauterman. Colossal for the medium: Meissen porcelain sculptures. *The Metropolitan Museum of Art Bulletin* 22, no. 1 (Summer 1963).

Dauterman 1970
Carl Christian Dauterman. *The Wrightsman Collection*, vol. 4: *Porcelain.* New York, 1970.

Davis 1991
John Davis. *Antique Garden Ornament.* Woodbridge, 1991.

Daxelmüller 1995
Christoph Daxelmüller. Von der Bedeutung und Kategorisierung der Dinge. Das gestaltete Objekt als Gegenstand gelehrter Traktate des 17. und 18. Jahrhunderts. In *Realität und Bedeutung der Dinge im zeitlichen Wandel. Referate der interdisziplinären Tagung, Nürnberg, Oktober 1993*, ed. Hermann Maué. From the Anzeiger des Germanischen Nationalmuseums 1995, 56–65. Nuremberg, 1995.

Donath 1919
Adolph Donath. Die jüngsten Preise für Meißener Porzellan. *Der Kunstwanderer*, October 1919, second issue: 69–72.

Donath 1920
Adolph Donath. Die Dresdener Porzellan-Auktion. *Der Kunstwanderer*, October 1920, second issue: 69–72.

Ducret 1946
Siegfried Ducret. Meissner Porzellanbauten des 18. Jahrhunderts. *Pro Arte* 5 (1946), no. 56: 359–362.

Ducret 1956
Siegfried Ducret. Zum 250. Geburtstag Johann Joachim Kändlers. *Keramikfreunde der Schweiz, Mitteilungsblatt* 36 (October 1956): 7–10.

Ducret 1962
Siegfried Ducret. *Deutsches Porzellan.* Baden-Baden, 1962. Translated as *German Porcelain and Faience* (London, 1963).

Ducret 1973
Siegfried Ducret. *Keramik und Graphik des 18. Jahrhunderts. Vorlagen für Maler und Modelleure.* Braunschweig, 1973.

Ehalt 1979
Hubert Ch. Ehalt. Zur Funktion des Zeremoniells im Absolutismus. In *Wolfenbütteler Arbeiten zur Barockforschung* 9, ed. Martin Bircher, 411–419. Hamburg, 1979.

Eichberg 1977
Henning Eichberg. Geometrie als barocke Verhaltensform. *Zeitschrift für historische Forschung* 4 (1977): 17–50.

Eissenhauer 1992
Michael Eissenhauer. Das Jagdgebiet als Landschaftsidylle. Der Fasaneriegarten beim Jagdschloß Moritzburg.

In *Vom Jagen*, Schloss Moritzburg exhibition catalog, 85–89. Moritzburg, 1992.

Elias 1997
Norbert Elias. *Die höfische Gesellschaft*. 8th ed. Frankfurt/Main, 1997. Trans. Edmund Jephcott as *The Court Society* (Oxford: Basil Blackwell, and New York: Pantheon, 1983).

Ermisch 1935
Hubert Georg Ermisch. Das Japanische Palais in Dresden-Neustadt. In *Geschichtliche Wanderfahrten* 40, ed. Arthur Brabant. Dresden, 1935.

Fichtner 1939–41
Fritz Fichtner. Von der kurfürstlichen Kunstkammer zur Porzellangalerie Dresden im Zwinger. In three parts in *Berichte der Deutschen Keramischen Gesellschaft* 20:293–309, 21:237–264, 22:330–370. Berlin, 1939–41.

Fichtner 1936.a
Fichtner, Fritz. *Meissener Porzellan* (Meyers bunte Bändchen 36). Leipzig, 1936.

Fichtner 1936 b
Fritz Fichtner. Phantastische Porzellanpläne Augusts des Starken und ihr Schicksal. Lecture delivered on 30 Nov 1935 to the Saxony branch of the Deutsche Keramische Gesellschaft. *Sprechsaal* 69, no. 14 (1936): 191–194.

Fichtner 1940
Fritz Fichtner. Meissner Porzellan für Polen und Russland. *Berichte der Deutschen Keramischen Gesellschaft* 21, no. 12 (1940): 487–520.

Fletcher 1988
John Fletcher. Athanasius Kircher und seine Beziehungen zum gelehrten Europa seiner Zeit. In *Wolfenbütteler Arbeiten zur Barockforschung* 17, ed. John Fletcher. Wiesbaden, 1988.

Forberger 1958
Rudolf Forberger. *Die Manufaktur in Sachsen vom Ende des 16. bis zum Anfang des 19. Jahrhunderts*. Berlin, 1958.

Franz 1953
Heinrich Gerhard Franz. *Zacharias Longuelune und die Baukunst des 18. Jahrhunderts in Dresden*. Berlin, 1953.

Fuhring 1998
Peter Fuhring. Juste-Aurèle Meissonier: The artist and his work. In the sale catalog *The Thyssen Meissonnier Tureen*, Sotheby's New York, 13 May 1998, 10–49.

Gibbons 1995
Mary Wetzel Gibbons. *Giambologna. Narrator of the Catholic Reformation*. Berkeley, 1995.

Gielke 2003
Dieter Gielke. *Meissener Porzellan des 18. und 19. Jahrhunderts*. Museum catalog, Grassimuseum Leipzig/Museum für Kunsthandwerk. Leipzig, 2003.

Giermann 2003
Giermann, Ralf. *"Mehr zum Staat als zum Gebrauche": Das Federzimmer im Schloß Moritzburg*. Dresden, 2003.

Glaser 1983
Gerhard Glaser. *Das Grüne Gewölbe im Dresdner Schloß als Weiterentwicklung der barocken Architekturidee des Spiegelkabinetts, als Spezialmuseum und als Ausgangspunkt gegenwärtiger Museumsgestaltung*. In Staatliche Kunstsammlungen Dresden, Jahrbuch 12 (1980), 7–67. Dresden, 1983.

Glassl 1989
Franz Glassl. Der Tiergarten Saraburg. *Gartenkunst* 1 (1989) no. 1: 47–66.

Goder 1978
Willi Goder. Über den Einfluß der Produktivkräfte des sächsischen Berg- und Hüttenwesens, insbesondere der Freiberger Montanwissenschaften, auf die Erfindung und technologische Entwicklung des Meissener Porzellans als Ausgangspunkt der europäischen Hartporzelanindustrie. Dissertation, Bergakademie Freiberg. Unpublished typescript, Staatliche Kunstsammlungen Dresden, Porzellansammlung.

Goder 1989
Willi Goder. Johann Friedrich Eberlein. Bildhauer und vielseitiger Gestalter Meissener Porzellanservice. *Keramos* 124 (1989): 105–116.

Gothein 1988
Marie-Luise Gothein. *Geschichte der Gartenkunst*. 2 vols. 2nd edition (Jena, 1926). Reprint: Munich, 1988.

Graesse 1873
Johann Gottfried Theodor Graesse. *Beschreibender Catalog der K. Porzellan- und Gefäss-Sammlung zu Dresden*. Dresden, 1873.

Gröger 1956
Helmuth Gröger. *Johann Joachim Kaendler, der Meister des Porzellans*. Dresden, 1956.

Grundmann 1989
Katharina Grundmann. Ein Fuchs so eine Henne frisst: eine Inkunabel der Meissner Grosstierplastik von J. G. Kirchner. *Kunst und Antiquitäten*, 1989, no. 6: 58–61.

Gurlitt 1903
Cornelius Gurlitt, ed. *Beschreibende Darstellung der älteren Bau- und Kunstdenkmäler des Königreichs Sachsen*, 23/III. Dresden, 1903.

Gurlitt 1924
Cornelius Gurlitt. *August der Starke*. 2 vols. Dresden, 1924.

Hackenbroch 1955
Yvonne Hackenbroch. A Renaissance bronze modelled in porcelain. *Connoisseur* 135 (1955): 208–210.

Hackenbroch 1962
Yvonne Hackenbroch. *Bronzes [and] other metalwork and sculpture in the Irwin Untermyer Collection*. London, 1962.

Handt 1954
Ingelore Handt. *Johann Joachim Kändler und die Meissner Porzellanplastik des 18. Jahrhunderts*. Das kleine Kunstheft 7. Dresden, 1954.

Handt/Rackebrand 1956
Ingelore Handt and Hilde Rackebrand. *Meissner Porzellan des achtzehnten Jahrhunderts 1710–1750*. Dresden, 1956.

Hannover/Rackham 1925
Emil Hannover and Bernard Rackham (translation and commentary). *Pottery and porcelain. A handbook for collectors*. 3 vols. London, 1925.

Hansmann 1983
Wilfried Hansmann. *Gartenkunst der Renaissance und des Barock*. Cologne, 1983.

Harran 2002
Jim Harran and Susan Harran. *Dresden Porcelain Studios*. Paducah, 2002.

Heckmann 1954
Hermann Heckmann. *Matthäus Daniel Pöppelmann als Zeichner*. Dresden, 1954.

Heckmann 1972
Hermann Heckmann. *Matthäus Daniel Pöppelmann. Leben und Werk*. Munich, 1972.

Heckmann 1986
Hermann Heckmann. *Matthäus Daniel Pöppelmann und die Barockbaukunst in Dresden*. Stuttgart, 1986.

Heckscher/Wirth 1967
William S. Heckscher and Karl-August Wirth. Emblem, Emblembuch. Entries in *Reallexikon zur Deutschen Kunstgeschichte*, vol. 5, cols. 85–228. Stuttgart, 1967.

Hensel 1992
Margitta Hensel. Die gebräuchlichsten Jagdmethoden in der Zeit vom 16. bis zum 18. Jahrhundert. In *Vom Jagen*, Schloss Moritzburg exhibition catalog, 29–41. Moritzburg, 1992.

Hensel 1995
Margitta Hensel. Die Fasanerie zu Moritzburg. *Dresdner Hefte* 13 (1995), no. 42/2 ("Die Moritzburger Kulturlandschaft"): 32–41.

Hensel 1998
Margitta Hensel. Die Menagerie zu Moritzburg. *Sächsische Heimatblätter* 44 (1998) no. 2: 61–70.

Hentschel 1960
Walter Hentschel. *Bibliographie zur sächsischen Kunstgeschichte*. Berlin, 1960.

Hentschel 1969
Walter Hentschel. *Die Zentralbauprojekte August des Starken: Ein Beitrag zur Rolle des Bauherrn im deutschen Barock*. Berlin, 1969.

Heres 1989
Gerald Heres. Die Museumsprojekte August des Starken. In *Jahrbuch für Regionalgeschichte 16* (1989), Part 1, 102–115. Weimar, 1989.

Heres 1991
Gerald Heres. *Dresdener Kunstsammlungen im 18. Jahrhundert*. Leipzig, 1991.

Hertel 1980
Rolf Hertel. Historische tiergärtnerische Anlagen in Dresden. In *Der*

zoologische Garten, NF 50 (1980), 82–88. Jena, 1980.

Historische Kommission der Sächsischen Akademie der Wissenschaften. *Bibliographie zur Geschichte der Stadt Dresden* (Supplement to Rudolf Bemmann and Jakob Jatzwank, *Bibliographie der sächsischen Geschichte* 3: Ortsgeschichte). 5 vols. Dresden, 1981–1984.

Hobusch 1992
Erich Hobusch. Sächsische Jagdordnungen und Jagdchroniken. In *Vom Jagen,* Schloss Moritzburg exhibition catalog, 59–65. Moritzburg, 1992.

Hofer 1956
Paul Hofer. Der barocke Raum in der Plastik. In *Die Kunstformen des Barockzeitalters: Vierzehn Vorträge,* ed. Rudolf Stamm, 144–168. Bern, 1956.

Hofmann/Tradler 2003
Cornelia Hofmann and Birgit Tradler. *Das Federzimmer August des Starken.* Dresden, 2003.

Hofmann 1980
Friedrich H. Hofmann. *Das Porzellan der europäischen Manufakturen.* Propyläen Kunstgeschichte, single volume. Frankfurt/Main, 1980.

Holenstein 1992
André Holenstein. Huldigung und Herrschaftszeremoniell im Zeitalter des Absolutismus und der Aufklärung. In *Zum Wandel von Zeremoniell und Gesellschaftsritualen in der Zeit der Aufklärung* (Aufklärung 6, no. 2), ed. Klaus Gerteis, 21–46. Hamburg, 1992.

Hoog 1982
Simone Hoog. *Louis XIV: Manière de montrer les Jardins de Versailles.* Paris, 1982.

Horschik 1977
Josef Horschik. Die vergessene Bemalung der großen Meissner Porzellantiere. *Keramos* 78 (1977): 13–18.

Howard/Ayers 1978
David Howard and John Ayers. China for the West: Chinese Porcelain and other Decorative Arts for Export, illustrated from the Mottahedeh Collection. 2 vols. London and New York, 1978.

Hsia 1985
Adrian Hsia, ed. *Deutsche Denker über China.* Frankfurt/Main, 1985.

Jedding 1974
Hermann Jedding. *Europäisches Porzellan,* vol. 1: *Von den Anfängen bis 1800.* 2nd corrected edition. Munich, 1974.

Jedding 1979
Hermann Jedding. *Meissener Porzellan des 18. Jahrhunderts.* Munich, 1979.

Jöchner 2001
Cornelia Jöchner. Der Große Garten als "Festort" in der Dresdner Residenzlandschaft. In *Der Große Garten zu Dresden: Gartenkunst in vier Jahrhunderten,* 73–88. Dresden: Sächsische Schlösserverwaltung, 2001.

Jong 1997
Erik A. de Jong. Gegensatz oder Zusammenhang? Gedanken zum Verhältnis zwischen Natur und Kunst in der klassischen Gartentheorie. *Gartenkunst* 9, no. 2 (1997): 239–254.

Jörg 1990
Christian J. A. Jörg. Der Porzellanhandel der VOC im 17. und 18. Jahrhundert. In *Porzellan aus China und Japan: Die Porzellangalerie der Landgrafen von Hessen-Kassel,* ed. Ulrich Schmidt, exhibition and permanet collection catalog of the Staatliche Kunstsammlungen Kassel, 143–156. Berlin, 1990.

Klappenbach 2001
Käthe Klappenbach. *Kronleuchter mit Behang aus Bergkristall und Glas sowie Glasarmkronleuchter bis 1810.* Catalog of holdings of the Stiftung Preußische Schlösser und Gärten Berlin-Brandenburg, ed. Burkhardt Göres. Berlin, 2001.

Köhler 2000
Bettina Köhler. "All white and gold and mirrors"; Lichträume oder: vom Licht in der Wand zum Licht im Raum. *Kunst und Architektur in der Schweiz* 1 (2000): 43–51. Bern, 2000.

Köllmann 1954
Erich Köllmann. Chinoiserie. Entry in *Reallexikon zur Deutschen Kunstgeschichte,* vol. 3, cols. 439–481. Stuttgart, 1954.

Köllmann 1961
Erich Köllmann. Porzellan und Fayence am Hofe Clemens Augusts. In *Kurfürst Clemens August. Landesherr und Mäzen des 18. Jahrhunderts,* Schloss Brühl exhibition catalog, 321–331. Cologne, 1961.

Kopplin/Haase 1998
Monika Kopplin and Gisela Haase, eds. *„Sächßisch Lacquirte Sachen": Lackkunst in Dresden unter August dem Starken.* Exhibition catalog of the Museum für Lackkunst. Münster, 1998.

Krahn 1995
Volker Krahn et al. *Von allen Seiten schön. Bronzen der Renaissance und des Barock.* Exhibition catalog of the Skulpturensammlung Berlin. Berlin, 1995.

Krüger 1995
Manuela Krüger. Die Sammlung der Meißner Porzellane des Kunstgewerbemuseums Berlin und ihr Schicksal: Die Kriegsverluste. Dissertation, Leipzig 1995. Typescript, Bibliothek Kunstgewerbemuseum Berlin.

Küas 1977
Herbert Küas. Die Brennhäuser der Meissner Porzellanmanufaktur auf der Albrechtsburg. *Sächsische Heimatblätter* 4 (1977): 153–159. Dresden, 1977.

Kuke 2002
Hans-Joachim Kuke. *Jean de Bodt 1670–1745: Architekt und Ingenieur im Zeitalter des Barock.* Worms, 2002.

Kunze 1982
Joachim Kunze. Die Bedeutung des "Englischen Handels" mit Porzellanen im "Altfranzösischen Geschmack" der Meißner Manufaktur in der ersten Hälfte des 19. Jahrhunderts. *Keramos* 95 (1982): 37–50.

Kunze-Köllensperger 1997
Melitta Kunze-Köllensperger. *Collection Franz E. Burda: Meissen. Figuren, Dosen und Tafelgerät aus dem 18. Jahrhundert.* St. Ottilien am Ammersee, 1997.

Langer 2002
Brigitte Langer, ed. *Pracht und Zeremoniell. Die Möbel der Residenz München.* Exhibition catalog of the Bayerische Verwaltung der Staatlichen Schlösser, Gärten und Seen, Residenz München. Munich, 2002.

Lehne 1985
Barbara Lehne. *Süddeutsche Tafelaufsätze vom Ende des 15. bis Anfang des 17. Jahrhunderts.* Munich, 1985.

Lieber 1979
Elfriede Lieber. *Verzeichnis der Inventare der Staalichen Kunstsammlungen Dresden 1568–1945.* Dresden, 1979.

Liebieghaus Frankfurt 1985
Natur und Antike in der Renaissance. Exhibition catalog of the Liebieghaus Frankfurt. Frankfurt/Main, 1985.

Lindemann 1989
Bernd Wolfgang Lindemann. *Ferdinand Tietz 1708–1777. Studien zu Werk, Stil und Ikonographie.* Weissendorn, 1989.

List 1993
Claudia List. *Tiere: Gestalt und Bedeutung in der Kunst.* Stuttgart, 1993.

Löffler 1962
Fritz Löffler. *Das alte Dresden. Geschichte seiner Bauten.* 4th edition. Dresden, 1962.

Lohneis 1985
Hans-Dieter Lohneis. *Die deutschen Spiegelkabinette. Studien zu den Räumen des späten 17. und des frühen 18. Jahrhunderts.* Schriften aus dem Institut für Kunstgeschichte an der Universität München 6. Munich, 1985.

Loibl 1989
Werner Loibl. Ideen im Spiegel: Die Spiegelkabinette in denfränkischen Schönborn-Schlössern. In *Die Grafen von Schönborn: Kirchenfürsten, Sammler, Mäzene,* ed. Gerhard Bott, exhibition catalog of the Germanisches Nationalmuseum, Nuremberg, 80–90. Nuremberg, 1989.

Loisel 1912
Gustave Loisel. *Histoire des ménageries de l'antiquité à nos jours.* 3 vols. Paris, 1912.

Lorenz 1998
Hellmut Lorenz, ed. *Berliner Baukunst der Barockzeit: Die Zeichnungen und Notizen aus dem Reisetagebuch des Architekten Christoph Pitzler (1657–1707).* Berlin, 1998.

Maué 1995
Claudia Maué. “Künstliche und artige Unordnung“. Naturalien und Naturimitationen in künstlichen Grotten des 16.–18. Jahrhunderts. In *Anzeiger des Germanischen Nationalmuseums 1995*, 76–92. Nuremberg, 1995.

May 1987
Walter May. Holländisches und Japanisches Palais. In *Matthäus Daniel Pöppelmann 1662–1736. Ein Architekt des Barocks in Dresden*, exhibition catalog of the Staatliche Kunstsammlungen Dresden, 90–96. Dresden, 1987.

May 1989
Walter May. Holländisches und Japanisches Palais. In *Matthäus Daniel Pöppelmann: Der Architekt des Dresdener Zwingers*, ed. Harald Marx, 198–207. Leipzig, 1989.

Meister/Reber 1980
Peter Wilhelm Meister and Horst Reber. *Europäisches Porzellan*. Stuttgart, 1980.

I. Menzhausen 1982.a
Ingelore Menzhausen. Das Älteste aus Meissen: Böttgersteinzeug und Bottgerporzellan. In *Johann Friedrich Böttger zum 300. Geburtstag*, exhibition catalog of the Staatliche Kunstsammlungen Dresden, 83–114. Leipzig, 1982.

I. Menzhausen 1982.b
Ingelore Menzhausen. “Das rothe und das weisse Porcellain“. In *Johann Friedrich Böttger. Die Erfindung des europäischen Porzellans*, ed. Rolf Sonnemann and Eberhard Wächtler, 143–315. Leipzig, 1982.

I. Menzhausen 1988
Ingelore Menzhausen. *Alt-Meissner Porzellan in Dresden*. Berlin, 1988.

J. Menzhausen 1980
Joachim Menzhausen. *Der Zwinger*. 10th edition. Dresden, 1980.

J. Menzhausen 1990
Joachim Menzhausen. Sinn und Wert des Mäzenatentums deutscher Fürsten im 18. Jahrhundert, speech delivered on 17 Feb 1989 at the opening of the exhibition “Die Grafen von Schönborn: Kirchenfürsten, Sammler, Mäzene“. In *Anzeiger des Germanischen Nationalmuseums 1989*, 167–175. Nuremberg, 1990.

J. Menzhausen 2002
Joachim Menzhausen. Werdegang und Stil des Bildhauers Kändler. *Keramos* 175/176 (2002): 3–16.

Miller 1998
Jonathan Miller. *Mirror-Image*. National Gallery exhibition catalog. London, 1998.

Möbius 1992
Ingrid Möbius. Moritzburg und die Jagd. Eine Einführung. In *Vom Jagen*, Schloss Moritzburg exhibition catalog, 9–11. Moritzburg, 1992.

Morley-Fletcher 1971
Hugo Morley-Fletcher. *Meissen*. London, 1971.

Morley-Fletcher 1975
Hugo Morley-Fletcher. Meissen beasts for Augustus the Strong. *Connoisseur*, June 1975: 95–99.

Morley-Fletcher 1993
Hugo Morley-Fletcher. *The Pflueger Collection*. 2 vols. London, 1993.

Morley-Fletcher 1996
Hugo Morley-Fletcher. The Meissen Menagerie. *Christie's international Magazine*, October 1996: 48–49.

Müllenmeister 1978
Kurt Müllenmeister. Tierdarstellungen in Werken niederländischer Künstler. In *Meer und Land im Licht des 17. Jahrhunderts*, vol. 2 (Artists A–M) and vol. 3 (Artists N–Z). Bremen, 1978.

Néto 1996
Isabelle Néto, ed. *L'animal. Miroir de l'homme*. Exhibition catalog of the Musée Cognacq-Jay. Paris, 1996.

Neuwirth 1970
Waltraud Neuwirth. Tier- und Jagddarstellungen auf frühem Wiener Porzellan. *Alte und moderne Kunst* 15/110 (1970).

Nickel 1996
Sieglinde Nickel. Ostra. Vom Dorf zum Gehege. *Dresdner Hefte* 14 (1996), no. 47/3 (“Grosses Ostragehege/Friedrichstadt”): 8–13.

Nissen 1966/78
Claus Nissen. *Die zoologische Buchillustration: Ihre Bibliographie und Geschichte*. 2 vols. Stuttgart, 1966/78.

Oettermann 1982
Stephan Oettermann. *Die Schaulust am Elefanten: Eine Elefantographia curiosa*. Frankfurt/Main, 1982.

Olbrich 1985
Harald Olbrich. Barock: Kunststil oder Epocheneinheit? In *Kunst der Bachzeit*, exhibition catalog of the Museum der bildenden Künste, Leipzig, 10–14. Leipzig, 1985.

Pallach 1987
Ulrich-Christian Pallach. Materielle Kultur und Mentalitäten im 18. Jahrhundert: Wirtschaftliche Entwicklung und politisch-sozialer Funktionswandel des Luxus in Frankreich und im Alten Reich am Ende des Ancien Régime. In *Ancien Régime, Aufklärung und Revolution*, ed. Rolf Reichardt and Eberhard Schmitt, vol. 14. Munich, 1987.

Paust 1996
Bettina Paust. *Studien zur barocken Menagerie im deutschsprachigen Raum*. Worms, 1996.

Pietsch 1996.a
Ulrich Pietsch. *Meissener Porzellan und seine ostasiatischen Vorbilder*. Leipzig, 1996.

Pietsch 1996.b
Ulrich Pietsch. *Johann Gregorius Höroldt (1696–1775) und die Meissener Porzellanmalerei: Zur dreihundertsten Wiederkehr seines Geburtstages*. Exhibition catalog of the Hetjens-Museum, Düsseldorf. Dresden: Staatliche Kunstsammlungen, 1996.

Pietsch 1997.a
Ulrich Pietsch. Johann Joachim Kaendlers “Maria Immaculata“ von 1738 aus Meissener Porzellan. *Dresdener Kunstblätter* 41 (1997), no. 3: 77–81.

Pietsch 1997.b
Ulrich Pietsch. Meissener Porzellandekore im Stile der Höroldtmalerei und Figuren von Johann Joachim Kändler. In *Frühes Meissener Porzellan: Kostbarkeiten aus deutschen Privatsammlungen*, exhibition catalog of the Hetjens-Museum Düsseldorf; Porzellansammlung Dresden. Munich, 1997.

Pietsch 1998
Ulrich Pietsch, ed. *Porzellansammlung Dresden*. Guide to the permanent exhibition. Dresden, 1998.

Pietsch 2000
Pietsch Ulrich, ed. *Schwanenservice: Meissener Porzellan für Heinrich Graf von Brühl*. Dresden, 2000.

Pietsch 2002
Ulrich Pietsch, ed. *Die Arbeitsberichte des Meissener Porzellanmodelleurs Johann Joachim Kaendler 1706–1775*. Leipzig, 2002.

Pincas 1996
Stéphane Pincas. *Versailles: The history of the gardens and their sculpture*. English translation of the original French edition (Paris, 1995). New York, 1996.

Piper 1921
Reinhard Piper. *Das Tier in der Kunst*. 2nd edition, enlarged. Munich, 1921.

Plaßmeyer 2001
Peter Plaßmeyer, ed. *Ehrenfried Walther von Tschirnhaus (1651–1708): Experimente mit dem Sonnenfeuer*. Exhibition catalog of the Staatliche Kunstsammlungen Dresden. Dresden, 2001.

Porstmann 1998
Gisbert Porstmann. Moses Mendelssohn und das Porzellan. *Keramos* 159 (1998): 61–68.

Raff 1994
Thomas Raff. *Die Sprache der Materialien: Anleitung zu einer Ikonologie der Werkstoffe*. Munich, 1994.

Rauda 1932
Fritz Rauda. Das Japanische Palais: Der Königstraum von einem Porzellanschloß. *Dresdner Anzeiger*, no. 361, 30 Dec 1932: 6.

Rauperich 1995
Susanne Rauperich. *Aspekte der Betrachtung und Rezeption von Plastik in der deutschen Kunstwissenschaft des 18. und 19. Jahrhunderts: Ein wissenschaftsgeschichtlicher Versuch*. Weimar, 1995.

Reichel 1964
Friedrich Reichel.... wie die Sperlinge im Porzellanschloß. *Dresdener Kunstblätter* 8 (1964), no. 9: 134–139.

Reichel 1972.a
Friedrich Reichel. Die Chinoiserie in Sachsen. 2 vols. Dissertation, Halle 1972. Typescript in the possession of the author.

Reichel 1972.b
Friedrich Reichel. Zur Geschichte des Turmzimmers im ehemaligen Dresdener Residenzschloß. *Dresdener Kunstblätter* 16 (1972), no. 5: 141–146.

Reichel 1995
Friedrich Reichel. Sächsische Chinoiserie-Kleinbauten. In *Denkmalkunde und Denkmalpflege*, Festschrift for Heinrich Magirius on his sixtieth birthday, 1 Feb 1994, ed. Ute Reupert, Thomas Trajkovits, and Winfried Werner, 393–399.
Dresden, 1995.

Reichel 2002
Friedrich Reichel. Stanislav Chometowski, ein polnischer Porzellansammler des frühen 18. Jahrhunderts. *Dresdener Kunstblätter* 46 (2002), no. 4: 127–131.
Dresden, 2002.

Reidemeister 1934
L. Reidemeister. Die Porzellankabinette der brandenburgisch-preußischen Schlösser. In *Jahrbuch der preußischen Kunstsammlungen* 50 (1934), 42–56. Berlin, 1934.

Reinheckel 1962
Günter Reinheckel. Nachrichten über eingeschickte Vorbilder und Modelle aus den Akten des Meissner Werkarchives von 1720–1745. *Keramik-Freunde der Schweiz, Mitteilungsblatt* 56 (1962): 23–24.

Reinheckel 1990
Günter Reinheckel. *Meissener Prunkservice*. Stuttgart, 1990.

Rieke-Müller 1995
Annelore Rieke-Müller. Tiere spielen Theater: Überlegungen zur Vorführung gezähmter Tiere vom 17. bis zum 19. Jahrhundert. *Mimos* 46 (1995): 2–7. Basel, 1995.

Rieke-Müller 2000
Annelore Rieke-Müller. "ein Kerl mit wilden Thieren": Zur sozialen Stellung und zum Selbstverständnis von Tierführern im 18. Jahrhundert. *Das achtzehnte Jahrhundert. Zeitschrift der Deutschen Gesellschaft für die Erforschung des 18. Jahrhunderts* 24 (2000), no. 2 ("Abenteuer und Abenteurer im 18. Jahrhundert"): 163–175.

Rietzsch 1987
Barbara Rietzsch. *Künstliche Grotten des 16. und 17. Jahrhunderts*. Augsburg, 1987.

Roda 1980
Burkard von Roda. *Adam Friedrich von Seinsheim: Auftraggeber zwischen Rokoko und Klassizismus*.
Neustadt/Aisch, 1980.

Röntgen 1984
Robert E. Röntgen. *The book of Meissen*. Exton, 1984.

Roth 1993
Gerhard Roth. *Eine Reise in das Innere von Wien*.
Frankfurt/Main, 1993.

Rückert 1966
Rainer Rückert. *Meissener Porzellan 1710–1810*. Exhibition catalog of the Bayerisches Nationalmuseum.
Munich, 1966.

Rückert 1990
Rainer Rückert. *Biographische Daten der Meissener Manufakturisten des 18. Jahrhunderts*.
Munich, 1990.

Rückert 1992/1993
Rainer Rückert. Christian Reinow und die großformatigen Tierfiguren aus Meißener Porzellan. In *Staatliche Kunstsammlungen Dresden, Jahrbuch 1989/1990*, 47–52.
Dresden, 1992/1993.

Rückert 1995–1997
Rainer Rückert. Zur Staffierung der Gesichter von Meissener Porzellanfiguren. In five parts, *Keramos* 149 (1995): 23–46; 150 (1995): 3–52; 151 (1996): 17–55; 153 (1996): 151–184; and 155 (1997): 37–87.

Rückert 1996
Rainer Rückert. Alchemistische Symbolzeichen als Meissener Masse-, Former-, Bossierer- und Drehermarken im vierten Jahrzehnt des 18. Jahrhunderts. *Keramos* 151 (1996): 57–108.

Rückert 1998
Rainer Rückert. *Der Hofnarr Joseph Fröhlich*. Offenbach, 1998.

Salmon 2001
Xavier Salmon. *Chefs-d'œuvre du cabinet d'Arts graphiques: Trésors cachés du château de Versailles*. Exhibition catalog of the Musée de la ville, Rouen, and Musée de la ville, Le Mans. Paris, 2001.

Scheicher 1995
Elisabeth Scheicher. Zur Ikonologie von Naturalien im Zusammenhang der enzyklopädischen Kunstkammer. In *Realität und Bedeutung der Dinge im zeitlichen Wandel*, ed. Hermann Maué, contributions to an interdisciplinary symposium held in Nuremberg in October 1993. From the *Anzeiger des Germanischen Nationalmuseums 1995*, 115–125. Nuremberg, 1995.

Schillinger 1992
Klaus Schillinger. *Solare Brenngeräte*. Catalog of the Mathematisch-Physikalischer Salon. Dresden, 1992.

Schillinger 1997
Klaus Schillinger. Naturwissenschaft und Instrumentenbau. In *Unter einer Krone: Kunst und Kultur der sächsisch-polnischen Union*, ed. Werner Schmidt and Dirk Syndram, exhibition catalog of the Staatliche Kunstsammlungen, Dresden, 141–142.
Leipzig, 1997.

Schlechte 1983
Monika Schlechte. Zu einer Entwurfsskizze August des Starken zu Moritzburg. *Sächsische Heimatblätter* 29 (1983), no. 6: 273–275.

Schlechte 1984
Monika Schlechte. Das barocke Architektur- und Landschaftsensemble Moritzburg: Die Umgestaltungsphase in der Regierungszeit August des Starken. Diss, TU Dresden, in 3 vols. Typescript, unpublished.
Dresden, 1984.

Schlechte 1985
Monika Schlechte. Der barocke Tiergarten Moritzburg. In *Staatliche Kunstsammlungen Dresden, Jahrbuch* 16 (1984): 23–42. Dresden, 1985.

Schlechte 1988
Monika Schlechte. Die barocke Schloßanlage und der Tiergarten Moritzburg. *Sächsische Heimatblätter* 34 (1988), no. 2: 48–54.

Schlechte 1990.a
Monika Schlechte. Afterword to the reprint of Julius Bernhard von Rohr, *Einleitung zur Ceremoniel-Wissenschafft der großen Herren* (2nd edition; Berlin, 1733).
Weinheim, 1990.

Schlechte 1990.b
Monika Schlechte. Die Dresdner Planetenfeste: Zur Ikonographie einer königlichen Tafel im Jahr 1719. *Kunst und Antiquitäten*, 1990, no. 9: 56–61.

Schlechte 1995
Monika Schlechte. "…dergleichen aber als in Moritzburg sey nirgends angetroffen": Die Schloßanlage im 18. Jahrhundert. *Dresdner Hefte* 13 (1995), no. 42/2 ("Die Moritzburger Kulturlandschaft"): 23–31.

Schmidberger 1990
Ekkehard Schmidberger. Porzellan aus China und Japan in Kassel: Zur Geschichte der ehemals landgräflichen Sammlung. In *Porzellan aus China und Japan: Die Porzellangalerie der Landgrafen von Hessen-Kassel*, ed. Ulrich Schmidt, exhibition and permanent collection catalog of the Staatliche Kunstsammlungen Kassel, 10–40. Berlin, 1990.

Schmid 1997
H. Rainer Schmid. Licht und Glanz an Kirchenausstattungen des 17. und 18. Jahrhunderts in Altbayern und Schwaben. In *Lacke des Barock und Rokoko*, ed. Katharina Walch and Johann Koller (Arbeitshefte des Bayerischen Landesamtes für Denkmalpflege 81), 11–20. Munich, 1997.

Schmidt 1970
Eva Schmidt. Tiersymbolik an Grabdenkmälern der Ernestiner. In *Jahrbuch der Coburger Landesstiftung 1970*, 303–316. Coburg, 1970.

Schmidt/Schnitzer 2002
Johannes Schmidt and Claudia Schnitzer. Die Arche: Streitfall, Ordnungsmythos und erste Kunstkammer. *Dresdener Kunstblätter* 46 (2002), no. 5: 154–169.

Schmidt/Syndram 1997
Werner Schmidt and Dirk Syndram, eds. *Unter einer Krone. Kunst und Kultur der sächsisch-polnischen Union*, exhibition catalog of the Staatliche Kunstsammlungen Dresden.
Leipzig, 1997.

Schnitzer 1995
Claudia Schnitzer. Königreiche, Wirtschaften, Bauernhochzeiten. Zeremonielltragende und -unterwandernde Spielformen höfischer Maskerade. In *Zeremoniell als höfische Ästhetik in Spätmittelalter und Früher Neuzeit*, ed. Jörg Jochen Berns and Thomas Rahn (Frühe Neuzeit 25), 80–331. Tübingen, 1995.

Schnitzer/Hölscher 2000
Claudia Schnitzer, and Petra Hölscher, eds. *Eine gute Figur machen: Kostüm und Fest am Dresdner Hof*, exhibition catalog of the Staatliche Kunstsammlungen Dresden. Dresden, 2000.

Schnitzler-Sekyra 1994
Andrea A. Schnitzler-Sekyra. Franz Anton Danreiter (1695–1760). *Dissertation, Salzburg 1994, in typescript.*

Schnorr von Carolsfeld 1928
Ludwig Schnorr von Carolsfeld. *Porzellansammlung Gustav von Klemperer: Sammlungskatalog.* Dresden, 1928.

Schnorr von Carolsfeld 1974
Ludwig Schnorr von Carolsfeld. *Porzellan der europäischen Fabriken.* Vol. 1. 6th edition, completely revised by Erich Köllman. Braunschweig, 1974.

Schnyder von Wartensee 1954/1955
Paul Schnyder von Wartensee. Ein königliches Geschenk für zwei Schweizer Adler. Published in two parts, *Keramik-Freunde der Schweiz, Mitteilungsblatt* 27 (April 1954): 11; and 30/31 (March 1955): 40–41.

Schumann 1885
Paul Schumann. *Barock und Rokoko: Studien zur Baugeschichte des 18. Jahrhunderts mit besonderem Bezug auf Dresden.* Leipzig, 1885.

Schurig 1907
Arthur Schurig. Friedrich August der Starke: Ein zeitgenössisches Charakterbild. Publikation eines Manuskripts von Graf Flemming 1722. *Frankfurter Zeitung* 52, 5 Sept 1907: 1.

Schwarm-Tomisch 2002.a
Elisabeth Schwarm-Tomisch. "...Wo hohe Potentaten ihr Plaisirs finden können...": Das Königlich Holländische Palais zu Altdresden bis zu seinem Umbau im Jahr 1727. *Dresdener Kunstblätter* 46 (2002), no. 2: 56–66.

Schwarm-Tomisch 2002.b
Elisabeth Schwarm-Tomisch. "...Das sehr kostbare Palais in Alt=Dreßden, so man das Japanische nennt...": Das Japanische Palais in der Zeit zwischen 1727 und 1763. *Dresdener Kunstblätter* 46 (2002), no. 5: 179–187.

Seelig 1995
Lorenz Seelig. Buffetwände des Spätbarocks in Berlin und Dresden. In *Höfische Pracht der Augsburger Goldschmiedekunst*, ed. Lorenz Seelig, 31–38. Munich, 1995.

Seyffarth 1959
Richard Seyffarth. Von der Arbeit des Restaurators in der Dresdener Porzellansammlung. *Kunstmuseen der Deutschen Demokratischen Republik, Mitteilungen und Berichte* 2 (1959): 80–84.

Simpson 1987
Jennifer Simpson, ed. *A European Journal: Two sisters abroad in 1847; [by] Mary Wilson with illustrations by Anne Wilson.* London, 1987.

Slitine 2002
Florence Slitine. *Samson, génie de l'imitation.* Paris, 2002.

Stimmel 1998
Folke Stimmel et al. *Stadtlexikon Dresden A–Z.* 2nd edition. Dresden, 1998.

Sponsel 1900
Jean Louis Sponsel. *Kabinettstücke der Meissner Porzellan-Manufaktur von Johann Joachim Kändler.* Leipzig, 1900.

Ströber 2002
Eva Ströber. Ostasiatika. *Sammlungskataloge des Herzog Anton Ulrich-Museums Braunschweig* 10. Braunschweig, 2002.

Ströber 2004
Eva Ströber. The earliest documented Ming-porcelain in Europe: A gift of chinese porcelain from Fernando De'Medici (1549–1609) to the Dresden court. In *The International Ceramics Fair and Seminar, Handbook 2004*, ed. Brian Haughton, 26–35. London, 2004.

Syndram 2001
Dirk Syndram. *Das Schloß zu Dresden: Von der Residenz zum Museum.* Munich and Berlin, 2001.

Temple 1990
Nigel Temple. Das chinesische Dorf der Landgrafen von Hessen-Kassel im Park von Wilhelmshöhe. In *Porzellan aus China und Japan: Die Porzellangalerie der Landgrafen von Hessen-Kassel*, ed. Ulrich Schmidt, exhibition and permanent collection catalog of the Staatliche Kunstsammlungen Kassel, 87–106. Berlin, 1990.

Thietje 1989
Gisela Thietje. Pflanzen und Tiere im französischen Garten der fürstbischöflichen Residenz Eutin im 18. Jahrhundert. *Gartenkunst* 1 (1989) no. 2: 206–246.

Tintelnot 1956
Hans Tintelnot. Zur Gewinnung unserer Barockbegriffe. In *Die Kunstformen des Barockzeitalters: Vierzehn Vorträge*, ed. Rudolf Stamm, 13–91. Bern, 1956.

Träger 1991
Susanne Träger. Das Japanische Palais in Dresden. Unpublished M.A. dissertation, Berlin 1991. Typescript, Staatliche Kunstsammlungen Dresden, Porzellansammlung.

Tralbaut 1946
Mark E. Tralbaut. *Michiel van der Voort de Oude als dierenbeelhouwer.* Antwerp, 1946.

Treue 1953
Wilhelm Treue. Porzellan im Handelsbereich der Niederl.-Ost-ind. Kompanie im 17. Jahrhundert. *Keramikfreunde der Schweiz, Mitteilungsblatt* 22 (Jan 1953): 12.

Treue 1954
Wilhelm Treue. Das Porzellan im Handelsbereich der Österreichischen Niederlande während des 18. Jahrhunderts. *Keramikfreunde der Schweiz, Mitteilungsblatt* 29 (Oct 1954): 18–23.

Treue 1958
Wilhelm Treue. Der japanische Porzellanhandel zur Zeit der ostindischen Kompagnien im 17. Jahrhundert. *Keramikfreunde der Schweiz, Mitteilungsblatt* 44 (Oct 1958): 21–25.

Vec 1998
Milos Vec. *Zeremonialwissenschaft im Fürstenstaat: Studien zur juristischen und politischen Theorie absolutistischer Herrschaftsrepräsentation.* Dissertation, Frankfurt/Main, published as Studien zur Europäischen Rechtsgeschichte Heft, Sonderhefte der Iuscommune-Veröffentlichungen des Max-Planck-Instituts für Europäische Rechtsgeschichte 106. Frankfurt/Main, 1998.

Vergoossen 1996
Manuela Vergoossen. Zeitstrukturen und Zeitmotive in Graphik und Malerei des französischen Rokoko. Dissertation, Aachen 1996.

Völkel 2001
Michaela Völkel. *Das Bild vom Schloß: Darstellung und Selbstdarstellung deutscher Höfe in Architekturstichserien 1600–1800.* Kunstwissenschaftliche Studien 92. Munich, 2001.

Vogel 1996
Gerd-Helge Vogel. Konfuzianismus und Chinoise Architekturen im Zeitalter der Aufklärung. *Gartenkunst* 8 (1996), no. 2: 188–212.

Wagner-Rieger 1979
Renate Wagner-Rieger. Zur Typologie des Barockschlosses. In *Wolfenbütteler Arbeiten zur Barockforschung* 9, ed. Martin Bircher, 57–67. Hamburg, 1979.

Walcha 1938
Otto Walcha. Die Bedeutung Kändlers in der sächsischen Barockplastik. Part 2 ("Sakralplastik") in the *Meissner Tagblatt und Anzeiger für Grossenhain, Weinböhla und Coswig*, no. 200, 27 Aug 1938; Part 3 ("Parkplastik") in no. 218, 17 Sept 1938; Part 4 ("Tierplastik") in no. 259, 5 Nov 1938).

Walcha 1961
Otto Walcha. Das Charakterbild Kirchners im Spiegel der Meissner Archivalien. *Keramikfreunde der Schweiz, Mitteilungsblatt* 53: 22–27; and *Mitteilungsblatt* 54: 18–27.

Walcha 1973
Otto Walcha. *Meissner Porzellan.* Dresden, 1973. Trans. Edmund Launert as *Meissen Porcelain* (London, 1981).

Walravens 1987
Hartmut Walravens. *China illustrata: Das europäische Chinaverständnis im Spiegel des 16. bis 18. Jahrhunderts.* Weinheim, 1987.

Warncke 1989
Carsten-Peter Warncke. Johann Melchior Dinglingers "Hofstaat des Grossmoguls": Form und Bedeutung

eines virtuosen Goldschmiedekunstwerkes. In *Anzeiger des Germanischen Nationalmuseums Nürnberg 1988*, 159–188. Nuremberg 1989.

Warner 2004
Roger Warner. Memoirs of a Twentieth-Century Antique Dealer. In *Regional Furniture Society* (annual society publication), 2004.

G. Weber 1985
Gerold Weber. *Brunnen und Wasserkünste in Frankreich im Zeitalter von Louis XIV., mit einem Überblick über die französischen Brunnen ab 1500*. Worms, 1985.

I. Weber 1985
Ingrid S. Weber. *Planetenfeste August des Starken zur Hochzeit des Kurprinzen 1719*. Munich, 1985.

M. Weber 1922
Max Weber. *Wirtschaft und Gesellschaft. Grundriß der Sozialökonomie*. Tübingen, 1922.

W. Weber 1981
Wolfhard Weber. Probleme des Technologietransfers in Europa im 18. Jahrhundert: Reisen und technologischer Transfer. In *Technologischer Wandel im 18. Jahrhundert* (Wolfenbütteler Forschungen 14, ed. Ulrich Troitzsch), 189–218. Wolfenbüttel, 1981.

Welzel 1997
Barbara Welzel. Galerien und Kunstkabinette als Orte des Gesprächs. In *Wolfenbütteler Arbeiten zur Barockforschung* 28, 495–504. Wiesbaden, 1997.

Wittwer 1999
Samuel Wittwer. Sinnliches Erleben von Macht: Chinoiserienmode im Dienste fürstlicher Repräsentation. In *Portikus* (special publication for the exhibition of the Stiftung Preußische Schlösser und Gärten Berlin-Brandenburg "Sophie Charlotte und ihr Schloß"), 13–14. Potsdam, 1999.

Wittwer 2000.a
Samuel Wittwer. Das Charlottenburger Porzellankabinett. Europäischer Herrschaftsanspruch im asiatischen Porzellanrausch. *MuseumsJournal* (Berlin) 14, no. 4: 46–49.

Wittwer 2000.b
Samuel Wittwer. *Ein königlicher Tiergarten. Tiere aus Meissener Porzellan*. Dossier 2 of the Rijksmuseum, Amsterdam. Zwolle, 2000. Trans. David McLintock as *A Royal Menagerie: Meissen Porcelain Animals* (Paul Getty Museum, 2001).

Wittwer 2001.a
Samuel Wittwer. Porzellan und Fayence im Schloß Oranienburg 1699 und 1743. In *Schloß Oranienburg: Ein Inventar aus dem Jahre 1743*, a publication of the Stiftung Preußische Schlösser und Gärten Berlin-Brandenburg, 34–52. Potsdam, 2001.

Wittwer 2001.b
Samuel Wittwer. Das Service Friedrichs I. von Preußen für den Schwarzen Adlerorden. In *Preußen 1701: eine europäische Geschichte*, Schloss Charlottenburg exhibition catalog, a publication of the Deutsches Historisches Museum and the Stiftung Preußische Schlösser und Gärten Berlin-Brandenburg, 127–128. Berlin, 2001.

Wittwer 2004
Samuel Wittwer. Fragile splendour and political representation: Baroque porcelain rooms as meaningful treasures. In *The International Ceramics Fair and Seminar, Handbook 2004*, ed. Brian Haughton, 36–44. London, 2004.

Wölfflin 1965
Heinrich Wölfflin. *Renaissance und Barock: Eine Untersuchung über Wesen und Entstehen des Barockstils in Italien*. 6th edition. Basel and Stuttgart, 1965.

Württemberg 1998
Philipp Herzog von Württemberg. *Das Lackkabinett im deutschen Schloßbau: zur Chinarezeption im 17. und 18. Jahrhundert*. Bern, 1998.

Zeitler 1994
Rudolf Zeitler. Handwerk, Kunsthandwerk, Kunst. Speech at the opening of the exhibition "Künstlerleben in Rom. Bertel Thorvaldsen" on 1 Dec 1991. In *Anzeiger des Germanischen Nationalmuseums 1994*, 20–24. Nuremberg, 1994.

Zimmermann o. J.
Ernst Zimmermann. Die Porzellanplastik Kändlers. In *Das Museum, eine Anleitung zum Genuß der Werke bildender Kunst*, vol. 8, 21–24. Stuttgart, n. d. (ca. 1900?).

Zimmermann 1905
Ernst Zimmermann. Das Porzellanzimmer im königlichen Schloß zu Dresden. In *Dresdener Jahrbuch 1905, Beilage zur bildenden Kunst*, vol. 1, 71–82. Dresden, 1905.

Zimmermann 1908
Ernst Zimmermann. *Erfindung und Frühzeit des Meissner Porzellans*. Berlin, 1908.

Zimmermann 1914
Ernst Zimmermann. Wer war der erste Plastiker der Meissner Manufaktur? *Mitteilungen aus den sächsischen Kunstsammlungen* 5 (1914): 71–76.

Zimmermann 1915
Ernst Zimmermann. Die Meissner Tiergroßplastik. *Mitteilungen aus den sächsischen Kunstsammlungen* 6 (1915), no. 6: 92–113.

Zimmermann 1926
Ernst Zimmermann. *Meissener Porzellan*. Leipzig, 1926.

Zimmermann 1929
Ernst Zimmermann. *Kirchner: Der Vorläufer Kändlers an der Meissner Manufaktur*. No. 5 of Keramik und Glasstudien, ed. Gustav E. Pazaurek. Berlin, 1929.

Catalog

Introduction

The following catalog has been compiled from the huge quantities of data on the animal figures that have accumulated in the course of the author's research. The catalog's format has been chosen with a view to minimizing tiresome factual enumerations in the running text, to presenting the entire corpus of information in a structured form, and to providing a reference work which will enable users to look up facts and figures with the greatest possible ease.

The catalog of the large Meissen animal figures produced for the Japanese Palace covers all the models referred to in connection with the furnishing of the Palace, the principal sources being the inventories, reports, and order and delivery lists from the period 1730 to 1736. While the Hoopoe, for instance, is mentioned by Kaendler in his work reports in July 1736, it is deliberately not included in the present catalog because it was neither ordered specifically for the Japanese Palace project, nor mentioned in the inventory of the royal collection at the palace. The best overall survey of all the eighteenth-century Meissen animals is still the book written by Carl Albiker.

Although the intention has been to present the data in as complete a form as possible, there are gaps which readers may care to fill themselves, particularly concerning the present-day whereabouts of certain figures.

The purpose of the following explanations is to help users to a better understanding of individual points in the catalog entries. They furthermore offer information about the sources from which the data has been derived and give consideration to fundamental problems related to how the data has been passed down to us, problems which raise questions particularly related to the deliveries and the holdings of animal and bird figures.

Explanatory notes on the individual sections of the Catalog

1. Name

"Historical name" contains: German-language terms and expressions used in the historical sources for the animal or bird, insofar as they are significantly different from the term used today. Differences only affecting single vowels and minor differences in spelling are not taken into consideration.

2. Model

"Modeler" contains: the name of the artist mentioned in the historical sources as having created the model (= "proven"). If the work has been attributed to a certain artist on stylistic or other grounds, then the name carries the annotation "attributed."

"Dating" contains: as exactly as possible, the date when the model was done, and not the date when the porcelain figures were produced. When the historical sources do not provide us with express information as to the date of the model (if they do, it is considered "proven"), they can often be used to show that it was created in a certain period (= "attributed"). Furthermore, a model can sometimes be attributed on stylistic grounds to a certain creative period of the artist in question. This is for instance true of the figure of two dogs fighting, which on account both of certain concrete details and of the "fighting" element can be attributed to Kaendler's initial phase at Meissen: it is almost certainly a creation from those three months of his first year for which there are no extant work reports. In many cases, approximate dating is facilitated by information related to the production process, here entered under "details of production." This is, for instance, the case with the Lion: two lions were made as early as December 1732, but the first delivery to the palace did not take place until one and a half years later.

"Work report/Rapport etc." contains: quotations from the Meissen manufactory records that shed light on the genesis of the model in question. In this case the source is usually a modeler's report, or one of the monthly reports submitted by the manufactory directorate to the Commission ("Rapport"). If the entry does not refer to the model itself but to a preparatory drawing or bozzetto, then there is an indication to this effect.

"Size" contains: average dimensions of the porcelain figures. Variations in the firing conditions and in the repairer's work sometimes led to differences in size of up to a few centimeters in the case of some large figures. The dimensions entered were compared with those in the historical sources and correspond to these to a very large extent.

"Revival of the model" contains: the date when the model in question was revived in the first half of the twentieth century, and the name of the modeler responsible. These pieces of information were taken from the manufactory model book, as was the additional data about other procedures necessitated by the revival, and are translated as follows here:
"Modellerneuerung": *revival of the model*
"kopiert nach altem Modell": *copied from an original figure*
"ergänzt nach altem Modell":
set of molds completed after an original figure
"ergänzt": *set of molds completed*
"erneuert" (= "aufrepariert"):
worn-down molds renewed (for procedure, see Glossary)

"Mold number" contains: the numbers allotted to the individual models in the current model book, which normally correspond to the numbers used in the eighteenth century. The problems related to the model numbers have been dealt in a number of publications. The main difficulty derives from the practice, particularly prevalent in the second half of the nineteenth century, of re-allotting the number of an old model to a new or newly reconstructed model once the old model was definitively no longer in production and its molds had been officially withdrawn ("kassiert"). If we did not know that the manufactory often re-allotted numbers formerly used for withdrawn models, we might assume that the numbering was done in strict chronological sequence and conclude from the mold numbers of some large-size figures that they were only done in the last quarter of the eighteenth century (e.g. Chamois, Lion, Nanny-Goat). Model numbers were thus primarily used as call numbers are used in library catalogs, and were intended to help the mold-master find the plaster molds belonging to a certain figure more efficiently in amongst the stock of molds at his disposal.

"Source of inspiration" contains: details about the modeler's sources of inspiration, insofar as they are known. These include studies made in the *Animaliengalerie* (natural history collection) or at the menageries in Dresden and at Moritzburg, and in a number of cases graphic works which may have served as models.

3. Orders/Deliveries

"Quantity ordered" contains: the number of copies of a given animal or bird ordered, as indicated in the "specifications," or order lists. In many cases the order remained numerically the same in later lists even when some of figures had already been delivered. The sources, which are only referred to with their abbreviations, are the following:

Early 1732 = "Specification was in dem Königl: Holländ: Pallais zu der fordern Gallerie in der Obern Etage an Porcellain erfordert wird" [Specification of the porcelain ordered for the front gallery of the upper story of the Royal Dutch Palace], (SächsHStA, loc. 1341, Varia die Porcelain-Manufactur betr., undated, loose leaves, paginated in pencil, fols. 29a–30a, printed here as Source 7); this list is more detailed in its enumeration of the animals ordered than a similar list dated 25 February 1732 (SächsHStA, loc. 1341, VI, Acta die Porcellän Manufactur betr. 1732, fols. 198a/b and 200a, here Source 6).

18 Nov 1732 = "Specification Dererjenigen Vasen, Terrinen, Thiere und Vogel, so in das Königl: Japanische Palais in die Obere Etage der fordern Gallerie, nach Ihro Königl: Majth. allergnädigsten Resolution und Befehl verfertiget werden sollen", (BA, IAa.17, fols. 332a–333a, here Source 9)

17 Dec 1732 = "Extract was von denjenigen Porcellain-Geschirren so ins Königl. Holländ. Pallais zuverfertigen anbefohlen worden, bereits geliefert, bis dato in Arbeit, und theils noch zu verfertigen sind" [List of which of the porcelain figures ordered for the Royal Dutch Palace have already been delivered, which are still in production, and which are still to be produced], (BA, IAa.17, fols. 335a–336a, here Source 10)

17 Nov 1733 = "Specificatio dererjenigen Porcelain Geschirre so auff Ihro Königl. May. allergnädigsten hohen mündlichen Befehl, und ferner hohen Anordnung des Herrn Geheimbden Raths und Ober-Stallmeisters Reichs-Graffen von Solcowsky Excellenz den 17. November 1733 bey Anwesenheit des Herrn Cammer-Rath von Pflugs, und Bettmeister Teufferts, in dem Königl. Meißnischen Porcelain Waaren-Lager zum ausmöbliren des Königl. Japanischen Palais befunden und ausgesezet worden" [Specification of the porcelain pieces that were found at the Meissen porcelain warehouse on 17 November 1733 in the presence of Councillor von Pflugk and Major-domo Teuffert and were reserved to be used for the furnishing of the Royal Japanese Palace in accordance with the verbal order of His most gracious Royal Majesty and delivered by Privy Councillor and Master of the Stables Reichsgraf von Sulkowski], (SächsHStA, loc. 1342, VII, Acta die Porcelaine Manufactur betr. 1733, fol. 8a/b, here Source 12; identical to BA, IAa.19, fols. 342a–343a)

26 Nov 1733 = "Specificatio dererjenigen Vasen, Thiere und Vögel, so in das Königl. Japanische Palais in die Obere Etage der fördern Gallerie auf Ihro Königl. Mayt. in Pohlen und ChurFürstl. Durchl. zu Sachßen allergnädigsten hohen mündlichen Befehl, und ferne hohen Anordnung Sr. Excellenz des Herrn Geheimbden Rath und Ober-StallMeisters, Reichs-Grafen von Sulkowsky in der Meißnischen Porcelain Fabrique verferttiget werden soll" (BA, IAa.19, fols. 347a–369a, here Source 13, identical to Sächs HStA, OHMA, *Pläne und Zeichnungen*, chap. II, no.15, Appendix on the ground plans and elevations, not dated)

18 Feb 1735 = "Specification was von denenjenigen Porcellain Geschirren so ins Königl. Japanische Palais zu verferttigen allergnädigst anbefohlen worden, breeits geliefert und noch zu verferttigen sind" (appended to the report of the Commission of February 18, 1735: SächsHStA, loc. 1342, VIII, Acta die Porcelaine Manufactur betr. 1734/1735, fols. 125a–127a, here Source 17; identical to BA, IAa.23, fols. 90a–92a)

9 Mar 1736 = "Specificatio Was von denenjenigen Porcellain-Geschirren, so in das Königl. Japanische Palais zu verferttigen allergnädigst anbefohlen worden, bereits bis und mit ult:Jan:1736 geliefert und noch zu liefern sind" [Specification of which of the porcelain figures most graciously ordered for the Royal Japanese Palace were delivered up to and including the last day of January 1736, and which are still to be delivered], (appended to the report of the Commission of March 9, 1736: SächsHStA, loc. 1342, IX, Acta die Porcelaine Manufactur betr. 1736/1737, fols. 41a–44a, here Source 19; identical to BA, IAa.25, fols. 48a–51a)

"Information on production" contains: such information about the genesis – particularly the dating – of models as goes beyond that contained in the order and delivery lists. This is derived partly from reports about the current state of affairs at the manufactory regarding the Japanese Palace project, or – insofar as they are extant – firing reports. Specific details such as the state of the figures mentioned (raw, low-fired, glazed, etc.) are also included, as are the original color indications, even though they often distinguish imprecisely or incorrectly between "painted" ("bemalt") and "enameled" ("emailliert"). The sources for the lists quoted are the following:

13 Dec 1731 = "Verzeichniß Derer nach Ihro Königl. Majth. hierzu absonderl. gegebenen Modellen und Rißen gefertigten großen Geschirre und dergl. so zum Verglühen mehrentheils parat stehen" [Catalog of the large porcelain pieces made in accordance with sketches and models provided by His Royal Majesty, the greater part of which now stand ready for low-firing], (appended to the report of the Commission of December 17, 1731. SächsHStA, loc. 1341, VI, Acta die Porcellän Manufactur betr. 1732, fol. 26a/b, here Source 5; identical to BA, IAa.15, fol. 522a/b)

18 Aug 1732 = "Specificatio Derjenigen Porcellain-Geschirren, welche theils emaillirt, theils gut gebrannt, theils aber noch roh und unverglühet bey der fabrique zu Meißen vorräthig und zum Königl: Holländischen Palais zuliefern dato fertig sind", (appended to the report of the Commission of September 2, 1732: SächsHStA, loc. 1341, VI, Acta die Porcellän Manufactur betr. 1732, fols. 353b–354a, here Source 8; identical to BA, IAa.17, fol. 234a/b, and to BA, IAa.18, fol. 188a/b, in the last case dated)

17 Dec 1732 = = "Extract was von denjenigen Porcellain-Geschirren so ins Königl. Holländ. Pallais zuverfertigen anbefohlen worden, bereits geliefert, bis dato in Arbeit, und theils noch zu verfertigen sind" [List of which of the porcelain figures ordered for the Royal Dutch Palace have already been delivered, which are still in production, and which are still to be produced], (BA, IAa.17, fols. 335a–336a, here Source 10)

17 Nov 1733 = "Specificatio dererjenigen Porcelain Geschirre so auff Ihro Königl. May. allergnädigsten hohen mündlichen Befehl, und ferner hohen Anordnung des Herrn Geheimbden Raths und Ober-Stallmeisters Reichs-Graffen von Solcowsky Excellenz den 17. November 1733 bey Anwesenheit des Herrn Cammer-Rath von Pflugs, und Bettmeister Teufferts, in dem Königl. Meißnischen Porcelain Waaren-Lager zum ausmöbliren des Königl. Japanischen Palais befunden und ausgesezet worden", (SächsHStA, loc. 1342, VII, Acta die Porcelaine Manufactur betr. 1733, fol. 8a/b, here Source 12; identical to BA, IAa.19, fols. 342a–343a)

4 Mar 1734 = "Rechnung des Lackierers Reinow" [Bill submitted by the lacquerer Reinow], (SächsHStA, loc. 520, *Porcelain Waaren Lager zu Dreßden Rechnung*, 1734, no indication of which volume (1 or 2), fol. 112b) (= Rückert 1992/1993)

Mar 1735 = Firing report ("Brennbericht") for March 1735 (BA, IAa.24, fols. 105a–106a)

Apr 1735 = Firing report for April 1735 (BA, IAa.24, fols. 198a–199a)

May 1735 = Firing report for May 1735 (BA, IAa.24, fols. 200a–201a)

June 1735 = Firing report for June 1735 (BA, IAa.24, fols. 206a–207a)

July 1735 = Firing report for July 1735 (BA, IAa.24, fols. 271a–272a)

Aug 1735 = Firing report for August 1735 (BA, IAa.24, fols. 312a–313a)

Sept 1735 = Firing report for September 1735 (BA, IAa.24, fols. 314a–315a)

Oct 1735 = Firing report for October 1735 (BA, IAa.24, fols. 326a–327a)

Nov 1735 = Firing report for November 1735 (BA, IAa. 24, fols. 348a–349a)

Jan 1736 = Firing report for January 1736 (BA, IAa.24b, fols. 7a–8a)

Mar 1736 = Firing report for March 1736 (BA, IAa.24b, fols. 71a–72a)

May 1736 = Firing report for May 1736 (BA, IAa.24b, fol. 189a)

"Deliveries" contains: Date and number of the copies delivered by the manufactory to the Japanese Palace. This is primarily based on delivery lists compiled by manufactory and palace officials, and in some cases also on firing reports and on the directorate's reports ("Rapport"). The fact that the quantity indications in the lists were as a rule very carefully recorded means that they allow us a correct picture of growth in the holdings. The lists, only referred to with their abbreviations, are the following:

1731/1732, or simply 1732 = "Specification Dererjenigen PorcellainGeschirre, welche in dem Jahre 1731 und 1732 aus der Königl. Porcellain Fabrique zu Meißen zum WaarenLager nacher Dreßden und ferner in das Holländische Palais nach und nach geliefert worden" [Specification of the porcelain pieces that were delivered in the course of the years 1731 and 1732 from the Royal Porcelain Factory in Meissen to the warehouse and then to Dresden and to the Dutch Palace] (BA, IAa.20, fols. 64a–65a, here Source 11)

1733 = "Specificatio Was vor Ihro Königl. Majestaet in Pohlen und Churfürstl Durchl. zu Sachßen, an emaillierten Porcelain-Geschirren in Dero Japanisches Palais zu Neustadt aus hiesiger manufactur Anno 1733 geliefert worden" [Specification of the enameled porcelain pieces that were delivered for His Royal Majesty in Poland and Highness the Elector of Saxony to the Japanese Palace in Neustadt from the manufactory here in the year 1733], (appended to the report of the Commission of April 2, 1734: Sächs HStA, loc. 1342, VIII, Acta die Porcellaine Manufactur betr. 1734/1735, fols. 20a–25b, here Source 14; identical to BA, IAa.21, fols. 16a–17a)

7 March 1733–22 October 1734 (or: 1733/1734) = "Specification Was vor Ihro Königl. Maj. in Pohlen undt Churfürstl. Durchl. zu Sachßen an allerhandt Porcelain-Wahren, sowohl ins Holl. Palais als auch sonsten geliefert worden als vom 7. Marty 1733 bis dato den 22. Oct. 1734" [Specification of what sundry porcelain pieces were delivered for His Royal Majesty in Poland and Highness the Elector of Saxony to the Dutch Palace and elsewhere from March 7, 1733 to October 22, 1734], (BA, IAe.3, fol. 236a/b, here Source 15)

1734, or 1734 in toto = "Anno 1734 in Dreßden, Vor Ihro Königl. Majestät in Pohlen und Chur-Fürstl. Durchl. zu Sachßen seynd dieses Jahr aus Dero Porcelaine Lager zum Japan. Palais in Unterthänigkeit geliefert worden:" [What has been duly delivered, for His Royal Majesty in Poland and Highness the Elector of Saxony, during this year 1734 from the porcelain warehouse to the Japanese Palace in Dresden], (SächsHStA, loc. 1342, VIII, Acta die Porcelaine Manufactur betr. 1734/1735, fols. 78/1a-78/7a, here Source 16; identical to SächsHStA, loc. 520, Porcelain Waaren Lagers zu Dreßden Rechnung vom 1. Jan. bis 31. Decembr. 1734, fols. 113b–114b)

Aug 1734 = "Acta Commissionis Die allergnädigst anbefohlene Beobachtung der Königl:Porcelain Manufactur auf dem Schloße zu Meißen [...] betr. 1734" [Deeds of the Commission, concerned with their due observation of the doings of the Royal Porcelain Manufactory in the castle at Meissen ... in the year 1734] (BA, IAa.21, fol. 144a/b)

November-December 1734 = the result of subtracting "1733/1734" from "1734 in toto"

1735, or 1735 in toto = "Anno1735 In Dreßden, Vor Ihro Königl. Majestaet in Pohlen und ChurFürstl. Durchl. zu Sachßen wurden zu Dero Japan. Palais vom 5. Marty bis 17. Decembr. a.c. in Unterthänigkeit geliefert:" (SächsHStA, loc. 520, Porcelain Waaren Lagers zu Dreßden Rechnung vom 1. Jan. bis 31. Decembr 1735, fols. 98b–99b, here Source 18)

before Feb 1735 = "Specificatio was von denenjenigen Porcellain Geschirren so ins Königl. Japanische Palais zu verferttigen allergnädigst anbefohlen worden, bereits geliefert und noch zu verferttigen sind", (appended as "E" to the report of the Commission of February 18, 1735: SächsHStA, loc. 1342, VIII, Acta die Porcelaine Manufactur betr. 1734/1735, fols. 125a–127a, here Source 17; identical to BA, IAa.23, fols. 90a–92a)

Feb 1735 = Firing report ("Brennbericht") for February 1735 (BA, IAa.24, fol.75a/b)

Mar 1735 = Firing report for March 1735 (BA, IAa.24, fols. 105a–106a)

Apr 1735 = Firing report for April 1735 (BA, IAa.24, fols. 198a–199a)

May 1735 = Firing report for May 1735 (BA, IAa.24, fols. 200a–201a)

June 1735 = Firing report for June 1735 (BA, IAa.24, fols. 206a–207a)

July 1735 = Firing report for July 1735 (BA, IAa.24, fols. 271a–272a)

Augt 1735 = Firing report for August 1735 (BA, IAa.24, fols. 312a–313a)

Sept 1735 = Firing report for September 1735 (BA, IAa.24, fols. 314a–315a)

Oct 1735 = Firing report for October 1735 (BA, IAa.24, fols. 326a–327a)

Nov 1735 = Firing report for November 1735 (BA, IAa.24, fols. 348a–349a)

1736 = "Specificatio Derjenigen Geschirre, welche anno1736 in das Königliche Jappanische Palais allergnädigst anbefohlenermaßen gefertiget und abgeliefert worden" [Specification of those pieces which were produced and delivered according to order to the Royal Japanese Palace in the year 1736], (appended to the report of the Commission of January 4, 1737: SächsHStA, loc. 1342, IX, Acta die Porcelaine Manufactur betr. 1736/1737, fols. 243b–245a, here Source 20; identical to BA, IAa.24c, fols. 8a–10a; and identical to SächsHStA, loc. 521, Porcelain Waaren Lagers zu Dreßden Rechnung vom 1. Jan. bis ult. Dec. 1736, unpaginated, with prices)

Jan 1736 = Firing report for January 1736 (BA, IAa.24b, fols. 7a–8a)

Mar 1736 = Firing report for March 1736 (BA, IAa.24b, fols. 71a–72a)

May 1736 = Firing report for May 1736 (BA, IAa.24b, fol.189a)

These lists do however have to be checked against each other: the five foxes, for example, that are recorded in the delivery of November 18, 1733, appear once again as five of the six foxes in the record of total deliveries for the whole of 1733 and 1734. Likewise, the two lions which arrived at the Palace in August 1734 are mentioned again together with three further lions in the overall deliveries report for 1734. And when the firing reports note the production of six she-wolves, but only five are recorded as having been delivered to the palace, then this can either be because one piece is referred to by two firing reports, or because one figure was broken before it could be delivered.

The total deliveries figure for 1734 contains several instances (the bustard, for instance) of figures which were in fact delivered before the end of 1733.

Mysterious discrepancies also occur in connection with a number of figures. The very vague and divergent statistics for monkeys, parrots and birds of prey, for example, make it impossible to come to any reliable conclusions. The entry for holdings from February 18, 1735 (see under "5. Holdings: Quantities in the Japanese Palace") likewise contains figures which according to the firing reports were only delivered in the following months, which very likely has to do with figures having already been packed and standing ready to be sent off, in which case it is understandable that the official included them in his listing.

The sometimes surprisingly long periods of time which elapsed between a model being finished, or even figures being completed, and the figure in question being recorded as having been incorporated into the holdings of the Japanese Palace are in some cases perhaps to be explained by packaging problems or difficulties related to transport. In the case of the group of somewhat unsubtle figures by Kirchner, there was a time lapse because Höroldt and Kaendler only released them when under pressure to increase deliveries. But no explanation is to be found as to why such a small figure as the Bird of Paradise was only sent to Dresden one whole year after it was ready.

"Historical price" contains: details of the sum on the bill submitted by the manufactory, as noted in some delivery lists. One taler was equal to 24 groschen. In 1736, Kaendler's annual salary as Modellmeister was 400 talers, and Höroldt's salary as director was 1,000 talers, while the repairer Friedrich August Albrecht and the molder Andreas Schiefer received 120 talers each; comparisons between these figures should however be made with a degree of caution as they were sometimes supplemented by payments in kind (firewood, lodgings and so on).

4. "Historical inventory number"

Under this rubric are entered the inventory number allotted in the inventories of 1770 and 1779, and the verbal entry in the inventory, quoted as a rule from the 1779 inventory. The inventory of 1779 has already been published (Boltz 1996). Where there are substantial differences between the inventory entries for a given figure, then both versions are quoted. The historical measurements have been omitted. The very sparing particulars contained in the 1769 inventory of the Tower Room of the Residence in Dresden are also included, quoted from Boltz 1996, although in some cases it is possible that figures were moved to and fro and thus make an appearance in two catalogs.

In several cases newly-delivered figures were given new numbers, even when copies of the same figure had already been entered in the inventory, but it did sometimes happen that the official noticed the precedent and gave the new accessions their correct number. If one compares the first certain delivery dates for all models with the inventory numbers allotted, the numbers rise relatively evenly, with the inventory numbers between 100 and 200 being given at the end of 1731 and in 1732, animals and birds delivered in 1733 and 1734 bearing numbers between 200 and 300, and those delivered in 1735 or 1736 numbers over 300.

5. Holdings

"Quantity at the Japanese Palace" contains: the number of copies of the model in question to be found at the given point in time in the Japanese Palace, or in the Tower Room of the Residency, as attested by the delivery reports including an interim total of pieces delivered to date, inventories and other publications. The following sources are used:

17 Dec 1732 = "Extract was von denjenigen Porcellain-Geschirren so ins Königl. Holländ. Pallais zuverfertigen anbefohlen worden, bereits geliefert, bis dato in Arbeit, und theils noch zu verfertigen sind", (BA, IAa.17, fols. 335a–336a, here Source 10)

18 Feb 1735 = Specification was von denenjenigen Porcellain Geschirren so ins Königl. Japanische Palais zu verferttigen allergnädigst anbefohlen worden, breeits geliefert und noch zu verferttigen sind" (appended to the report of the Commission of February 18, 1735: SächsHStA, loc. 1342, VIII, Acta die Porcelaine Manufactur betr. 1734/1735, fols. 125a–127a, here Source 17; identical to BA, IAa.23, fols. 90a–92a)

9 Mar 1736 = "Specificatio Was von denenjenigen Porcellain-Geschirren, so in das Königl. Japanische Palais zu verferttigen allergnädigst anbefohlen worden, bereits bis und mit ult:Jan:1736 geliefert und noch zu liefern sind" (appended to the report of the Commission of March 9, 1736: SächsHStA, loc. 1342, IX, Acta die Porcelaine Manufactur betr. 1736/1737, fols. 41a–44a, here Source 19; identical to BA, IAa.25, fols. 48a–51a)

Tower Room inventory 1769 = Wares in the "Buffetzimmer" (= Tower Room) of the show apartment in the Residency, quoted from Boltz 1996

Inv. 1770 = "Inventarium vom ChurFürstl. Sächßischen Japans. Palais zu Neustadt bey Dreßden und zwar über das Sächß. Porcellain 1770" [Inventory of the Japanese Palace of the Elector of Saxony at Neustadt, Dresden, concerning the Saxon porcelain 1770] = Vol. II (SächsHStA, Hausmarschallamt R, XVI, Nr. 55)

Inv. 1779 = "Inventarium vom ChurFürstl. Sächßischen Holländischen Palais zu Neustadt bey Dreßden und zwar über das Sächßis. Porcellain 1779" [Inventory of the Japanese Palace of the Elector of Saxony at Neustadt, Dresden, concerning the Saxon porcelain 1779] = Vol. II (Staatliche Kunstsammlungen Dresden, Porzellansammlung im Zwinger, Inventories No. 328)

Royal Collection 1900 = Holdings of the Collection in the Johanneum and in the Residency, quoted from Sponsel 1900

The three lists, of 1732, 1735, and 1736, recording the animal figures delivered to date are to be regarded as a kind of substitute for the entries never added to the inventory of 1721. However, close comparison of these lists does reveal problems to which there are no clear solutions. For example, two foxes listed in 1736 are missing in the 1770 inventory. As we know very little about cases of figures being removed to be used as gifts, figures being shifted around from one place to another, or breakages, we simply have to leave these figures as they stand. Smaller figures are more likely to have been used as gifts than larger ones, which was clearly the case with the Coot, two copies of which appear in the Kozel inventory of 1819 and were thus clearly given away probably before the end of the eighteenth century.

Difficult questions arise in connection with the holdings of three large-size figures in particular. What happened to the one pelican that appears in the 1770 inventory but not in that of 1779? As there is no reference to a breakage (as there normally was, in the case of the cassowary, for instance), it is possible that it was removed. Given that we now know of the actual existence of seven lions, why is it that only five can be deduced from the sources? It is very probable that the lion that turned bluish in the firing (now in the Metropolitan Museum of Arts, New York) was not delivered, but remained at the warehouse whence it was sold on in the 19th century. One further lion and the one lioness (lying) that is today's "one figure too many" as compared with inventory of 1779 may likewise have been used for the decoration of a sales warehouse (as attested in the sources) and then sold in the nineteenth century, never having been delivered to the Japanese Palace at all. This, however, is pure speculation.

"Sales/losses" contains: details of figures which were lost to the Royal Collection as a result of exchanges, direct sales, or auctions. In this case it was only possible to use the few sources which have any relevant information on this subject. If one compares the number of figures in the Royal Collection in 1779 with the number in 1900, or even today, then it is clear that there were far more losses than are documented in the sources.

"Present-day holdings" contains: details of their present whereabouts of historical figures, and if relevant, decoration and markings. This list reflects the state of the author's knowledge at the time of publication and thus makes no claims to being definitive or complete. Readers are invited to make further entries to cover other figures known to them. In the case of the smaller figures, particularly those birds which were sold on the open market from the 1730s onwards, no attempt has been made to perform the almost impossible task of counting the mass of copies in existence today, this being indicated by the entry "no record made." The path followed by a figure between leaving the Royal Collection and ending up in its present home has only been recorded if information to this effect has presented itself in the course of research; the information presented is thus incomplete in this respect and gaps may be filled in by readers who may have the missing information. The following historical firms of auctioneers are referred to with the following abbreviations: : Lepke = Auction-House Rudolph Lepke, Berlin; Ball/Graupe = Auction-House Hermann Ball and Paul Graupe, Berlin; Helbing = Auction-House Bruno Helbing, Frankfurt/M., with Cassirer/Helbing indicating the branch in Berlin.

I. Quadrupeds and creatures of fable

Badger

Name

1. Historical name	*Tachße, Taxe*
2. Latin name	Meles meles

Orders/Deliveries

1. Quantity ordered	18 Nov 1732	2
	17 Dec 1732	4
	26 Nov 1733	8
	18 Feb 1735	2
	9 Mar 1736	2
2. Information on production	Order not carried out	

Bear

Name

1. Latin name	Ursus arctos

Model

1. Modeler	Johann Gottlieb Kirchner (proven)
2. Dating	Oct 1732 (proven)
3. Work report/*Rapport* etc.	work report Oct 1732: "a large bear, life-size, Gottlieb Kirchner"[1]
	work report July 1734 (bozzetto only): "Specification of the foreign animals and exotic birds which . . . I, as named below, modeled and drew exactly and correctly, so that they . . . may here at the Royal Porcelain Factory be done large . . . In the Bear-House I made a model of . . . a bear, JJ Kändler"[2]
4. Size	L: 88.5 cm, H: 56.5 cm
5. Revival	Karl Stein, Apr – Aug 1924, copied from an original figure
6. Mold number	8

Orders/Deliveries

1. Quantity ordered	18 Nov 1732	4
	17 Dec 1732	8
	26 Nov 1733	8
	18 Feb 1735	4
	9 Mar 1736	4
2. Information on production	17 Dec 1732	3 in production at manufactory
3. Deliveries	1734	5
4. Historical price	209 talers 8 groschen	

Historical inventory number

N = 257-W [1770 and 1779 inventories]
"five bears, somewhat brown in color"

Holdings

1. Quantities	a) Japanese Palace:	
	17 Dec 1732	no reference
	18 Feb 1735	5
	9 Mar 1736	5
	Inv. 1770	5
	Inv. 1779	5
	b) Royal Collection 1900:	
	3	
2. Sales/losses	1836	exchange Sèvres 1
	9 Jan 1851	to Helena Wolfssohn 1
	1919	Lepke 1
3. Present-day holdings	Dresden Porcelain Collection 1 white	
	Sèvres, Musée National de Céramique 1 white	
	Lepke 1919, then Ball/Graupe 1931, now in Vienna, Museum of Applied Art 1 white	

Bear, small

Note

The model cannot be identified with certainty.

Name

1. Latin name	Ursus arctos

Model

1. Size	H: 7 cm

Orders/Deliveries

1. Deliveries	1735	3

Historical inventory number

N = 310-W [1770 and 1779 inventories] "three white bears with a somewhat brown tinge, two sitting and one standing"

Holdings

1. Quantities	a) Japanese Palace:	
	18 Feb 1735	3
	9 Mar 1736	3
	Inv. 1770	3
	Inv. 1779	3
2. Present-day holdings	no record made	

Camel

Name

1. historical	*Camehle*
2. Latin name	Camelus ferus

Orders/Deliveries

1. Quantity ordered	18 Nov 1732	4
	17 Dec 1732	8
	26 Nov 1733	8
	18 Feb 1735	4
	9 Mar 1736	4
2. Information on production	Order not carried out	
3. Work report/*Rapport* etc.	work report July 1734 (bozzetto only): "Specification of the foreign animals and exotic birds which . . . I, as named below, modeled and drew exactly and correctly, so that they . . . may here at the Royal Porcelain Factory be done large . . . In the *Kunstkammer*, from the stuffed animals, I made models of . . . a camel, JJ Kändler"[3]	

Cat

Name

1. Latin name	Felis domestica

Model

1. Modeler	Johann Gottlieb Kirchner (attributed)
2. Dating	before Aug 1732 (attributed)
3. Work report/*Rapport* etc.	no reference
4. Size	L: 27 cm, H: 46.5 cm
5. Revival	Karl Theodor Eichler, June 1924, copied from an original figure
6. Mold number	32

Orders/Deliveries

1. Quantity ordered	18 Nov 1732	2
	17 Dec 1732	4
	26 Nov 1733	4
	18 Feb 1735	2
	9 Mar 1736	2
2. Information on production	18 Aug 1732	3 unfired at manufactory, 2 low-fired at manufactory
	17 Dec 1732	3 in production at manufactory
3. Deliveries	1732	4
4. Historical price	no reference	

Historical inventory number

N = 251-W[4] [1770 and 1779 inventories] "one large cat with fire-cracks, white"

Holdings

1. Quantities	a) Japanese Palace:	
	17 Dec 1732	4
	18 Feb 1735	4
	9 Mar 1736	4
	Inv. 1770	1
	Inv. 1779	1
	b) Royal Collection 1900:	
	3 white	
2. Sales/losses	1920	Lepke 1 most likely not sold
3. Present-day holdings	Dresden Porcelain Collection 3 white	

Chameleon

Name

1. Historical name	*Gardeleons, Jardeleons*
2. Latin name	Chamaeleo chamaeleon

Orders/Deliveries

1. Quantity ordered	18 Nov 1732	4
	17 Dec 1732	8
	26 Nov 1733	8
	18 Feb 1735	4
	9 Mar 1736	4
2. Information on production	Order not carried out	

Chamois

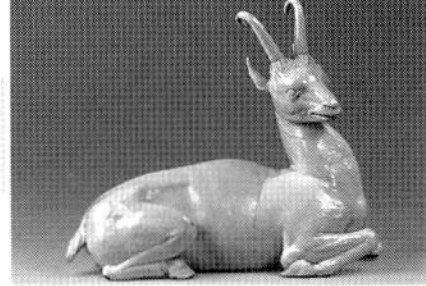

Name

1. Latin name	Rupicapra rupicapra

Model

1. Modeler	Johann Friedrich Eberlein (proven)
2. Dating	Apr – May 1735 (proven)
3. Work report/*Rapport* etc.	work report Aug 1735: "What I the undersigned have sculpted at the Royal Porcelain Manufactory from April 18 until the end of the month of May . . . a chamois buck, large, Johann Friedrich Eberlein, sculptor"[5]
	work report July 1735: "Made two large chamois models, Johann Friedrich Eberlein, sculptor"[6]
	work report Oct 1735: "Made four chamois bucks in paste, Johann Friedrich Eberlein, sculptor"[7]
4. Size	L: 58 cm, H: 52 cm
5. Revival	Karl Stein, June – July 1928, worn-down molds renewed
6. Mold number	A192

Orders/Deliveries

1. Quantity ordered	18 Nov 1732	4
	26 Nov 1733	8
	18 Feb 1735	4
	9 Mar 1736	4
2. Information on production	Aug 1735	1 finished, manufactory firing report
	Sept 1735	2 finished, manufactory firing report
	Jan 1736	1 finished, manufactory firing report
	Mar 1736	2 finished, manufactory firing report
3. Deliveries	Mar 1736	2
4. Historical price	32 talers	

Historical inventory number

N = 347-W [1770 and 1779 inventories]
"two chamois lying down, defective"

Holdings

1. Quantities	a) Japanese Palace:	
	9 Mar 1736	2
	Inv. 1770	2
	Inv. 1779	2
	b) Royal Collection 1900:	
	2 white	
2. Sales/losses	no reference	
3. Present-day holdings	Dresden Porcelain Collection 2 white	
	(Rouen, Musée de la Céramique 1 white)[8]	

Crocodile

Name

1. Historical name	*Crocodillo*
2. Latin name	Crocodylus porosus

Orders/Deliveries

1. Quantity ordered	no reference

Holdings

1. Quantities	a) Japanese Palace:	
	18 Feb 1735	4 probably small ones
	9 Mar 1736	4 probably small ones

Dog, Bolognese

Note

At first sight, certain stylistic features suggest that this figure was by Kirchner: parts of its coat are modeled in rather the same way as those of his monkey figures, or his Bear. Erich Hösel, however, has attributed the model to Kaendler, dating it to a part of 1734 for which there are no extant work reports. Given that the first copies were not delivered to the Japanese Palace until early 1735, there would seem to be more logic in this later dating. Moreover, some parts of the coat do have a certain ornamental quality in the curls that is more typical of Kaendler than of Kirchner. The fact, attested in work reports from after the expiry of the Japanese Palace, that Kaendler later made models for smaller Bolognese dog figures also speaks in favor of this attribution.

Name

1. Latin name	Canis familiaris

Model

1. Modeler	Johann Joachim Kaendler (attributed)	
2. Dating	Oct – Nov 1734 (attributed)[9]	
3. Work report/*Rapport* etc.	no reference	
4. Size	L: 42.0 cm, H: 43.0 cm	
5. Revival	Karl Stein, June – July 1919, set of molds completed from an original figure	
6. Mold number	129	

Orders/Deliveries

1. Quantity ordered	no reference	
2. Information on production	no reference	
3. Deliveries	Mar 1735	1 colored
	May 1735	4
4. Historical price	33 talers	

Historical inventory number

N = 305-W [1770 and 1779 inventories] "three Bolognese dogs, wearing collars with gilded edges"

Holdings

1. Quantities	a) Japanese Palace:	
	18 Feb 1735	5
	9 Mar 1736	5
	Inv. 1770	3
	Inv. 1779	3
	b) Royal Collection 1900:	
	3 enameled	
2. Sales/losses	no reference	
3. Present-day holdings	Dresden Porcelain Collection 2 enameled 1 enameled (war loss) (Ills: Albiker 1935, 256; 1959, 22)	
	Paris, Musée du Louvre 1 enameled	
	New York, Metropolitan Museum of Art 1 enameled	

Dogs

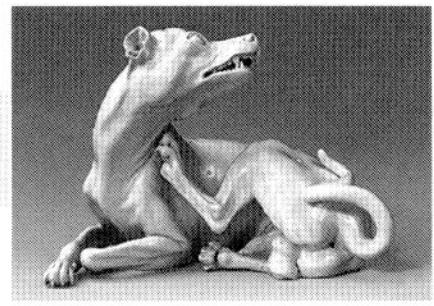

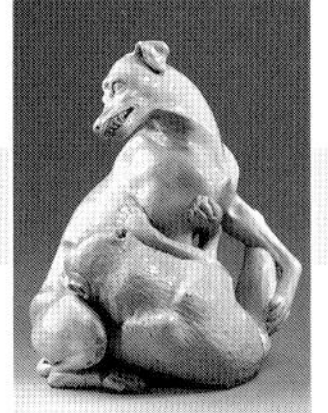

Note

In addition to the little Bolognese, there are also two other dog models, which are not distinguished in the order and delivery lists but are nevertheless very different from each other: a dog scratching itself, and a grayhound fighting with a bulldog. The latter figure is on stylistic grounds to be regarded as a work by Kaendler from the period when he was particularly fascinated by fighting animals (see, for example, Wisent Fighting with a Boar).

Name

1. Latin name	Canis familiaris

Model

1. Modeler	dogs fighting: Johann Joachim Kaendler (attributed)
	dog scratching itself: Johann Joachim Kaendler (proven)
2. Dating	fighting: Oct – Dec 1731 (attributed)
	scratching itself: Sept 1732 (proven)
3. Work report/*Rapport* etc.	scratching itself: *Rapport* Sept 1732: "Modeler Kentler, for his part, has modeled and made ready . . . a lying dog"[10]
4. Size	fighting: L: 36.0 cm, H: 47.5 cm
	scratching itself: L: 36.0 cm, H: 25.5 cm
5. Revival	fighting: Karl Stein, May – July 1926, copied from an original figure
	scratching itself: Karl Stein, June – July 1920, copied from an original figure
6. Mold number	fighting: 53
	scratching itself: 47

Orders/Deliveries

1. Quantity ordered	18 Nov 1732	2
	17 Dec 1732	4
	26 Nov 1733	8
	18 Feb 1735	2
	9 Mar 1736	2
2. Information on production	13 Dec 1731	1 unfired at manufactory (fighting), 2 low-fired at manufactory (fighting)
	4 Mar 1734	2 fighting, 1 scratching itself lacquered
3. Deliveries	1731/1732	4
4. Historical price	1 taler for lacquering (fighting)	
	16 groschen for lacquering (scratching itself)	

Historical inventory number

fighting: N = 170-W [1770 and 1779 inventories] "two pairs of white dogs, fighting tooth and nail, lacquered, defective"

scratching itself: N = 171-W [1770 and 1779 inventories] "two of the same [= dogs] lying, one defective"

Holdings

1. Quantities	a) Japanese Palace:	
	17 Dec 1732	4
	18 Feb 1735	5
	9 Mar 1736	5
	Inv. 1770	2 fighting
		2 scratching itself
	Inv. 1779	2 fighting
		2 scratching itself
	b) Royal Collection 1900:	
	2 fighting 2 scratching itself	
2. Sales/losses	no reference	
3. Present-day holdings	Dresden Porcelain Collection 2 white (fighting) 2 white (scratching itself)	

Dragon

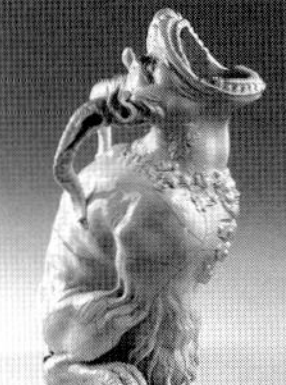

Note

The figure consistently referred to as a Dragon, both by the manufactory and in all lists and inventories, is without doubt to be identified with the work which has generally been known as an "Untier-Krug" or "Untier-Kanne" ("monster-jug," "grotesque jug") in literature on Meissen. There are two versions of this figure, one with front paws and one without.

Name

1. Historical name	*Trache*

Model

1. Modeler	Johann Gottlieb Kirchner (attributed)
2. Dating	1730 (attributed)
3. Work report/*Rapport* etc.	Report of the molder Friedrich Aug Albrecht: "All this time . . . I . . . have been encouraged to do work of this kind, even to the extent that Court Commissary Höroldt gave me a ducat from his own purse when I was doing the first pieces, the so-called Dragons . . ."[11]
4. Size	H: 56 cm (without front paws) H: 68 cm (with front paws)
5. Revival	no reference
6. Mold number	no record made
7. Source of inspiration	Bernard de Montfaucon: *L'Antiquité expliquée et représentée*, 1719/24, Vol. III, Plate 70

Orders/Deliveries

1. Quantity ordered	26 Nov 1733	11
2. Information on production	13 Dec 1731	3 unfired at manufactory
	18 Aug 1732	3 unfired at manufactory, 1 low-fired at manufactory, 1 finished at manufactory
	4 Mar 1734	3 lacquered by Reinow
3. Deliveries	1731/1732	11, two of which enameled
4. Historical price	no reference 2 talers for the lacquering by Reinow	

Historical inventory number

N = 156-W [1770 and 1779 inventories] "two colored dragons, with their mouths wide open" [with front paws]

N = 157-W [1770 and 1779 inventories] "nine of the same [= dragon] white, and lacquered, 4 1 ell 6 inches [= with front paws] 5 but only 1 ell high [= without front paws], 6 are defective"

Holdings

1. Quantities	a) Japanese Palace:	
	17 Dec 1732	no reference[12]
	18 Feb 1735	11 undifferentiated
	9 Mar 1736	11 undifferentiated
	Inv. 1770	2 with front paws 4 with front paws 5 without front paws
	Inv. 1779	2 with front paws 4 with front paws 5 without front paws
	b) Royal Collection 1900:	
	no reference	
2. Sales/losses	17. 4. 1847	to Teichert (branch of the manufactory) 1 undifferentiated
	1836	exchange Sèvres 1 (with front paws) enameled
	8. 1. 1851	to Helena Wolfssohn 2 undifferentiated
	9. 1. 1851	to Helena Wolfssohn 1 undifferentiated
	1919	Lepke 1 (without front paws) white

3. Present-day holdings	without front paws:
	Dresden Porcelain Collection 2 white, swords marks 1 lacquered, swords mark 1 enameled, swords mark
	Lepke 1919, then Siegfried Salz Collection then Kramarsky collection, now in a private collection, New York 1 white, swords mark
	with front paws:
	Sèvres, Musée National de Céramique 1 enameled, AR
	New York, Pflueger Collection (to go to Boston, Museum of Fine Arts) 1 white, with bottom missing
	Christie's London 2 July 1984 (lot 133) 2 white, AR marks
	Ball/Graupe 15 March 1933 (lot 13) 2 white, 1 with AR mark

Elephant

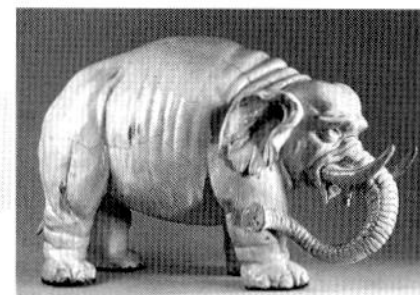

Name

1. Historical name	*Elephant*
2. Latin name	Loxodonta africana

Model

1. Modeler	Johann Gottlieb Kirchner (attributed)
2. Dating	Oct 1731 (proven)
3. Work report/*Rapport* etc.	*Rapport* Oct 1731: "Among the new figures is an elephant . . . modeled to a considerable size, and it is to be sent on to have molds made from it in the coming days."[13]
	Rapport Feb 1732: "A number of large elephant figures have now been made in paste"[14]
	18 Aug 1732: "On August 7th, the first Elephant was delivered from the firing house to the warehouse. Although it has a number of small cracks, Court Commissioner Höroldt is of the opinion that it is a passable piece and can be taken to be enameled"[15]
4. Size	H: 56.5 cm (one copy according to the 1770/1779 inventories)
	H: 61.5 cm, L: 93.5 cm
5. Revival	Karl Stein, Apr – May 1921, worn-down molds renewed, no longer in existence
6. Mold number	45
7. Source of inspiration	possibly Boremann, Thomas: *Threehundred animals.* Glasgow 1730

Orders/Deliveries

1. Quantity ordered	18 Nov 1732	4
	17 Dec 1732	8
	26 Nov 1733	8
	18 Feb 1735	4
	9 Mar 1736	4
2. Information on production	13 Dec 1731	clay model finished at manufactory
	18 Aug 1732	1 finished at manufactory, 1 unfired at manufactory
	4 Mar 1734	1 lacquered by Reinow
3. Deliveries	1732	1
	1733/1734	4
4. Historical price	197 talers	
	3 talers for the lacquering	

Historical inventory number

N = 179-W [1770 and 1779 inventories]
"one large white elephant, likewise lacquered, defective" [smaller version]

N = 255-W [1770 and 1779 inventories]
"three elephants, painted brown"

Holdings

1. Quantities	a) Japanese Palace:	
	17 Dec 1732	1
	18 Feb 1735	5
	9 Mar 1736	5
	Inv. 1770	1 of the smaller size
		3
	Inv. 1779	1 of the smaller size
		3
	b) Royal Collection 1900:	
	2 white	
2. Sales/losses	9 Jan 1851	to Helena Wolfssohn 1
3. Present-day holdings	Dresden Porcelain Collection 1 white 1 white, in pieces	
	Longleat, collection of the Marquess of Bath 1 white	
	Kuskowo, Museum 1 white[16]	

Fox

Name

1. Latin name	Vulpes vulpes

Model

1. Modeler	Johann Gottlieb Kirchner (proven)
2. Dating	Oct 1732 (proven)
3. Work report/*Rapport* etc.	work report Oct 1732: "A fox devouring a chicken, life-size, Gottlieb Kirchner"[17]
4. Size	L: 52 cm, H: 45 cm
5. Revival	Karl Stein, Nov 1920 – Feb 1921, copied from an original figure
6. Mold number	7
7. Literature	Grundmann 1989

Orders/Deliveries

1. Quantity ordered	18 Nov 1732	2
	17 Dec 1732	4
	26 Nov 1733	8
	18 Feb 1735	2
	9 Mar 1736	2
2. Information on production	17 Dec 1732	3 in production
	17 Nov 1733	4 enameled at manufactory
3. Deliveries	18 Nov 1733	5 colored
	1733/1734	6 altogether
4. Historical price	66 talers 8 groschen	

Historical inventory number

N = 260-W [1770 and 1779 inventories] "four figures of a fox, sitting with a young chicken in its mouth"

Holdings

1. Quantities	a) Japanese Palace:	
	17 Dec 1732	no reference
	18 Feb 1735	6
	9 Mar 1736	6
	Inv. 1770	4
	Inv. 1779	4
	b) Royal Collection 1900:	
	4	
2. Sales/losses	8 Jan 1851	to Helena Wolfssohn 1
	9 Jan 1851	to Helena Wolfssohn 1
	1920	Lepke 1

3. Present-day holdings	Dresden Porcelain Collection 3 white
	Lepke 1920, today in Nürnberg, Germanisches Nationalmuseum (on loan from a private collector) 1 white
	Longleat, collection of the Marquess of Bath 1 white
	Longleat, collection of the Marquess of Bath, then Christie's 13 June 2002 (lot 350), now Los Angeles, J. Paul Getty Museum 1 white

Goat (Billy-Goat)

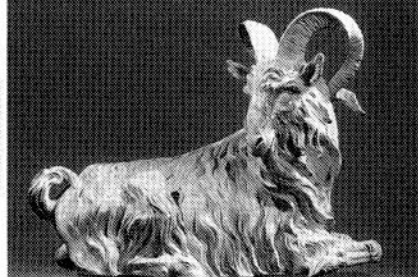

Name

1. Latin name	Capra

Model

1. Modeler	Johann Joachim Kaendler (attributed)
2. Dating	before Dec 1732 (proven)
3. Work report/*Rapport* etc.	no reference
4. Size	L: 74 cm, H: 56 cm
5. Revival	Karl Stein, Jan 1922, worn-down molds renewed
6. Mold number	126

Orders/Deliveries

1. Quantity ordered	18 Nov 1732	4
	17 Dec 1732	8
	26 Nov 1733	8
	18 Feb 1735	4
	9 Mar 1736	4
2. Information on production	17 Dec 1732	1 in production at manufactory
3. Deliveries	1732	3 white
	1734	2 altogether
	Aug 1734	1 colored
4. Historical price	134 talers	

Historical inventory number

N = 178-W [1770 and 1779 inventories] "three white lying billy-goats, lacquered, defective"

N = 262-W [1770 and 1779 inventories] "two black billy-goats, one defective"

Holdings

1. Quantities	a) Japanese Palace:	
	17 Dec 1732	3
	18 Feb 1735	5
	9 Mar 1736	5
	Inv. 1770	5
	Inv. 1779	5
	b) Royal Collection 1900:	
	3 white	
	1 lacquered	
2. Sales/losses	21. 6. 1850	to Marks, London 1
	1920	Lepke 1
3. Present-day holdings	Dresden Porcelain Collection 2 white	
	Lepke 1920, now London, Victoria and Albert Museum 1 white	
	Philadelphia, Museum of Art 1 white	

Goat (Nanny-Goat)

Name

1. Latin name	Capra

Model

1. Modeler	Johann Joachim Kaendler (proven)
2. Dating	Aug 1732 (proven)
3. Work report/*Rapport* etc.	*Rapport* Aug 1732: "Modeler Kentler, for his part, has modeled and made ready the following . . . a nanny-goat with a kid"[18]
4. Size	L: 65 cm, H: 48 cm
5. Revival	molds lost in war
6. Mold number	B 149

Orders/Deliveries

1. Quantity ordered	18 Nov 1732	4
	17 Dec 1732	4
	26 Nov 1733	8
	18 Feb 1735	4
	9 Mar 1736	4
2. Information on production		no reference
3. Deliveries	1732	2 white
	Aug 1734	2 colored
	Nov – Dec 1734	1
4. Historical price	132 talers 16 groschen	

Historical inventory number

N = 212-W [1770 and 1779 inventories] "two white nanny-goats, lying, each with a young one, lacquered at the time, damaged"

N = 261-W [1770 and 1779 inventories] "three nanny-goats, lying, each with a young one, one defective"

Holdings

1. Quantities	a) Japanese Palace:	
	17 Dec 1732	2
	18 Feb 1735	5
	9 Mar 1736	5
	Inv. 1770	5
	Inv. 1779	5
	b) Royal Collection 1900:	
	1 lacquered 3 white	
2. Sales/losses	8. 1. 1851	to Helena Wolfssohn 1
	1919	Lepke 1
	1920	Lepke 1
3. Present-day holdings	Dresden Porcelain Collection 1 lacquered 1 white	
	Lepke 1919, now Philadelphia, Museum of Art 1 white	
	Lepke 1920, now New York, Metropolitan Museum of Art 1 white	
	Waddesdon Manor 1 white	

Hare

Name

1. Latin name	Lepus europaeus

Orders/Deliveries

1. Quantity ordered	18 Nov 1732	4
	17 Dec 1732	4
	26 Nov 1733	8
	18 Feb 1735	4
	9 Mar 1736	4
2. Information on production	Order not carried out	

Horse

Name

1. Latin name	Equidae

Orders/Deliveries

1. Quantity ordered	18 Nov 1732	4
	17 Dec 1732	8
	26 Nov 1733	4
	18 Feb 1735	4
	9 Mar 1736	4
2. Information on production	Order not carried out	

"Indian deer"

Orders/Deliveries

1. Quantity ordered	18 Nov 1732	4
	18 Feb 1735	4
	9 Mar 1736	4
2. Information on production	Order not carried out	

Jerboa

Name

1. Historical name	*indianische Ratte, indianische Ratze*
2. Latin name	Jaculus jaculus

Model

1. Modeler	Johann Joachim Kaendler (proven)
2. Dating	Apr 1735 (proven)
3. Work report/*Rapport* etc.	work report July 1734 (bozzetto only): "Specification of the foreign animals and exotic birds which . . . I, as named below, modeled and drew exactly and correctly, so that they . . . may here at the Royal Porcelain Factory be done large . . . In the Lion-House I made a model of . . . an Indian rat, JJ Kändler"[19]
	work report Apr 1735: "An Indian rat, as can be seen alive in the Royal Lion-House, modeled with the pedestal done as a corn-sack open at the top, with the rat eating from it, Johann Joachim Kändler"[20]
4. Size	L: 18 cm, H: 21.4 cm
5. Revival	no name given, Aug 1913, most likely by renewing worn-down molds
6. Mold number	139
7. Source of inspiration	live specimen

Orders/Deliveries

1. Quantity ordered	18 Nov 1732	4
	26 Nov 1733	8
	18 Feb 1735	4
	9 Mar 1736	4
2. Information on production	July 1735	3 finished at manufactory, according to firing report
3. Deliveries	June 1735	1 enameled
	July 1735	7 enameled
	Sept 1735	1 enameled
	1735	9 altogether
4. Historical price	7 talers	

Historical inventory number

N = 309-W [Tower Room inventory 1769] four "Indian rats"

[1770 and 1779 inventories] "four of the same [= "Indian"] rats, painted in red and brown colors, each one sitting on a white sack filled with grain"

Holdings

1. Quantities	a) Japanese Palace:	
	9 Mar 1736	9
	Tower Room Inv. 1769	4
	Inv. 1770	4
	Inv. 1779	4

	b) Royal Collection 1900:
	4 enameled
2. Sales/losses	no reference
2. Present-day holdings	Dresden Porcelain Collection 1 enameled

Leopard

Name

1. Latin name	Panthera pardus

Model

1. Modeler	Johann Gottlieb Kirchner (proven)
2. Dating	Jan 1733 (proven)
3. Work report/*Rapport* etc.	work report Jan 1733: "In the month of January 1733, I made ready . . . a life-size leopard, Gottlieb Kirchner"[21]
4. Size	L: 73 cm, H: 71 cm
5. Revival	Karl Stein, Dec 1923 – Jan 1924, worn-down molds renewed, head and legs re-modeled
6. Mold number	13

Orders/Deliveries

1. Quantity ordered	18 Nov 1732	4
	17 Dec 1732	8
	26 Nov 1733	8
	18 Feb 1735	4
	9 Mar 1736	4
2. Information on production	no reference	
3. Deliveries	Aug 1734	2 colored, according to firing report
	1734	5 altogether
4. Historical price	66 talers 8 groschen	

Historical inventory number

N = 254-W [1770 and 1779 inventories] "five yellowish leopards with brown stripes"

Holdings

1. Quantities	a) Japanese Palace:	
	18 Feb 1735	5
	9 Mar 1736	5
	Inv. 1770	5
	Inv. 1779	5
	b) Royal Collection 1900:	
	3 white	
2. Sales/losses	21. 6. 1850	to Marks, London 1 (sold as a tiger)
	1920	Lepke 1
3. Present-day holdings	Dresden Porcelain Collection 3 white	
	Lepke 1920, then Lepke 1929, Baron v. Budapest, then Pietro Accorsi, now Turin, Museo Civico 1 white	
	(possibly Berlin, Kunstgewerbe-museum 1 war loss)[22]	

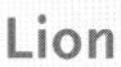

Lion

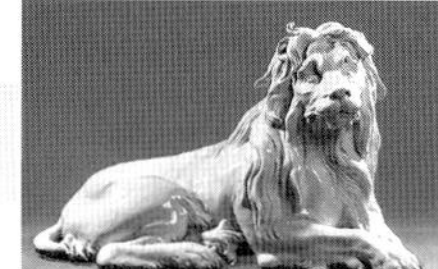

Name

1. Latin name	Panthera leo

Model

1. Modeler	Johann Gottlieb Kirchner (attributed)
2. Dating	before Aug 1732 (proven)
3. Work report/*Rapport* etc.	no reference
4. Size	L: 80 cm, H: 51 cm
5. Revival	Karl Theodor Eichler, April 1928, worn-down molds renewed
6. Mold number	A193

Orders/Deliveries

1. Quantity ordered	18 Nov 1732	4
	17 Dec 1732	4
	26 Nov 1733	8
	18 Feb 1735	4
	9 Mar 1736	4
2. Information on production	18 Aug 1732	2 unfired at manufactory
	17 Dec 1732	2 in production at manufactory
3. Deliveries	Aug 1734	2 colored, according to firing report
	1734	altogether 5
4. Historical price	106 talers	

Historical inventory number

N = 252-W [1770 and 1779 inventories] "five large brown lions"

Holdings

1. Quantities	a) Japanese Palace:	
	17 Dec 1732	no reference
	18 Feb 1735	5
	9 Mar 1736	5
	Inv. 1770	5
	Inv. 1779	5
	b) Royal Collection 1900:	
	4 white	
2. Sales/losses	8.1.1851	to Helena Wolfssohn 2
	9.1.1851	to Helena Wolfssohn 1
	1919	Lepke 1
3. Present-day holdings	Dresden Porcelain Collection 3 white	
	Lepke 1919, then Ole Olsen Collection, then Sotheby's 15 Nov 1955, now in a private collection 1 white	
	Longleat, Marquess of Bath 1 white	
	Edinburgh, Royal Museum of Scotland[23] 1 white	
	Tullynally Castle, Earl of Longford, now New York, Metropolitan Museum of Art 1 with some blue discoloring	

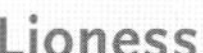

Lioness

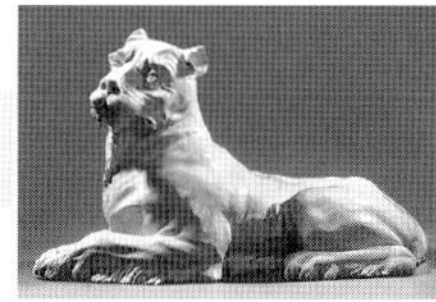

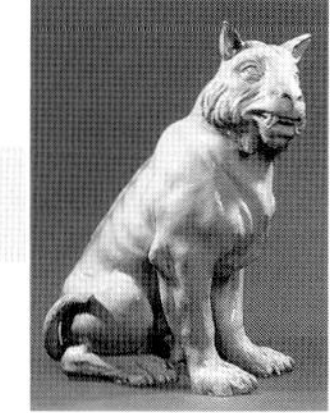

Note

In the order and delivery lists a distinction was always made between a sitting Lioness and a lying Lioness. Comparisons of the numbers of figures, measurements, and inventory numbers shows clearly that the model made by Kirchner as a tiger was wrongly identified by the compilers of the lists, and it was referred to as a sitting lioness. As almost all the references in the sources also make this mistake, the figure which Kirchner intended to be regarded as a tiger is listed here as a sitting lioness.

Name

1. Latin name	Panthera leo

Model

1. Modeler	Lioness, lying: Johann Gottlieb Kirchner (attributed)
	Lioness, sitting: Johann Gottlieb Kirchner (proven)
2. Dating	lying: before Dec 1732 (proven)
	sitting: Jan 1733
3. Work report/*Rapport* etc.	sitting: work report Jan 1733: "In the month of January 1733, I made ready the following . . . a tiger in the same size [= life-size], Gottlieb Kirchner"[24]
4. Size	lying: L: 77 cm; H: 48 cm
	sitting: L: 64.5 cm; H: 74 cm
5. Revival	lying: Karl Stein, Jan – Feb 1926, worn-down molds renewed, no case-molds in existence
	sitting: Karl Stein, Mar 1924, worn-down molds renewed
6. Mold number	lying: A191
	sitting: 12[25]

Orders/Deliveries

1. Quantity ordered	18 Nov 1732	4
	17 Dec 1732	4
	26 Nov 1733	8
	18 Feb 1735	4
	9 Mar 1736	4
2. Information on production	17 Dec 1732	4 in production, undifferentiated
3. Deliveries	Aug 1734	5 colored, according to firing report, undifferentiated
	1734	altogether 8 undifferentiated
4. Historical price	106 talers (undifferentiated)	

Historical inventory number

N = 253-W [1770 and 1779 inventories] "eight yellowish lionesses, 5 lying and 3 sitting"

Holdings

1. Quantities	a) Japanese Palace:	
	18 Feb 1735	8 undifferentiated
	9 Mar 1736	8 undifferentiated
	Inv. 1770	5 lying 3 sitting
	Inv. 1779	5 lying 3 sitting
	b) Royal Collection 1900:	
	details given unclear	
2. Sales/losses	9 Jan 1851	to Helena Wolfssohn 1 undifferentiated
	1919, Lepke	1 lying
	1919, Lepke	1 sitting
3. Present-day holdings	lying: Dresden Porcelain Collection 3 white	

Lepke 1919, then Berlin, Kunstgewerbe-museum, now war loss
1 white

Ole Olsen Collection, then Sotheby's 15.11.1955, now in a private collection
1 white

Tullynally Castle, Earl of Longford, now New York, Metropolitan Museum of Art
1 white

sitting:
Dresden Porcelain Collection
2 white

Lepke 1919, then Andreina Torré,[26] now Bayerisches Nationalmuseum, Schneider Collection, Lustheim
1 white

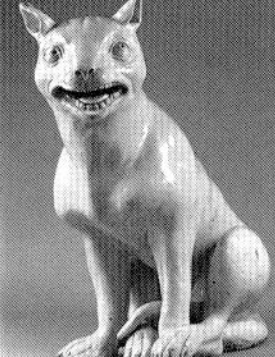

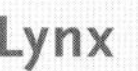

Lynx

Name

1. Historical name	*Luxe*
2. Latin name	Lynx lynx

Model

1. Modeler	Johann Gottlieb Kirchner (proven)
2. Dating	Jan 1733 (proven)
3. Work report/*Rapport* etc.	work report Jan 1733: "In the month of January 1733, I made ready the following . . . a lynx, life-size, Gottlieb Kirchner"[27]
	work report July 1734 (bozzetto only): "Specification of the foreign animals and exotic birds which . . . I, as named below, modeled and drew exactly and correctly, so that they . . . may here at the Royal Porcelain Factory be done large . . . In the Lion-House I made a model of . . . a lynx, JJ Kändler"[28]
4. Size	L: 53 cm, H: 61 cm
5. Revival	Karl Stein, Mar – Apr 1921, worn-down molds renewed
6. Mold number	14

Orders/Deliveries

1. Quantity ordered	18 Nov 1732	4
	17 Dec 1732	4
	26 Nov 1733	4
	18 Feb 1735	4
	9 Mar 1736	4
2. Information on production	no reference	
3. Deliveries	Aug 1734	2 colored, according to firing report
	1734	altogether 5
4. Historical price	60 talers	

Historical inventory number

N = 258-W [1770 and 1779 inventories]
"five lynxes with white and black patches"

Holdings

1. Quantities	a) Japanese Palace:	
	18 Feb 1735	5
	9 Mar 1736	5
	Inv. 1770	5
	Inv. 1779	5
	b) Royal Collection 1900:	
	4 white 1 lacquered	
2. Sales/losses	1920	Lepke 1
3. Present-day holdings	Dresden Porcelain Collection 3 white 1 with remains of lacquer	
	Lepke 1920, now Cologne, Museum für Angewandte Kunst 1 white	

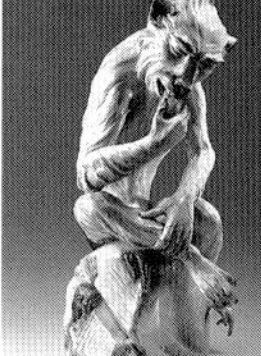

Mandrill

Note

This model is sometimes referred to as a "Pavian" (baboon), particularly in the order lists, and sometimes as a "Waldteufel" (lit. wood-devil), particularly in the delivery lists. Although one delivery list has the entry "8 baboons," the baboons are always entered as still outstanding in subsequent interim totals, and the "Waldteufel" appear as "delivered, but not ordered." Comparison of all the available data makes it reasonably clear that different expressions were used for one and the same figure by those compiling the lists, and that this figure was of a mandrill, which was still commonly referred to as a "Waldteufel" in the eighteenth century.

Name

1. Historical name	*Waldteufel* ("wood-devil"), rarely *indianischer Teufel;* also *Pavion, Bavian* (baboon)
2. Latin name	Mandrillus sphinx

Model

1. Modeler	Johann Gottlieb Kirchner (attributed)
2. Dating	before Dec 1731 (proven)
3. Work report/*Rapport* etc.	work report July 1734: "Specification of the foreign animals and exotic birds which . . . I, as named below, modeled and drew exactly and correctly, so that they . . . may here at the Royal Porcelain Factory be done large . . . which are to be seen stuffed in the *Kunstkammer* and of which I made drawings . . . an 'Indian devil,' JJ Kändler"[29]
4. Size	L: 43 cm, H: 67 cm
5. Revival	Karl Stein, Sept – Dec 1928, recreated with modifications from an original figure Karl Stein, Jan 1929
6. Mold number	40 (and 40x for the modified model)

Orders/Deliveries

1. Quantity ordered	18 Nov 1732	8 ("Pavian")
	17 Dec 1732	8 ("Pavian")
	26 Nov 1733	8 ("Pavian")
	18 Feb 1735	8 ("Pavian")
	9 Mar 1736	8 ("Pavian")
2. Information on production	13 Dec 1731	2 unfired at manufactory ("Waldteufel")
	18 Aug 1732	6 finished at manufactory ("Waldteufel"), 2 low-fired in manufactory ("Waldteufel"), 2 unfired at manufactory ("Waldteufel")
	4 Mar 1734	4 lacquered by Reinow ("Pavian")
3. Deliveries	1731/1732	7 ("Waldteufel")
4. Historical price	no reference 2 talers for lacquering by Reinow	

Historical inventory number

N = 158-W [1770 and 1779 inventories]
"six large 'wood-devils,'
all damaged"

Holdings

1. Quantities	a) Japanese Palace:	
	17 Dec 1732	8 "Pavian"
	18 Feb 1735	7 "Waldteufel"
	9 Mar 1736	7 "Waldteufel"
	Inv. 1770	6 "Waldteufel"
	b) Royal Collection 1900:	
	2 white 1 lacquered 1 enameled	
2. Sales/losses	21.6.1850	to Marks, London, 1 monkey, from the price probably a mandrill
	8.1.1851	to Helena Wolfssohn 1 monkey, from the price probably a mandrill
	1919	Lepke 1
3. Present-day holdings	Dresden Porcelain Collection 2 white, 1 lacquered, 1 enameled	
	Lepke 1919, now Hamburg, Museum für Kunst und Gewerbe 1 white	
	Helbing, 1936 1 with spots, without original pedestal	

Monkeys

Note

The monkey figures present particular problems, as there is as good as no differentiation made between the various models either in the order and delivery lists or in the other sources. The Mandrill, the largest of the monkey models, is the only one which can be dealt with independently, thanks to the fact of it having a name of its own. The inventories do sometimes make distinct references to the smallest model – the so-called Marmoset – and, because of its particular characteristics, the Mother-Monkey. Nevertheless, the degree of uncertainty is so great that the only statistics that can be given in the following five tables from the order and delivery lists are the ones that relate to all the monkey figures together. In spite of the great similarity in their postures, detailed comparison shows that the Monkey taking snuff and the Monkey with chain or grape were not made from the same model. Lack of source evidence means that the only criteria that can be used to attribute them to either Kaendler or Kirchner are stylistic ones, but close study makes this process easier than one would imagine from the confusing variety characteristic of the monkey figures.

Monkey, marmoset

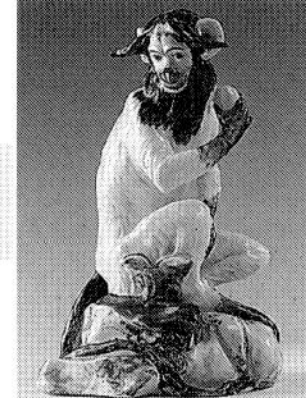

Name

1. Latin name	Callithrix jacchus

Model

1. Modeler	Johann Joachim Kaendler (attributed)
2. Dating	Oct–Dec 1731 (attributed)

3. Work report/*Rapport* etc.	no reference	
4. Size	L: 17.5 cm, H: 25 cm	
5. Revival	Karl Stein, May–Sept 1927, copied from an original figure	
6. Mold number	3	

Orders/Deliveries

1. Quantity ordered	18 Nov 1732	12 monkeys, undifferentiated
	17 Dec 1732	12 monkeys, undifferentiated
	26 Nov 1733	26 monkeys, undifferentiated
	18 Feb 1735	12 monkeys, undifferentiated
	9 Mar 1736	12 monkeys, undifferentiated
2. Information on production	13 Dec 1731	9 monkeys of various kinds finished at manufactory, 3 small monkeys (marmosets?) finished at manufactory, 3 monkeys of various kinds unfired at manufactory
	18 Aug 1732	11 monkeys of various kinds finished at manufactory, 5 of which enameled
	Mar 1735	1 monkey finished at manufactory, according to firing report
3. Deliveries	1731/1732	3 large monkeys of various kinds, white; 6 small monkeys, 17 various monkeys, enameled
	5 Mar – 17 Dec 1735	1 monkey
4. Historical price	86 talers 12 groschen ("Affe")	

Historical inventory number

N = 162-W [1770 and 1779 inventories] "one of the same [= monkey] very small, on a pedestal, defective"

Holdings

1. Quantities	a) Japanese Palace:	
	17 Dec 1732	12 monkeys, undifferentiated
	18 Feb 1735	26 monkeys, undifferentiated
	9 Mar 1736	27 monkeys, undifferentiated
	Inv. 1770	1
	Inv. 1779	1
	b) Royal Collection 1900:	
	1 enameled marmoset	
2. Sales/losses	no definite references	
3. Present-day holdings	Dresden Porcelain Collection 1 enameled marmoset as in illustration; and some further copies[30]	

Monkey, mother-monkey (macaque)

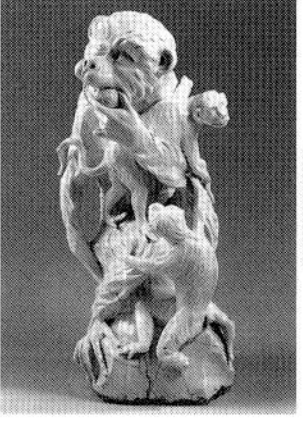

Name

1. Latin name	Macaca

Model

1. Modeler	Johann Gottlieb Kirchner (attributed)
2. Dating	1731 (attributed)
3. Work report/*Rapport* etc.	no reference
4. Size	L: 34 cm, H: 58 cm
5. Revival	Karl Theodor Eichler, 1927, copied from an original figure
6. Mold number	with one young: 23 with two young: 22

Orders/Deliveries

1. Quantity ordered	18 Nov 1732	12 monkeys, undifferentiated
	17 Dec 1732	12 monkeys, undifferentiated
	26 Nov 1733	26 monkeys, undifferentiated
	18 Feb 1735	12 monkeys, undifferentiated
	9 Mar 1736	12 monkeys, undifferentiated
2. Information on production	13 Dec 1731	9 monkeys of various kinds finished at manufactory, 3 small monkeys (marmosets?) finished at manufactory, 3 monkeys of various kinds unfired at manufactory
	18 Aug 1732	11 monkeys of various kinds finished at manufactory, 5 of which enameled
	Mar 1735	1 monkey finished at manufactory, according to firing report
3. Deliveries	1731/1732	3 large monkeys of various kinds, white 6 small monkeys, white 17 various enameled monkeys
	5 Mar – 17 Dec 1735	1 monkey
4. Historical price	86 talers 12 groschen ("Affe")	

Historical inventory number

N = 159-W [1770 and 1779 inventories] "five large monkeys with young, white, all defective"

Holdings

1. Quantities	a) Japanese Palace	
	17 Dec 1732	12 monkeys, undifferentiated

	18 Feb 1735	26 monkeys, undifferentiated
	9 Mar 1736	27 monkeys, undifferentiated
	Inv. 1770	5
	Inv. 1779	5
	b) Royal Collection 1900:	
	3 white mother-monkeys	
2. Sales/losses	no reference	
3. Present-day holdings	Dresden Porcelain Collection 3 mother-monkeys, white	

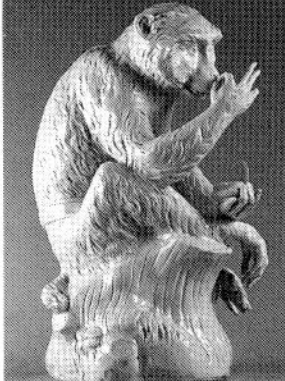

Monkey, taking snuff (macaque)

Name

1. Latin name	Macaca

Model

1. Modeler	Johann Joachim Kaendler (attributed)
2. Dating	Feb 1732 (attributed)
3. Work report/*Rapport* etc.	*Rapport* Feb 1732: "Modeler Kaendler also . . . modeled . . . a large monkey of a special kind."[31] (cf. Monkey with chain/grape)
4. Size	L: 31 cm, H: 48 cm
5. Revival	Erich Oehme, Nov 1926 – Feb 1927, copied from an original figure
6. Mold number	85

Orders/Deliveries

1. Quantity ordered	18 Nov 1732	12 monkeys, undifferentiated
	17 Dec 1732	12 monkeys, undifferentiated
	26 Nov 1733	26 monkeys, undifferentiated
	18 Feb 1735	12 monkeys, undifferentiated
	9 Mar 1736	12 monkeys, undifferentiated
2. Information on production	13 Dec 1731	9 monkeys of various kinds finished at manufactory, 3 small monkeys (marmosets?) finished at manufactory, 3 monkeys of various kinds unfired at manufactory
	18 Aug 1732	11 monkeys of various kinds finished at manufactory, 5 of which enameled
	Mar 1735	1 monkey finished at manufactory, according to firing report
3. Deliveries	1731/1732	3 large monkeys of various kinds, white 6 small monkeys, white 17 various enameled monkeys
	5 Mar – 17 Dec 1735	1 monkey
4. Historical price	86 talers 12 groschen ("Affe")	

Historical inventory number

N = 160-W [1770 and 1779 inventories] "four of the same [= large monkeys, white] without young, all damaged"

Holdings

1. Quantities	a) Japanese Palace:	
	17 Dec 1732	12 monkeys, undifferentiated
	18 Feb 1735	26 monkeys, undifferentiated
	9 Mar 1736	27 monkeys, undifferentiated
	Inv. 1770	4 monkeys (taking snuff?)
	Inv. 1779	4 monkeys (taking snuff?)
	b) Royal Collection 1900:	
	1 monkey taking snuff, white	
	1 monkey taking snuff, enameled	
2. Sales/losses	17. 4. 1849	to Teichert (branch of the manufactory) 1 monkey (taking snuff)
3. Present-day holdings	Dresden Porcelain Collection 1 monkey taking snuff, white	
	Amsterdam, Rijksmuseum 1 monkey taking snuff, enameled	

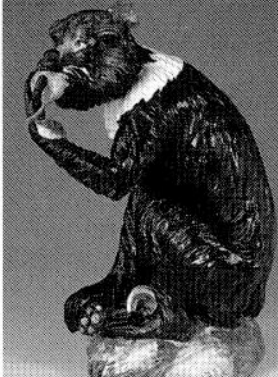

Monkey, wearing a ruff

Name

1. Latin name	Symphalangus syndactylus (siamang gibbon)

Model

1. Modeler	Johann Gottlieb Kirchner (attributed)
2. Dating	1731 (attributed)
3. Work report/*Rapport* etc.	no reference
4. Size	L: 34 cm, H: 39 cm
5. Revival	Herbert Hanke/Karl Theodor Eichler, Jan 1936, copied from a figure from Paris
6. Mold number	28

Orders/Deliveries

1. Quantity ordered	18 Nov 1732	12 monkeys, undifferentiated
	17 Dec 1732	12 monkeys, undifferentiated
	26 Nov 1733	26 monkeys, undifferentiated
	18 Feb 1735	12 monkeys, undifferentiated
	9 Mar 1736	12 monkeys, undifferentiated
2. Information on production	13 Dec 1731	9 monkeys of various kinds finished at manufactory, 3 small monkeys (marmosets?) finished at manufactory, 3 monkeys of various kinds unfired at manufactory
	18 Aug 1732	11 monkeys of various kinds finished at manufactory, 5 of which enameled
	Mar 1735	1 monkey finished at manufactory, according to firing report
3. Deliveries	1731/1732	3 white large monkeys of various kinds, 6 small monkeys, white 17 various monkeys, enameled
	5 Mar – 17 Dec 1735 1 monkey	
4. Historical price	86 talers 12 groschen ("Affe")	

Historical inventory number

N = 161-W [1770 and 1779 inventories] "six of the same [= large monkeys, white] in various postures 17 and 21 inches ["Zoll"] high"
[on grounds of size probably Monkey wearing a ruff, and Monkey with chain/grape]

Holdings

1. Quantities	a) Japanese Palace:	
	17 Dec 1732	12 monkeys, undifferentiated
	18 Feb 1735	26 monkeys, undifferentiated
	9 Mar 1736	27 monkeys, undifferentiated
	Inv. 1770	6 monkeys (with chain/grape and with ruff)
	Inv. 1779	6 monkeys (with chain/grape and with ruff)
	b) Royal Collection 1900:	
	1 monkey wearing a ruff, white 1 monkey wearing a ruff, enameled	
2. Sales/losses	no definite references	
3. Present-day holdings	Dresden Porcelain Collection 1 white, 1 enameled (war loss)[32]	
	Amsterdam, Rijksmuseum 1 monkey wearing a ruff, enameled	
	Pittsburgh, Carnegie Museum of Art 1 monkey wearing a ruff, enameled	
	Geneva, Musée Ariana, Schmidheiny Collection 1 monkey wearing a ruff, enameled	

Monkey, with chain/grape (macaque)

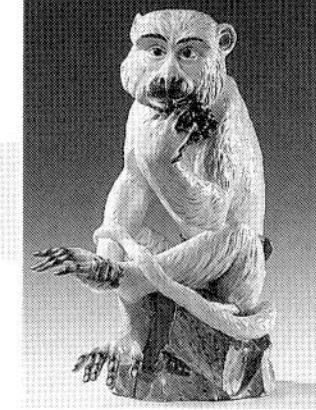

Name

1. Latin name	Macaca

Model

1. Modeler	Johann Joachim Kaendler (attributed)
2. Dating	Feb 1732 (attributed)
3. Work report/*Rapport* etc.	*Rapport* Feb 1732: "Modeler Kaendler also . . . modeled . . . a large monkey of a special kind"[33] (cf. Monkey taking snuff)
4. Size	L: 32 cm, H: 47 cm
5. Revival	Erich Oehme, Sept 1920 – Jan 1921, copied from an original figure
6. Mold number	84

Orders/Deliveries

1. Quantity ordered	18 Nov 1732	12 monkeys, undifferentiated
	17 Dec 1732	12 monkeys, undifferentiated
	26 Nov 1733	26 monkeys, undifferentiated
	18 Feb 1735	12 monkeys, undifferentiated
	9 Mar 1736	12 monkeys, undifferentiated
2. Information on production	13 Dec 1731	9 monkeys of various kinds finished at manufactory, 3 small monkeys (marmosets?) finished at manufactory, 3 monkeys of various kinds unfired at manufactory
	18 Aug 1732	11 monkeys of various kinds finished at manufactory, 5 of which enameled
	Mar 1735	1 monkey finished at manufactory, according to firing report
3. Deliveries	1731/1732	3 large monkeys of various kinds, white 6 small monkeys, white 17 various monkeys, enameled
	5 Mar-17 Dec 1735 1 monkey	
4. Historical price	86 talers 12 groschen ("Affe")	

Historical inventory number

N = 161-W [1770 and 1779 inventories] "six of the same [= large monkeys, white] in various postures 17 and 21 inches ["Zoll"] high"
[on grounds of size probably Monkey wearing a ruff, and Monkey with chain/grape]

Holdings

1. Quantities	a) Japanese Palace:	
	17 Dec 1732	12 monkeys, undifferentiated
	18 Feb 1735	26 monkeys, undifferentiated
	9 Mar 1736	27 monkeys, undifferentiated
	Inv. 1770	6 monkeys (with chain/grape, and with ruff?)
	Inv. 1779	6 monkeys (with chain/grape, and with ruff?)
	b) Royal Collection 1900:	
	5 enameled monkeys with grapes (?)[34]	
2. Sales/losses	1920	Lepke 1 monkey with chain, enameled
3. Present-day holdings	Monkey with grape Dresden Porcelain Collection 1 enameled	
	Monkey with chain Dresden Porcelain Collection 1 enameled (now lost in war)[35]	
	Lepke 1920, then Amsterdam, Rijksmuseum 1 enameled (same model, but without chain)	

Panther

Name

1. Latin name	Panthera pardus melas

Orders/Deliveries

1. Quantity ordered	18 Nov 1732	4
	26 Nov 1733	8
	18 Feb 1735	4
	9 Mar 1736	4
2. Information on production	Order not carried out	

Porcupine

Name

1. Latin name	Hystrix africaeaustralis

Orders/Deliveries

1. Quantity ordered	18 Nov 1732	4
	17 Dec 1732	8
	26 Nov 1733	8
	18 Feb 1735	4
	9 Mar 1736	4
2. Information on production	Order not carried out	
3. Work report/*Rapport* etc.	work report July 1734 (bozzetto only): "Specification of the foreign animals and exotic birds which . . . I, as named below, modeled and drew exactly and correctly, so that they . . . may here at the Royal Porcelain Factory be done large . . . In the Lion-House I made a model of . . . a porcupine, JJ Kändler"[36]	

Rhinoceros

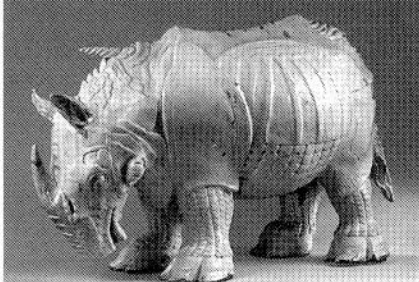

Name

1. Historical name	*Rinoceros, Rhenocerus, Renoceri, Reinocerus, Rheinoceros*
2. Latin name	Rhinoceros unicornis

Model

1. Modeler	Johann Gottlieb Kirchner (attributed)
2. Dating	Dec 1731 (proven)
3. Work report/*Rapport* etc.	*Rapport* Feb 1732: "A number of rhinoceros figures have now been made in paste"[37]
4. Size	L: 109.5 cm, H: 68 cm
5. Revival	Karl Stein, May – Sept 1921, copied from an original figure
6. Mold number	44
7. Source of inspiration	most probably: Boreman, Thomas: *Three-hundred animals*. Glasgow 1730 (in the tradition of Albrecht Dürer's woodcut)

Orders/Deliveries

1. Quantity ordered	18 Nov 1732	4
	17 Dec 1732	8
	26 Nov 1733	8
	18 Feb 1735	4
	9 Mar 1736	4
2. Information on production	13 Dec 1731	clay model finished at manufactory
	18 Aug 1732	2 unfired at manufactory
	17 Dec 1732	1 in production at manufactory
3. Deliveries	1734	4
4. Historical price	172 talers	

Historical inventory number

	N = 256-W [1770 and 1779 inventories] "four rhinoceroses with brown and white patches, damaged"

Holdings

1. Quantities	a) Japanese Palace:	
	17 Dec 1732	no reference
	18 Feb 1735	4
	9 Mar 1736	4
	Inv. 1770	4
	Inv. 1779	4
	b) Royal Collection 1900:	
	2 white 1 lacquered	
2. Sales/losses	1836	exchange Sèvres The lacquered figure was offered at Lepke's in 1920 but was not sold.
3. Present-day holdings	Dresden Porcelain Collection 2 white 1 lacquered	
	Sèvres, Musée National de Céramique 1 white	

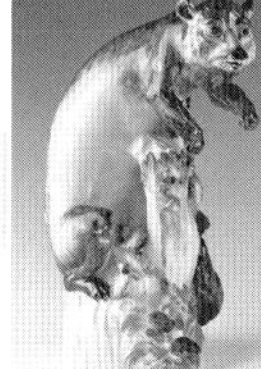

Sable

Name

1. Historical name	*Zobel, indianisches Zobel*
2. Latin name	Martes zibellina

Model

1. Modeler	Johann Joachim Kaendler (proven)
2. Dating	Apr 1735 (proven)
3. Work report/*Rapport* etc.	work report July 1734 (bozzetto only): "Specification of the foreign animals and exotic birds which . . . I, as named below, modeled and drew exactly and correctly, so that they . . . may here at the Royal Porcelain Factory be done large . . . In the *Kunstkammer*, from the stuffed animals, I made models of . . . a sable, JJ Kändler"[38] work report Apr 1735: "Likewise, an Indian sable has been done life-size, sitting on a tree-stump which is overgrown with branches and leaves, Johann Joachim Kändler"[39]
4. Size	L: 30 cm, H: 40 cm
5. Revival	Karl Stein, Jan – Feb 1915
6. Mold number	141
7. Source of inspiration	stuffed specimen

Orders/Deliveries

1. Quantity ordered	18 Nov 1732	2
	17 Dec 1732	4
	26 Nov 1733	8
	18 Feb 1735	2
	9 Mar 1736	2
2. Information on production	June 1735	2 finished at manufactory, according to firing report
	Aug 1735	2 finished at manufactory, according to firing report
3. Deliveries	July 1735	2 enameled
	Sept 1735	4 enameled
4. Historical price	48 talers 20 groschen	

Historical inventory number

	N = 307-W [1770 and 1779 inventories] "three figures of a sable, sitting on a pedestal covered with foliage, colored flowers and other embellishments"

Holdings

1. Quantities	a) Japanese Palace:	
	9 Mar 1736	6
	Inv. 1770	3
	Inv. 1779	3
	b) Royal Collection 1900:	
	2 enameled	
2. Sales/losses	1919	Lepke 1
3. Present-day holdings	Dresden Porcelain Collection 1 enameled	
	in a private collection in Munich 1 enameled	

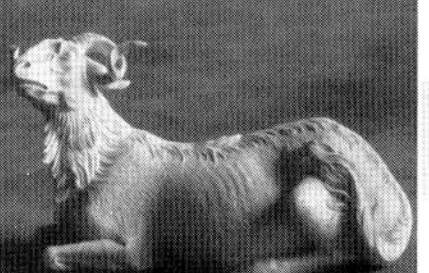

Scapegoat

Name

1. Historical name	*Versühnbock* ("goat of atonement")

Model

1. Modeler	Johann Joachim Kaendler (proven)

2. Dating	Jan 1735 (proven)
3. Work report/*Rapport* etc.	work report July 1734 (bozzetto only): "Specification of the foreign animals and exotic birds which . . . I, as named below, modeled and drew exactly and correctly, so that they . . . may here at the Royal Porcelain Factory be done large . . . . . . In the *Kunstkammer*, from the stuffed animals, I made models of . . . a goat of atonement or scapegoat, such as the Jews have, JJ Kändler"[40] work report Jan 1735: "A large piece done for the Palace, known as the Goat of Atonement or Scapegoat, modeled in clay in accordance with its wondrous appearance and kind, and in its natural size, Johann Joachim Kändler"[41]
4. Size	L: 49 cm
5. Revival	Karl Stein, Oct – Nov 1922, set of molds completed
6. Mold number	133
7. Source of inspiration	stuffed specimen

Orders/Deliveries

1. Quantity ordered	no reference	
2. Information on production	July 1735	1 finished at manufactory, according to firing report
3. Deliveries	no reference	
4. Historical price	no reference	

Holdings

1. Quantities	a) Japanese Palace:
	no reference
2. Sales/losses	no reference
3. Present-day holdings	Meissen, Museum Schauhalle 1 new execution of 1922

Sheep

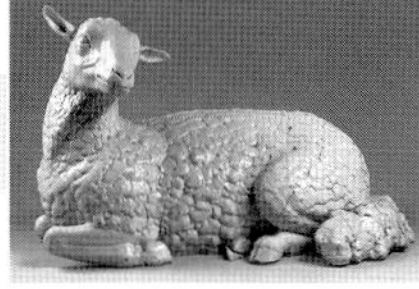

Note

In August 1735 Eberlein stated that he was working on a larger-than-life model of a sheep, and described as life-size the model that we now know to have been made shortly before. The larger-than-life model possibly never went into production.

Name

1. Latin name	Ovis ammon

Model

1. Modeler	Johann Friedrich Eberlein (proven)
2. Dating	June – July 1735 (proven)
3. Work report/*Rapport* etc.	work report July 1735: "A sheep, life-size and in clay, Johann Friedrich Eberlein, sculptor"[42] work report Aug 1735: "A sheep, all in clay and larger than life, Johann Friedrich Eberlein, sculptor"[43] work report Sept 1735: "Did a large sheep in paste, Johann Friedrich Eberlein, sculptor"[44] work report Oct 1735: "Did a large sheep in paste, Johann Friedrich Eberlein, sculptor"[45]
4. Size	L: 63 cm, H: 41 cm
5. Revival	Karl Stein, Dec 1922 – Apr 1923, copied from an original figure
6. Mold number	135

Orders/Deliveries

1. Quantity ordered	18 Nov 1732	4
	17 Dec 1732	8
	26 Nov 1733	8
	18 Feb 1735	4
	9 Mar 1736	4
2. Information on production	Nov 1735	1 finished at manufactory, according to firing report
	Jan 1736	1 finished at manufactory, according to firing report
	Mar 1736	1 finished at manufactory, according to firing report
	May 1736	1 finished at manufactory, according to firing report
3. Deliveries	Mar 1736	1 according to firing report
4. Historical price	27 talers (for a damaged figure, delivered)	

Historical inventory number

N = 348-W [1770 and 1779 inventories]
"one sheep, lying down, defective"

Holdings

1. Quantities	a) Japanese Palace:	
	9 Mar 1736	2 probably meaning one normal sheep and one exotic ("Indian") sheep
	Inv. 1770	1
	Inv. 1779	1
	b) Royal Collection 1900:	
	1 white	
2. Sales/losses	no reference	
3. Present-day holdings	Dresden Porcelain Collection 1 white	

Sheep ("Exotic Sheep")

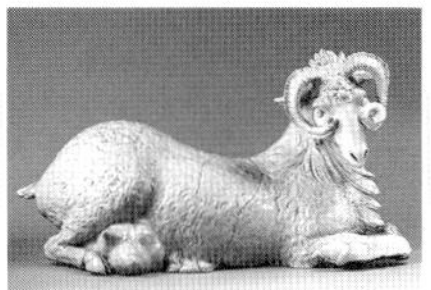

Note

The figure is the female counterpart of the Scapegoat ("goat of atonement").

Name

1. Historical name	*orientalisches Schaf, afrikanisches Schaf*

Model

1. Modeler	Johann Joachim Kaendler (proven)
2. Dating	Dec 1734 (proven)
3. Work report/*Rapport* etc.	work report July 1734 (bozzetto only): "Specification of the foreign animals and exotic birds which . . . I, as named below, modeled and drew exactly and correctly, so that they . . . may here at the Royal Porcelain Factory be done large . . . In the *Kunstkammer*, from the stuffed animals, I made models of . . . an Indian sheep, JJ Kändler"[46]
	work report Dec 1734: "A large Indian sheep with two horns growing most wondrously over the creature's eyes, Johann Joachim Kändler"[47]
4. Size	L: 92 cm, H: 48.2 cm
5. Revival	Karl Stein, May – Nov 1923, copied after an original figure
6. Mold number	130
7. Source of inspiration	stuffed specimen

Orders/Deliveries

1. Quantity ordered	26 Nov 1733	8 African sheep
2. Information on production	Mar 1735	1 oriental sheep finished at manufactory, according to firing report
3. Deliveries	Sept 1735	1 Indian sheep, enameled [most likely meaning painted with cold colors]
	1735	altogether 1 Indian sheep
4. Historical price	131 talers	

Historical inventory number

N = 308-W [1770 and 1779 inventories]
"an Indian sheep, lying down, painted brown, damaged and with large fire-cracks on the underside"

Holdings

1. Quantities	a) Japanese Palace:	
	9 Mar 1736	see note under Sheep
	Inv. 1770	1
	Inv. 1779	1
	b) Royal Collection 1900:	
	1 white (but referred to as a ram)	
2. Sales/losses	no reference	
3. Present-day holdings	Dresden Porcelain Collection 1 white	

Sphinx

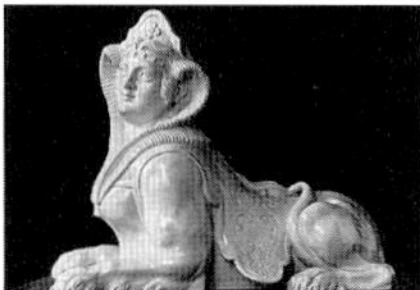

Note

The Dresden Porcelain Collection possesses one large sphinx and a number of small ones. When Kirchner refers to a sphinx in his work report, he is certainly talking about the large model, but the inventory of the Japanese Palace only mentions small ones. Siegfried Asche attributed the larger model, on account of stylistic features, to Christian Kirchner, Johann Gottlieb's brother (Asche 1970), explaining that as the former died in Dresden in 1732, all Johann Gottlieb did was to modify and prepare it for realization in porcelain.

Name

1. Historical name	*Sfinxe, Spinxhe, Spinxe*

Model

1. Modeler	large: Christian and und Johann Gottlieb Kirchner (attributed)
2. Dating	large: most likely after Oct 1732
	most likely small: before Dec 1731 (proven)
3. Work report/*Rapport* etc.	work report J. G. Kirchner Oct 1732: "Modified two sphinxes = large, Gottlieb Kirchner"[48]
4. Size	large: L: 58.5 cm, H: 51 cm
	small: H: 21
5. Revival	large: Karl Stein, 1926, copied (then mold no. 137)
	large: Karl Stein, June – Aug 1926, copied (then mold no. 142)
6. Mold number	B 147 (previously 137; looking to the left)
	B 148 (previously 142; looking to the right)

Orders/Deliveries

1. Quantity ordered	18 Nov 1732	4
	17 Dec 1732	8
	26 Nov 1733	8
	18 Feb 1735	4
	9 Mar 1736	4

2. Information on production	13 Dec 1731	4 finished at manufactory, most likely small ones 5 unfired in manufactory, most likely small ones
	17 Dec 1732	4 in production at manufactory, most likely large ones
	Oct 1735	1 finished at manufactory, according to firing report, most likely small
	May 1736	1 finished at manufactory, according to firing report, most likely small
3. Deliveries	1731/1732	5 most likely small
	5 Mar – 17 Dec 1735	8, from the price small ones
4. Historical price	16 talers 8 groschen (those delivered in 1735)	

Historical inventory number

N = 311-W [Tower Room inventory 1769] "four lying sphinxes, half man and half dog with green coverings, and gilded decorations in enamel colors" [= small sphinxes]

[1770 and 1779 inventories] "four lying sphinxes, half man and half dog with green coverings, and gilded decorations in enamel colors, with fire-cracks" [= small sphinxes]

Holdings

1. Quantities	a) Japanese Palace:	
	18 Feb 1735	8 without size (most likely small)
	9 Mar 1736	10 without size (most likely small)
	Tower Room Inv. 1769	4 small ones
	Inv. 1770	4 small ones
	Inv. 1779	4 small ones
	b) Royal Collection 1900:	
	no reference	
2. Sales/losses	no reference	
3. Present-day holdings	Dresden Porcelain Collection 1 large, white, looking to the right (small Sphinx: no record made)	

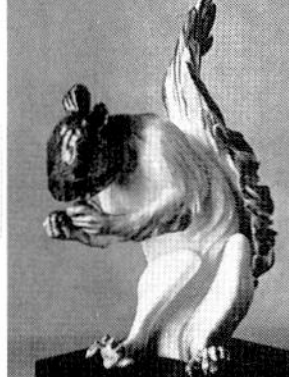

Squirrel (also as teapot)

Note

This model went into production a number of times in the period of the Japanese Palace order, both as a figure (produced as a matching pair) and also in the form of a teapot. But as squirrels were in 1734 already being delivered to the Palace as teapots, and Kaendler also refers to another such model in his work report for May 1735, it is not possible to distinguish the various versions with any degree of certainty in the sources.

Name

1. Historical name	*Eichhörnigen*
2. Latin name	Sciurus vulgaris

Model

1. Modeler	figure: Johann Joachim Kaendler (proven) teapot: Johann Joachim Kaendler (proven)
2. Dating	figure: Aug 1732 (proven) teapot: probably 1734 (see Note) teapot: May 1735 (proven)
3. Work report/*Rapport* etc.	Figure: *Rapport* Aug 1732: "The modeler Kaendler, for his part, has modeled and made ready . . . two squirrels"[49] teapot: work report May 1735: "A squirrel in the form of a teapot, done with two different tails: in one case, the tea is poured through the tail, and in the other the tea is poured where the squirrel has a ribbon with little bells on it around its neck, Johann Joachim Kändler"[50]
4. Size	H: 21.5 cm H: 14.5 cm (teapot)
5. Revival	no reference
6. Mold number	not recorded

Orders/Deliveries

1. Quantity ordered	18 Nov 1732	2
	17 Dec 1732	8
	26 Nov 1733	4
	18 Feb 1735	2
	9 Mar 1736	2
2. Information on production	no reference	
3. Deliveries	1732	2 enameled
	1734	2 as teapots
4. Historical price	teapot: 4 talers	

Historical inventory number

figure:	N = 194-W [1770 and 1779 inventories] "a squirrel"
teapot:	N = 263-W [1770 inventory] "a squirrel, made so that it can be used as a teapot [added later:] broken"

Holdings

1. Quantities	a) Japanese Palace:	
	17 Dec 1732	2
	18 Feb 1735	4 two as teapots
	9 Mar 1736	4 two as teapots
	Inv. 1770	1 1 as a teapot
	Inv. 1779	1
	b) Royal Collection 1900:	
	1 enameled	
2. Sales/losses	no reference	
3. Present-day holdings	not recorded	

Stag

Name

1. Latin name	Cervus elaphus

Orders/Deliveries

1. Quantity ordered	18 Nov 1732	4
	17 Dec 1732	8
	26 Nov 1733	8
	18 Feb 1735	4
	9 Mar 1736	4
2. Information on production	Order not carried out	

Tiger

Name

1. Latin name	Panthera tigris

Model

See Lioness (sitting).

Orders/Deliveries

1. Quantity ordered	18 Nov 1732	4
	17 Dec 1732	8
	26 Nov 1733	8
	18 Feb 1735	4
	9 Mar 1736	4

2. Work report/*Rapport* etc.	work report July 1734 (bozzetto only): "Specification of the foreign animals and exotic birds which . . . I, as named below, modeled and drew exactly and correctly, so that they . . . may here at the Royal Porcelain Factory be done large . . . In the Lion-House I made a model of . . . a tiger, JJ Kändler"[51]

Unicorn

Orders/Deliveries

1. Quantity ordered	26 Nov 1733	4
2. Information on production	Order not carried out	

Wisent Fighting with a Boar

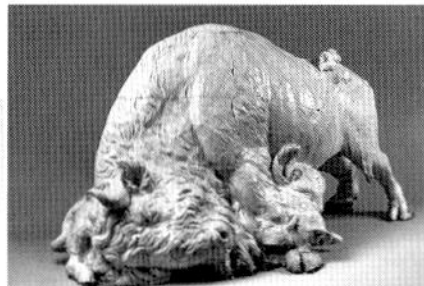

Name

1. Historical name	*Auer Thier* (aurochs)
2. Latin name	bison: Bison bonasus (wisent, or European bison) boar: Sus scrofa [aurochs: Bos taurus primigenius]

Model

1. Modeler	Johann Joachim Kaendler (proven)
2. Dating	Oct 1731 (proven)
3. Work report/*Rapport* etc.	work report June – Oct 1731: "At present being worked upon . . . an aurochs [= wisent] killing a wild boar"[52] *Rapport* Oct 1731: "recently . . . an aurochs of considerable size has been modeled, from which plaster molds are to be made in the days to come"[53] *Rapport* Sept/Oct 1734: "Modellmeister Kaendler claims, rightly, that in the year 1731 he, by order of a superior authority, had to do a drawing, from life, of an aurochs in Moritzburg"[54]
4. Size	L: 104 cm, H: 62 cm
5. Revival	Karl Stein, Aug to Dec 1920, set of molds completed from an original figure
6. Mold number	43
7. Source of inspiration	live specimen

Orders/Deliveries

1. Quantity ordered	18. Nov 1732	4
17 Dec 1732	8	
	26 Nov 1733	8
	18 Feb 1735	4
	9 Mar 1736	4
2. Information on production	13 Dec 1731	1 clay model at manufactory
	18 Aug 1732	1 low-fired at manufactory
	17 Dec 1732	2 being worked on at manufactory
3. Deliveries	1734	2
4. Historical price	265 talers	

Historical inventory number

N = 259-W [1770 and 1779 inventories] "two figures of an aurochs fighting with a wild boar"

Holdings

1. Quantities	a) Japanese Palace:	
	17 Dec 1732	no reference
	18 Feb 1735	2
	9 Mar 1736	2
	Inv. 1770	2
	Inv. 1779	2
	b) Royal Collection 1900:	
	2 white	
2. Sales/losses	no reference	
3. Present-day holdings	Dresden Porcelain Collection 1 white, assembled from the two defective figures after the Second World War (see Seyffarth 1959)	

Wolf (She-Wolf)

Name

1. Latin name	Canis lupus

Model

1. Modeler	Johann Joachim Kaendler (proven)
2. Dating	Apr 1735 (proven)
3. Work report/*Rapport* etc.	work report Apr 1735: "Another large piece for the Palace, this time a life-size she-wolf sitting on her hind legs, and holding her head up high as if howling so that one can see her fangs quite clearly in her mouth. She has two cubs sitting underneath her, one somewhat larger than the other, mainly done to stabilize the figure in the firing, Johann Joachim Kändler"[55]
4. Size	L: 44 cm, H: 66 cm
5. Revival	Karl Stein, July – Aug 1919, work begun but workpiece lost in war
6. Mold number	145

Orders/Deliveries

1. Quantity ordered	18 Nov 1732	4
	17 Dec 1732	4
	26 Nov 1733	8
	18 Feb 1735	4
	9 Mar 1736	4
2. Information on production	July 1735	1 finished at manufactory, according to firing report
	Aug 1735	1 finished at manufactory, according to firing report
	Sept 1735	2 finished at manufactory, according to firing report
	Oct 1735	1 finished at manufactory, according to firing report
	Jan 1736	1 finished at manufactory, according to firing report
3. Deliveries	Sept 1735	1 enameled [most likely meaning painted with cold colors]
	Mar 1736	4
4. Historical price	92 talers 8 groschen	

Historical inventory number

N = 345-W [1770 and 1779 inventories] "a she-wolf with two young sucklings"

N = 346-W [1770 and 1779 inventories] "four of the same, of the same height"

Holdings

1. Quantities	a) Japanese Palace:	
	9 Mar 1736	5
	Inv. 1770	5
	Inv. 1779	5
	b) Royal Collection 1900:	
	no reference	
2. Sales/losses	8 Jan 1851	to Helena Wolfssohn 1
3. Present-day holdings	Dresden Porcelain Collection 1 white 2 lacquered 1 with remains of lacquer, in pieces	
	Turin, Museo Civico 1 white	

Zebra

Name

1. Historical name	*Africanischer Esel*
2. Latin name	Equus quagga

Orders/Deliveries

1. Quantity ordered	18 Nov 1732	4
	17 Dec 1732	8
	26 Nov 1733	8
	18 Feb 1735	4
	9 Mar 1736	4
2. Information on production	Order not carried out	
3. Work report/*Rapport* etc.	work report July 1734 (bozzetto only): "Specification of the foreign animals and exotic birds which . . . I, as named below, modeled and drew exactly and correctly, so that they . . . may here at the Royal Porcelain Factory be done large . . . In the *Kunstkammer*, from the stuffed animals, I made models of . . . an African donkey ["Africanischer Esel"], JJ Kändler"[56]	

II. Birds

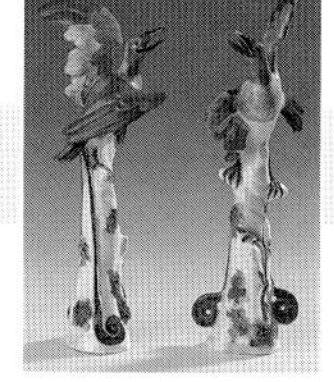

Bird of Paradise

Name

1. Latin name	Cicinnurus regius

Model

1. Modeler	Johann Joachim Kaendler (proven)
2. Dating	Jan 1733 (proven)
3. Work report/*Rapport* etc.	work report Jan 1733: "In the month of January 1733 the following new models were made ready . . . another small bird the size of a finch. It has two large and two small wings, and a long beak, and its tail consists of two long feathers which turn into a double ring at the end, Kändler"[57]
	work report July 1734: "Specification of the foreign animals and exotic birds which . . . I, as named below, modeled and drew exactly and correctly, so that they . . . may here at the Royal Porcelain Factory be done large . . . birds which are to be seen stuffed in the *Kunstkammer* and of which I made drawings . . . a bird of paradise . . . JJ Kändler"[58]
4. Size	H: 37.5 cm (Inv. no. N = 280-W)
	H: 32 cm (Inv. no. N = 318-W)
5. Revival	without name, Apr 1911
6. Mold number	39 x

Orders/Deliveries

1. Quantity ordered	no reference	
2. Information on production		no reference
3. Deliveries	1734	13
	5 Mar – 17 Dec 1735	4
4. Historical price	4 talers 8 groschen (delivery 1734)	
	4 talers 12 groschen (delivery 1735)	

Historical inventory number

N = 280-W [1770 and 1779 inventories] "twelve birds of paradise on high pedestals decorated with leaves, mostly defective"

N = 318-W [1770 and 1779 inventories] "four colored birds of paradise, on high decorated pedestals, all defective"

Holdings

1. Quantities	a) Japanese Palace:	
	18 Feb 1735	17
	9 Mar 1736	17
	Inv. 1770	16
	Inv. 1779	16
	b) Royal Collection 1900:	
	no reference	
2. Sales/losses	no reference	
3. Present-day holdings	no record made	

Bird with high pedestal/Indian bird

Note

The figures referred to by these names cannot be identified with certainty. Of all the models with a bird on a high pedestal with an overall height of about 75 cm (measurement quoted in the inventory), it is the Golden Pheasant which comes closest to the description, but in 1735 there were only four examples of this model in the Palace, which does not fit in with the seven birds on high pedestals recorded as being delivered in 1733/34. However, as no golden pheasant can be identified for certain in the Palace inventory, it could be that when the compiler made the entry "two birds on high pedestals" (Inv. no. N = 166-W) he was referring to two golden pheasants. As this is no more than speculation, the figures referred to with this expression are treated separately here. "Indian bird" could have referred to more or less any exotic bird, which is why the numerical statistics related to this term of reference are recorded here rather than being included in any specific catalog entry.

Name

1. Historical name	also: *Vögel auf hohem Podest* ("birds on high pedestals")

Model

1. Size	H: 74.5 cm (according to the 1770 inventory)

Orders/Deliveries

1. Quantity ordered	not ordered under this name; see Note	
2. Deliveries	1733	6 Indian birds on high pedestals
	7 Mar 1733 – 22 Oct 1734	7 birds on high pedestals 6 Indian birds
	Feb 1735	6 Indian birds

Historical inventory number

N = 166-W [1770 inventory] "two birds of prey, on pedestals one ell high, [later corrected to:] two birds on high pedestals, 1 ell 7 1/2 inches high"

[1779 inventory] "two birds on high pedestals, one ell high"[59]

Holdings

1. Quantities	a) Japanese Palace:	
	Inv. 1770	2
	Inv. 1779	2

Bird's nest

Note

There was never an order for a bird's nest as such and this term of reference only appears in one delivery list and two lists of figures delivered. It cannot refer to the canaries with nests as they are also referred to expressly in the same lists. The fact of the low price means that it cannot have been the dove with nest. It is thus not at all clear what figure was meant.

Orders/Deliveries

1. Quantity ordered	no reference	
2. Deliveries	1734	6
3. Historical price	4 talers	

Holdings

1. Quantities	a) Japanese Palace:	
	18 Feb 1735	6
	9 Mar 1736	6
	Inv. 1770	no reference
	Inv. 1779	no reference
	b) Royal Collection 1900:	
	no reference	
2. Present-day holdings	no record made	

Birds of Prey

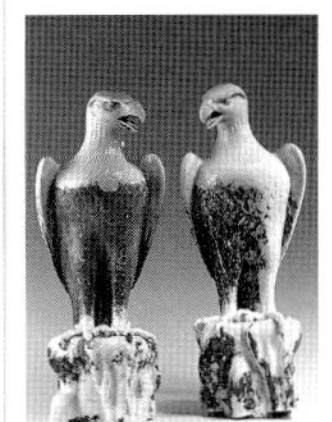
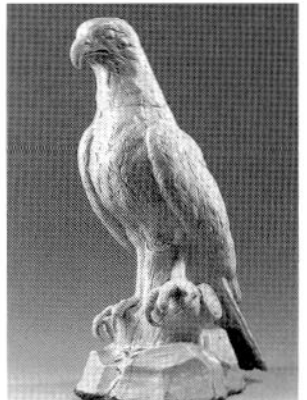
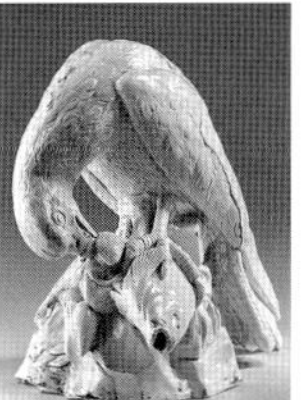
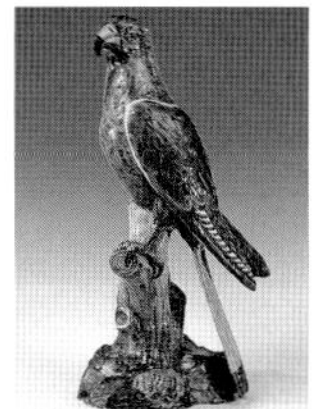

Note

As with the monkeys and parrots, the student of certain bird of prey figures is faced with the problem of ambiguous nomenclature in the sources, where they were often simply gathered under such collective terms as "birds of prey." Study of the extant figures makes it clear that the following figures fell into this category:

Eagle, copy of Japanese original
Osprey, sitting
Osprey, with carp
Kestrel ("Falke")

The terminology is often confusing and inconsistent. For instance, certain lists have references to deliveries of "Falken" (falcons), but when the Japanese Palace inventory says "Falken" it is quite clearly referring to the eagle copied from a Japanese original. Examination of the sources also throws up further expressions which must refer to figures from this group but cannot be narrowed down any further than that, such as:

"Raubvogel" (bird of prey)
"Indianischer Raubvogel" ("Indian" bird of prey)

The six "birds of prey" listed in the inventory are the only figures which, on grounds of size, can be identified either as kestrels made from Kaendler's model, or as sitting ospreys. As regards all the further information provided by the sources, there is no option but to record the figures with their historical terms of reference (in inverted commas), and their presumed or definite identification added in brackets.

Name

1. Historical name	*Fischadler: FischAhner* (from "Fischahr")
2. Latin name	osprey: Pandion haliaëtus
	kestrel: Falco tinnunculus

Model

1. Modeler	eagle, copy of Japanese original: Molds taken directly from a Far Eastern original, most likely by George Fritzsche
	osprey, sitting: Johann Joachim Kaendler (proven)
	osprey, with carp: Johann Joachim Kaendler (proven)
	kestrel: Johann Joachim Kaendler (proven)
2. Dating	eagle copied from a Japanese original: c. 1729/30[60]
	osprey, sitting: June – Oct 1731 (proven)
	osprey, with carp: June – Oct 1731 (proven)
	kestrel: June – Oct 1731 (proven)
3. Work report/*Rapport* etc.	eagle, copy of Japanese original: In 1735 Höroldt states, "that a number of years ago, his Royal Majesty gave the factory two Indian eagle figures, not big ones but rather about three quarters of an ell in height, to be copied,"[61]; and on April 7, 1731, "two large eagle figures, enameled," were found when a search was carried out on the house of Count Hoym.[62]
	osprey, sitting: work report June – Oct 1731: "A 'Fischahr' or 'Fischfreßer' one ell high which His Majesty has already received"[63]
	osprey, with carp: work report June – Oct 1731: "Another osprey tearing a carp apart, an impeccable piece of work"[64]
	kestrel: work report June – Oct 1731: "A kestrel, also on a pedestal of which a part has already been finished"[65]
4. Size	eagle, copy of Japanese original: H: 57 cm (Inv. nos. N = 128-W bis N = 130-W) H: 35.5 cm (Inv. no. N = 131-W)
	osprey, sitting: H: 55 cm
	osprey, with carp: H: 37 cm
	kestrel: L: 25 cm, H: 55 cm
5. Revival	eagle, copy of Japanese original: Franz Otto Stange, 1916, copied from an original figure in the museum
	osprey, sitting: no further information
	osprey, with carp: Karl Theodor Eichler, 1924, copied from an original figure
	kestrel: no further information
6. Mold number	eagle, copy of Japanese original: 1
	osprey, sitting: no information
	osprey, with carp: 41
	kestrel: 1773 (?)
7. Source of inspiration	eagle, copy of Japanese original: porcelain figure from Arita
8. Literature	eagle, copy of Japanese original: Baer 1979

Orders/Deliveries

1. Quantity ordered	18 Nov 1732	12 large birds of prey 4 kestrels
	17 Dec 1732	8 large birds of prey 4 kestrels 4 Indian birds of prey
	26 Nov 1733	18 large birds of prey 8 kestrels
	18 Feb 1735	12 large birds of prey 4 kestrels
	9 Mar 1736	12 large birds of prey 4 kestrels
2. Information on production	13 Dec 1731	3 "Fischahr" unfired at manufactory (identifiable as ospreys, sitting), 3 "FischAnher mit dem Karpffen" unfired at manufactory (identifiable as ospreys, with carp), 4 "Falcken" unfired at manufactory (eagle copied from Japanese original?), 1 kestrel, or "Stoßvogel", enameled in manufactory (presumably kestrel)
	18 Aug 1732	8 birds of prey finished at manufactory
	4 Mar 1734	1 "Falcke" lacquered by Reinow (eagle, copy of Japanese original?)

3. Deliveries	1731/1732	12 birds of prey, 6 birds of prey enameled
	5 Mar – 17 Dec 1735	6 kestrels
4. Historical price	no reference	

Historical inventory number

N = 128-W [1770 and 1779 inventories] "two white falcons with black beaks and brown feet, on the same kind of lacquered pedestal, with fire-cracks" [identifiable on grounds of size: eagle, copy of Japanese original]

N = 129-W [1770 and 1779 inventories] "two of the same, with brown coloring and white breasts, have fire-cracks" [identifiable on grounds of size: eagle, copy of Japanese original]

N = 130-W [1770 and 1779 inventories] "two of the same, light brown, defective" [identifiable on grounds of size: eagle copied from a Japanese original]

N = 131-W [1770 and 1779 inventories] "two of the same, even lighter" [identifiable on grounds of size: eagle copied from a Japanese original]

N = 167-W [1770 and 1779 inventories] "six of the same [= birds of prey[66]] 2 lacquered and 4 white, partly defective [identifiable on grounds of size: sitting osprey or kestrel]; [annotation in the 1779 inventory:] one, although its severe fire-cracks had already been filled, broke during transport from R. III to VIII on 15 Jan 1834"

Holdings

1. Quantities	a) Japanese Palace:	
	17 Dec 1732	8 birds of prey 3 kestrels 4 Indian birds of prey
	18 Feb 1735	18 birds of prey 18 kestrels
	9 Mar 1736	18 birds of prey 18 kestrels
	Inv. 1770	8 kestrels (identifiable as eagle copied from a Japanese original) 6 birds of prey (presumably sitting osprey or kestrel)
	Inv. 1779	8 kestrels, lacquered (identifiable as eagle copied from a Japanese original) 6 birds of prey (presumably sitting osprey or kestrel)
	b) Royal Collection 1900:	
	details unclear	
2. Sales/losses	7.7.1853	to Anatol Demidoff 2 kestrels
	1919	Lepke 1 kestrel
3. Present-day holdings	Eagle copied from a Japanese original: Dresden Porcelain Collection 6 (further examples: no record made)	
	osprey, sitting: Dresden Porcelain Collection 1 white	
	Schloss Moritzburg (loan from the Dresden Porcelain Collection) 1 white	
	England, private collection 1 white	
	osprey, with carp: Dresden Porcelain Collection 1 white 1 enameled	
	kestrel: Schloss Moritzburg (loan from the Dresden Porcelain Collection) 1 white	
	Lepke 1919, then Ole Olsen, then Christie's 30. 6.1975, now New York, Pflueger Collection (to go to the Museum of Fine Arts, Boston) 1 white	
	Amsterdam, Rijksmuseum 2 enameled	

Bittern

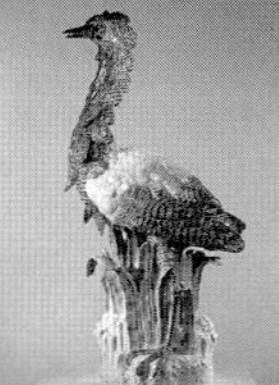

Note

In a small number of cases, it is clear that Kaendler corrected, or changed, the name he used in his reports for an animal or bird figure between making his preliminary study and finishing the model. This is particularly true of animals and birds for which he made bozzetti in Dresden and Moritzburg in July 1734. In the case of the bittern, he might well still have been using the expression "Indian heron" when he saw the stuffed specimen in the *Kunstkammer.*

Name

1. Historical name	*Rohrtummel, indianischer Fischreiher*
2. Latin name	Botaurus stellaris

Model

1. Modeler	Johann Joachim Kaendler (proven)
2. Dating	Mar 1735 (proven)
3. Work report/*Rapport* etc.	(possible reference to the Bittern) work report July 1734: "Specification of the foreign animals and exotic birds which . . . I, as named below, modeled and drew exactly and correctly, so that they . . . may here at the Royal Porcelain Factory be done large . . . birds which are to be seen stuffed in the *Kunstkammer* and of which I made drawings . . . an Indian Heron, JJ Kändler"[67]

	work report Mar 1735: "For the Palace, the bird known as the 'Rohrtummel' [*Rohrdommel*] which is the same size as a heron and on account of its thickly feathered breast and other features is wondrous to behold, done sitting in such reeds, rushes and grass as are wont to grow in ponds, Johann Joachim Kändler"[68]
4. Size	L: 35.5 cm, H: 68 cm
5. Revival	no name, 1907
	Karl Stein, Sept – Nov 1926, completion of the original case-molds
6. Mold number	138
7. Source of inspiration	Stuffed specimen

Orders/Deliveries

1. Quantity ordered	no reference	
2. Information on production	May 1735	3 finished at manufactory
	June 1735	3 finished at manufactory
3. Deliveries	June 1735	1 enameled
	July 1735	5 enameled
4. Historical price	33 talers 6 groschen	

Historical inventory number

N = 324-W [1770 and 1779 inventories] "two bitterns, brown and black on white pedestals decorated with colored rushes, defective"

Holdings

1. Quantities	a) Japanese Palace:	
	9 Mar 1736	6
	Inv. 1770	2
	Inv. 1779	2
	b) Royal Collection 1900:	
	2 enameled	
2. Sales/losses	24 Oct 1931 1 enameled	to Arthur Wittekind
3. Present-day holdings	Dresden Porcelain Collection 1 enameled	
	New York, privately owned 2 enameled	

Bullfinch

Name

1. Historical name	*Gümpel, Grümpel*
2. Latin name	Pyrrhula pyrrhula

Model

1. Modeler	Johann Joachim Kaendler (proven)
2. Dating	Feb 1733 (proven)
3. Work report/*Rapport* etc.	work report Feb 1733: "In the month of February 1733 the following new models were made ready . . . a bullfinch with a little baby bird sitting next to it, Kändler"[69]
4. Size	H: 15 cm
5. Revival	no reference
6. Mold number	no record made

Orders/Deliveries

1. Quantity ordered	no reference	
2. Information on production	no reference	
3. Deliveries	18 Nov 1733	2
	25 Nov 1733	4 enameled
4. Historical price	3 talers 6 groschen	

Historical inventory number

no reference

Holdings

1. Quantities	a) Japanese Palace:	
	18 Feb 1735	6
	9 Mar 1736	6
	Inv. 1770	no reference
	Inv. 1779	no reference
	b) Royal Collection 1900:	
	2 enameled	
2. Sales/losses	no reference	
3. Present-day holdings	no record made	

Bustard

Note

The three realizations of this model delivered in 1731/1732 are listed as herons, but cross-comparison of the production details and quantities delivered makes it clear that they must have been bustards (see Note under "Heron").

Name

1. Latin name	Otis tarda

Model

1. Modeler	Johann Gottlieb Kirchner (proven)
2. Dating	Nov 1732 (proven)
3. Work report/*Rapport* etc.	work report Nov 1732: "A large bird or bustard"[70]
4. Size	L: 45 cm, H: 85 cm
5. Revival	Karl Theodor Eichler, 1928, set of molds completed
6. Mold number	6
	the acorns on the stump of the Peacock, mold no. 50

Orders/Deliveries

1. Quantity ordered	18 Nov 1732	4
	17 Dec 1732	8
	26 Nov 1733	8
	18 Feb 1735	4
	9 Mar 1736	4
2. Information on production	17 Nov 1733	2 enameled [most likely meaning painted with cold colors], at manufactory
3. Deliveries	1731/32	3 enameled [most likely meaning painted with cold colors], referred to as herons
	18 Nov 1733	2 colored
	Aug 1734	1 colored
4. Historical price	99 talers 12 groschen	

Historical inventory number

N = 268-W [1770 and 1779 inventories] "six bustards, variously painted, two are damaged"

Holdings

1. Quantities	a) Japanese Palace:	
	17 Dec 1732	no reference
	18 Feb 1735	6
	9 Mar 1736	6
	Inv. 1770	6
	Inv. 1779	6
	b) Royal Collection 1900:	
	4 white	
2. Sales/losses	7 July 1853	to Anatol Demidoff 1
	1920	Lepke 1
3. Present-day holdings	Dresden Porcelain Collection 2 white	
	Lepke 1920, now New York, Arnhold Collection 1 white	
	Turin, Museo Civico 1 white	
	privately owned (Italy) 1 white	

Canary

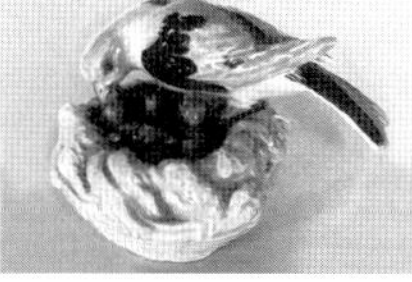

Note

There are two versions of the Canary, standing on its own, and as a bird in its nest. This distinction is made in the lists, but the two versions are recorded here under one title.

Name

1. Latin name	Serinus canaria

Model

1. Modeler	on its own: Johann Joachim Kaendler (proven)
	with nest: Johann Joachim Kaendler (proven)
2. Dating	on its own: Sept 1732 (proven)
	with nest: Jan 1733 (proven)
3. Work report/*Rapport* etc.	on its own: *Rapport* Sept 1732: "Modeler Kentler, for his part, has modeled and made ready . . . a canary"[71]
	with nest: work report Jan 1733: "In the month of January 1733 the following new models were made ready . . . a canary on its nest which contains three young and an egg not yet hatched, and another canary sitting on its nest and feeding its young, Kändler"[72]
4. Size	on its own: H: 10.5 cm
	with nest: H: 8.5 cm
5. Revival	no reference
6. Mold number	on its own: 227

Orders/Deliveries

1. Quantity ordered	no reference	
2. Information on production	no reference	
3. Deliveries	23 Dec 1733	6 with nests
4. Historical price	no reference	

Historical inventory number

N = 215-W [1770 inventory only] "three canaries of the same kind [on pedestals], [annotation when sold:] two to Count Marcolini"

N = 287-W [1770 and 1779 inventories] "two canaries with young and eggs"

Holdings

1. Quantities	a) Japanese Palace:	
	18 Feb 1735	5 undifferentiated
	9 Mar 1736	5 undifferentiated
	Inv. 1770	3 on their own 2 with nests
	Inv. 1779	2 with nests
	b) Royal Collection 1900:	
	no reference	
2. Sales/losses	no reference	
3. Present-day holdings	no record made	

Capercaillie

Name

1. Latin name	Tetrao urogallus

Orders/Deliveries

1. Quantity ordered	18 Nov 1732	4
	17 Dec 1732	4
	26 Nov 1733	8
	18 Feb 1735	4
	9 Mar 1736	4
2. Information on production	Order not carried out	

Cassowary

Name

1. Historical name	*Casuarios, Casuarius*
2. Latin name	Casuarius casuarius

Model

1. Modeler	Johann Joachim Kaendler (proven)
2. Dating	Sept 1732 (proven)
3. Work report/*Rapport* etc.	*Rapport* Sept 1732: "For his part, the modeler Kentler . . . has modeled and made ready the bird known as the cassowary, life-size"[73]
4. Size	L: 56 cm, H: 129 cm
5. Revival	Karl Stein, Feb – July 1925, copied from an original figure
6. Mold number	9

Orders/Deliveries

1. Quantity ordered	18 Nov 1732	4
	17 Dec 1732	8
	26 Nov 1733	8
	18 Feb 1735	4
	9 Mar 1736	4
2. Information on production	17 Dec 1732	4 in production
	17 Nov 1733	4 enameled at manufactory [most likely meaning painted with cold colors]
3. Deliveries	1732	1
	18 Nov 1733	4 colored
	Nov – Dec 1734	1
4. Historical price	309 talers	

Historical inventory number

N = 172-W [1770 and 1779 inventories] "one large white cassowary, lacquered, defective"

N = 267-W [1770 and 1779 inventories] "two cassowaries, painted with colors, three defective [annotation in the 1779 inventory:] one broke in two during cleaning"

Holdings

1. Quantities	a) Japanese Palace:	
	17 Dec 1732	1
	18 Feb 1735	6
	9 Mar 1736	6
	Inv. 1770	5
	Inv. 1779	5
	b) Royal Collection 1900:	
	4 white	
2. Sales/losses	no reference	
3. Present-day holdings	Dresden Porcelain Collection 2 white	
	Berlin, private collection 1 white	

Cockatoo

Name

1. Historical name	*Jakacou, indianischer Jakedow, Jackowie, Jackaciie*
2. Latin name	Kakatoe cacatua

Model

1. Modeler	Johann Joachim Kaendler (proven)
2. Dating	Aug 1734 (proven)
3. Work report/*Rapport* etc.	*Rapport* Sept/Oct 1734: "Specification of the models invented and made ready by the undersigned in the month of August 1734 . . . another fairly large bird named the cockatoo. It has a natural bonnet-shaped crest on its head which makes it look rather courtly, and it is resting on a pedestal grown over with branches and foliage, Johann Joachim Kändler"[74]
4. Size	L: 42 cm, H: 35.5 cm
5. Revival	no reference
6. Mold number	1780

Orders/Deliveries

1. Quantity ordered	no reference	
2. Information on production	no reference	
3. Deliveries	1734	5
	5 Mar – 17 Dec 1735	1
4. Historical price	24 talers (the five from 1734)	
	33 talers (the one from 1735)	

Historical inventory number

N = 276-W [Tower Room inventory 1769] "two cockatoos" [1770 and 1779 inventories] "two cockatoos on pedestals decorated with foliage"

Holdings

1. Quantities	a) Japanese Palace:	
	18 Feb 1735	6
	9 Mar 1736	6
	Tower Room Inv. 1769	2
	Inv. 1770	2
	Inv. 1779	2
	b) Royal Collection 1900:	
	2 enameled	
2. Sales/losses	no reference	
3. Present-day holdings	Dresden Porcelain Collection 1 enameled	
	Amsterdam, Rijksmuseum 1 enameled, and a number of others[75]	

Cockerel

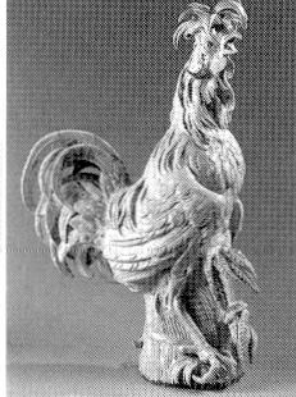

Note

Although this figure bears a number of different names, they all refer to executions of the same model, as is borne out by, among other things, the size data. Even though, for instance, the inventory of the Royal Collection uses two names, "Hahn auf Ähren" ("standing on ears of corn"), "Haushahn" ("domestic cockerel"), it is clear that the two terms refer to the same model, the two executions possibly finally differing in the way they were decorated.

Name

1. Historical name	*großer Hahn, Brabander Hahn, Haußhahn*
2. Latin name	Gallus domesticus

Model

1. Modeler	Johann Joachim Kaendler (proven)
2. Dating	Aug 1732 (proven)
3. Work report/*Rapport* etc.	*Rapport* Aug 1732: "Modeler Kentler, for his part, has modeled and made ready . . . a cockerel, life-size"[76]
4. Size	L: 44 cm, H: 73 cm
5. Revival	Erich Oehme, Apr 1921, set of molds completed, with amendments
6. Mold number	B144

Orders/Deliveries

1. Quantity ordered	18 Nov 1732	4
	17 Dec 1732	8
	26 Nov 1733	8
	18 Feb 1735	4
	9 Mar 1736	4
2. Information on production	17 Nov 1733	1 enameled at manufactory [most likely meaning painted with cold colors]
	4 Mar 1734	1 lacquered by Reinow
3. Deliveries	1732	1
	18 Nov 1733	1 colored
	1734	5
4. Historical price	48 talers 8 groschen	
	1 taler for lacquering	

Historical inventory number

N = 175-W [1770 and 1779 inventories] "a painted cockerel on a pedestal with ears of corn, defective, [annotation in the 1770 inventory:] was painted later"

	N = 272-W [1770 and 1779 inventories] "five domestic cockerels on high pedestals, two defective"

Holdings

1. Quantities	a) Japanese Palace:	
	17 Dec 1732	2
	18 Feb 1735	8
	9 Mar 1736	8
	Inv. 1770	6
	Inv. 1779	6
	b) Royal Collection 1900:	
	3 white	
2. Sales/losses	17 Apr 1851	to Teichert (branch of the manufactory) 1
	7 July 1853	to Anatol Demidof 1
	1919	Lepke 1
3. Present-day holdings	Dresden Porcelain Collection 2 white	
	1919 Lepke, now England, Raby Castle 1 white	
	St. Petersburg, Hermitage 1 white	
	Kopenhagen, Museum of Industrial Art 1 white	
	Warsaw, National Museum 1 white	

Coot

Name

1. Historical name	*BlassEndten, Blässgen, Waßerente, Waßer Huhn*
2. Latin name	Fulica atra

Model

1. Modeler	Johann Joachim Kaendler (attributed)
2. Dating	June – Oct 1731 (proven)
3. Work report/*Rapport* etc.	work report June – Oct 1731: "a coot sitting on a pedestal which is decorated with reeds and other things"[77]
4. Size	L: 20 cm, H: 41 cm
5. Revival	Karl Theodor Eichler, 1925, copied from an original figure
6. Mold number	42

Orders/Deliveries

1. Quantity ordered	26 Nov 1733	6
2. Information on production	13 Dec 1731	3 unfired at manufactory
3. Deliveries	1731/1732	3 without indication of condition 3 enameled
4. Historical price	no reference	

Historical inventory number

	N = 183-W [1770 and 1779 inventories] "two coots"
	N = 184-W [1770 and 1779 inventories] "one coot, lacquered but the lacquer has worn off"

Holdings

1. Quantities	a) Japanese Palace:	
	18 Feb 1735	6
	9 Mar 1736	6
	Tower Room Inv. 1769 Inv. nos. N = 183-W	 2
	Inv. 1770	no reference
	Inv. 1779 Inv. no. N = 183-W	1
	b) Royal Collection 1900:	
	no reference	
2. Sales/losses	no reference	
3. Present-day holdings	Dresden Porcelain Collection,	
	1919 restituted, then stolen[78] 1 enameled	
	Schloss Moritzburg, on loan from the Dresden Porcelain Collection 1 white, swords mark	
	Kozel, Czech Republic 2 white, swords marks[79]	

Crane

Name

1. Historical name	*Granige, Kraniche mit dem Steine*
2. Latin name	Grus grus

Model

1. Modeler	Johann Joachim Kaendler (proven)
2. Dating	Apr 1735 (proven)

3. Work report/*Rapport* etc.	work report June 1734 (bozzetto): "I was in Moritzburg for two days, where I . . . made a small model of the crane from life, Kändler"[80]
	work report Apr 1735: " . . . a crane, life-size, with a pedestal composed of an abundance of such reeds and rushes as grow in ponds, Johann Joachim Kändler"[81]
4. Size	L: 52 cm, H: 87 cm
5. Revival	no reference
6. Mold number	1769
7. Source of inspiration	live specimen

Orders/Deliveries

1. Quantity ordered	18 Nov 1732	4
	17 Dec 1732	8 with stone
	26 Nov 1733	8
	18 Feb 1735	4
	9 Mar 1736	4
2. Information on production	June 1735	2 finished at manufactory
	July 1735	4 finished at manufactory
3. Deliveries	Sept 1735	6 enameled [most likely meaning painted with cold colors]
4. Historical price	74 talers 6 groschen	

Historical inventory number

N = 331-W [1770 and 1779 inventories] "six cranes on white pedestals decorated with rushes, defective"

Holdings

1. Quantities	a) Japanese Palace:	
	9 Mar 1736	6
	Inv. 1770	6
	Inv. 1779	6
	b) Royal Collection 1900:	
	1 white	
2. Sales/losses	8 Jan 1851	to Helena Wolfssohn 3 referred to as herons, but distinguished from the "Fischreiher"
3. Present-day holdings	Dresden Porcelain Collection 1 with remains of lacquering	
	Longleat, collection of the Marquess of Bath 1 white	
	ca. 1935 private collection in Paris, then Arthur Wittekind, now Bayerisches Nationalmuseum, Schneider Collection, Lustheim 1 white	
	Sotheby's 6 June 1950, now Detroit, Institute of Arts 1 white	
	Sotheby's 6 June 1950 1 white	

Cuckoo

Note

The Cuckoo is mentioned in two lists under the interim totals of figures delivered to date; neither, however, is it clear which of the documented porcelain birds was being referred to, nor has any other evidence on this figure been thrown up in the course of research.

Name

1. Historical name	*indianische Gugucke, indianische Guckgucken*
2. Latin name	Cuculus canorus

Orders/Deliveries

1. Quantity ordered	no reference
2. Information on production	no reference

Holdings

1. Quantities	a) Japanese Palace:	
	18 Feb 1735	6
	9 Mar 1736	6

"Diver"

Note

It is not clear which figure the compiler of the lists was referring to when he used the term "Taucher" (diver). Simple equations such as "diver" = coot, gull, or osprey are ruled out on the grounds of internal evidence, as either these birds appear with their correct names in the very same lists, or their models did not come into being until later. It could even be the case that when "Taucher" appears in the various sources, it refers to a different species each time. When Kaendler spent time at the *Kunstkammer* in Dresden in July 1734, birds he made studies of included an "Indian duck with a ruff-like collar" (= Great Crested Grebe), an "African duck with curious feet," and an "Indian diver." In his work reports, on the other hand, he ends up describing an "African duck with a ruff-like collar." We are thus not on firm enough ground to be able to draw any conclusions as to what we are dealing with here, whether it is a genuine model in its own right (now lost), or simply a terminological variant.

Model

1. Work report/*Rapport* etc.	work report July 1734: "Specification of the foreign animals and exotic birds which . . . I, as named below, modeled and drew exactly and correctly, so that they . . . may here at the Royal Porcelain Factory be done large . . . birds which are to be seen stuffed in the *Kunstkammer* and of which I made drawings . . . an Indian diver, JJ Kändler"[82]

Orders/Deliveries

1. Quantity ordered	26 Nov 1733	4
2. Information on production	13 Dec 1731	1 enameled at manufactory
3. Deliveries	1731/1732	1 referred to as a "Waßer-Taucher"

Holdings

1. Quantities	a) Japanese Palace:	
	18 Feb 1735	4
	9 Mar 1736	7

Doves

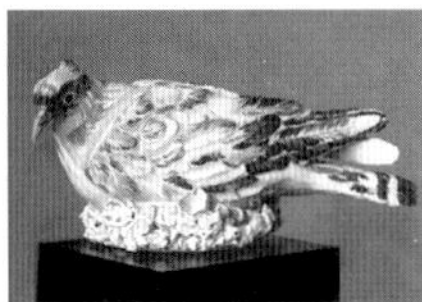
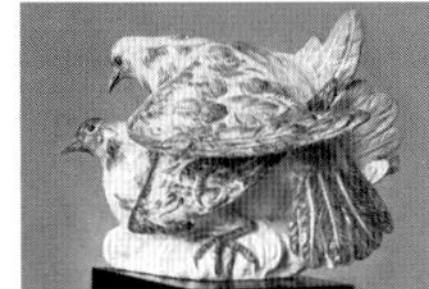
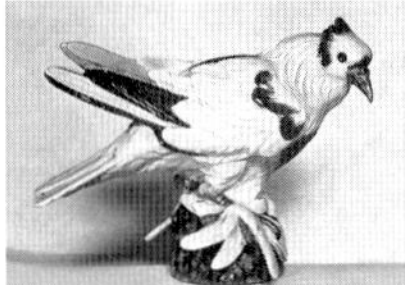

Note

Certain sources distinguish between the dove on its nest, the dove on a pedestal ("Trommeltaube" or, according to Erwin Hösel, "Turkish dove"), and pairs of doves. The information we have, however, is not sufficient to treat the models individually.

Name

1. Latin name	Streptopelia turtur (Turtle Dove)
	Columba palumbus (Wood Pigeon)

Model

1. Modeler	all three models: Johann Joachim Kaendler (proven)
2. Dating	"Trommeltaube": Sept 1732 (proven)
	dove on its nest: Oct 1732 (proven)
	doves at dalliance: Jan 1733 (proven)
3. Work report/*Rapport* etc.	"Trommeltaube": *Rapport* Sept 1732: "Modeler Kentler for his part has modeled and finished . . . a 'Trommeltaube'." [83]
	dove on its nest: *Rapport* Oct 1732: "The following new models have been finished . . . a dove sitting brooding on its nest"[84]
	pair of doves: work report Jan 1733: "In January 1733 the following new models were finished . . . a pair of doves at dalliance, Kändler"[85]
4. Size	"Trommeltaube": L: 23.5 cm
	dove on its nest: L: 29 cm, H: 15.5 cm
	doves at dalliance: H: 21 cm
5. Revival	"Trommeltaube": no name, Apr 1910, after an original figure, "extra"
	dove on its nest: Karl Theodor Eichler, Mar 1926, copied from an original figure
	doves at dalliance: Karl Theodor Eichler, Feb 1926, copied from an original figure
6. Mold number	"Trommeltaube": 827
	dove on its nest: 78
	doves at dalliance: 77

Orders/Deliveries

1. Quantity ordered	26 Nov 1733	24
2. Information on production	no reference	
3. Deliveries	1732	4 enameled
	11 Nov 1733	2 enameled
	1734	4
	5 Mar – 17 Dec 1735 doves at dalliance, 5	
4. Historical price	12 talers 6 groschen (no differentiation)	

Historical inventory number

	N = 193-W [1770 and 1779 inventories] "two doves"
	N = 278-W [1770 and 1779 inventories] "four colored doves of which two are on low pedestals and two on nests"
	N = 328-W [1770 and 1779 inventories] "two colored doves"

Holdings

1. Quantities	a) Japanese Palace:	
	17 Dec 1732	no reference
	18 Feb 1735	13
	9 Mar 1736	13
	Inv. 1770	6 "Trommeltauben" dove on nest, 2
	Inv. 1779	6 "Trommeltauben" dove on nest, 2
	b) Royal Collection 1900:	
	3 "Trommeltauben," enameled	

	dove on nest, 6, enameled
	doves at dalliance, 1, enameled
2. Sales/losses	no reference
3. Present-day holdings	no record made

Eagles (sitting, and beating one wing

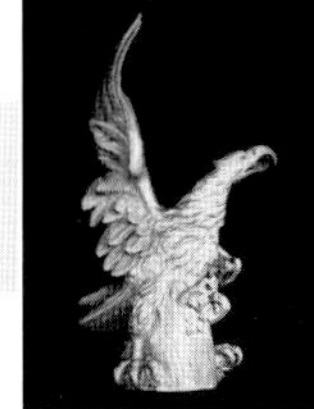

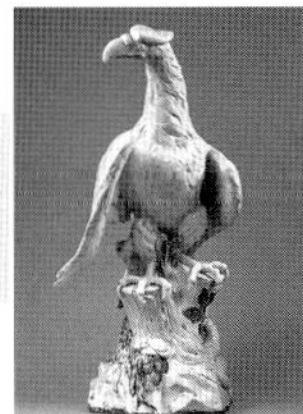

Note

There are two large eagle models, one of an eagle sitting, and one of an eagle beating one wing. Although no historical example of the latter has been preserved, possibly because the model was never successfully fired, a number of pieces of data related to it are recorded here, on the revival of the model, for instance. Differences in size and appearance make the two models easy to distinguish in the sources. The sitting eagle has two different heads, the one looking to the left and the other to the right. The other models of eagles and birds of prey which cannot be distinguished absolute clarity in the sources (Osprey, Kestrel etc.) are all dealt with together under "Birds of Prey."

Name

1. Latin name	Aquila chrysaetos

Model

1. Modeler	both: Johann Joachim Kaendler (proven)
2. Dating	sitting: June 1731 (proven)
	beating one wing: Oct 1732 (proven)
3. Work report/*Rapport* etc.	sitting: *Rapport* June 1731: "finished in particular a large eagle and a number of other models in clay; molds have recently been made from the models and the figures have been prepared in porcelain paste"[86]
	work report June – Oct 1731: "a large eagle two ells minus three inches in height with the pedestal, with wings slightly raised"[87]
	beating one wing: work report Oct 1732: "The following new models have been made ready . . . a large eagle spreading its right wing high into the air, at the same representing the graciousness of a great and noble lord, over two ells in height"[88]
	work report July 1734 (bozzetto only): "exotic birds which . . . I, as named below, modeled and drew exactly and correctly, so that they . . . may here at the Royal Porcelain Factory be done large . . . In the Bear-House I made a model . . . of a golden eagle, JJ Kändler"[89]
4. Size	sitting: L: 44 cm, H: 90 cm
	beating one wing: H: 135 cm
5. Revival	sitting: Karl Stein, Oct – Dec 1921, set of molds completed
	beating one wing: Karl Stein, Aug – Sept 1921, set of molds completed
6. Mold number	sitting: 19
	beating one wing: 31, Molds for decorative appendages identical with those for the Macaw (no. 24) and Cockatoo (no. 123)[90]

Orders/Deliveries

1. Quantity ordered	Early 1732	8
	18 Nov 1732	4
	17 Dec 1732	8
	26 Nov 1733	8
	18 Feb 1735	4
	9 Mar 1736	4
2. Information on production	13 Dec 1731	3 unfired at manufactory, sitting
	18 Aug 1732	3 unfired at manufactory, sitting, 1 low-fired at manufactory, sitting
	17 Dec 1732	1 in production, sitting or beating one wing
3. Deliveries	1731/1732	1 sitting
	1734	6 sitting
4. Historical price	136 talers (sitting)	

Historical inventory number

	N = 191-W [1770 and 1779 inventories] "a white eagle on a pedestal, subsequently lacquered" [delivery 1731/1732]
	N = 264-W [1770 and 1779 inventories] "six eagles colored in black and brown, on pedestals, two defective" [delivery 1734]

Holdings

1. Quantities	a) Japanese Palace:	
	17 Dec 1732	no reference
	18 Feb 1735	7
	9 Mar 1736	7
	Inv. 1770	7
	Inv. 1779	7
	b) Royal Collection 1900:	
	4 looking to the right	
	2 looking to the left	
2. Sales/losses	17 Apr 1849	to Teichert (branch of the manufactory) 1
	1919	Lepke 2
	16 July 1932	to Arthur Wittekind 1

3. Present-day holdings	Dresden Porcelain Collection 2 looking to the right, white 2 looking to the left, white
	Lepke 1919, then Ole Olsen Collection now Kopenhagen, Kunstindustriemuseum 2 as a complementary pair, white
	England, Raby Castle 1 looking to the left, white

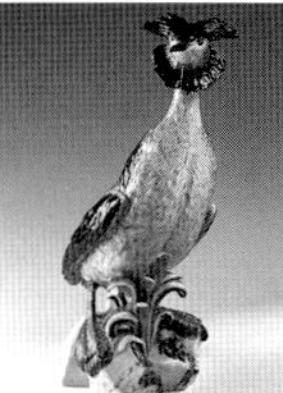

Great Crested Grebe

Note

There is no mention of a Great Crested Grebe in the sources, but evidence in Kaendler's work reports show that he did make a model of a grebe but referred to it as an African duck. Although an "afrikanische Ente" as such was never ordered, a "türkische Ente" was, which in its turn was constantly recorded as not having gone into production ("nicht ausgeführt"). Here, the data regarding both these terms of reference has been gathered under one title.

Name

1. Historical name	*indianische Ente, afrikanische Ente, Türcke Enden, Wasserente*
2. Latin name	Podiceps cristatus

Model

1. Modeler	Johann Joachim Kaendler (proven)
2. Dating	Oct 1734 (proven)
3. Work report/*Rapport* etc.	work report July 1734: "Specification of the foreign animals and exotic birds which . . . I, as named below, modeled and drew exactly and correctly, so that they . . . may here at the Royal Porcelain Factory be done large . . . birds which are to be seen stuffed in the *Kunstkammer* and of which I made drawings . . . an Indian Duck with a collar around its neck, JJ Kändler"[91]
	Rapport Sept/Oct 1734: "Specification of those models that were invented by . . . a large African Duck which is larger than our local ducks and has a remarkable appearance on account of the ruff and collar around its neck; it has a tail almost like a hen and is rendered in a similar fashion sitting in amongst an abundance of reeds and grass, Johann Joachim Kändler"[92]
4. Size	H: 48 cm
5. Revival	Karl Theodor Eichler, Feb – Mar 1926, copied from an original figure
6. Mold number	76
7. Source of inspiration	Stuffed specimen

Orders/Deliveries

1. Quantity ordered	18 Nov 1732	4 Turkish ducks
	17 Dec 1732	4 Turkish ducks
	26 Nov 1733	8 Turkish ducks
	18 Feb 1735	4 Turkish ducks
	9 Mar 1736	4 Turkish ducks
2. Information on production	Apr 1735	1 finished at manufactory, referred to as a "Wasserente" ("water duck")
3. Deliveries	Apr 1735	5 enameled
	5 Mar – 17 Dec 1735 6[93]	
	(of which: July 1735 1 enameled)	
4. Historical price	48 talers 12 groschen	

Historical inventory number

N = 185-W [Tower Room inventory 1769] "four divers"

Holdings

1. Quantities	a) Japanese Palace:	
	18 Feb 1735	5
	9 Mar 1736	11
	Tower Room Inv. 1769	4
	Inv. 1770	no reference
	Inv. 1779	no reference
	b) Royal Collection 1900:	
	no reference	
2. Sales/losses	no reference	
3. Present-day holdings	Dresden Porcelain Collection 1 white 2 enameled	

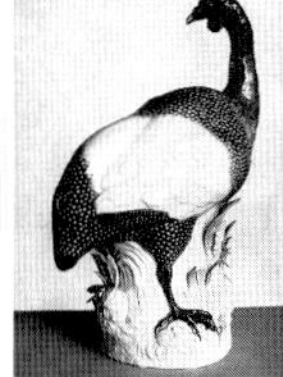

Guinea Fowl

Name

1. Historical name	*BerlHenne, indianisches Berghuhn*
2. Latin name	Numida meleagris

Model

1. Modeler	Johann Joachim Kaendler (proven)
2. Dating	Mar – Apr 1735 (proven)

3. Work report/*Rapport* etc.	work report Mar 1735: “Made a model of a guinea fowl, also for the Palace order, quite in accordance with its particular appearance, but there is still a little work to be done on it, Johann Joachim Kändler”[94]
	work report Apr 1735: “Finished the guinea fowl which still had a little work to be done on it last month, Johann Joachim Kändler”[95]
	work report Feb 1737: “Made a new neck and head for the guinea fowl, to vary it”[96]
4. Size	H: 43.5 cm
5. Revival	no reference
6. Mold number	140

Orders/Deliveries

1. Quantity ordered	18 Nov 1732	4
	17 Dec 1732	8 ordered as “indianische Berghühner”
	26 Nov 1733	8
	18 Feb 1735	4
	9 Mar 1736	4
2. Information on production	May 1735	7 finished at manufactory
3. Deliveries	June 1735	1 enameled
	July 1735	6 enameled
4. Historical price	21 talers 6 groschen	

Historical inventory number

N = 327-W [Tower Room inventory 1769] “two guinea fowls”

[1770 and 1779 inventories] “one guinea fowl on the same kind of pedestal [= decorated with green leaves and grass]”

Holdings

1. Quantities	a) Japanese Palace:	
	9 Mar 1736	7
	Tower Room Inv. 1769	2
	Inv. 1770	1
	Inv. 1779	1
	b) Royal Collection 1900: 1 enameled	
2. Sales/losses	no reference	
3. Present-day holdings	no record made	

Gull

Name

1. Historical name	*Seemerhe, Sehmehe, Seemeube*
2. Latin name	Larus ridibundus

Model

1. Modeler	Johann Joachim Kaendler (proven)
2. Dating	June – Oct 1731 (proven)
3. Work report/*Rapport* etc.	work report June – Oct 1731: “A seagull on a pedestal which is decorated with all sorts of seashells in the manner in which a number of different figures have been produced”[97]
4. Size	H: 34 cm
5. Revival	Karl Theodor Eichler, July 1926, copied
6. Mold number	74

Orders/Deliveries

1. Quantity ordered	26 Nov 1733	3
2. Information on production	13 Dec 1731	2 unfired at manufactory
	18 Aug 1732	1 finished at manufactory
3. Deliveries	1731/1732	2 without indications as to condition; 1 enameled
	5 Mar – 17 Dec 1735	“three gulls,” but the exact model is unclear, as after this date only one gull is mentioned in the lists of figures delivered to date
4. Historical price	no reference	

Historical inventory number

no reference

Holdings

1. Quantities	a) Japanese Palace:	
	17 Dec 1732	no reference
	18 Feb 1735	1
	9 Mar 1736	1
	Inv. 1770	no reference
	Inv. 1779	no reference
	b) Royal Collection 1900: 1	
2. Sales/losses	no reference	
3. Present-day holdings	(Dresden Porcelain Collection 1 war loss)	

Hen

Name

1. Historical name	*Gluckhüner mit Jungen,* *Hühner mit Coppen*
2. Latin name	Gallus domesticus

Model

1. Modeler	Johann Joachim Kaendler (proven)
2. Dating	Aug 1732 (proven)
3. Work report/*Rapport* etc.	*Rapport* Aug 1732: "Modeler Kentler, for his part, has modeled and made ready . . . a hen with its young"[98]
4. Size	L: 32 cm, H: 35 cm
5. Revival	no reference
6. Mold number	no record made

Orders/Deliveries

1. Quantity ordered	18 Nov 1732	4
	17 Dec 1732	8
	26 Nov 1733	8
	18 Feb 1735	4
	9 Mar 1736	4
2. Information on production	4 Mar 1734	2 lacquered by Reinow
3. Deliveries	1732	4
4. Historical price	1 talers for lacquering	

Historical inventory number

N = 165-W [1770 and 1779 inventories] "four hens with their young, of the same kind [= white and gray]"

Holdings

1. Quantities	a) Japanese Palace:	
	17 Dec 1732	4
	18 Feb 1735	4
	9 Mar 1736	4
	Inv. 1770	4
	Inv. 1779	4
	b) Royal Collection 1900:	
	no reference	
2. Sales/losses	17 Apr 1851	to Teichert (branch of the manufactory) 1 hen
	8 Jan 1851	to Helena Wolfssohn 2 hens with young
	7 July 1853	to Anatol Demidoff 1 hen
3. Present-day holdings	Dresden Porcelain Collection 1 white	

Heron

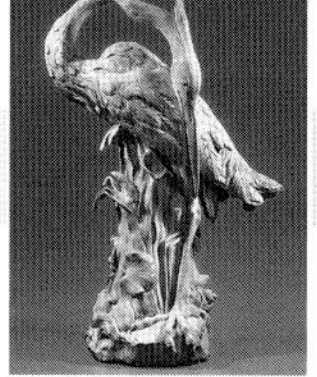

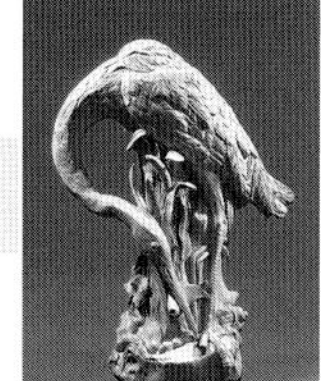

Note

The delivery list for 1731/1732 contains references to 14 herons, of which three are listed under the rubric "enameled." All other lists have only 11 herons, so that the three enameled figures may have been from another model. When size and shape are taken into consideration, the only model that comes into question is the Bustard, which Kirchner finished in autumn 1732. That this was the case is all the more likely as the synonymous use of the terms "enameled" and "colored" is particularly conspicuous in connection with the Bustard – the figures chosen by Sulkowski on 17 Nov 1733 included two "enameled" bustards, which are on the very next day then referred to as "colored" in a list drawn up prior to their being delivered, or set aside for delivery, to the Japanese Palace.
There are two variants of the heron model, one with a carp (or in some cases a frog) and one preening itself, and these are referred to as such here insofar as the sources make this possible.
For instances of this model being decorated as a stork, see under "Stork."

Name

1 Latin name	Ardea cinerea

Model

1. Modeler	Johann Joachim Kaendler (proven)
2. Dating	Mar 1732 (proven)
3. Work report/*Rapport* etc.	*Rapport* Mar 1732: "But modeler Kentler has modeled a large heron"[99]
4. Size	with carp: L: 45.5 cm, H. 61.5 cm
	preening itself: L: 45.5 cm, H: 74 cm
5. Revival	with carp: Karl Stein, July – Aug 1926, copied
	preening itself: Karl Stein, Aug – Dec 1925, copied[100]
6. Mold number	with carp: 51
	preening itself: 52
7. Source of inspiration	live specimen in the garden at the Residence

Orders/Deliveries

1. Quantity ordered	18 Nov 1732	4
	17 Dec 1732	8
	26 Nov 1733	12
	18 Feb 1735	4
	9 Mar 1736	4
2. Information on production	18 Aug 1732	12 finished at manufactory
3. Deliveries	1732	11, (3 enameled; see Note, and catalog entry for Bustard)
4. Historical price	93 talers	

Historical inventory number

N = 163-W [1770 and 1779 inventories] "eleven white and gray herons, on pedestals with an abundance of rushes, 3 defective"

Holdings

1. Quantities	a) Japanese Palace:	
	17 Dec 1732	11
	18 Feb 1735	11
	9 Mar 1736	11
	Inv. 1770	11
	Inv. 1779	11
	b) Royal Collection 1900:	
	1 with carp	
	4 preening their plumage	
2. Sales/losses	17 Apr 1849	to Teichert (branch of the manufactory) 2
	June 6 1850	to Moritz Meyer 2
	June 10 1850	to Mr Marks 1
	8 Jan 1851	to Helena Wolfssohn 1 Heron in the reeds
	7 July 1853	to Anatol Demidoff 2
	1920	Lepke 1 preening itself
3. Present-day holdings	with carp in its beak: Dresden Porcelain Collection 1 with small lacquer remains	
	with a frog in its beak: Private collection 1 white	
	preening itself: Dresden Porcelain Collection 2 white	
	New York, Pflueger Collection 1 white	
	private collection 1 white	

Heron, Indian

Note

The delivery list for the period March 5 to December 17, 1735, records "4 Indian Herons" as having being delivered to the palace, but it is not clear what figure is being referred to. All the bird figures to which the name "Indian Heron" might apply – such as the Heron, Crane, Bustard, Bittern, or even the Cassowary – are ruled out, either because the number of figures quoted up until then for the bird was not increased, or because the bird in question appears in the same delivery list under its correct name. Furthermore, no larger-size figures appear in the palace inventory to which this designation could be applied.

Orders/Deliveries

1. Quantity ordered	no reference	
2. Deliveries	5 Mar – 17 Dec 1735	4

Jay

Name

1. Historical name	*Eichel Gabicht* ("acorn hawk")
2. Latin name	Garrulus glandarius

Model

1. Modeler	Johann Joachim Kaendler (proven)
2. Dating	Oct 1735 (proven)
3. Work report/*Rapport* etc.	work report Oct 1735: "Modeled a jay which is to go to the Royal Palace, done sitting on a large oak branch thick with acorns and leaves, and eating an acorn, which is its food. Various insects which are to be found on oak-trees, such as a "Pöner" [= stag beetle?], are also included, Johann Joachim Kändler"[101]
	work report May 1740: "Modeled in clay a variety of oak leaves and other accessories for decorating the jays"[102]
4. Size	L: 24 cm, H: 39 cm
5. Revival	no reference
6. Mold number	167 without squirrel[103]
	1128 with squirrel

Orders/Deliveries

1. Quantity ordered	no reference
2. Information on production	no reference

3. Deliveries	May 1736	2
4. Historical price	12 talers	

Historical inventory number

not identifiable in the inventory

Holdings

1. Quantities	a) Japanese Palace:	
	9 Mar 1736	2
	Inv. 1770	no reference
	Inv. 1779	no reference
	b) Royal Collection 1900:	
	no reference	
2. Sales/losses	no reference	
3. Present-day holdings	no record made	

Kingfisher

Name

1. Latin name	Alcedo atthis

Model

1. Modeler	Johann Joachim Kaendler (proven)
2. Dating	Sept 1735 (proven)
3. Work report/*Rapport* etc.	work report Sept 1735: "Modeled a kingfisher sitting on a small stone precipice somewhat overgrown with leaves, Johann Joachim Kändler"[104]
4. Size	H: 23.5 cm
5. Revival	no reference
6. Mold number	170

Orders/Deliveries

1. Quantity ordered	no reference	
2. Information on production	no reference	
3. Deliveries	Mar 1736	4
4. Historical price	3 talers 12 groschen	

Historical inventory number

N = 353-W [1770 inventory] "two colored kingfishers on pedestals covered with reeds, [added later:] broken during cleaning"

Holdings

1. Quantities	a) Japanese Palace:	
	9 Mar 1736	4
	Inv. 1770	2
	Inv. 1779	no reference
	b) Royal Collection 1900:	
	no reference	
2. Sales/losses	no reference	
3. Present-day holdings	no record made	

"Krescher"

Note

In spite of the greatest efforts it has not been possible to identify a bird which answers to this or a similar name.

Name

1. Historical name	*Krescher, Krischer*

Orders/Deliveries

1. Quantity ordered	18 Nov 1732	4
	17 Dec 1732	4
	26 Nov 1733	12
	18 Feb 1735	4
	9 Mar 1736	4
2. Information on production	Order not carried out	

Macaw

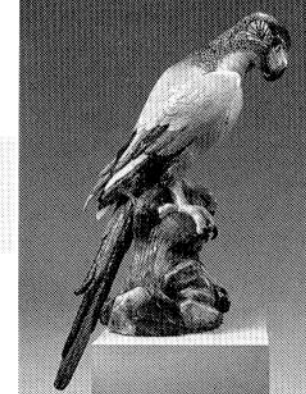

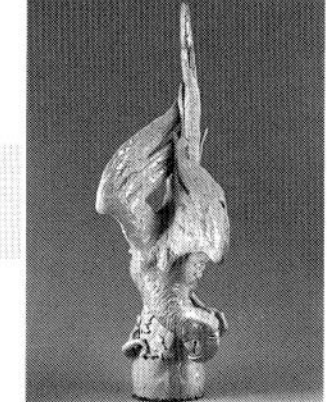

Note

The Macaw exists in two versions; when source data make it possible to distinguish the one from the other, they are referred to here as "sitting" and "climbing downwards." In addition, the Museum Schauhalle in Meissen has another macaw, 94 cm tall, sitting and eating a piece of fruit, a twentieth-century recreation recorded in the model book under the number 24 as follows: "Karl Stein, May – July 1921, completed from an original porcelain figure ["ergänzt nach altem Porzellanmodell"]." As the figure has no known eighteenth-century precedents, it remains unclear what "original porcelain figure" Karl Stein worked from. Under number 54 b, the model book has a smaller version of the Macaw, climbing downwards, created in 1944 by Vogel.

Name

1. Historical name	*indianischer Rabe* ("Indian raven")
2. Latin name	Ara ararauna / Ara macao

Model

1. Modeler	sitting: Johann Joachim Kaendler (attributed)
	climbing downwards: Johann Joachim Kaendler (proven)
2. Dating	sitting: Oct – Dec 1731 (attributed)
	climbing downwards: May 1732 (proven)
3. Work report/*Rapport* etc.	*Rapport* May 1732: "Modeler Kaendler, for his part, has modeled . . . a large raven of the Indian kind"[105]
4. Size	sitting: L: 42 cm, H: 70 cm
	climbing downwards: L: 40 cm, H: 123 cm
5. Revival	sitting: Herrmann, Apr 1908, copied from an original figure
	climbing downwards: Karl Stein, Apr 1920, set of molds completed
6. Mold number	sitting: 343
	climbing downwards: 54

Orders/Deliveries

1. Quantity ordered	Early 1732	8
	18 Nov 1732	4
	17 Dec 1732	8
	26 Nov 1733	14
	18 Feb 1735	4
	9 Mar 1736	4
2. Information on production	13 Dec 1731	4 unfired at manufactory
	18 Aug 1732	10 finished at manufactory, 4 unfired at manufactory
	17 Dec 1732	2 in production
	17 Nov 1733	1 enameled at manufactory
	4 Mar 1734	9 lacquered by Reinow
3. Deliveries	1731/1732	10 undifferentiated, 3 enameled
	18 Nov 1733	1 colored
4. Historical price	112 talers	
	2 talers for lacquering	

Historical inventory number

N = 173-W [1770 inventory] "three Indian ravens with long tails hanging down onto the pedestal, damaged"

[1779 inventory] "three Indian ravens with long tails hanging down onto the pedestal, damaged [later addition:] Nota. Holding their tails upwards"

N = 174-W [1770 and 1779 inventories] "nine of the same [= Indian ravens] mostly defective"

N = 270-W [1770 and 1779 inventories] "an Indian raven, with red and blue colors, on a high pedestal, badly damaged"

Holdings

1. Quantities	a) Japanese Palace:	
	17 Dec 1732	6
	18 Feb 1735	14
	9 Mar 1736	14
	Inv. 1770	13 no differentiation between the models, one enameled
	Inv. 1779	10 sitting, one enameled
		3 climbing downwards
	b) Royal Collection 1900:	
	4 sitting, white 1 sitting, enameled 2 climbing downwards, white	
2. Sales/losses	June 6 1850	to Moritz Meyer 2 sitting
	8.1.1851	to Helena Wolfssohn 1 climbing downwards 2 sitting
	1920	Lepke (sitting) 1
3. Present-day holdings	sitting: Dresden Porcelain Collection	
	3 white 2 enameled, in pieces	
	Amsterdam, Rijksmuseum 1 enameled	
	New York, Pflueger Collection (to go to the Museum of Fine Arts, Boston)[106] 1 white	
	Lepke 1920, then Sotheby's PB 27. 6. 1978, now Cologne, Museum für Angewandte Kunst 1 white	
	Christie's 26. 6. 1967, now Bayerisches Nationalmuseum, Schneider Collection, Lustheim 1 white	
	climbing downwards: Dresden Porcelain Collection 2 white	
	New York, Pflueger Collection (to go to the Museum of Fine Arts, Boston) 1 white	

Magpie

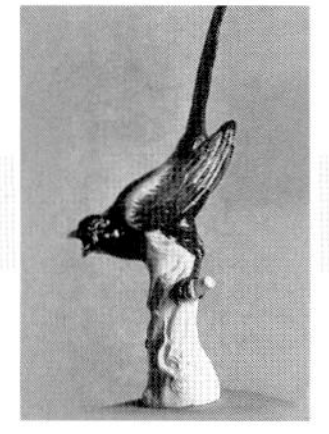

Name

1. Historical name	*Aelster, Aeltester*
2. Latin name	Pica pica

Model

1. Modeler	Johann Joachim Kaendler (proven)
2. Dating	Feb 1733 (proven)
3. Work report/*Rapport* etc.	work report Feb 1733: "In the month of February 1733 the following new models were made ready . . . a magpie, life-size, Kändler"[107]
4. Size	L: 21 cm, H: 56 cm
5. Revival	no indication of modeler, June 1913, with new base
6. Mold number	62a (looking to the right), 62b (looking to the left)

Orders/Deliveries

1. Quantity ordered	26 Nov 1733	8
2. Information on production	no reference	
3. Deliveries	31 Oct 1733	2 enameled
	25 Nov 1733	4 enameled
	1734	14
	5 Mar – 17 Dec 1735	5
4. Historical price	11 talers 6 groschen	

Historical inventory number

N = 281-W [Tower Room inventory 1769] "three magpies"

[1770 and 1779 inventories] "seven magpies with pedestals done in the same way [covered high with leaves], mainly damaged"

N = 313-W [1770 and 1779 inventories] "two magpies on pedestals covered high with leaves, very damaged"

Holdings

1. Quantities	a) Japanese Palace:	
	18 Feb 1735	18
	9 Mar 1736	19
	Tower Room Inv. 1769	3
	Inv. 1770	9
	Inv. 1779	9
	b) Royal Collection 1900: 7 enameled	
2. Sales/losses	no reference	
2. Present-day holdings	no record made	

Oriole

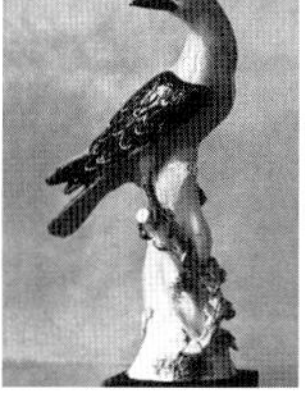

Note

Kaendler's model of an oriole was reworked several times by Reinicke and Ehder after 1740, and Reinicke went as far as making a completely new model in January 1747, by which time the figure was only being produced for the open market (see Albiker 1935/1959).

Name

1. Historical name	*Bier Eule, gelb und schwartze Vögel* ("black-and-yellow birds")
2. Latin name	Oriolus oriolus

Model

1. Modeler	Johann Joachim Kaendler (proven)
2. Dating	July 1733 und Mar 1734 (proven)
3. Work report/*Rapport* etc.	work report July 1733: "Specification of what new models were invented and finished in the month of July 1733 . . . a middle-size bird called a 'Bier-Eule' sitting on a pedestal, Kändler, Modellmeister"[108]
	work report Mar 1734: "In the month of March 1734 at this Porcelain Factory of the King in Poland and Elector of Saxony the following new models were finished . . . a middle-size bird known as a 'Bier-Eule,' Johann Joachim Kändler"[109]
4. Size	H: 30 cm
5. Revival	no reference
6. Mold number	1733 model: 820
	1734 model: 820x

Orders/Deliveries

1. Quantity ordered	no reference	
2. Information on production	no reference	
3. Deliveries	1734	6
	5 Mar – 17 Dec 1735	10
4. Historical price	6 talers	

Historical inventory number

	N = 283-W [1770 and 1779 inventories] "six golden orioles with black wings, on white pedestals decorated with leaves"
	N = 315-W [1770 and 1779 inventories] "ten orioles with black wings, 8 of which are standing on high pedestals decorated with leaves, but 2 of the pedestals are simply ["schlecht"[110]] done"

Holdings

1. Quantities	a) Japanese Palace:	
	18 Feb 1735	12
	9 Mar 1736	12
	Inv. 1770	16 yellow/black
	Inv. 1779	16 yellow/black
	b) Royal Collection 1900:	
	7 enameled, with wings hanging, H: 30 cm	
	5 enameled, with wings folded, H: 26.5 cm	
2. Sales/losses	no reference	
3. Present-day holdings	no record made	

Ostrich

Name

1. Latin name	Struthio camelus

Orders/Deliveries

1. Quantity ordered	18 Nov 1732	4
	17 Dec 1732	8
	26 Nov 1733	8
	18 Feb 1735	4
	9 Mar 1736	4
2. Information on production	Order not carried out	
3. Work report/*Rapport* etc.	work report June 1734 (bozzetto only): "Was in Moritzburg for two days, where I . . . did a small model of the ostrich[111] from life, Kändler"[112]	

Owl (Eagle Owl)

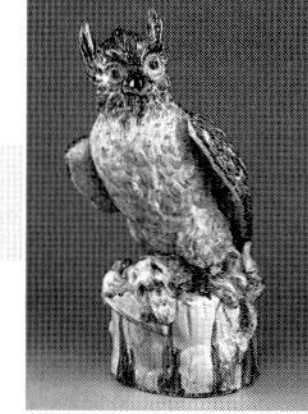

Name

1. Historical name	*Buhue*
2. Latin name	Bubo bubo

Model

1. Modeler	Johann Friedrich Eberlein (proven)
2. Dating	Apr – May 1735 (proven)
3. Work report/*Rapport* etc.	work report Apr – May 1735: "What I, the undersigned, sculpted at the Royal Porcelain Manufactory from April 18 until the end of the month of May . . . a large eagle owl with a dove, Johann Friedrich Eberlein, sculptor"[113]
4. Size	H: 52 cm
5. Revival	Karl Theodor Eichler, Feb 1725, copied
6. Mold number	146

Orders/Deliveries

1. Quantity ordered	18 Nov 1732	4
	17 Dec 1732	6
	26 Nov 1733	8
	18 Feb 1735	4
	9 Mar 1736	4
2. Information on production	Oct 1735	4 finished at manufactory
3. Deliveries	Mar 1736	4
4. Historical price	41 talers 16 groschen	

Historical inventory number

	N = 350-W [1770 and 1779 inventories] "two eagle owls, each with a dove in its claws, with fire-cracks"

Holdings

1. Quantities	a) Japanese Palace:	
	9 Mar 1736	5
	Inv. 1770	2
	Inv. 1779	2
	b) Royal Collection 1900:	
	2 enameled	
2. Sales/losses	no reference	

3. Present-day holdings	Dresden Porcelain Collection 1 enameled, in pieces New York, Metropolitan Museum of Art 1 enameled

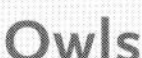

Owls

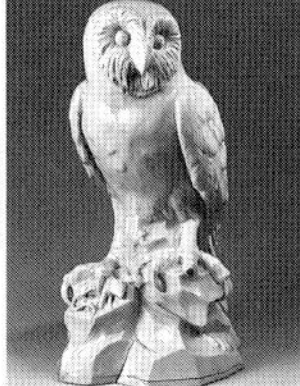

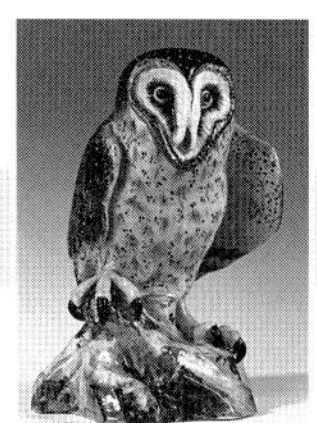

Note

Two owl figures exist, one of a large owl with a mouse in its claws, and one of a barn owl. As the lists do not distinguish between the two, but the inventories do, these two models are dealt with together here.

Name

1. Historical name	Eylen
2. Latin name	owl: Asio otus ("Waldohreule" = American Barn Owl, Long-eared Owl) barn owl: Tyto alba

Model

1. Modeler	Johann Joachim Kaendler (proven)
2. Dating	owl: July – Oct 1731 (proven) barn owl: Oct – Dec 1731 (attributed)
3. Work report/*Rapport* etc.	owl: work report June – Oct 1731: "A large owl on a pedestal which I have already received from His Majesty"[114]
4. Size	L: 32 cm, H: 47 cm (owl) L: 18 cm, H: 26 cm (barn owl)
5. Revival	owl: Karl Stein, Dec 1914, no further details barn owl: Karl Stein, Feb – Mar 1928, copied from an original figure in the Residence museum
6. Mold number	owl: 27 barn owl: 15

Orders/Deliveries

1. Quantity ordered	18 Nov 1732	4
	17 Dec 1732	8
	26 Nov 1733	12
	18 Feb 1735	4
	9 Mar 1736	4
2. Information on production	13 Dec 1731	2 large (owls) unfired at manufactory, 3 small (barn owls) finished at manufactory
	18 Aug 1732	2 white finished at manufactory, 2 enameled finished at manufactory
	4 Mar 1734	2 lacquered by Reinow
3. Deliveries	1731/1732	6 without indication as to condition, 5 enameled
4. Historical price	1 talers for lacquering by Reinow	

Historical inventory number

N = 181-W [1770 and 1779 inventories] "three owls on pedestals, each with a mouse in its mouth, one lacquered [added later:] Only one has a mouse in its mouth, the other two are lacquered" [from the size = owl]

N = 182-W [1770 and 1779 inventories] "two enameled owls" [from the size = barn owls]

Holdings

1. Quantities	a) Japanese Palace:	
	17 Dec 1732	5
	18 Feb 1735	11
	9 Mar 1736	11
	Tower Room Inv. 1769	2 barn owls
	Inv. 1770	3 owls
	Inv. 1779	3 owls
	b) Royal Collection 1900:	
	2 owls	
	1 enameled barn owl	
	1 enameled barn owl in the castle museum	
2. Sales/losses	no reference	
3. Present-day holdings	Dresden Porcelain Collection 1 white owl 1 owl with lacquer remains 1 enameled barn owl, AR mark Ball/Graupe 15. 3. 1933 (lot 19) 1 white barn owl, AR marks	

Parrots

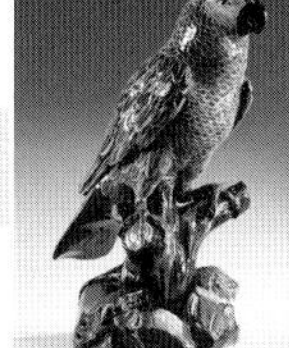

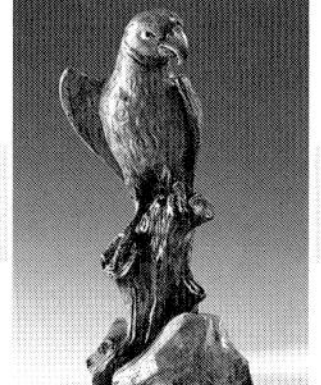

Note

Research related to the category "Parrots" faces the same problem as that which besets the monkey figures and the birds of prey; the only parrots which were called by their own name in the sources are the macaws, with the smaller parrot figures being lumped together under headings which were sometimes quite idiosyncratic. Furthermore, study of the lists reveals that the distinction made between parrots and parakeets does not accord with that followed in present-day zoological usage. The information provided below was arrived at by comparing the extant porcelain figures with the information

provided by the historical lists and with the descriptions and size data in the inventories, insofar as these exist. The numerical statistics make it possible to establish which figures were gray parrots and which rose-ringed parakeets.
The Dresden Porcelain Collection possesses two parakeets, one with the inventory number N = 188-W and the other N = 275-W, so that at least the figures listed in the 1770 and 1779 inventories cannot but have been of these birds; the sizes are right, but the color descriptions do not quite fit.
The German-language historical names are included in inverted commas as a complement to the numerical statistics, with identifications in brackets, qualified as hypothetical with "presumably," or as more or less certain with "most likely" ("wohl").

Name

1. Historical name	*Pappegoye, Papagey, Papogey; Manninchen* (presumably Gray Parrot)
2. Latin name	gray parrot: Psittacus erithacus
	rose-ringed parakeet: Psittacula krameri

Model

1. Modeler	gray parrot: Johann Joachim Kaendler (attributed)
	rose-ringed parakeet: Johann Gottlieb Kirchner (attributed)[115]
2. Dating	gray parrot: Oct – Dec 1731 (attributed)
	parakeet: 1731 (attributed)
3. Work report/*Rapport* etc.	no reference
4. Size	gray parrot: H: 34.5 cm
	parakeet: H: 40 cm
5. Revival	no reference
6. Mold number	no record made

Orders/Deliveries

1. Quantity ordered	Early 1732	8 gray parrots
	18 Nov 1732	4 gray parrots
	17 Dec 1732	12 gray parrots 12 "Manninchen" (presumably gray parrots)
	26 Nov 1733	13 gray parrots
	18 Feb 1735	4 gray parrots
	9 Mar 1736	4 gray parrots
2. Information on production	13 Dec 1731	9 gray parrots finished at manufactory, 5 gray parrots enameled, finished at manufactory
	18 Aug 1732	7 gray parrots enameled, finished at manufactory
3. Deliveries	1731/1732	2 gray parrots (no further information), 8 gray parrots enameled (presumably parakeets), 3 "Manincken" enameled (presumably gray parrots)
	7 Mar 1733 – 22 Oct 1734	6 large gray parrots, 3 small gray parrots
	1734	6 gray parrots altogether (presumably the six from the previous list)
	Mar 1736	2 gray parrots; in the 1736 delivery list referred to as "paroetgen" (= parakeets)
4. Historical price	14 talers (the 6 large ones from the 1734 delivery)	

Historical inventory number

N = 188-W [Tower Room inventory 1769]
"two parrots in many colors, on pedestals [later crossed out]"

[1770 and 1779 inventories]
"three parrots in many colors, on pedestals" [on grounds of size = parakeets]

N = 275-W [Tower Room inventory 1769]
"two parrots"

[1770 and 1779 inventories]
"two parrots with black-gray heads, on pedestals [later addition:] are green" [on grounds of size, most likely = parakeets]

Holdings

1. Quantities	a) Japanese Palace:	
	17 Dec 1732	12 gray parrots
	18 Feb 1735	16 gray parrots 3 "Manninchen" (presumably gray parrots)
	9 Mar 1736	16 gray parrots 3 "Manninchen" (presumably gray parrots)
	Tower Room Inv. 1769	4 gray parrots (two crossed out later)
	Inv. 1770	5 gray parrots
	Inv. 1779	5 gray parrots
	b) Royal Collection 1900:	
	4 rose-ringed parakeets 1 gray parrot	
	1 large Alexandrine parakeet (according to Sponsel) 6 "amazons" (according to Sponsel)	
2. Sales/losses	24 Oct 1931	to Arthur Wittekind 1 parakeet[116]
	30 Sept 1932	to Arthur Wittekind 1 parakeet[117]
3. Present-day holdings	parakeet: Dresden Porcelain Collection 4 enameled	
	gray parrot: Amsterdam, Rijksmuseum 1 enameled	

Peacock

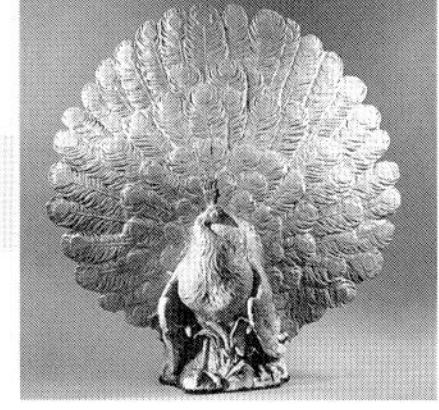

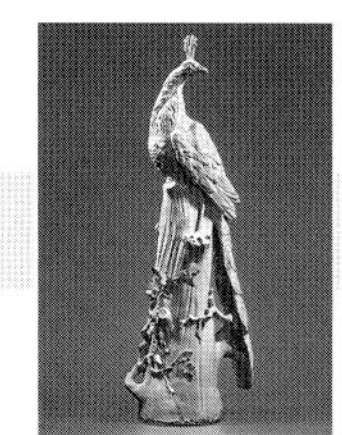

Note

There are two versions of the large Peacock – in one, it is sitting on a tall tree-stump, and in the other it is displaying its fan. The inventories are the only sources which distinguish between the two versions, which is why the two figures are catalogued under one heading here. In the inventories the sitting peacocks are also referred to as "Pfau Hühner."

Name

1. Latin name	Pavo cristatus

Model

1. Modeler	both: Johann Joachim Kaendler (proven)
2. Dating	displaying: Mar 1734 (proven)
	sitting: Apr 1734 (proven)
3. Work report/*Rapport* etc.	displaying: work report Mar 1734: "In the month of March 1734 at this Porcelain Factory of the King in Poland and Elector of Saxony the following new models were made ready . . . a peacock modeled as large as life, almost two and a half ells high with its train fanned out like a wheel. Its pedestal is only two ells broad but is done almost entirely as grass, which provides a good hold for the expansive fan, Johann Joachim Kändler"[118]
	sitting: work report Apr 1734: "In the month of April 1734 at this Porcelain Factory of the King in Poland and Elector of Saxony the following new models were made ready . . . a large peacock resting on a high pedestal decorated with a variety of green branches and foliage, 2 and a 1/2 ells high, Johann Joachim Kändler"[119]
4. Size	displaying: L: 47 cm, H: 102 cm
	sitting: L: 40 cm, H: 118 cm
5. Revival	displaying: Karl Stein, Jan – Mar 1921, set of molds completed (addition: set of case-molds incomplete)
	sitting: Karl Stein, June – July 1920, copied from an original figure
6. Mold number	displaying: 114
	sitting: 50

Orders/Deliveries

1. Quantity ordered	Early 1732	8
	18 Nov 1732	4
	17 Dec 1732	4 white[120] 4 colored
	26 Nov 1733	8
	18 Feb 1735	4
	9 Mar 1736	4
2. Information on production		no reference
3. Deliveries	Aug 1734	1 colored
	1734	altogether 4 displaying, 5 sitting
4. Historical price	displaying: 179 talers	
	sitting: 120 talers	

Historical inventory number

displaying: N = 266-W [1770 and 1779 inventories] "four of the same [= peacock] on low pedestals with trains fanned"

sitting: N = 265-W [1770 and 1779 inventories] "five peacocks on high pedestals wound about with green foliage, the crown missing on two of them"

Holdings

1. Quantities	a) Japanese Palace:	
	18 Feb 1735	9
	9 Mar 1736	9
	Inv. 1770	4 displaying 5 sitting
	Inv. 1779	4 displaying 5 sitting
	b) Royal Collection 1900:	
		3 displaying, white 5 sitting, white
2. Sales/losses	1836	exchange Sèvres 1 displaying
	22 Jan 1931	to Arthur Wittekind 1 sitting
3. Present-day holdings	displaying: Dresden Porcelain Collection 2 white	
	Schloss Moritzburg (on loan from the Dresden Porcelain Collection) 1 white	
	Sèvres, Musée National de Céramique 1 white	
	sitting: Dresden Porcelain Collection 3 white	
	Luzern, Otto Büel,[121] then New York, Winston Guest, now New York, Pflueger Collection (to go to Boston, Museum of Fine Arts) 1 white	

Pelican

Name

1. Historical name	*Löffel Gannß* ("spoon goose")
2. Latin name	Pelecanus onocrotalus

Model

1. Modeler	Johann Joachim Kaendler (proven)
2. Dating	Oct 1732 (proven)
3. Work report/*Rapport* etc.	*Rapport* Oct 1732: "The following new models have been finished . . . a large 'spoon goose' devouring a carp"[122]
4. Size	L: 80 cm, H: 82 cm
5. Revival	Erich Oehme, July – Aug 1921, set of molds completed
	Wünsche, 1964, set of molds completed from an original figure
6. Mold number	30

Orders/Deliveries

1. Quantity ordered	18 Nov 1732	4
	17 Dec 1732	8
	26 Nov 1733	8
	18 Feb 1735	4
	9 Mar 1736	4
2. Information on production	17 Dec 1732	1 in production
	17 Nov 1733	1 enameled, finished in manufactory [most likely meaning painted with cold colors]
3. Deliveries	18 Nov 1733	1 colored
	Aug 1734	1 colored
	Nov – Dec 1734	1
	Mar 1735	3 colored
4. Historical price	204 talers	

Historical inventory number

N = 269-W [1770 inventory] "three pelicans with colored beaks, have fire-cracks"

[1779 inventory] "two pelicans with colored beaks, have fire-cracks"

N = 319-W [1770 and 1779 inventories] "three pelicans colored black and light gray, with colored beaks, have fire-cracks"

Holdings

1. Quantities	a) Japanese Palace:	
	17 Dec 1732	no reference
	18 Feb 1735	6
	9 Mar 1736	6
	Inv. 1770	6
	Inv. 1779	5
	b) Royal Collection 1900:	
	2 white	
2. Sales/losses	1836	exchange Sèvres 1
	17 Apr 1849	to Teichert (branch of the manufactory) 1
	8 Jan 1851	to Helena Wolfssohn 1
	9 Jan 1851	to Helena Wolfssohn 1
3. Present-day holdings	Dresden Porcelain Collection 2 white 1 in pieces	
	Sèvres, Musée National de Céramique 1 white	
	England, Raby Castle 1 white	
	London, private collection 1 white	

Pheasant (Golden Pheasant)

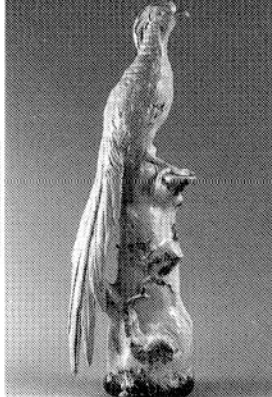

Note

As there is no mention, either in the lists or in any other sources, of a "Golden Pheasant," the figure was clearly recorded under another name. The quantities can however be deduced through comparison and cross-checking with other birds; as the lists record that "pheasants" were delivered before the year in which Kaendler created his normal pheasant model, namely 1735, the bird referred to must have been the Golden Pheasant, to which the expression "indianische Fasan" must also correspond. Strangely enough, the Golden Pheasants do not appear – as such – in the interim delivery totals of 1736. The dating can be derived clearly from stylistic features. Compare also the "Bird on a high pedestal."

Name

1. Historical name	*Fasan, indianischer Fasan*
2. Latin name	Chrysolophus pictus

Model

1. Modeler	Johann Joachim Kaendler (attributed)
2. Dating	Oct – Dec 1731 (attributed)
3. Work report/*Rapport* etc.	no reference
4. Size	L: 25 cm, H: 81 cm

5. Revival	no reference
6. Mold number	75

Orders/Deliveries

1. Quantity ordered	no reference, possibly ordered as "Pheasant" without any further distinction	
2. Information on production	13 Dec 1731 18 Aug 1732	2 unfired at manufactory 2 finished at manufactory
	4 Mar 1734	2 lacquered by Reinow
3. Deliveries	1731/1732	4
4. Historical price	1 taler for the lacquering by Reinow	

Historical inventory number

no reference[123]

Holdings

1. Quantities	a) Japanese Palace:	
	17 Dec 1732	6
	18 Feb 1735	4
	9 Mar 1736	no reference
	Inv. 1770	no reference
	Inv. 1779	no reference
	b) Royal Collection 1900:	
	no reference	
2. Sales/losses	1963	to A. van der Meer 1
3. Present-day holdings	Dresden Porcelain Collection 2 white with lacquer remains	
	Dresden Porcelain Collection, then (1964) A. van der Meer, now Amsterdam, Rijksmuseum 1 enameled	

Pheasants, cock and hen

Note

In the orders, and in some of the delivery lists, no distinction is made between cock and hen pheasant.

Name

1. Latin name	Phasianus colchicus

Model

1. Modeler	both: Johann Joachim Kaendler (proven)
2. Dating	cock: Feb 1735 (proven)
	hen: Mar 1735 (proven)
3. Work report/*Rapport* etc.	cock: work report Feb 1735: "Modeled a life-size cock pheasant, with the pedestal it is resting upon done as a sod of earth modeled with many ears of corn, grass and a variety of decorative leaves, Johann Joachim Kändler"[124]
	hen: work report Mar 1735: "I have done a hen pheasant for the Palace with three youngs chicks sittings by her, resting on a pedestal which I took the greatest trouble to decorate with ears of corn, grass, foliage, strawberries and the like, Johann Joachim Kändler"[125]
4. Size	cock: H: 75.5 cm
	hen: H: 49.5 cm
5. Revival	no reference
6. Mold number	cock: 1765
	hen: 1766

Orders/Deliveries

1. Quantity ordered	18 Nov 1732	4
	17 Dec 1732	12
	26 Nov 1733	8
	18 Feb 1735	4
	9 Mar 1736	4
2. Information on production	Apr 1735	1 finished at manufactory
	May 1735	10 cocks and hens finished at manufactory
3. Deliveries	1735	5 cocks altogether, 6 hens
	June 1735	2 enameled
	July 1735	8 cocks and hens, enameled
	Sept 1735	1 hen, enameled
4. Historical price	cock: 93 talers	
	hen: 96 talers	

Historical inventory number

N = 325-W [Tower Room inventory 1769] "one pheasant on a colored [= covered with undergrowth] pedestal"

[1770 and 1779 inventories] "a pheasant on the same kind of pedestal [= white, covered with undergrowth], the tail defective"

N = 326-W [Tower Room inventory 1769] "two hen pheasants with their young"

[1770 and 1779 inventories] "two of the same [cock pheasants], pedestals covered with green leaves and grass"

Holdings

1. Quantities		
a) Japanese Palace	9 Mar 1736	5 cocks 6 hens
	Tower Room Inv. 1769	2 cocks 2 hens
	Inv. 1770	1 cock 2 hens
	Inv. 1779	1 cock 2 hens
	b) Royal Collection 1900:	
	1 cock, enameled	
	2 hens, enameled	
2. Sales/losses	no reference	
3. Present-day holdings	no record made	

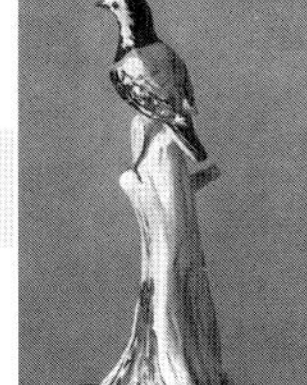

Pied Wagtail

Name

1. Latin name	Motacilla alba

Model

1. Modeler	Johann Gottlieb Kirchner (proven)
2. Dating	Feb 1733 (proven)
3. Work report/*Rapport* etc.	work report Feb 1733: "In the month of February 1733, I made ready the following models . . . a life-size pied wagtail sitting on a tree"[126]
4. Size	H: 26 cm
5. Revival	no reference
6. Mold number	58

Orders/Deliveries

1. Quantity ordered	no reference	
2. Information on production	no reference	
3. Deliveries	18 Nov 1733	4 enameled
	5 Mar – 17 Dec 1735	2
4. Historical price	5 talers 16 groschen (1733)	
	5 talers 12 groschen (1735)	

Historical inventory number

N = 284-W [1770 and 1779 inventories] "four pied wagtails on high pedestals, one defective" [delivery 1733]

N = 316-W [1770 and 1779 inventories] "two pied wagtails, colored, on high white pedestals" [delivery 1735]

Holdings

1. Quantities	a) Japanese Palace:	
	18 Feb 1735	6
	9 Mar 1736	6
	Inv. 1770	6
	Inv. 1779	6
	b) Royal Collection 1900:	
	6 enameled	
2. Sales/losses	no reference	
3. Present-day holdings	no record made	

Roller

Note

This model was sometimes decorated as a jay.

Name

1. Historical name	*Mandel Kraen, Mandel Grahnen*
2. Latin name	Coracias garrulus

Model

1. Modeler	Johann Joachim Kaendler (proven)
2. Dating	Sept 1735 (proven)
3. Work report/*Rapport* etc.	work report Aug 1735: "Started a roller for the Royal Palace order, but it still has some work to be done on it"[127]
	work report Sept 1735: " . . . the roller which still has to be finished, sitting on a tree-stump overgrown with much foliage on which a variety of beetles and caterpillars are to be seen, some being eaten by the roller, Johann Joachim Kändler"[128]
4. Size	H: 37.5 cm (Inv. no. 253)
	H: 33 cm (Inv. no. 352)
5. Revival	no reference
6. Mold number	953

Orders/Deliveries

1. Quantity ordered	18 Nov 1732	4
	17 Dec 1732	8
	26 Nov 1733	8

	18 Feb 1735	4
	9 Mar 1736	4
2. Information on production	no reference	
3. Deliveries	Mar 1736	4
	May 1736	2
4. Historical price	12 talers	

Historical inventory number

N = 253-W[129] [1770 and 1779 inventories]
"a roller, on a colored hill"

N = 352-W [1770 and 1779 inventories]
"two colored rollers, on pedestals with beetles and caterpillars"

Holdings

1. Quantities	a) Japanese Palace:	
	9 Mar 1736	6
	Inv. 1770	3
	Inv. 1779	3
	b) Royal Collection 1900:	
	no reference	
2. Sales/losses	no reference	
3. Present-day holdings	no record made	

Sparrowhawk

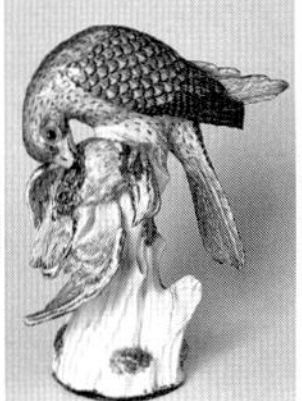

Name

1. Historical name	*Lerchenstösser* ("lark-basher"), *Lerchen Geyer* ("lark vulture"), *Rittelweibgen*
2. Latin name	Accipiter nisus (= Northern Sparrowhawk; not the American Kestrel, likewise known in the United States as the Sparrow Hawk)

Model

1. Modeler	Johann Joachim Kaendler (proven)
2. Dating	Apr 1734 (proven)
3. Work report/*Rapport* etc.	work report Apr 1734: "In the month of April 1734 at this Porcelain Factory of the King in Poland and Elector of Saxony the following new models were made ready . . . a 'Rittelweibgen' or 'Lerchen Geyer' done life-size eating a lark and resting on a decorated pedestal, Johann Joachim Kändler"[130]
4. Size	H: 30 cm
5. Revival	Karl Stein, Dec 1926 to Feb 1927, copied from an original figure
6. Mold number	196

Orders/Deliveries

1. Quantity ordered	no reference
2. Information on production	no reference
3. Deliveries	5 Mar – 17 Dec 1735, 3 of which Mar 1735: 2 colored
4. Historical price	10 talers 22 groschen

Historical inventory number

no reference

Holdings

1. Quantities	a) Japanese Palace:	
	18 Feb 1735	2
	9 Mar 1736	3
	Inv. 1770	no reference
	Inv. 1779	no reference
	b) Royal Collection 1900:	
	no reference	
2. Sales/losses	no reference	
3. Present-day holdings	Dresden Porcelain Collection (1?) enameled	

Stork

Note

Although there is no evidence for a stork model as such having been made for the Japanese Palace, the court lacquerer Reinow is in 1734 to be found stating that he has lacquered three storks. These must have been figures made from a different bird model, which he colored as storks. The Crane did not come into being until later, nor can they have been bustards, as at that point all the bustards in the palace had already been painted. We can thus assume that the figures Reinow painted in this instance must have been herons. What the Stork was (expressly referred to as "large") that Johann Friedrich Eberlein created in July 1735, and what figure the firing report of 1736 was referring to, are puzzling questions, firstly because all the long-legged birds (heron, crane, bustard and so on) were by that time already finished and installed in the Japanese Palace, and secondly because there is no trace of any further large stork-like figure whatsoever in any of the sources. Was this model perhaps a complete failure?

Name

1. Latin name	Ciconia ciconia

Orders/Deliveries

1. Quantity ordered	18 Nov 1732	4

	17 Dec 1732	4 black
	26 Nov 1733	8
	18 Feb 1735	4
	9 Mar 1736	4
2. Work report/*Rapport* etc.	work report July 1735: "One large stork, for which two necks, Johann Friedrich Eberlein, sculptor"[131]	
3. Information on production	4 Mar 1734	"1 as white stork lacquered by Reinow, 2 as black storks lacquered by Reinow"
	Jan 1736	4 finished at manufactory (firing report, see Note)

Swallow

Name

1. Latin name	Hirundo rustica

Model

1. Modeler	Johann Joachim Kaendler (proven)
2. Dating	Sept 1732 (proven)
3. Work report/*Rapport* etc.	*Rapport* Sept 1732: "For his part, the modeler Kentler has modeled and made ready . . . a swallow"[132]
4. Size	H: 10.5 cm (Inv. nos. N = 190-W and N = 214-W)
	H: 13 cm (Inv. no. N = 288-W)
5. Revival	no reference
6. Mold number	no record made

Orders/Deliveries

1. Quantity ordered	no reference	
2. Information on production	no reference	
3. Deliveries	1732	2
	18 Nov 1733	2
	1734	2
4. Historical price	2 talers 8 groschen	

Historical inventory number

N = 190-W [1770 and 1779 inventories] "a swallow on a pedestal, defective"

N = 214-W [1770 and 1779 inventories] "four swallows on pedestals, defective"

N = 288-W [1770 and 1779 inventories] "two colored swallows on pedestals, 1 defective"

Holdings

1. Quantities	a) Japanese Palace:	
	18 Feb 1735	8
	9 Mar 1736	8
	Inv. 1770	7
	Inv. 1779	7
	b) Royal Collection 1900:	
	6 enameled	
2. Sales/losses	no reference	
3. Present-day holdings	no record made	

Swan

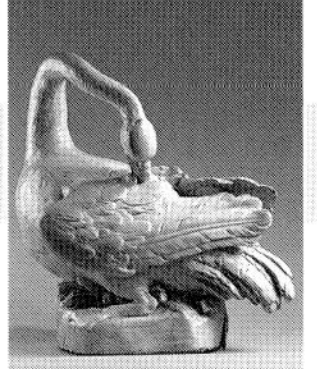

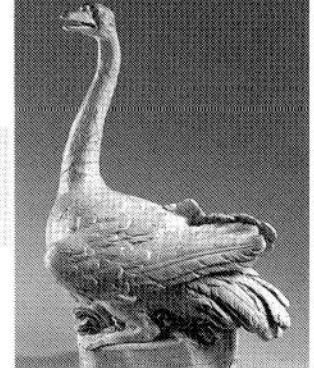

Note

Two necks were modeled for the large Swan, so that in one version it is holding its head up and in the other hiding it in its feathers. The sources make no distinction between the two versions.

Name

1. Latin name	Cygnus olor

Model

1. Modeler	Johann Friedrich Eberlein (proven)
2. Dating	Apr – May 1735 (proven)
3. Work report/*Rapport* etc.	work report Apr – May 1735: "What I, the undersigned, sculpted at the Royal Porcelain Manufactory from April 18 until the end of the month of May . . . a large swan with two necks, Johann Friedrich Eberlein, sculptor"[133]
	work report July 1735: "Did two large swans in paste, Johann Friedrich Eberlein, sculptor"[134]
4. Size	with raised head: L: 57 cm, H: 75 cm
	with head in its feathers: L: 57 cm, H: 56 cm
5. Revival	Karl Stein, Feb 1924, copied
6. Mold number	144

Orders/Deliveries

1. Quantity ordered	18 Nov 1732	4
	17 Dec 1732	4
	26 Nov 1733	8
	18 Feb 1735	4
	9 Mar 1736	4

2. Information on production	Aug 1735	1 finished at manufactory
	Oct 1735	1 finished at manufactory
	Nov 1735	1 finished at manufactory
3. Deliveries	Mar 1736	3
4. Historical price	81 talers 6 groschen	

Historical inventory number

N = 349-W [1770 and 1779 inventories] "three swans, with fire-cracks"

Holdings

1. Quantities	a) Japanese Palace:	
	9 Mar 1736	3
	Inv. 1770	3
	Inv. 1779	3
	b) Royal Collection 1900:	
	2 white, with raised heads	
	1 white, with its head in its feathers	
2. Sales/losses	no reference	
3. Present-day holdings	Dresden Porcelain Collection 2 white, with raised heads 1 white, with its head in its feathers	

Swan, small

Note

The small swan model was produced without being specifically ordered and only appears twice in the records, in the interim totals for figures delivered. They are not documented either in the inventory of the Japanese Palace or in that of the Tower Room.

Name

1. Latin name	Cygnus olor

Model

1. Modeler	Johann Friedrich Eberlein (proven)
2. Dating	Apr – May 1735 (proven)
3. Work report/*Rapport* etc.	work report Apr – May 1735: "What I, the undersigned, sculpted at the Royal Porcelain Manufactory from April 18 until the end of the month of May . . . a small one of the same [= swan], and two necks, Johann Friedrich Eberlein, sculptor"[135]
4. Size	L: 24 cm, H: 33 cm
5. Revival	no reference
6. Mold number	no record made

Orders/Deliveries

1. Quantity ordered	no reference
2. Information on production	no reference
3. Deliveries	before Feb 1735 16
4. Historical price	no reference

Historical inventory number

no reference

Holdings

1. Quantities	a) Japanese Palace:	
	18 Feb 1735	16
	9 Mar 1736	16
	Inv. 1770	no reference
	Inv. 1779	no reference
	b) Royal Collection 1900:	
	no reference	
2. Sales/losses	no reference	
3. Present-day holdings	Dresden Porcelain Collection 1 enameled	

Tit

Note

Kaendler's Tit was decorated in two different ways, and the delivery lists distinguish between a Blue Tit and a Great Tit.

Name

1. Latin name	Great Tit: Parus major Blue Tit: Parus caeruleus

Model

1. Modeler	Johann Joachim Kaendler (proven)
2. Dating	Sept 1732 und Feb 1733 (proven)
3. Work report/*Rapport* etc.	*Rapport* Sept 1732: "The modeler Kentler, for his part, has . . . modeled and finished a tit"[136] work report Feb 1733: "In the month of February 1733 the following new models were made ready . . . a 'Druten Meiße', Kändler"[137]
4. Size	H: 10.5 cm
5. Revival	no reference
6. Mold number	no record made

Orders/Deliveries

1. Quantity ordered	no reference	
2. Information on production	no reference	
3. Deliveries	18 Nov 1733	2 great tits, 2 blue tits
	25 Nov 1733	6 great tits
	1734	14 undifferentiated
	5 Mar – 17 Dec 1735	6 undifferentiated
4. Historical price	2 talers (delivery 1734)	
	1 talers 8 groschen (delivery 1735)	

Historical inventory number

N = 216-W [1770 and 1779 inventories] "two tits of the same kind [= on pedestals] each one cracking open a nut"

N = 286-W [1770 and 1779 inventories] "five tits, each cracking open a nut, defective"

N = 317-W [1770 and 1779 inventories] "four blue tits, partly defective"

Holdings

1. Quantities	a) Japanese Palace:	
	17 Dec 1732	no reference
	18 Feb 1735	23
	9 Mar 1736	23
	Inv. 1770	11
	Inv. 1779	11
	b) Royal Collection 1900:	
	7 enameled	
2. Sales/losses	no reference	
2. Present-day holdings	no record made	

Turkeycock

Name

1. Historical name	*Welscher Hahn, Calcuzscher Hahn*
2. Latin name	Meleagris gallopavo

Model

1. Modeler	Johann Joachim Kaendler (proven)
2. Dating	Jan 1733 (proven)
3. Work report/*Rapport* etc.	work report Jan 1733: "In January 1733, the following new models were finished . . . a life-size turkeycock, Kändler"[138]
4. Size	L: 44 cm, H: 56 cm
5. Revival	no reference
6. Mold number	B145

Orders/Deliveries

1. Quantity ordered	18 Nov 1732	4
	17 Dec 1732	4
	26 Nov 1733	8
	18 Feb 1735	4
	9 Mar 1736	4
2. Information on production	17 Nov 1733	3 enameled at manufactory [most likely meaning painted with cold colors]
3. Deliveries	18 Nov 1733	3 colored
	1734	2
4. Historical price	67 talers	

Historical inventory number

N = 271-W [1770 inventory] "five turkeycocks on low pedestals, 3 hens"

[1779 inventory] "five turkeycocks on low pedestals"[139]

Holdings

1. Quantities	a) Japanese Palace:	
	18 Feb 1735	5
	9 Mar 1736	5
	Inv. 1770	5
	Inv. 1779	5
	b) Royal Collection 1900:	
	1 white	
2. Sales/losses	17 Apr 1849	to Teichert (branch of the manufactory) 1
	8 Jan 1851	to Helena Wolfssohn 2
	9 Jan 1851	to Helena Wolfssohn 1
3. Present-day holdings	Dresden Porcelain Collection 1 white	
	England, Raby Castle 1 white	
	England, Waddesdon Manor[140] 1 white	
	Longleat, collection of the Marquess of Bath 1 white	
	Longleat, collection of the Marquess of Bath, then Christie's 13 June 2002 (lot 351), now Los Angeles, J. Paul Getty Museum 1 white	

Turkeyhen

Name

1. Historical name	*Welsche Hühner, Caloutsch-Hüner*
2. Latin name	Meleagris gallopavo

Model

1. Modeler	Johann Friedrich Eberlein (proven)
2. Dating	Aug 1735 (proven)
3. Work report/*Rapport* etc.	work report Aug 1735: "A turkeyhen, for which two necks, Johann Friedrich Eberlein, sculptor"[141]
	work report Sept 1735: "Three turkeyhens done large in paste, Johann Friedrich Eberlein, sculptor"[142]
4. Size	L: 33.5 cm, H: 47 cm
5. Revival	no reference
6. Mold number	B146

Orders/Deliveries

1. Quantity ordered	18 Nov 1732	4
	17 Dec 1732	4
	18 Feb 1735	4
	9 Mar 1736	4
2. Information on production	Nov 1735	3 finished at manufactory
	Jan 1736	1 finished at manufactory
3. Deliveries	1736	4
4. Historical price	58 talers 12 groschen	

Historical inventory number

N = 351-W [1770 and 1779 inventories] "three 'Welsche Hühner', one defective"

Holdings

1. Quantities	a) Japanese Palace:	
	9 Mar 1736	4
	Inv. 1770	3
	Inv. 1779	3
	b) Royal Collection 1900:	
	4 enameled	
2. Sales/losses	1919	Lepke
3. Present-day holdings	Dresden Porcelain Collection 1 enameled 2 enameled, in pieces	

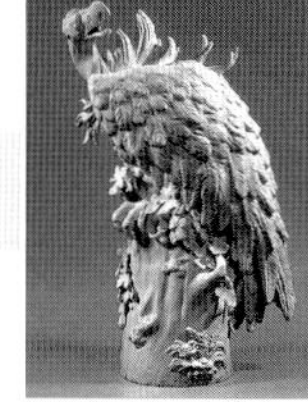

Vulture (Griffon Vulture)

Note

A total of three vulture figures were produced, although in fact only two were ordered, under the names current at the time. Comparisons should therefore be made with "Vulture, King Vulture 1731" and "Vulture, King Vulture 1734." Furthermore, the Griffon Vulture exists in two versions, the one described in detail by Kaendler in a work report as having a cockatoo in its clutches, and a variant created by the repairer without the cockatoo. The two versions are not distinguished in the sources.

Name

1. Historical name	*indianische Gayren* ("Indian vultures")
2. Latin name	Gyps fulvus

Model

1. Modeler	Johann Joachim Kaendler (proven)
2. Dating	Sept 1734 (proven)
3. Work report/*Rapport* etc.	work report June 1734 (bozzetto): "Was in Moritzburg for two days, where I made a small model from life of . . . the Indian vulture together with the cockatoo, Kändler"[143]
	work report Sept/Oct 1734: "Specification of those models which the undersigned invented and finished in August 1734 . . . I have made a model of the large Indian vulture that can be seen living in Moritzburg. Together with the pedestal, which I have done as a tree-stump overgrown with leaves and grass, it is one ell and twelve inches high, truly wondrous to behold on account both of its strange appearance and also of it having just caught a cockatoo, another exotic bird about as big as a large pigeon; it held the mortal remains of this bird torn apart at its feet, and in its beak the bird's innards as if it was on the point of eating them, Johann Joachim Kändler."[144]
4. Size	L: 45 cm, H: 80.5 cm
5. Revival	Karl Stein, Mar – Aug 1915, set of molds completed
6. Mold number	123
	with the same decorative molds as the Macaw (mold no. 24) and the Eagle (mold no. 31)
7. Modeled after	live specimen

Orders/Deliveries

1. Quantity ordered	no reference	
2. Information on production	no reference	
3. Deliveries	1734	1
	Apr 1735	4 enameled [most likely meaning painted with cold colors]
4. Historical price	95 talers	

Historical inventory number

N = 274-W [1770 and 1779 inventories] "a white Indian vulture with ash-colored beak, on a high pedestal covered with leaves" [delivery 1734]

N = 322-W [1770 and 1779 inventories] "four white Indian vultures with ash-colored beaks, on high pedestals covered with leaves, each one clutching and devouring a cockatoo, all damaged and ridden with fire-cracks" [delivery 1735]

Holdings

1. Quantities	a) Japanese Palace:	
	18 Feb 1735	5
	9 Mar 1736	5
	Inv. 1770	5
	Inv. 1779	5
	b) Royal Collection 1900:	
	details given unclear	
2. Sales/losses	1836	exchange Sèvres 1 with cockatoo
	8 Jan 1851	to Helena Wolfssohn 1 with cockatoo
3. Present-day holdings	Dresden Porcelain Collection 1 with cockatoo, white 1 without cockatoo, white	
	Sèvres, Musée National de Céramique 1 with cockatoo, white	
	England, Raby Castle 1 without cockatoo	

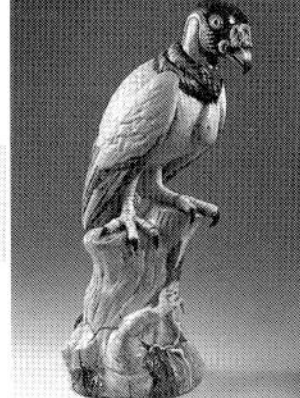

Vulture (King Vulture, 1731)

Note

Compare also especially the note to "Vulture, King Vulture, model of 1734." The king vulture model was realized in various different ways when it came to the repairing. At the stage when the paste had a leather-like texture, the bird's body was cut off at different heights before being placed onto the pedestal, so that some figures stand on stretched-out legs, some are rather more bent over with the legs well visible, and some are represented crouching low down on the tree-stump. It is interesting that the three groups thus identified with their different measurements are also recorded in the inventory as having been delivered at different times. It is however not quite clear whether the variants were made for the practical reason of minimizing firing damage, or simply for the sake of variety. The latter is more probable, principally because the vultures with their heads lowered were done first, and then the crouching ones and the ones standing upright together, and then finally one further one standing upright. This has been reflected as far as possible in the present entries. In the eighteenth century the parts of all the different figures were taken from the same basic molds and then varied when the repairers cut them to the size and shape they required; when the model was recreated in the twentieth century two sets of molds were created for two different-sized variants.

Name

1. Historical name	*KropffVogel, Grobvogel, Krob-Vogel, Krobgvogel* ("crop bird")
2. Latin name	Sarcorhamphus papa

Model

1. Modeler	Johann Joachim Kaendler (attributed)
2. Dating	Oct – Dec 1731 (attributed)
3. Work report/*Rapport* etc.	no reference
4. Size	crouching, Inv. no. 279, 4 copies: L: 35 cm, H: 60 cm
	with head down, Inv. no. 180, 2 copies: L: 35 cm, H: 64 cm
	standing upright, Inv. no. 279, 3 copies
	and Inv.no. 320, 1 Stück: L: 35 cm, H: 71 cm
5. Revival	crouching: Karl Stein, May – July 1927, copied from an original figure
	standing upright: Karl Stein, Feb – May 1927, copied from an original figure
6. Mold number	crouching: 125
	standing upright: 122

Orders/Deliveries

1. Quantity ordered	26 Nov 1733	2
2. Information on production	13 Dec 1731	1 finished at manufactory, 2 unfired at manufactory
3. Deliveries	1731/1732	2 enameled
	7 Mar 1733 – 22 Oct 1734	4
	Nov – Dec 1734	3
	Mar 1735	1 colored
4. Historical price	66 talers 8 groschen	

Historical inventory number

N = 180-W [1770 and 1779 inventories] "two 'crop birds' on pedestals, each one ell and three inches high" [deliveries 1731/1732]

N = 279-W [1770 and 1779 inventories] "seven 'crop birds'on high pedestals decorated with

	leaves, 3 of them 1 ell and 6 inches high, and the others 1 ell and 2 inches high, defective" [deliveries 1734]
	N = 320-W [1770 and 1779 inventories] "one 'crop bird' colored on a high pedestal decorated with leaves, damaged, 1 ell 6 inches high" [delivery 1735]

Holdings

1. Quantities	a) Japanese Palace:	
	17 Dec 1732	no reference
	18 Feb 1735	10
	9 Mar 1736	10
	Inv. 1770	10
	Inv. 1779	10
	b) Royal Collection 1900:	
	details given unclear	
2. Sales/losses	17 Apr 1849	to Teichert (branch of the manufactory) 1 Vulture
	7 July 1853	to Anatol Demidoff 1 Vulture
3. Present-day holdings	Dresden Porcelain Collection 1 crouching, white 1 standing upright, enameled	
	Kykuit, Rockefeller collection 2 crouching, white (= both: N = 180-W)	
	New York, Pflueger Collection (to go to the Museum of Fine Arts, Boston) 2 with head down	
	Longleat, collection of the Marquess of Bath 1 standing upright, with remains of lacquer	
	Longleat, collection of the Marquess of Bath, then Christie's 13. 6. 2002 (lot 353), now London,	
	Victoria & Albert Museum 1 crouching, remains of lacquer (= N = 320-W)	
	Longleat, collection of the Marquess of Bath, then Christie's 13. 6. 2002 (lot 352), now in the trade 1 standing upright, remains of lacquer	

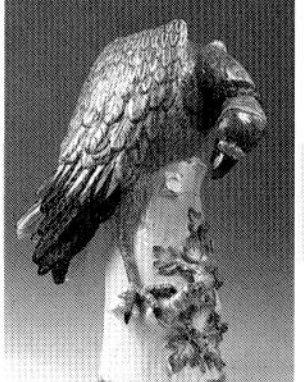

Vulture (King Vulture, 1734)

Note

Since Albiker's 1935 publication, this figure has normally been referred to – when the historical name has not been used – as the "Kronengeier." Interestingly enough, this name is not in fact used for any kind of vulture, nor was it in currency in the early twentieth century (information kindly supplied by Dr. Christiane Quaisser from the ornithological department of the Institut für Systematische Zoologie, Museum für Naturkunde, Berlin). It is unclear where Albiker got the name from is unclear, but this question need not be considered here: the shape and coloring of this bird tell us that it is a king vulture.
It is not hard to explain why Kaendler decided, in 1734, to make a new and very different model of a bird he had already modeled once three years earlier. The first model of 1731 (known historically as the "Kropfvogel" on account of its crop) must have been done from a print, and it is clear from its physical characteristics that it is definitely a king vulture. As Kaendler was in 1731 not familiar with the creature's natural appearance and behavior, the impression given by the figure he modeled is correspondingly stiff and unnatural, and its enamel decoration, far from being a true reflection of that of a real king vulture, is sheer exotic fantasy. Study of the Moritzburg king vulture in 1734, however, enabled Kaendler to come up with a quite new concept, which bore fruit in a vulture which, ogling down intently from its tree-stump, is very much more lifelike. Even the colors used in the decoration of this version have a closeness to those of a real mature king vulture – in itself an argument in favor of the enamel coloring being original, which has sometimes been doubted. Whether Kaendler was in 1734 aware that he was modeling a species of bird he had already modeled once from (probably) a print is unclear, but the name given to the second model suggests that it was only in 1734 that the manufactory realized what species they were dealing with; now the bird was called the "König von Wauwon" (a clear Germanization of "king of vultures" or "roi des vautours"), rather than just "Kropfvogel" ("crop-bird"), an appellation derived from one of its external features.

Name

1. Historical name	*König von Wawou, König Wouwou, König von Waiwou, König von Wawa*
2. Latin name	Sarcorhamphus papa

Model

1. Modeler	Johann Joachim Kaendler (proven)
2. Dating	June 1734 (proven)
3. Work report/*Rapport* etc.	work report June 1734 (bozzetto): "Was in Moritzburg for two days, where I made a small figure of the 'King of Vultures' from life, Kändler"[145]
	work report June 1734: "In the month of June, at this Porcelain Factory of the King in Poland and Elector of Saxony, the undersigned made ready the following new models . . . a large Indian bird by the name of the King of Vultures, its height with the pedestal being one and a quarter ells, and the pedestal being decorated with leafwork in the Indian fashion, Kändler"[146]
4. Size	L: 43 cm, H: 58 cm
5. Revival	no reference
6. Mold number	1768
7. Source of inspiration	live specimen

Orders/Deliveries

1. Quantity ordered	18 Nov 1732	4
	17 Dec 1732	8
	26 Nov 1733	12
	18 Feb 1735	4
	9 Mar 1736	4

2. Information on production	no reference	
3. Deliveries	1734	5
	Mar 1735	1 colored
4. Historical price	67 talers 16 groschen	
	67 talers 12 groschen (for the single figure delivered later)	

Historical inventory number

N = 273-W [1770 and 1779 inventories] "five black-gray king vultures, also reddish-painted on high white pedestals decorated with leaves" [delivery 1734]

N = 321-W [1770 and 1779 inventories] "a king-bird, known as a 'Wauwau', reddish and black-gray, on high white pedestals with leaves" [delivery 1735]

Holdings

1. Quantities	a) Japanese Palace:	
	18 Feb 1735	6
	9 Mar 1736	6
	Inv. 1770	6
	Inv. 1779	6
	b) Royal Collection 1900:	
	details unclear	
2. Sales/losses	1919	Lepke 1
	1920	to Ligner-Stiftung 1
3. Present-day holdings	Dresden Porcelain Collection 2 enameled	
	Lepke 1919, then Ole Olsen Collection now Kopenhagen, Kunstindustriemuseum 1 enameled	
	Sotheby's 6 June 1950, collection of Lord Hastings, now in a private collection in New York 1 enameled	
	Kykuit, Rockefeller collection 1 white	
	Ligner-Stiftung 1920, present whereabouts unknown 1	

Woodpecker

Name

1. Historical name	*Baumhacker*
2. Latin name	Green Woodpecker: Picus viridis
	Great Spotted Woodpecker: Dendrocopos major

Model

1. Modeler	Johann Joachim Kaendler (proven)
2. Dating	Jan 1733, Feb 1733, Mar 1734 (proven)
3. Work report/*Rapport* etc.	work report Jan 1733: "In January 1731, the following new models were made ready . . . a woodpecker with wings spread out, Kändler"[147]
	work report Feb 1733: "In February 1733 the following new models were made . . . a green woodpecker, Kändler"[148]
	work report Mar 1734: "In the month of March 1734 at this Porcelain Factory of the King in Poland and Elector of Saxony the following new models were made ready . . . a green woodpecker, also life-size and resting on a decorated pedestal, Johann Joachim Kändler"[149]
4. Size	H: 31 cm
5. Revival	no reference
6. Mold number	55 (1733 model)
	56 (1734 model)

Orders/Deliveries

1. Quantity ordered	no reference	
2. Information on production	no reference	
3. Deliveries	1734	7
	Mar 1736	2
4. Historical price	no reference	

Historical inventory number

N = 282-W [1770 inventory] "seven woodpeckers on white pedestals, mostly defective, [later addition:] one broken during cleaning"

[1779 inventory] "six woodpeckers on white pedestals, all defective"

N = 354-W [1770 and 1779 inventories] "one colored woodpecker on a high pedestal decorated with green foliage, defective"

Holdings

1. Quantities	a) Japanese Palace:	
	18 Feb 1735	7
	9 Mar 1736	7
	Inv. 1770	8
	Inv. 1779	7
	b) Royal Collection 1900:	
	10 of various kinds and sizes, enameled	
2. Sales/losses	no reference	
3. Present-day holdings	no record made	

Further bird models

Note

Two further birds fall into the period when bird figures were being produced for the Japanese Palace, but they cannot be made to correspond to the extant sources for orders and deliveries; for this reason, only the work reports are quoted here.

1. Nuthatch *Kleiber*

Name

1. Historical name	*BaumLäuffergen*
2. Latin name	Sitta europaea

Model

1. Modeler	Johann Joachim Kaendler (proven)
2. Dating	Jan 1733 (proven)
3. Work report/*Rapport* etc.	work report Jan 1733: "In January 1733 the following new models were made ready . . . another nuthatch the size of a wren, Kändler"[150]

2. Robin *Rotkehlchen*

Name

1. Historical name	*Roth Kählgen* ("redbreast")
2. Latin name	Erithacus rubecula

Model

1. Modeler	Johann Joachim Kaendler (proven)
2. Dating	Jan 1733 (proven)
3. Work report/*Rapport* etc.	work report Jan 1733: "In the month of January 1733 the following new models were finished . . . a robin, Kändler"[151]

NOTES

1 "Einen großen Bähren in Lebensgröße, Gottlieb Kirchner"; BA, IAa.18, fol. 322a.
2 BA, IAa.22, fol. 227a; see Source 25.
3 BA, IAa.22, fol. 227a; see Source 25.
4 Not, however, in the first chapter, "Aufsätze, Flaschen, Figuren etc," but in the third, "Schalen, Milchkannen, Butterbüchsen etc."
5 "Was ich Endes benander bey der Königl. Porcelain Manufactur von 18. April biß zu Ende des Monaths May vor Bildhauer Arbeit verfertiget, Alß . . . Einen Gemsbock, Groß, Johann Friedrich Eberlein, Bildhauer"; BA, IAa.24, fol. 264a.
6 "Zwey Große Gemßböcke verbotzet, Johann Friedrich Eberlein, Bildhauer"; BA, IAa.24, fol. 265a.
7 "Vier Gemß Böcke auch in Masse verbotzet, Johann Friedrich Eberlein, Bildhauer"; BA, IAa.24, fol. 325a.
8 The author has only seen this example of the figure in photographs. As there would seem to be one more figure in existence than is recorded by the inventories of the Royal Collections, it is also possible that the supernumerary example was produced in the nineteenth or early twentieth century, as is for instance the case with the chamois bearing the swords mark in the Museum für angewandte Kunst, Frankfurt am Main (see Hofmann 1980, fig. 48a).
9 See BA, IIIH. 121.
10 "hingegen [hat] der Modelirer Kentler . . . einen Hund liegend poussiret und gefertiget"; BA, IAa.18, fol. 263b.
11 "Alldieweil . . . ich . . . dergleichen Arbeit encouragiret worden bin, dergestalt, daß auch der Hoff-Commissarius Hörold mir einen Ducaten aus seinem eigenen Beutel bey denen erstern Stücken, als sogenannten Trachen . . . genießen lassen"; BA, IAb. 12, fol. 148a.
12 Strangely enough, there are none mentioned, although the list for 1731/32 records that a number had been delivered.
13 "ist voritzo aufs neue nicht nur ein Elephante . . . von ziemlicher Größe poussiret worden, so nechster Tage zum Abformen in Gipß befördert werden soll"; BA, IAa.16, fol. 109a.
14 "Es sind . . . von den großen Elephanten . . . nunmehro etliche Stücken aus Massa gefertiget worden"; BA, IAa.16, fol. 283b.
15 "Mann hat auch am 7 Aug den ersten Elephanten aus dem Brennhauße zum Waaren-Lager geliefert erhalten, ob er schon einige kleine Riße in sich hat, nach des Hr. Hoff-Commissarii Meynung dennoch vor ein gut Stück passiren und zum eMayllirен genommen werden könne"; BA, IAa.18, fol. 169b.
16 My thanks go to Claus Boltz for this piece of information.
17 "Einen Fuchß,so Eine Hünne frißt, Lebensgröße, Gottlieb Kirchner"; BA, IAa.18, fol. 322a.
18 "Hingegen hat der Modelirer Kentler zu einigen Modelen poussiret und gefertiget . . . eine alte nebst einer jungen Ziege"; BA, IAa.18, fol. 208a.
19 BA, IAa.22, fol. 227a; see Source 25.
20 "Eine Indianische Ratze, wie solche in Königl. Löwen Hauße am Leben sind gefertiget Deren postament worauf sie ruhet Stellet einen Korn Sack vor, wie er oben offen ist und die Ratze daraus frißet, Johann Joachim Kändler"; BA, IAa. 24, fol. 173a.
21 "In den Monath January des 1733. Jahres ist folgendes von mier verfertiget worden, als . . . Einen Leoparten Lebens Größe, Gottlieb Kirchner"; BA, IAa.20, fol. 49a.
22 The unpublished catalog of lost Meissen pieces from the Kunstgewerbemuseum, Berlin (see Krüger 1995) mentions an early Meissen "Lynx" under the number 233, but on a four-sided pedestal, which on account of its size (H: 89 cm including the pedestal) could have been a leopard; the numbers of extant figures mean that it cannot have been a lynx or a sitting lioness ("tiger").
23 This figure is mentioned in the memoirs of an English art-dealer who found the lion at a small auction, see Warner 2004, 125. I am indebted to John Whitehead for this piece of information.
24 "In den Monath January des 1733. Jahres ist folgendes von mier verfertiget worden, als . . . Ein Thieger dergl. Größe, Gottlieb Kirchner"; BA, IAa.20, fol. 49a.
25 Thus the same mold number as the deer copied in June 1919 by Karl Stein.
26 Published in: Keramik-Freunde der Schweiz, Mitteilungsblatt 44 (1958) 37.
27 "In den Monath January des 1733. Jahres ist folgendes von mier verfertiget worden, als . . . Einen Lux Lebens größe, Gottlieb Kirchner"; BA, IAa.20, fol. 49a.
28 BA, IAa.22, fol. 227a; see Source 25.
29 BA, IAa.22, fol. 227b; see Source 25.
30 The marmoset was produced in many different versions, as it was very probably offered for sale on the open market, like the smaller bird figures. For this reason, no attempt has been made here to list all the figures currently held by public or private collections, or dealers.
31 "So hat auch der Modelirer Kenntler . . . einen großen Affen von besonderer Arth . . . poussiret"; BA, IAa.16, fol. 283a.
32 Illustration in Albiker 1935, fig. 25.
33 "So hat auch der Modelirer Kenntler . . . einen großen Affen von besonderer Arth . . . poussiret"; BA, IAa.16, fol. 283a.
34 It is not clear how Sponsel came up with this figure.
35 Illustration in Albiker 1935, fig. 24.
36 BA, IAa.22, fol. 227a; see Source 25.
37 "Es sind . . . von dem Rhinoceros nunmehro etliche Stücken aus Massa gefertiget worden"; BA, IAa.16, fol. 283b.
38 BA, IAa.22, fol. 227b; see Source 25.
39 "Einen Indianischen Zobel Ebenfalls in Lebens Größe ist vorgestellet wie er auf einen Stock sitze welcher mit Ästen und Blättern bewachsen ist, Johann Joachim Kändler"; BA, IAa.24, fol. 173a.
40 BA, IAa.22, fol. 227b; see Source 25.
41 "Ein Groß Balläis Stück dem Versühn oder Sünden Bock genannt, Nach seiner wunderlich anzusehenden Gestalt und Arth in seiner Natürlichen Größe aus Thon possiret, Johann Joachim Kändler"; BA, IAa.24, fol. 32a.
42 "Ein Schaff in Lebens Größe von Dohn, Johann Friedrich Eberlein, Bildhauer"; BA, IAa.24, fol. 265a.
43 "Ein Schaff, alles von Thon über Lebens Größe, Johann Friedrich Eberlein, Bildhauer"; BA, IAa.24, fol. 264a.
44 "Ein Schaff groß in Masse verbotzet, Johann Friedrich Eberlein, Bildhauer"; BA, IAa.24, fol. 302a.
45 "Ein Schaff groß in Masse verbottzet, Johann Friedrich Eberlein, Bildhauer"; BA, IAa.24, fol. 325a.
46 BA, IAa.22, fol. 227b; see Source 25.
47 "Ein Indianisches großes Schaf mit 2 Hörnern welche wunderlich über des Schafes Augen gewachsen, Johann Joachim Kändler"; BA, IAa.22, fol. 373a.

48 "Zwey Spinxe Verändert = groß, Gottlieb Kirchner"; BA, IAa.18, fol. 322a.
49 "Hingegen hat der Modelirer Kentler zu einigen Modelen poussiret und gefertiget . . . zwey Eichhörngen"; BA, IAa.18, fol. 208.
50 "Ein Eich Hörngen in gestalt eines Thee Krügels mit zweyerley Schwäntzen gefertiget, in daß eine gießet man oben den Thee zum Schwantze hinein, in daß andere aber zu der Band Schleife welche am Halß Bande mit Schellen befindlich, Johann Joachim Kändler"; BA, IAa.24, fol. 175b.
51 BA, IAa.22, fol. 227a; see Source 25.
52 "Anitze aber sind in Arbeit . . . ein Auer Thier welcher ein wildes Schwein um bringet"; SächsHStA loc. 1341, Vol. VI, fol. 323b.
53 "ist voritzo . . . auch ein Auer-Ochße von ziemlicher Größe poussiret worden, so nechster Tage zum Abformen in Gipß befördert werden soll"; BA, IAa.16, fol. 109a.
54 "Wird von dem Modellmeister Kändler die gebührende Vorstellung gethan, wie daß er in dem Jahre 1731, vermöge hoher Anordnung . . . in Moritzburg einen Auer-Ochßen . . . nach dem Leben zeichnen müßen"; BA, IAa.22, fol. 264b.
55 "Wiederum Ein groß Balläis Stück Eine Wölffin in Lebens Größe, sitzet auf den hintern Läufften und hält den Kopff in die Höhe als heulete sie daß Mann den die in Rachen habenden großen Fänge gar deutlich sehen kann, Unter sich aber hat sie 2. Junge Wölffe einen etwas größer als den andern sitzen, welche die Haltung im Feuer hauptsächlich geben müßen, Johann Joachim Kändler"; BA, IAa.24, fol. 173b.
56 BA, IAa.22, fol. 227b; see Source 25.
57 "Im Monath Januario 1733 sind an neuen Modellen gefertiget worden folgende Stücken . . . Noch Einen kleinen Vogel in Größe eines Fincken. Hat Flügel 2 große und 2 kleine Einen langen Schnabel, und der Schwantz bestehet in 2 langen Federn, Welche sich am Ende in eine doppelte ring VerWandeln, Kändler"; BA, IAa.20, fol. 51a.
58 BA, IAa.22, fol. 227b; see Source 25.
59 For this entry, cf. the note on inventory number N = 167-W under "Birds of Prey."
60 Information kindly given by Claus Boltz; see also p. 120.
61 "daß vor etl. Jahren Ihro des höchstseel. Königs Majt. 2 Stk. Indianische Adler zur Fabrique gegeben, umb solche nachzumachen, welche zwar nicht groß, sondern nur ohngefehr 3/4 elln hoch gewesen"; BA, IAe.5, fol. 199a.
62 "zwey Stück große Adler eMayllirt"; SächsHStA loc. 32562, Nr. 120a, fol. 187a–196a, here 193a.
63 SächsHStA, loc. 1341, Vol. VI, fol. 323a/b; see Source 24.
64 SächsHStA, loc. 1341, Vol. VI, fol. 323a/b; see Source 24.
65 SächsHStA, loc. 1341, Vol. VI, fol. 323a/b; see Source 24.
66 In the 1770 inventory, the number 166 referred to here mentions two "Raubvögel" ("birds of prey") on high pedestals, with a later correction in which "Raub" ("prey") was deleted and the measurement (56. 6 cm) raised to 74. 3 cm (cf. the entry "Bird with high pedestal"). The subsequent inventory entry, numbered 167 and quoted here, which referred to the uncorrected term of reference "Raubvogel," was not changed. Given the equation 1 ell = 56. 6 cm, the measurements suggest that this number (167) relates to the sitting osprey or the kestrel.
67 BA, IAa.22, fol. 227b; see Source 25.
68 "Ein Balläis Stück Den Vogel Rohrtummel genannt ist in seiner Größe einem Fisch Reiher gleich, und wegen seines starck befederten Halßes und andern an sich habenden Eigenschafften wunderlich anzusehen, ist vorgestellet wie er in Schilff-Rohr, Binsen und Graß wie es in Teigten zu wachsen Pfleget sitzet, Johann Joachim Kändler"; BA, IAa.24, fol. 108a.
69 "Im Monath Februarii 1733 Sind an Neuen Modellen gefertiget Worden folgende . . . Einen Gimpel Welcher noch ein klein Vögelchen Neben sich zu sitzen hat, Kändler"; BA, IAa.20, fol. 116a.
70 "Einen großen Vogel oder Trappen"; BA, IAa.18, fol. 363a.
71 "hingegen [hat] der Modelirer Kentler . . . einen Canarienvogel poussiret und gefertiget"; BA, IAa.18, fol. 263b.
72 "Im Monath Januario 1733 sind an neuen Modellen gefertiget worden folgende Stücke . . . Ein Canari Vogel auf demNest Worinnen Sich 3 Junge Nebst einem unaus gebrüteten Ey befinden, und vder alte Canari Vogel auf dem Nest Sitzet und die Jungen füttert, Kändler"; BA, IAa.20, fol. 51a.
73 "hingegen [hat] der Modelirer Kentler . . . den Vogel Casuarium in LebensGröße poussiret und gefertiget"; BA, IAa.18, fol. 263b.
74 "Specificatio Dererjenigen Modelle so von Endes-Benannten im Monath Augusti 1734 sind Inventiret und gefertiget worden . . . Noch einen Vogel von ziemlicher Größe Nahmens Gackedu Hat eine sonderliche von Natur gewachsene Haube auf seinem Kopfe wes wegen er sehr artig anzusehen und ruhet auf einem mit Ästen und Laub bewachsenen Postamente, Johann Joachim Kändler"; BA, IAa.22, fol. 317b.
75 The author has not investigated any further examples of this model, which was also produced for the open market after 1736; on this subject, see Blaauwen 2000, 407.
76 "Hingegen hat der Modelirer Kentler zu einigen Modellen poussiret und gefertiget . . . einen Hahn in LebensGröße"; BA, IAa.18, fol. 208a.
77 SächsHStA, loc. 1341, Vol. VI, fol. 323 ab; see Source 24.
78 See Weltkunst 71/2001, 6, 1087.
79 I am grateful to Karel Bobek for the information that the existence of the two figures has been attested since 1816 through the inventory of the estate of the builder of Schloss Kozel, Imperial Master of the Hunt for the Kingdom of Bohemia Johann Adalbert Czernin von Chudenitz (1746–1816), which has been in Kozel since that year.
80 "Zwey Tage in Moritzburg gewesen, Alda . . . den Kranich . . . ins kleine nach dem leben Poussiret, Kändler"; BA, IAa.22, fol. 202a.
81 "Einen Kranich in Lebens Größe Deßen postament besteht in lauter Schilff und Rohr wie es in Teigen zu wachsen pfleget, Johann Joachim Kändler"; BA, IAa.24, fol. 173b.
82 BA, IAa.22, fol. 227b; see Source 25.
83 "hingegen [hat] der Modelirer Kentler . . . eine Trommel Taube poussiret und gefertiget"; BA, IAa.18, fol. 263b.
84 "Sind an Neuen Modellen gefertiget worden . . . Eine Taube Welche auf einen Nest sitzet und brüttet"; BA, IAa.18, fol. 323a.
85 "Im Monath Januario 1733 sind an neuen Modellen gefertiget worden folgende Stücken . . . Ein baar Tauben Welche mit Einander Cordisiren, Kändler"; BA, IAa.20, fol. 51a.
86 "insonderheit einen großen Adler und noch andere Stücke, aus Thon gefertiget, die aber nunmehro in Gips abgeformet und von Porcelain-Massa bereitet worden"; BA, IAa.16, fol. 5ab.
87 SächsHStA, loc. 1341, Vol. VI, fol. 323ab; see Source 24.
88 "Sind an neuen Modelen gefertiget worden . . . einen Großen Adler, Welcher den rechten Flügel in die Höhe Von Sich stecket, Deutet zugleich eines großen Herren Gnade an, Deßen Höhe über 2 elln"; BA, IAa.18, fol. 323a.
89 BA, IAa.22, fol. 227a; see Source 25.
90 The only existing set of molds, which had been completed in 1921, was thrown away when the attics of the Triebischtal manufactory were cleared out for the construction of an extra story. As the only completed realization of the wing-beating eagle (illustrations in Albiker 1935 & 1959, and Gröger 1956) has likewise disappeared, this time from the inner courtyard of the factory, it is now no longer possible to bring this outstanding sculpture of Kaendler's back into production.
91 BA, IAa.22, fol. 227b; see Source 25.
92 "Specificatio Dererjenigen Modelle so von Endes-Benannten im Monath Augusti 1734 sind Inventiret und gefertiget worden . . . Eine Große Africanische Ente groesser als die hiesigen EntVögel seynd Ist sonderlich wegen ihrer an Hals Habenden bunden Graußе und Kragen anzusehen Hat einen Schwantz fast wie eine Henne und ist vor gestellet wie selbige in alerhand Schilff und Graße sitzet, Johann Joachim Kändler"; BA, IAa.22, fol. 317b.
93 The five pieces from April are not included in these six, reflecting a procedure that can also be observed in connection with other animal figures. The interim total of February 1735 shows that the five figures are listed in the April firing report as ready for delivery but were in fact already at the Palace. The only one that is a valid entry is the one from July 1735.
94 "Eine Berl Henne Ebenfalls ins Balläis gehörig Nach ihrer sonderbaren Arth vorgebildet an welcher aber noch etwas weniges zu thun, Johann Joachim Kändler"; BA, IAa.24, fol. 108a.

95 "Die Berel Henne folends fertig gemacht an welcher in vorigen Monath noch etwas zu thun übrig Blieben, Johann Joachim Kändler"; BA, IAa.24, fol. 173a.
96 "Einen neuen Halß und Kopff zu der Perel Henne gefertiget um selbige zu verändern"; BA, IAb.9, fol. 35a.
97 SächsHStA, loc. 1341, Vol. VI, fol. 323a/b; see Source 24.
98 "Hingegen hat der Modelirer Kentler zu einigen Modellen poussiret und gefertiget . . . eine Gluckhenne mit Jungen"; BA, IAa.18, fol. 208a.
99 "Der Modelirer Kentler aber hat einen großen Fisch-Reyher poussiret"; BA, IAa.18, fol. 18a.
100 This information is not taken from the model book, but from BA III. 121, February 1926 (list by Erwin Hösel).
101 "Einen Eigelgabich poussiret welcher ins Königl. Balläis gehörig ist, vorgestellet wie er auf einem großen Eigel Ast sietzet welcher mit Eigeln und Blättern starck bewachsen ist, und sich eine Eigel abfrißet welches sein Futter ist, So sind auch unterschiedliche Raupen wie auch ein Pöner [= Hirschkäfer/stag beetle?], welche sich gerne auf den Eigel Bäumen aufhalten Daran Befindlich, Johann Joachim Kändler"; BA, IAa.24, fol. 343a.
102 "Annoch unterschiedliche Eigel Blätter nebst andern zu behör, Die Eigel Gabichte damit zu verziren in Thon poussiret"; BA, IAb. 14, fol. 102a.
103 According to Hösel, BA, IIIH. 121.
104 "Einen EißVogel possiret wie er auf einem kleinen Stein Klipgen sitzet Daran etwas Blätter Werck gewachßen ist, Johann Joachim Kändler"; BA, IAa.24, fol. 317a.
105 "Hingegen hat der Modelirer Kantlern einen großen Raben nach indianischer Arth . . . poussiret"; BA, IAa.18, fol. 100a.
106 Although the Pflueger Collection catalog by Hugo Morley-Fletcher gives the provenance as "Christie's 26 June 1967," this cannot be the case, on account of the position of the head and certain salient details (firing cracks and so on). The macaw auctioned in 1967 is now in the Schneider Collection, Lustheim, while the one in the Pflueger Collection was sold at "Sotheby's, Parke Bernet, 12 February 1962."
107 "Im Monath Febrarii 1733 Sind an Neuen Modellen gefertiget Worden folgende . . . Eine Aelster in lebens Größe, Kändler"; BA, IAa.20, fol. 116a.
108 "Specificatio Was in dem Monath July 1733 an Neuen Modellen Inventiret und gefertiget worden . . . Einen Vogel Von Mittel Mäßiger Größe Eine Bier Eule genannt auf einem Postament sitzend, Kandler, Modellmeister"; BA, IAa.20, fol. 265a.
109 "Im Monath Martio 1734 sind auf hiesiger Königl. Pohl. und Churfürstl. Sächß. Porcellain Fabrique an neuen Modellen gefertiget worden . . . Einen Vogel Von Mittel-Mäßiger Größe gefertiget welcher Eine Bier Eule genannt wird, Johann Joachim Kändler"; BA, IAa.22, fol. 99a.
110 In the usage of the time "schlecht" meant "simple" ("schlicht"), that is to say, without leaves; see Boltz 1996, 33.
111 In the same monthly report he also lists the model executed for the ostrich egg goblet now kept in the Green Vaults.
112 "Zwey Tage in Moritzburg gewesen Alda den Strauß . . . ins kleine nach dem leben Poussiret, Kändler"; BA, IAa.22, fol. 202a.
113 "Was ich Endes benander bey der Königl. Porcelain Manufactur von 18. April biß zu Ende des Monaths May vor Bildhauer Arbeit verfertiget, Alß . . . Einen Großen Puhu mit einer Taube, JohannFriedrich Eberlein, Bildhauer"; BA, IAa.24, fol. 264a.
114 SächsHStA, loc. 1341, Vol. VI, fol. 323a/b; see Source 24.
115 Compare for style with the Pied Wagtail.
116 According to Zimmermann 1931, three more in the Collection and two at the Residence; see Staatliche Kunstsammlungen Dresden, Archive, Records 36/1931–1933, I: fol. 188.
117 According to Zimmermann 1931, two more in the Collection and two at the Residence; see Staatliche Kunstsammlungen Dresden, Archive, Records 36/1931–1933, II: fol. 361.
118 "Im Monath Martio 1734 sind auf hiesiger Königl. Pohl. und Churfürstl. Sächß. Porcellain Fabrique an neuen Modellen gefertiget worden . . . Einen Pfau in Lebend Größe Modeliret, welcher mit seinem ausgebreiteten Rade förmigen Schwantze fast 2 elln und 1/2 hoch ist Die Breite aber nur **2** elln Deßen Postament Ist fast wie lauter Graß gemacht und giebet solches Graß Dem Groß umschweiffenden Schwantze gute Haltung, Johann Joachim Kändler"; BA, IAa.22, fol. 99a.
119 "Im Monath April 1734 sind an neuen Modellen auf hießiger Königl. Pohl. und Churfürstl. Sächß. Porcellain-Fabrique gefertiget worden . . . Einen großen Pfau welcher auf einem hohen Postament ruhet welches mit allerhand Grünen Zweigen verzieret Nebst andern Blätterwerck Deßen Höhe ist 2 und 1/2 ell, Johann Joachim Kändler"; BA, IAa.22, fol. 151a.
120 On November 22, 1732, Augustus the Strong had acquired two live white peacocks from a Tirolean; see p. 64.
121 According to information for which I am indebted to Prof. Dr. Rudolf Schnyder, this Peacock was shown as item 56 at the exhibition mounted in the Kunsthaus, Zürich, by the Keramik-Freunde der Schweiz, "Schönheit des 18. Jahrhunderts," and illustrated in the catalog; at that time the figure was the property of the Lucerne art-dealer Otto Büel.
122 "Sind an Neuen Modellen gefertiget worden . . . eine Große Löffel Ganß Welche einen Karpffen Verschlinget"; BA, IAa.18, fol. 323a.
123 See "Bird with high pedestal." N = 166-W is possibly the Golden Pheasant.
124 "Einen Faßan Hahn in lebens Größe poussiret, Deßen postament worauf er ruhet in gestalt eines Klumpens Erde, welcher mit vielen Korn Ähren Graß und unterschiedlichen zierlichen Laubblättern bewachsen vorgestellet ist, Johann Joachim Kändler"; BA, IAa.24, fol. 73a.
125 "Eine Faßan Hen als ein Balläis Stück ist vorgestellet wie sie 3 Stück junge Hüner bey sich sitzen hat, ruhet auf einen postament, welches aufs Mühsamste mit Korn Ähren Graß, Laubwerck, Erdbeeren und dergleichen verzieret ist, Johann Joachim Kändler"; BA, IAa.24, fol. 107a.
126 "In den Monath Februar 1733 sindt von mir Modelle verferdiget . . . Eine Bachsteltze auff Einen Baum sitzend Lebens größe, Gottlieb Kirchner"; BA, IAa.20, fol. 115a.
127 "Eine Mandel Krahe angefangen welche ins Königl. Balläis gehörigan welcher aber noch etwas zu fertigen übrig verblieben"; BA, IAa.24, fol. 262a.
128 "Die Mandel Krahe follend fertig gemacht wie sie auf einem mit vielen Laub bewachßenen Stocke sitzet darauf verschiedene Käfer und Raupe befindlich Davon sie welche frißet, Johann Joachim Kändler"; BA, IAa.24, fol. 316a.
129 Not, however, in the first chapter, "Aufsätze, Flaschen, Figuren etc," but in the third, "Schalen, Milchkannen, Butterbüchsen etc."
130 "Im Monath April 1734 sind an Neuen Modellen auf hießiger Königl. Pohl. und Churfürstl. Sächß. Porcellain-Fabrique gefertiget worden . . . Ein Rittelweibgen oder Lerchen Geyer welches vorgestellet in lebens Größe wie es Eine lerche frißt ruhet auf Einem verzierten Postament, Johann Joachim Kändler"; BA, IAa.22, fol. 151a.
131 "Ein Storch Groß worzu zwey Hälße, Johann Friedrich Eberlein, Bildhauer"; BA, IAa.24, fol. 265a.
132 "hingegen [hat] der Modelirer Kentler . . . eine Schwalbe poussiret und gefertiget"; BA, IAa.18, fol. 263a.
133 "Was ich Endes benander bey der Königl. Porcelin Manufactur von 18. April biß zu Ende des Monaths May vor Bildhauer Arbeit verfertiget, Alß . . . Einen Großen Schwan worzu zwey Helße, Johann Friedrich Eberlein, Bildhauer"; BA, IAa.24, fol. 264a.
134 "Zwey Große Schwane von Masse verbotzet, Johann Friedrich Eberlein, Bildhauer"; BA, IAa.24, fol. 265a.
135 "Was ich Endes benander bey der Königl. Porcelin Manufactur von 18. April biß zu Ende des Monaths May vor Bildhauer Arbeit verfertiget, Alß . . . Einen dergleichen [= swan] klein, nebst zwey Helßen, Johann Friedrich Eberlein, Bildhauer"; BA, IAa.24, fol. 264a.
136 "hingegen [hat] der Modelirer Kentler . . . eine Meiße poussiret und gefertiget"; BA, IAa.18, fol. 263b.
137 "Im Monath Febrarii 1733 Sind an neuen Modellen gefertiget Worden folgende . . . eine Druten Meiße, Kändler"; BA, IAa.20, fol. 116a.
138 "Im Monath Januario 1733 sind an neuen Modellen gefertiget worden folgende Stücken . . . Einen Truthahn in Lebens Größe, Kändler"; BA, IAa.20, fol. 51a.
139 When copying the information from the 1770 inventory, the writer included – wrongly – the "3 hens" added at the end of the inventory entry, and compounded his mistake by turning the five cockerels men-

tioned in the 1779 inventory into five hens.

140 This turkey was shown as item 57 at the exhibition mounted in the Kunsthaus, Zürich, by the Keramik-Freunde der Schweiz, "Schönheit des 18. Jahrhunderts," but was not accorded an illustration in the catalog.

141 "Eine Truthenne worzu zwey Hälße, Johann Friedrich Eberlein, Bildhauer"; BA, IAa.24, fol. 266a.

142 "Drey Truthüner groß in Masse verbotzet, Johann Friedrich Eberlein, Bildhauer"; BA, IAa.24, fol. 302a.

143 "Zwey Tage in Moritzburg gewesen Alda den ... Indianischen Geyer sammbt dem Gackedu ... ins kleine nach dem leben Poussiret, Kändler"; BA, IAa.22, fol 202a.

144 "Specificatio Dererjenigen Modelle so von Endes-Benannten im Monath Augusti 1734 sind Inventiret und gefertiget worden ... Einen großen Indianischen Geyer wie er in Moritzburg im Leben Befindlich ist poussiret hat in seiner Höhe mit sammbt den Postament welches in Gestalt eines mit Laub und Graß Bewachsenen Stockes 1 ell und 12 Zoll, und ist wegen seiner Seltsamen Gestaltwunderlich anzusehen zu mahlen er auch einen noch andern Ausländischen Vogel in Größe einer Starcken Tauben Gackedu genannt, geraubet und solchen als Todt neben sich zu seinen Füßen liegen Hat welchen er gantz zerrißen, und davon Das eingeweyde in seinem Schnabel Hat als wollte er es freßen, Johann Joachim Kändler"; BA, IAa.22, fol 315a.

145 "Zwey Tage in Moritzburg gewesen Alda den ... König von die Wawon ins kleine nach dem leben Poussiret, Kändler"; BA, IAa.22, fol. 202a.

146 "Im Monath Juneo sind auf hießiger Königl.Pohl. und Churfürstl. Sächßischer Porcellain-Fabrique von ein Endes benannten an Neuen Modellen gefertiget worden ... Einen Großen Indianischen Vogel Poussiret seines Nahmens dem Konig von die Wawon seine Höhe mit sammbt dem Postament 5e Viertel [= quarters of an ell] Deßen Postament ist mit Blätter Werck auf Indianische Art verzieret, Kändler"; BA, IAa.22, fol. 202a.

147 "Im Monath Januario 1733 sind an neuen Modellen gefertiget worden folgende Stücken ... Ein Baum-Hacker mit ausgesezeten Flügeln, Kändler"; BA, IAa.20, fol. 51a.

148 "Im Monath Februarii 1733 Sind an Neuen Modellen gefertiget Worden folgende ... Ein GrünSpecht, Kändler"; BA, IAa.20, fol. 116a.

149 "Im Monath Martio 1734 sind auf hiesiger Königl. Pohl. und Churfürstl. Sächß. Porcellain Fabrique an Neuen Modellen gefertiget worden ... Einen Grünspecht auch in Lebens Größe und ruhet auf Einem verzierten Postament, Johann Joachim Kändler"; BA, IAa.22, fol. 99a.

150 "Im Monath Januario 1733 sind an neuen Modellen gefertiget worden folgende Stücken ... Noch ein BaumLäuffergen in Größe Eines ZaunKönigs, Kändler"; BA, IAa.20, fol. 51a.

151 "Im Monath Januario 1733 sind an neuen Modellen gefertiget worden folgende Stücken ... Ein Roth Kählgen, Kändler"; BA, IAa.20, fol. 51a.

Glossary

abformen
→ mold-making

Administrator
Title given by Augustus the Strong to Böttger in 1710 when he put him in charge of the operations of the newly founded porcelain manufactory. In this function he was answerable to a directorate (later known as the → Manufactory Commission) that was responsible for the manufactory as an enterprise.

anbossieren
→ ornamenting

Arbeitsbericht
→ work report

Arbeitsform
→ mold, working mold

arcanist
→ arcanum

Arcanum
The entire corpus of knowledge relating to the production and decoration of porcelain, including the necessary raw materials and how they were to be processed and combined to make → paste and → glaze, the right way to construct firing-kilns, firing procedures and temperatures (→ firing), and color-recipes. As a whole it provided the key to the production of true porcelain; although espionage and voluntary and induced defections led to its gradual dissemination all over Europe it was one of the best kept secrets of the entire eighteenth century.

aufreparieren
The creation of a new set of → molds. If a set of molds has so much wear and tear that the fine detail is no longer visible, or if the set is incomplete through breakage, then → moldings are taken in normal modeler's clay from the molds still in existence, and then assembled. The repairer then sharpens the detail and outlines on the figure and fills in missing sections where necessary (→ repair). This clay figure is then treated like an original → model: plaster molds are made to produce a new set of molds with pristinely sharp outlines and detail.

Aufsatz
Historical term for a decorative piece. When used to refer to vases, *Aufsatz* can mean either one single larger vase or a set (or "garniture") composed of several vases. On a dining table, an *Aufsatz* is a thematically and formally coherent decorative composition, made up either of figurative or of non-figurative pieces.

aurochs
→ wisent

Bärenhaus
→ *Jägerhof*

base
→ *Sockel*

Bauamt
"Building Office": an administrative office for organizing building projects. Among other things, the *Bauamt* was responsible for drafting and enforcing building legislation. It was primarily staffed by architects, draughtsmen, and administrators. There were various building offices: the *Stadtbauamt* for the towns, the *Landesbauamt* for the country, and the *Hofbauamt* for court buildings. They were all subordinate to the *Oberbauamt*.

Bedeutung
→ meaning

bossieren
→ repair, → *poussieren*

building office
→ *Bauamt*

chamotte
Ground-down dead-burned fire-clay, used to make such things as bricks (for kilns); the historic sources sometimes say – not always correctly – "Kapselton" (→ sagger clay).

cold painting
Painting on porcelain with non-fired colors such as oils. As non-fired paints do not combine with the → glaze, *cold painting* is very vulnerable to scratches and can peel off easily. Most of the cold-painted animal figures had their paint washed off in the nineteenth century.

Commission
→ Manufactory Commission

Court Commissioner
→ *Hofkommissar*

denunciation affair
Also known as the Reinhardt affair, an occurrence at the Meissen manufactory in which accusations and criticisms were followed by a formal investigation.
In 1734, → Modellmeister Kaendler and → Inspektor Reinhardt filed an extensive list of charges against Höroldt, criticizing the structures of authority at the manufactory and charging Höroldt in particular with incompetence. The subsequent investigation and hearings carried out by a special commission brought forth a large number of reports that contain valuable statements by Meissen staff regarding the technical and human situation at the manufactory.

Dreher
→ thrower

ell
A historical unit of length. One Saxon *ell* was 24 "Zoll" ("inches") = 56.65 cm.

enamel firing
→ firing

feldspar
A component of porcelain → paste. Feldspathic rock (in Chinese, *petuntse*) is a very common mineral, the components of which include silicic acid and aluminum oxide.

fettling
The process of working over joins to remove surplus → slip. → repairing

filling material
A paste made principally from glue and wood shavings, used to fill the large → fire-cracks that appeared in the animal figures after the high → firing, in order to prevent the cracks from getting worse and the figures from falling apart.

fire-crack
A crack resulting from stresses in the body during high → firing. *Fire-cracks* have a variety of causes. A figure that has not dried thoroughly will be subject to stress as moisture leaves the body; uneven shaping and design also inevitably lead to tensions that can only be resolved by the paste tearing open when it softens at high temperature; over-hasty cooling is another cause of *fire-cracks*. The numerous *fire-cracks* in the Meissen large animal figures were mainly caused by the interaction of two conflicting forces: the sheer weight of the volume of → paste and the → shrinkage in the horizontal plane.

firing
A porcelain figure has to be subjected to as many as three different *firings*.
low firing (biscuit firing) Once a porcelain figure has been allowed time to dry out, it is subjected to a *low firing* at a temperature of 700–900°C. In this first firing the ceramic body contracts to such an extent that although it is still absorbent it is no longer soluble and does not turn into → slip if it comes into contact with water.
high firing (glost firing) After the low-fired body has been → glazed and has dried, it is subjected to the *high firing*. At ca. 1300–1450°C the ceramic body undergoes changes in its chemical composition and physical structure. It → sinters ("vitrifies"), acquiring the white color characteristic of porcelain. The → glaze combines inseparably with the → body, which ideally becomes somewhat translucent. The figure shrinks by about one sixth of its volume (→ shrinkage). When the highest temperature is reached, the kiln is sealed to block the influx of oxygen and prevent residual traces of iron in the paste from oxidizing and discoloring the body. In this firing the porcelain pieces have to be put in containers known as → saggers to protect them from direct contact with flame and flying ash.
enamel firing If the figure is to be decorated with → overglaze colors, it has to be given an *enamel firing* at a temperature of ca. 600–850°C. For this firing a special kiln is used that is smaller than those used for low and high firing. Its walls are covered with → chamotte bricks.

flux
An additive used to change the behavior of → overglaze colors during → firing. If the metallic oxides contained in the overglaze colors are to bind with the → glaze as perfectly as possible, their melting point has to be lowered. The painter adds the *flux* to the pigment and oil in proportions corresponding to pragmatical values derived from experiment. Different colors require different quantities of *flux* if they are to acquire an ideal shine in the firing. Too much flux makes the fine brushstrokes run, while too little results in dullness or in the colors not adhering properly to the glaze.

Former
→ molder

Garbrand
→ firing, high firing

garnieren
→ ornamenting

Geschirr
→ tableware

Glattbrand
→ firing, high firing

glaze
Porcelain's hard, transparent, shiny surface coating.
The *glaze* is made of almost the same raw materials as porcelain → paste, but in different proportions. The finely ground component parts are mixed in accordance with a recipe and stirred into water to form a runny suspension then used to coat the low-fired (→ firing) porcelain (→ glazing). In the high firing the glaze combines with the ceramic body and covers it with a thin and very shiny transparent coating.

glazer
→ glazing

glazing
The application of → glaze. When a low-fired (→ firing) figure is immersed in the liquid glaze, or when the glazer pours or sprays glaze over the figure, the water content is absorbed by the porcelain body (later simply to evaporate), while the surface becomes covered in the residual layer of fine powder that will be transformed into the glaze in the → high firing.

Green Vaults
Sequence of vaulted rooms in the → *Residenzschloss* in Dresden. With their thick walls and grated windows, these high-security rooms on the ground floor of the Residence served as the electoral treasury from the sixteenth century onwards. From 1721, under Augustus the Strong, the *Green Vaults* were turned into a magnificent set of exhibition rooms which could be visited under certain special conditions. The name comes from the green-painted ceilings of the vaulted rooms. The *Green Vaults* still exist in this form today and constitute one of Europe's oldest treasury museums.

Groschen
→ taler

high firing
→ firing

Hofkommissar
A title bestowed on individuals entrusted by the Court Administration with particular administrative or management tasks. Höroldt was appointed *Hofkommissar* in 1731 and at the same time *Malerei-Inspektor* (Inspector of Painting), a combination which effectively gave him the authority of a manufactory director.

hunting lodge
→ *Jagdschloss*

"Indian"
An eighteenth-century designation for things, plants, and animals from the Far East, and sometimes also from Africa.
By contrast with exactly defined geographical terms such as Chinese, Turkish, African, "indianisch" was often used in the seventeenth and eighteenth centuries as a general indication of non-European or "exotic" origin.

indianisch
→ Indian

Inspektor
Title of an administrative official at the Meissen manufactory; it first came into being after Böttger's death. The *Inspektor* conducted checks and submitted reports, was in charge of procuring many of the raw materials and of keeping the warehouse supplied with porcelain, and was responsible for the accounts.

iron spot
An imperfection in the porcelain paste resulting in a brownish-black spot. Most forms of → kaolin found in Europe also contain traces of iron. Even though the greatest care was taken over cleaning the kaolin in the eighteenth century, it was never possible to eliminate particles of iron entirely. Impurities of this kind are at first invisible, but if they are close to the surface of a piece they turn into dirty, brownish-black spots in the firing. On → tableware, spots of this kind were often painted over with little insects, leaves, and the like. In German: *Eisenfleck*.

iron-red
An enamel color made from ferric oxide; in German, *Eisenrot*, and in French, *rouge de fer*. Depending on its composition, *iron-red* can result in tones ranging from reddish-brown to orange. It was one of the first enamel colors to be fired on European porcelain (→ overglaze colors).

Jagdschloss
The *Jagdschloss* was one of the eighteenth century's least easily definable princely buildings. The importance of a *Jagdschloss* was not usually determined by its size or geographical location, but rather by its decoration and furnishings, and by the rank of its owner.
The term encompasses hunting lodges built to provide accommodation in hunting areas, country houses situated on estates specifically designed as locations for grand court hunts, and also stately homes incorporating iconography devoted to princely hunting. Under Augustus the Strong, Jagdschloss Moritzburg near Dresden was turned into a highly complex *Gesamtkunstwerk* with a landscaped estate and iconographically decorated and furnished interiors that specifically reflected his position as *Reichsoberjägermeister* (Supreme Imperial Master of the Hunt). Its symbolic identity and significance as "the Emperor's first hunting lodge" had to be made clear to all who set eyes upon it, which is why it was much more than a "hunting lodge": rather, a "hunting palace" or even a "hunting Residence."

Jägerhof
Building in Dresden Neustadt. Built in 1546, the *Jägerhof* not only accommodated the Saxon electors' hunting equipment but also had stables, workshops, rooms for festivities, and apartments for staff. This made it the center of hunting in Saxony. It also had reserves and outhouses for wild animals: among the buildings at the *Jägerhof* referred to in the records are the *Löwenhaus* (lion-house) and the *Bärenhaus* (bear-house), with the general term *Tierhaus* (animal-house) also being used.

joins
Visible seams marking the join between two halves of a → mold, or between single pieces. The pressing together of two paste-filled mold-halves usually results in the forma-

tion of a tiny ridge of → paste at the join. When the → molding has been taken from the molds, these ridges have to be removed and the marks smoothed over by the → repairer. This is particularly important when two pieces are bonded with → slip, as the pressure exerted squeezes out a small measure of excess fluid. If the procedures are not followed correctly, or if the slip is not of the right consistency, then these joins can become visible again after the high → firing even though they have been cleaned and smoothed away by the repairer.

Kaltbemalung
→ cold painting

kaolin
One of the principal components of porcelain *paste*. Also known as "china clay" (German: *Porzellanerde*), *kaolin* is a white, non-fusible (cannot be melted) clay earth extracted from open pits. The Meissen manufactory obtained its kaolin from the works in Aue bei Schneeberg, which is today still one of the biggest of its kind in Europe.

Kapsel
→ sagger

Kitt
→ filling material

low firing
→ firing

Löwenhaus
→ *Jägerhof*

Magerungsmittel
→ opening material

Manufactory Commission
The *Commission* was the manufactory's "board of directors." From 1719 onwards, the *Commission* functioned as a direct link between the minister entrusted with overall responsibility for the manufactory (Sulkowski, later Brühl) and those in charge of the everyday running of the enterprise (from 1731, Höroldt). It was principally concerned with checking the accounts and with matters related to staff and jurisdiction.

Masse
→ paste

meaning ("Bedeutung")
In his critical anthology of writings by art historians, *The Art of Art History* (Oxford, 1998), Donald Preziosi gives the following excellent general definition: "Meaning: generally, the significance or referential content of an art work; the values or issues, themes, or subject-matter which it may be said to 'contain' or point to." Erwin Panofsky – in his essay "Iconography and Iconology" in *Meaning in the Visual Arts*, (published in German as *Sinn und Deutung in der bildenden Kunst*) – identified three levels of "meaning" in works of art: (1) the natural, factual, expressional meaning, (2) the secondary, conventional meaning (as in allegory and symbolism), and (3) the intrinsic meaning or content. In the present volume, *meaning* is used in the third of these senses.
With regard to "content," Panofsky offers an illuminating definition (deriving from Pierce) in the introductory essay of *Meaning in the Visual Arts*, "The History of Art as a Humanistic Discipline": "that which a work betrays but does not parade."

model
The word *model* is used to refer either to the source of inspiration for a work in porcelain, or to the actual prototype created by the → modeler in clay, wax, or wood. As porcelain pieces are usually produced in series, the word *model* is also used to refer to a certain shape or composition, rather as it is used to refer to a certain "model" of car.

modeler
In a porcelain manufactory, a *modeler* is a creator of forms, who produces three-dimensional designs and makes the actual → models that constitute the point of departure for the production process. As a rule, modelers are trained sculptors. Their greatest challenge is to learn how to make models that take account of the specific behavioral characteristics of porcelain → paste, in particular its behavior in the heat of the → firing. This is why they have to be capable of performing the duties actually carried out by the → molder and the → repairer.

modeling
The process of shaping a piece in a plastic (easily shaped or molded) material. By contrast with the reproductive making of → molds or taking of → moldings, or the mechanical throwing or turning of pieces on the wheel, the modeling done by the → modeler is original work, done freehand in three dimensions.

Modellmeister
A porcelain manufactory can have a number of modelers working at the same time, under the supervision of a *Modellmeister* (variously translated as master sculptor, head modeler, modeler-in-chief, model master, or master modeler). At Meissen the *Modellmeister* was particularly important as he not only determined the forms and stylistic character of the porcelain, correcting other → modelers when necessary, but was also in charge of the other stages in the production of white wares.

mold (noun)
A hollow case consisting of two or more parts. *Molds* made to produce single parts of porcelain figures are as a rule made in plaster of Paris, and are produced from a → model. The *molds* necessary for a whole figure are known as a set.
Urform The first set of molds taken from a clay model is known as the *Urform* ("prototype mold"). When – as is usually the case – the production of this set of molds involves the clay model being cut up into sections, which are kneaded back into a formless lump of clay after the → mold-making to be used again, the *Urform* is the most immediate testimony to the → modeler's original work. In the eighteenth century, the moldings in porcelain paste were as a rule taken from the *Urform*. Inevitably, the *Urform* became worn down and the detail on the → moldings became so blurred and indistinct that it was scarcely even possible for the → repairer to recreate the detail through retouching (→ repair). When this happened, the usual solution was to create a new set of molds (→ *aufreparieren*).
working mold Later, the Meissen Manufactory introduced the distinction between *Urform* and *Arbeitsform* (working mold). The *Urform* was no longer used in the actual production process: instead, it was reserved for making moldings in clay that reproduced the → model exactly and were assembled to make a block-mold, which was in its turn used to make new sets of working molds. If one reckons that a block-mold recreated from the *Urform* could be used to produce ten sets of working molds, and that each set of working molds could produce a series of twenty porcelain pieces, it follows that one use of the *Urform* sufficed to produce two hundred porcelain figures.
Originalform In German there is a fine distinction between *Urform* and *Originalform*. If the *Urform* is irretrievably lost and the → *aufreparieren* procedure is used to make a replacement, then that replacement is known as an *Originalform*.

mold (verb)
In German: *ausformen*. The shaping of a component part of a figure by using porcelain → paste and a plaster → mold. In the eighteenth century, the component parts of figures were not shaped by casting but were hand-pressed in the mold. The *molder* presses a slab of porcelain paste into each of the two halves of the mold, coats the edges with → slip and fits the two halves together exactly. After a certain time the plaster will have absorbed so much water from the paste that when the two halves of the mold are separated the → molding can be removed without difficulty.

molder, mold-maker
Worker responsible both for making → molds (from the → model) and for taking moldings in → paste (from the molds).

molding (noun)
A part of a figure, once it has been taken from the → mold.

mold-making
In German: *abformen*. Production of plaster molds for the reproduction of a → model. The first step in the production of multiple copies of a porcelain figure is to make a negative of the clay model, i.e., a → mold. As a rule, a set of molds has to be made: no single mold can have any overhangs or awkward protrusions on the inside, as once the paste has been pressed in, overhangs make it impossible for the → molding to be removed satisfactorily when it has taken shape. The → molder therefore has to establish how many individual molds are needed in order to reproduce the entire surface of the clay → model. Having done so, the molder proceeds in one of two ways.

Either – less commonly – the still moist clay model is covered part-for-part with thick liquid plaster, which is then removed once it has hardened, or – the usual procedure – the clay model is cut up into well-judged sections, which are then used to make plaster molds.

Muffel
→ sagger

muffle
→ sagger

opening material
An additive used to stabilize clay or porcelain paste in the firing by making it less plastic (leaner, shorter). *Opening* (or "shortening") *material* is added to clay or porcelain → paste when there is a danger that the object will deform in the → firing, whether because it is particularly voluminous, or because the melting point of the clay or paste is too low. In the case of the Meissen large animal figures, ground high-fired porcelain shards were used as opening material.

ornamenting
The largely free application of additional decorative elements, also known as *sprigging*.
Once a figure has been assembled (→ repaired), it can be further embellished with elements cemented to the body with → slip. The technical term for the process is *luting*. These trimmings – leaves, flowers, ribbons and the like – were either freely modeled (→ modeling) or taken from small, flat → molds ("Belegformen," "ornamenting molds"), and ranged from small elements such as leaves to larger ones such as branches, birds, beetles, or putti.

overglaze colors
The colors used for the eye-catching decoration of white glazed porcelain. As a rule, overglaze colors are metal oxides in finely ground powder form, mixed with a → flux and stirred into an oil (usually thickened terpentine). In the eighteenth century, the manufactories produced their colors in their own laboratories, with the recipes forming part of the → arcanum.
They are also known as fusible (= "meltable") colors, or enamel colors. In the eighteenth-century records for Meissen, the practice of decorating with overglaze colors is referred to as "emaillieren" (enameling).

overglaze painting
Diluted in pure terpentine (or some other non-viscous oil), the colors are applied in thin coats rather in the same way as watercolors. The colors can be made deeper by superimposing further layers. Outlines and shading are generally effected by using darker tones. In the → enamel firing (ca. 700–850°C) the overglaze colors sink into the slightly softened → glaze, where they acquire both their characteristic radiant shine and also their final color.

paste
In German: *die Masse*. The material used for making porcelain. As no suitable composite is found naturally in Europe, the *paste* is a mixture of various raw materials. The essential ingredients of porcelain paste are → kaolin (40–60%), → feldspar, and quartz. The proportions vary according to the character of the piece in production; the historical proportions were sometimes written down in recipe-books. In the case of the large animal figures in particular, lengthy series of experiments were necessary before the ideal composition was found.

pedestal
→ *Sockel*

porcelain paste
→ paste

poussieren
Historical expression for sculpting in a plastic material. In the eighteenth century, the word *poussieren* was used in two ways, either meaning "to model" (the free shaping of a three-dimensional object in a plastic material such as clay, → modeling), or → "to repair" (assembling and putting finishing touches to a three-dimensional object made up of a number of parts made from molds).

puce
A reddish color. The colors referred to in German as *Purpur* were among the most precious and costly of all, because they were made from gold. There were various shades, all referred to as *Purpur* in the historic sources. In English the reddish shade of *Purpur* is known as *puce*, the blue-violet shade as "purple," and the strongly red-violet shade as "crimson." All these shades appear in porcelain-painting but *puce* is the most common.

Purpur
→ puce

Quartier
Historically, a measure of volume. In 1744, however, Johann Christian Müller used the term as a measure of length, most likely meaning a quarter of an → ell, or roughly 14.2 cm (see Source 27).

Registratur
A term for an administrative procedure. Documents to be archived first of all have to be "registered": put into order, paginated, and marked. A short summary report on an item put into the archives was likewise known as a *Registratur*. Those to do with items in the Meissen archive are of particular value today because they provide researchers with important facts in a highly compressed form.

Reinhardt affair
→ denunciation affair

repair, repairer
To *repair* means to assemble the parts of a figure and to prepare it for → firing.
Having received the → moldings from the → molder, the *repairer* puts them together into a figure using porcelain → slip, smoothing over ("verputzen") the joins and sharpening up the edges. Sometimes, the *repairer* incises surface structures such as hair or feathers, or does some → ornamenting. The *repairer* is also responsible for deciding when the figure is dry enough for the first firing. → *poussieren*

Residence
→ *Residenzschloss*

Residenzschloss
The Residence in Dresden was the principal seat of the electors of Saxony and the hub of the princely administration. Of all the elector's properties it was the most important "state" seat, comparable in present-day terms with a seat of government. It was here that the most important ceremonial events took place, such as the official reception of ambassadors. The electors had other castles, palaces and country seats at their disposition for festivities, excursions, hunts and the like; some of these were as important as the *Residenzschloss* from the artistic point of view, but none had such great political significance.

sagger
A simple lidded container (also known as a "muffle") made of high-fired clay (→ sagger clay), into which porcelain is put in the high firing to protect it from the direct heat of the flame and from flying ash.

sagger clay
A coarse clay with a high melting point (German: *Kapselton*), used to make → saggers. → chamotte

Schrühbrand
→ firing, low firing

shrinkage
The contraction of porcelain in the → firing.
The complete loss of water in the low firing brings about a certain contraction, but the shrinkage is relatively slight. Only in the high firing, when the body → sinters, does the body lose about a sixth of its volume. The contraction is somewhat greater in the vertical than in the horizontal plane. → Modelers have to take this *shrinkage* into account when making new → models. It was one of the greatest problems encountered in the firing of the large animal figures.

sinter (verb)
The physical and chemical change that takes place in the high → firing. The high firing brings about physical and chemical changes in the structure of porcelain paste. Put in simple terms, it contracts, vitrifies (fuses into a glass-like substance), and becomes watertight. It is only once this has happened that the piece can really be spoken of as porcelain.

slip
Clay or porcelain → paste diluted with water to form a fluid that is used in → repairing and → ornamenting.

Sockel
The eighteenth-century sources use the word *Sockel* with two different meanings. In some cases, it is used to refer to the lower part of a porcelain figure, which is an inseparable part of the whole and is designed to ensure that the figure stands up properly; in the present volume, this is referred to as the "pedestal" as in most cases it also provides the sur-

faces for the animal to stand upon. *Sockel* can also refer to the object known in English as a "socle": a stand, low or high, separate from the porcelain piece, designed for the piece to stand on and to make it look right in a given setting.

tableware
Vessels and instruments used in the preparation, storing, or consumption of food and drink. German: *Geschirr*. The plans for the Japanese Palace also included the decorative use of plates, dishes and bowls, cups and other vessels otherwise used at table. These items were known as *Geschirr* to distinguish them from figures, vases, and sets of vases (→ *Aufsatz*).

taler
Also spelt *thaler*, it was the usual unit of currency in the accounts of the Meissen manufactory. One *taler* (in full, "Reichstaler") = 24 *Groschen*. Attempts to estimate the present-day worth of the *taler* on the basis of the prices for basic foodstuffs are not really satisfactory, because prices in those days were determined by market forces different from those of our own day. In 1734, Höroldt's annual salary as director of the Meissen manufactory was 1,000 *talers*, while Kaendler received 300 and the molder Fritzsche 144, though it should be remembered that they also received payments in kind such as housing and firewood.

thrower
A craftsman who forms porcelain pieces at the wheel. The thrower shapes plates and vessels (tureens, pots, cups, vases, and the like) in porcelain paste on the potter's wheel, either with the free use of the hands or with a rotating plaster mold known as a "jigger" (for plates) or a "jolly" (for cups).

Tierhaus
→ *Jägerhof*

underglaze colors
Colors for the decoration of porcelain in the high → firing.
The best-known *underglaze color* is the Chinese blue that the Meissen arcanists (→ arcanum) were at great pains to imitate from the very beginning. It is made from cobalt oxide and is painted directly onto the low-fired body. After the glaze has been applied, *underglaze colors* have to withstand the temperatures of the high firing. Underglaze colors finally lie between the body and the → glaze and thus do not interfere with the high degree of shine on the surface, and in themselves have a pleasingly soft character. Physically and chemically speaking, they have to be extremely stable and resistant. In Europe, it was only in the nineteenth century that further colors were developed that did not burn in the high firing and were suitable for use in underglaze painting.

Verglühbrand
→ firing, low firing

verputzen
→ fettling

vessels
→ tableware

wisent / *Wisent*
Still to be found in Poland and Lithuania, the *wisent* is also known as the European bison (not to be confused with the better-known American bison, or buffalo). Even in the early eighteenth century the numbers of *wisents* had been so reduced, particularly by the princely hunts, that the Prussian king Wilhelm I was fond of giving wisent bulls as state presents to other courts, where they were proudly exhibited in menageries. Augustus the Strong had special reserves for his *wisents*, which were bred for use in court hunts and animal fights.
In the eighteenth century, and thus also in all the documents of the time relating to the Saxon court, the *wisent* is wrongly referred to as the "Auer-Ochs": the European aurochs (the Bos primogenius from which our cattle are probably descended) was in fact rendered extinct in the early seventeenth century.
Kaendler's *Wisent Fighting with a Boar* reflects the natural enmity between these two animals, which is also well captured in an impressive series of photographs of just such a fight taken recently in a wisent reserve in Poland: see *GEO* (German edition) 2005/2, 56–70. I am grateful to Prof. Fritz Jürgen Obst of Dresden for drawing my attention to these photographs.

work report
In German: *Arbeitsbericht*. The short reports that the → modelers at the Meissen manufactory had to submit (from 1731 onwards) on the work they had done in the past month.

Zwinger
Originally an orangerie by the architect Matthäus Daniel Pöppelmann, close to the → *Residenzschloss* in Dresden. Building began in 1709, considerable extensions were made from 1711 on, and from 1728 parts of the electoral collections were housed in the pavilions and galleries surrounding its spacious courtyard.

Indexes

Numbers in bold indicate illustrations

Index of places

Abadia 29
Africa 64–66, 69
Amsterdam 17, 18, 54, 228, 229, 232, 239
Ansbach 240
Antwerp 30
Aranjuez 29, 59
Athens 136
Augustusburg 62
Bath 229, 232
Berlin 18, 20, 44, 46, 228, 229
Bohemia 218
Bow 237
Calcutta 190
Caputh 18, 20, 46
Castello 27; **8**
Charlottenburg 18, 20, 23, 44, 46, 242; **6**
China 20, 22, 24, 56, 120, 137, 159, 163, 221, 225
Chiswick House 29
Colditz 78, 86
Cologne 229
Copenhagen 109, 228, 229, 235
Corbitz 78
Cossebaude 138
Detroit 229
Dresden (in general) 10, 14, 15, 18, 32–35, 37, 42, 45–47, 51–55, 58, 60–67, 69, 70–73, 98, 102, 108, 110, 123, 122, 128, 134, 135, 137, 138, 141–143, 150, 152, 156, 158, 164, 184, 218, 221, 225–229, 231, 237, 242, 244, 246, 256
Dresden, *Altmarkt* 141, 150
Dresden, court church 56
Dresden, court fish garden 59, 62, 141, 245
Dresden, Dutch Palace 18, 21, 32–34, 37, 39, 41, 47–49, 51, 53, 55, 58, 66, 68, 72, 74, 110, 131, 132, 134, 138, 164, 237, 241–242, 245, 246, 249, 254, 263, 264, 279; **16, 41, 137**
Dresden, Green Vaults 37, 47, 53, 190, 210, 212, 256, 257
Dresden, *Großer Garten* 62, 138, 141, 143, 156
Dresden, *Jägerhof* 62, 66, 122, 129, 141, 142, 174, 247, 253, 269, 270
Dresden, Japanese Palace 17, 18, 20, 24, 30, 32, 33, 35, 37, 39, 41, 42, 44–58, 63, 66–69, 70, 71, 73–77, 85, 87, 91, 93, 94, 96, 98, 100, 101, 103, 106–108, 110, 112, 117, 119–121, 125, 126, 129, 130–132, 134, 135, 137–139, 140, 144, 146, 151, 152, 155–158, 163–165, 167, 168, 172, 173, 176, 178, 184, 190, 206, 210–216, 218, 219, 221, 222, 223, 224, 225, 227, 228, 230, 232, 233, 235, 237–239, 254, 259, 263, 264, 279, 280; **17–22, 26–40, 42, 43, 139, 141**
Dresden, Johanneum 110, 221, 224; **199**
Dresden, *Kunstkammer* 17, 32, 48, 129, 227, 267
Dresden, *Löwenhaus* 62–64, 118, 119, 129, 144, 195, 278, 281
Dresden, Porcelain Collection 234–236, 239
Dresden, *Residenzschloss* 44, 48, 53, 56, 65, 68, 134, 155, 156, 199, 215, 219, 221; **198, 200**
Dresden, Royal Library 122
Dresden, *Schmeltzgarten* 62
Dresden, Taschenberg Palais 48, 258
Dresden, warehouse 222, 224, 225, 227, 260, 262, 265
Dresden, Zwinger 34, 35, 37, 53, 56, 65, 112, 134, 138, 139, 140, 156, 164, 176, 188, 210, 213, 215, 221, 227; **25**
Dresdner Heide, Saugarten (piggery) 62
Edinburgh 229
England 19, 138, 157, 163, 218, 229, 254, 256
Erzgebirge 14
Fischbach 70
Florence 27
France 14, 19, 20, 22, 24–27, 152, 157, 163, 172, 216, 218, 224
Frankenthal 218, 237
Freiberg 15
Freital, Potschappel manufactory 231, 235, 236; **211, 212**
Fulda 240
Geneva 229
Genoa 64
Germany 157, 224
Glasgow 123
Großsedlitz 62, 138, 254
Hamburg 65, 229, 235
Hildburghausen 240; **13**
Holland *See* Netherlands
Holländisches Palais *See* Dutch Palace
Hubertusburg 142, 143
India 19, 20, 48
Italy 26, 27
Japan 20, 120, 221
Kykuit 109, 111
Leipzig 14, 17, 64, 134, 135, 221
London 110, 226–229
Longleat Castle 93, 108, 109, 229
Los Angeles 229
Meissen, *Albrechtsburg* 15, 71, 87, 92, 98, 111, 130
Meissen, in general 59, 130, 221, 223, 228
Meissen, porcelain manufactory 10, 16–18, 36, 41, 45, 48–53, 55–57, 59, 66–77, 79, 84, 86, 87, 91, 93, 94, 96–98, 100, 101, 105, 106, 110–114, 119, 120, 122, 129, 130, 132, 135, 137, 146, 172, 176, 184, 190, 192, 210, 218, 219, 221, 223–226, 230, 232–237, 239, 247, 248, 251, 254, 258, 259
Meissen, warehouse 67, 221, 222, 223, 243, 259
Merseburg 240
Moritzburg 60–63, 68, 69, 77, 122, 128, 129, 138–140, 142–144, 146, 152, 168, 195, 215, 256, 281, 282
Moscow 229
Munich 229, 232, 239, 240
Nanking 24
Nantes 20
Netherlands 19, 21, 22, 25, 27, 32
Neustadt an der Dosse 22
New York 85, 109, 229, 237
Nuremberg 229
Nymphenburg 237; **190**
Oranienburg 18, 20, 22, 23, 46, 240, 242; **5**
Ostra 62, 141
Paris 18, 27, 62, 229, 230, 236
Paris, Achille Bloch manufactory 236, 237; **216**
Paris, Samson manufactory 232, 235, 237; **213, 214**
Philadelphia 229
Pillnitz 33, 34, 37, 39, 61, 138; **27**
Pittsburgh 229
Poland 14, 34
Pommersfelden 240
Portugal 19
Prussia 14, 24, 46, 248
Raby Castle 229
Residence *See* Dresden, *Residenzschloss*
Rome 64, 125
Rouen 229
Russia 256
Salzdahlum 44
Saxony 14, 15, 34, 36, 46, 57, 60, 62, 134–137, 139, 140, 143, 152, 164, 165
Schelde, Sankt Bernardusabtei 30
Sèvres 221, 225, 228, 229
Siebeneichen, Schloss 228
Siebenlehn 78, 79, 109
Spain 19, 157
St. Petersburg, 64, 229
Sternburg 138
Stockholm 233
Sweden 46
Thuringia 218
Tirol 64, 69
Tullynally Castle 229
Tunis 65, 276
Turin 229
Übigau 18
Veitshöchheim 29
Venice 19, 63, 64
Versailles, in general 23, 24, 26, 28, 37, 140, 155, 158; **140**
Versailles, labyrinth 27, 28, 30, 60, 148, 171, 246; **11, 12, 14**
Versailles, menagerie 60–63, 144, 245, 253; **45**
Versailles, *Trianon de Porcelaine* 24, 33, 164; **7**
Vienna 62, 142, 218, 229, 256
Vincennes 56

Waddesdon Manor 229
Warsaw 14, 15, 34, 39, 51, 52, 64, 66, 221, 222, 229
Weikersheim 240
Weimar 70, 74, 114
Wiesentheid 240
Wittenberg 135, 246
Würzburg 240
Zeithain 18

Index of artists and historical personages

Aesop (620–560 BC) 28, 141
Albani, Cardinal Alessandro (1692–1779) 54
Albrecht, Friedrich August sen. (most likely 1699–1761) 74, 75, 83, 126
Altheim, Count, Imperial Master of the Stables 222
Anna Ivanovna, Tsarina of Russia (1693–1740) 142
Anton Ulrich, Duke of Braunschweig-Wolfenbüttel (1633–1714) 18, 242
Aristotle (384–322 BC) 150
Augustus III, elector of Saxony and king in Poland (1696–1763) 14, 15, 17, 18, 32, 41, 48, 50–53, 56, 57, 58, 65, 67, 68, 73, 91, 96, 102, 103, 119, 129, 135–137, 141, 143, 164, 213, 215, 222, 223, 235, 245, 247, 278, 279; **2**
Augustus the Strong, elector of Saxony and king in Poland (1670–1733) 9, 11, 14, 15, 17, 18, 24, 28, 32–35, 37, 39, 41, 44, 46–54, 57, 59–70, 73, 75, 85, 93, 102, 103, 128, 131, 132, 134–143, 144, 151, 152, 156–158, 163, 176, 190, 192, 199, 200, 212, 213, 215, 216, 221, 228, 230, 235, 239, 240, 242, 243, 254–247, 254, 256, 278, 279; **1**, **30**
Aulicek, Dominikus (1734–1804) 190
Bailly, Jacques, the elder (1629–1679) 12
Ball, Hermann 228
Bassenge & Co., art dealers 227
Bassetouche, Elisabeth 18, 48
Bella, Stefano della (1610–1664) 125; **161**
Berling, Karl 68
Besser, Johann von (1654–1729) 46
Beutler, director of the *Kunstkammer* 240
Bodt, Jean de (1670–1745) 34, 42, 43, 46, 48, 136; **20**, **21**, **22**
Böhme, Christian Gottfried 74
Bologna, Giovanni da, known as Giambologna (1529–1608) 27, 60; **8**, **9**
Borck, Prussian lieutenant 64
Boreman, Thomas 123; 74, **126**
Böttger, Johann Friedrich (1682–1719) 15, 16, 59, 126, 131, 135, 137, 160
Bouzonnet, Claudine (1636–1697) 151
Bowes, John 231
Brinkmann, Julius 228
Briosco, Andres, known as Riccio (1470–1532) 26
Broebes, Jean Baptiste (ca. 1660–after 1720) **5**
Brongniart, Alexandre (1770–1847) 221
Brühl, Heinrich Graf von (1700–1763) 15, 52, 57, 58, 65, 72, 73, 103, 164, 222, 278
Buchner, Johann Heinrich 65
Cassel, Ernest (Collection) 228
Chemetowski, Stanislav (1673–1728) 18
Chladni, Samuel (most likely 1673–1753) 67, 71, 222, 265
Christian I, elector of Saxony (1560–1591) 134
Confucius (551–ca. 479 BC) 20
Corvinus, Johann August (1683–1738) 34, 132; **16**
Cotelle, Jean, the younger (1642–1708) 241
Danreiter, Franz Anton († 1760) 254
Decker, Paul, the elder (1677–1713) 22, 39; **4**
Demidoff, Anatol (1812–1870) 227
Diana, goddess of the hunt 60, 138, 139
Dinglinger, Johann Melchior (1664–1731) 212
Donath, Adolph 228
Dürer, Albrecht (1471–1528) 123
Eberlein, Johann Friedrich (1695–1749) 73, 74, 75, 82, 91, 112, 113, 173; **70**, **71**, **84**, **152**, **156**, **180**, **205**, **206**
Eggebrecht, Peter (before 1708–1738) 88
Ehder, Johann Gottlieb (1716–1750) 74
Emperor of China 20, 164
Eosander von Göthe, Johann Friedrich (1669–1728) 46
Escher vom Glas, Johannes 64
Eugene, Prince of Savoy (1663–1736) 62
Falke, David 227
Fäsch, Johann Rudolf (1680–1749) 241
Fassmann, David (1665–1744) 63, 64
Feige, Johann Christian, the elder (1689–1751) 70
Feist, Hermine († 1933) 228
Ferdinand I, grand duke of Tuscany (1549–1609) 134
Ferdinand II, archduke of Austria (1578–1637) 240
Fichtner, Fritz (1890–1969) 161, 228
Flemming, Count Jakob Heinrich (1667–1728) 18, 32, 33
Fleutner, Johann Friedrich (most likely 1692–1749) 57
Friedrich I, king in Prussia (1657–1713) 18, 46
Friedrich IV, king of Denmark (1671–1730) 46
Friedrich von Hessen-Kassel, king of Sweden 63, 64
Friedrich Wilhelm I, king in Prussia (1688–1740) 34, 46, 63, 64
Fritzsche, George, the elder (most likely 1697–1756) 70, 74, 75, 83, 108; **100**
Fröhlich, Joseph (1694–1757) 68, 227, 245
Fyt, Jan (1611–1661) 26
Gama, Vasco da (1469–1524) 19
Gebhardt, Gottfried 65, 112
Geithner, Peter sen. (1679–1760) 74
George IV of England (1762–1830) 224
Gerhard, Hubert (ca. 1550–1623) 27
Goldschmidt-Rothschild, Baron von 228
Gottsched, Johann Christoph (1700–1766) 166
Gracián, Baltasar (1601–1658) 166, 167
Graesse, Theodor (1814–1885) 132, 224
Grand Mogul of India, Aureng Zeb 20, 164, 212
Grund, Johann Elias (1703–1758) 74
Habermann, Franz Xaver (1721–1796) **157**, **158**, **197**
Hanway, Jonas 52, 55, 56, 131, 165, 276
Hasche, Johann Christian (1744–1827) 36, 53–55, 69
Hebenstreit, Johann Ernst (1702–1757) 64–66
Hercules 53, 139
Hermann, Christian (1708–1763) 222
Heymann, Johann George (most likely 1698–1747) 247, 271
Homann, Johann Baptist (1664–1724) 241; **13**
Hondekoeter, Melchior de (1636–1695) 26
Höroldt, Johann Gregorius (1696–1775) 16, 17, 53, 57–59, 71, 72, 74, 75, 77–79, 82, 83, 86–88, 90–93, 96–98, 101, 103, 105, 109–111, 116, 119, 120, 130, 190, 207, 245, 247–252, 258
Hoym, Count Carl Heinrich (1694–1736) 120

Huêt, Jean-Charles 222
Irminger, Johann Jacob (most likely 1635–1721) 59, 69, 98
Johann Georg III, elector of Saxony (1657–1691) 240
Johann Georg IV, elector of Saxony (1668–1694) 17, 240
Johann, king of Saxony (1801–1873) 224
Jonston, John 129
Kaendler, Johann Joachim (1706–1775) 17, 56–58, 66–68, 70–79, 81–83, 86–88, 90–93, 96–99, 106, 107, 112–117, 119–122, 125, 129, 131, 141, 146, 148–151, 168, 172–174, 176, 178–180, 182–184, 186–190, 192, 193, 195, 196, 199–204, 206–216, 218, 221, 222, 227, 228, 232, 233, 236, 239, 244, 246, 248–253, 257, 258, 260, 278–280, 283; **46, 50, 69, 77, 78, 82, 83, 85, 87, 88, 90–94, 96–99, 108–110, 112, 114–116, 122, 128, 136, 142–146, 148–151, 153–156, 162–165, 167–170, 172–175, 179, 181–183, 185–188, 193–196, 201, 202, 215**
Kaskel, Michael 225
Keil, Gottfried († 1732) 114, 200; **193**
Kessel, Jan van, the elder (1626–1679) 26
Keyssler, Johann Georg 34, 41, 50, 54, 55, 64, 66, 106, 110, 112, 132, 120, 230, 244, 254
Kirchner, Johann Christian († 1732) 37, 70, 241; **26**
Kirchner, Johann Gottlieb (b. 1706) 66, 70–74, 77, 90, 91, 112–120, 122, 123, 125, 126, 128, 129, 151, 173–176, 179–183, 187, 189, 192, 206–209, 211–215, 225, 228, 236, 241, 244, 247–249, 253, 257, 260; **23, 24, 53, 75, 76, 86, 89, 111, 113, 117–119, 125, 127, 130, 132, 133, 147, 159, 160, 166, 203, 204, 207, 208**
Klemm, Gustav (1802–1867) 223–227
Knöffel, Johann Christoph (1686–1752) 43
Kranenburg, Johan van Haersolte Heer van (1647–1716) 32
Krumbholz, Carl Friedrich (b. 1713) 73, 74, 83
La Fontaine, Jean de (1621–1695) 28
Lagnasco, Count Peter Robert Taparelli (1659–1735) 18, 64
Lairesse, Gérard de (1641–1711) 157
Le Clerc, Sébastien (1637–1714) 241; **14**
Leibniz, Gottfried Wilhelm Freiherr von (1646–1716) 173
LeNôtre, André (1613–1700) 28
Lepke, Rudolph 228, 235
LePlat, Raymond de (ca. 1664–1742) 17, 18, 32, 131; **41, 138**
Loen, Johann Michael von 60, 143, 152
Lohse, Gottfried sen. (1678–1745) 74
Longhi, Pietro (1702–1785) 63
Longuelune, Zacharias (1669–1748) 34, 41, 43–38, 50, 51, 53, 54, 73, 131, 136, 164, 165, 242; **28, 29, 37, 39, 40**
Louis XIV, of France (1638–1715) 24, 55, 61, 62, 155, 156
Lubomirski, Count Jerzy Ignazcy (1691–1753) 57
Lücke, Carl Friedrich 74
Lücke, Johann Christoph Ludwig 70
Ludwig, Christian Gottlieb (1709–1773) 65, 277
Luise Henriette von Nassau-Oranien, electress of Brandenburg (1627–1667) 22
Marcolini, Count Camillo (1739–1814) 56, 221
Maria Amalia, landgravine of Hessen-Kassel (1653–1711) 18
Maria Anna, princess of Saxony (1728–1797) 141
Maria Antonia, electress of Saxony (1724–1780) 258
Maria Josepha, electress of Saxony (1699–1757) 14, 32, 56, 215
Marks, English art-dealer 226
Marot, Daniel, the elder (ca. 1663–1752) 22; **3**
Mayer, Löw 224
Mehlhorn, Johann Gottfried (ca. 1695–1739) 249, 250, 252
Mehlhorn, Johann Gottlieb (before 1695–1769) 98
Meissonier, Juste-Aurèle (1693–1750) 43
Mendelssohn, family 232
Merian, Matthäus, the younger (1621–1687) 245; **129**
Meyer, Moritz 226
Miltitz, Freiherr von 228
Minerva 36, 136
Montespan, Françoise Athénaïs Marquise de (1641–1707) 24
Montfaucon, Bernard de (1655–1729) 125, 126; **131**
Moritz von Sachsen, Maréchal de France (1696–1750) 143, 222
Müller, Christoph (1687–1748) 74, 75
Müller, Johann Christian, preacher 55, 56, 131, 168, 279, 280
Neptune 136, 162
Nering, Johann Arnold (1659–1695) 142
Neuhof, Johann 24
Oberschall, Johann Matthäus (1688–1755) 241
Orpheus 26, 60, 125, 152
Oudry, Jean Baptiste (1686–1755) 26
Pabst von Ohain, Gottfried (1656–1729) 15
Palissy, Bernard (1510–1589) 27, 211
Pérelle, André 24; **7, 45**
Permoser, Balthasar (1651–1732) 37; **25**
Perrault, Charles 28, 241
Petzsch, Christoph Heinrich (1692–1756) 78, 79, 83–85, 87, 92, 108
Pfeiffer, Max Adolf 230, 232, 233, 239
Pflugk, Damian (most likely 1688–1741) 50, 58, 67
Pliny, the elder 150
Pöllnitz, Baron von (1692–1775) 54
Polo, Marco 159
Pöppelmann, Matthäus Daniel (1662–1736) 32, 34, 39, 43–45, 56, 62, 131, 132, 157; **36, 38, 137**
Raschke, War Councillor 18
Reinhardt, Johann David (ca. 1684–after 1760) 17, 71, 96
Reinicke, Peter (most likely 1711–1768) 74
Reinow, Christian (1685–1749) 93, 94, 98, 129, 130, 151
Rohr, Julius Bernhard von (1688–1735) 142, 155–157, 163, 164
Rost, Johann Christian (book-keeper of the manufactory's office in Dresden) (1700–1784) 67
Rothe, Johann Adam 42, 43
Savery, Roelant (1576–1639) 26
Saxonia 136
Schiefer, Andreas (most likely 1690–1761) 74, 75, 83, 108; **101**
Schlicke, Johann Georg (most likely 1711–1756) 75, 83
Schmahl, Johann Gottlieb sen. (b. most likely 1708) 74
Schmiedel, Gottfried 116, 227
Schmieder, Johann Friedrich (most likely 1715–1780) 73, 74, 83, 190
Schnell, Martin (ca. 1675–1740?) 242
Schramm, Carl Christian 54
Schwarze, Julius Heinrich 48
Seinsheim, Prince Adam Friedrich von (1708–1779) 132
Seyffahrth, Richard 236
Silvestre, Louis de (1675–1760) 53; **1, 2**
Snyders, Frans (1579–1657) 26
Springer, Johann Daniel 110
Stain zu Jettingen, Johanna Freifrau von (1723–1783) 57
Stella, Jacques (1596–1657) 37, 126; **23, 24**
Stöltzel, Samuel (1685–1737) 16, 59, 72, 78, 86, 92
Sturm, Leonhard Christan (1669–1719) 132

Sulkowski, Count Alexander Joseph (1695–1762) 15, 50–53, 57, 58, 67, 73, 77, 78, 96, 103, 107, 119, 135, 164, 171, 213; **46**
Susini, Antonio († 1624) 10
Tauschert, custodian of the Japanese Palace 226
Teichert, Johann Carl Friedrich 225, 226
Teuffert, Martin 48–51, 55–57, 67, 75, 96, 130, 137, 223, 243, 247, 259
Thiele, Alexander (1686–1752) 34, 254
Thielmann, Johann Friedrich 244
Thomae, Benjamin (1682–1751) 70, 176, 184
Tietz, Ferdinand (1708–1777) 15
Tschirnhaus, Ehrenfried Walther von (1651–1708) 15, 135
Vischer, Peter, the elder (1460–1529) 184; **171**
Voort, Michael, the elder, van der (1667–1737) 30
Wackerbarth, Count August Christoph (1662–1734) 18, 32–34, 64
Weenix, Jan (1640–1719) 26
Weinart, Benjamin Gottfried (1751–1813) 54, 56
Wentzel, Johann Georg 141, 228
Wichmannshausen, Rudolph Friedrich von 57, 137
Wietersheim, von 225
Wildenstein, Paul (most likely 1681–1744) 93
Wilson, Anne and Mary 225
Wittekind, Arthur (firm of art-dealers) 228
Wittich, Johann Christian (most likely 1714–1768) 74, 93
Wiwild, Isaak Augustin 47, 48
Wolf, court antiquary 226
Wolff, Count Sulkowski's master of the kitchen 57
Wolfssohn, Helena 226
Zedler, Johann Heinrich (1706–1751) 150, 158
Zimmermann, Ernst (1866–1940) 221, 227, 228

Index of animal names

afrikanische Ente *See* great crested grebe
afrikanischer Esel *See* zebra
arctic fox 63, 64
aurochs *See* wisent
badger 142
barn owl 105, 110, 113, 219, 230; **93–95, 105**
Barognittchen (*Parognitten*) 69
bear 68, 76, 113, 115, 125, 129, 141, 142, 146, 149, 158, 180, 182, 225, 226, 229, 230; **202, 203**
bear, dancing 63
beaver 143
billy-goat 110, 114, 115, 193, 202–204, 226, 229, 230, 233; **196**
bird of paradise 113, 219, 228; **201**
bird's nest 113
bittern 88, 101, 113, 143, 186–190, 193, 219, 228, 230, 236; **174, 175**
boar 27, 29; **10**
bull 27
bulldog 146
bullfinch 113, 219
bustard 74, 108, 113–116, 143, 149, 187, 189, 227, 229, 230; **173**
Calcuzscher Hahn *See* turkeycock
Caloutsch-Hühner *See* turkeyhen
camel 63, 69
canary 110, 113
capercaillie (cock) 143
carp 148, 196, 198, 199, 200, 230
cassowary 66, 68, 79, 113, 115, 116, 186, 187, 189, 190, 193, 219, 221, 230; **48, 172**
cat 25, 74, 83, 108, 114, 149, 150, 189, 219, 228, 230; **54, 101, 113**
chameleon 69
chamois 113, 151, 229, 230; **152**
chicken *See* hen
cockatoo 64, 77, 113, 129, 151, 168, 170, 171, 192, 206, 219, 225, 226, 229, 230
cockerel 113, 183, 184, 192, 208, 218, 219, 225–227, 229, 230, 233, 236, 237; **57, 168**
coot 103, 106, 110, 113, 219, 230; **91**
cow 142
crane 64, 77, 93, 113, 143, 149, 150, 229, 230; **14, 15, 151**
creature of fable (beasts of fable) 25, 30, 68, 125, 129
crocodile 65
deer 64, 65, 69, 91, 143, 158
dog 27, 113, 115, 117, 141, 149, 158, 181, 183, 184, 186, 193, 206, 208, 218, 219, 224, 229, 230; **142–144, 169–171**
dog, bolognese 105, 219, 224, 229, 230–232, 237; **92**
donkey 142
dove 113, 209, 219, 230
dragon 69, 75, 110, 113, 125, 126, 128, 225, 229; **104, 130–134**
eagle owl 101, 105, 113, 125, 229, 230; **84**
eagle 29, 64, 66, 67, 71, 81, 82, 90–92, 109, 113, 115, 120–122, 173, 174, 176, 178–180, 182, 195, 209, 219, 225, 227, 229, 230; **47, 121, 162–165**
elephant 63, 67, 69, 88, 101, 112, 115, 117, 121, 123, 158, 180, 188, 219, 225, 226, 229, 230; **125, 126**
exotic sheep *See* sheep
falcon *See* kestrel
fish 62, 65, 66, 76, 82, 90, 115, 148, 196, 198, 200–202, 227
flamingo 64
fox 91, 113–115, 143, 146, 148, 150–152, 180–182, 189, 207, 209, 219, 226, 227, 229, 230; **56, 67, 166**
frog 76, 199–201, 258; **192, 193**
gibbon *See* Monkey wearing a ruff
giraffe 63
golden pheasant 96, 101, 106, 107, 193, 229, 230, 238; **79, 98, 181**
gray parrot 106, 110, 114, 229; **96**
great crested grebe 103, 110, 113, 129, 183, 189, 230; **90**
green woodpecker 113
griffon vulture 72, 77, 110, 113, 129, 151, 168, 170, 171, 192, 206, 225–227, 229, 230, 233; **80, 153–155**
guinea fowl 113, 219, 222, 230, 235, 236
gull 113, 183, 230; **128**
hen 113, 131, 148, 168, 180, 181, 225–227; **148**
heron 76, 79, 82, 88, 90, 113, 148, 149, 183, 187, 189, 199, 200, 201, 202, 204, 215, 225, 226, 229, 230; **51, 52, 176, 187–192**
hoopoe 113, 121
horse 27, 29, 60, 75, 142, 143, 182
indianische Ratte *See* jerboa
indianischer Rabe *See* macaw
indianisches Schaf *See* sheep
jay 113, 222
jerboa 113, 129, 180, 182, 219; **167**
kestrel 106, 113, 121, 183, 189, 226, 227, 229, 135; **122**
kid 90, 131, 148, 202–204, 226
king vulture 77, 98, 100, 101, 109, 111, 113, 125, 151, 228–230, 233, 235; **72, 81–83, 102, 106, 107**
kingfisher 113, 221
Kletpapagei 69
König von Wauwau *See* king vulture
Krescher See *Kletpapagei*
Kropfvogel *See* king vulture
lark 113, 148
leopard 113, 118, 119, 129, 142, 229, 230; **58, 117, 204**
Lerchenstößer *See* sparrowhawk
lion 25, 29, 60, 63–67, 74, 85, 86, 92, 108, 115, 123, 125, 135, 141, 142, 150, 151, 158, 173–176, 179, 180–182, 206, 207, 209, 210, 213, 223, 225–227, 229, 230, 237; **61–63, 100, 159, 161**
lioness 63, 64, 113, 115, 118, 119, 142, 151, 180, 226, 229, 230; **64, 117, 160**
Löffelgans *See* pelican
lynx 113, 118, 119, 129, 142, 226, 229, 230; **60, 119**
macaque *See* monkey, Mother-Monkey
macaw 69, 81, 90, 91, 101, 106, 107, 113, 122, 125, 189, 193, 195, 196, 199, 206–209, 219, 226, 229, 230, 257; **49, 50, 65, 85, 123, 124, 177,182–184**
magpie 110, 113, 219, 222
Mandelkrähe *See* roller

mandrill 69, 100, 114, 115, 218, 219, 229–231, 235–238; **206–213**
marmoset 101–103, 110, 111, 114, 230, 236; **88**
marten 143
Monkey taking snuff 101–103, 113–115, 225, 229, 230, 232, 233, 236, 237, 239; **87, 215, 216**
Monkey wearing a ruff 101–103, 110, 113, 115, 229, 230; **59, 89**
Monkey with grape/chain 110, 113, 229, 230; **66**
monkey 27, 62, 63, 65, 66, 69, 74, 90, 113, 118, 141, 142, 189, 218, 219, 222, 223, 226–228, 230, 234; **9, 11–13**
monkey, Mother-Monkey 82, 113, 115, 148, 230; **53, 55, 147**
Mops *See* pug
mule 142
nanny-goat 90, 96, 110, 113, 114, 131, 148, 193, 202–204, 206, 226, 229, 230; **78, 194, 195**
oriole 113
osprey 103, 110, 113, 115, 121, 148, 183, 230, 236; **97, 114, 115**
ostrich 64, 65, 67
owl 110, 113, 125, 148, 183, 219, 222, 229, 230; **145**
Paduaner Hahn *See* cockerel
panther 142, 223
parakeet 219
parrot 60, 63, 64, 66, 69, 110, 113, 219, 221–223, 228, 229
Pavian(baboon) *See* mandrill
peacock 64, 66, 69, 90, 91, 109, 110, 113, 131, 149, 189, 224, 225, 227–230; **68, 103, 149, 150**
pelican 66, 68, 79, 88, 113, 148, 193, 196, 198, 199, 208, 221, 225–227, 229, 230; **185, 186**
pheasant 62, 107, 113, 141, 143, 189, 219, 230; **99**
pheasant, hen 148
pied wagtail 79, 113
pigeon 113, 125, 129
polar bear 64
porcupine 77, 129, 142
pug 27
ram 112; **205**
rhinoceros 63, 69, 88, 94, 123, 225–230; **44, 73–76**
Rittelweibgen *See* sparrowhawk
roller 113, 219
rose-ringed parakeet 103, 106, 110, 219, 228; **127**
sable 113, 129, 219, 230; **136**
scapegoat 112, 113, 129, 230; **108**
seagull *See* gull
sheep 112, 113, 129, 151, 158, 192, 219, 230, 235; **109, 206**
she-wolf 90, 93, 94, 113, 148, 226, 229, 230; **69, 77**
snail 200, 201
snake 69
sparrow 113
sparrowhawk 69, 113, 148, 219; **146**
sphinx 69, 230
squirrel 62, 113, 219, 221
stork 113, 227
swallow 113, 219
swan 82, 91, 113, 131, 143, 149, 230; **70, 71**
tiger 60, 63, 64, 66, 113, 118, 119, 129, 142, 226
tit 113, 228
toucan 64
turkeycock 69, 73, 113, 190, 192, 193, 225, 226, 229–231, 236; **178, 179**
turkeyhen 73, 110, 113, 190, 219, 236; **180**
türkische Ente *See* great crested grebe
turtledove 113
unicorn 60, 69
vulture *See* griffon vulture
Waldteufel *See* mandrill
Wasserhuhn *See* coot
Welsche Hühner *See* turkeyhen
Welscher Hahn *See* turkeycock
wild boar 90, 112, 113, 115, 117, 131, 142–144, 146, 184, 195, 230
wild cat 77
wisent 67, 68, 90, 91, 112, 113, 115–117, 128, 131, 142, 146, 183, 184, 188, 193, 230, 244; **116**
wolf 29, 65, 142; **14, 15**
woodpecker 113, 219, 221
zebra 66, 69, 91

Illustration credits

Angela Wallwitz 201
Author 7, 8, 10, 14, 44, 45, 47–49, 51–54, 57, 58, 60, 61, 72, 73, 79, 80, 81, 88, 95, 101, 102, 106, 107, 120, 140, 176–178, 184, 189, 191, 192, 212, 213
Hans Bach jacket and frontispiece, 23–26, 50, 55, 56, 59, 62, 64–68, 70, 71, 74, 75, 78, 82, 83, 90, 92–94, 97, 103–105, 109, 113–116, 119, 121, 123–125, 127, 130, 132, 134, 136, 139, 142–145, 147, 148, 150–1 52, 154, 155, 163, 166–170, 172, 179–183, 185, 186, 188, 193, 194, 203, 206–208, 215
Historisches Museum Basel, Peter Portner 1, 2, 46
Klaus Peter Arnold 211
Kunstbibliothek Berlin SPK 15, 131, 161, 171
Landesamt für Denkmalpflege Sachsen, Plansammlung Dresden 19, 27
Longleat Castle, Marquess of Bath 100
Marcus Köhler 216
Metropolitan Museum of Art, New York 63, 84, 86, 190
Musée Ariana, Geneva 89
Photothèque des Musées de la Ville de Paris 12
Réunion des Musées Nationaux de France 9, 11
Rijksmuseum Amsterdam, Peter Mookhoek 69, 77, 85, 87, 96, 98, 99, 117, 118, 122, 149, 153, 159, 160, 173–175, 187, 195, 196, 199
Sächsische Landesbibliothek, Staats- und Universitätsbibliothek, Deutsche Fotothek 17, 18, 141, 200
Sächsisches Hauptstaatsarchiv, Dresden 20–22, 28–40, 42, 43, 110, 137
Sotheby's 214
Staatliche Kunstsammlungen Dresden, Kupferstichkabinett 16, 41
Staatliche Kunstsammlungen Dresden, Porzellansammlung im Zwinger, Jürgen Karpinski 91, 111, 112, 135, 156
Staatsbibliothek Berlin SPK 129
Stiftung Preußische Schlösser und Gärten Berlin-Brandenburg 5, 6, 13, 146
Stiftung Preußische Schlösser und Gärten Berlin-Brandenburg, KPM-Archiv (Land Berlin) 3, 4, 157, 158, 197, 210
The New York Public Library, General Research Division, Astor, Lenox and Tilden Foundations 74, 126
from: Carl Albiker, *Die Meißener Porzellantiere im 18. Jahrhundert* (Berlin, 1959) 108, 128, 162, 164, 202, 204, 205
from: Helmuth Gröger, *Johann Joachim Kaendler, der Meister des Porzellans* (Dresden, 1956) 165

Jacket:
Johann Joachim Kaendler, Pelican, model 1732,
Dresden Porcelain Collection (fig. 185)

Frontispiece:
Johann Joachim Kaendler, Peacock displaying, model 1734,
Dresden Porcelain Collection (fig. 150)

Translation: John Nicholson, Vienna

Design: Peter Grassinger

Lithography: S. Zanotto/Brisotto, Tezze di Piave (color),
Repro Knopp, Inning (black and white)

Printing: Aumüller, Regensburg

Binding: Conzella, Pfarrkirchen

Original publication

Translated from *Die Galerie der Meißener Tiere: Die Menagerie Augusts des Starken für das Japanische Palais in Dresden*, published in 2004 by Hirmer, Munich, as the first number in the *Schriftenreihe der Gesellschaft der Keramikfreunde e. V. Düsseldorf.*

Bibliographical information of the Deutsche Bibliothek:
This publication is catalogued in the *Deutsche Nationalbibliographie*; detailed bibliographical details may be obtained from the Internet (http://dnb.ddb.de).

ISBN-10: 3-7774-2795-0
ISBN-13: 978-3-7774-2795-9

Printed in Germany